American Institute of Certified Public Accountants

Codification of Statements on Auditing Standards

(Including Statements on Standards for Attestation Engagements)

Numbers 1 to 85

Reprinted from
AICPA Professional Standards,
Auditing Part
(as of January 1, 1998)

1 2 3 4 5 6 7 8 9 0 PrP 9 9 8

ISBN 0-87051-201-3

FOREWORD

This volume, issued by the Auditing Standards Board, is a Codification of Statements on Auditing Standards. It includes the currently effective Statements on Auditing Standards Nos. 1 through 85, with superseded portions deleted and amendments included, the related auditing interpretations, Statements on Standards for Attestation Engagements Nos. 1 through 7, and the related attestation engagements interpretations.

The Auditing Standards Board is the AICPA's senior technical body on auditing matters. The origin of a senior technical committee on auditing in 1939 and its history are explained in Appendix A.

Rule 202 of the AICPA's Code of Professional Conduct requires adherence to generally accepted auditing standards, recognizes Statements on Auditing Standards as interpretations of those standards, and requires that members be prepared to justify departures.

The Accounting and Review Services Committee, Auditing Standards Board, and Management Consulting Services Executive Committee are the senior technical committees of the Institute designated to issue enforceable standards under Rules 201 and 202 of the AICPA's Code of Professional Conduct concerning attestation services in their respective areas of responsibility.

AUDITING STANDARDS BOARD

Deborah D. Lambert, Chair

Thomas Ray, Director—
Audit and Attest Standards

STANDARDS RECENTLY ISSUED

Statement	Title	Issue Date	Section
SAS No. 83	*Establishing an Understanding With the Client*	October 1997	Integrated into AU 310[1]
SAS No. 84	*Communications Between Predecessor and Successor Auditors*	October 1997	AU 315[2]
SAS No. 85	*Management Representations*	November 1997	AU 333[3]
SSAE No. 7	*Establishing an Understanding With the Client*	October 1997	Integrated into AT 100

Other changes to this edition of the *Codification of Statements on Auditing Standards (Including Statements on Standards for Attestation Engagements)* include:

Section	Change
AU 316A	Deletion of SAS No. 53, *The Auditor's Responsibility to Detect and Report Errors and Irregularities*, as originally issued in April 1988, as a result of SAS No. 82, *Consideration of Fraud in a Financial Statement Audit*, becoming effective
AU 9311.38–.47	Addition of Auditing Interpretation No. 4 of SAS No. 22, *Planning and Supervision*, titled "Audit Considerations for the Year 2000 Issue"
AU 9319	Addition of Auditing Interpretation No. 1 of SAS No. 55, *Consideration of Internal Control in a Financial Statement Audit*, titled "Audit Considerations for the Year 2000 Issue"
AU 9325	Addition of Auditing Interpretation No. 2 of SAS No. 60, *Communication of Internal Control Related Matters Noted in an Audit*, titled "Audit Considerations for the Year 2000 Issue"

---

[1] SAS No. 1, section 310, *Relationship Between the Auditor's Appointment and Planning*, as amended by SAS No. 45, *Omnibus Statement on Auditing Standards—1983*, "Substantive Tests Prior to the Balance-Sheet Date," has been moved to AU section 310A until the effective date of SAS No. 83.

[2] SAS No. 7, *Communications Between Predecessor and Successor Auditors*, as amended, as well as its related interpretations, have been moved to AU sections 315A and 9315A, respectively, until the effective date of SAS No. 84.

[3] SAS No. 19, *Client Representations*, as originally issued in June 1977, as well as its related interpretations, have been moved to AU sections 333A and 9333A, respectively, until the effective date of SAS No. 85. The former AU section 333A containing the appendix to SAS No. 19 has been incorporated into the new AU section 333A.14.

Section	Change
AU 9336.01–.18	Addition of Auditing Interpretation No. 1 of SAS No. 73, *Using the Work of a Specialist*, titled "The Use of Legal Interpretations as Evidential Matter to Support Management's Assertion That a Transfer of Financial Assets Has Met the Isolation Criterion in Paragraph 9(a) of Financial Accounting Standards Board Statement No. 125"
AU 9622.01–.02	Addition of Auditing Interpretation No. 1 of SAS No. 75, *Engagements to Apply Agreed-Upon Procedures to Specified Elements, Accounts, or Items of a Financial Statement*, titled "Applying Agreed-Upon Procedures to All, or Substantially All, of the Elements, Accounts, or Items of a Financial Statement"
AU 9623.88–.93	Addition of Auditing Interpretation No. 14 of SAS No. 62, *Special Reports*, titled "Evaluating the Adequacy of Disclosure in Financial Statements Prepared on the Cash, Modified Cash, or Income Tax Basis of Accounting"

In addition, conforming and editorial changes have been made throughout the literature to reflect the issuance of SAS No. 82 and SSAE No. 7.

TABLE OF CONTENTS

Section | Page

... How to Use This Volume 1

... Cross-References to SASs........................ 3

U.S. AUDITING

AU 100 Statements on Auditing Standards—Introduction 19
- 110—Responsibilities and Functions of the Independent Auditor
- 150—Generally Accepted Auditing Standards
- 161—The Relationship of Generally Accepted Auditing Standards to Quality Control Standards

AU 200 The General Standards 29
- 201—Nature of the General Standards
- 210—Training and Proficiency of the Independent Auditor
- 220—Independence
- 230—Due Professional Care in the Performance of Work

AU 300 The Standards of Field Work........................ 41
- 310—Appointment of the Independent Auditor
- 310A—Relationship Between the Auditor's Appointment and Planning
- 311—Planning and Supervision
- 9311—Planning and Supervision: Auditing Interpretations of Section 311
- 312—Audit Risk and Materiality in Conducting an Audit
- 313—Substantive Tests Prior to the Balance-Sheet Date
- 315—Communications Between Predecessor and Successor Auditors
- 315A—Communications Between Predecessor and Successor Auditors
- 9315A—Communications Between Predecessor and Successor Auditors: Auditing Interpretations of Section 315A
- 316—Consideration of Fraud in a Financial Statement Audit
- 317—Illegal Acts by Clients
- 9317—Illegal Acts by Clients: Auditing Interpretations of Section 317
- 319—Consideration of Internal Control in a Financial Statement Audit

Section Page

AU 300 The Standards of Field Work—continued

9319—Consideration of Internal Control in a Financial Statement Audit: Auditing Interpretations of Section 319

322—The Auditor's Consideration of the Internal Audit Function in an Audit of Financial Statements

324—Reports on the Processing of Transactions by Service Organizations

9324—Reports on the Processing of Transactions by Service Organizations: Auditing Interpretations of Section 324

325—Communication of Internal Control Related Matters Noted in an Audit

9325—Communication of Internal Control Related Matters Noted in an Audit: Auditing Interpretations of Section 325

326—Evidential Matter

9326—Evidential Matter: Auditing Interpretations of Section 326

329—Analytical Procedures

330—The Confirmation Process

331—Inventories

332—Auditing Investments

333—Management Representations

333A—Client Representations

9333—Management Representations: Auditing Interpretations of Section 333

9333A—Client Representations: Auditing Interpretations of Section 333A

334—Related Parties

9334—Related Parties: Auditing Interpretations of Section 334

336—Using the Work of a Specialist

9336—Using the Work of a Specialist: Auditing Interpretations of Section 336

337—Inquiry of a Client's Lawyer Concerning Litigation, Claims, and Assessments

9337—Inquiry of a Client's Lawyer Concerning Litigation, Claims, and Assessments: Auditing Interpretations of Section 337

339—Working Papers

9339—Working Papers: Auditing Interpretations of Section 339

341—The Auditor's Consideration of an Entity's Ability to Continue as a Going Concern

9341—The Auditor's Consideration of an Entity's Ability to Continue as a Going Concern: Auditing Interpretations of Section 341

Section | Page

AU 300 The Standards of Field Work—continued
- 342—Auditing Accounting Estimates
- 9342—Auditing Accounting Estimates: Auditing Interpretations of Section 342
- 350—Audit Sampling
- 9350—Audit Sampling: Auditing Interpretations of Section 350
- 380—Communication With Audit Committees
- 9380—Communication With Audit Committees: Auditing Interpretations of Section 380
- 390—Consideration of Omitted Procedures After the Report Date

AU 400 The First, Second, and Third Standards of Reporting 385
- 410—Adherence to Generally Accepted Accounting Principles
- 9410—Adherence to Generally Accepted Accounting Principles: Auditing Interpretations of Section 410
- 411—The Meaning of *Present Fairly in Conformity With Generally Accepted Accounting Principles* in the Independent Auditor's Report
- 9411—The Meaning of *Present Fairly in Conformity With Generally Accepted Accounting Principles* in the Independent Auditor's Report: Auditing Interpretations of Section 411
- 420—Consistency of Application of Generally Accepted Accounting Principles
- 9420—Consistency of Application of Generally Accepted Accounting Principles: Auditing Interpretations of Section 420
- 431—Adequacy of Disclosure in Financial Statements
- 435—Segment Information

AU 500 The Fourth Standard of Reporting 421
- 504—Association With Financial Statements
- 9504—Association With Financial Statements: Auditing Interpretations of Section 504
- 508—Reports on Audited Financial Statements
- 9508—Reports on Audited Financial Statements: Auditing Interpretations of Section 508
- 530—Dating of the Independent Auditor's Report
- 534—Reporting on Financial Statements Prepared for Use in Other Countries
- 9534—Reporting on Financial Statements Prepared for Use in Other Countries: Auditing Interpretations of Section 534

Section Page

AU 500 The Fourth Standard of Reporting—continued

543—Part of Audit Performed by Other Independent Auditors

9543—Part of Audit Performed by Other Independent Auditors: Auditing Interpretations of Section 543

544—Lack of Conformity With Generally Accepted Accounting Principles

550—Other Information in Documents Containing Audited Financial Statements

9550—Other Information in Documents Containing Audited Financial Statements: Auditing Interpretations of Section 550

551—Reporting on Information Accompanying the Basic Financial Statements in Auditor-Submitted Documents

552—Reporting on Condensed Financial Statements and Selected Financial Data

558—Required Supplementary Information

9558—Required Supplementary Information: Auditing Interpretations of Section 558

560—Subsequent Events

561—Subsequent Discovery of Facts Existing at the Date of the Auditor's Report

9561—Subsequent Discovery of Facts Existing at the Date of the Auditor's Report: Auditing Interpretations of Section 561

AU 600 Other Types of Reports 533

622—Engagements to Apply Agreed-Upon Procedures to Specified Elements, Accounts, or Items of a Financial Statement

9622—Engagements to Apply Agreed-Upon Procedures to Specified Elements, Accounts, or Items of a Financial Statement: Auditing Interpretations of Section 622

623—Special Reports

9623—Special Reports: Auditing Interpretations of Section 623

625—Reports on the Application of Accounting Principles

634—Letters for Underwriters and Certain Other Requesting Parties

9634—Letters for Underwriters and Certain Other Requesting Parties: Auditing Interpretations of Section 634

9642—Reporting on Internal Accounting Control: Auditing Interpretations of SAS No. 30

Section | Page

AU 700 Special Topics 661
711—Filings Under Federal Securities Statutes
9711—Filings Under Federal Securities Statutes: Auditing Interpretations of Section 711
722—Interim Financial Information

AU 800 Compliance Auditing 687
801—Compliance Auditing Considerations in Audits of Governmental Entities and Recipients of Governmental Financial Assistance

AU 900 Special Reports of the Committee on Auditing Procedure 697
901—Public Warehouses—Controls and Auditing Procedures for Goods Held

AU . . . Appendixes 707

AU . . . Topical Index 755

ATTESTATION ENGAGEMENTS

AT . . . Attestation Engagements—Contents 811

AT . . . Statements on Standards for Attestation Engagements—Introduction 813

AT . . . Statements on Standards for Attestation Engagements 815
100—Attestation Standards
9100—Attestation Standards: Attestation Engagements Interpretations of Section 100
200—Financial Forecasts and Projections
300—Reporting on Pro Forma Financial Information
400—Reporting on an Entity's Internal Control Over Financial Reporting
9400—Reporting on an Entity's Internal Control Over Financial Reporting: Attestation Engagements Interpretations of Section 400
500—Compliance Attestation
600—Agreed-Upon Procedures Engagements

AT . . . Topical Index 999

ATTESTATION ENGAGEMENTS

HOW TO USE THIS VOLUME

Scope of the Volume ...

This volume, which is a reprint of the auditing part of the looseleaf edition of *AICPA Professional Standards*, includes Statements on Auditing Standards Nos. 1 through 85 and Statements on Standards for Attestation Engagements Nos. 1 through 7, issued by the Auditing Standards Board, Accounting and Review Services Committee, and the Management Consulting Services Executive Committee, and Auditing Interpretations and Attestation Engagements Interpretations issued by the AICPA staff.

How This Volume Is Arranged ...

The contents of this volume are arranged as follows:

Cross-References to SASs

Statements on Auditing Standards and related Auditing Interpretations

AU § 100—Introduction

AU § 200—The General Standards

AU § 300—The Standards of Field Work

AU § 400—The First, Second, and Third Standards of Reporting

AU § 500—The Fourth Standard of Reporting

AU § 600—Other Types of Reports

AU § 700—Special Topics

AU § 800—Compliance Auditing

AU § 900—Special Reports of the Committee on Auditing Procedure

Appendixes

Topical Index

Statements on Standards for Attestation Engagements and related Attestation Engagements Interpretations

AT § 100—Attestation Standards

AT § 200—Financial Forecasts and Projections

AT § 300—Reporting on Pro Forma Financial Information

AT § 400—Reporting on an Entity's Internal Control Over Financial Reporting

AT § 500—Compliance Attestation

AT § 600—Agreed-Upon Procedures Engagements

Topical Index

How to Use This Volume ...

The arrangement of material in this volume is indicated in the general table of contents at the front of the volume. There is a detailed table of contents covering the material within each major division.

The cross-references to SASs section consists of three parts as follows:

Part I is a list of Statements on Auditing Procedure Nos. 1–54, Statements on Auditing Standards Nos. 1–85 and Statements on Standards for Attestation Engagements Nos. 1–7.

Part II provides a list of sources of sections in the current text.

Part III is a list of sections in Statement on Auditing Standards No. 1, *Codification of Auditing Standards and Procedures*.

The major divisions are divided into sections, each with its own section number. Each paragraph within a section is decimally numbered. For example, AU section 210.04 refers to the fourth paragraph of section 210, *Training and Proficiency of the Independent Auditor.*

Auditing Interpretations are numbered in the 9000 series with the last three digits indicating the section to which the Interpretation relates. Interpretations immediately follow their corresponding section. For example, Interpretations related to section 311 are numbered 9311 which directly follows section 311.

There are five appendixes as follows:

Appendix A provides the historical background for the present Statements on Auditing Standards.

Appendix B provides an analysis of International Standards on Auditing to AICPA Statements on Auditing Standards.

Appendix C indicates sections and paragraphs of the text cross-referenced to Auditing Interpretations.

Appendix D provides a list of AICPA Audit and Accounting Guides and Statements of Position.

Appendix E provides a schedule of changes in Statements on Auditing Standards since the issuance of Statement on Auditing Standards No. 1, *Codification of Auditing Standards and Procedures, Nos. 33 through 54*.

Statements on Standards for Attestation Engagements and Attestation Engagements Interpretations appear with the prefix AT in their section numbers. Attestation Engagements Interpretations are numbered in the 9000 series with the last three digits indicating the section to which the Interpretation relates. Interpretations immediately follow their corresponding section. For example, Interpretations relating to section 100 are numbered 9100 which directly follows section 100.

The AU topical index covers the Statements on Auditing Standards and Auditing Interpretations. The AT topical index covers the Statements on Standards for Attestation Engagements and Attestation Engagements Interpretations.

The topical indexes use the key word method to facilitate reference to the pronouncements. The indexes are arranged alphabetically by topic with references to major division, section and paragraph numbers.

AU

CROSS-REFERENCES TO SASs

. . . statements on auditing procedure/ standards/standards for attestation engagements . . . sources of sections in current text . . . sections in statement on auditing standards no. 1 . . .

TABLE OF CONTENTS

Part I

List of Statements on Auditing Procedure Nos. 1-54, Statements on Auditing Standards, and Statements on Standards for Attestation Engagements Issued to Date

Statements on Auditing Procedure

No.	*Date Issued*	*Title*
1	Oct. 1939	Extensions of Auditing Procedure
2	Dec. 1939	The Auditor's Opinion on the Basis of a Restricted Examination
3	Feb. 1940	Inventories and Receivables of Department Stores, Instalment Houses, Chain Stores, and Other Retailers
4	Mar. 1941	Clients' Written Representations Regarding Inventories, Liabilities, and Other Matters
5	Feb. 1941	The Revised SEC Rule on "Accountants' Certificates"
6	Mar. 1941	The Revised SEC Rule on "Accountants' Certificates" (continued)
7	Mar. 1941	Contingent Liability Under Policies With Mutual Insurance Companies
8	Sept. 1941	Interim Financial Statements and the Auditor's Report Thereon
9	Dec. 1941	Accountants' Reports on Examinations of Securities and Similar Investments Under the Investment Company Act
10	June 1942	Auditing Under Wartime Conditions
11	Sept. 1942	The Auditor's Opinion on the Basis of a Restricted Examination (No. 2)
12	Oct. 1942	Amendment to Extensions of Auditing Procedure
13	Dec. 1942	The Auditor's Opinion on the Basis of a Restricted Examination (No. 3)—Face-Amount Certificate Companies
14	Dec. 1942	Confirmation of Public Utility Accounts Receivable
15	Dec. 1942	Disclosure of the Effect of Wartime Uncertainties on Financial Statements
16	Dec. 1942	Case Studies on Inventories
17	Dec. 1942	Physical Inventories in Wartime
18	Jan. 1943	Confirmation of Receivables From the Government
19	Nov. 1943	Confirmation of Receivables (Positive and Negative Methods)
20	Dec. 1943	Termination of Fixed Price Supply Contracts
21	July 1944	Wartime Government Regulations

Statements on Auditing Procedure—continued

No.	*Date Issued*	*Title*
22	May 1945	References to the Independent Accountant in Securities Registrations
23	Dec. 1949	Clarification of Accountant's Report When Opinion is Omitted (Revised)
24	Oct. 1948	Revision in Short-Form Accountant's Report or Certificate
25	Oct. 1954	Events Subsequent to the Date of Financial Statements
26	April 1956	Reporting on Use of "Other Procedures"
27	July 1957	Long-Form Reports
28	Oct. 1957	Special Reports
29	Oct. 1958	Scope of the Independent Auditor's Review of Internal Control
30	Sept. 1960	Responsibilities and Functions of the Independent Auditor in the Examination of Financial Statements
31	Oct. 1961	Consistency
32	Sept. 1962	Qualifications and Disclaimers
33	Dec. 1963	Auditing Standards and Procedures (a codification)
34	Sept. 1965	Long-Term Investments
35	Nov. 1965	Letters for Underwriters
36	Aug. 1966	Revision of "Extensions of Auditing Procedure" Relating to Inventories
37	Sept. 1966	Special Report: Public Warehouses—Controls and Auditing Procedures for Goods Held
38	Sept. 1967	Unaudited Financial Statements
39	Sept. 1967	Working Papers
40	Oct. 1968	Reports Following a Pooling of Interests
41	Oct. 1969	Subsequent Discovery of Facts Existing at the Date of the Auditor's Report
42	Jan. 1970	Reporting When a Certified Public Accountant Is Not Independent
43	Sept. 1970	Confirmation of Receivables and Observation of Inventories
44	April 1971	Reports Following a Pooling of Interests
45	July 1971	Using the Work and Reports of Other Auditors
46	July 1971	Piecemeal Opinions
47	Sept. 1971	Subsequent Events
48	Oct. 1971	Letters for Underwriters
49	Nov. 1971	Reports on Internal Control
50	Nov. 1971	Reporting on the Statement of Changes in Financial Position
51	July 1972	Long-Term Investments
52	Oct. 1972	Reports on Internal Control Based on Criteria Established by Governmental Agencies
53	Nov. 1972	Reporting on Consistency and Accounting Changes
54	Nov. 1972	The Auditor's Study and Evaluation of Internal Control

Statements on Auditing Standards*

No.	Date Issued	Title	Section
1	**Nov. 1972**	**Codification of Auditing Standards and Procedures**	**See Part III**[1]
2	Oct. 1974	Reports on Audited Financial Statements [Superseded by SAS 58]	
3	Dec. 1974	The Effects of EDP on the Auditor's Study and Evaluation of Internal Control [Superseded by SAS 48]	
4	Dec. 1974	Quality Control Considerations for a Firm of Independent Auditors [Superseded by SAS 25]	
5	July 1975	The Meaning of "Present Fairly in Conformity With Generally Accepted Accounting Principles" in the Independent Auditor's Report [Superseded by SAS 69]	
6	July 1975	Related Party Transactions [Superseded by SAS 45]	
7	**Oct. 1975**	**Communications Between Predecessor and Successor Auditors**	**315A**[2]
8	**Dec. 1975**	**Other Information in Documents Containing Audited Financial Statements**	**550**
9	Dec. 1975	The Effect of an Internal Audit Function on the Scope of the Independent Auditor's Examination [Superseded by SAS 65]	
10	Dec. 1975	Limited Review of Interim Financial Information [Superseded by SAS 24]	
11	Dec. 1975	Using the Work of a Specialist [Superseded by SAS 73]	
12	**Jan. 1976**	**Inquiry of a Client's Lawyer Concerning Litigation, Claims, and Assessments**	**337**
13	May 1976	Reports on a Limited Review of Interim Financial Information [Superseded by SAS 24]	
14	Dec. 1976	Special Reports [Superseded by SAS 62]	
15	Dec. 1976	Reports on Comparative Financial Statements [Superseded by SAS 58]	
16	Jan. 1977	The Independent Auditor's Responsibility for the Detection of Errors or Irregularities [Superseded by SAS 53]	

* Outstanding Statements are indicated in **boldface** type.

[1] Portions of Statement on Auditing Standards No. 1 have been superseded by subsequent pronouncements.

[2] Statement on Auditing Standards No. 7 has been superseded by Statement on Auditing Standards No. 84 at section 315. Statement on Auditing Standards No. 7, as amended, has been moved to section 315A until the effective date of Statement on Auditing Standards No. 84.

Statements on Auditing Standards—continued

No.	Date Issued	Title	Section
17	Jan. 1977	Illegal Acts by Clients [Superseded by SAS 54]	
18	May 1977	Unaudited Replacement Cost Information [Withdrawn by the Auditing Standards Board]	
19	**June 1977**	**Client Representations**	**333A**[3]
20	Aug. 1977	Required Communication of Material Weaknesses in Internal Accounting Control [Superseded by SAS 60]	
21	**Dec. 1977**	**Segment Information**	**435**
22	**Mar. 1978**	**Planning and Supervision**	**311**
23	Oct. 1978	Analytical Review Procedures [Superseded by SAS 56]	
24	Mar. 1979	Review of Interim Financial Information [Superseded by SAS 36]	
25	**Nov. 1979**	**The Relationship of Generally Accepted Auditing Standards to Quality Control Standards**	**161**
26	**Nov. 1979**	**Association With Financial Statements**	**504**
27	Dec. 1979	Supplementary Information Required by the Financial Accounting Standards Board [Superseded by SAS 52]	
28	June 1980	Supplementary Information on the Effects of Changing Prices [Withdrawn by SAS 52]	
29	**July 1980**	**Reporting on Information Accompanying the Basic Financial Statements in Auditor-Submitted Documents**	**551**
30	July 1980	Reporting on Internal Accounting Control [Superseded by SSAE 2]	
31	**Aug. 1980**	**Evidential Matter**	**326**
32	**Oct. 1980**	**Adequacy of Disclosure in Financial Statements**	**431**
33	Oct. 1980	Supplementary Oil and Gas Reserve Information [Superseded by SAS 45]	
34	Mar. 1981	The Auditor's Considerations When a Question Arises About an Entity's Continued Existence [Superseded by SAS 59]	
35	April 1981	Special Reports—Applying Agreed-Upon Procedures to Specified Elements, Accounts, or Items of a Financial Statement [Superseded by SAS 75]	

[3] Statement on Auditing Standards No. 19 has been superseded by Statement on Auditing Standards No. 85 at section 333. Statement on Auditing Standards No. 19, as originally issued in June 1977, has been moved to section 333A until the effective date of Statement on Auditing Standards No. 85. The former section 333A containing the appendix to Statement on Auditing Standards No. 19 has been incorporated into the new section 333A.14.

Statements on Auditing Standards—continued

No.	Date Issued	Title	Section
36	April 1981	Review of Interim Financial Information [Superseded by SAS 71]	
37	**April 1981**	**Filings Under Federal Securities Statutes**	**711**
38	April 1981	Letters for Underwriters [Superseded by SAS 49]	
39	**June 1981**	**Audit Sampling**	**350**
40	Feb. 1982	Supplementary Mineral Reserve Information [Superseded by SAS 52]	
41	**April 1982**	**Working Papers**	**339**
42	**Sept. 1982**	**Reporting on Condensed Financial Statements and Selected Financial Data**	**552**
43	**Aug. 1982**	**Omnibus Statement on Auditing Standards**[4]	
44	Dec. 1982	Special-Purpose Reports on Internal Accounting Control at Service Organizations [Superseded by SAS 70]	
45	**Aug. 1983**	**Omnibus Statement on Auditing Standards—1983**[5]	
46	**Sept. 1983**	**Consideration of Omitted Procedures After the Report Date**	**390**
47	**Dec. 1983**	**Audit Risk and Materiality in Conducting an Audit**	**312**
48	**July 1984**	**The Effects of Computer Processing on the Audit of Financial Statements**[6]	
49	Sept. 1984	Letters for Underwriters [Superseded by SAS 72]	
50	**July 1986**	**Reports on the Application of Accounting Principles**	**625**
51	**July 1986**	**Reporting on Financial Statements Prepared for Use in Other Countries**	**534**
52	**April 1988**	**Omnibus Statement on Auditing Standards—1987**[7]	

[4] Statement on Auditing Standards No. 43 has been integrated within sections 150.06, 320.50–.56 (superseded by Statement on Auditing Standards No. 55), 320.59–.62 (superseded by Statement on Auditing Standards No. 55), 331.14, 350.46, 420.15, 901.01, 901.24, and 901.28.

[5] Statement on Auditing Standards No. 45 has created new sections 313, *Substantive Tests Prior to the Balance Sheet Date*; 334, *Related Parties*; and 557, *Supplementary Oil and Gas Reserve Information* (withdrawn by the issuance of Statement on Auditing Standards No. 52).

[6] Statement on Auditing Standards No. 48 has been integrated within sections 311.03, 311.09, 311.10, 318.07 (superseded by Statement on Auditing Standards No. 56), 320.33 and 320.34 (superseded by Statement on Auditing Standards No. 55), 320.37 (superseded by Statement on Auditing Standards No. 55), 320.57 and 320.58 (superseded by Statement on Auditing Standards No. 55), 320.65–.68 (superseded by Statement on Auditing Standards No. 55), and 326.12.

[7] Statement on Auditing Standards No. 52 has been integrated within sections 411.05–.08 (superseded by Statement on Auditing Standards No. 69) and 551.15 and has created a new section 558, *Required Supplementary Information*.

Statements on Auditing Standards—continued

No.	Date Issued	Title	Section
53	April 1988	The Auditor's Responsibility to Detect and Report Errors and Irregularities [Superseded by SAS 82]	
54	**April 1988**	**Illegal Acts by Clients**	**317**
55	**April 1988**	**Consideration of Internal Control in a Financial Statement Audit**	**319**
56	**April 1988**	**Analytical Procedures**	**329**
57	**April 1988**	**Auditing Accounting Estimates**	**342**
58	**April 1988**	**Reports on Audited Financial Statements**	**508**
59	**April 1988**	**The Auditor's Consideration of an Entity's Ability to Continue as a Going Concern**	**341**
60	**April 1988**	**Communication of Internal Control Related Matters Noted in an Audit**	**325**
61	**April 1988**	**Communication With Audit Committees**	**380**
62	**April 1989**	**Special Reports**	**623**
63	April 1989	Compliance Auditing Applicable to Governmental Entities and Other Recipients of Governmental Financial Assistance [Superseded by SAS 68]	
64	**Dec. 1990**	**Omnibus Statement on Auditing Standards—1990**[8]	
65	**April 1991**	**The Auditor's Consideration of the Internal Audit Function in an Audit of Financial Statements**	**322**
66	June 1991	Communication of Matters About Interim Financial Information Filed or to Be Filed With Specified Regulatory Agencies—An Amendment to SAS No. 36, *Review of Interim Financial Information* [Superseded by SAS 71]	
67	**Nov. 1991**	**The Confirmation Process**	**330**
68	Dec. 1991	Compliance Auditing Applicable to Governmental Entities and Other Recipients of Governmental Financial Assistance [Superseded by SAS 74]	
69	**Jan. 1992**	**The Meaning of *Present Fairly in Conformity With Generally Accepted Accounting Principles* in the Independent Auditor's Report**	**411**
70	**April 1992**	**Reports on the Processing of Transactions by Service Organizations**	**324**

[8] Statement on Auditing Standards No. 64 has been integrated within sections 341.12, 508.74 (formerly paragraph .83, renumbered and amended, effective for reports issued or reissued on or after February 29, 1996, by the issuance of Statement on Auditing Standards No. 79), and 543.16.

Statements on Auditing Standards—continued

No.	Date Issued	Title	Section
71	May 1992	Interim Financial Information	722
72	Feb. 1993	Letters for Underwriters and Certain Other Requesting Parties	634
73	July 1994	Using the Work of a Specialist	336
74	Feb. 1995	Compliance Auditing Considerations in Audits of Governmental Entities and Recipients of Governmental Financial Assistance	801
75	Sept. 1995	Engagements to Apply Agreed-Upon Procedures to Specified Elements, Accounts, or Items of a Financial Statement	622
76	Sept. 1995	Amendments to Statement on Auditing Standards No. 72, *Letters for Underwriters and Certain Other Requesting Parties*[9]	
77	Nov. 1995	Amendments to Statements on Auditing Standards No. 22, *Planning and Supervision*, No. 59, *The Auditor's Consideration of an Entity's Ability to Continue as a Going Concern*, and No. 62, *Special Reports*[10]	
78	Dec. 1995	Consideration of Internal Control in a Financial Statement Audit: An Amendment to Statement on Auditing Standards No. 55[11]	
79	Dec. 1995	Amendment to Statement on Auditing Standards No. 58, *Reports on Audited Financial Statements*[12]	
80	Dec. 1996	Amendment to Statement on Auditing Standards No. 31, *Evidential Matter*[13]	
81	Dec. 1996	Auditing Investments	332
82	Feb. 1997	Consideration of Fraud in a Financial Statement Audit	316
83	Oct. 1997	Establishing an Understanding With the Client[14]	

[9] Statement on Auditing Standards No. 76 has been integrated within section 634.01, 634.09, 634.10, 634.64, and AT section 300.01.

[10] Statement on Auditing Standards No. 77 has been integrated within sections 311.05, 341.13, 544.02, 544.04, 623.05, and 623.08.

[11] Statement on Auditing Standards No. 78 has been integrated within section 319.

[12] Statement on Auditing Standards No. 79 has been integrated within section 508.11, 508.19, 508.29–.32, 508.45–.49, 508.61, 508.62, and 508.74–.76.

[13] Statement on Auditing Standards No. 80 has been integrated within section 326.07, 326.12–.14, 326.16–.22, and 326.25.

[14] Statement on Auditing Standards No. 83 has been integrated within section 310.05–.07. Statement on Auditing Standards No. 1, section 310, as amended by Statement on Auditing Standards No. 45, *Omnibus Statement on Auditing Standards—1983*, "Substantive Tests Prior to the Balance-Sheet Date," has been moved to section 310A until the effective date of Statement on Auditing Standards No. 83.

Statements on Auditing Standards—continued

No.	Date Issued	Title	Section
84	Oct. 1997	**Communications Between Predecessor and Successor Auditors**	315
85	Nov. 1997	**Management Representations**	333

Statements on Standards for Attestation Engagements

No.	Date Issued	Title	Section
1[15]	Mar. 1986	**Attestation Standards**	100
1[15]	Dec. 1987	**Attest Services Related to MAS Engagements**	100.77–.81
1[15]	Oct. 1985	**Financial Forecasts and Projections**	200
1[15]	Sept. 1988	**Reporting on Pro Forma Financial Information**	300
2	May 1993	**Reporting on an Entity's Internal Control Over Financial Reporting**	400
3	Dec. 1993	**Compliance Attestation**	500
4	Sept. 1995	**Agreed-Upon Procedures Engagements**	600
5	Nov. 1995	**Amendment to Statement on Standards for Attestation Engagements No. 1, *Attestation Standards***	100.72–.76
6	Dec. 1995	**Reporting on an Entity's Internal Control Over Financial Reporting: An Amendment to Statement on Standards for Attestation Engagements**[16]	
7	Oct. 1997	**Establishing an Understanding With the Client**	100.32

[15] In January 1989, the Statements on Standards for Attestation Engagements *Attestation Standards* (AT section 100), *Financial Forecasts and Projections* (AT section 200), and *Reporting on Pro Forma Financial Information* (AT section 300), were codified in *Codification of Statements on Standards for Attestation Engagements*. In April 1993, the codified sections became Statement on Standards for Attestation Engagements No. 1, *Attestation Standards*.

[16] Statement on Standards for Attestation Engagements No. 6 has been integrated within AT section 400.

Part II

Sources of Sections in Current Text

Section	*Contents*	*Source*
100	**Introduction**	
110	Responsibilities and Functions of the Independent Auditor	SAS 1[*]
150	Generally Accepted Auditing Standards	SAS 1[*]
161	The Relationship of Generally Accepted Auditing Standards to Quality Control Standards	SAS 25
200	**The General Standards**	
201	Nature of the General Standards	SAS 1[*]
210	Training and Proficiency of the Independent Auditor	SAS 1[*]
220	Independence	SAS 1[*]
230	Due Professional Care in the Performance of Work	SAS 1[*]
300	**The Standards of Field Work**	
310	Appointment of the Independent Auditor	SAS 83[1]
310A	Relationship Between the Auditor's Appointment and Planning	SAS 1[*]
311	Planning and Supervision	SAS 22
312	Audit Risk and Materiality in Conducting an Audit	SAS 47
313	Substantive Tests Prior to the Balance-Sheet Date	SAS 45
315	Communications Between Predecessor and Successor Auditors	SAS 84[2]
315A	Communications Between Predecessor and Successor Auditors	SAS 7
316	Consideration of Fraud in a Financial Statement Audit	SAS 82
317	Illegal Acts By Clients	SAS 54
319	Consideration of Internal Control in a Financial Statement Audit	SAS 55
322	The Auditor's Consideration of the Internal Audit Function in an Audit of Financial Statements	SAS 65
324	Reports on the Processing of Transactions by Service Organizations	SAS 70
325	Communication of Internal Control Related Matters Noted in an Audit	SAS 60

[*] Portions of Statement on Auditing Standards No. 1 have been superseded by subsequent pronouncements. See Part III.

[1] Statement on Auditing Standards No. 1, section 310 has been amended by Statement on Auditing Standards No. 83, which has been integrated within section 310. Statement on Auditing Standards No. 1, section 310, as amended by Statement on Auditing Standards No. 45, *Omnibus Statement on Auditing Standards—1983*, "Substantive Tests Prior to the Balance-Sheet Date," has been moved to section 310A until the effective date of Statement on Auditing Standards No. 83.

[2] Statement on Auditing Standards No. 7 has been superseded by Statement on Auditing Standards No. 84 at section 315. Statement on Auditing Standards No. 7, as amended, has been moved to section 315A until the effective date of Statement on Auditing Standards No. 84.

Section	*Contents*	*Source*
326	Evidential Matter	SAS 31
329	Analytical Procedures	SAS 56
330	The Confirmation Process	SAS 67
331	Inventories	SAS 1*
332	Auditing Investments	SAS 81
333	Management Representations	SAS 85[3]
333A	Client Representations	SAS 19
334	Related Parties	SAS 45
336	Using the Work of a Specialist	SAS 73
337	Inquiry of a Client's Lawyer Concerning Litigation, Claims, and Assessments	SAS 12
339	Working Papers	SAS 41
341	The Auditor's Consideration of an Entity's Ability to Continue as a Going Concern	SAS 59
342	Auditing Accounting Estimates	SAS 57
350	Audit Sampling	SAS 39
380	Communications With Audit Committees	SAS 61
390	Consideration of Omitted Procedures After the Report Date	SAS 46
400	**The First, Second, and Third Standards of Reporting**	
410	Adherence to Generally Accepted Accounting Principles	SAS 1*
411	The Meaning of *Present Fairly in Conformity With Generally Accepted Accounting Principles* in the Independent Auditor's Report	SAS 69
420	Consistency of Application of Generally Accepted Accounting Principles	SAS 1*
431	Adequacy of Disclosure in Financial Statements	SAS 32
435	Segment Information	SAS 21
500	**The Fourth Standard of Reporting**	
504	Association With Financial Statements	SAS 26
508	Reports on Audited Financial Statements	SAS 58
530	Dating of the Independent Auditor's Report	SAS 1*
534	Reporting on Financial Statements Prepared for Use in Other Countries	SAS 51
543	Part of Audit Performed by Other Independent Auditors	SAS 1*
544	Lack of Conformity With Generally Accepted Accounting Principles	SAS 1*
550	Other Information in Documents Containing Audited Financial Statements	SAS 8

* Portions of Statement on Auditing Standards No. 1 have been superseded by subsequent pronouncements. See Part III.

[3] Statement on Auditing Standards No. 19 has been superseded by Statement on Auditing Standards No. 85 at section 333. Statement on Auditing Standards No. 19, as originally issued in June 1977, has been moved to section 333A until the effective date of Statement on Auditing Standards No. 85. The former section 333A containing the appendix to Statement on Auditing Standards No. 19 has been incorporated into the new section 333A.14.

Section	Contents	Source
551	Reporting on Information Accompanying the Basic Financial Statements in Auditor-Submitted Documents	SAS 29
552	Reporting on Condensed Financial Statements and Selected Financial Data	SAS 42
558	Required Supplementary Information	SAS 52
560	Subsequent Events	SAS 1*
561	Subsequent Discovery of Facts Existing at the Date of the Auditor's Report	SAS 1*
600	**Other Types of Reports**	
622	Engagements to Apply Agreed-Upon Procedures to Specified Elements, Accounts, or Items of a Financial Statement	SAS 75
623	Special Reports	SAS 62
625	Reports on the Application of Accounting Principles	SAS 50
634	Letters for Underwriters and Certain Other Requesting Parties	SAS 72
700	**Special Topics**	
711	Filings Under Federal Securities Statutes	SAS 37
722	Interim Financial Information	SAS 71
800	**Compliance Auditing**	
801	Compliance Auditing Considerations in Audits of Governmental Entities and Recipients of Governmental Financial Assistance	SAS 74
900	**Special Reports of the Committee on Auditing Procedure**	
901	Public Warehouses—Controls and Auditing Procedures for Goods Held	SAS 1*

Statements on Standards for Attestation Engagements

AT Section	Contents	Source
100	Attestation Standards	SSAE 1
100.32	Establishing an Understanding With the Client	SSAE 7
100.72–.76	Amendment to Statement on Standards for Attestation Engagements No. 1, *Attestation Standards*	SSAE 5
100.77–.81	Attest Services Related to MAS Engagements	SSAE 1
200	Financial Forecasts and Projections	SSAE 1
300	Reporting on Pro Forma Financial Information	SSAE 1
400	Reporting on an Entity's Internal Control Over Financial Reporting	SSAE 2
500	Compliance Attestation	SSAE 3
600	Agreed-Upon Procedures Engagements	SSAE 4

* Portions of Statement on Auditing Standards No. 1 have been superseded by subsequent pronouncements. See Part III.

Part III

List of Sections in Statement on Auditing Standards No. 1, Codification of Auditing Standards and Procedures*

Section	*Title*[1]
100	*Introduction*
110	**Responsibilities and Functions of the Independent Auditor**
150	**Generally Accepted Auditing Standards**
200	*The General Standards*
201	**Nature of the General Standards**
210	**Training and Proficiency of the Independent Auditor**
220	**Independence**
230	**Due Professional Care in the Performance of Work**[1]
300	*The Standards of Field Work*
310	**Appointment of the Independent Auditor**[1]
320	The Auditor's Study and Evaluation of Internal Control [Superseded by SAS 55]
320A	Appendix A—Relationship of Statistical Sampling to Generally Accepted Auditing Standards [Superseded by SAS 39]
320B	Appendix B—Precision and Reliability for Statistical Sampling in Auditing [Superseded by SAS 39]
330	Evidential Matter [Superseded by SAS 31]
331	**Inventories**[1]
332	Evidential Matter for Long-Term Investments [Superseded by SAS 81]
338	Working Papers [Superseded by SAS 41]
400	*The First, Second and Third Standards of Reporting*
410	**Adherence to Generally Accepted Accounting Principles**
420	**Consistency of Application of Generally Accepted Accounting Principles**
430	Adequacy of Informative Disclosure [Superseded by SAS 32]
500	*The Fourth Standard of Reporting*
510	Expression of Opinion in the Auditor's Report [Superseded by SAS 2]
511	Unqualified Opinion [Superseded by SAS 2]
512	Qualified Opinion [Superseded by SAS 2]
513	Adverse Opinion [Superseded by SAS 2]
514	Disclaimer of Opinion [Superseded by SAS 2]
515	Piecemeal Opinion [Superseded by SAS 2]
516	Unaudited Financial Statements [Superseded by SAS 26]
517	Reporting When a Certified Public Accountant Is Not Independent [Superseded by SAS 26]
518	Negative Assurance [Superseded by SAS 26]

* Outstanding sections are listed in **boldface** type.

[1] Current section titles are listed. Section titles reflect amendments and conforming changes resulting from subsequent pronouncements.

Section	*Title*[1]
530	**Dating of the Independent Auditor's Report**
535	Opinions on Prior Year's Statements [Superseded by SAS 2]
540	Circumstances Which Require a Departure From the Standard Short-Form Report [Superseded by SAS 2]
541	Restrictions Imposed by the Client [Superseded by SAS 2]
542	Other Conditions Which Preclude the Application of Necessary Auditing Procedures [Superseded by SAS 58]
543	**Part of Audit Performed by Other Independent Auditors**[1]
544	**Lack of Conformity With Generally Accepted Accounting Principles**
545	Inadequate Disclosure [Superseded by SAS 58]
546	Reporting on Inconsistency [Superseded by SAS 58]
547	Unusual Uncertainties as to the Effect of Future Developments on Certain Items [Superseded by SAS 2]
560	**Subsequent Events**
561	**Subsequent Discovery of Facts Existing at the Date of the Auditor's Report**
600	*Other Types of Reports*
610	Long-Form Reports [Superseded by SAS 29]
620	Special Reports [Superseded by SAS 14]
630	Letters for Underwriters [Superseded by SAS 38]
640	Reports on Internal Control [Superseded by SAS 30]
641	Reports on Internal Control Based on Criteria Established by Governmental Agencies [Superseded by SAS 30]
700	*Special Topics*
710	Filings Under Federal Securities Statutes [Superseded by SAS 37]
900	*Special Reports of the Committee on Auditing Procedure*
901	**Public Warehouses—Controls and Auditing Procedures for Goods Held**[1]

---

[1] Current section titles are listed. Section titles reflect amendments and conforming changes resulting from subsequent pronouncements.

AU Section 100

STATEMENTS ON AUDITING STANDARDS — Introduction

Statements on Auditing Standards are issued by the Auditing Standards Board, the senior technical body of the Institute designated to issue pronouncements on auditing matters. Rule 202 of the Institute's Code of Professional Conduct requires adherence to the applicable generally accepted auditing standards promulgated by the Institute. It recognizes Statements on Auditing Standards as interpretations of generally accepted auditing standards and requires that members be prepared to justify departures from such Statements.

Interpretations are issued by the Audit Issues Task Force of the Auditing Standards Board to provide timely guidance on the application of pronouncements of that Board. Interpretations are reviewed by the Auditing Standards Board. An interpretation is not as authoritative as a pronouncement of that Board, but members should be aware that they may have to justify a departure from an interpretation if the quality of their work is questioned.

. . . responsibilities and functions of independent auditor . . . generally accepted auditing standards . . . quality control standards . . .

TABLE OF CONTENTS

AU Section 110

Responsibilities and Functions of the Independent Auditor

Source: SAS No. 1, section 110; SAS No. 78; SAS No. 82.

Issue date, unless otherwise indicated: November, 1972.

.01 The objective of the ordinary audit of financial statements by the independent auditor is the expression of an opinion on the fairness with which they present, in all material respects, financial position, results of operations, and its cash flows in conformity with generally accepted accounting principles. The auditor's report is the medium through which he expresses his opinion or, if circumstances require, disclaims an opinion. In either case, he states whether his audit has been made in accordance with generally accepted auditing standards. These standards require him to state whether, in his opinion, the financial statements are presented in conformity with generally accepted accounting principles and to identify those circumstances in which such principles have not been consistently observed in the preparation of the financial statements of the current period in relation to those of the preceding period.

Distinction Between Responsibilities of Auditor and Management

.02 The auditor has a responsibility to plan and perform the audit to obtain reasonable assurance about whether the financial statements are free of material misstatement, whether caused by error or fraud.[1] Because of the nature of audit evidence and the characteristics of fraud, the auditor is able to obtain reasonable, but not absolute, assurance that material misstatements are detected.[2] The auditor has no responsibility to plan and perform the audit to obtain reasonable assurance that misstatements, whether caused by errors or fraud, that are not material to the financial statements are detected. [Paragraph added, effective for audits of financial statements for periods ending on or after December 15, 1997, by Statement on Auditing Standards No. 82.]

.03 The financial statements are management's responsibility. The auditor's responsibility is to express an opinion on the financial statements. Man-

---

[1] See section 312, *Audit Risk and Materiality in Conducting an Audit*, and section 316, *Consideration of Fraud in a Financial Statement Audit*. The auditor's consideration of illegal acts and responsibility for detecting misstatements resulting from illegal acts is defined in section 317, *Illegal Acts by Clients*. For those illegal acts that are defined in that section as having a direct and material effect on the determination of financial statement amounts, the auditor's responsibility to detect misstatements resulting from such illegal acts is the same as that for error or fraud. [Footnote added, effective for audits of financial statements for periods ending on or after December 15, 1997, by Statement on Auditing Standards No. 82.]

[2] See section 230, *Due Professional Care in the Performance of Work*, paragraphs .10 through .13. [Footnote added, effective for audits of financial statements for periods ending on or after December 15, 1997, by Statement on Auditing Standards No. 82.]

agement is responsible for adopting sound accounting policies and for establishing and maintaining internal control that will, among other things, record, process, summarize, and report transactions (as well as events and conditions) consistent with management's assertions embodied in the financial statements. The entity's transactions and the related assets, liabilities, and equity are within the direct knowledge and control of management. The auditor's knowledge of these matters and internal control is limited to that acquired through the audit. Thus, the fair presentation of financial statements in conformity with generally accepted accounting principles[3] is an implicit and integral part of management's responsibility. The independent auditor may make suggestions about the form or content of the financial statements or draft them, in whole or in part, based on information from management during the performance of the audit. However, the auditor's responsibility for the financial statements he or she has audited is confined to the expression of his or her opinion on them. [Paragraph amended to reflect the conforming changes necessary due to the issuance of Statement on Auditing Standards Nos. 53 through 62. As amended, effective for audits of financial statements for periods beginning on or after January 1, 1997, by Statement on Auditing Standards No. 78. Paragraph renumbered by the issuance of Statement on Auditing Standards No. 82, February 1997.]

Professional Qualifications

.04 The professional qualifications required of the independent auditor are those of a person with the education and experience to practice as such. They do not include those of a person trained for or qualified to engage in another profession or occupation. For example, the independent auditor, in observing the taking of a physical inventory, does not purport to act as an appraiser, a valuer, or an expert in materials. Similarly, although the independent auditor is informed in a general manner about matters of commercial law, he does not purport to act in the capacity of a lawyer and may appropriately rely upon the advice of attorneys in all matters of law. [Paragraph renumbered by the issuance of Statement on Auditing Standards No. 82, February 1997.]

.05 In the observance of generally accepted auditing standards, the independent auditor must exercise his judgment in determining which auditing procedures are necessary in the circumstances to afford a reasonable basis for his opinion. His judgment is required to be the informed judgment of a qualified professional person. [Paragraph renumbered by the issuance of Statement on Auditing Standards No. 82, February 1997.]

Detection of Fraud

[.06–.09] [Superseded January 1977 by Statement on Auditing Standards No. 16, as superseded by Statement on Auditing Standards No. 53, as superseded by section 316. Paragraphs renumbered by the issuance of Statement on Auditing Standards No. 82, February 1997.]

---

[3] The responsibilities and functions of the independent auditor are also applicable to financial statements presented in conformity with a comprehensive basis of accounting other than generally accepted accounting principles; references in this section to financial statements presented in conformity with generally accepted accounting principles also include those presentations. [Footnote added, effective for audits of financial statements for periods beginning on or after January 1, 1997, by Statement on Auditing Standards No. 78. Footnote renumbered by the issuance of Statement on Auditing Standards No. 82, February 1997.]

Responsibility to the Profession

.10 The independent auditor also has a responsibility to his profession, the responsibility to comply with the standards accepted by his fellow practitioners. In recognition of the importance of such compliance, the American Institute of Certified Public Accountants has adopted, as part of its Code of Professional Conduct, rules which support the standards and provide a basis for their enforcement. [Paragraph renumbered by the issuance of Statement on Auditing Standards No. 82, February 1997.]

AU Section 150

Generally Accepted Auditing Standards

Sources: SAS No. 1, section 150; SAS No. 43.

Issue date, unless otherwise indicated: November, 1972.

.01 Auditing standards differ from auditing procedures in that "procedures" relate to acts to be performed, whereas "standards" deal with measures of the quality of the performance of those acts and the objectives to be attained by the use of the procedures undertaken. *Auditing standards* as distinct from *auditing procedures* concern themselves not only with the auditor's professional qualities but also with the judgment exercised by him in the performance of his audit and in his report.

.02 The generally accepted auditing standards as approved and adopted by the membership of the American Institute of Certified Public Accountants are as follows:

General Standards

1. The audit is to be performed by a person or persons having adequate technical training and proficiency as an auditor.
2. In all matters relating to the assignment, an independence in mental attitude is to be maintained by the auditor or auditors.
3. Due professional care is to be exercised in the performance of the audit and the preparation of the report.

Standards of Field Work

1. The work is to be adequately planned and assistants, if any, are to be properly supervised.
2. A sufficient understanding of internal control is to be obtained to plan the audit and to determine the nature, timing, and extent of tests to be performed.
3. Sufficient competent evidential matter is to be obtained through inspection, observation, inquiries, and confirmations to afford a reasonable basis for an opinion regarding the financial statements under audit.

Standards of Reporting

1. The report shall state whether the financial statements are presented in accordance with generally accepted accounting principles.
2. The report shall identify those circumstances in which such principles have not been consistently observed in the current period in relation to the preceding period.
3. Informative disclosures in the financial statements are to be regarded as reasonably adequate unless otherwise stated in the report.

4. The report shall either contain an expression of opinion regarding the financial statements, taken as a whole, or an assertion to the effect that an opinion cannot be expressed. When an overall opinion cannot be expressed, the reasons therefor should be stated. In all cases where an auditor's name is associated with financial statements, the report should contain a clear-cut indication of the character of the auditor's work, if any, and the degree of responsibility the auditor is taking.

.03 These standards to a great extent are interrelated and interdependent. Moreover, the circumstances which are germane to a determination of whether one standard is met may apply equally to another. "Materiality" and "audit risk" underlie the application of all the standards, particularly the standards of field work and reporting.*

.04 The concept of materiality is inherent in the work of the independent auditor. There should be stronger grounds to sustain the independent auditor's opinion with respect to those items which are relatively more important and with respect to those in which the possibilities of material misstatement are greater than with respect to those of lesser importance or those in which the possibility of material misstatement is remote. For example, in an entity with few, but large, accounts receivable, the accounts individually are more important and the possibility of material misstatement is greater than in another entity that has a great number of small accounts aggregating the same total. In industrial and merchandising enterprises, inventories are usually of great importance to both financial position and results of operations and accordingly may require relatively more attention by the auditor than would the inventories of a public utility company. Similarly, accounts receivable usually will receive more attention than prepaid insurance.

.05 The consideration of audit risk has an important bearing on the nature of the audit.* Cash transactions are more susceptible to fraud than inventories, and the work undertaken on cash may therefore have to be carried out in a more conclusive manner without necessarily implying a greater expenditure of time. Arm's-length transactions with outside parties are usually subjected to less detailed scrutiny than intercompany transactions or transactions with officers and employees, where the same degree of disinterested dealing cannot be assumed. The effect of internal control on the scope of an audit is an outstanding example of the influence on auditing procedures of a greater or lesser degree of risk of misstatement; i.e., the more effective the internal control, the less the degree of control risk.

Services Other Than Audits of Financial Statements

.06 In addition to audits of financial statements, the ten generally accepted auditing standards, to the extent that they are relevant in the circumstances, apply to all other services governed by Statements on Auditing Standards unless the Statement specifies otherwise. [As amended, effective after August 31, 1982, by Statement on Auditing Standards No. 43.]

---

* Editor's Note: See section 312, *Audit Risk and Materiality in Conducting an Audit*.

AU Section 161

The Relationship of Generally Accepted Auditing Standards to Quality Control Standards

(Supersedes Statement on Auditing Standards No. 4, *Quality Control Considerations for a Firm of Independent Auditors*)[1]

Source: SAS No. 25.

Issue date, unless otherwise indicated: November, 1979.

.01 The independent auditor is responsible for compliance with generally accepted auditing standards in an audit engagement. Rule 202 [ET section 202.01] of the Rules of Conduct of the Code of Professional Conduct of the American Institute of Certified Public Accountants requires members to comply with such standards when associated with financial statements.

.02 A firm of independent auditors also needs to comply with generally accepted auditing standards in conducting an audit practice. Thus, a firm should establish quality control policies and procedures to provide it with reasonable assurance of conforming with generally accepted auditing standards in its audit engagements. The nature and extent of a firm's quality control policies and procedures depend on factors such as its size, the degree of operating autonomy allowed its personnel and its practice offices, the nature of its practice, its organization, and appropriate cost-benefit considerations.

.03 Generally accepted auditing standards relate to the conduct of individual audit engagements; quality control standards relate to the conduct of a firm's audit practice as a whole. Thus, generally accepted auditing standards and quality control standards are related, and the quality control policies and procedures that a firm adopts may affect both the conduct of individual audit engagements and the conduct of a firm's audit practice as a whole.

---

[1] The elements of quality control identified in SAS No. 4 have been incorporated in the body of Statement on Quality Control Standards (SQCS) No. 2, *System of Quality Control for a CPA Firm's Accounting and Auditing Practice* [QC section 20], issued by the Auditing Standards Board. Firms that are enrolled in an Institute-approved practice-monitoring program are obligated to adhere to quality control standards established by the Institute. (SQCS No. 1, *System of Quality Control for a CPA Firm*, was superseded by the issuance of SQCS No. 2 [QC section 20]). [Footnote revised, July 1997, by issuance of Statement on Quality Control Standards No. 2.]

AU Section 200

THE GENERAL STANDARDS

. . . nature of standards . . . training and proficiency of auditor . . . independence . . . performance of work . . .

TABLE OF CONTENTS

Section		Paragraph
201	Nature of the General Standards	.01
210	Training and Proficiency of the Independent Auditor	.01-.05
220	Independence	.01-.07
230	Due Professional Care in the Performance of Work	.01-.13
	Professional Skepticism	.07-.09
	Reasonable Assurance	.10-.13

AU Section 201

Nature of the General Standards

Source: SAS No. 1, section 201.

Issue date, unless otherwise indicated: November, 1972.

.01 The general standards are personal in nature and are concerned with the qualifications of the auditor and the quality of his work as distinct from those standards which relate to the performance of his field work and to his reporting. These personal, or general, standards apply alike to the areas of field work and reporting.

AU Section 210

Training and Proficiency of the Independent Auditor

Sources: SAS No. 1, section 210; SAS No. 5.

Issue date, unless otherwise indicated: November, 1972.

.01 The first general standard is:

> The audit is to be performed by a person or persons having adequate technical training and proficiency as an auditor.

.02 This standard recognizes that however capable a person may be in other fields, including business and finance, he cannot meet the requirements of the auditing standards without proper education and experience in the field of auditing.

.03 In the performance of the audit which leads to an opinion, the independent auditor holds himself out as one who is proficient in accounting and auditing. The attainment of that proficiency begins with the auditor's formal education and extends into his subsequent experience. The independent auditor must undergo training adequate to meet the requirements of a professional. This training must be adequate in technical scope and should include a commensurate measure of general education. The junior assistant, just entering upon an auditing career, must obtain his professional experience with the proper supervision and review of his work by a more experienced superior. The nature and extent of supervision and review must necessarily reflect wide variances in practice. The auditor charged with final responsibility for the engagement must exercise a seasoned judgment in the varying degrees of his supervision and review of the work done and judgment exercised by his subordinates, who in turn must meet the responsibility attaching to the varying gradations and functions of their work.

.04 The independent auditor's formal education and professional experience complement one another; each auditor exercising authority upon an engagement should weigh these attributes in determining the extent of his supervision of subordinates and review of their work. It should be recognized that the training of a professional man includes a continual awareness of developments taking place in business and in his profession. He must study, understand, and apply new pronouncements on accounting principles and auditing procedures as they are developed by authoritative bodies within the accounting profession.

.05 In the course of his day-to-day practice, the independent auditor encounters a wide range of judgment on the part of management, varying from true objective judgment to the occasional extreme of deliberate misstatement. He is retained to audit and report upon the financial statements of a business because, through his training and experience, he has become skilled in accounting and auditing and has acquired the ability to consider objectively and to exercise independent judgment with respect to the information recorded in books of account or otherwise disclosed by his audit. [As amended July, 1975 by Statement on Auditing Standards No. 5.]

AU Section 220

Independence

Source: SAS No. 1, section 220.

Issue date, unless otherwise indicated: November, 1972.

.01 The second general standard is:

> In all matters relating to the assignment, an independence in mental attitude is to be maintained by the auditor or auditors.

.02 This standard requires that the auditor be independent; aside from being in public practice (as distinct from being in private practice), he must be without bias with respect to the client since otherwise he would lack that impartiality necessary for the dependability of his findings, however excellent his technical proficiency may be. However, independence does not imply the attitude of a prosecutor but rather a judicial impartiality that recognizes an obligation for fairness not only to management and owners of a business but also to creditors and those who may otherwise rely (in part, at least) upon the independent auditor's report, as in the case of prospective owners or creditors.

.03 It is of utmost importance to the profession that the general public maintain confidence in the independence of independent auditors. Public confidence would be impaired by evidence that independence was actually lacking, and it might also be impaired by the existence of circumstances which reasonable people might believe likely to influence independence. To *be* independent, the auditor must be intellectually honest; to be *recognized* as independent, he must be free from any obligation to or interest in the client, its management, or its owners. For example, an independent auditor auditing a company of which he was also a director might be intellectually honest, but it is unlikely that the public would accept him as independent since he would be in effect auditing decisions which he had a part in making. Likewise, an auditor with a substantial financial interest in a company might be unbiased in expressing his opinion on the financial statements of the company, but the public would be reluctant to believe that he was unbiased. Independent auditors should not only be independent in fact; they should avoid situations that may lead outsiders to doubt their independence.

.04 The profession has established, through the AICPA's Code of Professional Conduct, precepts to guard against the *presumption* of loss of independence. "Presumption" is stressed because the possession of intrinsic independence is a matter of personal quality rather than of rules that formulate certain objective tests. Insofar as these precepts have been incorporated in the profession's code, they have the force of professional law for the independent auditor.

.05 The Securities and Exchange Commission has also adopted requirements for independence of auditors who report on financial statements filed with it that differ from the AICPA requirements in certain respects. [As modified, November 1979, by the Auditing Standards Board.]

.06 The independent auditor should administer his practice within the spirit of these precepts and rules if he is to achieve a proper degree of independence in the conduct of his work.

.07 To emphasize independence from management, many corporations follow the practice of having the independent auditor appointed by the board of directors or elected by the stockholders.

AU Section 230

*Due Professional Care in the Performance of Work**

Sources: SAS No. 1, section 230; SAS No. 41; SAS No. 82.

Issue date, unless otherwise indicated: November, 1972.

.01 The third general standard is:

> Due professional care is to be exercised in the planning and performance of the audit and the preparation of the report.[1]

[As amended, effective for audits of financial statements for periods ending on or after December 15, 1997, by Statement on Auditing Standards No. 82.]

.02 This standard requires the independent auditor to plan and perform his or her work with due professional care. Due professional care imposes a responsibility upon each professional within an independent auditor's organization to observe the standards of field work and reporting. [As amended, effective for audits of financial statements for periods ending on or after December 15, 1997, by Statement on Auditing Standards No. 82.]

.03 *Cooley on Torts*, a legal treatise, describes the obligation for due care as follows:

> Every man who offers his services to another and is employed assumes the duty to exercise in the employment such skill as he possesses with reasonable care and diligence. In all these employments where peculiar skill is requisite, if one offers his services, he is understood as holding himself out to the public as possessing the degree of skill commonly possessed by others in the same employment, and if his pretentions are unfounded, he commits a species of fraud upon every man who employs him in reliance on his public profession. But no man, whether skilled or unskilled, undertakes that the task he assumes shall be performed successfully, and without fault or error; he undertakes for good faith and integrity, but not for infallibility, and he is liable to his employer for negligence, bad faith, or dishonesty, but not for losses consequent upon pure errors of judgment.[2]

[As amended, effective for audits of financial statements for periods ending on or after December 15, 1997, by Statement on Auditing Standards No. 82.]

.04 The matter of due professional care concerns what the independent auditor does and how well he or she does it. The quotation from *Cooley on Torts*

---

* [Title amended, effective for audits of financial statements for periods ending on or after December 15, 1997, by Statement on Auditing Standards No. 82.]

[1] This amendment revises the third general standard of the ten generally accepted auditing standards. [Footnote added, effective for audits of financial statements for periods ending on or after December 15, 1997, by Statement on Auditing Standards No. 82.]

[2] D. Haggard, *Cooley on Torts*, 472 (4th ed., 1932). [Footnote added, effective for audits of financial statements for periods ending on or after December 15, 1997, by Statement on Auditing Standards No. 82.]

provides a source from which an auditor's responsibility for conducting an audit with due professional care can be derived. The remainder of the section discusses the auditor's responsibility in the context of an audit. [As amended, April 1982, by Statement on Auditing Standards No. 41 (see section 339). As amended, effective for audits of financial statements for periods ending on or after December 15, 1997, by Statement on Auditing Standards No. 82.]

.05 An auditor should possess "the degree of skill commonly possessed" by other auditors and should exercise it with "reasonable care and diligence" (that is, with due professional care). [Paragraph added, effective for audits of financial statements for periods ending on or after December 15, 1997, by Statement on Auditing Standards No. 82.]

.06 Auditors should be assigned to tasks and supervised commensurate with their level of knowledge, skill, and ability so that they can evaluate the audit evidence they are examining. The auditor with final responsibility for the engagement should know, at a minimum, the relevant professional accounting and auditing standards and should be knowledgeable about the client.[3] The auditor with final responsibility is responsible for the assignment of tasks to, and supervision of, assistants.[4] [Paragraph added, effective for audits of financial statements for periods ending on or after December 15, 1997, by Statement on Auditing Standards No. 82.]

Professional Skepticism

.07 Due professional care requires the auditor to exercise *professional skepticism*. Professional skepticism is an attitude that includes a questioning mind and a critical assessment of audit evidence. The auditor uses the knowledge, skill, and ability called for by the profession of public accounting to diligently perform, in good faith and with integrity, the gathering and objective evaluation of evidence. [Paragraph added, effective for audits of financial statements for periods ending on or after December 15, 1997, by Statement on Auditing Standards No. 82.]

.08 Gathering and objectively evaluating audit evidence requires the auditor to consider the competency and sufficiency of the evidence. Since evidence is gathered and evaluated throughout the audit, professional skepticism should be exercised throughout the audit process. [Paragraph added, effective for audits of financial statements for periods ending on or after December 15, 1997, by Statement on Auditing Standards No. 82.]

.09 The auditor neither assumes that management is dishonest nor assumes unquestioned honesty. In exercising professional skepticism, the auditor should not be satisfied with less than persuasive evidence because of a belief that management is honest. [Paragraph added, effective for audits of financial statements for periods ending on or after December 15, 1997, by Statement on Auditing Standards No. 82.]

Reasonable Assurance

.10 The exercise of due professional care allows the auditor to obtain *reasonable assurance* that the financial statements are free of material mis-

---

[3] See section 311, *Planning and Supervision*, paragraph .07. [Footnote added, effective for audits of financial statements for periods ending on or after December 15, 1997, by Statement on Auditing Standards No. 82.]

[4] See section 311.11. [Footnote added, effective for audits of financial statements for periods ending on or after December 15, 1997, by Statement on Auditing Standards No. 82.]

statement, whether caused by error or fraud. Absolute assurance is not attainable because of the nature of audit evidence and the characteristics of fraud. Therefore, an audit conducted in accordance with generally accepted auditing standards may not detect a material misstatement. [Paragraph added, effective for audits of financial statements for periods ending on or after December 15, 1997, by Statement on Auditing Standards No. 82.]

.11 The independent auditor's objective is to obtain sufficient competent evidential matter to provide him or her with a reasonable basis for forming an opinion. The nature of most evidence derives, in part, from the concept of selective testing of the data being audited, which involves judgment regarding both the areas to be tested and the nature, timing, and extent of the tests to be performed. In addition, judgment is required in interpreting the results of audit testing and evaluating audit evidence. Even with good faith and integrity, mistakes and errors in judgment can be made. Furthermore, accounting presentations contain accounting estimates, the measurement of which is inherently uncertain and depends on the outcome of future events. The auditor exercises professional judgment in evaluating the reasonableness of accounting estimates based on information that could reasonably be expected to be available prior to the completion of field work.[5] As a result of these factors, in the great majority of cases, the auditor has to rely on evidence that is persuasive rather than convincing.[6] [Paragraph added, effective for audits of financial statements for periods ending on or after December 15, 1997, by Statement on Auditing Standards No. 82.]

.12 Because of the characteristics of fraud, particularly those involving concealment and falsified documentation (including forgery), a properly planned and performed audit may not detect a material misstatement. For example, an audit conducted in accordance with generally accepted auditing standards rarely involves authentication of documentation, nor are auditors trained as or expected to be experts in such authentication. Also, auditing procedures may be ineffective for detecting an intentional misstatement that is concealed through collusion among client personnel and third parties or among management or employees of the client. [Paragraph added, effective for audits of financial statements for periods ending on or after December 15, 1997, by Statement on Auditing Standards No. 82.]

.13 Since the auditor's opinion on the financial statements is based on the concept of obtaining reasonable assurance, the auditor is not an insurer and his or her report does not constitute a guarantee. Therefore, the subsequent discovery that a material misstatement, whether from error or fraud, exists in the financial statements does not, in and of itself, evidence (*a*) failure to obtain reasonable assurance, (*b*) inadequate planning, performance, or judgment, (*c*) the absence of due professional care, or (*d*) a failure to comply with generally accepted auditing standards. [Paragraph added, effective for audits of financial statements for periods ending on or after December 15, 1997, by Statement on Auditing Standards No. 82.]

---

[5] See section 342, *Auditing Accounting Estimates*, paragraph .22. [Footnote added, effective for audits of financial statements for periods ending on or after December 15, 1997, by Statement on Auditing Standards No. 82.]

[6] See section 326, *Evidential Matter*. [Footnote added, effective for audits of financial statements for periods ending on or after December 15, 1997, by Statement on Auditing Standards No. 82.]

AU Section 300

THE STANDARDS OF FIELD WORK

. . . appointment of the independent auditor . . . auditor's appointment and planning . . . planning and supervision . . . audit risk and materiality . . . substantive tests prior to balance-sheet date . . . predecessor and successor auditors . . . fraud in a financial statement audit . . . errors and irregularities . . . illegal acts by clients . . . internal control . . . internal audit function . . . reports on the processing of transactions by service organizations . . . communication of internal control . . . evidential matter . . . analytical procedures . . . confirmation process . . . receivables and inventories . . . auditing investments . . . management representations . . . client representations . . . related parties . . . using work of specialist . . . inquiry of client's lawyer . . . working papers . . . entity's continued existence . . . auditing accounting estimates . . . audit sampling . . . communication with audit committees . . . omitted procedures after report date . . .

TABLE OF CONTENTS

Section		*Paragraph*
310	Appointment of the Independent Auditor	.01-.07
	Appointment of the Independent Auditor	.03
	Appointment of the Auditor Near or After the Year-End Date . . .	.04
	Establishing an Understanding With the Client	.05-.07
310A	Relationship Between the Auditor's Appointment and Planning	.01-.04
	Appointment of the Independent Auditor	.03
	Appointment of Auditor Near or After the Year-End Date	.04
311	Planning and Supervision	.01-.15
	Planning.	.03-.10
	Supervision	.11-.14
	Effective Date	.15
9311	Planning and Supervision: Auditing Interpretations of Section 311	
	1. Communications Between the Auditor and Firm Personnel Responsible for Non-Audit Services (2/80)	.01-.03

Section		Paragraph
9311	Planning and Supervision: Auditing Interpretations of Section 311—continued	
	[2.] Planning Considerations for an Audit of a Federally Assisted Program (4/81) [Withdrawn March, 1989]	[.04-.34]
	3. Responsibility of Assistance for the Resolution of Accounting and Auditing Issues (2/86)	.35-.37
	4. Audit Considerations for the Year 2000 Issue (1/98)	.38-.47
312	Audit Risk and Materiality in Conducting an Audit	.01-.41
	Planning the Audit	.12-.33
	Considerations at the Financial Statements Level	.13-.23
	Considerations at the Individual Account-Balance or Class-of-Transactions Level	.24-.33
	Evaluating Audit Findings	.34-.40
	Effective Date	.41
313	Substantive Tests Prior to the Balance-Sheet Date	.01-.10
	Factors to Be Considered Before Applying Principal Substantive Tests to the Details of Balance-Sheet Accounts at Interim Dates	.04-.07
	Extending Audit Conclusions to the Balance-Sheet Date	.08-.09
	Coordinating the Timing of Auditing Procedures	.10
315	Communications Between Predecessor and Successor Auditors	.01-.25
	Introduction	.01-.02
	Change of Auditors	.03-.11
	Communications Before Successor Auditor Accepts Engagement	.07-.10
	Other Communications	.11
	Successor Auditor's Use of Communications	.12-.13
	Audits of Financial Statements That Have Been Previously Audited	.14-.20
	Discovery of Possible Misstatements in Financial Statements Reported on by a Predecessor Auditor	.21-.22
	Effective Date	.23
	Appendix A: Illustrative Client Consent and Acknowledgment Letter	.24
	Appendix B: Illustrative Successor Auditor Acknowledgment Letter	.25
315A	Communications Between Predecessor and Successor Auditors	.01-.12
	Communications Before Successor Accepts Engagement	.04-.07
	Other Communications	.08-.09
	Financial Statements Reported on by Predecessor	.10
	Effective Date	.12

Section		Paragraph
9315A	Communications Between Predecessor and Successor Auditors: Auditing Interpretations of Section 315A	
	1. Determining the Predecessor Auditor (5/85)	.01-.05
	2. Restating Financial Statements Reported on by a Predecessor Auditor (9/86)	.06-.07
	3. Auditors of Financial Statements That Had Been Previously Audited by a Predecessor Auditor (4/95)	.08-.18
316	Consideration of Fraud in a Financial Statement Audit	.01-.41
	Introduction	.01-.02
	Description and Characteristics of Fraud	.03-.10
	Assessment of the Risk of Material Misstatement Due to Fraud	.11-.25
	Risk Factors Relating to Misstatements Arising From Fraudulent Financial Reporting	.16-.17
	Risk Factors Relating to Misstatements Arising From Misappropriation of Assets	.18-.20
	Consideration of Risk Factors in Assessing the Risk of Material Misstatement Due to Fraud	.21-.25
	The Auditor's Response to the Results of the Assessment	.26-.32
	Overall Considerations	.27-.28
	Considerations at the Account Balance, Class of Transactions, and Assertion Level	.29
	Specific Responses—Misstatements Arising From Fraudulent Financial Reporting	.30
	Specific Responses—Misstatements Arising From Misappropriations of Assets	.31-.32
	Evaluation of Audit Test Results	.33-.36
	Documentation of the Auditor's Risk Assessment and Response	.37
	Communications About Fraud to Management, the Audit Committee, and Others	.38-.40
	Effective Date	.41
317	Illegal Acts by Clients	.01-.25
	Definition of Illegal Acts	.02-.06
	Dependence on Legal Judgment	.03
	Relation to Financial Statements	.04-.06
	The Auditor's Consideration of the Possibility of Illegal Acts	.07-.11
	Audit Procedures in the Absence of Evidence Concerning Possible Illegal Acts	.08
	Specific Information Concerning Illegal Acts	.09
	Audit Procedures in Response to Possible Illegal Acts	.10-.11
	The Auditor's Response to Detected Illegal Acts	.12-.21
	The Auditor's Consideration of Financial Statement Effect	.13-.15
	Implications for Audit	.16

Section		Paragraph
317	Illegal Acts by Clients—continued	
	Communication With the Audit Committee	.17
	Effect on the Auditor's Report	.18-.21
	Other Considerations in an Audit in Accordance With Generally Accepted Auditing Standards	.22-.23
	Responsibilities in Other Circumstances	.24
	Effective Date	.25
9317	Illegal Acts by Clients: Auditing Interpretations of Section 317	
	1. Consideration of Internal Control in a Financial Statement Audit and the Foreign Corrupt Practices Act (10/78)	.01-.02
	2. Material Weaknesses in Internal Control and the Foreign Corrupt Practices Act (10/78)	.03-.06
319	Consideration of Internal Control in a Financial Statement Audit	.01-.84
	Introduction	.01-.05
	Definition of Internal Control	.06-.07
	Relationship Between Objectives and Components	.08-.13
	Financial Reporting Objective	.10
	Operations and Compliance Objectives	.11-.12
	Safeguarding of Assets	.13
	Application of Components to a Financial Statement Audit	.14-.15
	Limitations of an Entity's Internal Control	.16-.18
	Consideration of Internal Control in Planning an Audit	.19-.44
	Understanding Internal Control	.23-.40
	Control Environment	.25-.27
	Risk Assessment	.28-.31
	Control Activities	.32-.33
	Information and Communication	.34-.36
	Monitoring	.37-.39
	Application to Small and Midsized Entities	.40
	Procedures to Obtain Understanding	.41-.43
	Documentation of Understanding	.44
	Consideration of Internal Control in Assessing Control Risk	.45-.57
	Documentation of the Assessed Level of Control Risk	.57
	Relationship of Understanding to Assessing Control Risk	.58-.63
	Further Reduction in the Assessed Level of Control Risk	.61-.63
	Evidential Matter to Support the Assessed Level of Control Risk	.64-.78
	Type of Evidential Matter	.66-.67
	Source of Evidential Matter	.68-.69
	Timeliness of Evidential Matter	.70-.73
	Interrelationship of Evidential Matter	.74-.78
	Correlation of Control Risk With Detection Risk	.79-.82
	Effective Date	.83
	Appendix: Internal Control Components	.84

Section *Paragraph*

9319 Consideration of Internal Control in a Financial Statement Audit: Auditing Interpretations of Section 319
1. Audit Considerations for the Year 2000 Issue (1/98)

322 The Auditor's Consideration of the Internal Audit Function in an Audit of Financial Statements .01-.29
Roles of the Auditor and the Internal Auditors .02-.03
Obtaining an Understanding of the Internal Audit Function .04-.08
Assessing the Competence and Objectivity of the Internal Auditors .09-.11
Competence of the Internal Auditors .09
Objectivity of the Internal Auditors .10
Assessing Competence and Objectivity .11
Effect of the Internal Auditors' Work on the Audit .12-.17
Understanding of Internal Control .13
Risk Assessment .14-.16
Financial-Statement Level .15
Account-Balance or Class-of-Transaction Level .16
Substantive Procedures .17
Extent of the Effect of the Internal Auditors' Work .18-.22
Coordination of the Audit Work With Internal Auditors .23
Evaluating and Testing the Effectiveness of Internal Auditors' Work .24-.26
Using Internal Auditors to Provide Direct Assistance to the Auditor .27
Effective Date .28
Appendix: The Auditor's Consideration of the Internal Audit Function in an Audit of Financial Statements .29

324 Reports on the Processing of Transactions by Service Organizations .01-.59
Introduction and Applicability .01-.04
The User Auditor's Consideration of the Effect of the Service Organization on the User Organization's Internal Control and the Availability of Audit Evidence .05-.17
The Effect of a Service Organization on a User Organization's Internal Control .06
Planning the Audit .07-.10
Assessing Control Risk at the User Organization .11-.16
Audit Evidence From Substantive Audit Procedures Performed by Service Auditors .17
Considerations in Using a Service Auditor's Report .18-.21
Responsibilities of Service Auditors .22-.58
Reports on Controls Placed in Operation .25-.40
Reports on Controls Placed in Operation and Tests of Operating Effectiveness .41-.56
Written Representations of the Service Organization's Management .57
Reporting on Substantive Procedures .58
Effective Date .59

Section		Paragraph
9324	Reports on the Processing of Transactions by Service Organizations: Auditing Interpretations of Section 324	
	1. Describing Tests of Operating Effectiveness and the Results of Such Tests (4/95)	.01-.03
	2. Service Organizations That Use the Services of Other Service Organizations (Subservice Organizations) (4/95)	.04-.18
325	Communication of Internal Control Related Matters Noted in an Audit	.01-.21
	Reportable Conditions	.02-.03
	Identifying Reportable Conditions	.04-.06
	Agreed-Upon Criteria	.07-.08
	Reporting—Form and Content	.09-.19
	Effective Date	.20
	Appendix: Examples of Possible Reportable Conditions	.21
9325	Communication of Internal Control Related Matters Noted in an Audit: Auditing Interpretations of Section 325	
	1. Reporting on the Existence of Material Weaknesses (2/89)	.01-.07
	2. Audit Considerations for the Year 2000 Issue (1/98)	
326	Evidential Matter	.01-.26
	Nature of Assertions	.03-.08
	Use of Assertions in Developing Audit Objectives and Designing Substantive Tests	.09-.14
	Nature of Evidential Matter	.15-.20
	Competence of Evidential Matter	.21
	Sufficiency of Evidential Matter	.22-.24
	Evaluation of Evidential Matter	.25
	Appendix: Financial Statement Assertions, Illustrative Audit Objectives, and Examples of Substantive Tests	.26
9326	Evidential Matter: Auditing Interpretations of Section 326	
	1. Evidential Matter for an Audit of Interim Financial Statements (10/80)	.01-.05
	2. The Effect of an Inability to Obtain Evidential Matter Relating to Income Tax Accruals (3/81)	.06-.17
	3. The Auditor's Consideration of the Completeness Assertion (4/86)	.18-.21
329	Analytical Procedures	.01-.23
	Analytical Procedures in Planning the Audit	.06-.08
	Analytical Procedures Used as Substantive Tests	.09-.21
	Nature of Assertion	.12
	Plausibility and Predictability of the Relationship	.13-.14
	Availability and Reliability of Data	.15-.16
	Precision of the Expectation	.17-.19
	Investigation and Evaluation of Significant Differences	.20-.21
	Analytical Procedures Used in the Overall Review	.22
	Effective Date	.23

Section | Paragraph

9329 Analytical Procedures: Auditing Interpretations of Section 329
[1.] Corroboration of Replies to Inquiries in Applying Analytical Review Procedures (3/79) [Withdrawn March, 1989] .... [.01-.02]

330 The Confirmation Process .... .01-.36
Introduction and Applicability .... .01-.03
Definition of the Confirmation Process .... .04
Relationship of Confirmation Procedures to the Auditor's Assessment of Audit Risk .... .05-.14
Assertions Addressed by Confirmations .... .11-.14
The Confirmation Process .... .15-.30
Designing the Confirmation Request .... .16-.27
Form of Confirmation Request .... .17-.22
Prior Experience .... .23
Nature of Information Being Confirmed .... .24-.25
Respondent .... .26-.27
Performing Confirmation Procedures .... .28-.30
Alternative Procedures .... .31-.32
Evaluating the Results of Confirmation Procedures .... .33
Confirmation of Accounts Receivable .... .34-.35
Effective Date .... .36

331 Inventories .... .01-.15
Inventories .... .09-.13
Inventories Held in Public Warehouses .... .14
Effect on the Auditor's Report .... .15

9331 Inventories: Auditing Interpretations of Section 331
[1.] Evidential Matter for Inventories at Interim Dates (2/74) [Withdrawn December, 1992] .... [.01-.05]

332 Auditing Investments .... .01-.34
Introduction and Applicability .... .01
Audit Objectives and Approach .... .02-.33
Existence, Ownership, and Completeness .... .04
Appropriateness of Accounting Policy .... .05-.22
FASB Statement No. 115 .... .07-.11
FASB Statement No. 124 .... .12
Investments Accounted for Using the Equity Method .... .13-.22
Valuation and Presentation .... .23-.33
Cost .... .23
Fair Value .... .24-.30
Impairment .... .31-.33
Effective Date .... .34

Section | Paragraph

333 Management Representations .01-.19
Introduction .01
Reliance on Management Repesentations .02-.04
Obtaining Written Representations .05-.12
Scope Limitations .13-.14
Effective Date .15
Appendix A: Illustrative Management Representation Letter .16
Appendix B: Additional Illustrative Representations .17
Appendix C: Illustrative Updating Management Representation Letter .18
Appendix D: Amendment to Section 508, *Reports on Audited Financial Statements* .19

333A Client Representations .01-.14
Reliance on Management Representations .02-.03
Obtaining Written Representations .04-.10
Scope Limitations .11-.12
Effective Date .13
Appendix: Illustrative Representation Letter .14

9333 Management Representations: Auditing Interpretations of Section 333
1. Management Representations on Violations and Possible Violations of Laws and Regulations (3/79) .01-.04

9333A Client Representations: Auditing Interpretations of Section 333A
1. Management Representations on Violations and Possible Violations of Laws and Regulations (3/79) .01-.04
2. Management Representations When Current Management Was Not Present During the Period Under Audit (10/95) .05-.06

334 Related Parties .01-.12
Accounting Considerations .02-.03
Audit Procedures .04-.10
Determining the Existence of Related Parties .07
Identifying Transactions With Related Parties .08
Examining Identified Related Party Transactions .09-.10
Disclosure .11-.12

9334 Related Parties: Auditing Interpretations of Section 334
[1.] Evaluating the Adequacy of Disclosure of Related Party Transactions (3/76) [Withdrawn August, 1983] [.01-.05]
[2.] Disclosure of Commonly Controlled Parties (3/76) [Withdrawn August, 1983] [.06-.09]
[3.] Definition of "Immediate Family" (3/76) [Withdrawn August, 1983] [.10-.11]
4. Exchange of Information Between the Principal and Other Auditor on Related Parties (4/79) .12-.13

Section		Paragraph
9334	Related Parties: Auditing Interpretations of Section 334—continued	
	5. Examination of Identified Related Party Transactions With a Component (4/79)	.14-.15
	6. The Nature and Extent of Auditing Procedures for Examining Related Party Transactions (5/86)	.16-.21
336	Using the Work of a Specialist	.01-.17
	Introduction and Applicability	.01-.05
	Decision to Use the Work of a Specialist	.06-.07
	Qualifications and Work of a Specialist	.08-.09
	Relationship of the Specialist to the Client	.10-.11
	Using the Findings of the Specialist	.12
	Effect of the Specialist's Work on the Auditor's Report	.13-.14
	Reference to the Specialist in the Auditor's Report	.15-.16
	Effective Date	.17
9336	Using the Work of a Specialist: Auditing Interpretations of Section 336	
	1. The Use of Legal Interpretations As Evidential Matter to Support Management's Assertion That a Transfer of Financial Assets Has Met the Isolation Criterion in Paragraph 9(a) of Financial Accounting Standards Board Statement No. 125 (2/98)	.01-.18
337	Inquiry of a Client's Lawyer Concerning Litigation, Claims, and Assessments	.01-.14
	Accounting Considerations	.02-.03
	Auditing Considerations	.04-.14
	Audit Procedures	.05-.07
	Inquiry of a Client's Lawyer	.08-.11
	Limitations on the Scope of a Lawyer's Response	.12-.13
	Other Limitations on a Lawyer's Response	.14
337A	Appendix—Illustrative Audit Inquiry Letter to Legal Counsel	.01
337B	Exhibit I—Excerpts from Statement of Financial Accounting Standards No. 5: Accounting for Contingencies	
337C	Exhibit II—American Bar Association Statement of Policy Regarding Lawyers' Responses to Auditors' Requests for Information	
9337	Inquiry of a Client's Lawyer Concerning Litigation, Claims, and Assessments: Auditing Interpretations of Section 337	
	1. Specifying Relevant Dates in an Audit Inquiry Letter (3/77)	.01-.03
	2. Relationship Between Date of Lawyer's Response and Auditor's Report (3/77)	.04-.05
	3. Form of Audit Inquiry Letter When Client Represents That No Unasserted Claims and Assessments Exist (3/77)	.06-.07
	4. Documents Subject to Lawyer-Client Privilege (3/77)	.08-.09
	5. Alternative Wording of the Illustrative Audit Inquiry Letter to a Client's Lawyer (6/83)	.10-.14

Section		Paragraph
9337	Inquiry of a Client's Lawyer Concerning Litigation, Claims, and Assessments: Auditing Interpretations of Section 337—continued	
	6. Client Has Not Consulted a Lawyer (6/83)	.15-.17
	7. Assessment of a Lawyer's Evaluation of the Outcome of Litigation (6/83)	.18-.23
	8. Use of the Client's Inside Counsel in the Evaluation of Litigation, Claims, and Assessments (6/83)	.24-.27
	9. Use of Explanatory Language About the Attorney-Client Privilege or the Attorney Work-Product Privilege (2/90)	.28-.30
	10. Use of Explanatory Language Concerning Unasserted Possible Claims or Assessments in Lawyers' Responses to Audit Inquiry Letters (1/97)	.31-.32
339	Working Papers	.01-.09
	Functions and Nature of Working Papers	.02-.04
	Content of Working Papers	.05
	Ownership and Custody of Working Papers	.06-.08
	Effective Date	.09
9339	Working Papers: Auditing Interpretations of Section 339	
	1. Providing Access to or Photocopies of Working Papers to a Regulator (7/94)	.01-.15
341	The Auditor's Consideration of an Entity's Ability to Continue as a Going Concern	.01-.17
	The Auditor's Responsibility	.02-.04
	Audit Procedures	.05
	Consideration of Conditions and Events	.06
	Consideration of Management's Plans	.07-.09
	Consideration of Financial Statement Effects	.10-.11
	Consideration of the Effects on the Auditor's Report	.12-.16
	Effective Date	.17
9341	The Auditor's Consideration of an Entity's Ability to Continue as a Going Concern: Auditing Interpretations of Section 341	
	1. Eliminating a Going-Concern Explanatory Paragraph From a Reissued Report (8/95)	.01-.02
342	Auditing Accounting Estimates	.01-.16
	Developing Accounting Estimates	.05-.06
	Internal Control Related to Accounting Estimates	.06
	Evaluating Accounting Estimates	.07-.14
	Identifying Circumstances That Require Accounting Estimates	.08
	Evaluating Reasonableness	.09-.14
	Effective Date	.15
	Appendix: Examples of Accounting Estimates	.16

9342 Auditing Accounting Estimates: Auditing Interpretation of Section 342
1. Performance and Reporting Guidance Related to Fair Value Disclosures (2/93) .... .01-.10

350 Audit Sampling .... .01-.47
Uncertainty and Audit Sampling .... .07-.14
Sampling Risk .... .12-.14
Sampling in Substantive Tests of Details .... .15-.30
Planning Samples .... .15-.23
Sample Selection .... .24
Performance and Evaluation .... .25-.30
Sampling in Tests of Controls .... .31-.42
Planning Samples .... .31-.37
Sample Selection .... .38
Performance and Evaluation .... .39-.42
Dual-Purpose Samples .... .43
Selecting a Sampling Approach .... .44-.45
Effective Date .... .46
Appendix .... .47

9350 Audit Sampling: Auditing Interpretations of Section 350
1. Applicability (1/85) .... .01-.02

380 Communication With Audit Committees .... .01-.15
Matters to Be Communicated .... .06-.14
The Auditor's Responsibility Under Generally Accepted Auditing Standards .... .06
Significant Accounting Policies .... .07
Management Judgments and Accounting Estimates .... .08
Significant Audit Adjustments .... .09
Other Information in Documents Containing Audited Financial Statements .... .10
Disagreements With Management .... .11
Consultation With Other Accountants .... .12
Major Issues Discussed With Management Prior to Retention .... .13
Difficulties Encountered in Performing the Audit .... .14
Effective Date .... .15

9380 Communication With Audit Committees: Auditing Interpretations of Section 380
1. Applicability of Section 380 (8/93) .... .01-.03

390 Consideration of Omitted Procedures After the Report Date .... .01-.08
Effective Date .... .08

AU Section 310

Appointment of the Independent Auditor[*], [**]

Sources: SAS No. 1, section 310; SAS No. 45; SAS No. 83.

Issue date, unless otherwise indicated: November, 1972.

.01 The first standard of field work is:

The work is to be adequately planned and assistants, if any, are to be properly supervised.

.02 Aspects of supervising assistants are discussed in section 210, *Training and Proficiency of the Independent Auditor*, and section 311, *Planning and Supervision*. Aspects of planning the field work and the timing of auditing procedures are discussed in section 311 and section 313, *Substantive Tests Prior to the Balance-Sheet Date*. [As amended August 1983, by Statement on Auditing Standards No. 45.] (See section 313.)

Appointment of the Independent Auditor

.03 Consideration of the first standard of field work recognizes that early appointment of the independent auditor has many advantages to both the auditor and his client. Early appointment enables the auditor to plan his work so that it may be done expeditiously and to determine the extent to which it can be done before the balance-sheet date. [As amended August, 1983, by Statement on Auditing Standards No. 45.] (See section 313.)

Appointment of Auditor Near or After the Year-End Date

.04 Although early appointment is preferable, an independent auditor may accept an engagement near or after the close of the fiscal year. In such instances, before accepting the engagement, he should ascertain whether circumstances are likely to permit an adequate audit and expression of an unqualified opinion and, if they will not, he should discuss with the client the possible necessity for a qualified opinion or disclaimer of opinion. Sometimes the audit limitations present in such circumstances can be remedied. For example, the taking of the physical inventory can be postponed or another physical inventory can be taken which the auditor can observe. (See section 331.09–.13.)

Establishing an Understanding With the Client

.05 The auditor should establish an understanding with the client regarding the services to be performed for each engagement.[1] Such an understanding

---

* [Title amended, effective for engagements for periods ending on or after June 15, 1998, by Statement on Auditing Standards No. 83.]

** *Note:* Title originally amended and former paragraphs .05–.09 under the heading "Timing of Audit Work" superseded, August 1983, by Statement on Auditing Standards No. 45. (See section 313.)

1 See Statement on Quality Control Standards No. 2, *System of Quality Control for a CPA Firm's Accounting and Auditing Practice*, paragraph 16 [QC section 20.16]. [Footnote added, effective for engagements for periods ending on or after June 15, 1998, by Statement on Auditing Standards No. 83.]

reduces the risk that either the auditor or the client may misinterpret the needs or expectations of the other party. For example, it reduces the risk that the client may inappropriately rely on the auditor to protect the entity against certain risks or to perform certain functions that are the client's responsibility. The understanding should include the objectives of the engagement, management's responsibilities, the auditor's responsibilities, and limitations of the engagement.[2] The auditor should document the understanding in the working papers, preferably through a written communication with the client. If the auditor believes an understanding with the client has not been established, he or she should decline to accept or perform the engagement. [Paragraph added, effective for engagements for periods ending on or after June 15, 1998, by Statement on Auditing Standards No. 83.]

.06 An understanding with the client regarding an audit of the financial statements generally includes the following matters.

- The objective of the audit is the expression of an opinion on the financial statements.
- Management is responsible for the entity's financial statements.
- Management is responsible for establishing and maintaining effective internal control over financial reporting.
- Management is responsible for identifying and ensuring that the entity complies with the laws and regulations applicable to its activities.
- Management is responsible for making all financial records and related information available to the auditor.
- At the conclusion of the engagement, management will provide the auditor with a letter that confirms certain representations made during the audit.
- The auditor is responsible for conducting the audit in accordance with generally accepted auditing standards. Those standards require that the auditor obtain reasonable rather than absolute assurance about whether the financial statements are free of material misstatement, whether caused by error or fraud. Accordingly, a material misstatement may remain undetected. Also, an audit is not designed to detect error or fraud that is immaterial to the financial statements. If, for any reason, the auditor is unable to complete the audit or is unable to form or has not formed an opinion, he or she may decline to express an opinion or decline to issue a report as a result of the engagement.
- An audit includes obtaining an understanding of internal control sufficient to plan the audit and to determine the nature, timing, and

---

[2] The objectives of certain engagements may differ. The understanding should reflect the effects of those objectives on the responsibilities of management and the auditor, and on the limitations of the engagement. The following are examples:

- Reviews of interim financial information (see section 722, *Interim Financial Information*, paragraph .09)
- Audits of recipients of governmental financial assistance (see section 801, *Compliance Auditing Considerations in Audits of Governmental Entities and Recipients of Governmental Financial Assistance*, paragraph .10)
- Application of agreed-upon procedures to specified elements, accounts or items of a financial statement (see section 622, *Engagements to Apply Agreed-Upon Procedures to Specified Elements, Accounts, or Items of a Financial Statement*, paragraph .03)

[Footnote added, effective for engagements for periods ending on or after June 15, 1998, by Statement on Auditing Standards No. 83.]

extent of audit procedures to be performed. An audit is not designed to provide assurance on internal control or to identify reportable conditions. However, the auditor is responsible for ensuring that the audit committee or others with equivalent authority or responsibility are aware of any reportable conditions which come to his or her attention.

These matters may be communicated in the form of an engagement letter. [Paragraph added, effective for engagements for periods ending on or after June 15, 1998, by Statement on Auditing Standards No. 83.]

.07 An understanding with the client also may include other matters, such as the following:

- Arrangements regarding the conduct of the engagement (for example, timing, client assistance regarding the preparation of schedules, and the availability of documents)
- Arrangements concerning involvement of specialists or internal auditors, if applicable
- Arrangements involving a predecessor auditor
- Arrangements regarding fees and billing
- Any limitation of or other arrangements regarding the liability of the auditor or the client, such as indemnification to the auditor for liability arising from knowing misrepresentations to the auditor by management (Regulators, including the Securities and Exchange Commission, may restrict or prohibit such liability limitation arrangements.)
- Conditions under which access to the auditor's working papers may be granted to others
- Additional services to be provided relating to regulatory requirements
- Arrangements regarding other services to be provided in connection with the engagement

[Paragraph added, effective for engagements for periods ending on or after June 15, 1998, by Statement on Auditing Standards No. 83.]

AU Section 310A

*Relationship Between the Auditor's Appointment and Planning**

Sources: SAS No. 1, section 310; SAS No. 45.

Issue date, unless otherwise indicated: November, 1972.

.01 The first standard of field work is:

> The work is to be adequately planned and assistants, if any, are to be properly supervised.

.02 Aspects of supervising assistants are discussed in section 210, *Training and Proficiency of the Independent Auditor*, and section 311, *Planning and Supervision*. Aspects of planning the field work and the timing of auditing procedures are discussed in section 311 and section 313, *Substantive Tests Prior to the Balance-Sheet Date*. [As amended August 1983, by Statement on Auditing Standards No. 45.] (See section 313.)

Appointment of the Independent Auditor

.03 Consideration of the first standard of field work recognizes that early appointment of the independent auditor has many advantages to both the auditor and his client. Early appointment enables the auditor to plan his work so that it may be done expeditiously and to determine the extent to which it can be done before the balance-sheet date. [As amended August, 1983, by Statement on Auditing Standards No. 45.] (See section 313.)

Appointment of Auditor Near or After the Year-End Date

.04 Although early appointment is preferable, an independent auditor may accept an engagement near or after the close of the fiscal year. In such instances, before accepting the engagement, he should ascertain whether circumstances are likely to permit an adequate audit and expression of an unqualified opinion and, if they will not, he should discuss with the client the possible necessity for a qualified opinion or disclaimer of opinion. Sometimes the audit limitations present in such circumstances can be remedied. For example, the taking of the physical inventory can be postponed or another physical inventory can be taken which the auditor can observe. (See section 331.09–.13.)

Timing of Audit Work

[.05–.09] [Superseded August, 1983, by Statement on Auditing Standards No. 45.] (See section 313.)

---

* [Title amended August, 1983, by Statement on Auditing Standards No. 45.] (See section 313.)

AU Section 311

Planning and Supervision

Sources: SAS No. 22; SAS No. 47; SAS No. 48; SAS No. 77.

See section 9311 for interpretations of this section.

Effective for periods ending after September 30, 1978, unless otherwise indicated.

.01 The first standard of field work requires that "the work is to be adequately planned and assistants, if any, are to be properly supervised." This section provides guidance to the independent auditor conducting an audit in accordance with generally accepted auditing standards on the considerations and procedures applicable to planning and supervision, including preparing an audit program, obtaining knowledge of the entity's business, and dealing with differences of opinion among firm personnel. Planning and supervision continue throughout the audit, and the related procedures frequently overlap.

.02 The auditor with final responsibility for the audit may delegate portions of the planning and supervision of the audit to other firm personnel. For purposes of this section, (*a*) firm personnel other than the auditor with final responsibility for the audit are referred to as *assistants* and (*b*) the term *auditor* refers to either the auditor with final responsibility for the audit or assistants.

Planning

.03 Audit planning involves developing an overall strategy for the expected conduct and scope of the audit. The nature, extent, and timing of planning vary with the size and complexity of the entity, experience with the entity, and knowledge of the entity's business. In planning the audit, the auditor should consider, among other matters:

a. Matters relating to the entity's business and the industry in which it operates (see paragraph .07).

b. The entity's accounting policies and procedures.

c. The methods used by the entity to process significant accounting information (see paragraph .09), including the use of service organizations, such as outside service centers.

d. Planned assessed level of control risk. (See section 319.)

e. Preliminary judgment about materiality levels for audit purposes.

f. Financial statement items likely to require adjustment.

g. Conditions that may require extension or modification of audit tests, such as the risk of material error or fraud or the existence of related party transactions.

h. The nature of reports expected to be rendered (for example, a report on consolidated or consolidating financial statements, reports on financial statements filed with the SEC, or special reports such as those on compliance with contractual provisions).

[As amended, December, 1983, by Statement on Auditing Standards No. 47.] (See section 312.14.) [As amended, effective for periods beginning after August 31, 1984, by Statement on Auditing Standards No. 48.]

.04 Procedures that an auditor may consider in planning the audit usually involve review of his records relating to the entity and discussion with other firm personnel and personnel of the entity. Examples of those procedures include:

- *a.* Reviewing correspondence files, prior year's working papers, permanent files, financial statements, and auditor's reports.
- *b.* Discussing matters that may affect the audit with firm personnel responsible for non-audit services to the entity.
- *c.* Inquiring about current business developments affecting the entity.
- *d.* Reading the current year's interim financial statements.
- *e.* Discussing the type, scope, and timing of the audit with management of the entity, the board of directors, or its audit committee.
- *f.* Considering the effects of applicable accounting and auditing pronouncements, particularly new ones.
- *g.* Coordinating the assistance of entity personnel in data preparation.
- *h.* Determining the extent of involvement, if any, of consultants, specialists, and internal auditors.
- *i.* Establishing the timing of the audit work.
- *j.* Establishing and coordinating staffing requirements.

The auditor may wish to prepare a memorandum setting forth the preliminary audit plan, particularly for large and complex entities.

.05 In planning the audit, the auditor should consider the nature, extent, and timing of work to be performed and should prepare a written audit program (or set of written audit programs) for every audit. The audit program should set forth in reasonable detail the audit procedures that the auditor believes are necessary to accomplish the objectives of the audit. The form of the audit program and the extent of its detail will vary with the circumstances. In developing the program, the auditor should be guided by the results of the planning considerations and procedures. As the audit progresses, changed conditions may make it necessary to modify planned audit procedures. [As amended, effective for engagements beginning after December 15, 1995, by Statement on Auditing Standards No. 77.]

.06 The auditor should obtain a level of knowledge of the entity's business that will enable him to plan and perform his audit in accordance with generally accepted auditing standards. That level of knowledge should enable him to obtain an understanding of the events, transactions, and practices that, in his judgment, may have a significant effect on the financial statements. The level of knowledge customarily possessed by management relating to managing the entity's business is substantially greater than that which is obtained by the auditor in performing his audit. Knowledge of the entity's business helps the auditor in:

- *a.* Identifying areas that may need special consideration.
- *b.* Assessing conditions under which accounting data are produced, processed, reviewed, and accumulated within the organization.
- *c.* Evaluating the reasonableness of estimates, such as valuation of inventories, depreciation, allowances for doubtful accounts, and percentage of completion of long-term contracts.

d. Evaluating the reasonableness of management representations.

e. Making judgments about the appropriateness of the accounting principles applied and the adequacy of disclosures.[1]

.07 The auditor should obtain a knowledge of matters that relate to the nature of the entity's business, its organization, and its operating characteristics. Such matters include, for example, the type of business, types of products and services, capital structure, related parties, locations, and production, distribution, and compensation methods. The auditor should also consider matters affecting the industry in which the entity operates, such as economic conditions, government regulations, and changes in technology, as they relate to his audit. Other matters, such as accounting practices common to the industry, competitive conditions, and, if available, financial trends and ratios should also be considered by the auditor.

.08 Knowledge of an entity's business is ordinarily obtained through experience with the entity or its industry and inquiry of personnel of the entity. Working papers from prior years may contain useful information about the nature of the business, organizational structure, operating characteristics, and transactions that may require special consideration. Other sources an auditor may consult include AICPA accounting and audit guides, industry publications, financial statements of other entities in the industry, textbooks, periodicals, and individuals knowledgeable about the industry.

.09 The auditor should consider the methods the entity uses to process accounting information in planning the audit because such methods influence the design of the internal control. The extent to which computer processing is used in significant accounting applications,[2] as well as the complexity of that processing, may also influence the nature, timing, and extent of audit procedures. Accordingly, in evaluating the effect of an entity's computer processing on an audit of financial statements, the auditor should consider matters such as—

a. The extent to which the computer is used in each significant accounting application.

b. The complexity of the entity's computer operations, including the use of an outside service center.[3]

c. The organizational structure of the computer processing activities.

d. The availability of data. Documents that are used to enter information into the computer for processing, certain computer files, and other evidential matter that may be required by the auditor may exist only for a short period or only in computer-readable form. In some computer systems, input documents may not exist at all because information is directly entered into the system. An entity's data retention policies may require the auditor to request retention of some information for his review or to perform audit procedures at

---

[1] Footnote deleted to reflect the conforming changes necessary due to the issuance of Statement on Auditing Standards Nos. 53 through 62.

[2] Significant accounting applications are those that relate to accounting information that can materially affect the financial statements the auditor is auditing. [Footnote added by issuance of Statement on Auditing Standards No. 48.]

[3] See section 324, *Reports on the Processing of Transactions by Service Organizations*, for guidance concerning the use of a service center for computer processing of significant accounting applications. [Footnote revised, June 1992, by issuance of Statement on Auditing Standards No. 70.]

a time when the information is available. In addition, certain information generated by the computer for management's internal purposes may be useful in performing substantive tests (particularly analytical procedures).[4]

e. The use of computer-assisted audit techniques to increase the efficiency of performing audit procedures.[5] Using computer-assisted audit techniques may also provide the auditor with an opportunity to apply certain procedures to an entire population of accounts or transactions. In addition, in some accounting systems, it may be difficult or impossible for the auditor to analyze certain data or test specific control procedures without computer assistance.

[Paragraph added, effective for periods beginning after August 31, 1984, by Statement on Auditing Standards No. 48.]

.10 The auditor should consider whether specialized skills are needed to consider the effect of computer processing on the audit, to understand the controls, or to design and perform audit procedures. If specialized skills are needed, the auditor should seek the assistance of a professional possessing such skills, who may be either on the auditor's staff or an outside professional. If the use of such a professional is planned, the auditor should have sufficient computer-related knowledge to communicate the objectives of the other professional's work; to evaluate whether the specified procedures will meet the auditor's objectives; and to evaluate the results of the procedures applied as they relate to the nature, timing, and extent of other planned audit procedures. The auditor's responsibilities with respect to using such a professional are equivalent to those for other assistants.[6] [Paragraph added, effective for periods beginning after August 31, 1984, by Statement on Auditing Standards No. 48.]

Supervision

.11 Supervision involves directing the efforts of assistants who are involved in accomplishing the objectives of the audit and determining whether those objectives were accomplished. Elements of supervision include instructing assistants, keeping informed of significant problems encountered, reviewing the work performed, and dealing with differences of opinion among firm personnel. The extent of supervision appropriate in a given instance depends on many factors, including the complexity of the subject matter and the qualifications of persons performing the work. [Formerly paragraph .09, number changed by issuance of Statement on Auditing Standards No. 48, effective for periods beginning after August 31, 1984.]

.12 Assistants should be informed of their responsibilities and the objectives of the procedures that they are to perform. They should be informed of matters that may affect the nature, extent, and timing of procedures they are to perform, such as the nature of the entity's business as it relates to their

---

[4] Section 329, *Analytical Procedures*, provides guidance pertaining to such procedures. [Footnote added by issuance of Statement on Auditing Standards No. 48.]

[5] [Footnote deleted.]

[6] Since the use of a specialist who is effectively functioning as a member of the audit team is not covered by section 336, *Using the Work of a Specialist*, a computer audit specialist requires the same supervision and review as any assistant. [Footnote added by issuance of Statement on Auditing Standards No. 48.]

assignments and possible accounting and auditing problems. The auditor with final responsibility for the audit should direct assistants to bring to his attention significant accounting and auditing questions raised during the audit so that he may assess their significance. [Formerly paragraph .10, number changed by issuance of Statement on Auditing Standards No. 48, effective for periods beginning after August 31, 1984.]

.13 The work performed by each assistant should be reviewed to determine whether it was adequately performed and to evaluate whether the results are consistent with the conclusions to be presented in the auditor's report. [Formerly paragraph .11, number changed by issuance of Statement on Auditing Standards No. 48, effective for periods beginning after August 31, 1984.]

.14 The auditor with final responsibility for the audit and assistants should be aware of the procedures to be followed when differences of opinion concerning accounting and auditing issues exist among firm personnel involved in the audit. Such procedures should enable an assistant to document his disagreement with the conclusions reached if, after appropriate consultation, he believes it necessary to disassociate himself from the resolution of the matter. In this situation, the basis for the final resolution should also be documented. [Formerly paragraph .12, number changed by issuance of Statement on Auditing Standards No. 48, effective for periods beginning after August 31, 1984.]

Effective Date

.15 Statements on Auditing Standards generally are effective at the time of their issuance. However, since this section provides for practices that may differ in certain respects from practices heretofore considered acceptable, this section will be effective for audits made in accordance with generally accepted auditing standards for periods ending after September 30, 1978. [Formerly paragraph .13, number changed by issuance of Statement on Auditing Standards No. 48, effective for periods beginning after August 31, 1984.]

[illegible] and possible [illegible] and auditing problems. The auditor with final responsibility for the audit should direct assistants to bring to his attention significant accounting and auditing questions raised during the audit so that he may assess their significance. [Formerly paragraph 10, number changed by issuance of Statement on Auditing Standards No. 48, effective for periods beginning after August 31, 1984.]

.13 The work performed by each assistant should be reviewed to determine whether it was adequately performed and to evaluate whether the results are consistent with the conclusions to be presented in the auditor's report. [Formerly paragraph 12, number changed by issuance of Statement on Auditing Standards No. 48, effective for periods beginning after August 31, 1984.]

.14 The auditor with final responsibility for the audit and assistants should be aware of the procedures to be followed when differences of opinion concerning accounting and auditing issues exist among firm personnel involved in the audit. Such procedures should enable an assistant to document his disagreement with the conclusions reached if, after appropriate consultation, he believes it necessary to disassociate himself from the resolution of the matter. In this situation, the basis for the final resolution should also be documented. [Formerly paragraph 13, number changed by issuance of Statement on Auditing Standards No. 48, effective for periods beginning after August 31, 1984.]

Effective Date

.15 Statements on Auditing Standards generally are effective at the time of their issuance. However, since this Section provides for practices that may differ in certain respects from practices heretofore considered acceptable, this section will be effective for audits made in accordance with generally accepted auditing standards for periods ending after September 30, 1978. [Formerly paragraph 14, number changed by issuance of Statement on Auditing Standards No. 48, effective for periods beginning after August 31, 1984.]

AU Section 9311

Planning and Supervision: Auditing Interpretations of Section 311

1. Communications Between the Auditor and Firm Personnel Responsible for Non-Audit Services

.01 *Question*—Section 311, *Planning and Supervision*, paragraph .04*b*, lists the following procedure that an auditor may consider in planning an audit: "Discussing matters that may affect the audit with firm personnel responsible for non-audit services to the entity."

.02 What specific things should the auditor consider in performing this procedure?

.03 *Interpretation*—The auditor should consider the nature of non-audit services that have been performed. He should assess whether the services involve matters that might be expected to affect the entity's financial statements or the performance of the audit, for example, tax planning or recommendations on a cost accounting system. If the auditor decides that the performance of the non-audit services or the information likely to have been gained from it may have implications for his audit, he should discuss the matter with personnel who rendered the services and consider how the expected conduct and scope of his audit may be affected. In some cases, the auditor may find it useful to review the pertinent portions of the work papers prepared for the non-audit engagement as an aid in determining the nature of the services rendered or the possible audit implications.

[Issue Date: February, 1980.]

[2.] Planning Considerations for an Audit of a Federally Assisted Program

[.04–.34] [Withdrawn March, 1989.]

3. Responsibility of Assistants for the Resolution of Accounting and Auditing Issues

.35 *Question*—Section 311, *Planning and Supervision*, paragraph .14, states, "The auditor with final responsibility for the audit and assistants should be aware of the procedures to be followed when differences of opinion concerning accounting and auditing issues exist among firm personnel involved in the audit." What are the responsibilities of assistants when there are disagreements or concerns with respect to accounting and auditing issues of significance to the financial statements or auditor's report?

.36 *Response*—Rule 201 of the Code of Professional Conduct [ET section 201.01] states that a member shall "Exercise due professional care in the performance of professional services." The discussion of the third general standard [section 230, *Due Professional Care in the Performance of Work*, paragraph .02] states that "due care imposes a responsibility upon each person within an independent auditor's organization to observe the standards of field work and reporting." The first general standard requires assistants to meet the responsibility attached to the work assigned to them.

.37 Accordingly, each assistant has a professional responsibility to bring to the attention of appropriate individuals in the firm, disagreements or concerns the assistant might have with respect to accounting and auditing issues that he believes are of significance to the financial statements or auditor's report, however those disagreements or concerns may have arisen. In addition, each assistant should have a right to document his disagreement if he believes it is necessary to disassociate himself from the resolution of the matter.

[Issue Date: February, 1986.]

4. Audit Considerations for the Year 2000 Issue

.38 *Introduction*—Many computerized systems, including both hardware and software applications, use only two digits rather than four to record the year in a date field. These systems may recognize the year 2000, which is entered into the computer as "00," as the year 1900 or some other date, resulting in errors when the dates are used in computations and comparisons. In addition, some computerized systems do not properly perform calculations with dates beginning in 1999 because these systems use the digits "99" in date fields to represent something other than the year 1999. Such problems are known as the Year 2000 Issue. The Year 2000 Issue may manifest itself before, on, or after January 1, 2000, and its effects on operations and financial reporting may range from minor errors to catastrophic systems failure.

Auditor Responsibility Regarding the Year 2000 Issue

.39 *Question*—In an audit of financial statements conducted in accordance with generally accepted auditing standards, what is the auditor's responsibility regarding the Year 2000 Issue?

.40 *Interpretation*—The auditor has a responsibility to plan and perform the audit to obtain reasonable assurance that the financial statements are free of material misstatement, whether caused by error or fraud. Thus, the auditor's responsibility relates to the detection of material misstatements of the financial statements being audited, whether caused by the Year 2000 Issue or by some other cause.

.41 Management is responsible for the financial statements and, because of the widespread publicity the Year 2000 Issue has received, generally should be aware of the Year 2000 Issue. Management also should have knowledge about the systems used by the entity in its operations and in preparation of the financial statements. An auditor does not have a responsibility to detect current or future effects of the Year 2000 Issue on operational matters that do not affect the entity's ability to prepare financial statements in accordance with generally accepted accounting principles (or an other comprehensive basis of accounting).

Planning Considerations

.42 *Question*—How does the Year 2000 Issue affect the planning for an audit of financial statements conducted in accordance with generally accepted auditing standards?

.43 *Interpretation*—When an auditor is considering the methods the entity uses to process accounting information pursuant to the provisions of section 311, *Planning and Supervision*, paragraph .09, he or she may determine that it is necessary to consider whether data processing errors caused by the Year 2000 Issue could result in a material misstatement of the financial statements under audit. The results of the consideration may affect the auditor's assessed level of control risk, testing of internal control, and substantive procedures. An audit of financial statements conducted in accordance with generally accepted auditing standards does not contemplate that the auditor would need to assess whether data processing errors caused by the Year 2000 Issue could result in material misstatement of financial statements in periods subsequent to the period being audited.

.44 The extent to which the auditor considers the Year 2000 Issue requires professional judgment. If the auditor concludes that he or she should consider whether the Year 2000 Issue could result in a material misstatement of the financial statements currently under audit, either alone or in combination with other factors, ordinarily the auditor would undertake that consideration in the context of section 311.09, which discusses the auditor's consideration of the methods the entity uses to process accounting information, and section 319, *Consideration of Internal Control in a Financial Statement Audit*, paragraph .19, which discusses the auditor's responsibility to obtain an understanding of each of the five components of internal control sufficient to plan the audit.

Internal Control Deficiencies Related to the Year 2000 Issue

.45 *Question*—During the course of an audit, the auditor may become aware that, in some period after the period being audited, the Year 2000 Issue could, as discussed in section 325, *Communication of Internal Control Related Matters Noted in an Audit*, paragraph .02, "adversely affect the organization's ability to record, process, summarize, and report financial data consistent with the assertions of management in the financial statements." For example, during an audit of financial statements for the year ending December 31, 1997, an auditor may become aware that the entity's computer programs, which are correctly processing current data, would not function correctly if used to process data in the year 2000. In this situation, is the potential significant internal control deficiency in the year 2000 a reportable condition as of December 31, 1997?

.46 *Interpretation*—No. The computer programs are correctly processing current data and are not currently affecting the organization's ability to prepare financial statements. The potential internal control deficiency becomes a reportable condition only when, in the auditor's judgment, it could adversely affect the organization's ability to record, process, summarize, and report financial data consistent with the assertions of management in the financial statements.

.47 As discussed in section 325.03, the auditor also may identify matters that, in his or her judgment, are not reportable conditions but that the auditor nonetheless may choose to communicate. The example discussed in paragraph .45 above is a type of matter the auditor may wish to communicate for the benefit of management.

[Issue Date: January, 1998.]

AU Section 312

Audit Risk and Materiality in Conducting an Audit[*]

Source: SAS No. 47; SAS No. 82.

Effective for audits of financial statements for periods beginning after June 30, 1984, unless otherwise indicated.

.01 This section provides guidance on the auditor's consideration of audit risk and materiality when planning and performing an audit of financial statements in accordance with generally accepted auditing standards. Audit risk and materiality affect the application of generally accepted auditing standards, especially the standards of field work and reporting, and are reflected in the auditor's standard report. Audit risk and materiality, among other matters, need to be considered together in determining the nature, timing, and extent of auditing procedures and in evaluating the results of those procedures.

.02 The existence of audit risk is recognized in the description of the responsibilities and functions of the independent auditor that states, "Because of the nature of audit evidence and the characteristics of fraud, the auditor is able to obtain reasonable, but not absolute, assurance that material misstatements are detected."[1] Audit risk[2] is the risk that the auditor may unknowingly fail to appropriately modify his or her opinion on financial statements that are materially misstated.[3] [As amended, effective for audits of financial statements for periods ending on or after December 15, 1997, by Statement on Auditing Standards No. 82.]

.03 The concept of materiality recognizes that some matters, either individually or in the aggregate, are important for fair presentation of finan-

---

[*] This section has been amended to reflect the conforming changes necessary due to the issuance of Statement on Auditing Standards Nos. 53 through 62.

[1] See section 110, *Responsibilities and Functions of the Independent Auditor*, and section 230, *Due Professional Care in the Performance of Work*, for a further discussion of reasonable assurance. [As amended, effective for audits of financial statements for periods ending on or after December 15, 1997, by Statement on Auditing Standards No. 82.]

[2] In addition to audit risk, the auditor is also exposed to loss or injury to his or her professional practice from litigation, adverse publicity, or other events arising in connection with financial statements audited and reported on. This exposure is present even though the auditor has performed the audit in accordance with generally accepted auditing standards and has reported appropriately on those financial statements. Even if an auditor assesses this exposure as low, the auditor should not perform less extensive procedures than would otherwise be appropriate under generally accepted auditing standards.

[3] This definition of audit risk does not include the risk that the auditor might erroneously conclude that the financial statements are materially misstated. In such a situation, the auditor would ordinarily reconsider or extend auditing procedures and request that the client perform specific tasks to reevaluate the appropriateness of the financial statements. These steps would ordinarily lead the auditor to the correct conclusion. This definition also excludes the risk of an inappropriate reporting decision unrelated to the detection and evaluation of misstatements in the financial statements, such as an inappropriate decision regarding the form of the auditor's report because of a limitation on the scope of the audit. [As amended, effective for audits of financial statements for periods ending on or after December 15, 1997, by Statement on Auditing Standards No. 82.]

cial statements in conformity with generally accepted accounting principles,[4] while other matters are not important. The phrase in the auditor's standard report "present fairly, in all material respects, in conformity with generally accepted accounting principles" indicates the auditor's belief that the financial statements taken as a whole are not materially misstated. [As amended, effective for audits of financial statements for periods ending on or after December 15, 1997, by Statement on Auditing Standards No. 82.]

.04 Financial statements are materially misstated when they contain misstatements whose effect, individually or in the aggregate, is important enough to cause them not to be presented fairly, in all material respects, in conformity with generally accepted accounting principles. Misstatements can result from errors or fraud.[5] [As amended, effective for audits of financial statements for periods ending on or after December 15, 1997, by Statement on Auditing Standards No. 82.]

.05 In planning the audit, the auditor is concerned with matters that could be material to the financial statements. The auditor has no responsibility to plan and perform the audit to obtain reasonable assurance that misstatements, whether caused by errors or fraud, that are not material to the financial statements are detected. [Paragraph added, effective for audits of financial statements for periods ending on or after December 15, 1997, by Statement on Auditing Standards No. 82.]

.06 The term *errors* refers to unintentional misstatements or omissions of amounts or disclosures in financial statements. Errors may involve—

- Mistakes in gathering or processing data from which financial statements are prepared.
- Unreasonable accounting estimates arising from oversight or misinterpretation of facts.
- Mistakes in the application of accounting principles relating to amount, classification, manner of presentation, or disclosure.[6]

[Paragraph added, effective for audits of financial statements for periods ending on or after December 15, 1997, by Statement on Auditing Standards No. 82.]

.07 Although *fraud* is a broad legal concept, the auditor's interest specifically relates to fraudulent acts that cause a misstatement of financial statements. Two types of misstatements are relevant to the auditor's consideration

---

[4] The concepts of audit risk and materiality also are applicable to financial statements presented in conformity with a comprehensive basis of accounting other than generally accepted accounting principles; references in this section to financial statements presented in conformity with generally accepted accounting principles also include those presentations.

[5] The auditor's consideration of illegal acts and responsibility for detecting misstatements resulting from illegal acts is defined in section 317, *Illegal Acts by Clients*. For those illegal acts that are defined in that section as having a direct and material effect on the determination of financial statement amounts, the auditor's responsibility to detect misstatements resulting from such illegal acts is the same as that for errors or fraud. [Footnote added, effective for audits of financial statements for periods ending on or after December 15, 1997, by Statement on Auditing Standards No. 82.]

[6] Errors do not include the effect of accounting processes employed for convenience, such as maintaining accounting records on the cash basis or the tax basis and periodically adjusting those records to prepare financial statements in conformity with generally accepted accounting principles. [Footnote added, effective for audits of financial statements for periods ending on or after December 15, 1997, by Statement on Auditing Standards No. 82.]

in a financial statement audit—misstatements arising from fraudulent financial reporting and misstatements arising from misappropriation of assets. These two types of misstatements are further described in section 316, *Consideration of Fraud in a Financial Statement Audit*. The primary factor that distinguishes fraud from error is whether the underlying action that results in the misstatement in financial statements is intentional or unintentional. [Paragraph added, effective for audits of financial statements for periods ending on or after December 15, 1997, by Statement on Auditing Standards No. 82.]

.08 When considering the auditor's responsibility to obtain reasonable assurance that the financial statements are free from material misstatement, there is no important distinction between errors and fraud. There is a distinction, however, in the auditor's response to detected misstatements. Generally, an isolated, immaterial error in processing accounting data or applying accounting principles is not significant to the audit. In contrast, when fraud is detected, the auditor should consider the implications for the integrity of management or employees and the possible effect on other aspects of the audit. [Paragraph added, effective for audits of financial statements for periods ending on or after December 15, 1997, by Statement on Auditing Standards No. 82.]

.09 When concluding as to whether the effect of misstatements, individually or in the aggregate, is material, an auditor ordinarily should consider their nature and amount in relation to the nature and amount of items in the financial statements under audit. For example, an amount that is material to the financial statements of one entity may not be material to the financial statements of another entity of a different size or nature. Also, what is material to the financial statements of a particular entity might change from one period to another. [Paragraph renumbered by the issuance of Statement on Auditing Standards No. 82, February 1997.]

.10 The auditor's consideration of materiality is a matter of professional judgment and is influenced by his or her perception of the needs of a reasonable person who will rely on the financial statements. The perceived needs of a reasonable person are recognized in the discussion of materiality in Financial Accounting Standards Board Statement of Financial Accounting Concepts No. 2, *Qualitative Characteristics of Accounting Information*, which defines materiality as "the magnitude of an omission or misstatement of accounting information that, in the light of surrounding circumstances, makes it probable that the judgment of a reasonable person relying on the information would have been changed or influenced by the omission or misstatement." That discussion recognizes that materiality judgments are made in light of surrounding circumstances and necessarily involve both quantitative and qualitative considerations. [Paragraph renumbered by the issuance of Statement on Auditing Standards No. 82, February 1997.]

.11 As a result of the interaction of quantitative and qualitative considerations in materiality judgments, misstatements of relatively small amounts that come to the auditor's attention could have a material effect on the financial statements. For example, an illegal payment of an otherwise immaterial amount could be material if there is a reasonable possibility that it could lead to a material contingent liability or a material loss of revenue.[7] [Paragraph renumbered by the issuance of Statement on Auditing Standards No. 82, February 1997.]

---

[7] See section 317. [Footnote renumbered and amended, effective for audits of financial statements for periods ending on or after December 15, 1997, by Statement on Auditing Standards No. 82.]

Planning the Audit

.12 The auditor should consider audit risk and materiality both in (*a*) planning the audit and designing auditing procedures and (*b*) evaluating whether the financial statements taken as a whole are presented fairly, in all material respects, in conformity with generally accepted accounting principles. The auditor should consider audit risk and materiality in the first circumstance to obtain sufficient competent evidential matter on which to properly evaluate the financial statements in the second circumstance. [Paragraph renumbered by the issuance of Statement on Auditing Standards No. 82, February 1997.]

Considerations at the Financial Statements Level[8]

.13 The auditor should plan the audit so that audit risk will be limited to a low level that is, in his or her professional judgment, appropriate for expressing an opinion on the financial statements. Audit risk may be assessed in quantitative or nonquantitative terms. [Paragraph renumbered by the issuance of Statement on Auditing Standards No. 82, February 1997.]

.14 Section 311, *Planning and Supervision*, requires the auditor, in planning the audit, to take into consideration, among other matters, his or her preliminary judgment about materiality levels for audit purposes.[9] That judgment may or may not be quantified. [Paragraph renumbered by the issuance of Statement on Auditing Standards No. 82, February 1997.]

.15 According to section 311, the nature, timing, and extent of planning and thus of the considerations of audit risk and materiality vary with the size and complexity of the entity, the auditor's experience with the entity, and his or her knowledge of the entity's business. Certain entity-related factors also affect the nature, timing, and extent of auditing procedures with respect to specific account balances and classes of transactions and related assertions. (See paragraphs .24 through .33.) [Paragraph renumbered by the issuance of Statement on Auditing Standards No. 82, February 1997.]

.16 An assessment of the risk of material misstatement (whether caused by error or fraud) should be made during planning. The auditor's understanding of internal control may heighten or mitigate the auditor's concern about the risk of material misstatement.[10] In considering audit risk, the auditor should specifically assess the risk of material misstatement of the financial statements due to fraud.[11] The auditor should consider the effect of these assessments on the overall audit strategy and the expected conduct and scope of the audit. [Paragraph added, effective for audits of financial statements for periods ending on or after December 15, 1997, by Statement on Auditing Standards No. 82.]

---

[8] [Footnote renumbered and deleted by the issuance of Statement on Auditing Standards No. 82, February 1997.]

[9] This section amends section 311, *Planning and Supervision*, paragraph .03*e*, by substituting the words "Preliminary judgment about materiality levels" in place of the words "Preliminary estimates of materiality levels." [Reference changed by the issuance of Statement on Auditing Standards No. 48. Footnote renumbered by the issuance of Statement on Auditing Standards No. 82, February 1997.]

[10] See section 319, *Consideration of Internal Control in a Financial Statement Audit*. [Footnote added, effective for audits of financial statements for periods ending on or after December 15, 1997, by Statement on Auditing Standards No. 82.]

[11] See section 316. [Footnote added, effective for audits of financial statements for periods ending on or after December 15, 1997, by Statement on Auditing Standards No. 82.]

.17 Whenever the auditor has concluded that there is significant risk of material misstatement of the financial statements, the auditor should consider this conclusion in determining the nature, timing, or extent of procedures; assigning staff; or requiring appropriate levels of supervision. The knowledge, skill, and ability of personnel assigned significant engagement responsibilities should be commensurate with the auditor's assessment of the level of risk for the engagement. Ordinarily, higher risk requires more experienced personnel or more extensive supervision by the auditor with final responsibility for the engagement during both the planning and the conduct of the engagement. Higher risk may cause the auditor to expand the extent of procedures applied, apply procedures closer to or as of year end, particularly in critical audit areas, or modify the nature of procedures to obtain more persuasive evidence. [Paragraph added, effective for audits of financial statements for periods ending on or after December 15, 1997, by Statement on Auditing Standards No. 82.]

.18 In an audit of an entity with operations in multiple locations or components, the auditor should consider the extent to which auditing procedures should be performed at selected locations or components. The factors an auditor should consider regarding the selection of a particular location or component include (*a*) the nature and amount of assets and transactions executed at the location or component, (*b*) the degree of centralization of records or information processing, (*c*) the effectiveness of the control environment, particularly with respect to management's direct control over the exercise of authority delegated to others and its ability to effectively supervise activities at the location or component, (*d*) the frequency, timing, and scope of monitoring activities by the entity or others at the location or component, and (*e*) judgments about materiality of the location or component. [Paragraph added, effective for audits of financial statements for periods ending on or after December 15, 1997, by Statement on Auditing Standards No. 82.]

.19 In planning the audit, the auditor should use his or her judgment as to the appropriately low level of audit risk and his or her preliminary judgment about materiality levels in a manner that can be expected to provide, within the inherent limitations of the auditing process, sufficient evidential matter to obtain reasonable assurance about whether the financial statements are free of material misstatement. Materiality levels include an overall level for each statement; however, because the statements are interrelated, and for reasons of efficiency, the auditor ordinarily considers materiality for planning purposes in terms of the smallest aggregate level of misstatements that could be considered material to any one of the financial statements. For example, if the auditor believes that misstatements aggregating approximately $100,000 would have a material effect on income but that such misstatements would have to aggregate approximately $200,000 to materially affect financial position, it would not be appropriate for him or her to design auditing procedures that would be expected to detect misstatements only if they aggregate approximately $200,000. [Paragraph renumbered by the issuance of Statement on Auditing Standards No. 82, February 1997.]

.20 The auditor plans the audit to obtain reasonable assurance of detecting misstatements that he or she believes could be large enough, individually or in the aggregate, to be quantitatively material to the financial statements. Although the auditor should be alert for misstatements that could be qualitatively material, it ordinarily is not practical to design procedures to detect them. Section 326, *Evidential Matter*, states that "an auditor typically works within economic limits; his or her opinion, to be economically useful, must be formed within a reasonable length of time and at reasonable cost." [Paragraph renumbered by the issuance of Statement on Auditing Standards No. 82, February 1997.]

.21 In some situations, the auditor considers materiality for planning purposes before the financial statements to be audited are prepared. In other situations, planning takes place after the financial statements under audit have been prepared, but the auditor may be aware that they require significant modification. In both types of situations, the auditor's preliminary judgment about materiality might be based on the entity's annualized interim financial statements or financial statements of one or more prior annual periods, as long as recognition is given to the effects of major changes in the entity's circumstances (for example, a significant merger) and relevant changes in the economy as a whole or the industry in which the entity operates. [Paragraph renumbered by the issuance of Statement on Auditing Standards No. 82, February 1997.]

.22 Assuming, theoretically, that the auditor's judgment about materiality at the planning stage was based on the same information available at the evaluation stage, materiality for planning and evaluation purposes would be the same. However, it ordinarily is not feasible for the auditor, when planning an audit, to anticipate all of the circumstances that may ultimately influence judgments about materiality in evaluating the audit findings at the completion of the audit. Thus, the auditor's preliminary judgment about materiality ordinarily will differ from the judgment about materiality used in evaluating the audit findings. If significantly lower materiality levels become appropriate in evaluating audit findings, the auditor should reevaluate the sufficiency of the auditing procedures he or she has performed. [Paragraph renumbered by the issuance of Statement on Auditing Standards No. 82, February 1997.]

.23 In planning auditing procedures, the auditor should also consider the nature, cause (if known), and amount of misstatements that he or she is aware of from the audit of the prior period's financial statements. [Paragraph renumbered by the issuance of Statement on Auditing Standards No. 82, February 1997.]

Considerations at the Individual Account-Balance or Class-of-Transactions Level

.24 The auditor recognizes that there is an inverse relationship between audit risk and materiality considerations. For example, the risk that a particular account balance or class of transactions and related assertions could be misstated by an extremely large amount might be very low, but the risk that it could be misstated by an extremely small amount might be very high. Holding other planning considerations equal, either a decrease in the level of audit risk that the auditor judges to be appropriate in an account balance or a class of transactions or a decrease in the amount of misstatements in the balance or class that the auditor believes could be material would require the auditor to do one or more of the following: (*a*) select a more effective auditing procedure, (*b*) perform auditing procedures closer to year end, or (*c*) increase the extent of a particular auditing procedure. [Paragraph renumbered and amended, effective for audits of financial statements for periods ending on or after December 15, 1997, by Statement on Auditing Standards No. 82.]

.25 In determining the nature, timing, and extent of auditing procedures to be applied to a specific account balance or class of transactions, the auditor should design procedures to obtain reasonable assurance of detecting misstatements that he or she believes, based on the preliminary judgment about materiality, could be material, when aggregated with misstatements in other balances or classes, to the financial statements taken as a whole. Auditors use various methods to design procedures to detect such misstatements. In some cases, auditors explicitly estimate, for planning purposes, the maximum amount of misstatements in the balance or class that, when combined with misstatements in other balances or classes, could exist without causing the financial statements to be materially misstated. In other cases, auditors relate their preliminary judgment about materiality to a specific account balance or class of transactions without explicitly estimating such misstatements. [Paragraph renumbered by the issuance of Statement on Auditing Standards No. 82, February 1997.]

.26 The auditor needs to consider audit risk at the individual account-balance or class-of-transactions level because such consideration directly assists in determining the scope of auditing procedures for the balance or class and related assertions. The auditor should seek to restrict audit risk at the individual balance or class level in such a way that will enable him or her, at the completion of the examination, to express an opinion on the financial statements taken as a whole at an appropriately low level of audit risk. Auditors use various approaches to accomplish that objective. [Paragraph renumbered by the issuance of Statement on Auditing Standards No. 82, February 1997.]

.27 At the account-balance or class-of-transactions level, audit risk consists of (*a*) the risk (consisting of inherent risk and control risk) that the balance or class and related assertions contain misstatements (whether caused by error or fraud) that could be material to the financial statements when aggregated with misstatements in other balances or classes and (*b*) the risk (detection risk) that the auditor will not detect such misstatements. The discussion that follows describes audit risk in terms of three component risks.[12] The way the auditor considers these component risks and combines them involves professional judgment and depends on the audit approach.

a. *Inherent risk* is the susceptibility of an assertion to a material misstatement, assuming that there are no related controls. The risk of such misstatement is greater for some assertions and related balances or classes than for others. For example, complex calculations are more likely to be misstated than simple calculations. Cash is more susceptible to theft than an inventory of coal. Accounts consisting of amounts derived from accounting estimates pose greater risks than do accounts consisting of relatively routine, factual data. External factors also influence inherent risk. For example, technological developments might make a particular product obsolete, thereby causing inventory to be more susceptible to overstatement. In addition to those factors that are peculiar to a specific assertion for an account balance or a class of transactions, factors that relate to several or all of the balances or classes may influence the inherent risk related to an assertion for a specific balance or class. These latter factors include, for example, a lack of sufficient working capital to continue operations or a declining industry characterized by a large number of business failures.

b. *Control risk* is the risk that a material misstatement that could occur in an assertion will not be prevented or detected on a timely basis by

---

[12] The formula in the appendix [paragraph .48] to section 350, *Audit Sampling*, describes audit risk in terms of four component risks. Detection risk is presented in terms of two components: the risk that analytical procedures and other relevant substantive tests would fail to detect misstatements equal to tolerable misstatement, and the allowable risk of incorrect acceptance for the substantive test of details. [Footnote renumbered by the issuance of Statement on Auditing Standards No. 82, February 1997.]

the entity's internal control. That risk is a function of the effectiveness of the design and operation of internal control in achieving the entity's objectives relevant to preparation of the entity's financial statements. Some control risk will always exist because of the inherent limitations of internal control.

c. *Detection risk* is the risk that the auditor will not detect a material misstatement that exists in an assertion. Detection risk is a function of the effectiveness of an auditing procedure and of its application by the auditor. It arises partly from uncertainties that exist when the auditor does not examine 100 percent of an account balance or a class of transactions and partly because of other uncertainties that exist even if he or she were to examine 100 percent of the balance or class. Such other uncertainties arise because an auditor might select an inappropriate auditing procedure, misapply an appropriate procedure, or misinterpret the audit results. These other uncertainties can be reduced to a negligible level through adequate planning and supervision and conduct of a firm's audit practice in accordance with appropriate quality control standards.

[Paragraph renumbered and amended, effective for audits of financial statements for periods ending on or after December 15, 1997, by Statement on Auditing Standards No. 82.]

.28 Inherent risk and control risk differ from detection risk in that they exist independently of the audit of financial statements, whereas detection risk relates to the auditor's procedures and can be changed at his or her discretion. Detection risk should bear an inverse relationship to inherent and control risk. The less the inherent and control risk the auditor believes exists, the greater the detection risk that can be accepted. Conversely, the greater the inherent and control risk the auditor believes exists, the less the detection risk that can be accepted. These components of audit risk may be assessed in quantitative terms such as percentages or in nonquantitative terms that range, for example, from a minimum to a maximum. [Paragraph renumbered by the issuance of Statement on Auditing Standards No. 82, February 1997.]

.29 When the auditor assesses inherent risk for an assertion related to an account balance or a class of transactions, he or she evaluates numerous factors that involve professional judgment. In doing so, the auditor considers not only factors peculiar to the related assertion, but also, other factors pervasive to the financial statements taken as a whole that may also influence inherent risk related to the assertion. If an auditor concludes that the effort required to assess inherent risk for an assertion would exceed the potential reduction in the extent of auditing procedures derived from such an assessment, the auditor should assess inherent risk as being at the maximum when designing auditing procedures. [Paragraph renumbered by the issuance of Statement on Auditing Standards No. 82, February 1997.]

.30 The auditor also uses professional judgment in assessing control risk for an assertion related to the account balance or class of transactions. The auditor's assessment of control risk is based on the sufficiency of evidential matter obtained to support the effectiveness of internal control in preventing or detecting misstatements in financial statement assertions. If the auditor believes controls are unlikely to pertain to an assertion or are unlikely to be effective, or believes that evaluating their effectiveness would be inefficient, he or she would assess control risk for that assertion at the maximum. [Paragraph renumbered by the issuance of Statement on Auditing Standards No. 82, February 1997.]

.31 The auditor might make separate or combined assessments of inherent risk and control risk. If the auditor considers inherent risk or control risk, separately or in combination, to be less than the maximum, he or she should have an appropriate basis for these assessments. This basis may be obtained, for example, through the use of questionnaires, checklists, instructions, or similar generalized materials and, in the case of control risk, the understanding of internal control and the performance of suitable tests of controls. However, professional judgment is required in interpreting, adapting, or expanding such generalized material as appropriate in the circumstances. [Paragraph renumbered by the issuance of Statement on Auditing Standards No. 82, February 1997.]

.32 The detection risk that the auditor can accept in the design of auditing procedures is based on the level to which he or she seeks to restrict audit risk related to the account balance or class of transactions and on the assessment of inherent and control risks. As the auditor's assessment of inherent risk and control risk decreases, the detection risk that can be accepted increases. It is not appropriate, however, for an auditor to rely completely on assessments of inherent risk and control risk to the exclusion of performing substantive tests of account balances and classes of transactions where misstatements could exist that might be material when aggregated with misstatements in other balances or classes. [Paragraph renumbered by the issuance of Statement on Auditing Standards No. 82, February 1997.]

.33 An audit of financial statements is a cumulative process; as the auditor performs planned auditing procedures, the evidence obtained may cause him or her to modify the nature, timing, and extent of other planned procedures. As a result of performing auditing procedures or from other sources during the audit, information may come to the auditor's attention that differs significantly from the information on which the audit plan was based. For example, the extent of misstatements detected may alter the judgment about the levels of inherent and control risks, and other information obtained about the financial statements may alter the preliminary judgment about materiality. In such cases, the auditor may need to reevaluate the auditing procedures he or she plans to apply, based on the revised consideration of audit risk and materiality for all or certain of the account balances or classes of transactions and related assertions. [Paragraph renumbered and amended, effective for audits of financial statements for periods ending on or after December 15, 1997, by Statement on Auditing Standards No. 82.]

Evaluating Audit Findings

.34 In evaluating whether the financial statements are presented fairly, in all material respects, in conformity with generally accepted accounting principles, the auditor should aggregate misstatements that the entity has not corrected in a way that enables him or her to consider whether, in relation to individual amounts, subtotals, or totals in the financial statements, they materially misstate the financial statements taken as a whole. Qualitative considerations also influence the auditor in reaching a conclusion as to whether misstatements are material. [Paragraph renumbered by the issuance of Statement on Auditing Standards No. 82, February 1997.]

.35 The aggregation of misstatements should include the auditor's best estimate of the total misstatements in the account balances or classes of transactions that he or she has examined (hereafter referred to as likely misstatement[13]), not just the amount of misstatements specifically identified (hereafter referred to as known misstatement).[14] When the auditor tests an account balance or a class of transactions and related assertions by an analytical procedure, he or she ordinarily would not specifically identify misstatements but would only obtain an indication of whether misstatement might exist in the balance or class and possibly its approximate magnitude. If the analytical procedure indicates that a misstatement might exist, but not its approximate amount, the auditor ordinarily would have to employ other procedures to enable him or her to estimate the likely misstatement in the balance or class. When an auditor uses audit sampling to test an assertion for an account balance or a class of transactions, he or she projects the amount of known misstatements identified in the sample to the items in the balance or class from which the sample was selected. That projected misstatement, along with the results of other substantive tests, contributes to the auditor's assessment of likely misstatement in the balance or class. [Paragraph renumbered by the issuance of Statement on Auditing Standards No. 82, February 1997.]

.36 The risk of material misstatement of the financial statements is generally greater when account balances and classes of transactions include accounting estimates rather than essentially factual data because of the inherent subjectivity in estimating future events. Estimates, such as those for inventory obsolescence, uncollectible receivables, and warranty obligations, are subject not only to the unpredictability of future events but also to misstatements that may arise from using inadequate or inappropriate data or misapplying appropriate data. Since no one accounting estimate can be considered accurate with certainty, the auditor recognizes that a difference between an estimated amount best supported by the audit evidence and the estimated amount included in the financial statements may be reasonable, and such difference would not be considered to be a likely misstatement. However, if the auditor believes the estimated amount included in the financial statements is unreasonable, he or she should treat the difference between that estimate and the closest reasonable estimate as a likely misstatement and aggregate it with other likely misstatements. The auditor should also consider whether the difference between estimates best supported by the audit evidence and the estimates included in the financial statements, which are individually reasonable, indicate a possible bias on the part of the entity's management. For example, if each accounting estimate included in the financial statements was individually reasonable, but the effect of the difference between each estimate and the estimate best supported by the audit evidence was to increase income, the auditor should reconsider the estimates taken as a whole. [Paragraph renumbered by the issuance of Statement on Auditing Standards No. 82, February 1997.]

.37 In prior periods, likely misstatements may not have been corrected by the entity because they did not cause the financial statements for those periods to be materially misstated. Those misstatements might also affect the current

---

[13] See section 316.33–.35 for a further discussion of the auditor's consideration of differences between the accounting records and the underlying facts and circumstances. Those paragraphs provide specific guidance on the auditor's consideration of an audit adjustment that is, or may be, the result of fraud. [Footnote renumbered and amended, effective for audits of financial statements for periods ending on or after December 15, 1997, by Statement on Auditing Standards No. 82.]

[14] If the auditor were to examine all of the items in a balance or a class, the likely misstatement applicable to recorded transactions in the balance or class would be the amount of known misstatements specifically identified. [Footnote renumbered by the issuance of Statement on Auditing Standards No. 82, February 1997.]

period's financial statements.[15] If the auditor believes that there is an unacceptably high risk that the current period's financial statements may be materially misstated when those prior-period likely misstatements that affect the current period's financial statements are considered along with likely misstatements arising in the current period, the auditor should include in aggregate likely misstatement the effect on the current period's financial statements of those prior-period likely misstatements. [Paragraph renumbered by the issuance of Statement on Auditing Standards No. 82, February 1997.]

.38 If the auditor concludes, based on the accumulation of sufficient evidential matter, that the aggregation of likely misstatements causes the financial statements to be materially misstated, the auditor should request management to eliminate the material misstatement. If the material misstatement is not eliminated, the auditor should issue a qualified or an adverse opinion on the financial statements. Material misstatements may be eliminated by, for example, application of appropriate accounting principles, other adjustments in amounts, or the addition of appropriate disclosure of inadequately disclosed matters. Even though the aggregate effect of likely misstatements on the financial statements may be immaterial, the auditor should recognize that an accumulation of immaterial misstatements in the balance sheet could contribute to material misstatements of future financial statements. [Paragraph renumbered by the issuance of Statement on Auditing Standards No. 82, February 1997.]

.39 If the auditor concludes that the aggregation of likely misstatements does not cause the financial statements to be materially misstated, he or she should recognize that they could still be materially misstated because of further misstatement remaining undetected. As aggregate likely misstatement increases, the risk that the financial statements may be materially misstated also increases. The auditor generally reduces this risk of material misstatement in planning the audit by restricting the extent of detection risk he or she is willing to accept for an assertion related to an account balance or a class of transactions. The auditor can reduce this risk of material misstatement by modifying the nature, timing, and extent of planned auditing procedures on a continuous basis in performing the audit. (See paragraph .33.) Nevertheless, if the auditor believes that such risk is unacceptably high, he or she should perform additional auditing procedures or satisfy himself or herself that the entity has adjusted the financial statements to reduce the risk of material misstatement to an acceptable level. [Paragraph renumbered by the issuance of Statement on Auditing Standards No. 82, February 1997.]

.40 In aggregating known and likely misstatements that the entity has not corrected, pursuant to paragraphs .34 and .35, the auditor may designate an amount below which misstatements need not be accumulated. This amount should be set so that any such misstatements, either individually or when aggregated with other such misstatements, would not be material to the financial statements, after the possibility of further undetected misstatements is considered. [Paragraph added, effective for audits of financial statements for periods ending on or after December 15, 1997, by Statement on Auditing Standards No. 82.]

---

[15] The measurement of the effect, if any, on the current period's financial statements of misstatements uncorrected in prior periods involves accounting considerations and is therefore not addressed in this section. [Footnote renumbered by the issuance of Statement on Auditing Standards No. 82, February 1997.]

Effective Date

.41 This section is effective for audits of financial statements for periods beginning after June 30, 1984. [Paragraph renumbered by the issuance of Statement on Auditing Standards No. 82, February 1997.]

AU Section 313

Substantive Tests Prior to the Balance-Sheet Date

(Supersedes Statement on Auditing Standards No. 1, AICPA, *Professional Standards*, vol. 1, AU sec. 310.05–.09.)*

Source: SAS No. 45.

Effective for periods ended after September 30, 1983, unless otherwise indicated.

.01 This section provides guidance for audits of financial statements concerning—

a. Factors to be considered before applying principal substantive tests to the details of particular asset or liability accounts as of a date (*interim date*) that is prior to the balance-sheet date.

b. Auditing procedures to provide a reasonable basis for extending from an interim date to the balance-sheet date (*remaining period*) the audit conclusions from such principal substantive tests.

c. Coordinating the timing of auditing procedures.

Guidance concerning the timing of tests of controls is provided in section 319.73.

.02 Audit testing at interim dates may permit early consideration of significant matters affecting the year-end financial statements (for example, related party transactions, changed conditions, recent accounting pronouncements, and financial statement items likely to require adjustment). In addition, much of the audit planning, including obtaining an understanding of internal control, assessing control risk and the application of substantive tests to transactions can be conducted prior to the balance-sheet date.[1]

.03 Applying principal substantive tests to the details of an asset or liability account as of an interim date rather than as of the balance-sheet date potentially increases the risk that misstatements that may exist at the balance-sheet date will not be detected by the auditor. The potential for such increased audit risk tends to become greater as the remaining period is lengthened. This potential incremental audit risk can be controlled, however,

---

* Editor's note deleted to reflect the conforming changes necessary due to the issuance of Statement on Auditing Standards Nos. 53 through 62.

[1] Substantive tests such as the following can be applied to transactions through any selected date(s) prior to the balance-sheet date and completed as part of the year-end procedures: (1) tests of details of the additions to and reductions of accounts such as property, investments, and debt and equity capital; (2) tests of details of transactions affecting income and expense accounts; (3) tests of accounts that are not to be audited by testing the details of items composing the balance (for example, warranty reserves, clearing accounts, certain deferred charges); and (4) analytical procedures applied to income and expense accounts.

if the substantive tests to cover the remaining period can be designed in a way that will provide a reasonable basis for extending to the balance-sheet date the audit conclusions from the tests of details at the interim date.

Factors to Be Considered Before Applying Principal Substantive Tests to the Details of Balance-Sheet Accounts at Interim Dates

.04 Before applying principal substantive tests to the details of asset or liability accounts at an interim date, the auditor should assess the difficulty in controlling the incremental audit risk. Paragraphs .05 through .07 discuss considerations that affect that assessment. In addition, the auditor should consider the cost of the substantive tests that are necessary to cover the remaining period in a way that will provide the appropriate audit assurance at the balance-sheet date. Applying principal substantive tests to the details of asset and liability accounts at an interim date may not be cost-effective if substantive tests to cover the remaining period cannot be restricted due to the assessed level of control risk.

.05 Assessing control risk at below the maximum is not required in order to have a reasonable basis for extending audit conclusions from an interim date to the balance-sheet date; however, if the auditor assesses control risk at the maximum during the remaining period, he should consider whether the effectiveness of certain of the substantive tests to cover that period will be impaired. For example, effective controls may be lacking over the internal documents that provide indications of transactions that have been executed. Substantive tests that are based on such documents and relate to the completeness assertion for the remaining period may be ineffective because the documents may be incomplete. Likewise, substantive tests covering the remaining period that relate to the existence assertion at the balance-sheet date may be ineffective if effective controls over the custody and physical movement of assets are not present. In both of the above examples, if the auditor concludes that the effectiveness of such substantive tests would be impaired, additional assurance should be sought or the accounts should be examined as of the balance-sheet date.

.06 The auditor should consider whether there are rapidly changing business conditions or circumstances that might predispose management to misstate financial statements in the remaining period.[2] If such conditions or circumstances are present, the auditor might conclude that the substantive tests to cover the remaining period would not be effective in controlling the incremental audit risk associated with them. In those situations, the asset and liability accounts affected should ordinarily be examined as of the balance-sheet date.

.07 The auditor should consider whether the year-end balances of the particular asset or liability accounts that might be selected for interim examination are reasonably predictable with respect to amount, relative significance, and composition. He should also consider whether the entity's proposed procedures for analyzing and adjusting such accounts at interim dates and for establishing proper accounting cutoffs are appropriate. In addition, the auditor

[2] See section 316, *Consideration of Fraud in a Financial Statement Audit*, paragraphs .16 through .19.

should consider whether the accounting system will provide information concerning the balances at the balance-sheet date and the transactions in the remaining period that is sufficient to permit investigation of (*a*) significant unusual transactions or entries (including those at or near year-end); (*b*) other causes of significant fluctuations, or expected fluctuations that did not occur; and (*c*) changes in the composition of the account balances. If the auditor concludes that evidential matter related to the above would not be sufficient for purposes of controlling audit risk, the account should be examined as of the balance-sheet date.

Extending Audit Conclusions to the Balance-Sheet Date

.08 Substantive tests should be designed to cover the remaining period in such a way that the assurance from those tests and the substantive tests applied to the details of the balance as of an interim date, and any audit assurance provided from the assessed level of control risk, achieve the audit objectives at the balance-sheet date. Such tests ordinarily should include (*a*) comparison of information concerning the balance at the balance-sheet date with the comparable information at the interim date to identify amounts that appear unusual and investigation of any such amounts and (*b*) other analytical procedures or substantive tests of details, or a combination of both, to provide a reasonable basis for extending to the balance-sheet date the audit conclusions relative to the assertions tested directly or indirectly at the interim date.[3]

.09 If misstatements are detected in account balances at interim dates, the auditor may be required to modify the planned nature, timing, or extent of the substantive tests covering the remaining period that relate to such accounts or to reperform certain auditing procedures at the balance-sheet date. The assessment of possible misstatement as of the balance-sheet date should be based on the auditor's judgment of the state of the particular account(s) as of that date, after considering (*a*) the possible implications of the nature and cause of the misstatements detected at the interim date, (*b*) the possible relationship to other phases of the audit, (*c*) the corrections subsequently recorded by the entity, and (*d*) the results of auditing procedures covering the remaining period (including those that are responsive to the particular possibilities for misstatement). For example, the auditor might conclude that the estimate of unrecorded credit memos at an interim date is representative of such misstatements at the balance-sheet date, based on substantive tests covering the remaining period. On the other hand, the assessment of the possible effects at the balance-sheet date of other types of cutoff misstatements at an interim date might be based on the results of reperforming substantive tests of the cutoff.

Coordinating the Timing of Auditing Procedures

.10 The timing of auditing procedures also involves consideration of whether related auditing procedures are properly coordinated. This includes, for example—

a. Coordinating the auditing procedures applied to related party transactions and balances.[4]

---

[3] Factors to be considered in determining the relative mix of tests of details and analytical procedures include (1) the nature of the transactions and balances in relation to the assertions involved, (2) the availability of historical data or other criteria for use in analytical procedures, and (3) the availability of records required for effective tests of details and the nature of the tests to which they are susceptible.

[4] See section 334, *Related Parties*.

b. Coordinating the testing of interrelated accounts and accounting cutoffs.

c. Maintaining temporary audit control over assets that are readily negotiable and simultaneously testing such assets and cash on hand and in banks, bank loans, and other related items.

Decisions about coordinating related auditing procedures should be made in the light of the assessed level of control risk and of the particular auditing procedures that could be applied, either for the remaining period or at year-end, or both.

AU Section 315

Communications Between Predecessor and Successor Auditors

(Supersedes SAS No. 7)

Source: SAS No. 84.

Effective with respect to acceptance of an engagement after March 31, 1998.

Introduction

.01 This section provides guidance on communications between predecessor and successor auditors when a change of auditors is in process or has taken place. It also provides communications guidance when possible misstatements are discovered in financial statements reported on by a predecessor auditor. This section applies whenever an independent auditor is considering accepting an engagement to audit or reaudit (see paragraph .14 of this section) financial statements in accordance with generally accepted auditing standards, and after such auditor has been appointed to perform such an engagement.

.02 For the purposes of this section, the term *predecessor auditor* refers to an auditor who (*a*) has reported on the most recent audited financial statements[1] or was engaged to perform but did not complete an audit of any subsequent financial statements[2] and (*b*) has resigned, declined to stand for reappointment, or been notified that his or her services have been, or may be, terminated. The term *successor auditor* refers to an auditor who is considering accepting an engagement to audit financial statements but has not communicated with the predecessor auditor as provided in paragraphs .07 through .10 and to an auditor who has accepted such an engagement.

Change of Auditors

.03 An auditor should not accept an engagement until the communications described in paragraphs .07 through .10 have been evaluated.[3] However, an auditor may make a proposal for an audit engagement before communicating with the predecessor auditor. The auditor may wish to advise the prospec-

---

[1] The provisions of this section are not required if the most recent audited financial statements are more than two years prior to the beginning of the earliest period to be audited by the successor auditor.

[2] Occasionally, a successor auditor is replaced before completing an audit engagement and issuing a report. This auditor is also considered to be a predecessor auditor. In such situations, there are two predecessor auditors: the auditor who reported on the most recent audited financial statements and the auditor who was engaged to perform but did not complete an audit of any subsequent financial statements.

[3] When the most recent financial statements have been compiled or reviewed in accordance with the Statements on Standards for Accounting and Review Services, the accountant who reported on those financial statements is not a predecessor auditor. Although not required by this section, in these circumstances the successor auditor may find the matters described in paragraphs .08 and .09 useful in determining whether to accept the engagement.

tive client (for example, in a proposal) that acceptance cannot be final until the communications have been evaluated.

.04 Other communications between the successor and predecessor auditors, described in paragraph .11, are advisable to assist in the planning of the engagement. However, the timing of these other communications is more flexible. The successor auditor may initiate these other communications either prior to acceptance of the engagement or subsequent thereto.

.05 When more than one auditor is considering accepting an engagement, the predecessor auditor should not be expected to be available to respond to inquiries until a successor auditor has been selected by the prospective client and has accepted the engagement subject to the evaluation of the communications with the predecessor auditor as provided in paragraphs .07 through .10.

.06 The initiative for communicating rests with the successor auditor. The communication may be either written or oral. Both the predecessor and successor auditors should hold in confidence information obtained from each other. This obligation applies whether or not the successor auditor accepts the engagement.

Communications Before Successor Auditor Accepts Engagement

.07 Inquiry of the predecessor auditor is a necessary procedure because the predecessor auditor may be able to provide information that will assist the successor auditor in determining whether to accept the engagement. The successor auditor should bear in mind that, among other things, the predecessor auditor and the client may have disagreed about accounting principles, auditing procedures, or similarly significant matters.

.08 The successor auditor should request permission from the prospective client to make an inquiry of the predecessor auditor prior to final acceptance of the engagement. Except as permitted by the Rules of the Code of Professional Conduct, an auditor is precluded from disclosing confidential information obtained in the course of an engagement unless the client specifically consents. Thus, the successor auditor should ask the prospective client to authorize the predecessor auditor to respond fully to the successor auditor's inquiries. If a prospective client refuses to permit the predecessor auditor to respond or limits the response, the successor auditor should inquire as to the reasons and consider the implications of that refusal in deciding whether to accept the engagement.

.09 The successor auditor should make specific and reasonable inquiries of the predecessor auditor regarding matters that will assist the successor auditor in determining whether to accept the engagement. Matters subject to inquiry should include—

- Information that might bear on the integrity of management.
- Disagreements with management as to accounting principles, auditing procedures, or other similarly significant matters.
- Communications to audit committees or others with equivalent authority and responsibility[4] regarding fraud, illegal acts by clients, and internal-control-related matters.[5]

---

[4] For entities that do not have audit committees, the phrase "others with equivalent authority and responsibility" may include the board of directors, the board of trustees, or the owner in owner-managed entities.

[5] See section 316, *Consideration of Fraud in a Financial Statement Audit*; section 317, *Illegal Acts by Clients*; and section 325, *Communication of Internal Control Related Matters Noted in an Audit*.

- The predecessor auditor's understanding as to the reasons for the change of auditors.

The successor auditor may wish to consider other reasonable inquiries.

.10 The predecessor auditor should respond promptly and fully, on the basis of known facts, to the successor auditor's reasonable inquiries. However, should the predecessor auditor decide, due to unusual circumstances such as impending, threatened, or potential litigation; disciplinary proceedings; or other unusual circumstances, not to respond fully to the inquiries, the predecessor auditor should clearly state that the response is limited. If the successor auditor receives a limited response, its implications should be considered in deciding whether to accept the engagement.

Other Communications

.11 The successor auditor should request that the client authorize the predecessor auditor to allow a review of the predecessor auditor's working papers. The predecessor auditor may wish to request a consent and acknowledgment letter from the client to document this authorization in an effort to reduce misunderstandings about the scope of the communications being authorized.[6] It is customary in such circumstances for the predecessor auditor to make himself or herself available to the successor auditor and make available for review certain of the working papers. The predecessor auditor should determine which working papers are to be made available for review and which may be copied. The predecessor auditor should ordinarily permit the successor auditor to review working papers, including documentation of planning, internal control, audit results, and other matters of continuing accounting and auditing significance, such as the working paper analysis of balance sheet accounts, and those relating to contingencies. Also, the predecessor auditor should reach an understanding with the successor auditor as to the use of the working papers.[7] The extent, if any, to which a predecessor auditor permits access to the working papers is a matter of judgment.

Successor Auditor's Use of Communications

.12 The successor auditor must obtain sufficient competent evidential matter to afford a reasonable basis for expressing an opinion on the financial statements he or she has been engaged to audit, including evaluating the consistency of the application of accounting principles. The audit evidence used in analyzing the impact of the opening balances on the current-year financial statements and consistency of accounting principles is a matter of professional judgment. Such audit evidence may include the most recent audited financial statements, the predecessor auditor's report thereon,[8] the results of inquiry of the predecessor auditor, the results of the successor auditor's review of the predecessor auditor's working papers, and audit procedures performed on the

---

[6] Appendix A [paragraph .24] contains an illustrative client consent and acknowledgment letter.

[7] Before permitting access to the working papers, the predecessor auditor may wish to obtain a written communication from the successor auditor regarding the use of the working papers. Appendix B [paragraph .25] contains an illustrative successor auditor acknowledgment letter.

[8] The successor auditor may wish to make inquiries about the professional reputation and standing of the predecessor auditor. See section 543, *Part of Audit Performed by Other Independent Auditors*, paragraph 10*a*.

current period's transactions that may provide evidence about the opening balances or consistency. For example, evidence gathered during the current year's audit may provide information about the realizability and existence of receivables and inventory recorded at the beginning of the year. The successor auditor may also apply appropriate auditing procedures to account balances at the beginning of the period under audit and to transactions in prior periods.

.13 The successor auditor's review of the predecessor auditor's working papers may affect the nature, timing, and extent of the successor auditor's procedures with respect to the opening balances and consistency of accounting principles. However, the nature, timing, and extent of audit work performed and the conclusions reached in both these areas are solely the responsibility of the successor auditor. In reporting on the audit, the successor auditor should not make reference to the report or work of the predecessor auditor as the basis, in part, for the successor auditor's own opinion.

Audits of Financial Statements That Have Been Previously Audited

.14 If an auditor is asked to audit and report on financial statements that have been previously audited and reported on (henceforth referred to as a reaudit), the auditor considering acceptance of the reaudit engagement is also a successor auditor, and the auditor who previously reported is also a predecessor auditor. In addition to the communications described in paragraphs .07 through .10, the successor auditor should state that the purpose of the inquiries is to obtain information about whether to accept an engagement to perform a reaudit.

.15 If the successor auditor accepts the reaudit engagement, he or she may consider the information obtained from inquiries of the predecessor auditor and review of the predecessor auditor's report and working papers in planning the reaudit. However, the information obtained from those inquiries and any review of the predecessor auditor's report and working papers is not sufficient to afford a basis for expressing an opinion. The nature, timing, and extent of the audit work performed and the conclusions reached in the reaudit are solely the responsibility of the successor auditor performing the reaudit.

.16 The successor auditor should plan and perform the reaudit in accordance with generally accepted auditing standards. The successor auditor should not assume responsibility for the predecessor auditor's work or issue a report that reflects divided responsibility as described in section 543, *Part of Audit Performed by Other Independent Auditors*. Furthermore, the predecessor auditor is not a specialist as defined in section 336, *Using the Work of a Specialist*, or an internal auditor as defined in section 322, *The Auditor's Consideration of the Internal Audit Function in an Audit of Financial Statements*.

.17 If the successor auditor has audited the current period, the results of that audit may be considered in planning and performing the reaudit of the preceding period or periods and may provide evidential matter that is useful in performing the reaudit.

.18 If, in a reaudit engagement, the successor auditor is unable to obtain sufficient competent evidential matter to express an opinion on the financial statements, the successor auditor should qualify or disclaim an opinion because of the inability to perform procedures the successor auditor considers necessary in the circumstances.

.19 The successor auditor should request working papers for the period or periods under reaudit and the period prior to the reaudit period. However, the extent, if any, to which the predecessor auditor permits access to the working papers is a matter of judgment. (See paragraph .11 of this section.)

.20 In a reaudit, the successor auditor generally will be unable to observe inventory or make physical counts at the reaudit date or dates in the manner discussed in paragraphs .09 through .11 of section 331, *Inventories*. In such cases, the successor auditor may consider the knowledge obtained from his or her review of the predecessor auditor's working papers and inquiries of the predecessor auditor to determine the nature, timing, and extent of procedures to be applied in the circumstances. The successor auditor performing the reaudit should, if material, observe or perform some physical counts of inventory at a date subsequent to the period of the reaudit, in connection with a current audit or otherwise, and apply appropriate tests of intervening transactions. Appropriate procedures may include tests of prior transactions, reviews of records of prior counts, and the application of analytical procedures, such as gross profit tests.

Discovery of Possible Misstatements in Financial Statements Reported on by a Predecessor Auditor

.21 If during the audit or reaudit, the successor auditor becomes aware of information that leads him or her to believe that financial statements reported on by the predecessor auditor may require revision, the successor auditor should request that the client inform the predecessor auditor of the situation and arrange for the three parties to discuss this information and attempt to resolve the matter. The successor auditor should communicate to the predecessor auditor any information that the predecessor auditor may need to consider in accordance with section 561, *Subsequent Discovery of Facts Existing at the Date of the Auditor's Report*, which sets out the procedures that an auditor should follow when the auditor subsequently discovers facts that may have affected the audited financial statements previously reported on.[9]

.22 If the client refuses to inform the predecessor auditor or if the successor auditor is not satisfied with the resolution of the matter, the successor auditor should evaluate (*a*) possible implications on the current engagement and (*b*) whether to resign from the engagement. Furthermore, the successor auditor may wish to consult with his or her legal counsel in determining an appropriate course of further action.

Effective Date

.23 This section will be effective with respect to acceptance of an engagement after March 31, 1998. Earlier application is permitted.

---

[9] See section 508, *Reports on Audited Financial Statements*, paragraphs .70 through .74, for reporting guidance.

.24

Appendix A

Illustrative Client Consent and Acknowledgment Letter

1. Paragraph .11 of this section states, "The successor auditor should request that the client authorize the predecessor auditor to allow a review of the predecessor auditor's working papers. The predecessor auditor may wish to request a consent and acknowledgment letter from the client to document this authorization in an effort to reduce misunderstandings about the scope of the communications being authorized." The following letter is presented for illustrative purposes only and is not required by professional standards.

[*Date*]

ABC Enterprises
[*Address*]

You have given your consent to allow [*name of successor CPA firm*], as successor independent auditors for ABC Enterprises (ABC), access to our working papers for our audit of the December 31, 19X1, financial statements of ABC. You also have given your consent to us to respond fully to [*name of successor CPA firm*] inquiries. You understand and agree that the review of our working papers is undertaken solely for the purpose of obtaining an understanding about ABC and certain information about our audit to assist [*name of successor CPA firm*] in planning the audit of the December 31, 19X2, financial statements of ABC.

Please confirm your agreement with the foregoing by signing and dating a copy of this letter and returning it to us.

Attached is the form of the letter we will furnish [*name of successor CPA firm*] regarding the use of the working papers.

Very truly yours,

[*Predecessor Auditor*]

By: ______________________________

Accepted:

ABC Enterprises

By: ______________________________ Date: ____________________

.25

Appendix B

Illustrative Successor Auditor Acknowledgment Letter

1. Paragraph .11, footnote 7, of this section states, "Before permitting access to the working papers, the predecessor auditor may wish to obtain a written communication from the successor auditor regarding the use of the working papers." The following letter is presented for illustrative purposes only and is not required by professional standards.

[*Date*]

[*Successor Auditor*]
[*Address*]

We have previously audited, in accordance with generally accepted auditing standards, the December 31, 19X1, financial statements of ABC Enterprises (ABC). We rendered a report on those financial statements and have not performed any audit procedures subsequent to the audit report date. In connection with your audit of ABC's 19X2 financial statements, you have requested access to our working papers prepared in connection with that audit. ABC has authorized our firm to allow you to review those working papers.

Our audit, and the working papers prepared in connection therewith, of ABC's financial statements were not planned or conducted in contemplation of your review. Therefore, items of possible interest to you may not have been specifically addressed. Our use of professional judgment and the assessment of audit risk and materiality for the purpose of our audit mean that matters may have existed that would have been assessed differently by you. We make no representation as to the sufficiency or appropriateness of the information in our working papers for your purposes.

We understand that the purpose of your review is to obtain information about ABC and our 19X1 audit results to assist you in planning your 19X2 audit of ABC. For that purpose only, we will provide you access to our working papers that relate to that objective.

Upon request, we will provide copies of those working papers that provide factual information about ABC. You agree to subject any such copies or information otherwise derived from our working papers to your normal policy for retention of working papers and protection of confidential client information. Furthermore, in the event of a third-party request for access to your working papers prepared in connection with your audits of ABC, you agree to obtain our permission before voluntarily allowing any such access to our working papers or information otherwise derived from our working papers, and to obtain on our behalf any releases that you obtain from such third party. You agree to advise us promptly and provide us a copy of any subpoena, summons, or other court order for access to your working papers that include copies of our working papers or information otherwise derived therefrom.

Please confirm your agreement with the foregoing by signing and dating a copy of this letter and returning it to us.

Very truly yours,

[Predecessor Auditor]

By: ______________________

Accepted:

[Successor Auditor]

By: ______________________ Date: ____________

Even with the client's consent, access to the predecessor auditor's working papers may still be limited. Experience has shown that the predecessor auditor may be willing to grant broader access if given additional assurance concerning the use of the working papers. Accordingly, the successor auditor might consider agreeing to the following limitations on the review of the predecessor auditor's working papers in order to obtain broader access:

- The successor auditor will not comment, orally or in writing, to anyone as a result of the review as to whether the predecessor auditor's engagement was performed in accordance with generally accepted auditing standards.
- The successor auditor will not provide expert testimony or litigation support services or otherwise accept an engagement to comment on issues relating to the quality of the predecessor auditor's audit.
- The successor auditor will not use the audit procedures or results thereof documented in the predecessor auditor's working papers as evidential matter in rendering an opinion on the 19X2 financial statements of ABC Enterprises, except as contemplated in Statement on Auditing Standards No. 84.

The following paragraph illustrates the above:

> Because your review of our working papers is undertaken solely for the purpose described above and may not entail a review of all our working papers, you agree that (1) the information obtained from the review will not be used by you for any other purpose, (2) you will not comment, orally or in writing, to anyone as a result of that review as to whether our audit was performed in accordance with generally accepted auditing standards, (3) you will not provide expert testimony or litigation support services or otherwise accept an engagement to comment on issues relating to the quality of our audits, and (4) you will not use the audit procedures or results thereof documented in our working papers as evidential matter in rendering your opinion on the 19X2 financial statements of ABC, except as contemplated in Statement on Auditing Standards No. 84.

AU Section 315A

Communications Between Predecessor and Successor Auditors

(Supersedes section 543.18)

Source: SAS No. 7.

See section 9315A for interpretations of this section.

Effective November 30, 1975, unless otherwise indicated.*

.01 The purpose of this section is to provide guidance on communications between predecessor and successor auditors when a change of auditors has taken place or is in process. The term "predecessor auditor" refers to an auditor who has resigned or who has been notified that his services have been terminated. The term "successor auditor" refers to an auditor who has accepted an engagement or an auditor who has been invited to make a proposal for an engagement. This section applies whenever an independent auditor has been retained, or is to be retained, to audit the financial statements in accordance with generally accepted auditing standards.

.02 The initiative in communicating rests with the successor auditor. The communication may be either written or oral. Both the predecessor and successor auditors should hold in confidence information obtained from each other. This obligation applies whether or not the successor accepts the engagement.

.03 Prior to acceptance of the engagement, the successor auditor should attempt certain communications that are described in paragraphs .04 through .07. Other communications between the successor and the predecessor, described in paragraphs .08 and .09 are advisable. However, their timing is more flexible. The successor may attempt these other communications either prior to acceptance of the engagement or subsequent thereto.

Communications Before Successor Accepts Engagement

.04 Inquiry of the predecessor auditor is a necessary procedure because the predecessor may be able to provide the successor with information that will assist him in determining whether to accept the engagement. The successor should bear in mind that, among other things, the predecessor and the client may have disagreed about accounting principles, auditing procedures, or similarly significant matters.

.05 The successor auditor should explain to his prospective client the need to make an inquiry of the predecessor and should request permission to do so. Except as permitted by the Rules of the Code of Professional Conduct, an auditor is precluded from disclosing confidential information obtained in the

---

* See paragraph .12.

course of an audit engagement unless the client specifically consents. Thus, the successor auditor should ask the prospective client to authorize the predecessor to respond fully to the successor's inquiries. If a prospective client refuses to permit the predecessor to respond or limits the response, the successor auditor should inquire as to the reasons and consider the implications of that refusal in deciding whether to accept the engagement.

.06 The successor auditor should make specific and reasonable inquiries of the predecessor regarding matters that the successor believes will assist him in determining whether to accept the engagement. His inquiries should include specific questions regarding, among other things, facts that might bear on the integrity of management; on disagreements with management as to accounting principles, auditing procedures, or other similarly significant matters; and on the predecessor's understanding as to the reasons for the change of auditors.

.07 The predecessor auditor should respond promptly and fully, on the basis of facts known to him, to the successor's reasonable inquiries. However, should he decide, due to unusual circumstances such as impending litigation, not to respond fully to the inquiries, he should indicate that his response is limited. If the successor auditor receives a limited response, he should consider its implications in deciding whether to accept the engagement.

Other Communications

.08 When one auditor succeeds another, the successor auditor must obtain sufficient competent evidential matter to afford a reasonable basis for expressing his opinion on the financial statements he has been engaged to audit as well as for evaluating the consistency of the application of accounting principles in that year as compared with the preceding year. This may be done by applying appropriate auditing procedures to the account balances at the beginning of the period under audit and in some cases to transactions in prior periods. The successor auditor's audit may be facilitated by (*a*) making specific inquiries of the predecessor regarding matters that the successor believes may affect the conduct of his audit, such as audit areas that have required an inordinate amount of time or audit problems that arose from the condition of the accounting system and records and (*b*) reviewing the predecessor auditor's working papers. In reporting on his audit, however, the successor auditor should not make reference to the report or work of the predecessor auditor as the basis, in part, for his own opinion.

.09 The successor auditor should request the client to authorize the predecessor to allow a review of the predecessor's working papers. It is customary in such circumstances for the predecessor auditor to make himself available to the successor auditor for consultation and to make available for review certain of his working papers. The predecessor and successor auditors should agree on those working papers that are to be made available for review and those that may be copied. Ordinarily, the predecessor should permit the successor to review working papers relating to matters of continuing accounting significance, such as the working paper analysis of balance sheet accounts, both current and noncurrent, and those relating to contingencies. Valid business reasons, however, may lead the predecessor auditor to decide not to allow a review of his working papers. Further, when more than one successor auditor is considering acceptance of an engagement, the predecessor auditor should not be expected to make himself or his working papers available until the successor has accepted the engagement.

Financial Statements Reported on by Predecessor

.10 If during his audit the successor auditor becomes aware of information that leads him to believe that financial statements reported on by the predecessor auditor may require revision, he should request his client to arrange a meeting among the three parties to discuss this information and attempt to resolve the matter.[1] If the client refuses or if the successor is not satisfied with the result, the successor auditor may be well advised to consult with his attorney in determining an appropriate course of further action.

[.11] [Superseded by Statement on Auditing Standards No. 15, effective for periods ending after June 30, 1977, as superseded by section 508.]

Effective Date

.12 Statements on Auditing Standards generally are effective at the time of their issuance. However, since this Statement provides for practices that may differ in certain respects from practices heretofore considered acceptable it will be effective with respect to changes in auditors in which the successor auditor's consideration of acceptance of an engagement begins after November 30, 1975.

---

[1] See sections 561, *Subsequent Discovery of Facts Existing at the Date of the Auditor's Report*, and 711.11 and .12, *Filings Under Federal Securities Statutes*, for guidance on action to be taken by the predecessor auditor. [Reference changed by issuance of Statement on Auditing Standards No. 37.]

AU Section 9315A

Communications Between Predecessor and Successor Auditors: Auditing Interpretations of Section 315A

1. Determining the Predecessor Auditor

.01 *Question*—Section 315A, *Communications Between Predecessor and Successor Auditors*, requires that before accepting an audit engagement an auditor attempt certain communications with the predecessor auditor. Occasionally, a successor auditor is replaced before completing an audit engagement and issuing a report. In such cases, is another auditor who is considering accepting the engagement required to communicate with the original auditor, the successor auditor who is being replaced, or both?

.02 *Interpretation*—Both. The situation described is unusual and the auditor who is considering accepting the engagement needs complete information to help him decide whether to accept it. To obtain complete information, he should attempt to communicate with both the original auditor and the one he is replacing. That is, both auditors are considered to be predecessor auditors.

.03 In such circumstances, the second successor auditor should make specific and reasonable inquiries of each predecessor auditor regarding matters that the successor believes will assist him in determining whether to accept the engagement. Inquiring of only one of the predecessor auditors would not result in a full response because the circumstances surrounding each change in auditors may be different and the predecessor auditors, having served at different times and for different lengths of time, may have different knowledge about the potential client. In addition, inquiring of each predecessor is relevant since both auditor changes occurred during the period since the issuance of the most recent audit report.

.04 For a publicly held client, the successor should also review any SEC forms 8-K filed regarding auditor changes and any related letters filed with the SEC by the predecessor auditors.

.05 Each predecessor auditor should respond promptly and fully, on the basis of facts known to him, to the successor's reasonable inquiries. A predecessor auditor would not be responding fully when his response is evasive or omits significant information. If either predecessor auditor, due to unusual circumstances, limits his response, he should inform the successor auditor of the limitation and the successor should consider the implications of such a limitation in light of information of which he is aware.

[Issue Date: May, 1985.]

2. Restating Financial Statements Reported on by a Predecessor Auditor

.06 *Question*—Occasionally, a successor auditor becomes aware of information that leads him to believe that prior period financial statements reported on by a predecessor auditor require restatement. Is it necessary in such a situation for the successor auditor to discuss the information with the predecessor auditor before referring to the restatement adjustments made to the previously issued financial statements?

.07 *Answer*—Yes. The successor auditor should discuss with the predecessor auditor information that he believes requires statement of the financial statements because such information may have been considered by the predecessor auditor. The successor auditor should communicate to the predecessor any information that the predecessor auditor may need to consider in accordance with section 561, *Subsequent Discovery of Facts Existing at the Date of the Auditor's Report*, which sets out the procedures that an auditor should follow when he subsequently discovers facts which may have affected the audited financial statements previously reported on.

[Issue Date: September, 1986.]

3. Audits of Financial Statements That Had Been Previously Audited by a Predecessor Auditor

.08 *Question*—A successor auditor may be asked to audit and report on financial statements that had been previously audited and reported on by a predecessor auditor (henceforth, for convenience referred to as a *reaudit*). What communications should be attempted between the successor and predecessor before accepting such an engagement?

.09 *Interpretation*—In addition to the communications described in paragraphs .04 through .07 of section 315A, *Communications Between Predecessor and Successor Auditors*, the successor should attempt to communicate that the purpose of his or her inquiries is to obtain information about whether to accept an engagement to perform a reaudit.

.10 *Question*—Paragraph .08 of section 315A states that "when one auditor succeeds another, the successor auditor must obtain sufficient competent evidential matter to afford a reasonable basis for expressing his opinion on the financial statements he has been engaged to audit...." If the successor accepts the reaudit engagement, would the predecessor's report, working papers and inquiries of the predecessor in and of themselves be considered sufficient competent evidential matter to afford the successor a reasonable basis for expressing an opinion on the financial statements?

.11 *Interpretation*—No. Although the successor may consider the information obtained from inquiries of the predecessor and any review of the predecessor's report and working papers in planning his or her audit, the information obtained from those inquiries and any review of the predecessor's report and working papers is not sufficient to afford a basis for expressing an opinion. The audit work performed and the conclusions reached in the reaudit are solely the responsibility of the successor auditor.

.12 The successor should plan and perform the reaudit in accordance with generally accepted auditing standards. The successor should not assume responsibility for the work of the predecessor or issue a report that reflects divided responsibility for the reaudit as described in section 543, *Part of Audit Performed by Other Independent Auditors*. Furthermore, the predecessor is not a specialist as defined in section 336, *Using the Work of a Specialist*, or an internal auditor as defined in section 322, *The Auditor's Consideration of the Internal Audit Function in an Audit of Financial Statements.*

.13 If the successor has audited the current year, the results of such audit may be considered in planning and performing his or her reaudit and may provide evidential matter that is useful in performing the reaudit.

.14 If, in a reaudit engagement, the successor is unable to obtain sufficient competent evidential matter to express an opinion on the financial statements, the successor should qualify or disclaim an opinion because of the inability to perform procedures the successor considers necessary in the circumstances.

.15 *Question*—Paragraph .09 of section 315A states, "The predecessor and successor auditors should agree on those working papers that are to be made available for review...." What working papers of the predecessor should the successor request access to when he or she is planning the reaudit?

.16 *Interpretation*—The successor should request working papers for the period(s) under reaudit and the period prior to the reaudit period. However, valid business reasons may lead the predecessor auditor to decide not to allow a review of his or her working papers.

.17 *Question*—Observation of inventories is a generally accepted auditing procedure. In a reaudit, the successor generally will be unable to observe inventory or make physical counts at the reaudit date(s) in the manner discussed in paragraphs .09–.11 of section 331, *Inventories*. How may the successor become satisfied as to the existence of such inventories?

.18 *Interpretation*—In such cases, the successor should follow the guidance in section 331.12 and .13. The successor may consider the knowledge obtained from his or her review of the predecessor's working papers and inquiries of the predecessor to determine the nature, timing, and extent of procedures to be applied in the circumstances. It will always be necessary for the successor to make, or observe, some physical counts of inventory at a date subsequent to the period of the reaudit, in connection with a current audit or otherwise, and apply appropriate tests of intervening transactions. Appropriate procedures may include tests of prior transactions, reviews of records of prior counts, and the application of analytical procedures such as gross profit tests.

[Issue Date: April, 1995.]

AU Section 316

Consideration of Fraud in a Financial Statement Audit

(Supersedes SAS No. 53)

Source: SAS No. 82.

Effective for audits of financial statements for periods ending on or after December 15, 1997.

Introduction

.01 Section 110, *Responsibilities and Functions of the Independent Auditor*, states that "The auditor has a responsibility to plan and perform the audit to obtain reasonable assurance about whether the financial statements are free of material misstatement, whether caused by error or fraud."[1] This section provides guidance to auditors in fulfilling that responsibility, as it relates to fraud, in an audit of financial statements conducted in accordance with generally accepted auditing standards. Specifically, this section—

- Describes fraud and its characteristics (see paragraphs .03 through .10).
- Requires the auditor to specifically assess the risk of material misstatement due to fraud and provides categories of fraud risk factors to be considered in the auditor's assessment (see paragraphs .11 through .25).
- Provides guidance on how the auditor responds to the results of the assessment (see paragraphs .26 through .32).
- Provides guidance on the evaluation of audit test results as they relate to the risk of material misstatement due to fraud (see paragraphs .33 through .36).
- Describes related documentation requirements (see paragraph .37).
- Provides guidance regarding the auditor's communication about fraud to management, the audit committee, and others (see paragraphs .38 through .40).

.02 While this section focuses on the auditor's consideration of fraud in an audit of financial statements, management is responsible for the prevention

---

[1] The auditor's consideration of illegal acts and responsibility for detecting misstatements resulting from illegal acts is defined in section 317, *Illegal Acts by Clients*. For those illegal acts that are defined in that section as having a direct and material effect on the determination of financial statement amounts, the auditor's responsibility to detect misstatements resulting from such illegal acts is the same as that for errors (see section 312, *Audit Risk and Materiality in Conducting an Audit*) or fraud.

and detection of fraud.[2] That responsibility is described in section 110.03, which states, "Management is responsible for adopting sound accounting policies and for establishing and maintaining internal control that will, among other things, record, process, summarize, and report transactions consistent with management's assertions embodied in the financial statements."

Description and Characteristics of Fraud

.03 Although fraud is a broad legal concept, the auditor's interest specifically relates to fraudulent acts that cause a material misstatement of financial statements. The primary factor that distinguishes fraud from error is whether the underlying action that results in the misstatement in financial statements is intentional or unintentional.[3] Two types of misstatements are relevant to the auditor's consideration of fraud in a financial statement audit—misstatements arising from fraudulent financial reporting and misstatements arising from misappropriation of assets.[4] These two types of misstatements are described in the following paragraphs.

.04 *Misstatements arising from fraudulent financial reporting* are intentional misstatements or omissions of amounts or disclosures in financial statements to deceive financial statement users. Fraudulent financial reporting may involve acts such as the following:

- Manipulation, falsification, or alteration of accounting records or supporting documents from which financial statements are prepared
- Misrepresentation in, or intentional omission from, the financial statements of events, transactions, or other significant information
- Intentional misapplication of accounting principles relating to amounts, classification, manner of presentation, or disclosure

.05 *Misstatements arising from misappropriation of assets* (sometimes referred to as defalcation) involve the theft of an entity's assets where the effect of the theft causes the financial statements not to be presented in conformity with generally accepted accounting principles.[5] Misappropriation can be accomplished in various ways, including embezzling receipts, stealing assets,

---

[2] In its October 1987 report, the National Commission on Fraudulent Financial Reporting, also known as the Treadway Commission, noted that "The responsibility for reliable financial reporting resides first and foremost at the corporate level. Top management—starting with the chief executive officer—sets the tone and establishes the financial reporting environment. Therefore, reducing the risk of fraudulent financial reporting must start with the reporting company."

[3] Intent is often difficult to determine, particularly in matters involving accounting estimates and the application of accounting principles. For example, unreasonable accounting estimates may be unintentional or may be the result of an intentional attempt to misstate the financial statements. Although the auditor has no responsibility to determine intent, the auditor's responsibility to plan and perform the audit to obtain reasonable assurance about whether the financial statements are free of material misstatement is relevant in either case.

[4] Unauthorized transactions also are relevant to the auditor when they could cause a misstatement in financial statements. When such transactions are intentional and result in material misstatement of the financial statements, they would fall into one of the two types of fraud discussed in this section. Also see the guidance in section 317.

[5] Reference to generally accepted accounting principles includes, where applicable, a comprehensive basis of accounting other than generally accepted accounting principles as defined in section 623, *Special Reports*, paragraph .04.

or causing an entity to pay for goods or services not received. Misappropriation of assets may be accompanied by false or misleading records or documents and may involve one or more individuals among management, employees, or third parties.

.06 Fraud frequently involves the following: (*a*) a pressure or an incentive to commit fraud and (*b*) a perceived opportunity to do so. Although specific pressures and opportunities for fraudulent financial reporting may differ from those for misappropriation of assets, these two conditions usually are present for both types of fraud. For example, fraudulent financial reporting may be committed because management is under pressure to achieve an unrealistic earnings target. Misappropriation of assets may be committed because the individuals involved are living beyond their means. A perceived opportunity may exist in either situation because an individual believes he or she could circumvent internal control.

.07 Fraud may be concealed through falsified documentation, including forgery. For example, management that engages in fraudulent financial reporting might attempt to conceal misstatements by creating fictitious invoices, while employees or management who misappropriate cash might try to conceal their thefts by forging signatures or creating invalid electronic approvals on disbursement authorizations. An audit conducted in accordance with generally accepted auditing standards rarely involves authentication of documentation, nor are auditors trained as or expected to be experts in such authentication.

.08 Fraud also may be concealed through collusion among management, employees, or third parties. For example, through collusion, false evidence that control activities have been performed effectively may be presented to the auditor. As another example, the auditor may receive a false confirmation from a third party who is in collusion with management. Collusion may cause the auditor to believe that evidence is persuasive when it is, in fact, false.

.09 Although fraud usually is concealed, the presence of risk factors or other conditions may alert the auditor to a possibility that fraud may exist. For example, a document may be missing, a general ledger may be out of balance, or an analytical relationship may not make sense. However, these conditions may be the result of circumstances other than fraud. Documents may have been legitimately lost; the general ledger may be out of balance because of an unintentional accounting error; and unexpected analytical relationships may be the result of unrecognized changes in underlying economic factors. Even reports of alleged fraud may not always be reliable, because an employee or outsider may be mistaken or may be motivated to make a false allegation.

.10 An auditor cannot obtain absolute assurance that material misstatements in the financial statements will be detected. Because of (*a*) the concealment aspects of fraudulent activity, including the fact that fraud often involves collusion or falsified documentation, and (*b*) the need to apply professional judgment in the identification and evaluation of fraud risk factors and other conditions, even a properly planned and performed audit may not detect a material misstatement resulting from fraud. Accordingly, because of the above characteristics of fraud and the nature of audit evidence as discussed in section 230, *Due Professional Care in the Performance of Work*, the auditor is able to obtain only reasonable assurance that material misstatements in the financial statements, including misstatements resulting from fraud, are detected.

Assessment of the Risk of Material Misstatement Due to Fraud

.11 Section 311, *Planning and Supervision*, provides guidance as to the level of knowledge of the entity's business that will enable the auditor to plan and perform an audit of financial statements in accordance with generally accepted auditing standards. Section 312, *Audit Risk and Materiality in Conducting an Audit*, provides that determination of the scope of the auditing procedures is directly related to the consideration of audit risk and indicates that the risk of material misstatement of the financial statements due to fraud is part of audit risk.

.12 The auditor should specifically assess the risk of material misstatement of the financial statements due to fraud and should consider that assessment in designing the audit procedures to be performed. In making this assessment, the auditor should consider fraud risk factors that relate to both (*a*) misstatements arising from fraudulent financial reporting and (*b*) misstatements arising from misappropriation of assets in each of the related categories presented in paragraphs .16 and .18.[6] While such risk factors do not necessarily indicate the existence of fraud, they often have been observed in circumstances where frauds have occurred.

.13 As part of the risk assessment, the auditor also should inquire of management (*a*) to obtain management's understanding regarding the risk of fraud in the entity and (*b*) to determine whether they have knowledge of fraud that has been perpetrated on or within the entity. Information from these inquiries could identify fraud risk factors that may affect the auditor's assessment and related response. Some examples of matters that might be discussed as part of the inquiry are (*a*) whether there are particular subsidiary locations, business segments, types of transactions, account balances, or financial statement categories where fraud risk factors exist or may be more likely to exist and (*b*) how management may be addressing such risks.

.14 Although the fraud risk factors described in paragraphs .17 and .19 below cover a broad range of situations typically faced by auditors, they are only examples. Moreover, not all of these examples are relevant in all circumstances, and some may be of greater or lesser significance in entities of different size, with different ownership characteristics, in different industries, or because of other differing characteristics or circumstances. Accordingly, the auditor should use professional judgment when assessing the significance and relevance of fraud risk factors and determining the appropriate audit response.

.15 For example, in a small entity domination of management by a single individual generally does not, in and of itself, indicate a failure by management to display and communicate an appropriate attitude regarding internal control and the financial reporting process. As another example, there may be little

---

[6] The auditor should assess the risk of material misstatement due to fraud regardless of whether the auditor otherwise plans to assess inherent or control risk at the maximum (see section 312.29 and .30). An auditor may meet this requirement using different categories of risk factors as long as the assessment embodies the substance of each of the risk categories described in paragraphs .16 and .18. Also, since these risk categories encompass both inherent and control risk attributes, the specific assessment of the risk of material misstatement due to fraud may be performed in conjunction with the assessment of audit risk required by section 312.13 through .33, and section 319, *Consideration of Internal Control in a Financial Statement Audit*, paragraphs .27 through .38. Furthermore, the assessment of audit risk may identify the presence of additional fraud risk factors that the auditor should consider.

motivation for fraudulent financial reporting by management of a privately held business when the financial statements audited are used only in connection with seasonal bank borrowings, debt covenants are not especially burdensome, and the entity has a long history of financial success consistent with the industry in which it operates. Conversely, management of a small entity with unusually rapid growth or profitability may be motivated to avoid an interruption in its growth trends, especially compared with others in its industry.

Risk Factors Relating to Misstatements Arising From Fraudulent Financial Reporting

.16 Risk factors that relate to misstatements arising from fraudulent financial reporting may be grouped in the following three categories:

a. *Management's characteristics and influence over the control environment.* These pertain to management's abilities, pressures, style, and attitude relating to internal control and the financial reporting process.

b. *Industry conditions.* These involve the economic and regulatory environment in which the entity operates.

c. *Operating characteristics and financial stability.* These pertain to the nature and complexity of the entity and its transactions, the entity's financial condition, and its profitability.

.17 The following are examples of risk factors relating to misstatements arising from fraudulent financial reporting for each of the three categories described above:

a. *Risk factors relating to management's characteristics and influence over the control environment.* Examples include—

- A motivation for management to engage in fraudulent financial reporting. Specific indicators might include—
  - — A significant portion of management's compensation represented by bonuses, stock options, or other incentives, the value of which is contingent upon the entity achieving unduly aggressive targets for operating results, financial position, or cash flow.
  - — An excessive interest by management in maintaining or increasing the entity's stock price or earnings trend through the use of unusually aggressive accounting practices.
  - — A practice by management of committing to analysts, creditors, and other third parties to achieve what appear to be unduly aggressive or clearly unrealistic forecasts.
  - — An interest by management in pursuing inappropriate means to minimize reported earnings for tax-motivated reasons.
- A failure by management to display and communicate an appropriate attitude regarding internal control and the financial reporting process. Specific indicators might include—

- — An ineffective means of communicating and supporting the entity's values or ethics, or communication of inappropriate values or ethics.
- — Domination of management by a single person or small group without compensating controls such as effective oversight by the board of directors or audit committee.
- — Inadequate monitoring of significant controls.
- — Management failing to correct known reportable conditions on a timely basis.
- — Management setting unduly aggressive financial targets and expectations for operating personnel.
- — Management displaying a significant disregard for regulatory authorities.
- — Management continuing to employ an ineffective accounting, information technology, or internal auditing staff.

- Nonfinancial management's excessive participation in, or preoccupation with, the selection of accounting principles or the determination of significant estimates.
- High turnover of senior management, counsel, or board members.
- Strained relationship between management and the current or predecessor auditor. Specific indicators might include—
  - — Frequent disputes with the current or predecessor auditor on accounting, auditing, or reporting matters.
  - — Unreasonable demands on the auditor including unreasonable time constraints regarding the completion of the audit or the issuance of the auditor's reports.
  - — Formal or informal restrictions on the auditor that inappropriately limit his or her access to people or information or his or her ability to communicate effectively with the board of directors or the audit committee.
  - — Domineering management behavior in dealing with the auditor, especially involving attempts to influence the scope of the auditor's work.
- Known history of securities law violations or claims against the entity or its senior management alleging fraud or violations of securities laws.

b. *Risk factors relating to industry conditions.* Examples include—

- New accounting, statutory, or regulatory requirements that could impair the financial stability or profitability of the entity.
- High degree of competition or market saturation, accompanied by declining margins.
- Declining industry with increasing business failures and significant declines in customer demand.

- Rapid changes in the industry, such as high vulnerability to rapidly changing technology or rapid product obsolescence

c. *Risk factors relating to operating characteristics and financial stability*. Examples include—

- Inability to generate cash flows from operations while reporting earnings and earnings growth.
- Significant pressure to obtain additional capital necessary to stay competitive considering the financial position of the entity—including need for funds to finance major research and development or capital expenditures.
- Assets, liabilities, revenues, or expenses based on significant estimates that involve unusually subjective judgments or uncertainties, or that are subject to potential significant change in the near term in a manner that may have a financially disruptive effect on the entity—such as ultimate collectibility of receivables, timing of revenue recognition, realizability of financial instruments based on the highly subjective valuation of collateral or difficult-to-assess repayment sources, or significant deferral of costs.
- Significant related-party transactions not in the ordinary course of business or with related entities not audited or audited by another firm.
- Significant, unusual, or highly complex transactions, especially those close to year end, that pose difficult "substance over form" questions.
- Significant bank accounts or subsidiary or branch operations in tax-haven jurisdictions for which there appears to be no clear business justification.
- Overly complex organizational structure involving numerous or unusual legal entities, managerial lines of authority, or contractual arrangements without apparent business purpose.
- Difficulty in determining the organization or individual(s) that control(s) the entity.
- Unusually rapid growth or profitability, especially compared with that of other companies in the same industry.
- Especially high vulnerability to changes in interest rates.
- Unusually high dependence on debt or marginal ability to meet debt repayment requirements; debt covenants that are difficult to maintain.
- Unrealistically aggressive sales or profitability incentive programs.
- Threat of imminent bankruptcy or foreclosure, or hostile takeover.
- Adverse consequences on significant pending transactions, such as a business combination or contract award, if poor financial results are reported.

- Poor or deteriorating financial position when management has personally guaranteed significant debts of the entity.

Risk Factors Relating to Misstatements Arising From Misappropriation of Assets

.18 Risk factors that relate to misstatements arising from misappropriation of assets may be grouped in the two categories below. The extent of the auditor's consideration of the risk factors in category *b* is influenced by the degree to which risk factors in category *a* are present.

a. *Susceptibility of assets to misappropriation.* These pertain to the nature of an entity's assets and the degree to which they are subject to theft.

b. *Controls.* These involve the lack of controls designed to prevent or detect misappropriations of assets.

.19 The following are examples of risk factors relating to misstatements arising from misappropriation of assets for each of the two categories described above:

a. *Risk factors relating to susceptibility of assets to misappropriation*

- Large amounts of cash on hand or processed
- Inventory characteristics, such as small size, high value, or high demand
- Easily convertible assets, such as bearer bonds, diamonds, or computer chips
- Fixed asset characteristics, such as small size, marketability, or lack of ownership identification

b. *Risk factors relating to controls*

- Lack of appropriate management oversight (for example, inadequate supervision or monitoring of remote locations)
- Lack of job applicant screening procedures relating to employees with access to assets susceptible to misappropriation
- Inadequate recordkeeping with respect to assets susceptible to misappropriation
- Lack of appropriate segregation of duties or independent checks
- Lack of appropriate system of authorization and approval of transactions (for example, in purchasing)
- Poor physical safeguards over cash, investments, inventory, or fixed assets
- Lack of timely and appropriate documentation for transactions (for example, credits for merchandise returns)
- Lack of mandatory vacations for employees performing key control functions

.20 The auditor is not required to plan the audit to discover information that is indicative of financial stress of employees or adverse relationships between the entity and its employees. Nevertheless, the auditor may become aware of such information. Some examples of such information include (*a*) anticipated future employee layoffs that are known to the workforce, (*b*) employees with access to assets susceptible to misappropriation who are known to be dissatisfied, (*c*) known unusual changes in behavior or lifestyle of employees with access to assets susceptible to misappropriation, and (*d*) known personal financial pressures affecting employees with access to assets susceptible to misappropriation. If the auditor becomes aware of the existence of such information, he or she should consider it in assessing the risk of material misstatement arising from misappropriation of assets.

Consideration of Risk Factors in Assessing the Risk of Material Misstatement Due to Fraud

.21 Fraud risk factors cannot easily be ranked in order of importance or combined into effective predictive models. The significance of risk factors varies widely. Some of these factors will be present in entities where the specific conditions do not present a risk of material misstatement. Accordingly, the auditor should exercise professional judgment when considering risk factors individually or in combination and whether there are specific controls that mitigate the risk. For example, an entity may not screen newly hired employees having access to assets susceptible to theft. This factor, by itself, might not significantly affect the assessment of the risk of material misstatement due to fraud. However, if it were coupled with a lack of appropriate management oversight and a lack of physical safeguards over such assets as readily marketable inventory or fixed assets, the combined effect of these related factors might be significant to that assessment.

.22 The size, complexity, and ownership characteristics of the entity have a significant influence on the consideration of relevant risk factors. For example, in the case of a large entity, the auditor ordinarily would consider factors that generally constrain improper conduct by senior management, such as the effectiveness of the board of directors, the audit committee or others with equivalent authority and responsibility, and the internal audit function. The auditor also would consider what steps had been taken to enforce a formal code of conduct and the effectiveness of the budgeting or reporting system. Furthermore, risk factors evaluated at a country-specific or business segment operating level may provide different insights than the evaluation at an entity-wide level.[7] In the case of a small entity, some or all of these considerations might be inapplicable or less important. For example, a smaller entity might not have a written code of conduct but, instead, develop a culture that emphasizes the importance of integrity and ethical behavior through oral communication and by management example.

.23 Section 319, *Consideration of Internal Control in a Financial Statement Audit*, requires the auditor to obtain a sufficient understanding of the entity's internal control over financial reporting to plan the audit. It also notes that such knowledge should be used to identify types of potential misstatements, consider factors that affect the risk of material misstatement, and design substantive tests. The understanding often will affect the auditor's con-

[7] Section 312.18 provides guidance on the auditor's consideration of the extent to which auditing procedures should be performed at selected locations or components.

sideration of the significance of fraud risk factors. In addition, when considering the significance of fraud risk factors, the auditor may wish to assess whether there are specific controls that mitigate the risk or whether specific control deficiencies may exacerbate the risk.[8]

.24 If the entity has established a program that includes steps to prevent, deter, and detect fraud, the auditor may consider its effectiveness. The auditor also should inquire of those persons overseeing such programs as to whether the program has identified any fraud risk factors.

.25 The assessment of the risk of material misstatement due to fraud is a cumulative process that includes a consideration of risk factors individually and in combination. In addition, fraud risk factors may be identified while performing procedures relating to acceptance or continuance of clients and engagements,[9] during engagement planning or while obtaining an understanding of an entity's internal control, or while conducting fieldwork.[10] Also, other conditions may be identified during fieldwork that change or support a judgment regarding the assessment—such as the following:

- *Discrepancies in the accounting records*, including—
  - — Transactions not recorded in a complete or timely manner or improperly recorded as to amount, accounting period, classification, or entity policy.
  - — Unsupported or unauthorized balances or transactions.
  - — Last-minute adjustments by the entity that significantly affect financial results.
- *Conflicting or missing evidential matter*, including—
  - — Missing documents.
  - — Unavailability of other than photocopied documents when documents in original form are expected to exist.
  - — Significant unexplained items on reconciliations.
  - — Inconsistent, vague, or implausible responses from management or employees arising from inquiries or analytical procedures.
  - — Unusual discrepancies between the entity's records and confirmation replies.
  - — Missing inventory or physical assets of significant magnitude.
- *Problematic or unusual relationships between the auditor and client*, including—
  - — Denied access to records, facilities, certain employees, customers, vendors, or others from whom audit evidence might be sought.[11]
  - — Undue time pressures imposed by management to resolve complex or contentious issues.

---

[8] Section 319.47 states that assessing control risk at below the maximum level involves identifying specific controls that are likely to prevent or detect material misstatements in those assertions, and performing tests of controls to evaluate their effectiveness.

[9] See Statement on Quality Control Standards No. 2, *System of Quality Control for a CPA Firm's Accounting and Auditing Practice*, paragraphs .14 through 16 [QC section 20.14–.16].

[10] The auditor also ordinarily obtains written representations from management concerning irregularities involving management and employees that could have a material effect on the financial statements (see section 333A, *Client Representations*).

[11] Denial of access to information may constitute a limitation on the scope of the audit that may require the auditor to consider qualifying or disclaiming an opinion on the financial statements (see section 508, *Reports on Audited Financial Statements*, paragraphs .22 through .32).

— Unusual delays by the entity in providing requested information.
— Tips or complaints to the auditor about fraud.

The Auditor's Response to the Results of the Assessment

.26 A risk of material misstatement due to fraud is always present to some degree. The auditor's response to the foregoing assessment is influenced by the nature and significance of the risk factors identified as being present. In some cases, even though fraud risk factors have been identified as being present, the auditor's judgment may be that audit procedures otherwise planned are sufficient to respond to the risk factors. In other circumstances, the auditor may conclude that the conditions indicate a need to modify procedures.[12] In these circumstances, the auditor should consider whether the assessment of the risk of material misstatement due to fraud calls for an overall response, one that is specific to a particular account balance, class of transactions or assertion, or both. The auditor also may conclude that it is not practicable to modify the procedures that are planned for the audit of the financial statements sufficiently to address the risk. In that case withdrawal from the engagement with communication to the appropriate parties may be an appropriate course of action (see paragraph .36).

Overall Considerations

.27 Judgments about the risk of material misstatement due to fraud may affect the audit in the following ways:

- *Professional skepticism.* Due professional care requires the auditor to exercise professional skepticism—that is, an attitude that includes a questioning mind and critical assessment of audit evidence (see section 230.07 through .09). Some examples demonstrating the application of professional skepticism in response to the auditor's assessment of the risk of material misstatement due to fraud include (*a*) increased sensitivity in the selection of the nature and extent of documentation to be examined in support of material transactions, and (*b*) increased recognition of the need to corroborate management explanations or representations concerning material matters—such as further analytical procedures, examination of documentation, or discussion with others within or outside the entity.
- *Assignment of personnel.* The knowledge, skill, and ability of personnel assigned significant engagement responsibilities should be commensurate with the auditor's assessment of the level of risk of the engagement (see section 210, *Training and Proficiency of the Independent Auditor*, paragraph .03). In addition, the extent of supervision should recognize the risk of material misstatement due to fraud and the qualifications of persons performing the work (see section 311.11).
- *Accounting principles and policies.* The auditor may decide to consider further management's selection and application of significant

[12] Section 312 requires the auditor to limit audit risk to a low level that is, in the auditor's professional judgment, appropriate for expressing an opinion on the financial statements.

accounting policies, particularly those related to revenue recognition, asset valuation, or capitalizing versus expensing. In this respect, the auditor may have a greater concern about whether the accounting principles selected and policies adopted are being applied in an inappropriate manner to create a material misstatement of the financial statements.

- *Controls.* When a risk of material misstatement due to fraud relates to risk factors that have control implications, the auditor's ability to assess control risk below the maximum may be reduced. However, this does not eliminate the need for the auditor to obtain an understanding of the components of the entity's internal control sufficient to plan the audit (see section 319). In fact, such an understanding may be of particular importance in further understanding and considering any controls (or lack thereof) the entity has in place to address the identified fraud risk factors. However, this consideration also would need to include an added sensitivity to management's ability to override such controls.

.28 The nature, timing, and extent of procedures may need to be modified in the following ways:

- The *nature* of audit procedures performed may need to be changed to obtain evidence that is more reliable or to obtain additional corroborative information. For example, more evidential matter may be needed from independent sources outside the entity. Also, physical observation or inspection of certain assets may become more important. (See section 326, *Evidential Matter*, paragraphs .19 through .22.)
- The *timing* of substantive tests may need to be altered to be closer to or at year end. For example, if there are unusual incentives for management to engage in fraudulent financial reporting, the auditor might conclude that substantive testing should be performed near or at year end because it would not otherwise be possible to control the incremental audit risk associated with that risk factor. (See section 313, *Substantive Tests Prior to the Balance-Sheet Date*, paragraph .06.)
- The *extent* of the procedures applied should reflect the assessment of the risk of material misstatement due to fraud. For example, increased sample sizes or more extensive analytical procedures may be appropriate. (See section 350, *Audit Sampling*, paragraph .23, and section 329, *Analytical Procedures*.)

Considerations at the Account Balance, Class of Transactions, and Assertion Level

.29 Specific responses to the auditor's assessment of the risk of material misstatement due to fraud will vary depending upon the types or combinations of fraud risk factors or conditions identified and the account balances, classes of transactions, and assertions they may affect. If these factors or conditions indicate a particular risk applicable to specific account balances or types of transactions, audit procedures addressing these specific areas should be considered that will, in the auditor's judgment, limit audit risk to an appropriate level in light of the risk factors or conditions identified. The following are specific examples of responses:

- Visit locations or perform certain tests on a surprise or unannounced basis—for example, observing inventory at locations where auditor attendance has not been previously announced or counting cash at a particular date on a surprise basis.

- Request that inventories be counted at a date closer to year end.
- Alter the audit approach in the current year—for example, contacting major customers and suppliers orally in addition to written confirmation, sending confirmation requests to a specific party within an organization, or seeking more and different information.
- Perform a detailed review of the entity's quarter-end or year-end adjusting entries and investigate any that appear unusual as to nature or amount.
- For significant and unusual transactions, particularly those occurring at or near year end, investigate (*a*) the possibility of related parties and (*b*) the sources of financial resources supporting the transactions.[13]
- Perform substantive analytical procedures at a detailed level. For example, compare sales and cost of sales by location and line of business to auditor-developed expectations.[14]
- Conduct interviews of personnel involved in areas in which a concern about the risk of material misstatement due to fraud is present, to obtain their insights about the risk and whether or how controls address the risk.
- When other independent auditors are auditing the financial statements of one or more subsidiaries, divisions, or branches, consider discussing with them the extent of work necessary to be performed to ensure that the risk of material misstatement due to fraud resulting from transactions and activities among these components is adequately addressed.
- If the work of a specialist becomes particularly significant with respect to its potential impact on the financial statements, perform additional procedures with respect to some or all of the specialist's assumptions, methods, or findings to determine that the findings are not unreasonable or engage another specialist for that purpose. (See section 336, *Using the Work of a Specialist*, paragraph .12.)

Specific Responses—Misstatements Arising From Fraudulent Financial Reporting

.30 Some examples of responses to the auditor's assessment of the risk of material misstatements arising from fraudulent financial reporting are—

- ***Revenue recognition.*** If there is a risk of material misstatement due to fraud that may involve or result in improper revenue recognition, it may be appropriate to confirm with customers certain relevant contract terms and the absence of side agreements—inasmuch as the appropriate accounting is often influenced by such terms or agree-

---

[13] Section 334, *Related Parties*, provides guidance with respect to the identification of related-party relationships and transactions, including transactions that may be outside the ordinary course of business (see section 334.06).

[14] Section 329, *Analytical Procedures*, provides guidance on performing analytical procedures used as substantive tests.

ments.[15] For example, acceptance criteria, delivery and payment terms and the absence of future or continuing vendor obligations, the right to return the product, guaranteed resale amounts, and cancellation or refund provisions often are relevant in such circumstances.

- ***Inventory quantities.*** If a risk of material misstatement due to fraud exists in inventory quantities, reviewing the entity's inventory records may help to identify locations, areas, or items for specific attention during or after the physical inventory count. Such a review may lead to a decision to observe inventory counts at certain locations on an unannounced basis (see paragraph .29). In addition, where the auditor has a concern about the risk of material misstatement due to fraud in the inventory area, it may be particularly important that the entity counts are conducted at all locations subject to count on the same date. Furthermore, it also may be appropriate for the auditor to apply additional procedures during the observation of the count—for example, examining more rigorously the contents of boxed items, the manner in which the goods are stacked (for example, hollow squares) or labeled, and the quality (that is, purity, grade, or concentration) of liquid substances such as perfumes or specialty chemicals. Finally, additional testing of count sheets, tags or other records, or the retention of copies may be warranted to minimize the risk of subsequent alteration or inappropriate compilation.

Specific Responses—Misstatements Arising From Misappropriations of Assets

.31 The auditor may have identified a risk of material misstatement due to fraud relating to misappropriation of assets. For example, the auditor may conclude that such a risk of asset misappropriation at a particular operating location is significant. This may be the case when a specific type of asset is particularly susceptible to such a risk of misappropriation—for example, a large amount of easily accessible cash, or inventory items such as jewelry, that can be easily moved and sold. Control risk may be evaluated differently in each of these situations. Thus, differing circumstances necessarily would dictate different responses.

.32 Usually the audit response to a risk of material misstatement due to fraud relating to misappropriation of assets will be directed toward certain account balances and classes of transactions. Although some of the audit responses noted in paragraphs .29 and .30 may apply in such circumstances, the scope of the work should be linked to the specific information about the misappropriation risk that has been identified. For example, where a particular asset is highly susceptible to misappropriation that is potentially material to the financial statements, obtaining an understanding of the control activi-

---

[15] Section 330, *The Confirmation Process*, provides guidance about the confirmation process in audits performed in accordance with generally accepted auditing standards. Among other considerations, that guidance discusses the types of respondents from whom confirmations may be requested, and what the auditor should consider if information about the respondent's competence, knowledge, motivation, ability, or willingness to respond, or about the respondent's objectivity and freedom from bias with respect to the audited entity comes to his or her attention (section 330.27). It also provides that the auditor maintain control over the confirmation requests and responses in order to minimize the possibility that the results will be biased because of interception and alteration of the confirmation requests or responses (section 330.28). Further, when confirmation responses are other than in written communications mailed to the auditor, additional evidence, such as verifying the source and contents of a facsimile response in a telephone call to the purported sender, may be required to support their validity (section 330.29).

ties related to the prevention and detection of such misappropriation and testing the operating effectiveness of such controls may be warranted. In certain circumstances, physical inspection of such assets (for example, counting cash or securities) at or near year end may be appropriate. In addition, the use of substantive analytical procedures, including the development by the auditor of an expected dollar amount, at a high level of precision, to be compared with a recorded amount, may be effective in certain circumstances.

Evaluation of Audit Test Results

.33 As indicated in paragraph .25, the assessment of the risk of material misstatement due to fraud is a cumulative process and one that should be ongoing throughout the audit. At the completion of the audit, the auditor should consider whether the accumulated results of audit procedures and other observations (for example, conditions noted in paragraph .25) affect the assessment of the risk of material misstatement due to fraud he or she made when planning the audit. This accumulation is primarily a qualitative matter based on the auditor's judgment. Such an accumulation may provide further insight into the risk of material misstatement due to fraud and whether there is a need for additional or different audit procedures to be performed.

.34 When audit test results identify misstatements in the financial statements, the auditor should consider whether such misstatements may be indicative of fraud.[16] If the auditor has determined that misstatements are or may be the result of fraud, but the effect of the misstatements is not material to the financial statements, the auditor nevertheless should evaluate the implications, especially those dealing with the organizational position of the person(s) involved. For example, fraud involving misappropriations of cash from a small petty cash fund normally would be of little significance to the auditor in assessing the risk of material misstatement due to fraud because both the manner of operating the fund and its size would tend to establish a limit on the amount of potential loss and the custodianship of such funds is normally entrusted to a relatively low-level employee.[17] Conversely, when the matter involves higher level management, even though the amount itself is not material to the financial statements, it may be indicative of a more pervasive problem. In such circumstances, the auditor should reevaluate the assessment of the risk of material misstatement due to fraud and its resulting impact on (*a*) the nature, timing, and extent of the tests of balances or transactions, (*b*) the assessment of the effectiveness of controls if control risk was assessed below the maximum, and (*c*) the assignment of personnel that may be appropriate in the circumstances.

.35 If the auditor has determined that the misstatement is, or may be, the result of fraud, and either has determined that the effect could be material to the financial statements or has been unable to evaluate whether the effect is material, the auditor should—

a. Consider the implications for other aspects of the audit (see previous paragraph).

b. Discuss the matter and the approach to further investigation with an appropriate level of management that is at least one level above those involved and with senior management.

---

[16] See footnote 3.

[17] However, see paragraph .38 for a discussion of the auditor's communication responsibilities.

c. Attempt to obtain additional evidential matter to determine whether material fraud has occurred or is likely to have occurred, and, if so, its effect on the financial statements and the auditor's report thereon.[18]

d. If appropriate, suggest that the client consult with legal counsel.

.36 The auditor's consideration of the risk of material misstatement due to fraud and the results of audit tests may indicate such a significant risk of fraud that the auditor should consider withdrawing from the engagement and communicating the reasons for withdrawal to the audit committee or others with equivalent authority and responsibility (hereafter referred to as the audit committee).[19, 20] Whether the auditor concludes that withdrawal from the engagement is appropriate may depend on the diligence and cooperation of senior management or the board of directors in investigating the circumstances and taking appropriate action. Because of the variety of circumstances that may arise, it is not possible to describe definitively when withdrawal is appropriate. The auditor may wish to consult with his or her legal counsel when considering withdrawal from an engagement.

Documentation of the Auditor's Risk Assessment and Response

.37 In planning the audit, the auditor should document in the working papers evidence of the performance of the assessment of the risk of material misstatement due to fraud (see paragraphs .12 through .14). Where risk factors are identified as being present, the documentation should include (*a*) those risk factors identified and (*b*) the auditor's response (see paragraphs .26 through .32) to those risk factors, individually or in combination. In addition, if during the performance of the audit fraud risk factors or other conditions are identified that cause the auditor to believe that an additional response is required (paragraph .33), such risk factors or other conditions, and any further response that the auditor concluded was appropriate, also should be documented.

Communications About Fraud to Management, the Audit Committee,[21] and Others[22]

.38 Whenever the auditor has determined that there is evidence that fraud may exist, that matter should be brought to the attention of an appropriate level of management. This is generally appropriate even if the matter

[18] However, see paragraph .38 for a discussion of the auditor's communication responsibilities.

[19] Examples of "others with equivalent authority and responsibility" may include the board of directors, the board of trustees, or the owner in owner-managed entities, as appropriate.

[20] If the auditor, subsequent to the date of the report on the audited financial statements, becomes aware that facts existed at that date which might have affected the report had the auditor then been aware of such facts, the auditor should refer to section 561, *Subsequent Discovery of Facts Existing at the Date of the Auditor's Report*, for guidance. Furthermore, section 315A, *Communications Between Predecessor and Successor Auditors*, paragraph .10, provides guidance regarding communication to the predecessor auditor.

[21] See footnote 19.

[22] The requirements to communicate noted in paragraphs .38 through .40 extend to any intentional misstatement of financial statements (see paragraph .03). However, the communication may utilize terms other than *fraud*—for example, *irregularity, intentional misstatement, misappropriation, defalcation*—if there is possible confusion with a legal definition of fraud or other reason to prefer alternative terms.

might be considered inconsequential, such as a minor defalcation by an employee at a low level in the entity's organization. Fraud involving senior management and fraud (whether caused by senior management or other employees) that causes a material misstatement of the financial statements should be reported directly to the audit committee. In addition, the auditor should reach an understanding with the audit committee regarding the expected nature and extent of communications about misappropriations perpetrated by lower-level employees.

.39 When the auditor, as a result of the assessment of the risk of material misstatement due to fraud, has identified risk factors that have continuing control implications (whether or not transactions or adjustments that could be the result of fraud have been detected), the auditor should consider whether these risk factors represent reportable conditions relating to the entity's internal control that should be communicated to senior management and the audit committee.[23] (See section 325, *Communication of Internal Control Related Matters Noted in an Audit.*) The auditor also may wish to communicate other risk factors identified when actions can be reasonably taken by the entity to address the risk.

.40 The disclosure of possible fraud to parties other than the client's senior management and its audit committee ordinarily is not part of the auditor's responsibility and ordinarily would be precluded by the auditor's ethical or legal obligations of confidentiality unless the matter is reflected in the auditor's report. The auditor should recognize, however, that in the following circumstances a duty to disclose outside the entity may exist:

a. To comply with certain legal and regulatory requirements[24]

b. To a successor auditor when the successor makes inquiries in accordance with section 315A, *Communications Between Predecessor and Successor Auditors*[25]

c. In response to a subpoena

d. To a funding agency or other specified agency in accordance with requirements for the audits of entities that receive governmental financial assistance

Because potential conflicts with the auditor's ethical and legal obligations for confidentiality may be complex, the auditor may wish to consult with legal counsel before discussing matters covered by paragraphs .38 through .40 with parties outside the client.

Effective Date

.41 This section is effective for audits of financial statements for periods ending on or after December 15, 1997. Early application of the provisions of this section is permissible.

---

[23] Alternatively, the auditor may decide to communicate solely with the audit committee.

[24] These requirements include reports in connection with the termination of the engagement, such as when the entity reports an auditor change under the appropriate securities law on Form 8-K and the fraud or related risk factors constitute a "reportable event" or is the source of a "disagreement," as these terms are defined in Item 304 of Regulation S-K. These requirements also include reports that may be required, under certain circumstances, pursuant to the Private Securities Litigation Reform Act of 1995 (codified in section 10A(b)1 of the Securities Exchange Act of 1934) relating to an illegal act that has a material effect on the financial statements.

[25] In accordance with section 315A, communication between predecessor and successor auditors requires the specific permission of the client.

AU Section 317

Illegal Acts by Clients

(Supersedes section 328)

Source: SAS No. 54.

See section 9317 for interpretations of this section.

Effective for audits of financial statements for periods beginning on or after January 1, 1989, unless otherwise indicated.

.01 This section prescribes the nature and extent of the consideration an independent auditor should give to the possibility of illegal acts by a client in an audit of financial statements in accordance with generally accepted auditing standards. The section also provides guidance on the auditor's responsibilities when a possible illegal act is detected.

Definition of Illegal Acts

.02 The term *illegal acts*, for purposes of this section, refers to violations of laws or governmental regulations. Illegal acts by clients are acts attributable to the entity whose financial statements are under audit or acts by management or employees acting on behalf of the entity. Illegal acts by clients do not include personal misconduct by the entity's personnel unrelated to their business activities.

Dependence on Legal Judgment

.03 Whether an act is, in fact, illegal is a determination that is normally beyond the auditor's professional competence. An auditor, in reporting on financial statements, presents himself as one who is proficient in accounting and auditing. The auditor's training, experience, and understanding of the client and its industry may provide a basis for recognition that some client acts coming to his attention may be illegal. However, the determination as to whether a particular act is illegal would generally be based on the advice of an informed expert qualified to practice law or may have to await final determination by a court of law.

Relation to Financial Statements

.04 Illegal acts vary considerably in their relation to the financial statements. Generally, the further removed an illegal act is from the events and transactions ordinarily reflected in financial statements, the less likely the auditor is to become aware of the act or to recognize its possible illegality.

.05 The auditor considers laws and regulations that are generally recognized by auditors to have a direct and material effect on the determination of financial statement amounts. For example, tax laws affect accruals and the amount recognized as expense in the accounting period; applicable laws and regulations may affect the amount of revenue accrued under government contracts. However, the auditor considers such laws or regulations from the perspective of their known relation to audit objectives derived from financial statements assertions rather than from the perspective of legality *per se*. The auditor's responsibility to detect and report misstatements resulting from illegal acts having a direct and material effect on the determination of financial statement amounts is the same as that for misstatements caused by error or fraud as described in section 110, *Responsibilities and Functions of the Independent Auditor*.

.06 Entities may be affected by many other laws or regulations, including those related to securities trading, occupational safety and health, food and drug administration, environmental protection, equal employment, and price-fixing or other antitrust violations. Generally, these laws and regulations relate more to an entity's operating aspects than to its financial and accounting aspects, and their financial statement effect is indirect. An auditor ordinarily does not have sufficient basis for recognizing possible violations of such laws and regulations. Their indirect effect is normally the result of the need to disclose a contingent liability because of the allegation or determination of illegality. For example, securities may be purchased or sold based on inside information. While the direct effects of the purchase or sale may be recorded appropriately, their indirect effect, the possible contingent liability for violating securities laws, may not be appropriately disclosed. Even when violations of such laws and regulations can have consequences material to the financial statements, the auditor may not become aware of the existence of the illegal act unless he is informed by the client, or there is evidence of a governmental agency investigation or enforcement proceeding in the records, documents, or other information normally inspected in an audit of financial statements.

The Auditor's Consideration of the Possibility of Illegal Acts

.07 As explained in paragraph .05, certain illegal acts have a direct and material effect on the determination of financial statement amounts. Other illegal acts, such as those described in paragraph .06, may, in particular circumstances, be regarded as having material but indirect effects on financial statements. The auditor's responsibility with respect to detecting, considering the financial statement effects of, and reporting these other illegal acts is described in this section. These other illegal acts are hereinafter referred to simply as *illegal acts*. The auditor should be aware of the possibility that such illegal acts may have occurred. If specific information comes to the auditor's attention that provides evidence concerning the existence of possible illegal acts that could have a material indirect effect on the financial statements, the auditor should apply audit procedures specifically directed to ascertaining whether an illegal act has occurred. However, because of the characteristics of illegal acts explained above, an audit made in accordance with generally accepted auditing standards provides no assurance that illegal acts will be detected or that any contingent liabilities that may result will be disclosed.

Audit Procedures in the Absence of Evidence Concerning Possible Illegal Acts

.08 Normally, an audit in accordance with generally accepted auditing standards does not include audit procedures specifically designed to detect illegal acts. However, procedures applied for the purpose of forming an opinion on the financial statements may bring possible illegal acts to the auditor's attention. For example, such procedures include reading minutes; inquiring of the client's management and legal counsel concerning litigation, claims, and assessments; performing substantive tests of details of transactions or balances. The auditor should make inquiries of management concerning the client's compliance with laws and regulations. Where applicable, the auditor should also inquire of management concerning—

- The client's policies relative to the prevention of illegal acts.
- The use of directives issued by the client and periodic representations obtained by the client from management at appropriate levels of authority concerning compliance with laws and regulations.

The auditor also ordinarily obtains written representations from management concerning the absence of violations or possible violations of laws or regulations whose effects should be considered for disclosure in the financial statements or as a basis for recording a loss contingency. (See section 333A, *Client Representations.*) The auditor need perform no further procedures in this area absent specific information concerning possible illegal acts.

Specific Information Concerning Possible Illegal Acts

.09 In applying audit procedures and evaluating the results of those procedures, the auditor may encounter specific information that may raise a question concerning possible illegal acts, such as the following:

- Unauthorized transactions, improperly recorded transactions, or transactions not recorded in a complete or timely manner in order to maintain accountability for assets
- Investigation by a governmental agency, an enforcement proceeding, or payment of unusual fines or penalties
- Violations of laws or regulations cited in reports of examinations by regulatory agencies that have been made available to the auditor
- Large payments for unspecified services to consultants, affiliates, or employees
- Sales commissions or agents' fees that appear excessive in relation to those normally paid by the client or to the services actually received
- Unusually large payments in cash, purchases of bank cashiers' checks in large amounts payable to bearer, transfers to numbered bank accounts, or similar transactions
- Unexplained payments made to government officials or employees
- Failure to file tax returns or pay government duties or similar fees that are common to the entity's industry or the nature of its business

Audit Procedures in Response to Possible Illegal Acts

.10 When the auditor becomes aware of information concerning a possible illegal act, the auditor should obtain an understanding of the nature of the act, the circumstances in which it occurred, and sufficient other information to evaluate the effect on the financial statements. In doing so, the auditor should inquire of management at a level above those involved, if possible. If management does not provide satisfactory information that there has been no illegal act, the auditor should—

a. Consult with the client's legal counsel or other specialists about the application of relevant laws and regulations to the circumstances and the possible effects on the financial statements. Arrangements for such consultation with client's legal counsel should be made by the client.

b. Apply additional procedures, if necessary, to obtain further understanding of the nature of the acts.

.11 The additional audit procedures considered necessary, if any, might include procedures such as the following:

a. Examine supporting documents, such as invoices, canceled checks, and agreements and compare with accounting records.

b. Confirm significant information concerning the matter with the other party to the transaction or with intermediaries, such as banks or lawyers.

c. Determine whether the transaction has been properly authorized.

d. Consider whether other similar transactions or events may have occurred, and apply procedures to identify them.

The Auditor's Response to Detected Illegal Acts

.12 When the auditor concludes, based on information obtained and, if necessary, consultation with legal counsel, that an illegal act has or is likely to have occurred, the auditor should consider the effect on the financial statements as well as the implications for other aspects of the audit.

The Auditor's Consideration of Financial Statement Effect

.13 In evaluating the materiality of an illegal act that comes to his attention, the auditor should consider both the quantitative and qualitative materiality of the act. For example, section 312, *Audit Risk and Materiality in Conducting an Audit*, paragraph .11, states that "an illegal payment of an otherwise immaterial amount could be material if there is a reasonable possibility that it could lead to a material contingent liability or a material loss of revenue."

.14 The auditor should consider the effect of an illegal act on the amounts presented in financial statements including contingent monetary effects, such as fines, penalties and damages. Loss contingencies resulting from illegal acts that may be required to be disclosed should be evaluated in the same manner as other loss contingencies. Examples of loss contingencies that may arise from an illegal act are: threat of expropriation of assets, enforced discontinuance of operations in another country, and litigation.

.15 The auditor should evaluate the adequacy of disclosure in the financial statements of the potential effects of an illegal act on the entity's operations. If material revenue or earnings are derived from transactions involving illegal acts, or if illegal acts create significant unusual risks associated with material revenue or earnings, such as loss of a significant business relationship, that information should be considered for disclosure.

Implications for Audit

.16 The auditor should consider the implications of an illegal act in relation to other aspects of the audit, particularly the reliability of representations of management. The implications of particular illegal acts will depend on the relationship of the perpetration and concealment, if any, of the illegal act to specific control procedures and the level of management or employees involved.

Communication With the Audit Committee

.17 The auditor should assure himself that the audit committee, or others with equivalent authority and responsibility, is adequately informed with respect to illegal acts that come to the auditor's attention.[1] The auditor need not communicate matters that are clearly inconsequential and may reach agreement in advance with the audit committee on the nature of such matters to be communicated. The communication should describe the act, the circumstances of its occurrence, and the effect on the financial statements. Senior management may wish to have its remedial actions communicated to the audit committee simultaneously. Possible remedial actions include disciplinary action against involved personnel, seeking restitution, adoption of preventive or corrective company policies, and modifications of specific control activities. If senior management is involved in an illegal act, the auditor should communicate directly with the audit committee. The communication may be oral or written. If the communication is oral, the auditor should document it.

Effect on the Auditor's Report

.18 If the auditor concludes that an illegal act has a material effect on the financial statements, and the act has not been properly accounted for or disclosed, the auditor should express a qualified opinion or an adverse opinion on the financial statements taken as a whole, depending on the materiality of the effect on the financial statements.

.19 If the auditor is precluded by the client from obtaining sufficient competent evidential matter to evaluate whether an illegal act that could be material to the financial statements has, or is likely to have, occurred, the auditor generally should disclaim an opinion on the financial statements.

.20 If the client refuses to accept the auditor's report as modified for the circumstances described in paragraphs .18 and .19, the auditor should withdraw from the engagement and indicate the reasons for withdrawal in writing to the audit committee or board of directors.

.21 The auditor may be unable to determine whether an act is illegal because of limitations imposed by the circumstances rather than by the client or because of uncertainty associated with interpretation of applicable laws or regulations or surrounding facts. In these circumstances, the auditor should consider the effect on his report.[2]

---

[1] For entities that do not have audit committees, the phrase "others with equivalent authority and responsibility" may include the board of directors, the board of trustees, or the owner in owner-managed entities.

[2] See section 508, *Reports on Audited Financial Statements*.

Other Considerations in an Audit in Accordance With Generally Accepted Auditing Standards

.22 In addition to the need to withdraw from the engagement, as described in paragraph .20, the auditor may conclude that withdrawal is necessary when the client does not take the remedial action that the auditor considers necessary in the circumstances even when the illegal act is not material to the financial statements. Factors that should affect the auditor's conclusion include the implications of the failure to take remedial action, which may affect the auditor's ability to rely on management representations, and the effects of continuing association with the client. In reaching a conclusion on such matters, the auditor may wish to consult with his own legal counsel.

.23 Disclosure of an illegal act to parties other than the client's senior management and its audit committee or board of directors is not ordinarily part of the auditor's responsibility, and such disclosure would be precluded by the auditor's ethical or legal obligation of confidentiality, unless the matter affects his opinion on the financial statements. The auditor should recognize, however, that in the following circumstances a duty to notify parties outside the client may exist:[3]

a. When the entity reports an auditor change under the appropriate securities law on Form 8-K[4]

b. To a successor auditor when the successor makes inquiries in accordance with section 315A, *Communications Between Predecessor and Successor Auditors*[5]

c. In response to a subpoena

d. To a funding agency or other specified agency in accordance with requirements for the audits of entities that receive financial assistance from a government agency

Because potential conflicts with the auditor's ethical and legal obligations for confidentiality may be complex, the auditor may wish to consult with legal counsel before discussing illegal acts with parties outside the client.

Responsibilities in Other Circumstances

.24 An auditor may accept an engagement that entails a greater responsibility for detecting illegal acts than that specified in this section. For example, a governmental unit may engage an independent auditor to perform an audit in accordance with the Single Audit Act of 1984. In such an engagement,

---

[3] Auditors may be required, under certain circumstances, pursuant to the Private Securities Litigation Reform Act of 1995 (codified in section 10A(b)1 of the Securities Exchange Act of 1934) to make a report to the Securities and Exchange Commission relating to an illegal act that has a material effect on the financial statements. [Footnote added, July 1997, to reflect conforming changes necessary due to the issuance of the Private Securities Litigation Reform Act of 1995.]

[4] Disclosure to the Securities and Exchange Commission may be necessary if, among other matters, the auditor withdraws because the board of directors has not taken appropriate remedial action. Such failure may be a reportable disagreement on Form 8-K. [Footnote renumbered, July 1997, to reflect conforming changes necessary due to the issuance of the Private Securities Litigation Reform Act of 1995.]

[5] In accordance with section 315A, communications between predecessor and successor auditors require the specific permission of the client. [Footnote renumbered, July 1997, to reflect conforming changes necessary due to the issuance of the Private Securities Litigation Reform Act of 1995.]

the independent auditor is responsible for testing and reporting on the governmental unit's compliance with certain laws and regulations applicable to Federal financial assistance programs. Also, an independent auditor may undertake a variety of other special engagements. For example, a corporation's board of directors or its audit committee may engage an auditor to apply agreed-upon procedures and report on compliance with the corporation's code of conduct under the attestation standards.

Effective Date

.25 This section is effective for audits of financial statements for periods beginning on or after January 1, 1989. Early application of the provisions of this section is permissible.

[illegible]

Effective Date

[illegible] This section is effective for [illegible] 1996 [illegible]

AU Section 9317

Illegal Acts by Clients: Auditing Interpretations of Section 317

1. Consideration of Internal Control in a Financial Statement Audit and the Foreign Corrupt Practices Act

.01 *Question*—The second standard of field work requires the auditor to obtain a sufficient understanding of internal control to plan the audit and to determine the nature, timing, and extent of tests to be performed. Is the auditor of an entity subject to the Securities Exchange Act of 1934 required, because of the *Foreign Corrupt Practices Act of 1977* and the provisions of section 317, to expand his consideration of internal control beyond that which is required by the second standard of field work?

.02 *Interpretation*—No. There is nothing in the Act or the related legislative history that purports to alter the auditor's duty to his client or the purpose of his consideration of internal control. The Act creates express new duties only for companies subject to the Securities Exchange Act of 1934, not for auditors.

[Issue Date: October, 1978.]

2. Material Weaknesses in Internal Control and the Foreign Corrupt Practices Act

.03 *Question*—What course of action should be followed by the auditor of an entity subject to the internal accounting control provision of the *Foreign Corrupt Practices Act of 1977* to comply with section 317 when a material weakness in internal control comes to his attention?

.04 *Interpretation*—The standards applied by an auditor in determining a material weakness in internal control may differ from the standards for determining a violation of the Act. Nevertheless, a specific material weakness may ultimately be determined to be a violation and, hence, an illegal act. Therefore, the auditor should inquire of the client's management and consult with the client's legal counsel as to whether the material weakness is a violation of the Act.

.05 In consultation with management and legal counsel, consideration should be given to corrective action taken or in process. If management has concluded that corrective action for a material weakness is not practicable, consideration should be given to the reasons underlying that conclusion, including management's evaluation of the costs of correction in relation to the expected benefit to be derived.[1] If it is determined that there has been a viola-

---

[1] The legislative history of the Act indicates that cost-benefit considerations are appropriate in determining compliance with the accounting provisions of the Act. For example, the Senate committee report stated that "the size of the business, diversity of operations, degree of centralization of financial and operating management, amount of contact by top management with day-to-day operations, and numerous other circumstances are factors which management must consider in establishing and maintaining an internal accounting control system."

tion of the Act and appropriate consideration is not given to the violation, the auditor should consider withdrawing from the current engagement or dissociating himself from any future relationship with the client (see section 317.22).

.06 A violation of the internal accounting control provision of the Act would not, in and of itself, have a direct effect on amounts presented in audited financial statements. However, the contingent monetary effect on an entity ultimately determined to have willfully violated the internal accounting control provision of the Act could be fines of up to $10,000 for the violation. The auditor should consider the materiality of such contingent monetary effect in relation to the audited financial statements taken as a whole. Other loss contingencies, as defined by FASB Statement No. 5 [AC section C59], ordinarily would not result from a weakness in internal control which gives rise to such a violation of the Act.

[Issue Date: October, 1978.]

AU Section 319

Consideration of Internal Control in a Financial Statement Audit

Source: SAS No. 55; SAS No. 78[*]

See section 9319 for interpretations of this section.

Effective for audits of financial statements for periods beginning on or after January 1, 1990, unless otherwise indicated.

Introduction

.01 This section provides guidance on the independent auditor's consideration of an entity's internal control in an audit of financial statements in accordance with generally accepted auditing standards. It defines internal control,[1] describes the objectives and components of internal control, and explains how an auditor should consider internal control in planning and performing an audit. In particular, this section provides guidance about implementing the second standard of field work[2]: "A sufficient understanding of internal control is to be obtained to plan the audit and to determine the nature, timing, and extent of tests to be performed."

.02 In all audits, the auditor should obtain an understanding of internal control sufficient to plan the audit by performing procedures to understand the design of controls relevant to an audit of financial statements, and whether they have been placed in operation.

.03 After obtaining this understanding, the auditor assesses control risk for the assertions embodied in the account balance, transaction class, and disclosure components of the financial statements. The auditor may assess control risk at the maximum level (the greatest probability that a material misstatement that could occur in an assertion will not be prevented or detected on a timely basis by an entity's internal control) because he or she believes controls are unlikely to pertain to an assertion, are unlikely to be effective, or because evaluating their effectiveness would be inefficient. Alternatively, the auditor may obtain evidential matter about the effectiveness of both the design

---

[*] This section has been revised to reflect the amendments and conforming changes necessary due to the issuance of Statement on Auditing Standards No. 78, effective for audits of financial statements for periods beginning on or after January 1, 1997. The amendments are made to recognize the definition and description of internal control contained in *Internal Control—Integrated Framework*, published by the Committee of Sponsoring Organizations of the Treadway Commission (COSO Report). Specifically, the amendments are to paragraph .01, the replacement of paragraphs .02 through .22 with new paragraphs .02 through .40 (subsequent paragraphs and footnotes have been renumbered accordingly), the addition of a new appendix [paragraph .84], and deletion of the former appendixes A, B, C, and D [paragraphs .66–.69]. In addition, conforming changes to terminology and cross references have been made throughout this section.

[1] Internal control *also may be referred to as internal control structure*.

[2] This section revises the second standard of fieldwork of the ten generally accepted auditing standards.

and operation of a control that supports a lower assessed level of control risk. Such evidential matter may be obtained from tests of controls planned or performed concurrently with obtaining the understanding or from procedures performed to obtain the understanding that were not specifically planned as tests of controls.

.04 After obtaining the understanding and assessing control risk, the auditor may desire to seek a further reduction in the assessed level of control risk for certain assertions. In such cases, the auditor considers whether evidential matter sufficient to support a further reduction is likely to be available and whether performing additional tests of controls to obtain such evidential matter would be efficient.

.05 The auditor uses the knowledge provided by the understanding of internal control and the assessed level of control risk in determining the nature, timing, and extent of substantive tests for financial statement assertions.

Definition of Internal Control

.06 *Internal control* is a process—effected by an entity's board of directors, management, and other personnel—designed to provide reasonable assurance regarding the achievement of objectives in the following categories: (*a*) reliability of financial reporting, (*b*) effectiveness and efficiency of operations, and (*c*) compliance with applicable laws and regulations.

.07 Internal control consists of five interrelated components, which are:

a. *Control environment* sets the tone of an organization, influencing the control consciousness of its people. It is the foundation for all other components of internal control, providing discipline and structure.

b. *Risk assessment* is the entity's identification and analysis of relevant risks to achievement of its objectives, forming a basis for determining how the risks should be managed.

c. *Control activities* are the policies and procedures that help ensure that management directives are carried out.

d. *Information and communication* are the identification, capture, and exchange of information in a form and time frame that enable people to carry out their responsibilities.

e. *Monitoring* is a process that assesses the quality of internal control performance over time.

Relationship Between Objectives and Components

.08 There is a direct relationship between objectives, which are what an entity strives to achieve, and components, which represent what is needed to achieve the objectives. In addition, internal control is relevant to the entire entity, or to any of its operating units or business functions. This relationship is depicted as follows:

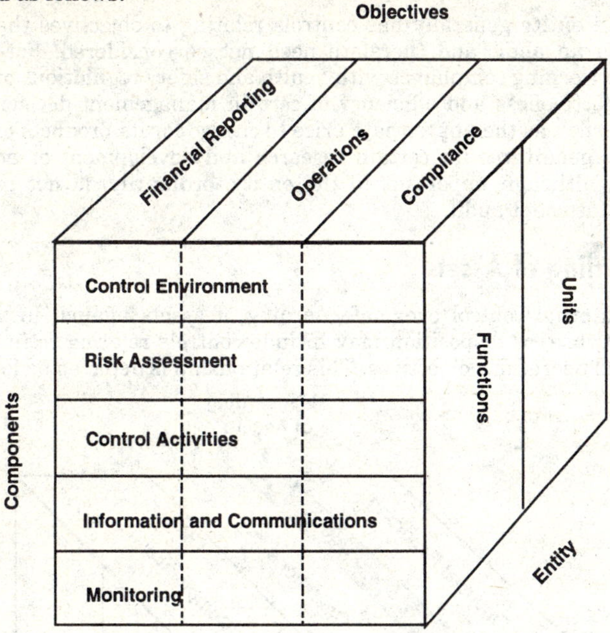

Objectives
Financial Reporting
Operations
Compliance
Units
Functions
Components
Control Environment
Risk Assessment
Control Activities
Information and Communications
Monitoring
Entity

.09 Although an entity's internal control addresses objectives in each of the categories referred to in paragraph .06, not all of these objectives and related controls are relevant to an audit of the entity's financial statements. Also, although internal control is relevant to the entire entity or to any of its operating units or business functions, an understanding of internal control relevant to each of the entity's operating units and business functions may not be necessary.

Financial Reporting Objective

.10 Generally, controls that are relevant to an audit pertain to the entity's objective of preparing financial statements for external purposes that are fairly presented in conformity with generally accepted accounting principles or a comprehensive basis of accounting other than generally accepted accounting principles.[3]

Operations and Compliance Objectives

.11 The controls relating to operations and compliance[4] objectives may be relevant to an audit if they pertain to data the auditor evaluates or uses in

---

[3] The term *comprehensive basis of accounting other than generally accepted accounting principles* is defined in section 623, *Special Reports*, paragraph .04. Hereafter, reference to generally accepted accounting principles in this section includes, where applicable, an other comprehensive basis of accounting.

[4] An auditor may need to consider controls relevant to compliance objectives when performing an audit in accordance with section 801, *Compliance Auditing Considerations in Audits of Governmental Entities and Recipients of Governmental Financial Assistance*.

applying auditing procedures. For example, controls pertaining to nonfinancial data that the auditor uses in analytical procedures, such as production statistics, or pertaining to detecting noncompliance with laws and regulations that may have a direct and material effect on the financial statements, such as controls over compliance with income tax laws and regulations used to determine the income tax provision, may be relevant to an audit.

.12 An entity generally has controls relating to objectives that are not relevant to an audit and therefore need not be considered. For example, controls concerning compliance with health and safety regulations or concerning the effectiveness and efficiency of certain management decision-making processes (such as the appropriate price to charge for its products or whether to make expenditures for certain research and development or advertising activities), although important to the entity, ordinarily do not relate to a financial statement audit.

Safeguarding of Assets

.13 Internal control over safeguarding of assets against unauthorized acquisition, use, or disposition may include controls relating to financial reporting and operations objectives. This relationship is depicted as follows:

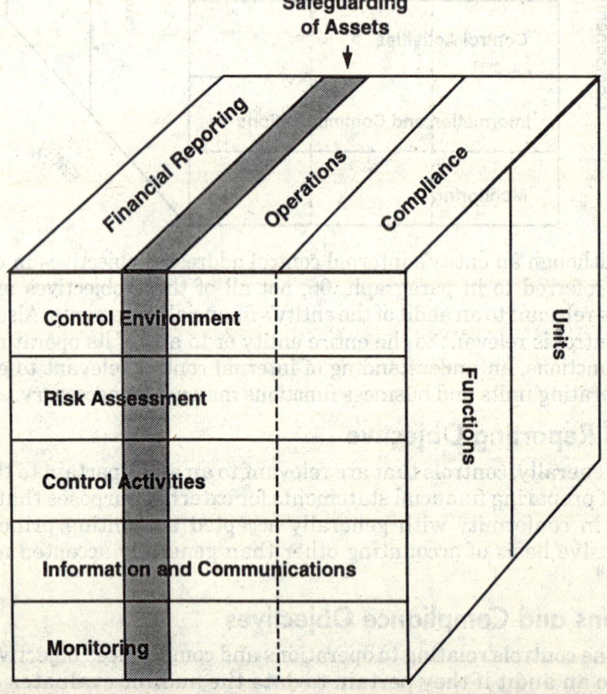

In obtaining an understanding of each of the components of internal control to plan the audit, the auditor's consideration of safeguarding controls is generally limited to those relevant to the reliability of financial reporting. For example, use of a lockbox system for collecting cash or passwords for limiting access to accounts receivable data files may be relevant to a financial statement audit. Conversely, controls to prevent the excess use of materials in production generally are not relevant to a financial statement audit.

Application of Components to a Financial Statement Audit

.14 The division of internal control into five components provides a useful framework for auditors to consider the impact of an entity's internal control in an audit. However, it does not necessarily reflect how an entity considers and implements internal control. Also, the auditor's primary consideration is whether a specific control affects financial statement assertions rather than its classification into any particular component.

.15 The five components of internal control are applicable to the audit of every entity. The components should be considered in the context of—

- The entity's size.
- The entity's organization and ownership characteristics.
- The nature of the entity's business.
- The diversity and complexity of the entity's operations.
- The entity's methods of transmitting, processing, maintaining, and accessing information.
- Applicable legal and regulatory requirements.

Limitations of an Entity's Internal Control

.16 Internal control, no matter how well designed and operated, can provide only reasonable assurance to management and the board of directors regarding achievement of an entity's control objectives. The likelihood of achievement is affected by limitations inherent to internal control. These include the realities that human judgment in decision-making can be faulty and that breakdowns in internal control can occur because of such human failures as simple error or mistake. Additionally, controls can be circumvented by the collusion of two or more people or management override of internal control.

.17 Another limiting factor is that the cost of an entity's internal control should not exceed the benefits that are expected to be derived. Although the cost-benefit relationship is a primary criterion that should be considered in designing internal control, the precise measurement of costs and benefits usually is not possible. Accordingly, management makes both quantitative and qualitative estimates and judgments in evaluating the cost-benefit relationship.

.18 Custom, culture, and the corporate governance system may inhibit irregularities by management, but they are not absolute deterrents. An effective control environment, too, may help mitigate the probability of such irregularities. For example, an effective board of directors, audit committee, and internal audit function may constrain improper conduct by management. Alternatively, the control environment may reduce the effectiveness of other components. For example, when the presence of management incentives creates an environment that could result in material misstatement of financial statements, the effectiveness of control activities may be reduced. The effectiveness of an entity's internal control might also be adversely affected by such factors as a change in ownership or control, changes in management or other personnel, or developments in the entity's market or industry.

Consideration of Internal Control in Planning an Audit

.19 In all audits, the auditor should obtain an understanding of each of the five components of internal control sufficient to plan the audit by performing procedures to understand the design of controls relevant to an audit of financial statements, and whether they have been placed in operation. In planning the audit, such knowledge should be used to—

- Identify types of potential misstatement.
- Consider factors that affect the risk of material misstatement.
- Design substantive tests.

.20 The nature, timing, and extent of procedures the auditor chooses to perform to obtain the understanding will vary depending on the size and complexity of the entity, previous experience with the entity, the nature of the specific controls involved, and the nature of the entity's documentation of specific controls. For example, the understanding of risk assessment needed to plan an audit for an entity operating in a relatively stable environment may be limited. Also, the understanding of monitoring needed to plan an audit for a small, noncomplex entity may be limited.

.21 Whether a control has been *placed in operation* is different from its *operating effectiveness*. In obtaining knowledge about whether controls have been placed in operation, the auditor determines that the entity is using them. Operating effectiveness, on the other hand, is concerned with how the control was applied, the consistency with which it was applied, and by whom it was applied. For example, a budgetary reporting system may provide adequate reports, but the reports may not be analyzed and acted on. This section does not require the auditor to obtain knowledge about operating effectiveness as part of the understanding of internal control.

.22 The auditor's understanding of internal control may sometimes raise doubts about the auditability of an entity's financial statements. Concerns about the integrity of the entity's management may be so serious as to cause the auditor to conclude that the risk of management misrepresentation in the financial statements is such that an audit cannot be conducted. Concerns about the nature and extent of an entity's records may cause the auditor to conclude that it is unlikely that sufficient competent evidential matter will be available to support an opinion on the financial statements.

Understanding Internal Control

.23 In making a judgment about the understanding of internal control necessary to plan the audit, the auditor considers the knowledge obtained from other sources about the types of misstatement that could occur, the risk that such misstatements may occur, and the factors that influence the design of substantive tests. Other sources of such knowledge include previous audits and the understanding of the industry in which the entity operates. The auditor also considers his or her assessment of inherent risk, judgments about materiality, and the complexity and sophistication of the entity's operations and systems, including whether the method of controlling information processing is based on manual procedures independent of the computer or is highly dependent on computerized controls. As an entity's operations and systems become more complex and sophisticated, it may be necessary to devote more attention to internal control components to obtain the understanding of them that is necessary to design effective substantive tests.

.24 Paragraphs .25 through .40 provide an overview of the five internal control components and the auditor's understanding of the components relating to a financial statement audit. A more detailed discussion of these components is provided in appendix A [paragraph .84].

Control Environment

.25 The control environment sets the tone of an organization, influencing the control consciousness of its people. It is the foundation for all other components of internal control, providing discipline and structure. Control environment factors include the following:

a. Integrity and ethical values

b. Commitment to competence

c. Board of directors or audit committee participation

d. Management's philosophy and operating style

e. Organizational structure

f. Assignment of authority and responsibility

g. Human resource policies and practices

.26 The auditor should obtain sufficient knowledge of the control environment to understand management's and the board of directors' attitude, awareness, and actions concerning the control environment, considering both the substance of controls and their collective effect. The auditor should concentrate on the substance of controls rather than their form, because controls may be established but not acted upon. For example, management may establish a formal code of conduct but act in a manner that condones violations of that code.

.27 When obtaining an understanding of the control environment, the auditor considers the collective effect on the control environment of strengths and weaknesses in various control environment factors. Management's strengths and weaknesses may have a pervasive effect on internal control. For example, owner-manager controls may mitigate a lack of segregation of duties in a small business, or an active and independent board of directors may influence the philosophy and operating style of senior management in larger entities. However, human resource policies and practices directed toward hiring competent financial and accounting personnel may not mitigate a strong bias by top management to overstate earnings.

Risk Assessment

.28 An entity's risk assessment for financial reporting purposes is its identification, analysis, and management of risks relevant to the preparation of financial statements that are fairly presented in conformity with generally accepted accounting principles. For example, risk assessment may address how the entity considers the possibility of unrecorded transactions or identifies and analyzes significant estimates recorded in the financial statements. Risks relevant to reliable financial reporting also relate to specific events or transactions.

.29 Risks relevant to financial reporting include external and internal events and circumstances that may occur and adversely affect an entity's ability to record, process, summarize, and report financial data consistent with the assertions of management in the financial statements.[5] Risks can arise or change due to circumstances such as the following

- Changes in operating environment
- New personnel
- New or revamped information systems
- Rapid growth
- New technology
- New lines, products, or activities
- Corporate restructurings
- Foreign operations
- Accounting pronouncements

.30 The auditor should obtain sufficient knowledge of the entity's risk assessment process to understand how management considers risks relevant to financial reporting objectives and decides about actions to address those risks. This knowledge might include understanding how management identifies risks, estimates the significance of the risks, assesses the likelihood of their occurrence, and relates them to financial reporting.

.31 An entity's risk assessment differs from the auditor's consideration of audit risk in a financial statement audit. The purpose of an entity's risk assessment is to identify, analyze, and manage risks that affect entity objectives. In a financial statement audit, the auditor assesses inherent and control risks to evaluate the likelihood that material misstatements could occur in the financial statements.

Control Activities

.32 Control activities are the policies and procedures that help ensure that management directives are carried out. They help ensure that necessary actions are taken to address risks to achievement of the entity's objectives. Control activities have various objectives and are applied at various organizational and functional levels. Generally, control activities that may be relevant to an audit may be categorized as policies and procedures that pertain to the following

- Performance reviews
- Information processing
- Physical controls
- Segregation of duties

---

[5] These assertions are discussed in section 326, *Evidential Matter*.

.33 The auditor should obtain an understanding of those control activities relevant to planning the audit. As the auditor obtains an understanding of the other components he or she is also likely to obtain knowledge about some control activities. For example, in obtaining an understanding of the documents, records, and processing steps in the financial reporting information system that pertain to cash, the auditor is likely to become aware of whether bank accounts are reconciled. The auditor should consider the knowledge about the presence or absence of control activities obtained from the understanding of the other components in determining whether it is necessary to devote additional attention to obtaining an understanding of control activities to plan the audit. Ordinarily, audit planning does not require an understanding of the control activities related to each account balance, transaction class, and disclosure component in the financial statements or to every assertion relevant to them.

Information and Communication

.34 The information system relevant to financial reporting objectives, which includes the accounting system, consists of the methods and records established to record, process, summarize, and report entity transactions (as well as events and conditions) and to maintain accountability for the related assets, liabilities, and equity. The quality of system-generated information affects management's ability to make appropriate decisions in controlling the entity's activities and to prepare reliable financial reports.

.35 Communication involves providing an understanding of individual roles and responsibilities pertaining to internal control over financial reporting.

.36 The auditor should obtain sufficient knowledge of the information system relevant to financial reporting to understand—

- The classes of transactions in the entity's operations that are significant to the financial statements.
- How those transactions are initiated.
- The accounting records, supporting information, and specific accounts in the financial statements involved in the processing and reporting of transactions.
- The accounting processing involved from the initiation of a transaction to its inclusion in the financial statements, including electronic means (such as computers and electronic data interchange) used to transmit, process, maintain, and access information.
- The financial reporting process used to prepare the entity's financial statements, including significant accounting estimates and disclosures.

In addition, the auditor should obtain sufficient knowledge of the means the entity uses to communicate financial reporting roles and responsibilities and significant matters relating to financial reporting.

Monitoring

.37 An important management responsibility is to establish and maintain internal control. Management monitors controls to consider whether they are operating as intended and that they are modified as appropriate for changes in conditions.

.38 Monitoring is a process that assesses the quality of internal control performance over time. It involves assessing the design and operation of controls on a timely basis and taking necessary corrective actions. This process is accomplished through ongoing activities, separate evaluations or by various combinations of the two. In many entities, internal auditors or personnel performing similar functions contribute to the monitoring of an entity's activities. Monitoring activities may include using information from communications from external parties such as customer complaints and regulator comments that may indicate problems or highlight areas in need of improvement.

.39 The auditor should obtain sufficient knowledge of the major types of activities the entity uses to monitor internal control over financial reporting, including how those activities are used to initiate corrective actions. When obtaining an understanding of the internal audit function, the auditor should follow the guidance in paragraphs .04 through .08 of section 322, *The Auditor's Consideration of the Internal Audit Function in an Audit of Financial Statements.*

Application to Small and Midsized Entities

.40 As indicated in paragraph .15, the way internal control components apply will vary based on an entity's size and complexity, among other considerations. Specifically, small and midsized entities may use less formal means to ensure that internal control objectives are achieved. For example, smaller entities with active management involvement in the financial reporting process may not have extensive descriptions of accounting procedures, sophisticated information systems, or written policies. Smaller entities may not have a written code of conduct but, instead, develop a culture that emphasizes the importance of integrity and ethical behavior through oral communication and by management example. Similarly, smaller entities may not have an independent or outside member on their board of directors. However, these conditions may not affect the auditor's assessment of control risk. When small or midsized entities are involved in complex transactions or are subject to legal and regulatory requirements also found in larger entities, more formal means of ensuring that internal control objectives are achieved may be present.

Procedures to Obtain Understanding

.41 In obtaining an understanding of controls that are relevant to audit planning, the auditor should perform procedures to provide sufficient knowledge of the design of the relevant controls pertaining to each of the five internal control components and whether they have been placed in operation. This knowledge is ordinarily obtained through previous experience with the entity and procedures such as inquiries of appropriate management, supervisory, and staff personnel; inspection of entity documents and records; and observation of entity activities and operations. The nature and extent of the procedures performed generally vary from entity to entity and are influenced by the size and complexity of the entity, the auditor's previous experience with the entity, the nature of the particular control, and the nature of the entity's documentation of specific controls.

.42 For example, the auditor's prior experience with the entity may provide an understanding of its classes of transactions. Inquiries of appropriate entity personnel and inspection of documents and records, such as source documents, journals, and ledgers, may provide an understanding of the accounting records designed to process those transactions and whether they have been placed in operation. Similarly, in obtaining an understanding of the design of computer-programmed control activities and whether they have been placed in operation, the auditor may make inquiries of appropriate entity personnel and inspect relevant systems documentation to understand control activity design and may inspect exception reports generated as a result of such control activities to determine that they have been placed in operation.

.43 The auditor's assessments of inherent risk and judgments about materiality for various account balances and transaction classes also affect the nature and extent of the procedures performed to obtain the understanding. For example, the auditor may conclude that planning the audit of the prepaid insurance account does not require specific procedures to be included in obtaining the understanding of internal control.

Documentation of Understanding

.44 The auditor should document the understanding of the entity's internal control components obtained to plan the audit. The form and extent of this documentation is influenced by the size and complexity of the entity, as well as the nature of the entity's internal control. For example, documentation of the understanding of internal control of a large complex entity may include flowcharts, questionnaires, or decision tables. For a small entity, however, documentation in the form of a memorandum may be sufficient. Generally, the more complex internal control and the more extensive the procedures performed, the more extensive the auditor's documentation should be.

Consideration of Internal Control in Assessing Control Risk

.45 Section 326, *Evidential Matter*, states that most of the independent auditor's work in forming an opinion on financial statements consists of obtaining and evaluating evidential matter concerning the assertions in such financial statements. These assertions are embodied in the account balance, transaction class, and disclosure components of financial statements and are classified according to the following broad categories:

- Existence or occurrence
- Completeness
- Rights and obligations
- Valuation or allocation
- Presentation and disclosure

In planning and performing an audit, an auditor considers these assertions in the context of their relationship to a specific account balance or class of transactions.

.46 The risk of material misstatement[6] in financial statement assertions consists of inherent risk, control risk, and detection risk. Inherent risk is the susceptibility of an assertion to a material misstatement assuming there are

---

[6] For purposes of this section, a material misstatement in a financial statement assertion is a misstatement whether caused by error or fraud as discussed in section 312, *Audit Risk and Materiality in Conducting an Audit*, that either individually or when aggregated with other misstatements in other assertions would be material to the financial statements taken as a whole.

no related controls. Control risk is the risk that a material misstatement that could occur in an assertion will not be prevented or detected on a timely basis by the entity's internal control. Detection risk is the risk that the auditor will not detect a material misstatement that exists in an assertion.

.47 Assessing control risk is the process of evaluating the effectiveness of an entity's internal control in preventing or detecting material misstatements in the financial statements. Control risk should be assessed in terms of financial statement assertions. After obtaining the understanding of internal control, the auditor may assess control risk at the maximum level for some or all assertions because he or she believes controls are unlikely to pertain to an assertion, are unlikely to be effective, or because evaluating their effectiveness would be inefficient.[7]

.48 Assessing control risk at below the maximum level involves—

- Identifying specific controls relevant to specific assertions that are likely to prevent or detect material misstatements in those assertions.
- Performing tests of controls to evaluate the effectiveness of such controls.

.49 In identifying controls relevant to specific financial statement assertions, the auditor should consider that the controls can have either a pervasive effect on many assertions or a specific effect on an individual assertion, depending on the nature of the particular internal control component involved. For example, the conclusion that an entity's control environment is highly effective may influence the auditor's decision about the number of an entity's locations at which auditing procedures are to be performed or whether to perform certain auditing procedures for some account balances or transaction classes at an interim date. Either decision affects the way in which auditing procedures are applied to specific assertions, even though the auditor may not have specifically considered each individual assertion that is affected by such decisions.

.50 Conversely, some control activities often have a specific effect on an individual assertion embodied in a particular account balance or transaction class. For example, the control activities that an entity established to ensure that its personnel are properly counting and recording the annual physical inventory relate directly to the existence assertion for the inventory account balance.

.51 Controls can be either directly or indirectly related to an assertion. The more indirect the relationship, the less effective that control may be in reducing control risk for that assertion. For example, a sales manager's review of a summary of sales activity for specific stores by region ordinarily is indirectly related to the completeness assertion for sales revenue. Accordingly, it may be less effective in reducing control risk for that assertion than controls more directly related to that assertion, such as matching shipping documents with billing documents.

.52 Procedures directed toward either the effectiveness of the design or operation of a control are referred to as tests of controls. Tests of controls dir-

---

[7] Control risk may be assessed in quantitative terms, such as percentages, or in nonquantitative terms that range, for example, from a maximum to a minimum. The term *maximum level* is used in this section to mean the greatest probability that a material misstatement that could occur in a financial statement assertion will not be prevented or detected on a timely basis by an entity's internal control.

ected toward the effectiveness of the design of a control are concerned with whether that control is suitably designed to prevent or detect material misstatements in specific financial statement assertions. Tests to obtain such evidential matter ordinarily include procedures such as inquiries of appropriate entity personnel, inspection of documents and reports, and observation of the application of specific controls. For entities with complex internal control, the auditor should consider that the use of flowcharts, questionnaires, or decision tables might facilitate the application of tests of design.

.53 Tests of controls directed toward the operating effectiveness of a control are concerned with how the control was applied, the consistency with which it was applied during the audit period, and by whom it was applied. These tests ordinarily include procedures such as inquiries of appropriate entity personnel; inspection of documents, reports, or electronic files, indicating performance of the control; observation of the application of the control; and reperformance of the application of the control by the auditor. In some circumstances, a specific procedure may address the effectiveness of both design and operation. However, a combination of procedures may be necessary to evaluate the effectiveness of the design or operation of a control.

.54 The conclusion reached as a result of assessing control risk is referred to as the assessed level of control risk. In determining the evidential matter necessary to support a specific assessed level of control risk at below the maximum level, the auditor should consider the characteristics of evidential matter about control risk discussed in paragraphs .64 through .78. Generally, however, the lower the assessed level of control risk, the greater the assurance the evidential matter must provide that the controls relevant to an assertion are designed and operating effectively.

.55 The auditor uses the assessed level of control risk (together with the assessed level of inherent risk) to determine the acceptable level of detection risk for financial statement assertions. The auditor uses the acceptable level of detection risk to determine the nature, timing, and extent of the auditing procedures to be used to detect material misstatements in the financial statement assertions. Auditing procedures designed to detect such misstatements are referred to in this section as substantive tests.

.56 As the acceptable level of detection risk decreases, the assurance provided from substantive tests should increase. Consequently, the auditor may do one or more of the following:

- Change the nature of substantive tests from a less effective to a more effective procedure, such as using tests directed toward independent parties outside the entity rather than tests directed toward parties or documentation within the entity.
- Change the timing of substantive tests, such as performing them at year end rather than at an interim date.
- Change the extent of substantive tests, such as using a larger sample size.

Documentation of the Assessed Level of Control Risk

.57 In addition to the documentation of the understanding of internal control discussed in paragraph .44, the auditor should document the basis for his or her conclusions about the assessed level of control risk. Conclusions about the assessed level of control risk may differ as they relate to various account balances or classes of transactions. However, for those financial statement assertions where control risk is assessed at the maximum level, the auditor should document his or her conclusion that control risk is at the maximum level but need not document the basis for that conclusion. For those assertions where the assessed level of control risk is below the maximum level, the auditor should document the basis for his or her conclusion that the effectiveness of the design and operation of controls supports that assessed level. The nature and extent of the auditor's documentation are influenced by the assessed level of control risk used, the nature of the entity's internal control, and the nature of the entity's documentation of internal control.

Relationship of Understanding to Assessing Control Risk

.58 Although understanding internal control and assessing control risk are discussed separately in this section, they may be performed concurrently in an audit. The objective of procedures performed to obtain an understanding of internal control (discussed in paragraphs .41 through .43) is to provide the auditor with knowledge necessary for audit planning. The objective of tests of controls (discussed in paragraphs .52 and .53) is to provide the auditor with evidential matter to use in assessing control risk. However, procedures performed to achieve one objective may also pertain to the other objective.

.59 Based on the assessed level of control risk the auditor expects to support and audit efficiency considerations, the auditor often plans to perform some tests of controls concurrently with obtaining the understanding of internal control. In addition, even though some of the procedures performed to obtain the understanding may not have been specifically planned as tests of controls, they may also provide evidential matter about the effectiveness of both the design and operation of the controls relevant to certain assertions and, consequently, serve as tests of controls. For example, in obtaining an understanding of the control environment, the auditor may have made inquiries about management's use of budgets, observed management's comparison of monthly budgeted and actual expenses, and inspected reports pertaining to the investigation of variances between budgeted and actual amounts. Although these procedures provide knowledge about the design of the entity's budgeting policies and whether they have been placed in operation, they may also provide evidential matter about the effectiveness of the design and operation of budgeting policies in preventing or detecting material misstatements in the classification of expenses. In some circumstances, that evidential matter may be sufficient to support an assessed level of control risk that is below the maximum level for the presentation and disclosure assertions pertaining to expenses in the income statement.

.60 When the auditor concludes that procedures performed to obtain the understanding of internal control also provide evidential matter for assessing control risk, he or she should consider the guidance in paragraphs .64 through .78 in judging the degree of assurance provided by that evidential matter. Although such evidential matter may not provide sufficient assurance to support an assessed level of control risk that is below the maximum level for certain assertions, it may do so for other assertions and thus provide a basis for modifying the nature, timing, or extent of the substantive tests that the auditor plans for those assertions. However, such procedures are not sufficient to support an assessed level of control risk below the maximum level if they do not provide sufficient evidential matter to evaluate the effectiveness of both the design and operation of a control relevant to an assertion.

Further Reduction in the Assessed Level of Control Risk

.61 After obtaining the understanding of internal control and assessing control risk, the auditor may desire to seek a further reduction in the assessed level of control risk for certain assertions. In such cases, the auditor considers whether additional evidential matter sufficient to support a further reduction is likely to be available, and whether it would be efficient to perform tests of controls to obtain that evidential matter. The results of the procedures performed to obtain the understanding of the internal control, as well as pertinent information from other sources, help the auditor to evaluate those two factors.

.62 In considering efficiency, the auditor recognizes that additional evidential matter that supports a further reduction in the assessed level of control risk for an assertion would result in less audit effort for the substantive tests of that assertion. The auditor weighs the increase in audit effort associated with the additional tests of controls that is necessary to obtain such evidential matter against the resulting decrease in audit effort associated with the reduced substantive tests. When the auditor concludes it is inefficient to obtain additional evidential matter for specific assertions, the auditor uses the assessed level of control risk based on the understanding of internal control in planning the substantive tests for those assertions.

.63 For those assertions for which the auditor performs additional tests of controls, the auditor determines the assessed level of control risk that the results of those tests will support. This assessed level of control risk is used in determining the appropriate detection risk to accept for those assertions and, accordingly, in determining the nature, timing, and extent of substantive tests for such assertions.

Evidential Matter to Support the Assessed Level of Control Risk

.64 When the auditor assesses control risk at below the maximum level, he or she should obtain sufficient evidential matter to support that assessed level. The evidential matter[8] that is sufficient to support a specific assessed level of control risk is a matter of auditing judgment. Evidential matter varies substantially in the assurance it provides to the auditor as he or she develops an assessed level of control risk. The type of evidential matter, its source, its timeliness, and the existence of other evidential matter related to the conclusion to which it leads all bear on the degree of assurance evidential matter provides.

.65 These characteristics influence the nature, timing, and extent of the tests of controls that the auditor applies to obtain evidential matter about control risk. The auditor selects such tests from a variety of techniques such as inquiry, observation, inspection, and reperformance of a control that pertains to an assertion. No one specific test of controls is always necessary, applicable, or equally effective in every circumstance.

---

[8] See also section 326 for guidance on evidential matter.

Type of Evidential Matter

.66 The nature of the particular controls that pertain to an assertion influences the type of evidential matter that is available to evaluate the effectiveness of the design or operation of those controls. For some controls, documentation of design or operation may exist. In such circumstances, the auditor may decide to inspect the documentation to obtain evidential matter about the effectiveness of design or operation.

.67 For other controls, however, such documentation may not be available or relevant. For example, documentation of design or operation may not exist for some factors in the control environment, such as assignment of authority and responsibility, or for some types of control activities, such as segregation of duties or some control activities performed by a computer. In such circumstances, evidential matter about the effectiveness of design or operation may be obtained through observation or the use of computer-assisted audit techniques to reperform the application of relevant controls.

Source of Evidential Matter

.68 Generally, evidential matter about the effectiveness of the design and operation of controls obtained directly by the auditor, such as through observation, provides more assurance than evidential matter obtained indirectly or by inference, such as through inquiry. For example, evidential matter about the proper segregation of duties that is obtained by the auditor's direct personal observation of the individual who applies a control generally provides more assurance than making inquiries about the individual. The auditor should consider, however, that the observed application of a control might not be performed in the same manner when the auditor is not present.

.69 Inquiry alone generally will not provide sufficient evidential matter to support a conclusion about the effectiveness of design or operation of a specific control. When the auditor determines that a specific control may have a significant effect in reducing control risk to a low level for a specific assertion, he or she ordinarily needs to perform additional tests to obtain sufficient evidential matter to support the conclusion about the effectiveness of the design or operation of that control.

Timeliness of Evidential Matter

.70 The timeliness of the evidential matter concerns when it was obtained and the portion of the audit period to which it applies. In evaluating the degree of assurance that is provided by evidential matter, the auditor should consider that the evidential matter obtained by some tests of controls, such as observation, pertains only to the point in time at which the auditing procedure was applied. Consequently, such evidential matter may be insufficient to evaluate the effectiveness of the design or operation of controls for periods not subjected to such tests. In such circumstances, the auditor may decide to supplement these tests with other tests of controls that are capable of providing evidential matter about the entire audit period. For example, for a control activity performed by a computer program, the auditor may test the operation of the control at a particular point in time to obtain evidential matter about whether the program executes the control effectively. The auditor may then perform tests of controls directed toward the design and operation of other control activities pertaining to the modification and the use of that computer program during the audit period to obtain evidential matter about whether the programmed control activity operated consistently during the audit period.

.71 Evidential matter about the effective design or operation of controls that was obtained in prior audits may be considered by the auditor in assessing control risk in the current audit. To evaluate the use of such evidential matter for the current audit, the auditor should consider the significance of the assertion involved, the specific controls that were evaluated during the prior audits, the degree to which the effective design and operation of those controls were evaluated, the results of the tests of controls used to make those evaluations, and the evidential matter about design or operation that may result from substantive tests performed in the current audit. The auditor should also consider that the longer the time elapsed since the performance of tests of controls to obtain evidential matter about control risk, the less assurance it may provide.

.72 When considering evidential matter obtained from prior audits, the auditor should obtain evidential matter in the current period about whether changes have occurred in internal control, including its policies, procedures, and personnel, subsequent to the prior audits, as well as the nature and extent of any such changes. Consideration of evidential matter about these changes, together with the considerations in the preceding paragraph, may support either increasing or decreasing the additional evidential matter about the effectiveness of design and operation to be obtained in the current period.

.73 When the auditor obtains evidential matter about the design or operation of controls during an interim period, he or she should determine what additional evidential matter should be obtained for the remaining period. In making that determination, the auditor should consider the significance of the assertion involved, the specific controls that were evaluated during the interim period, the degree to which the effective design and operation of those controls were evaluated, the results of the tests of controls used to make that evaluation, the length of the remaining period, and the evidential matter about design or operation that may result from the substantive test performed in the remaining period. The auditor should obtain evidential matter about the nature and extent of any significant changes in internal control, including its policies, procedures, and personnel, that occur subsequent to the interim period.

Interrelationship of Evidential Matter

.74 The auditor should consider the combined effect of various types of evidential matter relating to the same assertion in evaluating the degree of assurance that evidential matter provides. In some circumstances, a single type of evidential matter may not be sufficient to evaluate the effective design or operation of a control. To obtain sufficient evidential matter in such circumstances, the auditor may perform other tests of controls pertaining to that control. For example, an auditor may observe that programmers are not authorized to operate the computer. Because an observation is pertinent only at the point in time at which it is made, the auditor may supplement the observation with inquiries about the frequency and circumstances under which programmers may have access to the computer and may inspect documentation of past instances when programmers attempted to operate the computer to determine how such attempts were prevented or detected.

.75 In addition, when evaluating the degree of assurance provided by evidential matter, the auditor should consider the interrelationship of an entity's control environment, risk assessment, control activities, information and communication, and monitoring. Although an individual internal control component may affect the nature, timing, or extent of substantive tests for a specific financial statement assertion, the auditor should consider the evidential matter about an individual component in relation to the evidential matter about the other components in assessing control risk for a specific assertion.

.76 Generally, when various types of evidential matter support the same conclusion about the design or operation of a control, the degree of assurance provided increases. Conversely, if various types of evidential matter lead to different conclusions about the design or operation of a control, the assurance provided decreases. For example, based on the evidential matter that the control environment is effective, the auditor may have reduced the number of locations at which auditing procedures will be performed. If, however, when evaluating specific control activities, the auditor obtains evidential matter that such activities are ineffective, he or she may reevaluate his or her conclusion about the control environment and, among other things, decide to perform auditing procedures at additional locations.

.77 Similarly, evidential matter indicating that the control environment is ineffective may adversely affect an otherwise effective control for a particular assertion. For example, a control environment that is likely to permit unauthorized changes in a computer program may reduce the assurance provided by evidential matter obtained from evaluating the effectiveness of the program at a particular point in time. In such circumstances, the auditor may decide to obtain additional evidential matter about the design and operation of that program during the audit period. For example, the auditor might obtain and control a copy of the program and use computer-assisted audit techniques to compare that copy with the program that the entity uses to process data.

.78 An audit of financial statements is a cumulative process; as the auditor assesses control risk, the information obtained may cause him or her to modify the nature, timing, or extent of the other planned tests of controls for assessing control risk. In addition, information may come to the auditor's attention as a result of performing substantive tests or from other sources during the audit that differs significantly from the information on which his or her planned tests of controls for assessing control risk were based. For example, the extent of misstatements that the auditor detects by performing substantive tests may alter his or her judgment about the assessed level of control risk. In such circumstances, the auditor may need to reevaluate the planned substantive procedures, based on a revised consideration of the assessed level of control risk for all or some of the financial statement assertions.

Correlation of Control Risk With Detection Risk

.79 The ultimate purpose of assessing control risk is to contribute to the auditor's evaluation of the risk that material misstatements exist in the financial statements. The process of assessing control risk (together with assessing inherent risk) provides evidential matter about the risk that such misstatements may exist in the financial statements. The auditor uses this evidential matter as part of the reasonable basis for an opinion referred to in the third standard of field work, which follows:

> Sufficient competent evidential matter is to be obtained through inspection, observation, inquiries, and confirmations to afford a reasonable basis for an opinion regarding the financial statements under audit.

.80 After considering the level to which he or she seeks to restrict the risk of a material misstatement in the financial statements and the assessed levels of inherent risk and control risk, the auditor performs substantive tests to restrict detection risk to an acceptable level. As the assessed level of control risk decreases, the acceptable level of detection risk increases. Accordingly, the auditor may alter the nature, timing, and extent of the substantive tests performed.

.81 Although the inverse relationship between control risk and detection risk may permit the auditor to change the nature or the timing of substantive tests or limit their extent, ordinarily the assessed level of control risk cannot be sufficiently low to eliminate the need to perform any substantive tests to restrict detection risk for all of the assertions relevant to significant account balances or transaction classes. Consequently, regardless of the assessed level of control risk, the auditor should perform substantive tests for significant account balances and transaction classes.

.82 The substantive tests that the auditor performs consist of tests of details of transactions and balances, and analytical procedures. In assessing control risk, the auditor also may use tests of details of transactions as tests of controls. The objective of tests of details of transactions performed as substantive tests is to detect material misstatements in the financial statements. The objective of tests of details of transactions performed as tests of controls is to evaluate whether a control operated effectively. Although these objectives are different, both may be accomplished concurrently through performance of a test of details on the same transaction. The auditor should recognize, however, that careful consideration should be given to the design and evaluation of such tests to ensure that both objectives will be accomplished.

Effective Date

.83 This section is effective for audits of financial statements for periods beginning on or after January 1, 1990. Paragraphs .01 to .40 and the appendix [paragraph .84] are effective for audits of financial statements for periods beginning on or after January 1, 1997. Early application of the provisions of this section is permissible.

.84

Appendix

Internal Control Components

1. This appendix discusses the five internal control components set forth in paragraph .07 and briefly described in paragraphs .25 through .40 as they relate to a financial statement audit.

Control Environment

2. The control environment sets the tone of an organization, influencing the control consciousness of its people. It is the foundation for all other components of internal control, providing discipline and structure.

3. The control environment encompasses the following factors:

a. *Integrity and ethical values.* The effectiveness of controls cannot rise above the integrity and ethical values of the people who create, administer, and monitor them. Integrity and ethical values are essential elements of the control environment, affecting the design, administration, and monitoring of other components. Integrity and ethical behavior are the product of the entity's ethical and behavioral standards, how they are communicated, and how they are reinforced in practice. They include management's actions to remove or reduce incentives and temptations that might prompt personnel to engage in dishonest, illegal, or unethical acts. They also include the communication of entity values and behavioral standards to personnel through policy statements and codes of conduct and by example.

b. *Commitment to competence.* Competence is the knowledge and skills necessary to accomplish tasks that define the individual's job. Commitment to competence includes management's consideration of the competence levels for particular jobs and how those levels translate into requisite skills and knowledge.

c. *Board of directors or audit committee participation.* An entity's control consciousness is influenced significantly by the entity's board of directors or audit committee. Attributes include the board or audit committee's independence from management, the experience and stature of its members, the extent of its involvement and scrutiny of activities, the appropriateness of its actions, the degree to which difficult questions are raised and pursued with management, and its interaction with internal and external auditors.

d. *Management's philosophy and operating style.* Management's philosophy and operating style encompass a broad range of characteristics. Such characteristics may include the following: management's approach to taking and monitoring business risks; management's attitudes and actions toward financial reporting (conservative or aggressive selection from available alternative accounting principles, and conscientiousness and conservatism with which accounting estimates are developed); and management's attitudes toward information processing and accounting functions and personnel.

e. *Organizational structure*. An entity's organizational structure provides the framework within which its activities for achieving entity-wide objectives are planned, executed, controlled, and monitored. Establishing a relevant organizational structure includes considering key areas of authority and responsibility and appropriate lines of reporting. An entity develops an organizational structure suited to its needs. The appropriateness of an entity's organizational structure depends, in part, on its size and the nature of its activities.

f. *Assignment of authority and responsibility.* This factor includes how authority and responsibility for operating activities are assigned and how reporting relationships and authorization hierarchies are established. It also includes policies relating to appropriate business practices, knowledge and experience of key personnel, and resources provided for carrying out duties. In addition, it includes policies and communications directed at ensuring that all personnel understand the entity's objectives, know how their individual actions interrelate and contribute to those objectives, and recognize how and for what they will be held accountable.

g. *Human resource policies and practices.* Human resource policies and practices relate to hiring, orientation, training, evaluating, counseling, promoting, compensating, and remedial actions. For example, standards for hiring the most qualified individuals—with emphasis on educational background, prior work experience, past accomplishments, and evidence of integrity and ethical behavior—demonstrate an entity's commitment to competent and trustworthy people. Training policies that communicate prospective roles and responsibilities and include practices such as training schools and seminars illustrate expected levels of performance and behavior. Promotions driven by periodic performance appraisals demonstrate the entity's commitment to the advancement of qualified personnel to higher levels of responsibility.

Application to Small and Midsized Entities

4. Small and midsized entities may implement the control environment factors differently than larger entities. For example, smaller entities might not have a written code of conduct but, instead, develop a culture that emphasizes the importance of integrity and ethical behavior through oral communication and by management example. Similarly, smaller entities may not have an independent or outside member on their board of directors. However, these conditions may not affect the auditor's assessment of control risk.

Risk Assessment

5. An entity's risk assessment for financial reporting purposes is its identification, analysis, and management of risks relevant to the preparation of financial statements that are fairly presented in conformity with generally accepted accounting principles. For example, risk assessment may address how the entity considers the possibility of unrecorded transactions or identifies and analyzes significant estimates recorded in the financial statements. Risks relevant to reliable financial reporting also relate to specific events or transactions.

6. Risks relevant to financial reporting include external and internal events and circumstances that may occur and adversely affect an entity's ability to record, process, summarize, and report financial data consistent with the assertions of management in the financial statements. Once risks are identified, management considers their significance, the likelihood of their occurrence, and how they should be managed. Management may initiate plans, programs, or actions to address specific risks or it may decide to accept a risk because of cost or other considerations. Risks can arise or change due to circumstances such as the following:

- *Changes in operating environment.* Changes in the regulatory or operating environment can result in changes in competitive pressures and significantly different risks.
- *New personnel.* New personnel may have a different focus on or understanding of internal control.
- *New or revamped information systems.* Significant and rapid changes in information systems can change the risk relating to internal control.
- *Rapid growth.* Significant and rapid expansion of operations can strain controls and increase the risk of a breakdown in controls.
- *New technology.* Incorporating new technologies into production processes or information systems may change the risk associated with internal control.
- *New lines, products, or activities.* Entering into business areas or transactions with which an entity has little experience may introduce new risks associated with internal control.
- *Corporate restructurings.* Restructurings may be accompanied by staff reductions and changes in supervision and segregation of duties that may change the risk associated with internal control.
- *Foreign operations.* The expansion or acquisition of foreign operations carries new and often unique risks that may impact internal control, for example, additional or changed risks from foreign currency transactions.
- *Accounting pronouncements.* Adoption of new accounting principles or changing accounting principles may affect risks in preparing financial statements.

Application to Small and Midsized Entities

7. The basic concepts of the risk assessment process should be present in every entity, regardless of size, but the risk assessment process is likely to be less formal and less structured in small and midsized entities than in larger ones. All entities should have established financial reporting objectives, but they may be recognized implicitly rather than explicitly in smaller entities. Management may be able to learn about risks related to these objectives through direct personal involvement with employees and outside parties.

Control Activities

8. Control activities are the policies and procedures that help ensure that necessary actions are taken to address risks to achievement of the entity's objectives. Control activities have various objectives and are applied at various organizational and functional levels.

9. Generally, control activities that may be relevant to an audit may be categorized as policies and procedures that pertain to the following:

- *Performance reviews.* These control activities include reviews of actual performance versus budgets, forecasts, and prior period performance; relating different sets of data—operating or financial—to one another, together with analyses of the relationships and investigative and corrective actions; and review of functional or activity performance, such as a bank's consumer loan manager's review of reports by branch, region, and loan type for loan approvals and collections.
- *Information processing.* A variety of controls are performed to check accuracy, completeness, and authorization of transactions. The two broad groupings of information systems control activities are general controls and application controls. General controls commonly include controls over data center operations, system software acquisition and maintenance, access security, and application system development and maintenance. These controls apply to mainframe, minicomputer, and end-user environments. Application controls apply to the processing of individual applications. These controls help ensure that transactions are valid, properly authorized, and completely and accurately processed.
- *Physical controls.* These activities encompass the physical security of assets, including adequate safeguards such as secured facilities, over access to assets and records; authorization for access to computer programs and data files; and periodic counting and comparison with amounts shown on control records. The extent to which physical controls intended to prevent theft of assets are relevant to the reliability of financial statement preparation, and therefore the audit, depends on the circumstances such as when assets are highly susceptible to misappropriation. For example, these controls would ordinarily not be relevant when any inventory losses would be detected pursuant to periodic physical inspection and recorded in the financial statements. However, if for financial reporting purposes management relies solely on perpetual inventory records, the physical security controls would be relevant to the audit.
- *Segregation of duties.* Assigning different people the responsibilities of authorizing transactions, recording transactions, and maintaining custody of assets is intended to reduce the opportunities to allow any person to be in a position to both perpetrate and conceal errors or irregularities in the normal course of his or her duties.

Application to Small and Midsized Entities

10. The concepts underlying control activities in small or midsized organizations are likely to be similar to those in larger entities, but the formality with which they operate varies. Further, smaller entities may find that certain types of control activities are not relevant because of controls applied by management. For example, management's retention of authority for approving credit sales, significant purchases, and draw-downs on lines of credit can provide strong control over those activities, lessening or removing the need for more detailed control activities. An appropriate segregation of duties often appears to present difficulties in smaller organizations. Even companies that have only a few employees, however, may be able to assign their responsibilities to achieve appropriate segregation or, if that is not possible, to use management oversight of the incompatible activities to achieve control objectives.

Information and Communication

11. The information system relevant to financial reporting objectives, which includes the accounting system, consists of the methods and records established to record, process, summarize, and report entity transactions (as well as events and conditions) and to maintain accountability for the related assets, liabilities, and equity. The quality of system-generated information affects management's ability to make appropriate decisions in managing and controlling the entity's activities and to prepare reliable financial reports.

12. An information system encompasses methods and records that—

- Identify and record all valid transactions.
- Describe on a timely basis the transactions in sufficient detail to permit proper classification of transactions for financial reporting.
- Measure the value of transactions in a manner that permits recording their proper monetary value in the financial statements.
- Determine the time period in which transactions occurred to permit recording of transactions in the proper accounting period.
- Present properly the transactions and related disclosures in the financial statements.

13. Communication involves providing an understanding of individual roles and responsibilities pertaining to internal control over financial reporting. It includes the extent to which personnel understand how their activities in the financial reporting information system relate to the work of others and the means of reporting exceptions to an appropriate higher level within the entity. Open communication channels help ensure that exceptions are reported and acted on.

14. Communication takes such forms as policy manuals, accounting and financial reporting manuals, and memoranda. Communication also can be made orally and through the actions of management.

Application to Small and Midsized Entities

15. Information systems in small or midsized organizations are likely to be less formal than in larger organizations, but their role is just as significant. Smaller entities with active management involvement may not need extensive descriptions of accounting procedures, sophisticated accounting records, or written policies. Communication may be less formal and easier to achieve in a small or midsized company than in a larger enterprise due to the smaller organization's size and fewer levels as well as management's greater visibility and availability.

Monitoring

16. Monitoring is a process that assesses the quality of internal control performance over time. It involves assessing the design and operation of controls on a timely basis and taking necessary corrective actions. This process is accomplished through ongoing monitoring activities, separate evaluations, or a combination of the two.

17. Ongoing monitoring activities are built into the normal recurring activities of an entity and include regular management and supervisory activities. Managers of sales, purchasing, and production at divisional and corporate levels are in touch with operations and may question reports that differ significantly from their knowledge of operations.

18. In many entities, internal auditors or personnel performing similar functions contribute to the monitoring of an entity's activities through separate evaluations. They regularly provide information about the functioning of internal control, focusing considerable attention on evaluating the design and operation of internal control. They communicate information about strengths and weaknesses and recommendations for improving internal control.

19. Monitoring activities may include using information from communications from external parties. Customers implicitly corroborate billing data by paying their invoices or complaining about their charges. In addition, regulators may communicate with the entity concerning matters that affect the functioning of internal control, for example, communications concerning examinations by bank regulatory agencies. Also, management may consider communications relating to internal control from external auditors in performing monitoring activities.

Application to Small and Midsized Entities

20. Ongoing monitoring activities of small and midsized entities are more likely to be informal and are typically performed as a part of the overall management of the entity's operations. Management's close involvement in operations often will identify significant variances from expectations and inaccuracies in financial data.

AU Section 9319

Consideration of Internal Control in a Financial Statement Audit: Auditing Interpretations of Section 319

1. Audit Considerations for the Year 2000 Issue

Note: The full text of this interpretation is included as Interpretation No. 4, "Audit Considerations for the Year 2000 Issue," in section 9311, *Planning and Supervision: Auditing Interpretations of Section 311*, paragraphs .38 through .47.

AU Section 322

The Auditor's Consideration of the Internal Audit Function in an Audit of Financial Statements

(Supersedes SAS No. 9)

Source: SAS No. 65.

Effective for audits of financial statements for periods ending after December 15, 1991, unless otherwise indicated.

.01 The auditor considers many factors in determining the nature, timing, and extent of auditing procedures to be performed in an audit of an entity's financial statements. One of the factors is the existence of an internal audit function.[1] This section provides the auditor with guidance on considering the work of internal auditors and on using internal auditors to provide direct assistance to the auditor in an audit performed in accordance with generally accepted auditing standards.

Roles of the Auditor and the Internal Auditors

.02 One of the auditor's responsibilities in an audit conducted in accordance with generally accepted auditing standards is to obtain sufficient competent evidential matter to provide a reasonable basis for the opinion on the entity's financial statements. In fulfilling this responsibility, the auditor maintains independence from the entity.[2]

.03 Internal auditors are responsible for providing analyses, evaluations, assurances, recommendations, and other information to the entity's management and board of directors or to others with equivalent authority and responsibility. To fulfill this responsibility, internal auditors maintain objectivity with respect to the activity being audited.

Obtaining an Understanding of the Internal Audit Function

.04 An important responsibility of the internal audit function is to monitor the performance of an entity's controls. When obtaining an understanding of internal control,[3] the auditor should obtain an understanding of the internal

---

[1] An *internal audit function* may consist of one or more individuals who perform internal auditing activities within an entity. This section is not applicable to personnel who have the title *internal auditor* but who do not perform internal auditing activities as described herein.

[2] Although internal auditors are not independent from the entity, The Institute of Internal Auditors' *Standards for the Professional Practice of Internal Auditing* defines internal auditing as an independent appraisal function and requires internal auditors to be independent of the activities they audit. This concept of independence is different from the independence the auditor maintains under the AICPA Code of Professional Conduct.

[3] Section 319, *Consideration of Internal Control in a Financial Statement Audit*, describes the procedures the auditor follows to obtain an understanding of internal control and indicates that the internal audit function is part of the entity's control environment.

audit function sufficient to identify those internal audit activities that are relevant to planning the audit. The extent of the procedures necessary to obtain this understanding will vary, depending on the nature of those activities.

.05 The auditor ordinarily should make inquiries of appropriate management and internal audit personnel about the internal auditors'—

a. Organizational status within the entity.

b. Application of professional standards (see paragraph .11).

c. Audit plan, including the nature, timing, and extent of audit work.

d. Access to records and whether there are limitations on the scope of their activities.

In addition, the auditor might inquire about the internal audit function's charter, mission statement, or similar directive from management or the board of directors. This inquiry will normally provide information about the goals and objectives established for the internal audit function.

.06 Certain internal audit activities may not be relevant to an audit of the entity's financial statements. For example, the internal auditors' procedures to evaluate the efficiency of certain management decision-making processes are ordinarily not relevant to a financial statement audit.

.07 Relevant activities are those that provide evidence about the design and effectiveness of controls that pertain to the entity's ability to record, process, summarize, and report financial data consistent with the assertions embodied in the financial statements or that provide direct evidence about potential misstatements of such data. The auditor may find the results of the following procedures helpful in assessing the relevancy of internal audit activities:

a. Considering knowledge from prior-year audits

b. Reviewing how the internal auditors allocate their audit resources to financial or operating areas in response to their risk-assessment process

c. Reading internal audit reports to obtain detailed information about the scope of internal audit activities

.08 If, after obtaining an understanding of the internal audit function, the auditor concludes that the internal auditors' activities are not relevant to the financial statement audit, the auditor does not have to give further consideration to the internal audit function unless the auditor requests direct assistance from the internal auditors as described in paragraph .27. Even if some of the internal auditors' activities are relevant to the audit, the auditor may conclude that it would not be efficient to consider further the work of the internal auditors. If the auditor decides that it would be efficient to consider how the internal auditors' work might affect the nature, timing, and extent of audit procedures, the auditor should assess the competence and objectivity of the internal audit function in light of the intended effect of the internal auditors' work on the audit.

Assessing the Competence and Objectivity of the Internal Auditors

Competence of the Internal Auditors

.09 When assessing the internal auditors' competence, the auditor should obtain or update information from prior years about such factors as—

- Educational level and professional experience of internal auditors.

- Professional certification and continuing education.
- Audit policies, programs, and procedures.
- Practices regarding assignment of internal auditors.
- Supervision and review of internal auditors' activities.
- Quality of working-paper documentation, reports, and recommendations.
- Evaluation of internal auditors' performance.

Objectivity of the Internal Auditors

.10 When assessing the internal auditors' objectivity, the auditor should obtain or update information from prior years about such factors as—

- The organizational status of the internal auditor responsible for the internal audit function, including—
  - — Whether the internal auditor reports to an officer of sufficient status to ensure broad audit coverage and adequate consideration of, and action on, the findings and recommendations of the internal auditors.
  - — Whether the internal auditor has direct access and reports regularly to the board of directors, the audit committee, or the owner-manager.
  - — Whether the board of directors, the audit committee, or the owner-manager oversees employment decisions related to the internal auditor.
- Policies to maintain internal auditors' objectivity about the areas audited, including—
  - — Policies prohibiting internal auditors from auditing areas where relatives are employed in important or audit-sensitive positions.
  - — Policies prohibiting internal auditors from auditing areas where they were recently assigned or are scheduled to be assigned on completion of responsibilities in the internal audit function.

Assessing Competence and Objectivity

.11 In assessing competence and objectivity, the auditor usually considers information obtained from previous experience with the internal audit function, from discussions with management personnel, and from a recent external quality review, if performed, of the internal audit function's activities. The auditor may also use professional internal auditing standards[4] as criteria in making the assessment. The auditor also considers the need to test the effectiveness of the factors described in paragraphs .09 and .10. The extent of such testing will vary in light of the intended effect of the internal auditors' work on the audit. If the auditor determines that the internal auditors are sufficiently

---

[4] Standards have been developed for the professional practice of internal auditing by The Institute of Internal Auditors and the General Accounting Office. These standards are meant to (*a*) impart an understanding of the role and responsibilities of internal auditing to all levels of management, boards of directors, public bodies, external auditors, and related professional organizations; (*b*) permit measurement of internal auditing performance; and (*c*) improve the practice of internal auditing.

competent and objective, the auditor should then consider how the internal auditors' work may affect the audit.

Effect of the Internal Auditors' Work on the Audit

.12 The internal auditors' work may affect the nature, timing, and extent of the audit, including—

- Procedures the auditor performs when obtaining an understanding of the entity's internal control (paragraph .13).
- Procedures the auditor performs when assessing risk (paragraphs .14 through .16).
- Substantive procedures the auditor performs (paragraph .17).

When the work of the internal auditors is expected to affect the audit, the guidance in paragraphs .18 through .26 should be followed for considering the extent of the effect, coordinating audit work with internal auditors, and evaluating and testing the effectiveness of internal auditors' work.

Understanding of Internal Control

.13 The auditor obtains a sufficient understanding of the design of controls relevant to the audit of financial statements to plan the audit and to determine whether they have been placed in operation. Since a primary objective of many internal audit functions is to review, assess, and monitor controls, the procedures performed by the internal auditors in this area may provide useful information to the auditor. For example, internal auditors may develop a flowchart of a new computerized sales and receivables system. The auditor may review the flowchart to obtain information about the design of the related controls. In addition, the auditor may consider the results of procedures performed by the internal auditors on related controls to obtain information about whether the controls have been placed in operation. [Revised, February 1997, to reflect conforming changes necessary due to the issuance of Statement on Auditing Standards No. 78.]

Risk Assessment

.14 The auditor assesses the risk of material misstatement at both the financial-statement level and the account-balance or class-of-transaction level.

Financial-Statement Level

.15 At the financial-statement level, the auditor makes an overall assessment of the risk of material misstatement. When making this assessment, the auditor should recognize that certain controls may have a pervasive effect on many financial statement assertions. The control environment and accounting system often have a pervasive effect on a number of account balances and transaction classes and therefore can affect many assertions. The auditor's assessment of risk at the financial-statement level often affects the overall audit strategy. The entity's internal audit function may influence this overall assessment of risk as well as the auditor's resulting decisions concerning the nature, timing, and extent of auditing procedures to be performed. For example, if the internal auditors' plan includes relevant audit work at various locations, the auditor may coordinate work with the internal auditors (see paragraph .23) and reduce the number of the entity's locations at which the auditor would otherwise need to perform auditing procedures.

Account-Balance or Class-of-Transaction Level

.16 At the account-balance or class-of-transaction level, the auditor performs procedures to obtain and evaluate evidential matter concerning management's assertions. The auditor assesses control risk for each of the significant assertions and performs tests of controls to support assessments below the maximum. When planning and performing tests of controls, the auditor may consider the results of procedures planned or performed by the internal auditors. For example, the internal auditors' scope may include tests of controls for the completeness of accounts payable. The results of internal auditors' tests may provide appropriate information about the effectiveness of controls and change the nature, timing, and extent of testing the auditor would otherwise need to perform.

Substantive Procedures

.17 Some procedures performed by the internal auditors may provide direct evidence about material misstatements in assertions about specific account balances or classes of transactions. For example, the internal auditors, as part of their work, may confirm certain accounts receivable and observe certain physical inventories. The results of these procedures can provide evidence the auditor may consider in restricting detection risk for the related assertions. Consequently, the auditor may be able to change the timing of the confirmation procedures, the number of accounts receivable to be confirmed, or the number of locations of physical inventories to be observed.

Extent of the Effect of the Internal Auditors' Work

.18 Even though the internal auditors' work may affect the auditor's procedures, the auditor should perform procedures to obtain sufficient, competent, evidential matter to support the auditor's report. Evidence obtained through the auditor's direct personal knowledge, including physical examination, observation, computation, and inspection, is generally more persuasive than information obtained indirectly.[5]

.19 The responsibility to report on the financial statements rests solely with the auditor. Unlike the situation in which the auditor uses the work of other independent auditors,[6] this responsibility cannot be shared with the internal auditors. Because the auditor has the ultimate responsibility to express an opinion on the financial statements, judgments about assessments of inherent and control risks, the materiality of misstatements, the sufficiency of tests performed, the evaluation of significant accounting estimates, and other matters affecting the auditor's report should always be those of the auditor.

.20 In making judgments about the extent of the effect of the internal auditors' work on the auditor's procedures, the auditor considers—

a. The materiality of financial statement amounts—that is, account balances or classes of transactions.

b. The risk (consisting of inherent risk and control risk) of material misstatement of the assertions related to these financial statement amounts.

---

[5] See section 326, *Evidential Matter,* paragraph .19c.

[6] See section 543, *Part of Audit Performed by Other Independent Auditors.*

c. The degree of subjectivity involved in the evaluation of the audit evidence gathered in support of the assertions.[7]

As the materiality of the financial statement amounts increases and either the risk of material misstatement or the degree of subjectivity increases, the need for the auditor to perform his or her own tests of the assertions increases. As these factors decrease, the need for the auditor to perform his or her own tests of the assertions decreases.

.21 For assertions related to material financial statement amounts where the risk of material misstatement or the degree of subjectivity involved in the evaluation of the audit evidence is high, the auditor should perform sufficient procedures to fulfill the responsibilities described in paragraphs .18 and .19. In determining these procedures, the auditor gives consideration to the results of work (either tests of controls or substantive tests) performed by internal auditors on those particular assertions. However, for such assertions, the consideration of internal auditors' work cannot alone reduce audit risk to an acceptable level to eliminate the necessity to perform tests of those assertions directly by the auditor. Assertions about the valuation of assets and liabilities involving significant accounting estimates, and about the existence and disclosure of related-party transactions, contingencies, uncertainties, and subsequent events, are examples of assertions that might have a high risk of material misstatement or involve a high degree of subjectivity in the evaluation of audit evidence.

.22 On the other hand, for certain assertions related to less material financial statement amounts where the risk of material misstatement or the degree of subjectivity involved in the evaluation of the audit evidence is low, the auditor may decide, after considering the circumstances and the results of work (either tests of controls or substantive tests) performed by internal auditors on those particular assertions, that audit risk has been reduced to an acceptable level and that testing of the assertions directly by the auditor may not be necessary. Assertions about the existence of cash, prepaid assets, and fixed-asset additions are examples of assertions that might have a low risk of material misstatement or involve a low degree of subjectivity in the evaluation of audit evidence.

Coordination of the Audit Work With Internal Auditors

.23 If the work of the internal auditors is expected to have an effect on the auditor's procedures, it may be efficient for the auditor and the internal auditors to coordinate their work by—

- Holding periodic meetings.
- Scheduling audit work.
- Providing access to internal auditors' working papers.
- Reviewing audit reports.
- Discussing possible accounting and auditing issues.

Evaluating and Testing the Effectiveness of Internal Auditors' Work

.24 The auditor should perform procedures to evaluate the quality and effectiveness of the internal auditors' work, as described in paragraphs .12

[7] For some assertions, such as existence and occurrence, the evaluation of audit evidence is generally objective. More subjective evaluation of the audit evidence is often required for other assertions, such as the valuation and disclosure assertions.

through .17, that significantly affects the nature, timing, and extent of the auditor's procedures. The nature and extent of the procedures the auditor should perform when making this evaluation are a matter of judgment depending on the extent of the effect of the internal auditors' work on the auditor's procedures for significant account balances or classes of transactions.

.25 In developing the evaluation procedures, the auditor should consider such factors as whether the internal auditors'—

- Scope of work is appropriate to meet the objectives.
- Audit programs are adequate.
- Working papers adequately document work performed, including evidence of supervision and review.
- Conclusions are appropriate in the circumstances.
- Reports are consistent with the results of the work performed.

.26 In making the evaluation, the auditor should test some of the internal auditors' work related to the significant financial statement assertions. These tests may be accomplished by either (*a*) examining some of the controls, transactions, or balances that the internal auditors examined or (*b*) examining similar controls, transactions, or balances not actually examined by the internal auditors. In reaching conclusions about the internal auditors' work, the auditor should compare the results of his or her tests with the results of the internal auditors' work. The extent of this testing will depend on the circumstances and should be sufficient to enable the auditor to make an evaluation of the overall quality and effectiveness of the internal audit work being considered by the auditor.

Using Internal Auditors to Provide Direct Assistance to the Auditor

.27 In performing the audit, the auditor may request direct assistance from the internal auditors. This direct assistance relates to work the auditor specifically requests the internal auditors to perform to complete some aspect of the auditor's work. For example, internal auditors may assist the auditor in obtaining an understanding of internal control or in performing tests of controls or substantive tests, consistent with the guidance about the auditor's responsibility in paragraphs .18 through .22. When direct assistance is provided, the auditor should assess the internal auditors' competence and objectivity (see paragraphs .09 through .11) and supervise,[8] review, evaluate, and test the work performed by internal auditors to the extent appropriate in the circumstances. The auditor should inform the internal auditors of their responsibilities, the objectives of the procedures they are to perform, and matters that may affect the nature, timing, and extent of audit procedures, such as possible accounting and auditing issues. The auditor should also inform the internal auditors that all significant accounting and auditing issues identified during the audit should be brought to the auditor's attention.

Effective Date

.28 This section is effective for audits of financial statements for periods ending after December 15, 1991. Early application of the provisions of this section is permissible.

---

[8] See section 311, *Planning and Supervision*, paragraphs .11 through .14, for the type of supervisory procedures to apply.

.29

Appendix

The Auditor's Consideration of the Internal Audit Function in an Audit of Financial Statements

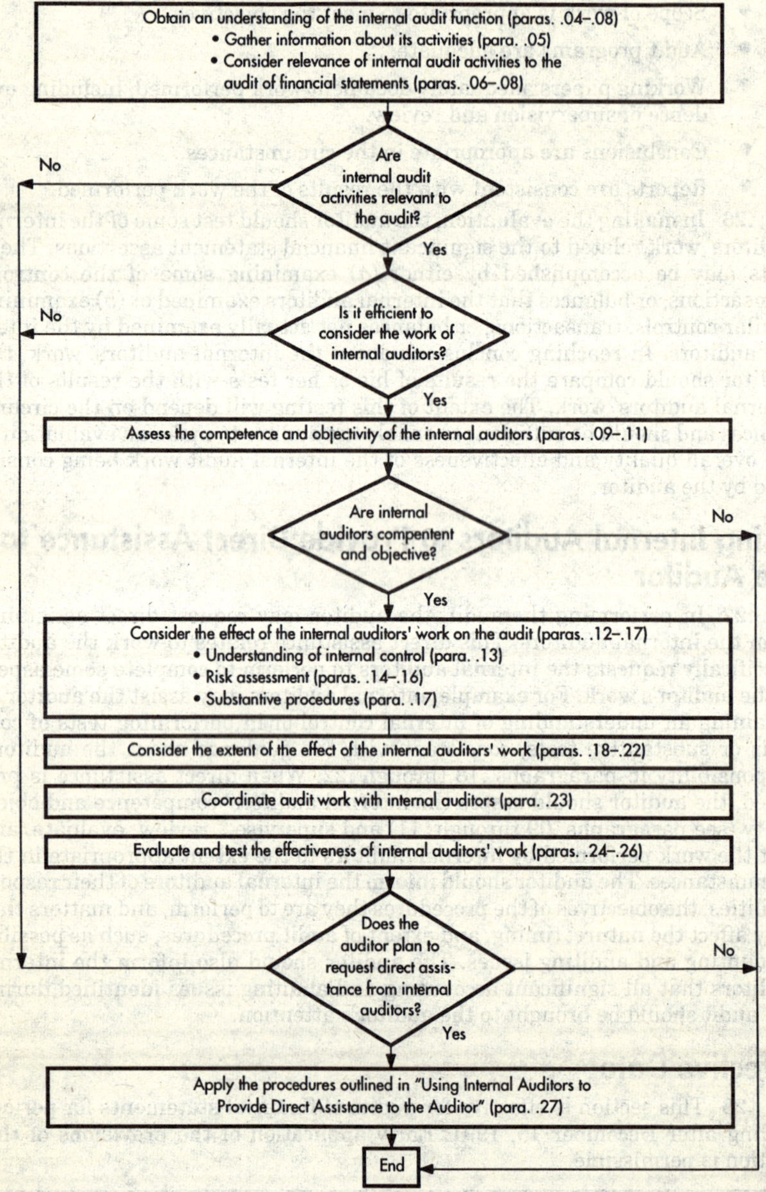

Obtain an understanding of the internal audit function (paras. .04–.08)
• Gather information about its activities (para. .05)
• Consider relevance of internal audit activities to the audit of financial statements (paras. .06–.08)
Are internal audit activities relevant to the audit?
No
Yes
Is it efficient to consider the work of internal auditors?
No
Yes
Assess the competence and objectivity of the internal auditors (paras. .09–.11)
Are internal auditors compentent and objective?
No
Yes
Consider the effect of the internal auditors' work on the audit (paras. .12–.17)
• Understanding of internal control (para. .13)
• Risk assessment (paras. .14–.16)
• Substantive procedures (para. .17)
Consider the extent of the effect of the internal auditors' work (paras. .18–.22)
Coordinate audit work with internal auditors (para. .23)
Evaluate and test the effectiveness of internal auditors' work (paras. .24–.26)
Does the auditor plan to request direct assistance from internal auditors?
No
Yes
Apply the procedures outlined in "Using Internal Auditors to Provide Direct Assistance to the Auditor" (para. .27)
End

AU Section 324

*Reports on the Processing of Transactions by Service Organizations**

(Supersedes SAS No. 44)

Source: SAS No. 70; SAS No. 78.

See section 9324 for interpretations of this section.

Effective for service auditors' reports dated after March 31, 1993, unless otherwise indicated. Earlier application is encouraged.

Introduction and Applicability

.01 This section provides guidance on the factors an independent auditor should consider when auditing the financial statements of an entity that uses a service organization to process certain transactions. This section also provides guidance for independent auditors who issue reports on the processing of transactions by a service organization for use by other auditors.

.02 For purposes of this section, the following definitions apply:

- *User organization*—The entity the has engaged a service organization and whose financial statements are being audited
- *User auditor*—The auditor who reports on the financial statements of the user organization
- *Service organization*—The entity (or segment of an entity) that provides services to the user organization
- *Service auditor*—The auditor who reports on the processing of transactions by a service organization
- *Report on controls placed in operation*—A service auditor's report on a service organization's description of its controls that may be relevant to a user organization's internal control as it relates to an audit of financial statements, on whether such controls were suitably designed to achieve specified control objectives, and on whether they had been placed in operation as of a specific date
- *Report on controls placed in operation and tests of operating effectiveness*—A service auditor's report on a service organization's description of its controls that may be relevant to a user organization's internal control as it relates to an audit of financial statements,[1] on whether such controls were suitably designed to achieve specified control objectives, on whether they had been placed in operation as of a specific

---

* This section has been revised to reflect the amendments and conforming changes necessary due to the issuance of Statement on Auditing Standards No. 78, effective for service auditor's reports covering descriptions as of or after January 1, 1997.

[1] In this section, a service organization's controls that may be relevant to a user organization's internal control as it relates to an audit of financial statements will be referred to as a service organization's *controls*.

date, and on whether the controls that were tested were operating with sufficient effectiveness to provide reasonable, but not absolute, assurance that the related control objectives were achieved during the period specified.

.03 The guidance in this section is applicable to the audit of the financial statements of an entity that obtains either or both of the following services from another organization:

- Executing transactions and maintaining the related accountability
- Recording transactions and processing related data

Service organizations that provide such services include, for example, bank trust departments that invest and hold assets for employee benefit plans or for others, mortgage bankers that service mortgages for others, and electronic data processing (EDP) service centers that process transactions and related data for others. The guidance in this section may also be relevant to situations in which an organization develops, provides, and maintains the software used by client organizations. The provisions of this section are not intended to apply to situations in which the services provided are limited to executing client organization transactions that are specifically authorized by the client, such as the processing of checking account transactions by a bank or the execution of securities transactions by a broker. This section also is not intended to apply to the audit of transactions arising from financial interests in partnerships, corporations, and joint ventures, such as working interests in oil and gas ventures, when proprietary interests are accounted for and reported to interest holders.

.04 This section is organized into the following sections:

a. The user auditor's consideration of the effect of the service organization on the user organization's internal control and the availability of evidence to—
   - Obtain the necessary understanding of the user organization's internal control to plan the audit
   - Assess control risk at the user organization
   - Perform substantive procedures

b. Considerations in using a service auditor's report

c. Responsibilities of service auditors

The User Auditor's Consideration of the Effect of the Service Organization on the User Organization's Internal Control and the Availability of Audit Evidence

.05 The user auditor should consider the discussion in paragraphs .06 through .21 when planning and performing the audit of an entity that uses a service organization to process its transactions.

The Effect of a Service Organization on a User Organization's Internal Control

.06 When a user organization uses a service organization, transactions that affect the user organization's financial statements are subjected to controls that are, at least in part, physically and operationally separate from the user organization. The relationship of the controls of the service organization to those of the user organization depends primarily on the nature of the services provided by the service organization. For example, when those services are limited to recording user transactions and processing the related data, and the user organization retains responsibility for authorizing transactions and maintaining the related accountability, there is a high degree of interaction between the controls at the service organization and those at the user organization. In these circumstances, it may be possible for the user organization to implement effective controls for those transactions. When the service organization executes the user organization's transactions and maintains the related accountability, there is a lower degree of interaction and it may not be practicable for the user organization to implement effective controls for those transactions. The degree of interaction, as well as the nature and materiality of the transactions processed by the service organization, are the most important factors in determining the significance of the service organization's controls to the user organization's internal control.

Planning the Audit

.07 Section 319, *Consideration of Internal Control in a Financial Statement Audit*, states that an auditor should obtain an understanding of each of the five components of the entity's internal control sufficient to plan the audit. This understanding should include knowledge about the design of controls relevant to the audit of financial statements and whether they have been placed in operation by the entity. In planning the audit, such knowledge should be used to—

- Identify types of potential misstatements.
- Consider factors that affect the risk of material misstatement.
- Design substantive tests.

[As amended, effective for service auditor's reports covering descriptions as of or after January 1, 1997, by Statement on Auditing Standards No. 78.]

.08 If an entity uses a service organization, certain controls and records of the service organization may be relevant to the user organization's ability to record, process, summarize, and report financial data consistent with the assertions embodied in the entity's financial statements. In determining the significance of these controls and records to planning the audit, the user should consider factors such as—

- The significance of the financial statement assertions that are affected by the controls of the service organization.
- The inherent risk associated with the assertions affected by the controls of the service organization.
- The nature of the services provided by the service organization and whether they are highly standardized and used extensively by many user organizations or unique and used only by a few.
- The extent to which the user organization's controls interact with the controls of the service organization.
- The user organization's controls that are applied to the transactions affected by the service organization's activities.

- The terms of the contract between the user organization and the service organization (for example, their respective responsibilities and the extent of the service organization's discretion to initiate transactions).
- The service organization's capabilities, including its—
  - — Record of performance.
  - — Insurance coverage.
  - — Financial stability.
- The user auditor's prior experience with the service organization.
- The extent of auditable data in the user organization's possession.
- The existence of specific regulatory requirements that may dictate the application of audit procedures beyond those required to comply with generally accepted auditing standards.

.09 The user auditor should also consider the available information about the service organization's controls, including *(a)* the information in the user organization's possession, such as user manuals, system overviews, and technical manuals, and *(b)* the existence of reports on the service organization's controls, such as reports by service auditors, internal auditors (the user organization's or the service organization's), or regulatory authorities.

.10 After considering the above factors and evaluating the available information, the user auditor may conclude that he or she has the means to obtain a sufficient understanding of internal control to plan the audit. If the user auditor concludes that information is not available to obtain a sufficient understanding to plan the audit, he or she may consider contacting the service organization, through the user organization, to obtain specific information or request that a service auditor be engaged to perform procedures that will supply the necessary information, or the user auditor may visit the service organization and perform such procedures. If the user auditor is unable to obtain sufficient evidence to achieve his or her audit objectives, the user auditor should qualify his or her opinion or disclaim an opinion on the financial statements because of a scope limitation.

Assessing Control Risk at the User Organization

.11 After obtaining an understanding of the internal control, the user auditor assesses control risk for the assertions embodied in the account balances and classes of transactions, including those that are affected by the activities of the service organization. In doing so, the user auditor may identify certain user organization controls that, if effective, would permit the user auditor to assess control risk below the maximum for particular assertions. Such controls may be applied at either the user organization or the service organization. The user auditor may conclude that it would be efficient to obtain evidential matter about the operating effectiveness of controls to provide a basis for assessing control risk below the maximum.

.12 A service auditor's report on controls placed in operation at the service organization should be helpful in providing a sufficient understanding to plan the audit of the user organization. Such a report, however, is not intended to provide any evidence of the operating effectiveness of the relevant controls that would allow the user auditor to reduce the assessed level of control risk below the maximum. Such evidential matter should be derived from one or more of the following:

a. Tests of the user organization's controls over the activities of the service organization (for example, the user auditor may test the user organization's independent reperformance of selected items processed by an EDP service center or test the user organization's reconciliation of output reports with source documents)

b. A service auditor's report on controls placed in operation and tests of operating effectiveness, or a report on the application of agreed-upon procedures that describes relevant tests of controls

c. Appropriate tests of controls performed by the user auditor at the service organization

.13 The user organization may establish effective controls over the service organization's activities that may be tested and that may enable the user auditor to reduce the assessed level of control risk below the maximum for some or all of the related assertions. If a user organization, for example, uses an EDP service center to process payroll transactions, the user organization may establish controls over input and output data to prevent or detect material misstatements. The user organization might reperform the service organization's payroll calculations on a test basis. In this situation, the user auditor may perform tests of the user organization's controls over data processing that would provide a basis for assessing control risk below the maximum for the assertions related to payroll transactions. The user auditor may decide that obtaining evidence of the operating effectiveness of the service organization's controls, such as those over changes in payroll programs, is not necessary or efficient.

.14 The user auditor may find that controls relevant to assessing control risk below the maximum for particular assertions are applied only at the service organization. If the user auditor plans to assess control risk below the maximum for those assertions, he or she should evaluate the operating effectiveness of those controls by obtaining a service auditor's report that describes the results of the service auditor's tests of those controls (that is, a report on controls placed in operation and tests of operating effectiveness, or an agreed-upon procedures report) or by performing tests of controls at the service organization. If the user auditor decides to use a service auditor's report, the user auditor should consider the extent of the evidence provided by the report about the effectiveness of controls intended to prevent or detect material misstatements in the particular assertions. The user auditor remains responsible for evaluating the evidence presented by the service auditor and for determining its effect on the assessment of control risk at the user organization.

.15 The user auditor's assessments of control risk regarding assertions about account balances or classes of transactions are based on the combined evidence provided by the service auditor's report and the user auditor's own procedures. In making these assessments, the user auditor should consider the nature, source, and interrelationships among the evidence, as well as the period covered by the tests of controls. The user auditor uses the assessed levels of control risk, as well as his or her understanding of internal control, in determining the nature, timing, and extent of substantive tests for particular assertions.

.16 The guidance in section 319.64 through .73, regarding the auditor's consideration of the sufficiency of evidential matter to support a specific assessed level of control risk is applicable to user auditors considering evidential matter provided by a service auditor's report on controls placed in operation and tests of operating effectiveness. Because the report may be intended to satisfy the needs of several different user auditors, a user auditor should determine whether the specific tests of controls and results in the service auditor's report are relevant to assertions that are significant in the user organization's financial statements. For those tests of controls and results that are relevant, a user auditor should consider whether the nature, timing, and extent of such tests of controls and results provide appropriate evidence about the effectiveness of the controls to support the user auditor's desired assessed level of control risk. In evaluating these factors, user auditors should also keep in mind that, for certain assumptions, the shorter the period covered by a specific test and the longer the time elapsed since the performance of the test, the less support for control risk reduction the test may provide.

Audit Evidence From Substantive Audit Procedures Performed by Service Auditors

.17 Service auditors may be engaged to perform procedures that are substantive in nature for the benefit of user auditors. Such engagements may involve the performance, by the service auditor, of procedures agreed upon by the user organization and its auditor and by the service organization and its auditor. In addition, there may be requirements imposed by governmental authorities or through contractual arrangements whereby service auditors perform designated procedures that are substantive in nature. The results of the application of the required procedures to balances and transactions processed by the service organization may be used by user auditors as part of the evidence necessary to support their opinions.

Considerations in Using a Service Auditor's Report

.18 In considering whether the service auditor's report is satisfactory for his or her purposes, the user auditor should make inquiries concerning the service auditor's professional reputation. Appropriate sources of information concerning the professional reputation of the service auditor are discussed in section 543, *Part of Audit Performed by Other Independent Auditors*, paragraph .10*a*.

.19 In considering whether the service auditor's report is sufficient to meet his or her objectives, the user auditor should give consideration to the guidance in section 543.12. If the user auditor believes that the service auditor's report may not be sufficient to meet his or her objectives, the user auditor may supplement his or her understanding of the service auditor's procedures and conclusions by discussing with the service auditor the scope and results of the service auditor's work. Also, if the user auditor believes it is necessary, he or she may contact the service organization, through the user organization, to request that the service auditor perform agreed-upon procedures at the service organization, or the user auditor may perform such procedures.

.20 When assessing a service organization's controls and how they interact with a user organization's controls, the user auditor may become aware of the existence of reportable conditions. In such circumstances, the user auditor should consider the guidance provided in section 325, *Communication of Internal Control Related Matters Noted in an Audit.*

.21 The user auditor should not make reference to the report of the service auditor as a basis, in part, for his or her own opinion on the user organization's financial statements. The service auditor's report is used in the audit, but the service auditor is not responsible for examining any portion of the financial statements as of any specific date or for any specified period. Thus, there cannot be a division of responsibility for the audit of the financial statements.

Responsibilities of Service Auditors

.22 The service auditor is responsible for the representations in his or her report and for exercising due care in the application of procedures that support those representations. Although a service auditor's engagement differs from an audit of financial statements conducted in accordance with generally accepted auditing standards, it should be performed in accordance with the general standards and with the relevant fieldwork and reporting standards. Although the service auditor should be independent from the service organization, it is not necessary for the service auditor to be independent from each user organization.

.23 As a result of procedures performed at the service organization, the service auditor may become aware of illegal acts, fraud, or uncorrected errors attributable to the service organization's management or employees that may affect one or more user organizations. The terms *errors*, *fraud*, and *illegal acts* are discussed in section 312, *Audit Risk and Materiality in Conducting an Audit*, and section 317, *Illegal Acts by Clients*; the discussions therein are relevant to this section. When the service auditor becomes aware of such matters, he or she should determine from the appropriate level of management of the service organization whether this information has been communicated appropriately to affected user organizations, unless those matters are clearly inconsequential. If the management of the service organization has not communicated the information to affected user organizations and is unwilling to do so, the service auditor should inform the service organization's audit committee or others with equivalent authority or responsibility. If the audit committee does not respond appropriately to the service auditor's communication, the service auditor should consider whether to resign from the engagement. The service auditor may wish to consult with his or her attorney in making this decision.

.24 The type of engagement to be performed and the related report to be prepared should be established by the service organization. However, when circumstances permit, discussions between the service organization and the user organizations are advisable to determine the type of report that will be most suitable for the user organizations' needs. This section provides guidance on the two types of reports that may be issued:

a. *Reports on controls placed in operation*—A service auditor's report on a service organization's description of the controls that may be relevant to a user organization's internal control as it relates to an audit of financial statements, on whether such controls were suitably designed to achieve specified control objectives, and on whether they had been placed in operation as of a specific date. Such reports may be useful in providing a user auditor with an understanding of the controls necessary to plan the audit and to design effective tests of controls and substantive tests at the user organization, but they are not intended to provide the user auditor with a basis for reducing his or her assessments of control risk below the maximum.

b. *Reports on controls placed in operation and tests of operating effectiveness*—A service auditor's report on a service organization's description of the controls that may be relevant to a user organization's internal control as it relates to an audit of financial statements, on whether such controls were suitably designed to achieve specified control objectives, on whether they had been placed in operation as of a specific date, and on whether the controls that were tested were operating with sufficient effectiveness to provide reasonable, but not absolute, assurance that the related control objectives were achieved during the period specified. Such reports may be useful in providing the user auditor with an understanding of the controls necessary to plan the audit and may also provide the user auditor with a basis for reducing his or her assessments of control risk below the maximum.

Reports on Controls Placed in Operation

.25 The information necessary for a report on controls placed in operation ordinarily is obtained through discussions with appropriate service organization personnel and through reference to various forms of documentation, such as system flowcharts and narratives.

.26 After obtaining a description of the relevant controls, the service auditor should determine whether the description provides sufficient information for user auditors to obtain an understanding of those aspects of the service organization's controls that may be relevant to a user organization's internal control. The description should contain a discussion of the features of the service organization's controls that would have an effect on a user organization's internal control. Such features are relevant when they directly affect the service provided to the user organization. They may include controls within the control environment, risk assessment, control activities, information and communication, and monitoring components of internal control. The control environment may include hiring practices and key areas of authority and responsibility. Risk assessment may include the identification of risks associated with processing specific transactions. Control activities may include policies and procedures over the modification of computer programs and are ordinarily designed to meet specific control objectives. The specific control objectives of the service organization should be set forth in the service organization's description of controls. Information and communication may include ways in which user transactions are initiated and processed. Monitoring may include the involvement of internal auditors. [As amended, effective for service auditor's reports covering descriptions as of or after January 1, 1997, by Statement on Auditing Standards No. 78.]

.27 Evidence of whether controls have been placed in operation is ordinarily obtained through previous experience with the service organization and through procedures such as inquiry of appropriate management, supervisory, and staff personnel; inspection of service organization documents and records; and observation of service organization activities and operations. For the type of report described in paragraph .24*a*, these procedures need not be supplemented by tests of the operating effectiveness of the service organization's controls.

.28 Although a service auditor's report on controls placed in operation is as of a specified date, the service auditor should inquire about changes in the service organization's controls that may have occurred before the beginning of fieldwork. If the service auditor believes that the changes would be considered significant by user organizations and their auditors, those changes should be included in the description of the service organization's controls. If the service auditor concludes that the changes would be considered significant by user organization's and their auditors and the changes are not included in the description of the service organization's controls, the service auditor should describe the changes in his or her report. Such changes might include—

- Procedural changes made to accommodate provisions of a new FASB Statement of Financial Accounting Standards.
- Major changes in an application to permit on-line processing.
- Procedural changes to eliminate previously identified deficiencies.

Changes that occurred more than twelve months before the date being reported on normally would not be considered significant, because they generally would not affect user auditors' considerations.

.29 A service auditor's report expressing an opinion on a description of controls placed in operation at a service organization should contain—

a. A specific reference to the applications, services, products, or other aspects of the service organization covered.

b. A description of the scope and nature of the service auditor's procedures.

c. Identification of the party specifying the control objectives.

d. An indication that the purpose of the service auditor's engagement was to obtain reasonable assurance about whether (1) the service organization's description presents fairly, in all material respects, the aspects of the service organization's controls that may be relevant to a user organization's internal control as it relates to an audit of financial statements, (2) the controls were suitably designed to achieve specified control objectives, and (3) such controls had been placed in operation as of a specific date.

e. A disclaimer of opinion on the operating effectiveness of the controls.

f. The service auditor's opinion on whether the description presents fairly, in all material respects, the relevant aspects of the service organization's controls that had been placed in operation as of a specific date and whether, in the service auditor's opinion, the controls were suitably designed to provide reasonable assurance that the specified control objectives would be achieved if those controls were complied with satisfactorily.

g. A statement of the inherent limitations of the potential effectiveness of controls at the service organization and of the risk of projecting to future periods any evaluation of the description.

h. Identification of the parties for whom the report is intended.

.30 If the service auditor believes that the description is inaccurate or insufficiently complete for user auditors, the service auditor's report should so state and should contain sufficient detail to provide user auditors with an appropriate understanding.

.31 It may become evident to the service auditor, when considering the service organization's description of controls placed in operation, that the system was designed with the assumption that certain controls would be implemented by the user organization. If the service auditor is aware of the need for such complementary user organization controls, these should be delineated in the description of controls. If the application of controls by user organizations is necessary to achieve the stated control objectives, the service auditor's report should be modified to include the phrase "and user organizations applied the controls contemplated in the design of the Service Organization's controls" following the words "complied with satisfactorily" in the scope and opinion paragraphs.

.32 The service auditor should consider conditions that come to his or her attention that, in the service auditor's judgment, represent significant deficiencies in the design or operation of the service organization's controls that preclude the service auditor from obtaining reasonable assurance that specified control objectives would be achieved. The service auditor should also consider whether any other information, irrespective of specified control objectives, has come to his or her attention that causes him or her to conclude (*a*) that design deficiencies exist that could adversely affect the ability to record, process, summarize, or report financial data to user organizations without error, and (*b*) that user organizations would not generally be expected to have controls in place to mitigate such design deficiencies.

.33 The description of controls and control objectives required for these reports may be prepared by the service organization. If the service auditor prepares the description of controls and control objectives, the representations in the description remain the responsibility of the service organization.

.34 For the service auditor to express an opinion on whether the controls were suitably designed to achieve the specified control objectives, it is necessary that—

a. The service organization identify and appropriately describe such control objectives and the relevant controls.

b. The service auditor consider the linkage of the controls to the stated control objectives.

c. The service auditor obtain sufficient evidence to reach an opinion.

.35 The control objectives may be designated by the service organization or by outside parties such as regulatory authorities, a user group, or others. When the control objectives are not established by outside parties, the service auditor should be satisfied that the control objectives, as set forth by the service organization, are reasonable in the circumstances and consistent with the service organization's contractual obligations.

.36 The service auditor's report should state whether the controls were suitably designed to achieve the specified control objectives. The report should not state whether they were suitably designed to achieve objectives beyond the specifically identified control objectives.

.37 The service auditor's opinion on whether the controls were suitably designed to achieve the specified control objectives is not intended to provide evidence of operating effectiveness or to provide the user auditor with a basis for concluding that control risk may be assessed below the maximum.

.38 The following is a sample report on controls placed in operation at a service organization. The report should have, as an attachment, a description of the service organization's controls that may be relevant to a user organization's internal control as it relates to an audit of financial statements. This report is illustrative only and should be modified as appropriate to suit the circumstances of individual engagements.

> To XYZ Service Organization:
>
> We have examined the accompanying description of controls related to the ______ application of XYZ Service Organization. Our examination included procedures to obtain reasonable assurance about whether (1) the accompanying description presents fairly, in all material respects, the aspects of XYZ Service Organization's controls that may be relevant to a user organization's internal control as it relates to an audit of financial statements, (2) the controls included in the description were suitably designed to achieve the control objectives specified in the description, if those controls were complied with satisfactorily,[2] and (3) such controls had been placed in operation as of ______. The control objectives were specified by ______. Our examination was performed in accordance with standards established by the American Institute of Certified Public Accountants and included those procedures we considered necessary in the circumstances to obtain a reasonable basis for rendering our opinion.
>
> We did not perform procedures to determine the operating effectiveness of controls for any period. Accordingly, we express no opinion on the operating effectiveness of any aspects of XYZ Service Organization's controls, individually or in the aggregate.
>
> In our opinion, the accompanying description of the aforementioned application presents fairly, in all material respects, the relevant aspects of XYZ Service Organization's controls that had been placed in operation as of ______. Also, in our opinion, the controls, as described, are suitably designed to provide reasonable assurance that the specified control objectives would be achieved if the described controls were complied with satisfactorily.
>
> The description of controls at XYZ Service Organization is as of ______ and any projection of such information to the future is subject to the risk that, because of change, the description may no longer portray the controls in existence. The potential effectiveness of specific controls at the Service Organization is subject to inherent limitations and, accordingly, errors or fraud may occur and not be detected. Furthermore, the projection of any conclusions, based on our findings, to future periods is subject to the risk that changes may alter the validity of such conclusions.
>
> This report is intended solely for use by the management of XYZ Service Organization, its customers, and the independent auditors of its customers.

.39 If the service auditor concludes that the description is inaccurate or insufficiently complete for user auditors, the service auditor should so state in

[2] If the application of controls by user organizations is necessary to achieve the stated control objectives, the service auditor's report should be modified to include the phrase "and user organizations applied the controls contemplated in the design of XYZ Service Organization's controls" following the words "complied with satisfactorily" in the scope and opinion paragraphs.

an explanatory paragraph preceding the opinion paragraph. An example of such an explanatory paragraph follows:

> The accompanying description states that XYZ Service Organization uses operator identification numbers and passwords to prevent unauthorized access to the system. Based on inquiries of staff personnel and inspections of activities, we determined that such procedures are employed in Applications A and B but are not required to access the system in Applications C and D.

In addition, the first sentence of the opinion paragraph would be modified to read as follows:

> In our opinion, except for the matter referred to in the preceding paragraph, the accompanying description of the aforementioned application presents fairly, in all material respects, the relevant aspects of XYZ Service Organization's controls that had been placed in operation as of ______.

.40 If, after applying the criteria in paragraph .32, the service auditor concludes that there are significant deficiencies in the design or operation of the service organization's controls, the service auditor should report those conditions in an explanatory paragraph preceding the opinion paragraph. An example of an explanatory paragraph describing a significant deficiency in the design or operation of the service organization's controls follows:

> As discussed in the accompanying description, from time to time the Service Organization makes changes in application programs to correct deficiencies or to enhance capabilities. The procedures followed in determining whether to make changes, in designing the changes, and in implementing them do not include review and approval by authorized individuals who are independent from those involved in making the changes. There are also no specified requirements to test such changes or provide test results to an authorized reviewer prior to implementing the changes.

In addition, the second sentence of the opinion paragraph would be modified to read as follows:

> Also in our opinion, except for the deficiency referred to in the preceding paragraph, the controls, as described, are suitably designed to provide reasonable assurance that the specified control objectives would be achieved if the described controls were complied with satisfactorily.

Reports on Controls Placed in Operation and Tests of Operating Effectiveness

Paragraphs .41 through .56 repeat some of the information contained in paragraphs .25 through .40 to provide readers with a comprehensive, stand-alone presentation of the relevant considerations for each type of report.

.41 The information necessary for a report on controls placed in operation and tests of operating effectiveness ordinarily is obtained through discussions with appropriate service organization personnel, through reference to various forms of documentation, such as system flowcharts and narratives, and through the performance of tests of controls. Evidence of whether controls have been placed in operation is ordinarily obtained through previous experience with the service organization and through procedures such as inquiry of appropriate management, supervisory, and staff personnel; inspection of service organization documents and records; and observation of service organization activities and operations. The service auditor applies tests of controls to determine whether specific controls are operating with sufficient effectiveness to achieve specified control objectives. Section 350, *Audit Sampling*, provides guidance on the application and evaluation of audit sampling in performing tests of controls.

.42 After obtaining a description of the relevant controls, the service auditor should determine whether the description provides sufficient information for user auditors to obtain an understanding of those aspects of the service organization's controls that may be relevant to a user organization's internal control. The description should contain a discussion of the features of the service organization's controls that would have an effect on a user organization's internal control. Such features are relevant when they directly affect the service provided to the user organization. They may include controls within the control environment, risk assessment, control activities, information and communication, and monitoring components of internal control. The control environment may include hiring practices and key areas of authority and responsibility. Risk assessment may include the identification of risks associated with processing specific transactions. Control activities may include policies and procedures over the modification of computer programs and are ordinarily designed to meet specific control objectives. The specific control objectives of the service organization should be set forth in the service organization's description of controls. Information and communication may include ways in which user transactions are initiated and processed. Monitoring may include the involvement of internal auditors. [As amended, effective for service auditor's reports covering descriptions as of or after January 1, 1997, by Statement on Auditing Standards No. 78.]

.43 The service auditor should inquire about changes in the service organization's controls that may have occurred before the beginning of fieldwork. If the service auditor believes the changes would be considered significant by user organizations and their auditors, those changes should be included in the description of the service organization's controls. If the service auditor concludes that the changes would be considered significant by user organizations and their auditors and the changes are not included in the description of the service organization's controls, the service auditor should describe the changes in his or her report. Such changes might include—

- Procedural changes made to accommodate provisions of a new FASB Statement of Financial Accounting Standards.
- Major changes in an application to permit on-line processing.
- Procedural changes to eliminate previously identified deficiencies.

Changes that occurred more than twelve months before the date being reported on normally would not be considered significant, because they generally would not affect user auditors' considerations.

.44 A service auditor's report expressing an opinion on a description of controls placed in operation at a service organization and tests of operating effectiveness should contain—

a. A specific reference to the applications, services, products, or other aspects of the service organization covered.

b. A description of the scope and nature of the service auditor's procedures.

c. Identification of the party specifying the control objectives.

d. An indication that the purpose of the service auditor's engagement was to obtain reasonable assurance about whether (1) the service organization's description presents fairly, in all material respects, the aspects of the service organization's controls that may be relevant to a user organization's internal control as it relates to an audit of financial statements, (2) the controls were suitably designed to achieve specified control objectives, and (3) such controls had been placed in operation as of a specific date.

e. The service auditor's opinion on whether the description presents fairly, in all material respects, the relevant aspects of the service organization's controls that had been placed in operation as of a specific date and whether, in the service auditor's opinion, the controls were suitably designed to provide reasonable assurance that the specified control objectives would be achieved if those controls were complied with satisfactorily.

f. A reference to a description of tests of specific service organization controls designed to obtain evidence about the operating effectiveness of those controls in achieving specified control objectives. The description should include the controls that were tested, the control objectives the controls were intended to achieve, the tests applied, and the results of the tests. The description should include an indication of the nature, timing, and extent of the tests, as well as sufficient detail to enable user auditors to determine the effect of such tests on user auditors' assessments of control risk. To the extent that the service auditor identified causative factors for exceptions, determined the current status of corrective actions, or obtained other relevant qualitative information about exceptions noted, such information should be provided.

g. A statement of the period covered by the service auditor's report on the operating effectiveness of the specific controls tested.

h. The service auditor's opinion on whether the controls that were tested were operating with sufficient effectiveness to provide reasonable, but not absolute, assurance that the related control objectives were achieved during the period specified.

i. When all of the control objectives listed in the description of controls placed in operation are not covered by tests of operating effectiveness, a statement that the service auditor does not express an opinion on control objectives not listed in the description of tests performed at the service organization.

j. A statement that the relative effectiveness and significance of specific service organization controls and their effect on assessments of control risk at user organizations are dependent on their interaction with the controls and other factors present at individual user organizations.

k. A statement that the service auditor has performed no procedures to evaluate the effectiveness of controls at individual user organizations.

l. A statement of the inherent limitations of the potential effectiveness of controls at the service organization and of the risk of projecting to the future any evaluation of the description or any conclusions about the effectiveness of controls in achieving control objectives.

m. Identification of the parties for whom the report is intended.

.45 If the service auditor believes that the description is inaccurate or insufficiently complete for user auditors, the service auditor's report should so state and should contain sufficient detail to provide user auditors with an appropriate understanding.

.46 It may become evident to the service auditor, when considering the service organization's description of controls placed in operation, that the system was designed with the assumption that certain controls would be implemented by the user organization. If the service auditor is aware of the need for such complementary user organization controls, these should be delineated in the description of controls. If the application of controls by user organizations is necessary to achieve the stated control objectives, the service auditor's report should be modified to include the phrase "and user organizations applied the controls contemplated in the design of the Service Organization's controls" following the words "complied with satisfactorily" in the scope and opinion paragraphs. Similarly, if the operating effectiveness of controls at the service organization is dependent on the application of controls at user organizations, this should be delineated in the description of tests performed.

.47 The service auditor should consider conditions that come to his or her attention that, in the service auditor's judgment, represent significant deficiencies in the design or operation of the service organization's controls that preclude the service auditor from obtaining reasonable assurance that specified control objectives would be achieved. The service auditor should also consider whether any other information, irrespective of specified control objectives, has come to his or her attention that causes him or her to conclude (*a*) that design deficiencies exist that could adversely affect the ability to record, process, summarize, or report financial data to user organizations without error, and (*b*) that user organizations would not generally be expected to have controls in place to mitigate such design deficiencies.

.48 The description of controls and control objectives required for these reports may be prepared by the service organization. If the service auditor prepares the description of controls and control objectives, the representations in the description remain the responsibility of the service organization.

.49 For the service auditor to express an opinion on whether the controls were suitably designed to achieve the specified control objectives, it is necessary that—

a. The service organization identify and appropriately describe such control objectives and the relevant controls.

b. The service auditor consider the linkage of the controls to the stated control objectives.

c. The service auditor obtain sufficient evidence to reach an opinion.

.50 The control objectives may be designated by the service organization or by outside parties such as regulatory authorities, a user group, or others. When the control objectives are not established by outside parties, the service auditor should be satisfied that the control objectives, as set forth by the service organization, are reasonable in the circumstances and consistent with the service organization's contractual obligations.

.51 The service auditor's report should state whether the controls were suitably designed to achieve the specified control objectives. The report should not state whether they were suitably designed to achieve objectives beyond the specifically identified control objectives.

.52 The service auditor's opinion on whether the controls were suitably designed to achieve the specified control objectives is not intended to provide evidence of operating effectiveness or to provide the user auditor with a basis for concluding that control risk may be assessed below the maximum. Evidence that may enable the user auditor to conclude that control risk may be assessed below the maximum may be obtained from the results of specific tests of operating effectiveness.

.53 The management of the service organization specifies whether all or selected applications and control objectives will be covered by the tests of operating effectiveness. The service auditor determines which controls are, in his or her judgment, necessary to achieve the control objectives specified by management. The service auditor then determines the nature, timing, and extent of the tests of controls needed to evaluate operating effectiveness. Testing should be applied to controls in effect throughout the period covered by the report. To be useful to user auditors, the report should ordinarily cover a minimum reporting period of six months.

.54 The following is a sample report on controls placed in operation at a service organization and tests of operating effectiveness. It should be assumed that the report has two attachments: (*a*) a description of the service organizations's controls that may be relevant to a user organization's internal control as it relates to an audit of financial statements and (*b*) a description of controls for which tests of operating effectiveness were performed, the control objectives the controls were intended to achieve, the tests applied, and the results of those tests. This report is illustrative only and should be modified as appropriate to suit the circumstances of individual engagements.

To XYZ Service Organization:

We have examined the accompanying description of controls related to the _____ application of XYZ Service Organization. Our examination included procedures to obtain reasonable assurance about whether (1) the accompanying description presents fairly, in all material respects, the aspects of XYZ Service Organization's controls that may be relevant to a user organization's internal control as it relates to an audit of financial statements, (2) the controls included in the description were suitably designed to achieve the control objectives specified in the description, if those controls were complied with satisfactorily,[3] and (3) such controls had been placed in operation as of _____. The control objectives were specified by _____. Our examination was performed in accordance with standards established by the American Institute of Certified Public Accountants and included those procedures we considered necessary in the circumstances to obtain a reasonable basis for rendering our opinion.

In our opinion, the accompanying description of the aforementioned application presents fairly, in all material respects, the relevant aspects of XYZ Service Organization's controls that had been placed in operation as of _____. Also, in our opinion, the controls, as described, are suitably designed to provide reasonable assurance that the specified control objectives would be achieved if the described controls were complied with satisfactorily.

---

[3] If the application of controls by user organizations is necessary to achieve the stated control objectives, the service auditor's report should be modified to include the phrase "and user organizations applied the controls contemplated in the design of XYZ Service Organization's controls" following the words "complied with satisfactorily" in the scope and opinion paragraphs.

In addition to the procedures we considered necessary to render our opinion as expressed in the previous paragraph, we applied tests to specific controls, listed in Schedule X, to obtain evidence about their effectiveness in meeting the control objectives, described in Schedule X, during the period from_____ to _____. The specific controls and the nature, timing, extent, and results of the tests are listed in Schedule X. This information has been provided to user organizations of XYZ Service Organization and to their auditors to be taken into consideration, along with information about the internal control at user organizations, when making assessments of control risk for user organizations. In our opinion the controls that were tested, as described in Schedule X, were operating with sufficient effectiveness to provide reasonable, but not absolute, assurance that the control objectives specified in Schedule X were achieved during the period from_____to_____. [However, the scope of our engagement did not include tests to determine whether control objectives not listed in Schedule X were achieved; accordingly, we express no opinion on the achievement of control objectives not included in Schedule X.][4]

The relative effectiveness and significance of specific controls at XYZ Service Organization and their effect on assessments of control risk at user organizations are dependent on their interaction with the controls and other factors present at individual user organizations. We have performed no procedures to evaluate the effectiveness of controls at individual user organizations.

The description of controls at XYZ Service Organization is as of _____, and information about tests of the operating effectiveness of specific controls covers the period from _____ to _____. Any projection of such information to the future is subject to the risk that, because of change, the description may no longer portray the controls in existence. The potential effectiveness of specific controls at the Service Organization is subject to inherent limitations and, accordingly, errors or fraud may occur and not be detected. Furthermore, the projection of any conclusions, based on our findings, to future periods is subject to the risk that changes may alter the validity of such conclusions.

This report is intended solely for use by the management of XYZ Service Organization, its customers, and the independent auditors of its customers.

.55 If the service auditor concludes that the description is inaccurate or insufficiently complete for user auditors, the service auditor should so state in an explanatory paragraph preceding the opinion paragraph. An example of such an explanatory paragraph follows:

The accompanying description states that XYZ Service Organization uses operator identification numbers and passwords to prevent unauthorized access to the system. Based on inquiries of staff personnel and inspection of activities, we determined that such procedures are employed in Applications A and B but are not required to access the system in Applications C and D.

In addition, the first sentence of the opinion paragraph would be modified to read as follows:

In our opinion, except for the matter referred to in the preceding paragraph, the accompanying description of the aforementioned application presents fairly, in all material respects, the relevant aspects of XYZ Service Organization's controls that had been placed in operation as of _____.

---

[4] This sentence should be added when all of the control objectives listed in the description of controls placed in operation are not covered by the tests of operating effectiveness. This sentence would be omitted when all of the control objectives listed in the description of controls placed in operation are included in the tests of operating effectiveness.

.56 If, after applying the criteria in paragraph .47, the service auditor concludes that there are significant deficiencies in the design or operation of the service organization's controls, the service auditor should report those conditions in an explanatory paragraph preceding the opinion paragraph. An example of an explanatory paragraph describing a significant deficiency in the design or operation of the service organization's controls follows:

> As discussed in the accompanying description, from time to time the Service Organization makes changes in application programs to correct deficiencies or to enhance capabilities. The procedures followed in determining whether to make changes, in designing the changes, and in implementing them do not include review and approval by authorized individuals who are independent from those involved in making the changes. There are also no specified requirements to test such changes or provide test results to an authorized reviewer prior to implementing the changes.

In addition, the second sentence of the opinion paragraph would be modified to read as follows:

> Also in our opinion, except for the deficiency referred to in the preceding paragraph, the controls, as described, are suitably designed to provide reasonable assurance that the related control objectives would be achieved if the described controls were complied with satisfactorily.

Written Representations of the Service Organization's Management

.57 Regardless of the type of report issued, the service auditor should obtain written representations from the service organization's management that—

- Acknowledge management's responsibility for establishing and maintaining appropriate controls relating to the processing of transactions for user organizations.
- Acknowledge the appropriateness of the specified control objectives.
- State that the description of controls presents fairly, in all material respects, the aspects of the service organization's controls that may be relevant to a user organization's internal control.
- State that the controls, as described, had been placed in operation as of a specific date.
- State that management believes its controls were suitably designed to achieve the specified control objectives.
- State that management has disclosed to the service auditor any significant changes in controls that have occurred since the service organization's last examination.
- State that management has disclosed to the service auditor any illegal acts, fraud, or uncorrected errors attributable to the service organization's management or employees that may affect one or more user organizations.
- State that management has disclosed to the service auditor all design deficiencies in controls of which it is aware, including those for which management believes the cost of corrective action may exceed the benefits.

If the scope of the work includes tests of operating effectiveness, the service auditor should obtain a written representation from the service organization's management stating that management has disclosed to the service auditor all instances, of which it is aware, when controls have not operated with sufficient effectiveness to achieve the specified control objectives.

Reporting on Substantive Procedures

.58 The service auditor may be requested to apply substantive procedures to user transactions or assets at the service organization. In such circumstances, the service auditor may make specific reference in his or her report to having carried out the designated procedures or may provide a separate report in accordance with section 622, *Engagements to Apply Agreed-Upon Procedures to Specified Elements, Accounts, or Items of a Financial Statement*. Either form of reporting should include a description of the nature, timing, extent, and results of the procedures in sufficient detail to be useful to user auditors in deciding whether to use the results as evidence to support their opinions.

Effective Date

.59 This section is effective for service auditors' reports dated after March 31, 1993. Earlier application of this section is encouraged.

AU Section 9324

Reports on the Processing of Transactions by Service Organizations: Auditing Interpretations of Section 324

1. Describing Tests of Operating Effectiveness and the Results of Such Tests

.01 *Question*—Paragraph .44*f* of section 324, *Reports on the Processing of Transactions by Service Organizations*, specifies the elements that should be included in a description of tests of operating effectiveness, which is part of a report on controls placed in operation and tests of operating effectiveness. Paragraph .44*f* states:

> "...The description should include the controls that were tested, the control objectives the controls were intended to achieve, the tests applied and the results of the tests. The description should include an indication of the nature, timing, and extent of the tests, as well as sufficient detail to enable user auditors to determine the effect of such tests on user auditors' assessments of control risk. To the extent that the service auditor identified causative factors for exceptions, determined the current status of corrective actions, or obtained other relevant qualitative information about exceptions noted, such information should be provided."

When a service auditor performs an engagement that includes tests of operating effectiveness, what information and how much detail should be included in the description of the "tests applied" and the "results of the tests"?

.02 *Interpretation*—In all cases, for each control objective tested, the description of tests of operating effectiveness should include all of the elements listed in paragraph .44*f* of section 324, whether or not the service auditor concludes that the control objective has been achieved. The description should provide sufficient information to enable user auditors to assess control risk for financial statement assertions affected by the service organization. The description need not be a duplication of the service auditor's detailed audit program, which in some cases would make the report too voluminous for user auditors and would provide more than the required level of detail.

.03 In describing the nature, timing, and extent of the tests applied, the service auditor also should indicate whether the items tested represent a sample or all of the items in the population, but need not indicate the size of the population. In describing the results of the tests, the service auditor should include exceptions and other information that in the service auditor's judgment could be relevant to user auditors. Such exceptions and other information should be included for each control objective, whether or not the service auditor concludes that the control objective has been achieved. When exceptions that could be relevant to user auditors are noted, the description also should include the following information:

- The size of the sample, when sampling has been used
- The number of exceptions noted

- The nature of the exceptions

If no exceptions or other information that could be relevant to user auditors are identified by the tests, the service auditor should indicate that finding (for example, "No relevant exceptions noted").

[Issue Date: April, 1995.]

2. Service Organizations That Use the Services of Other Service Organizations (Subservice Organizations)

.04 *Question*—A service organization may use the services of another service organization, such as a bank trust department that uses an independent computer processing service organization to perform its data processing. In this situation, the bank trust department is a service organization and the computer processing service organization is considered a subservice organization. How are a user auditor's and a service auditor's procedures affected when a service organization uses a subservice organization?

.05 *Interpretation*—When a service organization uses a subservice organization, the user auditor should determine whether the processing performed by the subservice organization affects assertions in the user organization's financial statements and whether those assertions are significant to the user organization's financial statements. To plan the audit and assess control risk, a user auditor may need to consider the controls at both the service organization and the subservice organization. Paragraphs .06–.16 of section 324 provide guidance to user auditors on considering the effect of a service organization on a user organization's internal control. Although paragraphs .06–.16 do not specifically refer to subservice organizations, when a subservice organization provides services to a service organization, the guidance in these paragraphs should be interpreted to include the subservice organization. For example, in situations where subservice organizations are used, the interaction between the user organization and the service organization described in paragraph .06 of section 324 would be expanded to include the interaction between the user organization, the service organization and the subservice organization.

.06 Similarly, a service auditor engaged to examine the controls of a service organization and issue a service auditor's report may need to consider functions performed by the subservice organization and the effect of the subservice organization's controls on the service organization.

.07 The degree of interaction and the nature and materiality of the transactions processed by the service organization and the subservice organization are the most important factors to consider in determining the significance of the subservice organization's controls to the user organization's internal control. Paragraphs .11–.16 of section 324 describe how a user auditor's assessment of control risk is affected when a user organization uses a service organization. When a subservice organization is involved, the user auditor may need to consider activities at both the service organization and the subservice organization in applying the guidance in these paragraphs.

.08 *Question*—How does a user auditor obtain information about controls at a subservice organization?

.09 *Interpretation*—If a user auditor concludes that he or she needs information about the subservice organization to plan the audit or to assess control risk, the user auditor (*a*) may contact the service organization through the user organization and may contact the subservice organization either through the user organization or the service organization to obtain specific information or (*b*) may request that a service auditor be engaged to perform procedures that will supply the necessary information. Alternatively, the user auditor may visit the service organization or subservice organization and perform such procedures.

.10 *Question*—When a service organization uses a subservice organization, what information about the subservice organization should be included in the service organization's description of controls?

.11 *Interpretation*—A service organization's description of controls should include a description of the functions and nature of the processing performed by the subservice organization in sufficient detail for user auditors to understand the significance of the subservice organization's functions to the processing of the user organizations' transactions. Ordinarily, disclosure of the identity of the subservice organization is not required. However, if the service organization determines that the identity of the subservice organization would be relevant to user organizations, the name of the subservice organization may be included in the description. The purpose of the description of the functions and nature of the processing performed by the subservice organization is to alert user organizations and their auditors to the fact that another entity (that is, the subservice organization) is involved in the processing of the user organizations' transactions and to summarize the functions the subservice organization performs.

.12 When a subservice organization performs services for a service organization, there are two alternative methods of presenting the description of controls. The service organization determines which method will be used.

a. *The Carve-Out Method*—The subservice organization's relevant control objectives and controls are excluded from the description and from the scope of the service auditor's engagement. The service organization states in the description that the subservice organization's control objectives and related controls are omitted from the description and that the control objectives in the report include only the objectives the service organization's controls are intended to achieve.

b. *The Inclusive Method*—The subservice organization's relevant controls are included in the description and in the scope of the engagement. The description should clearly differentiate between controls of the service organization and controls of the subservice organization. The set of control objectives includes all of the objectives a user auditor would expect both the service organization and the subservice organization to achieve. To accomplish this, the service organization should coordinate the preparation and presentation of the description of controls with the subservice organization.

In either method, the service organization includes in its description of controls a description of the functions and nature of the processing performed by the subservice organization, as set forth in paragraph .11.

.13 If the functions and processing performed by the subservice organization are significant to the processing of user organization transactions, and the service organization does not disclose the existence of the subservice organization and the functions it performs, the service auditor may need to issue a qualified or adverse opinion as to the fairness of the presentation of the description of controls.

.14 *Question*—How is the service auditor's report affected by the method of presentation selected?

.15 *Interpretation*—If the service organization has adopted the carve-out method, the service auditor should modify the scope paragraph of the service auditor's report to briefly summarize the functions and nature of the processing performed by the subservice organization. This summary ordinarily would be briefer than the information provided by the service organization in its description of the functions and nature of the processing performed by the subservice organization. The service auditor should include a statement in the scope paragraph of the service auditor's report indicating that the description of controls includes only the control objectives and related controls of the service organization; accordingly, the service auditor's examination does not extend to controls at the subservice organization.

.16 An example of the scope paragraph of a service auditor's report using the carve-out method is presented below. Additional or modified report language is shown in ***boldface italics***.

Sample Scope Paragraph of a Service Auditor's Report Using the Carve-Out Method

Independent Service Auditor's Report

To the Board of Directors of Example Trust Company:

We have examined the accompanying description of the controls of Example Trust Company applicable to the processing of transactions for users of the Institutional Trust Division. Our examination included procedures to obtain reasonable assurance about whether (1) the accompanying description presents fairly, in all material respects, the aspects of Example Trust Company's controls that may be relevant to a user organization's internal control as it relates to an audit of financial statements; (2) the controls included in the description were suitably designed to achieve the control objectives specified in the description, if those controls were complied with satisfactorily, and user organizations applied the controls contemplated in the design of Example Trust Company's policies and procedures; and (3) such controls had been placed in operation as of June 30, 19XX. ***Example Trust Company uses a computer processing service organization for all of its computerized application processing. The accompanying description includes only those control objectives and related controls of Example Trust Company and does not include control objectives and related controls of the computer processing service organization. Our examination did not extend to controls of the computer processing service organization.*** The control objectives were specified by the management of Example Trust Company. Our examination was performed in accordance with standards established by the American Institute of Certified Public Accountants and included those procedures we considered necessary in the circumstances to obtain a reasonable basis for rendering our opinion.

[The remainder of the report is the same as the standard service auditor's report illustrated in paragraphs .48 and .54 of section 324.]

.17 If the service organization has used the inclusive method, the service auditor should perform procedures comparable to those described in paragraph .12 of section 324. Such procedures may include performing tests of the service organization's controls over the activities of the subservice organization or performing procedures at the subservice organization. If the service auditor will be performing procedures at the subservice organization, the service organization should arrange for such procedures. The service auditor should recognize that the subservice organization generally is not the client for the engagement. Accordingly, in these circumstances the service auditor should determine whether it will be possible to obtain the required evidence to support the portion of the opinion covering the subservice organization and whether it will be possible to obtain an appropriate letter of representations regarding the subservice organization's controls.

.18 An example of a service auditor's report using the inclusive method is presented below. Additional or modified report language is shown in ***boldface italics***.

Sample Service Auditor's Report Using the Inclusive Method

Independent Service Auditor's Report

To the Board of Directors of Example Trust Company:

We have examined the accompanying description of the controls of Example Trust Company ***and Computer Processing Service Organization, an independent service organization that provides computer processing services to Example Trust Company,*** applicable to the processing of transactions for users of the Institutional Trust Division. Our examination included procedures to obtain reasonable assurance about whether (1) the accompanying description presents fairly, in all material respects, the aspects of Example Trust Company's ***and Computer Processing Service Organization's*** controls that may be relevant to a user organization's internal control as it relates to an audit of financial statements; (2) the controls included in the description were suitably designed to achieve the control objectives specified in the description, if those controls were complied with satisfactorily, and user organizations applied the controls contemplated in the design of Example Trust Company's controls; and (3) the controls had been placed in operation as of June 30, 19XX. The control objectives were specified by the management of Example Trust Company. Our examination was performed in accordance with standards established by the American Institute of Certified Public Accountants and included those procedures we considered necessary in the circumstances to obtain a reasonable basis for rendering our opinion.

In our opinion, the accompanying description of the aforementioned controls presents fairly, in all material respects, the relevant aspects of Example Trust Company's ***and Computer Processing Service Organization's*** controls that had been placed in operation as of June 30, 19XX. Also, in our opinion, the controls, as described, are suitably designed to provide reasonable assurance that the specified control objectives would be achieved if the described controls were complied with satisfactorily and user organizations applied the controls contemplated in the design of Example Trust Company's controls.

In addition to the procedures we considered necessary to render our opinion as expressed in the previous paragraph, we applied tests to specific controls, listed in Schedule X to obtain evidence about their effectiveness in meeting the control objectives, described in Schedule X, during the period from January 1, 19XX, to June 30, 19XX. The specific controls and the nature, timing, extent, and results of the tests are listed in Schedule X. This information has been provided to user organizations of Example Trust Company and to their auditors to be taken into consideration, along with information about internal control at user organizations, when making assessments of control risk for user organizations. In our opinion the controls that were tested, as described in Schedule X, were operating with sufficient effectiveness to provide reasonable, but not absolute, assurance that the control objectives specified in Schedule X were achieved during the period from January 1, 19XX, to June 30, 19XX.

The relative effectiveness and significance of specific controls at Example Trust Company ***and Computer Processing Service Organization***, and their effect on assessments of control risk at user organizations are dependent on their interaction with the controls and other factors present at individual user organizations. We have performed no procedures to evaluate the effectiveness of controls at individual user organizations.

The description of controls at Example Trust Company ***and Computer Processing Service Organization*** is as of June 30, 19XX, and information about tests of the operating effectiveness of specific controls covers the period from January 1, 19XX, to June 30, 19XX. Any projection of such information to the future is subject to the risk that, because of change, the description may no longer portray the controls in existence. The potential effectiveness of specific controls at the Service Organization ***and Computer Processing Service Organization*** is subject to inherent limitations and, accordingly, errors or fraud may occur and not be detected. Furthermore, the projection of any conclusions, based on our findings, to future periods is subject to the risk that changes may alter the validity of such conclusions.

This report is intended solely for use by the management of Example Trust Company, its users, and the independent auditors of its users.

July 10, 19XX

[Issue Date: April, 1995; Revised: February, 1997.]

AU Section 325

Communication of Internal Control Related Matters Noted in an Audit[*]

(Supersedes AU sections 323 and 642.47—.53)

Source: SAS No. 60; SAS No. 78.

See section 9325 for interpretations of this section.

Effective for audits of financial statements for periods beginning on or after January 1, 1989, unless otherwise indicated.

.01 This section provides guidance in identifying and reporting conditions that relate to an entity's internal control observed during an audit of financial statements. It is contemplated that the communication would generally be to the audit committee or to individuals with a level of authority and responsibility equivalent to an audit committee in organizations that do not have one, such as the board of directors, the board of trustees, an owner in an owner-managed enterprise, or others who may have engaged the auditor. For the purpose of this section, the term *audit committee* is used to refer to the appropriate recipient of the communication. This section also provides guidance on establishing, between the auditor and client, agreed-upon criteria for identifying and reporting additional matters beyond those required by this section.

Reportable Conditions

.02 During the course of an audit, the auditor may become aware of matters relating to internal control that may be of interest to the audit committee. The matters that this section requires for reporting to the audit committee are referred to as *reportable conditions*.[1] Specifically, these are matters coming to the auditor's attention that, in his judgment, should be communicated to the audit committee because they represent significant deficiencies in the design or operation of internal control, which could adversely affect the organization's ability to record, process, summarize, and report financial data consistent with the assertions of management in the financial statements.[2] Such deficiencies may involve aspects of the five internal control components[3] of (*a*) the control environment, (*b*) risk assessment, (*c*) control ac-

---

[*] This section has been revised to reflect the amendments and conforming changes necessary due to the issuance of Statement on Auditing Standards No. 78, effective for audits of financial statements for periods beginning on or after January 1, 1997.

[1] This section supersedes section 323, *Required Communication of Material Weaknesses in Internal Accounting Control*, and section 642, *Reporting on Internal Accounting Control*, paragraphs .47 through .53, and related auditing interpretations. This section does not affect the reporting of material weaknesses noted in an engagement to report on an entity's internal control.

[2] The auditor should also consider matters coming to his attention that relate to interim financial reporting outside the entity in the communication contemplated by this section.

[3] *Internal control* refers to the controls established to provide reasonable assurance that specific entity objectives will be achieved. (See section 319, *Consideration of Internal Control in a Financial Statement Audit*, for additional key definitions.) [Footnote transferred from paragraph .04 to paragraph .02, February 1997.]

tivities, (*d*) information and communication, and (*e*) monitoring. (See paragraph .21 for examples of reportable conditions.) [As amended, effective for audits of financial statements for periods beginning on or after January 1, 1997, by Statement on Auditing Standards No. 78.]

.03 The auditor may also identify matters that, in his judgment, are not reportable conditions as defined in paragraph .02; however, the auditor may choose to communicate such matters for the benefit of management (and other recipients, as appropriate).

Identifying Reportable Conditions

.04 The auditor's objective in an audit of financial statements is to form an opinion on the entity's financial statements taken as a whole. The auditor is not obligated to search for reportable conditions. However, the auditor may become aware of possible reportable conditions through consideration of the components of internal control, application of audit procedures to balances and transactions, or otherwise during the course of the audit. The auditor's awareness of reportable conditions varies with each audit and is influenced by the nature, timing, and extent of audit procedures and numerous other factors, such as an entity's size, its complexity, and the nature and diversity of its business activities. [As amended, effective for audits of financial statements for periods beginning on or after January 1, 1997, by Statement on Auditing Standards No. 78.]

.05 In making the judgment as to which matters are reportable conditions, the auditor should take into consideration various factors relating to the entity, such as its size, complexity and diversity of activities, organizational structure, and ownership characteristics.

.06 The existence of reportable conditions related to internal control design or operation may already be known and, in fact, may represent a conscious decision by management—a decision of which the audit committee is aware—to accept that degree of risk because of cost or other considerations. It is the responsibility of management to make the decisions concerning costs to be incurred and related benefits. Provided the audit committee has acknowledged its understanding and consideration of such deficiencies and the associated risks, the auditor may decide the matter does not need to be reported. Periodically, the auditor should consider whether, because of changes in management, the audit committee, or simply because of the passage of time, it is appropriate and timely to report such matters.

Agreed-Upon Criteria

.07 The auditor and client may discuss internal control and concerns regarding its functioning when making arrangements for the audit. Clients may request the auditor to be alert to matters and to report conditions that go beyond those contemplated by this section. The auditor is not precluded from reporting matters that he views to be of value to management in the absence of any specific request to do so.

.08 Agreed-upon arrangements between the auditor and the client to report conditions noted may include, for example, the reporting of matters of less significance than provided for by this section, the existence of conditions specified by the client, or the results of further investigation of matters noted to identify underlying causes. Under these arrangements, it is possible that the auditor may be requested to visit specific locations, assess specific controls, or undertake specific procedures not otherwise planned.

Reporting—Form and Content

.09 Conditions noted by the auditor that are considered reportable under this section or that are the result of agreement with the client should be reported, preferably in writing. If information is communicated orally, the auditor should document the communication by appropriate memoranda or notations in the working papers.

.10 The report should state that the communication is intended solely for the information and the use of the audit committee, management, and others within the organization. When there are requirements established by governmental authorities to furnish such reports, specific reference to such regulatory authorities may be made.

.11 Any report issued on reportable conditions should—

- Indicate that the purpose of the audit was to report on the financial statements and not to provide assurance on internal control.
- Include the definition of reportable conditions.
- Include the restriction on distribution as discussed in paragraph .10.

.12 The following is an illustration of the sections of a report encompassing the above requirements.

> In planning and performing our audit of the financial statements of the ABC Corporation for the year ended December 31, 19XX, we considered its internal control in order to determine our auditing procedures for the purpose of expressing our opinion on the financial statements and not to provide assurance on the internal control. However, we noted certain matters involving the internal control and its operation that we consider to be reportable conditions under standards established by the American Institute of Certified Public Accountants. Reportable conditions involve matters coming to our attention relating to significant deficiencies in the design or operation of the internal control that, in our judgment, could adversely affect the organization's ability to record, process, summarize, and report financial data consistent with the assertions of management in the financial statements.
>
> [*Include paragraphs to describe the reportable conditions noted.*]
>
> This report is intended solely for the information and use of the audit committee (board of directors, board of trustees, or owners in owner-managed enterprises), management, and others within the organization (or specified regulatory agency or other specified third party).

.13 In some circumstances, the auditor may wish to include additional statements in the report regarding the inherent limitations of internal control in general, the specific extent and nature of his consideration of internal control during the audit, or other matters regarding the basis for the comments made.

.14 In a communication that contains both observations deemed by the auditor to be reportable conditions, as defined, and other comments, it may be appropriate to indicate which comments are in each category.

.15 A reportable condition may be of such magnitude as to be considered a material weakness. A *material weakness* in internal control is a reportable condition in which the design or operation of one or more of the internal control components does not reduce to a relatively low level the risk that misstatements caused by error or fraud in amounts that would be material in relation to the financial statements being audited may occur and not be detected within a timely period by employees in the normal course of performing their assigned functions. Although this section does not require that the auditor separately identify and communicate material weaknesses, the auditor may choose or the client may request the auditor to separately identify and communicate as material weaknesses those reportable conditions that, in the auditor's judgment, are considered to be material weaknesses. [As modified, June 1990, by the Audit Issues Task Force.]

.16 The following is an illustration of the sections of a report that may be used when the auditor wishes, or has been requested, to advise the audit committee in writing that one or more reportable conditions have been identified, but none is deemed to be a material weakness.

> [*Include the first paragraph in the report illustrated in paragraph .12.*]
>
> [*Include paragraphs to describe the reportable conditions noted.*]
>
> A material weakness is a reportable condition in which the design or operation of one or more of the internal control components does not reduce to a relatively low level the risk that misstatements caused by error or fraud in amounts that would be material in relation to the financial statements being audited may occur and not be detected within a timely period by employees in the normal course of performing their assigned functions.
>
> Our consideration of internal control would not necessarily disclose all matters in internal control that might be reportable conditions and, accordingly, would not necessarily disclose all reportable conditions that are also considered to be material weaknesses as defined above. However, none of the reportable conditions described above is believed to be a material weakness.
>
> [*Include the final paragraph in the report illustrated in paragraph .12.*]

.17 Because of the potential for misinterpretation of the limited degree of assurance associated with the auditor issuing a written report representing that no reportable conditions were noted during an audit, the auditor should not issue such representations.

.18 Because timely communication may be important, the auditor may choose to communicate significant matters during the course of the audit rather than after the audit is concluded. The decision on whether an interim communication should be issued would be influenced by the relative significance of the matters noted and the urgency of corrective follow-up action.

.19 The provisions in this section should not be viewed as precluding an auditor from communicating to a client a variety of observations and suggestions regarding its activities that go beyond internal control related matters. Such matters may deal with operational or administrative efficiencies, business strategies, and other items of perceived benefit to the client.

Effective Date

.20 This section is effective for audits of financial statements for periods beginning on or after January 1, 1989, with early application permissible.

.21

Appendix

Examples of Possible Reportable Conditions

1. As indicated in paragraph .02 of this section reportable conditions involve matters coming to the auditor's attention that relate to significant deficiencies in the design or operation of internal control that, in the auditor's judgment, could adversely affect the organization's ability to record, process, summarize, and report financial data consistent with the assertions of management in the financial statements.

2. The following are examples of matters that may be reportable conditions. They are grouped by categories of conditions and within categories by specific examples of conditions. Certain of these matters may also require communications under the provisions of other statements on auditing standards.

Deficiencies in internal control design

- Inadequate overall internal control design
- Absence of appropriate segregation of duties consistent with appropriate control objectives
- Absence of appropriate reviews and approvals of transactions, accounting entries, or systems output
- Inadequate procedures for appropriately assessing and applying accounting principles
- Inadequate provisions for the safeguarding of assets
- Absence of other controls considered appropriate for the type and level of transaction activity
- Evidence that a system fails to provide complete and accurate output that is consistent with objectives and current needs because of design flaws

Failures in the operation of internal control

- Evidence of failure of identified controls in preventing or detecting misstatements of accounting information
- Evidence that a system fails to provide complete and accurate output consistent with the entity's control objectives because of the misapplication of controls
- Evidence of failure to safeguard assets from loss, damage or misappropriation
- Evidence of intentional override of internal control by those in authority to the detriment of the overall objectives of the system
- Evidence of failure to perform tasks that are part of internal control, such as reconciliations not prepared or not timely prepared
- Evidence of willful wrongdoing by employees or management
- Evidence of manipulation, falsification, or alteration of accounting records or supporting documents
- Evidence of intentional misapplication of accounting principles

- Evidence of misrepresentation by client personnel to the auditor
- Evidence that employees or management lack the qualifications and training to fulfill their assigned functions

Others

- Absence of a sufficient level of control consciousness within the organization
- Failure to follow up and correct previously identified internal control deficiencies
- Evidence of significant or extensive undisclosed related party transactions
- Evidence of undue bias or lack of objectivity by those responsible for accounting decisions

---

AU Section 9325

Communication of Internal Control Related Matters Noted in an Audit: Auditing Interpretations of Section 325

1. Reporting on the Existence of Material Weaknesses

.01 *Question*—Section 325 requires the auditor to report to the audit committee or to individuals with equivalent authority and responsibility reportable conditions noted during an audit of financial statements. It permits the issuance of reports that include a statement about whether any of the reportable conditions identified are material weaknesses. In connection with an audit, may the auditor issue a written report on material weaknesses separate from the report on reportable conditions?

.02 *Interpretation*—Yes. Section 325 does not preclude the auditor from issuing a separate report stating whether he or she noted any material weaknesses during the audit. Reports on material weaknesses should—

- Indicate that the purpose of the audit was to report on the financial statements and not to provide assurance on internal control.
- Include the definition of a material weakness.
- State that the communication is intended solely for the information and the use of the audit committee, management, and others within the organization. When there are requirements established by governmental agencies to furnish such reports, specific reference to such regulatory authorities may be made.

.03 Section 325 prohibits the auditor from issuing a written report representing that no reportable conditions were noted during the audit. Therefore, in issuing a report stating that no material weaknesses were noted, the auditor should not imply that no reportable conditions were noted.

.04 The following is an illustration of a report encompassing the above requirements:

> In planning and performing our audit of the financial statements of ABC Corporation for the year ended December 31, 19XX, we considered its internal control in order to determine our auditing procedures for the purpose of expressing our opinion on the financial statements and not to provide assurance on the internal control. Our consideration of the internal control would not necessarily disclose all matters in the internal control that might be material weaknesses under standards established by the American Institute of Certified Public Accountants. A material weakness is a condition in which the design or operation of one or more of the internal control components does not reduce to a relatively low level the risk that misstatements caused by error or fraud in amounts that would be material in relation to the financial statements being audited may occur and not be detected within a timely period by employees in the normal course of performing their assigned functions. However, we noted no matters involving the internal control and its operation that we consider to be material weaknesses as defined above.

> This report is intended solely for the information and use of the audit committee (board of directors, board of trustees, or owners in owner-managed enterprises), management, and others within the organization (or specified regulatory agency or other specified third party).

.05 If conditions believed to be material weaknesses are disclosed, the report should describe the weaknesses that have come to the auditor's attention. The last sentence of the first paragraph of the report illustrated in paragraph .04 should be modified as follows and paragraphs describing the material weaknesses should follow the first paragraph:

> However, we noted the following matters involving internal control and its operation that we consider to be material weaknesses as defined above.

.06 In some cases reports on material weaknesses may include comments on specific aspects of internal control or on additional matters. For example, a regulatory agency may require comments on the accounting system and controls (but not on the control environment) or on compliance with certain provisions in contracts or regulations. In such cases the language in paragraph .04 should be modified to:

a. identify clearly the specific aspects of internal controls or the additional matters covered by the report

b. distinguish any additional matters from internal control

c. describe in reasonable detail the scope of the review and tests concerning the additional matters

d. express conclusions in language comparable to that in paragraph .04 or .05, as appropriate

.07 The identification of the specific aspects of internal control or additional matters covered in the report should be as specific as the auditor considers necessary to prevent misunderstanding in this respect. Such identification can be made in some cases by reference to specific portions of other documents such as contracts or regulations.

[Issue Date: February, 1989.]

2. Audit Considerations for the Year 2000 Issue

Note: The full text of this interpretation is included as Interpretation No. 4, "Audit Considerations for the Year 2000 Issue," in section 9311, *Planning and Supervision: Auditing Interpretations of Section 311*, paragraphs .38 through .47.

AU Section 326
Evidential Matter

(Supersedes section 330, "Evidential Matter")

Sources: SAS No. 31; SAS No. 48; SAS No. 80.

See section 9326 for interpretations of this section.

Issue date, unless otherwise indicated: August, 1980

.01 The third standard of field work is:

> Sufficient competent evidential matter is to be obtained through inspection, observation, inquiries, and confirmations to afford a reasonable basis for an opinion regarding the financial statements under audit.

.02 Most of the independent auditor's work in forming his or her opinion on financial statements consists of obtaining and evaluating evidential matter[1] concerning the assertions in such financial statements. The measure of the validity of such evidence for audit purposes lies in the judgment of the auditor; in this respect audit evidence differs from legal evidence, which is circumscribed by rigid rules. Evidential matter varies substantially in its influence on the auditor as he or she develops an opinion with respect to financial statements under audit. The pertinence of the evidence, its objectivity, its timeliness, and the existence of other evidential matter corroborating the conclusions to which it leads all bear on its competence.

Nature of Assertions

.03 Assertions are representations by management that are embodied in financial statement components. They can be either explicit or implicit and can be classified according to the following broad categories:

- Existence or occurrence
- Completeness
- Rights and obligations
- Valuation or allocation
- Presentation and disclosure

.04 Assertions about existence or occurrence address whether assets or liabilities of the entity exist at a given date and whether recorded transactions have occurred during a given period. For example, management asserts that finished goods inventories in the balance sheet are available for sale. Similarly, management asserts that sales in the income statement represent the exchange of goods or services with customers for cash or other consideration.

---

[1] See section 319, *Consideration of Internal Control in a Financial Statement Audit*, paragraphs .64 through .78, for further guidance on evidential matter. [Footnote added, May 1994, to cross-reference guidance on evidential matter to section 319.]

.05 Assertions about completeness address whether all transactions and accounts that should be presented in the financial statements are so included. For example, management asserts that all purchases of goods and services are recorded and are included in the financial statements. Similarly, management asserts that notes payable in the balance sheet include all such obligations of the entity.

.06 Assertions about rights and obligations address whether assets are the rights of the entity and liabilities are the obligations of the entity at a given date. For example, management asserts that amounts capitalized for leases in the balance sheet represent the cost of the entity's rights to leased property and that the corresponding lease liability represents an obligation of the entity.

.07 Assertions about valuation or allocation address whether asset, liability, equity, revenue, and expense components have been included in the financial statements at appropriate amounts. For example, management asserts that property is recorded at historical cost and that such cost is systematically allocated to appropriate accounting periods. Similarly, management asserts that trade accounts receivable included in the balance sheet are stated at net realizable value. [As amended, effective for engagements beginning on or after January 1, 1997, by Statement on Auditing Standards No. 80.]

.08 Assertions about presentation and disclosure address whether particular components of the financial statements are properly classified, described, and disclosed. For example, management asserts that obligations classified as long-term liabilities in the balance sheet will not mature within one year. Similarly, management asserts that amounts presented as extraordinary items in the income statement are properly classified and described.

Use of Assertions in Developing Audit Objectives and Designing Substantive Tests

.09 In obtaining evidential matter in support of financial statement assertions, the auditor develops specific audit objectives in the light of those assertions. In developing the audit objectives of a particular engagement, the auditor should consider the specific circumstances of the entity, including the nature of its economic activity and the accounting practices unique to its industry. For example, one audit objective related to the assertion about completeness that an auditor might develop for inventory balances is that inventory quantities include all products, materials, and supplies on hand.

.10 There is not necessarily a one-to-one relationship between audit objectives and procedures. Some auditing procedures may relate to more than one objective. On the other hand, a combination of auditing procedures may be needed to achieve a single objective. Paragraph .26 provides illustrative audit objectives for inventories of a manufacturing company for each of the broad categories of assertions listed in paragraph .03 and examples of substantive tests that may achieve those audit objectives.

.11 In selecting particular substantive tests to achieve the audit objectives he or she has developed, an auditor considers, among other things, the risk of material misstatement of the financial statements, including the assessed levels of control risk, and the expected effectiveness and efficiency of such tests. These considerations include the nature and materiality of the items being tested, the kinds and competence of available evidential matter, and the nature of the audit objective to be achieved. For example, in designing substantive tests to achieve an objective related to the assertion of existence or occurrence, the auditor selects from items contained in a financial statement amount and searches for relevant evidential matter. On the other hand, in designing procedures to achieve an objective related to the assertion of completeness, the auditor selects from evidential matter indicating that an item should be included in the relevant financial statement amount and investigates whether that item is so included.

.12 The auditor's specific audit objectives do not change whether information is processed manually or electronically. However, the methods of applying audit procedures to gather evidence may be influenced by the method of processing. The auditor may use either manual auditing procedures, information technology-assisted audit techniques, or a combination of both to obtain sufficient competent evidential matter. Because of the growth in the use of computers and other information technology, many entities process significant information electronically. Accordingly, it may be difficult or impossible for the auditor to access certain information for inspection, inquiry, or confirmation without using information technology. [Paragraph added, effective for periods beginning after August 31, 1984, by Statement on Auditing Standards No. 48. As amended, effective for engagements beginning on or after January 1, 1997, by Statement on Auditing Standards No. 80.]

.13 The nature, timing, and extent of the procedures to be applied on a particular engagement are a matter of professional judgment to be determined by the auditor, based on the specific circumstances. However, the procedures adopted should be adequate to achieve the auditor's specific objectives and reduce detection risk to a level acceptable to the auditor. The evidential matter obtained should be sufficient for the auditor to form conclusions concerning the validity of the individual assertions embodied in the components of financial statements. The evidential matter provided by the combination of the auditor's assessment of inherent risk and control risk and on substantive tests should provide a reasonable basis for his or her opinion (see section 319, *Consideration of Internal Control in a Financial Statement Audit*, paragraphs .79 through .82. [Paragraph renumbered by the issuance of Statement on Auditing Standards No. 48, July 1984. As amended, effective for engagements beginning on or after January 1, 1997, by Statement on Auditing Standards No. 80.]

.14 In entities where significant information is transmitted, processed, maintained, or accessed electronically, the auditor may determine that it is not practical or possible to reduce detection risk to an acceptable level by performing only substantive tests for one or more financial statement assertions. For example, the potential for improper initiation or alteration of information to occur and not be detected may be greater if information is produced, maintained, or accessed only in electronic form. In such circumstances, the auditor should perform tests of controls to gather evidential matter to use in assessing control risk,[2] or consider the effect on his or her report (see paragraph .25 of this section). [Paragraph added, effective for engagements beginning on or after January 1, 1997, by Statement on Auditing Standards No. 80.]

---

[2] Section 319.81 states that ordinarily the assessed level of control risk cannot be sufficiently low to eliminate the need to perform any substantive tests for significant account balances and transaction classes and, consequently, the auditor should perform substantive tests for such balances and classes regardless of the assessed level of control risk. [Footnote added, effective for engagements beginning on or after January 1, 1997, by Statement on Auditing Standards No. 80.]

Nature of Evidential Matter

.15 Evidential matter supporting the financial statements consists of the underlying accounting data and all corroborating information available to the auditor. [Paragraph renumbered by the issuance of Statement on Auditing Standards No. 48, July 1984. Paragraph subsequently renumbered by the issuance of Statement on Auditing Standards No. 80, December 1996.]

.16 The books of original entry, the general and subsidiary ledgers, related accounting manuals, and records such as work sheets and spreadsheets supporting cost allocations, computations, and reconciliations all constitute evidence in support of the financial statements. These accounting data are often in electronic form. Accounting data alone cannot be considered sufficient support for financial statements; on the other hand, without adequate attention to the propriety and accuracy of the underlying accounting data, an opinion on financial statements would not be warranted. [Paragraph renumbered by the issuance of Statement on Auditing Standards No. 48, July 1984. Paragraph subsequently renumbered and amended, effective for engagements beginning on or after January 1, 1997, by the issuance of Statement on Auditing Standards No. 80.]

.17 Corroborating evidential matter includes both written and electronic information such as checks; records of electronic fund transfers; invoices; contracts; minutes of meetings; confirmations and other written representations by knowledgeable people; information obtained by the auditor from inquiry, observation, inspection, and physical examination; and other information developed by, or available to, the auditor which permits him or her to reach conclusions through valid reasoning. [Paragraph renumbered by the issuance of Statement on Auditing Standards No. 48, July 1984. Paragraph subsequently renumbered and amended, effective for engagements beginning on or after January 1, 1997, by the issuance of Statement on Auditing Standards No. 80.]

.18 In certain entities, some of the accounting data and corroborating evidential matter are available only in electronic form. Source documents such as purchase orders, bills of lading, invoices, and checks are replaced with electronic messages. For example, entities may use Electronic Data Interchange (EDI) or image processing systems. In EDI, the entity and its customers or suppliers use communication links to transact business electronically. Purchase, shipping, billing, cash receipt, and cash disbursement transactions are often consummated entirely by the exchange of electronic messages between the parties. In image processing systems, documents are scanned and converted into electronic images to facilitate storage and reference, and the source documents may not be retained after conversion. Certain electronic evidence may exist at a certain point in time. However, such evidence may not be retrievable after a specified period of time if files are changed and if backup files do not exist. Therefore, the auditor should consider the time during which information exists or is available in determining the nature, timing, and extent of his or her substantive tests, and, if applicable, tests of controls. [Paragraph added, effective for engagements beginning on or after January 1, 1997, by Statement on Auditing Standards No. 80.]

.19 The auditor tests underlying accounting data by (*a*) analysis and review, (*b*) retracing the procedural steps followed in the accounting process and in developing the allocations involved, (*c*) recalculation, and (*d*) reconciling related types and applications of the same information. Through the performance of such procedures, the auditor may determine that the accounting records are internally consistent. Such internal consistency ordinarily provides evidence about the fairness of presentation of the financial statements. [Paragraph renumbered by the issuance of Statement on Auditing Standards No. 48, July 1984. Paragraph subsequently renumbered and amended, effective for engagements beginning on or after January 1, 1997, by the issuance of Statement on Auditing Standards No. 80.]

.20 The pertinent accounting data and corroborating evidential matter to support entries in the accounts and assertions in the financial statements ordinarily are available from the entity's files and accessible to the auditor for examination at certain points or periods in time. Both within the entity's organization and outside it are knowledgeable people to whom the auditor can direct inquiries. Assets having physical existence are available to the auditor for his or her inspection. Activities of the entity's personnel can be observed. Based on observations of these or other conditions or circumstances, the auditor may reach conclusions about the validity of various assertions in the financial statements. [Paragraph renumbered by the issuance of Statement on Auditing Standards No. 48, July 1984. Paragraph subsequently renumbered and amended, effective for engagements beginning on or after January 1, 1997, by the issuance of Statement on Auditing Standards No. 80.]

Competence of Evidential Matter

.21 To be competent, evidence, regardless of its form, must be both valid and relevant. The validity of evidential matter is so dependent on the circumstances under which it is obtained that generalizations about the reliability of various kinds of evidence are subject to important exceptions. If the possibility of important exceptions is recognized, however, the following presumptions, which are not mutually exclusive, about the validity of evidential matter in auditing have some usefulness:

a. When evidential matter can be obtained from independent sources outside an entity, it provides greater assurance of reliability for the purposes of an independent audit than that secured solely within the entity.

b. The more effective the internal control, the more assurance it provides about the reliability of the accounting data and financial statements.

c. The independent auditor's direct personal knowledge, obtained through physical examination, observation, computation, and inspection, is more persuasive than information obtained indirectly.

[Paragraph renumbered by the issuance of Statement on Auditing Standards No. 48, July 1984. Paragraph subsequently renumbered and amended, effective for engagements beginning on or after January 1, 1997, by the issuance of Statement on Auditing Standards No. 80.]

Sufficiency of Evidential Matter

.22 The independent auditor's objective is to obtain sufficient competent evidential matter to provide him or her with a reasonable basis for forming an opinion. The amount and kinds of evidential matter required to support an informed opinion are matters for the auditor to determine in the exercise of his or her professional judgment after a careful study of the circumstances in the particular case. However, in the great majority of cases, the auditor has to rely on evidence that is persuasive rather than convincing. Both the individual assertions in financial statements and the overall proposition that the financial statements as a whole are fairly presented are of such a nature that even an experienced auditor is seldom convinced beyond all doubt with respect to all aspects of the statements being audited. [Paragraph renumbered by the issuance of Statement on Auditing Standards No. 48, July 1984. Paragraph subsequently renumbered and amended, effective for engagements beginning on or after January 1, 1997, by the issuance of Statement on Auditing Standards No. 80.]

.23 An auditor typically works within economic limits; the auditor's opinion, to be economically useful, must be formed within a reasonable length of time and at reasonable cost. The auditor must decide, again exercising professional judgment, whether the evidential matter available to him or her within the limits of time and cost is sufficient to justify expression of an opinion. [Paragraph renumbered by the issuance of Statement on Auditing Standards No. 48, July 1984. Paragraph subsequently renumbered by the issuance of Statement on Auditing Standards No. 80, December 1996.]

.24 As a guiding rule, there should be a rational relationship between the cost of obtaining evidence and the usefulness of the information obtained. The matter of difficulty and expense involved in testing a particular item is not in itself a valid basis for omitting the test. [Paragraph renumbered by the issuance of Statement on Auditing Standards No. 48, July 1984. Paragraph subsequently renumbered by the issuance of Statement on Auditing Standards No. 80, December 1996.]

Evaluation of Evidential Matter

.25 In evaluating evidential matter, the auditor considers whether specific audit objectives have been achieved. The independent auditor should be thorough in his or her search for evidential matter and unbiased in its evaluation. In designing audit procedures to obtain competent evidential matter, he or she should recognize the possibility that the financial statements may not be fairly presented in conformity with generally accepted accounting principles or a comprehensive basis of accounting other than generally accepted accounting principles.[3] In developing his or her opinion, the auditor should consider relevant evidential matter regardless of whether it appears to corroborate or to contradict the assertions in the financial statements. To the extent the auditor remains in substantial doubt about any assertion of material significance, he or she must refrain from forming an opinion until he or she has obtained sufficient competent evidential matter to remove such substantial doubt, or the auditor must express a qualified opinion or a disclaimer of opinion.[4] [Paragraph renumbered by the issuance of Statement on Auditing Standards No. 48, July 1984. Paragraph subsequently renumbered and amended, effective for engagements beginning on or after January 1, 1997, by the issuance of Statement on Auditing Standards No. 80.]

---

[3] The term *comprehensive basis of accounting other than generally accepted accounting principles* is defined in section 623, *Special Reports*, paragraph .04. [Footnote added, effective for engagements beginning on or after January 1, 1997, by Statement on Auditing Standards No. 80.]

[4] See section 508, *Reports on Audited Financial Statements*, paragraphs .20 through .34 and .61 through .63, for further guidance on expression of a qualified opinion or a disclaimer of opinion. [Footnote added, effective for engagements beginning on or after January 1, 1997, by Statement on Auditing Standards No. 80.]

.26

Appendix

Financial Statement Assertions, Illustrative Audit Objectives, and Examples of Substantive Tests

Illustrations for Inventories of a Manufacturing Company

This appendix illustrates the use of assertions in developing audit objectives and designing substantive tests. The following examples of substantive tests are not intended to be all-inclusive nor is it expected that all of the procedures would be applied in an audit.

Illustrative Audit Objectives	*Examples of Substantive Tests*
	Existence or Occurrence
Inventories included in the balance sheet physically exist	• Observing physical inventory counts • Obtaining confirmation of inventories at locations outside the entity. • Testing of inventory transactions between a preliminary physical inventory date and the balance sheet date.
Inventories represent items held for sale or use in the normal course of business.	• Reviewing perpetual inventory records, production records, and purchasing records for indications of current activity. • Comparing inventories with a current sales catalog and subsequent sales and delivery reports. • Using the work of specialists to corroborate the nature of specialized products.
	Completeness
Inventory quantities include all products, materials, and supplies on hand	• Observing physical inventory counts • Analytically comparing the relationship of inventory balances to recent purchasing, production, and sales activities. • Testing shipping and receiving cutoff procedures.
Inventory quantities include all products, materials, and supplies owned by the company that are in transit or stored at outside locations.	• Obtaining confirmation of inventories at locations outside the entity. • Analytically comparing the relationship of inventory balances to recent purchasing, production, and sales activities. • Testing shipping and receiving cutoff procedures.

Illustrative Audit Objectives	*Examples of Substantive Tests*
Inventory listings are accurately compiled and the totals are properly included in the inventory accounts.	• Tracing test counts recorded during the physical inventory observation to the inventory listing. • Accounting for all inventory tags and count sheets used in recording the physical inventory counts. • Testing the clerical accuracy of inventory listings. • Reconciling physical counts to perpetual records and general ledger balances and investigating significant fluctuations.
	Rights and Obligations
The entity has legal title or similar rights of ownership to the inventories.	• Observing physical inventory counts. • Obtaining confirmation of inventories at locations outside the entity. • Examining paid vendors' invoices, consignment agreements, and contracts.
Inventories exclude items billed to customers or owned by others.	• Examining paid vendors' invoices, consignment agreements, and contracts. • Testing shipping and receiving cutoff procedures.
	Valuation or Allocation
Inventories are properly stated at cost (except when market is lower).	• Examining paid vendors' invoices. • Reviewing direct labor rates. • Testing the computation of standard overhead rates. • Examining analyses of purchasing and manufacturing standard cost variances.
Slow-moving, excess, defective, and obsolete items included in inventories are properly identified.	• Examining an analysis of inventory turnover. • Reviewing industry experience and trends. • Analytically comparing the relationship of inventory balances to anticipated sales volume. • Touring the plant. • Inquiring of production and sales personnel concerning possible excess or obsolete inventory items.
Inventories are reduced, when appropriate, to replacement cost or net realizable value.	• Obtaining current market value quotations. • Reviewing current production costs.

Illustrative Audit Objectives	*Examples of Substantive Tests*
	• Examining sales after year-end and open purchase order commitments.
Presentation and Disclosure	
Inventories are properly classified in the balance sheet as current assets.	• Reviewing drafts of the financial statements.
The major categories of inventories and their bases of valuation are adequately disclosed in the financial statements.	• Reviewing drafts of the financial statements. • Comparing the disclosures made in the financial statements to the requirements of generally accepted accounting principles.
The pledge or assignment of any inventories is appropriately disclosed.	• Obtaining confirmation of inventories pledged under loan agreements.

[Paragraph renumbered by the issuance of Statement on Auditing Standards No. 48, July 1984. Paragraph subsequently renumbered by the issuance of Statement on Auditing Standards No. 80, December 1996.]

AU Section 9326

Evidential Matter: Auditing Interpretations of Section 326

1. Evidential Matter for an Audit of Interim Financial Statements

.01 *Question*—APB Opinion No. 28 [AC section I73] concluded that certain accounting principles and practices followed for annual reporting purposes may require modification at interim report dates. Paragraph 10 of Opinion No. 28 [AC section I73.103] states that the modifications are needed "so that the reported results for the interim period may better relate to the results of operations for the annual period." The modifications introduce a need for estimates to a greater extent than is necessary for annual financial information. Does this imply a relaxation of the third standard of field work, which requires that sufficient competent evidential matter be obtained to afford a reasonable basis for an opinion regarding the financial statements under audit?

.02 *Interpretation*—No. The third standard of field work applies to all engagements leading to an expression of opinion on financial statements or financial information.

.03 The objective of the independent auditor's engagement is to obtain sufficient competent evidential matter to provide him with a reasonable basis for forming an opinion. The auditor develops specific audit objectives in light of assertions by management that are embodied in financial statement components. Section 326.11 states, "In selecting particular substantive tests to achieve the audit objectives he has developed, an auditor considers, among other things, the risk of material misstatement of the financial statements, including the assessed level of control risk, and the expected effectiveness and efficiency of such tests. His considerations include the nature and materiality of the items being tested, the kinds and competence of available evidential matter, and the nature of the audit objective to be achieved."

.04 Evidential matter obtained for an audit of annual financial statements may also be useful in an audit of interim financial statements, and evidential matter obtained for an audit of interim financial statements may also be useful in an audit of annual financial statements. Section 313.02 indicates that "Audit testing at interim dates may permit early consideration of significant matters affecting the year-end financial statements (for example, related party transactions, changed conditions, recent accounting pronouncements, and financial statement items likely to require adjustment)" and that "much of the audit planning, including obtaining an understanding of internal control and assessing control risk, and the application of substantive tests to transactions can be conducted prior to the balance-sheet date."[1] [As amended August, 1983, by issuance of Statement on Auditing Standards No. 45.] (See section 313.)

---

[1] See section 313, *Substantive Tests Prior to the Balance-Sheet Date* for guidance on the auditor's considerations before applying substantive tests to the details of asset or liability accounts at interim dates, including the relationship between the assessed level of control risk and such tests, and on extending the audit conclusions from such tests to the balance-sheet date. [Footnote added August 1983, by issuance of Statement on Auditing Standards No. 45.]

.05 The introduction by Opinion No. 28 [AC section I73] of a need for additional estimates in measuring certain items for interim financial information may lead to a need for evidence in examining those items that differs from the evidence required in an audit of annual financial information. For example, computing the provision for federal income taxes in interim information involves estimating the effective tax rate expected to be applicable for the full fiscal year, and the auditor should examine evidence as to the basis for estimating that rate. Since the effective tax rate for the full year ordinarily is known at year-end, similar evidence is not usually required in examining annual information.

[Issue Date: February, 1974; Modified: October, 1980.]

2. The Effect of an Inability to Obtain Evidential Matter Relating to Income Tax Accruals

.06 *Question*—The Internal Revenue Service's audit manual instructs its examiners on how to secure from corporate officials "tax accrual workpapers" or the "tax liability contingency analysis," including, "a memorandum discussing items reflected in the financial statements as income or expense where the ultimate tax treatment is unclear." The audit manual states that the examiner may question or summons a corporate officer or manager concerning the "knowledge of the items that make up the corporation's contingent reserve accounts." It also states that "in unusual circumstances, access may be had to the audit or tax workpapers" of an independent accountant or an accounting firm after attempting to obtain the information from the taxpayer. (Internal Revenue Manual, section 4024.2–.5, 5/14/81).

.07 Concern over IRS access to tax accrual working papers might cause some clients to not prepare or maintain appropriate documentation of the calculation or contents of the accrual for income taxes included in the financial statement, or to deny the independent auditor access to such information.

.08 What effect does this situation have on the auditor's opinion on the financial statements?

.09 *Interpretation*—Limitations on the auditor's access to information he considers necessary to audit the tax accrual will affect his ability to issue an unqualified opinion on the financial statements. Thus, if the client does not have appropriate documentation of the calculation or contents of the accrual for income taxes and denies the auditor access to client personnel responsible for making the judgments and estimates relating to the accrual, the auditor should assess the importance of that inadequacy in the accounting records and the client imposed limitation on his ability to form an opinion on the financial statements. Also, if the client has appropriate documentation but denies the auditor access to it and to client personnel who possess the information the auditor should assess the importance of the client-imposed scope limitation on his ability to form an opinion.

.10 The third standard of field work requires the auditor to obtain sufficient competent evidential matter through, among other things, inspection and inquiries to afford a reasonable basis for an opinion on the financial statements. Section 326, *Evidential Matter*, paragraph .25, requires the auditor to obtain sufficient competent evidential matter about assertions in the financial statements of material significance or else to qualify or disclaim his opinion on the statements. Section 508, *Reports on Audited Financial Statements*, paragraph .24, states that, "When restrictions that significantly limit the scope of the audit are imposed by the client, ordinarily the auditor should disclaim an opinion on the financial statements." Also, section 333A on *Client Representations* requires the auditor to obtain written representations from management. Section 333A.04 states that the representations ordinarily include, among other matters, "availability of all financial records and related data," and section 333A.05 states that a materiality limit does not apply to that representation. Section 333A.11 states that "management's refusal to furnish a written representation" constitutes a limitation on the scope of the audit sufficient to preclude an unqualified opinion.

.11 *Question*—A client may allow the auditor to inspect its tax accrual workpapers, but may request that he not retain copies for his audit working papers, particularly of the tax liability contingency analysis. The client may also suggest that the auditor not prepare and maintain similar documentation of his own. What should the auditor consider in deciding a response to such a request?

.12 *Interpretation*—Section 326, *Evidential Matter*, paragraph .17, states that corroborating information includes information obtained by the auditor from inquiry, observation, inspection, and physical examination. Section 339 gives guidance on "Working Papers," and states that they provide the principal record of conclusions the auditor has reached concerning significant matters and that ordinarily they should include, among other things, documentation showing that the audit evidence obtained afforded a reasonable basis for an opinion. The section also states that working papers may take the form of memoranda. The nature and extent of audit working paper documentation that is necessary to meet those requirements is a matter of the auditor's professional judgment in light of the circumstances and his needs on the specific engagement. [As modified by the issuance of Statement on Auditing Standards No. 41.] (See section 339.)

.13 *Question*—In some situations a client may furnish its outside legal counsel or in-house legal or tax counsel with information concerning the tax contingencies covered by the accrual for income taxes included in the financial statements and ask counsel to give the auditor an opinion on the adequacy of the accrual for those contingencies.

.14 In such circumstances, instead of inspecting the client's tax liability contingency analysis and making inquiries of the client, may the auditor consider the counsel as a specialist within the meaning of section 336, *Using the Work of a Specialist*, and rely solely on counsel's opinion as an appropriate procedure for obtaining evidential matter to support his opinion on the financial statements?

.15 *Interpretation*—No. The opinion of legal counsel in this situation would not provide sufficient competent evidential matter to afford a reasonable basis for an opinion on the financial statements.

.16 Section 336.01 defines a specialist as "a person (or firm) possessing special skill or knowledge in a particular field other than accounting or auditing." It is intended to apply to situations requiring special knowledge of matters about which the auditor does not have adequate technical training and proficiency. The auditor's education, training and experience on the other hand, do enable him to be knowledgeable concerning income tax matters and competent to assess their presentation in the financial statements.

.17 The opinion of legal counsel on specific tax issues that he is asked to address and to which he has devoted substantive attention, as contemplated by section 337, *Inquiry of a Client's Lawyer Concerning Litigation, Claims, and Assessments*, can be useful to the auditor in forming his own opinion. However, the audit of income tax accounts requires a combination of tax expertise and knowledge about the client's business that is accumulated during all aspects of an audit. Therefore, as stated above, it is not appropriate for the auditor to rely solely on such legal opinion.

[Issue Date: March, 1981.]

3. The Auditor's Consideration of the Completeness Assertion

.18 *Question*—Section 326, *Evidential Matter*, paragraph .03, identifies five categories of assertions that are embodied in financial statement components. In obtaining audit evidence about four of these categories—existence or occurrence, rights and obligations, valuation or allocation, and presentation and disclosure—the auditor considers transactions and accounts that are included in the financial statements. In contrast, in obtaining audit evidence about the completeness assertion, the auditor considers whether transactions and accounts have been improperly excluded from the financial statements. May management's written representations and the auditor's assessment of control risk constitute sufficient audit evidence about the completeness assertion?

.19 *Interpretation*—Written representations from management are a part of the evidential matter the auditor obtains in an audit performed in accordance with generally accepted auditing standards. Management's representations about the completeness assertion, whether considered alone or in combination with the auditor's assessment of control risk, do not constitute sufficient audit evidence to support that assertion. Obtaining such representations complements but does not replace other auditing procedures that the auditor should perform.

.20 In planning audit procedures to obtain evidence about the completeness assertion, the auditor should consider the inherent risk that transactions and accounts have been improperly omitted from the financial statements. When the auditor assesses the inherent risk of omission for a particular account balance or class of transactions to be such that he believes omissions could exist that might be material when aggregated with errors in other balances or classes, he should restrict the audit risk of omission by performing substantive tests designed to obtain evidence about the completeness assertion. Substantive tests designed primarily to obtain evidence about the completeness assertion include analytical procedures and tests of details of *related populations*.[2]

.21 The extent of substantive tests of completeness may properly vary in relation to the assessed level of control risk. Because of the unique nature of the completeness assertion, an assessed level of control risk below the maximum may be an effective means for the auditor to obtain evidence about that assertion. Although an assessed level of control risk below the maximum is not required to satisfy the auditor's objectives with respect to

---

[2] For purposes of this interpretation, a related population is a population other than the recorded account balance or class of transactions being audited that would be expected to contain evidence of whether all accounts or transactions that should be presented in that balance or class are so included.

the completeness assertion, the auditor should consider that for some transactions (e.g., revenues that are received primarily in cash, such as those of a casino or of some charitable organizations) it may be difficult to limit audit risk for those assertions to an acceptable level without an assessed level of control risk below the maximum.

[Issue Date: April, 1986.]

AU Section 329
Analytical Procedures

(Supersedes section 318)

Source: SAS No. 56.

Effective for audits of financial statements for periods beginning on or after January 1, 1989, unless otherwise indicated.

.01 This section provides guidance on the use of analytical procedures and requires the use of analytical procedures in the planning and overall review stages of all audits.

.02 Analytical procedures are an important part of the audit process and consist of evaluations of financial information made by a study of plausible relationships among both financial and nonfinancial data. Analytical procedures range from simple comparisons to the use of complex models involving many relationships and elements of data. A basic premise underlying the application of analytical procedures is that plausible relationships among data may reasonably be expected to exist and continue in the absence of known conditions to the contrary. Particular conditions that can cause variations in these relationships include, for example, specific unusual transactions or events, accounting changes, business changes, random fluctuations, or misstatements.

.03 Understanding financial relationships is essential in planning and evaluating the results of analytical procedures, and generally requires knowledge of the client and the industry or industries in which the client operates. An understanding of the purposes of analytical procedures and the limitations of those procedures is also important. Accordingly, the identification of the relationships and types of data used, as well as conclusions reached when recorded amounts are compared to expectations, requires judgment by the auditor.

.04 Analytical procedures are used for the following purposes:

a. To assist the auditor in planning the nature, timing, and extent of other auditing procedures

b. As a substantive test to obtain evidential matter about particular assertions related to account balances or classes of transactions

c. As an overall review of the financial information in the final review stage of the audit

Analytical procedures should be applied to some extent for the purposes referred to in (*a*) and (*c*) above for all audits of financial statements made in accordance with generally accepted auditing standards. In addition, in some cases, analytical procedures can be more effective or efficient than tests of details for achieving particular substantive testing objectives.

.05 Analytical procedures involve comparisons of recorded amounts, or ratios developed from recorded amounts, to expectations developed by the auditor. The auditor develops such expectations by identifying and using plausible relationships that are reasonably expected to exist based on the auditor's understanding of the client and of the industry in which the client operates. Following are examples of sources of information for developing expectations:

- *a.* Financial information for comparable prior period(s) giving consideration to known changes
- *b.* Anticipated results—for example, budgets, or forecasts including extrapolations from interim or annual data
- *c.* Relationships among elements of financial information within the period
- *d.* Information regarding the industry in which the client operates—for example, gross margin information
- *e.* Relationships of financial information with relevant nonfinancial information

Analytical Procedures in Planning the Audit

.06 The purpose of applying analytical procedures in planning the audit is to assist in planning the nature, timing, and extent of auditing procedures that will be used to obtain evidential matter for specific account balances or classes of transactions. To accomplish this, the analytical procedures used in planning the audit should focus on (*a*) enhancing the auditor's understanding of the client's business and the transactions and events that have occurred since the last audit date, and (*b*) identifying areas that may represent specific risks relevant to the audit. Thus, the objective of the procedures is to identify such things as the existence of unusual transactions and events, and amounts, ratios and trends that might indicate matters that have financial statement and audit planning ramifications.

.07 Analytical procedures used in planning the audit generally use data aggregated at a high level. Furthermore, the sophistication, extent and timing of the procedures, which are based on the auditor's judgment, may vary widely depending on the size and complexity of the client. For some entities, the procedures may consist of reviewing changes in account balances from the prior to the current year using the general ledger or the auditor's preliminary or unadjusted working trial balance. In contrast, for other entities, the procedures might involve an extensive analysis of quarterly financial statements. In both cases, the analytical procedures, combined with the auditor's knowledge of the business, serve as a basis for additional inquiries and effective planning.

.08 Although analytical procedures used in planning the audit often use only financial data, sometimes relevant nonfinancial information is considered as well. For example, number of employees, square footage of selling space, volume of goods produced, and similar information may contribute to accomplishing the purpose of the procedures.

Analytical Procedures Used as Substantive Tests

.09 The auditor's reliance on substantive tests to achieve an audit objective related to a particular assertion[1] may be derived from tests of details, from

---

[1] Assertions are representations by management that are embodied in financial statement components. See section 326, *Evidential Matter*.

analytical procedures, or from a combination of both. The decision about which procedure or procedures to use to achieve a particular audit objective is based on the auditor's judgment on the expected effectiveness and efficiency of the available procedures.

.10 The auditor considers the level of assurance, if any, he wants from substantive testing for a particular audit objective and decides, among other things, which procedure, or combination of procedures, can provide that level of assurance. For some assertions, analytical procedures are effective in providing the appropriate level of assurance. For other assertions, however, analytical procedures may not be as effective or efficient as tests of details in providing the desired level of assurance.

.11 The expected effectiveness and efficiency of an analytical procedure in identifying potential misstatements depends on, among other things, (*a*) the nature of the assertion, (*b*) the plausibility and predictability of the relationship, (*c*) the availability and reliability of the data used to develop the expectation, and (*d*) the precision of the expectation.

Nature of Assertion

.12 Analytical procedures may be effective and efficient tests for assertions in which potential misstatements would not be apparent from an examination of the detailed evidence or in which detailed evidence is not readily available. For example, comparisons of aggregate salaries paid with the number of personnel may indicate unauthorized payments that may not be apparent from testing individual transactions. Differences from expected relationships may also indicate potential omissions when independent evidence that an individual transaction should have been recorded may not be readily available.

Plausibility and Predictability of the Relationship

.13 It is important for the auditor to understand the reasons that make relationships plausible because data sometimes appear to be related when they are not, which could lead the auditor to erroneous conclusions. In addition, the presence of an unexpected relationship can provide important evidence when appropriately scrutinized.

.14 As higher levels of assurance are desired from analytical procedures, more predictable relationships are required to develop the expectation. Relationships in a stable environment are usually more predictable than relationships in a dynamic or unstable environment. Relationships involving income statement accounts tend to be more predictable than relationships involving only balance sheet accounts since income statement accounts represent transactions over a period of time, whereas balance sheet accounts represent amounts as of a point in time. Relationships involving transactions subject to management discretion are sometimes less predictable. For example, management may elect to incur maintenance expense rather than replace plant and equipment, or they may delay advertising expenditures.

Availability and Reliability of Data

.15 Data may or may not be readily available to develop expectations for some assertions. For example, to test the completeness assertion, expected sales for some entities might be developed from production statistics or square feet of selling space. For other entities, data relevant to the assertion of completeness of sales may not be readily available, and it may be more effective or efficient to use the details of shipping records to test that assertion.

.16 The auditor obtains assurance from analytical procedures based upon the consistency of the recorded amounts with expectations developed from data derived from other sources. The reliability of the data used to develop the expectations should be appropriate for the desired level of assurance from the analytical procedure. The auditor should assess the reliability of the data by considering the source of the data and the conditions under which it was gathered, as well as other knowledge the auditor may have about the data. The following factors influence the auditor's consideration of the reliability of data for purposes of achieving audit objectives:

- Whether the data was obtained from independent sources outside the entity or from sources within the entity
- Whether sources within the entity were independent of those who are responsible for the amount being audited
- Whether the data was developed under a reliable system with adequate controls
- Whether the data was subjected to audit testing in the current or prior year
- Whether the expectations were developed using data from a variety of sources

Precision of the Expectation

.17 The expectation should be precise enough to provide the desired level of assurance that differences that may be potential material misstatements, individually or when aggregated with other misstatements, would be identified for the auditor to investigate (see paragraph .20). As expectations become more precise, the range of expected differences becomes narrower and, accordingly, the likelihood increases that significant differences from the expectations are due to misstatements. The precision of the expectation depends on, among other things, the auditor's identification and consideration of factors that significantly affect the amount being audited and the level of detail of data used to develop the expectation.

.18 Many factors can influence financial relationships. For example, sales are affected by prices, volume and product mix. Each of these, in turn, may be affected by a number of factors, and offsetting factors can obscure misstatements. More effective identification of factors that significantly affect the relationship is generally needed as the desired level of assurance from analytical procedures increases.

.19 Expectations developed at a detailed level generally have a greater chance of detecting misstatement of a given amount than do broad comparisons. Monthly amounts will generally be more effective than annual amounts and comparisons by location or line of business usually will be more effective than company-wide comparisons. The level of detail that is appropriate will be influenced by the nature of the client, its size and its complexity. Generally, the risk that material misstatement could be obscured by offsetting factors increases as a client's operations become more complex and more diversified. Disaggregation helps reduce this risk.

Investigation and Evaluation of Significant Differences

.20 In planning the analytical procedures as a substantive test, the auditor should consider the amount of difference from the expectation that can be accepted without further investigation. This consideration is influenced primarily by materiality and should be consistent with the level of assurance desired from the procedures. Determination of this amount involves considering the possibility that a combination of misstatements in the specific account balances, or class of transactions, or other balances or classes could aggregate to an unacceptable amount.[2]

.21 The auditor should evaluate significant unexpected differences. Reconsidering the methods and factors used in developing the expectation and inquiry of management may assist the auditor in this regard. Management responses, however, should ordinarily be corroborated with other evidential matter. In those cases when an explanation for the difference cannot be obtained, the auditor should obtain sufficient evidence about the assertion by performing other audit procedures to satisfy himself as to whether the difference is a likely misstatement.[3] In designing such other procedures, the auditor should consider that unexplained differences may indicate an increased risk of material misstatement. (See section 316, *Consideration of Fraud in a Financial Statement Audit.)*

Analytical Procedures Used in the Overall Review

.22 The objective of analytical procedures used in the overall review stage of the audit is to assist the auditor in assessing the conclusions reached and in the evaluation of the overall financial statement presentation. A wide variety of analytical procedures may be useful for this purpose. The overall review would generally include reading the financial statements and notes and considering (*a*) the adequacy of evidence gathered in response to unusual or unexpected balances identified in planning the audit or in the course of the audit and (*b*) unusual or unexpected balances or relationships that were not previously identified. Results of an overall review may indicate that additional evidence may be needed.

Effective Date

.23 This section is effective for audits of financial statements for periods beginning on or after January 1, 1989. Early application of the provisions of this section is permissible.

---

[2] See section 312, *Audit Risk and Materiality in Conducting an Audit*, paragraphs .24 through .26.

[3] See section 312.35.

AU Section 330

The Confirmation Process

(Supersedes section 331.03–.08)

Source: SAS No. 67.

Effective for audits of fiscal periods ending after June 15, 1992, unless otherwise indicated.

Introduction and Applicability

.01 This section provides guidance about the confirmation process in audits performed in accordance with generally accepted auditing standards. This section—

- Defines the confirmation process (see paragraph .04).
- Discusses the relationship of confirmation procedures to the auditor's assessment of audit risk (see paragraphs .05 through .10).
- Describes certain factors that affect the reliability of confirmations (see paragraphs .16 through .27).
- Provides guidance on performing alternative procedures when responses to confirmation requests are not received (see paragraphs .31 and .32).
- Provides guidance on evaluating the results of confirmation procedures (see paragraph .33).
- Specifically addresses the confirmation of accounts receivable and supersedes section 331, *Inventories*, paragraphs .03–.08 and the portion of section 331.01 that addresses the confirmation of receivables (see paragraphs .34 and .35). This section does not supersede the portion of section 331.01 that addresses the observation of inventories.

.02 This section does not address the extent or timing of confirmation procedures. Guidance on the extent of audit procedures (that is, considerations involved in determining the number of items to confirm) is found in section 350, *Audit Sampling*, and section 312, *Audit Risk and Materiality in Conducting an Audit*. Guidance on the timing of audit procedures is included in section 313, *Substantive Tests Prior to the Balance-Sheet Date*.

.03 In addition, this section does not address matters described in section 336, *Using the Work of a Specialist*, or in section 337, *Inquiry of a Client's Lawyer Concerning Litigation, Claims, and Assessments*.

Definition of the Confirmation Process

.04 Confirmation is the process of obtaining and evaluating a direct communication from a third party in response to a request for information about a particular item affecting financial statement assertions. The process includes—

- Selecting items for which confirmations are to be requested.

- Designing the confirmation request.
- Communicating the confirmation request to the appropriate third party.
- Obtaining the response from the third party.
- Evaluating the information, or lack thereof, provided by the third party about the audit objectives, including the reliability of that information.

Relationship of Confirmation Procedures to the Auditor's Assessment of Audit Risk

.05 Section 312 discusses the audit risk model. It describes the concept of assessing inherent and control risks, determining the acceptable level of detection risk, and designing an audit program to achieve an appropriately low level of audit risk. The auditor uses the audit risk assessment in determining the audit procedures to be applied, including whether they should include confirmation.

.06 Confirmation is undertaken to obtain evidence from third parties about financial statement assertions made by management. Section 326, *Evidential Matter*, states that, in general, it is presumed that "When evidential matter can be obtained from independent sources outside an entity, it provides greater assurance of reliability for the purposes of an independent audit than that secured solely within the entity."

.07 The greater the combined assessed level of inherent and control risk, the greater the assurance that the auditor needs from substantive tests related to a financial statement assertion. Consequently, as the combined assessed level of inherent and control risk increases, the auditor designs substantive tests to obtain more or different evidence about a financial statement assertion. In these situations, the auditor might use confirmation procedures rather than or in conjunction with tests directed toward documents or parties within the entity.

.08 Unusual or complex transactions may be associated with high levels of inherent risk and control risk. If the entity has entered into an unusual or complex transaction and the combined assessed level of inherent and control risk is high, the auditor should consider confirming the terms of the transaction with the other parties in addition to examining documentation held by the entity. For example, if the combined assessed level of inherent and control risk over the occurrence of revenue related to an unusual, year-end sale is high, the auditor should consider confirming the terms of that sale.

.09 The auditor should assess whether the evidence provided by confirmations reduces audit risk for the related assertions to an acceptably low level. In making that assessment, the auditor should consider the materiality of the account balance and his or her inherent and control risk assessments. When the auditor concludes that evidence provided by confirmations alone is not sufficient, additional procedures should be performed. For example, to achieve an appropriately low level of audit risk related to the completeness and existence assertions for accounts receivable, an auditor may perform sales cutoff tests in addition to confirming accounts receivable.

.10 The lower the combined assessed level of inherent and control risk, the less assurance the auditor needs from substantive tests to form a conclusion about a financial statement assertion. Consequently, as the combined assessed level of inherent and control risk decreases for a particular assertion, the auditor may modify substantive tests by changing their nature from more effective (but costly) tests to less effective (and less costly) tests. For example, if the combined assessed level of inherent and control risk over the existence of cash is low, the auditor might limit substantive procedures to inspecting client-provided bank statements rather than confirming cash balances.

Assertions Addressed by Confirmations

.11 For the evidence obtained to be competent, it must be reliable and relevant. Factors affecting the reliability of confirmations are discussed in paragraphs .16 through .27. The relevance of evidence depends on its relationship to the financial statement assertion being addressed. Section 326 classifies financial statement assertions into five categories:

a. Existence or occurrence

b. Completeness

c. Rights and obligations

d. Valuation or allocation

e. Presentation and disclosure

.12 Confirmation requests, if properly designed by the auditor, may address any one or more of those assertions. However, confirmations do not address all assertions equally well. Confirmation of goods held on consignment with the consignee would likely be more effective for the existence and the rights-and-obligations assertions than for the valuation assertion. Accounts receivable confirmations are likely to be more effective for the existence assertion than for the completeness and valuation assertions. Thus, when obtaining evidence for assertions not adequately addressed by confirmations, auditors should consider other audit procedures to complement confirmation procedures or to be used instead of confirmation procedures.

.13 Confirmation requests can be designed to elicit evidence that addresses the completeness assertion: that is, if properly designed, confirmations may provide evidence to aid in assessing whether all transactions and accounts that should be included in the financial statements are included. Their effectiveness in addressing the completeness assertion depends, in part, on whether the auditor selects from an appropriate population for testing. For example, when using confirmations to provide evidence about the completeness assertion for accounts payable, the appropriate population might be a list of vendors rather than the amounts recorded in the accounts payable subsidiary ledger.

.14 Some confirmation requests are not designed to elicit evidence regarding the completeness assertion. For example, the AICPA Standard Form to Confirm Account Balance Information With Financial Institutions is designed to substantiate information that is stated on the confirmation request; the form is not designed to provide assurance that information about accounts not listed on the form will be reported.

The Confirmation Process

.15 The auditor should exercise an appropriate level of professional skepticism throughout the confirmation process (see section 230, *Due Professional*

Care in the Performance of Work). Professional skepticism is important in designing the confirmation request, performing the confirmation procedures, and evaluating the results of the confirmation procedures.

Designing the Confirmation Request

.16 Confirmation requests should be tailored to the specific audit objectives. Thus, when designing the confirmation requests, the auditor should consider the assertion(s) being addressed and the factors that are likely to affect the reliability of the confirmations. Factors such as the form of the confirmation request, prior experience on the audit or similar engagements, the nature of the information being confirmed, and the intended respondent should affect the design of the requests because these factors have a direct effect on the reliability of the evidence obtained through confirmation procedures.

Form of Confirmation Request

.17 There are two types of confirmation requests: the positive form and the negative form. Some positive forms request the respondent to indicate whether he or she agrees with the information stated on the request. Other positive forms, referred to as blank forms, do not state the amount (or other information) on the confirmation request, but request the recipient to fill in the balance or furnish other information.

.18 Positive forms provide audit evidence only when responses are received from the recipients; nonresponses do not provide audit evidence about the financial statement assertions being addressed.

.19 Since there is a risk that recipients of a positive form of confirmation request with the information to be confirmed contained on it may sign and return the confirmation without verifying that the information is correct, blank forms may be used as one way to mitigate this risk. Thus, the use of blank confirmation requests may provide a greater degree of assurance about the information confirmed. However, blank forms might result in lower response rates because additional effort may be required of the recipients; consequently, the auditor may have to perform more alternative procedures.

.20 The negative form requests the recipient to respond only if he or she disagrees with the information stated on the request. Negative confirmation requests may be used to reduce audit risk to an acceptable level when (*a*) the combined assessed level of inherent and control risk is low, (*b*) a large number of small balances is involved, and (*c*) the auditor has no reason to believe that the recipients of the requests are unlikely to give them consideration. For example, in the examination of demand deposit accounts in a financial institution, it may be appropriate for an auditor to include negative confirmation requests with the customers' regular statements when the combined assessed level of inherent and control risk is low and the auditor has no reason to believe that the recipients will not consider the requests. The auditor should consider performing other substantive procedures to supplement the use of negative confirmations.

.21 Negative confirmation requests may generate responses indicating misstatements, and are more likely to do so if the auditor sends a large number of negative confirmation requests and such misstatements are widespread. The auditor should investigate relevant information provided on negative confirmations that have been returned to the auditor to determine the effect such information may have on the audit. If the auditor's investigation of responses to negative confirmation requests indicates a pattern of misstatements, the auditor should reconsider his or her combined assessed level of inherent and control risk and consider the effect on planned audit procedures.

.22 Although returned negative confirmations may provide evidence about the financial statement assertions, unreturned negative confirmation requests rarely provide significant evidence concerning financial statement assertions other than certain aspects of the existence assertion. For example, negative confirmations may provide some evidence of the existence of third parties if they are not returned with an indication that the addressees are unknown. However, unreturned negative confirmations do not provide explicit evidence that the intended third parties received the confirmation requests and verified that the information contained on them is correct.

Prior Experience

.23 In determining the effectiveness and efficiency of employing confirmation procedures, the auditor may consider information from prior years' audits or audits of similar entities. This information includes response rates, knowledge of misstatements identified during prior years' audits, and any knowledge of inaccurate information on returned confirmations. For example, if the auditor has experienced poor response rates to properly designed confirmation requests in prior audits, the auditor may instead consider obtaining audit evidence from other sources.

Nature of Information Being Confirmed

.24 When designing confirmation requests, the auditor should consider the types of information respondents will be readily able to confirm, since the nature of the information being confirmed may directly affect the competence of the evidence obtained as well as the response rate. For example, certain respondents' accounting systems may facilitate the confirmation of single transactions rather than of entire account balances. In addition, respondents may not be able to confirm the balances of their installment loans, but they may be able to confirm whether their payments are up-to-date, the amount of the payment, and the key terms of their loans.

.25 The auditor's understanding of the client's arrangements and transactions with third parties is key to determining the information to be confirmed. The auditor should obtain an understanding of the substance of such arrangements and transactions to determine the appropriate information to include on the confirmation request. The auditor should consider requesting confirmation of the terms of unusual agreements or transactions, such as bill and hold sales,[1] in addition to the amounts. The auditor also should consider whether there may be oral modifications to agreements, such as unusual payment terms or liberal rights of return. When the auditor believes there is a moderate or high degree of risk that there may be significant oral modifications, he or she should inquire about the existence and details of any such modifications to written agreements. One method of doing so is to confirm both the terms of the agreements and whether any oral modifications exist.

Respondent

.26 The auditor should direct the confirmation request to a third party who the auditor believes is knowledgeable about the information to be con-

---

[1] Bill and hold sales are sales of merchandise that are billed to customers before delivery and are held by the entity for the customers.

firmed. For example, to confirm a client's oral and written guarantees with a financial institution, the auditor should direct the request to a financial institution official who is responsible for the financial institution's relationship with the client or is knowledgeable about the transactions or arrangements.

.27 If information about the respondent's competence, knowledge, motivation, ability, or willingness to respond, or about the respondent's objectivity and freedom from bias with respect to the audited entity[2] comes to the auditor's attention, the auditor should consider the effects of such information on designing the confirmation request and evaluating the results, including determining whether other procedures are necessary. In addition, there may be circumstances (such as for significant, unusual year-end transactions that have a material effect on the financial statements or where the respondent is the custodian of a material amount of the audited entity's assets) in which the auditor should exercise a heightened degree of professional skepticism relative to these factors about the respondent. In these circumstances, the auditor should consider whether there is sufficient basis for concluding that the confirmation request is being sent to a respondent from whom the auditor can expect the response will provide meaningful and competent evidence.

Performing Confirmation Procedures

.28 During the performance of confirmation procedures, the auditor should maintain control over the confirmation requests and responses. Maintaining control[3] means establishing direct communication between the intended recipient and the auditor to minimize the possibility that the results will be biased because of interception and alteration of the confirmation requests or responses.

.29 There may be situations in which the respondent, because of timeliness or other considerations, responds to a confirmation request other than in a written communication mailed to the auditor. When such responses are received, additional evidence may be required to support their validity. For example, facsimile responses involve risks because of the difficulty of ascertaining the sources of the responses. To restrict the risks associated with facsimile responses and treat the confirmations as valid audit evidence, the auditor should consider taking certain precautions, such as verifying the source and contents of a facsimile response in a telephone call to the purported sender. In addition, the auditor should consider requesting the purported sender to mail the *original* confirmation directly to the auditor. Oral confirmations should be documented in the workpapers. If the information in the oral confirmations is significant, the auditor should request the parties involved to submit written confirmation of the specific information directly to the auditor.

.30 When using confirmation requests other than the negative form, the auditor should generally follow up with a second and sometimes a third request to those parties from whom replies have not been received.

---

[2] Section 334, *Related Parties*, paragraphs .09 and .10, provide guidance on examining related-party transactions that have been identified by the auditor.

[3] The need to maintain control does not preclude the use of internal auditors in the confirmation process. Section 322, *The Auditor's Consideration of the Internal Audit Function in an Audit of Financial Statements*, provides guidance on considering the work of internal auditors and on using internal auditors to provide direct assistance to the auditor.

Alternative Procedures

.31 When the auditor has not received replies to positive confirmation requests, he or she should apply alternative procedures to the nonresponses to obtain the evidence necessary to reduce audit risk to an acceptably low level. However, the omission of alternative procedures may be acceptable (*a*) when the auditor has not identified unusual qualitative factors or systematic characteristics related to the nonresponses, such as that all nonresponses pertain to year-end transactions, and (*b*) when testing for overstatement of amounts, the nonresponses in the aggregate, when projected as 100 percent misstatements to the population and added to the sum of all other unadjusted differences, would not affect the auditor's decision about whether the financial statements are materially misstated.

.32 The nature of alternative procedures varies according to the account and assertion in question. In the examination of accounts receivable, for example, alternative procedures may include examination of subsequent cash receipts (including matching such receipts with the actual items being paid), shipping documents, or other client documentation to provide evidence for the existence assertion. In the examination of accounts payable, for example, alternative procedures may include examination of subsequent cash disbursements, correspondence from third parties, or other records to provide evidence for the completeness assertion.

Evaluating the Results of Confirmation Procedures

.33 After performing any alternative procedures, the auditor should evaluate the combined evidence provided by the confirmations and the alternative procedures to determine whether sufficient evidence has been obtained about all the applicable financial statement assertions. In performing that evaluation, the auditor should consider (*a*) the reliability of the confirmations and alternative procedures; (*b*) the nature of any exceptions, including the implications, both quantitative and qualitative, of those exceptions; (*c*) the evidence provided by other procedures; and (*d*) whether additional evidence is needed. If the combined evidence provided by the confirmations, alternative procedures, and other procedures is not sufficient, the auditor should request additional confirmations or extend other tests, such as tests of details or analytical procedures.

Confirmation of Accounts Receivable

.34 For the purpose of this section, *accounts receivable* means—

a. The entity's claims against customers that have arisen from the sale of goods or services in the normal course of business, and

b. A financial institution's loans.

Confirmation of accounts receivable is a generally accepted auditing procedure. As discussed in paragraph .06, it is generally presumed that evidence obtained from third parties will provide the auditor with higher-quality audit evidence than is typically available from within the entity. Thus, there is a presumption that the auditor will request the confirmation of accounts receivable during an audit unless one of the following is true:

- Accounts receivable are immaterial to the financial statements.

- The use of confirmations would be ineffective.[4]
- The auditor's combined assessed level of inherent and control risk is low, and the assessed level, in conjunction with the evidence expected to be provided by analytical procedures or other substantive tests of details, is sufficient to reduce audit risk to an acceptably low level for the applicable financial statement assertions. In many situations, both confirmation of accounts receivable and other substantive tests of details are necessary to reduce audit risk to an acceptably low level for the applicable financial statement assertions.

.35 An auditor who has not requested confirmations in the examination of accounts receivable should document how he or she overcame this presumption.

Effective Date

.36 This section is effective for audits of fiscal periods ending after June 15, 1992. Early application of this section is permissible.

---

[4] For example, if, based on prior years' audit experience or on experience with similar engagements, the auditor concludes that response rates to properly designed confirmation requests will be inadequate, or if responses are known or expected to be unreliable, the auditor may determine that the use of confirmations would be ineffective.

AU Section 331

*Inventories**

Sources: SAS No. 1, section 331; SAS No. 43; SAS No. 67.

Issue date, unless otherwise indicated: November, 1972.

.01 Observation of inventories is a generally accepted auditing procedure. The independent auditor who issues an opinion when he has not employed them must bear in mind that he has the burden of justifying the opinion expressed. [As amended, effective for fiscal periods ending after June 15, 1992, by Statement on Auditing Standards No. 67.] (See section 330.)

.02 The purpose of this section is to provide guidelines for the independent auditor in observing inventories. This section relates only to observation of inventories and does not deal with other important auditing procedures which generally are required for the independent auditor to satisfy himself as to these assets. [Modified, December 1991, to reflect conforming changes necessary due to the issuance of Statement on Auditing Standards No. 67.] (See section 330.)

Receivables

[.03—.08] [Superseded November 1991 by Statement on Auditing Standards No. 67.] (See section 330.)[1], [2]

Inventories

.09 When inventory quantities are determined solely by means of a physical count, and all counts are made as of the balance-sheet date or as of a single date within a reasonable time before or after the balance-sheet date, it is ordinarily necessary for the independent auditor to be present at the time of count and, by suitable observation, tests, and inquiries, satisfy himself respecting the effectiveness of the methods of inventory-taking and the measure of reliance which may be placed upon the client's representations about the quantities and physical condition of the inventories.

.10 When the well-kept perpetual inventory records are checked by the client periodically by comparisons with physical counts, the auditor's observation procedures usually can be performed either during or after the end of the period under audit.

.11 In recent years, some companies have developed inventory controls or methods of determining inventories, including statistical sampling, which are highly effective in determining inventory quantities and which are sufficiently reliable to make unnecessary an annual physical count of each item of inventory. In such circumstances, the independent auditor must satisfy himself that

---

* [Title amended, December 1991, by Statement on Auditing Standards No. 67.] (See section 330.)

[1] [Superseded November 1991, by Statement on Auditing Standards No. 67.] (See section 330.)

[2] [Superseded November 1991, by Statement on Auditing Standards No. 67.] (See section 330.)

the client's procedures or methods are sufficiently reliable to produce results substantially the same as those which would be obtained by a count of all items each year. The auditor must be present to observe such counts as he deems necessary and must satisfy himself as to the effectiveness of the counting procedures used. If statistical sampling methods are used by the client in the taking of the physical inventory, the auditor must be satisfied that the sampling plan is reasonable and statistically valid, that it has been properly applied, and that the results are reasonable in the circumstances. [As modified by the issuance of SAS No. 39.] (See section 350.)

.12 When the independent auditor has not satisfied himself as to inventories in the possession of the client through the procedures described in paragraphs .09–.11, tests of the accounting records alone will not be sufficient for him to become satisfied as to quantities; it will always be necessary for the auditor to make, or observe, some physical counts of the inventory and apply appropriate tests of intervening transactions. This should be coupled with inspection of the records of any client's counts and procedures relating to the physical inventory on which the balance-sheet inventory is based.

.13 The independent auditor may be asked to audit financial statements covering the current period and one or more periods for which he had not observed or made some physical counts of prior inventories. He may, nevertheless, be able to become satisfied as to such prior inventories through appropriate procedures, such as tests of prior transactions, reviews of the records of prior counts, and the application of gross profit tests, provided that he has been able to become satisfied as to the current inventory.

Inventories Held in Public Warehouses[3]

.14 If inventories are in the hands of public warehouses or other outside custodians, the auditor ordinarily would obtain direct confirmation in writing from the custodian. If such inventories represent a significant proportion of current or total assets, to obtain reasonable assurance with respect to their existence, the auditor should apply one or more of the following procedures as he considers necessary in the circumstances.

a. Test the owner's procedures for investigating the warehouseman and evaluating the warehouseman's performance.

b. Obtain an independent accountant's report on the warehouseman's control procedures relevant to custody of goods and, if applicable, pledging of receipts, or apply alternative procedures at the warehouse to gain reasonable assurance that information received from the warehouseman is reliable.

c. Observe physical counts of the goods, if practicable and reasonable.

d. If warehouse receipts have been pledged as collateral, confirm with lenders pertinent details of the pledged receipts (on a test basis, if appropriate).

[As amended, (by replacing paragraphs .14 and .15 with a new paragraph .14), effective after August 31, 1982 by Statement on Auditing Standards No. 43.]

---

[3] See section 901 for Special Report of Committee on Auditing Procedure.

Effect on the Auditor's Report

.15 For a discussion of the circumstances relating to receivables and inventories affecting the independent auditor's report, see sections 508.24 and 508.67. [As amended, effective for periods ending on or after December 31, 1974, by Statement on Auditing Standards No. 2. Formerly paragraph .16, number changed by issuance of Statement on Auditing Standards No. 43, effective after August 31, 1982.]

Effect on the Auditor's Report

[illegible]

AU Section 332

Auditing Investments

(Supersedes SAS No. 1, section 332)

Source: SAS No. 81.

Effective for audits of financial statements for periods ending on or after December 15, 1997.

Introduction and Applicability

.01 This section provides guidance to auditors in auditing investments in *securities*, that is, *debt securities* and *equity securities*,[1] investments accounted for under Accounting Principles Board (APB) Opinion No. 18, *The Equity Method of Accounting for Investments in Common Stock* [AC section I82].

Audit Objectives and Approach

.02 The auditor should ascertain whether investments are accounted for in conformity with generally accepted accounting principles,[2] including adequate disclosure of material matters. Section 312, *Audit Risk and Materiality in Conducting an Audit*, provides guidance on the auditor's consideration of audit risk when planning and performing an audit of financial statements. The auditor considers audit risk in determining the nature, timing, and extent of the auditing procedures to be performed for financial statement assertions about investments.

.03 Section 326, *Evidential Matter*, states that most of the auditor's work in forming an opinion on financial statements consists of obtaining and evaluating evidential matter related to assertions in the financial statements. This section provides guidance concerning substantive auditing procedures to be performed in gathering evidential matter related to assertions about investments.

Existence, Ownership,[3] and Completeness

.04 The procedures the auditor performs to obtain evidence about the existence, ownership, and completeness of investments will vary depending on the types of investments involved and the auditor's assessment of audit risk. These procedures should include one or more of the following:

---

[1] The terms *securities, debt securities,* and *equity securities* are defined in Financial Accounting Standards Board (FASB) Statement of Financial Accounting Standards No. 115, *Accounting for Certain Investments in Debt and Equity Securities* [AC section I80].

[2] The guidance in this section is also applicable to audits of presentations covered by section 623, *Special Reports*, that include assertions about investments.

[3] Section 326, *Evidential Matter*, uses the terminology *rights and obligations* in describing financial statement assertions about ownership.

- Physical inspection
- Confirmation[4] with the issuer
- Confirmation with the custodian
- Confirmation of unsettled transactions with the broker-dealer
- Confirmation with the counterparty
- Reading executed partnership or similar agreements

Furthermore, the auditor should consider the guidance in section 324, *Reports on the Processing of Transactions by Service Organizations*, if the entity obtains either or both of the following services from another organization:

a. Executing investment transactions and maintaining the related accountability

b. Recording investment transactions and processing the related data

Appropriateness of Accounting Policy

.05 The auditor should ascertain whether the accounting policies adopted by the entity for investments are in conformity with generally accepted accounting principles. Certain investments require the application of Financial Accounting Standards Board (FASB) Statement of Financial Accounting Standards No. 115, *Accounting for Certain Investments in Debt and Equity Securities* [AC section I80], or FASB Statement No. 124, *Accounting for Certain Investments Held by Not-for-Profit Organizations* [AC section No5]. Other investments may require the application of the cost or equity methods of accounting.

.06 Certain entities, such as state and local governmental entities, follow accounting standards issued by the Governmental Accounting Standards Board and certain other pronouncements issued by the American Institute of Certified Public Accountants. Also, certain entities, such as broker-dealers, employee benefit plans, and investment companies follow specialized industry accounting policies.

FASB Statement No. 115

.07 For entities required to follow FASB Statement No. 115 [AC section I80], the accounting policy for an investment in a security depends on its classification. Specifically, the Summary of FASB Statement No. 115 [AC section I80] states the following:

> Debt securities that the enterprise has the positive intent and ability to hold to maturity are classified as *held-to-maturity securities* and reported at amortized cost.
>
> Debt and equity securities that are bought and held principally for the purpose of selling them in the near term are classified as *trading securities* and reported at fair value, with unrealized gains and losses included in earnings.
>
> Debt and equity securities not classified as either held-to-maturity securities or trading securities are classified as *available-for-sale securities* and reported at fair value, with unrealized gains and losses excluded from earnings and reported in a separate component of shareholders' equity.

---

[4] Section 330, *The Confirmation Process*, provides guidance to the auditor concerning the use of confirmations in audits of financial statements.

.08 The appropriate classification of investments depends on management's intent in purchasing and holding the investment, on the entity's actual investment activities, and, for certain debt securities, on the entity's ability to hold the investment to maturity. In determining the nature, timing, and extent of the auditor's substantive procedures, the auditor should obtain an understanding of the process used by management to classify investments.

.09 In evaluating management's intent related to an investment, the auditor should consider whether investment activities corroborate or conflict with management's stated intent. For example, sales of investments classified in the held-to-maturity category, for reasons other than those identified in paragraphs 8 and 11 of FASB Statement No. 115 [AC section I80.105 and 108], should cause the auditor to question the appropriateness of management's classification of other investments classified in that category, as well as future classifications of investments into that category. When considering investment activities, the auditor ordinarily should examine evidence such as written and approved records of investment strategies, records of investment activities, instructions to portfolio managers, and minutes of meetings of the board of directors or the investment committee.

.10 In evaluating an entity's ability to hold a debt security to maturity, the auditor gathers evidence that tends to either corroborate or conflict with such ability. The auditor should consider factors such as the entity's financial position, working capital needs, operating results, debt agreements, guarantees, and other relevant contractual obligations, as well as laws and regulations. The auditor also should consider whether existing operating and cash flow projections or forecasts provide relevant information about an entity's ability to hold an investment to maturity.

.11 In addition to performing other auditing procedures, the auditor ordinarily should obtain written representations from management confirming that the entity has properly classified securities as held-to-maturity, trading, or available-for-sale, and, with respect to held-to-maturity debt securities, that management has the intent and the entity has the ability to hold such investments to maturity.[5]

FASB Statement No. 124

.12 For entities required to follow FASB Statement No. 124 [AC section No5], the accounting policy for investments in equity securities with readily determinable fair values and all investments in debt securities is that they be measured at fair value.

Investments Accounted for Using the Equity Method

.13 Paragraph 17 of APB Opinion 18 [AC section I82.104] states that the equity method of accounting for an investment in common stock should be used by an investor whose investment in voting stock gives it the ability to exercise significant influence, but not control, over an investee. That paragraph also provides criteria to be considered in determining whether an investor has the ability to exercise significant influence.

.14 The auditor should obtain evidence about the appropriateness of the accounting method adopted for investments in common stock of an in-

---

[5] Section 333A, *Client Representations*, provides guidance to the auditor concerning written representations from management in an audit of an entity's financial statements.

vestee.[6] Inquiry should be made of the investor's management as to (*a*) whether the investor has the ability to exercise significant influence over the operating and financial policies of the investee under the criteria set forth in paragraph 17 of APB Opinion 18 [AC section I82.104][7] and (*b*) the attendant circumstances that serve as a basis for management's conclusion. The auditor should evaluate the information received on the basis of facts otherwise obtained by him or her in the course of the audit.

.15 If an investor accounts for an investment in an investee contrary to the applicable presumption contained in paragraph 17 of APB Opinion 18 [AC section I82.104], the auditor should obtain sufficient competent evidential matter about whether that presumption has been overcome and whether appropriate disclosure is made regarding the reasons for not accounting for the investment in keeping with the presumption.[8]

.16 The refusal of an investee to furnish necessary financial data to the investor is evidence (but not necessarily conclusive evidence) that the investor does not have the ability to exercise significant influence over the investee to justify the application of the equity method of accounting.

.17 Financial statements of the investee generally constitute sufficient evidential matter as to the equity in the underlying net assets and the results of operations of the investee if such statements have been audited by an auditor whose report is satisfactory, for this purpose, to the investor's auditor. Section 543, *Part of Audit Performed by Other Independent Auditors*, paragraph .14, provides guidance to the investor's auditor in determining (*a*) whether to make reference to the report of the other auditor and (*b*) what additional procedures may be necessary.

.18 Unaudited financial statements, reports issued on examination by regulatory bodies and taxing authorities, and similar data provide evidence but are not by themselves sufficient as evidential matter. An investor may include its proportionate share of the results of operations of an investee based on the investee's unaudited interim financial statements. An example of this would be a situation in which an investor whose year ends on June 30 includes its equity in earnings of an investee based on the investee's financial statements for the six-month period ended December 31 and the six-month period ended June 30. In such situations, the auditor for the investor should recognize that, although the investee's financial statements for the year ended December 31 may have been audited, the financial statements as of June 30 and for the year then ended represent unaudited data because neither six-month period is covered by an auditor's report. If the financial statements of the investee are not audited, the auditor should apply, or should request that the investor arrange with the investee to have the investee's auditor apply, appropriate auditing procedures to such financial statements, considering the materiality of the investment in relation to the financial statements of the investor.

---

[6] Although APB Opinion 18 [AC section I82] applies to investments in common stock, Interpretation No. 2, *Investments in Partnerships and Ventures*, of APB Opinion 18 indicates that many of the provisions of APB Opinion 18 [AC section I82] are appropriate in accounting for investments in partnerships and unincorporated joint ventures.

[7] Paragraph 17 of APB Opinion 18 [AC section I82.104] states that "an investment (direct or indirect) of 20% or more of the voting stock of an investee should lead to a presumption that in the absence of evidence to the contrary an investor has the ability to exercise significant influence over an investee. Conversely, an investment of less than 20% of the voting stock of an investee should lead to a presumption that an investor does not have the ability to exercise significant influence unless such ability can be demonstrated."

[8] See footnotes 13 and 14 of paragraph 20 in APB Opinion 18 [AC section I82.110].

.19 If the carrying amount of an investment reflects (*a*) factors (such as goodwill or other intangibles) that are not recognized in the financial statements of the investee or (*b*) fair values of assets that are materially different from the investee's carrying amounts, the auditor should consider obtaining current evaluations of these amounts. Although evaluations made by persons within the investor or within the investee may be acceptable, evaluations made by persons independent of these companies usually provide greater assurance of reliability. If such evaluations are made by third parties, the auditor should consider the applicability of section 336, *Using the Work of a Specialist*.

.20 There may be a time lag in reporting between the date of the financial statements of the investor and that of the investee. A time lag in reporting should be consistent from period to period. If a change in time lag occurs that has a material effect on the investor's financial statements, an explanatory paragraph should be added to the auditor's report because of the change in reporting period.[9]

.21 With respect to subsequent events and transactions of the investee occurring after the date of the investee's financial statements but before the date of the report of the investor's auditor, the auditor should read available interim financial statements of the investee and make appropriate inquiries of the investor to identify subsequent events and transactions that are material to the investor's financial statements. Such events or transactions of the type contemplated in section 560, *Subsequent Events*, paragraphs .05 and .06, should be disclosed in the notes to the investor's financial statements and (where applicable) labeled as unaudited information. For the purpose of recording the investor's share of the investee's results of operations, recognition should be given to events or transactions of the type contemplated in section 560.03.

.22 Evidence relating to material transactions between the investor and investee should be obtained to evaluate the propriety of the elimination of unrealized intercompany profits and losses and the adequacy of the disclosures about material related-party transactions. Normally, information about unrealized intercompany profits and losses is not shown separately in the investee's financial statements and, therefore, may have to be obtained from the investee. If the amounts of unrealized intercompany profits or losses are or could reasonably be expected to be material in relation to the investor's financial position or results of operations, unaudited data obtained from the investee ordinarily should be subjected to auditing procedures.

Valuation and Presentation

Cost

.23 The auditor should obtain evidence about the cost of investments if the entity carries its investments at cost or amortized cost or is required to make certain disclosures about the cost basis of investments carried at fair value and realized and unrealized gains and losses. The procedures performed to obtain evidence about cost may include inspection of documentation indicating the purchase price of the security, confirmation with the issuer or custodian, and recomputation of discount or premium amortization.

---

[9] See section 508, *Reports on Audited Financial Statements*, paragraphs .16 through .18.

Fair Value

.24 If investments are carried at fair value or if fair value is disclosed for investments carried at other than fair value, the auditor should obtain evidence corroborating the fair value. In some cases, the method for determining fair value is specified by generally accepted accounting principles. For example, generally accepted accounting principles may require that the fair value of an investment be determined using quoted market prices or quotations as opposed to estimation techniques. In those cases, the auditor should evaluate whether the determination of fair value is consistent with the required valuation method. The following paragraphs provide guidance on audit evidence that may be used to corroborate assertions about fair value; the guidance should be considered in the context of specific accounting requirements.

.25 Quoted market prices for investments listed on national exchanges or over-the-counter markets are available from sources such as financial publications, the exchanges, or the National Association of Securities Dealers Automated Quotations System (NASDAQ). For certain other investments, quoted market prices may be obtained from broker-dealers who are market makers in those investments. If quoted market prices are not available, estimates of fair value frequently can be obtained from third-party sources based on proprietary models or from the entity based on internally developed or acquired models.

.26 Quoted market prices obtained from financial publications or from national exchanges and NASDAQ are generally considered to provide sufficient evidence of the fair value of investments. However, for certain investments, such as securities that do not trade regularly, the auditor should consider obtaining estimates of fair value from broker-dealers or other third-party sources. In some situations, the auditor may determine that it is necessary to obtain fair-value estimates from more than one pricing source. For example, this may be appropriate if a pricing source has a relationship with an entity that might impair its objectivity.

.27 For fair-value estimates obtained from broker-dealers and other third-party sources, the auditor should consider the applicability of the guidance in section 336 or section 324. The auditor's decision as to whether such guidance is applicable and which guidance is applicable will depend on the circumstances. The guidance in section 336 may be applicable if the third-party source derives the fair value of a security by using modeling or similar techniques. If an entity uses a pricing service to obtain prices of listed securities in the entity's portfolio, the guidance in section 324 may be appropriate.

.28 In the case of investments valued by the entity using a valuation model, the auditor does not function as an appraiser and is not expected to substitute his or her judgment for that of the entity's management. Rather, the auditor generally should assess the reasonableness and appropriateness of the model. The auditor also should determine whether the market variables and assumptions used are reasonable and appropriately supported. Estimates of expected future cash flows should be based on reasonable and supportable assumptions. Further, the auditor should determine whether the entity has made appropriate disclosures about the method(s) and significant assumptions used to estimate the fair values of such investments.

.29 The evaluation of the appropriateness of valuation models and each of the variables and assumptions used in the models may require considerable judgment and knowledge of valuation techniques, market factors that affect value, and market conditions, particularly in relation to similar investments that are traded. Accordingly, in some circumstances, the auditor may consider it necessary to involve a specialist in assessing the entity's fair-value estimates or related models.

.30 Negotiable securities, real estate, chattels, or other property is often assigned as collateral for investments in debt securities. If the collateral is an important factor in evaluating fair value and collectibility of the investment, the auditor should obtain evidence regarding the existence, fair value, and transferability of such collateral as well as the investor's rights to the collateral.

Impairment

.31 Generally accepted accounting principles require management to determine whether a decline in fair value below the amortized cost basis of certain investments is other than temporary. Such determinations often involve estimation of the outcome of future events. Accordingly, judgment is required in determining whether an other-than-temporary impairment condition exists at the date of the financial statements. These judgments are based on subjective as well as objective factors, including knowledge and experience about past and current events and assumptions about future events.

.32 The auditor should evaluate whether management has considered relevant information in determining whether an other-than-temporary impairment condition exists. Examples of factors that may indicate an other-than-temporary impairment condition include the following:

- Fair value is significantly below cost.
- The decline in fair value is attributable to specific adverse conditions affecting a particular investment.
- The decline in fair value is attributable to specific conditions, such as conditions in an industry or in a geographic area.
- Management does not possess both the intent and the ability to hold the investment for a period of time sufficient to allow for any anticipated recovery in fair value.
- The decline in fair value has existed for an extended period of time.
- A debt security has been downgraded by a rating agency.
- The financial condition of the issuer has deteriorated.
- Dividends have been reduced or eliminated, or scheduled interest payments on debt securities have not been made.

.33 The auditor should evaluate management's conclusions about the existence of an other-than-temporary impairment condition. In evaluating management's conclusions, the auditor should obtain evidence about conditions, such as those listed in paragraph .32, that tend to corroborate or conflict with such conclusions.

Effective Date

.34 This section is effective for audits of financial statements for periods ending on or after December 15, 1997. Early application of the provisions of this section is permissible.

---

31. Generally accepted accounting principles require [illegible] whether a decline in fair value [illegible] other than temporary [illegible]. Accordingly, judgment [illegible] determining whether [illegible] other than temporary [illegible]. These judgments are based on subjective as well as objective factors, including knowledge and experience about past and current events and assumptions about future events.

- The decline is attributable to adverse conditions specifically related to the security or to specific conditions in an industry or in a geographic area.

33. The auditor should evaluate [illegible] the need to recognize an impairment loss. [illegible] the auditor should obtain evidence [illegible].

AU Section 333

*Management Representations**

(Supersedes SAS No. 19)

Source: SAS No. 85.

See section 9333 for interpretations of this section.

Effective for audits of financial statements for periods ending on or after June 30, 1998.

Introduction

.01 This section establishes a requirement that the independent auditor obtain written representations from management as a part of an audit of financial statements performed in accordance with generally accepted auditing standards and provides guidance concerning the representations to be obtained.

Reliance on Management Representations

.02 During an audit, management makes many representations to the auditor, both oral and written, in response to specific inquiries or through the financial statements. Such representations from management are part of the evidential matter the independent auditor obtains, but they are not a substitute for the application of those auditing procedures necessary to afford a reasonable basis for an opinion regarding the financial statements under audit. Written representations from management ordinarily confirm representations explicitly or implicitly given to the auditor, indicate and document the continuing appropriateness of such representations, and reduce the possibility of misunderstanding concerning the matters that are the subject of the representations.[1]

.03 The auditor obtains written representations from management to complement other auditing procedures. In many cases, the auditor applies auditing procedures specifically designed to obtain evidential matter concerning matters that also are the subject of written representations. For example, after the auditor performs the procedures prescribed in section 334, *Related*

---

* Any reference to section 508, *Reports on Audited Financial Statements*, "as amended by this section" reflects the amendment that appears in appendix D [paragraph .19]. The amendment and any necessary conforming changes to section 508 will be made closer to the effective date of this section.

[1] Section 230, *Due Care in the Performance of Work*, states, "The auditor neither assumes that management is dishonest nor assumes unquestioned honesty. In exercising professional skepticism, the auditor should not be satisfied with less than persuasive evidence because of a belief that management is honest."

Parties, even if the results of those procedures indicate that transactions with related parties have been properly disclosed, the auditor should obtain a written representation to document that management has no knowledge of any such transactions that have not been properly disclosed. In some circumstances, evidential matter that can be obtained by the application of auditing procedures other than inquiry is limited; therefore, the auditor obtains written representations to provide additional evidential matter. For example, if an entity plans to discontinue a line of business and the auditor is not able to obtain sufficient information through other auditing procedures to corroborate the plan or intent, the auditor obtains a written representation to provide evidence of management's intent.

.04 If a representation made by management is contradicted by other audit evidence, the auditor should investigate the circumstances and consider the reliability of the representation made. Based on the circumstances, the auditor should consider whether his or her reliance on management's representations relating to other aspects of the financial statements is appropriate and justified.

Obtaining Written Representations

.05 Written representations from management should be obtained for all financial statements and periods covered by the auditor's report.[2] For example, if comparative financial statements are reported on, the written representations obtained at the completion of the most recent audit should address all periods being reported on. The specific written representations obtained by the auditor will depend on the circumstances of the engagement and the nature and basis of presentation of the financial statements.

.06 In connection with an audit of financial statements presented in accordance with generally accepted accounting principles, specific representations should relate to the following matters:[3]

Financial Statements

a. Management's acknowledgment of its responsibility for the fair presentation in the financial statements of financial position, results of operations, and cash flows in conformity with generally accepted accounting principles

b. Management's belief that the financial statements are fairly presented in conformity with generally accepted accounting principles

Completeness of Information

c. Availability of all financial records and related data

d. Completeness and availability of all minutes of meetings of stockholders, directors, and committees of directors

---

[2] An illustrative representation letter from management is contained in appendix A, "Illustrative Management Representation Letter" [paragraph .16].

[3] Specific representations also are applicable to financial statements presented in conformity with a comprehensive basis of accounting other than generally accepted accounting principles. The specific representations to be obtained should be based on the nature and basis of presentation of the financial statements being audited.

e. Communications from regulatory agencies concerning noncompliance with or deficiencies in financial reporting practices

f. Absence of unrecorded transactions

Recognition, Measurement, and Disclosure

g. Information concerning fraud involving (1) management, (2) employees who have significant roles in internal control, or (3) others where the fraud could have a material effect on the financial statements.[4]

h. Plans or intentions that may affect the carrying value or classification of assets or liabilities.

i. Information concerning related-party transactions and amounts receivable from or payable to related parties.[5]

j. Guarantees, whether written or oral, under which the entity is contingently liable.

k. Significant estimates and material concentrations known to management that are required to be disclosed in accordance with the AICPA's Statement of Position 94-6, *Disclosure of Certain Significant Risks and Uncertainties.*

l. Violations or possible violations of laws or regulations whose effects should be considered for disclosure in the financial statements or as a basis for recording a loss contingency.[6]

m. Unasserted claims or assessments that the entity's lawyer has advised are probable of assertion and must be disclosed in accordance with Financial Accounting Standards Board (FASB) Statement No. 5, *Accounting for Contingencies* [AC section C59].[7]

n. Other liabilities and gain or loss contingencies that are required to be accrued or disclosed by FASB Statement No. 5 [AC section C59].[8]

o. Satisfactory title to assets, liens or encumbrances on assets, and assets pledged as collateral.

p. Compliance with aspects of contractual agreements that may affect the financial statements.

Subsequent Events

q. Information concerning subsequent events[9]

.07 The representation letter ordinarily should be tailored to include additional appropriate representations from management relating to matters

---

[4] See section 316, *Consideration of Fraud in a Financial Statement Audit.*

[5] See section 334.

[6] See section 317, *Illegal Acts by Clients.*

[7] See section 337, *Inquiry of a Client's Lawyer Concerning Litigation, Claims, and Assessments,* paragraph .05*d.* If the entity has not consulted a lawyer regarding litigation, claims, and assessments, the auditor normally would rely on the review of internally available information and obtain a written representation by management regarding the lack of litigation, claims, and assessments; see auditing Interpretation No. 6, "Client Has Not Consulted a Lawyer" (section 9337.15–.17).

[8] See section 337.05*b.*

[9] See section 560, *Subsequent Events,* paragraph .12, section 711, *Filings Under Federal Securities Statutes,* paragraph .10, and section 634, *Letters for Underwriters and Certain Other Requesting Parties,* paragraph .45, footnote 29.

specific to the entity's business or industry.[10] Examples of additional representations that may be appropriate are provided in appendix B, "Additional Illustrative Representations" [paragraph .17].

.08 Management's representations may be limited to matters that are considered either individually or collectively material to the financial statements, provided management and the auditor have reached an understanding on materiality for this purpose. Materiality may be different for different representations. A discussion of materiality may be included explicitly in the representation letter, in either qualitative or quantitative terms. Materiality considerations would not apply to those representations that are not directly related to amounts included in the financial statements, for example, items (*a*), (*c*), (*d*), and (*e*) above. In addition, because of the possible effects of fraud on other aspects of the audit, materiality would not apply to item (*g*) above with respect to management or those employees who have significant roles in internal control.

.09 The written representations should be addressed to the auditor. Because the auditor is concerned with events occurring through the date of his or her report that may require adjustment to or disclosure in the financial statements, the representations should be made as of a date no earlier than the date of the auditor's report. [If the auditor "dual dates" his or her report, the auditor should consider whether obtaining additional representations relating to the subsequent event is appropriate. See section 530, *Dating of the Independent Auditor's Report*, paragraph .05]. The letter should be signed by those members of management with overall responsibility for financial and operating matters whom the auditor believes are responsible for and knowledgeable about, directly or through others in the organization, the matters covered by the representations. Such members of management normally include the chief executive officer and chief financial officer or others with equivalent positions in the entity.

.10 If current management was not present during all periods covered by the auditor's report, the auditor should nevertheless obtain written representations from current management on all such periods. The specific written representations obtained by the auditor will depend on the circumstances of the engagement and the nature and basis of presentation of the financial statements. As discussed in paragraph .08, management's representations may be limited to matters that are considered either individually or collectively material to the financial statements.

.11 In certain circumstances, the auditor may want to obtain written representations from other individuals. For example, he or she may want to obtain written representations about the completeness of the minutes of the meetings of stockholders, directors, and committees of directors from the person responsible for keeping such minutes. Also, if the independent auditor performs an audit of the financial statements of a subsidiary but does not audit those of the parent company, he or she may want to obtain representations from management of the parent company concerning matters that may affect the subsidiary, such as related-party transactions or the parent company's intention to provide continuing financial support to the subsidiary.

.12 There are circumstances in which an auditor should obtain updating representation letters from management. If a predecessor auditor is requested

---

[10] Certain AICPA Audit Guides recommend that the auditor obtain written representations concerning matters that are unique to a particular industry.

by a former client to reissue (or consent to the reuse of) his or her report on the financial statements of a prior period, and those financial statements are to be presented on a comparative basis with audited financial statements of a subsequent period, the predecessor auditor should obtain an updating representation letter from the management of the former client.[11] Also, when performing subsequent events procedures in connection with filings under the Securities Act of 1933, the auditor should obtain certain written representations.[12] The updating management representation letter should state (*a*) whether any information has come to management's attention that would cause them to believe that any of the previous representations should be modified, and (*b*) whether any events have occurred subsequent to the balance-sheet date of the latest financial statements reported on by the auditor that would require adjustment to or disclosure in those financial statements.[13]

Scope Limitations

.13 Management's refusal to furnish written representations constitutes a limitation on the scope of the audit sufficient to preclude an unqualified opinion and is ordinarily sufficient to cause an auditor to disclaim an opinion or withdraw from the engagement.[14] However, based on the nature of the representations not obtained or the circumstances of the refusal, the auditor may conclude that a qualified opinion is appropriate. Further, the auditor should consider the effects of the refusal on his or her ability to rely on other management representations.

.14 If the auditor is precluded from performing procedures he or she considers necessary in the circumstances with respect to a matter that is material to the financial statements, even though management has given representations concerning the matter, there is a limitation on the scope of the audit, and the auditor should qualify his or her opinion or disclaim an opinion.

Effective Date

.15 This section is effective for audits of financial statements for periods ending on or after June 30, 1998. Earlier application is permitted.

---

[11] See section 508, *Reports on Audited Financial Statements*, paragraph .71, as amended by this section [appendix D (paragraph .19)].

[12] See section 711.10.

[13] An illustrative updating management representation letter is contained in appendix C, "Illustrative Updating Management Representation Letter" [paragraph .18].

[14] See section 508.22–.34.

.16

Appendix A

Illustrative Management Representation Letter

1. The following letter, which relates to an audit of financial statements prepared in conformity with generally accepted accounting principles, is presented for illustrative purposes only. The introductory paragraph should specify the financial statements and periods covered by the auditor's report, for example, "balance sheets of XYZ Company as of December 31, 19X1 and 19X0, and the related statements of income and retained earnings and cash flows for the years then ended." The written representations to be obtained should be based on the circumstances of the engagement and the nature and basis of presentation of the financial statements being audited. (See appendix B [paragraph .17]).

2. If matters exist that should be disclosed to the auditor, they should be indicated by listing them following the representation. For example, if an event subsequent to the date of the balance sheet has been disclosed in the financial statements, the final paragraph could be modified as follows: "To the best of our knowledge and belief, except as discussed in Note X to the financial statements, no events have occurred. . . ." Similarly, in appropriate circumstances, item 6 could be modified as follows: "The company has no plans or intentions that may materially affect the carrying value or classification of assets and liabilities, except for our plans to dispose of segment A, as disclosed in footnote X to the financial statements, which are discussed in the minutes of the December 7, 19X1, meeting of the board of directors."

3. The qualitative discussion of materiality used in the illustrative letter is adapted from FASB Statement of Financial Accounting Concepts No. 2, *Qualitative Characteristics of Accounting Information.*

4. Certain terms are used in the illustrative letter that are described elsewhere in authoritative literature. Examples are fraud, in section 316, and related parties, in section 334, footnote 1. To avoid misunderstanding concerning the meaning of such terms, the auditor may wish to furnish those definitions to management or request that the definitions be included in the written representations.

5. The illustrative letter assumes that management and the auditor have reached an understanding on the limits of materiality for purposes of the written representations. However, it should be noted that a materiality limit would not apply for certain representations, as explained in paragraph .08 of this section.

6.

[Date]

To *[Independent Auditor]*

We are providing this letter in connection with your audit(s) of the *[identification of financial statements]* of *[name of entity]* as of *[dates]* and for the *[periods]* for the purpose of expressing an opinion as to whether the *[consolidated]* financial statements present fairly, in all material respects, the financial position, results of operations, and cash flows of *[name of entity]* in conformity with generally accepted accounting principles. We confirm that we are responsible for the fair presentation in the *[consolidated]* financial statements of financial position, results of operations, and cash flows in conformity with generally accepted accounting principles.

Certain representations in this letter are described as being limited to matters that are material. Items are considered material, regardless of size, if they involve an omission or misstatement of accounting information that, in the light of surrounding circumstances, makes it probable that the judgment of a reasonable person relying on the information would be changed or influenced by the omission or misstatement.

We confirm, to the best of our knowledge and belief, *[as of (date of auditor's report),]* the following representations made to you during your audit(s).

1. The financial statements referred to above are fairly presented in conformity with generally accepted accounting principles.
2. We have made available to you all—
   a. Financial records and related data.
   b. Minutes of the meetings of stockholders, directors, and committees of directors, or summaries of actions of recent meetings for which minutes have not yet been prepared.
3. There have been no communications from regulatory agencies concerning noncompliance with or deficiencies in financial reporting practices.
4. There are no material transactions that have not been properly recorded in the accounting records underlying the financial statements.
5. There has been no—
   a. Fraud involving management or employees who have significant roles in internal control.
   b. Fraud involving others that could have a material effect on the financial statements.
6. The company has no plans or intentions that may materially affect the carrying value or classification of assets and liabilities.
7. The following have been properly recorded or disclosed in the financial statements:
   a. Related-party transactions, including sales, purchases, loans, transfers, leasing arrangements, and guarantees, and amounts receivable from or payable to related parties.
   b. Guarantees, whether written or oral, under which the company is contingently liable.
   c. Significant estimates and material concentrations known to management that are required to be disclosed in accordance with the AICPA's Statement of Position 94-6, *Disclosure of Certain Significant Risks and Uncertainties.* *[Significant estimates are estimates*

at the balance sheet date that could change materially within the next year. Concentrations refer to volumes of business, revenues, available sources of supply, or markets or geographic areas for which events could occur that would significantly disrupt normal finances within the next year.]

8. There are no—

   a. Violations or possible violations of laws or regulations whose effects should be considered for disclosure in the financial statements or as a basis for recording a loss contingency.

   b. Unasserted claims or assessments that our lawyer has advised us are probable of assertion and must be disclosed in accordance with Financial Accounting Standards Board (FASB) Statement No. 5, *Accounting for Contingencies.*[1]

   c. Other liabilities or gain or loss contingencies that are required to be accrued or disclosed by FASB Statement No. 5.

9. The company has satisfactory title to all owned assets, and there are no liens or encumbrances on such assets nor has any asset been pledged as collateral.

10. The company has complied with all aspects of contractual agreements that would have a material effect on the financial statements in the event of noncompliance.

[*Add additional representations that are unique to the entity's business or industry. See paragraph .07 and appendix B [paragraph .17] of this section.*]

To the best of our knowledge and belief, no events have occurred subsequent to the balance-sheet date and through the date of this letter that would require adjustment to or disclosure in the aforementioned financial statements.

____

[*Name of Chief Executive Officer and Title*]

____

[*Name of Chief Financial Officer and Title*]

---

[1] In the circumstance discussed in footnote 7 of this section, this representation might be worded as follows:

> We are not aware of any pending or threatened litigation, claims, or assessments or unasserted claims or assessments that are required to be accrued or disclosed in the financial statements in accordance with Financial Accounting Standards Board Statement No. 5, *Accounting for Contingencies,* and we have not consulted a lawyer concerning litigation, claims, or assessments.

.17

Appendix B

Additional Illustrative Representations

1. As discussed in paragraph .07 of this section, representation letters ordinarily should be tailored to include additional appropriate representations from management relating to matters specific to the entity's business or industry. The auditor also should be aware that certain AICPA Audit Guides recommend that the auditor obtain written representations concerning matters that are unique to a particular industry. The following is a list of additional representations that may be appropriate in certain situations. This list is not intended to be all-inclusive. The auditor also should consider the effects of pronouncements issued subsequent to the issuance of this section.

General

Condition	*Illustrative Example*
Unaudited interim information accompanies the financial statements.	The unaudited interim financial information accompanying [*presented in Note X to*] the financial statements for the [*identify all related periods*] has been prepared and presented in conformity with generally accepted accounting principles applicable to interim financial information [*and with Item 302(a) of Regulation S-K*]. The accounting principles used to prepare the unaudited interim financial information are consistent with those used to prepare the audited financial statements.
The impact of a new accounting principle is not known.	We have not completed the process of evaluating the impact that will result from adopting Financial Accounting Standards Board (FASB) Statement No. [*XXX, Name*], as discussed in Note [*X*]. The company is therefore unable to disclose the impact that adopting FASB Statement No. [*XXX*] will have on its financial position and the results of operations when such Statement is adopted.
There is justification for a change in accounting principles.	We believe that [*describe the newly adopted accounting principle*] is preferable to [*describe the former accounting principle*] because [*describe management's justification for the change in accounting principles*].

(continued)

Condition	Illustrative Example
Financial circumstances are strained, with disclosure of management's intentions and the entity's ability to continue as a going concern.	Note [*X*] to the financial statements discloses all of the matters of which we are aware that are relevant to the company's ability to continue as a going concern, including significant conditions and events, and management's plans.
The possibility exists that the value of specific significant long-lived assets or certain identifiable intangibles may be impaired.	We have reviewed long-lived assets and certain identifiable intangibles to be held and used for impairment whenever events or changes in circumstances have indicated that the carrying amount of its assets might not be recoverable and have appropriately recorded the adjustment.
The work of a specialist has been used by the entity.	We agree with the findings of specialists in evaluating the [*describe assertion*] and have adequately considered the qualifications of the specialist in determining the amounts and disclosures used in the financial statements and underlying accounting records. We did not give or cause any instructions to be given to specialists with respect to the values or amounts derived in an attempt to bias their work, and we are not otherwise aware of any matters that have had an impact on the independence or objectivity of the specialists.

Assets

Condition	Illustrative Example
Cash	
Disclosure is required of compensating balances or other arrangements involving restrictions on cash balances, line of credit, or similar arrangements.	Arrangements with financial institutions involving compensating balances or other arrangements involving restrictions on cash balances, line of credit, or similar arrangements have been properly disclosed.
Financial Instruments	
Management intends to and has the ability to hold to maturity debt securities classified as held-to-maturity.	Debt securities that have been classified as held-to-maturity have been so classified due to the company's intent to hold such securities

Condition	*Illustrative Example*
	to maturity and the company's ability to do so. All other debt securities have been classified as available-for-sale or trading.
Management considers the decline in value of debt or equity securities to be temporary.	We consider the decline in value of debt or equity securities classified as either available-for-sale or held-to-maturity to be temporary.
Management has determined the fair value of significant financial instruments that do not have readily determinable market values.	The methods and significant assumptions used to determine fair values of financial instruments are as follows: [*describe methods and significant assumptions used to determine fair values of financial instruments*]. The methods and significant assumptions used result in a measure of fair value appropriate for financial statement measurement and disclosure purposes.
There are financial instruments with off-balance-sheet risk and financial instruments with concentrations of credit risk.	The following information about financial instruments with off-balance-sheet risk and financial instruments with concentrations of credit risk has been properly disclosed in the financial statements: 1. The extent, nature, and terms of financial instruments with off-balance-sheet risk 2. The amount of credit risk of financial instruments with off-balance-sheet risk and information about the collateral supporting such financial instruments 3. Significant concentrations of credit risk arising from all financial instruments and information about the collateral supporting such financial instruments
Receivables	
Receivables have been recorded in the financial statements.	Receivables recorded in the financial statements represent valid claims against debtors for sales or other charges arising on or before the balance-sheet date and have been appropriately reduced to their estimated net realizable value.

(continued)

Condition	*Illustrative Example*
Inventories Excess or obsolete inventories exist.	Provision has been made to reduce excess or obsolete inventories to their estimated net realizable value.
Investments There are unusual considerations involved in determining the application of equity accounting.	[*For investments in common stock that are either nonmarketable or of which the entity has a 20 percent or greater ownership interest, select the appropriate representation from the following:*] • The equity method is used to account for the company's investment in the common stock of [*investee*] because the company has the ability to exercise significant influence over the investee's operating and financial policies. • The cost method is used to account for the company's investment in the common stock of [*investee*] because the company does not have the ability to exercise significant influence over the investee's operating and financial policies.
Deferred Charges Material expenditures have been deferred.	We believe that all material expenditures that have been deferred to future periods will be recoverable.
Deferred Tax Assets A deferred tax asset exists at the balance-sheet date.	The valuation allowance has been determined pursuant to the provisions of FASB Statement No. 109, *Accounting for Income Taxes,* including the company's estimation of future taxable income, if necessary, and is adequate to reduce the total deferred tax asset to an amount that will more likely than not be realized. [*Complete with appropriate wording detailing how the entity determined the valuation allowance against the deferred tax asset.*] or

Condition	Illustrative Example
	A valuation allowance against deferred tax assets at the balance-sheet date is not considered necessary because it is more likely than not the deferred tax asset will be fully realized.

Liabilities

Condition	Illustrative Example
Debt	
Short-term debt could be refinanced on a long-term basis and management intends to do so.	The company has excluded short-term obligations totaling $[*amount*] from current liabilities because it intends to refinance the obligations on a long-term basis. [*Complete with appropriate wording detailing how amounts will be refinanced as follows*:] • The company has issued a long-term obligation [*debt security*] after the date of the balance sheet but prior to the issuance of the financial statements for the purpose of refinancing the short-term obligations on a long-term basis. • The company has the ability to consummate the refinancing, by using the financing agreement referred to in Note [*X*] to the financial statements.
Tax-exempt bonds have been issued.	Tax-exempt bonds issued have retained their tax-exempt status.
Taxes	
Management intends to reinvest undistributed earnings of a foreign subsidiary.	We intend to reinvest the undistributed earnings of [*name of foreign subsidiary*].
Contingencies	
Estimates and disclosures have been made of environmental remediation liabilities and related loss contingencies.	Provision has been made for any material loss that is probable from environmental remediation liabilities associated with [*name of site*]. We believe that such estimate is reasonable based on available information and that the liabilities and related loss contingencies and the ex-

(continued)

Condition	*Illustrative Example*
	pected outcome of uncertainties have been adequately described in the company's financial statements.
Agreements may exist to repurchase assets previously sold.	Agreements to repurchase assets previously sold have been properly disclosed.
Pension and Postretirement Benefits	
An actuary has been used to measure pension liabilities and costs.	We believe that the actuarial assumptions and methods used to measure pension liabilities and costs for financial accounting purposes are appropriate in the circumstances.
There is involvement with a multiemployer plan.	We are unable to determine the possibility of a withdrawal liability in a multiemployer benefit plan. or We have determined that there is the possibility of a withdrawal liability in a multiemployer plan in the amount of $[*XX*].
Postretirement benefits have been eliminated.	We do not intend to compensate for the elimination of postretirement benefits by granting an increase in pension benefits. or We plan to compensate for the elimination of postretirement benefits by granting an increase in pension benefits in the amount of $[*XX*].
Employee layoffs that would otherwise lead to a curtailment of a benefit plan are intended to be temporary.	Current employee layoffs are intended to be temporary.
Management intends to either continue to make or not make frequent amendments to its pension or other postretirement benefit plans, which may affect the amortization period of prior service cost, or has expressed a substantive commitment to increase benefit obligations.	We plan to continue to make frequent amendments to its pension or other postretirement benefit plans, which may affect the amortization period of prior service cost. or We do not plan to make frequent amendments to its pension or other postretirement benefit plans.

Equity

Condition	*Illustrative Example*
There are capital stock repurchase options or agreements or capital stock reserved for options, warrants, conversions, or other requirements.	Capital stock repurchase options or agreements or capital stock reserved for options, warrants, conversions, or other requirements have been properly disclosed.

Income Statement

Condition	*Illustrative Example*
There may be a loss from sales commitments.	Provisions have been made for losses to be sustained in the fulfillment of or from inability to fulfill any sales commitments.
There may be losses from purchase commitments.	Provisions have been made for losses to be sustained as a result of purchase commitments for inventory quantities in excess of normal requirements or at prices in excess of prevailing market prices.
Nature of the product or industry indicates the possibility of undisclosed sales terms.	We have fully disclosed to you all sales terms, including all rights of return or price adjustments and all warranty provisions.

.18

Appendix C

Illustrative Updating Management Representation Letter

1. The following letter is presented for illustrative purposes only. It may be used in the circumstances described in paragraph .12 of this section. Management need not repeat all of the representations made in the previous representation letter.

2. If matters exist that should be disclosed to the auditor, they should be indicated by listing them following the representation. For example, if an event subsequent to the date of the balance sheet has been disclosed in the financial statements, the final paragraph could be modified as follows: "To the best of our knowledge and belief, except as discussed in Note X to the financial statements, no events have occurred. . . ."

3.

[*Date*]

To [*Auditor*]

In connection with your audit(s) of the [*identification of financial statements*] of [*name of entity*] as of [*dates*] and for the [*periods*] for the purpose of expressing an opinion as to whether the [*consolidated*] financial statements present fairly, in all material respects, the financial position, results of operations, and cash flows of [*name of entity*] in conformity with generally accepted accounting principles, you were previously provided with a representation letter under date of [*date of previous representation letter*]. No information has come to our attention that would cause us to believe that any of those previous representations should be modified.

To the best of our knowledge and belief, no events have occurred subsequent to [*date of latest balance sheet reported on by the auditor*] and through the date of this letter that would require adjustment to or disclosure in the aforementioned financial statements.

____

[*Name of Chief Executive Officer and Title*]

____

[*Name of Chief Financial Officer and Title*]

.19

Appendix D

Amendment to Section 508, *Reports on Audited Financial Statements*

(Amends section 508.71.)

[*Explanation*]

1. This amendment requires the predecessor auditor to obtain a representation letter from management, in addition to the representation letter from the successor auditor, before reissuing a report previously issued on financial statements of a prior period. New language is shown in boldface; deleted language is shown by strike-through. The amendment is effective for reports reissued on or after June 30, 1998. Earlier application of the provisions of this amendment is permissible.

[*Text of Proposed Change*]

.71 Before reissuing (or consenting to the reuse of) a report previously issued on the financial statements of a prior period, **when those financial statements are to be presented on a comparative basis with audited financial statements of a subsequent period,** a predecessor auditor should consider whether his previous report on those statements is still appropriate. Either the current form or manner of presentation of the financial statements of the prior period or one or more subsequent events might make a predecessor auditor's previous report inappropriate. Consequently, a predecessor auditor should (*a*) read the financial statements of the current period, (*b*) compare the prior-period financial statements that he reported on with the financial statements to be presented for comparative purposes, and (*c*) obtain ~~a letter~~ representation~~s~~ **letters** from **management of the former client and from** the successor auditor. **The representation letter from management of the former client should state (*a*) whether any information has come to management's attention that would cause them to believe that any of the previous representations should be modified, and (*b*) whether any events have occurred subsequent to the balance-sheet date of the latest prior-period financial statements reported on by the predecessor auditor that would require adjustment to or disclosure in those financial statements.**[27] The ~~letter of~~ representation~~s~~ **letter from the successor auditor** should state whether the successor's audit revealed any matters that, in the successor's opinion, might have a material effect on, or require disclosure in, the financial statements reported on by the predecessor auditor. Also, the predecessor auditor may wish to consider the matters described in section 543, *Part of Audit Performed by Other Independent Auditors,* paragraphs .10 through .12. However, the predecessor auditor should not refer in his reissued report to the report or work of the successor auditor.

---

[27] **See section 333, *Management Representations*, appendix C, "Illustrative Updating Management Representation Letter" [paragraph .18].**

AU Section 333A

Client Representations[*]

Source: SAS No. 19.

See section 9333A for interpretations of this section.

Effective for periods ending on or after September 30, 1977, unless otherwise indicated.

.01 This section establishes a requirement that the independent auditor obtain written representations from management as a part of an audit performed in accordance with generally accepted auditing standards and provides guidance concerning the representations to be obtained.

Reliance on Management Representations

.02 During an audit, management makes many representations to the auditor, both oral and written, in response to specific inquiries or through the financial statements. Such representations from management are part of the evidential matter the independent auditor obtains, but they are not a substitute for the application of those auditing procedures necessary to afford a reasonable basis for his opinion on the financial statements. Written representations from management ordinarily confirm oral representations given to the auditor, indicate and document the continuing appropriateness of such representations, and reduce the possibility of misunderstanding concerning the matters that are the subject of the representations.

.03 The auditor obtains written representations from management to complement his other auditing procedures. In many cases, the auditor applies auditing procedures specifically designed to obtain corroborating information concerning matters that are also the subject of written representations. For example, after the auditor performs the procedures prescribed in section 334, *Related Parties*, even if the results of those procedures indicate that transactions with related parties have been properly disclosed, he should obtain a written representation to document that management has no knowledge of any such transactions that have not been disclosed. In some cases involving written representations, the corroborating information that can be obtained by the application of auditing procedures other than inquiry is limited. When a client plans to discontinue a line of business, for example, the auditor may not be able to obtain information through other auditing procedures to corroborate the plan or intent. Accordingly, the auditor should obtain a written representation

---

[*] Prior to the issuance of Statement on Auditing Standards No. 85, *Management Representations*, this section was entitled *Appendix—Illustrative Representation Letter* and contained only the appendix to Statement on Auditing Standards No. 19, *Client Representations*. Statement on Auditing Standards No. 19 has been superseded by Statement on Auditing Standards No. 85 at section 333. Statement on Auditing Standards No. 19, as originally issued in June 1977, has been moved and incorporated into this section until the effective date of Statement on Auditing Standards No. 85.

to provide confirmation of management's intent.[1] [Reference changed August, 1983, by the issuance of Statement on Auditing Standards No. 45.] (See section 334.)

Obtaining Written Representations[2]

.04 The specific written representations obtained by the auditor will depend on the circumstances of the engagement and the nature and basis of presentation of the financial statements. They ordinarily include the following matters, if applicable:

a. Management's acknowledgment of its responsibility for the fair presentation in the financial statements of financial position, results of operations, and cash flows in conformity with generally accepted accounting principles or other comprehensive basis of accounting.

b. Availability of all financial records and related data.

c. Completeness and availability of all minutes of meetings of stockholders, directors, and committees of directors.

d. Absence of errors in the financial statements and unrecorded transactions.

e. Information concerning related party transactions and related amounts receivable or payable.[3]

f. Noncompliance with aspects of contractual agreements that may affect the financial statements.

g. Information concerning subsequent events.[4]

h. Fraud involving management or employees.[5]

i. Communications from regulatory agencies concerning noncompliance with, or deficiencies in, financial reporting practices.

j. Plans or intentions that may affect the carrying value or classification of assets or liabilities.

k. Disclosure of compensating balance or other arrangements involving restrictions on cash balances, and disclosure of line-of-credit or similar arrangements.

l. Reduction of excess or obsolete inventories to net realizable value.

m. Losses from sales commitments.

n. Satisfactory title to assets, liens on assets, and assets pledged as collateral.

o. Agreements to repurchase assets previously sold.

---

[1] See section 316A.16, which states: "... The auditor neither assumes that management is dishonest nor assumes unquestioned honesty. Rather, the auditor recognizes that conditions observed and evidential matter obtained, including information from prior audits, need to be objectively evaluated to determine whether the financial statements are free of material misstatement."

[2] An illustrative representation letter from management is contained in the appendix [paragraph .14].

[3] See section 334. [Reference changed August, 1983, by the issuance of Statement on Auditing Standards No. 45.]

[4] See sections 560.12 and 711.10. [Reference changed by issuance of Statement on Auditing Standards No. 37.]

[5] See section 316.

p. Losses from purchase commitments for inventory quantities in excess of requirements or at prices in excess of market.

q. Violations or possible violations of laws or regulations whose effects should be considered for disclosure in the financial statements or as a basis for recording a loss contingency.[6]

r. Other liabilities and gain or loss contingencies that are required to be accrued or disclosed by Statement of Financial Accounting Standards No. 5 [AC section C59].[7]

s. Unasserted claims or assessments that the client's lawyer has advised are probable of assertion and must be disclosed in accordance with Statement of Financial Accounting Standards No. 5 [AC section C59].[8]

t. Capital stock repurchase options or agreements or capital stock reserved for options, warrants, conversions, or other requirements.

.05 Management's representations may be limited to matters that are considered either individually or collectively material to the financial statements, provided management and the auditor have reached an understanding on the limits of materiality for this purpose. Such limitations would not apply to those representations that are not directly related to amounts included in the financial statements, for example, items (*a*), (*b*), and (*c*) above. In addition, because of the possible effects of irregularities on other aspects of the audit, a materiality limit would not apply to item (*h*) above with respect to management and those personnel who have significant roles in the internal control structure.

.06 In addition to matters such as those indicated above, the auditor may determine, based on the circumstances of the engagement, that other matters should be specifically included in written representations from management.[9] For example, if a company excludes a short-term obligation from current liabilities because it intends to refinance the obligation on a long-term basis, the auditor should obtain a specific representation of management's intent to consummate the refinancing.[10] Also, the auditor should obtain written representations concerning interim financial information accompanying audited financial statements. [As modified, May 1981, by the Auditing Standards Board.]

.07 In certain instances, the auditor may request other written representations from management in addition to evidential matter obtained through other procedures. For example, although the auditor may be satisfied with the method of pricing inventories, he may ask management to furnish a representation concerning inventory pricing.

.08 If the independent auditor is reporting on consolidated financial statements, the written representations obtained from the parent company's

---

6 See section 317.

7 See section 337.05.

8 See section 337.05.

9 Certain AICPA audit guides require or recommend that the auditor obtain written representations concerning matters that are unique to a particular industry. This section does not supersede those requirements or recommendations.

10 See Statement of Financial Accounting Standards No. 6, paragraphs 9 through 11 [AC section B05.113].

management should specify that they pertain to the consolidated financial statements and, if applicable, to the separate financial statements of the parent company.

.09 The written representations should be addressed to the auditor. Because the auditor is concerned with events occurring through the date of his report that may require adjustment to or disclosure in the financial statements, the representations should be dated as of the date of the auditor's report. They should be signed by members of management whom the auditor believes are responsible for and knowledgeable, directly or through others in the organization, about the matters covered by the representations. Normally, the chief executive officer and chief financial officer should sign the representations.

.10 In certain circumstances, the auditor may want to obtain written representations from other individuals. For example, he may want to obtain written representations about the completeness of the minutes of the meetings of stockholders, directors, and committees of directors from the person responsible for keeping such minutes. Also, if the independent auditor performs an audit of the financial statements of a subsidiary but does not audit those of the parent company, he may want to obtain representations from management of the parent company concerning matters that may affect the subsidiary, such as related party transactions or the parent company's intention to provide continuing financial support to the subsidiary.

Scope Limitations[11]

.11 Management's refusal to furnish written representations constitutes a limitation on the scope of the audit sufficient to preclude an unqualified opinion. Further, the auditor should consider the effects of the refusal on his ability to rely on other management representations.

.12 If the auditor is precluded from performing procedures he considers necessary in the circumstances with respect to a matter that is material to the financial statements, even though he has been given representations from management concerning the matter, there is a limitation on the scope of his audit, and he should qualify his opinion or disclaim an opinion.

Effective Date

.13 Statements on Auditing Standards generally are effective at the time of their issuance. However, since this section provides for practices that may differ in certain respects from practices heretofore considered acceptable, this section will be effective for audits made in accordance with generally accepted auditing standards for periods ending on or after September 30, 1977.

---

[11] See section 508.40–.48.

.14

Appendix

Illustrative Representation Letter

1. The following letter is presented for illustrative purposes only. The written representations to be obtained should be based on the circumstances of the engagement and the nature and basis of presentation of the financial statements being audited. The introductory paragraph should specify the financial statements and periods covered by the auditor's report, for example, "balance sheets of XYZ Company as of December 31, 19X1 and 19X0, and the related statements of income and retained earnings and cash flows for the years then ended." Similarly, representations concerning inventories and sales and purchase commitments would not be obtained if such items are not material to the company's financial position and results of operations or if they are not recorded in the financial statements under a comprehensive basis of accounting other than generally accepted accounting principles, for example, financial statements prepared on the cash basis of accounting.

2. The illustrative letter assumes that there are no matters requiring specific disclosure to the auditor. If such matters exist, they should be indicated by listing them following the representation, by reference to accounting records or financial statements, or by other similar means. For example, if an event subsequent to the date of the balance sheet has been disclosed in the financial statements, item 14 could be modified as follows: "Except as discussed in Note X to the financial statements, no events have occurred. . . ." Similarly, in appropriate circumstances, item 4 could be modified as follows: "We have no plans or intentions that may materially affect the carrying value or classification of assets and liabilities, except that certain marketable securities have been excluded from current assets based on our intention not to dispose of them, which is supported by the minutes of the December 7, 19X1, meeting of the board of directors."

3. Certain terms are used in the illustrative letter that are defined elsewhere in authoritative literature, for example, irregularities (section 316A) and related parties (section 334.01, footnote 1). To avoid misunderstanding concerning the meaning of such terms, the auditor may wish to furnish those definitions to the client and request that the client include the definitions in the written representations. [Reference changed August, 1983, by issuance of Statement on Auditing Standards No. 45.] (See section 334.)

4. The illustrative letter assumes that management and the auditor have reached an understanding on the limits of materiality for purposes of the written representations. However, it should be noted that a materiality limit would not apply for certain representations, as explained in section 333A.05.

5.

(Date of Auditor's Report)

(To Independent Auditor)

In connection with your audit of the (identification of financial statements) of (name of client) as of (date) and for the (period of examination) for the purpose of expressing an opinion as to whether the (consolidated) financial statements present fairly, in all material respects, the financial position, results of operations, and cash flows of (name of client) in conformity with generally accepted accounting principles (other comprehensive basis of accounting), we confirm, to the best of our knowledge and belief, the following representations made to you during your audit.

1. We are responsible for the fair presentation in the (consolidated) financial statements of financial position, results of operations, and cash flows in conformity with generally accepted accounting principles (other comprehensive basis of accounting).
2. We have made available to you all—
   a. Financial records and related data.

   b. Minutes of the meetings of stockholders, directors, and committees of directors, or summaries of actions of recent meetings for which minutes have not yet been prepared.
3. There has been no—
   a. Fraud involving management or employees who have significant roles in internal control.

   b. Fraud involving other employees that could have a material effect on the financial statements.
4. There have been no communications from regulatory agencies concerning noncompliance with, or deficiencies in, financial reporting practices that could have a material effect on the financial statements.
5. We have no plans or intentions that may materially affect the carrying value or classification of assets and liabilities.
6. The following have been properly recorded or disclosed in the financial statements:
   a. Related party transactions and related amounts receivable or payable, including sales, purchases, loans, transfers, leasing arrangements, and guarantees.

   b. Capital stock repurchase options or agreements or capital stock reserved for options, warrants, conversions, or other requirements.

   c. Arrangements with financial institutions involving compensating balances or other arrangements involving restrictions on cash balances and line-of-credit or similar arrangements.

   d. Agreements to repurchase assets previously sold.
7. There are no—
   a. Violations or possible violations of laws or regulations whose effects should be considered for disclosure in the financial statements or as a basis for recording a loss contingency.

b. Other material liabilities or gain or loss contingencies that are required to be accrued or disclosed by Statement of Financial Accounting Standards No. 5.

8. There are no unasserted claims or assessments that our lawyer has advised us are probable of assertion and must be disclosed in accordance with Statement of Financial Accounting Standards No. 5.

9. There are no material transactions that have not been properly recorded in the accounting records underlying the financial statements.

10. Provision, when material, has been made to reduce excess or obsolete inventories to their estimated net realizable value.

11. The company has satisfactory title to all owned assets, and there are no liens or encumbrances on such assets nor has any asset been pledged.

12. Provision has been made for any material loss to be sustained in the fulfillment of, or from inability to fulfill, any sales commitments.

13. Provision has been made for any material loss to be sustained as a result of purchase commitments for inventory quantities in excess of normal requirements or at prices in excess of the prevailing market prices.

14. We have complied with all aspects of contractual agreements that would have a material effect on the financial statements in the event of noncompliance.

15. No events have occurred subsequent to the balance sheet date that would require adjustment to, or disclosure in, the financial statements.

____

(Name of Chief Executive Officer and Title)

____

(Name of Chief Executive Officer and Title)

AU Section 9333

Management Representations: Auditing Interpretations of Section 333

1. Management Representations on Violations and Possible Violations of Laws and Regulations

.01 *Question*—Section 333, *Management Representations*, lists matters for which the auditor ordinarily obtains written representations from management. One of those matters is: Violations or possible violations of laws or regulations whose effects should be considered for disclosure in financial statements or as a basis for recording a loss contingency.

.02 Guidance on evaluating the need to disclose litigation, claims, and assessments that may result from possible violations is provided by FASB Statement No. 5, *Accounting for Contingencies* [AC section C59]. Section 317, *Illegal Acts By Clients*, provides guidance on evaluating the materiality of illegal acts. Does the representation regarding "possible violations" include matters beyond those described in FASB Statement No. 5 [AC section C59] and section 317?

.03 *Interpretation*—No. Section 333 did not change the relevant criteria for evaluating the need for disclosure of violations and possible violations of laws or regulations. In requesting the representation on possible violations, the auditor is not asking for management's speculation on all possibilities of legal challenges to its actions.

.04 The representation concerns matters that have come to management's attention and that are significant enough that they should be considered in determining whether financial statement disclosures are necessary. It recognizes that these are matters of judgment and that the need for disclosure is not always readily apparent.

[Issue Date: March, 1979.]

AU Section 9333A

Client Representations: Auditing Interpretations of Section 333A

1. Management Representations on Violations and Possible Violations of Laws and Regulations

.01 *Question*—Section 333A, *Client Representations*, lists matters for which the auditor ordinarily obtains written representations from management. One of those matters is: Violations or possible violations of laws or regulations whose effects should be considered for disclosure in financial statements or as a basis for recording a loss contingency.

.02 Guidance on evaluating the need to disclose litigation, claims, and assessments that may result from possible violations is provided by FASB Statement No. 5, *Accounting for Contingencies* [AC section C59]. Section 317, *Illegal Acts By Clients*, provides guidance on evaluating the materiality of illegal acts. Does the representation regarding "possible violations" include matters beyond those described in FASB Statement No. 5 [AC section C59] and section 317?

.03 *Interpretation*—No. Section 333A did not change the relevant criteria for evaluating the need for disclosure of violations and possible violations of laws or regulations. In requesting the representation on possible violations, the auditor is not asking for management's speculation on all possibilities of legal challenges to its actions.

.04 The representation concerns matters that have come to management's attention and that are significant enough that they should be considered in determining whether financial statement disclosures are necessary. It recognizes that these are matters of judgment and that the need for disclosure is not always readily apparent.

[Issue Date: March, 1979.]

2. Management Representations When Current Management Was Not Present During the Period Under Audit

.05 *Question*—How is the auditor's responsibility for obtaining a written management representation letter affected when current management was not present during the period under audit?

.06 *Interpretation*—Section 333A, *Client Representations*, paragraph .09, states that the written representations "should be signed by members of management whom the auditor believes are responsible for and knowledgeable, directly or through others in the organization, about the matters covered by the representations." In an audit engagement, the auditor should obtain written representations from current management on all periods covered in the auditor's report. The specific written representations obtained by the auditor will depend on the circumstances of the engagement and the nature and basis of presentation of the financial statements. Management's representations may be limited to matters that are considered either individually or collectively material to the financial statements. If current management is unable or unwilling to provide such written representations, the auditor should follow the guidance in section 333A.11.

[Issue Date: October, 1995.]

AU Section 334

Related Parties

(Supersedes Statement on Auditing Standards No. 6, AICPA, Professional Standards, vol. 1, AU sec. 335.01–.19)*

Source: SAS No. 45.

See section 9334 for interpretations of this section.

Effective for periods ended after September 30, 1983, unless otherwise indicated.

.01 This section provides guidance on procedures that should be considered by the auditor when he is performing an audit of financial statements in accordance with generally accepted auditing standards to identify related party relationships and transactions and to satisfy himself concerning the required financial statement accounting and disclosure.[1] The procedures set forth in this section should not be considered all-inclusive. Also, not all of them may be required in every audit.

Accounting Considerations

.02 FASB Statement No. 57, *Related Party Disclosures* [AC section R36], gives the requirements for related party disclosures. Certain accounting pronouncements prescribe the accounting treatment when related parties are involved; however, established accounting principles ordinarily do not require transactions with related parties to be accounted for on a basis different from

---

* This section also withdraws the following auditing interpretations dated March 1976 (AICPA, *Professional Standards*, vol. 1, AU sec. 9335.01–.11):

- Evaluating the Adequacy of Disclosure of Related Party Transactions
- Disclosure of Commonly Controlled Parties
- Definition of "Immediate Family"

[1] Financial Accounting Standards Board Statement No. 57, *Related Party Disclosures*, paragraphs 2 through 4 [AC section R36.102–.104], contains the disclosure requirements for related party relationships and transactions. The glossary of that Statement [AC section R36.406] defines related parties as follows:

> Affiliates of the enterprise; entities for which investments are accounted for by the equity method by the enterprise; trusts for the benefit of employees, such as pension and profit-sharing trusts that are managed by or under the trusteeship of management; principal owners of the enterprise; its management; members of the immediate families of principal owners of the enterprise and its management; and other parties with which the enterprise may deal if one party controls or can significantly influence the management or operating policies of the other to an extent that one of the transacting parties might be prevented from fully pursuing its own separate interests. Another party also is a related party if it can significantly influence the management or operating policies of the transacting parties or if it has an ownership interest in one of the transacting parties and can significantly influence the other to an extent that one or more of the transacting parties might be prevented from fully pursuing its own separate interests.

The glossary also gives definitions of the terms "affiliate," "control," "immediate family," "management," and "principal owners" [AC section R36.401–.405]. Paragraph 1 of the FASB Statement [AC section R36.101] gives examples of related party transactions.

that which would be appropriate if the parties were not related. The auditor should view related party transactions within the framework of existing pronouncements, placing primary emphasis on the adequacy of disclosure. In addition, the auditor should be aware that the substance of a particular transaction could be significantly different from its form and that financial statements should recognize the substance of particular transactions rather than merely their legal form.[2]

.03 Transactions that because of their nature may be indicative of the existence of related parties include[3]—

a. Borrowing or lending on an interest-free basis or at a rate of interest significantly above or below market rates prevailing at the time of the transaction.

b. Selling real estate at a price that differs significantly from its appraised value.

c. Exchanging property for similar property in a nonmonetary transaction.

d. Making loans with no scheduled terms for when or how the funds will be repaid.

Audit Procedures

.04 An audit performed in accordance with generally accepted auditing standards cannot be expected to provide assurance that all related party transactions will be discovered. Nevertheless, during the course of his audit, the auditor should be aware of the possible existence of material related party transactions that could affect the financial statements and of common ownership or management control relationships for which FASB Statement No. 57 [AC section R36] requires disclosure even though there are no transactions. Many of the procedures outlined in the following paragraphs are normally performed in an audit in accordance with generally accepted auditing standards, even if the auditor has no reason to suspect that related party transactions or control relationships exist. Other audit procedures set forth in this section are specifically directed to related party transactions.

.05 In determining the scope of work to be performed with respect to possible transactions with related parties, the auditor should obtain an understanding of management responsibilities and the relationship of each component to the total entity. He should consider controls over management

---

[2] Some pronouncements specify criteria for determining, presenting, and accounting for the substance of certain transactions and events. Examples include (1) presenting consolidated financial statements instead of separate statements of the component legal entities (Accounting Research Bulletin No. 51 [AC section C51]); (2) capitalizing leases (FASB Statement No. 13 [AC section L10]); and (3) imputing an appropriate interest rate when the face amount of a note does not reasonably represent the present value of the consideration given or received in exchange for it (Accounting Principles Board Opinion No. 21 [AC section I69]; FASB Statement No. 94 [AC section C51]). [Footnote revised, June 1993, to reflect conforming changes necessary due to the issuance of Statement of Position 93-3.]

[3] FASB Statement No. 57, paragraph 1 [AC section R36.101], gives other examples of common types of transactions with related parties, and it states that "transactions between related parties are considered to be related party transactions even though they may not be given accounting recognition."

activities, and he should consider the business purpose served by the various components of the entity. Normally, the business structure and style of operating are based on the abilities of management, tax and legal considerations, product diversification, and geographical location. Experience has shown, however, that business structure and operating style are occasionally deliberately designed to obscure related party transactions.

.06 In the absence of evidence to the contrary, transactions with related parties should not be assumed to be outside the ordinary course of business. The auditor should, however, be aware of the possibility that transactions with related parties may have been motivated solely, or in large measure, by conditions similar to the following:

a. Lack of sufficient working capital or credit to continue the business

b. An urgent desire for a continued favorable earnings record in the hope of supporting the price of the company's stock

c. An overly optimistic earnings forecast

d. Dependence on a single or relatively few products, customers, or transactions for the continuing success of the venture

e. A declining industry characterized by a large number of business failures

f. Excess capacity

g. Significant litigation, especially litigation between stockholders and management

h. Significant obsolescence dangers because the company is in a high-technology industry

Determining the Existence of Related Parties

.07 The auditor should place emphasis on testing material transactions with parties he knows are related to the reporting entity. Certain relationships, such as parent-subsidiary or investor-investee, may be clearly evident. Determining the existence of others requires the application of specific audit procedures, which may include the following:

a. Evaluate the company's procedures for identifying and properly accounting for related party transactions.

b. Request from appropriate management personnel the names of all related parties and inquire whether there were any transactions with these parties during the period.

c. Review filings by the reporting entity with the Securities and Exchange Commission and other regulatory agencies for the names of related parties and for other businesses in which officers and directors occupy directorship or management positions.

d. Determine the names of all pension and other trusts established for the benefit of employees and the names of their officers and trustees.[4]

---

[4] According to FASB Statement No. 57, paragraph 24(f) [AC section R36.406] "trusts for the benefit of employees, such as pension and profit-sharing trusts that are managed by or under the trusteeship of management," are related parties.

e. Review stockholder listings of closely held companies to identify principal stockholders.

f. Review prior years' working papers for the names of known related parties.

g. Inquire of predecessor, principal, or other auditors of related entities concerning their knowledge of existing relationships and the extent of management involvement in material transactions.

h. Review material investment transactions during the period under audit to determine whether the nature and extent of investments during the period create related parties.

Identifying Transactions With Related Parties

.08 The following procedures are intended to provide guidance for identifying material transactions with parties known to be related and for identifying material transactions that may be indicative of the existence of previously undetermined relationships:

a. Provide audit personnel performing segments of the audit or auditing and reporting separately on the accounts of related components of the reporting entity with the names of known related parties so that they may become aware of transactions with such parties during their audits.

b. Review the minutes of meetings of the board of directors and executive or operating committees for information about material transactions authorized or discussed at their meetings.

c. Review proxy and other material filed with the Securities and Exchange Commission and comparable data filed with other regulatory agencies for information about material transactions with related parties.

d. Review conflict-of-interests statements obtained by the company from its management.[5]

e. Review the extent and nature of business transacted with major customers, suppliers, borrowers, and lenders for indications of previously undisclosed relationships.

f. Consider whether transactions are occurring, but are not being given accounting recognition, such as receiving or providing accounting, management or other services at no charge or a major stockholder absorbing corporate expenses.

g. Review accounting records for large, unusual, or nonrecurring transactions or balances, paying particular attention to transactions recognized at or near the end of the reporting period.

h. Review confirmations of compensating balance arrangements for indications that balances are or were maintained for or by related parties.

---

[5] Conflict-of-interests statements are intended to provide the board of directors with information about the existence or nonexistence of relationships between the reporting persons and parties with whom the company transacts business.

i. Review invoices from law firms that have performed regular or special services for the company for indications of the existence of related parties or related party transactions.

j. Review confirmations of loans receivable and payable for indications of guarantees. When guarantees are indicated, determine their nature and the relationships, if any, of the guarantors to the reporting entity.

Examining Identified Related Party Transactions

.09 After identifying related party transactions, the auditor should apply the procedures he considers necessary to obtain satisfaction concerning the purpose, nature, and extent of these transactions and their effect on the financial statements. The procedures should be directed toward obtaining and evaluating sufficient competent evidential matter and should extend beyond inquiry of management. Procedures that should be considered include the following:

a. Obtain an understanding of the business purpose of the transaction.[6]

b. Examine invoices, executed copies of agreements, contracts, and other pertinent documents, such as receiving reports and shipping documents.

c. Determine whether the transaction has been approved by the board of directors or other appropriate officials.

d. Test for reasonableness the compilation of amounts to be disclosed, or considered for disclosure, in the financial statements.

e. Arrange for the audits of intercompany account balances to be performed as of concurrent dates, even if the fiscal years differ, and for the examination of specified, important, and representative related party transactions by the auditors for each of the parties, with appropriate exchange of relevant information.

f. Inspect or confirm and obtain satisfaction concerning the transferability and value of collateral.

.10 When necessary to fully understand a particular transaction, the following procedures, which might not otherwise be deemed necessary to comply with generally accepted auditing standards, should be considered.[7]

a. Confirm transaction amount and terms, including guarantees and other significant data, with the other party or parties to the transaction.

b. Inspect evidence in possession of the other party or parties to the transaction.

---

[6] Until the auditor understands the business sense of material transactions, he cannot complete his audit. If he lacks sufficient specialized knowledge to understand a particular transaction, he should consult with persons who do have the requisite knowledge.

[7] Arrangements for certain procedures should be made or approved in advance by appropriate client officials.

c. Confirm or discuss significant information with intermediaries, such as banks, guarantors, agents, or attorneys, to obtain a better understanding of the transaction.

d. Refer to financial publications, trade journals, credit agencies, and other information sources when there is reason to believe that unfamiliar customers, suppliers, or other business enterprises with which material amounts of business have been transacted may lack substance.

e. With respect to material uncollected balances, guarantees, and other obligations, obtain information about the financial capability of the other party or parties to the transaction. Such information may be obtained from audited financial statements, unaudited financial statements, income tax returns, and reports issued by regulatory agencies, taxing authorities, financial publications, or credit agencies. The auditor should decide on the degree of assurance required and the extent to which available information provides such assurance.

Disclosure

.11 For each material related party transaction (or aggregation of similar transactions) or common ownership or management control relationship for which FASB Statement No. 57 [AC section R36] requires disclosure, the auditor should consider whether he has obtained sufficient competent evidential matter to understand the relationship of the parties and, for related party transactions, the effects of the transaction on the financial statements. He should then evaluate all the information available to him concerning the related party transaction or control relationship and satisfy himself on the basis of his professional judgment that it is adequately disclosed in the financial statements.[8]

.12 Except for routine transactions, it will generally not be possible to determine whether a particular transaction would have taken place if the parties had not been related, or assuming it would have taken place, what the terms and manner of settlement would have been. Accordingly, it is difficult to substantiate representations that a transaction was consummated on terms equivalent to those that prevail in arm's-length transactions.[9] If such a representation is included in the financial statements and the auditor believes that the representation is unsubstantiated by management, he should express a qualified or adverse opinion because of a departure from generally accepted accounting principles, depending on materiality (see section 508.35 and .36).

---

[8] The disclosure standards are contained in FASB Statement No. 57, paragraphs 2 through 4 [AC section R36.102–.104]. Also, see section 431, *Adequacy of Disclosure in Financial Statements*.

[9] FASB Statement No. 57, paragraph 3 [AC section R36.103], states that if representations are made about transactions with related parties, the representations "shall not imply that the related party transactions were consummated on terms equivalent to those that prevail in arm's-length transactions unless such representations can be substantiated."

AU Section 9334*

Related Parties: Auditing Interpretations of Section 334

[1.] Evaluating the Adequacy of Disclosure of Related Party Transactions

[.01–.05] [Withdrawn August, 1983, by SAS No. 45.] (See section 334.)

[2.] Disclosure of Commonly Controlled Parties

[.06–.09] [Withdrawn August, 1983, by SAS No. 45.] (See Section 334.)

[3.] Definition of "Immediate Family"

[.10–.11] [Withdrawn August, 1983, by SAS No. 45.] (See section 334.)

4. Exchange of Information Between the Principal and Other Auditor on Related Parties

.12 *Question*—Section 334, *Related Parties*, paragraphs .04 and .07, states that "during the course of his audit, the auditor should be aware of the possible existence of material related party transactions," and that determining the existence of related party transactions may require the inquiry of the "principal, or other auditors of related entities concerning their knowledge of existing relationships and the extent of management involvement in material transactions." When should that inquiry be made? [Reference changed August, 1983, by issuance of Statement on Auditing Standards No. 45.] (See section 334.)

.13 *Interpretation*—The principal auditor and the other auditor should each obtain from the other the names of known related parties and the other information referred to above. Ordinarily, that exchange of information should be made at an early stage of the audit.

[Issue Date: April, 1979.]

5. Examination of Identified Related Party Transactions with a Component

.14 *Question*—According to section 334.09, once related party transactions have been identified, "the auditor should apply the procedures he considers necessary to obtain satisfaction concerning the purpose, nature and extent of these transactions and their effect on the financial statements." When there is a principal auditor-other auditor relationship, how may the auditors obtain that satisfaction regarding transactions that may involve not only the components[1] they are auditing, but also, other components? [Reference changed August, 1983, by issuance of Statement on Auditing Standards No. 45.] (See section 334.)

---

* [Section number changed August, 1983, to correspond to section 334, *Related Parties*.]

[1] For the purpose of this interpretation, the entities whose separate financial statements collectively comprise the consolidated or other financial statements are referred to as components.

.15 *Interpretation*—Audit procedures may sometimes have to be applied to records of components being audited by the other. One auditor may arrange to perform those procedures himself, or he may request the other to do so.[2] There may be circumstances when there are unusual or complex related party transactions and an auditor believes that access to relevant portions of the other's work papers is essential to his understanding of the effects of those transactions on the financial statements he is auditing. In those circumstances, access ordinarily should be provided.[3]

[Issue Date: April, 1979.]

6. The Nature and Extent of Auditing Procedures for Examining Related Party Transactions

.16 *Question*—Section 334, *Related Parties*, provides general guidance about the types of procedures an auditor might apply to identified related party transactions. How extensive should the auditor's procedures be to examine related party transactions?

.17 *Interpretation*—The auditor's procedures should be sufficient to provide reasonable assurance that related party transactions are adequately disclosed and that identified related party transactions do not contain misstatements that, when aggregated with misstatements in other balances or classes of transactions, could be material to the financial statements taken as a whole. As in examining any other material account balance or class of transactions, the auditor needs to consider audit risk[4] and design and apply appropriate substantive tests to evaluate management's assertions.

.18 The risk associated with management's assertions about related party transactions is often assessed as higher than for many other types of transactions because of the possibility that the parties to the transaction are motivated by reasons other than those that exist for most business transactions.[5]

.19 The higher the auditor's assessment of risk regarding related party transactions, the more extensive or effective the audit tests should be. For example, the auditor's tests regarding valuation of a receivable from an entity under common control might be more extensive than for a trade receivable of the same size because the common parent may be motivated to obscure the substance of the transaction. In assessing the risk of the related party transactions the auditor obtains an understanding of the business purpose of the transactions. Until the auditor understands the business sense of material transactions, he cannot complete his audit. If he lacks sufficient specialized knowledge to obtain that understanding for a particular transaction, he should consult with persons who do have the requisite knowledge. In addition, to un-

---

[2] In this case, the auditor should follow the guidance in the interpretation titled *Specific Procedures Performed by Other Auditors at the Principal Auditor's Request*, section 9543.01–.03.

[3] There is no intention in this interpretation to modify section 543.12c regarding the principal auditor's consideration of review of the other auditor's workpapers when he decides not to make reference to the other auditor.

[4] Audit risk and its components are described in section 312, *Audit Risk and Materiality in Conducting an Audit*.

[5] See section 334.06.

derstand the transaction, or obtain evidence regarding it, the auditor may have to refer to audited or unaudited financial statements of the related party, apply procedures at the related party, or in some cases audit the financial statements of the related party.

.20 *Question*—Section 334, *Related Parties*, paragraph .07, states that specific audit procedures should be applied to determine if related parties exist. That paragraph also suggests some specific audit procedures to identify related parties that the auditor should consider. What other audit procedures for determining the existence of related parties should the auditor consider?

.21 *Interpretation*—The auditor should consider obtaining representations from the entity's senior management and its board of directors about whether they or any other related parties engaged in any transactions with the entity during the period.

[Issue Date: May, 1986.]

---

understanding the transaction or obtain evidence regarding it, the auditor may have to refer to audited or unaudited financial statements of the related party, apply procedures at the related party, or in some cases audit the financial statements of the related party.

.22 *Question*—Section 334, *Related Parties*, paragraph .07, states that specific audit procedures should be applied to determine if related parties exist. What paragraph .08 suggests some specific audit procedures to identify related parties that the auditor should consider. What other audit procedures in determining the existence of related parties should the auditor consider?

.23 *Interpretation*—The auditor should consider obtaining representations from the entity's senior management and its board of directors about whether they or any other related parties engaged in any transactions with the entity during the period.

[Issue Date: May, 1986.]

AU Section 336

Using the Work of a Specialist

(Supersedes SAS No. 11)

Source: SAS No. 73.

See section 9336 for interpretations of this section.

Effective for audits of periods ending on or after December 15, 1994.

Introduction and Applicability

.01 The purpose of this section is to provide guidance to the auditor who uses the work of a specialist in performing an audit in accordance with generally accepted auditing standards. For purposes of this section, a specialist is a person (or firm) possessing special skill or knowledge in a particular field other than accounting or auditing.[1]

.02 Specialists to which this section applies include, but are not limited to, actuaries, appraisers, engineers, environmental consultants, and geologists. This section also applies to attorneys engaged as specialists in situations other than to provide services to a client concerning litigation, claims, or assessments to which section 337, *Inquiry of a Client's Lawyer Concerning Litigation, Claims, and Assessments*, applies. For example, attorneys may be engaged by a client or by the auditor as specialists in a variety of other circumstances, including interpreting the provisions of a contractual agreement.

.03 The guidance in this section is applicable when—

a. Management engages or employs a specialist and the auditor uses that specialist's work as evidential matter in performing substantive tests to evaluate material financial statement assertions.

b. Management engages a specialist employed by the auditor's firm to provide advisory services[2] and the auditor uses that specialist's work as evidential matter in performing substantive tests to evaluate material financial statement assertions.

c. The auditor engages a specialist and uses that specialist's work as evidential matter in performing substantive tests to evaluate material financial statement assertions.

.04 The guidance provided in this section applies to audits of financial statements prepared in conformity with generally accepted accounting principles (GAAP)[3] and to engagements performed under section 623, *Special Reports*, including a comprehensive basis of accounting other than GAAP.

---

[1] In general, the auditor's education, training, and experience enable him or her to be knowledgeable concerning income tax matters and to be competent to assess their presentation in the financial statements.

[2] The auditor should consider the effect, if any, that using the work of a specialist employed by the auditor's firm has on independence.

[3] References in this section to "financial statements" and to "generally accepted accounting principles" include special reports covered under section 623, *Special Reports*.

.05 This section does not apply to situations covered by section 311, *Planning and Supervision*, in which a specialist employed by the auditor's firm participates in the audit.

Decision to Use the Work of a Specialist

.06 The auditor's education and experience enable him or her to be knowledgeable about business matters in general, but the auditor is not expected to have the expertise of a person trained for or qualified to engage in the practice of another profession or occupation. During the audit, however, an auditor may encounter complex or subjective matters potentially material to the financial statements. Such matters may require special skill or knowledge and in the auditor's judgment require using the work of a specialist to obtain competent evidential matter.

.07 Examples of the types of matters that the auditor may decide require him or her to consider using the work of a specialist include, but are not limited to, the following:

a. Valuation (for example, special-purpose inventories, high-technology materials or equipment, pharmaceutical products, complex financial instruments, real estate, restricted securities, works of art, and environmental contingencies)

b. Determination of physical characteristics relating to quantity on hand or condition (for example, quantity or condition of minerals, mineral reserves, or materials stored in stockpiles)

c. Determination of amounts derived by using specialized techniques or methods (for example, actuarial determinations for employee benefits obligations and disclosures, and determinations for insurance loss reserves[4])

d. Interpretation of technical requirements, regulations, or agreements (for example, the potential significance of contracts or other legal documents or legal title to property)

Qualifications and Work of a Specialist

.08 The auditor should consider the following to evaluate the professional qualifications of the specialist in determining that the specialist possesses the necessary skill or knowledge in the particular field:

a. The professional certification, license, or other recognition of the competence of the specialist in his or her field, as appropriate

b. The reputation and standing of the specialist in the views of peers and others familiar with the specialist's capability or performance

c. The specialist's experience in the type of work under consideration

.09 The auditor should obtain an understanding of the nature of the work performed or to be performed by the specialist. This understanding should cover the following:

a. The objectives and scope of the specialist's work

[4] In the specific situation involving the audit of an insurance entity's loss reserves, an outside loss reserve specialist—that is, one who is not an employee or officer of the insurance entity—should be used. When the auditor has the requisite knowledge and experience, the auditor may serve as the loss reserve specialist. (See Statement of Position 92-4, *Auditing Insurance Entities' Loss Reserves*.)

b. The specialist's relationship to the client (see paragraphs .10 and .11)

c. The methods or assumptions used

d. A comparison of the methods or assumptions used with those used in the preceding period

e. The appropriateness of using the specialist's work for the intended purpose[5]

f. The form and content of the specialist's findings that will enable the auditor to make the evaluation described in paragraph .12

Relationship of the Specialist to the Client

.10 The auditor should evaluate the relationship[6] of the specialist to the client, including circumstances that might impair the specialist's objectivity. Such circumstances include situations in which the client has the ability—through employment, ownership, contractual right, family relationship, or otherwise—to directly or indirectly control or significantly influence the specialist.

.11 When a specialist does not have a relationship with the client, the specialist's work usually will provide the auditor with greater assurance of reliability. However, the work of a specialist who has a relationship with the client may be acceptable under certain circumstances. If the specialist has a relationship with the client, the auditor should assess the risk that the specialist's objectivity might be impaired. If the auditor believes the relationship might impair the specialist's objectivity, the auditor should perform additional procedures with respect to some or all of the specialist's assumptions, methods, or findings to determine that the findings are not unreasonable or should engage another specialist for that purpose.

Using the Findings of the Specialist

.12 The appropriateness and reasonableness of methods and assumptions used and their application are the responsibility of the specialist. The auditor should (*a*) obtain an understanding of the methods and assumptions used by the specialist, (*b*) make appropriate tests of data provided to the specialist, taking into account the auditor's assessment of control risk, and (*c*) evaluate whether the specialist's findings support the related assertions in the financial statements. Ordinarily, the auditor would use the work of the specialist unless the auditor's procedures lead him or her to believe the findings are unreasonable in the circumstances. If the auditor believes the findings are unreasonable, he or she should apply additional procedures, which may include obtaining the opinion of another specialist.

Effect of the Specialist's Work on the Auditor's Report

.13 If the auditor determines that the specialist's findings support the related assertions in the financial statements, he or she reasonably may con-

---

[5] In some cases, the auditor may decide it is necessary to contact the specialist to determine that the specialist is aware that his or her work will be used for evaluating the assertions in the financial statements.

[6] The term *relationship* includes, but is not limited to, those situations discussed in section 334, *Related Parties*, footnote 1.

clude that sufficient competent evidential matter has been obtained. If there is a material difference between the specialist's findings and the assertions in the financial statements, he or she should apply additional procedures. If after applying any additional procedures that might be appropriate the auditor is unable to resolve the matter, the auditor should obtain the opinion of another specialist, unless it appears to the auditor that the matter cannot be resolved. A matter that has not been resolved ordinarily will cause the auditor to conclude that he or she should qualify the opinion or disclaim an opinion because the inability to obtain sufficient competent evidential matter as to an assertion of material significance in the financial statements constitutes a scope limitation. (See section 508, *Reports on Audited Financial Statements*, paragraphs .22 and .23.)

.14 The auditor may conclude after performing additional procedures, including possibly obtaining the opinion of another specialist, that the assertions in the financial statements are not in conformity with GAAP. In that event, the auditor should express a qualified or adverse opinion. (See section 508.35, .36, and .41.)

Reference to the Specialist in the Auditor's Report

.15 Except as discussed in paragraph .16, the auditor should not refer to the work or findings of the specialist. Such a reference might be misunderstood to be a qualification of the auditor's opinion or a division of responsibility, neither of which is intended. Further, there may be an inference that the auditor making such reference performed a more thorough audit than an auditor not making such reference.

.16 The auditor may, as a result of the report or findings of the specialist, decide to add explanatory language to his or her standard report or depart from an unqualified opinion. Reference to and identification of the specialist may be made in the auditor's report if the auditor believes such reference will facilitate an understanding of the reason for the explanatory paragraph or the departure from the unqualified opinion.

Effective Date

.17 This section is effective for audits of periods ending on or after December 15, 1994. Early application of the provisions of this section is encouraged.

AU Section 9336

Using the Work of a Specialist: Auditing Interpretations of Section 336

1. The Use of Legal Interpretations As Evidential Matter to Support Management's Assertion That a Transfer of Financial Assets Has Met the Isolation Criterion in Paragraph 9(a) of Financial Accounting Standards Board Statement No. 125

.01 *Introduction*—Financial Accounting Standards Board (FASB) Statement No. 125, *Accounting for Transfers and Servicing of Financial Assets and Extinguishments of Liabilities* [AC section F38], requires that a transferor of financial assets must surrender control over the financial assets to account for the transfer as a sale. Paragraph 9(a) [AC section F38.103] states one of several conditions that must be met to provide evidence of surrender of control:

> The transferred assets have been isolated from the transferor—put presumptively beyond the reach of the transferor and its creditors, even in bankruptcy or other receivership.

Paragraph 23 of FASB Statement No. 125 [AC section F38.111] describes in greater detail the evidence required to support management's assertion that transferred financial assets have been isolated:

> The nature and extent of supporting evidence required for an assertion in financial statements that transferred financial assets have been isolated—put presumptively beyond the reach of the transferor and its creditors, either by a single transaction or a series of transactions taken as a whole—depend on the facts and circumstances. All available evidence that either supports or questions an assertion shall be considered. That consideration includes making judgments about whether the contract or circumstances permit the transferor to revoke the transfer. It also may include making judgments about the kind of bankruptcy or other receivership into which a transferor or special-purpose entity might be placed, whether a transfer of financial assets would likely be deemed a true sale at law, whether the transferor is affiliated with the transferee, and other factors pertinent under applicable law. Derecognition of transferred assets is appropriate only if the available evidence provides reasonable assurance that the transferred assets would be beyond the reach of the powers of a bankruptcy trustee or other receiver for the transferor or any of its affiliates, except for an affiliate that is a qualifying special-purpose entity designed to make remote the possibility that it would enter bankruptcy or other receivership.

A determination about whether the isolation criterion has been met to support a conclusion regarding surrender of control is largely a matter of law. This aspect of surrender of control, therefore, is assessed primarily from a legal perspective.

.02 *Effective Date and Applicability*—This interpretation is effective for auditing procedures related to transactions required to be accounted for under FASB Statement No. 125 [AC section F38] that are entered into on or after January 1, 1998. This interpretation does not apply to transfers of financial assets by banks for which a receiver, if appointed, would be the Federal Deposit Insurance Corporation or its designee as referred to in paragraph 58 of FASB Statement No. 125 [AC section F38.142].

.03 *Question*—What should the auditor consider in determining whether to use the work of a legal specialist[1] to obtain persuasive evidence to support management's assertion that a transfer of financial assets meets the isolation criterion of FASB Statement No. 125 [AC section F38]?

.04 *Interpretation*—Section 336, *Using the Work of a Specialist*, paragraph .06, states that "during the audit . . . an auditor may encounter complex or subjective matters potentially material to the financial statements. Such matters may require special skill or knowledge and in the auditor's judgment require using the work of a specialist to obtain competent evidential matter."

.05 Use of a legal specialist may not be necessary to obtain competent evidential matter to support management's assertion that the isolation criterion is met in certain situations, such as when there is a routine transfer of financial assets that does not result in any continuing involvement by the transferor (e.g., the transferor does not provide full or limited recourse, retain servicing of the transferred assets, retain any other interest in the transferred assets, or have an equity interest in the transferee).

.06 Many transfers of financial assets involve complex legal structures, continuing involvement by the transferor, or other legal issues that, in the auditor's judgment, make it difficult to determine whether the isolation criterion is met. In these situations, use of a legal specialist usually is necessary. A legal specialist formulating an opinion as to whether a transfer isolates the transferred assets beyond the reach of the transferor and its creditors may consider, among other things, the structure of the transaction taken as a whole, the nature of the transferor's continuing involvement, if any, the type of insolvency or other receivership proceedings to which the transferor might be subject if it fails, and other factors pertinent under applicable law.

.07 If a legal opinion is used as evidence to support the accounting conclusion related to multiple transfers under a single structure, and such transfers occur over an extended period of time under that structure, the auditor should evaluate the need for management to obtain periodic updates of that opinion to confirm that there have been no subsequent changes in relevant law that may change the applicability of the previous opinion to such transfers.[2]

.08 If management's assertion with respect to a new transaction is that the transaction structure is the same as a prior structure for which a legal opinion that complies with this interpretation was used as evidence to support an assertion that the transfer of assets met the isolation criterion, the auditor should evaluate the need for management to obtain an update of that opinion to confirm that there have been no changes in relevant law or in the pertinent facts of the transaction that may affect the applicability of the previous opinion to the new transaction.

---

[1] Client's internal or external attorney who is knowledgeable about relevant sections of the U.S. Bankruptcy Code and other federal, state, or foreign law, as applicable.

[2] For structures that include ongoing transfers, such as revolving structures, this interpretation applies to transfers occurring on or after January 1, 1998.

.09 *Question*—If the auditor determines that the use of a legal specialist is required, what should he or she consider in assessing the adequacy of the legal opinion?

.10 *Interpretation*—In assessing the adequacy of the legal opinion, the auditor should consider whether the legal specialist has experience with relevant matters, including knowledge of the U.S. Bankruptcy Code, and other federal, state, or foreign law, as applicable, as well as knowledge of the transaction upon which management's assertion is based. The auditor should obtain an understanding of the assumptions that are used by the legal specialist, and make appropriate tests of any information that management provides to the legal specialist and upon which the specialist indicates it relied.

.11 The auditor also should consider the form and content of the documentation that the legal specialist provides and evaluate whether the legal specialist's findings support management's assertions with respect to the isolation criterion. Section 336.13 states that "if the auditor determines that the specialist's findings support the related assertions in the financial statements, he or she reasonably may conclude that sufficient competent evidential matter has been obtained." FASB Statement No. 125's [AC section F38] requirement regarding reasonable assurance that the transferred assets would be isolated provides the basis for what auditors should consider in evaluating the work of a legal specialist.

.12 Findings of a legal specialist that relate to the isolation of transferred financial assets are often in the form of a reasoned legal opinion that is restricted to particular facts and circumstances relevant to the specific transaction. The reasoning of such opinion may rely upon analogy to legal precedents that may not involve facts and circumstances that are comparable to that specific transaction.

.13 An example of the conclusions in a legal opinion for an entity that is subject to the U.S. Bankruptcy Code that provides persuasive evidence, in the absence of contradictory evidence, to support management's assertion that the transferred financial assets have been put presumptively beyond the reach of the entity and its creditors, even in bankruptcy or other receivership, follows:

> "*We believe (or it is our opinion) that* in a properly presented and argued case, as a legal matter, in the event the Seller were to become a Debtor, the transfer of the Financial Assets from the Seller to the Purchaser *would be considered to be a sale* (or a true sale) of the Financial Assets from the Seller to the Purchaser and not a loan and, accordingly, the Financial Assets and the proceeds thereof transferred to the Purchaser by the Seller in accordance with the Purchase Agreement would not be deemed to be property of the Seller's estate for purposes of (the relevant sections) of the U.S. Bankruptcy Code. . . .
>
> * * *
>
> ". . . Based upon the assumptions of fact and the discussion set forth above, and on a reasoned analysis of analogous case law, we are of the opinion that in a properly presented and argued case, as a legal matter, in a proceeding under the U.S. Bankruptcy Code,[3] in which the Seller is a Debtor, a court would not grant an order consolidating the assets and liabilities of the Purchaser with

[3] For an entity subject to additional regulation (e.g., a broker-dealer subject to the Securities Investor Protection Act), the legal opinion also generally should address the effect of such regulation and the policies of the regulators implementing such regulations (e.g., the Securities Investor Protection Corporation).

those of the Seller in a case involving the insolvency of the Seller under the doctrine of substantive consolidation."[4]

In the case of a transferor that is not entitled to become a debtor under the U.S. Bankruptcy Code, a legal opinion regarding whether the isolation criterion is met would consider whether isolation is satisfactorily achieved under the insolvency or receivership laws that apply to the transferor.

.14 A legal opinion that includes an inadequate opinion or a disclaimer of opinion, or that effectively limits the scope of the opinion to facts and circumstances that are not applicable to the transaction, does not provide persuasive evidence to support the entity's assertion that the transferred assets have been put presumptively beyond the reach of the transferor and its creditors, even in bankruptcy or other receivership. Likewise, a legal letter that includes conclusions that are expressed using some of the following language would not provide persuasive evidence that a transfer of financial assets has met the isolation criterion of FASB Statement No. 125 [AC section F38] (see paragraphs .17 and .18 of this interpretation):

- "We are unable to express an opinion . . ."
- "It is our opinion, based upon limited facts . . ."
- "We are of the view . . ." or "it appears . . ."
- "There is a reasonable basis to conclude that . . ."
- "In our opinion, the transfer would *either* be a sale *or* . . ."[5]
- "In our opinion, there is a reasonable possibility . . ."
- "In our opinion, the transfer *should* be considered a sale . . ."
- "It is our opinion that the company will be able to assert meritorious arguments . . ."
- "In our opinion, it is more likely than not . . ."
- "In our opinion, the transfer would *presumptively* be . . ."
- "In our opinion, it is probable that . . ."

Furthermore, conclusions about hypothetical transactions may not be relevant to the transaction that is the subject of management's assertions. Section 326, *Evidential Matter*, paragraph .21, states that "to be competent, evidence, regardless of its form, must be both valid and relevant." Additionally, conclusions about hypothetical transactions may not contemplate all of the facts and circumstances or the provisions in the agreements of the transaction that is the subject of management's assertions, and generally would not provide persuasive evidence.[6]

---

[4] The second paragraph in the sample opinion addressing non-consolidation is not applicable in all cases and may, therefore, not be included. The auditor should evaluate whether such exclusion is appropriate. Further, when an affiliate of the transferor has entered into transactions with the transferee that could affect the issue of substantive consolidation, the opinion should address such issue.

[5] Certain transferors are subject *only* to receivership (and not to proceedings under the U.S. Bankruptcy Code) under laws that do not allow a receiver to reach assets in which a security interest has been granted. In such circumstances, an opinion that concludes that the transfer would either be a sale or a grant of a security interest that puts the transferred assets beyond the reach of such receiver would provide persuasive evidence.

[6] For example, a memorandum of law from a legal specialist usually analyzes (and may make conclusions about) a transaction that may be completed subsequently. Such memorandum generally would not provide persuasive evidence unless the conclusions conform with this interpretation and a legal specialist opines that such conclusions apply to a completed transaction that is the subject of management's assertion.

.15 *Question*—Are legal opinions that restrict the use of the opinion to the client, or to third parties other than the auditor, acceptable audit evidence?

.16 *Interpretation*—No. Footnote 5 to section 336.09 states: "In some cases, the auditor may decide it is necessary to contact the specialist to determine that the specialist is aware that his or her work will be used for evaluating the assertions in the financial statements." Given the importance of the legal opinion to the assertion in this case, and the precision that legal specialists use in drafting such opinions, an auditor should not use as evidence a legal opinion that he or she deems otherwise adequate if the letter restricts use of the findings expressed therein to the client or to third parties other than the auditor. In that event, the auditor should request that the client obtain the legal specialist's written permission for the auditor to use the opinion for the purpose of evaluating management's assertion that a transfer of financial assets meets the isolation criterion of FASB Statement No. 125 [AC section F38].

.17 *Question*—If the auditor determines that it is appropriate to use the work of a legal specialist, and either the resulting legal response does not provide persuasive evidence that a transfer of assets has met the isolation criterion, or the legal specialist does not grant permission for the auditor to use a legal opinion that is restricted to the client or to third parties other than the auditor, what other steps might an auditor consider?

.18 *Interpretation*—When other relevant evidential matter exists, the auditor should consider it before reaching a conclusion about the appropriateness of management's accounting for a transfer.[7] However, since the isolation aspect of surrender of control is assessed primarily from a legal perspective, the auditor usually will not be able to obtain persuasive evidence in a form other than a legal opinion. In the absence of persuasive evidence that a transfer has met the isolation criterion, derecognition of the transferred assets is not in conformity with generally accepted accounting principles and the auditor should consider the need to express a qualified or adverse opinion in accordance with section 508, *Reports on Audited Financial Statements*, paragraphs .35 through .60. However, if permission for the auditor to use a legal opinion that he or she deems otherwise adequate is not granted, this would be a scope limitation and the auditor should consider the need to express a qualified opinion or to disclaim an opinion in accordance with section 508.22–.26 and .61–.63.

[Issue Date: February 1998.]

---

[7] See section 336.13 as to additional procedures that may be applied.

AU Section 337

Inquiry of a Client's Lawyer Concerning Litigation, Claims, and Assessments[1]

Source: SAS No. 12.

See section 9337 for interpretations of this section.

Issue date, unless otherwise indicated: January, 1976.

.01 This section provides guidance on the procedures an independent auditor should consider for identifying litigation, claims, and assessments and for satisfying himself as to the financial accounting and reporting for such matters when he is performing an audit in accordance with generally accepted auditing standards.

Accounting Considerations

.02 Management is responsible for adopting policies and procedures to identify, evaluate, and account for litigation, claims, and assessments as a basis for the preparation of financial statements in conformity with generally accepted accounting principles.

.03 The standards of financial accounting and reporting for loss contingencies, including those arising from litigation, claims, and assessments, are set forth in Statement of Financial Accounting Standards No. 5 [AC section C59], *Accounting for Contingencies*.[2]

Auditing Considerations

.04 With respect to litigation, claims, and assessments, the independent auditor should obtain evidential matter relevant to the following factors:

a. The existence of a condition, situation, or set of circumstances indicating an uncertainty as to the possible loss to an entity arising from litigation, claims, and assessments.

b. The period in which the underlying cause for legal action occurred.

c. The degree of probability of an unfavorable outcome.

d. The amount or range of potential loss.

---

[1] This section supersedes the commentary, "Lawyers' Letters," January 1974 (section 1001), and auditing interpretations of section 560.12 on lawyers' letters, January 1975 (section 9560.01–.26). It amends section 560.12(*d*) to read as follows: "Inquire of client's legal counsel concerning litigation, claims, and assessments (see section 337)."

[2] Pertinent portions are reprinted in Exhibit I, section 337B. FASB Statement No. 5 [AC section C59], also describes the standards of financial accounting and reporting for gain contingencies. The auditor's procedures with respect to gain contingencies are parallel to those described in this SAS for loss contingencies.

Audit Procedures

.05 Since the events or conditions that should be considered in the financial accounting for and reporting of litigation, claims, and assessments are matters within the direct knowledge and, often, control of management of an entity, management is the primary source of information about such matters. Accordingly, the independent auditor's procedures with respect to litigation, claims, and assessments should include the following:

a. Inquire of and discuss with management the policies and procedures adopted for identifying, evaluating, and accounting for litigation, claims, and assessments.

b. Obtain from management a description and evaluation of litigation, claims, and assessments that existed at the date of the balance sheet being reported on, and during the period from the balance sheet date to the date the information is furnished, including an identification of those matters referred to legal counsel, and obtain assurances from management, ordinarily in writing, that they have disclosed all such matters required to be disclosed by Statement of Financial Accounting Standards No. 5 [AC section C59].

c. Examine documents in the client's possession concerning litigation, claims, and assessments, including correspondence and invoices from lawyers.

d. Obtain assurance from management, ordinarily in writing, that it has disclosed all unasserted claims that the lawyer has advised them are probable of assertion and must be disclosed in accordance with Statement of Financial Accounting Standards No. 5 [AC section C59]. Also the auditor, with the client's permission, should inform the lawyer that the client has given the auditor this assurance. This client representation may be communicated by the client in the inquiry letter or by the auditor in a separate letter.[3]

.06 An auditor ordinarily does not possess legal skills and, therefore, cannot make legal judgments concerning information coming to his attention. Accordingly, the auditor should request the client's management to send a letter of inquiry to those lawyers with whom management consulted concerning litigation, claims, and assessments.

.07 The audit normally includes certain other procedures undertaken for different purposes that might also disclose litigation, claims, and assessments. Examples of such procedures are as follows:

a. Reading minutes of meetings of stockholders, directors, and appropriate committees held during and subsequent to the period being audited.

b. Reading contracts, loan agreements, leases, and correspondence from taxing or other governmental agencies, and similar documents.

---

[3] An example of a separate letter is as follows: We are writing to inform you that (name of company) has represented to us that (except as set forth below and excluding any such matters listed in the letter of audit inquiry) there are no unasserted possible claims that you have advised are probable of assertion and must be disclosed in accordance with Statement of Financial Accounting Standards No. 5 [AC section C59] in its financial statements at (balance sheet date) and for the (period) then ended. (List unasserted possible claims, if any.) Such a letter should be signed and sent by the auditor.

c. Obtaining information concerning guarantees from bank confirmation forms.

d. Inspecting other documents for possible guarantees by the client.

Inquiry of a Client's Lawyer[4]

.08 A letter of audit inquiry to the client's lawyer is the auditor's primary means of obtaining corroboration of the information furnished by management concerning litigation, claims, and assessments.[5] Evidential matter obtained from the client's inside general counsel or legal department may provide the auditor with the necessary corroboration. However, evidential matter obtained from inside counsel is not a substitute for information outside counsel refuses to furnish.

.09 The matters that should be covered in a letter of audit inquiry include, but are not limited to, the following:

a. Identification of the company, including subsidiaries, and the date of the audit.

b. A list prepared by management (or a request by management that the lawyer prepare a list) that describes and evaluates pending or threatened litigation, claims, and assessments with respect to which the lawyer has been engaged and to which he has devoted substantive attention on behalf of the company in the form of legal consultation or representation.

c. A list prepared by management that describes and evaluates unasserted claims and assessments that management considers to be probable of assertion, and that, if asserted, would have at least a reasonable possibility of an unfavorable outcome, with respect to which the lawyer has been engaged and to which he has devoted substantive attention on behalf of the company in the form of legal consultation or representation.

d. As to each matter listed in item *b*, a request that the lawyer either furnish the following information or comment on those matters as to which his views may differ from those stated by management, as appropriate:

(1) A description of the nature of the matter, the progress of the case to date, and the action the company intends to take (for example, to contest the matter vigorously or to seek an out-of-court settlement).

(2) An evaluation of the likelihood of an unfavorable outcome and an estimate, if one can be made, of the amount or range of potential loss.

(3) With respect to a list prepared by management, an identification of the omission of any pending or threatened litigation, claims, and assessments or a statement that the list of such matters is complete.

---

[4] An illustrative inquiry letter to legal counsel is contained in the Appendix (section 337A).

[5] It is not intended that the lawyer be requested to undertake a reconsideration of all matters upon which he was consulted during the period under audit for the purpose of determining whether he can form a conclusion regarding the probability of assertion of any possible claim inherent in any of the matters so considered.

e. As to each matter listed in item *c*, a request that the lawyer comment on those matters as to which his views concerning the description or evaluation of the matter may differ from those stated by management.

f. A statement by the client that the client understands that whenever, in the course of performing legal services for the client with respect to a matter recognized to involve an unasserted possible claim or assessment that may call for financial statement disclosure, the lawyer has formed a professional conclusion that the client should disclose or consider disclosure concerning such possible claim or assessment, the lawyer, as a matter of professional responsibility to the client, will so advise the client and will consult with the client concerning the question of such disclosure and the applicable requirements of Statement of Financial Accounting Standards No. 5 [AC section C59].

g. A request that the lawyer confirm whether the understanding described in item *f* is correct.

h. A request that the lawyer specifically identify the nature of and reasons for any limitation on his response.

Inquiry need not be made concerning matters that are not considered material, provided the client and the auditor have reached an understanding on the limits of materiality for this purpose.

.10 In special circumstances, the auditor may obtain a response concerning matters covered by the audit inquiry letter in a conference, which offers an opportunity for a more detailed discussion and explanation than a written reply. A conference may be appropriate when the evaluation of the need for accounting for or disclosure of litigation, claims, and assessments involves such matters as the evaluation of the effect of legal advice concerning unsettled points of law, the effect of uncorroborated information, or other complex judgments. The auditor should appropriately document conclusions reached concerning the need for accounting for or disclosure of litigation, claims, and assessments.

.11 In some circumstances, a lawyer may be required by his Code of Professional Responsibility to resign his engagement if his advice concerning financial accounting and reporting for litigation, claims, and assessments is disregarded by the client. When the auditor is aware that a client has changed lawyers or that a lawyer engaged by the client has resigned, the auditor should consider the need for inquiries concerning the reasons the lawyer is no longer associated with the client.

Limitations on the Scope of a Lawyer's Response[6]

.12 A lawyer may appropriately limit his response to matters to which he has given substantive attention in the form of legal consultation or representation. Also, a lawyer's response may be limited to matters that are consid-

---

[6] The American Bar Association has approved a "Statement of Policy Regarding Lawyers' Responses to Auditors' Requests for Information," which explains the concerns of lawyers and the nature of the limitations an auditor is likely to encounter. That Statement of Policy is reprinted as Exhibit II (section 337C) for the convenience of readers, but is not an integral part of this Statement.

ered individually or collectively material to the financial statements, provided the lawyer and auditor have reached an understanding on the limits of materiality for this purpose. Such limitations are not limitations on the scope of the audit.

.13 A lawyer's refusal to furnish the information requested in an inquiry letter either in writing or orally (see paragraphs .09 and .10) would be a limitation on the scope of the audit sufficient to preclude an unqualified opinion (see section 508.22 and .23).[7] A lawyer's response to such an inquiry and the procedures set forth in paragraph .05 provide the auditor with sufficient evidential matter to satisfy himself concerning the accounting for and reporting of pending and threatened litigation, claims and assessments. The auditor obtains sufficient evidential matter to satisfy himself concerning reporting for those unasserted claims and assessments required to be disclosed in financial statements from the foregoing procedures and the lawyer's specific acknowledgement of his responsibility to his client in respect of disclosure obligations (see paragraph .09*g*). This approach with respect to unasserted claims and assessments is necessitated by the public interest in protecting the confidentiality of lawyer-client communications.

Other Limitations on a Lawyer's Response

.14 A lawyer may be unable to respond concerning the likelihood of an unfavorable outcome of litigation, claims, and assessments or the amount or range of potential loss, because of inherent uncertainties. Factors influencing the likelihood of an unfavorable outcome may sometimes not be within a lawyer's competence to judge; historical experience of the entity in similar litigation or the experience of other entities may not be relevant or available; and the amount of the possible loss frequently may vary widely at different stages of litigation. Consequently, a lawyer may not be able to form a conclusion with respect to such matters. In such circumstances, the auditor ordinarily will conclude that the financial statements are affected by an uncertainty concerning the outcome of a future event which is not susceptible of reasonable estimation, and should look to the guidance in section 508.45 through .49 to determine the effect, if any, of the lawyer's response on the auditor's report. [Revised, February 1997, to reflect conforming changes necessary due to the issuance of Statement on Auditing Standards No. 79.]

---

[7] A refusal to respond should be distinguished from an inability to form a conclusion with respect to certain matters of judgment (see paragraph .14). Also, lawyers outside the United States sometimes follow practices at variance with those contemplated by this section to the extent that different procedures from those outlined herein may be necessary. In such circumstances, the auditor should exercise judgment in determining whether alternative procedures are adequate to comply with the requirements of this section.

AU Section 337A

Appendix—Illustrative Audit Inquiry Letter to Legal Counsel

Source: SAS No. 12.

Issue date, unless otherwise indicated: January, 1976.

.01 In connection with an audit of our financial statements at (balance sheet date) and for the (period) then ended, management of the Company has prepared, and furnished to our auditors (name and address of auditors), a description and evaluation of certain contingencies, including those set forth below involving matters with respect to which you have been engaged and to which you have devoted substantive attention on behalf of the Company in the form of legal consultation or representation. These contingencies are regarded by management of the Company as material for this purpose (management may indicate a materiality limit if an understanding has been reached with the auditor). Your response should include matters that existed at (balance sheet date) and during the period from that date to the date of your response.

Pending or Threatened Litigation (excluding unasserted claims)

[Ordinarily the information would include the following: (1) the nature of the litigation, (2) the progress of the case to date, (3) how management is responding or intends to respond to the litigation (for example, to contest the case vigorously or to seek an out-of-court settlement), and (4) an evaluation of the likelihood of an unfavorable outcome and an estimate, if one can be made, of the amount or range of potential loss.] Please furnish to our auditors such explanation, if any, that you consider necessary to supplement the foregoing information, including an explanation of those matters as to which your views may differ from those stated and an identification of the omission of any pending or threatened litigation, claims, and assessments or a statement that the list of such matters is complete.

Unasserted Claims and Assessments (considered by management to be probable of assertion, and that, if asserted, would have at least a reasonable possibility of an unfavorable outcome)

[Ordinarily management's information would include the following: (1) the nature of the matter, (2) how management intends to respond if the claim is asserted, and (3) an evaluation of the likelihood of an unfavorable outcome and an estimate, if one can be made, of the amount or range of potential loss.] Please furnish to our auditors such explanation, if any, that you consider necessary to supplement the foregoing information, including an explanation of those matters as to which your views may differ from those stated.

We understand that whenever, in the course of performing legal services for us with respect to a matter recognized to involve an unasserted possible claim or assessment that may call for financial statement disclosure, if you have formed a professional conclusion that we should disclose or consider disclosure concerning such possible claim or assessment, as a matter of professional responsibility to us, you will so advise us and will consult with us concerning the question of such disclosure and the applicable requirements of Statement of Financial Accounting Standards No. 5. Please specifically confirm to our auditors that our understanding is correct.

Please specifically identify the nature of and reasons for any limitation on your response.

[The auditor may request the client to inquire about additional matters, for example, unpaid or unbilled charges or specified information on certain contractually assumed obligations of the company, such as guarantees of indebtedness of others.]

AU Section 337B

Exhibit I—Excerpts from Statement of Financial Accounting Standards No. 5: Accounting for Contingencies

Source: SAS No. 12.

March, 1975.

The following excerpts are reprinted with the permission of the Financial Accounting Standards Board.

Introduction

1. For the purpose of this Statement, a contingency is defined as an existing condition, situation, or set of circumstances involving uncertainty as to possible gain (hereinafter a "gain contingency") or loss[1] (hereinafter a "loss contingency") to an enterprise that will ultimately be resolved when one or more future events occur or fail to occur. Resolution of the uncertainty may confirm the acquisition of an asset or the reduction of a liability or the loss or impairment of an asset or the incurrence of a liability. . . .

3. When a loss contingency exists, the likelihood that the future event or events will confirm the loss or impairment of an asset or the incurrence of a liability can range from probable to remote. This Statement uses the terms *probable*, *reasonably possible*, and *remote* to identify three areas within that range, as follows:

a. *Probable.* The future event or events are likely to occur.

b. *Reasonably possible.* The chance of the future event or events occurring is more than remote but less than likely.

c. *Remote.* The chance of the future event or events occurring is slight. . . .

Standards of Financial Accounting and Reporting

Accrual of Loss Contingencies

8. An estimated loss from a loss contingency (as defined in paragraph 1) shall be accrued by a charge to income[3] if *both* of the following conditions are met:

a. Information available prior to issuance of the financial statements indicates that it is probable that an asset had been impaired or a liability had been incurred at the date of the financial statements.[4]

---

[1] The term *loss* is used for convenience to include many charges against income that are commonly referred to as *expenses* and others that are commonly referred to as *losses*.

[3] [Superseded, effective for financial statements for fiscal years beginning after October 15, 1977, by FASB Statement No. 16.]

[4] *Date of the financial statements* means the end of the most recent accounting period for which financial statements are being presented.

It is implicit in this condition that it must be probable that one or more future events will occur confirming the fact of the loss.

b. The amount of loss can be reasonably estimated.

Disclosure of Loss Contingencies

9. Disclosure of the nature of an accrual[5] made pursuant to the provisions of paragraph 8, and in some circumstances the amount accrued, may be necessary for the financial statements not to be misleading.

10. If no accrual is made for a loss contingency because one or both of the conditions in paragraph 8 are not met, or if an exposure to loss exists in excess of the amount accrued pursuant to the provisions of paragraph 8, disclosure of the contingency shall be made when there is at least a reasonable possibility that a loss or an additional loss may have been incurred.[6] The disclosure shall indicate the nature of the contingency and shall give an estimate of the possible loss or range of loss or state that such an estimate cannot be made. Disclosure is not required of a loss contingency involving an unasserted claim or assessment when there has been no manifestation by a potential claimant of an awareness of a possible claim or assessment unless it is considered probable that a claim will be asserted and there is a reasonable possibility that the outcome will be unfavorable.

11. After the date of an enterprise's financial statements but before those financial statements are issued, information may become available indicating that an asset was impaired or a liability was incurred after the date of the financial statements or that there is at least a reasonable possibility that an asset was impaired or a liability was incurred after that date. The information may relate to a loss contingency that existed at the date of the financial statements, e.g., an asset that was not insured at the date of the financial statements. On the other hand, the information may relate to a loss contingency that did not exist at the date of the financial statements, e.g., threat of expropriation of assets after the date of the financial statements or the filing for bankruptcy by an enterprise whose debt was guaranteed after the date of the financial statements. In none of the cases cited in this paragraph was an asset impaired or a liability incurred at the date of the financial statements, and the condition for accrual in paragraph 8(*a*) is, therefore, not met. Disclosure of those kinds of losses or loss contingencies may be necessary, however, to keep the financial statements from being misleading. If disclosure is deemed necessary, the financial statements shall indicate the nature of the loss or loss contingency and give an estimate of the amount or range of loss or possible loss or state that such an estimate cannot be made. Occasionally, in the case of a loss arising after the date of the financial statements where the amount of asset impairment or liability incurrence can be reasonably estimated, disclosure may best be made by supplementing the historical financial statements with pro forma financial data giving effect to the loss as if it had occurred at the date of

---

[5] Terminology used shall be descriptive of the nature of the accrual (see paragraphs 57–64 of *Accounting Terminology Bulletin No. 1*, "Review and Resume").

[6] For example, disclosure shall be made of any loss contingency that meets the condition in paragraph 8(*a*) but that is not accrued because the amount of loss cannot be reasonably estimated (paragraph 8(*b*)). Disclosure is also required of some loss contingencies that do not meet the condition in paragraph 8(*a*)—namely, those contingencies for which there is a *reasonable possibility* that a loss may have been incurred even though information may not indicate that it is *probable* that an asset had been impaired or a liability had been incurred at the date of the financial statements.

the financial statements. It may be desirable to present pro forma statements, usually a balance sheet only, in columnar form on the face of the historical financial statements. . . .

Litigation, Claims, and Assessments

33. The following factors, among others, must be considered in determining whether accrual and/or disclosure is required with respect to pending or threatened litigation and actual or possible claims and assessments:

a. The period in which the underlying cause (i.e., the cause for action) of the pending or threatened litigation or of the actual or possible claim or assessment occurred.

b. The degree of probability of an unfavorable outcome.

c. The ability to make a reasonable estimate of the amount of loss.

34. As a condition for accrual of a loss contingency, paragraph 8(*a*) requires that information available prior to the issuance of financial statements indicate that it is probable that an asset had been impaired or a liability had been incurred at the date of the financial statements. Accordingly, accrual would clearly be inappropriate for litigation, claims, or assessments whose underlying cause is an event or condition occurring after the date of financial statements but before those financial statements are issued, for example, a suit for damages alleged to have been suffered as a result of an accident that occurred after the date of the financial statements. Disclosure may be required, however, by paragraph 11.

35. On the other hand, accrual may be appropriate for litigation, claims, or assessments whose underlying cause is an event occurring on or before the date of an enterprise's financial statements even if the enterprise does not become aware of the existence or possibility of the lawsuit, claim, or assessment until after the date of the financial statements. If those financial statements have not been issued, accrual of a loss related to the litigation, claim, or assessment would be required if the probability of loss is such that the condition in paragraph 8(*a*) is met and the amount of loss can be reasonably estimated.

36. If the underlying cause of the litigation, claim, or assessment is an event occurring before the date of an enterprise's financial statements, the probability of an outcome unfavorable to the enterprise must be assessed to determine whether the condition in paragraph 8(*a*) is met. Among the factors that should be considered are the nature of the litigation, claim, or assessment, the progress of the case (including progress after the date of the financial statements but before those statements are issued), the opinions or views of legal counsel and other advisers, the experience of the enterprise in similar cases, the experience of other enterprises, and any decision of the enterprise's management as to how the enterprise intends to respond to the lawsuit, claim, or assessment (for example, a decision to contest the case vigorously or a decision to seek an out-of-court settlement). The fact that legal counsel is unable to express an opinion that the outcome will be favorable to the enterprise should not necessarily be interpreted to mean that the condition for accrual of a loss in paragraph 8(*a*) is met.

37. The filing of a suit or formal assertion of a claim or assessment does not automatically indicate that accrual of a loss may be appropriate. The degree of probability of an unfavorable outcome must be assessed. The condition for accrual in paragraph 8(*a*) would be met if an unfavorable outcome is determined

to be probable. If an unfavorable outcome is determined to be reasonably possible but not probable, or if the amount of loss cannot be reasonably estimated, accrual would be inappropriate, but disclosure would be required by paragraph 10 of this Statement.

38. With respect to unasserted claims and assessments, an enterprise must determine the degree of probability that a suit may be filed or a claim or assessment may be asserted and the possibility of an unfavorable outcome. For example, a catastrophe, accident, or other similar physical occurrence predictably engenders claims for redress, and in such circumstances their assertion may be probable; similarly, an investigation of an enterprise by a governmental agency, if enforcement proceedings have been or are likely to be instituted, is often followed by private claims for redress, and the probability of their assertion and the possibility of loss should be considered in each case. By way of further example, an enterprise may believe there is a possibility that it has infringed on another enterprise's patent rights, but the enterprise owning the patent rights has not indicated an intention to take any action and has not even indicated an awareness of the possible infringement. In that case, a judgment must first be made as to whether the assertion of a claim is probable. If the judgment is that assertion is not probable, no accrual or disclosure would be required. On the other hand, if the judgment is that assertion is probable, then a second judgment must be made as to the degree of probability of an unfavorable outcome. If an unfavorable outcome is probable and the amount of loss can be reasonably estimated, accrual of a loss is required by paragraph 8. If an unfavorable outcome is probable but the amount of loss cannot be reasonably estimated, accrual would not be appropriate, but disclosure would be required by paragraph 10. If an unfavorable outcome is reasonably possible but not probable, disclosure would be required by paragraph 10.

39. As a condition for accrual of a loss contingency, paragraph 8(*b*) requires that the amount of loss can be reasonably estimated. In some cases, it may be determined that a loss was incurred because an unfavorable outcome of the litigation, claim, or assessment is probable (thus satisfying the condition in paragraph 8(*a*)), but the range of possible loss is wide. For example, an enterprise may be litigating an income tax matter. In preparation for the trial, it may determine that, based on recent decisions involving one aspect of the litigation, it is probable that it will have to pay additional taxes of $2 million. Another aspect of the litigation may, however, be open to considerable interpretation, and depending on the interpretation by the court the enterprise may have to pay taxes of $8 million over and above the $2 million. In that case, paragraph 8 requires accrual of the $2 million if that is considered a reasonable estimate of the loss. Paragraph 10 requires disclosure of the additional exposure to loss if there is a reasonable possibility that additional taxes will be paid. Depending on the circumstances, paragraph 9 may require disclosure of the $2 million that was accrued.

AU Section 337C

Exhibit II—American Bar Association Statement of Policy Regarding Lawyers' Responses to Auditors' Requests for Information

Source: SAS No. 12.

Preamble

The public interest in protecting the confidentiality of lawyer-client communications is fundamental. The American legal, political and economic systems depend heavily upon voluntary compliance with the law and upon ready access to a respected body of professionals able to interpret and advise on the law. The expanding complexity of our laws and governmental regulations increases the need for prompt, specific and unhampered lawyer-client communication. The benefits of such communication and early consultation underlie the strict statutory and ethical obligations of the lawyer to preserve the confidences and secrets of the client, as well as the long-recognized testimonial privilege for lawyer-client communication.

Both the Code of Professional Responsibility and the cases applying the evidentiary privilege recognize that the privilege against disclosure can be knowingly and voluntarily waived by the client. It is equally clear that disclosure to a third party may result in loss of the "confidentiality" essential to maintain the privilege. Disclosure to a third party of the lawyer-client communication on a particular subject may also destroy the privilege as to other communications on that subject. Thus, the mere disclosure by the lawyer to the outside auditor, with due client consent, of the substance of communications between the lawyer and client may significantly impair the client's ability in other contexts to maintain the confidentiality of such communications.

Under the circumstances a policy of audit procedure which requires clients to give consent and authorize lawyers to respond to general inquiries and disclose information to auditors concerning matters which have been communicated in confidence is essentially destructive of free and open communication and early consultation between lawyer and client. The institution of such a policy would inevitably discourage management from discussing potential legal problems with counsel for fear that such discussion might become public and precipitate a loss to or possible liability of the business enterprise and its stockholders that might otherwise never materialize.

It is also recognized that our legal, political and economic systems depend to an important extent on public confidence in published financial statements.

Note: This document, in the form herein set forth, was approved by the Board of Governors of the American Bar Association in December 1975, which official action permitted its release to lawyers and accountants as the standard recommended by the American Bar Association for the lawyer's response to letters of audit inquiry.

To meet this need the accounting profession must adopt and adhere to standards and procedures that will command confidence in the auditing process. It is not, however, believed necessary, or sound public policy, to intrude upon the confidentiality of the lawyer-client relationship in order to command such confidence. On the contrary, the objective of fair disclosure in financial statements is more likely to be better served by maintaining the integrity of the confidential relationship between lawyer and client, thereby strengthening corporate management's confidence in counsel and encouraging its readiness to seek advice of counsel and to act in accordance with counsel's advice.

Consistent with the foregoing public policy considerations, it is believed appropriate to distinguish between, on the one hand, litigation which is pending or which a third party has manifested to the client a present intention to commence and, on the other hand, other contingencies of a legal nature or having legal aspects. As regards the former category, unquestionably the lawyer representing the client in a litigation matter may be the best source for a description of the claim or claims asserted, the client's position (e.g., denial, contest, etc.), and the client's possible exposure in the litigation (to the extent the lawyer is in a position to do so). As to the latter category, it is submitted that, for the reasons set forth above, it is not in the public interest for the lawyer to be required to respond to general inquiries from auditors concerning possible claims.

It is recognized that the disclosure requirements for enterprises subject to the reporting requirements of the Federal securities laws are a major concern of managements and counsel, as well as auditors. It is submitted that compliance therewith is best assured when clients are afforded maximum encouragement, by protecting lawyer-client confidentiality, freely to consult counsel. Likewise, lawyers must be keenly conscious of the importance of their clients being competently advised in these matters.

Statement of Policy

NOW, THEREFORE, BE IT RESOLVED that it is desirable and in the public interest that this Association adopt the following Statement of Policy regarding the appropriate scope of the lawyer's response to the auditor's request, made by the client at the request of the auditor, for information concerning matters referred to the lawyer during the course of his representation of the client:

(1) *Client Consent to Response.* The lawyer may properly respond to the auditor's requests for information concerning loss contingencies (the term and concept established by Statement of Financial Accounting Standards No. 5, promulgated by the Financial Accounting Standards Board in March 1975 and discussed in Paragraph 5.1 of the accompanying Commentary), to the extent hereinafter set forth, subject to the following:

a. Assuming that the client's initial letter requesting the lawyer to provide information to the auditor is signed by an agent of the client having apparent authority to make such a request, the lawyer may provide to the auditor information requested, without further consent, unless such information discloses a confidence or a secret or requires an evaluation of a claim.

b. In the normal case, the initial request letter does not provide the necessary consent to the disclosure of a confidence or secret or to the evaluation of a claim since that consent may only be given after full disclosure to the client of the legal consequences of such action.

c. Lawyers should bear in mind, in evaluating claims, that an adverse party may assert that any evaluation of potential liability is an admission.

d. In securing the client's consent to the disclosure of confidences or secrets, or the evaluation of claims, the lawyer may wish to have a draft of his letter reviewed and approved by the client before releasing it to the auditor; in such cases, additional explanation would in all probability be necessary so that the legal consequences of the consent are fully disclosed to the client.

(2) *Limitation on Scope of Response.* It is appropriate for the lawyer to set forth in his response, by way of limitation, the scope of his engagement by the client. It is also appropriate for the lawyer to indicate the date as of which information is furnished and to disclaim any undertaking to advise the auditor of changes which may thereafter be brought to the lawyer's attention. *Unless the lawyer's response indicates otherwise, (a) it is properly limited to matters which have been given substantive attention by the lawyer in the form of legal consultation and, where appropriate, legal representation since the beginning of the period or periods being reported upon, and (b) if a law firm or a law department, the auditor may assume that the firm or department has endeavored, to the extent believed necessary by the firm or department, to determine from lawyers currently in the firm or department who have performed services for the client since the beginning of the fiscal period under audit whether such services involved substantive attention in the form of legal consultation concerning those loss contingencies referred to in Paragraph 5(a) below but, beyond that, no review has been made of any of the client's transactions or other matters for the purpose of identifying loss contingencies to be described in the response.*[*]

(3) *Response may be Limited to Material Items.* In response to an auditor's request for disclosure of loss contingencies of a client, it is appropriate for the lawyer's response to indicate that the response is limited to items which are considered individually or collectively material to the presentation of the client's financial statements.

(4) *Limited Responses.* Where the lawyer is limiting his response in accordance with the Statement of Policy, his response should so indicate (see Paragraph 8). If in any other respect the lawyer is not undertaking to respond to or comment on particular aspects of the inquiry when responding to the auditor, he should consider advising the auditor that his response is limited, in order to avoid any inference that the lawyer has responded to all aspects; otherwise, he may be assuming a responsibility which he does not intend.

(5) *Loss Contingencies.* When properly requested by the client, it is appropriate for the lawyer to furnish to the auditor information concerning the following matters if the lawyer has been engaged by the client to represent or advise the client professionally with respect thereto and he has devoted substantive attention to them in the form of legal representation or consultation:

a. *overtly threatened or pending litigation*, whether or not specified by the client;

b. *a contractually assumed obligation* which the client has specifically identified and upon which the client has specifically requested, in the inquiry letter or a supplement thereto, comment to the auditor;

---

[*] As contemplated by Paragraph 8 of this Statement of Policy, this sentence is intended to be the subject of incorporation by reference as therein provided.

c. *an unasserted possible claim or assessment* which the client has specifically identified and upon which the client has specifically requested, in the inquiry letter or a supplement thereto, comment to the auditor.

With respect to clause (*a*), overtly threatened litigation means that a potential claimant has manifested to the client an awareness of and present intention to assert a possible claim or assessment unless the likelihood of litigation (or of settlement when litigation would normally be avoided) is considered remote. With respect to clause (*c*), where there has been no manifestation by a potential claimant of an awareness of and present intention to assert a possible claim or assessment, consistent with the considerations and concerns outlined in the Preamble and Paragraph 1 hereof, the client should request the lawyer to furnish information to the auditor only if the client has determined that it is probable that a possible claim will be asserted, that there is a reasonable possibility that the outcome (assuming such assertion) will be unfavorable, and that the resulting liability would be material to the financial condition of the client. Examples of such situations might (depending in each case upon the particular circumstances) include the following: (i) a catastrophe, accident or other similar physical occurrence in which the client's involvement is open and notorious, or (ii) an investigation by a government agency where enforcement proceedings have been instituted or where the likelihood that they will not be instituted is remote, under circumstances where assertion of one or more private claims for redress would normally be expected, or (iii) a public disclosure by the client acknowledging (and thus focusing attention upon) the existence of one or more probable claims arising out of an event or circumstance. In assessing whether or not the assertion of a possible claim is probable, it is expected that the client would normally employ, by reason of the inherent uncertainties involved and insufficiency of available data, concepts parallel to those used by the lawyer (discussed below) in assessing whether or not an unfavorable outcome is probable; thus, assertion of a possible claim would be considered probable only when the prospects of its being asserted seem reasonably certain (i.e., supported by extrinsic evidence strong enough to establish a presumption that it will happen) and the prospects of nonassertion seem slight.

It would not be appropriate, however, for the lawyer to be requested to furnish information in response to an inquiry letter or supplement thereto if it appears that (*a*) the client has been required to specify unasserted possible claims without regard to the standard suggested in the preceding paragraph, or (*b*) the client has been required to specify all or substantially all unasserted possible claims as to which legal advice may have been obtained, since, in either case, such a request would be in substance a general inquiry and would be inconsistent with the intent of this Statement of Policy.

The information that lawyers may properly give to the auditor concerning the foregoing matters would include (to the extent appropriate) an identification of the proceedings or matter, the stage of proceedings, the claim(s) asserted, and the position taken by the client.

In view of the inherent uncertainties, the lawyer should normally refrain from expressing judgments as to outcome except in those relatively few clear cases where it appears to the lawyer that an unfavorable outcome is either "probable" or "remote"; for purposes of any such judgment it is appropriate to use the following meanings:

(i) *probable*—an unfavorable outcome for the client is probable if the prospects of the claimant not succeeding are judged to be extremely doubtful and the prospects for success by the client in its defense are judged to be slight.

(ii) *remote*—an unfavorable outcome is remote if the prospects for the client not succeeding in its defense are judged to be extremely doubtful and the prospects of success by the claimant are judged to be slight.

If, in the opinion of the lawyer, considerations within the province of his professional judgment bear on a particular loss contingency to the degree necessary to make an informed judgment, he may in appropriate circumstances communicate to the auditor his view that an unfavorable outcome is "probable" or "remote," applying the above meanings. No inference should be drawn, from the absence of such a judgment, that the client will not prevail.

The lawyer also may be asked to estimate, in dollar terms, the potential amount of loss or range of loss in the event that an unfavorable outcome is not viewed to be "remote." In such a case, the amount or range of potential loss will normally be as inherently impossible to ascertain, with any degree of certainty, as the outcome of the litigation. Therefore, it is appropriate for the lawyer to provide an estimate of the amount or range of potential loss (if the outcome should be unfavorable) only if he believes that the probability of inaccuracy of the estimate of the amount or range of potential loss is slight.

The considerations bearing upon the difficulty in estimating loss (or range of loss) where pending litigation is concerned are obviously even more compelling in the case of unasserted possible claims. In most cases, the lawyer will not be able to provide any such estimate to the auditor.

As indicated in Paragraph 4 hereof, the auditor may assume that all loss contingencies specified by the client in the manner specified in clauses (*b*) and (*c*) above have received comment in the response, unless otherwise therein indicated. The lawyer should not be asked, nor need the lawyer undertake, to furnish information to the auditor concerning loss contingencies except as contemplated by this Paragraph 5.

(6) *Lawyer's Professional Responsibility.* Independent of the scope of his response to the auditor's request for information, the lawyer, depending upon the nature of the matters as to which he is engaged, may have as part of his professional responsibility to his client an obligation to advise the client concerning the need for or advisability of public disclosure of a wide range of events and circumstances. The lawyer has an obligation not knowingly to participate in any violation by the client of the disclosure requirements of the securities laws. In appropriate circumstances, the lawyer also may be required under the Code of Professional Responsibility to resign his engagement if his advice concerning disclosures is disregarded by the client. The auditor may properly assume that whenever, in the course of performing legal services for the client with respect to a matter recognized to involve an unasserted possible claim or assessment which may call for financial statement disclosure, the lawyer has formed a professional conclusion that the client must disclose or consider disclosure concerning such possible claim or assessment, the lawyer, as a matter of professional responsibility to the client, will so advise the client and will consult with the client concerning the question of such disclosure and the applicable requirements* of FAS 5.

---

* Under FAS 5, when there has been no manifestation by a potential claimant of an awareness of a possible claim or assessment, disclosure of an unasserted possible claim is required only if the enterprise concludes that (i) it is probable that a claim will be asserted, (ii) there is a reasonable possibility, if the claim is in fact asserted, that the outcome will be unfavorable, and (iii) the liability resulting from such unfavorable outcome would be material to its financial condition.

(7) *Limitation on Use of Response. Unless otherwise stated in the lawyer's response, it shall be solely for the auditor's information in connection with his audit of the financial condition of the client and is not to be quoted in whole or in part or otherwise referred to in any financial statements of the client or related documents, nor is it to be filed with any governmental agency or other person, without the lawyer's prior written consent.*† *Notwithstanding such limitation, the response can properly be furnished to others in compliance with court process or when necessary in order to defend the auditor against a challenge of the audit by the client or a regulatory agency, provided that the lawyer is given written notice of the circumstances at least twenty days before the response is so to be furnished to others, or as long in advance as possible if the situation does not permit such period of notice.*†

(8) *General.* This Statement of Policy, together with the accompanying Commentary (which is an integral part hereof), has been developed for the general guidance of the legal profession. In a particular case, the lawyer may elect to supplement or modify the approach hereby set forth. If desired, this Statement of Policy may be incorporated by reference in the lawyer's response by the following statement: "This response is limited by, and in accordance with, the ABA Statement of Policy Regarding Lawyers' Responses to Auditors' Requests for Information (December 1975); without limiting the generality of the foregoing, the limitations set forth in such Statement on the scope and use of this response (Paragraphs 2 and 7) are specifically incorporated herein by reference, and any description herein of any 'loss contingencies' is qualified in its entirety by Paragraph 5 of the Statement and the accompanying Commentary (which is an integral part of the Statement)."

The accompanying Commentary is an integral part of this Statement of Policy.

Commentary

Paragraph 1 (Client Consent to Response)

In responding to any aspect of an auditor's inquiry letter, the lawyer must be guided by his ethical obligations as set forth in the Code of Professional Responsibility. Under Canon 4 of the Code of Professional Responsibility a lawyer is enjoined to preserve the client's confidences (defined as information protected by the attorney-client privilege under applicable law) and the client's secrets (defined as other information gained in the professional relationship that the client has requested be held inviolate or the disclosure of which would be embarrassing or would be likely to be detrimental to the client). The observance of this ethical obligation, in the context of public policy, "... not only facilitates the full development of facts essential to proper representation of the client but also encourages laymen to seek early legal assistance." (Ethical Consideration 4-1).

The lawyer's ethical obligation therefore includes a much broader range of information than that protected by the attorney-client privilege. As stated in Ethical Consideration 4-4: "The attorney-client privilege is more limited than the ethical obligation of a lawyer to guard the confidences and secrets of his

† As contemplated by Paragraph 8 of this Statement of Policy, this sentence is intended to be the subject of incorporation by reference as therein provided.

client. This ethical precept, unlike the evidentiary privilege, exists without regard to the nature or source of information or the fact that others share the knowledge."

In recognition of this ethical obligation, the lawyer should be careful to disclose fully to his client any confidence, secret or evaluation that is to be revealed to another, including the client's auditor, and to satisfy himself that the officer or agent of a corporate client consenting to the disclosure understands the legal consequences thereof and has authority to provide the required consent.

The law in the area of attorney-client privilege and the impact of statements made in letters to auditors upon that privilege has not yet been developed. Based upon cases treating the attorney-client privilege in other contexts, however, certain generalizations can be made with respect to the possible impact of statements in letters to auditors.

It is now generally accepted that a corporation may claim the attorney-client privilege. Whether the privilege extends beyond the control group of the corporation (a concept found in the existing decisional authority), and if so, how far, is yet unresolved.

If a client discloses to a third party a part of any privileged communication he has made to his attorney, there may have been a waiver as to the whole communication; further, it has been suggested that giving accountants *access* to privileged statements made to attorneys may waive any privilege as to those statements. Any disclosure of privileged communications relating to a particular subject matter may have the effect of waiving the privilege on other communications with respect to the same subject matter.

To the extent that the lawyer's knowledge of unasserted possible claims is obtained by means of confidential communications from the client, any disclosure thereof might constitute a waiver as fully as if the communication related to pending claims.

A further difficulty arises with respect to requests for evaluation of either pending or unasserted possible claims. It might be argued that any evaluation of a claim, to the extent based upon a confidential communication with the client, waives any privilege with respect to that claim.

Another danger inherent in a lawyer's placing a value on a claim, or estimating the likely result, is that such a statement might be treated as an admission or might be otherwise prejudicial to the client.

The Statement of Policy has been prepared in the expectation that judicial development of the law in the foregoing areas will be such that useful communication between lawyers and auditors in the manner envisaged in the Statement will not prove prejudicial to clients engaged in or threatened with adversary proceedings. If developments occur contrary to this expectation, appropriate review and revision of the Statement of Policy may be necessary.

Paragraph 2 (Limitation on Scope of Response)

In furnishing information to an auditor, the lawyer can properly limit himself to loss contingencies which he is handling on a substantive basis for the client in the form of legal consultation (advice and other attention to matters not in litigation by the lawyer in his professional capacity) or legal representation (counsel of record or other direct professional responsibility for a matter in litigation). Some auditors' inquiries go further and ask for information on matters of which the lawyer "has knowledge." Lawyers are concerned that such a broad request may be deemed to include information coming from a variety of sources including social contact and thirdparty contacts as well as professional engagement and that the lawyer might be criticized or subjected to liability if some of this information is forgotten at the time of the auditor's request.

It is also believed appropriate to recognize that the lawyer will not necessarily have been authorized to investigate, or have investigated, all legal problems of the client, even when on notice of some facts which might conceivably constitute a legal problem upon exploration and development. Thus, consideration in the form of preliminary or passing advice, or regarding an incomplete or hypothetical state of facts, or where the lawyer has not been requested to give studied attention to the matter in question, would not come within the concept of "substantive attention" and would therefore be excluded. Similarly excluded are matters which may have been mentioned by the client but which are not actually being handled by the lawyer. Paragraph 2 undertakes to deal with these concerns.

Paragraph 2 is also intended to recognize the principle that the appropriate lawyer to respond as to a particular loss contingency is the lawyer having charge of the matter for the client (e.g., the lawyer representing the client in a litigation matter and/or the lawyer having overall charge and supervision of the matter), and that the lawyer not having that kind of role with respect to the matter should not be expected to respond merely because of having become aware of its existence in a general or incidental way.

The internal procedures to be followed by a law firm or law department may vary based on factors such as the scope of the lawyer's engagement and the complexity and magnitude of the client's affairs. Such procedures could, but need not, include use of a docket system to record litigation, consultation with lawyers in the firm or department having principal responsibility for the client's affairs or other procedures which, in light of the cost to the client, are not disproportionate to the anticipated benefit to be derived. Although these procedures may not necessarily identify all matters relevant to the response, the evolution and application of the lawyer's customary procedures should constitute a reasonable basis for the lawyer's response.

As the lawyer's response is limited to matters involving his professional engagement as counsel, such response should not include information concerning the client which the lawyer receives in another role. In particular, a lawyer who is also a director or officer of the client would not include information which he received as a director or officer unless the information was also received (or, absent the dual role, would in the normal course be received) in his capacity as legal counsel in the context of his professional engagement. Where the auditor's request for information is addressed to a law firm as a firm, the law firm may properly assume that its response is not expected to include any information which may have been communicated to the particular individual by reason of his serving in the capacity of director or officer of the client. The question of the individual's duty, in his role as a director or officer, is not here addressed.

Paragraph 3 (Response May Cover only Material Items in Certain Cases)

Paragraph 3 makes it clear that the lawyer may optionally limit his responses to those items which are individually or collectively material to the auditor's inquiry. If the lawyer takes responsibility for making a determination that a matter is not material for the purposes of his response to the audit inquiry, he should make it clear that his response is so limited. The auditor, in such circumstance, should properly be entitled to rely upon the lawyer's response as providing him with the necessary corroboration. It should be emphasized that the employment of inside general counsel by the client should not detract from the acceptability of his response since inside general counsel is as fully bound by the professional obligations and responsibilities contained in the Code of Professional Responsibility as outside counsel. If the audit inquiry sets forth a definition of materiality but the lawyer utilizes a different test of materiality, he should specifically so state. The lawyer may wish to reach an understanding with the auditor concerning the test of materiality to be used in his response, but he need not do so if he assumes responsibility for the criteria used in making materiality determinations. Any such understanding with the auditor should be referred to or set forth in the lawyer's response. In this connection, it is assumed that the test of materiality so agreed upon would not be so low in amount as to result in a disservice to the client and an unreasonable burden on counsel.

Paragraph 4 (Limited Responses)

The Statement of Policy is designed to recognize the obligation of the auditor to complete the procedures considered necessary to satisfy himself as to the fair presentation of the company's financial condition and results, in order to render a report which includes an opinion not qualified because of a limitation on the scope of the audit. In this connection, reference is made to SEC Accounting Series Release No. 90 [Financial Reporting Release No. 1, section 607.01(b)], in which it is stated:

> "A 'subject to' or 'except for' opinion paragraph in which these phrases refer to the scope of the audit, indicating that the accountant has not been able to satisfy himself on some significant element in the financial statements, is not acceptable in certificates filed with the Commission in connection with the public offering of securities. The 'subject to' qualification is appropriate when the reference is to a middle paragraph or to footnotes explaining the status of matters which cannot be resolved at statement date."

Paragraph 5 (Loss Contingencies)

Paragraph 5 of the Statement of Policy summarizes the categories of "loss contingencies" about which the lawyer may furnish information to the auditor. The term loss contingencies and the categories relate to concepts of accounting accrual and disclosure specified for the accounting profession in Statement of Financial Accounting Standards No. 5 ("FAS 5") issued by the Financial Accounting Standards Board in March, 1975.

5.1 Accounting Requirements

To understand the significance of the auditor's inquiry and the implications of any response the lawyer may give, the lawyer should be aware of the following accounting concepts and requirements set out in FAS 5:*

(a) A "loss contingency" is an existing condition, situation or set of circumstances involving uncertainty as to possible loss to an enter-

* Citations are to paragraph numbers of FAS 5.

prise that will ultimately be resolved when one or more events occur or fail to occur. Resolutions of the uncertainty may confirm the loss or impairment of an asset or the incurrence of a liability.

(Para. 1)

(b) When a "loss contingency" exists, the likelihood that a future event or events will confirm the loss or impairment of an asset or the incurrence of a liability can range from probable to remote. There are three areas within that range, defined as follows:

(i) *Probable*—"The future event or events are likely to occur."

(ii) *Reasonably possible*—"The chance of the future event or events occurring is more than remote but less than likely."

(iii) *Remote*—"The chance of the future event or events occurring is slight."

(Para. 3)

(c) *Accrual* in a client's financial statements by a charge to income of the period will be required if *both* the following conditions are met:

(i) "Information available prior to issuance of the financial statements indicates that it is *probable* that an asset had been impaired or a liability had been incurred at the date of the financial statements. It is implicit in this condition that it must be *probable* that one or more future events will occur confirming the fact of the loss." (emphasis added; footnote omitted)

(ii) "The amount of loss can be reasonably estimated."

(Para. 8)

(d) If there is no *accrual* of the loss contingency in the client's financial statements because one of the two conditions outlined in (*c*) above are not met, *disclosure* may be required as provided in the following:

> "If no accrual is made for a loss contingency because one or both of the conditions in paragraph 8 are not met, or if an exposure to loss exists in excess of the amount accrued pursuant to the provisions of paragraph 8, *disclosure* of the contingency *shall be made when there is at least a reasonable possibility* that a loss or an additional loss may have been incurred. *The disclosure shall indicate the nature of the contingency and shall give an estimate of the possible loss or range of loss or state that such an estimate cannot be made. Disclosure is not required of* a loss contingency involving *an unasserted claim* or assessment *when there has been no manifestation by potential claimant of an awareness of a possible claim or assessment unless it is considered probable that a claim will be asserted and there is a reasonable possibility that the outcome will be unfavorable.*" (emphasis added; footnote omitted)

(Para. 10)

(e) The accounting requirements recognize or specify that (i) the opinions or views of counsel are not the sole source of evidential matter in making determinations about the accounting recognition or treatment to be given to litigation, and (ii) the fact that the lawyer is not

able to express an opinion that the outcome will be favorable does not necessarily require an accrual of a loss. Paragraphs 36 and 37 of FAS 5 state as follows:

"If the underlying cause of the litigation, claim, or assessment is an event occurring before the date of an enterprise's financial statements, the probability of an outcome unfavorable to the enterprise must be assessed to determine whether the condition in paragraph 8(*a*) is met. Among the factors that should be considered are the nature of the litigation, claim, or assessment, the progress of the case (including progress after the date of the financial statements but before those statements are issued), the opinions or views of legal counsel and other advisers, the experience of the enterprise in similar cases, the experience of other enterprises, and any decision of the enterprise's management as to how the enterprise intends to respond to the lawsuit, claim, or assessment (for example, a decision to contest the case vigorously or a decision to seek an out-of-court settlement). The fact that legal counsel is unable to express an opinion that the outcome will be favorable to the enterprise should not necessarily be interpreted to mean that the condition for accrual of a loss in paragraph 8(*a*) is met.

"The filing of a suit or formal assertion of a claim or assessment does not automatically indicate that accrual of a loss may be appropriate. The degree of probability of an unfavorable outcome must be assessed. The condition for accrual in paragraph 8(*a*) would be met if an unfavorable outcome is determined to be probable. If an unfavorable outcome is determined to be reasonably possible but not probable, or if the amount of loss cannot be reasonably estimated, accrual would be inappropriate, but disclosure would be required by paragraph 10 of this Statement."

(f) Paragraph 38 of FAS 5 focuses on certain examples concerning the determination by the enterprise whether an assertion of an *unasserted possible claim* may be considered probable:

"With respect to unasserted claims and assessments, an enterprise must determine the degree of probability that a suit may be filed or a claim or assessment may be asserted and the possibility of an unfavorable outcome. For example, a catastrophe, accident, or other similar physical occurrence predictably engenders claims for redress, and in such circumstances their assertion may be probable; similarly, an investigation of an enterprise by a governmental agency, if enforcement proceedings have been or are likely to be instituted, is often followed by private claims for redress, and the probability of their assertion and the possibility of loss should be considered in each case. By way of further example, an enterprise may believe there is a possibility that it has infringed on another enterprise's patent rights, but the enterprise owning the patent rights has not indicated an intention to take any action and has not even indicated an awareness of the possible infringement. In that case, a judgment must first be made as to whether the assertion of a claim is probable. If the judgment is that assertion is not probable, no accrual or disclosure would be required. On the other hand, if the judgment is that assertion is probable, then a second judgment must be made as to the degree of probability of an unfavorable outcome. If an unfavorable outcome is probable and the amount of loss can be reasonably estimated, accrual of a loss is required by paragraph 8. If an unfavorable outcome is probable but the amount of loss cannot be reasonably estimated, accrual would not be appropriate, but disclosure would be required by paragraph 10. If an unfavorable outcome is reasonably possible but not probable, disclosure would be required by paragraph 10."

For a more complete presentation of FAS 5, reference is made to Exhibit I, section 337B, in which are set forth excerpts selected by the AICPA as relevant to a Statement on Auditing Standards, issued by its Auditing Standards Executive Committee, captioned "Inquiry of a Client's Lawyer Concerning Litigation, Claims, and Assessments."

5.2 Lawyer's Response

Concepts of probability inherent in the usage of terms like "probable" or "reasonably possible" or "remote" mean different things in different contexts. Generally, the outcome of, or the loss which may result from, litigation cannot be assessed in any way that is comparable to a statistically or empirically determined concept of "probability" that may be applicable when determining such matters as reserves for warranty obligations or accounts receivable or loan losses when there is a large number of transactions and a substantial body of known historical experience for the enterprise or comparable enterprises. While lawyers are accustomed to counseling clients during the progress of litigation as to the possible amount required for settlement purposes, the estimated risks of the proceedings at particular times and the possible application or establishment of points of law that may be relevant, such advice to the client is not possible at many stages of the litigation and may change dramatically depending upon the development of the proceedings. Lawyers do not generally quantify for clients the "odds" in numerical terms; if they do, the quantification is generally only undertaken in an effort to make meaningful, for limited purposes, a whole host of judgmental factors applicable at a particular time, without any intention to depict "probability" in any statistical, scientific or empirically-grounded sense. Thus, for example, statements that litigation is being defended vigorously and that the client has meritorious defenses do not, and do not purport to, make a statement about the probability of outcome in any measurable sense.

Likewise, the "amount" of loss—that is, the total of costs and damages that ultimately might be assessed against a client—will, in most litigation, be a subject of wide possible variance at most stages; it is the rare case where the amount is precise and where the question is whether the client against which claim is made is liable either for all of it or none of it.

In light of the foregoing considerations, it must be concluded that, as a general rule, it should not be anticipated that meaningful quantifications of "probability" of outcome or amount of damages can be given by lawyers in assessing litigation. To provide content to the definitions set forth in Paragraph 5 of the Statement of Policy, this Commentary amplifies the meanings of the terms under discussion, as follows:

"probable"—An unfavorable outcome is normally "probable" if, but only if, investigation, preparation (including development of the factual data and

legal research) and progress of the matter have reached a stage where a judgment can be made, taking all relevant factors into account which may affect the outcome, that it is extremely doubtful that the client will prevail.

"remote"—The prospect for an unfavorable outcome appears, at the time, to be slight; i.e., it is extremely doubtful that the client will not prevail. Normally, this would entail the ability to make an unqualified judgment, taking into account all relevant factors which may affect the outcome, that the client may confidently expect to prevail on a motion for summary judgment on all issues due to the clarity of the facts and the law.

In other words, for purposes of the lawyer's response to the request to advise auditors about litigation, an unfavorable outcome will be "probable" only if the chances of the client prevailing appear slight and of the claimant losing appear extremely doubtful; it will be "remote" when the client's chances of losing appear slight and of not winning appear extremely doubtful. It is, therefore, to be anticipated that, in most situations, an unfavorable outcome will be neither "probable" nor "remote" as defined in the Statement of Policy.

The discussion above about the very limited basis for furnishing judgments about the outcome of litigation applies with even more force to a judgment concerning whether or not the assertion of a claim not yet asserted is "probable." That judgment will infrequently be one within the professional competence of lawyers and therefore the lawyer should not undertake such assessment except where such judgment may become meaningful because of the presence of special circumstances, such as catastrophes, investigations and previous public disclosure as cited in Paragraph 5 of the Statement of Policy, or similar extrinsic evidence relevant to such assessment. Moreover, it is unlikely, absent relevant extrinsic evidence, that the client or anyone else will be in a position to make an informed judgment that assertion of a possible claim is "probable" as opposed to "reasonably possible" (in which event disclosure is not required). In light of the legitimate concern that the public interest would not be well served by resolving uncertainties in a way that invites the assertion of claims or otherwise causes unnecessary harm to the client and its stockholders, a decision to treat an unasserted claim as "probable" of assertion should be based only upon compelling judgment.

Consistent with these limitations believed appropriate for the lawyer, he should not represent to the auditor, nor should any inference from his response be drawn, that the unasserted possible claims identified by the client (as contemplated by Paragraph 5(*c*) of the Statement of Policy) represent all such claims of which the lawyer may be aware or that he necessarily concurs in his client's determination of which unasserted possible claims warrant specification by the client; within proper limits, this determination is one which the client is entitled to make—and should make—and it would be inconsistent with his professional obligations for the lawyer to volunteer information arising from his confidential relationship with his client.

As indicated in Paragraph 5, the lawyer also may be asked to estimate the potential loss (or range) in the event that an unfavorable outcome is not viewed to be "remote." In such a case, the lawyer would provide an estimate only if he believes that the probability of inaccuracy of the estimate of the range or amount is slight. What is meant here is that the estimate of amount of loss presents the same difficulty as assessment of outcome and that the same formulation of "probability" should be used with respect to the determination of estimated loss amounts as should be used with respect to estimating the outcome of the matter.

In special circumstances, with the proper consent of the client, the lawyer may be better able to provide the auditor with information concerning loss contingencies through conferences where there is opportunity for more detailed discussion and interchange. However, the principles set forth in the Statement of Policy and this Commentary are fully applicable to such conferences.

Subsumed throughout this discussion is the ongoing responsibility of the lawyer to assist his client, at the client's request, in complying with the requirements of FAS 5 to the extent such assistance falls within his professional competence. This will continue to involve, to the extent appropriate, privileged discussions with the client to provide a better basis on which the client can make accrual and disclosure determinations in respect of its financial statements.

In addition to the considerations discussed above with respect to the making of any judgment or estimate by the lawyer in his response to the auditor, including with respect to a matter specifically identified by the client, the lawyer should also bear in mind the risk that the furnishing of such a judgment or estimate to any one other than the client might constitute an admission or be otherwise prejudicial to the client's position in its defense against such litigation or claim (see Paragraph 1 of the Statement of Policy and of this Commentary).

Paragraph 6 (Lawyer's Professional Responsibility)

The client must satisfy whatever duties it has relative to timely disclosure, including appropriate disclosure concerning material loss contingencies, and, to the extent such matters are given substantive attention in the form of legal consultation, the lawyer, when his engagement is to advise his client concerning a disclosure obligation, has a responsibility to advise his client concerning its obligations in this regard. Although lawyers who normally confine themselves to a legal specialty such as tax, antitrust, patent or admiralty law, unlike lawyers consulted about SEC or general corporate matters, would not be expected to advise generally concerning the client's disclosure obligations in respect of a matter on which the lawyer is working, the legal specialist should counsel his client with respect to the client's obligations under FAS 5 to the extent contemplated herein. Without regard to legal specialty, the lawyer should be mindful of his professional responsibility to the client described in Paragraph 6 of the Statement of Policy concerning disclosure.

The lawyer's responsibilities with respect to his client's disclosure obligations have been a subject of considerable discussion and there may be, in due course, clarification and further guidance in this regard. In any event, where in the lawyer's view it is clear that (i) the matter is of material importance and seriousness, and (ii) there can be no reasonable doubt that its non-disclosure in the client's financial statements would be a violation of law giving rise to material claims, rejection by the client of his advice to call the matter to the attention of the auditor would almost certainly require the lawyer's withdrawal from employment in accordance with the Code of Professional Responsibility. (See, e.g., Disciplinary Rule 7-102 (A)(3) and (7), and Disciplinary Rule 2-110 (B)(2).) Withdrawal under such circumstances is obviously undesirable and might present serious problems for the client. Accordingly, in the context of financial accounting and reporting for loss contingencies arising from unasserted claims, the standards for which are contained in FAS 5, clients should be urged to disclose to the auditor information concerning an unasserted possible claim or assessment (not otherwise specifically identified by the client) where in the course of the services performed for the client it has become clear to the lawyer that (i) the client has no reasonable basis to conclude that assertion of the claim is not probable (employing the concepts hereby enunciated) and (ii) given the probability of assertion, disclosure of the loss contingency in the client's financial statements is beyond reasonable dispute required.

Paragraph 7 (Limitation on Use of Response)

Some inquiry letters make specific reference to, and one might infer from others, an intention to quote verbatim or include the substance of the lawyer's reply in footnotes to the client's financial statements. Because the client's prospects in pending litigation may shift as a result of interim developments, and because the lawyer should have an opportunity, if quotation is to be made, to review the footnote in full, it would seem prudent to limit the use of the lawyer's reply letter. Paragraph 7 sets out such a limitation.

Paragraph 7 also recognizes that it may be in the client's interest to protect information contained in the lawyer's response to the auditor, if and to the extent possible, against unnecessary further disclosure or use beyond its intended purpose of informing the auditor. For example, the response may contain information which could prejudice efforts to negotiate a favorable settlement of a pending litigation described in the response. The requirement of consent to further disclosure, or of reasonable advance notice where disclosure may be required by court process or necessary in defense of the audit, is designed to give the lawyer an opportunity to consult with the client as to whether consent should be refused or limited or, in the case of legal process or the auditor's defense of the audit, as to whether steps can and should be taken to challenge the necessity of further disclosure or to seek protective measures in connection therewith. It is believed that the suggested standard of twenty days advance notice would normally be a minimum reasonable time for this purpose.

Paragraph 8 (General)

It is reasonable to assume that the Statement of Policy will receive wide distribution and will be readily available to the accounting profession. Specifically, the Statement of Policy has been reprinted as Exhibit II to the Statement on Auditing Standards, "Inquiry of a Client's Lawyer Concerning Litigation, Claims, and Assessments," issued by the Auditing Standards Executive Committee of the American Institute of Certified Public Accountants. Accordingly, the mechanic for its incorporation by reference will facilitate lawyer-auditor communication. The incorporation is intended to include not only limitations, such as those provided by Paragraphs 2 and 7 of the Statement of Policy, but also the explanatory material set forth in this Commentary.

Annex A

[Illustrative forms of letters for full response by outside practitioner or law firm and inside general counsel to the auditor's inquiry letter. These illustrative forms, which are not part of the Statement of Policy, have been prepared by the Committee on Audit Inquiry Responses solely in order to assist those who may wish to have, for reference purposes, a form of response which incorporates the principles of the Statement of Policy and accompanying Commentary. Other forms of response letters will be appropriate depending on the circumstances.]

Illustrative form of letter for use by outside practitioner or law firm:

[Name and Address of Accounting Firm]

Re: [Name of Client] [and Subsidiaries]

Dear Sirs:

By letter date [*insert date of request*] Mr. [*insert name and title of officer signing request*] of [*insert name of client*] [(the "Company") or (together with its subsidiaries, the "Company")] has requested us to furnish you with certain information in connection with your examination of the accounts of the Company as at [*insert fiscal year-end*].

[Insert description of the scope of the lawyer's engagement; the following are sample descriptions:]

While this firm represents the Company on a regular basis, our engagement has been limited to specific matters as to which we were consulted by the Company.

[or]

We call your attention to the fact that this firm has during the past year represented the Company only in connection with certain [*Federal income tax matters*] [*litigation*] [*real estate transactions*] [*describe other specific matters, as appropriate*] and has not been engaged for any other purpose.

Subject to the foregoing and to the last paragraph of this letter, we advise you that since [*insert date of beginning of fiscal period under audit*] we have not been engaged to give substantive attention to, or represent the Company in connection with, [*material*]* loss contingencies coming within the scope of clause (*a*) of Paragraph 5 of the Statement of Policy referred to in the last paragraph of this letter, except as follows:

[Describe litigation and claims which fit the foregoing criteria.]

> [If the inquiry letter requests information concerning specified unasserted possible claims or assessments and/or contractually assumed obligations:]

With respect to the matters specifically identified in the Company's letter and upon which comment has been specifically requested, as contemplated by clauses (*b*) or (*c*) of Paragraph 5 of the ABA Statement of Policy, we advise you, subject to the last paragraph of this letter, as follows:

[Insert information as appropriate]

The information set forth herein is [as of the date of this letter] [as of [*insert date*], the date on which we commenced our internal review procedures for purposes of preparing this response], except as otherwise noted, and we disclaim any undertaking to advise you of changes which thereafter may be brought to our attention.

[Insert information with respect to outstanding bills for services and disbursements.]

---

* ***Note:*** See Paragraph 3 of the Statement of Policy and the accompanying Commentary for guidance where the response is limited to material items.

This response is limited by, and in accordance with, the ABA Statement of Policy Regarding Lawyers' Responses to Auditors' Requests for Information (December 1975); without limiting the generality of the foregoing, the limitations set forth in such Statement on the scope and use of this response (Paragraphs 2 and 7) are specifically incorporated herein by reference, and any description herein of any "loss contingencies" is qualified in its entirety by Paragraph 5 of the Statement and the accompanying Commentary (which is an integral part of the Statement). Consistent with the last sentence of Paragraph 6 of the ABA Statement of Policy and pursuant to the Company's request, this will confirm as correct the Company's understanding as set forth in its audit inquiry letter to us that whenever, in the course of performing legal services for the Company with respect to a matter recognized to involve an unasserted possible claim or assessment that may call for financial statement disclosure, we have formed a professional conclusion that the Company must disclose or consider disclosure concerning such possible claim or assessment, we, as a matter of professional responsibility to the Company, will so advise the Company and will consult with the Company concerning the question of such disclosure and the applicable requirements of Statement of Financial Accounting Standards No. 5. [Describe any other or additional limitation as indicated by Paragraph 4 of the Statement]

Very truly yours,

Illustrative form of letter for use by inside general counsel:

[Name and Address of Accounting Firm]

Re: [Name of Company] [and Subsidiaries]

Dear Sirs:

As General Counsel* of [*insert name of client*] [(the "Company")] [(together with its subsidiaries, the "Company")], I advise you as follows in connection with your examination of the accounts of the Company as at [*insert fiscal year-end*].

I call your attention to the fact that as General Counsel* for the Company I have general supervision of the Company's legal affairs. [*If the general legal supervisory responsibilities of the person signing the letter are limited, set forth here a clear description of those legal matters over which such person exercises general supervision, indicating exceptions to such supervision and situations where primary reliance should be placed on other sources.*] In such capacity, I have reviewed litigation and claims threatened or asserted involving the Company and have consulted with outside legal counsel with respect thereto where I have deemed appropriate.

Subject to the foregoing and to the last paragraph of this letter, I advise you that since [*insert date of beginning of fiscal period under audit*] neither I, nor any of the lawyers over whom I exercise general legal supervision, have given substantive attention to, or represented the Company in connection with, [material]** loss contingencies coming within the scope of clause (*a*) of Paragraph 5 of the Statement of Policy referred to in the last paragraph of this letter, except as follows:

[Describe litigation and claims which fit the foregoing criteria.]

[If information concerning specified unasserted possible claims or assessments and/or contractually assumed obligations is to be supplied:]

With respect to matters which have been specifically identified as contemplated by clauses (*b*) or (*c*) of Paragraph 5 of the ABA Statement of Policy, I advise you, subject to the last paragraph of this letter, as follows:

[Insert information as appropriate]

The information set forth herein is [as of the date of this letter] as of [*insert date*], the date on which we commenced our internal review procedures for purposes of preparing this response], except as otherwise noted, and I disclaim any undertaking to advise you of changes which thereafter may be brought to my attention or to the attention of the lawyers over whom I exercise general legal supervision.

This response is limited by, and in accordance with, the ABA Statement of Policy Regarding Lawyers' Responses to Auditors' Requests for Information (December 1975); without limiting the generality of the foregoing, the limitations set forth in such Statement on the scope and use of this response (Paragraphs 2 and 7) are specifically incorporated herein by reference, and any description herein of any "loss contingencies" is qualified in its entirety by

---

* It may be appropriate in some cases for the response to be given by inside counsel other than inside general counsel in which event this letter should be appropriately modified.

** *Note:* See Paragraph 3 of the Statement of Policy and the accompanying Commentary for guidance where the response is limited to material items.

Paragraph 5 of the Statement and the accompanying Commentary (which is an integral part of the Statement). Consistent with the last sentence of Paragraph 6 of the ABA Statement of Policy, this will confirm as correct the Company's understanding that whenever, in the course of performing legal services for the Company with respect to a matter recognized to involve an unasserted possible claim or assessment that may call for financial statement disclosure, I have formed a professional conclusion that the Company must disclose or consider disclosure concerning such possible claim or assessment, I, as a matter of professional responsibility to the Company, will so advise the Company and will consult with the Company concerning the question of such disclosure and the applicable requirements of Statement of Financial Accounting Standards No. 5. [Describe any other or additional limitation as indicated by Paragraph 4 of the Statement.]

Very truly yours,

____

AU Section 9337

Inquiry of a Client's Lawyer Concerning Litigation, Claims, and Assessments: Auditing Interpretations of Section 337

1. Specifying Relevant Date in an Audit Inquiry Letter

.01 *Question*—Should the auditor request the client to specify, in his audit inquiry letter to a lawyer prepared in accordance with section 337, *Inquiry of a Client's Lawyer Concerning Litigation, Claims, and Assessments*, the date by which the lawyer's response should be sent to the auditor. Also, should the letter request the lawyer to specify in his response the latest date covered by his review (the "effective date")?

.02 *Interpretation*—Yes. It should be recognized that, to adequately respond to an audit inquiry letter, lawyers will ordinarily employ some internal review procedures which will be facilitated by specifying the earliest acceptable effective date of the response and the latest date by which it should be sent to the auditor. Ordinarily, a two-week period should be allowed between the specified effective date of the lawyer's response and the latest date by which the response should be sent to the auditor. Clearly stating the relevant dates in the letter and specifying these dates to the lawyer in a timely manner will allow the responding lawyer an adequate amount of time to complete his review procedures and assist the auditor in coordinating the timing of the completion of his field work with the latest date covered by the lawyer's review.

.03 Further, the lawyer should be requested to specify the effective date of his response. If the lawyer's response does not specify an effective date, the auditor can assume that the date of the lawyer's response is the effective date.

[Issue Date: March, 1977.]

2. Relationship Between Date of Lawyer's Response and Auditor's Report

.04 *Question*—The illustrative form of audit inquiry letter included in the Appendix [section 337A] to section 337, *Inquiry of a Client's Lawyer Concerning Litigation, Claims, and Assessments*, requests a response as to matters that existed at the balance sheet date and during the period from that date to the date of the response. What is the relationship between the effective date of the lawyer's response and the date of the auditor's report, which is generally the date of the completion of field work?

.05 *Interpretation*—Section 560.10 through .12 indicates that the auditor is concerned with events, which may require adjustment to, or disclosure in, the financial statements, occurring through the date of his report. Therefore, the latest date of the period covered by the lawyer's response (the "effective date") should be as close to the completion of field work as is practicable in the circumstances. Consequently, specifying the effective date of the lawyer's response to reasonably approximate the expected date of the completion of the field work will in most instances obviate the need for an updated response from the lawyer.

[Issue Date: March, 1977.]

3. Form of Audit Inquiry Letter When Client Represents That No Unasserted Claims and Assessments Exist

.06 *Question*—The illustrative audit inquiry letter included in the Appendix [section 337A] to section 337, *Inquiry of a Client's Lawyer Concerning Litigation, Claims, and Assessments*, assumes that the client specifies certain unasserted claims and assessments. However, in some cases, clients have stated that there are no such claims or assessments (to be specified to the lawyer for comment) that are probable of assertion and that, if asserted, would have a reasonable possibility of an unfavorable outcome. What appropriate revision to the wording of the letter can be used in such situations?

.07 *Interpretation*—Wording that could be used in an audit inquiry letter, instead of the heading and first paragraph in the section relating to unasserted claims and assessments included in the Appendix [section 337A] to section 337, when the client believes that there are no unasserted claims or assessments (to be specified to the lawyer for comment) that are probable of assertion and that, if asserted, would have a reasonable possibility of an unfavorable outcome as specified by FASB Statement No. 5, *Accounting for Contingencies* [AC section C59], is as follows:

> *Unasserted claims and assessments*—We have represented to our auditors that there are no unasserted possible claims that you have advised us are probable of assertion and must be disclosed, in accordance with Statement of Financial Accounting Standards No. 5. (The second paragraph in the section relating to unasserted claims and assessments would not be altered.)

[Issue Date: March, 1977.]

4. Documents Subject to Lawyer-Client Privilege

.08 *Question*—Section 337, *Inquiry of a Client's Lawyer Concerning Litigation, Claims, and Assessments*, paragraph .05c, states: "Examine documents in the client's possession concerning litigation, claims, and assessments, including correspondence and invoices from lawyers." Would this include a review of documents at the client's location considered by the lawyer and the client to be subject to the lawyer-client privilege?

.09 *Interpretation*—No. Although ordinarily an auditor would consider the inability to review information that could have a significant bearing on his audit as a scope restriction, in recognition of the public interest in protecting the confidentiality of lawyer-client communications (see section 337.13), section 337.05c is not intended to require an auditor to examine documents that the client identifies as subject to the lawyer-client privilege. In the event of questions concerning the applicability of this privilege, the auditor may request confirmation from the client's counsel that the information is subject to that privilege and that the information was considered by the lawyer in responding to the audit inquiry letter or, if the matters are being handled by another lawyer, an identification of such lawyer for the purpose of sending him an audit inquiry letter.

[Issue Date: March, 1977.]

5. Alternative Wording of the Illustrative Audit Inquiry Letter to a Client's Lawyer

.10 *Question*—The Appendix [section 337A] of section 337, *Inquiry of a Client's Lawyer Concerning Litigation, Claims, and Assessments*, provides an illustrative audit inquiry letter to legal counsel. That inquiry letter is based on the assumptions that (1) management of the company has prepared and furnished to the auditor and has set forth in the audit inquiry letter a description and evaluation of pending or threatened litigation, claims, and assessments and (2) management has identified and specified for comment in the audit inquiry letter unasserted claims or assessments that are probable of assertion and that, if asserted, would have at least a reasonable possibility of an unfavorable outcome. In many engagements, circumstances may render certain portions of the illustrative letter inappropriate. For instance, many clients ask their lawyers to prepare the list that describes and evaluates pending or threatened litigation, claims, and assessments rather than have management furnish such information. How can the wording of the inquiry letter be modified to recognize circumstances that differ from those assumed in the illustrative letter and to be more specific regarding the timing of the lawyer's response?

.11 *Interpretation*—Section 337.09, outlines the matters that should be covered in a letter of audit inquiry. Although section 337 provides an illustrative audit inquiry letter to legal counsel, it should be modified, if necessary, to fit the circumstances. The modified illustrative audit inquiry letter that follows is based on a typical situation: management requests the lawyer to prepare the list that describes and evaluates pending or threatened litigation, claims, and assessments, and also represents that there are no unasserted claims or assessments that are probable of assertion and that, if asserted, would have a reasonable possibility of an unfavorable outcome as specified by FASB Statement No. 5, *Accounting for Contingencies* [AC section C59]. It also includes a separate response section with language that clarifies the auditor's expectations regarding the timing of the lawyer's response.

"In connection with an audit of our financial statements as of (balance-sheet date) and for the (period) then ended, please furnish our auditors, (name and address of auditors), with the information requested below concerning certain contingencies involving matters with respect to which you have devoted substantive attention on behalf of the Company in the form of legal consultation or representation." [When a materiality limit has been established based on an understanding between management and the auditor, the following sentence should be added: This request is limited to contingencies amounting to (amount) individually or items involving lesser amounts that exceed (amount) in the aggregate.]

.12 Pending or Threatened Litigation, Claims, and Assessments

"Regarding pending or threatened litigation, claims, and assessments, please include in your response: (1) the nature of each matter, (2) the progress of each matter to date, (3) how the Company is responding or intends to respond (for example, to contest the case vigorously or seek an out-of-court settlement), and (4) an evaluation of the likelihood of an unfavorable outcome and an estimate, if one can be made, of the amount or range of potential loss."

.13 Unasserted Claims and Assessments

"We have represented to our auditors that there are no unasserted possible claims or assessments that you have advised us are probable of assertion and must be disclosed in accordance with FASB Statement No. 5 [AC section C59].[1] We understand that whenever, in the course of performing legal services for us with respect to a matter recognized to involve an unasserted possible claim or assessment that may call for financial statement disclosure, you have formed a professional conclusion that we should disclose or consider disclosure concerning such possible claim or assessment, as a matter of professional responsibility to us, you will so advise us and will consult with us concerning the question of such disclosure and the applicable requirements of FASB Statement No. 5 [AC section C59]. Please specifically confirm to our auditors that our understanding is correct."

.14 Response

"Your response should include matters that existed as of (balance-sheet date) and during the period from that date to the effective date of your response."

"Please specifically identify the nature of and reasons for any limitations on your response."

"Our auditors expect to have the audit completed about (expected completion date). They would appreciate receiving your reply by that date with a specified effective date no earlier than (ordinarily two weeks before expected completion date)."[2]

[Issue Date: June 1983.]

6. Client Has Not Consulted a Lawyer

.15 *Question*—Section 337.06 requires an auditor to request that the client's management send a letter of inquiry to those lawyers with whom management has consulted concerning litigation, claims, or assessments. In some instances, management may not have consulted a lawyer. In such circumstances, what should the auditor do to obtain sufficient, competent evidential matter regarding litigation, claims, and assessments?

.16 *Interpretation*—Section 337 is expressly limited to inquiry of lawyers with whom management has consulted. If the client has not consulted a lawyer, the auditor normally would rely on the review of internally available information as outlined in section 337.05 and .07, and the written repre-

---

[1] A parenthetical statement such as "(excerpts of which can be found in the ABA's *Auditor's Letter Handbook*)" might be added here if the auditor believes that it would be helpful to the lawyer's understanding of the requirements of FASB Statement No. 5 [AC section C59]. *The Auditor's Letter Handbook* contains, among other things, a copy of section 337, the ABA's *Statement of Policy Regarding Lawyers' Responses to Auditors' Requests for Information* [section 337C], and excerpts from FASB Statement No. 5 [AC section C59].

[2] Two auditing interpretations (see sections 9337.01–.05) address relevant dates in an audit inquiry letter and the relationship between the date of the lawyer's response and the audit report date.

sentation of management regarding litigation, claims, and assessments as required by section 333A, *Client Representations*, paragraph 4*r* and *s*. In those circumstances, the representation regarding litigation, claims, and assessments might be worded as follows:

"We are not aware of any pending or threatened litigation, claims, or assessments or unasserted claims or assessments that are required to be accrued or disclosed in the financial statements in accordance with FASB Statement No. 5 [AC section C59], and we have not consulted a lawyer concerning litigation, claims, or assessments."

.17 If information comes to the auditor's attention that may indicate potentially material litigation, claims, and assessments, the auditor should discuss with the client its possible need to consult legal counsel so that the client may evaluate its responsibility under FASB Statement No. 5 [AC section C59] to accrue or disclose loss contingencies. Depending on the severity of the matter, refusal by the client to consult legal counsel in those circumstances may result in a scope limitation, and the auditor should consider the effect of such a limitation on his audit report.

[Issue Date: June 1983.]

7. Assessment of a Lawyer's Evaluation of the Outcome of Litigation

.18 *Question*—Section 337, *Inquiry of a Client's Lawyer Concerning Litigation, Claims, and Assessments*, paragraph .09*d*(2), states that a letter of audit inquiry should include a request for the lawyer's evaluation of the likelihood of an unfavorable outcome of pending or threatened litigation, claims, and assessments to which he has devoted substantive attention. However, written responses from lawyers vary considerably and may contain evaluation wording that is vague or ambiguous and, thus, of limited use to the auditor. What constitutes a clear response and what should the auditor do if he considers the response unclear?

.19 *Interpretation*—The American Bar Association's *Statement of Policy Regarding Lawyers' Responses to Auditors' Requests for Information* (ABA Statement) is reprinted as Exhibit II [section 337C] to section 337. While Paragraph 5 of the ABA Statement [section 337C] states that the lawyer "may in appropriate circumstances communicate to the auditor his view that an unfavorable outcome is 'probable' or 'remote'," he is not required to use those terms in communicating his evaluation to the auditor. The auditor may find other wording sufficiently clear as long as the terms can be used to classify the outcome of the uncertainty under one of the three probability classifications established in FASB Statement No. 5, *Accounting for Contingencies* [AC section C59].[3]

.20 Some examples of evaluations concerning litigation that may be considered to provide sufficient clarity that the likelihood of an unfavorable outcome is "remote" even though they do not use that term are:

- ☐ "We are of the opinion that this action will not result in any liability to the company."

---

[3] FASB Statement No. 5 [AC section C59] uses the terms "probable," "reasonably possible," and "remote" to describe different degrees of likelihood that future events will confirm a loss or an impairment of an asset or incurrence of a liability, and the accounting standards for accrual and disclosure are based on those terms.

- ☐ "It is our opinion that the possible liability to the company in this proceeding is nominal in amount."
- ☐ "We believe the company will be able to defend this action successfully."
- ☐ "We believe that the plaintiff's case against the company is without merit."
- ☐ "Based on the facts known to us, after a full investigation, it is our opinion that no liability will be established against the company in these suits."

.21 Absent any contradictory information obtained by the auditor either in other parts of the lawyer's letter or otherwise, the auditor need not obtain further clarification of evaluations such as the foregoing.

.22 Because of inherent uncertainties described in section 337.14 and in the ABA Policy Statement [section 337C], an evaluation furnished by the lawyer may indicate significant uncertainties or stipulations as to whether the client will prevail. The following are examples of lawyers' evaluations that are unclear as to the likelihood of an unfavorable outcome:

- ☐ "This action involves unique characteristics wherein authoritative legal precedents do not seem to exist. We believe that the plaintiff will have serious problems establishing the company's liability under the act; nevertheless, if the plaintiff is successful, the award may be substantial."
- ☐ "It is our opinion that the company will be able to assert meritorious defenses to this action." (The term "meritorious defenses" indicates that the company's defenses will not be summarily dismissed by the court; it does not necessarily indicate counsel's opinion that the company will prevail.)
- ☐ "We believe the action can be settled for less than the damages claimed."
- ☐ "We are unable to express an opinion as to the merits of the litigation at this time. The company believes there is absolutely no merit to the litigation." (If client's counsel, with the benefit of all relevant information, is unable to conclude that the likelihood of an unfavorable outcome is "remote," it is unlikely that management would be able to form a judgment to that effect.)
- ☐ "In our opinion, the company has a substantial chance of prevailing in this action." (A "substantial chance," a "reasonable opportunity," and similar terms indicate more uncertainty than an opinion that the company will prevail.)

.23 If the auditor is uncertain as to the meaning of the lawyer's evaluation, he should request clarification either in a follow-up letter or a conference with the lawyer and client, appropriately documented. If the lawyer is still unable to give an unequivocal evaluation of the likelihood of an unfavorable outcome in writing or orally, the auditor should look to the guidance in section 508.45 through .49 to determine the effect, if any, of the lawyer's response on the auditor's report.

[Issue Date: June, 1983; Revised: February, 1997.]

8. Use of the Client's Inside Counsel in the Evaluation of Litigation, Claims, and Assessments

.24 *Question*—Section 337.06 requires an auditor to request that the client's management send a letter of inquiry to those lawyers with whom management has consulted concerning litigation, claims, and assessments. Sometimes, the client's inside general counsel or legal department (hereinafter referred to as "inside counsel") is handling litigation, claims, and assessments either exclusive of or in conjunction with outside lawyers. In such circumstances, when does inside counsel's response constitute sufficient, competent evidential matter regarding litigation, claims, and assessments?

.25 *Interpretation*—Section 337.08 states that "Evidential matter obtained from the client's inside general counsel or legal department may provide the auditor with the necessary corroboration." Inside counsel can range from one lawyer to a large staff, with responsibilities ranging from specific internal matters to a comprehensive coverage of all of the client's legal needs, including litigation with outside parties. Because both inside counsel and outside lawyers are bound by the ABA's Code of Professional Responsibilities, there is no difference in their professional obligations and responsibilities. In some circumstances, outside lawyers, if used at all, may be used only for limited purposes, such as data accumulation or account collection activity. In such circumstances, inside counsel has the primary responsibility for corporate legal matters and is in the best position to know and precisely describe the status of all litigation, claims, and assessments or to corroborate information furnished by management.

.26 Audit inquiry letters should be sent to those lawyers, which may be either inside counsel or outside lawyers, who have the primary responsibility for, and knowledge about, particular litigation, claims, and assessments. If inside counsel in handling litigation, claims, and assessments exclusively, their evaluation and response ordinarily would be considered adequate. Similarly, if both inside counsel and outside lawyers have been involved in the matters, but inside counsel has assumed the primary responsibility for the matters, inside counsel's evaluation may well be considered adequate.[4] However, there may be circumstances when litigation, claims, or assessments involving substantial overall participation by outside lawyers are of such significance to the financial statements that the auditor should consider obtaining the outside lawyers' response that they have not formulated a substantive conclusion that differs in any material respect from inside counsel's evaluation, even though inside counsel may have primary responsibility.

.27 If both inside counsel and outside lawyers have devoted substantive attention to a legal matter, but their evaluations of the possible outcome differ, the auditor should discuss the differences with the parties involved. Failure to reach agreement between the lawyers may require the auditor to consider appropriate modification of his audit report.

[Issue Date: June 1983.]

9. Use of Explanatory Language About the Attorney-Client Privilege or the Attorney Work-Product Privilege

.28 *Question*—In some cases, in order to emphasize the preservation of the attorney-client privilege or the attorney work-product privilege, some cli-

---

[4] This does not alter the caveat in section 337.08 that "evidential matter obtained from inside counsel is not a substitute for information outside counsel refuses to furnish."

ents have included the following or substantially similar language in the audit inquiry letter to legal counsel:

> We do not intend that either our request to you to provide information to our auditor or your response to our auditor should be construed in any way to constitute a waiver of the attorney-client privilege or the attorney work-product privilege.

For the same reason, some lawyers have included the following or substantially similar language in their response letters to auditors:

> The Company [OR OTHER DEFINED TERM] has advised us that, by making the request set forth in its letter to us, the Company [OR OTHER DEFINED TERM] does not intend to waive the attorney-client privilege with respect to any information which the Company [OR OTHER DEFINED TERM] has furnished to us. Moreover, please be advised that our response to you should not be construed in any way to constitute a waiver of the protection of the attorney work-product privilege with respect to any of our files involving the Company [OR OTHER DEFINED TERM].

Does the explanatory language about the attorney-client privilege or the attorney work-product privilege result in a limitation on the scope of the audit?

.29 *Answer*—No. According to the *Report by the American Bar Association's Subcommittee on Audit Inquiry Responses*, explanatory language similar to the foregoing in the letters of the client or the lawyer is not a limitation on the scope of the lawyer's response. The report states that such language simply makes explicit what has always been implicit, namely, the language states clearly that neither the client nor the lawyer intended a waiver. The report further states that non-inclusion of either or both of the foregoing statements by the client or the lawyer in their respective letters at any time in the past or the future would not constitute an expression of intent to waive the privileges. The *Report by the American Bar Association's Subcommittee on Audit Inquiry Responses* is reprinted in paragraph .30.

.30 Report of the Subcommittee on Audit Inquiry Responses*

Because of a recent court case and other judicial decisions involving lawyers' responses to auditors' requests for information, an area of uncertainty or concern has been brought to the Subcommittee's attention and is the subject of the following comment:

This Committee's report does not modify the ABA Statement of Policy, nor does it constitute an interpretation thereof. The Preamble to the ABA Statement of Policy states as follows:

> Both the Code of Professional Responsibility and the cases applying the evidentiary privilege recognize that the privilege against disclosure can be knowingly and voluntarily waived by the client. It is equally clear that disclosure to a third party may result in loss of the "confidentiality" essential to maintain the privilege. Disclosure to a third party of the lawyer-client communication on a particular subject may also destroy the privilege as to other communications on that subject. Thus, the mere disclosure by the lawyer to the outside auditor, with due client consent, of the substance of communications between the lawyer and client may significantly impair the client's ability in other contexts to maintain the confidentiality of such communications.

---

* "Excerpted from 'Statement of Policy Regarding Lawyers' Responses to Auditors' Requests for Information,' *The Business Lawyer*, vol. 31, no. 3, April 1976, copyright 1976 American Bar Association, reprinted by permission of the American Bar Association."

Under the circumstances a policy of audit procedure which requires clients to give consent and authorize lawyers to respond to general inquiries and disclose information to auditors concerning matters which have been communicated in confidence is essentially destructive of free and open communication and early consultation between lawyer and client. The institution of such a policy would inevitably discourage management from discussing potential legal problems with counsel for fear that such discussion might become public and precipitate a loss to or possible liability of the business enterprise and its stockholders that might otherwise never materialize.

It is also recognized that our legal, political, and economic systems depend to an important extent on public confidence in published financial statements. To meet this need the accounting profession must adopt and adhere to standards and procedures that will command confidence in the auditing process. It is not, however, believed necessary, or sound public policy, to intrude upon the confidentiality of the lawyer-client relationship in order to command such confidence. On the contrary, the objective of fair disclosure in financial statements is more likely to be better served by maintaining the integrity of the confidential relationship between lawyer and client, thereby strengthening corporate management's confidence in counsel and to act in accordance with counsel's advice.

Paragraph (1) of the ABA Statement of Policy provides as follows:

(1) *Client Consent to Response.* The lawyer may properly respond to the auditor's requests for information concerning loss contingencies (the term and concept established by Statement of Financial Accounting Standards No. 5, promulgated by the Financial Accounting Standards Board in March 1975 and discussed in Paragraph 5.1 of the accompanying commentary), to the extent hereinafter set forth, subject to the following:

(a) Assuming that the client's initial letter requesting the lawyer to provide information to the auditor is signed by an agent of the client having apparent authority to make such a request, the lawyer may provide to the auditor information requested, without further consent, unless such information discloses a confidence or a secret or requires an evaluation of a claim.

(b) In the normal case, the initial request letter does not provide the necessary consent to the disclosure of a confidence or secret or to the evaluation of a claim since that consent may only be given after full disclosure to the client of the legal consequences of such action.

(c) Lawyers should bear in mind, in evaluating claims, that an adverse party may assert that any evaluation of potential liability is an admission.

(d) In securing the client's consent to the disclosure of confidences or secrets, or the evaluation of claims, the lawyer may wish to have a draft of his letter reviewed and approved by the client before releasing it to the auditor; in such cases, additional explanation would in all probability be necessary so that the legal consequences of the consent are fully disclosed to the client.

In order to preserve explicitly the evidentiary privileges, some lawyers have suggested that clients include language in the following or substantially similar form:

We do not intend that either our request to you to provide information to our auditor or your response to our auditor should be construed in any way to constitute a waiver of the attorney-client privilege or the attorney work-product privilege.

If client's request letter does not contain language similar to that in the preceding paragraph, the lawyer's statement that the client has so advised him or her may be based upon the fact that the client has in fact so advised the lawyer, in writing or orally, in other communications or in discussions.

For the same reason, the response letter from some lawyers also includes language in the following or substantially similar form:

> The Company [OR OTHER DEFINED TERM] has advised us that, by making the request set forth in its letter to us, the Company [OR OTHER DEFINED TERM] does not intend to waive the attorney-client privilege with respect to any information which the Company [OR OTHER DEFINED TERM] has furnished to us. Moreover, please be advised that our response to you should not be construed in any way to constitute a waiver of the protection of the attorney work-product privilege with respect to any of our files involving the Company [OR OTHER DEFINED TERM].

We believe that language similar to the foregoing in letters of the client or the lawyer simply makes explicit what has always been implicit, namely, it expressly states clearly that neither the client nor the lawyer intended a waiver. It follows that non-inclusion of either or both of the foregoing statements by the client or the lawyer in their respective letters at any time in the past or the future would not constitute an expression of intent to waive the privileges.

On the other hand, the inclusion of such language does not necessarily assure the client that, depending on the facts and circumstances, a waiver may not be found by a court of law to have occurred.

We do not believe that the foregoing types of inclusions cause a negative impact upon the public policy considerations described in the Preamble to the ABA Statement of Policy nor do they intrude upon the arrangements between the legal profession and the accounting profession contemplated by the ABA Statement of Policy. Moreover, we do not believe that such language interferes in any way with the standards and procedures of the accounting profession in the auditing process nor should it be construed as a limitation upon the lawyer's reply to the auditors. We have been informed that the Auditing Standards Board of the AICPA has adopted an interpretation of SAS 12 recognizing the propriety of these statements.

Lawyers, in any case, should be encouraged to have their draft letters to auditors reviewed and approved by the client before releasing them to the auditors and may wish to explain to the client the legal consequences of the client's consent to lawyer's response as contemplated by sub-paragraph 1(*d*) of the Statement of Policy.

December 1989

[Issue Date: February, 1990.]

10. Use of Explanatory Language Concerning Unasserted Possible Claims or Assessments in Lawyers' Responses to Audit Inquiry Letters

.31 *Question*—In order to emphasize the preservation of the attorney-client privilege with respect to unasserted possible claims or assessments, some lawyers include the following or substantially similar language in their responses to audit inquiry letters:

> "Please be advised that pursuant to clauses (*b*) and (*c*) of Paragraph 5 of the ABA Statement of Policy [American Bar Association's *Statement of Policy Regarding Lawyers' Responses to Auditors' Requests for Information*] and related Commentary referred to in the last paragraph of this letter, it would be

> inappropriate for this firm to respond to a general inquiry relating to the existence of unasserted possible claims or assessments involving the Company. We can only furnish information concerning those unasserted possible claims or assessments upon which the Company has specifically requested in writing that we comment. We also cannot comment upon the adequacy of the Company's listing, if any, of unasserted possible claims or assessments or its assertions concerning the advice, if any, about the need to disclose same."

Does the inclusion of this or similar language result in a limitation on the scope of the audit?

.32 *Interpretation*—No. Additional language similar to the foregoing in a letter of a lawyer is not a limitation on the scope of the audit. However, the ABA Statement of Policy [section 337C] and the understanding between the legal and accounting professions assumes that the lawyer, under certain circumstances, will advise and consult with the client concerning the client's obligation to make financial statement disclosure with respect to unasserted possible claims or assessments.[5] Confirmation of this understanding should be included in the lawyer's response.

[Issue Date: January, 1997.]

---

[5] See Paragraph 6 of the ABA Statement of Policy [section 337C] and its Commentary [section 337C]. In addition, Annex A to the ABA Statement of Policy [section 337C] contains the following illustrative language in the lawyers' response letter to the auditors:

> "Consistent with the last sentence of Paragraph 6 of the ABA Statement of Policy and pursuant to the Company's request, this will confirm as correct the Company's understanding as set forth in its audit inquiry letter to us that whenever, in the course of performing legal services for the Company with respect to a matter recognized to involve an unasserted possible claim or assessment that may call for financial statement disclosure, we have formed a professional conclusion that the Company must disclose or consider disclosure concerning such possible claim or assessment, we, as a matter of professional responsibility to the Company, will so advise the Company and will consult with the Company concerning the question of such disclosure and the applicable requirements of FASB Statement No. 5, *Accounting for Contingencies* [AC section C59]."

AU Section 339

Working Papers

(Supersedes Statement on Auditing Standards No. 1, section 338, "Working Papers.")[1]

Source: SAS No. 41.

See section 9339 for interpretations of this section.

Issue date, unless otherwise indicated: April 1, 1982.

.01 The auditor should prepare and maintain working papers, the form and content of which should be designed to meet the circumstances of a particular engagement.[2] The information contained in working papers constitutes the principal record of the work that the auditor has done and the conclusions that he has reached concerning significant matters.[3]

Functions and Nature of Working Papers

.02 Working papers serve mainly to—

a. Provide the principal support for the auditor's report, including his representation regarding observance of the standards of field work, which is implicit in the reference in his report to generally accepted auditing standards.

b. Aid the auditor in the conduct and supervision of the audit.

---

[1] This section amends section 230, *Due Professional Care in the Performance of Work*, paragraph .04, by deleting the second sentence of that paragraph.

[2] This section does not modify the guidance in other Statements on Auditing Standards, including the following:

- The letter of audit inquiry to the client's lawyer required by section 337, *Inquiry of a Client's Lawyer Concerning Litigation, Claims, and Assessments*, paragraphs .08–.09, or the documentation required by paragraph .10 when a response to the audit inquiry letter is received in a conference
- The written representations from management required by section 333A, *Client Representations*
- The notation in the working papers required by section 325, *Communication of Internal Control Related Matters Noted in an Audit*, paragraph .09, if conditions relating to internal control observed during an audit of financial statements are communicated orally to the audit committee or others with equivalent authority and responsibility
- The written audit program or set of written audit programs required by section 311, *Planning and Supervision*, paragraph .05
- The representation letter from a successor auditor required by section 711, *Filings Under Federal Securities Statutes*, paragraph .11*b*, when an auditor has audited the financial statements for prior periods but has not audited the financial statements for the most recent audited period included in a registration statement
- The understanding of internal control components obtained to plan the audit, and the basis for conclusions about the assessed level of control risk required by section 319.44 and 319.57 *Consideration of Internal Control in a Financial Statement Audit*
- The notation in the working papers required by section 317, *Illegal Acts by Clients*, if illegal acts are communicated orally to the audit committee or others with equivalent authority and responsibility
- The notation in the working papers required by section 380, *Communication With Audit Committees* (if applicable), paragraph .03, if matters regarding the scope and results of the audit are communicated orally to the committee

[3] However, there is no intention to imply that the auditor would be precluded from supporting his report by other means in addition to working papers.

.03 Working papers are records kept by the auditor of the procedures applied, the tests performed, the information obtained, and the pertinent conclusions reached in the engagement. Examples of working papers are audit programs, analyses, memoranda, letters of confirmation and representation, abstracts of company documents, and schedules or commentaries prepared or obtained by the auditor. Working papers also may be in the form of data stored on tapes, films, or other media.

.04 Factors affecting the auditor's judgment about the quantity, type, and content of the working papers for a particular engagement include (*a*) the nature of the engagement, (*b*) the nature of the auditor's report, (*c*) the nature of the financial statements, schedules, or other information on which the auditor is reporting, (*d*) the nature and condition of the client's records, (*e*) the assessed level of control risk, and (*f*) the needs in the particular circumstances for supervision and review of the work.

Content of Working Papers

.05 The quantity, type, and content of working papers vary with the circumstances (see paragraph .04), but they should be sufficient to show that the accounting records agree or reconcile with the financial statements or other information reported on and that the applicable standards of field work have been observed. Working papers ordinarily should include documentation showing that—

a. The work has been adequately planned and supervised, indicating observance of the first standard of field work.

b. A sufficient understanding of internal control has been obtained to plan the audit and to determine the nature, timing, and extent of tests to be performed.

c. The audit evidence obtained, the auditing procedures applied, and the testing performed have provided sufficient competent evidential matter to afford a reasonable basis for an opinion, indicating observance of the third standard of field work.

Ownership and Custody of Working Papers

.06 Working papers are the property of the auditor, and some states have statutes that designate the auditor as the owner of the working papers. The auditor's rights of ownership, however, are subject to ethical limitations relating to the confidential relationship with clients.

.07 Certain of the auditor's working papers may sometimes serve as a useful reference source for his client, but the working papers should not be regarded as a part of, or a substitute for, the client's accounting records.

.08 The auditor should adopt reasonable procedures for safe custody of his working papers and should retain them for a period sufficient to meet the needs of his practice and to satisfy any pertinent legal requirements of records retention.

Effective Date

.09 This section is effective for engagements beginning after May 31, 1982.

AU Section 9339

Working Papers: Auditing Interpretations of Section 339

1. Providing Access to or Photocopies of Working Papers to a Regulator[1, 2]

.01 *Question*—Section 339, *Working Papers*, paragraph .06, states that "working papers are the property of the auditor and some states have statutes that designate the auditor as the owner of the working papers. The auditor's rights of ownership, however, are subject to ethical limitations relating to the confidential relationship with clients." In addition, section 339.08 states that, "The auditor should adopt reasonable procedures for safe custody of his working papers and should retain them for a period sufficient to meet the needs of his practice and to satisfy any pertinent legal requirements of records retention."

Notwithstanding the provisions of section 339.06 and .08, auditors are sometimes required by law, regulation or audit contract,[3] to provide a regulator, or a duly appointed representative, access to working papers. For example, a regulator may request access to the working papers to fulfill a quality review requirement or to assist in establishing the scope of a regulatory examination. Furthermore, as part of the regulator's review of the working papers, the regulator may request photocopies of all or selected portions of the working papers during or after the review. The regulator may intend, or decide, to make photocopies (or information derived from the original working papers) available to others, including other governmental agencies, for their particular purposes, with or without the knowledge of the auditor or the client. When a regulator requests the auditor to provide access to (and possibly photocopies of) working papers pursuant to law, regulation or audit contract, what steps should the auditor take?

.02 *Interpretation*—When a regulator requests access to working papers pursuant to law, regulation or audit contract, the auditor should take the following steps:

---

[1] The term "regulator(s)" includes federal, state and local government officials with legal oversight authority over the entity. Examples of regulators who may request access to working papers include, but are not limited to, state insurance and utility regulators, various health care authorities, and federal agencies such as the Federal Deposit Insurance Corporation, the Office of Thrift Supervision, the Department of Housing and Urban Development, the Department of Labor, and the Rural Electrification Administration.

[2] The guidance in this Interpretation does not apply to requests from the Internal Revenue Service, firm practice-monitoring programs to comply with AICPA or state professional requirements such as peer or quality reviews, proceedings relating to alleged ethics violations, or subpoenas.

[3] For situations in which the auditor is not required by law, regulation or audit contract to provide a regulator access to the working papers, reference should be made to the guidance in paragraphs .11–.15 of this Interpretation.

a. Consider advising the client that the regulator has requested access to (and possibly photocopies of) the working papers and that the auditor intends to comply with such request.[4]

b. Make appropriate arrangements with the regulator for the review.

c. Maintain control over the original working papers, and

d. Consider submitting the letter described in paragraph .05 of this Interpretation to the regulator.

.03 The auditor should make appropriate arrangements with the regulator. These arrangements ordinarily would include the specific details such as the date, time and location of the review. The working papers may be made available to a regulator at the offices of the client, the auditor, or a mutually agreed-upon location, so long as the auditor maintains control. Furthermore, the auditor should take appropriate steps to maintain custody of the original working papers. For example, the auditor (or his or her representative) should consider being present when the original working papers are reviewed by the regulator. Maintaining control of the working papers is necessary to ensure the continued integrity of the working papers and to ensure confidentiality of client information.

.04 Ordinarily, the auditor should not agree to transfer ownership of the working papers to a regulator. Furthermore, the auditor should not agree, without client authorization, that the information contained therein about the client may be communicated to or made available to any other party. In this regard, the action of an auditor providing access to, or photocopies of, the working papers shall not constitute transfer of ownership or authorization to make them available to any other party.

.05 An audit performed in accordance with generally accepted auditing standards is not intended to, and does not, satisfy a regulator's oversight responsibilities. To avoid any misunderstanding, prior to allowing a regulator access to the working papers, the auditor should consider submitting a letter to the regulator that:

a. Sets forth the auditor's understanding of the purpose for which access is being requested

b. Describes the audit process and the limitations inherent in a financial statement audit

c. Explains the purpose for which the working papers were prepared, and that any individual conclusions must be read in the context of the auditor's report on the financial statements

d. States, except when not applicable, that the audit was not planned or conducted in contemplation of the purpose for which access is being granted or to assess the entity's compliance with laws and regulations

---

[4] The auditor may wish (and in some cases may be required by law, regulation, or audit contract) to confirm in writing with the client that the auditor may be required to provide a regulator access to the working papers. Sample language that may be used follows:

"The working papers for this engagement are the property of (*name of auditor*) and constitute confidential information. However, we may be requested to make certain working papers available to (*name of regulator*) pursuant to authority given to it by law or regulation. If requested, access to such working papers will be provided under the supervision of (*name of auditor*) personnel. Furthermore, upon request, we may provide photocopies of selected working papers to (*name of regulator*). The (*name of regulator*) may intend, or decide, to distribute the photocopies or information contained therein to others, including other governmental agencies."

e. States that the audit and the working papers should not supplant other inquiries and procedures that should be undertaken by the regulator for its purposes

f. Requests confidential treatment under the Freedom of Information Act or similar laws and regulations,[5] when a request for the working papers is made, and that written notice be given to the auditor before transmitting any information contained in the working papers to others, including other governmental agencies, except when such transfer is required by law or regulation, and

g. States that if any photocopies are to be provided, they will be identified as "Confidential Treatment Requested by (*name of auditor, address, telephone number*)."

The auditor may wish to obtain a signed acknowledgment copy of the letter as evidence of the regulator's receipt of the letter.

.06 An example of a letter containing the elements described in paragraph .05 of this Interpretation is presented below:

Illustrative Letter to Regulator[6]

(*Date*)

(*Name and Address of Regulatory Agency*)

Your representatives have requested access to our working papers in connection with our audit of the December 31, 19XX financial statements of (*name of client*). It is our understanding that the purpose of your request is (*state purpose: for example, "to facilitate your regulatory examination"*).[7]

Our audit of (*name of client*) December 31, 19XX financial statements was conducted in accordance with generally accepted auditing standards,[8] the objective[9] of which is to form an opinion as to whether the financial statements, which are the responsibility and representations of management, present fairly, in all material respects, the financial position, results of operations and cash flows in conformity with generally accepted accounting principles.[10] Under generally accepted auditing standards, we have the re-

---

[5] The auditor may need to consult the regulations of individual agencies and, if necessary, consult with legal counsel regarding the specific procedures and requirements necessary to gain confidential treatment.

[6] The auditor should appropriately modify this letter when the audit has been performed in accordance with generally accepted auditing standards and also in accordance with additional auditing requirements specified by a regulatory agency (for example, the requirements specified in *Government Auditing Standards* issued by the Comptroller General of the United States).

[7] If the auditor is not required by law, regulation, or audit contract to provide a regulator access to the working papers but otherwise intends to provide such access (see paragraphs .11–.15 of this Interpretation), the letter should include a statement that: "Management of (*name of client*) has authorized us to provide you access to our working papers for (*state purpose*)."

[8] Refer to footnote 6.

[9] In an audit performed in accordance with the *Single Audit Act of 1984*, and certain other federal audit requirements, an additional objective of the audit is to assess compliance with laws and regulations applicable to federal financial assistance. Accordingly, in these situations, the above letter should be modified to include the additional objective.

[10] If the financial statements have been prepared in conformity with regulatory accounting practices, the phrase "financial position, results of operations and cash flows in conformity with generally accepted accounting principles" should be replaced with appropriate wording such as, in the case of an insurance company, the "admitted assets, liabilities... of the XYZ Insurance Company in conformity with accounting practices prescribed or permitted by the state of... insurance department."

sponsibility, within the inherent limitations of the auditing process, to design our audit to provide reasonable assurance that errors and irregularities that have a material effect on the financial statements will be detected, and to exercise due care in the conduct of our audit. The concept of selective testing of the data being audited, which involves judgment both as to the number of transactions to be audited and as to the areas to be tested, has been generally accepted as a valid and sufficient basis for an auditor to express an opinion on financial statements. Thus, our audit, based on the concept of selective testing, is subject to the inherent risk that material errors or irregularities, if they exist, would not be detected. In addition, an audit does not address the possibility that material errors or irregularities may occur in the future. Also, our use of professional judgment and the assessment of materiality for the purpose of our audit means that matters may have existed that would have been assessed differently by you.

The working papers were prepared for the purpose of providing the principal support for our report on (*name of client*) December 31, 19XX financial statements and to aid in the conduct and supervision of our audit. The working papers document the procedures performed, the information obtained and the pertinent conclusions reached in the engagement. The audit procedures that we performed were limited to those we considered necessary under generally accepted auditing standards[11] to enable us to formulate and express an opinion on the financial statements[12] taken as a whole. Accordingly, we make no representation as to the sufficiency or appropriateness, for your purposes, of either the information contained in our working papers or our audit procedures. In addition, any notations, comments, and individual conclusions appearing on any of the working papers do not stand alone, and should not be read as an opinion on any individual amounts, accounts, balances or transactions.

Our audit of (*name of client*) December 31, 19XX financial statements was performed for the purpose stated above and has not been planned or conducted in contemplation of your (*state purpose: for example, "regulatory examination"*) or for the purpose of assessing (*name of client*) compliance with laws and regulations.[13] Therefore, items of possible interest to you may not have been specifically addressed. Accordingly, our audit and the working papers prepared in connection therewith, should not supplant other inquiries and procedures that should be undertaken by the (*name of regulatory agency*) for the purpose of monitoring and regulating the financial affairs of the (*name of client*). In addition, we have not audited any financial statements of (*name of client*) since (*date of audited balance sheet referred to in the first paragraph above*) nor have we performed any audit procedures since (*date*), the date of our auditor's report, and significant events or circumstances may have occurred since that date.

The working papers constitute and reflect work performed or information obtained by (*name of auditor*) in its capacity as independent auditor for (*name of client*). The documents contain trade secrets and confidential commercial and financial information of our firm and (*name of client*) that is privileged and confidential, and we expressly reserve all rights with respect to disclosures to third parties. Accordingly, we request confidential treatment under the Freedom of Information Act or similar laws and regulations[14] when requests are

---

[11] Refer to footnote 6.

[12] Refer to footnote 9.

[13] Refer to footnote 9.

[14] This illustrative paragraph may not in and of itself be sufficient to gain confidential treatment under the rules and regulations of certain regulatory agencies. The auditor should consider tailoring this paragraph to the circumstances after consulting the regulations of each applicable regulatory agency and, if necessary, consult with legal counsel regarding the specific procedures and requirements to gain confidential treatment.

made for the working papers or information contained therein or any documents created by the (*name of regulatory agency*) containing information derived therefrom. We further request that written notice be given to our firm before distribution of the information in the working papers (or photocopies thereof) to others, including other governmental agencies, except when such distribution is required by law or regulation.

[*If it is expected that photocopies will be requested, add:*

Any photocopies of our working papers we agree to provide you will be identified as "Confidential Treatment Requested by (*name of auditor, address, telephone number*)."]

Firm signature

.07 *Question*—A regulator may request access to the working papers before the audit has been completed and the report released. May the auditor allow access in such circumstances?

.08 *Interpretation*—When the audit has not been completed, the working papers are necessarily incomplete because (*a*) additional information may be added as a result of further tests and review by supervisory personnel and (*b*) any audit results and conclusions reflected in the incomplete working papers may change. Accordingly, it is preferable that access be delayed until all audit procedures have been completed and all internal reviews have been performed. If access is provided prior to completion of the audit, the auditor should consider issuing the letter referred to in paragraph .05 of this Interpretation, appropriately modified, and including additional language along the following lines:

"We have been engaged to audit in accordance with generally accepted auditing standards the December 31, 19XX, financial statements of XYZ Company, but have not as yet completed our audit. Accordingly, at this time we do not express any opinion on the Company's financial statements. Furthermore, the contents of the working papers may change as a result of additional audit procedures and review of the working papers by supervisory personnel of our firm. Accordingly, our working papers are incomplete."

Because the working papers may change prior to completion of the audit, the auditor ordinarily should not provide photocopies of the working papers until the audit has been completed.

.09 *Question*—Some regulators may engage an independent party, such as another independent public accountant, to perform the working paper review on behalf of the regulatory agency. Are there any special precautions the auditor should observe in these circumstances?

.10 *Interpretation*—The auditor should be satisfied that the party engaged by the regulator is subject to the same confidentiality restrictions as the regulatory agency itself. This can be accomplished by obtaining acknowledgment, preferably in writing, from the regulator stating that the third party is acting on behalf of the regulator and agreement from the third party that he or she is subject to the same restrictions on disclosure and use of working papers and the information contained therein as the regulator.

.11 *Question*—When a regulator requests the auditor to provide access to (and possibly photocopies of) working papers and the auditor is not otherwise required by law, regulation or audit contract to provide such access, what steps should the auditor take?

.12 *Interpretation*—The auditor should obtain an understanding of the reasons for the regulator's request for access to the working papers and may wish to consider consulting with legal counsel regarding the request. If the auditor decides to provide such access, the auditor should obtain the client's consent, preferably in writing, to provide the regulator access to the working papers.

.13 Following is an example of language that may be used in the written communication to the client:

> "The working papers for this engagement are the property of (*name of auditor*) and constitute confidential information. However, we have been requested to make certain working papers available to (*name of regulator*) for (*describe the regulator's basis for its request*). Access to such working papers will be provided under the supervision of (*name of auditor*) personnel. Furthermore, upon request, we may provide photocopies of selected working papers to (*name of regulator*).
>
> "You have authorized (*name of auditor*) to allow (*name of regulator*) access to the working papers in the manner discussed above. Please confirm your agreement to the above by signing below and returning to (*name of auditor, address*)."
>
> Firm signature
>
> ______________________
>
> Agreed and acknowledged:
>
> ______________________
>
> (Name and title)
>
> ______________________
>
> (Date)

.14 If the client requests to review the working papers before allowing the regulator access, the auditor may provide the client with the opportunity to obtain an understanding of the nature of the information about its financial statements contained in the working papers that are being made available to the regulator. When a client reviews the working papers, the auditor should maintain control of the working papers as discussed in paragraph .03 of this Interpretation.

.15 The auditor should also refer to the guidance in paragraphs .03–.10 of this Interpretation which provide guidance on making arrangements with the regulator for access to the working papers, maintaining control over the original working papers and submitting a letter describing various matters to the regulator.

[Issue Date: July, 1994; Revised: June, 1996.]

AU Section 341

The Auditor's Consideration of an Entity's Ability to Continue as a Going Concern

(Supersedes section 340)

Source: SAS No. 59; SAS No. 64; SAS No. 77.

See section 9341 for interpretations of this section.

Effective for audits of financial statements for periods beginning on or after January 1, 1989, unless otherwise indicated.

.01 This section provides guidance to the auditor in conducting an audit of financial statements in accordance with generally accepted auditing standards with respect to evaluating whether there is substantial doubt about the entity's ability to continue as a going concern.[1, 2] Continuation of an entity as a going concern is assumed in financial reporting in the absence of significant information to the contrary. Ordinarily, information that significantly contradicts the going concern assumption relates to the entity's inability to continue to meet its obligations as they become due without substantial disposition of assets outside the ordinary course of business, restructuring of debt, externally forced revisions of its operations, or similar actions.

The Auditor's Responsibility

.02 The auditor has a responsibility to evaluate whether there is substantial doubt about the entity's ability to continue as a going concern for a reasonable period of time, not to exceed one year beyond the date of the financial statements being audited (hereinafter referred to as *a reasonable period of time*). The auditor's evaluation is based on his knowledge of relevant conditions and events that exist at or have occurred prior to the completion of fieldwork. Information about such conditions or events is obtained from the application of auditing procedures planned and performed to achieve audit objectives that are related to management's assertions embodied in the financial statements being audited, as described in section 326, *Evidential Matter*.

---

[1] This section does not apply to an audit of financial statements based on the assumption of liquidation (for example, when [*a*] an entity is in the process of liquidation, [*b*] the owners have decided to commence dissolution or liquidation, or [*c*] legal proceedings, including bankruptcy, have reached a point at which dissolution or liquidation is probable). See Auditing Interpretation, "Reporting on Financial Statements Prepared on a Liquidation Basis of Accounting" (section 9508.33–.38).

[2] The guidance provided in this section applies to audits of financial statements prepared either in accordance with generally accepted accounting principles or in accordance with a comprehensive basis of accounting other than generally accepted accounting principles. References in this section to generally accepted accounting principles are intended to include a comprehensive basis of accounting other than generally accepted accounting principles (excluding liquidation basis).

.03 The auditor should evaluate whether there is substantial doubt about the entity's ability to continue as a going concern for a reasonable period of time in the following manner:

a. The auditor considers whether the results of his procedures performed in planning, gathering evidential matter relative to the various audit objectives, and completing the audit identify conditions and events that, when considered in the aggregate, indicate there could be substantial doubt about the entity's ability to continue as a going concern for a reasonable period of time. It may be necessary to obtain additional information about such conditions and events, as well as the appropriate evidential matter to support information that mitigates the auditor's doubt.

b. If the auditor believes there is substantial doubt about the entity's ability to continue as a going concern for a reasonable period of time, he should (1) obtain information about management's plans that are intended to mitigate the effect of such conditions or events, and (2) assess the likelihood that such plans can be effectively implemented.

c. After the auditor has evaluated management's plans, he concludes whether he has substantial doubt about the entity's ability to continue as a going concern for a reasonable period of time. If the auditor concludes there is substantial doubt, he should (1) consider the adequacy of disclosure about the entity's possible inability to continue as a going concern for a reasonable period of time, and (2) include an explanatory paragraph (following the opinion paragraph) in his audit report to reflect his conclusion. If the auditor concludes that substantial doubt does not exist, he should consider the need for disclosure.

.04 The auditor is not responsible for predicting future conditions or events. The fact that the entity may cease to exist as a going concern subsequent to receiving a report from the auditor that does not refer to substantial doubt, even within one year following the date of the financial statements, does not, in itself, indicate inadequate performance by the auditor. Accordingly, the absence of reference to substantial doubt in an auditor's report should not be viewed as providing assurance as to an entity's ability to continue as a going concern.

Audit Procedures

.05 It is not necessary to design audit procedures solely to identify conditions and events that, when considered in the aggregate, indicate there could be substantial doubt about the entity's ability to continue as a going concern for a reasonable period of time. The results of auditing procedures designed and performed to achieve other audit objectives should be sufficient for that purpose. The following are examples of procedures that may identify such conditions and events:

- Analytical procedures
- Review of subsequent events
- Review of compliance with the terms of debt and loan agreements
- Reading of minutes of meetings of stockholders, board of directors, and important committees of the board

- Inquiry of an entity's legal counsel about litigation, claims, and assessments
- Confirmation with related and third parties of the details of arrangements to provide or maintain financial support

Consideration of Conditions and Events

.06 In performing audit procedures such as those presented in paragraph .05, the auditor may identify information about certain conditions or events that, when considered in the aggregate, indicate there could be substantial doubt about the entity's ability to continue as a going concern for a reasonable period of time. The significance of such conditions and events will depend on the circumstances, and some may have significance only when viewed in conjunction with others. The following are examples of such conditions and events:

- *Negative trends*—for example, recurring operating losses, working capital deficiencies, negative cash flows from operating activities, adverse key financial ratios
- *Other indications of possible financial difficulties*—for example, default on loan or similar agreements, arrearages in dividends, denial of usual trade credit from suppliers, restructuring of debt, noncompliance with statutory capital requirements, need to seek new sources or methods of financing or to dispose of substantial assets
- *Internal matters*—for example, work stoppages or other labor difficulties, substantial dependence on the success of a particular project, uneconomic long-term commitments, need to significantly revise operations
- *External matters that have occurred*—for example, legal proceedings, legislation, or similar matters that might jeopardize an entity's ability to operate; loss of a key franchise, license, or patent; loss of a principal customer or supplier; uninsured or underinsured catastrophe such as a drought, earthquake, or flood

Consideration of Management's Plans

.07 If, after considering the identified conditions and events in the aggregate, the auditor believes there is substantial doubt about the ability of the entity to continue as a going concern for a reasonable period of time, he should consider management's plans for dealing with the adverse effects of the conditions and events. The auditor should obtain information about the plans and consider whether it is likely the adverse effects will be mitigated for a reasonable period of time and that such plans can be effectively implemented. The auditor's considerations relating to management plans may include the following:

- Plans to dispose of assets
  - Restrictions on disposal of assets, such as covenants limiting such transactions in loan or similar agreements or encumbrances against assets
  - Apparent marketability of assets that management plans to sell
  - Possible direct or indirect effects of disposal of assets

- Plans to borrow money or restructure debt
  - Availability of debt financing, including existing or committed credit arrangements, such as lines of credit or arrangements for factoring receivables or sale-leaseback of assets
  - Existing or committed arrangements to restructure or subordinate debt or to guarantee loans to the entity
  - Possible effects on management's borrowing plans of existing restrictions on additional borrowing or the sufficiency of available collateral
- Plans to reduce or delay expenditures
  - Apparent feasibility of plans to reduce overhead or administrative expenditures, to postpone maintenance or research and development projects, or to lease rather than purchase assets
  - Possible direct or indirect effects of reduced or delayed expenditures
- Plans to increase ownership equity
  - Apparent feasibility of plans to increase ownership equity, including existing or committed arrangements to raise additional capital
  - Existing or committed arrangements to reduce current dividend requirements or to accelerate cash distributions from affiliates or other investors

.08 When evaluating management's plans, the auditor should identify those elements that are particularly significant to overcoming the adverse effects of the conditions and events and should plan and perform auditing procedures to obtain evidential matter about them. For example, the auditor should consider the adequacy of support regarding the ability to obtain additional financing or the planned disposal of assets.

.09 When prospective financial information is particularly significant to management's plans, the auditor should request management to provide that information and should consider the adequacy of support for significant assumptions underlying that information. The auditor should give particular attention to assumptions that are—

- Material to the prospective financial information.
- Especially sensitive or susceptible to change.
- Inconsistent with historical trends.

The auditor's consideration should be based on knowledge of the entity, its business, and its management and should include (*a*) reading of the prospective financial information and the underlying assumptions and (*b*) comparing prospective financial information in prior periods with actual results and comparing prospective information for the current period with results achieved to date. If the auditor becomes aware of factors, the effects of which are not reflected in such prospective financial information, he should discuss those factors with management and, if necessary, request revision of the prospective financial information.

Consideration of Financial Statement Effects

.10 When, after considering management's plans, the auditor concludes there is substantial doubt about the entity's ability to continue as a going concern for a reasonable period of time, the auditor should consider the possible effects on the financial statements and the adequacy of the related disclosure. Some of the information that might be disclosed includes—

- Pertinent conditions and events giving rise to the assessment of substantial doubt about the entity's ability to continue as a going concern for a reasonable period of time.
- The possible effects of such conditions and events.
- Management's evaluation of the significance of those conditions and events and any mitigating factors.
- Possible discontinuance of operations.
- Management's plans (including relevant prospective financial information).[3]
- Information about the recoverability or classification of recorded asset amounts or the amounts or classification of liabilities.

.11 When, primarily because of the auditor's consideration of management's plans, he concludes that substantial doubt about the entity's ability to continue as a going concern for a reasonable period of time is alleviated, he should consider the need for disclosure of the principal conditions and events that initially caused him to believe there was substantial doubt. The auditor's consideration of disclosure should include the possible effects of such conditions and events, and any mitigating factors, including management's plans.

Consideration of the Effects on the Auditor's Report

.12 If, after considering identified conditions and events and management's plans, the auditor concludes that substantial doubt about the entity's ability to continue as a going concern for a reasonable period of time remains, the audit report should include an explanatory paragraph (following the opinion paragraph) to reflect that conclusion.[4] The auditor's conclusion about the entity's ability to continue as a going concern should be expressed through the use of the phrase "substantial doubt about its (the entity's) ability to continue as a going concern" [or similar wording that includes the terms substantial doubt *and* going concern] as illustrated in paragraph .13. [As amended, effective for reports issued after December 31, 1990, by Statement on Auditing Standards No. 64.]

.13 An example follows of an explanatory paragraph (following the opinion paragraph) in the auditor's report describing an uncertainty about the entity's ability to continue as a going concern for a reasonable period of time.[5]

---

[3] It is not intended that such prospective financial information constitute prospective financial statements meeting the minimum presentation guidelines set forth in AT section 200, *Financial Forecasts and Projections*, nor that the inclusion of such information require any consideration beyond that normally required by generally accepted auditing standards.

[4] The inclusion of an explanatory paragraph (following the opinion paragraph) in the auditor's report contemplated by this section should serve adequately to inform the users of the financial statements. Nothing in this section, however, is intended to preclude an auditor from declining to express an opinion in cases involving uncertainties. If he disclaims an opinion, the uncertainties and their possible effects on the financial statements should be disclosed in an appropriate manner (see paragraph .10), and the auditor's report should give all the substantive reasons for his disclaimer of opinion (see section 508, *Reports on Audited Financial Statements*).

[5] In a going-concern explanatory paragraph, the auditor should not use conditional language in expressing a conclusion concerning the existence of substantial doubt about the entity's ability to continue as a going concern. Examples of inappropriate wording in the explanatory paragraph would be, "If the Company continues to suffer recurring losses from operations and continues to have a net capital deficiency, there may be substantial doubt about its ability to continue as a going concern" or "The Company has been unable to renegotiate its expiring credit agreements. Unless the Company is able to obtain financial support, there is substantial doubt about its ability to continue as a going concern." [Footnote added, effective for reports issued after December 15, 1995, by Statement on Auditing Standards No. 77.]

> The accompanying financial statements have been prepared assuming that the Company will continue as a going concern. As discussed in Note X to the financial statements, the Company has suffered recurring losses from operations and has a net capital deficiency that raise substantial doubt about its ability to continue as a going concern. Management's plans in regard to these matters are also described in Note X. The financial statements do not include any adjustments that might result from the outcome of this uncertainty.

[As amended, effective for reports issued after December 31, 1990, by Statement on Auditing Standards No. 64.]

.14 If the auditor concludes that the entity's disclosures with respect to the entity's ability to continue as a going concern for a reasonable period of time are inadequate, a departure from generally accepted accounting principles exists. This may result in either a qualified (except for) or an adverse opinion. Reporting guidance for such situations is provided in section 508, *Reports on Audited Financial Statements*.

.15 Substantial doubt about the entity's ability to continue as a going concern for a reasonable period of time that arose in the current period does not imply that a basis for such doubt existed in the prior period and, therefore, should not affect the auditor's report on the financial statements of the prior period that are presented on a comparative basis. When financial statements of one or more prior periods are presented on a comparative basis with financial statements of the current period, reporting guidance is provided in section 508.

.16 If substantial doubt about the entity's ability to continue as a going concern for a reasonable period of time existed at the date of prior period financial statements that are presented on a comparative basis, and that doubt has been removed in the current period, the explanatory paragraph included in the auditor's report (following the opinion paragraph) on the financial statements of the prior period should not be repeated.

Effective Date

.17 This section is effective for audits of financial statements for periods beginning on or after January 1, 1989. Early application of the provisions of this section is permissible.

AU Section 9341

The Auditor's Consideration of an Entity's Ability to Continue as a Going Concern: Auditing Interpretations of Section 341

1. Eliminating a Going-Concern Explanatory Paragraph From a Reissued Report

.01 *Question*—An auditor may be asked to reissue his or her report on financial statements and eliminate the going-concern explanatory paragraph that appeared in the original report. Such requests ordinarily occur after the conditions that gave rise to substantial doubt about the entity's ability to continue as a going concern have been resolved. For example, subsequent to the date of the auditor's original report, an entity might obtain needed financing. In such circumstances, may the auditor reissue his or her report and eliminate the going-concern explanatory paragraph that appeared in the original report?

.02 *Interpretation*—An auditor has no obligation to reissue his or her report.[1] However, if the auditor decides to reissue the report,[2] the auditor should perform the following procedures when determining whether to reissue the report without the going-concern explanatory paragraph that appeared in the original report:

- Audit the event or transaction that prompted the request to reissue the report without the going-concern explanatory paragraph.
- Perform the procedures listed in section 560, *Subsequent Events*, paragraph .12, at or near the date of reissuance.
- Consider the factors described in section 341, *The Auditor's Consideration of an Entity's Ability to Continue as a Going Concern*, paragraphs .06 through .11, based on the conditions and circumstances at the date of reissuance.

The auditor may perform any other procedures that he or she deems necessary in the circumstances. Based on the information that the auditor becomes aware of as a result of performing the procedures mentioned above, the auditor should reassess the going-concern status of the entity.

[Issue Date: August, 1995.]

---

[1] If the auditor decides not to reissue his or her report, the auditor may agree to be engaged to audit the financial statements for a period subsequent to that covered by the original report. This might be the case, for example, if the entity is experiencing profitable operations.

[2] Section 530, *Dating of the Independent Auditor's Report*, paragraph .05, states that an auditor may either "dual-date" or "later-date" his or her reissued report.

AU Section 9341

The Auditor's Consideration of an Entity's Ability to Continue as a Going Concern: Auditing Interpretations of Section 341

[illegible]

AU Section 342

Auditing Accounting Estimates

Source: SAS No. 57.

See section 9342 for interpretations of this section.

Effective for audits of financial statements for periods beginning on or after January 1, 1989, unless otherwise indicated.

.01 This section provides guidance to auditors on obtaining and evaluating sufficient competent evidential matter to support significant accounting estimates in an audit of financial statements in accordance with generally accepted auditing standards. For purposes of this section, an *accounting estimate* is an approximation of a financial statement element, item, or account. Accounting estimates are often included in historical financial statements because—

a. The measurement of some amounts or the valuation of some accounts is uncertain, pending the outcome of future events.

b. Relevant data concerning events that have already occurred cannot be accumulated on a timely, cost-effective basis.

.02 Accounting estimates in historical financial statements measure the effects of past business transactions or events, or the present status of an asset or liability. Examples of accounting estimates include net realizable values of inventory and accounts receivable, property and casualty insurance loss reserves, revenues from contracts accounted for by the percentage-of-completion method, and pension and warranty expenses.[1]

.03 Management is responsible for making the accounting estimates included in the financial statements. Estimates are based on subjective as well as objective factors and, as a result, judgment is required to estimate an amount at the date of the financial statements. Management's judgment is normally based on its knowledge and experience about past and current events and its assumptions about conditions it expects to exist and courses of action it expects to take.

.04 The auditor is responsible for evaluating the reasonableness of accounting estimates made by management in the context of the financial statements taken as a whole. As estimates are based on subjective as well as objective factors, it may be difficult for management to establish controls over them. Even when management's estimation process involves competent personnel using relevant and reliable data, there is potential for bias in the subjective factors. Accordingly, when planning and performing procedures to evaluate accounting estimates, the auditor should consider, with an attitude of professional skepticism, both the subjective and objective factors.

---

[1] Additional examples of accounting estimates included in historical financial statements are presented in paragraph .16.

Developing Accounting Estimates

.05 Management is responsible for establishing a process for preparing accounting estimates. Although the process may not be documented or formally applied, it normally consists of—

a. Identifying situations for which accounting estimates are required.

b. Identifying the relevant factors that may affect the accounting estimate.

c. Accumulating relevant, sufficient, and reliable data on which to base the estimate.

d. Developing assumptions that represent management's judgment of the most likely circumstances and events with respect to the relevant factors.

e. Determining the estimated amount based on the assumptions and other relevant factors.

f. Determining that the accounting estimate is presented in conformity with applicable accounting principles and that disclosure is adequate.

The risk of material misstatement of accounting estimates normally varies with the complexity and subjectivity associated with the process, the availability and reliability of relevant data, the number and significance of assumptions that are made, and the degree of uncertainty associated with the assumptions.

Internal Control Related to Accounting Estimates

.06 An entity's internal control may reduce the likelihood of material misstatements of accounting estimates. Specific relevant aspects of internal control include the following:

a. Management communication of the need for proper accounting estimates

b. Accumulation of relevant, sufficient, and reliable data on which to base an accounting estimate

c. Preparation of the accounting estimate by qualified personnel

d. Adequate review and approval of the accounting estimates by appropriate levels of authority, including—
   1. Review of sources of relevant factors
   2. Review of development of assumptions
   3. Review of reasonableness of assumptions and resulting estimates
   4. Consideration of the need to use the work of specialists
   5. Consideration of changes in previously established methods to arrive at accounting estimates

e. Comparison of prior accounting estimates with subsequent results to assess the reliability of the process used to develop estimates

f. Consideration by management of whether the resulting accounting estimate is consistent with the operational plans of the entity.

Evaluating Accounting Estimates

.07 The auditor's objective when evaluating accounting estimates is to obtain sufficient competent evidential matter to provide reasonable assurance that—

a. All accounting estimates that could be material to the financial statements have been developed.

b. Those accounting estimates are reasonable in the circumstances.

c. The accounting estimates are presented in conformity with applicable accounting principles[2] and are properly disclosed.[3]

Identifying Circumstances That Require Accounting Estimates

.08 In evaluating whether management has identified all accounting estimates that could be material to the financial statements, the auditor considers the circumstances of the industry or industries in which the entity operates, its methods of conducting business, new accounting pronouncements, and other external factors. The auditor should consider performing the following procedures:

a. Consider assertions embodied in the financial statements to determine the need for estimates. (See paragraph .16 for examples of accounting estimates included in financial statements.)

b. Evaluate information obtained in performing other procedures, such as—

1. Information about changes made or planned in the entity's business, including changes in operating strategy, and the industry in which the entity operates that may indicate the need to make an accounting estimate (section 311, *Planning and Supervision*).
2. Changes in the methods of accumulating information.
3. Information concerning identified litigation, claims, and assessments (section 337, *Inquiry of a Client's Lawyer Concerning Litigation, Claims, and Assessments*), and other contingencies.
4. Information from reading available minutes of meetings of stockholders, directors, and appropriate committees.
5. Information contained in regulatory or examination reports, supervisory correspondence, and similar materials from applicable regulatory agencies.

c. Inquire of management about the existence of circumstances that may indicate the need to make an accounting estimate.

Evaluating Reasonableness

.09 In evaluating the reasonableness of an estimate, the auditor normally concentrates on key factors and assumptions that are—

a. Significant to the accounting estimate.

b. Sensitive to variations.

c. Deviations from historical patterns.

d. Subjective and susceptible to misstatement and bias.

The auditor normally should consider the historical experience of the entity in making past estimates as well as the auditor's experience in the industry. How-

---

[2] Section 411, *The Meaning of* Present Fairly in Conformity With Generally Accepted Accounting Principles *in the Independent Auditor's Report*, discusses the auditor's responsibility for evaluating conformity with generally accepted accounting principles.

[3] Section 431, *Adequacy of Disclosure in Financial Statements*, discusses the auditor's responsibility to consider whether the financial statements include adequate disclosures of material matters in light of the circumstances and facts of which he is aware.

ever, changes in facts, circumstances, or entity's procedures may cause factors different from those considered in the past to become significant to the accounting estimate.[4]

.10 In evaluating reasonableness, the auditor should obtain an understanding of how management developed the estimate. Based on that understanding, the auditor should use one or a combination of the following approaches:

a. Review and test the process used by management to develop the estimate.

b. Develop an independent expectation of the estimate to corroborate the reasonableness of management's estimate.

c. Review subsequent events or transactions occurring prior to completion of fieldwork.

.11 Review and test management's process. In many situations, the auditor assesses the reasonableness of an accounting estimate by performing procedures to test the process used by management to make the estimate. The following are procedures the auditor may consider performing when using this approach:

a. Identify whether there are controls over the preparation of accounting estimates and supporting data that may be useful in the evaluation.

b. Identify the sources of data and factors that management used in forming the assumptions, and consider whether such data and factors are relevant, reliable, and sufficient for the purpose based on information gathered in other audit tests.

c. Consider whether there are additional key factors or alternative assumptions about the factors.

d. Evaluate whether the assumptions are consistent with each other, the supporting data, relevant historical data, and industry data.

e. Analyze historical data used in developing the assumptions to assess whether the data is comparable and consistent with data of the period under audit, and consider whether such data is sufficiently reliable for the purpose.

f. Consider whether changes in the business or industry may cause other factors to become significant to the assumptions.

g. Review available documentation of the assumptions used in developing the accounting estimates and inquire about any other plans, goals, and objectives of the entity, as well as consider their relationship to the assumptions.

h. Consider using the work of a specialist regarding certain assumptions (section 336, *Using the Work of a Specialist*).

i. Test the calculations used by management to translate the assumptions and key factors into the accounting estimate.

.12 *Develop an expectation.* Based on the auditor's understanding of the facts and circumstances, he may independently develop an expectation as to the estimate by using other key factors or alternative assumptions about those factors.

---

[4] In addition to other evidential matter about the estimate, in certain instances, the auditor may wish to obtain written representation from management regarding the key factors and assumptions.

.13 *Review subsequent events or transactions.* Events or transactions sometimes occur subsequent to the date of the balance sheet, but prior to the completion of fieldwork, that are important in identifying and evaluating the reasonableness of accounting estimates or key factors or assumptions used in the preparation of the estimate. In such circumstances, an evaluation of the estimate or of a key factor or assumption may be minimized or unnecessary as the event or transaction can be used by the auditor in evaluating their reasonableness.

.14 As discussed in section 312, *Audit Risk and Materiality in Conducting an Audit*, paragraph .36, the auditor evaluates the reasonableness of accounting estimates in relationship to the financial statements taken as a whole:

> Since no one accounting estimate can be considered accurate with certainty, the auditor recognizes that a difference between an estimated amount best supported by the audit evidence and the estimated amount included in the financial statements may be reasonable, and such difference would not be considered to be a likely misstatement. However, if the auditor believes the estimated amount included in the financial statements is unreasonable, he should treat the difference between that estimate and the closest reasonable estimate as a likely misstatement and aggregate it with other likely misstatements. The auditor should also consider whether the difference between estimates best supported by the audit evidence and the estimates included in the financial statements, which are individually reasonable, indicate a possible bias on the part of the entity's management. For example, if each accounting estimate included in the financial statements was individually reasonable, but the effect of the difference between each estimate and the estimate best supported by the audit evidence was to increase income, the auditor should reconsider the estimates taken as a whole.

Effective Date

.15 This section is effective for audits of financial statements for periods beginning on or after January 1, 1989. Early application of the provisions of this section is permissible.

.16

Appendix

Examples of Accounting Estimates

The following are examples of accounting estimates that are included in financial statements. The list is presented for information only. It should not be considered all-inclusive.

Receivables:
- Uncollectible receivables
- Allowance for loan losses
- Uncollectible pledges

Inventories:
- Obsolete inventory
- Net realizable value of inventories where future selling prices and future costs are involved
- Losses on purchase commitments

Financial instruments:
- Valuation of securities
- Trading versus investment security classification
- Probability of high correlation of a hedge
- Sales of securities with puts and calls

Productive facilities, natural resources and intangibles:
- Useful lives and residual values
- Depreciation and amortization methods
- Recoverability of costs
- Recoverable reserves

Accruals:
- Property and casualty insurance company loss reserves
- Compensation in stock option plans and deferred plans
- Warranty claims
- Taxes on real and personal property
- Renegotiation refunds
- Actuarial assumptions in pension costs

Revenues:
- Airline passenger revenue
- Subscription income
- Freight and cargo revenue
- Dues income
- Losses on sales contracts

Contracts:
- Revenue to be earned
- Costs to be incurred
- Percent of completion

Leases:
- Initial direct costs
- Executory costs
- Residual values

Litigation:
- Probability of loss
- Amount of loss

Rates:
- Annual effective tax rate in interim reporting
- Imputed interest rates on receivables and payables
- Gross profit rates under program method of accounting

Other:
- Losses and net realizable value on disposal of segment or restructuring of a business
- Fair values in nonmonetary exchanges
- Interim period costs in interim reporting
- Current values in personal financial statements

AU Section 9342

Auditing Accounting Estimates: Auditing Interpretations of Section 342

1. Performance and Reporting Guidance Related to Fair Value Disclosures

.01 *Question*—In December 1991, the Financial Accounting Standards Board (FASB) issued Statement No. 107, *Disclosures about Fair Value of Financial Instruments* [AC section F25], which requires all entities to disclose the fair value of certain financial instruments for which it is practicable to estimate fair value. Some entities may disclose the information required by FASB Statement No. 107 and also disclose voluntarily the fair value of assets and liabilities not encompassed by FASB Statement No. 107. What are the auditor's responsibilities in situations in which entities are disclosing required or both required and voluntary fair value financial information?

.02 *Interpretation*—The auditor should determine whether the fair value disclosures represent only those required by FASB Statement No. 107 or whether additional voluntary fair value information has been disclosed by the entity. When auditing management's estimate of both required and voluntary fair value information, the auditor should obtain sufficient competent evidential matter to reasonably assure that—

- the valuation principles are acceptable, are being consistently applied, and are supported by the underlying documentation, and
- the method of estimation and significant assumptions used are properly disclosed.

If such assurance cannot be obtained, the auditor should evaluate whether the financial statements are materially affected by the departure from generally accepted accounting principles.

.03 *Required Information Presented*—When an entity discloses in its basic financial statements only information required by FASB Statement No. 107, the auditor may issue a standard unqualified opinion (assuming no other report modifications are necessary). The auditor may add an emphasis-of-matter paragraph describing the nature and possible range of such fair value information especially when management's best estimate of value is used in the absence of quoted market values (FASB Statement No. 107, paragraph 11 [AC section F25.115D]) and the range of possible values is significant. If the entity has not disclosed required fair value information, the auditor should evaluate whether the financial statements are materially affected by the departure from generally accepted accounting principles.

.04 *Required and Voluntary Information Presented*—When voluntary information is presented in addition to required information the auditor may audit the voluntary information only if both the following conditions exist:

- the measurement and disclosure criteria used to prepare the fair value financial information are reasonable

- competent persons using the measurement and disclosure criteria would ordinarily obtain materially similar measurements or disclosures.

In applying this guidance to fair value disclosures, the intention is that another auditor would reach similar conclusions regarding the reasonableness of the valuation or estimation techniques and methods used by the entity.

.05 Voluntary disclosures may supplement required disclosures in such a fashion as to constitute either a complete balance sheet (the fair value of all material items in the balance sheet) or a presentation of less than a complete balance sheet.

.06 When the audited disclosures constitute a complete balance sheet presentation, the auditor should add a paragraph to the report, similar to the following:

> We have also audited in accordance with generally accepted auditing standards the supplemental fair value balance sheet of ABC Company as of December 31, 19XX. As described in Note X, the supplemental fair value balance sheet has been prepared by management to present relevant financial information that is not provided by the historical-cost balance sheets and is not intended to be a presentation in conformity with generally accepted accounting principles. In addition, the supplemental fair value balance sheet does not purport to present the net realizable, liquidation, or market value of ABC Company as a whole. Furthermore, amounts ultimately realized by ABC Company from the disposal of assets may vary significantly from the fair values presented. In our opinion, the supplemental fair value balance sheet referred to above presents fairly, in all material respects, the information set forth therein as described in Note X.

.07 When the audited disclosures do not constitute a complete balance sheet presentation and are located on the face of the financial statements or in the footnotes, the auditor may issue a standard unqualified opinion and need not mention the disclosures in the report. When the audited disclosures do not constitute a complete balance sheet presentation and are included in a supplemental schedule or exhibit, the auditor should add an additional paragraph to the report as discussed in section 551, *Reporting on Information Accompanying the Basic Financial Statements in the Auditor-Submitted Documents*, paragraph .12.

.08 In some situations, the auditor may not be engaged to audit the voluntary information or may be unable to audit it because it does not meet both conditions in paragraph .04 of this interpretation. When the unaudited voluntary disclosures are included in an auditor-submitted document and located on the face of the financial statements, the footnotes, or in a supplemental schedule to the basic financial statements, the voluntary disclosures should be labelled "unaudited" and the auditor should disclaim an opinion on the unaudited information as discussed in section 551.13.

.09 When the unaudited voluntary disclosures are included in a client-prepared document and are located on the face of the financial statements, the footnotes, or in a supplemental schedule, the voluntary disclosures should be labelled "unaudited." When such unaudited information is not presented on the face of the financial statements, the footnotes, or in a supplemental schedule, the auditor should consider the guidance in section 550, *Other Information in Documents Containing Audited Financial Statements*.

.10 The auditing guidance related to each of these alternatives is presented in the following flowcharts:

AUDITING GUIDANCE FOR FAIR VALUE INFORMATION
Required* Information Only

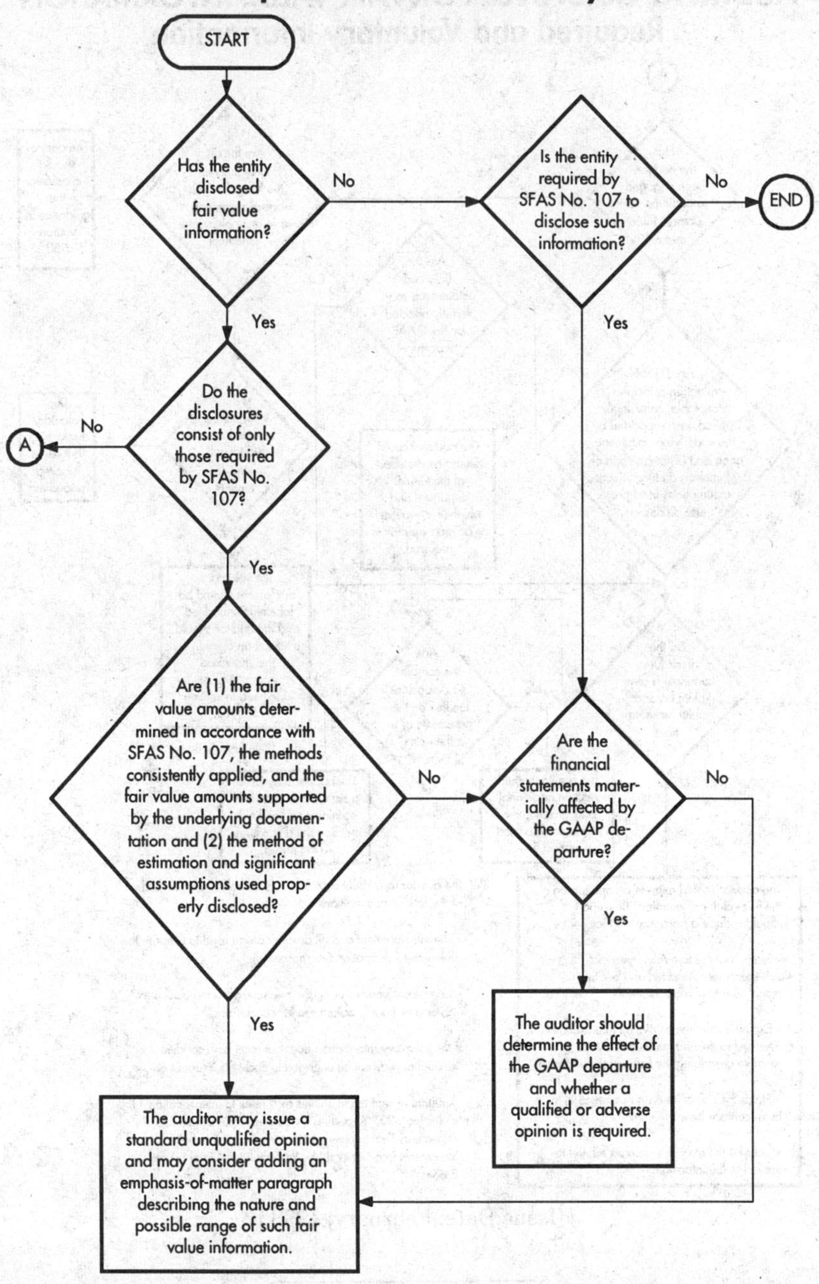
START
Has the entity disclosed fair value information?
No
Is the entity required by SFAS No. 107 to disclose such information?
No
END
Yes
Yes
Do the disclosures consist of only those required by SFAS No. 107?
No
A
Yes
Are (1) the fair value amounts determined in accordance with SFAS No. 107, the methods consistently applied, and the fair value amounts supported by the underlying documentation and (2) the method of estimation and significant assumptions used properly disclosed?
No
Are the financial statements materially affected by the GAAP departure?
No
Yes
Yes
The auditor should determine the effect of the GAAP departure and whether a qualified or adverse opinion is required.
The auditor may issue a standard unqualified opinion and may consider adding an emphasis-of-matter paragraph describing the nature and possible range of such fair value information.

* Required by Statement of Financial Accounting Standards (SFAS) No. 107, *Disclosures about Fair Value of Financial Instruments.*

AUDITING GUIDANCE FOR FAIR VALUE INFORMATION
Required and Voluntary Information

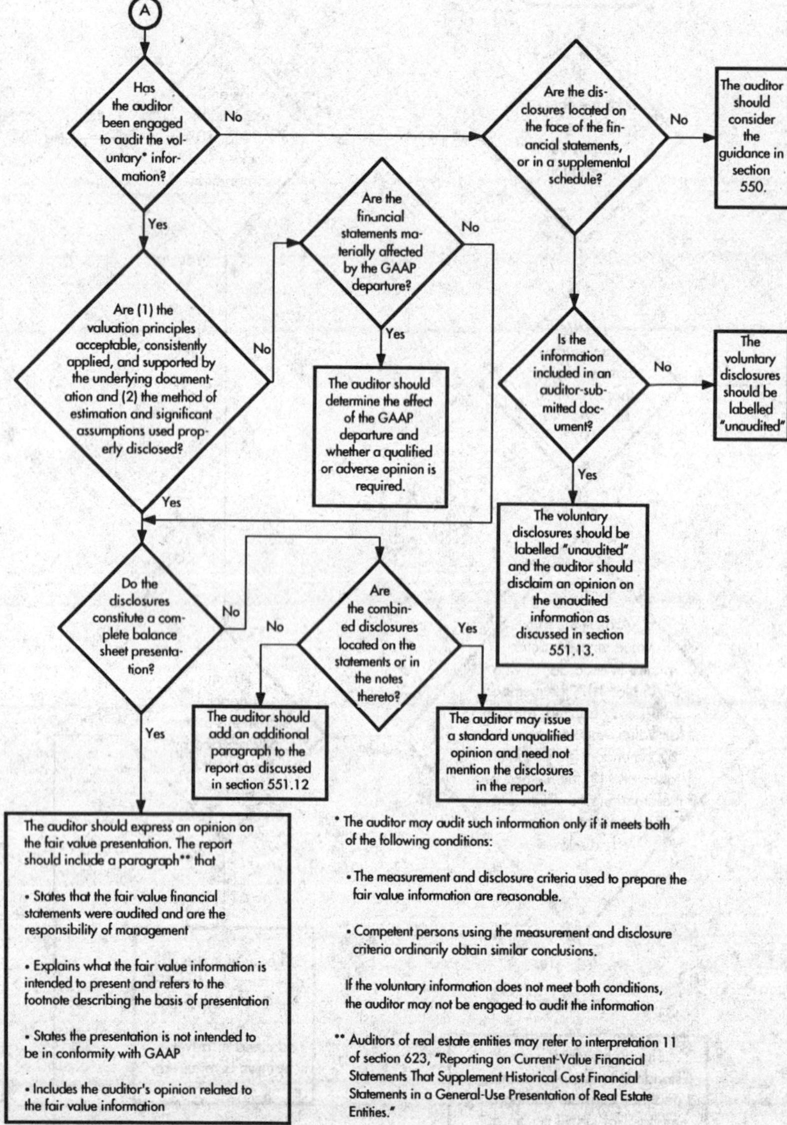
A
Has the auditor been engaged to audit the voluntary* information?
No
Yes
Are the disclosures located on the face of the financial statements, or in a supplemental schedule?
No
The auditor should consider the guidance in section 550.
Is the information included in an auditor-submitted document?
No
The voluntary disclosures should be labelled "unaudited"
Yes
The voluntary disclosures should be labelled "unaudited" and the auditor should disclaim an opinion on the unaudited information as discussed in section 551.13.
Are (1) the valuation principles acceptable, consistently applied, and supported by the underlying documentation and (2) the method of estimation and significant assumptions used properly disclosed?
No
Yes
Are the financial statements materially affected by the GAAP departure?
No
Yes
The auditor should determine the effect of the GAAP departure and whether a qualified or adverse opinion is required.
Do the disclosures constitute a complete balance sheet presentation?
No
Yes
Are the combined disclosures located on the statements or in the notes thereto?
No
Yes
The auditor should add an additional paragraph to the report as discussed in section 551.12
The auditor may issue a standard unqualified opinion and need not mention the disclosures in the report.
The auditor should express an opinion on the fair value presentation. The report should include a paragraph** that
• States that the fair value financial statements were audited and are the responsibility of management
• Explains what the fair value information is intended to present and refers to the footnote describing the basis of presentation
• States the presentation is not intended to be in conformity with GAAP
• Includes the auditor's opinion related to the fair value information
* The auditor may audit such information only if it meets both of the following conditions:
• The measurement and disclosure criteria used to prepare the fair value information are reasonable.
• Competent persons using the measurement and disclosure criteria ordinarily obtain similar conclusions.
If the voluntary information does not meet both conditions, the auditor may not be engaged to audit the information
** Auditors of real estate entities may refer to interpretation 11 of section 623, "Reporting on Current-Value Financial Statements That Supplement Historical Cost Financial Statements in a General-Use Presentation of Real Estate Entities."

[Issue Date: February, 1993.]

AU Section 350

Audit Sampling

(Supersedes Statement on Auditing Standards No. 1, sections 320A, and 320B.)

Sources: SAS No. 39; SAS No. 43; SAS No. 45.

See section 9350 for interpretations of this section.

Effective for periods ended on or after June 25, 1983, unless otherwise indicated.

.01 Audit sampling is the application of an audit procedure to less than 100 percent of the items within an account balance or class of transactions for the purpose of evaluating some characteristic of the balance or class.[1] This section provides guidance for planning, performing, and evaluating audit samples.

.02 The auditor often is aware of account balances and transactions that may be more likely to contain misstatements.[2] He considers this knowledge in planning his procedures, including audit sampling. The auditor usually will have no special knowledge about other account balances and transactions that, in his judgment, will need to be tested to fulfill his audit objectives. Audit sampling is especially useful in these cases.

.03 There are two general approaches to audit sampling: nonstatistical and statistical. Both approaches require that the auditor use professional judgment in planning, performing, and evaluating a sample and in relating the evidential matter produced by the sample to other evidential matter when forming a conclusion about the related account balance or class of transactions. The guidance in this section applies equally to nonstatistical and statistical sampling.

.04 The third standard of field work states, "Sufficient competent evidential matter is to be obtained through inspection, observation, inquiries, and confirmations to afford a reasonable basis for an opinion regarding the financial statements under audit." Either approach to audit sampling, when properly applied, can provide sufficient evidential matter.

.05 The sufficiency of evidential matter is related to the design and size of an audit sample, among other factors. The size of a sample necessary to provide sufficient evidential matter depends on both the objectives and the efficiency of the sample. For a given objective, the efficiency of the sample relates to its design; one sample is more efficient than another if it can achieve the same objectives with a smaller sample size. In general, careful design can produce more efficient samples.

---

[1] There may be other reasons for an auditor to examine less than 100 percent of the items comprising an account balance or class of transactions. For example, an auditor may examine only a few transactions from an account balance or class of transactions to (*a*) gain an understanding of the nature of an entity's operations or (*b*) clarify his understanding of the entity's internal control. In such cases, the guidance in this statement is not applicable.

[2] For purposes of this section the use of the term misstatement can include both errors and fraud as appropriate for the design of the sampling application. Errors and fraud are discussed in section 312, *Audit Risk and Materiality in Conducting an Audit*.

.06 Evaluating the competence of evidential matter is solely a matter of auditing judgment and is not determined by the design and evaluation of an audit sample. In a strict sense, the sample evaluation relates only to the likelihood that existing monetary misstatements or deviations from prescribed controls are proportionately included in the sample, not to the auditor's treatment of such items. Thus, the choice of nonstatistical or statistical sampling does not directly affect the auditor's decisions about the auditing procedures to be applied, the competence of the evidential matter obtained with respect to individual items in the sample, or the actions that might be taken in light of the nature and cause of particular misstatements.

Uncertainty and Audit Sampling

.07 Some degree of uncertainty is implicit in the concept of "a reasonable basis for an opinion" referred to in the third standard of field work. The justification for accepting some uncertainty arises from the relationship between such factors as the cost and time required to examine all of the data and the adverse consequences of possible erroneous decisions based on the conclusions resulting from examining only a sample of the data. If these factors do not justify the acceptance of some uncertainty, the only alternative is to examine all of the data. Since this is seldom the case, the basic concept of sampling is well established in auditing practice.

.08 The uncertainty inherent in applying audit procedures is referred to as audit risk. Audit risk consists of (*a*) the risk (consisting of inherent risk and control risk) that the balance or class and related assertions contain misstatements that could be material to the financial statements when aggregated with misstatements in other balances or classes and (*b*) the risk (detection risk) that the auditor will not detect such misstatement. The risk of these adverse events occurring jointly can be viewed as a function of the respective individual risks. Using professional judgment, the auditor evaluates numerous factors to assess inherent risk and control risk (assessing control risk at less than the maximum level involves performing tests of controls), and performs substantive tests (analytical procedures and test of details of account balances or classes of transactions) to restrict detection risk.

.09 Audit risk includes both uncertainties due to sampling and uncertainties due to factors other than sampling. These aspects of audit risk are sampling risk and nonsampling risk, respectively. [As amended August, 1983, by Statement on Auditing Standards No. 45.] (See section 313.)

.10 Sampling risk arises from the possibility that, when a test of controls or a substantive test is restricted to a sample, the auditor's conclusions may be different from the conclusions he would reach if the test were applied in the same way to all items in the account balance or class of transactions. That is, a particular sample may contain proportionately more or less monetary misstatements or deviations from prescribed controls than exist in the balance or class as a whole. For a sample of a specific design, sampling risk varies inversely with sample size: the smaller the sample size, the greater the sampling risk.

.11 Nonsampling risk includes all the aspects of audit risk that are not due to sampling. An auditor may apply a procedure to all transactions or balances and still fail to detect a material misstatement. Nonsampling risk includes the possibility of selecting audit procedures that are not appropriate to achieve the specific objective. For example, confirming recorded receivables cannot be relied on to reveal unrecorded receivables. Nonsampling risk also arises because the auditor may fail to recognize misstatements included in documents that he examines, which would make that procedure ineffective even if he were to examine all items. Nonsampling risk can be reduced to a negligible level through such factors as adequate planning and supervision (see section 311, *Planning and Supervision*) and proper conduct of a firm's audit practice (see section 161, *The Relationship of Generally Accepted Auditing Standards to Quality Control Standards*). [As amended August, 1983, by Statement on Auditing Standards No. 45.] (See section 313.)

Sampling Risk

.12 The auditor should apply professional judgment in assessing sampling risk. In performing substantive tests of details the auditor is concerned with two aspects of sampling risk:

- *The risk of incorrect acceptance* is the risk that the sample supports the conclusion that the recorded account balance is not materially misstated when it is materially misstated.
- *The risk of incorrect rejection* is the risk that the sample supports the conclusion that the recorded account balance is materially misstated when it is not materially misstated.

The auditor is also concerned with two aspects of sampling risk in performing tests of controls when sampling is used:

- *The risk of assessing control risk too low* is the risk that the assessed level of control risk based on the sample is less than the true operating effectiveness of the control.
- *The risk of assessing control risk too high* is the risk that the assessed level of control risk based on the sample is greater than the true operating effectiveness of the control.

.13 The risk of incorrect rejection and the risk of assessing control risk too high relate to the efficiency of the audit. For example, if the auditor's evaluation of an audit sample leads him to the initial erroneous conclusion that a balance is materially misstated when it is not, the application of additional audit procedures and consideration of other audit evidence would ordinarily lead the auditor to the correct conclusion. Similarly, if the auditor's evaluation of a sample leads him to unnecessarily assess control risk too high for an assertion, he would ordinarily increase the scope of substantive tests to compensate for the perceived ineffectiveness of the controls. Although the audit may be less efficient in these circumstances, the audit is, nevertheless, effective.

.14 The risk of incorrect acceptance and the risk of assessing control risk too low relate to the effectiveness of an audit in detecting an existing material misstatement. These risks are discussed in the following paragraphs.

Sampling in Substantive Tests of Details

Planning Samples

.15 Planning involves developing a strategy for conducting an audit of financial statements. For general guidance on planning, see section 311, *Planning and Supervision*.

.16 When planning a particular sample for a substantive test of details, the auditor should consider

- The relationship of the sample to the relevant audit objective (see section 326, *Evidential Matter*).
- Preliminary judgments about materiality levels.
- The auditor's allowable risk of incorrect acceptance.
- Characteristics of the population, that is, the items comprising the account balance or class of transactions of interest.

.17 When planning a particular sample, the auditor should consider the specific audit objective to be achieved and should determine that the audit procedure, or combination of procedures, to be applied will achieve that objective. The auditor should determine that the population from which he draws the sample is appropriate for the specific audit objective. For example, an auditor would not be able to detect understatements of an account due to omitted items by sampling the recorded items. An appropriate sampling plan for detecting such understatements would involve selecting from a source in which the omitted items are included. To illustrate, subsequent cash disbursements might be sampled to test recorded accounts payable for understatement because of omitted purchases, or shipping documents might be sampled for understatement of sales due to shipments made but not recorded as sales.

.18 Evaluation in monetary terms of the results of a sample for a substantive test of details contributes directly to the auditor's purpose, since such an evaluation can be related to his judgment of the monetary amount of misstatements that would be material. When planning a sample for a substantive test of details, the auditor should consider how much monetary misstatement in the related account balance or class of transactions may exist without causing the financial statements to be materially misstated. This maximum monetary misstatement for the balance or class is called *tolerable misstatement* for the sample. Tolerable misstatement is a planning concept and is related to the auditor's preliminary judgments about materiality levels in such a way that tolerable misstatement, combined for the entire audit plan, does not exceed those estimates.

.19 The second standard of field work states, "A sufficient understanding of the internal control structure is to be obtained to plan the audit and to determine the nature, timing, and extent of tests to be performed." After assessing and considering the levels of inherent and control risks, the auditor performs substantive tests to restrict detection risk to an acceptable level. As the assessed levels of inherent risk, control risk, and detection risk for other substantive procedures directed toward the same specific audit objective decreases, the auditor's allowable risk of incorrect acceptance for the substantive tests of details increases and, thus, the smaller the required sample size for the substantive tests of details. For example, if inherent and control risks are assessed at the maximum, and no other substantive tests directed toward the same specific audit objectives are performed, the auditor should allow for a low risk of incorrect acceptance for the substantive tests of details.[3] Thus, the auditor would select a larger sample size for the tests of details than if he allowed a higher risk of incorrect acceptance.

---

[3] Some auditors prefer to think of risk levels in quantitative terms. For example, in the circumstances described, an auditor might think in terms of a 5 percent risk of incorrect acceptance for the substantive test of details. Risk levels used in sampling applications in other fields are not necessarily relevant in determining appropriate levels for applications in auditing because an audit includes many interrelated tests and sources of evidence.

.20 The Appendix illustrates how the auditor may relate the risk of incorrect acceptance for a particular substantive test of details to his assessments of inherent risk, control risk, and the risk that analytical procedures and other relevant substantive tests would fail to detect material misstatement.

.21 As discussed in section 326, the sufficiency of tests of details for a particular account balance or class of transactions is related to the individual importance of the items examined as well as to the potential for material misstatement. When planning a sample for a substantive test of details, the auditor uses his judgment to determine which items, if any, in an account balance or class of transactions should be individually examined and which items, if any, should be subject to sampling. The auditor should examine those items for which, in his judgment, acceptance of some sampling risk is not justified. For example, these may include items for which potential misstatements could individually equal or exceed the tolerable misstatement. Any items that the auditor has decided to examine 100 percent are not part of the items subject to sampling. Other items that, in the auditor's judgment, need to be tested to fulfill the audit objective but need not be examined 100 percent, would be subject to sampling.

.22 The auditor may be able to reduce the required sample size by separating items subject to sampling into relatively homogeneous groups on the basis of some characteristic related to the specific audit objective. For example, common bases for such groupings are the recorded or book value of the items, the nature of controls related to processing the items, and special considerations associated with certain items. An appropriate number of items is then selected from each group.

.23 To determine the number of items to be selected in a sample for a particular substantive test of details, the auditor should consider the tolerable misstatement, the allowable risk of incorrect acceptance, and the characteristics of the population. An auditor applies professional judgment to relate these factors in determining the appropriate sample size. The Appendix illustrates the effect these factors may have on sample size.

Sample Selection

.24 Sample items should be selected in such a way that the sample can be expected to be representative of the population. Therefore, all items in the population should have an opportunity to be selected. For example, haphazard and random-based selection of items represents two means of obtaining such samples.[4]

Performance and Evaluation

.25 Auditing procedures that are appropriate to the particular audit objective should be applied to each sample item. In some circumstances the auditor may not be able to apply the planned audit procedures to selected sample items because, for example, supporting documentation may be missing. The auditor's treatment of unexamined items will depend on their effect on his evaluation of the sample. If the auditor's evaluation of the sample results would not be altered by considering those unexamined items to be misstated, it is not necessary to examine the items. However, if considering those unex-

---

[4] Random-based selection includes, for example, random sampling, stratified random sampling, sampling with probability proportional to size, and systematic sampling (for example, every hundredth item) with one or more random starts.

amined items to be misstated would lead to a conclusion that the balance or class contains material misstatement, the auditor should consider alternative procedures that would provide him with sufficient evidence to form a conclusion. The auditor should also consider whether the reasons for his inability to examine the items have implications in relation to his planned assessed level of control risk or his degree of reliance on management representations.

.26 The auditor should project the misstatement results of the sample to the items from which the sample was selected.[5, 6] There are several acceptable ways to project misstatements from a sample. For example, an auditor may have selected a sample of every twentieth item (50 items) from a population containing one thousand items. If he discovered overstatements of $3,000 in that sample, the auditor could project a $60,000 overstatement by dividing the amount of misstatement in the sample by the fraction of total items from the population included in the sample. The auditor should add that projection to the misstatements discovered in any items examined 100 percent. This total projected misstatement should be compared with the tolerable misstatement for the account balance or class of transactions, and appropriate consideration should be given to sampling risk. If the total projected misstatement is less than tolerable misstatement for the account balance or class of transactions, the auditor should consider the risk that such a result might be obtained even though the true monetary misstatement for the population exceeds tolerable misstatement. For example, if the tolerable misstatement in an account balance of $1 million is $50,000 and the total projected misstatement based on an appropriate sample (see paragraph .23) is $10,000, he may be reasonably assured that there is an acceptably low sampling risk that the true monetary misstatement for the population exceeds tolerable misstatement. On the other hand, if the total projected misstatement is close to the tolerable misstatement, the auditor may conclude that there is an unacceptably high risk that the actual misstatements in the population exceed the tolerable misstatement. An auditor uses professional judgment in making such evaluations.

.27 In addition to the evaluation of the frequency and amounts of monetary misstatements, consideration should be given to the qualitative aspects of the misstatements. These include (*a*) the nature and cause of misstatements, such as whether they are differences in principle or in application, are errors or irregularities, or are due to misunderstanding of instructions or to carelessness, and (*b*) the possible relationship of the misstatements to other phases of the audit. The discovery of an irregularity ordinarily requires a broader consideration of possible implications than does the discovery of an error.

.28 If the sample results suggest that the auditor's planning assumptions were incorrect, he should take appropriate action. For example, if monetary misstatements are discovered in a substantive test of details in amounts or frequency that is greater than is consistent with the assessed levels of inherent and control risk, the auditor should alter his risk assessments. The auditor should also consider whether to modify the other audit tests that were designed based upon the inherent and control risk assessments. For example, a large number of misstatements discovered in confirmation of receivables may indi-

---

[5] If the auditor has separated the items subject to sampling into relatively homogeneous groups (see paragraph .22), he separately projects the misstatement results of each group and sums them.

[6] See section 316, *Consideration of Fraud in a Financial Statement Audit*, paragraph .34, for a further discussion of the auditor's consideration of differences between the accounting records and the underlying facts and circumstances. This section provides specific guidance on the auditor's consideration of an audit adjustment that is, or may be, fraud.

cate the need to reconsider the control risk assessment related to the assertions that impacted the design of substantive tests of sales or cash receipts.

.29 The auditor should relate the evaluation of the sample to other relevant audit evidence when forming a conclusion about the related account balance or class of transactions.

.30 Projected misstatement results for all audit sampling applications and all known misstatements from nonsampling applications should be considered in the aggregate along with other relevant audit evidence when the auditor evaluates whether the financial statements taken as a whole may be materially misstated.

Sampling in Tests of Controls

Planning Samples

.31 When planning a particular audit sample for a test of controls, the auditor should consider

- The relationship of the sample to the objective of the test of controls.
- The maximum rate of deviations from prescribed controls that would support his planned assessed level of control risk.
- The auditor's allowable risk of assessing control risk too low.
- Characteristics of the population, that is, the items comprising the account balance or class of transactions of interest.

.32 For many tests of controls, sampling does not apply. Procedures performed to obtain an understanding of internal control sufficient to plan an audit do not involve sampling.[7] Sampling generally is not applicable to tests of controls that depend primarily on appropriate segregation of duties or that otherwise provide no documentary evidence of performance. In addition, sampling may not apply to tests of certain documented controls. Sampling may not apply to tests directed toward obtaining evidence about the design or operation of the control environment or the accounting system. For example, inquiry or observation of explanation of variances from budgets when the auditor does not desire to estimate the rate of deviation from the prescribed control.

.33 When designing samples for tests of controls the auditor ordinarily should plan to evaluate operating effectiveness in terms of deviations from prescribed controls, as to either the rate of such deviations or the monetary amount of the related transactions.[8] In this context, pertinent controls are ones that, had they not been included in the design of internal control would have adversely affected the auditor's planned assessed level of control risk. The auditor's overall assessment of control risk for a particular assertion involves combining judgments about the prescribed controls, the deviations from prescribed controls, and the degree of assurance provided by the sample and other tests of controls.

---

[7] The auditor often plans to perform tests of controls concurrently with obtaining an understanding of internal control (see section 319.59) for the purpose of estimating the rate of deviation from the prescribed controls, as to either the rate of such deviations or monetary amount of the related transactions. Sampling, as defined in this section, applies to such tests of controls.

[8] For simplicity the remainder of this section will refer to only the rate of deviations.

.34 The auditor should determine the maximum rate of deviations from the prescribed control that he would be willing to accept without altering his planned assessed level of control risk. This is the *tolerable rate*. In determining the tolerable rate, the auditor should consider (*a*) the planned assessed level of control risk, and (*b*) the degree of assurance desired by the evidential matter in the sample. For example, if the auditor plans to assess control risk at a low level, and he desires a high degree of assurance from the evidential matter provided by the sample for tests of controls (i.e., not perform other tests of controls for the assertion), he might decide that a tolerable rate of 5 percent or possibly less would be reasonable. If the auditor either plans to assess control risk at a higher level, or he desires assurance from other tests of controls along with that provided by the sample (such as inquiries of appropriate entity personnel or observation of the application of the policy or procedure), the auditor might decide that a tolerable rate of 10 percent or more is reasonable.

.35 In assessing the tolerable rate of deviations, the auditor should consider that, while deviations from pertinent controls increase the risk of material misstatements in the accounting records, such deviations do not necessarily result in misstatements. For example, a recorded disbursement that does not show evidence of required approval may nevertheless be a transaction that is properly authorized and recorded. Deviations would result in misstatements in the accounting records only if the deviations and the misstatements occurred on the same transactions. Deviations from pertinent controls at a given rate ordinarily would be expected to result in misstatements at a lower rate.

.36 In some situations, the risk of material misstatement for an assertion may be related to a combination of controls. If a combination of two or more controls is necessary to affect the risk of material misstatement for an assertion, those controls should be regarded as a single procedure, and deviations from any controls in combination should be evaluated on that basis.

.37 Samples taken to test the operating effectiveness of controls are intended to provide a basis for the auditor to conclude whether the controls are being applied as prescribed. When the degree of assurance desired by the evidential matter in the sample is high, the auditor should allow for a low level of sampling risk (that is, the risk of assessing control risk too low).[9]

.38 To determine the number of items to be selected for a particular sample for a test of controls, the auditor should consider the tolerable rate of deviation from the controls being tested, the likely rate of deviations, and the allowable risk of assessing control risk too low. An auditor applies professional judgment to relate these factors in determining the appropriate sample size.

Sample Selection

.39 Sample items should be selected in such a way that the sample can be expected to be representative of the population. Therefore, all items in the population should have an opportunity to be selected. Random-based selection of items represents one means of obtaining such samples. Ideally, the auditor should use a selection method that has the potential for selecting items from

---

[9] The auditor who prefers to think of risk levels in quantitative terms might consider, for example, a 5 percent to 10 percent risk of assessing control risk too low.

the entire period under audit. Section 319.73 provides guidance applicable to the auditor's use of sampling during interim and remaining periods.

Performance and Evaluation

.40 Auditing procedures that are appropriate to achieve the objective of the test of controls should be applied to each sample item. If the auditor is not able to apply the planned audit procedures or appropriate alternative procedures to selected items, he should consider the reasons for this limitation, and he should ordinarily consider those selected items to be deviations from the prescribed policy or procedure for the purpose of evaluating the sample.

.41 The deviation rate in the sample is the auditor's best estimate of the deviation rate in the population from which it was selected. If the estimated deviation rate is less than the tolerable rate for the population, the auditor should consider the risk that such a result might be obtained even though the true deviation rate for the population exceeds the tolerable rate for the population. For example, if the tolerable rate for a population is 5 percent and no deviations are found in a sample of 60 items, the auditor may conclude that there is an acceptably low sampling risk that the true deviation rate in the population exceeds the tolerable rate of 5 percent. On the other hand, if the sample includes, for example, two or more deviations, the auditor may conclude that there is an unacceptably high sampling risk that the rate of deviations in the population exceeds the tolerable rate of 5 percent. An auditor applies professional judgment in making such an evaluation.

.42 In addition to the evaluation of the frequency of deviations from pertinent procedures, consideration should be given to the qualitative aspects of the deviations. These include (*a*) the nature and cause of the deviations, such as whether they are errors or irregularities or are due to misunderstanding of instructions or to carelessness, and (*b*) the possible relationship of the deviations to other phases of the audit. The discovery of an irregularity ordinarily requires a broader consideration of possible implications than does the discovery of an error.

.43 If the auditor concludes that the sample results do not support the planned assessed level of control risk for an assertion, he should reevaluate the nature, timing, and extent of substantive procedures based on a revised consideration of the assessed level of control risk for the relevant financial statement assertions.

Dual-Purpose Samples

.44 In some circumstances the auditor may design a sample that will be used for dual purposes: assessing control risk and testing whether the recorded monetary amount of transactions is correct. In general, an auditor planning to use a dual-purpose sample would have made a preliminary assessment that there is an acceptably low risk that the rate of deviations from the prescribed control in the population exceeds the tolerable rate. For example, an auditor designing a test of a control procedure over entries in the voucher register may plan a related substantive test at a risk level that anticipates an assessment level of control risk below the maximum. The size of a sample designed for dual purposes should be the larger of the samples that would otherwise have been designed for the two separate purposes. In evaluating such tests, deviations from pertinent procedures and monetary misstatements should be evaluated separately using the risk levels applicable for the respective purposes.

Selecting a Sampling Approach

.45 As discussed in paragraph .04, either a nonstatistical or statistical approach to audit sampling, when properly applied, can provide sufficient evidential matter.

.46 Statistical sampling helps the auditor (*a*) to design an efficient sample, (*b*) to measure the sufficiency of the evidential matter obtained, and (*c*) to evaluate the sample results. By using statistical theory, the auditor can quantify sampling risk to assist himself in limiting it to a level he considers acceptable. However, statistical sampling involves additional costs of training auditors, designing individual samples to meet the statistical requirements, and selecting the items to be examined. Because either nonstatistical or statistical sampling can provide sufficient evidential matter, the auditor chooses between them after considering their relative cost and effectiveness in the circumstances.

Effective Date

.47 This section is effective for audits of financial statements for periods ended on or after June 25, 1983. Earlier application is encouraged. [As amended, effective retroactively to June 25, 1982, by Statement on Auditing Standards No. 43.]

.48

Appendix

Relating the Risk of Incorrect Acceptance for a Substantive Test of Details to Other Sources of Audit Assurance

1. Audit risk, with respect to a particular account balance or class of transactions, is the risk that there is a monetary misstatement greater than tolerable misstatement affecting an assertion in an account balance or class of transactions that the auditor fails to detect. The auditor uses professional judgment in determining the allowable risk for a particular audit after he consider such factors as the risk of material misstatement in the financial statements, the cost to reduce the risk, and the effect of the potential misstatements on the use and understanding of the financial statements.

2. An auditor assesses inherent and control risk, and plans and performs substantive tests (analytical procedures and substantive tests of details) in whatever combination to reduce audit risk to an appropriate level. However, the second standard of field work contemplates that ordinarily the assessed level of control risk cannot be sufficiently low to eliminate the need to perform any substantive tests to restrict detection risk for all of the assertions relevant to significant account balances or transactions classes.

3. The sufficiency of audit sample sizes, whether nonstatistical or statistical, is influenced by several factors. Table 1 illustrates how several of these factors may affect sample sizes for a substantive test of details. Factors *a, b* and *c* in table 1 should be considered together (see paragraph .08). For example, high inherent risk, the lack of effective controls, and the absence of other substantive tests related to the same audit objective ordinarily require larger sample sizes for related substantive tests of details than if there were other sources to provide the basis for assessing inherent or control risks below the maximum, or if other substantive tests related to the same objective were performed. Alternatively, low inherent risk, effective controls, or effective analytical procedures and other relevant substantive tests may lead the auditor to conclude that the sample, if any, needed for an additional test of details can be small.

4. The following model expresses the general relationship of the risks associated with the auditor's assessment of inherent and control risks, and the effectiveness of analytical procedures (including other relevant substantive tests) and substantive tests of details. The model is not intended to be a mathematical formula including all factors that may influence the determination of individual risk components; however, some auditors find such a model to be useful when planning appropriate risk levels for audit procedures to achieve the auditor's desired audit risk.

$$AR = IR \times CR \times AP \times TD$$

An auditor might use this model to obtain an understanding of an appropriate risk of incorrect acceptance for a substantive test of details as follows:

$$TD = AR/(IR \times CR \times AP)$$

AR = The allowable audit risk that monetary misstatements equal to tolerable misstatement might remain undetected for the account balance or class of transactions and related assertions after the auditor has completed all audit procedures deemed necessary.[1] The auditor uses his professional judgment to determine the allowable audit risk after considering factors such as those discussed in paragraph 1 of this appendix.

IR = Inherent risk is the susceptibility of an assertion to a material misstatement assuming there are no related internal control structure policies or procedures.

CR = Control risk is the risk that a material misstatement that could occur in an assertion will not be prevented or detected on a timely basis by the entity's controls. The auditor may assess control risk at the maximum, or assess control risk below the maximum based on the sufficiency of evidential matter obtained to support the effectiveness of controls. The quantification for this model relates to the auditor's evaluation of the overall effectiveness of those controls that would prevent or detect material misstatements equal to tolerable misstatement in the related account balance or class of transactions. For example, if the auditor believes that pertinent controls would prevent or detect misstatements equal to tolerable misstatement about half the time, he would assess this risk as 50 percent. (CR is not the same as the risk of assessing control risk too low.)

AP = The auditor's assessment of the risk that analytical procedures and other relevant substantive tests would fail to detect misstatements that could occur in an assertion equal to tolerable misstatement, given that such misstatements occur and are not detected by the internal control structure.

TD = The allowable risk of incorrect acceptance for the substantive test of details, given that misstatements equal to tolerable misstatement occur in an assertion and are not detected by internal control or analytical procedures and other relevant substantive tests.

5. The auditor planning a statistical sample can use the relationship in paragraph 4 of this Appendix to assist in planning his allowable risk of incorrect acceptance for a specific substantive test of details. To do so, he selects an acceptable audit risk (AR), and substantively quantifies his judgment of risks IR, CR and AP. Some levels of these risks are implicit in evaluating audit evidence and reaching conclusions. Auditors using the relationship prefer to evaluate these judgment risks explicitly.

6. The relationships between these independent risks are illustrated in table 2. In table 2 it is assumed, for illustrative purposes, that the auditor has chosen an audit risk of 5 percent for an assertion where inherent risk has been assessed at the maximum. Table 2 incorporates the premise that no internal control can be expected to be completely effective in detecting aggregate misstatements equal to tolerable misstatement that might occur. The table also illustrates the fact that the risk level for substantive tests for particular assertions is not an isolated decision. Rather, it is a direct consequence of the auditor's assessments of inherent and control risks, and judgments about the effectiveness of analytical procedures and other relevant substantive tests, and it cannot be properly considered out of this context. [As amended August, 1983, by Statement on Auditing Standards No. 45.] (See section 313.)

---

[1] For purposes of this Appendix, the nonsampling risk aspect of audit risk is assumed to be negligible, based on the level of quality controls in effect. [Footnote amended August, 1983, by Statement on Auditing Standards No. 45.] (See section 313.)

Table 1

Factors Influencing Sample Sizes for a Substantive Test of Details in Sample Planning

Factor	*Conditions leading to* Smaller sample size	*Conditions leading to* Larger sample size	*Related factor for substantive sample planning*
a. Assessment of inherent risk.	Low assessed level of inherent risk.	High assessed level of inherent risk.	Allowable risk of incorrect acceptance.
b. Assessment of control risk.	Low assessed level of control risk.	High assessed level of control risk.	Allowable risk of incorrect acceptance.
c. Assessment of risk for other substantive tests related to the same assertion (including analytical procedures and other relevant substantive tests).	Low assessment of risk associated with other relevant substantive tests.	High assessment of risk associated with other relevant substantive tests.	Allowable risk of incorrect acceptance.
d. Measure of tolerable misstatement for a specific account.	Larger measure of tolerable misstatement.	Smaller measure of tolerable misstatement.	Tolerable misstatement.
e. Expected size and frequency of misstatements.	Smaller misstatements or lower frequency.	Larger misstatements or higher frequency.	Assessment of population characteristics.
f. Number of items in the population.	Virtually no effect on sample size unless population is very small.		

Table 2

Allowable Risk of Incorrect Acceptance (TD) for Various Assessments of CR and AP; for AR = .05 and IR = 1.0

Auditor's subjective assessment control risk.	Auditor's subjective assessment of risk that analytical procedures and other relevant substantive tests might fail to detect aggregate misstatements equal to tolerable misstatement.			
CR	*AP*			
	10%	*30%*	*50%*	*100%*
	TD			
10%	*	*	*	50%
30%	*	55%	33%	16%
50%	*	33%	20%	10%
100%	50%	16%	10%	5%

* The allowable level of AR of 5 percent exceeds the product of IR, CR, and AP, and thus, the planned substantive test of details may not be necessary.

Note: The table entries for TD are computed from the illustrated model: TD equals AR/(IR x CR x AP). For example, for IR = 1.0, CR = .50, AP = .30, TD = .05/(1.0 x .50 x .30) or .33 (equals 33%).

AU Section 9350

Audit Sampling: Auditing Interpretations of Section 350

1. Applicability

.01 *Question*—Section 350, *Audit Sampling*, paragraph .01, footnote 1, states that there may be reasons other than sampling for an auditor to examine less than 100 percent of the items comprising an account balance or class of transactions. For what reasons might an auditor's examination of less than 100 percent of the items comprising an account balance or class of transactions *not* be considered audit sampling?

.02 *Interpretation*—The auditor's examination of less than 100 percent of the items comprising an account balance or class of transactions would not be considered to be an audit sampling application under the following circumstances.

a. *It is not the auditor's intent to extend the conclusion that he reaches by examining the items to the remainder of the items in the account balance or class.* Audit sampling is defined as the application of an audit procedure to less than 100 percent of the items within an account balance or class of transactions for the purpose of evaluating some characteristic of the balance or class. Thus, if the purpose of the auditor's application of an auditing procedure to less than 100 percent of the items in an account balance or class of transactions is something other than evaluating a trait of the entire balance or class, he is not using audit sampling.

For example, an auditor might trace several transactions through an entity's accounting system to gain an understanding of the nature of the entity's operations or clarify his understanding of the design of the entity's internal control. In such cases the auditor's intent is to gain a general understanding of the accounting system or other relevant parts of the internal control, rather than the evaluation of a characteristic of all transactions processed. As a result, the auditor is not using audit sampling.

Occasionally auditors perform procedures such as checking arithmetical calculations or tracing journal entries into ledger accounts on a test basis. When such procedures are applied to less than 100 percent of the arithmetical calculations or ledger postings that affect the financial statements, audit sampling may not be involved if the procedure is not a test to evaluate a characteristic of an account balance or class of transactions, but is intended only to provide limited knowledge that supplements the auditor's other evidential matter regarding a financial statement assertion.

b. *Although he might not be examining all the items in an account balance or class of transactions, the auditor might be examining 100 percent of the items in a given population.* A "population" for audit sampling purposes does not necessarily need to be an entire account balance or class of transactions. For example, in some circumstances, an auditor might examine all of the items that comprise an account balance or class of transactions that exceed a given amount or that have an unusual characteristic and either apply other auditing procedures (e.g., analytical procedures) to those items that do not exceed the given amount or possess the unusual characteristic or apply no auditing procedures to them because of their insignificance. Again, the auditor is not using audit sampling. Rather, he has broken the account balance or class of transactions into two groups. One group is tested 100 percent, the other group is either tested by analytical procedures or considered insignificant. The auditor would be using audit sampling only if he applied an auditing procedure to less than all of the items in the second group to form a conclusion about that group. For the same reason, cutoff tests often do not involve audit sampling applications. In performing cutoff tests auditors often examine all significant transactions for a period surrounding the cutoff date and, as a result, such tests do not involve the application of audit sampling.

c. *The auditor is testing controls that are not documented.* Auditors choose from a variety of methods including inquiry, observation, and examination of documentary evidence in testing controls. For example, observation of a client's physical inventory count procedures is a test that is performed primarily through the auditor's observation of controls over such things as inventory movement, counting procedures and other procedures used by the client to control the count of the inventory. The procedures that the auditor uses to observe the client's physical inventory count generally do not require use of audit sampling. However, audit sampling may be used in certain tests of controls or substantive tests of details of inventory, for example, in tracing selected test counts into inventory records.

d. *The auditor is not performing a substantive test of details.* Substantive tests consist of tests of details of transactions and balances, analytical review and or from a combination of both. In performing substantive tests, audit sampling is generally used only in testing details of transactions and balances.

[Issue Date: January, 1985.]

AU Section 380

Communication With Audit Committees

Source: SAS No. 61.

See section 9380 for interpretations of this section.

Effective for audits of financial statements for periods beginning on or after January 1, 1989, unless otherwise indicated.

.01 This section establishes a requirement for the auditor to determine that certain matters related to the conduct of an audit are communicated to those who have responsibility for oversight of the financial reporting process.[1] For purposes of this document, the recipient of the communications is referred to as the *audit committee*. The communications required by this section are applicable to (1) entities that either have an audit committee or that have otherwise formally designated oversight of the financial reporting process to a group equivalent to an audit committee (such as a finance committee or budget committee) and (2) all Securities and Exchange Commission (SEC) engagements.[2]

.02 This section requires the auditor to ensure that the audit committee receives additional information regarding the scope and results of the audit that may assist the audit committee in overseeing the financial reporting and disclosure process for which management is responsible. This section does not

---

[1] Communication with the audit committee by the independent auditor on certain specified matters when they arise in the conduct of an audit is required by other standards, including—

- Section 325, *Communication of Internal Control Related Matters Noted in an Audit*.
- Section 316, *Consideration of Fraud in a Financial Statement Audit*.
- Section 317, *Illegal Acts by Clients*.
- Section 801, *Compliance Auditing Considerations in Audits of Governmental Entities and Recipients of Governmental Financial Assistance*.

In addition, section 722, *Interim Financial Information*, requires that certain information be communicated to audit committees as a result of performing a review of interim financial information or assisting an entity in preparing such information.

[2] For purposes of this section, an SEC engagement is defined as one that involves the audit of the financial statements of—

1. An issuer making an initial filing, including amendments, under the Securities Act of 1933 and the Securities Exchange Act of 1934.
2. A registrant that files periodic reports with the SEC under the Investment Company Act of 1940 or the Securities Exchange Act of 1934 (except a broker or dealer registered only because of section 15(*a*) of the 1934 Act).
3. A bank or other lending institution that files periodic reports with the Comptroller of the Currency, the Federal Reserve System, the Federal Deposit Insurance Corporation, or the Federal Home Loan Bank Board because the powers, functions, and duties of the SEC to enforce its periodic reporting provisions are vested, pursuant to section 12(*i*) of the 1934 Act, in those agencies. (Section 12(*g*) of the Securities Exchange Act of 1934 provides an exemption from periodic reporting to the SEC to [1] entities with less than $5 million in total assets on the last day of each of the entity's three most recent fiscal years and fewer than 500 shareholders and [2] entities with fewer than 300 shareholders. Accordingly, such entities are not encompassed within the scope of this definition.)
4. A company whose financial statements appear in the annual report or proxy statement of any investment fund because it is a sponsor or manager of such a fund, but which is not itself a registrant required to file periodic reports under the 1940 Act or section 13 or 15(*d*) of the Securities Exchange Act of 1934.

require communications with management; however, it does not *preclude* communications with management or other individuals within the entity who may, in the auditor's judgment, benefit from the communications.

.03 The communications may be oral or written. If information is communicated orally, the auditor should document the communication by appropriate memoranda or notations in the working papers. When the auditor communicates in writing, the report should indicate that it is intended solely for the use of the audit committee or the board of directors and, if appropriate, management.

.04 The communications specified by this section are incidental to the audit. Accordingly, they are not required to occur before the issuance of the auditor's report on the entity's financial statements so long as the communications occur on a timely basis. There may be occasions, however, when discussion of certain of the matters (specified by paragraphs .06 through .14 below) with the audit committee prior to the issuance of the report may, in the auditor's judgment, be desirable.

.05 It may be appropriate for management to communicate to the audit committee certain of the matters specified in this section. In such circumstances, the auditor should be satisfied that such communications have, in fact, occurred. Generally, it is not necessary to repeat the communication of recurring matters each year. Periodically, however, the auditor should consider whether, because of changes in the audit committee or simply because of the passage of time, it is appropriate and timely to report such matters. Finally, this section is not intended to restrict the communication of other matters.

Matters to Be Communicated

The Auditor's Responsibility Under Generally Accepted Auditing Standards

.06 An audit performed in accordance with generally accepted auditing standards may address many matters of interest to an audit committee. For example, an audit committee is usually interested in internal control and in whether the financial statements are free of material misstatement. In order for the audit committee to understand the nature of the assurance provided by an audit, the auditor should communicate the level of responsibility assumed for these matters under generally accepted auditing standards. It is also important for the audit committee to understand that an audit conducted in accordance with generally accepted auditing standards is designed to obtain reasonable, rather than absolute, assurance about the financial statements.

Significant Accounting Policies

.07 The auditor should determine that the audit committee is informed about the initial selection of and changes in significant accounting policies or their application. The auditor should also determine that the audit committee is informed about the methods used to account for significant unusual transactions and the effect of significant accounting policies in controversial or emerging areas for which there is a lack of authoritative guidance or consensus. For example, significant accounting issues may exist in areas such as revenue recognition, off-balance-sheet financing, and accounting for equity investments.

Management Judgments and Accounting Estimates

.08 Accounting estimates are an integral part of the financial statements prepared by management and are based upon management's current judgments. Those judgments are normally based on knowledge and experience about past and current events and assumptions about future events. Certain accounting estimates are particularly sensitive because of their significance to the financial statements and because of the possibility that future events affecting them may differ markedly from management's current judgments. The auditor should determine that the audit committee is informed about the process used by management in formulating particularly sensitive accounting estimates and about the basis for the auditor's conclusions regarding the reasonableness of those estimates.

Significant Audit Adjustments

.09 The auditor should inform the audit committee about adjustments arising from the audit that could, in his judgment, either individually or in the aggregate, have a significant effect on the entity's financial reporting process. For purposes of this section, an audit adjustment, whether or not recorded by the entity, is a proposed correction of the financial statements that, in the auditor's judgment, may not have been detected except through the auditing procedures performed. Matters underlying adjustments proposed by the auditor but not recorded by the entity could potentially cause future financial statements to be materially misstated, even though the auditor has concluded that the adjustments are not material to the current financial statements.

Other Information in Documents Containing Audited Financial Statements

.10 The audit committee often considers information prepared by management that accompanies the entity's financial statements. An example of information of this nature would be the "Management's Discussion and Analysis of Financial Condition and Results of Operations" that certain entities that file reports with the SEC are required to present in annual reports to shareholders. Section 550, *Other Information in Documents Containing Audited Financial Statements*, establishes the auditor's responsibility for such information.[3] The auditor should discuss with the audit committee his responsibility for other information in documents containing audited financial statements, any procedures performed, and the results.

Disagreements With Management

.11 Disagreements with management may occasionally arise over the application of accounting principles to the entity's specific transactions and events and the basis for management's judgments about accounting estimates. Disagreements may also arise regarding the scope of the audit, disclosures to be included in the entity's financial statements, and the wording of the auditor's report. The auditor should discuss with the audit committee any disagree-

---

[3] Guidance on the auditor's consideration of other information is also provided by section 558, *Required Supplementary Information*; section 551, *Reporting on Information Accompanying the Basic Financial Statements in Auditor-Submitted Documents*; and section 711, *Filings Under Federal Securities Statutes*.

ments with management,[4] whether or not satisfactorily resolved, about matters that individually or in the aggregate could be significant to the entity's financial statements or the auditor's report. For purposes of this section, disagreements do not include differences of opinion based on incomplete facts or preliminary information that are later resolved.

Consultation With Other Accountants

.12 In some cases, management may decide to consult with other accountants about auditing and accounting matters. When the auditor is aware that such consultation has occurred, he should discuss with the audit committee his views about significant matters that were the subject of such consultation.[5]

Major Issues Discussed With Management Prior to Retention

.13 The auditor should discuss with the audit committee any major issues that were discussed with management in connection with the initial or recurring retention of the auditor including, among other matters, any discussions regarding the application of accounting principles and auditing standards.

Difficulties Encountered in Performing the Audit

.14 The auditor should inform the audit committee of any serious difficulties he encountered in dealing with management related to the performance of the audit. This may include, among other things, unreasonable delays by management in permitting the commencement of the audit or in providing needed information, and whether the timetable set by management was unreasonable under the circumstances. Other matters that the auditor may encounter include the unavailability of client personnel and the failure of client personnel to complete client-prepared schedules on a timely basis. If the auditor considers these matters significant, he should inform the audit committee.

Effective Date

.15 This section is effective for audits of financial statements for periods beginning on or after January 1, 1989. Early application of the provisions of this section is permissible.

---

[4] The glossary to Financial Accounting Standards Board (FASB) Statement No. 57, *Related Party Disclosures* [AC section R36], defines management as follows:

> Persons who are responsible for achieving the objectives of the enterprise and who have the authority to establish policies and make decisions by which those objectives are to be pursued. Management normally includes members of the board of directors, the chief executive officer, chief operating officer, vice presidents in charge of principal business functions (such as sales, administration, or finance), and other persons who perform similar policy-making functions. Persons without formal titles also may be members of management.

[5] Circumstances in which the auditor should be informed of such consultations are described in section 625, *Reports on the Application of Accounting Principles*, paragraph .07.

AU Section 9380

Communication With Audit Committees: Auditing Interpretations of Section 380

1. Applicability of Section 380

.01 *Question*—Section 380, *Communication With Audit Committees*, requires the auditor to determine that certain matters related to the conduct of an audit are communicated to those who have responsibility for oversight of the financial reporting process. Paragraph .01 indicates that the section is applicable to "(1) entities that either have an audit committee or that have otherwise formally designated oversight of the financial reporting process to a group equivalent to an audit committee (such as a finance committee or budget committee) and (2) all Securities and Exchange Commission (SEC) engagements."[1]

.02 When a non-SEC client has no designated group equivalent to an audit committee with formal responsibility for the financial reporting process, does the auditor have a responsibility to communicate section 380 matters to the governing or oversight body or person(s)?

.03 *Interpretation*—No. If a governing or oversight body, such as a board of directors or a board of trustees, has not established an audit committee or formally designated a group with equivalent responsibility for the financial reporting process, the auditor is not required to make the communications. Similarly, the auditor has no responsibility to communicate section 380 matters if the client has no governing or oversight body (for example, a small owner-managed entity). However, the auditor is not precluded from communicating any or all matters described in section 380 in such cases.

[Issue Date: August, 1993.]

---

[1] See section 380.01, footnote 2.

AU Section 390

Consideration of Omitted Procedures After the Report Date

Source: SAS No. 46.

Effective, unless otherwise indicated: October 31, 1983.

.01 This section provides guidance on the considerations and procedures to be applied by an auditor who, subsequent to the date of his report on audited financial statements, concludes that one or more auditing procedures considered necessary at the time of the audit in the circumstances then existing were omitted from his audit of the financial statements, but there is no indication that those financial statements are not fairly presented in conformity with generally accepted accounting principles or with another comprehensive basis of accounting.[1] This circumstance should be distinguished from that described in section 561, which applies if an auditor, subsequent to the date of his report on audited financial statements, becomes aware that facts regarding those financial statements may have existed at that date that might have affected his report had he then been aware of them.

.02 Once he has reported on audited financial statements, an auditor has no responsibility to carry out any retrospective review of his work. However, reports and working papers relating to particular engagements may be subjected to postissuance review in connection with a firm's internal inspection program,[2] peer review, or otherwise, and the omission of a necessary auditing procedure may be disclosed.

.03 A variety of conditions might be encountered in which an auditing procedure considered necessary at the time of the audit in the circumstances then existing has been omitted; therefore, the considerations and procedures described herein necessarily are set forth only in general terms. The period of time during which the auditor considers whether this section applies to the circumstances of a particular engagement and then takes the actions, if any, that are required hereunder may be important. Because of legal implications that may be involved in taking the actions contemplated herein, the auditor would be well advised to consult with his attorney when he encounters the circumstances to which this section may apply, and, with the attorney's advice and assistance, determine an appropriate course of action.

.04 When the auditor concludes that an auditing procedure considered necessary at the time of the audit in the circumstances then existing was omitted from his audit of financial statements, he should assess the importance of the omitted procedure to his present ability to support his previously ex-

---

[1] The provisions of this section are not intended to apply to an engagement in which an auditor's work is at issue in a threatened or pending legal proceeding or regulatory investigation. (A *threatened legal proceeding* means that a potential claimant has manifested to the auditor an awareness of, and present intention to assert, a possible claim.)

[2] See section 161, *The Relationship of Generally Accepted Auditing Standards to Quality Control Standards*, paragraph .02, and related quality control standards regarding the quality control function of inspection.

pressed opinion regarding those financial statements taken as a whole. A review of his working papers, discussion of the circumstances with engagement personnel and others, and a reevaluation of the overall scope of his audit may be helpful in making this assessment. For example, the results of other procedures that were applied may tend to compensate for the one omitted or make its omission less important. Also, subsequent audits may provide audit evidence in support of the previously expressed opinion.

.05 If the auditor concludes that the omission of a procedure considered necessary at the time of the audit in the circumstances then existing impairs his present ability to support his previously expressed opinion regarding the financial statements taken as a whole, and he believes there are persons currently relying, or likely to rely, on his report, he should promptly undertake to apply the omitted procedure or alternative procedures that would provide a satisfactory basis for his opinion.

.06 When as a result of the subsequent application of the omitted procedure or alternative procedures, the auditor becomes aware that facts regarding the financial statements existed at the date of his report that would have affected that report had he been aware of them, he should be guided by the provisions of section 561.05–.09.

.07 If in the circumstances described in paragraph .05, the auditor is unable to apply the previously omitted procedure or alternative procedures, he should consult his attorney to determine an appropriate course of action concerning his responsibilities to his client, regulatory authorities, if any, having jurisdiction over the client, and persons relying, or likely to rely, on his report.

Effective Date

.08 This section is effective as of October 31, 1983.

AU Section 400

THE FIRST, SECOND, AND THIRD STANDARDS OF REPORTING

. . . adherence to principles . . . meaning of present fairly . . . consistency . . . adequacy of disclosure . . . segment information . . .

TABLE OF CONTENTS

Section		Paragraph
410	Adherence to Generally Accepted Accounting Principles	.01-.02
9410	Adherence to Generally Accepted Accounting Principles: Auditing Interpretations of Section 410	
	[1.] Accounting Principles Recommended by Trade Associations (11/74) [Withdrawn August, 1982]	[.01-.03]
	[2.] The Impact of FASB Statement No. 2 on Auditor's Report Issued Prior to the Statement's Effective Date (1/75) [Superseded October, 1979]	[.04-.12]
	3. The Impact on an Auditor's Report on an FASB Statement Prior to the Statement's Effective Date (10/79). . . .	.13-.18
411	The Meaning of *Present Fairly in Conformity With Generally Accepted Accounting Principles* in the Independent Auditor's Report	.01-.16
	Application to Nongovernmental Entities	.10-.11
	Application to State and Local Governmental Entities	.12-.13
	Effective Date	.14
	Transition	.15
	GAAP Hierarchy Summary	.16
9411	The Meaning of *Present Fairly in Conformity With Generally Accepted Accounting Principles* in the Independent Auditor's Report: Auditing Interpretations of Section 411	
	[1.] The Auditor's Consideration of Accounting Principles Set Forth in Industry Audit and Accounting Guides (9/80) [Deleted September, 1984]	[.01-.04]
	[2.] The Auditor's Consideration of Accounting Principles Promulgated by the Governmental Accounting Standards Board (12/84) [Withdrawn April, 1988].	[.05-.10]
	3. The Auditor's Consideration of Management's Adoption of Accounting Principles for New Transactions or Events (3/95)	.11-.15
420	Consistency of Application of Generally Accepted Accounting Principles	.01-.24
	Accounting Changes Affecting Consistency.	.06-.13

Section		Paragraph
420	Consistency of Application of Generally Accepted Accounting Principles—continued	
	Change in Accounting Principle	.06
	Change in the Reporting Entity	.07
	Reports Following a Pooling of Interests	.08-.10
	Correction of an Error in Principle	.11
	Change in Principle Inseparable From Change in Estimate	.12
	Changes in Presentation of Cash Flows	.13
	Changes Not Affecting Consistency	.14-.20
	Change in Accounting Estimate	.14
	Error Correction Not Involving Principle	.15
	Changes in Classification and Reclassifications	.16
	Variations in Presentation of Statement of Changes in Financial Position	.17
	Substantially Different Transactions or Events	.18
	Changes Expected to Have a Material Future Effect	.19
	Disclosure of Changes Not Affecting Consistency	.20
	Periods to Which the Consistency Standard Relates	.21
	Consistency Expression	.22
	First Year Audits	.23-.24
9420	Consistency of Application of Generally Accepted Accounting Principles: Auditing Interpretations of Section 420	
	[1.] The Effect of APB Opinion No. 30 on Consistency (1/74) [Superseded October, 1979]	[.01-.10]
	2. The Effect of APB Opinion No. 28 on Consistency (2/74)	.11-.15
	3. Impact on the Auditor's Report of FIFO to LIFO Change in Comparative Financial Statements (1/75)	.16-.23
	[4.] The Effect of FASB Statement No. 13 on Consistency (1/78) [Withdrawn March, 1989]	[.24-.27]
	[5.] The Effects of Changes in Accounting Principles and Classification on Consistency (10/79) [Withdrawn December, 1992]	[.28-.31]
	[6.] The Effect of FASB Statement No. 34 on Consistency (2/80) [Withdrawn March, 1989]	[.32-.43]
	[7.] The Effect of FASB Statement No. 31 on Consistency (3/80) [Withdrawn March, 1989]	[.44-.51]
	8. The Effect of Accounting Changes by an Investee on Consistency (7/80)	.52-.57
	[9.] The Effect of Adoption of FASB Statement No. 35 on Consistency (12/80) [Withdrawn March, 1989]	[.58-.63]

Section		Paragraph
9420	Consistency of Application of Generally Accepted Accounting Principles: Auditing Interpretations of Section 420—continued	
	10. Change in Presentation of Accumulated Benefit Information in the Financial Statements of a Defined Benefit Pension Plan (12/80)	.64-.65
	[11.] The Effect of the Adoption of FASB Statement No. 36 on Consistency (12/80) [Withdrawn March, 1989]	[.66-.68]
431	Adequacy of Disclosure in Financial Statements	.01-.04
435	Segment Information	.01-.18
	Auditor's Objective	.03
	Auditing Procedures	.04-.07
	Reporting	.08-.16
	Misstatement or Omission of Segment Information	.09-.10
	Consistency	.11-.14
	Scope Limitation	.15-.16
	Reporting Separately on Segment Information	.17-.18
9435	Segment Information: Auditing Interpretations of Section 435	
	[1.] Applicability of Section 435 to Nonpublic Companies (5/78) [Deleted May, 1980]	[.01-.07]

AU Section 410

Adherence to Generally Accepted Accounting Principles

Sources: SAS No. 1, section 410; SAS No. 62.

See section 9410 for interpretations of this section.

Issue date, unless otherwise indicated: November, 1972.

.01 The first standard of reporting is:

> The report shall state whether the financial statements are presented in accordance with generally accepted accounting principles.

.02 The term "generally accepted accounting principles" as used in reporting standards is construed to include not only accounting principles and practices but also the methods of applying them. The first reporting standard is construed not to require a statement of fact by the auditor but an opinion as to whether the financial statements are presented in conformity with such principles.[1] If limitations on the scope of the audit make it impossible for the auditor to form an opinion as to such conformity, appropriate qualification of his report is required. [Amended by Statement on Auditing Standards No. 14, effective with respect to engagements to issue special reports on data for periods beginning after December 31, 1976.]

[.03–.04] [Superseded July 1975 by Statement on Auditing Standards No. 5, as superseded by section 411.]

---

[1] When an auditor reports on financial statements prepared in accordance with a comprehensive basis of accounting other than generally accepted accounting principles, the first standard of reporting is satisfied by disclosing in the auditor's report that the statements have been prepared in conformity with another comprehensive basis of accounting other than generally accepted accounting principles and by expressing an opinion (or disclaiming an opinion) on whether the financial statements are presented in conformity with the comprehensive basis of accounting used (see section 623, *Special Reports*, paragraphs .02–.10).

AU Section 9410

Adherence to Generally Accepted Accounting Principles: Auditing Interpretations of Section 410

[1.] Accounting Principles Recommended by Trade Associations[1]

[.01–.03] [Withdrawn August, 1982 by Statement on Auditing Standards No. 43.]

[2.] The Impact of FASB Statement No. 2 on Auditor's Report Issued Prior to the Statement's Effective Date[2]

[.04–.12] [Superseded October, 1979 by Interpretation No. 3, paragraphs .13–.18.]

3. The Impact on an Auditor's Report of an FASB Statement Prior to the Statement's Effective Date

.13 *Question*—What is the impact on the auditor's report when he is reporting on financial statements issued before the effective date of a Statement of Financial Accounting Standards and the financial statements will have to be restated in the future because the FASB statement will require retroactive application of its provisions by prior period adjustment?

.14 *Interpretation*—Where the accounting principles being followed are currently acceptable, the auditor should not qualify his opinion if a company does not adopt before an FASB Statement becomes effective accounting principles that will be prescribed by that Statement. For example, Financial Accounting Standards Board Statement No. 2 [AC section R50], *Accounting for Research and Development Costs*, was issued in October 1974, but was effective for fiscal years beginning on or after January 1, 1975. This Statement requires companies to expense research and development costs encompassed by the Statement in the period they are incurred. Companies that had deferred research and development costs were required to restate their financial statements by prior period adjustment in the period in which FASB Statement No. 2 [AC section R50] became effective. Deferring research and development costs before FASB Statement No. 2 [AC section R50] became effective was an acceptable alternative principle under GAAP, although FASB Statement No. 2 [AC section R50] proscribed such treatment for fiscal years beginning on or after January 1, 1975. Other reporting considerations are addressed in the following paragraphs.

.15 Section 508, *Reports on Audited Financial Statements*, paragraph .41 states: "Information essential for a fair presentation in conformity with generally accepted accounting principles should be set forth in the financial statements (which include related notes)." For financial statements that are prepared on the basis of accounting principles that are acceptable at the financial-statement date but that will not be acceptable in the future, the auditor should con-

---

[1] [Footnote deleted.]

[2] Originally issued under the title "Effect on the Auditor's Opinion of FASB Statement on Research and Development Costs" (*Journal of Accountancy*, Jan. '75, p. 74).

sider whether disclosure of the impending change in principle and the resulting restatement are essential data. If he decides that the matter should be disclosed and it is not, the auditor should express a qualified or adverse opinion as to conformity with GAAP, as required by section 508.41.

.16 To evaluate the adequacy of disclosure of the prospective change in principle, the auditor should assess the potential effect on the financial statements. Using the research and development cost example given above, the effect of the anticipated prior period adjustment to write off previously deferred research and development costs would in some instances be so material that disclosure would be essential for an understanding of the financial statements. In cases such as this, where the estimated impact is so material, disclosure can best be made by supplementing the historical financial statements with pro forma financial data that give effect to the future adjustment as if it had occurred on the date of the balance sheet. (See section 560.05.) The pro forma data may be presented in columnar form alongside the historical statements, in the notes to the historical statements, or in separate pro forma statements presented with the historical statements.

.17 The auditor also should consider whether disclosure is needed for other effects that may result upon the required future adoption of an accounting principle. For example, the future adoption of such a principle may result in a reduction to stockholders' equity that may cause the company to be in violation of its debt covenants, which in turn may accelerate the due date for repayment of debt.

.18 Even if the auditor decides that the disclosure of the forthcoming change and its effects are adequate and, consequently, decides not to qualify his opinion, he nevertheless may decide to include an explanatory paragraph in his report if the effects of the change are expected to be unusually material. The explanatory paragraph should not be construed as a qualification of the auditor's opinion; it is intended to highlight circumstances of particular importance and to aid in interpreting the financial statements (see section 508.19).

[Issue Date: October, 1979; Revised: December, 1992; Revised: June, 1993; Revised: February, 1997.]

AU Section 411

The Meaning of Present Fairly in Conformity With Generally Accepted Accounting Principles *in the Independent Auditor's Report*

(Supersedes SAS No. 5)

Source: SAS No. 69.

See section 9411 for interpretations of this section.

Effective for audits of financial statements for periods ending after March 15, 1992.

.01 An independent auditor's unqualified opinion usually reads as follows:

> In our opinion, the financial statements referred to above present fairly, in all material respects, the financial position of X Company as of (at) December 31, 19XX, and the results of its operations and its cash flows for the year then ended, in conformity with generally accepted accounting principles.

The purpose of this section is to explain the meaning of the phrase "present fairly . . . in conformity with generally accepted accounting principles" in the independent auditor's report.

.02 The first standard of reporting requires an auditor who has audited financial statements in accordance with generally accepted auditing standards to state in the auditor's report whether the statements are presented in accordance with generally accepted accounting principles. The phrase "generally accepted accounting principles" is a technical accounting term that encompasses the conventions, rules, and procedures necessary to define accepted accounting practice at a particular time. It includes not only broad guidelines of general application, but also detailed practices and procedures. Those conventions, rules, and procedures provide a standard by which to measure financial presentations. [Revised, June 1993, to reflect conforming changes necessary due to the issuance of Statement of Position 93-3.]

.03 The independent auditor's judgment concerning the "fairness" of the overall presentation of financial statements should be applied within the framework of generally accepted accounting principles. Without that framework, the auditor would have no uniform standard for judging the presentation of financial position, results of operations, and cash flows in financial statements.

.04 The auditor's opinion that financial statements present fairly an entity's financial position, results of operations, and cash flows in conformity with generally accepted accounting principles should be based on his or her judgment as to whether (*a*) the accounting principles selected and applied have general acceptance; (*b*) the accounting principles are appropriate in the circumstances; (*c*) the financial statements, including the related notes, are informative of matters that may affect their use, understanding, and interpretation (see section 431); (*d*) the information presented in the financial statements is classified and summarized in a reasonable manner, that is, neither too detailed nor too condensed (see section 431); and (*e*) the financial statements reflect the underlying transactions and events in a manner that presents the financial position, results of operations, and cash flows stated within a range of acceptable limits, that is, limits that are reasonable and practicable to attain in financial statements.[1]

.05 Independent auditors agree on the existence of a body of generally accepted accounting principles, and they are knowledgeable about these principles and in the determination of their general acceptance. Nevertheless, the determination that a particular accounting principle is generally accepted may be difficult because no single reference source exists for all such principles. The sources of established accounting principles that are generally accepted in the United States are—

a. Accounting principles promulgated by a body designated by the AICPA Council to establish such principles, pursuant to rule 203 [ET section 203.01] of the AICPA Code of Professional Conduct. Rule 203 [ET section 203.01] provides that an auditor should not express an unqualified opinion if the financial statements contain a material departure from such pronouncements unless, due to unusual circumstances, adherence to the pronouncements would make the statements misleading. Rule 203 [ET section 203.01] implies that application of officially established accounting principles almost always results in the fair presentation of financial position, results of operations, and cash flows, in conformity with generally accepted accounting principles. Nevertheless, rule 203 [ET section 203.01] provides for the possibility that literal application of such a pronouncement might, in unusual circumstances, result in misleading financial statements. (See section 508, *Reports on Audited Financial Statements*, paragraphs .14 and .15.)

b. Pronouncements of bodies, composed of expert accountants, that deliberate accounting issues in public forums for the purpose of establishing accounting principles or describing existing accounting practices that are generally accepted, provided those pronouncements have been exposed for public comment and have been cleared by a body referred to in category (*a*).[2]

c. Pronouncements of bodies, organized by a body referred to in category (*a*) and composed of expert accountants, that deliberate accounting issues in public forums for the purpose of interpreting or establishing accounting principles or describing existing accounting practices that are generally accepted, or pronouncements referred to in category (*b*) that have been cleared by a body referred to in category (*a*) but have not been exposed for public comment.

d. Practices or pronouncements that are widely recognized as being generally accepted because they represent prevalent practice in a particular industry, or the knowledgeable application to specific circumstances of pronouncements that are generally accepted.

.06 Generally accepted accounting principles recognize the importance of reporting transactions and events in accordance with their substance. The auditor should consider whether the substance of transactions or events differs materially from their form.

---

[1] The concept of materiality is inherent in the auditor's judgments. That concept involves qualitative as well as quantitative judgments (see sections 150.04, 312.10, and 508.36).

[2] For purposes of this section, the word *cleared* means that a body referred to in subparagraphs (*a*) has indicated that it does not object to the issuance of the proposed pronouncement.

.07 If the accounting treatment of a transaction or event is not specified by a pronouncement covered by rule 203 [ET section 203.01], the auditor should consider whether the accounting treatment is specified by another source of established accounting principles. If an established accounting principle from one or more sources in category (*b*), (*c*), or (*d*) is relevant to the circumstances, the auditor should be prepared to justify a conclusion that another treatment is generally accepted. If there is a conflict between accounting principles relevant to the circumstances from one or more sources in category (*b*), (*c*), or (*d*), the auditor should follow the treatment specified by the source in the higher category—for example, follow category (*b*) treatment over category (*c*)—or be prepared to justify a conclusion that a treatment specified by a source in the lower category better presents the substance of the transaction in the circumstances.

.08 The auditor should be aware that the accounting requirements adopted by regulatory agencies for reports filed with them may differ from generally accepted accounting principles in certain respects. Section 544, *Lack of Conformity With Generally Accepted Accounting Principles*, paragraph .04 and section 623, *Special Reports* provide guidance if the auditor is reporting on financial statements prepared in conformity with a comprehensive basis of accounting other than generally accepted accounting principles.

.09 Because of developments such as new legislation or the evolution of a new type of business transaction, there sometimes are no established accounting principles for reporting a specific transaction or event. In those instances, it might be possible to report the event or transaction on the basis of its substance by selecting an accounting principle that appears appropriate when applied in a manner similar to the application of an established principle to an analogous transaction or event.

Application to Nongovernmental Entities

.10 For financial statements of entities other than governmental entities—[3]

a. Category (*a*), officially established accounting principles, consists of Financial Accounting Standards Board (FASB) Statements of Financial Accounting Standards and Interpretations, Accounting Principles Board (APB) Opinions, and AICPA Accounting Research Bulletins.

b. Category (*b*) consists of FASB Technical Bulletins and, if cleared[4] by the FASB, AICPA Industry Audit and Accounting Guides and AICPA Statements of Position.

c. Category (*c*) consists of AICPA Accounting Standards Executive Committee (AcSEC) Practice Bulletins that have been cleared[4] by the FASB and consensus positions of the FASB Emerging Issues Task Force.

---

[3] Rules and interpretive releases of the Securities and Exchange Commission (SEC) have an authority similar to category (*a*) pronouncements for SEC registrants. In addition, the SEC staff issues Staff Accounting Bulletins that represent practices followed by the staff in administering SEC disclosure requirements. Also, the Introduction to the FASB's *EITF Abstracts* states that the Securities and Exchange Commission's Chief Accountant has said that the SEC staff would challenge any accounting that differs from a consensus of the FASB Emerging Issues Task Force, because the consensus position represents the best thinking on areas for which there are no specific standards.

[4] The auditor should assume that such pronouncements have been cleared by the FASB unless the pronouncement indicates otherwise.

d. Category (*d*) includes AICPA accounting interpretations and implementation guides ("Qs and As") published by the FASB staff, and practices that are widely recognized and prevalent either generally or in the industry.

.11 In the absence of a pronouncement covered by rule 203 [ET section 203.01] or another source of established accounting principles, the auditor of financial statements of entities other than governmental entities may consider other accounting literature, depending on its relevance in the circumstances. Other accounting literature includes, for example, FASB Statements of Financial Accounting Concepts; AICPA Issues Papers; International Accounting Standards of the International Accounting Standards Committee; Governmental Accounting Standards Board (GASB) Statements, Interpretations, and Technical Bulletins; pronouncements of other professional associations or regulatory agencies; Technical Information Service Inquiries and Replies included in AICPA Technical Practice Aids; and accounting textbooks, handbooks, and articles. The appropriateness of other accounting literature depends on its relevance to particular circumstances, the specificity of the guidance, and the general recognition of the issuer or author as an authority. For example, FASB Statements of Financial Accounting Concepts would normally be more influential than other sources in this category. [Revised, June 1993, to reflect conforming changes necessary due to the issuance of Statement of Position 93-3.]

Application to State and Local Governmental Entities

.12 For financial statements of state and local governmental entities—[5]

a. Category (*a*), officially established accounting principles, consists of GASB Statements and Interpretations, as well as AICPA and FASB pronouncements specifically made applicable to state and local governmental entities by GASB Statements or Interpretations. GASB Statements and Interpretations are periodically incorporated in the *Codification of Governmental Accounting and Financial Reporting Standards*.

b. Category (*b*) consists of GASB Technical Bulletins and, if specifically made applicable to state and local governmental entities by the AICPA and cleared[6] by the GASB, AICPA Industry Audit and Accounting Guides and AICPA Statements of Position.

c. Category (*c*) consists of AICPA AcSEC Practice Bulletins if specifically made applicable to state and local governmental entities and cleared[6] by the GASB, as well as consensus positions of a group of accountants organized by the GASB that attempts to reach consensus positions on accounting issues applicable to state and local governmental entities.[7]

d. Category (*d*) includes implementation guides ("Qs and As") published by the GASB staff, as well as practices that are widely recognized and prevalent in state and local government.

---

[5] State and local governmental entities include public benefit corporations and authorities; public employee retirement systems; and governmental utilities, hospitals and other health care providers, and colleges and universities.

[6] The auditor should assume that such pronouncements specifically made applicable to state and local governments have been cleared by the GASB unless the pronouncement indicates otherwise.

[7] As of the date of this section, the GASB had not organized such a group.

.13 In the absence of a pronouncement covered by rule 203 [ET section 203.01] or another source of established accounting principles, the auditor of financial statements of state and local governmental entities may consider other accounting literature, depending on its relevance in the circumstances. Other accounting literature includes, for example, GASB Concepts Statements; the pronouncements referred to in categories (*a*) through (*d*) of paragraph .10 when not specifically made applicable to state and local governmental entities either by the GASB or by the organization issuing them; FASB Concepts Statements; AICPA Issues Papers; International Accounting Standards of the International Accounting Standards Committee; pronouncements of other professional associations or regulatory agencies; Technical Information Service Inquiries and Replies included in AICPA Technical Practice Aids; and accounting textbooks, handbooks, and articles. The appropriateness of other accounting literature depends on its relevance to particular circumstances, the specificity of the guidance, and the general recognition of the issuer or author as an authority. For example, GASB Concepts Statements would normally be more influential than other sources in this category. [Revised, June 1993, to reflect conforming changes necessary due to the issuance of Statement of Position 93-3.]

Effective Date

.14 This section is effective for audits of financial statements for periods ending after March 15, 1992.

Transition

.15 Most of the pronouncements or practices in categories (*b*), (*c*), and (*d*) of paragraphs .10 and .12 had equal authoritative standing prior to the issuance of this section. An entity following an accounting treatment in category (*c*) or (*d*) as of March 15, 1992, need not change to an accounting treatment in a category (*b*) or category (*c*) pronouncement whose effective date is before March 15, 1992. For example, a nongovernmental entity that followed a prevalent industry practice (category (*d*)) as of March 15, 1992, need not change to an accounting treatment included in a pronouncement in category (*b*) or (*c*) (for example, an accounting principle in a cleared AICPA Statement of Position or AcSEC Practice Bulletin) whose effective date is before March 15, 1992. For pronouncements whose effective date is subsequent to March 15, 1992, and for entities initially applying an accounting principle after March 15, 1992 (except for FASB Emerging Issues Task Force consensus positions issued before March 16, 1992, which become effective in the hierarchy for initial application of an accounting principle after March 15, 1993), the auditor should follow the applicable hierarchy established by paragraphs .10 and .12 in determining whether an entity's financial statements are fairly presented in conformity with generally accepted accounting principles.

.16 GAAP Hierarchy Summary*

Nongovernmental Entities	*State and Local Governments*
Established Accounting Principles	
.10*a* FASB Statements and Interpretations, APB Opinions, and AICPA Accounting Research Bulletins	.12*a* GASB Statements and Interpretations, plus AICPA and FASB pronouncements if made applicable to state and local governments by a GASB Statement or Interpretation
.10*b* FASB Technical Bulletins, AICPA Industry Audit and Accounting Guides, and AICPA Statements of Position	.12*b* GASB Technical Bulletins, and the following pronouncements if specifically made applicable to state and local governments by the AICPA: AICPA Industry Audit and Accounting Guides and AICPA Statements of Position
.10*c* Consensus positions of the FASB Emerging Issues Task Force and AICPA Practice Bulletins	.12*c* Consensus positions of the GASB Emerging Issues Task Force ‡ and AICPA Practice Bulletins if specifically made applicable to state and local governments by the AICPA
.10*d* AICPA accounting interpretations, "Qs and As" published by the FASB staff, as well as industry practices widely recognized and prevalent	.12*d* "Qs and As" published by the GASB staff, as well as industry practices widely recognized and prevalent
Other Accounting Literature †	
.11 Other accounting literature, including FASB Concepts Statements; AICPA Issues Papers; International Accounting Standards Committee Statements; GASB Statements, Interpretations, and Technical Bulletins; pronouncements of other professional associations or regulatory agencies; AICPA *Technical Practice Aids*, and accounting textbooks, handbooks, and articles	.13 Other accounting literature, including GASB Concepts Statements; pronouncements in categories (*a*) through (*d*) of the hierarchy for nongovernmental entities when not specifically made applicable to state and local governments; FASB Concepts Statements; AICPA Issues Papers; International Accounting Standards Committee Statements; pronouncements of other professional associations or regulatory agencies; AICPA *Technical Practice Aids*; and accounting textbooks, handbooks, and articles

[Revised, June 1993, to reflect conforming changes necessary due to the issuance of Statement of Position 93-3.]

---

* Paragraph references correspond to the paragraphs of this section that describe the categories of the GAAP hierarchy.

† In the absence of established accounting principles, the auditor may consider other accounting literature, depending on its relevance in the circumstances.

‡ As of the date of this section, the GASB had not organized such a group.

AU Section 9411

The Meaning of Present Fairly in Conformity With Generally Accepted Accounting Principles *in the Independent Auditor's Report:* Auditing Interpretations of Section 411

[1.] The Auditor's Consideration of Accounting Principles Set Forth in Industry Audit and Accounting Guides

[.01–.04] [Deleted September, 1984.]

[2.] The Auditor's Consideration of Accounting Principles Promulgated by the Governmental Accounting Standards Board

[.05–.10] [Withdrawn April, 1988 by SAS No. 52.]

3. The Auditor's Consideration of Management's Adoption of Accounting Principles for New Transactions or Events

.11 *Question*—When an entity engages in new types of transactions or encounters new events that are material and for which there are no established sources of accounting principles, what should the auditor consider in formulating a judgment about the general acceptance and appropriateness in the circumstances of the accounting principles selected by management?

.12 *Interpretation*—When an entity adopts accounting principles in response to new types of transactions or events that are material and for which there are no established sources of accounting principles, the auditor should understand the basis used by management to select the particular accounting principle. In assessing the appropriateness of the accounting principle selected by management, the auditor may consider whether there are analogous transactions or events for which there are established accounting principles. If the auditor has identified analogous transactions or events for which there are established accounting principles, he or she should follow the guidance in section 411, *The Meaning of* Present Fairly in Conformity With Generally Accepted Accounting Principles *in the Independent Auditor's Report*, paragraph .09. Section 411.09 states that "there sometimes are no established accounting principles for reporting a specific transaction or event. In those instances, it might be possible to report the event or transaction on the basis of its substance by selecting an accounting principle that appears appropriate when applied in a manner similar to the application of an established principle to an analogous transaction or event."

.13 In addition, the auditor also may consider the appropriateness of other accounting literature, as discussed in section 411.11 for nongovernmental entities or section 411.13 for governmental entities. The appropriateness of other accounting literature depends on its relevance to particular circumstances, the specificity of the guidance, and the general recognition of the issuer or author as an authority.

.14 Section 411.04 recognizes that an auditor's opinion that financial statements are presented fairly in conformity with generally accepted accounting principles should be based on his or her judgment as to whether the accounting principles selected and applied have general acceptance and are appropriate in the circumstances.

.15 Furthermore, in engagements where section 380, *Communication With Audit Committees*, applies, the auditor should determine that the audit committee (or its equivalent) is informed about the initial selection of and changes in significant accounting policies or their application. The auditor should also determine that the audit committee (or its equivalent) is informed about the methods used to account for significant unusual transactions and the effect of significant accounting policies in controversial or emerging areas for which there is a lack of authoritative guidance or consensus.

[Issue Date: March, 1995.]

AU Section 420

Consistency of Application of Generally Accepted Accounting Principles

Sources: SAS No. 1, section 420; SAS No. 43.

See section 9420 for interpretations of this section.

Issue date, unless otherwise indicated: November, 1972.

.01 The second standard of reporting (referred to herein as the consistency standard) is:

> The report shall identify those circumstances in which such principles have not been consistently observed in the current period in relation to the preceding period.

.02 The objective of the consistency standard is to ensure that if comparability of financial statements between periods has been materially affected by changes in accounting principles, there will be appropriate reporting by the independent auditor regarding such changes.[1] It is also implicit in the objective that such principles have been consistently observed within each period. The auditor's standard report implies that the auditor is satisfied that the comparability of financial statements between periods has not been materially affected by changes in accounting principles and that such principles have been consistently applied between or among periods because either (*a*) no change in accounting principles has occurred, or (*b*) there has been a change in accounting principles or in the method of their application, but the effect of the change on the comparability of the financial statements is not material. In these cases, the auditor would not refer to consistency in his report.

.03 Proper application of the consistency standard by the independent auditor requires an understanding of the relationship of consistency to comparability. Although lack of consistency may cause lack of comparability, other factors unrelated to consistency may also cause lack of comparability.[2]

.04 A comparison of the financial statements of an entity between years may be affected by (*a*) accounting changes, (*b*) an error in previously issued financial statements, (*c*) changes in classification, and (*d*) events or transactions substantially different from those accounted for in previously issued statements. Accounting change, as defined in APB Opinion No. 20 [AC section

---

[1] The appropriate form of reporting on a lack of consistency is discussed in section 508.16–.18. [Footnote added to reflect the conforming changes necessary due to the issuance of Statement on Auditing Standards Nos. 53 through 62.]

[2] For a discussion of comparability of financial statements of a single enterprise, see paragraphs 111 through 119 of FASB Statement of Financial Accounting Concepts No. 2, "Qualitative Characteristics of Accounting Information." [Footnote renumbered to reflect the conforming changes necessary due to the issuance of Statement on Auditing Standards Nos. 53 through 62; Revised, June, 1993, to reflect conforming changes necessary due to the issuance of Statement of Position 93-3.]

A06], means a change in (1) an accounting principle, (2) an accounting estimate, or (3) the reporting entity (which is a special type of change in accounting principle).

.05 Changes in accounting principle having a material effect on the financial statements require recognition in the independent auditor's report through the addition of an explanatory paragraph (following the opinion paragraph). Other factors affecting comparability in financial statements may require disclosure, but they would not ordinarily be commented upon in the independent auditor's report.

Accounting Changes Affecting Consistency

Change in Accounting Principle

.06 "A change in accounting principle results from adoption of a generally accepted accounting principle different from the one used previously for reporting purposes. The term *accounting principle* includes not only accounting principles and practices but also the methods of applying them."[3] A change in accounting principle includes, for example, a change from the straight-line method to the declining balance method of depreciation for all assets in a class or for all newly acquired assets in a class. The consistency standard is applicable to this type of change and requires recognition in the auditor's report through the addition of an explanatory paragraph. [As modified, effective January 1, 1975, by FASB Statement No. 2 (AC section R50).]

Change in the Reporting Entity

.07 Since a change in the reporting entity is a special type of change in accounting principle, the consistency standard is applicable. Changes in reporting entity that require recognition in the auditor's report include:

a. Presenting consolidated or combined statements in place of statements of individual companies.

b. Changing specific subsidiaries comprising the group of companies for which consolidated statements are presented.

c. Changing the companies included in combined financial statements.

d. Changing among the cost, equity, and consolidation methods of accounting for subsidiaries or other investments in common stock.

Reports Following a Pooling of Interests

.08 When companies have merged or combined in accordance with the accounting concept known as a "pooling of interests," appropriate effect of the pooling should be given in the presentation of financial position, results of operations, cash flows, and other historical financial data of the continuing business for the year in which the combination is consummated and, in comparative financial statements, for years prior to the year of pooling, as de-

[3] Accounting Principles Board Opinion No. 20, paragraph 7 [AC section A06.105]. [Footnote renumbered to reflect the conforming changes necessary due to the issuance of Statement on Auditing Standards Nos. 53 through 62.]

scribed in APB Opinion No. 16, *Business Combinations* [AC section B50]. If prior year financial statements, presented in comparison with current year financial statements, are not restated to give appropriate recognition to a pooling of interests, the comparative financial statements are not presented on a consistent basis. In this case, the inconsistency arises not from a change in the application of an accounting principle in the current year, but from the lack of such application to prior years. Such inconsistency would require the auditor to add an explanatory paragraph to the report. In addition, failure to give appropriate recognition to the pooling in comparative financial statements is a departure from generally accepted accounting principles. [Paragraph added to reflect the conforming changes necessary due to the issuance of Statement on Auditing Standards Nos. 53 through 62.]

.09 When single-year statements only are presented for the year in which a combination is consummated, a note to the financial statements should adequately disclose the pooling transaction and state the revenues, extraordinary items, and net income of the constituent companies for the preceding year on a combined basis. In such instances, the disclosure and consistency standards are met. Omission of disclosure of the pooling transaction and its effect on the preceding year would require the auditor to qualify the opinion because of the lack of disclosure and may also require the auditor to add an explanatory paragraph to the report because of the inconsistency (see footnote 16 of section 508.52). [Paragraph added to reflect the conforming changes necessary due to the issuance of Statement on Auditing Standards Nos. 53 through 62.]

.10 For purposes of application of the consistency standard, a change in reporting entity does not result from the creation, cessation, purchase, or disposition of a subsidiary or other business unit. [Paragraph renumbered to reflect the conforming changes necessary due to the issuance of Statement on Auditing Standards Nos. 53 through 62.]

Correction of an Error in Principle

.11 A change from an accounting principle that is not generally accepted to one that is generally accepted, including correction of a mistake in the application of a principle, is a correction of an error. Although this type of change in accounting principle should be accounted for as the correction of an error,[4] the change requires recognition in the auditor's report through the addition of an explanatory paragraph. [Paragraph renumbered to reflect the conforming changes necessary due to the issuance of Statement on Auditing Standards Nos. 53 through 62.][5]

Change in Principle Inseparable From Change in Estimate

.12 The effect of a change in accounting principle may be inseparable from the effect of a change in estimate.[6] Although the accounting for such a change is the same as that accorded a change only in estimate, a change in principle is involved. Accordingly, this type of change requires recognition in the inde-

---

[4] See paragraphs 13, 36, and 37 of Accounting Principles Board Opinion No. 20 [AC section A35.104–.105]. [Footnote renumbered to reflect the conforming changes necessary due to the issuance of Statement on Auditing Standards Nos. 53 through 62.]

[5] Footnote deleted to reflect the conforming changes necessary due to the issuance of Statement on Auditing Standards Nos. 53 through 62.

[6] See paragraph 11 of Accounting Principles Board Opinion No. 20 [AC section A06.110]. [Footnote renumbered to reflect the conforming changes necessary due to the issuance of Statement on Auditing Standards Nos. 53 through 62.]

pendent auditor's report through the addition of an explanatory paragraph. [Paragraph renumbered to reflect the conforming changes necessary due to the issuance of Statement on Auditing Standards Nos. 53 through 62.]

Changes in Presentation of Cash Flows

.13 For purposes of presenting cash flows, FASB Statement No. 95, *Statement of Cash Flows* [AC section C25], states that, "An enterprise shall disclose its policy for determining which items are treated as cash equivalents. Any change to that policy is a change in accounting principle that shall be effected by restating financial statements for earlier years presented for comparative purposes." Accordingly, this type of change in presentation of cash flows requires recognition in the independent auditor's report through the addition of an explanatory paragraph. [Paragraph added to reflect the conforming changes necessary due to the issuance of Statement on Auditing Standards Nos. 53 through 62.]

Changes Not Affecting Consistency

Change in Accounting Estimate

.14 Accounting estimates (such as service lives and salvage values of depreciable assets and provisions for warranty costs, uncollectible receivables, and inventory obsolescence) are necessary in the preparation of financial statements. Accounting estimates change as new events occur and as additional experience and information are acquired. This type of accounting change is required by altered conditions that affect comparability but do not involve the consistency standard. The independent auditor, in addition to satisfying himself with respect to the conditions giving rise to the change in accounting estimate, should satisfy himself that the change does not include the effect of a change in accounting principle. Provided he is so satisfied, he need not comment on the change in his report.[7] However, an accounting change of this type having a material effect on the financial statements may require disclosure in a note to the financial statements.[8] [Paragraph renumbered to reflect the conforming changes necessary due to the issuance of Statement on Auditing Standards Nos. 53 through 62.]

Error Correction Not Involving Principle

.15 Correction of an error in previously issued financial statements resulting from mathematical mistakes, oversight, or misuse of facts that existed at the time the financial statements were originally prepared does not involve the consistency standard if no element of accounting principles or their application is included. Accordingly, the independent auditor need not recognize the correction in his report.[9] [Paragraph renumbered to reflect the conforming changes necessary due to the issuance of Statement on Auditing Standards Nos. 53 through 62.]

---

[7] Footnote deleted. [Footnote renumbered to reflect the conforming changes necessary due to the issuance of Statement on Auditing Standards Nos. 53 through 62.]

[8] See paragraph 33 of Accounting Principles Board Opinion No. 20 [AC section A06.132]. [Footnote renumbered to reflect the conforming changes necessary due to the issuance of Statement on Auditing Standards Nos. 53 through 62.]

[9] If the independent auditor had previously reported on the financial statements containing the error, he should refer to section 561, *Subsequent Discovery of Facts Existing at the Date of the Auditor's Report*. [Footnote renumbered to reflect the conforming changes necessary due to the issuance of Statement on Auditing Standards Nos. 53 through 62.]

Changes in Classification and Reclassifications

.16 Classifications in the current financial statements may be different from classifications in the prior year's financial statements. Although changes in classification are usually not of sufficient importance to necessitate disclosure, material changes in classification should be indicated and explained in the financial statements or notes. These changes and material reclassifications made in previously issued financial statements to enhance comparability with current financial statements ordinarily would not need to be referred to in the independent auditor's report. [Paragraph renumbered to reflect the conforming changes necessary due to the issuance of Statement on Auditing Standards Nos. 53 through 62.]

Variations in Presentation of Statement of Changes in Financial Position

.17 [Paragraph renumbered and deleted to reflect the conforming changes necessary due to the issuance of Statement on Auditing Standards Nos. 53 through 62.]

Substantially Different Transactions or Events

.18 Accounting principles are adopted when events or transactions first become material in their effect. Such adoption, as well as modification or adoption of an accounting principle necessitated by transactions or events that are clearly different in substance from those previously occurring, do not involve the consistency standard although disclosure in the notes to the financial statements may be required. [Formerly paragraph .17, number changed by issuance of Statement on Auditing Standards No. 43, effective after August 31, 1982. Paragraph renumbered to reflect the conforming changes necessary due to the issuance of Statement on Auditing Standards Nos. 53 through 62.]

Changes Expected to Have a Material Future Effect

.19 If an accounting change has no material effect on the financial statements in the current year, but the change is reasonably certain to have substantial effect in later years, the change should be disclosed in the notes to the financial statements whenever the statements of the period of change are presented, but the independent auditor need not recognize the change in his report. [Formerly paragraph .18, number changed by issuance of Statement on Auditing Standards No. 43, effective after August 31, 1982. Paragraph renumbered to reflect the conforming changes necessary due to the issuance of Statement on Auditing Standards Nos. 53 through 62.]

Disclosure of Changes Not Affecting Consistency

.20 While the matters do not require the addition of an explanatory paragraph about consistency in the independent auditor's report, the auditor should qualify his opinion as to the disclosure matter if necessary disclosures are not made. (See section 431.) [Reference changed by issuance of Statement on Auditing Standards No. 32. Formerly paragraph .19, number changed by issuance of Statement on Auditing Standards No. 43, effective after August 31, 1982. Paragraph renumbered to reflect the conforming changes necessary due to the issuance of Statement on Auditing Standards Nos. 53 through 62.]

Periods to Which the Consistency Standard Relates

.21 When the independent auditor reports only on the current period, he should obtain sufficient, competent evidential matter about consistency of the application of accounting principles, regardless of whether financial statements for the preceding period are presented. (The term "current period" means the most recent year, or period of less than one year, upon which the independent auditor is reporting.) When the independent auditor reports on two or more years, he should address the consistency of the application of accounting principles between such years and the consistency of such years with the year prior thereto if such prior year is presented with the financial statements being reported upon. [Formerly paragraph .20, number changed by issuance of Statement on Auditing Standards No. 43, effective after August 31, 1982. Paragraph renumbered to reflect the conforming changes necessary due to the issuance of Statement on Auditing Standards Nos. 53 through 62.]

Consistency Expression

[.22] [Paragraph renumbered and deleted to reflect the conforming changes necessary due to the issuance of Statement on Auditing Standards Nos. 53 through 62.]

First Year Audits

.23 When the independent auditor has not audited the financial statements of a company for the preceding year, he should adopt procedures that are practicable and reasonable in the circumstances to assure himself that the accounting principles employed are consistent between the current and the preceding year. Where adequate records have been maintained by the client, it is usually practicable and reasonable to extend auditing procedures to gather sufficient competent evidential matter about consistency.

.24 Inadequate financial records or limitations imposed by the client may preclude the independent auditor from obtaining sufficient, competent evidential matter about the consistent application of accounting principles between the current and the prior year, as well as to the amounts of assets or liabilities at the beginning of the current year. Where such amounts could materially affect current operating results, the independent auditor would also be unable to express an opinion on the current year's results of operations and cash flows.

AU Section 9420

Consistency of Application of Generally Accepted Accounting Principles: Auditing Interpretations of Section 420

[1.] The Effect of APB Opinion No. 30 on Consistency[1]

[.01–.10] [Superseded October, 1979 by Interpretation No. 5, paragraphs .28–.31.]

2. The Effect of APB Opinion No. 28 on Consistency

.11 *Question*—Independent auditors may be engaged to report on financial information for an annual period and a subsequent interim period. Should the auditor add an explanatory paragraph (following the opinion paragraph) to his report in those circumstances where accounting principles and practices used in preparing the annual financial information have been modified in accordance with APB Opinion No. 28 [AC section I73] in preparing the interim financial statements?

.12 *Interpretation*—No. The auditor should not add an explanatory paragraph to his report because of these modifications. Although the modifications deemed appropriate under Opinion No. 28 [AC section I73] may appear to be changes in the methods of applying accounting principles, they differ from changes in methods that require an explanatory paragraph since the modifications are made in order to recognize a difference in circumstances, that is, a difference between presenting financial information for a year and presenting financial information for only a part of a year.

.13 Section 420, *Consistency of Application of Generally Accepted Accounting Principles*, paragraph .02, states: "The objective of the consistency standard is to ensure that if comparability of financial statements between periods has been materially affected by changes in accounting principles there will be appropriate reporting by the independent auditor regarding such changes." Section 420.02 refers to changes in methods that lessen the usefulness of financial statements in comparing the financial information of one period with that of an earlier period. Thus, the purpose of an explanatory paragraph about consistency in the auditor's report is to alert readers of the report not to make an unqualified comparison of the financial information for the two periods.

.14 The modifications introduced by Opinion No. 28 [AC section I73], however, do not lessen the comparability of the financial information of an interim period with that of a preceding annual period. On the contrary, those modifications are intended to enhance comparability between the two sets of financial information. As paragraph 10 of Opinion No. 28 [AC section I73.103] states, the modifications are needed "so that the reported results for the interim period may better relate to the results of operations for the annual period."

---

[1] Originally issued under the title "Reporting on Consistency and Extraordinary Items" (*Journal of Accountancy*, Jan. '74, p. 67).

.15 Thus the modifications introduced by Opinion No. 28 [AC section I73] are not of the type that would require an explanatory paragraph (following the opinion paragraph) in the auditor's report. Independent auditors should, of course, add an explanatory paragraph if changes of the type that lessen comparability are introduced in the interim financial information.

[Issue Date: February, 1974.]

3. Impact on the Auditor's Report of FIFO to LIFO Change in Comparative Financial Statements

.16 *Question*—Changing economic conditions have caused some companies to change their inventory pricing methods from the first-in, first-out (FIFO) method to the last in, first out (LIFO) method. When a company presents comparative financial statements and the year of the FIFO to LIFO change is the earliest year both presented and reported on, should the auditor refer to that change in accounting principle in his report?

.17 *Interpretation*—The auditor would not be required to refer in his report to a FIFO to LIFO change in the circumstances described above.

.18 A change in accounting principle usually results in including the cumulative effect of the change in net income of the period of the change. A change in inventory pricing method from FIFO to LIFO, however, is a change in accounting principle that ordinarily does not affect retained earnings at the beginning of the period in which the change was made. (See APB Opinion No. 20, paragraphs 14(d) and 26.)[2]

.19 An example of typical disclosure of a FIFO to LIFO change in the year of the change is as follows:

> "In 1974, the company adopted the last in, first out (LIFO) method of costing inventory. Previously, the first in, first out (FIFO) method of costing inventory was used. Management believes that the LIFO method has the effect of minimizing the impact of price level changes on inventory valuations and generally matches current costs against current revenues in the income statement. The effect of the change was to reduce net income by $xxxx ($.xx per share) from that which would otherwise have been reported. There is no cumulative effect on prior years since the ending inventory as previously reported (1973) is the beginning inventory for LIFO purposes. Accordingly, pro forma results of operations for the prior year had LIFO been followed is not determinable."

.20 Section 420, *Consistency of Application of Generally Accepted Accounting Principles*, paragraph .21 discusses the periods to which the consistency standard relates: "When the independent auditor reports on two or more years, he should address the consistency of the application of accounting principles between such years. . . ." For a FIFO to LIFO change made in the earliest year presented and reported on, there is no inconsistency in the application of accounting principles, and comparability between the earliest year and subsequent years is not affected since no cumulative effect is reported in the year of the change. Consequently, the independent auditor need not refer to the change in inventory pricing methods.

[.21–.23] [Paragraphs deleted to reflect the conforming changes necessary due to the issuance of Statement on Auditing Standards Nos. 53 through 62.]

---

[2] AC section A06.122.

[Interpretation amended to reflect the conforming changes necessary due to the issuance of Statement on Auditing Standards Nos. 53 through 62.]

[Issue Date: January, 1975.]

[4.] The Effect of FASB Statement No. 13 on Consistency[3]

[.24–.27] [Withdrawn March, 1989 by the Auditing Standards Board.]

[5.] The Effects of Changes in Accounting Principles and Classification on Consistency

[.28–.31] [Withdrawn December, 1992 by the Audit Issues Task Force.]

[6.] The Effect of FASB Statement No. 34 on Consistency

[.32–.43] [Withdrawn March, 1989 by the Auditing Standards Board.]

[7.] The Effect of FASB Statement No. 31 on Consistency

[.44–.51] [Withdrawn March, 1989 by the Auditing Standards Board.]

8. The Effect of Accounting Changes by an Investee on Consistency

.52 *Question*—Does a change in accounting principle by an investee accounted for by the equity method require the auditor to add an explanatory paragraph (following the opinion paragraph) to his report on the financial statements of the investor?

.53 *Interpretation*—Changes in accounting principle affect the comparability of financial statements regardless of whether such changes originate at the investor level or are made solely by an investee.[4] Section 420, *Consistency of Application of Generally Accepted Accounting Principles*, paragraph .02, states: "The objective of the consistency standard is to ensure that if comparability of financial statements between periods has been materially affected by changes in accounting principles there will be appropriate reporting by the independent auditor regarding such changes."

.54 Thus, the auditor would need to add an explanatory paragraph (following the opinion paragraph) to his report when there has been a change in accounting principle by an investee accounted for by the equity method that causes a material lack of comparability in the financial statements of an investor.

[.55–.57] [Paragraphs deleted to reflect the conforming changes necessary due to the issuance of Statement on Auditing Standards Nos. 53 through 62.]

[Issue Date: July, 1980; Revised: June, 1993.]

[9.] The Effect of Adoption of FASB Statement No. 35 on Consistency

[.58–.63] [Withdrawn March, 1989 by the Auditing Standards Board.]

10. Change in Presentation of Accumulated Benefit Information in the Financial Statements of a Defined Benefit Pension Plan

.64 *Question*—FASB Statement No. 35, *Accounting and Reporting by Defined Benefit Pension Plans* [AC section Pe5] requires the presentation of

---

[3] [Footnote deleted.]

[4] For a discussion of comparability of financial statements of a single enterprise, see paragraphs 111 through 119 of FASB Statement of Financial Accounting Concepts No. 2, "Qualitative Characteristics of Accounting Information."

information regarding the actuarial present value of accumulated plan benefits and year-to-year changes therein of a defined benefit pension plan but permits certain flexibility in presenting such information. The information may be included on the face of a financial statement (a separate statement or one that combines accumulated benefit information with asset information), or it may be included in the notes to the financial statements. Furthermore, the benefit information may be as of the beginning of the period being reported upon or as of the end of that period. Does a change in the format of presentation of accumulated benefit information or a change in the date as of which such information is presented require the auditor to add an explanatory paragraph (after the opinion paragraph) to his report because of the change?

.65 *Interpretation*—Such changes in the presentation of information regarding accumulated benefits are considered reclassifications or variations in the nature of information presented. Changes such as these that are material should be explained in the financial statements or notes, but these changes ordinarily would not require the auditor to add this explanatory paragraph to his report (see section 420.16).

[Issue Date: December, 1980.]

11. The Effect of the Adoption of FASB Statement No. 36 on Consistency

[.66–.68] [Withdrawn March, 1989 by the Auditing Standards Board.]

AU Section 431

Adequacy of Disclosure in Financial Statements

(Supersedes Statement on Auditing Standards No. 1, section 430)

Source: SAS No. 32.

Issue date, unless otherwise indicated: October, 1980.

.01 The third standard of reporting is:

> Informative disclosures in the financial statements are to be regarded as reasonably adequate unless otherwise stated in the report.

.02 The presentation of financial statements in conformity with generally accepted accounting principles includes adequate disclosure of material matters. These matters relate to the form, arrangement, and content of the financial statements and their appended notes, including, for example, the terminology used, the amount of detail given, the classification of items in the statements, and the bases of amounts set forth. An independent auditor considers whether a particular matter should be disclosed in light of the circumstances and facts of which he is aware at the time.

.03 If management omits from the financial statements, including the accompanying notes, information that is required by generally accepted accounting principles, the auditor should express a qualified or an adverse opinion and should provide the information in his report, if practicable, unless its omission from the auditor's report is recognized as appropriate by a specific Statement on Auditing Standards.[1] In this context, *practicable* means that the information is reasonably obtainable from management's accounts and records and that providing the information in his report does not require the auditor to assume the position of a preparer of financial information. For example, the auditor would not be expected to prepare a basic financial statement or segment information and include it in his report when management omits such information.

.04 In considering the adequacy of disclosure, and in other aspects of his audit, the auditor uses information received in confidence from the client. Without such confidence, the auditor would find it difficult to obtain information necessary for him to form an opinion on financial statements. Thus, the auditor should not ordinarily make available, without the client's consent, information that is not required to be disclosed in financial statements to comply with generally accepted accounting principles (see AICPA Code of Professional Conduct, Rule 301 [ET section 301.01]).

---

[1] An independent auditor may participate in preparing financial statements, including accompanying notes. The financial statements, including accompanying notes, however, remain the representations of management, and such participation by the auditor does not require him to modify his report (see section 110.03).

AU Section 435

Segment Information[*][1]

Source: SAS No. 21.

Issue date, unless otherwise indicated: December, 1977.

.01 Statement of Financial Accounting Standards No. 14 [AC section S20], *Financial Reporting for Segments of a Business Enterprise*, requires the inclusion of certain information about an entity's operations in different industries, its foreign operations and export sales, and its major customers (referred to in this section as "segment information") in annual financial statements that are intended to present financial position, results of operations, and cash flows in conformity with generally accepted accounting principles. Disclosure of segment information requires the disaggregation of certain significant elements of an entity's financial statements, such as revenue, operating profit or loss, identifiable assets, depreciation, and capital expenditures. This section provides guidance to an auditor in auditing and reporting on financial statements that are required to include segment information in conformity with FASB Statement No. 14 [AC section S20].

.02 Segment information is one of the disclosures required by generally accepted accounting principles as an integral part of financial statements. The purpose of segment information is stated in paragraph 5 of FASB Statement No. 14 [AC section S20.106]:

> The purpose of the information required to be reported by this Statement is to assist financial statement users in analyzing and understanding the enterprise's financial statements by permitting better assessment of the enterprise's past performance and future prospects .... information prepared in conformity with this Statement may be of limited usefulness for comparing a segment of one enterprise with a similar segment of another enterprise.

Auditor's Objective

.03 The objective of auditing procedures applied to segment information is to provide the auditor with a reasonable basis for concluding whether the information is presented in conformity with FASB Statement No. 14 [AC section S20] in relation to the financial statements taken as a whole. The auditor performing an audit of financial statements in accordance with generally accepted auditing standards considers segment information, as other informative disclosures, in relation to the financial statements taken as a whole, and is not required to apply auditing procedures that would be necessary to express a separate opinion on the segment information.

---

[*] See FASB Statement No. 21 [AC section S20.101–.103 and S20.407], *Suspension of the Reporting of Earnings per Share and Segment Information by Nonpublic Enterprises*.

[1] The meaning of the term "segment information" in this section differs from that of the term "segment" in section 623, *Special Reports*, paragraph .02.

Auditing Procedures

.04 Paragraphs .05–.07 of this section provide guidance as to auditing procedures when financial statements include segment information. If an entity represents to the auditor that it does not have industry segments, foreign operations, export sales, or major customers required to be disclosed by FASB Statement No. 14 [AC section S20], the auditor should follow the guidance in paragraph .15 of this section.

.05 The auditor applies the concept of materiality, discussed in section 150.04, in determining the nature, timing, and extent of auditing procedures to be applied in an audit of financial statements. Materiality of segment information is evaluated primarily by relating the dollar magnitude of the information to the financial statements taken as a whole. However, as with other elements of financial statements, the materiality of segment information does not depend entirely on relative size; the concept involves qualitative as well as quantitative judgments. (A discussion of materiality as it relates to the auditor's report is included in paragraph .08 of this section.)

.06 In planning his audit, it may be necessary for the auditor to modify or redirect selected audit tests to be applied to the financial statements taken as a whole. For example, the auditor may decide to select inventories for physical observation on the basis of industry segments or geographic areas. Factors such as the following should be considered by the auditor in determining whether his procedures should be modified or redirected:

a. Internal control and the degree of integration, centralization, and uniformity of the accounting records.

b. The nature, number, and relative size of industry segments and geographic areas.

c. The nature and number of subsidiaries or divisions in each industry segment and geographic area.

d. The accounting principles used for the industry segments and geographic areas.

In any event, the tests of underlying accounting records normally applied in an audit of financial statements should include a consideration of whether the entity's revenue, operating expenses, and identifiable assets are appropriately classified among industry segments and geographic areas.

.07 In addition, the auditor should apply the following procedures to segment information presented in financial statements:

a. Inquire of management concerning its methods of determining segment information, and evaluate the reasonableness of those methods in relation to the factors identified in FASB Statement No. 14 [AC section S20] for making those determinations.[2]

b. Inquire as to the bases of accounting for sales or transfers between industry segments and between geographic areas, and test, to the extent considered necessary, those sales or transfers for conformity with the bases of accounting disclosed.

---

[2] Paragraphs 11–21 and Appendix D of FASB Statement No. 14 [AC sections S20.113–.127 and S20.409] discuss how an entity's industry segments and reportable segments should be determined. Paragraph 34 of that Statement [AC section S20.140] describes factors to be considered in grouping the countries in which an entity operates into geographic areas, and paragraphs 36 and 39 [AC section S20.142] describe criteria for disclosing export sales and major customers, respectively.

c. Test the disaggregation of the entity's financial statements into segment information. The tests should include (1) an evaluation of the entity's application of the various percentage tests specified in paragraphs 15–20 and 31–39 of FASB Statement No. 14 [AC sections S20.119–.126 and S20.137–.144], and (2) application of analytical procedures to the segment information to identify and provide a basis for inquiry about relationships and individual items that appear to be unusual. Analytical procedures, for purposes of this section, consist of (*a*) comparison of the segment information with comparable information for the immediately preceding year, (*b*) comparison of the segment information with any available related budgeted information for the current year, and (*c*) study of the relationships of elements of the segment information that would be expected to conform to a predictable pattern based on the entity's experience (for example, operating profit as a percentage of both total revenue and identifiable assets by industry segment or geographic area). In applying these procedures, the auditor should consider the types of matters that in the preceding year have required accounting adjustments of segment information. [As modified, November 1979, by the Auditing Standards Board.]

d. Inquire as to the methods of allocating operating expenses incurred and identifiable assets used jointly by two or more segments, evaluate whether those methods are reasonable, and test the allocations to the extent considered necessary.

e. Determine whether the segment information has been presented consistently from period to period and, if not, whether the nature and effect of the inconsistency are disclosed and, if applicable, whether the information has been retroactively restated in conformity with paragraph 40 of FASB Statement No. 14 [AC section S20.146].

Reporting

.08 The auditor's standard report on financial statements prepared in conformity with generally accepted accounting principles implicitly applies to segment information included in those statements in the same manner that it applies to other informative disclosures in the financial statements that are not clearly marked as "unaudited."[3] The auditor's standard report would not refer to segment information unless his audit revealed a misstatement or omission, or a change in accounting principle, relating to the segment information that is material in relation to the financial statements taken as a whole, or the auditor was unable to apply the auditing procedures that he considered necessary in the circumstances. The auditor should consider qualitative as well as quantitative factors in evaluating whether such a matter is material to the financial statements taken as a whole. The significance of a matter to a particular entity (for example, a misstatement of the revenue and operating

---

[3] If an entity discloses comparative segment information for fiscal years beginning prior to December 15, 1976, that information should be clearly marked as "unaudited" unless the auditor has applied to that segment information the auditing procedures set forth in this section. If the auditor concludes, on the basis of facts known to him, that segment information marked "unaudited" is not in conformity with FASB Statement No. 14 [AC section S20] in relation to the financial statements taken as a whole, he should follow the guidance in section 504. [Reference changed by the issuance of Statement on Auditing Standards No. 26, *Association With Financial Statements*.]

profit of a relatively small segment that is represented by management to be important to the future profitability of the entity), the pervasiveness of a matter (for example, whether it affects the amounts and presentation of numerous items in the segment information), and the impact of a matter (for example, whether it distorts the trends reflected in the segment information) should all be considered in judging whether a matter relating to segment information is material to the financial statements taken as a whole. Accordingly, situations may arise in practice where the auditor will conclude that a matter relating to segment information is material to the financial statements taken as a whole even though, in his judgment, it is quantitatively immaterial to those financial statements.

Misstatement or Omission of Segment Information

.09 If the audit reveals a misstatement in the segment information that is material in relation to the financial statements taken as a whole and that misstatement is not corrected, the auditor should modify[4] his opinion on the financial statements because of a departure from generally accepted accounting principles. The following is an example of an auditor's report qualified because of a misstatement of segment information.

Independent Auditor's Report

[*Same first and second paragraphs as the standard report*]

(Explanatory paragraph)

With respect to the segment information in Note X , $...... of the operating expenses of Industry A were incurred jointly by Industries A and B. In our opinion, generally accepted accounting principles require that those operating expenses be allocated between Industries A and B. The effect of the failure to allocate those operating expenses has been to understate the operating profit of Industry A and to overstate the operating profit of Industry B by an amount that has not been determined.

(Opinion paragraph)

In our opinion, except for the effects of not allocating certain common operating expenses between Industries A and B, as discussed in the preceding paragraph, the financial statements referred to above present fairly . . .

.10 If the entity declines to include in the financial statements part or all of the segment information that the auditor believes, based on his knowledge of the entity's business, is required to be disclosed, the auditor should modify his opinion on the financial statements because of inadequate disclosure and should describe the type of information omitted.[5] The auditor is not required to provide the omitted information in his report.[6], [7] The following is an example of an auditor's report qualified because of an omission of segment information.

[4] The term "modify" in this context means to express a qualified or an adverse opinion.

[5] [Footnote deleted to reflect the conforming changes necessary due to the issuance of Statement on Auditing Standards Nos. 53 through 62.]

[6] [Footnote deleted to reflect the conforming changes necessary due to the issuance of Statement on Auditing Standards Nos. 53 through 62.]

[7] See section 508.41–.44 for further discussion of the auditor's responsibility in these circumstances. [Footnote added to reflect the conforming changes necessary due to the issuance of Statement on Auditing Standards Nos. 53 through 62.]

Independent Auditor's Report

[*Same first and second paragraphs as the standard report*]

(Explanatory paragraph)

The Company declined to present segment information for the year ended December 31, 19XX. In our opinion, presentation of segment information concerning the Company's operations in different industries, its foreign operations and export sales, and its major customers is required by generally accepted accounting principles. The omission of segment information results in an incomplete presentation of the Company's financial statements.

(Opinion paragraph)

In our opinion, except for the omission of segment information, as discussed in the preceding paragraph, the financial statements referred to above present fairly . . .

Consistency

.11 Paragraph 67 of FASB Statement No. 14, states:

> . . . consistency from period to period in the methods by which an enterprise's segment information is prepared and presented is as important as consistency in the application of the accounting principles used in preparing the enterprise's consolidated financial statements.

An inconsistency in segment information may occur because of—

a. A change in the bases of accounting for sales or transfers between industry segments or between geographic areas, or in the methods of allocating operating expenses or identifiable assets among industry segments or geographic areas (paragraphs 23, 24, and 35a of FASB Statement No. 14 [AC sections S20.129–.130 and S20.141a]).

b. A change in the method of determining or presenting a measure of profitability for some or all of the segments (paragraphs 25 and 35b of FASB Statement No. 14 [AC sections S20.131 and S20.141b]).

c. A change in accounting principle as discussed in APB Opinion No. 20 [AC section A06], *Accounting Changes* (paragraph 27d of FASB Statement No. 14 [AC section S20.133d]).

d. A change requiring retroactive restatement as discussed in paragraph .12 of this section.

.12 Paragraph 40 of FASB Statement No. 14 [AC section S20.146] requires that segment information for prior periods that is disclosed in comparative financial statements be retroactively restated if—

a. The financial statements of the entity as a whole have been retroactively restated.

b. The method of grouping products and services into industry segments or of grouping foreign operations into geographic areas is changed and the change affects the segment information disclosed.

.13 FASB Statement No. 14 [AC section S20] requires that the nature and effect of the changes indicated in paragraphs .11 and .12 be disclosed in the period of the change. If the nature and effect of a change are not disclosed or, if applicable, the segment information is not retroactively restated, the auditor should modify his opinion because of the departure from generally accepted accounting principles. The following is an example of an auditor's report qualified because of an entity's failure to disclose the nature and effect of a change in the basis of accounting for sales between industry segments.

Independent Auditor's Report

[*Same first and second paragraphs as the standard report*]

(Explanatory paragraph)

In 19XX, the Company changed the basis of accounting for sales between its industry segments from the market price method to the negotiated price method, but declined to disclose the nature and effect of this change on its segment information. In our opinion, disclosure of the nature and effect of this change, which has not been determined, is required by generally accepted accounting principles.

(Opinion paragraph)

In our opinion, except for the omission of the information discussed in the preceding paragraph, the financial statements referred to above present fairly . . .

.14 The addition of an explanatory paragraph (following the opinion paragraph) to the auditor's report because of lack of consistency is not required for the changes indicated in paragraphs .11 and .12 except for a change in accounting principle that affects the financial statements taken as a whole (paragraph .11*c*), in which case the auditor should also follow the guidance in sections 420 and 508.

Scope Limitation

.15 An entity may represent to the auditor that it does not have industry segments, foreign operations, export sales, or major customers required to be disclosed by FASB Statement No. 14 [AC section S20]. The auditor ordinarily would be able to conclude, based on his knowledge of the entity's business, whether the entity has such industry segments, foreign operations, export sales, or major customers. If the auditor is unable to reach a conclusion based on that knowledge and the entity declines to develop the information he considers necessary to reach a conclusion, the auditor should indicate in the scope paragraph of his report the limitation on his audit and should qualify his opinion on the financial statements taken as a whole. The following is an example of an auditor's report qualified because of the auditor's inability to conclude whether the entity is required to present segment information.

Independent Auditor's Report

[*Same first paragraph as the standard report*]

(Scope paragraph)

. . . Except as discussed in the following paragraph, we conducted our audit in accordance with . . .

(Explanatory paragraph)

The Company has not developed the information we consider necessary to reach a conclusion as to whether the presentation of segment information concerning the Company's operations in different industries, its foreign operations and export sales, and its major customers is necessary to conform to generally accepted accounting principles.

(Opinion paragraph)

In our opinion, except for the possible omission of segment information, the financial statements referred to above present fairly . . .

.16 The auditor should also qualify his opinion on the financial statements taken as a whole if he is unable to apply to reported segment information the auditing procedures that he considers necessary in the circumstances. The following is an example of an auditor's report qualified because the entity has specified that the auditor should not apply to reported segment information the auditing procedures that he considered necessary in the circumstances.

Independent Auditor's Report

[*Same first paragraph as the standard report*]

(Scope paragraph)

. . . Except as discussed in the following paragraph, we conducted our audit in accordance with . . .

(Explanatory paragraph)

In accordance with the Company's request, our audit of the financial statements did not include the segment information presented in Note X concerning the Company's operations in different industries, its foreign operations and export sales, and its major customers.

(Opinion paragraph)

In our opinion, except for the effects of such adjustments or disclosures, if any, as might have been determined to be necessary had we applied to the segment information the procedures we considered necessary in the circumstances, the financial statements referred to above present fairly . . .

Reporting Separately on Segment Information

.17 The auditor may be requested to report separately on segment information, either in a special report or as part of his report on the financial statements taken as a whole. In such an engagement, the measurement of materiality should be related to the segment information itself rather than to the financial statements taken as a whole. Consequently, an audit of segment information for the purpose of reporting on it separately is more extensive than if the same information were considered in conjunction with an audit of the financial statements taken as a whole.

.18 Paragraphs .11–.17 of section 623, *Special Reports*, provide guidance that is applicable to reporting separately on segment information. However, all of the generally accepted auditing standards, including the first and second standards of reporting, are applicable because FASB Statement No. 14 [AC section S20] establishes generally accepted accounting principles for the presentation of segment information. Thus, whether segment information is presented voluntarily or because it is required, the auditor's report on such information should state whether it is presented in accordance with generally accepted accounting principles.

AU Section 500

THE FOURTH STANDARD OF REPORTING

. . . association with financial statements . . . reports on audited financial statements . . . dating of independent auditor's report . . . reporting on financial statements prepared for use in other countries . . . part of audit made by other independent auditors . . . lack of conformity with GAAP . . . other information in documents containing audited financial statements . . . reporting on information in auditor-submitted documents . . . reporting on condensed financial statements and selected financial data . . . supplementary information . . . subsequent events . . . subsequent discovery of facts . . .

TABLE OF CONTENTS

Section		Paragraph
504	Association With Financial Statements	.01-.19
	Disclaimer of Opinion on Unaudited Financial Statements	.05-.06
	Disclaimer of Opinion on Unaudited Financial Statements Prepared on a Comprehensive Basis of Accounting	.07
	Disclaimer of Opinion When Not Independent	.08-.10
	Circumstances Requiring a Modified Disclaimer	.11-.13
	Reporting on Audited and Unaudited Financial Statements in Comparative Form.	.14-.17
	Negative Assurance	.18-.19
9504	Association With Financial Statements: Auditing Interpretations of Section 504	
	1. Annual Report Disclosure of Unaudited Fourth Quarter Interim Data (11/79).	.01-.07
	[2.] Association of the Auditor of an Acquired Company With Unaudited Statements in a Listing Application (11/79) [Deleted May, 1980]	[.08-.12]
	[3.] Association of the Auditor of the Acquiring Company With Unaudited Statements in a Listing Application (11/79) [Deleted May, 1980]	[.13-.14]
	4. Auditor's Identification With Condensed Financial Data (11/79)	.15-.18
	5. Applicability of Guidance on Reporting When Not Independent (11/79)	.19-.22
	[6.] Reporting on Solvency (12/84) [Rescinded May, 1988]....	[.23-.35]

Section		Paragraph
508	Reports on Audited Financial Statements	.01-.76
	Introduction	.01-.06
	The Auditor's Standard Report	.07-.10
	Explanatory Language Added to the Auditor's Standard Report	.11-.19
	Opinion Based in Part on Report of Another Auditor	.12-.13
	Departure From a Promulgated Accounting Principle	.14-.15
	Lack of Consistency	.16-.18
	Emphasis of a Matter	.19
	Departures From Unqualified Opinions	.20-.63
	Qualified Opinions	.20-.57
	Scope Limitations	.22-.34
	Departure From a Generally Accepted Accounting Principle	.35-.57
	Adverse Opinions	.58-.60
	Disclaimer of Opinion	.61-.63
	Piecemeal Opinions	.64
	Reports on Comparative Financial Statements	.65-.74
	Different Reports on Comparative Financial Statements Presented	.67
	Opinion on Prior-Period Financial Statements Different From the Opinion Previously Expressed	.68-.69
	Report of Predecessor Auditor	.70-.74
	Predecessor Auditor's Report Reissued	.71-.73
	Predecessor Auditor's Report Not Presented	.74
	Effective Date and Transition	.75-.76
9508	Reports on Audited Financial Statements: Auditing Interpretations of Section 508	
	1. Report of an Outside Inventory-Taking Firm as an Alternative Procedure for Observing Inventories (7/75)	.01-.06
	[2.] Reporting on Comparative Financial Statements of Nonprofit Organizations [Superseded December, 1976]	[.07-.10]
	[3.] Reporting on Loss Contingencies (1/76) [Superseded April, 1988]	[.11-.14]
	[4.] Reports on Consolidated Financial Statements That Include Supplementary Consolidating Information (3/79) [Superseded December, 1980]	[.15-.20]
	[5.] Disclosures of Subsequent Events (7/79) [Superseded April, 1988]	[.21-.24]
	[6.] The Materiality of Uncertainties (10/79) [Superseded April, 1988]	[.25-.28]

Section *Paragraph*

9508 Reports on Audited Financial Statements: Auditing Interpretations of Section 508—continued
[7.] Reporting on an Uncertainty (10/79) [Withdrawn August, 1982] ..... [.29-.32]
8. Reporting on Financial Statements Prepared on a Liquidation Basis of Accounting (12/84) ..... .33-.38
[9.] Quantifying Departures From Generally Accepted Accounting Principles (4/86) [Superseded April, 1988] ..... [.39-.43]
[10.] Updated Reports Resulting From the Retroactive Suspension of Earnings per Share and Segment Information Disclosure Requirements (3/79) [Withdrawn March, 1989] ..... [.44-.48]
11. Restating Financial Statements Reported on by a Predecessor Auditor (9/86) ..... .49-.50
12. Reference in Auditor's Standard Report to Management's Report (1/89) ..... .51-.52

530 Dating of the Independent Auditor's Report ..... .01-.08
Events Occurring After Completion of Field Work but Before Issuance of Report ..... .03-.05
Reissuance of the Independent Auditor's Report ..... .06-.08

534 Reporting on Financial Statements Prepared for Use in Other Countries ..... .01-.16
Purpose and Use of Financial Statements ..... .02
General and Fieldwork Standards ..... .03-.05
Compliance With Auditing Standards of Another Country ..... .06
Reporting Standards ..... .07-.15
Use Only Outside the United States ..... .09-.13
Use in the United States ..... .14-.15
Effective Date ..... .16

9534 Reporting on Financial Statements Prepared for Use in Other Countries: Auditing Interpretations of Section 534
1. Financial Statements for General Use Only Outside of the United States in Accordance With International Accounting Standards and International Standards on Auditing (5/96) ..... .01-.04

543 Part of Audit Performed by Other Independent Auditors ..... .01-.17
Principal Auditor's Course of Action ..... .02-.03
Decision Not to Make Reference ..... .04-.05
Decision to Make Reference ..... .06-.09
Procedures Applicable to Both Methods of Reporting ..... .10-.11
Additional Procedures Under Decision Not to Make Reference ..... .12-.13
Long-Term Investments ..... .14

Section		Paragraph
543	Part of Audit Performed by Other Independent Auditors—continued	
	Qualifications in Other Auditor's Report	.15
	Restated Financial Statements of Prior Years Following a Pooling of Interests	.16-.17
9543	Part of Audit Performed by Other Independent Auditors: Auditing Interpretations of Section 543	
	1. Specific Procedures Performed by the Other Auditor at the Principal Auditor's Request (4/79)	.01-.03
	2. Inquiries of the Principal Auditor by the Other Auditor (4/79)	.04-.07
	3. Form of Inquiries of the Principal Auditor Made by the Other Auditor (4/79)	.08-.10
	4. Form of Principal Auditor's Response to Inquiries From Other Auditors (4/79)	.11-.14
	5. Procedures of the Principal Auditor (4/79)	.15-.17
	6. Application of Additional Procedures Concerning the Audit Performed by the Other Auditor (12/81)	.18-.20
	[7.] Reporting on Financial Statements Presented on a Comprehensive Annual Financial Report of a Governmental Entity When One Fund Has Been Audited by Another Auditor (10/89) [Withdrawn December, 1992]	[.21-.24]
544	Lack of Conformity With Generally Accepted Accounting Principles	.02-.04
	Regulated Companies	.02-.04
9544	Lack of Conformity With Generally Accepted Accounting Principles: Auditing Interpretations of Section 544	
	[1.] Auditors' Reports Solely for Purposes of Filing With Insurance Regulatory Agencies (7/75) [Superseded October, 1979]	[.01-.09]
	[2.] Reports in Filings Other Than With the Regulatory Agency on Financial Statements Prepared Using FHLBB Accounting Practices—Savings and Loan Associations (4/82) [Withdrawn March, 1989]	[.10-.14]
550	Other Information in Documents Containing Audited Financial Statements	.01-.06
9550	Other Information in Documents Containing Audited Financial Statements: Auditing Interpretations of Section 550	
	[1.] Reports by Management of Internal Accounting Control (1/81) [Superseded May, 1994]	[.01-.06]
	2. Reports by Management on Internal Control Over Financial Reporting (5/94)	.07-.11
	3. Other References by Management to Internal Control Over Financial Reporting, Including References to the Independent Auditor (5/94)	.12-.15
	4. Other Information in Electronic Sites Containing Audited Financial Statements (3/97)	.16-.18

Section *Paragraph*

551 Reporting on Information Accompanying the Basic Financial Statements in Auditor-Submitted Documents .01-.22
- Reporting Responsibility .04-.11
- Reporting Examples .12-.14
- Supplementary Information Required by FASB or GASB Pronouncements .15
- Consolidating Information .16-.19
- Additional Commentary Concerning the Audit .20
- Co-Existing Financial Statements .21
- Effective Date .22

552 Reporting on Condensed Financial Statements and Selected Financial Data .01-.12
- Condensed Financial Statements .03-.08
- Selected Financial Data .09-.11
- Effective Date .12

558 Required Supplementary Information .01-.10
- Applicability .02-.03
- Involvement With Information Outside Financial Statements .04-.05
- Involvement With Required Supplementary Information .06
- Procedures .07
- Circumstances Requiring Reporting on Required Supplementary Information .08-.10

9558 Required Supplementary Information: Auditing Interpretations of Section 558
- 1. Supplementary Oil and Gas Reserve Information (2/89) .01-.06

560 Subsequent Events .01-.12
- Auditing Procedures in the Subsequent Period .10-.12

9560 Subsequent Events: Auditing Interpretations of Section 560
- [1.–4.] Lawyers' Letters [Superseded January, 1976] [.01-.26]

561 Subsequent Discovery of Facts Existing at the Date of the Auditor's Report .01-.10

9561 Subsequent Discovery of Facts Existing at the Date of the Auditor's Report: Auditing Interpretations of Section 561
- 1. Auditor's Association With Subsequently Discovered Information When the Auditor Has Resigned or Been Discharged (2/89) .01-.02

AU Section 504

Association With Financial Statements

(Supersedes Statement on Auditing Standards No. 1, Sections 516, 517, and 518 and Statement on Auditing Standards No. 15, paragraphs 13–15)[1]

Sources: SAS No. 26; SAS No. 35; SAS No. 72.

See section 9504 for interpretations of this section.

Issue date, unless otherwise indicated: November, 1979.

.01 The fourth standard of reporting is:

> The report shall either contain an expression of opinion regarding the financial statements, taken as a whole, or an assertion to the effect that an opinion cannot be expressed. When an overall opinion cannot be expressed, the reasons therefor should be stated. In all cases where an auditor's name is associated with financial statements, the report should contain a clear-cut indication of the character of the auditor's work, if any, and the degree of responsibility the auditor is taking.

The objective of the fourth reporting standard is to prevent misinterpretation of the degree of responsibility the accountant assumes when his name is associated with financial statements.

.02 This section defines *association* as that term is used in the fourth reporting standard. It provides guidance to an accountant associated with the financial statements of a public entity or with a nonpublic entity's financial statements that he has been engaged to audit in accordance with generally accepted auditing standards.[2]

.03 An accountant is associated with financial statements when he has consented to the use of his name in a report, document, or written communication containing the statements.[3] Also, when an accountant submits to his client or others financial statements that he has prepared or assisted in preparing, he is deemed to be associated even though the accountant does not append his name to the statements. Although the accountant may participate in the preparation of financial statements, the statements are representations of management, and the fairness of their presentation in conformity with generally accepted accounting principles is management's responsibility.

---

[1] [Footnote deleted to reflect the conforming changes necessary due to the issuance of Statement on Auditing Standards Nos. 53 through 62.]

[2] For purposes of this section, a public entity is any entity (*a*) whose securities trade in a public market either on a stock exchange (domestic or foreign) or in the over-the-counter market, including securities quoted only locally or regionally, (*b*) that makes a filing with a regulatory agency in preparation for the sale of any class of its securities in a public market, or (*c*) a subsidiary, corporate joint venture, or other entity controlled by an entity covered by (*a*) or (*b*). Statements on Standards for Accounting and Review Services provide guidance in connection with the unaudited financial statements or other unaudited financial information of a nonpublic entity.

[3] However, this section does not apply to data, such as tax returns, prepared solely for submission to taxing authorities.

.04 An accountant may be associated with audited or unaudited financial statements. Financial statements are audited if the accountant has applied auditing procedures sufficient to permit him to report on them as described in section 508, *Reports on Audited Financial Statements*. The unaudited interim financial statements (or financial information) of a public entity are reviewed when the accountant has applied procedures sufficient to permit him to report on them as described in section 722, *Interim Financial Information*.

Disclaimer of Opinion on Unaudited Financial Statements

.05 When an accountant is associated with the financial statements of a public entity, but has not audited or reviewed[4] such statements, the form of report to be issued is as follows:

> The accompanying balance sheet of X Company as of December 31, 19X1, and the related statements of income, retained earnings, and cash flows for the year then ended were not audited by us and, accordingly, we do not express an opinion on them.
>
> (Signature and date)

This disclaimer of opinion is the means by which the accountant complies with the fourth standard of reporting when associated with unaudited financial statements in these circumstances. The disclaimer may accompany the unaudited financial statements or it may be placed directly on them. In addition, each page of the financial statements should be clearly and conspicuously marked as unaudited. When an accountant issues this form of disclaimer of opinion, he has no responsibility to apply any procedures beyond reading the financial statements for obvious material misstatements. Any procedures that may have been applied should not be described, except in the limited circumstances set forth in paragraphs .18–.20. Describing procedures that may have been applied might cause the reader to believe the financial statements have been audited or reviewed.

.06 If the accountant is aware that his name is to be included in a client-prepared written communication of a public entity containing financial statements that have not been audited or reviewed, he should request (*a*) that his name not be included in the communication or (*b*) that the financial statements be marked as unaudited and that there be a notation that he does not express an opinion on them. If the client does not comply, the accountant should advise the client that he has not consented to the use of his name and should consider what other actions might be appropriate.[5]

Disclaimer of Opinion on Unaudited Financial Statements Prepared on a Comprehensive Basis of Accounting

.07 When an accountant is associated with unaudited financial statements of a public entity prepared in accordance with a comprehensive basis of

---

[4] When a public entity does not have its annual financial statements audited, an accountant may be requested to review its annual or interim financial statements. In those circumstances, an accountant may make a review and look to the guidance in Statements on Standards for Accounting and Review Services for the standards and procedures and form of report applicable to such an engagement.

[5] In considering what actions, if any, may be appropriate in the circumstances, the accountant may wish to consult his legal counsel.

accounting other than generally accepted accounting principles, he should follow the guidance provided by paragraph .05, except that he should modify the identification of financial statements in his disclaimer of opinion (see section 623.02–.10, *Special Reports*).[6] For example, a disclaimer of opinion on cash-basis statements might be worded as follows:

> The accompanying statement of assets and liabilities resulting from cash transactions of XYZ Corporation as of December 31, 19X1, and the related statement of revenues collected and expenses paid during the year then ended were not audited by us and, accordingly, we do not express an opinion on them.
>
> (Signature and date)

A note to the financial statements should describe how the basis of presentation differs from generally accepted accounting principles, but the monetary effect of such differences need not be stated.

Disclaimer of Opinion When Not Independent

.08 The second general standard requires that "In all matters relating to the assignment, an independence in mental attitude is to be maintained by the auditor or auditors." The independent public accountant must be without bias with respect to the client; otherwise, he would lack that impartiality necessary for the dependability of his findings. Whether the accountant is independent is something he must decide as a matter of professional judgment.

.09 When an accountant is not independent, any procedures he might perform would not be in accordance with generally accepted auditing standards, and he would be precluded from expressing an opinion on such statements. Accordingly, he should disclaim an opinion with respect to the financial statements and should state specifically that he is not independent.

.10 If the financial statements are those of a nonpublic entity, the accountant should look to the guidance in Statements on Standards for Accounting and Review Services. In all other circumstances, regardless of the extent of procedures applied, the accountant should follow the guidance in paragraph .05, except that the disclaimer of opinion should be modified to state specifically that he is not independent. The reasons for lack of independence and any procedures he has performed should not be described; including such matters might confuse the reader concerning the importance of the impairment of independence. An example of such a report is as follows:

> We are not independent with respect to XYZ Company, and the accompanying balance sheet as of December 31, 19X1, and the related statements of income, retained earnings, and cash flows for the year then ended were not audited by us and, accordingly, we do not express an opinion on them.
>
> (Signature and date)

Circumstances Requiring a Modified Disclaimer

.11 If the accountant concludes on the basis of facts known to him that the unaudited financial statements on which he is disclaiming an opinion are not in conformity with generally accepted accounting principles, which include adequate disclosure, he should suggest appropriate revision; failing that, he should describe the departure in his disclaimer of opinion. This description should refer specifically to the nature of the departure and, if practicable, state the effects on the financial statements or include the necessary information for adequate disclosure.

---

[6] Reference to generally accepted accounting principles in this section includes, where applicable, another comprehensive basis of accounting.

.12 When the effects of the departure on the financial statements are not reasonably determinable, the disclaimer of opinion should so state. When a departure from generally accepted accounting principles involves inadequate disclosure, it may not be practicable for the accountant to include the omitted disclosures in his report. For example, when management has elected to omit substantially all of the disclosures, the accountant should clearly indicate that in his report, but the accountant would not be expected to include such disclosures in his report.

.13 If the client will not agree to revision of the financial statements or will not accept the accountant's disclaimer of opinion with the description of the departure from generally accepted accounting principles, the accountant should refuse to be associated with the statements and, if necessary, withdraw from the engagement.

Reporting on Audited and Unaudited Financial Statements in Comparative Form

.14 When unaudited financial statements are presented in comparative form with audited financial statements in documents filed with the Securities and Exchange Commission, such statements should be clearly marked as "unaudited" but should not be referred to in the auditor's report.

.15 When unaudited financial statements are presented in comparative form with audited financial statements in any other document, the financial statements that have not been audited should be clearly marked to indicate their status and either (*a*) the report on the prior period should be reissued (see section 530.06–.08)[7] or (*b*) the report on the current period should include as a separate paragraph an appropriate description of the responsibility assumed for the financial statements of the prior period (see paragraphs .16 and .17). Either reissuance or reference in a separate paragraph is acceptable; in both circumstances, the accountant should consider the current form and manner of presentation of the financial statements of the prior period in light of the information of which he has become aware during his current engagement.

.16 When the financial statements of the prior period have been audited and the report on the current period is to contain a separate paragraph, it should indicate (*a*) that the financial statements of the prior period were audited previously, (*b*) the date of the previous report, (*c*) the type of opinion expressed previously, (*d*) if the opinion was other than unqualified, the substantive reasons therefor, and (*e*) that no auditing procedures were performed after the date of the previous report. An example of such a separate paragraph is as follows:

> The financial statements for the year ended December 31, 19X1, were audited by us (other accountants) and we (they) expressed an unqualified opinion on them in our (their) report dated March 1, 19X2, but we (they) have not performed any auditing procedures since that date.

.17 When the financial statements of the prior period have not been audited and the report on the current period is to contain a separate paragraph, it should include (*a*) a statement of the service performed in the prior period, (*b*) the date of the report on that service, (*c*) a description of any material modifications noted in that report, and (*d*) a statement that the service was less in scope than an audit and does not provide the basis for the

---

[7] For reissuance of a compilation or review report, see Statements on Standards for Accounting and Review Services.

expression of an opinion on the financial statements taken as a whole. When the financial statements are those of a public entity, the separate paragraph should include a disclaimer of opinion (see paragraph .05) or a description of a review. When the financial statements are those of a nonpublic entity and the financial statements were compiled or reviewed, the separate paragraph should contain an appropriate description of the compilation or review. For example, a separate paragraph describing a review might be worded as follows:

> The 19X1 financial statements were reviewed by us (other accountants) and our (their) report thereon, dated March 1, 19X2, stated we (they) were not aware of any material modifications that should be made to those statements for them to be in conformity with generally accepted accounting principles. However, a review is substantially less in scope than an audit and does not provide a basis for the expression of an opinion on the financial statements taken as a whole.

A separate paragraph describing a compilation might be worded as follows:

> The 19X1 financial statements were compiled by us (other accountants) and our (their) report thereon, dated March 1, 19X2, stated we (they) did not audit or review those financial statements and, accordingly, express no opinion or other form of assurance on them.

Negative Assurance

.18 When an accountant, for whatever reason, disclaims an opinion on financial statements his disclaimer should not be contradicted by the inclusion of expressions of assurance on the absence of knowledge of departures from generally accepted accounting principles except as specifically recognized as appropriate in applicable standards established by the American Institute of Certified Public Accountants.

.19 Negative assurances, for example, are permissible in letters for underwriters in which the independent auditor reports on limited procedures followed with respect to unaudited financial statements or other financial data pertinent to a registration statement filed with the Securities and Exchange Commission (see section 634, *Letters for Underwriters and Certain Other Requesting Parties*[*]).

[.20] [Superseded, February 1993, by Statement on Auditing Standards No. 72.] (See section 634.)

---

[*] [Reference number 631, formerly 630, changed by the issuance of Statement on Auditing Standards No. 38 (superseded). Reference number 634, formerly 631, changed by the issuance of Statement on Auditing Standards No. 49 (superseded). Title of section 634 changed, February 1993, to reflect the issuance of Statement on Auditing Standards No. 72.] (See section 634.)

AU Section 9504

Association With Financial Statements: Auditing Interpretations of Section 504

1. Annual Report Disclosure of Unaudited Fourth Quarter Interim Data

.01 *Question*—APB Opinion No. 28, paragraph 31 [AC section I73.147], which applies to publicly traded companies, states: "If interim financial data and disclosures are not separately reported for the fourth quarter, security holders often make inferences about that quarter by subtracting data based on the third quarter interim report from the annual results. In the absence of a separate fourth quarter report or disclosure of the results . . . for that quarter in the annual report, disposals of segments of a business and extraordinary, unusual, or infrequently occurring items recognized in the fourth quarter, as well as the aggregate effect of year-end adjustments which are material to the results of that quarter . . . shall be disclosed in the annual report in a note to the annual financial statements." Does the auditor have an obligation, arising from the disclosure requirements of paragraph 31 of Opinion No. 28 [AC section I73.147], to audit interim data?

.02 *Interpretation*—No. If the auditor has not been specifically engaged to audit interim information, he does not have an obligation to audit interim data as a result of his audit of the annual financial statements.

.03 Disclosure of fourth quarter adjustments and other disclosures required by paragraph 31 [AC section I73.147] would appear in a note to the annual financial statements of a publicly traded company only if fourth quarter data were not separately distributed or did not appear elsewhere in the annual report. Consequently, such disclosures are not essential for a fair presentation of the annual financial statements in conformity with generally accepted accounting principles.

.04 If interim financial data and disclosures are not separately reported (as outlined in paragraph 30 of Opinion No. 28 [AC section I73.146]) for the fourth quarter, the independent auditor, during his audit of the annual financial statements, should inquire as to whether there are fourth quarter items that need to be disclosed in a note to the annual financial statements.

.05 Information on fourth quarter adjustments and similar items that appear in notes to the annual financial statements to comply with paragraph 31 of Opinion No. 28 [AC section I73.147] would ordinarily not be audited separately and, therefore, the information would be labeled "unaudited" or "not covered by auditor's report."

.06 If a publicly traded company fails to comply with the provisions of paragraph 31 of Opinion No. 28 [AC section I73.147], the auditor should suggest appropriate revision; failing that, he should call attention in his report to the omission of the information. The auditor need not qualify his opinion on the annual financial statements since the disclosure is not essential for a fair presentation of those statements in conformity with generally accepted accounting principles.

.07 Reference should be made to section 722 for guidance with respect to reviews of interim financial information of public entities.

[Issue Date: November, 1979.]

[2.] Association of the Auditor of an Acquired Company With Unaudited Statements in a Listing Application

[.08–.12] [Deleted May, 1980.]

[3.] Association of the Auditor of the Acquiring Company With Unaudited Statements in a Listing Application

[.13–.14] [Deleted May, 1980.]

4. Auditor's Identification With Condensed Financial Data

.15 *Question*—Section 150.02 states in part: "In all cases where an auditor's name is associated with financial statements, the report should contain a clear-cut indication of the character of the auditor's work, if any, and the degree of responsibility the auditor is taking." Section 504.03 states that "An accountant is associated with financial statements when he has consented to the use of his name in a report, document, or written communication containing the statements." Is the auditor "associated" with condensed financial data when he is identified by a financial reporting service as being a company's independent auditor or when his report is reproduced and presented with such data?

.16 *Interpretation*—No. The accountant has not consented to the use of his name when it is published by a financial reporting service. Financial data released to the public by a company and the name of its auditor are public information. Accordingly, neither the auditor nor his client has the ability to require a financial reporting service to withhold publishing such information.

.17 Financial reporting services, such as Dun & Bradstreet and Moody's Investors Service, furnish to subscribers information and ratings concerning commercial enterprises as a basis for credit, insurance, marketing and other business purposes. Those reports frequently include condensed financial data and other data such as payments to trade creditors, loan experience with banks, a brief history of the entity and a description of its operations. Also, as part of its report, the financial service often discloses the names of the officers and directors or principals or owners of the company and the name of the company's auditor.

.18 In the context in which the auditor's name appears, it is doubtful that readers will assume that he has audited the information presented. However, the AICPA has suggested to certain financial reporting services that they identify data as "unaudited" if the data has been extracted from unaudited financial statements. Also, the AICPA has suggested that when summarized financial data is presented together with an auditor's report on complete financial statements (including notes), the financial reporting services state that the auditor's report applies to the complete financial statements which are not presented.

[Issue Date: November, 1979.]

5. Applicability of Guidance on Reporting When Not Independent

.19 *Question*—Section 504 describes the reporting responsibilities of the certified public accountant who has determined that he is not independent with respect to financial statements with which he is associated. That section, however, does not indicate how he should determine whether he is independent. What should the certified public accountant consider in determining whether he is independent? Also, should his consideration be any different for an engagement to prepare unaudited financial statements?

.20 *Interpretation*—Section 504 explains the certified public accountant's reporting responsibilities when he is not independent. However, it does not attempt to explain how the certified public accountant determines whether he is independent because that is a question of professional ethics. Section 220.04 states: "The profession has established, through the AICPA Code of Professional Conduct, precepts to guard against the . . . loss of independence." The AICPA, state CPA societies and state boards of accountancy have issued pronouncements to provide the certified public accountant with guidance to aid him in determining whether he is independent.

.21 The certified public accountant should consider the AICPA's Code of Professional Conduct in determining whether he is independent and whether the reporting requirements of section 504 apply. He should also consider the ethical requirements of his state CPA society or state board of accountancy.

.22 Section 504.10 states that the reporting guidance applies, *regardless of the extent of procedures applied*, (emphasis added) in all circumstances other than when the financial statements are those of a non-public entity.[1] Thus, the accountant's consideration of whether he is independent should be the same whether the financial statements are audited or unaudited.

[Issue Date: November, 1979.]

[6.] Reporting on Solvency

[.23–.35] [Rescinded May, 1988 by the issuance of attestation interpretation, "Responding to Requests for Reports on Matters Relating to Solvency."] (See AT section 9100.33–.46.)

---

[1] If the financial statements are those of a non-public entity, the accountant should look to the guidance in Statements on Standards for Accounting and Review Services.

AU Section 508

Reports on Audited Financial Statements[*]

(Supersedes sections 505, 509, 542, 545, and 546)

Source: SAS No. 58; SAS No. 64; SAS No. 79.

See section 9508 for interpretations of this section.

Effective for reports issued or reissued on or after January 1, 1989, unless otherwise indicated.

Introduction

.01 This section applies to auditors' reports issued in connection with audits[1] of historical financial statements that are intended to present financial position, results of operations, and cash flows in conformity with generally accepted accounting principles. It distinguishes the types of reports, describes the circumstances in which each is appropriate, and provides example reports.

.02 This section does not apply to unaudited financial statements as described in section 504, *Association With Financial Statements*, nor does it apply to reports on incomplete financial information or other special presentations as described in section 623, *Special Reports*.

.03 Justification for the expression of the auditor's opinion rests on the conformity of his audit with generally accepted auditing standards and on his findings. Generally accepted auditing standards include four standards of reporting.[2] This section is concerned primarily with the relationship of the fourth reporting standard to the language of the auditor's report.

.04 The fourth standard of reporting is as follows:

> The report shall either contain an expression of opinion regarding the financial statements, taken as a whole, or an assertion to the effect that an opinion cannot be expressed. When an overall opinion cannot be expressed, the reasons therefor

---

[*] Statement on Auditing Standards No. 85, *Management Representations*, which is effective for audits of financial statements for periods ending on or after June 30, 1998, amends this section. The amendment and any necessary conforming changes to this section will be made closer to the effective date of Statement on Auditing Standards No. 85. See section 333.19.

[1] An audit, for purposes of this section, is defined as an examination of historical financial statements performed in accordance with generally accepted auditing standards in effect at the time the audit is performed. Generally accepted auditing standards include the ten standards as well as the Statements on Auditing Standards that interpret those standards. In some cases, regulatory authorities may have additional requirements applicable to entities under their jurisdiction and auditors of such entities should consider those requirements.

[2] This section revises the second standard of reporting as follows:

> The report shall identify those circumstances in which such principles have not been consistently observed in the current period in relation to the preceding period.

Previously, the second standard required the auditor's report to state whether accounting principles had been consistently applied. As revised, the second standard requires the auditor to add an explanatory paragraph to his report only if accounting principles have not been applied consistently. (See section 420, *Consistency of Application of Generally Accepted Accounting Principles*.) Paragraphs .16–.18 of this section provide reporting guidance under these circumstances.

should be stated. In all cases where an auditor's name is associated with financial statements, the report should contain a clear-cut indication of the character of the auditor's work, if any, and the degree of responsibility the auditor is taking.

.05 The objective of the fourth standard is to prevent misinterpretation of the degree of responsibility the auditor is assuming when his name is associated with financial statements. Reference in the fourth reporting standard to the financial statements "taken as a whole" applies equally to a complete set of financial statements and to an individual financial statement (for example, to a balance sheet) for one or more periods presented. (Paragraph .65 discusses the fourth standard of reporting as it applies to comparative financial statements.) The auditor may express an unqualified opinion on one of the financial statements and express a qualified or adverse opinion or disclaim an opinion on another if the circumstances warrant.

.06 The auditor's report is customarily issued in connection with an entity's basic financial statements—balance sheet, statement of income, statement of retained earnings and statement of cash flows. Each financial statement audited should be specifically identified in the introductory paragraph of the auditor's report. If the basic financial statements include a separate statement of changes in stockholders' equity accounts, it should be identified in the introductory paragraph of the report but need not be reported on separately in the opinion paragraph since such changes are part of the presentation of financial position, results of operations, and cash flows.

The Auditor's Standard Report

.07 The auditor's standard report states that the financial statements present fairly, in all material respects, an entity's financial position, results of operations, and cash flows in conformity with generally accepted accounting principles. This conclusion may be expressed only when the auditor has formed such an opinion on the basis of an audit performed in accordance with generally accepted auditing standards.

.08 The auditor's standard report identifies the financial statements audited in an opening (introductory) paragraph, describes the nature of an audit in a scope paragraph, and expresses the auditor's opinion in a separate opinion paragraph. The basic elements of the report are the following:

a. A title that includes the word *independent*[3]

b. A statement that the financial statements identified in the report were audited

c. A statement that the financial statements are the responsibility of the Company's management[4] and that the auditor's responsibility is to express an opinion on the financial statements based on his audit

d. A statement that the audit was conducted in accordance with generally accepted auditing standards

e. A statement that generally accepted auditing standards require that the auditor plan and perform the audit to obtain reasonable assurance about whether the financial statements are free of material misstatement

---

[3] This section does not require a title for an auditor's report if the auditor is not independent. See section 504, *Association With Financial Statements*, for guidance on reporting when the auditor is not independent.

[4] In some instances, a document containing the auditor's report may include a statement by management regarding its responsibility for the presentation of the financial statements. Nevertheless, the auditor's report should state that the financial statements are management's responsibility.

f. A statement that an audit includes—

(1) Examining, on a test basis, evidence supporting the amounts and disclosures in the financial statements

(2) Assessing the accounting principles used and significant estimates made by management

(3) Evaluating the overall financial statement presentation[5]

g. A statement that the auditor believes that his audit provides a reasonable basis for his opinion

h. An opinion as to whether the financial statements present fairly, in all material respects, the financial position of the Company as of the balance sheet date and the results of its operations and its cash flows for the period then ended in conformity with generally accepted accounting principles

i. The manual or printed signature of the auditor's firm

j. The date[6] of the audit report

The form of the auditor's standard report on financial statements covering a single year is as follows:

Independent Auditor's Report

We have audited the accompanying balance sheet of X Company as of December 31, 19XX, and the related statements of income, retained earnings, and cash flows for the year then ended. These financial statements are the responsibility of the Company's management. Our responsibility is to express an opinion on these financial statements based on our audit.

We conducted our audit in accordance with generally accepted auditing standards. Those standards require that we plan and perform the audit to obtain reasonable assurance about whether the financial statements are free of material misstatement. An audit includes examining, on a test basis, evidence supporting the amounts and disclosures in the financial statements. An audit also includes assessing the accounting principles used and significant estimates made by management, as well as evaluating the overall financial statement presentation. We believe that our audit provides a reasonable basis for our opinion.

In our opinion, the financial statements referred to above present fairly, in all material respects, the financial position of X Company as of [at] December 31, 19XX, and the results of its operations and its cash flows for the year then ended in conformity with generally accepted accounting principles.

[*Signature*]

[*Date*]

The form of the auditor's standard report on comparative financial statements[7] is as follows:

---

[5] Section 411, *The Meaning of* Present Fairly in Conformity With Generally Accepted Accounting Principles *in the Independent Auditor's Report*, paragraphs .03 and .04, discuss the auditor's evaluation of the overall presentation of the financial statements.

[6] For guidance on dating the auditor's report, see section 530, *Dating of the Independent Auditor's Report*.

[7] If statements of income, retained earnings, and cash flows are presented on a comparative basis for one or more prior periods, but the balance sheet(s) as of the end of one (or more) of the prior period(s) is not presented, the phrase "for the years then ended" should be changed to indicate that the auditor's opinion applies to each period for which statements of income, retained earnings, and cash flows are presented, such as "for each of the three years in the period ended [date of latest balance sheet]."

Independent Auditor's Report

We have audited the accompanying balance sheets of X Company as of December 31, 19X2 and 19X1, and the related statements of income, retained earnings, and cash flows for the years then ended. These financial statements are the responsibility of the Company's management. Our responsibility is to express an opinion on these financial statements based on our audits.

We conducted our audits in accordance with generally accepted auditing standards. Those standards require that we plan and perform the audit to obtain reasonable assurance about whether the financial statements are free of material misstatement. An audit includes examining, on a test basis, evidence supporting the amounts and disclosures in the financial statements. An audit also includes assessing the accounting principles used and significant estimates made by management, as well as evaluating the overall financial statement presentation. We believe that our audits provide a reasonable basis for our opinion.

In our opinion, the financial statements referred to above present fairly, in all material respects, the financial position of X Company as of [at] December 31, 19X2 and 19X1, and the results of its operations and its cash flows for the years then ended in conformity with generally accepted accounting principles.

[*Signature*]

[*Date*]

.09 The report may be addressed to the company whose financial statements are being audited or to its board of directors or stockholders. A report on the financial statements of an unincorporated entity should be addressed as circumstances dictate, for example, to the partners, to the general partner, or to the proprietor. Occasionally, an auditor is retained to audit the financial statements of a company that is not his client; in such a case, the report is customarily addressed to the client and not to the directors or stockholders of the company whose financial statements are being audited.

.10 This section also discusses the circumstances that may require the auditor to depart from the standard report and provides reporting guidance in such circumstances. This section is organized by type of opinion that the auditor may express in each of the various circumstances presented; this section describes what is meant by the various audit opinions:

- *Unqualified opinion.* An unqualified opinion states that the financial statements present fairly, in all material respects, the financial position, results of operations, and cash flows of the entity in conformity with generally accepted accounting principles. This is the opinion expressed in the standard report discussed in paragraph .08.
- *Explanatory language added to the auditor's standard report.* Certain circumstances, while not affecting the auditor's unqualified opinion on the financial statements, may require that the auditor add an explanatory paragraph (or other explanatory language) to his report.
- *Qualified opinion.* A qualified opinion states that, except for the effects of the matter(s) to which the qualification relates, the financial statements present fairly, in all material respects, the financial position, results of operations, and cash flows of the entity in conformity with generally accepted accounting principles.
- *Adverse opinion.* An adverse opinion states that the financial statements do not present fairly the financial position, results of operations, or cash flows of the entity in conformity with generally accepted accounting principles.

- *Disclaimer of opinion.* A disclaimer of opinion states that the auditor does not express an opinion on the financial statements.

These opinions are discussed in greater detail throughout the remainder of this section.

Explanatory Language Added to the Auditor's Standard Report

.11 Certain circumstances, while not affecting the auditor's unqualified opinion, may require that the auditor add an explanatory[8] paragraph (or other explanatory language) to his standard report.[9] These circumstances include:

a. The auditor's opinion is based in part on the report of another auditor (paragraphs .12 and .13).

b. To prevent the financial statements from being misleading because of unusual circumstances, the financial statements contain a departure from an accounting principle promulgated by a body designated by the AICPA Council to establish such principles (paragraphs .14 and .15).

c. There is substantial doubt about the entity's ability to continue as a going concern.[10]

d. There has been a material change between periods in accounting principles or in the method of their application (paragraphs .16–.18).

e. Certain circumstances relating to reports on comparative financial statements exist (paragraphs .68, .69, and .72–.74).

f. Selected quarterly financial data required by SEC Regulation S-K has been omitted or has not been reviewed. (See section 722, *Interim Financial Information*, paragraph .41.) [Reference changed by the issuance of Statement on Auditing Standards No. 71.]

g. Supplementary information required by the Financial Accounting Standards Board (FASB) or the Governmental Accounting Standards Board (GASB) has been omitted, the presentation of such information departs materially from FASB or GASB guidelines, the auditor is unable to complete prescribed procedures with respect to such information, or the auditor is unable to remove substantial doubts about whether the supplementary information conforms to FASB or GASB guidelines. (See section 558, *Required Supplementary Information*, paragraph .02.)

h. Other information in a document containing audited financial statements is materially inconsistent with information appearing in the financial statements. (See section 550, *Other Information in Documents Containing Audited Financial Statements*, paragraph .04.)

In addition, the auditor may add an explanatory paragraph to emphasize a matter regarding the financial statements (paragraph .19). [As amended, effective for reports issued or reissued on or after February 29, 1996, by Statement on Auditing Standards No. 79.]

---

[8] Unless otherwise required by the provisions of this section, an explanatory paragraph may precede or follow the opinion paragraph in the auditor's report.

[9] See footnote 3.

[10] Section 341, *The Auditor's Consideration of an Entity's Ability to Continue as a Going Concern*, describes the auditor's responsibility to evaluate whether there is substantial doubt about the entity's ability to continue as a going concern for a reasonable period of time and, when applicable, to consider the adequacy of financial statement disclosure and to include an explanatory paragraph in his report to reflect his conclusions.

Opinion Based in Part on Report of Another Auditor

.12 When the auditor decides to make reference to the report of another auditor as a basis, in part, for his opinion, he should disclose this fact in the introductory paragraph of his report and should refer to the report of the other auditor in expressing his opinion. These references indicate division of responsibility for performance of the audit. (See section 543, *Part of Audit Performed by Other Independent Auditors*.)

.13 An example of a report indicating a division of responsibility follows:

Independent Auditor's Report

We have audited the consolidated balance sheets of ABC Company and subsidiaries as of December 31, 19X2 and 19X1, and the related consolidated statements of income, retained earnings, and cash flows for the years then ended. These financial statements are the responsibility of the Company's management. Our responsibility is to express an opinion on these financial statements based on our audits. We did not audit the financial statements of B Company, a wholly-owned subsidiary, which statements reflect total assets of $______ and $______ as of December 31, 19X2 and 19X1, respectively, and total revenues of $______ and $______ for the years then ended. Those statements were audited by other auditors whose report has been furnished to us, and our opinion, insofar as it relates to the amounts included for B Company, is based solely on the report of the other auditors.

We conducted our audits in accordance with generally accepted auditing standards. Those standards require that we plan and perform the audit to obtain reasonable assurance about whether the financial statements are free of material misstatement. An audit includes examining, on a test basis, evidence supporting the amounts and disclosures in the financial statements. An audit also includes assessing the accounting principles used and significant estimates made by management, as well as evaluating the overall financial statement presentation. We believe that our audits and the report of other auditors provide a reasonable basis for our opinion.

In our opinion, based on our audits and the report of other auditors, the consolidated financial statements referred to above present fairly, in all material respects, the financial position of ABC Company and subsidiaries as of December 31, 19X2 and 19X1, and the results of their operations and their cash flows for the years then ended in conformity with generally accepted accounting principles.

Departure From a Promulgated Accounting Principle

.14 Rule 203 [ET section 203.01] of the Code of Professional Conduct of the AICPA states:

A member shall not (1) express an opinion or state affirmatively that the financial statements or other financial data of any entity are presented in conformity with generally accepted accounting principles or (2) state that he or she is not aware of any material modifications that should be made to such statements or data in order for them to be in conformity with generally accepted accounting principles, if such statements or data contain any departure from an accounting principle promulgated by bodies designated by Council to establish such principles that has a material effect on the statements or data taken as a whole. If, however, the statements or data contain such a departure and the member can demonstrate that due to unusual circumstances the financial statements or data would otherwise have been misleading, the member can comply with the rule by describing the departure, its approximate effects, if practicable, and the reasons why compliance with the principle would result in a misleading statement.

.15 When the circumstances contemplated by Rule 203 [ET section 203.01] are present, the auditor's report should include, in a separate paragraph or paragraphs, the information required by the rule. In such a case, it is appropriate for him to express an unqualified opinion with respect to the conformity of the financial statements with generally accepted accounting principles unless there are other reasons, not associated with the departure from a promulgated principle, not to do so. (See section 411, *The Meaning of* Present Fairly in Conformity With Generally Accepted Accounting Principles *in the Independent Auditor's Report*.)

Former paragraphs .16 through .33 and related footnotes have been deleted and all subsequent paragraphs and footnotes renumbered by the issuance of Statement on Auditing Standards No. 79, effective for reports issued or reissued on or after February 29, 1996.

Lack of Consistency

.16 The auditor's standard report implies that the auditor is satisfied that the comparability of financial statements between periods has not been materially affected by changes in accounting principles and that such principles have been consistently applied between or among periods because either (*a*) no change in accounting principles has occurred, or (*b*) there has been a change in accounting principles or in the method of their application, but the effect of the change on the comparability of the financial statements is not material. In these cases, the auditor should not refer to consistency in his report. If, however, there has been a change in accounting principles or in the method of their application that has a material effect on the comparability of the company's financial statements, the auditor should refer to the change in an explanatory paragraph of his report. Such explanatory paragraph (following the opinion paragraph) should identify the nature of the change and refer the reader to the note in the financial statements that discusses the change in detail. The auditor's concurrence with a change is implicit unless he takes exception to the change in expressing his opinion as to fair presentation of the financial statements in conformity with generally accepted accounting principles.[11] When there is a change in accounting principles, there are also other matters that the auditor should consider (see paragraphs .50 through .57). [Paragraph renumbered by the issuance of Statement on Auditing Standards No. 79, December 1995.]

.17 Following is an example of an appropriate explanatory paragraph:

> As discussed in Note X to the financial statements, the Company changed its method of computing depreciation in 19X2.

[Paragraph renumbered by the issuance of Statement on Auditing Standards No. 79, December 1995.]

---

[11] With respect to the method of accounting for the effect of a change in accounting principle, see Accounting Principles Board Opinion No. 20, *Accounting Changes*, including paragraph 4 [AC section A06.103], which states that methods of accounting for changes in principles resulting from the implementation of new pronouncements is provided in those pronouncements. [Footnote renumbered by the issuance of Statement on Auditing Standards No. 79, December 1995.]

.18 The addition of this explanatory paragraph in the auditor's report is required in reports on financial statements of subsequent years as long as the year of the change is presented and reported on.[12] However, if the accounting change is accounted for by retroactive restatement of the financial statements affected, the additional paragraph is required only in the year of the change since, in subsequent years, all periods presented will be comparable. [Paragraph renumbered by the issuance of Statement on Auditing Standards No. 79, December 1995.]

Emphasis of a Matter

.19 In any report on financial statements, the auditor may emphasize a matter regarding the financial statements. Such explanatory information should be presented in a separate paragraph of the auditor's report. Phrases such as "with the foregoing [following] explanation" should not be used in the opinion paragraph if an emphasis paragraph is included in the auditor's report. Emphasis paragraphs are never required; they may be added solely at the auditor's discretion. Examples of matters the auditor may wish to emphasize are—

- That the entity is a component of a larger business enterprise.
- That the entity has had significant transactions with related parties.
- Unusually important subsequent events.
- Accounting matters, other than those involving a change or changes in accounting principles, affecting the comparability of the financial statements with those of the preceding period.

[Paragraph renumbered and amended, effective for reports issued or reissued on or after February 29, 1996, by the issuance of Statement on Auditing Standards No. 79.]

Departures From Unqualified Opinions

Qualified Opinions

.20 Certain circumstances may require a qualified opinion. A qualified opinion states that, *except for* the effects of the matter to which the qualification relates, the financial statements present fairly, in all material respects, financial position, results of operations, and cash flows in conformity with generally accepted accounting principles. Such an opinion is expressed when—

a. There is a lack of sufficient competent evidential matter or there are restrictions on the scope of the audit that have led the auditor to conclude that he cannot express an unqualified opinion and he has concluded not to disclaim an opinion (paragraphs .22–.34).

b. The auditor believes, on the basis of his audit, that the financial statements contain a departure from generally accepted accounting principles, the effect of which is material, and he has concluded not to express an adverse opinion (paragraphs .35–.57).

---

[12] An exception to this requirement occurs when a change in accounting principle that does not require a cumulative effect adjustment is made at the beginning of the earliest year presented and reported on. That exception is addressed in the auditing interpretation of section 420, *Consistency of Application of Generally Accepted Accounting Principles*, titled "Impact on the Auditor's Report of FIFO to LIFO Change in Comparative Financial Statements," (section 9420.16–.23). [Footnote renumbered by the issuance of Statement on Auditing Standards No. 79, December 1995.]

[Paragraph renumbered by the issuance of Statement on Auditing Standards No. 79, December 1995.]

.21 When the auditor expresses a qualified opinion, he should disclose all of the substantive reasons in one or more separate explanatory paragraph(s) preceding the opinion paragraph of his report. He should also include, in the opinion paragraph, the appropriate qualifying language and a reference to the explanatory paragraph. A qualified opinion should include the word *except* or *exception* in a phrase such as *except for* or *with the exception of*. Phrases such as *subject to* and *with the foregoing explanation* are not clear or forceful enough and should not be used. Since accompanying notes are part of the financial statements, wording such as *fairly presented, in all material respects, when read in conjunction with Note 1* is likely to be misunderstood and should not be used. [Paragraph renumbered by the issuance of Statement on Auditing Standards No. 79, December 1995.]

Scope Limitations

.22 The auditor can determine that he is able to express an unqualified opinion only if his audit has been conducted in accordance with generally accepted auditing standards and if he has therefore been able to apply all the procedures he considers necessary in the circumstances. Restrictions on the scope of his audit, whether imposed by the client or by circumstances, such as the timing of his work, the inability to obtain sufficient competent evidential matter, or an inadequacy in the accounting records, may require him to qualify his opinion or to disclaim an opinion. In such instances, the reasons for the auditor's qualification of opinion or disclaimer of opinion should be described in his report. [Paragraph renumbered by the issuance of Statement on Auditing Standards No. 79, December 1995.]

.23 The auditor's decision to qualify his opinion or disclaim an opinion because of a scope limitation depends on his assessment of the importance of the omitted procedure(s) to his ability to form an opinion on the financial statements being audited. This assessment will be affected by the nature and magnitude of the potential effects of the matters in question and by their significance to the financial statements. If the potential effects relate to many financial statement items, this significance is likely to be greater than if only a limited number of items is involved. [Paragraph renumbered by the issuance of Statement on Auditing Standards No. 79, December 1995.]

.24 Common restrictions on the scope of the audit include those applying to the observation of physical inventories and the confirmation of accounts receivable by direct communication with debtors.[13] Another common scope restriction involves accounting for long-term investments when the auditor has not been able to obtain audited financial statements of an investee. Restrictions on the application of these or other audit procedures to important elements of the financial statements require the auditor to decide whether he has examined sufficient competent evidential matter to permit him to express an unqualified or qualified opinion, or whether he should disclaim an opinion.

---

[13] Circumstances such as the timing of his work may make it impossible for the auditor to accomplish these procedures. In this case, if he is able to satisfy himself as to inventories or accounts receivable by applying alternative procedures, there is no significant limitation on the scope of his work, and his report need not include a reference to the omission of the procedures or the use of alternative procedures. It is important to understand, however, that section 331, *Inventories*, states that "it will always be necessary for the auditor to make, or observe, some physical counts of the inventory and apply appropriate tests of intervening transactions." [Footnote renumbered by the issuance of Statement on Auditing Standards No. 79, December 1995.]

When restrictions that significantly limit the scope of the audit are imposed by the client, ordinarily the auditor should disclaim an opinion on the financial statements. [Paragraph renumbered by the issuance of Statement on Auditing Standards No. 79, December 1995.]

.25 When a qualified opinion results from a limitation on the scope of the audit or an insufficiency of evidential matter, the situation should be described in an explanatory paragraph preceding the opinion paragraph and referred to in both the scope and opinion paragraphs of the auditor's report. It is not appropriate for the scope of the audit to be explained in a note to the financial statements, since the description of the audit scope is the responsibility of the auditor and not that of his client. [Paragraph renumbered by the issuance of Statement on Auditing Standards No. 79, December 1995.]

.26 When an auditor qualifies his opinion because of a scope limitation, the wording in the opinion paragraph should indicate that the qualification pertains to the possible effects on the financial statements and not to the scope limitation itself. Wording such as "In our opinion, except for the above-mentioned limitation on the scope of our audit . . ." bases the exception on the restriction itself, rather than on the possible effects on the financial statements and, therefore, is unacceptable. An example of a qualified opinion related to a scope limitation concerning an investment in a foreign affiliate (assuming the effects of the limitation are such that the auditor has concluded that a disclaimer of opinion is not appropriate) follows:

Independent Auditor's Report

[*Same first paragraph as the standard report*]

Except as discussed in the following paragraph, we conducted our audits in accordance with generally accepted auditing standards. Those standards require that we plan and perform the audit to obtain reasonable assurance about whether the financial statements are free of material misstatement. An audit includes examining, on a test basis, evidence supporting the amounts and disclosures in the financial statements. An audit also includes assessing the accounting principles used and significant estimates made by management, as well as evaluating the overall financial statement presentation. We believe that our audits provide a reasonable basis for our opinion.

We were unable to obtain audited financial statements supporting the Company's investment in a foreign affiliate stated at $______ and $______ at December 31, 19X2 and 19X1, respectively, or its equity in earnings of that affiliate of $______ and $______, which is included in net income for the years then ended as described in Note X to the financial statements; nor were we able to satisfy ourselves as to the carrying value of the investment in the foreign affiliate or the equity in its earnings by other auditing procedures.

In our opinion, except for the effects of such adjustments, if any, as might have been determined to be necessary had we been able to examine evidence regarding the foreign affiliate investment and earnings, the financial statements referred to in the first paragraph above present fairly, in all material respects, the financial position of X Company as of December 31, 19X2 and 19X1, and the results of its operations and its cash flows for the years then ended in conformity with generally accepted accounting principles.

[Paragraph renumbered by the issuance of Statement on Auditing Standards No. 79, December 1995.]

.27 ***Other scope limitations.*** Sometimes, notes to financial statements may contain unaudited information, such as pro forma calculations or other similar disclosures. If the unaudited information (for example, an investor's share, material in amount, of an investee's earnings recognized on the equity method) is such that it should be subjected to auditing procedures in order for the auditor to form an opinion with respect to the financial statements taken as a whole, the auditor should apply the procedures he deems necessary to the unaudited information. If the auditor has not been able to apply the procedures he considers necessary, he should qualify his opinion or disclaim an opinion because of a limitation on the scope of his audit. [Paragraph renumbered by the issuance of Statement on Auditing Standards No. 79, December 1995.]

.28 If, however, these disclosures are not necessary to fairly present the financial position, operating results, or cash flows on which the auditor is reporting, such disclosures may be identified as *unaudited* or as *not covered by the auditor's report*. For example, the pro forma effects of a business combination or of a subsequent event may be labelled unaudited. Therefore, while the event or transaction giving rise to the disclosures in these circumstances should be audited, the pro forma disclosures of that event or transaction would not be. The auditor should be aware, however, that section 530, *Dating of the Independent Auditor's Report*, states that, if the auditor is aware of a material subsequent event that has occurred after the completion of fieldwork but before issuance of the report that should be disclosed, his only options are to dual date the report or date the report as of the date of the subsequent event and extend the procedures for review of subsequent events to that date. Labelling the note unaudited is not an acceptable alternative in these circumstances. [Paragraph renumbered by the issuance of Statement on Auditing Standards No. 79, December 1995.]

.29 ***Uncertainties and scope limitations.*** A matter involving an uncertainty is one that is expected to be resolved at a future date, at which time conclusive evidential matter concerning its outcome would be expected to become available. Uncertainties include, but are not limited to, contingencies covered by Financial Accounting Standards Board (FASB) Statement of Financial Accounting Standards No. 5, *Accounting for Contingencies*, and matters related to estimates covered by Statement of Position 94-6, *Disclosure of Certain Significant Risks and Uncertainties*. [Paragraph added, effective for reports issued or reissued on or after February 29, 1996, by Statement on Auditing Standards No. 79.]

.30 Conclusive evidential matter concerning the ultimate outcome of uncertainties cannot be expected to exist at the time of the audit because the outcome and related evidential matter are prospective. In these circumstances, management is responsible for estimating the effect of future events on the financial statements, or determining that a reasonable estimate cannot be made and making the required disclosures, all in accordance with generally accepted accounting principles, based on management's analysis of existing conditions. An audit includes an assessment of whether the evidential matter is sufficient to support management's analysis. Absence of the existence of information related to the outcome of an uncertainty does not necessarily lead to a conclusion that the evidential matter supporting management's assertion is not sufficient. Rather, the auditor's judgment regarding the sufficiency of the evidential matter is based on the evidential matter that is, or should be, available. If, after considering the existing conditions and available evidence, the auditor concludes that sufficient evidential matter supports management's assertions about the nature of a matter involving an uncertainty and its presentation or disclosure in the financial statements, an unqualified opinion ordinarily is appropriate. [Paragraph added, effective for reports issued or reissued on or after February 29, 1996, by Statement on Auditing Standards No. 79.]

.31 If the auditor is unable to obtain sufficient evidential matter to support management's assertions about the nature of a matter involving an uncertainty and its presentation or disclosure in the financial statements, the auditor should consider the need to express a qualified opinion or to disclaim an opinion because of a scope limitation. A qualification or disclaimer of opinion because of a scope limitation is appropriate if sufficient evidential matter related to an uncertainty does or did exist but was not available to the auditor for reasons such as management's record retention policies or a restriction imposed by management. [Paragraph added, effective for reports issued or reissued on or after February 29, 1996, by Statement on Auditing Standards No. 79.]

.32 Scope limitations related to uncertainties should be differentiated from situations in which the auditor concludes that the financial statements are materially misstated due to departures from generally accepted accounting principles related to uncertainties. Such departures may be caused by inadequate disclosure concerning the uncertainty, the use of inappropriate accounting principles, or the use of unreasonable accounting estimates. Paragraphs .45 to .49 provide guidance to the auditor when financial statements contain departures from generally accepted accounting principles related to uncertainties. [Paragraph added, effective for reports issued or reissued on or after February 29, 1996, by Statement on Auditing Standards No. 79.]

.33 ***Limited reporting engagements.*** The auditor may be asked to report on one basic financial statement and not on the others. For example, he may be asked to report on the balance sheet and not on the statements of income, retained earnings or cash flows. These engagements do not involve scope limitations if the auditor's access to information underlying the basic financial statements is not limited and if he applies all the procedures he considers necessary in the circumstances; rather, such engagements involve limited reporting objectives. [Paragraph renumbered by the issuance of Statement on Auditing Standards No. 79, December 1995.]

.34 An auditor may be asked to report on the balance sheet only. In this case, the auditor may express an opinion on the balance sheet only. An example of an unqualified opinion on a balance-sheet-only audit follows (the report assumes that the auditor has been able to satisfy himself regarding the consistency of application of accounting principles):

Independent Auditor's Report

> We have audited the accompanying balance sheet of X Company as of December 31, 19XX. This financial statement is the responsibility of the Company's management. Our responsibility is to express an opinion on this financial statement based on our audit.
>
> We conducted our audit in accordance with generally accepted auditing standards. Those standards require that we plan and perform the audit to obtain reasonable assurance about whether the balance sheet is free of material misstatement. An audit includes examining, on a test basis, evidence supporting the amounts and disclosures in the balance sheet. An audit also includes assessing the accounting principles used and significant estimates made by management, as well as evaluating the overall balance sheet presentation. We believe that our audit of the balance sheet provides a reasonable basis for our opinion.

> In our opinion, the balance sheet referred to above presents fairly, in all material respects, the financial position of X Company as of December 31, 19XX, in conformity with generally accepted accounting principles.

[Paragraph renumbered by the issuance of Statement on Auditing Standards No. 79, December 1995.]

Departure From a Generally Accepted Accounting Principle

.35 When financial statements are materially affected by a departure from generally accepted accounting principles and the auditor has audited the statements in accordance with generally accepted auditing standards, he should express a qualified (paragraphs .36 through .57) or an adverse (paragraphs .58 through .60) opinion. The basis for such opinion should be stated in his report. [Paragraph renumbered by the issuance of Statement on Auditing Standards No. 79, December 1995.]

.36 In deciding whether the effects of a departure from generally accepted accounting principles are sufficiently material to require either a qualified or adverse opinion, one factor to be considered is the dollar magnitude of such effects. However, the concept of materiality does not depend entirely on relative size; it involves qualitative as well as quantitative judgments. The significance of an item to a particular entity (for example, inventories to a manufacturing company), the pervasiveness of the misstatement (such as whether it affects the amounts and presentation of numerous financial statement items), and the effect of the misstatement on the financial statements taken as a whole are all factors to be considered in making a judgment regarding materiality. [Paragraph renumbered by the issuance of Statement on Auditing Standards No. 79, December 1995.]

.37 When the auditor expresses a qualified opinion, he should disclose, in a separate explanatory paragraph(s) preceding the opinion paragraph of his report, all of the substantive reasons that have led him to conclude that there has been a departure from generally accepted accounting principles. Furthermore, the opinion paragraph of his report should include the appropriate qualifying language and a reference to the explanatory paragraph(s). [Paragraph renumbered by the issuance of Statement on Auditing Standards No. 79, December 1995.]

.38 The explanatory paragraph(s) should also disclose the principal effects of the subject matter of the qualification on financial position, results of operations, and cash flows, if practicable.[14] If the effects are not reasonably determinable, the report should so state. If such disclosures are made in a note to the financial statements, the explanatory paragraph(s) may be shortened by referring to it. [Paragraph renumbered by the issuance of Statement on Auditing Standards No. 79, December 1995.]

.39 An example of a report in which the opinion is qualified because of the use of an accounting principle at variance with generally accepted accounting principles follows (assuming the effects are such that the auditor has concluded that an adverse opinion is not appropriate):

---

[14] Section 431, *Adequacy of Disclosure in the Financial Statements*, defines *practicable* as "... the information is reasonably obtainable from management's accounts and records and that providing the information in his report does not require the auditor to assume the position of a preparer of financial information." For example, if the information can be obtained from the accounts and records without the auditor substantially increasing the effort that would normally be required to complete the audit, the information should be presented in his report. [Footnote renumbered by the issuance of Statement on Auditing Standards No. 79, December 1995.]

Independent Auditor's Report

[*Same first and second paragraphs as the standard report*]

The Company has excluded, from property and debt in the accompanying balance sheets, certain lease obligations that, in our opinion, should be capitalized in order to conform with generally accepted accounting principles. If these lease obligations were capitalized, property would be increased by $______ and $______, long-term debt by $______ and $______, and retained earnings by $______ and $______ as of December 31, 19X2 and 19X1, respectively. Additionally, net income would be increased (decreased) by $______ and $______ and earnings per share would be increased (decreased) by $______ and $______, respectively, for the years then ended.

In our opinion, except for the effects of not capitalizing certain lease obligations as discussed in the preceding paragraph, the financial statements referred to above present fairly, in all material respects, the financial position of X Company as of December 31, 19X2 and 19X1, and the results of its operations and its cash flows for the years then ended in conformity with generally accepted accounting principles.

[Paragraph renumbered by the issuance of Statement on Auditing Standards No. 79, December 1995.]

.40 If the pertinent facts are disclosed in a note to the financial statements, a separate paragraph (preceding the opinion paragraph) of the auditor's report in the circumstances illustrated in paragraph .39 might read as follows:

As more fully described in Note X to the financial statements, the Company has excluded certain lease obligations from property and debt in the accompanying balance sheets. In our opinion, generally accepted accounting principles require that such obligations be included in the balance sheets.

[Paragraph renumbered by the issuance of Statement on Auditing Standards No. 79, December 1995.]

.41 ***Inadequate disclosure.*** Information essential for a fair presentation in conformity with generally accepted accounting principles should be set forth in the financial statements (which include the related notes). When such information is set forth elsewhere in a report to shareholders, or in a prospectus, proxy statement, or other similar report, it should be referred to in the financial statements. If the financial statements, including accompanying notes, fail to disclose information that is required by generally accepted accounting principles, the auditor should express a qualified or adverse opinion because of the departure from those principles and should provide the information in his report, if practicable,[15] unless its omission from the auditor's report is recognized as appropriate by a specific Statement on Auditing Standards. [Paragraph renumbered by the issuance of Statement on Auditing Standards No. 79, December 1995.]

.42 Following is an example of a report qualified for inadequate disclosure (assuming the effects are such that the auditor has concluded an adverse opinion is not appropriate):

Independent Auditor's Report

[*Same first and second paragraphs as the standard report*]

The Company's financial statements do not disclose [*describe the nature of the omitted disclosures*]. In our opinion, disclosure of this information is required by generally accepted accounting principles.

[15] See footnote 14. [Footnote renumbered by the issuance of Statement on Auditing Standards No. 79, December 1995.]

In our opinion, except for the omission of the information discussed in the preceding paragraph, . . .

[Paragraph renumbered by the issuance of Statement on Auditing Standards No. 79, December 1995.]

.43 If a company issues financial statements that purport to present financial position and results of operations but omits the related statement of cash flows, the auditor will normally conclude that the omission requires qualification of his opinion. [Paragraph renumbered by the issuance of Statement on Auditing Standards No. 79, December 1995.]

.44 The auditor is not required to prepare a basic financial statement (for example, a statement of cash flows for one or more periods) and include it in his report if the company's management declines to present the statement. Accordingly, in these cases, the auditor should ordinarily qualify his report in the following manner:

Independent Auditor's Report

We have audited the accompanying balance sheets of X Company as of December 31, 19X2 and 19X1, and the related statements of income and retained earnings for the years then ended. These financial statements are the responsibility of the Company's management. Our responsibility is to express an opinion on these financial statements based on our audit.

[*Same second paragraph as the standard report*]

The Company declined to present a statement of cash flows for the years ended December 31, 19X2 and 19X1. Presentation of such statement summarizing the Company's operating, investing, and financing activities is required by generally accepted accounting principles.

In our opinion, except that the omission of a statement of cash flows results in an incomplete presentation as explained in the preceding paragraph, the financial statements referred to above present fairly, in all material respects, the financial position of X Company as of December 31, 19X2 and 19X1, and the results of its operations for the years then ended in conformity with generally accepted accounting principles.

[Paragraph renumbered by the issuance of Statement on Auditing Standards No. 79, December 1995.]

.45 ***Departures from generally accepted accounting principles involving risks or uncertainties, and materiality considerations.*** Departures from generally accepted accounting principles involving risks or uncertainties generally fall into one of the following categories:

- Inadequate disclosure (paragraphs .46 and .47)
- Inappropriate accounting principles (paragraph .48)
- Unreasonable accounting estimates (paragraph .49)

[Paragraph added, effective for reports issued or reissued on or after February 29, 1996, by Statement on Auditing Standards No. 79.]

.46 If the auditor concludes that a matter involving a risk or an uncertainty is not adequately disclosed in the financial statements in conformity with generally accepted accounting principles, the auditor should express a qualified or an adverse opinion. [Paragraph added, effective for reports issued or reissued on or after February 29, 1996, by Statement on Auditing Standards No. 79.]

.47 The auditor should consider materiality in evaluating the adequacy of disclosure of matters involving risks or uncertainties in the financial statements in the context of the financial statements taken as a whole. The auditor's consideration of materiality is a matter of professional judgment and is influenced by his perception of the needs of a reasonable person who will rely on the financial statements. Materiality judgments involving risks or uncertainties are made in light of the surrounding circumstances. The auditor evaluates the materiality of reasonably possible losses that may be incurred upon the resolution of uncertainties both individually and in the aggregate. The auditor performs the evaluation of reasonably possible losses without regard to his evaluation of the materiality of known and likely misstatements in the financial statements. [Paragraph added, effective for reports issued or reissued on or after February 29, 1996, by Statement on Auditing Standards No. 79.]

.48 In preparing financial statements, management estimates the outcome of certain types of future events. For example, estimates ordinarily are made about the useful lives of depreciable assets, the collectibility of accounts receivable, the realizable value of inventory items, and the provision for product warranties. FASB Statement No. 5, *Accounting for Contingencies*, paragraphs 23 and 25, describes situations in which the inability to make a reasonable estimate may raise questions about the appropriateness of the accounting principles used. If, in those or other situations, the auditor concludes that the accounting principles used cause the financial statements to be materially misstated, he should express a qualified or an adverse opinion. [Paragraph added, effective for reports issued or reissued on or after February 29, 1996, by Statement on Auditing Standards No. 79.]

.49 Usually, the auditor is able to satisfy himself regarding the reasonableness of management's estimate of the effects of future events by considering various types of evidential matter, including the historical experience of the entity. If the auditor concludes that management's estimate is unreasonable (see section 312, *Audit Risk and Materiality*, and section 342, *Auditing Accounting Estimates*) and that its effect is to cause the financial statements to be materially misstated, he should express a qualified or an adverse opinion. [Paragraph added, effective for reports issued or reissued on or after February 29, 1996, by Statement on Auditing Standards No. 79.]

.50 ***Accounting changes.*** The auditor should evaluate a change in accounting principle to satisfy himself that (*a*) the newly adopted accounting principle is a generally accepted accounting principle, (*b*) the method of accounting for the effect of the change is in conformity with generally accepted accounting principles, and (*c*) management's justification for the change is reasonable. If a change in accounting principle does not meet these conditions, the auditor's report should so indicate, and his opinion should be appropriately qualified as discussed in paragraphs .51 and .52. [Paragraph renumbered by the issuance of Statement on Auditing Standards No. 79, December 1995.]

.51 If (*a*) a newly adopted accounting principle is not a generally accepted accounting principle, (*b*) the method of accounting for the effect of the change is not in conformity with generally accepted accounting principles, or (*c*) management has not provided reasonable justification for the change in accounting principle, the auditor should express a qualified opinion or, if the effect of the change is sufficiently material, the auditor should express an adverse opinion on the financial statements. [Paragraph renumbered by the issuance of Statement on Auditing Standards No. 79, December 1995.]

.52 Accounting Principles Board Opinion No. 20, *Accounting Changes*, paragraph 16 [AC section A06.112], states: "The presumption that an entity should not change an accounting principle may be overcome only if the enterprise justifies the use of an alternative acceptable accounting principle on the basis that it is preferable." If management has not provided reasonable justification for the change in accounting principles, the auditor should express an exception to the change having been made without reasonable justification. An example of a report qualified for this reason follows:

Independent Auditor's Report

[*Same first and second paragraphs as the standard report*]

As disclosed in Note X to the financial statements, the Company adopted, in 19X2, the first-in, first-out method of accounting for its inventories, whereas it previously used the last-in, first-out method. Although use of the first-in, first-out method is in conformity with generally accepted accounting principles, in our opinion the Company has not provided reasonable justification for making this change as required by generally accepted accounting principles.[16]

In our opinion, except for the change in accounting principle discussed in the preceding paragraph, the financial statements referred to above present fairly, in all material respects, the financial position of X Company as of December 31, 19X2 and 19X1, and the results of its operations and its cash flows for the years then ended in conformity with generally accepted accounting principles.

[Paragraph renumbered by the issuance of Statement on Auditing Standards No. 79, December 1995.]

.53 Whenever an accounting change results in an auditor expressing a qualified or adverse opinion on the conformity of financial statements with generally accepted accounting principles for the year of change, he should consider the possible effects of that change when reporting on the entity's financial statements for subsequent years, as discussed in paragraphs .54 through .57. [Paragraph renumbered by the issuance of Statement on Auditing Standards No. 79, December 1995.]

.54 If the financial statements for the year of such change are presented and reported on with a subsequent year's financial statements, the auditor's report should disclose his reservations with respect to the statements for the year of change. [Paragraph renumbered by the issuance of Statement on Auditing Standards No. 79, December 1995.]

.55 If an entity has adopted an accounting principle that is not a generally accepted accounting principle, its continued use might have a material effect on the statements of a subsequent year on which the auditor is reporting. In this situation, the independent auditor should express either a qualified opinion or an adverse opinion, depending on the materiality of the departure in relation to the statements of the subsequent year. [Paragraph renumbered by the issuance of Statement on Auditing Standards No. 79, December 1995.]

---

[16] Section 420, *Consistency of Application of Generally Accepted Accounting Principles*, states that a change from an accounting principle that is not generally accepted to one that is generally accepted is a correction of an error and that such a change requires recognition in the auditor's report as to consistency. Therefore, the auditor should add an explanatory paragraph to his report discussing the accounting change.

However, because the middle paragraph included in the example presented contains all of the information required in an explanatory paragraph on consistency, a separate explanatory paragraph (following the opinion paragraph) as required by paragraphs .16 through .18 of this section is not necessary in this instance. A separate paragraph that identifies the change in accounting principle would be required if the substance of the disclosure did not fulfill the requirements outlined in these paragraphs. [Footnote renumbered by the issuance of Statement on Auditing Standards No. 79, December 1995.]

.56 If an entity accounts for the effect of a change prospectively when generally accepted accounting principles require restatement or the inclusion of the cumulative effect of the change in the year of change, a subsequent year's financial statements could improperly include a charge or credit that is material to those statements. This situation also requires that the auditor express a qualified or an adverse opinion. [Paragraph renumbered by the issuance of Statement on Auditing Standards No. 79, December 1995.]

.57 If management has not provided reasonable justification for a change in accounting principles, the auditor's opinion should express an exception to the change having been made without reasonable justification, as previously indicated. In addition, the auditor should continue to express his exception with respect to the financial statements for the year of change as long as they are presented and reported on. However, the auditor's exception relates to the accounting change and does not affect the status of a newly adopted principle as a generally accepted accounting principle. Accordingly, while expressing an exception for the year of change, the independent auditor's opinion regarding the subsequent years' statements need not express an exception to use of the newly adopted principle. [Paragraph renumbered by the issuance of Statement on Auditing Standards No. 79, December 1995.]

Adverse Opinions

.58 An adverse opinion states that the financial statements do not present fairly the financial position or the results of operations or cash flows in conformity with generally accepted accounting principles. Such an opinion is expressed when, in the auditor's judgment, the financial statements taken as a whole are not presented fairly in conformity with generally accepted accounting principles. [Paragraph renumbered by the issuance of Statement on Auditing Standards No. 79, December 1995.]

.59 When the auditor expresses an adverse opinion, he should disclose in a separate explanatory paragraph(s) preceding the opinion paragraph of his report (*a*) all the substantive reasons for his adverse opinion, and (*b*) the principal effects of the subject matter of the adverse opinion on financial position, results of operations, and cash flows, if practicable.[17] If the effects are not reasonably determinable, the report should so state.[18] [Paragraph renumbered by the issuance of Statement on Auditing Standards No. 79, December 1995.]

.60 When an adverse opinion is expressed, the opinion paragraph should include a direct reference to a separate paragraph that discloses the basis for the adverse opinion, as shown below:

Independent Auditor's Report

[*Same first and second paragraphs as the standard report*]

As discussed in Note X to the financial statements, the Company carries its property, plant and equipment accounts at appraisal values, and provides depreciation on the basis of such values. Further, the Company does not provide for income taxes with respect to differences between financial income and taxable income arising because of the use, for income tax purposes, of the in-

---

[17] See footnote 14 [Footnote renumbered by the issuance of Statement on Auditing Standards No. 79, December 1995.]

[18] When the auditor expresses an adverse opinion, he should also consider the need for an explanatory paragraph under the circumstances identified in paragraph .11, subsections (*c*), (*d*), and (*e*) of this section. [Footnote renumbered by the issuance of Statement on Auditing Standards No. 79, December 1995.]

stallment method of reporting gross profit from certain types of sales. Generally accepted accounting principles require that property, plant and equipment be stated at an amount not in excess of cost, reduced by depreciation based on such amount, and that deferred income taxes be provided.

Because of the departures from generally accepted accounting principles identified above, as of December 31, 19X2 and 19X1, inventories have been increased $______ and $______ by inclusion in manufacturing overhead of depreciation in excess of that based on cost; property, plant and equipment, less accumulated depreciation, is carried at $______ and $______ in excess of an amount based on the cost to the Company; and deferred income taxes of $______ and $______ have not been recorded; resulting in an increase of $______ and $______ in retained earnings and in appraisal surplus of $______ and $______, respectively. For the years ended December 31, 19X2 and 19X1, cost of goods sold has been increased $______ and $______, respectively, because of the effects of the depreciation accounting referred to above and deferred income taxes of $______ and $______ have not been provided, resulting in an increase in net income of $______ and $______, respectively.

In our opinion, because of the effects of the matters discussed in the preceding paragraphs, the financial statements referred to above do not present fairly, in conformity with generally accepted accounting principles, the financial position of X Company as of December 31, 19X2 and 19X1, or the results of its operations or its cash flows for the years then ended.

[Paragraph renumbered by the issuance of Statement on Auditing Standards No. 79, December 1995.]

Disclaimer of Opinion

.61 A disclaimer of opinion states that the auditor does not express an opinion on the financial statements. An auditor may decline to express an opinion whenever he is unable to form or has not formed an opinion as to the fairness of presentation of the financial statements in conformity with generally accepted accounting principles. If the auditor disclaims an opinion, the auditor's report should give all of the substantive reasons for the disclaimer. [Paragraph renumbered and amended, effective for reports issued or reissued on or after February 29, 1996, by the issuance of Statement on Auditing Standards No. 79.]

.62 A disclaimer is appropriate when the auditor has not performed an audit sufficient in scope to enable him to form an opinion on the financial statements.[19] A disclaimer of opinion should not be expressed because the auditor believes, on the basis of his audit, that there are material departures from generally accepted accounting principles (see paragraphs .35 through .57). When disclaiming an opinion because of a scope limitation, the auditor should state in a separate paragraph or paragraphs all of the substantive reasons for the disclaimer. He should state that the scope of his audit was not sufficient to warrant the expression of an opinion. The auditor should not identify the procedures that were performed nor include the paragraph describ-

---

[19] If an accountant is engaged to conduct an audit of the financial statements of a nonpublic entity in accordance with generally accepted auditing standards, but is requested to change the engagement to a review or a compilation of the statements, he should look to the guidance in paragraphs 44 to 49 of Statement on Standards for Accounting and Review Services 1, *Compilation and Review of Financial Statements* [AR section 100.44–.49]. Section 504, *Association With Financial Statements*, paragraph .05, provides guidance to an accountant who is associated with the financial statements of a public entity, but has not audited such statements. [Footnote renumbered and amended, effective for reports issued or reissued on or after February 29, 1996, by the issuance of Statement on Auditing Standards No. 79.]

ing the characteristics of an audit (that is, the scope paragraph of the auditor's standard report); to do so may tend to overshadow the disclaimer. In addition, he should also disclose any other reservations he has regarding fair presentation in conformity with generally accepted accounting principles. [Paragraph renumbered and amended, effective for reports issued or reissued on or after February 29, 1996, by the issuance of Statement on Auditing Standards No. 79.]

.63 An example of a report disclaiming an opinion resulting from an inability to obtain sufficient competent evidential matter because of the scope limitation follows:

Independent Auditor's Report

> We were engaged to audit the accompanying balance sheets of X Company as of December 31, 19X2 and 19X1, and the related statements of income, retained earnings, and cash flows for the years then ended. These financial statements are the responsibility of the Company's management.[20]
>
> [*Second paragraph of standard report should be omitted*]
>
> The Company did not make a count of its physical inventory in 19X2 or 19X1, stated in the accompanying financial statements at $______ as of December 31, 19X2, and at $______ as of December 31, 19X1. Further, evidence supporting the cost of property and equipment acquired prior to December 31, 19X1, is no longer available. The Company's records do not permit the application of other auditing procedures to inventories or property and equipment.
>
> Since the Company did not take physical inventories and we were not able to apply other auditing procedures to satisfy ourselves as to inventory quantities and the cost of property and equipment, the scope of our work was not sufficient to enable us to express, and we do not express, an opinion on these financial statements.

[Paragraph renumbered by the issuance of Statement on Auditing Standards No. 79, December 1995.]

Piecemeal Opinions

.64 Piecemeal opinions (expressions of opinion as to certain identified items in financial statements) should not be expressed when the auditor has disclaimed an opinion or has expressed an adverse opinion on the financial statements *taken as a whole* because piecemeal opinions tend to overshadow or contradict a disclaimer of opinion or an adverse opinion. [Paragraph renumbered by the issuance of Statement on Auditing Standards No. 79, December 1995.]

Reports on Comparative Financial Statements

.65 The fourth standard of reporting requires that an auditor's report contain either an expression of opinion regarding the financial statements *taken as a whole* or an assertion to the effect that an opinion cannot be expressed. Reference in the fourth reporting standard to the financial statements *taken as a whole* applies not only to the financial statements of the cur-

---

[20] The wording in the first paragraph of the auditor's standard report is changed in a disclaimer of opinion because of a scope limitation. The first sentence now states that "we were engaged to audit" rather than "we have audited" since, because of the scope limitation, the auditor was not able to perform an audit in accordance with generally accepted auditing standards. In addition, the last sentence of the first paragraph is also deleted, because of the scope limitation, to eliminate the reference to the auditor's responsibility to express an opinion. [Footnote renumbered by the issuance of Statement on Auditing Standards No. 79, December 1995.]

rent period but also to those of one or more prior periods that are presented on a comparative basis with those of the current period. Therefore, a continuing auditor[21] should update[22] his report on the individual financial statements of the one or more prior periods presented on a comparative basis with those of the current period.[23] Ordinarily, the auditor's report on comparative financial statements should be dated as of the date of completion of his most recent audit. (See section 530, *Dating of the Independent Auditor's Report*, paragraph .01.) [Paragraph renumbered by the issuance of Statement on Auditing Standards No. 79, December 1995.]

.66 During his audit of the current-period financial statements, the auditor should be alert for circumstances or events that affect the prior-period financial statements presented (see paragraph .68) or the adequacy of informative disclosures concerning those statements. (See section 431, *Adequacy of Disclosure in Financial Statements*, and ARB No. 43, Chapter 2A [AC section F43].) In updating his report on the prior-period financial statements, the auditor should consider the effects of any such circumstances or events coming to his attention. [Paragraph renumbered by the issuance of Statement on Auditing Standards No. 79, December 1995.]

Different Reports on Comparative Financial Statements Presented

.67 Since the auditor's report on comparative financial statements applies to the individual financial statements presented, an auditor may express a qualified or adverse opinion, disclaim an opinion, or include an explanatory paragraph with respect to one or more financial statements for one or more periods, while issuing a different report on the other financial statements presented. Following are examples of reports on comparative financial statements (excluding the standard introductory and scope paragraphs, where applicable) with different reports on one or more financial statements presented.

---

[21] A *continuing auditor* is one who has audited the financial statements of the current period and of one or more consecutive periods immediately prior to the current period.

If one firm of independent auditors merges with another firm and the new firm becomes the auditor of a former client of one of the former firms, the new firm may accept responsibility and express an opinion on the financial statements for the prior period(s), as well as for those of the current period. In such circumstances, the new firm should follow the guidance in paragraphs .65 through .69 and may indicate in its report or signature that a merger took place and may name the firm of independent auditors that was merged with it. If the new firm decides not to express an opinion on the prior-period financial statements, the guidance in paragraphs .70 through .74 should be followed. [Footnote renumbered by the issuance of Statement on Auditing Standards No. 79, December 1995.]

[22] An updated report on prior-period financial statements should be distinguished from a reissuance of a previous report (see section 530, *Dating of the Independent Auditor's Report*, paragraphs .06 through .08), since in issuing an updated report the continuing auditor considers information that he has become aware of during his audit of the current-period financial statements (see paragraph .68) and because an updated report is issued in conjunction with the auditor's report on the current-period financial statements. [Footnote renumbered by the issuance of Statement on Auditing Standards No. 79, December 1995.]

[23] A continuing auditor need not report on the prior-period financial statements if only summarized comparative information of the prior period(s) is presented. For example, entities such as state and local governmental units and not-for-profit organizations frequently present total-all-funds information for the prior period(s) rather than information by individual funds because of space limitations or to avoid cumbersome or confusing formats. In some circumstances, the client may request the auditor to express an opinion on the prior period(s) as well as the current period. In those circumstances, the auditor should consider whether the information included for the prior period(s) contains sufficient detail to constitute a fair presentation in conformity with generally accepted accounting principles. In most cases, this will necessitate including additional columns or separate detail by fund, or the auditor would need to modify his report. [Footnote renumbered by the issuance of Statement on Auditing Standards No. 79, December 1995.]

Standard Report on the Prior-Year Financial Statements and a Qualified Opinion on the Current-Year Financial Statements

Independent Auditor's Report

[*Same first and second paragraphs as the standard report*]

The Company has excluded, from property and debt in the accompanying 19X2 balance sheet, certain lease obligations that were entered into in 19X2 which, in our opinion, should be capitalized in order to conform with generally accepted accounting principles. If these lease obligations were capitalized, property would be increased by $______, long-term debt by $______, and retained earnings by $______ as of December 31, 19X2, and net income and earnings per share would be increased (decreased) by $______ and $______, respectively, for the year then ended.

In our opinion, except for the effects on the 19X2 financial statements of not capitalizing certain lease obligations as described in the preceding paragraph, the financial statements referred to above present fairly, in all material respects, the financial position of ABC Company as of December 31, 19X2 and 19X1, and the results of its operations and its cash flows for the years then ended in conformity with generally accepted accounting principles.

Standard Report on the Current-Year Financial Statements With a Disclaimer of Opinion on the Prior-Year Statements of Income, Retained Earnings, and Cash Flows

Independent Auditor's Report

[*Same first paragraph as the standard report*]

Except as explained in the following paragraph, we conducted our audits in accordance with generally accepted auditing standards. Those standards require that we plan and perform our audit to obtain reasonable assurance about whether the financial statements are free of material misstatement. An audit includes examining, on a test basis, evidence supporting the amounts and disclosures in the financial statements. An audit also includes assessing the accounting principles used and significant estimates made by management, as well as evaluating the overall financial statement presentation. We believe that our audits provide a reasonable basis for our opinion.

We did not observe the taking of the physical inventory as of December 31, 19X0, since that date was prior to our appointment as auditors for the Company, and we were unable to satisfy ourselves regarding inventory quantities by means of other auditing procedures. Inventory amounts as of December 31, 19X0, enter into the determination of net income and cash flows for the year ended December 31, 19X1.[24]

Because of the matter discussed in the preceding paragraph, the scope of our work was not sufficient to enable us to express, and we do not express, an opinion on the results of operations and cash flows for the year ended December 31, 19X1.

---

[24] It is assumed that the independent auditor has been able to satisfy himself as to the consistency of application of generally accepted accounting principles. See section 420, *Consistency of Application of Generally Accepted Accounting Principles*, for a discussion of consistency. [Footnote renumbered by the issuance of Statement on Auditing Standards No. 79, December 1995; the former footnote 29 has been deleted and subsequent footnotes renumbered by the issuance of Statement on Auditing Standards No. 79, December 1995.]

> In our opinion, the balance sheets of ABC Company as of December 31, 19X2 and 19X1, and the related statements of income, retained earnings, and cash flows for the year ended December 31, 19X2, present fairly, in all material respects, the financial position of ABC Company as of December 31, 19X2 and 19X1, and the results of its operations and its cash flows for the year ended December 31, 19X2, in conformity with generally accepted accounting principles.

[Paragraph renumbered by the issuance of Statement on Auditing Standards No. 79, December 1995.]

Opinion on Prior-Period Financial Statements Different From the Opinion Previously Expressed

.68 If, during his current audit, an auditor becomes aware of circumstances or events that affect the financial statements of a prior period, he should consider such matters when updating his report on the financial statements of the prior period. For example, if an auditor has previously qualified his opinion or expressed an adverse opinion on financial statements of a prior period because of a departure from generally accepted accounting principles, and the prior-period financial statements are restated in the current period to conform with generally accepted accounting principles, the auditor's updated report on the financial statements of the prior period should indicate that the statements have been restated and should express an unqualified opinion with respect to the restated financial statements. [Paragraph renumbered by the issuance of Statement on Auditing Standards No. 79, December 1995.]

.69 If, in an updated report, the opinion is different from the opinion previously expressed on the financial statements of a prior period, the auditor should disclose all the substantive reasons for the different opinion in a separate explanatory paragraph(s) preceding the opinion paragraph of his report.[29] The explanatory paragraph(s) should disclose (*a*) the date of the auditor's previous report, (*b*) the type of opinion previously expressed, (*c*) the circumstances or events that caused the auditor to express a different opinion, and (*d*) that the auditor's updated opinion on the financial statements of the prior period is different from his previous opinion on those statements. The following is an example of an explanatory paragraph that may be appropriate when an auditor issues an updated report on the financial statements of a prior period that contains an opinion different from the opinion previously expressed:

> Independent Auditor's Report
>
> [*Same first and second paragraphs as the standard report*]
>
> In our report dated March 1, 19X2, we expressed an opinion that the 19X1 financial statements did not fairly present financial position, results of operations, and cash flows in conformity with generally accepted accounting principles because of two departures from such principles: (1) the Company carried its property, plant, and equipment at appraisal values, and provided for depreciation on the basis of such values, and (2) the Company did not provide for deferred income taxes with respect to differences between income for financial reporting purposes and taxable income. As described in Note X, the Company has changed its method of accounting for these items and restated its 19X1 financial statements to conform with generally accepted accounting principles. Accordingly, our present opinion on the 19X1 financial statements, as presented herein, is different from that expressed in our previous report.[25]

[25] See footnote 16. [Footnote renumbered by the issuance of Statement on Auditing Standards No. 79, December 1995.]

In our opinion, the financial statements referred to above present fairly, in all material respects, the financial position of X Company as of December 31, 19X2 and 19X1, and the results of its operations and its cash flows for the years then ended in conformity with generally accepted accounting principles.

[Paragraph renumbered by the issuance of Statement on Auditing Standards No. 79, December 1995.]

Report of Predecessor Auditor

.70 A predecessor auditor ordinarily would be in a position to reissue his report on the financial statements of a prior period at the request of a former client if he is able to make satisfactory arrangements with his former client to perform this service and if he performs the procedures described in paragraph .71.[26] [Paragraph renumbered by the issuance of Statement on Auditing Standards No. 79, December 1995.]

Predecessor Auditor's Report Reissued

.71 Before reissuing (or consenting to the reuse of) a report previously issued on the financial statements of a prior period, a predecessor auditor should consider whether his previous report on those statements is still appropriate. Either the current form or manner of presentation of the financial statements of the prior period or one or more subsequent events might make a predecessor auditor's previous report inappropriate. Consequently, a predecessor auditor should (*a*) read the financial statements of the current period, (*b*) compare the prior-period financial statements that he reported on with the financial statements to be presented for comparative purposes, and (*c*) obtain a letter of representations from the successor auditor. The letter of representations should state whether the successor's audit revealed any matters that, in the successor's opinion, might have a material effect on, or require disclosure in, the financial statements reported on by the predecessor auditor. Also, the predecessor auditor may wish to consider the matters described in section 543, *Part of Audit Performed by Other Independent Auditors*, paragraphs .10 through .12. However, the predecessor auditor should not refer in his reissued report to the report or work of the successor auditor. [Paragraph renumbered by the issuance of Statement on Auditing Standards No. 79, December 1995.]

.72 A predecessor auditor who has agreed to reissue his report may become aware of events or transactions occurring subsequent to the date of his previous report on the financial statements of a prior period that may affect his previous report (for example, the successor auditor might indicate in his response that certain matters have had a material effect on the prior-period financial statements reported on by the predecessor auditor). In such circumstances, the predecessor auditor should make inquiries and perform other procedures that he considers necessary (for example, reviewing the working papers of the successor auditor as they relate to the matters affecting the prior-period financial statements). He should then decide, on the basis of the evidential matter obtained, whether to revise his report. If a predecessor auditor concludes that his report should be revised, he should follow the guidance in paragraphs .68, .69, and .73 of this section. [Paragraph renumbered by the issuance of Statement on Auditing Standards No. 79, December 1995.]

---

[26] It is recognized that there may be reasons why a predecessor auditor's report may not be reissued and this section does not address the various situations that could arise. [Footnote renumbered by the issuance of Statement on Auditing Standards No. 79, December 1995.]

.73 A predecessor auditor's knowledge of the current affairs of his former client is obviously limited in the absence of a continuing relationship. Consequently, when reissuing his report on prior-period financial statements, a predecessor auditor should use the date of his previous report to avoid any implication that he has examined any records, transactions, or events after that date. If the predecessor auditor revises his report or if the financial statements are restated, he should dual-date his report. (See section 530, *Dating of the Independent Auditor's Report*, paragraph .05.) [Paragraph renumbered by the issuance of Statement on Auditing Standards No. 79, December 1995.]

Predecessor Auditor's Report Not Presented

.74 If the financial statements of a prior period have been audited by a predecessor auditor whose report is not presented, the successor auditor should indicate in the introductory paragraph of his report (*a*) that the financial statements of the prior period were audited by another auditor,[27] (*b*) the date of his report, (*c*) the type of report issued by the predecessor auditor, and (*d*) if the report was other than a standard report, the substantive reasons therefor.[28] An example of a successor auditor's report when the predecessor auditor's report is not presented is shown below:

Independent Auditor's Report

> We have audited the balance sheet of ABC Company as of December 31, 19X2, and the related statements of income, retained earnings, and cash flows for the year then ended. These financial statements are the responsibility of the Company's management. Our responsibility is to express an opinion on these financial statements based on our audit. The financial statements of ABC Company as of December 31, 19X1, were audited by other auditors whose report dated March 31, 19X2, expressed an unqualified opinion on those statements.
>
> [*Same second paragraph as the standard report*]
>
> In our opinion, the 19X2 financial statements referred to above present fairly, in all material respects, the financial position of ABC Company as of December 31, 19X2, and the results of its operations and its cash flows for the year then ended in conformity with generally accepted accounting principles.

If the predecessor auditor's report was other than a standard report, the successor auditor should describe the nature of and reasons for the explanatory paragraph added to the predecessor's report or his opinion qualification. Following is an illustration of the wording that may be included in the successor auditor's report:

> . . . were audited by other auditors whose report dated March 1, 19X2, on those statements included an explanatory paragraph that described the change in the Company's method of computing depreciation discussed in Note X to the financial statements.

---

[27] The successor auditor should not name the predecessor auditor in his report; however, the successor auditor may name the predecessor auditor if the predecessor auditor's practice was acquired by, or merged with, that of the successor auditor. [Footnote renumbered by the issuance of Statement on Auditing Standards No. 79, December, 1995.]

[28] If the predecessor's report was issued before the effective date of this section and contained an uncertainties explanatory paragraph, a successor auditor's report issued or reissued after the effective date hereof should not make reference to the predecessor's previously required explanatory paragraph. [Footnote added, effective for reports issued or reissued on or after February 29, 1996, by Statement on Auditing Standards No. 79.]

If the financial statements have been restated, the introductory paragraph should indicate that a predecessor auditor reported on the financial statements of the prior period before restatement. In addition, if the successor auditor is engaged to audit and applies sufficient procedures to satisfy himself as to the appropriateness of the restatement adjustments, he may also include the following paragraph in his report:

> We also audited the adjustments described in Note X that were applied to restate the 19X1 financial statements. In our opinion, such adjustments are appropriate and have been properly applied.

[Paragraph renumbered and amended, effective for reports issued or reissued on or after February 29, 1996, by the issuance of Statement on Auditing Standards No. 79.]

Effective Date and Transition

.75 This section is effective for reports issued or reissued on or after February 29, 1996. Earlier application of the provisions of this section is permissible. [Paragraph renumbered and amended, effective for reports issued or reissued on or after February 29, 1996, by the issuance of Statement on Auditing Standards No. 79.]

.76 An auditor who previously included an uncertainties explanatory paragraph in a report should not repeat that paragraph and is not required to include an emphasis paragraph related to the uncertainty in a reissuance of that report or in a report on subsequent periods' financial statements, even if the uncertainty has not been resolved. If the auditor decides to include an emphasis paragraph related to the uncertainty, the paragraph may include an explanation of the change in reporting standards.[29] [Paragraph renumbered and amended, effective for reports issued or reissued on or after February 29, 1996, by the issuance of Statement on Auditing Standards No. 79.]

---

[29] [Footnote renumbered and deleted by the issuance of Statement on Auditing Standards No. 79, December 1995.]

AU Section 9508

Reports on Audited Financial Statements: Auditing Interpretations of Section 508

1. Report of an Outside Inventory-Taking Firm as an Alternative Procedure for Observing Inventories

.01 *Question*—Section 508, *Reports on Audited Financial Statements*, paragraph .24 states that "Common restrictions on the scope of the audit include those applying to the observation of physical inventories and the confirmation of accounts receivable by direct communication with debtors. . . ." A footnote to that paragraph states: "Circumstances such as the timing of his work may make it impossible for the auditor to accomplish these procedures. In this case, if he is able to satisfy himself as to inventories or accounts receivable by applying alternative procedures, there is no significant limitation on the scope of his work, and his report need not include reference to the omission of the procedures or to the use of alternative procedures." Outside firms of nonaccountants specializing in the taking of physical inventories are used at times by some companies, such as retail stores, hospitals, and automobile dealers, to count, list, price and subsequently compute the total dollar amount of inventory on hand at the date of the physical count. Would obtaining the report of an outside inventory-taking firm be an acceptable alternative procedure to the independent auditor's own observation of physical inventories?

.02 *Interpretation*—Sufficient competent evidential matter for inventories is discussed in section 331, *Inventories*, paragraphs .09–.12. Section 331.09 states that ". . . it is ordinarily necessary for the independent auditor to be present at the time of count and, by suitable observation, tests, and inquiries, satisfy himself respecting the effectiveness of the methods of inventory-taking and the measure of reliance which may be placed upon the client's representations about the quantities and physical condition of the inventories."

.03 Section 331.10 and .11 discusses two variations of that procedure when the client has well-kept perpetual records that are checked periodically by comparisons with physical counts or when the client uses statistical sampling to determine inventories. In such instances, the auditor may vary the timing and extent of his observation of physical counts, but he "must be present to observe such counts as he deems necessary and must satisfy himself as to the effectiveness of the counting procedures used."

.04 Section 331.12 deals with circumstances in which the auditor has not satisfied himself as to inventories in the possession of the client through procedures described in section 331.09–.11. In those circumstances, the general requirement for satisfactory alternative procedures is that ". . . tests of the accounting records alone will not be sufficient for him to become satisfied as to quantities; it will always be necessary for the auditor to make, or observe, some physical counts of the inventory and apply appropriate tests of intervening transactions."

.05 The fact that the inventory is counted by an outside inventory firm of nonaccountants is not, by itself, a satisfactory substitute for the auditor's own observation or taking of some physical counts. The auditor's concern, in this respect, is to satisfy himself as to the effectiveness of the counting procedures used. If the client engages an outside inventory firm to take the physical inventory, the auditor's primary concern would be to evaluate the effectiveness of the procedures used by the outside firm and his auditing procedures would be applied accordingly.

.06 Thus, the auditor would examine the outside firm's program, observe its procedures and controls, make or observe some physical counts of the inventory, recompute calculations of the submitted inventory on a test basis and apply appropriate tests to the intervening transactions. The independent auditor ordinarily may reduce the extent of his work on the physical count of inventory because of the work of an outside inventory firm, but any restriction on the auditor's judgment concerning the extent of his contact with the inventory would be a scope restriction.

[Issue Date: July, 1975.]

[2.] Reporting on Comparative Financial Statements of Nonprofit Organizations

[.07–.10] [Superseded by Statement on Auditing Standards No. 15, effective for periods ending after June 30, 1977.]

[3.] Reporting on Loss Contingencies

[.11–.14] [Superseded by Statement on Auditing Standards No. 58, effective for reports issued or reissued on or after January 1, 1989.] (See section 508.)

[4.] Reports on Consolidated Financial Statements That Include Supplementary Consolidating Information

[.15–.20] [Superseded December 31, 1980, by SAS No. 29.] (See section 551.)

[5.] Disclosures of Subsequent Events

[.21–.24] [Superseded by Statement on Auditing Standards No. 58, effective for reports issued or reissued on or after January 1, 1989.] (See section 508.)

[6.] The Materiality of Uncertainties

[.25–.28] [Superseded by Statement on Auditing Standards No. 58, effective for reports issued or reissued on or after January 1, 1989.] (See section 508.)

[7.] Reporting on an Uncertainty

[.29–.32] [Withdrawn August, 1982 by Statement on Auditing Standards No. 43.]

8. Reporting on Financial Statements Prepared on a Liquidation Basis of Accounting

.33 *Question*—Footnote 6 of Statement of Position 93-3, *Rescission of Accounting Principles Board Statements*, states that an enterprise is not viewed as a going concern if liquidation appears imminent. How should the auditor report on financial statements that are prepared on a liquidation basis of accounting for an entity in liquidation or for which liquidation appears imminent?

.34 *Answer*—A liquidation basis of accounting may be considered generally accepted accounting principles for entities in liquidation or for which liquidation appears imminent. Therefore, the auditor should issue an unqualified opinion on such financial statements, provided that the liquidation basis of accounting has been properly applied, and that adequate disclosures are made in the financial statements.

.35 Typically, the financial statements of entities that adopt a liquidation basis of accounting are presented along with financial statements of a period prior to adoption of a liquidation basis that were prepared on the basis of generally accepted accounting principles for going concerns. In such circumstances, the auditor's report ordinarily should include an explanatory paragraph that states that the entity has changed the basis of accounting used to determine the amounts at which assets and liabilities are carried from the going concern basis to a liquidation basis.

.36 Examples of auditor's reports with such an explanatory paragraph follow.

Report on Single Year Financial Statements in Year of Adoption of Liquidation Basis

"We have audited the statement of net assets in liquidation of XYZ Company as of December 31, 19X2, and the related statement of changes in net assets in liquidation for the period from April 26, 19X2 to December 31, 19X2. In addition, we have audited the statements of income, retained earnings, and cash flows for the period from January 1, 19X2 to April 25, 19X2. These financial statements are the responsibility of the Company's management. Our responsibility is to express an opinion on these financial statements based on our audit.

"We conducted our audit in accordance with generally accepted auditing standards. Those standards require that we plan and perform the audit to obtain reasonable assurance about whether the financial statements are free of material misstatement. An audit includes examining, on a test basis, evidence supporting the amounts and disclosures in the financial statements. An audit also includes assessing the accounting principles used and significant estimates made by management, as well as evaluating the overall financial statement presentation. We believe that our audit provides a reasonable basis for our opinion.

"As described in Note X to the financial statements, the stockholders of XYZ Company approved a plan of liquidation on April 25, 19X2, and the company commenced liquidation shortly thereafter. As a result, the company has changed its basis of accounting for periods subsequent to April 25, 19X2 from the going-concern basis to a liquidation basis.

"In our opinion, the financial statements referred to above present fairly, in all material respects, the net assets in liquidation of XYZ Company as of December 31, 19X2, the changes in its net assets in liquidation for the period from April 26, 19X2 to December 31, 19X2, and the results of its operations and its cash flows for the period from January 1, 19X2 to April 25, 19X2, in conformity with generally accepted accounting principles applied on the bases described in the preceding paragraph."

Report on Comparative Financial Statements in Year of Adoption of Liquidation Basis

"We have audited the balance sheet of XYZ Company as of December 31, 19X1, the related statements of income, retained earnings, and cash flows for the year then ended, and the statements of income, retained earnings, and cash flows for the period from January 1, 19X2 to April 25, 19X2. In addition, we have audited the statement of net assets in liquidation as of December 31, 19X2, and the related statement of changes in net assets in liquidation for the period from April 26, 19X2 to December 31, 19X2. These financial statements are the responsibility of the Company's management. Our responsibility is to express an opinion on these financial statements based on our audits.

"We conducted our audits in accordance with generally accepted auditing standards. Those standards require that we plan and perform the audit to obtain reasonable assurance about whether the financial statements are free of material misstatements. An audit includes examining, on a test basis, evidence supporting the amounts and disclosures in the financial statements. An audit also includes assessing the accounting principles used and significant estimates made by management, as well as evaluating the overall financial statement presentation. We believe that our audits provide a reasonable basis for our opinion.

"As described in Note X to the financial statements, the stockholders of XYZ Company approved a plan of liquidation on April 25, 19X2, and the company commenced liquidation shortly thereafter. As a result, the company has changed its basis of accounting for periods subsequent to April 25, 19X2 from the going-concern basis to a liquidation basis.

"In our opinion, the financial statements referred to above present fairly, in all material respects, the financial position of XYZ Company as of December 31, 19X1, the results of its operations and its cash flows for the year then ended and for the period from January 1, 19X2 to April 25, 19X2, its net assets in liquidation as of December 31, 19X2, and the changes in its net assets in liquidation for the period from April 26, 19X2 to December 31, 19X2, in conformity with generally accepted accounting principles applied on the bases described in the preceding paragraph."

.37 The auditor may, in subsequent years, continue to include an explanatory paragraph in his report to emphasize that the financial statements are presented on a liquidation basis of accounting.

[.38] [Paragraph deleted to reflect conforming changes necessary due to the issuance of Statement on Auditing Standards No. 79.]

[Issue Date: December, 1984; Revised: June, 1993; Revised: February, 1997.]

[9.] Quantifying Departures From Generally Accepted Accounting Principles

[.39–.43] [Superseded by Statement on Auditing Standards No. 58, effective for reports issued or reissued on or after January 1, 1989.] (See section 508.)

[10.] Updated Reports Resulting From the Retroactive Suspension of Earnings per Share and Segment Information Disclosure Requirements

[.44–.48] [Withdrawn March, 1989 by the Auditing Standards Board.]

11. Restating Financial Statements Reported on by a Predecessor Auditor

[.49–.50] [An Interpretation of section 315A, *Communications Between Predecessor and Successor Auditors*, and section 508, *Reports on Audited Financial Statements*, paragraph entitled *Restating Financial Statements Reported on by a Predecessor Auditor*, can be found in section 9315A.06–.07.]

12. Reference in Auditor's Standard Report to Management's Report

.51 *Question*—One of the basic elements of the auditor's standard report is a statement that the financial statements are the responsibility of the Company's management. That statement is required in the auditor's report even when a document containing the auditor's report includes a statement by management regarding its responsibility for the presentation of the financial statements. When an annual shareholders' report (or other client-prepared document that includes audited financial statements) contains a management report that states the financial statements are the responsibility of management, is it permissible for the auditor's report to include a reference to the management report?

.52 *Interpretation*—No. The statement about management's responsibilities for the financial statements required by section 508, *Reports on Audited Financial Statements*, should not be further elaborated upon in the auditor's standard report or referenced to management's report. Such modifications to the standard auditor's report may lead users to erroneously believe that the auditor is providing assurances about representations made by management about their responsibility for financial reporting, internal controls and other matters that might be discussed in the management report.

[Issue Date: January, 1989.]

AU Section 530

Dating of the Independent Auditor's Report

Sources: SAS No. 1, section 530; SAS No. 29.

Issue date, unless otherwise indicated: November, 1972.

.01 Generally, the date of completion of the field work should be used as the date of the independent auditor's report. Paragraph .05 describes the procedure to be followed when a subsequent event occurring after the completion of the field work is disclosed in the financial statements.

.02 The auditor has no responsibility to make any inquiry or carry out any auditing procedures for the period after the date of his report.[1] However, with respect to filings under the Securities Act of 1933, reference should be made to section 711.10–.13.[*]

Events Occurring After Completion of Field Work But Before Issuance of Report

.03 In case a subsequent event of the type requiring adjustment of the financial statements (as discussed in section 560.03) occurs after the date of the independent auditor's report but before its issuance, and the event comes to the attention of the auditor, the financial statements should be adjusted or the auditor should qualify his opinion.[2] When the adjustment is made without disclosure of the event, the report ordinarily should be dated in accordance with paragraph .01. However, if the financial statements are adjusted and disclosure of the event is made, or if no adjustment is made and the auditor qualifies his opinion,[3] the procedures set forth in paragraph .05 should be followed.

.04 In case a subsequent event of the type requiring disclosure (as discussed in section 560.05) occurs after the date of the auditor's report but before issuance of his report, and the event comes to the attention of the auditor, it should be disclosed in a note to the financial statements or the auditor should qualify his opinion.[4] If disclosure of the event is made, either in a note or in the auditor's report, the auditor would date his report as set forth in the following paragraph.

.05 The independent auditor has two methods available for dating his report when a subsequent event disclosed in the financial statements occurs after completion of his field work but before issuance of his report. He may use "dual dating," for example, "February 16, 19 , except for Note , as to which

---

[1] See section 561 regarding procedures to be followed by the auditor who, subsequent to the date of his report upon audited financial statements, becomes aware that facts may have existed at that date which might have affected his report had he then been aware of such facts.

[*] Reference changed by issuance of Statement on Auditing Standards No. 37.

[2] In some cases, a disclaimer of opinion or an adverse opinion may be appropriate.

[3] Ibid.

[4] Ibid.

the date is March 1, 19 ," or he may date his report as of the later date. In the former instance, his responsibility for events occurring subsequent to the completion of his field work is limited to the specific event referred to in the note (or otherwise disclosed). In the latter instance, the independent auditor's responsibility for subsequent events extends to the date of his report and, accordingly, the procedures outlined in section 560.12 generally should be extended to that date.

Reissuance of the Independent Auditor's Report

.06 An independent auditor may reissue his report on financial statements contained in annual reports filed with the Securities and Exchange Commission or other regulatory agencies or in a document he submits to his client or to others that contains information in addition to the client's basic financial statements subsequent to the date of his original report on the basic financial statements. An independent auditor may also be requested by his client to furnish additional copies of a previously issued report. Use of the original report date in a reissued report removes any implication that records, transactions, or events after that date have been examined or reviewed. In such cases, the independent auditor has no responsibility to make further investigation or inquiry as to events which may have occurred during the period between the original report date and the date of the release of additional reports. However, see section 711* as to an auditor's responsibility when his report is included in a registration statement filed under the Securities Act of 1933 and see section 508.70–.73, for the predecessor auditor's responsibility when reissuing or consenting to the reuse of a report previously issued on the financial statements of a prior period. [As modified, effective December 31, 1980, by SAS No. 29.] (See section 551.)

.07 In some cases, it may not be desirable for the independent auditor to reissue his report in the circumstances described in paragraph .06 because he has become aware of an event that occurred subsequent to the date of his original report that requires adjustment or disclosure in the financial statements. In such cases, adjustment with disclosure or disclosure alone should be made as described in section 560.08. The independent auditor should consider the effect of these matters on his opinion and he should date his report in accordance with the procedures described in paragraph .05.

.08 However, if an event of the type requiring disclosure only (as discussed in sections 560.05 and 560.08) occurs between the date of the independent auditor's original report and the date of the reissuance of such report, and if the event comes to the attention of the independent auditor, the event may be disclosed in a separate note to the financial statements captioned somewhat as follows:

Event (Unaudited) Subsequent to the Date of the
Independent Auditor's Report

Under these circumstances, the report of the independent auditor would carry the same date used in the original report.

---

* Reference changed by issuance of Statement on Auditing Standards No. 37.

AU Section 534

Reporting on Financial Statements Prepared for Use in Other Countries

Source: SAS No. 51.

See section 9534 for interpretations of this section.

Effective for audits of financial statements for periods beginning after July 31, 1986, unless otherwise indicated.

.01 This section provides guidance for an independent auditor practicing in the United States who is engaged to report on the financial statements of a U.S. entity that have been prepared in conformity with accounting principles generally accepted in another country for use outside the United States.[1] A "U.S. entity" is an entity that is either organized or domiciled in the United States.

Purpose and Use of Financial Statements

.02 A U.S. entity ordinarily prepares financial statements for use in the United States in conformity with accounting principles generally accepted in the United States, but it may also prepare financial statements that are intended for use outside the United States and are prepared in conformity with accounting principles generally accepted in another country. For example, the financial statements of a U.S. entity may be prepared for inclusion in the consolidated financial statements of a non-U.S. parent. A U.S. entity may also have non-U.S. investors or may decide to raise capital in another country. Before reporting on financial statements prepared in conformity with the accounting principles of another country, the auditor should have a clear understanding of, and obtain written representations from management regarding, the purpose and uses of such financial statements. If the auditor uses the standard report of another country, and the financial statements will have general distribution in that country, he should consider whether any additional legal responsibilities are involved.

General and Fieldwork Standards

.03 When auditing the financial statements of a U.S. entity prepared in conformity with accounting principles generally accepted in another country, the auditor should perform the procedures that are necessary to comply with the general and fieldwork standards of U.S. generally accepted auditing standards (GAAS).

---

[1] See paragraph .07, however, for a discussion of financial statements prepared in conformity with accounting principles generally accepted in another country for limited distribution in the United States.

.04 The auditing procedures generally performed under U.S. GAAS may need to be modified, however. The assertions embodied in financial statements prepared in conformity with accounting principles generally accepted in another country may differ from those prepared in conformity with U.S. generally accepted accounting principles. For example, accounting principles generally accepted in another country may require that certain assets be revalued to adjust for the effects of inflation—in which case, the auditor should perform procedures to test the revaluation adjustments. On the other hand, another country's accounting principles may not require or permit recognition of deferred taxes; consequently, procedures for testing deferred tax balances would not be applicable. As another example, the accounting principles of some countries do not require or permit disclosure of related party transactions. Determining that such transactions are properly disclosed, therefore, would not be an audit objective in such cases. Other objectives, however, would remain relevant—such as identifying related parties in order to fully understand the business purpose, nature, and extent of the transactions and their effects on the financial statements.

.05 The auditor should understand the accounting principles generally accepted in the other country. Such knowledge may be obtained by reading the statutes or professional literature (or codifications thereof) that establish or describe the accounting principles generally accepted in the other country. Application of accounting principles to a particular situation often requires practical experience; the auditor should consider, therefore, consulting with persons having such expertise in the accounting principles of the other country. If the accounting principles of another country are not established with sufficient authority or by general acceptance, or a broad range of practices is acceptable, the auditor may nevertheless be able to report on financial statements for use in such countries if, in the auditor's judgment, the client's principles and practices are appropriate in the circumstances and are disclosed in a clear and comprehensive manner. In determining the appropriateness of the accounting principles used, the auditor may consider, for example, International Accounting Standards established by the International Accounting Standards Committee.

Compliance With Auditing Standards of Another Country

.06 In those circumstances in which the auditor is requested to apply the auditing standards of another country when reporting on financial statements prepared in conformity with accounting principles generally accepted in that country, the auditor should comply with the general and fieldwork standards of that country as well as with those standards in U.S. GAAS. This may require the auditor to perform certain procedures required by auditing standards of the other country in addition to those required by U.S. GAAS. The auditor will need to read the statutes or professional literature, or codifications thereof, that establish or describe the auditing standards generally accepted in the other country. He should understand, however, that such statutes or professional literature may not be a complete description of auditing practices and, therefore, should consider consulting with persons having expertise in the auditing standards of the other country.

Reporting Standards

.07 If financial statements prepared in conformity with accounting principles generally accepted in another country are prepared for use only outside the United States, the auditor may report using either (*a*) a U.S.-style report modified to report on the accounting principles of another country (see paragraphs .09 and .10) or (*b*) if appropriate, the report form of the other country (see paragraphs .11 and .12). This is not intended to preclude limited distribution of the financial statements to parties (such as banks, institutional investors, and other knowledgeable parties that may choose to rely on the report) within the United States that deal directly with the entity, if the financial statements are to be used in a manner that permits such parties to discuss differences from U.S. accounting and reporting practices and their significance with the entity.

.08 Financial statements prepared in conformity with accounting principles generally accepted in another country ordinarily are not useful to U.S. users. Therefore, if financial statements are needed for use both in another country and within the United States, the auditor may report on two sets of financial statements for the entity—one prepared in conformity with accounting principles generally accepted in another country for use outside the United States, and the other prepared in accordance with accounting principles generally accepted in the United States (see paragraph .13). If dual statements are not prepared, or for some other reason the financial statements prepared in conformity with accounting principles generally accepted in another country will have more than limited distribution in the United States, the auditor should report on them using the U.S. standard form of report, modified as appropriate for departures from accounting principles generally accepted in the United States (see paragraph .14).

Use Only Outside the United States

.09 A U.S.-style report modified to report on financial statements prepared in conformity with accounting principles generally accepted in another country that are intended for use only outside the United States should include—

a. A title that includes the word "independent."[2]

b. A statement that the financial statements identified in the report were audited.

c. A statement that refers to the note to the financial statements that describes the basis of presentation of the financial statements on which the auditor is reporting, including identification of the nationality of the accounting principles.

d. A statement that the financial statements are the responsibility of the Company's management[3] and that the auditor's responsibility is to express an opinion on the financial statements based on his audit.

e. A statement that the audit was conducted in accordance with auditing standards generally accepted in the United States (and, if appropriate, with the auditing standards of the other country).

---

[2] This statement does not require a title for an auditor's report if the auditor is not independent. See section 504, *Association With Financial Statements*, for guidance on reporting when the auditor is not independent. [Footnote added to reflect conforming changes necessary due to the issuance of Statement on Auditing Standards Nos. 53 through 62.]

[3] In some instances, a document containing the auditor's report may include a statement by management regarding its responsibility for the presentation of the financial statements. Nevertheless, the auditor's report should state that the financial statements are management's responsibility. [Footnote added to reflect conforming changes necessary due to the issuance of Statement on Auditing Standards Nos. 53 through 62.]

f. A statement that U.S. standards require that the auditor plan and perform the audit to obtain reasonable assurance about whether the financial statements are free of material misstatement.

g. A statement that an audit includes:

(1) Examining, on a test basis, evidence supporting the amounts and disclosures in the financial statements,

(2) Assessing the accounting principles used and significant estimates made by management, and

(3) Evaluating the overall financial statement presentation.[4]

h. A statement that the auditor believes that his audit provides a reasonable basis for his opinion.

i. A paragraph that expresses the auditor's opinion on whether the financial statements are presented fairly, in all material respects, in conformity with the basis of accounting described. If the auditor concludes that the financial statements are not fairly presented on the basis of accounting described, all substantive reasons for that conclusion should be disclosed in an additional explanatory paragraph (preceding the opinion paragraph) of the report, and the opinion paragraph should include appropriate modifying language as well as a reference to the explanatory paragraph.

j. If the auditor is auditing comparative financial statements and the described basis of accounting has not been applied in a manner consistent with that of the preceding period and the change has had a material effect on the comparability of the financial statements, the auditor should add an explanatory paragraph to his report (following the opinion paragraph) that describes the change in accounting principle and refers to the note to the financial statements that discusses the change and its effect on the financial statements.

k. The manual or printed signature of the auditor's firm.

l. Date.[5]

[Paragraph amended to reflect conforming changes necessary due to the issuance of Statement on Auditing Standards Nos. 53 through 62.]

.10 The following is an illustration of such a report:

Independent Auditor's Report

We have audited the accompanying balance sheet of International Company as of December 31, 19XX and the related statements of income, retained earnings, and cash flows for the year then ended which, as described in Note X, have been prepared on the basis of accounting principles accepted in [*name of country*]. These financial statements are the responsibility of the Company's management. Our responsibility is to express an opinion on these financial statements based on our audit.

---

[4] Section 411, *The Meaning of* Present Fairly in Conformity With Generally Accepted Accounting Principles *in the Independent Auditor's Report*, paragraphs .03 and .04, discuss the auditor's evaluation of the overall presentation of the financial statements. [Footnote added to reflect conforming changes necessary due to the issuance of Statement on Auditing Standards Nos. 53 through 62.]

[5] For guidance on dating the independent auditor's report, see section 530, *Dating of the Independent Auditor's Report*. [Footnote added to reflect conforming changes necessary due to the issuance of Statement on Auditing Standards Nos. 53 through 62.]

We conducted our audit in accordance with auditing standards generally accepted in the United States (and in [*name of country*]). U.S. standards require that we plan and perform the audit to obtain reasonable assurance about whether the financial statements are free of material misstatement. An audit includes examining, on a test basis, evidence supporting the amounts and disclosures in the financial statements. An audit also includes assessing the accounting principles used and significant estimates made by management, as well as evaluating the overall financial statement presentation. We believe that our audit provides a reasonable basis for our opinion.

In our opinion, the financial statements referred to above present fairly, in all material respects, the financial position of International Company as of [at] December 31, 19XX, and the results of its operations and its cash flows for the year then ended in conformity with accounting principles generally accepted in [*name of country*].

[Paragraph amended to reflect conforming changes necessary due to the issuance of Statement on Auditing Standards Nos. 53 through 62.]

.11 The independent auditor may also use the auditor's standard report of another country, provided that—

a. Such a report would be used by auditors in the other country in similar circumstances.

b. The auditor understands, and is in a position to make, the attestations contained in such a report (see paragraph .12).

The auditor should consider whether the standard report of another country or the financial statements may be misunderstood because they resemble those prepared in conformity with U.S. standards. When the auditor believes there is a risk of misunderstanding, he should identify the other country in the report.

.12 When the auditor uses the standard report of the other country, the auditor should comply with the reporting standards of that country. The auditor should recognize that the standard report used in another country, even when it appears similar to that used in the United States, may convey a different meaning and entail a different responsibility on the part of the auditor due to custom or culture. Use of a standard report of another country may also require the auditor to provide explicit or implicit assurance of statutory compliance or otherwise require understanding of local law. When using the auditor's standard report of another country, the auditor needs to understand applicable legal responsibilities, in addition to the auditing standards and the accounting principles generally accepted in the other country. Accordingly, depending on the nature and extent of the auditor's knowledge and experience, he should consider consulting with persons having expertise in the audit reporting practices of the other country to attain the understanding needed to issue that country's standard report.

.13 A U.S. entity that prepares financial statements in conformity with U.S. generally accepted accounting principles also may prepare financial statements in conformity with accounting principles generally accepted in another country for use outside the United States. In such circumstances, the auditor may report on the financial statements that are in conformity with accounting principles of the other country by following the guidance in paragraphs .09 and .10. The auditor may wish to include, in one or both of the reports, a statement that another report has been issued on the financial statements for the entity that have been prepared in accordance with accounting principles generally accepted in another country. The auditor may also wish to reference any note describing significant differences between the accounting principles used and U.S. GAAP. An example of such a statement follows.

> We also have reported separately on the financial statements of International Company for the same period presented in accordance with accounting principles generally accepted in [*name of country*]. (The significant differences between the accounting principles accepted in [*name of country*] and those generally accepted in the United States are summarized in Note X.)

Use in the United States

.14 If the auditor is requested to report on the fair presentation of financial statements, prepared in conformity with the accounting principles generally accepted in another country, that will have more than limited distribution in the United States, he should use the U.S. standard form of report (see section 508, *Reports on Audited Financial Statements*, paragraph .08), modified as appropriate (see section 508.35–.57), because of departures from accounting principles generally accepted in the United States.[6] The auditor may also, in a separate paragraph to the report, express an opinion on whether the financial statements are presented in conformity with accounting principles generally accepted in another country.

.15 The auditor may also report on the same set of financial statements, prepared in conformity with accounting principles generally accepted in another country, that will have more than limited distribution in the United States by using both the standard report of the other country or a U.S.-style report (described in paragraph .09) for distribution outside the United States, and a U.S. form of report (described in paragraph .14) for distribution in the United States.

Effective Date

.16 This section is effective for audits of financial statements for periods beginning after July 31, 1986.

---

[6] This section does not apply to reports on financial statements of U.S. subsidiaries of foreign registrants presented in SEC filings of foreign parent companies where the subsidiaries' financial statements have been prepared on the basis of accounting principles used by the parent company. [Footnote renumbered to reflect the conforming changes necessary due to the issuance of Statement on Auditing Standards Nos. 53 through 62.]

AU Section 9534

Reporting on Financial Statements Prepared for Use in Other Countries: Auditing Interpretations of Section 534

1. Financial Statements for General Use Only Outside of the United States in Accordance With International Accounting Standards and International Standards on Auditing

.01 *Question*—Section 534, *Reporting on Financial Statements Prepared for Use in Other Countries*, provides guidance for the independent auditor practicing in the United States who is engaged to report on the financial statements of a U.S. entity[1] for general use only outside of the United States in conformity with accounting principles generally accepted in another country. May an independent auditor practicing in the United States report on the financial statements of a U.S. entity presented in conformity with the International Accounting Standards for general use only outside of the United States?

.02 *Interpretation*—Yes. In these circumstances, the auditor should follow the guidance in section 534 in planning and performing the engagement.

.03 *Question*—If the financial statements are presented in conformity with the International Accounting Standards, may a U.S. auditor perform the audit in accordance with the International Standards on Auditing?

.04 *Interpretation*—Yes. In these circumstances, the auditor should follow the guidance in section 534 in planning and performing the engagement. Section 534 requires the U.S. auditor, in these circumstances, to comply with the general and fieldwork standards of U.S. generally accepted auditing standards as well as any additional requirements of the International Standards on Auditing. The auditor may use either a U.S.-style report (section 534.09) or the report form set forth in the International Standards on Auditing.

[Issue Date: May, 1996.]

---

[1] A U.S. entity is an entity that is either organized or domiciled in the United States.

AU Section 543

Part of Audit Performed by Other Independent Auditors

Source: SAS No. 1, section 543; SAS No. 64.

See section 9543 for interpretations of this section.

Issue date, unless otherwise indicated: November, 1972.

.01 This section provides guidance on the professional judgments the independent auditor makes in deciding (*a*) whether he may serve as principal auditor and use the work and reports of other independent auditors who have audited the financial statements of one or more subsidiaries, divisions, branches, components, or investments included in the financial statements presented and (*b*) the form and content of the principal auditor's report in these circumstances.[1] Nothing in this section should be construed to require or imply that an auditor, in deciding whether he may properly serve as principal auditor without himself auditing particular subsidiaries, divisions, branches, components, or investments of his client, should make that decision on any basis other than his judgment regarding the professional considerations as discussed in paragraphs .02 and .10; nor should an auditor state or imply that a report that makes reference to another auditor is inferior in professional standing to a report without such a reference. [As modified, September 1981, by the Auditing Standards Board.]

Principal Auditor's Course of Action

.02 The auditor considering whether he may serve as principal auditor may have performed all but a relatively minor portion of the work, or significant parts of the audit may have been performed by other auditors. In the latter case, he must decide whether his own participation is sufficient to enable him to serve as the principal auditor and to report as such on the financial statements. In deciding this question, the auditor should consider, among other things, the materiality of the portion of the financial statements he has audited in comparison with the portion audited by other auditors, the extent of his knowledge of the overall financial statements, and the importance of the components he audited in relation to the enterprise as a whole. [As modified, September 1981, by the Auditing Standards Board.]

.03 If the auditor decides that it is appropriate for him to serve as the principal auditor, he must then decide whether to make reference in his report[2] to the audit performed by another auditor. If the principal auditor decides to assume responsibility for the work of the other auditor insofar as

---

[1] Section 315A applies if an auditor uses the work of a predecessor auditor in expressing an opinion on financial statements.

[2] See paragraph .09 for example of appropriate reporting when reference is made to the audit of other auditors.

that work relates to the principal auditor's expression of an opinion on the financial statements taken as a whole, no reference should be made to the other auditor's work or report. On the other hand, if the principal auditor decides not to assume that responsibility, his report should make reference to the audit of the other auditor and should indicate clearly the division of responsibility between himself and the other auditor in expressing his opinion on the financial statements. Regardless of the principal auditor's decision, the other auditor remains responsible for the performance of his own work and for his own report.

Decision Not to Make Reference

.04 If the principal auditor is able to satisfy himself as to the independence and professional reputation of the other auditor (see paragraph .10) and takes steps he considers appropriate to satisfy himself as to the audit performed by the other auditor (see paragraph .12), he may be able to express an opinion on the financial statements taken as a whole without making reference in his report to the audit of the other auditor. If the principal auditor decides to take this position, he should not state in his report that part of the audit was made by another auditor because to do so may cause a reader to misinterpret the degree of responsibility being assumed.

.05 Ordinarily, the principal auditor would be able to adopt this position when:

a. Part of the audit is performed by another independent auditor which is an associated or correspondent firm and whose work is acceptable to the principal auditor based on his knowledge of the professional standards and competence of that firm; or

b. The other auditor was retained by the principal auditor and the work was performed under the principal auditor's guidance and control; or

c. The principal auditor, whether or not he selected the other auditor, nevertheless takes steps he considers necessary to satisfy himself as to the audit performed by the other auditor and accordingly is satisfied as to the reasonableness of the accounts for the purpose of inclusion in the financial statements on which he is expressing his opinion; or

d. The portion of the financial statements audited by the other auditor is not material to the financial statements covered by the principal auditor's opinion.

Decision to Make Reference

.06 On the other hand, the principal auditor may decide to make reference to the audit of the other auditor when he expresses his opinion on the financial statements. In some situations, it may be impracticable for the principal auditor to review the other auditor's work or to use other procedures which in the judgment of the principal auditor would be necessary for him to satisfy himself as to the audit performed by the other auditor. Also, if the financial statements of a component audited by another auditor are material in relation to the total, the principal auditor may decide, regardless of any other considerations, to make reference in his report to the audit of the other auditor.

.07 When the principal auditor decides that he will make reference to the audit of the other auditor, his report should indicate clearly, in both the introductory, scope and opinion paragraphs, the division of responsibility as between that portion of the financial statements covered by his own audit and that covered by the audit of the other auditor. The report should disclose the magnitude of the portion of the financial statements audited by the other auditor. This may be done by stating the dollar amounts or percentages of one or more of the following: total assets, total revenues, or other appropriate criteria, whichever most clearly reveals the portion of the financial statements audited by the other auditor. The other auditor may be named but only with his express permission and provided his report is presented together with that of the principal auditor.[3]

.08 Reference in the report of the principal auditor to the fact that part of the audit was made by another auditor is not to be construed as a qualification of the opinion but rather as an indication of the divided responsibility between the auditors who conducted the audits of various components of the overall financial statements. [As modified, September 1981, by the Auditing Standards Board.]

.09 An example of appropriate reporting by the principal auditor indicating the division of responsibility when he makes reference to the audit of the other auditor follows:

Independent Auditor's Report

> We have audited the consolidated balance sheet of X Company and subsidiaries as of December 31, 19...., and the related consolidated statements of income and retained earnings and cash flows for the year then ended. These financial statements are the responsibility of the Company's management. Our responsibility is to express an opinion on these financial statements based on our audits. We did not audit the financial statements of B Company, a wholly-owned subsidiary, which statements reflect total assets and revenues constituting 20 percent and 22 percent, respectively, of the related consolidated totals. Those statements were audited by other auditors whose report has been furnished to us, and our opinion, insofar as it relates to the amounts included for B Company, is based solely on the report of the other auditors.
>
> We conducted our audit in accordance with generally accepted auditing standards. Those standards require that we plan and perform the audit to obtain reasonable assurance about whether the financial statements are free of material misstatement. An audit includes examining, on a test basis, evidence supporting the amounts and disclosures in the financial statements. An audit also includes assessing the accounting principles used and significant estimates made by management, as well as evaluating the overall financial statement presentation. We believe that our audit and the report of the other auditors provide a reasonable basis for our opinion.
>
> In our opinion, based on our audit and the report of the other auditors, the consolidated financial statements referred to above present fairly, in all material respects, the financial position of X Company as of [at] December 31, 19...., and the results of its operations and its cash flows for the year then ended in conformity with generally accepted accounting principles.

When two or more auditors in addition to the principal auditor participate in the audit, the percentages covered by the other auditors may be stated in the aggregate. [Paragraph amended to reflect the conforming changes necessary due to the issuance of Statement on Auditing Standards Nos. 53 through 62.]

---

[3] As to filings with the Securities and Exchange Commission, see Rule 2-05 of Regulation S-X.

Procedures Applicable to Both Methods of Reporting

.10 Whether or not the principal auditor decides to make reference to the audit of the other auditor, he should make inquiries concerning the professional reputation and independence of the other auditor. He also should adopt appropriate measures to assure the coordination of his activities with those of the other auditor in order to achieve a proper review of matters affecting the consolidating or combining of accounts in the financial statements. These inquiries and other measures may include procedures such as the following:

a. Make inquiries as to the professional reputation and standing of the other auditor to one or more of the following:

(i) The American Institute of Certified Public Accountants,[4] the applicable state society of certified public accountants and/or the local chapter, or in the case of a foreign auditor, his corresponding professional organization.

(ii) Other practitioners.

(iii) Bankers and other credit grantors.

(iv) Other appropriate sources.

b. Obtain a representation from the other auditor that he is independent under the requirements of the American Institute of Certified Public Accountants and, if appropriate, the requirements of the Securities and Exchange Commission.

c. Ascertain through communication with the other auditor:

(i) That he is aware that the financial statements of the component which he is to audit are to be included in the financial statements on which the principal auditor will report and that the other auditor's report thereon will be relied upon (and, where applicable, referred to) by the principal auditor.

(ii) That he is familiar with accounting principles generally accepted in the United States and with the generally accepted auditing standards promulgated by the American Institute of Certified Public Accountants and will conduct his audit and will report in accordance therewith.

(iii) That he has knowledge of the relevant financial reporting requirements for statements and schedules to be filed with regulatory agencies such as the Securities and Exchange Commission, if appropriate.

---

[4] The AICPA Professional Ethics Division can respond to inquiries about whether individuals are members of the American Institute of Certified Public Accountants and whether complaints against members have been adjudicated by the Joint Trial Board. The division cannot respond to inquiries about public accounting firms or provide information about letters of required corrective action issued by the division or pending disciplinary proceedings or investigations. The AICPA Division for CPA Firms can respond to inquiries about whether specific public accounting firms are members of either the Private Companies Practice Section (PCPS) or the SEC Practice Section (SECPS), and can indicate whether a firm had a peer review in compliance with the Section's membership requirements and whether any sanctions against the firm have been publicly announced. In addition, the division will supply copies of peer-review reports that have been accepted by the applicable section of the division and information submitted by member firms on applications for membership and annual updates. The AICPA Practice Monitoring staff or the appropriate state CPA society can respond to inquiries as to whether specific public accounting firms are enrolled in the AICPA Peer Review Program and can indicate whether a firm had a peer review in compliance with the AICPA *Standards for Performing and Reporting on Peer Reviews* [PR section 100]. [Footnote amended by the Auditing Standards Board, June 1990.]

(iv) That a review will be made of matters affecting elimination of intercompany transactions and accounts and, if appropriate in the circumstances, the uniformity of accounting practices among the components included in the financial statements.

(Inquiries as to matters under *a*, and *c* (ii) and (iii) ordinarily would be unnecessary if the principal auditor already knows the professional reputation and standing of the other auditor and if the other auditor's primary place of practice is in the United States.)

[As modified, September 1981, by the Auditing Standards Board.]

.11 If the results of inquiries and procedures by the principal auditor with respect to matters described in paragraph .10 lead him to the conclusion that he can neither assume responsibility for the work of the other auditor insofar as that work relates to the principal auditor's expression of an opinion on the financial statements taken as a whole, nor report in the manner set forth in paragraph .09, he should appropriately qualify his opinion or disclaim an opinion on the financial statements taken as a whole. His reasons therefor should be stated, and the magnitude of the portion of the financial statements to which his qualification extends should be disclosed.

Additional Procedures Under Decision Not to Make Reference

.12 When the principal auditor decides not to make reference to the audit of the other auditor, in addition to satisfying himself as to the matters described in paragraph .10, he should also consider whether to perform one or more of the following procedures:

a. Visit the other auditor and discuss the audit procedures followed and results thereof.

b. Review the audit programs of the other auditor. In some cases, it may be appropriate to issue instructions to the other auditor as to the scope of his audit work.

c. Review the working papers of the other auditor, including the understanding of internal control and the assessment of control risk.

.13 In some circumstances the principal auditor may consider it appropriate to participate in discussions regarding the accounts with management personnel of the component whose financial statements are being audited by other auditors and/or to make supplemental tests of such accounts. The determination of the extent of additional procedures, if any, to be applied rests with the principal auditor alone in the exercise of his professional judgment and in no way constitutes a reflection on the adequacy of the other auditor's work. Because the principal auditor in this case assumes responsibility for his opinion on the financial statements on which he is reporting without making reference to the audit performed by the other auditor, his judgment must govern as to the extent of procedures to be undertaken.

Long-Term Investments

.14 With respect to investments accounted for under the equity method, the auditor who uses another auditor's report for the purpose of reporting on the investor's equity in underlying net assets and its share of earnings or losses and other transactions of the investee is in the position of a principal auditor using the work and reports of other auditors. Under these circumstances, the auditor may decide that it would be appropriate to refer to the work and report of the other auditor in his report on the financial statements of the investor. (See paragraphs .06–.11.) When the work and reports of other auditors constitute a major element of evidence with respect to investments accounted for under the cost method, the auditor may be in a position analogous to that of a principal auditor.

Other Auditor's Report Departs From Standard Report

.15 If the report of the other auditor is other than a standard report, the principal auditor should decide whether the reason for the departure from the standard report is of such nature and significance in relation to the financial statements on which the principal auditor is reporting that it would require recognition in his own report. If the reason for the departure is not material in relation to such financial statements and the other auditor's report is not presented, the principal auditor need not make reference in his report to such departure, if the other auditor's report is presented, the principal auditor may wish to make reference to such departure and its disposition.

Restated Financial Statements of Prior Years Following a Pooling of Interests

.16 Following a pooling-of-interests transaction, an auditor may be asked to report on restated financial statements for one or more prior years when other auditors have audited one or more of the entities included in such financial statements. In some of these situations the auditor may decide that he has not audited a sufficient portion of the financial statements for such prior year or years to enable him to serve as principal auditor (see paragraph .02). Also, in such cases, it often is not possible or it may not be appropriate or necessary for the auditor to satisfy himself with respect to the restated financial statements. In these circumstances it may be appropriate for him to express his opinion solely with respect to the combining of such statements; however, no opinion should be expressed unless the auditor has audited the statements of at least one of the entities included in the restatement for at least the latest period presented. The following is an illustration of appropriate reporting on such combination that can be presented in an additional paragraph of the auditor's report following the standard introductory, scope and opinion paragraphs covering the consolidated financial statements for the current year:*

> We previously audited and reported on the consolidated statements of income and cash flows of XYZ Company and subsidiaries for the year ended December 31, 19X1, prior to their restatement for the 19X2 pooling of interests. The contribution of XYZ Company and subsidiaries to revenues and net income represented . . . . . percent and . . . . . percent of the respective restated totals. Separate financial statements of the other companies included in the 19X1 restated consolidated statements of income and cash flows were audited and reported on separately by other auditors. We also audited the combination of the accompanying consolidated statements of income and cash flows for the year ended December 31, 19X1, after restatement for the 19X2 pooling of interests; in our opinion, such consolidated statements have been properly combined on the basis described in Note A of notes to consolidated financial statements.

---

* If restated consolidated balance sheets are also presented, the auditor may also express his opinion with respect to the combination of the consolidated balance sheets.

[As modified, October 1980, by the Auditing Standards Board. As amended, effective for reports issued after December 31, 1990, by Statement on Auditing Standards No. 64.]

.17 In reporting on restated financial statements as described in the preceding paragraph, the auditor does not assume responsibility for the work of other auditors nor the responsibility for expressing an opinion on the restated financial statements taken as a whole. He should apply procedures which will enable him to express an opinion only as to proper combination of the financial statements. These procedures include testing the combination for clerical accuracy and the methods used to combine the restated financial statements for conformity with generally accepted accounting principles. For example, the auditor should make inquiries and apply procedures regarding such matters as the following:

a. Elimination of intercompany transactions and accounts.

b. Combining adjustments and reclassifications.

c. Adjustments to treat like items in a comparable manner, if appropriate.

d. The manner and extent of presentation of disclosure matters in the restated financial statements and notes thereto.

The auditor should also consider the application of procedures contained in paragraph .10.

[As modified, October 1980, by the Auditing Standards Board.]

Predecessor Auditor

[.18] [Superseded by Statement on Auditing Standards No. 7, effective November 30, 1975.] (See section 315A.)

AU Section 9543

Part of Audit Performed by Other Independent Auditors: Auditing Interpretations of Section 543

1. Specific Procedures Performed by the Other Auditor at the Principal Auditor's Request

.01 *Question*—An independent auditor is auditing the financial statements of a component[1] in accordance with generally accepted auditing standards and is issuing a report to his client that will also be used by another independent auditor who is acting as a principal auditor.[2] The principal auditor requests the other auditor to perform specific procedures, for example, to furnish or test amounts to be eliminated in consolidation, such as intercompany profits, or to read other information in documents containing audited financial statements. In those circumstances, who is responsible to determine the extent of the procedures to be performed?

.02 *Interpretation*—Section 543, *Part of Audit Performed by Other Independent Auditors*, paragraph .10, states that the principal auditor "should adopt appropriate measures to assure the coordination of his activities with those of the other auditor in order to achieve a proper review of matters affecting the consolidating or combining of accounts in the financial statements." Section 543.10*c*(iv) further states that those measures may include procedures such as ascertaining through communication with the other auditor "that a review will be made of matters affecting elimination of intercompany transactions and accounts."

.03 Thus, when the principal auditor requests the other auditor to perform procedures, the principal auditor is responsible for determining the extent of the procedures to be performed. The principal auditor should provide specific instructions on procedures to be performed, materiality considerations for that purpose, and other information that may be necessary in the circumstances. The other auditor should perform the requested procedures in accordance with the principal auditor's instructions and report the findings solely for the use of the principal auditor.

[Issue Date: April, 1979; As Revised, November 1996, by the Audit Issues Task Force.]

2. Inquiries of the Principal Auditor by the Other Auditor

.04 *Question*—Section 543, *Part of Audit Performed by Other Independent Auditors*, gives guidance to a principal auditor on making inquiries of the other auditor. Section 543.03 also states that "the other auditor remains responsible for the performance of his own work and for his own report." Should the other auditor also make inquiries of the principal auditor to fulfill that responsibility?

---

[1] For the purposes of this interpretation, the entities whose separate financial statements collectively comprise the consolidated or other financial statements are referred to as components.

[2] See section 543 for the definition of a principal auditor. For the purposes of this interpretation, the auditor whose work is used by a principal auditor is referred to as the other auditor.

.05 *Interpretation*—Section 334, *Related Parties*, states that there may be inquiry of the principal auditor regarding related parties. In addition, before issuing his report, the other auditor should consider whether he should inquire of the principal auditor as to matters that may be significant to his own audit. [Reference changed August, 1983, by issuance of Statement on Auditing Standards No. 45.] (See section 334.)

.06 The other auditor's consideration of whether to make the inquiry should be based on factors such as his awareness that there are transactions or relationships which are unusual or complex between the component he is auditing and the component the principal auditor is auditing, or his knowledge that in the past matters relating to his audit have arisen that were known to the principal auditor but not to him.

.07 If the other auditor believes inquiry is appropriate he may furnish the principal auditor with a draft of the financial statements expected to be issued and of his report solely for the purpose of aiding the principal auditor to respond to the inquiry. The inquiry would concern transactions, adjustments, or other matters that have come to the principal auditor's attention that he believes require adjustment to or disclosure in the financial statements of the component being audited by the other auditor. Also, the other auditor should inquire about any relevant limitation on the scope of the audit performed by the principal auditor.

[Issue Date: April, 1979.]

3. Form of Inquiries of the Principal Auditor Made by the Other Auditor

.08 *Question*—In those circumstances when the other auditor believes an inquiry of the principal auditor is appropriate, what form should the inquiry take and when should it be made?

.09 *Interpretation*—The other auditor's inquiry ordinarily should be in writing. It should indicate whether the response should be in writing, and should specify the date as of which the principal auditor should respond. Ordinarily, that date should be near the anticipated date of the other auditor's report. An example of a written inquiry from the other auditor is as follows:

> "We are auditing the financial statements of (name of client) as of (date) and for the (period of audit) for the purpose of expressing an opinion as to whether the financial statements present fairly, in all material respects, the financial position, results of operations, and cash flows of (name of client) in conformity with generally accepted accounting principles.
>
> A draft of the financial statements referred to above and a draft of our report are enclosed solely to aid you in responding to this inquiry. Please provide us (in writing) (orally) with the following information in connection with your current examination of the consolidated financial statements of (name of parent company):
>
> 1. Transactions or other matters (including adjustments made during consolidation or contemplated at the date of your reply) that have come to your attention that you believe require adjustment to or disclosure in the financial statements of (name of client) being audited by us.
>
> 2. Any limitation on the scope of your audit that is related to the financial statements of (name of client) being audited by us, or that limits your ability to provide us with the information requested in this inquiry.

Please make your response as of a date near (expected date of the other auditor's report)."

.10 The principal auditor's reply will often be made as of a date when his audit is still in progress; however, the other auditor should expect that ordinarily the response should satisfy his need for information. However, there may be instances when the principal auditor's response explains that it is limited because his audit has not progressed to a point that enables him to provide a response that satisfies the other auditor's need for information. If the principal auditor's response is limited in that manner, the other auditor should consider whether to apply acceptable alternative procedures, delay the issuance of his report until the principal auditor can respond, or qualify his opinion or disclaim an opinion for a limitation on the scope of his audit.

[Issue Date: April, 1979]

4. Form of Principal Auditor's Response to Inquiries from Other Auditors

.11 *Question*—An independent auditor acting in the capacity of a principal auditor may receive an inquiry from another independent auditor performing the audit of the financial statements of a component concerning transactions, adjustments, or limitations on his audit.[3] What should be the form of the principal auditor's response?

.12 *Interpretation*—The principal auditor should respond promptly to the other auditor's inquiry, based on his audit, and if applicable, on his reading of the draft financial statements and report furnished by the other auditor. His response may be written or oral, as requested by the other auditor. However, the principal auditor's response ordinarily should be in writing if it contains information that may have a significant effect on the other auditor's audit.

.13 The principal auditor should identify the stage of completion of his audit as of the date of his reply. He should also indicate that no audit procedures were performed for the purpose of identifying matters that would not affect his audit and report, and therefore, not all the information requested would necessarily be revealed. If the principal auditor has been furnished with a draft of the financial statements being audited by the other auditor and a draft of his report, the principal auditor should state that he has read the draft only to aid him in making his reply.

.14 An example of a written response from the principal auditor is as follows:

"This letter is furnished to you in response to your request that we provide you with certain information in connection with your audit of the financial statements of (name of component), a (subsidiary, division, branch or investment) of Parent Company for the year ended (date).

We are in the process of performing an audit of the consolidated financial statements of Parent Company for the year ended (date) (but have not completed our work as of this date). The objective of our audit is to enable us to express an opinion on the consolidated financial statements of Parent Company and, accordingly, we have performed no procedures directed toward identifying matters that would not affect our audit or our report. However, solely for the purpose of responding to your inquiry, we have read the draft of the financial statements of (name of component) as of (date) and for the (period of audit) and the draft of your report on them, included with your inquiry dated (date of inquiry).

---

[3] See section 9543.04–.07, "Inquiries of the Principal Auditor by the Other Auditor," above.

Based solely on the work we have performed (to date) in connection with our audit of the consolidated financial statements, which would not necessarily reveal all or any of the matters covered in your inquiry, we advise you that:

1. No transactions or other matters (including adjustments made during consolidation or contemplated at this date) have come to our attention that we believe require adjustment to or disclosure in the financial statements of (name of component) being audited by you.

2. No limitation has been placed by Parent Company on the scope of our audit that, to our knowledge, is related to the financial statements of (name of component) being audited by you, that has limited our ability to provide you with the information requested in your inquiry."

[Issue Date: April, 1979.]

5. Procedures of the Principal Auditor

.15 *Question*—What steps, if any, should the principal auditor take in responding to an inquiry such as that described in section 9543.11?

.16 *Interpretation*—The principal auditor's response should ordinarily be made by the auditor with final responsibility for the engagement. He should take those steps that he considers reasonable under the circumstances to be informed of known matters pertinent to the other auditor's inquiry. For example, the auditor with final responsibility may inquire of principal assistants[4] responsible for various aspects of the engagement or he may direct assistants to bring to his attention any significant matters of which they become aware during the audit. The principal auditor is not required to perform any procedures directed toward identifying matters that would not affect his audit or his report.

.17 If between the date of his response and the completion of his audit, the principal auditor becomes aware of information that he would have included in his response to the other auditor's inquiry had he been aware of it, the principal auditor should promptly communicate such information to the other auditor.[5]

[Issue Date: April, 1979.]

6. Application of Additional Procedures Concerning the Audit Performed by the Other Auditor

.18 *Question*—If a principal auditor decides not to make reference to the audit of another auditor, section 543 requires him to consider whether to apply procedures to obtain information about the adequacy of the audit performed by the other auditor. In making a decision about (*a*) whether to apply one or more of the procedures listed in section 543.12 and (*b*), if applicable, the extent of those procedures, may the principal auditor consider his knowledge of the other auditor's compliance with quality control policies and procedures?

.19 *Interpretation*—Yes. The principal auditor's judgment about the extent of additional procedures, if any, to be applied in the circumstances may be affected by various factors including his knowledge of the other auditor's qua-

---

[4] See section 311, *Planning and Supervision*, for the definition of "assistants."

[5] See section 561, *Subsequent Discovery of Facts Existing at the Date of the Auditor's Report*, concerning procedures to be followed by the other auditor if he receives the information after the issuance of his report.

lity control policies and procedures that provide the other auditor with reasonable assurance of conformity with generally accepted auditing standards in his audit engagements.

.20 Other factors that the principal auditor may wish to consider in making that decision include his previous experience with the other auditor, the materiality of the portion of the financial statements audited by the other auditor, the control exercised by the principal auditor over the conduct of the audit performed by the other auditor, and the results of the principal auditor's other procedures that may indicate whether additional evidential matter is necessary.

[Issue Date: December, 1981.]

[7.] Reporting on Financial Statements Presented on a Comprehensive Annual Financial Report of a Governmental Entity When One Fund Has Been Audited by Another Auditor

[.21–.24] [Withdrawn December, 1992 by the Audit Issues Task Force.][6], [7]

---

[6] [Footnote deleted.]

[7] [Footnote deleted.]

AU Section 544

Lack of Conformity With Generally Accepted Accounting Principles

Sources: SAS No. 1, section 544; SAS No. 2; SAS No. 62; SAS No. 77.

Issue date, unless otherwise indicated: November, 1972.

[.01] [Superseded by Statement on Auditing Standards No. 2, effective December 31, 1974.]

Regulated Companies

.02 The basic postulates and broad principles of accounting comprehended in the term "generally accepted accounting principles" which pertain to business enterprises in general apply also to companies whose accounting practices are prescribed by governmental regulatory authorities or commissions. (For example, public utilities and insurance companies.) Accordingly, the first reporting standard is equally applicable to opinions on financial statements of such regulated companies presented for purposes other than filings with their respective supervisory agencies; and material variances from generally accepted accounting principles, and their effects, should be dealt with in the independent auditor's report in the same manner followed for companies which are not regulated.[1] Ordinarily, this will require either a qualified or an adverse opinion on such statements. An adverse opinion may be accompanied by an opinion on supplementary data which are presented in conformity with generally accepted accounting principles. [As amended, effective periods ending on or after December 31, 1974, by Statement on Auditing Standards No. 2. As amended by Statement on Auditing Standards No. 62, effective for reports issued on or after July 1, 1989.]

.03 It should be recognized, however, that appropriate differences exist with respect to the application of generally accepted accounting principles as between regulated and nonregulated businesses because of the effect in regulated businesses of the rate-making process, a phenomenon not present in nonregulated businesses (FASB Statement No. 71, *Accounting for the Effects of Certain Types of Regulations* [AC section Re6]). Such differences usually concern mainly the time at which various items enter into the determination of net income in accordance with the principle of matching costs and revenues.

---

[1] When reporting on financial statements of a regulated entity that are prepared in accordance with the requirements of financial reporting provisions of a government regulatory agency to whose jurisdiction the entity is subject, the auditor may report on the financial statements as being prepared in accordance with a comprehensive basis of accounting other than generally accepted accounting principles (see section 623, *Special Reports*, paragraphs .02 and .10). Reports of this nature, however, should be issued only if the financial statements are intended solely for filing with one or more regulatory agencies to whose jurisdiction the entity is subject. [As amended, effective for audits of financial statements for periods ended on or after December 31, 1996, by Statement on Auditing Standards No. 77.]

It should also be recognized that accounting requirements not directly related to the rate-making process commonly are imposed on regulated businesses and that the imposition of such accounting requirements does not necessarily mean that they conform with generally accepted accounting principles.

.04 When financial statements of a regulated entity are prepared in accordance with a basis of accounting prescribed by one or more regulatory agencies or the financial reporting provisions of another agency, the independent auditor may also be requested to report on their fair presentation in conformity with such prescribed basis of accounting in presentations for distribution in other than filings with the entity's regulatory agency. In those circumstances, the auditor should use the standard form of report (see section 508, *Reports on Audited Financial Statements*, paragraph .08), modified as appropriate (see section 508.35–.60) because of the departures from generally accepted accounting principles, and then, in an additional paragraph to the report, express an opinion on whether the financial statements are presented in conformity with the prescribed basis of accounting. [As amended by Statement on Auditing Standards No. 62, effective for reports issued on or after July 1, 1989. As amended, effective for audits of financial statements for periods ended on or after December 31, 1996, by Statement on Auditing Standards No. 77.]

AU Section 550

Other Information in Documents Containing Audited Financial Statements

Source: SAS No. 8.

See section 9550 for interpretations of this section.

Issue date, unless otherwise indicated: December, 1975.

.01 An entity may publish various documents that contain information (hereinafter, "other information") in addition to audited financial statements and the independent auditor's report thereon. This section provides guidance for the auditor's consideration of other information included in such documents.

.02 This section is applicable only to other information contained in (*a*) annual reports to holders of securities or beneficial interests, annual reports of organizations for charitable or philanthropic purposes distributed to the public, and annual reports filed with regulatory authorities under the Securities Exchange Act of 1934 or (*b*) other documents to which the auditor, at the client's request, devotes attention.

.03 This section is not applicable when the financial statements and report appear in a registration statement filed under the Securities Act of 1933. The auditor's procedures with respect to 1933 Act filings are unaltered by this section (see sections 634[†] and 711[††]). Also, this section is not applicable to other information on which the auditor is engaged to express an opinion.[1] The guidance applicable to auditing and reporting on certain information other than financial statements intended to be presented in conformity with generally accepted accounting principles is unaltered by this section (see sections 551[*] and 623[**]).

.04 Other information in a document may be relevant to an audit performed by an independent auditor or to the continuing propriety of his report. The auditor's responsibility with respect to information in a document does not extend beyond the financial information identified in his report, and the auditor has no obligation to perform any procedures to corroborate other information contained in a document. However, he should read the other information and consider whether such information, or the manner of its presentation, is materially inconsistent with information, or the manner of its presentation, appearing in the financial statements.[2] If the auditor concludes

---

† [Reference number 631, formerly 630, changed by the issuance of Statement on Auditing Standards No. 38 (superseded). Reference number 634, formerly 631, changed by the issuance of Statement on Auditing Standards No. 49.] (See section 634.)

†† [Reference changed by issuance of Statement on Auditing Standards No. 37.] (See section 711.)

1 Mere reading of other information is an inadequate basis for expressing an opinion on that information.

* [Reference changed by issuance of Statement on Auditing Standards No. 29.] (See section 551.)

** [Reference changed by issuance of Statement on Auditing Standards No. 62.] (See section 623.)

2 In fulfilling his responsibility under this section, a principal auditor may also request the other auditor or auditors involved in the engagement to read the other information. If a predecessor auditor's report appears in a document to which this section applies, he should read the other information for the reasons described in this paragraph.

that there is a material inconsistency, he should determine whether the financial statements, his report, or both require revision. If he concludes that they do not require revision, he should request the client to revise the other information. If the other information is not revised to eliminate the material inconsistency, he should consider other actions such as revising his report to include an explanatory paragraph describing the material inconsistency, withholding the use of his report in the document, and withdrawing from the engagement. The action he takes will depend on the particular circumstances and the significance of the inconsistency in the other information.

.05 If, while reading the other information for the reasons set forth in paragraph .04, the auditor becomes aware of information that he believes is a material misstatement of fact that is not a material inconsistency as described in paragraph .04, he should discuss the matter with the client. In connection with this discussion, the auditor should consider that he may not have the expertise to assess the validity of the statement, that there may be no standards by which to assess its presentation, and that there may be valid differences of judgment or opinion. If the auditor concludes he has a valid basis for concern he should propose that the client consult with some other party whose advice might be useful to the client, such as the client's legal counsel.

.06 If, after discussing the matter as described in paragraph .05, the auditor concludes that a material misstatement of fact remains, the action he takes will depend on his judgment in the particular circumstances. He should consider steps such as notifying his client in writing of his views concerning the information and consulting his legal counsel as to further appropriate action in the circumstances.

AU Section 9550

Other Information in Documents Containing Audited Financial Statements: Auditing Interpretations of Section 550

[1.] Reports by Management on Internal Accounting Control[1–4]

[.01–.06] [Superseded May, 1994 by Interpretation Nos. 2 and 3, paragraphs .07–.15.]

2. Reports by Management on Internal Control Over Financial Reporting

.07 *Question*—Communications to various parties specified in section 550, *Other Information in Documents Containing Audited Financial Statements*, paragraph .02 may include a separate report by management containing an assertion about the effectiveness of the entity's internal control over financial reporting. What is the auditor's responsibility concerning such report?

.08 *Interpretation*—If the auditor has been engaged to examine and report on management's assertion, the guidance in AT section 400, *Reporting on an Entity's Internal Control Over Financial Reporting*, should be followed.

.09 If the auditor has not been engaged to examine and report on management's assertion, the auditor should follow the guidance in section 550, which states that "the auditor has no obligation to perform any procedures to corroborate other information contained in [such] a document." Under section 550, the auditor is required to read the report by management and consider whether it is materially inconsistent with information appearing in the financial statements and, as a result, he or she may become aware of a material misstatement of fact.[5]

.10 Although not required, the auditor may consider adding the following paragraph to the standard auditor's report: "We were not engaged to examine management's assertion about the effectiveness of [*name of entity's*] internal control over financial reporting as of [*date*] included in the accompanying [*title of management's report*] and, accordingly, we do not express an opinion thereon."

.11 Because an auditor is required to consider internal control in an audit of the financial statements, he or she would often be familiar with matters covered in a management report on internal control over financial reporting. As a result, the auditor may become aware of information that causes him or her to believe that management's assertion on the effectiveness of internal control over financial reporting contains a material misstatement of fact as described in section 550.[6] If the auditor becomes aware of information in the

---

[1–4] [Superseded May, 1994 by Interpretation Nos. 2 and 3, paragraphs .07–.15.]

[5] Unless information on internal control over financial reporting appears in the financial statements, which is not common, a management assertion on the effectiveness of internal control over financial reporting could not be inconsistent with information appearing in financial statements.

[6] For example, the auditor has communicated to management a material weakness in internal control over financial reporting and management states or implies there are no material weaknesses.

report by management that conflicts with his or her knowledge or understanding of such matters, he or she should discuss the information with the client. If, after discussions with the client, the auditor concludes that a material misstatement of fact exists, the auditor should follow the guidance in section 550.06.

[Issue Date: May, 1994.]

3. Other References by Management to Internal Control Over Financial Reporting, Including References to the Independent Auditor

.12 *Question*—Communications to various parties specified in section 550, *Other Information in Documents Containing Audited Financial Statements*, paragraph .02 may include a statement by management about the entity's internal control over financial reporting. Such documents may also refer to the independent auditor in circumstances other than when the auditor has been engaged to examine and report on management's assertion about the effectiveness of internal control over financial reporting. What is the auditor's responsibility in such circumstances?

.13 *Interpretation*—The auditor should follow the guidance in section 550, which states that "the auditor has no obligation to perform any procedures to corroborate other information contained in [such] a document." Under section 550, the auditor is required to read other information in documents containing audited financial statements and consider whether it is materially inconsistent with information appearing in the financial statements and, as a result, he or she may become aware of a material misstatement of fact. If the auditor becomes aware of information in the report by management that conflicts with his or her knowledge or understanding of such matters, he or she should discuss the information with the client. If, after discussions with the client, the auditor concludes that a material misstatement of fact exists, the auditor should follow the guidance in section 550.06.

.14 Generally, management may discuss its responsibility for internal control over financial reporting and report on its effectiveness. In reading such information, the auditor should evaluate specific references by management that deal with the auditor's consideration of internal control in planning and performing the audit of the financial statements, particularly if such reference would lead the reader to assume the auditor had performed more work than required under generally accepted auditing standards or would lead the reader to believe that the auditor was giving assurances on internal control. The auditor should also consider whether management's comment or statement uses the auditor's name in such a way as to indicate or imply that the auditor's involvement is greater than is supported by the facts.[7] If management misstates the auditor's responsibility for consideration of internal control over financial reporting, the auditor should discuss the matter with the client and consider whether any further action is needed in accordance with section 550.06.

.15 The auditing interpretation of section 325, *Communication of Internal Control Related Matters Noted in an Audit*, titled "Reporting on the Exis-

---

[7] For instance, management may report that "X Company's external auditors have reviewed the company's internal control in connection with their audit of the financial statements." Because AT section 400, *Reporting on an Entity's Internal Control Over Financial Reporting*, prohibits an engagement to review and report on management's assertion about the effectiveness of the entity's internal control over financial reporting, a statement by management that the auditors had "reviewed" the company's internal control would be inappropriate.

tence of Material Weaknesses" (section 9325.01–.07), permits an auditor to report to management that he or she has not become aware of any material weaknesses[8] during his or her audit of the financial statements, but requires such reports to be solely for the information and use of the entity's audit committee, management and others within the organization. If, however, management decides to include or refer to this communication in a general use document, the auditor should communicate to management the restrictions on use of the communication and the potential for such a statement to be misunderstood. For example, the fact that an audit has not disclosed any material weaknesses does not necessarily mean none exist since an audit of the financial statements does not constitute an examination of a management assertion about the effectiveness of internal control over financial reporting. If management refuses to make appropriate changes to the report, the auditor should advise management that he or she has not consented to the use of his or her name and should consider what other actions might be appropriate. In considering what actions, if any, may be appropriate in the circumstances, the auditor may wish to consult legal counsel.

[Issue Date: May, 1994.]

4. Other Information in Electronic Sites Containing Audited Financial Statements

.16 *Question*—An entity may make information available in public computer networks, such as the World Wide Web area of the Internet, an electronic bulletin board, the Securities and Exchange Commission's EDGAR system, or similar electronic venues (hereinafter, "electronic sites"). Information in electronic sites may include annual reports to shareholders, financial statements and other financial information, as well as press releases, product information and promotional material. When audited financial statements and the independent auditor's report thereon are included in an electronic site, what is the auditor's responsibility with respect to other information included in the electronic site?

.17 *Interpretation*—Electronic sites are a means of distributing information and are not "documents," as that term is used in section 550, *Other Information in Documents Containing Audited Financial Statements*. Thus, auditors are not required by section 550 to read information contained in electronic sites, or to consider the consistency of other information (as that term is used in section 550) in electronic sites with the original documents.

.18 Auditors may be asked by their clients to render professional services with respect to information in electronic sites. Such services, which might take different forms, are not contemplated by section 550. Other auditing or attestation standards may apply, for example, agreed-upon procedures pursuant to section 622, *Engagements to Apply Agreed-Upon Procedures to Specified Elements, Accounts, or Items of a Financial Statement*, or AT section 600, *Agreed-Upon Procedures Engagements*, depending on the nature of the service requested.

[Issue Date: March, 1997.]

---

[8] Section 325.17 prohibits a written communication that no reportable conditions were noted during the audit. If management reports that an auditor made an oral communication that no reportable conditions were noted during the audit, the auditor should follow the guidance in this paragraph.

.16 Question—An entity may make information available in electronic sites, such as the World Wide Web, and include in that information the audited financial statements. [illegible] electronic sites [illegible] information [illegible] in electronic [illegible] financial statements [illegible] other information [illegible] with respect to other information contained in the electronic site.

.18 Auditors may be asked by their clients to render professional services with respect to information in electronic sites. Such services, which might take various forms, are not contemplated by section 550. Other professional standards may apply, [illegible] depending on the nature of the service requested.

[Issue Date: March, 1997.]

[1] [illegible]

AU Section 551

Reporting on Information Accompanying the Basic Financial Statements in Auditor-Submitted Documents

(Supersedes section 610, "Long-Form Reports")[1]

Source: SAS No. 29; SAS No. 52.

Effective for auditors' reports dated on or after December 31, 1980, unless otherwise indicated.

.01 This section provides guidance on the form and content of reporting when an auditor submits to his client or to others a document that contains information in addition to the client's basic financial statements and the auditor's report thereon.

.02 The auditor's standard report covers the basic financial statements: balance sheet, statement of income, statement of retained earnings or changes in stockholders' equity, and statement of cash flows. The following presentations are considered part of the basic financial statements: descriptions of accounting policies, notes to financial statements, and schedules and explanatory material that are identified as being part of the basic financial statements. For purposes of this section, basic financial statements also include an individual basic financial statement, such as a balance sheet or statement of income and financial statements prepared in accordance with a comprehensive basis of accounting other than generally accepted accounting principles.

.03 The information covered by this section is presented outside the basic financial statements and is not considered necessary for presentation of financial position, results of operations, or cash flows in conformity with generally accepted accounting principles. Such information includes additional details or explanations of items in or related to the basic financial statements, consolidating information, historical summaries of items extracted from the basic financial statements, statistical data, and other material, some of which may be from sources outside the accounting system or outside the entity.

Reporting Responsibility

.04 When an auditor submits a document containing audited financial statements to his client or to others, he has a responsibility to report on all the information included in the document. On the other hand, when the auditor's report is included in a client-prepared document[2] and the auditor is not engaged to report on information accompanying the basic financial statements, his responsibility with respect to such information is described in (*a*) section

---

[1] This section also supersedes the March 1979 auditing interpretation, "Reports on Consolidated Financial Statements That Include Supplementary Consolidating Information".

[2] Client-prepared documents include financial reports prepared by the client but merely reproduced by the auditor on the client's behalf.

550, *Other Information in Documents Containing Audited Financial Statements*, and (*b*) other sections covering particular types of information or circumstances, such as section 558, *Required Supplementary Information*.

.05 An auditor's report on information accompanying the basic financial statements in an auditor-submitted document has the same objective as an auditor's report on the basic financial statements: to describe clearly the character of the auditor's work and the degree of responsibility the auditor is taking. Although the auditor may participate in the preparation of the accompanying information as well as the basic financial statements, both the statements and the accompanying information are representations of management.

.06 The following guidelines apply to an auditor's report on information accompanying the basic financial statements in an auditor-submitted document:

a. The report should state that the audit has been performed for the purpose of forming an opinion on the basic financial statements taken as a whole.

b. The report should identify the accompanying information. (Identification may be by descriptive title or page number of the document.)

c. The report should state that the accompanying information is presented for purposes of additional analysis and is not a required part of the basic financial statements.[3]

d. The report should include either an opinion on whether the accompanying information is fairly stated in all material respects in relation to the basic financial statements taken as a whole or a disclaimer of opinion, depending on whether the information has been subjected to the auditing procedures applied in the audit of the basic financial statements. The auditor may express an opinion on a portion of the accompanying information and disclaim an opinion on the remainder.

e. The report on the accompanying information may be added to the auditor's report on the basic financial statements or may appear separately in the auditor-submitted document.

.07 The purpose of an audit of basic financial statements in accordance with generally accepted auditing standards is to form an opinion on those statements taken as a whole. Nevertheless, an audit of basic financial statements often encompasses information accompanying those statements in an auditor-submitted document. Also, although an auditor has no obligation to apply auditing procedures to information presented outside the basic financial statements, he may choose to modify or redirect certain of the procedures to be applied in the audit of the basic financial statements so that he may express an opinion on the accompanying information in the manner described in paragraph .06.

.08 When reporting in this manner, the measurement of materiality is the same as that used in forming an opinion on the basic financial statements taken as a whole. Accordingly, the auditor need not apply procedures as extensive as would be necessary to express an opinion on the information taken by itself. Guidance applicable to the expression of an opinion on specified elements, accounts, or items of financial statements for the purpose of a separate presentation is provided in section 623.11–.18, *Special Reports*.

---

[3] The auditor may refer to any regulatory agency requirements applicable to the information presented.

.09 If the auditor concludes, on the basis of facts known to him, that any accompanying information is materially misstated in relation to the basic financial statements taken as a whole, he should discuss the matter with the client and propose appropriate revision of the accompanying information.[4] If the client will not agree to revision of the accompanying information, the auditor should either modify his report on the accompanying information and describe the misstatement or refuse to include the information in the document.

.10 The auditor should consider the effect of any modifications in his standard report when reporting on accompanying information. When the auditor expresses a qualified opinion on the basic financial statements, he should make clear the effects upon any accompanying information as well (see paragraph .14). When the auditor expresses an adverse opinion, or disclaims an opinion, on the basic financial statements, he should not express the opinion described in paragraph .06 on any accompanying information.[5] An expression of such an opinion in these circumstances would be inappropriate because, like a piecemeal opinion, it may tend to overshadow or contradict the disclaimer of opinion or adverse opinion on the basic financial statements. (See section 508.64 and section 623.14.)

.11 A client may request that nonaccounting information and certain accounting information not directly related to the basic financial statements be included in an auditor-submitted document. Ordinarily, such information would not have been subjected to the auditing procedures applied in the audit of the basic financial statements, and, accordingly, the auditor would disclaim an opinion on it. In some circumstances, however, such information may have been obtained or derived from accounting records that have been tested by the auditor (for example, number of units produced related to royalties under a license agreement or number of employees related to a given payroll period). Accordingly, the auditor may be in a position to express an opinion on such information in the manner described in paragraph .06.

Reporting Examples

.12 An example of reporting on information accompanying the basic financial statements in an auditor-submitted document follows:

> Our audit was conducted for the purpose of forming an opinion on the basic financial statements taken as a whole. The (identify accompanying information) is presented for purposes of additional analysis and is not a required part of the basic financial statements. Such information has been subjected to the auditing procedures applied in the audit of the basic financial statements and, in our opinion, is fairly stated in all material respects in relation to the basic financial statements taken as a whole.[6]

.13 When the auditor disclaims an opinion on all or part of the accompanying information in a document that he submits to his client or to others, such

---

[4] See paragraph .10 for guidance when there is a modification of the auditor's standard report on the basic financial statements.

[5] The provisions of this paragraph do not change the guidance, concerning companies whose accounting practices are prescribed by governmental regulatory authorities or commissions, in the last sentence of section 544.02, "Regulated Companies," which reads: "An adverse opinion may be accompanied by an opinion on supplementary data which are presented in conformity with generally accepted accounting principles."

[6] This form of reporting is not appropriate with respect to supplementary information required by the FASB (see paragraph .15).

information should either be marked as unaudited or should include a reference to the auditor's disclaimer of opinion. The wording of the disclaimer will vary according to the circumstances. Two examples follow.

Disclaimer on All of the Information

> Our audit was conducted for the purpose of forming an opinion on the basic financial statements taken as a whole. The (identify the accompanying information) is presented for purposes of additional analysis and is not a required part of the basic financial statements. Such information has not been subjected to the auditing procedures applied in the audit of the basic financial statements, and, accordingly, we express no opinion on it.

Disclaimer on Part of the Information

> Our audit was conducted for the purpose of forming an opinion on the basic financial statements taken as a whole. The information on pages XX—YY is presented for purposes of additional analysis and is not a required part of the basic financial statements. Such information, except for that portion marked "unaudited," on which we express no opinion, has been subjected to the auditing procedures applied in the audit of the basic financial statements; and, in our opinion, the information is fairly stated in all material respects in relation to the basic financial statements taken as a whole.

.14 An example follows of reporting on accompanying information to which a qualification in the auditor's report on the basic financial statements applies.

> Our audit was conducted for the purpose of forming an opinion on the basic financial statements taken as a whole. The schedules of investments (page 7), property (page 8), and other assets (page 9) as of December 31, 19XX, are presented for purposes of additional analysis and are not a required part of the basic financial statements. The information in such schedules has been subjected to the auditing procedures applied in the audit of the basic financial statements; and, in our opinion, except for the effects on the schedule of investments of not accounting for the investments in certain companies by the equity method as explained in the second preceding paragraph [second paragraph of our report on page 1], such information is fairly stated in all material respects in relation to the basic financial statements taken as a whole.

Supplementary Information Required by FASB or GASB Pronouncements

.15 When supplementary information required by the FASB or GASB is presented outside the basic financial statements in an auditor-submitted document, the auditor should disclaim an opinion on the information unless he has been engaged to examine and express an opinion on it.[7] The following is an example of a disclaimer an auditor might use in these circumstances:

> The [*identify the supplementary information*] on page XX is not a required part of the basic financial statements but is supplementary information required by the (Financial or Governmental) Accounting Standards Board. We have applied certain limited procedures, which consisted principally of inquiries of management regarding the methods of measurement and presentation of the supplementary information. However, we did not audit the information and express no opinion on it.

---

[7] The guidance in subsection (*b*) of this paragraph applies to GASB required supplementary information, such as that required by GASB Statement No. 5, *Disclosure of Pension Information by Public Employee Retirement Systems and State and Local Governmental Employers*. The auditor should refer to section 552, *Reporting on Condensed Financial Statements and Selected Financial Data*, paragraphs .09–.10, for an example of a report on GASB required supplementary information.

Also, the auditor's report should be expanded in accordance with section 558, *Required Supplementary Information*, paragraph .08, if (*a*) supplementary information that the FASB or GASB requires to be presented in the circumstances is omitted, (*b*) the auditor has concluded that the measurement or presentation of the supplementary information departs materially from guidelines prescribed by the FASB or GASB, (*c*) the auditor is unable to complete the procedures prescribed by section 558, or (*d*) the auditor is unable to remove substantial doubts about whether the supplementary information conforms to prescribed guidelines. [As amended, April 1988, by Statement on Auditing Standards No. 52.]

Consolidating Information

.16 Consolidated financial statements may include consolidating information or consolidating schedules presenting separate financial statements of one or more components of the consolidated group.[8] In some cases, the auditor is engaged to express an opinion on the financial statements of the components as well as on the consolidated financial statements. In other cases, the auditor is engaged to express an opinion only on the consolidated financial statements but consolidating information or schedules accompany the basic consolidated financial statements.

.17 When the auditor is engaged to express an opinion only on the consolidated financial statements and consolidating information is also included, the auditor should be satisfied that the consolidating information is suitably identified. For example, when the consolidated financial statements include columns of information about the components of the consolidated group, the balance sheets might be titled, "Consolidated Balance Sheet—December 31, 19X1, with Consolidated Information," and the columns including the consolidating information might be marked, "Consolidating Information." When the consolidating information is presented in separate schedules, the schedules presenting balance sheet information of the components might be titled, for example, "Consolidating Schedule, Balance Sheet Information, December 31, 19X1."

.18 When the consolidated financial statements include consolidating information that has not been separately audited, the auditor's report on the consolidating information might read

> Our audit was conducted for the purpose of forming an opinion on the consolidated financial statements taken as a whole. The consolidating information is presented for purposes of additional analysis of the consolidated financial statements rather than to present the financial position, results of operations, and cash flows of the individual companies. The consolidating information has been subjected to the auditing procedures applied in the audit of the consolidated financial statements and, in our opinion, is fairly stated in all material respects in relation to the consolidated financial statements taken as a whole.

.19 When the auditor is engaged to express an opinion on both the consolidated financial statements and the separate financial statements of the components presented in consolidating financial statements, the auditor's reporting responsibilities with respect to the separate financial statements are the same as his responsibilities with respect to the consolidated financial state-

---

[8] This section [paragraphs .16–.19] is also applicable to combined and combining financial statements.

ments. In such cases, the consolidating financial statements and accompanying notes should include all the disclosures that would be necessary for presentation in conformity with generally accepted accounting principles of separate financial statements of each component.

Additional Commentary Concerning the Audit

.20 The auditor may be requested to describe the procedures applied to specific items in the financial statements. Additional comments of this nature should not contradict or detract from the description of the scope of his audit in the standard report. Also, they should be set forth separately rather than interspersed with the information accompanying the basic financial statements to maintain a clear distinction between management's representations and the auditor's representations.

Co-existing Financial Statements

.21 More than one type of document containing the audited financial statements may exist. For example, the auditor may submit to his client or others a document containing the basic financial statements, other information, and his report thereon, and the client may issue a separate document containing only the basic financial statements and the auditor's report. The basic financial statements should include all the information considered necessary for presentation in conformity with generally accepted accounting principles in all co-existing documents. The auditor should be satisfied that information accompanying the basic financial statements in an auditor-submitted document would not support a contention that the basic financial statements in the other document were not presented in conformity with generally accepted accounting principles because of inadequate disclosure of material information known to the auditor.

Effective Date

.22 This section will be effective for auditors' reports dated on or after December 31, 1980.

AU Section 552

Reporting on Condensed Financial Statements and Selected Financial Data

Source: SAS No. 42; SAS No. 71.*

Effective for reports issued or reissued on or after January 1, 1989, on condensed financial statements or selected financial data unless otherwise indicated.

.01 This section provides guidance on reporting in a client-prepared document on—

a. Condensed financial statements (either for an annual or an interim period) that are derived from audited financial statements of a public entity[1] that is required to file, at least annually, complete audited financial statements with a regulatory agency.

b. Selected financial data that are derived from audited financial statements of either a public or a nonpublic entity and that are presented in a document that includes audited financial statements (or, with respect to a public entity, that incorporates audited financial statements by reference to information filed with a regulatory agency).

Guidance on reporting on condensed financial statements or selected financial data that accompany audited financial statements in an auditor-submitted document is provided in section 551, *Reporting on Information Accompanying the Basic Financial Statements in Auditor-Submitted Documents*.

.02 In reporting on condensed financial statements or selected financial data in circumstances other than those described in paragraph .01, the auditor should follow the guidance in section 508, *Reports on Audited Financial Statements*, paragraphs .41 through .44, section 623, *Special Reports*, or other applicable Statements on Auditing Standards.[2]

Condensed Financial Statements

.03 Condensed financial statements are presented in considerably less detail than complete financial statements that are intended to present financial position, results of operations, and cash flows in conformity with generally accepted accounting principles. For this reason, they should be read in conjunction with the entity's most recent complete financial statements that include all the disclosures required by generally accepted accounting principles.

---

* Section amended to reflect the conforming changes necessary due to the issuance of Statement on Auditing Standards Nos. 53 through 62.

[1] *Public entity* is defined in section 504, *Association With Financial Statements*, footnote 2.

[2] An auditor who has audited and reported on complete financial statements of a nonpublic entity may subsequently be requested to compile financial statements for the same period that omit substantially all disclosures required by generally accepted accounting principles. Reporting on comparative financial statements in those circumstances is described in SSARS 2, paragraphs 29–30 [AR section 200.29–.30].

.04 An auditor may be engaged to report on condensed financial statements that are derived from audited financial statements. Because condensed financial statements do not constitute a fair presentation of financial position, results of operations, and cash flows in conformity with generally accepted accounting principles, an auditor should not report on condensed financial statements in the same manner as he reported on the complete financial statements from which they are derived. To do so might lead users to assume, erroneously, that the condensed financial statements include all the disclosures necessary for complete financial statements. For the same reason, it is desirable that the condensed financial statements be so marked.

.05 In the circumstances described in paragraph .01(*a*),[3] the auditor's report on condensed financial statements that are derived from financial statements that he has audited should indicate (*a*) that the auditor has audited and expressed an opinion on the complete financial statements, (*b*) the date of the auditor's report on the complete financial statements,[4] (*c*) the type of opinion expressed, and (*d*) whether, in the auditor's opinion, the information set forth in the condensed financial statements is fairly stated in all material respects in relation to the complete financial statements from which it has been derived.[5]

.06 The following is an example of wording that an auditor may use in the circumstances described in paragraph .01(*a*) to report on condensed financial statements that are derived from financial statements that he has audited and on which he has issued a standard report:

Independent Auditor's Report

> We have audited, in accordance with generally accepted auditing standards, the consolidated balance sheet of X Company and subsidiaries as of December 31, 19X0, and the related consolidated statements of income, retained earnings, and cash flows for the year then ended (not presented herein); and in our report dated February 15, 19X1, we expressed an unqualified opinion on those consolidated financial statements.
>
> In our opinion, the information set forth in the accompanying condensed consolidated financial statements is fairly stated, in all material respects, in relation to the consolidated financial statements from which it has been derived.

---

[3] SEC regulations require certain registrants to include in filings, as a supplementary schedule to the consolidated financial statements, condensed financial information of the parent company. The auditor should report on such condensed financial information in the same manner as he reports on other supplementary schedules.

[4] Reference to the date of the original report removes any implication that records, transactions, or events after that date have been examined. The auditor does not have a responsibility to investigate or inquire further into events that may have occurred during the period between the date of the report on the complete financial statements and the date of the report on the condensed financial statements. (However, see section 711, *Filings Under Federal Securities Statutes*, regarding the auditor's responsibility when his report is included in a registration statement filed under the Securities Act of 1933.)

[5] If the auditor's opinion on the complete financial statements was other than unqualified, the report should describe the nature of, and the reasons for, the qualification. The auditor should also consider the effect that any modification of the report on the complete financial statements might have on the report on the condensed financial statements or selected financial data. For example, if the auditor's report on the complete financial statements referred to another auditor or included an explanatory paragraph because of a material uncertainty, a going concern matter, or an inconsistency in the application of accounting principles, the report on the condensed financial statements should state that fact. However, no reference to the inconsistency is necessary if a change in accounting referred to in the auditor's report on the complete financial statements does not affect the comparability of the information being presented.

.07 A client might make a statement in a client-prepared document that names the auditor and also states that condensed financial statements have been derived from audited financial statements. Such a statement does not, in itself, require the auditor to report on the condensed financial statements, provided that they are included in a document that contains audited financial statements (or that incorporates such statements by reference to information filed with a regulatory agency). However, if such a statement is made in a client-prepared document of a public entity that is required to file, at least annually, complete audited financial statements with a regulatory agency and that document does not include audited financial statements (or does not incorporate such statements by reference to information filed with a regulatory agency),[6] the auditor should request that the client either (*a*) not include the auditor's name in the document or (*b*), include the auditor's report on the condensed financial statements, as described in paragraph .05. If the client will neither delete the reference to the auditor nor allow the appropriate report to be included, the auditor should advise the client that he does not consent to either the use of his name or the reference to him, and he should consider what other actions might be appropriate.[7]

.08 Condensed financial statements derived from audited financial statements of a public entity may be presented on a comparative basis with interim financial information as of a subsequent date that is accompanied by the auditor's review report. In that case, the auditor should report on the condensed financial statements of each period in a manner appropriate for the type of service provided for each period. The following is an example of a review report on a condensed balance sheet as of March 31, 19X1, and the related con-

---

[6] If such a statement is made in a client-prepared document that does not include audited financial statements and the client is not a public entity that is required to file complete audited financial statements with a regulatory agency (at least annually), the auditor would ordinarily express an adverse opinion on the condensed financial statements because of inadequate disclosure. (See section 508, *Reports on Audited Financial Statements*, paragraphs .41 through .44.) The auditor would not be expected to provide the disclosure in his report. The following is an example of an auditor's report on condensed financial statements in such circumstances when the auditor had previously audited and reported on the complete financial statements:

Independent Auditor's Report

We have audited the consolidated balance sheet of X Company and subsidiaries as of December 31, 19X0, and the related earnings, and cash flows for the year then ended (not presented herein). These financial statements are the responsibility of the Company's management. Our responsibility is to express an opinion on these financial statements based on our audit.

We conducted our audit in accordance with generally accepted auditing standards. Those standards require that we plan and perform the audit to obtain reasonable assurance about whether the financial statements are free of material misstatement. An audit includes examining, on a test basis, evidence supporting the amounts and disclosures in the financial statements. An audit also includes assessing the accounting principles used and significant estimates made by management, as well as evaluating the overall financial statement presentation. We believe that our audit provides a reasonable basis for our opinion.

The condensed consolidated balance sheet as of December 31, 19X0, and the related condensed statements of income, retained earnings, and cash flows for the year then ended, presented on pages xx-xx, are presented as a summary and therefore do not include all of the disclosures required by generally accepted accounting principles.

In our opinion, because of the significance of the omission of the information referred to in the preceding paragraph, the condensed consolidated financial statements referred to above do not present fairly, in conformity with generally accepted accounting principles, the financial position of X Company and subsidiaries as of December 31, 19X0, or the results of its operations or its cash flows for the year then ended.

[7] In considering what other actions, if any, may be appropriate in these circumstances, the auditor may wish to consult his legal counsel.

densed statements of income and cash flows for the three-month periods ended March 31, 19X1 and 19X0, together with a report on a condensed balance sheet derived from audited financial statements as of December 31, 19X0, included in Form 10-Q:[8]

> We have reviewed the condensed consolidated balance sheet of ABC Company and subsidiaries as of March 31, 19X1, and the related condensed consolidated statements of income and cash flows for the three-month periods ended March 31, 19X1 and 19X0. These financial statements are the responsibility of the company's management.
>
> We conducted our review in accordance with standards established by the American Institute of Certified Public Accountants. A review of interim financial information consists principally of applying analytical procedures to financial data and making inquiries of persons responsible for financial and accounting matters. It is substantially less in scope than an audit conducted in accordance with generally accepted auditing standards, the objective of which is the expression of an opinion regarding the financial statements taken as a whole. Accordingly, we do not express such an opinion.
>
> Based on our review, we are not aware of any material modifications that should be made to the condensed consolidated financial statements referred to above for them to be in conformity with generally accepted accounting principles.
>
> We have previously audited, in accordance with generally accepted auditing standards, the consolidated balance sheet as of December 31, 19X0, and the related consolidated statements of income, retained earnings, and cash flows for the year then ended (not presented herein); and in our report dated February 15, 19X1, we expressed an unqualified opinion on those consolidated financial statements. In our opinion, the information set forth in the accompanying condensed consolidated balance sheet as of December 31, 19X0, is fairly stated, in all material respects, in relation to the consolidated balance sheet from which it has been derived.

[Paragraph amended to reflect the conforming changes necessary due to the issuance of Statement on Auditing Standards No. 71.]

Selected Financial Data

.09 An auditor may be engaged to report on selected financial data that are included in a client-prepared document that contains audited financial statements (or, with respect to a public entity, that incorporates such statements by reference to information filed with a regulatory agency). Selected financial data are not a required part of the basic financial statements, and the entity's management is responsible for determining the specific selected finan-

---

[8] Regulation S-X specifies that the following financial information should be provided in filings on Form 10-Q:

a. An interim balance sheet as of the end of the most recent fiscal quarter and a balance sheet (which may be condensed to the same extent as the interim balance sheet) as of the end of the preceding fiscal year.

b. Interim condensed statements of income for the most recent fiscal quarter, for the period between the end of the preceding fiscal year and the end of the most recent fiscal quarter, and for the corresponding periods of the preceding fiscal year.

c. Interim condensed cash flow statements for the period between the end of the preceding fiscal year and the end of the most recent fiscal quarter and for the corresponding period for the preceding fiscal year.

This financial information need not be audited, and, accordingly, there is no requirement for an auditor to report on condensed financial statements contained in Form 10-Q. If the auditor has made a review of interim financial information, however, he may agree to the reference to his name and the inclusion of his review report in a Form 10-Q. (See section 722, *Interim Financial Information*, paragraph .35.) [Reference changed by the issuance of Statement on Auditing Standards No. 71.]

cial data to be presented.[9] If the auditor is engaged to report on the selected financial data, his report should be limited to data that are derived from audited financial statements (which may include data that are calculated from amounts presented in the financial statements, such as working capital). If the selected financial data that management presents include both data derived from audited financial statements and other information (such as number of employees or square footage of facilities), the auditor's report should specifically identify the data on which he is reporting. The report should indicate (*a*) that the auditor has audited and expressed an opinion on the complete financial statements, (*b*) the type of opinion expressed,[10] and (*c*) whether, in the auditor's opinion, the information set forth in the selected financial data is fairly stated in all material respects in relation to the complete financial statements from which it has been derived.[11] If the selected financial data for any of the years presented are derived from financial statements that were audited by another independent auditor, the report on the selected financial data should state that fact, and the auditor should not express an opinion on that data.

.10 The following is an example of an auditor's report that includes an additional paragraph because he is also engaged to report on selected financial data for a five-year period ended December 31, 19X5, in a client-prepared document that includes audited financial statements:

Independent Auditor's Report

> We have audited the consolidated balance sheets of ABC Company and subsidiaries as of December 31, 19X5 and 19X4, and the related consolidated statements of income, retained earnings, and cash flows for each of the three years in the period ended December 31, 19X5. These financial statements are the responsibility of the Company's management. Our responsibility is to express an opinion on these financial statements based on our audit.
>
> We conducted our audits in accordance with generally accepted auditing standards. Those standards require that we plan and perform the audit to obtain reasonable assurance about whether the financial statements are free of material misstatement. An audit includes examining, on a test basis, evidence supporting the amounts and disclosures in the financial statements. An audit also includes assessing the accounting principles used and significant estimates made by management, as well as evaluating the overall financial statement presentation. We believe that our audits provided a reasonable basis for our opinion.
>
> In our opinion, the consolidated financial statements referred to above present fairly, in all material respects, the financial position of the ABC Company and subsidiaries as of December 31, 19X5 and 19X4, and the results of their operations and their cash flows for each of the three years in the period ended December 31, 19X5, in conformity with generally accepted accounting principles.

---

[9] Under regulations of the SEC, certain reports must include, for each of the last five fiscal years, selected financial data in accordance with regulation S-K, including net sales or operating revenues, income or loss from continuing operations, income or loss from continuing operations per common share, total assets, long-term obligations and redeemable preferred stock and cash dividends declared per common share. Registrants may include additional items that they believe may be useful. There is no SEC requirement for the auditor to report on selected financial data.

[10] See footnote 5.

[11] Nothing in this section is intended to preclude an auditor from expressing an opinion on one or more specified elements, accounts, or items of a financial statement, providing the provisions of section 623, *Special Reports*, are observed.

We have also previously audited, in accordance with generally accepted auditing standards, the consolidated balance sheets as of December 31, 19X3, 19X2, and 19X1, and the related statements of income, retained earnings, and cash flows for the years ended December 31, 19X2, and 19X1 (none of which are presented herein); and we expressed unqualified opinions on those consolidated financial statements. In our opinion, the information set forth in the selected financial data for each of the five years in the period ended December 31, 19X5, appearing on page xx, is fairly stated, in all material respects, in relation to the consolidated financial statements from which it has been derived.

.11 In introductory material regarding the selected financial data included in a client-prepared document, an entity might name the independent auditor and state that the data are derived from financial statements that he audited. Such a statement does not, in itself, require the auditor to report on the selected financial data, provided that the selected financial data are presented in a document that contains audited financial statements (or, with respect to a public entity, that incorporates such statements by reference to information filed with a regulatory agency). If such a statement is made in a document that does not include (or incorporate by reference) audited financial statements, the auditor should request that neither his name nor reference to him be associated with the information, or he should disclaim an opinion on the selected financial data and request that the disclaimer be included in the document. If the client does not comply, the auditor should advise the client that he does not consent to either the use of his name or the reference to him, and he should consider what other actions might be appropriate.[12]

Effective Date

.12 This section is effective for reports issued or reissued on or after January 1, 1989. Earlier application of the provision of this section is permissible.

---

[12] See footnote 7.

AU Section 558

Required Supplementary Information

(Supersedes section 553)*

Source: SAS No. 52.

See section 9558 for interpretations of this section.

Issue date, unless otherwise indicated: April, 1988.

.01 The Financial Accounting Standards Board (FASB) and Governmental Accounting Standards Board (GASB) develop standards for financial reporting, including standards for financial statements and for certain other information supplementary to financial statements.[1] This section provides the independent auditor with guidance on the nature of procedures to be applied to supplementary information required by the FASB or GASB, and describes the circumstances that would require the auditor to report such information.

Applicability

.02 This section is applicable in an audit in accordance with generally accepted auditing standards of financial statements included in a document that should contain supplementary information required by the FASB or GASB

---

* This section also withdraws the following Statements on Auditing Standards:

- Statement on Auditing Standards No. 28, *Supplementary Information on the Effects of Changing Prices* [Formerly section 554].
- Statement on Auditing Standards No. 40, *Supplementary Mineral Reserve Information* [Formerly section 556].
- Statement on Auditing Standards No. 45, *Supplementary Oil and Gas Reserve Information* [Formerly section 557].

SAS No. 45 was reissued as an auditing interpretation, see section 9558.01–.06.

[1] The FASB and GASB's roles in setting standards for financial reporting have been recognized by the AICPA Council. The FASB's authority to establish standards for disclosure of financial information outside of the basic financial statements is described in the following resolution:

> That as of (September 19, 1987), the FASB, in respect of statements of financial accounting standards finally adopted by such board in accordance with its rules of procedure and the bylaws of the Financial Accounting Foundation, be, and hereby is, designated by this Council as the body to establish accounting principles pursuant to rule 203 and standards on disclosure of financial information for such entities outside financial statements in published financial reports containing financial statements under rule 202 of the *Rules of the Code of Professional Conduct* of the American Institute of Certified Public Accountants provided, however, any accounting research bulletins, or opinions of the accounting principles board issued or approved for exposure by the accounting principles board prior to April 1, 1973, and finally adopted by such board on or before June 30, 1973, shall constitute statements of accounting principles promulgated by a body designated by Council as contemplated in rule 203 of the *Rules of the Code of Professional Conduct* unless and until such time as they are expressly superseded by action of the FASB.

The GASB's authority to establish standards for financial reporting is described in the following resolution:

> That as of (September 19, 1987), the GASB, with respect to statements of governmental accounting standards adopted and issued in July 1984 and subsequently in accordance with its rules of procedure and the bylaws of the FASB, be, and hereby is, designated by the Council of the American Institute of Certified Public Accountants as the body to establish financial accounting principles for state and local governmental entities pursuant to rule 203, and standards on disclosure of financial information for such entities outside financial statements in published financial reports containing financial statements under rule 202.

However, this section is not applicable if the auditor has been engaged to audit such supplementary information.[2]

.03 Some entities may voluntarily include, in documents containing audited financial statements, certain supplementary information that is required of other entities. When an entity voluntarily includes such information as a supplement to the financial statements or in an unaudited note to the financial statements, the provisions of this section are applicable unless either the entity indicates that the auditor has not applied the procedures described in this section or the auditor includes in an explanatory paragraph in his report on the audited financial statements a disclaimer on the information.[3] The following is an example of a disclaimer an auditor might use in these circumstances:

> The [*identify the supplementary information*] on page XX (or in Note XX) is not a required part of the basic financial statements, and we did not audit or apply limited procedures to such information and do not express any assurances on such information.

When the auditor does not apply the procedures described in this section to a voluntary presentation of required supplementary information required for other entities, the provisions of section 550, apply.

Involvement With Information Outside Financial Statements

.04 The objective of an audit of financial statements in accordance with generally accepted auditing standards is the expression of an opinion on such statements. The auditor has no responsibility to audit information outside the basic financial statements in accordance with generally accepted auditing standards. However, the auditor does have certain responsibilities with respect to information outside the financial statements. The nature of the auditor's responsibility varies with the nature of both the information and the document containing the financial statements.

.05 The auditor's responsibility for other information not required by the FASB or GASB but included in certain annual reports—which are client-prepared documents[4]—is specified in section 550. The auditor's responsibility for information outside the basic financial statements in documents that the auditor submits to the client or to others is specified in section 551. The auditor's responsibility for supplementary information required by the FASB or GASB (called *required supplementary information*) is discussed in the paragraphs that follow.

Involvement With Required Supplementary Information

.06 Required supplementary information differs from other types of information outside the basic financial statements because the FASB or GASB con-

---

[2] This section is not applicable to entities that voluntarily present supplementary information not required by the FASB or GASB. For example, entities that voluntarily present supplementary information on the effects of inflation and changes in specific prices, formerly required by FASB Statement No. 33, *Financial Reporting and Changing Prices*, are guided by section 550, *Other Information in Documents Containing Audited Financial Statements*.

[3] When supplementary information is presented in an auditor-submitted document outside the basic financial statements, the guidance in section 551, *Reporting on Information Accompanying the Basic Financial Statements in Auditor-Submitted Documents*, as amended by SAS No. 52, *Omnibus Statement on Auditing Standards—1987*, should be followed.

[4] Client-prepared documents include financial reports prepared by the client but merely reproduced by the auditor on the client's behalf.

siders the information an essential part of the financial reporting of certain entities and because authoritative guidelines for the measurement and presentation of the information have been established. Accordingly, the auditor should apply certain limited procedures to required supplementary information and should report deficiencies in, or the omission of, such information.

Procedures

.07 The auditor should consider whether supplementary information is required by the FASB or GASB in the circumstances. If supplementary information is required, the auditor ordinarily should apply the following procedures to the information.[5]

a. Inquire of management about the methods of preparing the information, including (1) whether it is measured and presented within prescribed guidelines, (2) whether methods of measurement or presentation have been changed from those used in the prior period and the reasons for any such changes, and (3) any significant assumptions or interpretations underlying the measurement or presentation.

b. Compare the information for consistency with (1) management's responses to the foregoing inquiries, (2) audited financial statements,[6] and (3) other knowledge obtained during the examination of the financial statements.

c. Consider whether representations on required supplementary information should be included in specific written representations obtained from management (section 333A, *Client Representations*).

d. Apply additional procedures, if any, that other statements, interpretations, guides, or statements of position prescribe for specific types of required supplementary information.

e. Make additional inquiries if application of the foregoing procedures causes the auditor to believe that the information may not be measured or presented within applicable guidelines.

Circumstances Requiring Reporting on Required Supplementary Information

.08 Since the supplementary information is not audited and is not a required part of the basic financial statements, the auditor need not add an explanatory paragraph to his report on the audited financial statements to refer to the supplementary information or to his limited procedures, except in any of the following circumstances:[7] (*a*) the supplementary information that

---

[5] These procedures are also appropriate when the auditor is involved with voluntary presentations of such information required for other entities (see paragraph .03).

[6] GASB Statement No. 5, *Disclosure of Pension Information by Public Employee Retirement Systems and State and Local Governmental Employers*, requires presentation of certain 10-year historical trend information relating to pension activities as supplementary information outside the basic financial statements. Such information is generally derived from financial statements. If such required supplementary information has been derived from audited financial statements and is presented outside the basic financial statements in an auditor-submitted document, the auditor may report on this information as indicated in section 552, *Reporting on Condensed Financial Statements and Selected Financial Data*, paragraph .10.

[7] When required supplementary information is presented outside the basic financial statements in an auditor-submitted document, the auditor should disclaim an opinion on the information unless he has been engaged to examine and express an opinion on it (see section 551.15).

the FASB or GASB requires to be presented in the circumstances is omitted; (*b*) the auditor has concluded that the measurement or presentation of the supplementary information departs materially from prescribed guidelines; (*c*) the auditor is unable to complete the prescribed procedures; (*d*) the auditor is unable to remove substantial doubts about whether the supplementary information conforms to prescribed guidelines. Since the required supplementary information does not change the standards of financial accounting and reporting used for the preparation of the entity's basic financial statements, the circumstances described above do not affect the auditor's opinion on the fairness of presentation of such financial statements in conformity with generally accepted accounting principles. Furthermore, the auditor need not present the supplementary information if it is omitted by the entity. The following are examples of additional explanatory paragraphs an auditor might use in these circumstances.

Omission of Required Supplementary Information

The (Company or Governmental Unit) has not presented [*describe the supplementary information required by the FASB or GASB in the circumstances*] that the (Financial or Governmental) Accounting Standards Board has determined is necessary to supplement, although not required to be part of, the basic financial statements.

Material Departures From Guidelines

The [*specifically identify the supplementary information*] on page XX is not a required part of the basic financial statements, and we did not audit and do not express an opinion on such information. However, we have applied certain limited procedures, which consisted principally of inquiries of management regarding the methods of measurement and presentation of the supplementary information. As a result of such limited procedures, we believe that the [*specifically identify the supplementary information*] is not in conformity with guidelines established by the (Financial or Governmental) Accounting Standards Board because [*describe the material departure(s) from the FASB or GASB guidelines*].

Prescribed Procedures Not Completed

The [*specifically identify the supplementary information*] on page XX is not a required part of the basic financial statements, and we did not audit and do not express an opinion on such information. Further, we were unable to apply to the information certain procedures prescribed by professional standards because [*state the reasons*].

Unresolved Doubts About Adherence to Guidelines

The [*specifically identify the supplementary information*] on page XX is not a required part of the basic financial statements, and we did not audit and do not express an opinion on such information. However, we have applied certain limited procedures prescribed by professional standards that raised doubts that we were unable to resolve regarding whether material modifications should be made to the information for it to conform with guidelines established by the (Financial or Governmental) Accounting Standards Board. [*The auditor should consider including in his report the reason(s) he was unable to resolve his substantial doubts.*]

Even though he is unable to complete the prescribed procedures, if, on the basis of facts known to him, the auditor concludes that the supplementary information has not been measured or presented within prescribed guidelines, he should suggest appropriate revision; failing that, he should describe the nature of any material departure(s) in his report.

.09 If the entity includes with the supplementary information an indication that the auditor performed any procedures regarding the information without also indicating that the auditor does not express an opinion on the information presented, the auditor's report on the audited financial statements should be expanded to include a disclaimer on the information.

.10 Ordinarily, the required supplementary information should be distinct from the audited financial statements and distinguished from other information outside the financial statements that is not required by the FASB or GASB. However, management may choose not to place the required supplementary information outside the basic financial statements. In such circumstances, the information should be clearly marked as unaudited. If the information is not clearly marked as unaudited, the auditor's report on the audited financial statements should be expanded to include a disclaimer on the supplementary information.

AU Section 9558

Required Supplementary Information: Auditing Interpretations of Section 558

1. Supplementary Oil and Gas Reserve Information

.01 *Question*—FASB Statement No. 69, *Disclosures about Oil and Gas Producing Activities* [AC section Oi5], which amended FASB Statement No. 19, *Financial Accounting and Reporting by Oil and Gas Producing Companies* [AC section Oi5], and FASB Statement No. 25, *Suspension of Certain Accounting Requirements for Oil and Gas Producing Companies* [AC section Oi5], requires publicly traded entities that have significant oil and gas producing activities to include, with complete sets of annual financial statements, disclosures of proved oil and gas reserve quantities, changes in reserve quantities, a standardized measure of discounted future net cash flows relating to reserve quantities, and changes in the standardized measure. In documents filed with the Securities and Exchange Commission (SEC), Regulation S-K requires that the disclosures related to annual periods be presented for each annual period for which an income statement is required and the disclosures as of the end of an annual period be presented as of the date of each audited balance sheet required. These disclosures are considered to be supplementary information and may be presented outside the basic financial statements. In these circumstances, should the auditor consider the provisions of section 558, *Required Supplementary Information*?

.02 *Interpretation*—Yes. Also, in addition to the provisions of section 558, the auditor should also consider the provisions of this Interpretation.

.03 Estimating oil and gas reserves is a complex process requiring the knowledge and experience of a reservoir engineer. In general, the quality of the estimate of proved reserves for an individual reservoir depends on the availability, completeness, and accuracy of data needed to develop the estimate and on the experience and judgment of the reservoir engineer. Estimates of proved reserves inevitably change over time as additional data become available and are taken into account. The magnitude of changes in these estimates is often substantial. Because oil and gas reserve estimates are more imprecise than most estimates that are made in preparing financial statements, entities are encouraged to explain the imprecise nature of such reserve estimates.

.04 In applying the procedures specified in section 558, the auditor's inquiries should be directed to management's understanding of the specific requirements for disclosure of the supplementary oil and gas reserve information, including—

a. The factors considered in determining the reserve quantity information to be reported, such as including in the information (1) quantities of all domestic and foreign proved oil and gas reserves owned by the entity net of interests of others, (2) reserves attributable to consolidated subsidiaries, (3) a proportionate share of reserves of investees that are proportionately consolidated, and (4) reserves relating to royalty interests owned.

b. The separate disclosure of items such as (1) the entity's share of oil and gas produced from royalty interests for which reserve quantity information is unavailable, (2) reserves subject to long-term agreements with governments or authorities in which the entity participates in the operation or otherwise serves as producer, (3) the entity's proportional interest in reserves of investees accounted for by the equity method, (4) subsequent events, important economic factors, or significant uncertainties affecting particular components of the reserve quantity information, (5) whether the entity's reserves are located entirely within its home country, and (6) whether certain named governments restrict the disclosure of reserves or require that the reserve estimates include reserves other than proved.

c. The factors considered in determining the standardized measure of discounted future net cash flows to be reported.

.05 In addition, the auditor should also—

a. Inquire about whether the person who estimated the entity's reserve quantity information has appropriate qualifications.[1]

b. Compare the entity's recent production with its reserve estimates for properties that have significant production or significant reserve quantities and inquire about disproportionate ratios.

c. Compare the entity's reserve quantity information with the corresponding information used for depletion and amortization, and make inquiries when differences exist.

d. Inquire about the calculation of the standardized measure of discounted future net cash flows. These inquiries might include matters such as whether—

i. The prices used to develop future cast inflows from estimated production of the proved reserves are based on prices received at the end of the entity's fiscal year, and whether the calculation of future cash inflows appropriately reflects the terms of sales contracts and applicable governmental laws and regulations.

ii. The entity's estimate of the nature and timing of future development of the proved reserves and the future rates of production are consistent with available development plans.

iii. The entity's estimates of future development and production costs are based on year-end costs and assumed continuation of existing economic conditions.

iv. Future income tax expenses have been computed using the appropriate year-end statutory tax rates, with consideration of future tax rates already legislated, after giving effect to the tax basis of the properties involved, permanent differences, and tax credits and allowances.

v. The future net cash flows have been appropriately discounted.

vi. With respect to full cost companies, the estimated future development costs are consistent with the corresponding amounts used for depletion and amortization purposes.

---

[1] For example, the Society of Petroleum Engineers has prepared "Standards Pertaining to the Estimating and Auditing of Oil and Gas Reserve Information," which indicate that a reserve estimator would normally be considered to be qualified if he or she (1) has a minimum of three years' practical experience in petroleum engineering or petroleum production geology, with at least one year of such experience being in the estimation and evaluation of reserve information; and (2) either (*a*) has obtained, from a college or university of recognized stature, a bachelor's or advanced degree in petroleum engineering, geology, or other discipline of engineering or physical science or (*b*) has received, and is maintaining in good standing, a registered or certified professional engineer's license or a registered or certified professional geologist's license, or the equivalent thereof, from an appropriate governmental authority or professional organization.

vii. With respect to the disclosure of changes in the standardized measure of discounted future net cash flows, the entity has computed and presented the sources of the changes in conformity with the requirements of FASB Statement No. 69 [AC section Oi5].

e. Inquire about whether the methods and bases for estimating the entity's reserve information are documented and whether the information is current.

.06 If the auditor believes that the information may not be presented within the applicable guidelines, section 558 indicates that he ordinarily should make additional inquires. However, because of the nature of estimates of oil and gas reserve information, the auditor may not be in a position to evaluate the responses to such additional inquiries and, thus, will need to report this limitation on the procedures prescribed by professional standards. The following is an example that illustrates reporting on oil and gas reserve information in that event.

> The oil and gas reserve information is not a required part of the basic financial statements, and we did not audit and do not express an opinion on such information. However, we have applied certain limited procedures prescribed by professional standards that raised doubts that we were unable to resolve regarding whether material modifications should be made to the information for it to conform with guidelines established by the Financial Accounting Standards Board. [The auditor should consider including in his report the reason(s) why he was unable to resolve his doubts. For example, the auditor may wish to state that the information was estimated by a person lacking appropriate qualifications.]

[Issue Date: February, 1989.]

AU Section 560

Subsequent Events

Sources: SAS No. 1, section 560; SAS No. 12.

Issue date, unless otherwise indicated: November, 1972.

.01 An independent auditor's report ordinarily is issued in connection with historical financial statements that purport to present financial position at a stated date and results of operations and cash flows for a period ended on that date. However, events or transactions sometimes occur subsequent to the balance-sheet date, but prior to the issuance of the financial statements and auditor's report, that have a material effect on the financial statements and therefore require adjustment or disclosure in the statements. These occurrences hereinafter are referred to as "subsequent events."

.02 Two types of subsequent events require consideration by management and evaluation by the independent auditor.

.03 The first type consists of those events that provide additional evidence with respect to conditions that existed at the date of the balance sheet and affect the estimates inherent in the process of preparing financial statements. All information that becomes available prior to the issuance of the financial statements should be used by management in its evaluation of the conditions on which the estimates were based. The financial statements should be adjusted for any changes in estimates resulting from the use of such evidence.

.04 Identifying events that require adjustment of the financial statements under the criteria stated above calls for the exercise of judgment and knowledge of the facts and circumstances. For example, a loss on an uncollectible trade account receivable as a result of a customer's deteriorating financial condition leading to bankruptcy subsequent to the balance-sheet date would be indicative of conditions existing at the balance-sheet date, thereby calling for adjustment of the financial statements before their issuance. On the other hand, a similar loss resulting from a customer's major casualty such as a fire or flood subsequent to the balance-sheet date would not be indicative of conditions existing at the balance-sheet date and adjustment of the financial statements would not be appropriate. The settlement of litigation for an amount different from the liability recorded in the accounts would require adjustment of the financial statements if the events, such as personal injury or patent infringement, that gave rise to the litigation had taken place prior to the balance-sheet date.

.05 The second type consists of those events that provide evidence with respect to conditions that did not exist at the date of the balance sheet being reported on but arose subsequent to that date. These events should not result in adjustment of the financial statements.[1] Some of these events, however, may be of such a nature that disclosure of them is required to keep the financial statements from being misleading. Occasionally such an event may be so significant that disclosure can best be made by supplementing the historical fi-

---

[1] This paragraph is not intended to preclude giving effect in the balance sheet, with appropriate disclosure, to stock dividends or stock splits or reverse splits consummated after the balance-sheet date but before issuance of the financial statements.

nancial statements with pro forma financial data giving effect to the event as if it had occurred on the date of the balance sheet. It may be desirable to present pro forma statements, usually a balance sheet only, in columnar form on the face of the historical statements.

.06 Examples of events of the second type that require disclosure to the financial statements (but should not result in adjustment) are:

a. Sale of a bond or capital stock issue.

b. Purchase of a business.

c. Settlement of litigation when the event giving rise to the claim took place subsequent to the balance-sheet date.

d. Loss of plant or inventories as a result of fire or flood.

e. Losses on receivables resulting from conditions (such as a customer's major casualty) arising subsequent to the balance-sheet date.

.07 Subsequent events affecting the realization of assets such as receivables and inventories or the settlement of estimated liabilities ordinarily will require adjustment of the financial statements (see paragraph .03) because such events typically represent the culmination of conditions that existed over a relatively long period of time. Subsequent events such as changes in the quoted market prices of securities ordinarily should not result in adjustment of the financial statements (see paragraph .05) because such changes typically reflect a concurrent evaluation of new conditions.

.08 When financial statements are reissued, for example, in reports filed with the Securities and Exchange Commission or other regulatory agencies, events that require disclosure in the reissued financial statements to keep them from being misleading may have occurred subsequent to the original issuance of the financial statements. Events occurring between the time of original issuance and reissuance of financial statements should not result in adjustment of the financial statements[2] unless the adjustment meets the criteria for the correction of an error or the criteria for prior period adjustments set forth in Opinions of the Accounting Principles Board[*] Similarly, financial statements reissued in comparative form with financial statements of subsequent periods should not be adjusted for events occurring subsequent to the original issuance unless the adjustment meets the criteria stated above.

.09 Occasionally, a subsequent event of the second type has such a material impact on the entity that the auditor may wish to include in his report an explanatory paragraph directing the reader's attention to the event and its effects. (See section 508.19.)

Auditing Procedures in the Subsequent Period

.10 There is a period after the balance-sheet date with which the auditor must be concerned in completing various phases of his audit. This period is known as the "subsequent period" and is considered to extend to the date of the auditor's report. Its duration will depend upon the practical requirements of each audit and may vary from a relatively short period to one of several months. Also, all auditing procedures are not carried out at the same time and some phases of an audit will be performed during the subsequent period, whereas other phases will be substantially completed on or before the balance-

[2] However, see paragraph .05 as to the desirability of presenting pro forma financial statements to supplement the historical financial statements in certain circumstances.

[*] See also Statement of Financial Accounting Standards No. 16, *Prior Period Adjustments* (AC section A35).

sheet date. As an audit approaches completion, the auditor will be concentrating on the unresolved auditing and reporting matters and he is not expected to be conducting a continuing review of those matters to which he has previously applied auditing procedures and reached satisfaction.

.11 Certain specific procedures are applied to transactions occurring after the balance-sheet date such as (*a*) the examination of data to assure that proper cutoffs have been made and (*b*) the examination of data which provide information to aid the auditor in his evaluation of the assets and liabilities as of the balance-sheet date.

.12 In addition, the independent auditor should perform other auditing procedures with respect to the period after the balance-sheet date for the purpose of ascertaining the occurrence of subsequent events that may require adjustment or disclosure essential to a fair presentation of the financial statements in conformity with generally accepted accounting principles. These procedures should be performed at or near the completion of the field work. The auditor generally should:

a. Read the latest available interim financial statements; compare them with the financial statements being reported upon; and make any other comparisons considered appropriate in the circumstances. In order to make these procedures as meaningful as possible for the purpose expressed above, the auditor should inquire of officers and other executives having responsibility for financial and accounting matters as to whether the interim statements have been prepared on the same basis as that used for the statements under audit.

b. Inquire of and discuss with officers and other executives having responsibility for financial and accounting matters (limited where appropriate to major locations) as to:

  (i) Whether any substantial contingent liabilities or commitments existed at the date of the balance sheet being reported on or at the date of inquiry.

  (ii) Whether there was any significant change in the capital stock, long-term debt, or working capital to the date of inquiry.

  (iii) The current status of items, in the financial statements being reported on, that were accounted for on the basis of tentative, preliminary, or inconclusive data.

  (iv) Whether any unusual adjustments had been made during the period from the balance-sheet date to the date of inquiry.

c. Read the available minutes of meetings of stockholders, directors, and appropriate committees; as to meetings for which minutes are not available, inquire about matters dealt with at such meetings.

d. Inquire of client's legal counsel concerning litigation, claims, and assessments. [As amended, January 1976, by Statement on Auditing Standards No. 12.] (See section 337.)

e. Obtain a letter of representations, dated as of the date of the auditor's report, from appropriate officials, generally the chief executive officer and chief financial officer, as to whether any events occurred subsequent to the date of the financial statements being reported on by the independent auditor that in the officer's opinion would require adjustment or disclosure in these statements. The auditor may elect to have the client include representations as to significant matters disclosed to the auditor in his performance of the procedures in subparagraphs (*a*) to (*d*) above and (*f*) below. (See section 333A, *Client Representations*.)

f. Make such additional inquiries or perform such procedures as he considers necessary and appropriate to dispose of questions that arise in carrying out the foregoing procedures, inquiries, and discussions.

AU Section 561

Subsequent Discovery of Facts Existing at the Date of the Auditor's Report

Source: SAS No. 1, section 561.

See section 9561 for interpretations of this section.

Issue date, unless otherwise indicated: November, 1972.

.01 The procedures described in this section should be followed by the auditor who, subsequent to the date of his report upon audited financial statements, becomes aware that facts may have existed at that date which might have affected his report had he then been aware of such facts.

.02 Because of the variety of conditions which might be encountered, some of these procedures are necessarily set out only in general terms; the specific actions to be taken in a particular case may vary somewhat in the light of the circumstances. The auditor would be well advised to consult with his attorney when he encounters the circumstances to which this section may apply because of legal implications that may be involved in actions contemplated herein, including, for example, the possible effect of state statutes regarding confidentiality of auditor-client communications.

.03 After he has issued his report, the auditor has no obligation[1] to make any further or continuing inquiry or perform any other auditing procedures with respect to the audited financial statements covered by that report, unless new information which may affect his report comes to his attention. In addition, this section does not apply to situations arising from developments or events occurring after the date of the auditor's report; neither does it apply to situations where, after issuance of the auditor's report, final determinations or resolutions are made of contingencies or other matters which had been disclosed in the financial statements or which had resulted in a departure from the auditor's standard report.

.04 When the auditor becomes aware of information which relates to financial statements previously reported on by him, but which was not known to him at the date of his report, and which is of such a nature and from such a source that he would have investigated it had it come to his attention during the course of his audit, he should, as soon as practicable, undertake to determine whether the information is reliable and whether the facts existed at the date of his report. In this connection, the auditor should discuss the matter with his client at whatever management levels he deems appropriate, including the board of directors, and request cooperation in whatever investigation may be necessary.

.05 When the subsequently discovered information is found both to be reliable and to have existed at the date of the auditor's report, the auditor should take action in accordance with the procedures set out in subsequent

---

[1] However, see section 711.10–.13 as to an auditor's obligation with respect to audited financial statements included in registration statements filed under the Securities Act of 1933 between the date of the auditor's report and the effective date of the registration statement. [Reference changed by issuance of Statement on Auditing Standards No. 37.]

paragraphs if the nature and effect of the matter are such that (*a*) his report would have been affected if the information had been known to him at the date of his report and had not been reflected in the financial statements and (*b*) he believes there are persons currently relying or likely to rely on the financial statements who would attach importance to the information. With respect to (*b*), consideration should be given, among other things, to the time elapsed since the financial statements were issued.

.06 When the auditor has concluded, after considering (*a*) and (*b*) in paragraph .05, that action should be taken to prevent future reliance on his report, he should advise his client to make appropriate disclosure of the newly discovered facts and their impact on the financial statements to persons who are known to be currently relying or who are likely to rely on the financial statements and the related auditor's report. When the client undertakes to make appropriate disclosure, the method used and the disclosure made will depend on the circumstances.

a. If the effect on the financial statements or auditor's report of the subsequently discovered information can promptly be determined, disclosure should consist of issuing, as soon as practicable, revised financial statements and auditor's report. The reasons for the revision usually should be described in a note to the financial statements and referred to in the auditor's report. Generally, only the most recently issued audited financial statements would need to be revised, even though the revision resulted from events that had occurred in prior years.[2]

b. When issuance of financial statements accompanied by the auditor's report for a subsequent period is imminent, so that disclosure is not delayed, appropriate disclosure of the revision can be made in such statements instead of reissuing the earlier statements pursuant to subparagraph (*a*).[3]

c. When the effect on the financial statements of the subsequently discovered information cannot be determined without a prolonged investigation, the issuance of revised financial statements and auditor's report would necessarily be delayed. In this circumstance, when it appears that the information will require a revision of the statements, appropriate disclosure would consist of notification by the client to persons who are known to be relying or who are likely to rely on the financial statements and the related report that they should not be relied upon, and that revised financial statements and auditor's report will be issued upon completion of an investigation. If applicable, the client should be advised to discuss with the Securities and Exchange Commission, stock exchanges, and appropriate regulatory agencies the disclosure to be made or other measures to be taken in the circumstances.

.07 The auditor should take whatever steps he deems necessary to satisfy himself that the client has made the disclosures specified in paragraph .06.

.08 If the client refuses to make the disclosures specified in paragraph .06, the auditor should notify each member of the board of directors of such refusal and of the fact that, in the absence of disclosure by the client, the audi-

---

[2] See paragraphs 26 and 27 of Accounting Principles Board Opinion No. 9 [AC section A35.107–.108] and paragraphs 36 and 37 of Opinion No. 20 [AC section A35.105] regarding disclosure of adjustments applicable to prior periods.

[3] Ibid.

tor will take steps as outlined below to prevent future reliance upon his report. The steps that can appropriately be taken will depend upon the degree of certainty of the auditor's knowledge that there are persons who are currently relying or who will rely on the financial statements and the auditor's report, and who would attach importance to the information, and the auditor's ability as a practical matter to communicate with them. Unless the auditor's attorney recommends a different course of action, the auditor should take the following steps to the extent applicable:

a. Notification to the client that the auditor's report must no longer be associated with the financial statements.

b. Notification to regulatory agencies having jurisdiction over the client that the auditor's report should no longer be relied upon.

c. Notification to each person known to the auditor to be relying on the financial statements that his report should no longer be relied upon. In many instances, it will not be practicable for the auditor to give appropriate individual notification to stockholders or investors at large, whose identities ordinarily are unknown to him; notification to a regulatory agency having jurisdiction over the client will usually be the only practicable way for the auditor to provide appropriate disclosure. Such notification should be accompanied by a request that the agency take whatever steps it may deem appropriate to accomplish the necessary disclosure. The Securities and Exchange Commission and the stock exchanges are appropriate agencies for this purpose as to corporations within their jurisdictions.

.09 The following guidelines should govern the content of any disclosure made by the auditor in accordance with paragraph .08 to persons other than his client:

a. If the auditor has been able to make a satisfactory investigation of the information and has determined that the information is reliable:

(i) The disclosure should describe the effect the subsequently acquired information would have had on the auditor's report if it had been known to him at the date of his report and had not been reflected in the financial statements. The disclosure should include a description of the nature of the subsequently acquired information and of its effect on the financial statements.

(ii) The information disclosed should be as precise and factual as possible and should not go beyond that which is reasonably necessary to accomplish the purpose mentioned in the preceding subparagraph (*i*). Comments concerning the conduct or motives of any person should be avoided.

b. If the client has not cooperated and as a result the auditor is unable to conduct a satisfactory investigation of the information, his disclosure need not detail the specific information but can merely indicate that information has come to his attention which his client has not cooperated in attempting to substantiate and that, if the information is true, the auditor believes that his report must no longer be relied upon or be associated with the financial statements. No such disclosure should be made unless the auditor believes that the financial statements are likely to be misleading and that his report should not be relied on.

.10 The concepts embodied in this section are not limited solely to corporations but apply in all cases where financial statements have been audited and reported on by independent auditors.

AU Section 9561

Subsequent Discovery of Facts Existing at the Date of the Auditor's Report: Auditing Interpretations of Section 561

1. Auditor Association With Subsequently Discovered Information When the Auditor Has Resigned or Been Discharged

.01 *Question*—New information may come to an auditor's attention subsequent to the date of his report on audited financial statements that might affect the previously issued audit report. Is the auditor's responsibility with respect to that information different if the auditor has resigned or been discharged prior to undertaking or completing his investigation than if he were the continuing auditor?

.02 *Interpretation*—No. Section 561, *Subsequent Discovery of Facts Existing at the Date of the Auditor's Report*, requires the auditor to undertake to determine whether the information is reliable and whether the facts existed at the date of his report. This undertaking must be performed even when the auditor has resigned or been discharged.

[Issue Date: February, 1989.]

AU Section 600
OTHER TYPES OF REPORTS

. . . engagements to apply agreed-upon procedures . . . special reports . . . reports on the application of accounting principles . . . letters for underwriters and certain other requesting parties . . .

TABLE OF CONTENTS

Section		Paragraph
622	Engagements to Apply Agreed-Upon Procedures to Specified Elements, Accounts, or Items of a Financial Statement	.01-49
	Introduction and Applicability	.01-.02
	Engagements to Apply Agreed-Upon Procedures	.03-.04
	Applicability of Generally Accepted Auditing Standards	.05
	Specified Elements, Accounts, or Items of a Financial Statement and Related Subject Matter	.06-.08
	Conditions for Engagement Performance	.09-.11
	Agreement on and Sufficiency of Procedures	.10
	Engagement Letters	.11
	Nature, Timing, and Extent of Procedures	.12-.25
	Users' Responsibility	.12
	Accountant's Responsibility	.13-.15
	Procedures to Be Performed	.16-.19
	Procedures on Internal Control	.20
	Involvement of a Specialist	.21-.23
	Internal Auditors and Other Personnel	.24-.25
	Findings	.26-.28
	Working Papers	.29-.32
	Reporting	.33-.38
	Required Elements	.33
	Illustrative Report	.34
	Explanatory Language	.35
	Dating of Report	.36
	Restrictions on the Performance of Procedures	.37
	Adding Parties as Specified Users (Nonparticipant Parties)	.38
	Representation Letter	.39-.40
	Knowledge of Matters Outside Agreed-Upon Procedures	.41
	Change to an Engagement to Apply Agreed-Upon Procedures From Another Form of Engagement	.42-.46
	Combined or Included Reports	.47
	Effective Date	.48

Section		Paragraph
622	Engagements to Apply Agreed-Upon Procedures to Specified Elements, Accounts, or Items of a Financial Statement—continued	
	Appendix A: Additional Illustrative Reports	.49
9622	Engagements to Apply Agreed-Upon Procedures to Specified Elements, Accounts, or Items of a Financial Statement: Auditing Interpretations of Section 622	
	1. Applying Agreed-Upon Procedures to All, or Substantially All, of the Elements, Accounts, or Items of a Financial Statement (11/97)	.01-.02
623	Special Reports	.01-.34
	Introduction	.01
	Financial Statements Prepared in Conformity With a Comprehensive Basis of Accounting Other Than Generally Accepted Accounting Principles	.02-.10
	Reporting on Financial Statements Prepared in Conformity With an Other Comprehensive Basis of Accounting (OCBOA)	.05-.08
	Evaluating the Adequacy of Disclosure in Financial Statements Prepared in Conformity With an Other Comprehensive Basis of Accounting	.09-.10
	Specified Elements, Accounts, or Items of a Financial Statement	.11-.18
	Reports on One or More Specified Elements, Accounts, or Items of a Financial Statement	.15-.18
	Compliance With Aspects of Contractual Agreements or Regulatory Requirements Related to Audited Financial Statements	.19-.21
	Special-Purpose Financial Presentations to Comply With Contractual Agreements or Regulatory Provisions	.22-.30
	Financial Statements Prepared on a Basis of Accounting Prescribed in a Contractual Agreement or Regulatory Provision That Results in an Incomplete Presentation But One That is Otherwise in Conformity With Generally Accepted Accounting Principles or an Other Comprehensive Basis of Accounting	.23-.26
	Financial Statements Prepared on a Basis of Accounting Prescribed in an Agreement That Results in a Presentation That is Not in Conformity With Generally Accepted Accounting Principles or an Other Comprehensive Basis of Accounting	.27-.30
	Circumstances Requiring Explanatory Language in an Auditor's Special Report	.31
	Financial Information Presented in Prescribed Forms or Schedules	.32-.33
	Effective Date	.34

Section | Paragraph

9623 Special Reports: Auditing Interpretations of Section 623
[1.] Auditor's Report Under Employee Retirement Income Security Act of 1974 (1/77) [Withdrawn February, 1983] . . [.01-.08]
[2.] Reports on Elements, Accounts, or Items of a Financial Statement That Are Presented in Conformity With GAAP (7/78) [Withdrawn March, 1989] . . . . . [.09-.10]
[3.] Compliance With the Foreign Corrupt Practices Act of 1977 (10/78) [Transferred to AU section 9642; Deleted October, 1993] . . . . . [.11-.14]
[4.] Reports on Engagements Solely to Meet State Regulatory Examination Requirements (10/79) [Deleted April, 1981] . . . [.15-.16]
[5.] Financial Statements Prepared in Accordance With Accounting Practices Specified in an Agreement (2/80) [Withdrawn March, 1989] . . . . . [.17-.25]
[6.] Reporting on Special-Purpose Financial Presentations (2/80) [Withdrawn March, 1989] . . . . . [.26-.31]
[7.] Understanding of Agreed-Upon Procedures (2/80) [Deleted April, 1981] . . . . . [.32-.33]
[8.] Adequacy of Disclosure in Financial Statements Prepared on a Comprehensive Basis of Accounting Other Than Generally Accepted Accounting Principles (2/80) [Withdrawn March, 1989] . . . . . [.34-.39]
9. Auditors' Special Reports on Property and Liability Insurance Companies' Loss Reserves (5/81) 40-.46
10. Reports on the Financial Statements Included in Internal Revenue Form 990, "Return of Organizations Exempt from Income Tax" (7/82) 47-.54
11. Reporting on Current-Value Financial Statements That Supplement Historical-Cost Financial Statements in a General-Use Presentation of Real Estate Entities (6/90) 55-.59
12. Evaluation of the Appropriateness of Informative Disclosures in Insurance Enterprises' Financial Statements Prepared on a Statutory Basis (12/91) 60-.79
13. Reporting on a Special-Purpose Financial Statement That Results in an Incomplete Presentation But is Otherwise in Conformity With Generally Accepted Accounting Principles (5/95) 80-.87
14. Evaluating the Adequacy of Disclosure in Financial Statements Prepared on the Cash, Modified Cash, or Income Tax Basis of Accounting (1/98) 88-.93

625 Reports on the Application of Accounting Principles .01-.09
Applicability 02-.04
Performance Standards 05-.07
Reporting Standards 08-.09

634 Letters for Underwriters and Certain Other Requesting Parties .01-.64
Introduction 01-.02
Applicability 03-.10

Section | Paragraph

634 Letters for Underwriters and Certain Other Requesting Parties—continued
General .... .11-.21
Guidance on the Format and Contents of Comfort Letters .... .22-.62
Dating .... .23-.24
Addressee .... .25
Introductory Paragraph .... .26-.30
Independence .... .31-.32
Compliance With SEC Requirements .... .33-.34
Commenting in a Comfort Letter on Information Other Than Audited Financial Statements .... .35-.53
General .... .35
Knowledge of Internal Control .... .36
Unaudited Condensed Interim Financial Information .... .37-.38
Capsule Financial Information .... .39-.41
Pro Forma Financial Information .... .42-.43
Financial Forecasts .... .44
Subsequent Changes .... .45-.53
Tables, Statistics, and Other Financial Information .... .54-.60
Concluding Paragraph .... .61
Disclosure of Subsequently Discovered Matters .... .62
Effective Date .... .63
Appendix—Examples .... .64
Example A: Typical Comfort Letter
Example B: Letter When a Short-Form Registration Statement Is Filed Incorporating Previously Filed Forms 10-K and 10-Q by Reference
Example C: Letter Reaffirming Comments in Example A as of a Later Date
Example D: Comments on Pro Forma Financial Information
Example E: Comments on a Financial Forecast
Example F: Comments on Tables, Statistics, and Other Financial Information—Complete Description of Procedures and Findings
Example G: Comments on Tables, Statistics, and Other Financial Information—Summarized Description of Procedures and Findings Regarding Tables, Statistics, and Other Financial Information
Example H: Comments on Tables, Statistics, and Other Financial Information: Descriptions of Procedures and Findings Regarding Tables, Statistics, and Other Financial Information—Attached Registration Statement (or Selected Pages) Identifies With Designated Symbols Items to Which Procedures Were Applied

Section *Paragraph*

634 Letters for Underwriters and Certain Other Requesting Parties—continued
- Example I: Alternate Wording When Accountants' Report on Audited Financial Statements Contains an Explanatory Paragraph
- Example J: Alternate Wording When More Than One Accountant Is Involved
- Example K: Alternate Wording When the SEC Has Agreed to a Departure From Its Published Accounting Requirements
- Example L: Alternate Wording When Recent Earnings Data Are Presented in Capsule Form
- Example M: Alternate Wording When Accountants Are Aware of a Decrease in a Specified Financial Statement Item
- Example N: Alternate Wording of the Letter for Companies That Are Permitted to Present Interim Earnings Data for a Twelve-Month Period
- Example O: Alternate Wording When the Procedures That the Underwriter Has Requested the Accountant to Perform on Interim Financial Information Are Less Than an SAS No. 71 Review
- Example P: A Typical Comfort Letter in a Non-1933 Act Offering, Including the Required Underwriter Representations
- Example Q: Letter to a Requesting Party That Has Not Provided the Representation Letter Described in Paragraphs .06 and .07

9634 Letters for Underwriters and Certain Other Requesting Parties: Auditing Interpretations of Section 634
- 1. Letters to Directors Relating to Annual Reports on For 10-K (5/81) .... .01-.09
- [2.] Negative Assurance on Unaudited Condensed Interim Financial Statements Attached to Comfort Letters (7/86) [Deleted April, 1993] .... [.10-.12]

9642 Reporting on Internal Accounting Control: Auditing Interpretations of SAS No. 30
- [1.] Pre-Award Surveys (8/80) [Deleted October, 1993] .... [.01-.03]
- [2.] Award Survey Made in Conjunction With an Audit (8/80) [Deleted October, 1993] .... [.04-.05]
- [3.] Reporting on Matters Not Covered by Government-Established Criteria (8/80) [Deleted October, 1993] .... [.06-.07]
- [4.] Limited Scope (8/80) [Deleted October, 1993] .... [.08-.09]
- [5.] Compliance With the Foreign Corrupt Practices Act of 1977 (8/80) [Deleted October, 1993] .... [.10-.13]
- [6.] Reports on Internal Accounting Control of Trust Departments of Banks (1/81) [Deleted October, 1993] .... [.14-.17]

AU Section 622

Engagements to Apply Agreed-Upon Procedures to Specified Elements, Accounts, or Items of a Financial Statement

(Supersedes SAS No. 35)

Source: SAS No. 75.

See section 9622 for interpretations of this section.

Effective for reports on engagements to apply agreed-upon procedures dated after April 30, 1996.

Introduction and Applicability

.01 This section sets forth standards and provides guidance to an accountant[1] concerning performance and reporting in all engagements to apply agreed-upon procedures to specified elements, accounts, or items of a financial statement, except as noted in paragraph .02.

.02 This section does not apply to[2]—

a. Situations in which an accountant reports on an engagement to apply agreed-upon procedures to other than specified elements, accounts, or items of a financial statement[3] pursuant to AT section 600, *Agreed-Upon Procedures Engagements.*[4]

b. Situations in which an accountant reports on specified compliance requirements based solely on an audit of financial statements, as addressed in section 623, *Special Reports*, paragraphs .19 through .21.

c. Engagements for which the objective is to report in accordance with section 801, *Compliance Auditing Considerations in Audits of Governmental Entities and Recipients of Governmental Financial Assistance*.

d. Circumstances covered by section 324, *Reports on the Processing of Transactions by Service Organizations*, paragraph .58, when the ser-

---

[1] For purposes of this section, the term *accountant* refers to a person possessing the professional qualifications required to practice as an independent auditor. See section 110, *Responsibilities and Functions of the Independent Auditor*, paragraph .04. An accountant performing an engagement to apply agreed-upon procedures to specified elements, accounts, or items of a financial statement is not required to be the auditor of the financial statements to which the specified elements, accounts, or items relate. Throughout this section, the term *auditor* may be used interchangeably with the term *accountant*.

[2] The attest interpretation "Responding to Requests on Matters Relating to Solvency" (AT section 9100.33–.44) prohibits the accountant's report on agreed-upon procedures from providing any assurances on matters relating to solvency or any financial presentation of matters relating to solvency.

[3] When engaged to perform agreed-upon procedures on prospective financial information, the accountant should follow the guidance in AT section 200, *Financial Forecasts and Projections*, and AT section 600, *Agreed-Upon Procedures Engagements*.

[4] The accountant may issue combined reports on engagements to apply agreed-upon procedures pursuant to paragraph .47 of this section and AT section 600.48.

vice auditor is requested to apply substantive procedures to user transactions or assets at the service organization and he or she makes specific reference in his or her service auditor's report to having carried out designated procedures. (However, this section would apply when the service auditor provides a separate report on the performance of applying agreed-upon procedures to specified elements, accounts, or items of a financial statement.)

e. Engagements covered by section 634, *Letters for Underwriters and Certain Other Requesting Parties.*

Engagements to Apply Agreed-Upon Procedures

.03 An engagement to apply agreed-upon procedures is one in which an accountant is engaged by a client to issue a report of findings based on specific procedures performed on the specific subject matter of specified elements, accounts, or items of a financial statement, as defined in paragraph .06. The client engages the accountant to assist users in evaluating specified elements, accounts, or items of a financial statement as a result of a need or needs of the users of the report. Because users require that findings be independently derived, the services of an accountant are obtained to perform procedures and report his or her findings. The users and the accountant agree upon the procedures to be performed by the accountant that the users believe are appropriate. Because users' needs may vary widely, the nature, timing, and extent of the agreed-upon procedures may vary as well; consequently, the users assume responsibility for the sufficiency of the procedures since they best understand their own needs. In an engagement performed under this section, the accountant does not perform an audit[5] and does not provide an opinion or negative assurance (see paragraph .26) relating to the fair presentation of the specified elements, accounts, or items of a financial statement. Instead, the accountant's report on agreed-upon procedures should be in the form of procedures and findings. (See paragraph .33.)

.04 As a consequence of the users' role in agreeing upon the procedures performed or to be performed, an accountant's report on such engagements should clearly indicate that its use is restricted to those users. Those users, including the client, are hereinafter referred to as *specified users*.

Applicability of Generally Accepted Auditing Standards

.05 The general standards (adequate technical training and proficiency, independence, due care) and the first standard of fieldwork (planning and supervision) should be followed by an accountant in an engagement to apply agreed-upon procedures to specified elements, accounts, or items of a financial statement. The accountant also should follow the interpretative guidance relating to the application of the third standard of fieldwork, and also should follow the reporting standards as addressed in this section.[6]

---

[5] For guidance on expressing an opinion on specified elements, accounts, or items of a financial statement based on an audit, see section 623.11 through .18. For guidance when reporting on a review of specified elements, accounts, or items of a financial statement, see AT section 100, *Attestation Standards*, paragraphs .57 through .59.

[6] In an engagement to apply agreed-upon procedures, an accountant is not obligated to follow any standards that would apply in an audit of financial statements or of specified elements, accounts, or items thereof other than the standards and interpretative guidance contained in or referred to in this section.

Specified Elements, Accounts, or Items of a Financial Statement and Related Subject Matter

.06 *Specified elements, accounts, or items of a financial statement* refers to accounting information that is a part of, but significantly less than, a financial statement. Specified elements, accounts, or items of a financial statement may be directly identified in a financial statement or notes thereto; or they may be derived therefrom by analysis, aggregation, summarization, or mathematical computation.[7] Specified elements, accounts, or items of a financial statement contain assertions that are embodied in financial statements. These assertions can be either implicit or explicit. An identified basis of accounting for a specified element, account, or item of a financial statement defines the particular aspects of those assertions applicable in a given circumstance, such as when the basis of accounting is generally accepted accounting principles. In an engagement to apply agreed-upon procedures, it is the subject matter underlying the assertions to which the accountant's procedures are applied (referred to in this section as *specific subject matter*). The procedures enumerated or referred to in the accountant's report generally recite the criteria against which the specific subject matter is to be measured in deriving a finding.

.07 The specified element, account, or item of a financial statement[8] may be presented in a schedule or statement, or in the accountant's report, appropriately identifying what is being presented and the point in time or the period of time covered. A specified element, account, or item of a financial statement also may be identified in accounting records (for example, a general ledger account or a computer printout) maintained for preparation of financial statements.

.08 Examples of specified elements, accounts, and items of a financial statement include—

- The cash accounts, as of a certain date, included in an entity's general ledger maintained for the purpose of preparing financial statements represented as being in accordance with generally accepted accounting principles.
- A schedule of accounts receivable of an entity, as of a certain date, that reflects the accounts receivable presented in conformity with generally accepted accounting principles.
- The amounts included in the caption "property and equipment" identified in a Statement of Assets, Liabilities, and Capital, as of a certain date, presented on an income-tax basis.
- The gross income component of a Statement of Operations for a period of time presented in accordance with the rules of a regulatory agency.

---

[7] Accounting information generally is expressed in monetary amounts (or percentages derived from such monetary amounts), but it also may include quantitative information derived from accounting records that is not expressed in monetary terms.

[8] The term *financial statement* refers to a presentation of financial data, including accompanying notes, derived from accounting records and intended to communicate an entity's economic resources or obligations at a point in time or the changes therein for a period of time. In this section, the term includes any financial statements that are prepared either in accordance with generally accepted accounting principles or in conformity with an other comprehensive basis of accounting. See section 623.02. The term also includes special-purpose financial presentations to comply with contractual agreements or regulatory provisions as discussed in section 623.22 through .30.

Conditions for Engagement Performance

.09 The accountant may perform an engagement under this section provided that—

a. The accountant is *independent*.

b. The accountant and the specified users agree upon the procedures performed or to be performed by the accountant.

c. The specified users take responsibility for the sufficiency of the agreed-upon procedures for their purposes.

d. The procedures to be performed are expected to result in reasonably consistent findings.

e. The basis of accounting of the specified elements, accounts, or items of a financial statement is clearly evident to the specified users and the accountant.

f. The specific subject matter to which the procedures are to be applied is subject to reasonably consistent estimation or measurement.

g. Evidential matter related to the specific subject matter to which the procedures are applied is expected to exist to provide a reasonable basis for expressing the findings in the accountant's report.

h. Where applicable, the accountant and the specified users agree on any materiality limits for reporting purposes. (See paragraph .27.)

i. Use of the report is restricted to the specified users.[9]

Agreement on and Sufficiency of Procedures

.10 To satisfy the requirements that the accountant and the specified users agree upon the procedures performed or to be performed and that the specified users take responsibility for the sufficiency of the agreed-upon procedures for their purposes, ordinarily the accountant should communicate directly with and obtain affirmative acknowledgment from each of the specified users. For example, this may be accomplished by meeting with the specified users or by distributing a draft of the anticipated report or a copy of an engagement letter to the specified users and obtaining their agreement. If the accountant is not able to communicate directly with all of the specified users, the accountant may satisfy these requirements by applying any one or more of the following or similar procedures:

- Compare the procedures to be applied to written requirements of the specified users.
- Discuss the procedures to be applied with appropriate representatives of the specified users involved.
- Review relevant contracts with or correspondence from the specified users.

The accountant should not report on an engagement when specified users do not agree upon the procedures performed or to be performed and do not take responsibility for the sufficiency of the procedures for their purposes. (See paragraph .38 for guidance on satisfying these requirements when the accountant is requested to add parties as specified users after the date of completion of the agreed-upon procedures.)

---

[9] An accountant may perform an engagement pursuant to which his or her report will be a matter of public record. (See paragraph .33.)

Engagement Letters

.11 The accountant should establish a clear understanding regarding the terms of engagement, preferably in an engagement letter. Engagement letters should be addressed to the client, and in some circumstances also to all specified users. Matters that might be included in such an engagement letter follow:

- Nature of the engagement
- Identification of or reference to the specified elements, accounts, or items of a financial statement and the party responsible for them
- Identification of specified users (see paragraph .38)
- Specified users' acknowledgment of their responsibility for the sufficiency of the procedures
- Responsibilities of the accountant (see paragraphs .13 through .15 and .41)
- Basis of accounting of the specified elements, accounts, or items of a financial statement
- Reference to applicable AICPA standards
- Agreement on procedures by enumerating (or referring to) the procedures (see paragraphs .16 through .19)
- Disclaimers expected to be included in the accountant's report
- Use restrictions
- Assistance to be provided to the accountant (see paragraph .24)
- Involvement of a specialist (see paragraphs .21 through .23)
- Agreed-upon materiality limits (see paragraph .27)

Nature, Timing, and Extent of Procedures

Users' Responsibility

.12 Specified users are responsible for the sufficiency (nature, timing, and extent) of the agreed-upon procedures, because they best understand their own needs. The specified users assume the risk that such procedures might be insufficient for their purposes. In addition, the specified users assume the risk that they might misunderstand or otherwise inappropriately use findings properly reported by the accountant.

Accountant's Responsibility

.13 The responsibility of the accountant is to carry out the procedures and report the findings in accordance with the applicable general, fieldwork, and reporting standards as discussed and interpreted in this section. The accountant assumes the risk that misapplication of the procedures may result in inappropriate findings being reported. Furthermore, the accountant assumes the risk that appropriate findings may not be reported or may be reported inaccurately. The accountant's risks can be reduced through adequate planning and supervision and due professional care in performing the procedures, determining the findings, and preparing the report.

.14 The accountant should have adequate knowledge in the specific subject matter of the specified elements, accounts, or items of a financial statement, including the basis of accounting. He or she may obtain such knowledge through formal or continuing education, practical experience, or consultation with others.

.15 The accountant has no responsibility to determine the differences between the agreed-upon procedures to be performed and the procedures that the accountant would have determined to be necessary had he or she been engaged to perform another form of engagement. The procedures that the accountant agrees to perform pursuant to an engagement to apply agreed-upon procedures may be more or less extensive than the procedures that the accountant would determine to be necessary had he or she been engaged to perform another form of engagement.

Procedures to Be Performed

.16 The procedures that the accountant and specified users agree upon may be as limited or as extensive as the specified users desire. However, mere reading of an assertion or specified information does not constitute a procedure sufficient to permit an accountant to report on the results of applying agreed-upon procedures. In some circumstances, the procedures agreed upon evolve or are modified over the course of the engagement. In general, there is flexibility in determining the procedures as long as the specified users acknowledge responsibility for the sufficiency of such procedures for their purposes. Matters that would be agreed upon include the nature, timing, and extent of the procedures.

.17 The accountant should not agree to perform procedures that are overly subjective and thus possibly open to varying interpretations. Terms of uncertain meaning (such as *general review, limited review, reconcile, check,* or *test*) should not be used in describing the procedures unless such terms are defined within the agreed-upon procedures. The accountant should obtain evidential matter from applying the agreed-upon procedures to provide a reasonable basis for the finding or findings expressed in his or her report, but need not perform additional procedures outside the scope of the engagement to gather additional evidential matter.

.18 Examples of appropriate procedures include—

- Execution of a sampling application after agreeing on relevant parameters.
- Inspection of specified documents evidencing certain types of transactions or detailed attributes thereof.
- Confirmation of specific information with third parties.
- Comparison of documents, schedules, or analyses with certain specified attributes.
- Performance of specific procedures on work performed by others (including the work of internal auditors—see paragraphs .24 and .25).
- Performance of mathematical computations.

.19 Examples of inappropriate procedures include—

- Mere reading of the work performed by others solely to describe their findings.
- Evaluating the competency or objectivity of another party.

- Obtaining an understanding about a particular subject.
- Interpreting documents outside the scope of the accountant's professional expertise.

Procedures on Internal Control

.20 As part of an engagement to apply agreed-upon procedures to specified elements, accounts, or items of a financial statement, an accountant also may perform agreed-upon procedures on part of an entity's internal control over financial reporting. The accountant's report on such procedures should be part of the accountant's report on applying agreed-upon procedures to the specified elements, accounts, or items and should follow the reporting guidance in paragraph .33. As noted in paragraph .26, the accountant should not provide negative assurance about the effectiveness of internal control over financial reporting or any part thereof.

Involvement of a Specialist[10]

.21 The accountant's education and experience enable him or her to be knowledgeable about business matters in general, but he or she is not expected to have the expertise of a person trained for or qualified to engage in the practice of another profession or occupation. In certain circumstances it may be appropriate to involve a specialist to assist the accountant in the performance of one or more procedures. For example—

- An environmental engineer may provide assistance in interpreting environmental remedial action regulatory directives that may affect the agreed-upon procedures applied to an environmental liabilities account in a financial statement.
- A geologist may provide assistance in distinguishing between varying physical characteristics of a generic minerals group related to information disclosed in a note to the financial statements to which the agreed-upon procedures are applied.

.22 The accountant and the specified users should explicitly agree to the involvement of the specialist in assisting an accountant in the performance of an engagement to apply agreed-upon procedures. This agreement may be reached when obtaining agreement on the procedures performed or to be performed and acknowledgment of responsibility for the sufficiency of the procedures, as discussed in paragraph .10. The accountant's report should describe the nature of the assistance provided by the specialist.

.23 An accountant may agree to apply procedures to the report or work product of a specialist that does not constitute assistance by the specialist to the accountant in an engagement to apply agreed-upon procedures. For example, the accountant may make reference to information contained in a report of a specialist in describing an agreed-upon procedure. However, it is inappropriate for the accountant to agree to merely read the specialist's report solely to describe or repeat the findings, or to take responsibility for all or a portion of any procedures performed by a specialist or the specialist's work product.

---

[10] A *specialist* is a person (or firm) possessing special skill or knowledge in a particular field other than accounting or auditing. As used herein, *specialist* does not include a person employed by the accountant's firm who participates in the agreed-upon procedures engagement.

Internal Auditors and Other Personnel[11]

.24 The agreed-upon procedures to be enumerated or referred to in the accountant's report are to be performed entirely by the accountant, except as discussed in paragraphs .21 through .23. However, internal auditors or other personnel may prepare schedules and accumulate data or provide other information for the accountant's use in performing the agreed-upon procedures. Also, internal auditors may perform and report separately on procedures that they have carried out. Such procedures may be similar to those that an accountant may perform under this section.

.25 An accountant may agree to perform procedures on the information documented in working papers of internal auditors. For example, the accountant may agree to—

- Repeat all or some of the procedures.
- Determine whether the internal auditors' working papers contain documentation of procedures performed and whether the findings documented in the working papers are presented in a report by the internal auditors.

However, it is inappropriate for the accountant to—

- Agree to merely read the internal auditors' report solely to describe or repeat their findings.
- Take responsibility for all or a portion of any procedures performed by the internal auditors by reporting those findings as the accountant's own.
- Report in any manner that implies shared responsibility for the procedures with the internal auditors.

Findings

.26 An accountant should present the results of applying agreed-upon procedures to specific subject matter in the form of findings. The accountant should not provide negative assurance about whether the specified elements, accounts, or items of a financial statement are fairly stated in relation to established or stated criteria such as generally accepted accounting principles. For example, the accountant should not include a statement in his or her report that "nothing came to my attention that caused me to believe that the specified element, account, or item of a financial statement is not fairly stated in accordance with generally accepted accounting principles."

.27 The accountant should report all findings from application of the agreed-upon procedures. The concept of materiality does not apply to findings to be reported in an engagement to apply agreed-upon procedures unless the definition of materiality is agreed to by the specified users. Any agreed-upon materiality limits should be described in the accountant's report.

.28 The accountant should avoid vague or ambiguous language in reporting findings. Examples of appropriate and inappropriate descriptions of findings resulting from the application of certain agreed-upon procedures follow:

---

[11] Section 322, *The Auditor's Consideration of the Internal Audit Function in an Audit of Financial Statements*, does not apply to agreed-upon procedures engagements.

Procedures Agreed Upon	*Appropriate Description of Findings*	*Inappropriate Description of Findings*
Trace all outstanding checks appearing on a bank reconciliation as of a certain date to checks cleared in the bank statement of the subsequent month.	All outstanding checks appearing on the bank reconciliation were cleared in the subsequent month's bank statement except for the following: [*List all exceptions.*]	Nothing came to my attention as a result of applying the procedure.
Compare the amounts of the invoices included in the "over ninety days" column shown in an identified schedule of aged accounts receivable of a specific customer as of a certain date to the amount and invoice date shown on the outstanding invoice, and determine whether or not the amounts agree and whether or not the invoice dates precede the date indicated on the schedule by more than ninety days.	All outstanding invoice amounts agreed with the amounts shown on the schedule in the "over ninety days" column, and the dates shown on such invoices preceded the date indicated on the schedule by more than ninety days.	The outstanding invoice amounts agreed within an approximation of the amounts shown on the schedule in the "over ninety days" column, and nothing came to our attention that the dates shown on such invoices preceded the date indicated on the schedule by more than ninety days.

Working Papers

.29 The accountant should prepare and maintain working papers in connection with an engagement to apply agreed-upon procedures; such working papers should be appropriate to the circumstance and the accountant's needs on the engagement to which they apply.[12] Although the quantity, type, and content of working papers vary with the circumstances, ordinarily they should indicate that—

a. The work was adequately planned and supervised.

b. Evidential matter was obtained to provide a reasonable basis for the finding or findings expressed in the accountant's report.

.30 Working papers are the property of the accountant, and some states have statutes or regulations that designate the accountant as the owner of the working papers. The accountant's rights of ownership, however, are subject to ethical limitations relating to confidentiality.[13]

.31 Certain of the accountant's working papers may sometimes serve as a useful reference source for his or her client, but the working papers should not be regarded as a part of, or a substitute for, the client's records.

.32 The accountant should adopt reasonable procedures for safe custody of his or her working papers and should retain them for a period of time sufficient to meet the needs of his or her practice and satisfy any pertinent legal requirements of records retention.

---

[12] There is no intention to imply that the accountant would be precluded from supporting his or her report by other means in addition to working papers.

[13] For guidance on requests from regulators for access to working papers, see the interpretation "Providing Access to or Photocopies of Working Papers to a Regulator" (section 9339.01–.15).

Reporting

Required Elements

.33 The accountant's report on applying agreed-upon procedures to specified elements, accounts, or items of a financial statement should be in the form of procedures and findings. The accountant's report should contain the following elements:

a. A title that includes the word *independent*

b. Reference to the specified elements, accounts, or items of a financial statement of an identified entity and the character of the engagement

c. Identification of specified users (see paragraph .38)

d. The basis of accounting of the specified elements, accounts, or items of a financial statement unless clearly evident

e. A statement that the procedures performed were those agreed to by the specified users identified in the report

f. Reference to standards established by the American Institute of Certified Public Accountants

g. A statement that the sufficiency of the procedures is solely the responsibility of the specified users and a disclaimer of responsibility for the sufficiency of those procedures

h. A list of the procedures performed (or reference thereto) and related findings (the accountant should not provide negative assurance—see paragraph .26)

i. Where applicable, a description of any agreed-upon materiality limits (see paragraph .27)

j. A statement that the accountant was not engaged to, and did not, perform an audit[14] of the specified elements, accounts, or items; a disclaimer of opinion on the specified elements, accounts, or items; and a statement that if the accountant had performed additional procedures, other matters might have come to his or her attention that would have been reported[15]

k. A disclaimer of opinion on the effectiveness of the internal control over financial reporting or any part thereof when the accountant has performed procedures pursuant to paragraph .20

---

[14] Alternatively, the wording may be: "These agreed-upon procedures do not constitute an audit or review of financial statements or any part thereof, the objective of which is the expression of opinion or limited assurance on the financial statements or a part thereof."

[15] When the accountant consents to the inclusion of his or her report on applying agreed-upon procedures in a document or written communication containing the entity's financial statements, he or she should refer to section 504, *Association With Financial Statements*, or to Statement on Standards for Accounting and Review Services (SSARS) 1, *Compilation and Review of Financial Statements* [AR section 100], as appropriate, for guidance on his or her responsibility pertaining to the financial statements.

The accountant should follow (*a*) section 504.04 when the financial statements of a public or a nonpublic entity are audited (or reviewed in accordance with section 722, *Interim Financial Information*) or (*b*) section 504.05 when the financial statements of a public entity are unaudited. The accountant should follow SSARS 1, paragraph 6 [AR section 100.06] when (*a*) the financial statements of a nonpublic entity are reviewed or compiled or (*b*) the financial statements of a nonpublic entity are *not* reviewed or compiled and are not submitted by the accountant (as defined in SSARS 1, paragraph 7 [AR section 100.07]).

In addition, including or combining a report that is restricted to specified users with a report for general distribution results in restriction of all included reports to the specified users (see paragraph .47).

l. A statement of restrictions on the use of the report because it is intended to be used solely by the specified users[16] (However, if the report is a matter of public record, the accountant should include the following sentence: "However, this report is a matter of public record and its distribution is not limited.")

m. Where applicable, reservations or restrictions concerning procedures or findings as discussed in paragraphs .35, .37, .40, and .41

n. Where applicable, a description of the nature of the assistance provided by a specialist as discussed in paragraphs .21 and .22

Illustrative Report

.34 The following is an illustration of a report on applying agreed-upon procedures to specified elements, accounts, or items of a financial statement. (See appendix A [paragraph .49] for additional illustrations.)

Independent Accountant's Report
on Applying Agreed-Upon Procedures

We have performed the procedures enumerated below, which were agreed to by [*list specified users*], solely to assist you with respect to [*refer to the specified elements, accounts, or items of a financial statement for an identified entity and the character of the engagement*]. This engagement to apply agreed-upon procedures was performed in accordance with standards established by the American Institute of Certified Public Accountants. The sufficiency of the procedures is solely the responsibility of the specified users of the report. Consequently, we make no representation regarding the sufficiency of the procedures described below either for the purpose for which this report has been requested or for any other purpose.

[*Include paragraphs to enumerate procedures and findings.*]

We were not engaged to, and did not, perform an audit, the objective of which would be the expression of an opinion on the specified elements, accounts, or items. Accordingly, we do not express such an opinion. Had we performed additional procedures, other matters might have come to our attention that would have been reported to you.

This report is intended solely for the use of the specified users listed above and should not be used by those who have not agreed to the procedures and taken responsibility for the sufficiency of the procedures for their purposes.

Explanatory Language

.35 The accountant also may include explanatory language about matters such as the following:

- Disclosure of stipulated facts, assumptions, or interpretations (including the source thereof) used in the application of agreed-upon procedures
- Description of the condition of records, controls, or data to which the procedures were applied

---

[16] The purpose of the restriction on use of an accountant's report on applying agreed-upon procedures is to limit its use to only those parties that have agreed upon the procedures performed and taken responsibility for the sufficiency of the procedures. Paragraph .38 describes the process for adding parties who were not originally contemplated in the agreed-upon procedures engagement.

- Explanation that the accountant has no responsibility to update his or her report
- Explanation of sampling risk

Dating of Report

.36 The date of completion of the agreed-upon procedures should be used as the date of the accountant's report.

Restrictions on the Performance of Procedures

.37 When circumstances impose restrictions on the performance of the agreed-upon procedures, the accountant should attempt to obtain agreement from the specified users for modification of the agreed-upon procedures. When such agreement cannot be obtained (for example, when the agreed-upon procedures are published by a regulatory agency that will not modify the procedures), the accountant should describe any restrictions on the performance of procedures in his or her report or withdraw from the engagement.

Adding Parties as Specified Users (Nonparticipant Parties)

.38 Subsequent to the completion of the agreed-upon procedures engagement, an accountant may be requested to consider the addition of another party as a specified user (a nonparticipant party). The accountant may agree to add a nonparticipant party as a specified user, based on consideration of such factors as the identity of the nonparticipant party and the intended use of the report.[17] If the accountant does agree to add the nonparticipant party, he or she should obtain affirmative acknowledgment, normally in writing, from the nonparticipant party agreeing to the procedures performed and of its taking responsibility for the sufficiency of the procedures. If the nonparticipant party is added after the accountant has issued his or her report, the report may be reissued or the accountant may provide other written acknowledgment that the nonparticipant party has been added as a specified user. If the report is reissued, the report date should not be changed. If the accountant provides written acknowledgment that the nonparticipant party has been added as a specified user, such written acknowledgment ordinarily should state that no procedures have been performed subsequent to the date of the report.

Representation Letter

.39 An accountant may find a representation letter to be a useful and practical means of obtaining representations from the parties responsible for the specified elements, accounts, or items of a financial statement. The need for such a letter may depend on the nature of the engagement and the specified users. Examples of matters that might appear in a representation letter include a statement that a responsible party has disclosed to the accountant—

- All known matters contradicting the basis of accounting for the specified elements, accounts, or items of a financial statement.
- Any communication from regulatory agencies affecting the specified elements, accounts, or items of a financial statement.

.40 The responsible party's refusal to furnish written representations determined by the accountant to be appropriate for the engagement constitutes a limitation on the performance of the engagement. In such circumstances, the accountant should do one of the following:

---

[17] When considering whether to add a nonparticipant party, the guidance in section 530, *Dating of the Independent Auditor's Report*, paragraphs .06 and .07, may be helpful.

a. Disclose in his or her report the inability to obtain representations from the responsible party.

b. Withdraw from the engagement.

c. Change the engagement to another form of engagement.

Knowledge of Matters Outside Agreed-Upon Procedures

.41 The accountant need not perform procedures beyond the agreed-upon procedures. However, if, in connection with the application of agreed-upon procedures, matters come to the accountant's attention by other means that significantly contradict the basis of accounting for the specified elements, accounts, or items of a financial statement referred to in the accountant's report, the accountant should include this matter in his or her report.[18] For example, if, in connection with the application of agreed-upon procedures, the accountant becomes aware of a potentially material adjustment to that account by means other than performance of the agreed-upon procedures, the accountant should include this matter in his or her report.

Change to an Engagement to Apply Agreed-Upon Procedures From Another Form of Engagement

.42 An accountant who has been engaged to perform another form of engagement may, before the engagement's completion, be requested to change the engagement to an engagement to apply agreed-upon procedures under this section. A request to change the engagement may result from a change in circumstances affecting the client's requirements, a misunderstanding about the nature of the original services or the alternative services originally available, or a restriction on the performance of the original engagement, whether imposed by the client or caused by circumstances.

.43 Before an accountant who was engaged to perform another form of engagement agrees to change the engagement to an engagement to apply agreed-upon procedures, he or she should consider the following:

a. The possibility that certain procedures performed as part of another type of engagement are not appropriate for inclusion in an engagement to apply agreed-upon procedures

b. The reason given for the request, particularly the implications of a restriction on the scope of the original engagement or the matters to be reported

c. The additional effort required to complete the original engagement

d. If applicable, the reasons for changing from a general-distribution report to a restricted-use report

.44 If the specified users acknowledge agreement to the procedures performed or to be performed and assume responsibility for the sufficiency of the procedures to be included in the agreed-upon procedures engagement, either of the following would be considered a reasonable basis for requesting a change in the engagement:

---

[18] If the accountant has performed (or has been engaged to perform) an audit of the entity's financial statements to which a specified element, account, or item of a financial statement relates and the auditor's report on such financial statements includes a departure from a standard report (section 508, *Reports on Audited Financial Statements*), he or she should consider including a reference to the auditor's report and the departure from the standard report in his or her agreed-upon procedures report.

a. A change in circumstances that requires another form of engagement

b. A misunderstanding concerning the nature of the original engagement or the available alternatives

.45 In all circumstances, if the original engagement procedures are substantially complete or the effort to complete such procedures is relatively insignificant, the accountant should consider the propriety of accepting a change in the engagement.

.46 If the accountant concludes, based on his or her professional judgment, that there is reasonable justification to change the engagement, and provided he or she complies with the standards applicable to an engagement to apply agreed-upon procedures, the accountant should issue an appropriate agreed-upon procedures report. The report should not include reference to either the original engagement or performance limitations that resulted in the changed engagement. (See paragraph .41.)

Combined or Included Reports

.47 When an accountant performs services pursuant to an engagement to apply agreed-upon procedures to specified elements, accounts, or items of a financial statement as part of or in addition to another form of service, this section applies only to those services described herein; other Standards would apply to the other services. Other services may include an audit, review, or compilation of a financial statement, attest services performed pursuant to the Statements on Standards for Attestation Engagements, or a nonattest service. Reports on applying agreed-upon procedures to specified elements, accounts, or items of a financial statement may be included or combined with reports on such other services, provided the types of services can be clearly distinguished and the applicable standards for each service are followed. However, since an accountant's report on applying agreed-upon procedures to specified elements, accounts, or items of a financial statement is restricted to the specified users, including or combining such a report with reports on other services results in restriction of all the included reports to the specified users.

Effective Date

.48 The effective date for this section is for reports on engagements to apply agreed-upon procedures dated after April 30, 1996. Earlier application is encouraged.

.49

Appendix A

Additional Illustrative Reports

The following are additional illustrations of reporting on applying agreed-upon procedures to specified elements, accounts, or items of a financial statement:

Report in Connection With a Proposed Acquisition

Independent Accountant's Report
on Applying Agreed-Upon Procedures

To the Board of Directors and Management of X Company:

We have performed the procedures enumerated below, which were agreed to by the Board of Directors and Management of X Company, solely to assist you in connection with the proposed acquisition of Y Company as of December 31, 19XX. This engagement to apply agreed-upon procedures was performed in accordance with standards established by the American Institute of Certified Public Accountants. The sufficiency of these procedures is solely the responsibility of the Board of Directors and Management of X Company. Consequently, we make no representation regarding the sufficiency of the procedures described below either for the purpose for which this report has been requested or for any other purpose.

The procedures and the associated findings are as follows:

Cash

1. We obtained confirmation of the cash on deposit from the following banks, and we agreed the confirmed balance to the amount shown on the bank reconciliations maintained by Y Company. We mathematically checked the bank reconciliations and compared the resultant cash balances per book to the respective general ledger account balances.

Bank	*General Ledger Account Balances as of December 31, 19XX*
ABC National Bank	$ 5,000
DEF State Bank	13,776
XYZ Trust Company—regular account	86,912
XYZ Trust Company—payroll account	5,000
	$110,688

We found no exceptions as a result of the procedures.

Accounts Receivable

2. We added the individual customer account balances shown in an aged trial balance of accounts receivable (identified as exhibit A) and compared the resultant total with the balance in the general ledger account.

   We found no difference.

3. We compared the individual customer account balances shown in the aged trial balance of accounts receivable (exhibit A) as of December 31, 19XX, to the balances shown in the accounts receivable subsidiary ledger.

   We found no exceptions as a result of the comparisons.

4. We traced the aging (according to invoice dates) for 50 customer account balances shown in exhibit A to the details of outstanding invoices in the accounts receivable subsidiary ledger. The balances selected for tracing were determined by starting at the eighth item and selecting every fifteenth item thereafter.

   We found no exceptions in the aging of the amounts of the 50 customer account balances selected. The sample size traced was 9.8 percent of the aggregate amount of the customer account balances.

5. We mailed confirmations directly to the customers representing the 150 largest customer account balances selected from the accounts receivable trial balance, and we received responses as indicated below. We also traced the items constituting the outstanding customer account balance to invoices and supporting shipping documents for customers from which there was no reply. As agreed, any individual differences in a customer account balance of less than $300 were to be considered minor, and no further procedures were performed.

   Of the 150 customer balances confirmed, we received responses from 140 customers; 10 customers did not reply. No exceptions were identified in 120 of the confirmations received. The differences disclosed in the remaining 20 confirmation replies were either minor in amount (as defined above) or were reconciled to the customer account balance without proposed adjustment thereto. A summary of the confirmation results according to the respective aging categories is as follows:

	Accounts Receivable December 31, 19XX		
Aging Categories	*Customer Account Balances*	*Confirmations Requested*	*Confirmation Replies Received*
Current	$156,000	$ 76,000	$ 65,000
Past due:			
Less than one month	60,000	30,000	19,000
One to three months	36,000	18,000	10,000
Over three months	48,000	48,000	8,000
	$300,000	$172,000	$102,000

We were not engaged to, and did not, perform an audit, the objective of which would be the expression of an opinion on the specified elements, accounts, or items. Accordingly, we do not express such an opinion. Had we performed additional procedures, other matters might have come to our attention that would have been reported to you.

This report is intended solely for the use of the Board of Directors and Management of X Company and should not be used by those who have not agreed to the procedures and taken responsibility for the sufficiency of the procedures for their purposes.

Report in Connection With Claims of Creditors

Independent Accountant's Report
on Applying Agreed-Upon Procedures

To the Trustee of XYZ Company:

We have performed the procedures described below, which were agreed to by the Trustee of XYZ Company, with respect to the claims of creditors to determine the validity of claims of XYZ Company as of May 31, 19XX, as set forth in accompanying Schedule A. This engagement to apply agreed-upon procedures was performed in accordance with standards established by the American Institute of Certified Public Accountants. The sufficiency of these procedures is solely the responsibility of the Trustee of XYZ Company. Consequently, we make no representation regarding the sufficiency of the procedures described below either for the purpose for which this report has been requested or for any other purpose.

The procedures and associated findings are as follows:

1. Compare the total of the trial balance of accounts payable at May 31, 19XX, prepared by XYZ Company, to the balance in the related general ledger account.

   The total of the accounts payable trial balance agreed with the balance in the related general ledger account.

2. Compare the amounts for claims received from creditors (as shown in claim documents provided by XYZ Company) to the respective amounts shown in the trial balance of accounts payable. Using the data included in the claims documents and in XYZ Company's accounts payable detail records, reconcile any differences found to the accounts payable trial balance.

   All differences noted are presented in column 3 of Schedule A. Except for those amounts shown in column 4 of Schedule A, all such differences were reconciled.

3. Examine the documentation submitted by creditors in support of the amounts claimed and compare it to the following documentation in XYZ Company's files: invoices, receiving reports, and other evidence of receipt of goods or services.

   No exceptions were found as a result of these comparisons.

We were not engaged to, and did not, perform an audit, the objective of which would be the expression of an opinion on the specified elements, accounts, or items. Accordingly, we do not express such an opinion. Had we performed additional procedures, other matters might have come to our attention that would have been reported to you.

This report is intended solely for the use of the Trustee of XYZ Company and should not be used by those who have not agreed to the procedures and taken responsibility for the sufficiency of the procedures for their purposes.

AU Section 9622

Engagements to Apply Agreed-Upon Procedures to Specified Elements, Accounts, or Items of a Financial Statement: Auditing Interpretations of Section 622

1. Applying Agreed-Upon Procedures to All, or Substantially All, of the Elements, Accounts, or Items of a Financial Statement

.01 *Question*—Section 622, *Engagements to Apply Agreed-Upon Procedures to Specified Elements, Accounts, or Items of a Financial Statement*, paragraph .06, defines specified elements, accounts, or items of a financial statement as accounting information that is "a part of, but significantly less than, a financial statement." Does that definition preclude applying procedures to all, or substantially all, of the elements, accounts, or items of a financial statement?

.02 *Interpretation*—No. Section 622.06 defines what constitutes an individual element, account, or item of a financial statement to which agreed-upon procedures are applied. It is not intended to limit the number of elements, accounts, or items to which such procedures are applied. Agreed-upon procedures may be applied to all, or substantially all, of the elements, accounts, or items of a financial statement, and section 622.16 states that the procedures may be "as limited or as extensive as the specified users desire." However, section 622.26 requires that the results of applying the procedures be presented in the form of findings and prohibits the accountant from providing negative assurance about whether the specified elements, accounts, or items are fairly stated in relation to established or stated criteria such as generally accepted accounting principles. In addition, if the report on applying agreed-upon procedures to specified elements, accounts, or items of a financial statement is presented along with the financial statements, the accountant should follow the guidance in footnote 15 in section 622 for his or her responsibility pertaining to the financial statements.

[Issue Date: November, 1997.]

AU Section 9622

Engagements to Apply Agreed-Upon Procedures to Specified Elements, Accounts, or Items of a Financial Statement: Auditing Interpretations of Section 622

1. Applying Agreed-Upon Procedures to All or Substantially All of the Elements, Accounts, or Items of a Financial Statement

[illegible]

AU Section 623

Special Reports

(Supersedes section 621)

Source: SAS No. 62; SAS No. 77.

See section 9623 for interpretations of this section.

Effective for reports issued on or after July 1, 1989, unless otherwise indicated.

Introduction

.01 This section applies to auditors' reports issued in connection with the following:

a. Financial statements that are prepared in conformity with a comprehensive basis of accounting other than generally accepted accounting principles (paragraphs .02 through .10)

b. Specified elements, accounts, or items of a financial statement (paragraphs .11 through .18)

c. Compliance with aspects of contractual agreements or regulatory requirements related to audited financial statements (paragraphs .19 through .21)

d. Financial presentations to comply with contractual agreements or regulatory provisions (paragraphs .22 through .30)

e. Financial information presented in prescribed forms or schedules that require a prescribed form of auditor's reports (paragraphs .32 and .33)

Financial Statements Prepared in Conformity With a Comprehensive Basis of Accounting Other Than Generally Accepted Accounting Principles

.02 Generally accepted auditing standards are applicable when an auditor conducts an audit of and reports on any financial statement. A financial statement may be, for example, that of a corporation, a consolidated group of corporations, a combined group of affiliated entities, a not-for-profit organization, a governmental unit, an estate or trust, a partnership, a proprietorship, a segment of any of these, or an individual. The term *financial statement* refers to a presentation of financial data, including accompanying notes, derived from accounting records and intended to communicate an entity's economic resources or obligations at a point in time or the changes therein for a period of time in conformity with a comprehensive basis of accounting. For reporting purposes, the independent auditor should consider each of the following types of financial presentations to be a financial statement:

a. Balance sheet

b. Statement of income or statement of operations

c. Statement of retained earnings

d. Statement of cash flows

e. Statement of changes in owners' equity

f. Statement of assets and liabilities that does not include owners' equity accounts

g. Statement of revenue and expenses

h. Summary of operations

i. Statement of operations by product lines

j. Statement of cash receipts and disbursements

.03 An independent auditor's judgment concerning the overall presentation of financial statements should be applied within an identifiable framework (see section 411, *The Meaning of* Present Fairly in Conformity With Generally Accepted Accounting Principles *in the Independent Auditor's Report*). Normally, the framework is provided by generally accepted accounting principles, and the auditor's judgment in forming an opinion is applied accordingly (see section 411.05). In some circumstances, however, a comprehensive basis of accounting other than generally accepted accounting principles may be used. [Reference deleted by the issuance of Statement on Auditing Standards No. 69, January 1992.]

.04 For purposes of this section, a comprehensive basis of accounting other than generally accepted accounting principles is one of the following—

a. A basis of accounting that the reporting entity uses to comply with the requirements or financial reporting provisions of a governmental regulatory agency to whose jurisdiction the entity is subject. An example is a basis of accounting insurance companies use pursuant to the rules of a state insurance commission.

b. A basis of accounting that the reporting entity uses or expects to use to file its income tax return for the period covered by the financial statements.

c. The cash receipts and disbursements basis of accounting, and modifications of the cash basis having substantial support, such as recording depreciation on fixed assets or accruing income taxes.

d. A definite set of criteria having substantial support that is applied to all material items appearing in financial statements, such as the price-level basis of accounting.

Unless one of the foregoing descriptions applies, reporting under the provisions of paragraph .05 is not permitted.

Reporting on Financial Statements Prepared in Conformity With an Other Comprehensive Basis of Accounting (OCBOA)

.05 When reporting on financial statements prepared in conformity with a comprehensive basis of accounting other than generally accepted accounting principles, as defined in paragraph .04, an independent auditor should include in the report—

a. A title that includes the word *independent*.[1]

---

[1] This section does not require a title for an auditor's report if the auditor is not independent. See section 504, *Association With Financial Statements*, for guidance on reporting when the auditor is not independent.

b. A paragraph that—

(1) States that the financial statements identified in the report were audited.

(2) States that the financial statements are the responsibility of the Company's management[2] and that the auditor is responsible for expressing an opinion on the financial statements based on the audit.

c. A paragraph that—

(1) States that the audit was conducted in accordance with generally accepted auditing standards.

(2) States that generally accepted auditing standards require that the auditor plan and perform the audit to obtain reasonable assurance about whether the financial statements are free of material misstatement.

(3) States that an audit includes—

(a) Examining, on a test basis, evidence supporting the amounts and disclosures in the financial statements,

(b) Assessing the accounting principles used and significant estimates made by management, and

(c) Evaluating the overall financial statement presentation (see paragraph .09).

(4) States that the auditor believes that his or her audit provides a reasonable basis for the opinion.

d. A paragraph that—

(1) States the basis of presentation and refers to the note to the financial statements that describes the basis (see paragraphs .09 and .10).

(2) States that the basis of presentation is a comprehensive basis of accounting other than generally accepted accounting principles.

e. A paragraph that expresses the auditor's opinion (or disclaims an opinion) on whether the financial statements are presented fairly, in all material respects, in conformity with the basis of accounting described. If the auditor concludes that the financial statements are not presented fairly on the basis of accounting described or if there has been a limitation on the scope of the audit, he or she should disclose all the substantive reasons for the conclusion in an explanatory paragraph(s) (preceding the opinion paragraph) of the report and should include in the opinion paragraph the appropriate modifying language and a reference to such explanatory paragraph(s).[3]

---

[2] In some instances, a document containing the auditor's report may include a statement by management regarding its responsibility for the presentation of the financial statements. Nevertheless, the auditor's report should state that the financial statements are management's responsibility. However, the statement about management's responsibility should not be further elaborated upon in the auditor's standard report or referenced to management's report.

[3] Paragraph .31 discusses other circumstances that may require that the auditor add additional explanatory language to the special report.

f. If the financial statements are prepared in conformity with the requirements or financial reporting provisions of a governmental regulatory agency (see paragraph .04*a*), a paragraph that restricts the use of the report solely to those within the entity and for filing with the regulatory agency. Such a restrictive paragraph is appropriate, even though by law or regulation the auditor's report may be made a matter of public record.[4] However, the auditor may use this form of report only if the financial statements and report are intended solely for filing with one or more regulatory agencies to whose jurisdiction the entity is subject.[5]

g. The manual or printed signature of the auditor's firm.

h. The date.[6]

[As amended, effective for audits of financial statements for periods ended on or after December 31, 1996, by Statement on Auditing Standards No. 77.]

.06 Unless the financial statements meet the conditions for presentation in conformity with a "comprehensive basis of accounting other than generally accepted accounting principles" as defined in paragraph .04, the auditor should use the standard form of report (see section 508, *Reports on Audited Financial Statements*, paragraph .08) modified as appropriate because of the departures from generally accepted accounting principles.

.07 Terms such as *balance sheet, statement of financial position, statement of income, statement of operations*, and *statement of cash flows*, or similar unmodified titles are generally understood to be applicable only to financial statements that are intended to present financial position, results of operations, or cash flows in conformity with generally accepted accounting principles. Consequently, the auditor should consider whether the financial statements that he or she is reporting on are suitably titled. For example, cash basis financial statements might be titled *statement of assets and liabilities arising from cash transactions*, or *statement of revenue collected and expenses paid*, and a financial statement prepared on a statutory or regulatory basis might be titled *statement of income—statutory basis*. If the auditor believes that the financial statements are not suitably titled, the auditor should disclose his or her reservations in an explanatory paragraph of the report and qualify the opinion.

.08 Following are illustrations of reports on financial statements prepared in conformity with a comprehensive basis of accounting other than generally accepted accounting principles.[7]

---

[4] Public record, for purposes of auditor's reports on financial statements of a regulated entity that are prepared in accordance with the financial reporting provisions of a government regulatory agency, includes circumstances in which specific requests must be made by the public to obtain access to or copies of the report. In contrast, the auditor would be precluded from using this form of report in circumstances in which the entity distributes the financial statements to parties other than the regulatory agency either voluntarily or upon specific request. [Footnote added, effective for audits of financial statements for periods ended on or after December 31, 1996, by Statement on Auditing Standards No. 77.]

[5] If the financial statements and report are intended for use other than for filing with one or more regulatory agencies to whose jurisdiction the entity is subject, the auditor should follow the guidance in section 544, *Lack of Conformity With Generally Accepted Accounting Principles*. [Footnote renumbered and amended, effective for audits of financial statements for periods ended on or after December 31, 1996, by the issuance of Statement on Auditing Standards No. 77.]

[6] For guidance on dating the auditor's report, see section 530, *Dating of the Independent Auditor's Report*. [Footnote renumbered by the issuance of Statement on Auditing Standards No. 77, November 1995.]

[7] If the report is a matter of public record, the following sentence may be added: "However, this report is a matter of public record and its distribution is not limited." [Footnote added, effective for audits of financial statements for periods ended on or after December 31, 1996, by Statement on Auditing Standards No. 77.]

Financial Statements Prepared on a Basis Prescribed by a Regulatory Agency Solely for Filing With That Agency

Independent Auditor's Report

We have audited the accompanying statements of admitted assets, liabilities, and surplus—statutory basis of XYZ Insurance Company as of December 31, 19X2 and 19X1, and the related statements of income and cash flows—statutory basis and changes in surplus—statutory basis for the years then ended. These financial statements are the responsibility of the Company's management. Our responsibility is to express an opinion on these financial statements based on our audits.

We conducted our audits in accordance with generally accepted auditing standards. Those standards require that we plan and perform the audit to obtain reasonable assurance about whether the financial statements are free of material misstatement. An audit includes examining, on a test basis, evidence supporting the amounts and disclosures in the financial statements. An audit also includes assessing the accounting principles used and significant estimates made by management, as well as evaluating the overall financial statement presentation. We believe that our audits provide a reasonable basis for our opinion.

As described in Note X, these financial statements were prepared in conformity with the accounting practices prescribed or permitted by the Insurance Department of [*State*], which is a comprehensive basis of accounting other than generally accepted accounting principles.

In our opinion, the financial statements referred to above present fairly, in all material respects, the admitted assets, liabilities, and surplus of XYZ Insurance Company as of December 31, 19X2 and 19X1, and the results of its operations and its cash flows for the years then ended, on the basis of accounting described in Note X.

This report is intended solely for the information and use of the board of directors and management of XYZ Insurance Company and for filing with the [*name of regulatory agency*] and should not be used for any other purpose.

Financial Statements Prepared on the Entity's Income Tax Basis

Independent Auditor's Report

We have audited the accompanying statements of assets, liabilities, and capital—income tax basis of ABC Partnership as of December 31, 19X2 and 19X1, and the related statements of revenue and expenses—income tax basis and of changes in partners' capital accounts—income tax basis for the years then ended. These financial statements are the responsibility of the Partnership's management. Our responsibility is to express an opinion on these financial statements based on our audits.

We conducted our audits in accordance with generally accepted auditing standards. Those standards require that we plan and perform the audit to obtain reasonable assurance about whether the financial statements are free of material misstatement. An audit includes examining, on a test basis, evidence supporting the amounts and disclosures in the financial statements. An audit also includes assessing the accounting principles used and significant estimates made by management, as well as evaluating the overall financial statement presentation. We believe that our audits provide a reasonable basis for our opinion.

As described in Note X, these financial statements were prepared on the basis of accounting the Partnership uses for income tax purposes, which is a comprehensive basis of accounting other than generally accepted accounting principles.

In our opinion, the financial statements referred to above present fairly, in all material respects, the assets, liabilities, and capital of ABC Partnership as of [at] December 31, 19X2 and 19X1, and its revenue and expenses and changes in partners' capital accounts for the years then ended, on the basis of accounting described in Note X.

Financial Statements Prepared on the Cash Basis

Independent Auditor's Report

We have audited the accompanying statements of assets and liabilities arising from cash transactions of XYZ Company as of December 31, 19X2 and 19X1, and the related statements of revenue collected and expenses paid for the years then ended. These financial statements are the responsibility of the Company's management. Our responsibility is to express an opinion on these financial statements based on our audits.

We conducted our audits in accordance with generally accepted auditing standards. Those standards require that we plan and perform the audit to obtain reasonable assurance about whether the financial statements are free of material misstatement. An audit includes examining, on a test basis, evidence supporting the amounts and disclosures in the financial statements. An audit also includes assessing the accounting principles used and significant estimates made by management, as well as evaluating the overall financial statement presentation. We believe that our audits provide a reasonable basis for our opinion.

As described in Note X, these financial statements were prepared on the basis of cash receipts and disbursements, which is a comprehensive basis of accounting other than generally accepted accounting principles.

In our opinion, the financial statements referred to above present fairly, in all material respects, the assets and liabilities arising from cash transactions of XYZ Company as of December 31, 19X2 and 19X1, and its revenue collected and expenses paid during the years then ended, on the basis of accounting described in Note X.

Evaluating the Adequacy of Disclosure in Financial Statements Prepared in Conformity With an Other Comprehensive Basis of Accounting

.09 When reporting on financial statements prepared on a comprehensive basis of accounting other than generally accepted accounting principles, the auditor should consider whether the financial statements (including the accompanying notes) include all informative disclosures that are appropriate for the basis of accounting used. The auditor should apply essentially the same criteria to financial statements prepared on an other comprehensive basis of accounting as he or she does to financial statements prepared in conformity with generally accepted accounting principles. Therefore, the auditor's opinion should be based on his or her judgment regarding whether the financial statements, including the related notes, are informative of matters that may affect their use, understanding, and interpretation as discussed in section 411, *The Meaning of* Present Fairly in Conformity With Generally Accepted Accounting Principles *in the Independent Auditor's Report*, paragraph .04.

.10 Financial statements prepared on an other comprehensive basis of accounting should include, in the accompanying notes, a summary of significant accounting policies that discusses the basis of presentation and describes how that basis differs from generally accepted accounting principles. However, the effects of the differences between generally accepted accounting principles and the basis of presentation of the financial statements that the auditor is reporting on need not be quantified. In addition, when the financial statements contain items that are the same as, or similar to, those in financial statements prepared in conformity with generally accepted accounting principles, similar informative disclosures are appropriate. For example, financial statements prepared on an income tax basis or a modified cash basis of accounting usually reflect depreciation, long-term debt and owners' equity. Thus, the informative disclosures for depreciation, long-term debt and owners' equity in such financial statements should be comparable to those in financial statements prepared in conformity with generally accepted accounting principles. When evaluating the adequacy of disclosures, the auditor should also consider disclosures related to matters that are not specifically identified on the face of the financial statements, such as (*a*) related party transactions, (*b*) restrictions on assets and owners' equity, (*c*) subsequent events, and (*d*) uncertainties.

Specified Elements, Accounts, or Items of a Financial Statement

.11 An independent auditor may be requested to express an opinion on one or more specified elements, accounts, or items of a financial statement. In such an engagement, the specified element(s), account(s), or item(s) may be presented in the report or in a document accompanying the report. Examples of one or more specified elements, accounts, or items of a financial statement that an auditor may report on based on an audit made in accordance with generally accepted auditing standards include rentals, royalties, a profit participation, or a provision for income taxes.[8]

.12 When expressing an opinion on one or more specified elements, accounts, or items of a financial statement, the auditor should plan and perform the audit and prepare his or her report with a view to the purpose of the engagement. With the exception of the first standard of reporting, the ten generally accepted auditing standards are applicable to any engagement to express an opinion on one or more specified elements, accounts, or items of a financial statement. The first standard of reporting, which requires that the auditor's report state whether the financial statements are presented in conformity with generally accepted accounting principles, is applicable only when the specified elements, accounts, or items of a financial statement are intended to be presented in conformity with generally accepted accounting principles.

---

[8] See section 622, *Engagements to Apply Agreed-Upon Procedures to Specified Elements, Accounts, or Items of a Financial Statement*, for guidance when reporting on the results of applying agreed-upon procedures to one or more specified elements, accounts, or items of a financial statement and AT section 100, *Attestation Standards*, for guidance when reporting on a review of one or more specified elements, accounts or items of a financial statement. [Footnote renumbered by the issuance of Statement on Auditing Standards No. 77, November 1995.]

.13 An engagement to express an opinion on one or more specified elements, accounts, or items of a financial statement may be undertaken as a separate engagement or in conjunction with an audit of financial statements. In either case, an auditor expresses an opinion on each of the specified elements, accounts, or items encompassed by the auditor's report; therefore, the measurement of materiality must be related to each individual element, account, or item reported on rather than to the aggregate thereof or to the financial statements taken as a whole. Consequently, an audit of a specified element, account, or item for purposes of reporting thereon is usually more extensive than if the same information were being considered in conjunction with an audit of financial statements taken as a whole. Also, many financial statement elements are interrelated, for example, sales and receivables; inventory and payables; and buildings and equipment and depreciation. The auditor should be satisfied that elements, accounts, or items that are interrelated with those on which he or she has been engaged to express an opinion have been considered in expressing an opinion.

.14 The auditor should not express an opinion on specified elements, accounts, or items included in financial statements on which he or she has expressed an adverse opinion or disclaimed an opinion based on an audit, if such reporting would be tantamount to expressing a piecemeal opinion on the financial statements (see section 508, *Reports on Audited Financial Statements*, paragraph .64). However, an auditor would be able to express an opinion on one or more specified elements, accounts, or items of a financial statement provided that the matters to be reported on and the related scope of the audit were not intended to and did not encompass so many elements, accounts, or items as to constitute a major portion of the financial statements. For example, it may be appropriate for an auditor to express an opinion on an entity's accounts receivable balance even if the auditor has disclaimed an opinion on the financial statements taken as a whole. However, the report on the specified element, account, or item should be presented separately from the report on the financial statements of the entity.

Reports on One or More Specified Elements, Accounts, or Items of a Financial Statement

.15 When an independent auditor is engaged to express an opinion on one or more specified elements, accounts, or items of a financial statement, the report should include—

a. A title that includes the word *independent*.[9]

b. A paragraph that—

(1) States that the specified elements, accounts, or items identified in the report were audited. If the audit was made in conjunction with an audit of the company's financial statements, the paragraph should so state and indicate the date of the auditor's report on those financial statements. Furthermore, any departure from the standard report on those statements should also be disclosed if considered relevant to the presentation of the specified element, account or item.

(2) States that the specified elements, accounts, or items are the responsibility of the Company's management and that the auditor is responsible for expressing an opinion on the specified elements, accounts or items based on the audit.

---

[9] See footnote 1. [Footnote renumbered by the issuance of Statement on Auditing Standards No. 77, November 1995.]

c. A paragraph that—

(1) States that the audit was conducted in accordance with generally accepted auditing standards.

(2) States that generally accepted auditing standards require that the auditor plan and perform the audit to obtain reasonable assurance about whether the specified elements, accounts, or items are free of material misstatement.

(3) States that an audit includes—

(*a*) Examining, on a test basis, evidence supporting the amounts and disclosures in the presentation of the specified elements, accounts, or items,

(*b*) Assessing the accounting principles used and significant estimates made by management, and

(*c*) Evaluating the overall presentation of the specified elements, accounts, or items.

(4) States that the auditor believes that his or her audit provides a reasonable basis for the auditor's opinion.

d. A paragraph[10] that—

(1) Describes the basis on which the specified elements, accounts, or items are presented (see paragraphs .09 and .10) and, when applicable, any agreements specifying such basis if the presentation is not prepared in conformity with generally accepted accounting principles.[11]

(2) If considered necessary, includes a description and the source of significant interpretations, if any, made by the Company's management, relating to the provisions of a relevant agreement.

e. A paragraph that expresses the auditor's opinion (or disclaims an opinion) on whether the specified elements, accounts, or items are fairly presented, in all material respects, in conformity with the basis of accounting described. If the auditor concludes that the specified elements, accounts, or items are not presented fairly on the basis of accounting described or if there has been a limitation on the scope of the audit, the auditor should disclose all the substantive reasons for that conclusion in an explanatory paragraph(s) (preceding the opinion paragraph) of the report and should include in the opinion paragraph appropriate modifying language and a reference to such explanatory paragraph(s).[12]

f. If the specified element, account, or item is prepared to comply with the requirements or financial reporting provisions of a contract or

---

[10] Alternatively, this requirement can be met by incorporating the description in the introductory paragraph discussed in paragraph .15*b* above. [Footnote renumbered by the issuance of Statement on Auditing Standards No. 77, November 1995.]

[11] When the specified element, account, or item is presented in conformity with an other comprehensive basis of accounting, see paragraph .05*d*(2). [Footnote renumbered by the issuance of Statement on Auditing Standards No. 77, November 1995.]

[12] Paragraph .31 discusses other circumstances that may require that the auditor add additional explanatory language to the special report. [Footnote renumbered by the issuance of Statement on Auditing Standards No. 77, November 1995.]

agreement that results in a presentation that is not in conformity with either generally accepted accounting principles or an other comprehensive basis of accounting, a paragraph that restricts the use of the report to those within the entity and the parties to the contract or agreement.[13] Such a restriction is necessary because the basis of presentation is determined by reference to a document that would not generally be available to other third parties.

g. The manual or printed signature of the auditor's firm.

h. The date.[14]

When expressing an opinion on one or more specified elements, accounts, or items of a financial statement, the auditor, to provide more information as to the scope of the audit, may wish to describe in a separate paragraph certain other auditing procedures applied. However, no modification in the content of paragraph .15*c* above should be made.

.16 If a specified element, account, or item is, or is based upon, an entity's net income or stockholders' equity or the equivalent thereof, the auditor should have audited the complete financial statements to express an opinion on the specified element, account, or item.

.17 The auditor should consider the effect that any departure, including additional explanatory language because of the circumstances discussed in section 508, *Reports on Audited Financial Statements*, paragraph .11, from the standard report on the audited financial statements might have on the report on a specified element, account, or item thereof.

.18 Following are illustrations of reports expressing an opinion on one or more specified elements, accounts, or items of a financial statement.

Report Relating to Accounts Receivable

Independent Auditor's Report

We have audited the accompanying schedule of accounts receivable of ABC Company as of December 31, 19X2. This schedule is the responsibility of the Company's management. Our responsibility is to express an opinion on this schedule based on our audit.

We conducted our audit in accordance with generally accepted auditing standards. Those standards require that we plan and perform the audit to obtain reasonable assurance about whether the schedule of accounts receivable is free of material misstatement. An audit includes examining, on a test basis, evidence supporting the amounts and disclosures in the schedule of accounts receivable. An audit also includes assessing the accounting principles used and significant estimates made by management, as well as evaluating the overall schedule presentation. We believe that our audit provides a reasonable basis for our opinion.

---

[13] If the presentation is prepared on a basis prescribed by a governmental regulatory agency (which is also OCBOA), the auditor should restrict the distribution of the report on such presentation. See paragraph .05*f* for further reporting guidance in this situation. [Footnote renumbered by the issuance of Statement on Auditing Standards No. 77, November 1995.]

[14] See footnote 6. [Footnote renumbered by the issuance of Statement on Auditing Standards No. 77, November 1995.]

In our opinion, the schedule of accounts receivable referred to above presents fairly, in all material respects, the accounts receivable of ABC Company as of December 31, 19X2, in conformity with generally accepted accounting principles.[15]

Report Relating to Amount of Sales for the Purpose of Computing Rental

Independent Auditor's Report

We have audited the accompanying schedule of gross sales (as defined in the lease agreement dated March 4, 19XX, between ABC Company, as lessor, and XYZ Stores Corporation, as lessee) of XYZ Stores Corporation at its Main Street store, [*City*], [*State*], for the year ended December 31, 19X2. This schedule is the responsibility of XYZ Stores Corporation's management. Our responsibility is to express an opinion on this schedule based on our audit.

We conducted our audit in accordance with generally accepted auditing standards. Those standards require that we plan and perform the audit to obtain reasonable assurance about whether the schedule of gross sales is free of material misstatement. An audit includes examining, on a test basis, evidence supporting the amounts and disclosures in the schedule of gross sales. An audit also includes assessing the accounting principles used and significant estimates made by management, as well as evaluating the overall schedule presentation. We believe that our audit provides a reasonable basis for our opinion.

In our opinion, the schedule of gross sales referred to above presents fairly, in all material respects, the gross sales of XYZ Stores Corporation at its Main Street store, [*City*], [*State*], for the year ended December 31, 19X2, as defined in the lease agreement referred to in the first paragraph.

This report is intended solely for the information and use of the boards of directors and managements of XYZ Stores Corporation and ABC Company and should not be used for any other purpose.

Report Relating to Royalties

Independent Auditor's Report

We have audited the accompanying schedule of royalties applicable to engine production of the Q Division of XYZ Corporation for the year ended December 31, 19X2, under the terms of a license agreement dated May 14, 19XX, between ABC Company and XYZ Corporation. This schedule is the responsibility of XYZ Corporation's management. Our responsibility is to express an opinion on this schedule based on our audit.

We conducted our audit in accordance with generally accepted auditing standards. Those standards require that we plan and perform the audit to obtain reasonable assurance about whether the schedule of royalties is free of material misstatement. An audit includes examining, on a test basis, evidence supporting the amounts and disclosures in the schedule of gross sales. An audit also includes assessing the accounting principles used and significant estimates made by management, as well as evaluating the overall schedule presentation. We believe that our audit provides a reasonable basis for our opinion.

---

[15] Since this presentation was prepared in conformity with generally accepted accounting principles, the report need not be restricted. [Footnote renumbered by the issuance of Statement on Auditing Standards No. 77, November 1995.]

We have been informed that, under XYZ Corporation's interpretation of the agreement referred to in the first paragraph, royalties were based on the number of engines produced after giving effect to a reduction for production retirements that were scrapped, but without a reduction for field returns that were scrapped, even though the field returns were replaced with new engines without charge to customers.

In our opinion, the schedule of royalties referred to above presents fairly, in all material respects, the number of engines produced by the Q Division of XYZ Corporation during the year ended December 31, 19X2, and the amount of royalties applicable thereto, under the license agreement referred to above.

This report is intended solely for the information and use of the boards of directors and managements of XYZ Corporation and ABC Company and should not be used for any other purpose.

Report on a Profit Participation[16]

Independent Auditor's Report

We have audited, in accordance with generally accepted auditing standards, the financial statements of XYZ Company for the year ended December 31, 19X1, and have issued our report thereon dated March 10, 19X2. We have also audited XYZ Company's schedule of John Smith's profit participation for the year ended December 31, 19X1. This schedule is the responsibility of the Company's management. Our responsibility is to express an opinion on this schedule based on our audit.

We conducted our audit of the schedule in accordance with generally accepted auditing standards. Those standards require that we plan and perform the audit to obtain reasonable assurance about whether the schedule of profit participation is free of material misstatement. An audit includes examining, on a test basis, evidence supporting the amounts and disclosures in the schedule. An audit also includes assessing the accounting principles used and significant estimates made by management, as well as evaluating the overall schedule presentation. We believe that our audit provides a reasonable basis for our opinion.

We have been informed that the documents that govern the determination of John Smith's profit participation are (*a*) the employment agreement between John Smith and XYZ Company dated February 1, 19X0, (*b*) the production and distribution agreement between XYZ Company and Television Network Incorporated dated March 1, 19X0, and (*c*) the studio facilities agreement between XYZ Company and QRX Studios dated April 1, 19X0, as amended November 1, 19X0.

In our opinion, the schedule of profit participation referred to above presents fairly, in all material respects, John Smith's participation in the profits of XYZ Company for the year ended December 31, 19X1, in accordance with the provisions of the agreements referred to above.

This report is intended solely for the information and use of the boards of directors and managements of XYZ Company and John Smith and should not be used for any other purpose.

[16] See paragraph .16. [Footnote renumbered by the issuance of Statement on Auditing Standards No. 77, November 1995.]

Report on Federal and State Income Taxes Included in Financial Statements[17]

Independent Auditor's Report

We have audited, in accordance with generally accepted auditing standards, the financial statements of XYZ Company, Inc., for the year ended June 30, 19XX, and have issued our report thereon dated August 15, 19XX. We have also audited the current and deferred provision for the Company's federal and state income taxes for the year ended June 30, 19XX, included in those financial statements, and the related asset and liability tax accounts as of June 30, 19XX. This income tax information is the responsibility of the Company's management. Our responsibility is to express an opinion on it based on our audit.

We conducted our audit of the income tax information in accordance with generally accepted auditing standards. Those standards require that we plan and perform the audit to obtain reasonable assurance about whether the federal and state income tax accounts are free of material misstatement. An audit includes examining, on a test basis, evidence supporting the amounts and disclosures related to the federal and state income tax accounts. An audit also includes assessing the accounting principles used and significant estimates made by management, as well as evaluating the overall presentation of the federal and state income tax accounts. We believe that our audit provides a reasonable basis for our opinion.

In our opinion, the Company has paid or, in all material respects, made adequate provision in the financial statements referred to above for the payment of all federal and state income taxes and for related deferred income taxes that could be reasonably estimated at the time of our audit of the financial statements of XYZ Company, Inc., for the year ended June 30, 19XX.

Compliance With Aspects of Contractual Agreements or Regulatory Requirements Related to Audited Financial Statements

.19 Entities may be required by contractual agreements, such as certain bond indentures and loan agreements, or by regulatory agencies to furnish compliance reports by independent auditors.[18] For example, loan agreements often impose on borrowers a variety of obligations involving matters such as payments into sinking funds, payments of interest, maintenance of current ratios, and restrictions of dividend payments. They usually also require the borrower to furnish annual financial statements that have been audited by an independent auditor. In some instances, the lenders or their trustees may request assurance from the independent auditor that the borrower has complied with certain covenants of the agreement relating to accounting matters. The independent auditor may satisfy this request by giving negative assurance relative to the applicable covenants based on the audit of the financial statements. This assurance may be given in a separate report or in one or more par-

---

[17] See paragraph .16. [Footnote renumbered by the issuance of Statement on Auditing Standards No. 77, November 1995.]

[18] When the auditor is engaged to test compliance with laws and regulations in accordance with *Government Auditing Standards* issued by the Comptroller General of the United States (Yellow Book), he or she should follow guidance contained in section 801, *Compliance Auditing Applicable to Governmental Entities and Other Specified Recipients of Governmental Financial Assistance*. [Footnote renumbered by the issuance of Statement on Auditing Standards No. 77, November 1995.]

agraphs of the auditor's report accompanying the financial statements. Such assurance, however, should not be given unless the auditor has audited the financial statements to which the contractual agreements or regulatory requirements relate and should not extend to covenants that relate to matters that have not been subjected to the audit procedures applied in the audit of the financial statements.[19] In addition, such assurance should not be given if the auditor has expressed an adverse opinion or disclaimed an opinion on the financial statements to which these covenants relate.

.20 When an auditor's report on compliance with contractual agreements or regulatory provisions is being given in a separate report, the report should include—

a. A title that includes the word *independent*.[20]

b. A paragraph that states the financial statements were audited in accordance with generally accepted auditing standards and that includes the date of the auditor's report on those financial statements. Furthermore, any departure from the standard report on those statements should also be disclosed.

c. A paragraph that includes a reference to the specific covenants or paragraphs of the agreement, provides negative assurance relative to compliance with the applicable covenants of the agreement insofar as they relate to accounting matters, and specifies that the negative assurance is being given in connection with the audit of the financial statements. The auditor should ordinarily state that the audit was not directed primarily toward obtaining knowledge regarding compliance.

d. A paragraph that includes a description and the source of significant interpretations, if any, made by the Company's management relating to the provisions of a relevant agreement.

e. A paragraph that restricts the use of the report to those within the entity and the parties to the contract or agreement or for filing with the regulatory agency, since the matters on which the auditor is reporting are set forth in a document that would not generally be available to other third parties.

f. The manual or printed signature of the auditor's firm.

g. The date.[21]

.21 When an auditor's report on compliance with contractual agreements or regulatory provisions is included in the report that expresses the auditor's opinion on the financial statements, the auditor should include a paragraph, after the opinion paragraph, that provides negative assurance relative to compliance with the applicable covenants of the agreement, insofar as they relate to accounting matters, and that specifies the negative assurance is being given in connection with the audit of the financial statements. The auditor should also ordinarily state that the audit was not directed primarily toward obtaining knowledge regarding compliance. In addition, the report should in-

---

[19] When the auditor is engaged to provide assurance on compliance with contractual agreements or regulatory provisions that relate to matters that have not been subjected to the audit procedures applied in the audit of the financial statements, the auditor should refer to the guidance in AT section 500, *Compliance Attestation*. [Footnote renumbered by the issuance of Statement on Auditing Standards No. 77, November 1995; Reference changed, February 1997, to AT section 500, to reflect the issuance of Statement on Standards for Attestation Engagements No. 3.]

[20] See footnote 1. [Footnote renumbered by the issuance of Statement on Auditing Standards No. 77, November 1995.]

[21] See footnote 6. [Footnote renumbered by the issuance of Statement on Auditing Standards No. 77, November 1995.]

clude a paragraph that includes a description and source of any significant interpretations made by the entity's management as discussed in paragraph .20*d* as well as a paragraph that restricts its distribution as discussed in paragraph .20*e*. Following are examples of reports that might be issued:

Report on Compliance With Contractual Provisions Given in a Separate Report[22]

Independent Auditor's Report

We have audited, in accordance with generally accepted auditing standards, the balance sheet of XYZ Company as of December 31, 19X2, and the related statement of income, retained earnings, and cash flows for the year then ended, and have issued our report thereon dated February 16, 19X3.

In connection with our audit, nothing came to our attention that caused us to believe that the Company failed to comply with the terms, covenants, provisions, or conditions of sections XX to XX, inclusive, of the Indenture dated July 21, 19X0, with ABC Bank insofar as they relate to accounting matters. However, our audit was not directed primarily toward obtaining knowledge of such noncompliance.

This report is intended solely for the information and use of the boards of directors and management of XYZ Company and ABC Bank and should not be used for any other purpose.

Report on Compliance With Regulatory Requirements Given in a Separate Report When the Auditor's Report on the Financial Statements Included an Explanatory Paragraph Because of an Uncertainty

Independent Auditor's Report

We have audited, in accordance with generally accepted auditing standards, the balance sheet of XYZ Company as of December 31, 19X2, and the related statement of income, retained earnings, and cash flows for the year then ended, and have issued our report thereon dated March 5, 19X3, which included an explanatory paragraph that described the litigation discussed in Note X of those statements.

In connection with our audit, nothing came to our attention that caused us to believe that the Company failed to comply with the accounting provisions in sections (1), (2) and (3) of the [name of state regulatory agency]. However, our audit was not directed primarily toward obtaining knowledge of such noncompliance.

This report is intended solely for the information and use of the board of directors and managements of XYZ Company and the [name of state regulatory agency] and should not be used for any other purpose.

---

[22] When the auditor's report on compliance with contractual agreements or regulatory provisions is included in the report that expresses the auditor's opinion on the financial statements, the last two paragraphs of this report are examples of the paragraphs that should follow the opinion paragraph of the auditor's report on the financial statements. [Footnote renumbered by the issuance of Statement on Auditing Standards No. 77, November 1995.]

Special-Purpose Financial Presentations to Comply With Contractual Agreements or Regulatory Provisions

.22 An auditor is sometimes asked to report on special-purpose financial statements prepared to comply with a contractual agreement[23] or regulatory provisions. In most circumstances, these types of presentations are intended solely for the use of the parties to the agreement, regulatory bodies, or other specified parties. This section discusses reporting on these types of presentations, which include the following:

a. A special-purpose financial presentation prepared in compliance with a contractual agreement or regulatory provision that does not constitute a complete presentation of the entity's assets, liabilities, revenues and expenses, but is otherwise prepared in conformity with generally accepted accounting principles or an other comprehensive basis of accounting (paragraphs .23 through .26).

b. A special-purpose financial presentation (may be a complete set of financial statements or a single financial statement) prepared on a basis of accounting prescribed in an agreement that does not result in a presentation in conformity with generally accepted accounting principles or an other comprehensive basis of accounting (paragraphs .27 through .30).

Financial Statements Prepared on a Basis of Accounting Prescribed in a Contractual Agreement or Regulatory Provision That Results in an Incomplete Presentation But One That is Otherwise in Conformity With Generally Accepted Accounting Principles or an Other Comprehensive Basis of Accounting

.23 A governmental agency may require a schedule of gross income and certain expenses of an entity's real estate operation in which income and expenses are measured in conformity with generally accepted accounting principles, but expenses are defined to exclude certain items such as interest, depreciation, and income taxes. Such a schedule may also present the excess of gross income over defined expenses. Also, a buy-sell agreement may specify a schedule of gross assets and liabilities of the entity measured in conformity with generally accepted accounting principles, but limited to the assets to be sold and liabilities to be transferred pursuant to the agreement.

.24 Paragraph .02 of this section defines the term *financial statement* and includes a list of financial presentations that an auditor should consider to be financial statements for reporting purposes. The concept of specified elements, accounts, or items of a financial statement discussed in paragraphs .11 through .18, on the other hand, refers to accounting information that is part of, but significantly less than, a financial statement. The financial presentations described above and similar presentations should generally be regarded as financial statements, even though, as indicated above, certain items may be excluded. Thus, when the auditor is asked to report on these types of presentations, the measurement of materiality for purposes of expressing an opinion

---

[23] A contractual agreement as discussed in this section is an agreement between the client and one or more third parties other than the auditor. [Footnote renumbered by the issuance of Statement on Auditing Standards No. 77, November 1995.]

should be related to the presentations taken as a whole (see section 312, *Audit Risk and Materiality in Conducting an Audit*). Further, the presentations should differ from complete financial statements only to the extent necessary to meet special purposes for which they were prepared. In addition, when these financial presentations contain items that are the same as, or similar to, those contained in a full set of financial statements prepared in conformity with generally accepted accounting principles, similar informative disclosures are appropriate (see paragraphs .09 and .10). The auditor should also be satisfied that the financial statements presented are suitably titled to avoid any implication that the special-purpose financial statements on which he or she is reporting are intended to present financial position, results of operations, or cash flows.

.25 When the auditor is asked to report on financial statements prepared on a basis of accounting prescribed in a contractual agreement or regulatory provision that results in an incomplete presentation but one that is otherwise in conformity with generally accepted accounting principles or an other comprehensive basis of accounting, the auditor's report should include—

a. A title that includes the word *independent*.[24]

b. A paragraph that—

(1) States that the financial statements identified in the report were audited.

(2) States that the financial statements are the responsibility of the Company's management[25] and that the auditor is responsible for expressing an opinion on the financial statements based on the audit.[26]

c. A paragraph that—

(1) States that the audit was conducted in accordance with generally accepted auditing standards.

(2) States that generally accepted auditing standards require that the auditor plan and perform the audit to obtain reasonable assurance about whether the financial statements are free of material misstatement.

(3) States that an audit includes—

(a) Examining, on a test basis, evidence supporting the amounts and disclosures in the financial statements,

(b) Assessing the accounting principles used and significant estimates made by management, and

(c) Evaluating the overall financial statement presentation.

---

[24] See footnote 1. [Footnote renumbered by the issuance of Statement on Auditing Standards No. 77, November 1995.]

[25] Sometimes the auditor's client may not be the person responsible for the financial statements on which the auditor is reporting. For example, when the auditor is engaged by the buyer to report on the seller's financial statements prepared in conformity with a buy-sell agreement, the person responsible for the financial statements may be the seller's management. In this case, the wording of this statement should be changed to clearly identify the party that is responsible for the financial statements reported on. [Footnote renumbered by the issuance of Statement on Auditing Standards No. 77, November 1995.]

[26] See footnote 2. [Footnote renumbered by the issuance of Statement on Auditing Standards No. 77, November 1995.]

(4) States that the auditor believes that the audit provides a reasonable basis for his or her opinion.

d. A paragraph that—

(1) Explains what the presentation is intended to present and refers to the note to the special-purpose financial statements that describes the basis of presentation (see paragraphs .09 and .10).

(2) If the basis of presentation is in conformity with generally accepted accounting principles, states that the presentation is not intended to be a complete presentation of the entity's assets, liabilities, revenues and expenses.[27]

e. A paragraph that expresses the auditor's opinion (or disclaims an opinion) related to the fair presentation, in all material respects, of the information the presentation is intended to present in conformity with generally accepted accounting principles or an other comprehensive basis of accounting. If the auditor concludes that the information the presentation is intended to present is not presented fairly on the basis of accounting described or if there has been a limitation on the scope of the audit, the auditor should disclose all the substantive reasons for that conclusion in an explanatory paragraph(s) (preceding the opinion paragraph) of the report and should include in the opinion paragraph appropriate modifying language and a reference to such explanatory paragraph(s).[28]

f. A paragraph that restricts the use of the report to those within the entity, to the parties to the contract or agreement, for filing with a regulatory agency or to those with whom the entity is negotiating directly. However, a restrictive paragraph is not appropriate when the report and related financial presentation are to be filed with a regulatory agency, such as the Securities and Exchange Commission, and are to be included in a document (such as a prospectus) that is distributed to the general public.

g. The manual or printed signature of the auditor's firm.

h. The date.[29]

.26 The following examples illustrate reports expressing an opinion on such special-purpose financial statements:

Report on a Schedule of Gross Income and Certain Expenses to Meet a Regulatory Requirement and to Be Included in a Document Distributed to the General Public

Independent Auditor's Report

We have audited the accompanying Historical Summaries of Gross Income and Direct Operating Expenses of ABC Apartments, City, State (Historical Sum-

---

[27] If the basis of presentation is an other comprehensive basis of accounting, the paragraph should state that the basis of presentation is a comprehensive basis of accounting other than generally accepted accounting principles and that it is not intended to be a complete presentation of the entity's assets, liabilities, revenues and expenses on the basis described. [Footnote renumbered by the issuance of Statement on Auditing Standards No. 77, November 1995.]

[28] Paragraph .31 discusses other circumstances that may require that the auditor add additional explanatory language to the special report. [Footnote renumbered by the issuance of Statement on Auditing Standards No. 77, November 1995.]

[29] See footnote 6. [Footnote renumbered by the issuance of Statement on Auditing Standards No. 77, November 1995.]

maries), for each of the three years in the period ended December 31, 19XX. These Historical Summaries are the responsibility of the Apartments' management. Our responsibility is to express an opinion on the Historical Summaries based on our audits.

We conducted our audits in accordance with generally accepted auditing standards. Those standards require that we plan and perform the audit to obtain reasonable assurance about whether the Historical Summaries are free of material misstatement. An audit includes examining, on a test basis, evidence supporting the amounts and disclosures in the Historical Summaries. An audit also includes assessing the accounting principles used and significant estimates made by management, as well as evaluating the overall presentation of the Historical Summaries. We believe that our audits provide a reasonable basis for our opinion.

The accompanying Historical Summaries were prepared for the purpose of complying with the rules and regulations of the Securities and Exchange Commission (for inclusion in the registration statement on Form S-11 of DEF Corporation) as described in Note X and are not intended to be a complete presentation of the Apartments' revenues and expenses.

In our opinion, the Historical Summaries referred to above present fairly, in all material respects, the gross income and direct operating expenses described in Note X of ABC Apartments for each of the three years in the period ended December 31, 19XX, in conformity with generally accepted accounting principles.

Report on a Statement of Assets Sold and Liabilities Transferred to Comply With a Contractual Agreement

Independent Auditor's Report

We have audited the accompanying statement of net assets sold of ABC Company as of June 8, 19XX. This statement of net assets sold is the responsibility of ABC Company's management. Our responsibility is to express an opinion on the statement of net assets sold based on our audit.

We conducted our audit in accordance with generally accepted auditing standards. Those standards require that we plan and perform the audit to obtain reasonable assurance about whether the statement of net assets sold is free of material misstatement. An audit includes examining, on a test basis, evidence supporting the amounts and disclosures in the statement. An audit also includes assessing the accounting principles used and significant estimates made by management, as well as evaluating the overall presentation of the statement of net assets sold. We believe that our audit provides a reasonable basis for our opinion.

The accompanying statement was prepared to present the net assets of ABC Company sold to XYZ Corporation pursuant to the purchase agreement described in Note X, and is not intended to be a complete presentation of ABC Company's assets and liabilities.

In our opinion, the accompanying statement of net assets sold presents fairly, in all material respects, the net assets of ABC Company as of June 8, 19XX sold pursuant to the purchase agreement referred to in Note X, in conformity with generally accepted accounting principles.

This report is intended solely for the information and use of the boards of directors and managements of ABC Company and XYZ Corporation and should not be used for any other purpose.

Financial Statements Prepared on a Basis of Accounting Prescribed in an Agreement That Results in a Presentation That is not in Conformity With Generally Accepted Accounting Principles or an Other Comprehensive Basis of Accounting

.27 The auditor may be asked to report on special-purpose financial statements prepared in conformity with a basis of accounting that departs from generally accepted accounting principles or an other comprehensive basis of accounting. A loan agreement, for example, may require the borrower to prepare consolidated financial statements in which assets, such as inventory, are presented on a basis that is not in conformity with generally accepted accounting principles or an other comprehensive basis of accounting. An acquisition agreement may require the financial statements of the entity being acquired (or a segment of it) to be prepared in conformity with generally accepted accounting principles except for certain assets, such as receivables, inventories, and properties for which a valuation basis is specified in the agreement.

.28 Financial statements prepared under a basis of accounting as discussed above are not considered to be prepared in conformity with a "comprehensive basis of accounting" as contemplated by paragraph .04 of this section because the criteria used to prepare such financial statements do not meet the requirement of being "criteria having substantial support," even though the criteria are definite.

.29 When an auditor is asked to report on these types of financial presentations, the report should include—

a. A title that includes the word *independent*.[30]

b. A paragraph that—

(1) States that the special-purpose financial statements identified in the report were audited.

(2) States that the financial statements are the responsibility of the Company's management[31] and that the auditor is responsible for expressing an opinion on the financial statements based on the audit.[32]

c. A paragraph that—

(1) States that the audit was conducted in accordance with generally accepted auditing standards.

(2) States that generally accepted auditing standards require that the auditor plan and perform the audit to obtain reasonable as-

---

[30] See footnote 1. [Footnote renumbered by the issuance of Statement on Auditing Standards No. 77, November 1995.]

[31] See footnote 25. [Footnote renumbered by the issuance of Statement on Auditing Standards No. 77, November 1995.]

[32] See footnote 2. [Footnote renumbered by the issuance of Statement on Auditing Standards No. 77, November 1995.]

surance about whether the financial statements are free of material misstatement.

(3) States that an audit includes—

(*a*) Examining, on a test basis, evidence supporting the amounts and disclosures in the financial statements,

(*b*) Assessing the accounting principles used and significant estimates made by management, and

(*c*) Evaluating the overall financial statement presentation.

(4) States that the auditor believes that the audit provides a reasonable basis for the auditor's opinion.

d. A paragraph that—

(1) Explains what the presentation is intended to present and refers to the note to the special-purpose financial statements that describes the basis of presentation (see paragraphs .09 and .10).

(2) States that the presentation is not intended to be a presentation in conformity with generally accepted accounting principles.

e. A paragraph that includes a description and the source of significant interpretations, if any, made by the Company's management relating to the provisions of a relevant agreement.

f. A paragraph that expresses the auditor's opinion (or disclaims an opinion) related to the fair presentation, in all material respects, of the information the presentation is intended to present on the basis of accounting specified. If the auditor concludes that the information the presentation is intended to present is not presented fairly on the basis of accounting described or if there has been a limitation on the scope of the audit, the auditor should disclose all the substantive reasons for that conclusion in an explanatory paragraph(s) (preceding the opinion paragraph) of the report and should include in the opinion paragraph appropriate modifying language and a reference to such explanatory paragraph(s).[33]

g. A paragraph that restricts the use of the report to those within the entity, the parties to the contract or agreement, for filing with a regulatory agency, or to those with whom the entity is negotiating directly. For example, when the financial statements have been prepared for the specified purpose of obtaining bank financing, the restriction should limit distribution to the various banks with whom the entity is negotiating the proposed financing.

h. The manual or printed signature of the auditor's firm.

i. The date.[34]

.30 The following example illustrates reporting on special-purpose financial statements that have been prepared pursuant to a loan agreement:

---

[33] Paragraph .31 discusses other circumstances that may require that the auditor add additional explanatory language to the special report. [Footnote renumbered by the issuance of Statement on Auditing Standards No. 77, November 1995.]

[34] See footnote 6. [Footnote renumbered by the issuance of Statement on Auditing Standards No. 77, November 1995.]

Report on Financial Statements Prepared Pursuant to a Loan Agreement That Results in a Presentation not in Conformity With Generally Accepted Accounting Principles or an Other Comprehensive Basis of Accounting

Independent Auditor's Report

We have audited the special-purpose statement of assets and liabilities of ABC Company as of December 31, 19X2 and 19X1, and the related special-purpose statements of revenues and expenses and of cash flows for the years then ended. These financial statements are the responsibility of the Company's management. Our responsibility is to express an opinion on these financial statements based on our audits.

We conducted our audits in accordance with generally accepted auditing standards. Those standards require that we plan and perform the audit to obtain reasonable assurance about whether the financial statements are free of material misstatement. An audit includes examining, on a test basis, evidence supporting the amounts and disclosures in the financial statements. An audit also includes assessing the accounting principles used and significant estimates made by management, as well as evaluating the overall financial statement presentation. We believe that our audits provide a reasonable basis for our opinion.

The accompanying special-purpose financial statements were prepared for the purpose of complying with Section 4 of a loan agreement between DEF Bank and the Company as discussed in Note X, and are not intended to be a presentation in conformity with generally accepted accounting principles.

In our opinion, the special-purpose financial statements referred to above present fairly, in all material respects, the assets and liabilities of ABC Company at December 31, 19X2 and 19X1, and the revenues, expenses and cash flows for the years then ended, on the basis of accounting described in Note X.

This report is intended solely for the information and use of the boards of directors and management of ABC Company and DEF Bank and should not be used for any other purpose.

Circumstances Requiring Explanatory Language in an Auditor's Special Report

.31 Certain circumstances, while not affecting the auditor's unqualified opinion, may require that the auditor add additional explanatory language to the special report. These circumstances include the following:

a. *Lack of Consistency in Accounting Principles.* If there has been a change in accounting principles or in the method of their application,[35] the auditor should add an explanatory paragraph to the report (following the opinion paragraph) that describes the change and refers to the note to the financial presentation (or specified elements, accounts, or items thereof) that discusses the change and its effect

---

[35] When financial statements (or specified elements, accounts, or items thereof) have been prepared in conformity with generally accepted accounting principles in prior years, and the entity changes its method of presentation in the current year by preparing its financial statements in conformity with an other comprehensive basis of accounting, the auditor need not follow the reporting guidance in this subparagraph. However, the auditor may wish to add an explanatory paragraph to the report to highlight (1) a difference in the basis of presentation from that used in prior years or (2) that another report has been issued on the entity's financial statements prepared in conformity with another basis of presentation (for example, when cash basis financial statements are issued in addition to GAAP financial statements). [Footnote renumbered by the issuance of Statement on Auditing Standards No. 77, November 1995.]

thereon[36] if the accounting change is considered relevant to the presentation. Guidance on reporting in this situation is contained in section 508, *Reports on Audited Financial Statements*, paragraphs .16 through .18.[37],[38]

b. *Going Concern Uncertainties.* If the auditor has substantial doubt about the entity's ability to continue as a going concern for a reasonable period of time not to exceed one year beyond the date of the financial statement, the auditor should add an explanatory paragraph after the opinion paragraph of the report only if the auditor's substantial doubt is relevant to the presentation.[39]

c. *Other Auditors.* When the auditor decides to make reference to the report of another auditor as a basis, in part, for his or her opinion, the auditor should disclose that fact in the introductory paragraph of the report and should refer to the report of the other auditors in expressing his or her opinion. Guidance on reporting in this situation is contained in section 508, *Reports on Audited Financial Statements*, paragraphs .12 and .13.

d. *Comparative Financial Statements (or Specified Elements, Accounts, or Items Thereof).* If the auditor expresses an opinion on prior-period financial statements (or specified elements, accounts, or items thereof) that is different from the opinion he or she previously expressed on that same information, the auditor should disclose all of the substantive reasons for the different opinion in a separate explanatory paragraph preceding the opinion paragraph of the report. Guidance on reporting in this situation is contained in section 508, *Reports on Audited Financial Statements*, paragraphs .68 and .69.

As in reports on financial statements prepared in conformity with generally accepted accounting principles, the auditor may add an explanatory paragraph to emphasize a matter regarding the financial statements (or specified elements, accounts, or items thereof). [Revised, February 1997, to reflect conforming changes necessary due to the issuance of Statement on Auditing Standards No. 79.]

Financial Information Presented in Prescribed Forms or Schedules

.32 Printed forms or schedules designed or adopted by the bodies with which they are to be filed often prescribe the wording of an auditor's report. Many of these forms are not acceptable to independent auditors because the prescribed form of auditor's report does not conform to the applicable professional reporting standards. For example, the prescribed language of the report may call for statements by the auditor that are not consistent with the auditor's function or responsibility.

---

[36] A change in the tax law is not considered to be a change in accounting principle for which the auditor would need to add an explanatory paragraph, although disclosure may be necessary. [Footnote renumbered by the issuance of Statement on Auditing Standards No. 77, November 1995.]

[37] [Footnote deleted to reflect conforming changes necessary due to the issuance of Statement on Auditing Standards No. 79.]

[38] [Footnote deleted to reflect conforming changes necessary due to the issuance of Statement on Auditing Standards No. 79.]

[39] See section 341, *The Auditor's Consideration of an Entity's Ability to Continue as a Going Concern*, for a report example when the auditor has substantial doubt about the entity's ability to continue as a going concern. [Footnote renumbered by the issuance of Statement on Auditing Standards No. 77, November 1995.]

.33 Some report forms can be made acceptable by inserting additional wording; others can be made acceptable only by complete revision. When a printed report form calls upon an independent auditor to make a statement that he or she is not justified in making, the auditor should reword the form or attach a separate report. In those situations, the reporting provisions of paragraph .05 may be appropriate.

Effective Date

.34 This section is effective for reports issued on or after July 1, 1989. Early application of the provisions of this section is permissible.

AU Section 9623

Special Reports: Auditing Interpretations of Section 623

[1.] Auditor's Report Under Employee Retirement Income Security Act of 1974

[.01–.08] [Withdrawn February 1983.*]

[2.] Reports on Elements, Accounts, or Items of a Financial Statement That Are Presented in Conformity with GAAP

[.09–.10] [Withdrawn March 1989, by SAS No. 62. (See section 623.)]

[3.] Compliance with the Foreign Corrupt Practices Act of 1977

[.11–.14] [Transferred to section 9642; Deleted October 1993.] (See the guidance provided in SSAE No. 2, paragraph 88 (AT section 400.83).)

[4.] Reports on Engagements Solely to Meet State Regulatory Examination Requirements

[.15–.16] [Deleted April 1981 by SAS No. 35, as superseded by SAS No. 75.] (See section 622.)

[5.] Financial Statements Prepared in Accordance with Accounting Practices Specified in an Agreement

[.17–.25] [Withdrawn March 1989, by SAS No. 62. (See section 623.)]

[6.] Reporting on Special-Purpose Financial Presentations[3], [4]

[.26–.31] [Withdrawn March 1989, by SAS No. 62. (See section 623.)]

[7.] Understanding of Agreed-Upon Procedures

[.32–.33] [Deleted April 1981 by SAS No. 35, as superseded by SAS No. 75.] (See section 622.)

[8.] Adequacy of Disclosure in Financial Statements Prepared on a Comprehensive Basis of Accounting Other Than Generally Accepted Accounting Principles

[.34–.39] [Withdrawn March 1989, by SAS No. 62. (See section 623.)]

9. Auditors' Special Reports on Property and Liability Insurance Companies' Loss Reserves

---

* See Audit and Accounting Guide *Audits of Employee Benefit Plans.*

[3] [Footnote deleted.]

[4] [Footnote deleted.]

.40 *Question*—The instructions to the statutory annual statement to be filed by property and liability insurance companies with state regulatory agencies include the following:

If a company is required by its domiciliary commissioner, there is to be submitted to the commissioner as an addendum to the Annual Statement by April 1 of the subsequent year a statement of a qualified loss reserve specialist setting forth his or her opinion relating to loss and loss adjustment expense reserves.

The term "qualified loss reserve specialist" includes an independent auditor who has competency in loss reserve evaluation.

.41 If an independent auditor who has made an audit of the insurance company's financial statements in accordance with generally accepted auditing standards is engaged to express a separate opinion on the company's loss and loss adjustment expense reserves for the purpose of compliance with the above instruction, what form of report should be used by the independent auditor?

.42 *Interpretation*—Section 623.11 through .18 provides guidance on auditors' reports expressing an opinion on one or more specified elements, accounts, or items of a financial statement. Following are illustrations of the auditor's report expressing an opinion on a company's loss and loss adjustment expense reserves and the schedule of liabilities for losses and loss adjustment expenses that would accompany the report.[5]

Illustrative report

Board of Directors

X Insurance Company

We are members of the American Institute of Certified Public Accountants (AICPA) and are the independent public accountants of X Insurance Company. We acknowledge our responsibility under the AICPA's Code of Professional Conduct to undertake only those engagements which we can complete with professional competence.

We have audited the financial statements prepared in conformity with generally accepted accounting principles [or prepared in conformity with accounting practices prescribed or permitted by the Insurance Department of the State of ....] of X Insurance Company as of December 31, 19X0, and have issued our report thereon dated March 1, 19X1. In the course of our audit, we have audited the estimated liabilities for unpaid losses and unpaid loss adjustment expenses of X Insurance Company as of December 31, 19X0, as set forth in the accompanying schedule including consideration of the assumptions and methods relating to the estimation of such liabilities.

In our opinion, the accompanying schedule presents fairly, in all material respects, the estimated unpaid losses and unpaid loss adjustment expenses of X Insurance Company that could be reasonably estimated at December 31, 19X0, in conformity with accounting practices prescribed or permitted by the Insurance Department of the State of .... on a basis consistent with that of the preceding year.

This report is intended solely for filing with regulatory agencies and is not intended for any other purpose.

Signature

Date

---

[5] If a significant period of time has elapsed between the date of the report on the financial statements and the date he is reporting on the loss and loss adjustment expense reserves, the auditor may wish to include the following paragraph after the opinion paragraph: Because we have not audited any financial statements of X Insurance Company as of any date or for any period subsequent to December 31, 19X0, we have no knowledge of the effects, if any, on the liability for unpaid losses and unpaid loss adjustment expenses of events that may have occurred subsequent to the date of our audit.

X Insurance Company

Schedule of Liabilities for Losses

and Loss Adjustment Expenses

December 31, 19X0

Liability for losses	$xx,xxx,xxx
Liability for loss adjustment expenses	x,xxx,xxx
Total	$xx,xxx,xxx

Note 1—Basis of presentation

The above schedule has been prepared in conformity with accounting practices prescribed or permitted by the Insurance Department of the State of .... (Significant differences between statutory practices and generally accepted accounting principles for the calculation of the above amounts should be described but the monetary effect of any such differences need not be stated.)

Losses and loss adjustment expenses are provided for when incurred in accordance with the applicable requirements of the insurance laws [and/or regulations] of the State of .... Such provisions include (1) individual case estimates for reported losses, (2) estimates received from other insurers with respect to reinsurance assumed, (3) estimates for unreported losses based on past experience modified for current trends, and (4) estimates of expenses for investigating and settling claims.

Note 2—Reinsurance

The Company reinsures certain portions of its liability insurance coverages to limit the amount of loss on individual claims and purchases catastrophe insurance to protect against aggregate single occurrence losses. Certain portions of property insurance are reinsured on a quota share basis.

The liability for losses and the liability for loss adjustment expenses were reduced by $xxx,xxx and $xxx,xxx, respectively, for reinsurance ceded to other companies.

Contingent liability exists with respect to reinsurance which would become an actual liability in the event the reinsuring companies, or any of them, might be unable to meet their obligations to the Company under existing reinsurance agreements.

.43 *Question*—The instructions to the statutory annual statement also include the following:

> If there has been any material change in the assumptions and/or methods from those previously employed, that change should be described in the statement of opinion by inserting a phrase such as:
>
> A material change in assumptions (and/or methods) was made during the past year, but such change accords with accepted loss reserving standards.

A brief description of the change should follow.

.44 In what circumstances is it appropriate for the independent auditor to modify his special report on loss and loss adjustment expense reserves for material changes in assumptions and/or methods?

.45 *Interpretation*—Section 420.06 states that changes in accounting principles and methods of applying them affect consistency and require the addition of an explanatory paragraph (following the opinion paragraph) in the auditor's report on the audited financial statements. Section 623.15 states that, if applicable, any departures from the auditor's standard report on the related financial statements should be indicated in the special report on an element, account, or item of a financial statement.

.46 Section 420.14 states that a change in accounting estimate is not a change affecting consistency requiring recognition in the auditor's report. However, such changes in estimates that are disclosed in the financial statements on which the auditor has reported should also be disclosed in the notes to the schedule of liabilities for unpaid losses and unpaid loss adjustment expenses accompanying the auditor's special report. (See APB Opinion No. 20, *Accounting Changes*, paragraph 33 [AC section A06.132].)

[Issue Date: May, 1981.]

10. Reports on the Financial Statements Included in Internal Revenue Form 990, "Return of Organizations Exempt from Income Tax"

.47 *Question*—Internal Revenue Form 990, "Return of Organizations Exempt from Income Tax," may be used as a uniform annual report by charitable organizations in some states for reporting to both state and federal governments. Many states require an auditor's opinion on whether the financial statements included in the report[6] are presented fairly in conformity with generally accepted accounting principles. Ordinarily, financial statements included in a Form 990 used by a charitable organization as a uniform annual report may be expected to contain certain material departures from the accounting principles in the AICPA industry audit guides, "Audits of Colleges and Universities," "Hospital Audit Guide," "Audits of Voluntary Health and Welfare Organizations," and AICPA Statement of Position 78-10, "Accounting Principles and Reporting Practices for Certain Nonprofit Organizations."

.48 In most states the report is used primarily to satisfy statutory requirements, but regulatory authorities make the financial statements and the accompanying auditor's report a matter of public record. In some situations, however, there may be public distribution of the report. What should be the form of the auditor's report in each of the above situations?

.49 *Interpretation*—In both situations, the auditor should first consider whether the financial statements (including appropriate notes to financial statements) are in conformity with generally accepted accounting principles. If they are, the auditor can express an unqualified opinion.

.50 If the financial statements are not in conformity with generally accepted accounting principles, the auditor should consider the distribution of the report to determine whether it is appropriate to issue a special report (as illustrated in section 623, *Special Reports*, paragraph .08, for reporting on financial statements prepared in accordance with the requirements or financial reporting provisions of a government regulatory agency).

.51 Section 623 permits this type of special report only if the financial statements are intended solely for filing with one or more regulatory agencies to whose jurisdiction the entity is subject. However, section 623 makes this

---

[6] As used in this interpretation, the report refers to a Form 990 report by a charitable organization in a filing with a government agency.

form of reporting appropriate, even though by law or regulation the accountant's report may be made a matter of public record.[7]

.52 The following example illustrates a report expressing an opinion on such special purpose financial statements:

Independent Auditor's Report

We have audited the balance sheet (Part V) of XYZ Charity as of December 31, 19XX, and the related statement of support, revenue and expenses and changes in fund balances (Part I) and statement of functional expenses (Part II) for the year then ended included in the accompanying Internal Revenue Service Form 990. These financial statements are the responsibility of Charity's management. Our responsibility is to express an opinion on these financial statements based on our audit.

We conducted our audit in accordance with generally accepted auditing standards. Those standards require that we plan and perform the audit to obtain reasonable assurance about whether the financial statements are free of material misstatement. An audit includes examining, on a test basis, evidence supporting the amounts and disclosures in the financial statements. An audit also includes assessing the accounting principles used and significant estimates made by management, as well as evaluating the overall financial statement presentation. We believe that our audit provides a reasonable basis for our opinion.

As described in Note X, these financial statements were prepared in conformity with the accounting practices prescribed by the Internal Revenue Service and the Office of the State of ......, which is a comprehensive basis of accounting other than generally accepted accounting principles.

In our opinion, the financial statements referred to above present fairly, in all material respects, the assets, liabilities and fund balances of XYZ Charity as of December 31, 19XX and its support, revenue and expenses and changes in fund balances for the year then ended on the basis of accounting described in Note X.[8]

Our audit was made for the purpose of forming an opinion on the above financial statements taken as a whole. The accompanying information on pages ...... to ...... is presented for purposes of additional analysis and is not a required part of the above financial statements. Such information, except for that portion marked "unaudited," on which we express no opinion, has been subjected to the auditing procedures applied in the audit of the above financial statements; and, in our opinion, the information is fairly stated in all material respects in relation to the financial statements taken as a whole.

This report is intended solely for the information and use of the board of directors and management of XYZ Charity and for filing with the Internal Revenue Service and the Office of the State of ...... and should not be used for any other purpose.

[*Signature*]

[*Date*]

---

[7] *Public record*, for purposes of auditors' reports in state with exempt organizations, includes circumstances in which specific requests must be made by the public to obtain access to or copies of the report, notwithstanding the fact that some states may advertise or require the exempt organization to advertise the availability of Form 990. In contrast, *public distribution*, for purposes of auditors' reports in state filings on various Forms 990 dealing with exempt organizations, includes circumstances in which the regulatory agency or the exempt organization, either because of regulatory requirements or voluntarily, distributes copies of Form 990 to contributors or others without receiving a specific request for such distribution.

[8] [Footnote deleted.]

.53 If there is public distribution[9] of the report, because the law requires it or otherwise (copies of Form 990 are distributed to contributors or others without receiving a specific request for such distribution) and the financial statements included in it are not in conformity with generally accepted accounting principles, a special report (as illustrated in section 623.08) is not appropriate. In such cases, the auditor should express a qualified or adverse opinion and disclose the effects on the financial statements of the departures from generally accepted accounting principles if the effects are reasonably determinable. If the effects are not reasonably determinable, the report should so state.

.54 Uniform generally accepted accounting principles for nonprofit organizations, including those filing Form 990, are still in the developmental stage. Therefore, auditors should recognize that the use of a special purpose report on Form 990 is only an interim solution until the reporting issues have been resolved by the Financial Accounting Standards Board.

[Issue Date: July, 1982; Revised: February, 1997.]

11. Reporting on Current-Value Financial Statements That Supplement Historical-Cost Financial Statements in a General-Use Presentation of Real Estate Entities

.55 *Question*—A real estate entity presents current-value financial statements[10] to supplement historical-cost financial statements in a general-use presentation. When engaged to report on these current-value financial statements, how should an auditor report?

.56 *Interpretation*—An auditor should accept an engagement to report on current-value financial statements that supplement historical-cost financial statements in a general-use presentation of a real estate entity only if the auditor believes the following two conditions exist—

- the measurement and disclosure criteria used to prepare the current-value financial statements are reasonable, and
- competent persons using the measurement and disclosure criteria would ordinarily obtain materially similar measurements or disclosures.

.57 If these conditions are satisfied, an auditor may report on such current-value financial statements in a manner similar to that discussed in section 623, *Special Reports*, paragraph .29. However, because the current-value financial statements only supplement the historical-cost financial statements and are not presented as a stand-alone presentation, it is not necessary to restrict the distribution of the auditor's report on the presentation as required by that paragraph.

---

[9] Auditors should consider whether there is a public distribution requirement by reference to the relevant state law. However, at this time (April 1982), most state laws do not contain a public distribution requirement and a special report is ordinarily appropriate. For example, the laws of New York, New Jersey and Connecticut do not presently require public distribution as defined by this interpretation.

[10] Generally accepted accounting principles require the use of current-value accounting for financial statements of certain types of entities (for example, investment companies, employee benefit plans, personal financial statements, and mutual and common trust funds). This interpretation does not apply to reports on current-value financial statements of such entities. The auditor engaged to report on current-value financial statements of such entities should follow the guidance in section 508, *Reports on Audited Financial Statements*, and the applicable industry audit guide.

.58 The following is an example of a report an auditor might issue when reporting on current-value financial statements that supplement historical-cost financial statements in a general-use presentation of a real estate entity:

Independent Auditor's Report

We have audited the accompanying historical cost-balance sheets of X Company as of December 31, 19X3 and 19X2, and the related historical-cost statements of income, shareholders' equity and cash flows for each of the three years in the period ended December 31, 19X3. We also have audited the supplemental current-value balance sheets of X Company as of December 31, 19X3 and 19X2, and the related supplemental current-value statements of income and shareholders' equity for each of the three years in the period ended December 31, 19X3. These financial statements are the responsibility of the Company's management. Our responsibility is to express an opinion on these financial statements based on our audits.

We conducted our audits in accordance with generally accepted auditing standards. Those standards require that we plan and perform the audit to obtain reasonable assurance about whether the financial statements are free of material misstatement. An audit includes examining, on a test basis, evidence supporting the amounts and disclosures in the financial statements. An audit also includes assessing the accounting principles used and significant estimates made by management, as well as evaluating the overall financial statement presentation. We believe that our audits provide a reasonable basis for our opinion.

In our opinion, the historical-cost financial statements referred to above present fairly, in all material respects, the financial position of X Company as of December 31, 19X3 and 19X2, and the results of its operations and its cash flows for each of the three years in the period ended December 31, 19X3, in conformity with generally accepted accounting principles.

As described in Note 1, the supplemental current-value financial statements have been prepared by management to present relevant financial information that is not provided by the historical-cost financial statements and are not intended to be a presentation in conformity with generally accepted accounting principles. In addition, the supplemental current-value financial statements do not purport to present the net realizable, liquidation, or market value of the Company as a whole. Furthermore, amounts ultimately realized by the Company from the disposal of properties may vary significantly from the current values presented.

In our opinion, the supplemental current-value financial statements referred to above present fairly, in all material respects, the information set forth in them on the basis of accounting described in Note 1.

[Signature]

[Date]

.59 The auditor should also consider the adequacy of disclosures relating to the current value financial statements. Such disclosures should describe the accounting policies applied and such matters as the basis of presentation, nature of the reporting entity's properties, status of construction-in-process, valuation bases used for each classification of assets and liabilities, and sources of valuation. These matters should be disclosed in the notes in a sufficiently clear and comprehensive manner that enables a knowledgeable reader to understand the current-value financial statements.

[Issue Date: July, 1990.]

12. Evaluation of the Appropriateness of Informative Disclosures in Insurance Enterprises' Financial Statements Prepared on a Statutory Basis

.60 *Question*—Insurance enterprises issue financial statements prepared in accordance with accounting practices prescribed or permitted by insurance regulators (a "statutory basis") in addition to, or instead of, financial statements prepared in accordance with generally accepted accounting principles (GAAP). How should auditors evaluate whether informative disclosures in financial statements prepared on a statutory basis are appropriate?

.61 *Interpretation*—Financial statements prepared on a statutory basis are financial statements prepared on a comprehensive basis of accounting other than GAAP according to section 623, *Special Reports*, paragraph .04. Section 623.09 states that "When reporting on financial statements prepared on a comprehensive basis of accounting other than generally accepted accounting principles, the auditor should consider whether the financial statements (including the accompanying notes) include all informative disclosures that are appropriate for the basis of accounting used. The auditor should apply essentially the same criteria to financial statements prepared on an other comprehensive basis of accounting as he or she does to financial statements prepared in conformity with generally accepted accounting principles. Therefore, the auditor's opinion should be based on his or her judgment regarding whether the financial statements, including the related notes, are informative of matters that may affect their use, understanding, and interpretation as discussed in section 411, *The Meaning of* Present Fairly in Conformity With Generally Accepted Accounting Principles *in the Independent Auditor's Report*, paragraph .04."

.62 Section 623.02 states that generally accepted auditing standards apply when an auditor conducts an audit of and reports on financial statements prepared on an other comprehensive basis of accounting. Thus, in accordance with the third standard of reporting, "informative disclosures in the financial statements are to be regarded as reasonably adequate unless otherwise stated in the report."

.63 *Question*—What types of items or matters should auditors consider in evaluating whether informative disclosures are reasonably adequate?

.64 *Interpretation*—Section 623.09 and .10 indicates that financial statements prepared on a comprehensive basis of accounting other than GAAP should include all informative disclosures that are appropriate for the basis of accounting used, including a summary of significant accounting policies that discusses the basis of presentation and describes how that basis differs from GAAP. Section 623.10 also states that when "the financial statements [prepared on an other comprehensive basis of accounting] contain items that are the same as, or similar to, those in financial statements prepared in conformity with generally accepted accounting principles, similar informative disclosures are appropriate."

.65 In addition, in 1991, the National Association of Insurance Commissioners (NAIC) adopted a new Annual Statement instruction, *Annual Audited Financial Reports*, under which insurance enterprises are required to include in their statutory basis financial statements those disclosures that "are appropriate to a CPA audited financial report, based on applicability, materiality and significance, taking into account the subjects covered in the instructions to and illustrations of how to report information in the notes to the financial statements section of [the] Annual Statement instructions and any other notes required by generally accepted accounting principles. . . ." The laws and regulations of some individual states contain similar requirements.

.66 Therefore, the auditor should also consider the disclosures and illustrations of how to report information in the notes to financial statements section of the Annual Statement instructions.

.67 *Question*—How does the auditor evaluate whether "similar informative disclosures" are appropriate for—

a. Items and transactions that are accounted for essentially the same or in a similar manner under a statutory basis as under GAAP

b. Items and transactions that are accounted for differently under a statutory basis than under GAAP

.68 *Interpretation*—Disclosures in statutory basis financial statements for items and transactions that are accounted for essentially the same or in a similar manner under a statutory basis as under GAAP should be the same as, or similar to, the disclosures required by GAAP. Other disclosures considered necessary upon review of the Annual Statement instructions should also be made to the extent that such disclosures are significant to the statutory basis financial statements.

.69 For example, disclosures in statutory basis financial statements concerning financial instruments should include the applicable disclosures required by FASB Statement No. 60, *Accounting and Reporting by Insurance Enterprises* [AC section In6], FASB Statement No. 105, *Disclosure of Information about Financial Instruments with Off-Balance-Sheet Risk and Financial Instruments with Concentrations of Credit Risk* [AC section F25], FASB Statement No. 107, *Disclosures about Fair Value of Financial Instruments* [AC section F25], and FASB Statement No. 115, *Accounting for Certain Investments in Debt and Equity Securities* [AC section I80].

.70 Disclosures in statutory basis financial statements for items that are accounted for differently under a statutory basis than under GAAP should be the same as the disclosures required by GAAP that are relevant to the statutory basis of accounting for that item. Such disclosures can be separated into two general categories, which are discussed in paragraphs .71–.76 of this Interpretation. The examples presented are for illustrative purposes only and are not intended to be all-inclusive.

.71 Specific disclosures are stated in GAAP literature for the accounting method used in the statutory basis financial statements, even though the item would be accounted for differently under GAAP. In such instances, the applicable GAAP disclosures should be made in addition to those disclosures considered necessary upon review of the Annual Statement instructions.

.72 For example, certain leases entered into by a lessee insurance enterprise that would be accounted for as capital leases under GAAP are accounted for as operating leases by insurance enterprises in their statutory basis financial statements. In such instances, the applicable disclosures for operating leases required by FASB Statement No. 13, *Accounting for Leases* [AC section L10], should be made in the statutory basis financial statements.

.73 Another example is reinsurance transactions. Certain reinsurance contracts are permitted to be accounted for as reinsurance transactions in statutory basis financial statements but would be accounted for as financing transactions under GAAP. In such instances, the applicable disclosures for the contracts accounted for as reinsurance transactions that are required by FASB Statement No. 113, *Accounting and Reporting for Reinsurance of Short-Duration and Long-Duration Contracts* [AC section In6], should be made in statutory basis financial statements.

.74 Specific disclosures are not stated in current GAAP literature for the accounting method used in the statutory basis financial statements. If statutory accounting principles (SAP) permit insurance enterprises to use an accounting method that has been superseded under GAAP literature, disclosures that were required under the superseded GAAP literature should be made.

.75 For example, some insurance companies are permitted to account for pensions in their statutory basis financial statements using the same method as required under APB Opinion No. 8, *Accounting for the Cost of Pension Plans*, which was amended by FASB Statement No. 36, *Disclosure of Pension Information*. (APB Opinion No. 8 and FASB Statement No. 36 were superseded by FASB Statement No. 87, *Employers' Accounting for Pensions* [AC section P16], for fiscal years that began after December 15, 1986.) In addition to disclosing the accounting policy for pensions, insurance companies should make the disclosures contained in APB Opinion No. 8 and FASB Statement No. 36 in their statutory basis financial statements. If a company is accounting for pensions using another method of measurement, such as tax, it should make informative disclosures, at a minimum, such as type of benefit formula, funding policy, fair value of plan assets, and amount of pension costs.

.76 A final example is deferred acquisition costs (DAC). Acquisition costs are expensed when paid under SAP and are capitalized and amortized under GAAP. FASB Statement No. 60 [AC section In6] requires certain disclosures about DAC—the nature of acquisition costs capitalized, the method of amortizing those costs, and the amount of those costs amortized for the period. Because DAC are not capitalized under SAP, such disclosures, other than a description of the accounting policy used, are unapplicable.

.77 When evaluating the adequacy of disclosures, the auditor should also consider disclosures related to matters that are not specifically identified on the face of the financial statements, such as (*a*) related party transactions, (*b*) restrictions on assets and owners' equity, (*c*) subsequent events, and (*d*) uncertainties. Other matters should be disclosed if such disclosures are necessary to keep the financial statements from being misleading.

[.78–.79] [Paragraphs deleted to reflect conforming changes necessary due to the issuance of FASB Statement No. 120, *Accounting and Reporting by Mutual Life Insurance Enterprises and by Insurance Enterprises for Certain Long-Duration Participating Contracts*, and FASB Interpretation No. 40, *Applicability of Generally Accepted Accounting Principles to Mutual Life Insurance and Other Enterprises*.]

[Issue Date: December, 1991; Revised: February, 1997.]

13. Reporting on a Special-Purpose Financial Statement That Results in an Incomplete Presentation But is Otherwise in Conformity With Generally Accepted Accounting Principles

.80 *Question*—An auditor may be requested to report on a special-purpose financial statement that results in an incomplete presentation but otherwise is in conformity with generally accepted accounting principles. For example, an entity wishing to sell a division or product line may prepare an offering memorandum that includes a special-purpose financial statement that presents certain assets and liabilities, revenues and expenses relating to the division or product line being sold. Section 623, *Special Reports*, paragraph .22 states that the auditor may report on a special-purpose financial statement prepared to comply with a contractual agreement. Does an offering memorandum (not including a filing with a regulatory agency) constitute a contractual agreement for purposes of issuing an auditor's report under this section?

.81 *Interpretation*—No. An offering memorandum generally is a document providing information as the basis for negotiating an offer to sell certain assets or businesses or to raise funds. Normally, parties to an agreement or other specified parties for whom the special-purpose financial presentation is intended have not been identified. Accordingly, the auditor should follow the reporting guidance in section 508, *Reports on Audited Financial Statements*, paragraphs .35–.44 and .58–.60.

.82 *Question*—Does an agreement between a client and one or more third parties other than the auditor to prepare financial statements using a special-purpose presentation constitute a contractual agreement for purposes of issuing an auditor's report under this section?

.83 *Interpretation*—Yes. In such cases, the auditor should follow the guidance in section 623.22–.26, and the auditor's report should be restricted to those within the entity, to the parties to the contract or agreement or to those with whom the entity is negotiating directly.

.84 If there is no such agreement, the auditor should follow the guidance in section 508.35–.44 and .58–.60.

.85 *Question*—The auditor may be requested to add to the restricted distribution of his or her report additional third parties that were not parties to the original contract or agreement. What guidance should the auditor follow in such cases?

.86 *Interpretation*—The auditor may add additional parties to the restricted distribution of his or her report provided such parties agree to the special-purpose financial statements. The auditor should obtain acknowledgment, normally in writing, from such parties concerning their acceptance of the incomplete presentation for their purposes. The auditor also may acknowledge that a party has been added to the distribution of his or her report or may reissue the report indicating all the parties to whom it is restricted.

.87 Alternatively, when it is likely that such requests may arise involving a specific class of parties, such as potential purchasers of a division or product line, the auditor may restrict his or her report to those parties that are presently known and have agreed to the special-purpose presentation and to those additional third parties that are expected to agree to the special-purpose presentation (for example, this may be accomplished by including in the restricted distribution those additional third parties agreeing to the special-purpose presentation by such additional parties signing a confidentiality agreement or similar document).

[Issue Date: May, 1995.]

14. Evaluating the Adequacy of Disclosure in Financial Statements Prepared on the Cash, Modified Cash, or Income Tax Basis of Accounting

.88 *Question*—Section 623, *Special Reports*, paragraph .10, requires that financial statements prepared on a comprehensive basis of accounting other than generally accepted accounting principles (GAAP) include a summary of significant accounting policies that discusses the basis of presentation and describes how that basis differs from GAAP. It also states that when such financial statements contain items that are the same as, or similar to, those in statements prepared in conformity with GAAP, "similar informative disclosures are appropriate." To illustrate how to apply that statement, section 623.10 says that the disclosures for depreciation, long-term debt, and owners' equity should be "comparable to" those in financial statements prepared in conformity with GAAP. That paragraph then states that the auditor "should also consider" the need for disclosure of matters that are not specifically identified on the face of the statements, such as (*a*) related party transactions, (*b*) restrictions on assets and owners' equity, (*c*) subsequent events, and (*d*) uncertainties. How should the guidance in section 623.10 be applied in evaluating the adequacy of disclosure in financial statements prepared on the cash, modified cash, or income tax basis of accounting?

.89 *Interpretation*—The discussion of the basis of presentation may be brief; for example: "The accompanying financial statements present financial results on the accrual basis of accounting used for federal income tax reporting." Only the primary differences from GAAP need to be described. To illustrate, assume that several items are accounted for differently than they would be under GAAP, but that only the differences in depreciation calculations are significant. In that situation, a brief description of the depreciation differences is all that would be necessary, and the remaining differences need not be described. Quantifying differences is not required.

.90 If cash, modified cash, or income tax basis financial statements contain elements, accounts, or items for which GAAP would require disclosure, the statements should either provide the relevant disclosure that would be required for those items in a GAAP presentation or provide information that communicates the substance of that disclosure. That may result in substituting qualitative information for some of the quantitative information required for GAAP presentations. For example, disclosing the repayment terms of significant long-term borrowings may sufficiently communicate information about future principal reduction without providing the summary of principal reduction during each of the next five years that would be required for a GAAP presentation. Similarly, disclosing estimated percentages of revenues, rather than amounts that GAAP presentations would require, may sufficiently convey the significance of sales or leasing to related parties. GAAP disclosure requirements that are not relevant to the measurement of the element, account, or item need not be considered. To illustrate:

a. The fair value information that FASB Statement No. 115, *Accounting for Certain Investments in Debt and Equity Securities* [AC section I80], would require disclosing for debt and equity securities reported in GAAP presentations would not be relevant when the basis of presentation does not adjust the cost of such securities to their fair value.

b. The information based on actuarial calculations that FASB Statement No. 87, *Employers' Accounting for Pensions* [AC section P16], would require disclosing for contributions to defined benefit plans reported in GAAP presentations would not be relevant in income tax or cash basis financial statements.

.91 If GAAP sets forth requirements that apply to the presentation of financial statements, then cash, modified cash, and income tax basis statements should either comply with those requirements or provide information that communicates the substance of those requirements. The substance of GAAP presentation requirements may be communicated using qualitative information and without modifying the financial statement format. For example:

a. Information about the effects of accounting changes, discontinued operations, and extraordinary items could be disclosed in a note to the financial statements without following the GAAP presentation requirements in the statement of results of operations, using those terms, or disclosing net-of-tax effects.

b. Instead of showing expenses by their functional classifications, the income tax basis statement of activities of a trade organization could present expenses according to their natural classifications, and a note to the statement could use estimated percentages to communicate information about expenses incurred by the major program and supporting services. A voluntary health and welfare organization could take such an approach instead of presenting the matrix of natural and functional expense classifications that would be required for a GAAP presentation, or, if information has been gathered for the Form 990 matrix required for such organizations, it could be presented either in the form of a separate statement or in a note to the financial statements.

c. Instead of showing the amounts of, and changes in, the unrestricted and temporarily and permanently restricted classes of net assets, which would be required for a GAAP presentation, the income tax basis statement of financial position of a voluntary health and welfare organization could report total net assets or fund balances, the related statement of activities could report changes in those totals, and a note to the financial statements could provide information, using estimated or actual amounts or percentages, about the restrictions on those amounts and on any deferred restricted amounts, describe the major restrictions, and provide information about significant changes in restricted amounts.

.92 Presentations using the cash basis of accounting, the modified cash basis, or the cash basis used for income tax reporting often include a presentation consisting entirely or mainly of cash receipts and disbursements. Such presentations need not conform with the requirements for a statement of cash flows that would be included in a GAAP presentation. While a statement of cash flows is not required in presentations using the cash, modified cash, or income tax basis of accounting, if a presentation of cash receipts and disbursements is presented in a format similar to a statement of cash flows or if the entity chooses to present such a statement, for example in a presentation on the accrual basis of accounting used for federal income tax reporting, the statement should either conform to the requirements for a GAAP presentation or communicate their substance. As an example, the statement of cash flows might disclose noncash acquisitions through captions on its face.

.93 If GAAP would require disclosure of other matters, the auditor should consider the need for that same disclosure or disclosure that communicates the substance of those requirements. Some examples are contingent liabilities, going concern considerations, and significant risks and uncertainties. However, the disclosures need not include information that is not relevant to the basis of accounting. To illustrate, the general information about the use of estimates that is required to be disclosed in GAAP presentations by Statement of Position 94-6, *Disclosure of Certain Significant Risks and Uncertainties*, would not be relevant in a presentation that has no estimates, such as one based on cash receipts and disbursements.

[Issue Date: January, 1998.]

AU Section 625

Reports on the Application of Accounting Principles

Source: SAS No. 50.

Issue date, unless otherwise indicated: July, 1986.

.01 Accounting principles evolve in response to changing economic conditions and to new transactions and financial products.[1] Agreement frequently does not exist about how accounting principles should be applied to those transactions and products. Management, accountants, and intermediaries often consult with professionals, including other accountants, on the application of accounting principles to those transactions and products or to increase their knowledge of specific financial reporting issues.[2] Such consultations are often useful because they may provide information and insights not otherwise available.

Applicability

.02 This section provides guidance that an accountant in public practice ("reporting accountant"), either in connection with a proposal to obtain a new client or otherwise, should apply[3]—

a. When preparing a written report on the application of accounting principles to specified transactions, either completed or proposed ("specific transactions").

b. When requested to provide a written report on the type of opinion that may be rendered on a specific entity's financial statements.

c. When preparing a written report to intermediaries on the application of accounting principles not involving facts or circumstances of a particular principal ("hypothetical transactions").

This section also applies to oral advice on the application of accounting principles to a specific transaction, or the type of opinion that may be rendered on an entity's financial statements, when the reporting accountant concludes the advice is intended to be used by a principal to the transaction as an important factor considered in reaching a decision.

---

[1] Accounting principles include generally accepted accounting principles and other comprehensive bases of accounting. See section 623, *Special Reports*, paragraph .04 for a description of other comprehensive bases of accounting.

[2] "Intermediaries" refers to those parties who may advise one or more principals to a transaction, and may include, but are not limited to, attorneys and investment, merchant, and commercial bankers.

[3] See ET section 92.09 of the AICPA Code of Professional Conduct for a definition of "practice of public accounting."

.03 This section does not apply to an accountant ("continuing accountant") who has been engaged to report on financial statements, to engagements either to assist in litigation involving accounting matters or to provide expert testimony in connection with such litigation, or to professional advice given to another accountant in public practice.

.04 This section also does not apply to communications such as position papers prepared by an accountant for the purpose of presenting views on an issue involving the application of accounting principles or the type of opinion that may be rendered on an entity's financial statements. Position papers include newsletters, articles, speeches and texts thereof, lectures and other forms of public presentations, and letters for the public record to professional and governmental standard-setting bodies. However, if communications of the type discussed in this paragraph are intended to provide guidance on the application of accounting principles to a specific transaction, or on the type of opinion that may be rendered on a specific entity's financial statements, the provisions of this section should be followed.

Performance Standards

.05 The reporting accountant should exercise due professional care in performing the engagement and should have adequate technical training and proficiency. The reporting accountant should also plan the engagement adequately, supervise the work of assistants, if any, and accumulate sufficient information to provide a reasonable basis for the professional judgment described in the report. The reporting accountant should consider who is the requester of the report, the circumstances under which the request is made, the purpose of the request, and the requester's intended use of the report.

.06 To aid in forming a judgment, the reporting accountant should perform the following procedures: (*a*) obtain an understanding of the form and substance of the transaction(s); (*b*) review applicable generally accepted accounting principles (see section 411, *The Meaning of* Present Fairly in Conformity with Generally Accepted Accounting Principles *in the Independent Auditor's Report*); (*c*) if appropriate, consult with other professionals or experts; and (*d*) if appropriate, perform research or other procedures to ascertain and consider the existence of creditable precedents or analogies.

.07 When evaluating accounting principles or determining the type of opinion that may be rendered on an entity's financial statements at the request of a principal, or an intermediary acting for a principal, that relate to a specific transaction, or to a specific entity's financial statements, the reporting accountant should consult with the continuing accountant of the principal to ascertain all the available facts relevant to forming a professional judgment. The continuing accountant may provide information not otherwise available to the reporting accountant regarding, for example, the following: the form and substance of the transaction; how management has applied accounting principles to similar transactions; whether the method of accounting recommended by the continuing accountant is disputed by management; or whether the continuing accountant has reached a different conclusion on the application of accounting principles or the type of opinion that may be rendered on the entity's financial statements. The reporting accountant should explain to the principal or intermediary the need to consult with the continuing accountant, request permission to do so, and request the principal to authorize the continuing accountant to respond fully to the reporting accountant's inquiries. The responsibilities of a principal's continuing accountant to respond to inquiries by the reporting accountant are the same as the responsibilities of a predecessor auditor to respond to inquiries by a successor auditor. See section 315A, *Communications Between Predecessor and Successor Auditors*, paragraph .07.

Reporting Standards

.08 The accountant's written report should be addressed to the principal to the transaction or to the intermediary, and should ordinarily include the following:[4]

a. A brief description of the nature of the engagement and a statement that the engagement was performed in accordance with applicable AICPA standards.

b. A description of the transaction(s), a statement of the relevant facts, circumstances, and assumptions, and a statement about the source of the information. Principals to specific transactions should be identified, and hypothetical transactions should be described as involving nonspecific principals (for example, Company A, Company B).

c. A statement describing the appropriate accounting principle(s) to be applied or type of opinion that may be rendered on the entity's financial statements, and, if appropriate, a description of the reasons for the reporting accountant's conclusion.

d. A statement that the responsibility for the proper accounting treatment rests with the preparers of the financial statements, who should consult with their continuing accountants.

e. A statement that any difference in the facts, circumstances, or assumptions presented may change the report.

.09 The following is an illustration of sections of the report described in paragraph .08.

Introduction

We have been engaged to report on the appropriate application of generally accepted accounting principles to the specific (hypothetical) transaction described below. This report is being issued to the ABC Company (XYZ Intermediaries) for assistance in evaluating accounting principles for the described specific (hypothetical) transaction. Our engagement has been conducted in accordance with standards established by the American Institute of Certified Public Accountants.

Description of Transaction

The facts, circumstances, and assumptions relevant to the specific (hypothetical) transaction as provided to us by the management of the ABC Company (XYZ Intermediaries) are as follows:

Appropriate Accounting Principles

[*Text discussing principles*]

---

[4] Although the reporting standards in this section apply only to written reports, accountants may find this guidance useful in presenting oral advice.

Concluding Comments

The ultimate responsibility for the decision on the appropriate application of generally accepted accounting principles for an actual transaction rests with the preparers of financial statements, who should consult with their continuing accountants. Our judgment on the appropriate application of generally accepted accounting principles for the described specific (hypothetical) transaction is based solely on the facts provided to us as described above; should these facts and circumstances differ, our conclusion may change.

AU Section 634

Letters for Underwriters and Certain Other Requesting Parties

(Supersedes SAS No. 49)

Source: SAS No. 72; SAS No. 76.

See section 9634 for interpretations of this section.

Effective for comfort letters issued on or after June 30, 1993, unless otherwise indicated.

Introduction

.01 This section[1] provides guidance to accountants for performing and reporting on the results of engagements to issue letters for underwriters and certain other requesting parties described in and meeting the requirements of paragraph .03, .04, or .05 (commonly referred to as "comfort letters") in connection with financial statements and financial statement schedules contained in registration statements filed with the Securities and Exchange Commission (SEC) under the Securities Act of 1933 (the Act) and other securities offerings. In paragraph .09, this section also provides guidance to accountants for performing and reporting on the results of engagements to issue letters for certain requesting parties, other than underwriters or other parties with a due diligence defense under section 11 of the Act, that are described in, but do not meet the requirements of, paragraph .03, .04, or .05. [As amended, effective for letters issued pursuant to paragraph .09 of this section after April 30, 1996, by Statement on Auditing Standards No. 76.]

.02 The service of accountants providing letters for underwriters developed following enactment of the Act. Section 11 of the Act provides that underwriters, among others, could be liable if any part of a registration statement contains material omissions or misstatements. The Act also provides for an affirmative defense for underwriters if it can be demonstrated that, after a reasonable investigation, the underwriter has reasonable grounds to believe that there were no material omissions or misstatements. Consequently, underwriters request accountants to assist them in developing a record of reasonable investigation. An accountant issuing a comfort letter is one of a number of procedures that may be used to establish that an underwriter has conducted a reasonable investigation.

Applicability

.03 Accountants may provide a comfort letter to underwriters,[2] or to other parties with a statutory due diligence defense under section 11 of the Act,

---

[1] [Footnote deleted by the issuance of Statement on Auditing Standards No. 76, September 1995.]

[2] The term *underwriter* is defined in section 2 of the Act as "any person who has purchased from an issuer with a view to, or offers or sells for an issuer in connection with, the distribution of any security, or participates or has a participation in the direct or indirect participation in any such un-

(footnote continued)

in connection with financial statements and financial statement schedules included (incorporated by reference) in registration statements filed with the SEC under the Act. A comfort letter may be addressed to parties with a statutory due diligence defense under section 11 of the Act, other than a named underwriter, only when a law firm or attorney for the requesting party issues a written opinion to the accountants that states that such party has a due diligence defense under section 11 of the Act.[3] An attorney's letter indicating that a party "may" be deemed to be an underwriter or has liability substantially equivalent to that of an underwriter under the securities laws would not meet this requirement. If the requesting party, in a securities offering registered pursuant to the Act, other than a named underwriter (such as a selling shareholder or sales agent) cannot provide such a letter, he or she must provide the representation letter described in paragraphs .06 and .07 for the accountants to provide them with a comfort letter.

.04 Accountants may also issue a comfort letter to a broker-dealer or other financial intermediary, acting as principal or agent in an offering or a placement of securities, in connection with the following types of securities offerings:

- Foreign offerings, including Regulation S, Eurodollar, and other offshore offerings
- Transactions that are exempt from the registration requirements of section 5 of the Act, including those pursuant to Regulation A, Regulation D, and Rule 144A
- Offerings of securities issued or backed by governmental, municipal, banking, tax-exempt, or other entities that are exempt from registration under the Act

In these situations the accountants may provide a comfort letter to a broker-dealer or other financial intermediary in connection with a securities offering only if the broker-dealer or other financial intermediary provides in writing the representations described in paragraphs .06 and .07.

.05 Accountants may also issue a comfort letter in connection with acquisition transactions (for example, cross-comfort letters in a typical Form S-4 or merger proxy situation) in which there is an exchange of stock and such comfort letters are requested by the buyer or seller, or both, as long as the representation letter described in paragraphs .06 and .07 is provided. An accountants' report on a preliminary investigation in connection with a proposed transaction (for example, a merger, an acquisition, or a financing) is not covered by this section; accountants should refer to the guidance in section 622.

.06 The required elements of the representation letter from a broker-dealer or other financial intermediary, or of other requesting parties described in paragraphs .03 and .05, are as follows:

- The letter should be addressed to the accountants.

---

dertaking or participates or has a participation in the direct or indirect underwriting of any such undertaking; but such term shall not include a person whose interest is limited to a commission from an underwriter or dealer not in excess of the usual and customary distributors' or sellers' commission. As used in this paragraph, the term *issuer* shall include, in addition to an issuer, any person directly or indirectly controlling or controlled by the issuer, of any person under direct or indirect common control with the issuer."

[3] This section is not intended to preclude accountants from providing to the client's board of directors, when appropriate, a letter addressed to the board of directors similar in content to a comfort letter. See the auditing interpretation "Letters to Directors Relating to Annual Reports on Form 10-K" (section 9634.01–.09).

- The letter should contain the following:

  "This review process, applied to the information relating to the issuer, is (will be) substantially consistent[4] with the due diligence review process that we would perform if this placement of securities (or issuance of securities in an acquisition transaction) were being registered pursuant to the Securities Act of 1933 (the Act). We are knowledgeable with respect to the due diligence review process that would be performed if this placement of securities were being registered pursuant to the Act."[5]

- The letter should be signed by the requesting party.

.07 An example of a letter, setting forth the required elements specified in paragraph .06, from a party requesting a comfort letter follows:

> [*Date*]
>
> Dear ABC Accountants:
>
> [*Name of financial intermediary*], as principal or agent, in the placement of [*identify securities*] to be issued by [*name of issuer*], will be reviewing certain information relating to [*issuer*] that will be included (incorporated by reference) in the document [*if appropriate, the document should be identified*], which may be delivered to investors and utilized by them as a basis for their investment decision. This review process, applied to the information relating to the issuer, is (will be) substantially consistent with the due diligence review process that we would perform if this placement of securities[6] were being registered pursuant to the Securities Act of 1933 (the Act). We are knowledgeable with respect to the due diligence review process that would be performed if this placement of securities were being registered pursuant to the Act. We hereby request that you deliver to us a "comfort" letter concerning the financial statements of the issuer and certain statistical and other data included in the offering document. We will contact you to identify the procedures we wish you to follow and the form we wish the comfort letter to take.
>
> Very truly yours,
>
> [*Name of Financial Intermediary*]

.08 When one of the parties identified in paragraphs .03, .04, and .05 requests a comfort letter and has provided the accountants with the representation letter described above, the accountants should refer in the comfort letter to the requesting party's representations (see example P [paragraph .64]).

---

[4] It is recognized that what is "substantially consistent" may vary from situation to situation and may not be the same as that done in a registered offering of the same securities for the same issuer; whether the procedures being, or to be, followed will be "substantially consistent" will be determined by the requesting party on a case-by-case basis.

[5] If a nonunderwriter requests a comfort letter in connection with a securities offering pursuant to the Act, the wording of the representation letter should be revised as follows:

> "This review process . . . is substantially consistent with the due diligence review process that an underwriter would perform in connection with this placement of securities. We are knowledgeable with respect to the due diligence review process that an underwriter would perform in connection with a placement of securities registered pursuant to the Securities Act of 1933."

[6] In an acquisition of securities, this sentence could be reworded to refer to "issuance of securities." See paragraph .05.

.09 When one of the parties identified in paragraphs .03, .04, or .05, other than an underwriter or other party with a due diligence defense under section 11 of the Act, requests a comfort letter but does not provide the representation letter described in paragraphs .06 and .07, accountants should not provide a comfort letter but may provide another form of letter. In such a letter, the accountants should not provide negative assurance on the financial statements as a whole, or on any of the specified elements, accounts, or items thereof. The other guidance in this section is applicable to performing procedures in connection with a letter and on the form of the letter (see paragraphs .36 through .43 and .54 through .60). Example Q in the Appendix [paragraph .64] provides an example of a letter issued in such a situation. Any such letter should include the following statements:

a. It should be understood that we have no responsibility for establishing (and did not establish) the scope and nature of the procedures enumerated in the paragraphs above; rather, the procedures enumerated therein are those the requesting party asked us to perform. Accordingly, we make no representations regarding questions of legal interpretation[7] or regarding the sufficiency for your purposes of the procedures enumerated in the preceding paragraphs; also, such procedures would not necessarily reveal any material misstatement of the amounts or percentages listed above as set forth in the offering circular. Further, we have addressed ourselves solely to the foregoing data and make no representations regarding the adequacy of disclosures or whether any material facts have been omitted. This letter relates only to the financial statement items specified above and does not extend to any financial statement of the company taken as a whole.

b. The foregoing procedures do not constitute an audit conducted in accordance with generally accepted auditing standards. Had we performed additional procedures or had we conducted an audit or a review of the company's [*give dates of any interim financial statements*] consolidated financial statements in accordance with standards established by the American Institute of Certified Public Accountants, other matters might have come to our attention that would have been reported to you.

c. These procedures should not be taken to supplant any additional inquiries or procedures that you would undertake in your consideration of the proposed offering.

d. This letter is solely for your information and to assist you in your inquiries in connection with the offering of the securities covered by the offering circular, and it is not to be used, circulated, quoted, or otherwise referred to for any other purpose, including but not limited to the registration, purchase, or sale of securities, nor is it to be filed with or referred to in whole or in part in the offering document or any other document, except that reference may be made to it in any list of closing documents pertaining to the offering of the securities covered by the offering document.

---

[7] If this letter is requested in connection with a secured debt offering, the accountants should also refer to the attest interpretation "Responding to Requests for Reports on Matters Relating to Solvency" (AT section 9100.33–.44) for inclusion of additional statements. [Footnote added, effective for letters issued pursuant to paragraph .09 of this section after April 30, 1996, by Statement on Auditing Standards No. 76.]

e. We have no responsibility to update this letter for events and circumstances occurring after [*cutoff date*].

[As amended, effective for letters issued pursuant to this paragraph after April 30, 1996, by Statement on Auditing Standards No. 76.]

.10 When a party other than those described in paragraphs .03, .04, or .05 requests a comfort letter, the accountants should not provide that party with a comfort letter or the letter described in paragraph .09 or example Q [paragraph .64]. The accountants may instead provide that party with a report on agreed-upon procedures and should refer to section 622, *Engagements to Apply Agreed-Upon Procedures to Specified Elements, Accounts, or Items of a Financial Statement*, or AT section 600, *Agreed-Upon Procedures Engagements*, as applicable, for guidance. [Paragraph added, effective for letters issued pursuant to paragraph .09 of this section after April 30, 1996, by Statement on Auditing Standards No. 76.]

General

.11 The services of independent accountants include audits of financial statements and financial statement schedules included (incorporated by reference) in registration statements filed with the SEC under the Act. In connection with this type of service, accountants are often called upon to confer with clients, underwriters, and their respective counsel concerning the accounting and auditing requirements of the Act and the SEC and to perform other services. One of these other services is the issuance of letters for underwriters, which generally address the subjects described in paragraph .22. [Paragraph renumbered by the issuance of Statement on Auditing Standards No. 76, September 1995.]

.12 Much of the uncertainty, and consequent risk of misunderstanding, with regard to the nature and scope of comfort letters has arisen from a lack of recognition of the necessarily limited nature of the comments that accountants can properly make with respect to financial information, in a registration statement or other offering document (hereafter referred to as a registration statement), that has not been audited in accordance with generally accepted auditing standards and, accordingly, is not covered by their opinion. In requesting comfort letters, underwriters are generally seeking assistance on matters of importance to them. They wish to perform a "reasonable investigation" of financial and accounting data not "expertized"[8] (that is, covered by a report of independent accountants, who consent to be named as experts, based on an audit performed in accordance with generally accepted auditing standards) as a defense against possible claims under section 11 of the Act.[9] What constitutes a reasonable investigation of unaudited financial information sufficient to satisfy an underwriter's purposes has never been authoritatively established. Consequently, only the underwriter can determine what is sufficient for his or her purposes. Accountants will normally be willing to assist the

---

[8] See the auditing interpretation "Consenting to Be Named as an Expert in an Offering Document in Connection With Securities Offerings Other Than Those Registered Under the Securities Act of 1933" (section 9711.12–.15). [Footnote renumbered by the issuance of Statement on Auditing Standards No. 76, September 1995.]

[9] See section 711, *Filings Under Federal Securities Statutes*, for a discussion of certain responsibilities of accountants that result from the inclusion of their reports in registration statements. [Footnote renumbered by the issuance of Statement on Auditing Standards No. 76, September 1995.]

underwriter, but the assistance accountants can provide by way of comfort letters is subject to limitations. One limitation is that independent accountants can properly comment in their professional capacity only on matters to which their professional expertise is substantially relevant. Another limitation is that procedures short of an audit, such as those contemplated in a comfort letter, provide the accountants with a basis for expressing, at the most, negative assurance.[10] Such limited procedures may bring to the accountants' attention significant matters affecting the financial information, but they do not provide assurance that the accountants will become aware of any or all significant matters that would be disclosed in an audit. Accordingly, there is necessarily a risk that the accountants may have provided negative assurance of the absence of conditions or matters that may prove to have existed. [Paragraph renumbered by the issuance of Statement on Auditing Standards No. 76, September 1995.]

.13 This section deals with several different kinds of matters. First, it addresses whether, in a number of areas involving professional standards, it is proper for independent accountants, acting in their professional capacity, to comment in a comfort letter on specified matters, and, if so, the form such a comment should take. Second, practical suggestions are offered on which form of comfort letter is suitable in a given circumstance, procedural matters, the dating of letters, and what steps may be taken when information that may require special mention in a letter comes to the accountants' attention.[11] Third, it suggests ways of reducing or avoiding the uncertainties, described in the preceding paragraph, regarding the nature and extent of accountants' responsibilities in connection with a comfort letter. Accountants who have been requested to follow a course other than what has been recommended, with regard to points not involving professional standards, would do well to consult their legal counsel. [Paragraph renumbered by the issuance of Statement on Auditing Standards No. 76, September 1995.]

.14 Comfort letters are not required under the Act, and copies are not filed with the SEC. It is nonetheless a common condition of an underwriting agreement in connection with the offering for sale of securities registered with the SEC under the Act that the accountants are to furnish a comfort letter. Some underwriters do not make the receipt of a comfort letter a condition of the underwriting agreement or purchase agreement (hereafter referred to as the underwriting agreement) but nevertheless ask for such a letter.[12] [Para-

---

[10] Negative assurance consists of a statement by accountants that, as a result of performing specified procedures, nothing came to their attention that caused them to believe that specified matters do not meet a specified standard (for example, that nothing came to their attention that caused them to believe that any material modifications should be made to the unaudited financial statements or unaudited condensed financial statements for them to be in conformity with generally accepted accounting principles). [Footnote renumbered by the issuance of Statement on Auditing Standards No. 76, September 1995.]

[11] It is important to note that although the illustrations in this section describe procedures that may be followed by accountants as a basis for their comments in comfort letters, this section does not necessarily prescribe such procedures. [Footnote renumbered by the issuance of Statement on Auditing Standards No. 76, September 1995.]

[12] Except when the context otherwise requires, the word underwriter (or certain other requesting parties, as described in paragraphs .03, .04, and .05), as used in this section refers to the managing, or lead, underwriter, who typically negotiates the underwriting agreement for a group of underwriters whose exact composition is not determined until shortly before a registration statement becomes effective. In competitive bidding situations in which legal counsel for the underwriters acts as the underwriters' representative prior to opening and acceptance of the bid, the accountants should carry out the discussions and other communications contemplated by this section with the legal counsel until the underwriter is selected. [Footnote renumbered by the issuance of Statement on Auditing Standards No. 76, September 1995.]

graph renumbered by the issuance of Statement on Auditing Standards No. 76, September 1995.]

.15 The accountants should suggest to the underwriter that they meet together with the client to discuss the procedures to be followed in connection with a comfort letter; during this meeting, the accountants may describe procedures that are frequently followed (see the examples in the appendix [paragraph .64]). Because of the accountants' knowledge of the client, such a meeting may substantially assist the underwriter in reaching a decision about procedures to be followed by the accountants. However, any discussion of procedures should be accompanied by a clear statement that the accountants cannot furnish any assurance regarding the sufficiency of the procedures for the underwriter's purposes, and the appropriate way of expressing this is shown in paragraph 4 of example A [paragraph .64]. [Paragraph renumbered by the issuance of Statement on Auditing Standards No. 76, September 1995.]

.16 Because the underwriter will expect the accountants to furnish a comfort letter of a scope to be specified in the underwriting agreement, a draft of that agreement should be furnished to the accountants so that they can indicate whether they will be able to furnish a letter in acceptable form. It is desirable practice for the accountants, promptly after they have received the draft of the agreement (or have been informed that a letter covering specified matters, although not a condition of the agreement, will nonetheless be requested), to prepare a draft of the form of the letter they expect to furnish. To the extent possible, the draft should deal with all matters to be covered in the final letter and should use exactly the same terms as those to be used in the final letter (subject, of course, to the understanding that the comments in the final letter cannot be determined until the procedures underlying it have been performed). The draft letter should be identified as a draft to avoid giving the impression that the procedures described therein have been performed. This practice of furnishing a draft letter at an early point permits the accountants to make clear to the client and the underwriter what they may expect the accountants to furnish. Thus furnished with a draft letter, the underwriter is afforded the opportunity to discuss further with the accountants the procedures that the accountants have indicated they expect to follow and to request any additional procedures that the underwriter may desire. If the additional procedures pertain to matters relevant to the accountants' professional competence, the accountants would ordinarily be willing to perform them, and it is desirable for them to furnish the underwriter with an appropriately revised draft letter. The accountants may reasonably assume that the underwriter, by indicating his or her acceptance of the draft comfort letter, and subsequently, by accepting the letter in final form, considers the procedures described sufficient for his or her purposes. It is important, therefore, that the procedures[13] to be followed by the accountants be clearly set out in the comfort letter, in both draft and final form, so that there will be no misunderstanding about the basis on which the accountants' comments have been made and so that the underwriter can decide whether the procedures performed are sufficient for his or her purposes. For reasons explained in paragraph .12, statements or implications that the accountants are carrying out such procedures as they consider necessary should be avoided, since this may lead to misunderstanding about

---

[13] When the accountants have been requested to provide negative assurance on interim financial information or capsule financial information and the procedures required for an SAS No. 71 [section 722] review have been performed, those procedures need not be specified. See paragraphs .37 through .41. [Footnote renumbered by the issuance of Statement on Auditing Standards No. 76, September 1995.]

the responsibility for the sufficiency of the procedures for the underwriter's purposes. The following is a suggested form of legend that may be placed on the draft letter for identification and explanation of its purposes and limitations.

> This draft is furnished solely for the purpose of indicating the form of letter that we would expect to be able to furnish [*name of underwriter*] in response to their request, the matters expected to be covered in the letter, and the nature of the procedures that we would expect to carry out with respect to such matters. Based on our discussions with [*name of underwriter*], it is our understanding that the procedures outlined in this draft letter are those they wish us to follow.[14] Unless [*name of underwriter*] informs us otherwise, we shall assume that there are no additional procedures they wish us to follow. The text of the letter itself will depend, of course, on the results of the procedures, which we would not expect to complete until shortly before the letter is given and in no event before the cutoff date indicated therein.

[Paragraph renumbered by the issuance of Statement on Auditing Standards No. 76, September 1995.]

.17 Comfort letters are occasionally requested from more than one accountant (for example, in connection with registration statements to be used in the subsequent sale of shares issued in recently effected mergers and from predecessor auditors). At the earliest practicable date, the client should advise any other accountants who may be involved about any letter that may be required from them and should arrange for them to receive a draft of the underwriting agreement so that they may make arrangements at an early date for the preparation of a draft of their letter (a copy of which should be furnished to the principal accountants) and for the performance of their procedures. In addition, the underwriter may wish to meet with the other accountants for the purposes discussed in paragraph .15. [Paragraph renumbered by the issuance of Statement on Auditing Standards No. 76, September 1995.]

.18 There may be situations in which more than one accountant is involved in the audit of the financial statements of a business and in which the reports of more than one accountant appear in the registration statement. For example, certain significant divisions, branches, or subsidiaries may be audited by other accountants. The principal accountants (that is, those who report on the consolidated financial statements and, consequently, are asked to give a comfort letter with regard to information expressed on a consolidated basis) should read the letters of the other accountants reporting on significant units. Such letters should contain statements similar to those contained in the comfort letter prepared by the principal accountants, including statements about their independence. The principal accountants should state in their comfort letters that (*a*) reading letters of the other accountants was one of the procedures followed, and (*b*) the procedures performed by the principal accountants (other than reading the letters of the other accountants) relate solely to companies audited by the principal accountants and to the consolidated financial statements. [Paragraph renumbered by the issuance of Statement on Auditing Standards No. 76, September 1995.]

.19 Regulations under the Act permit companies, in certain circumstances, to register a designated amount of securities for continuous or delayed

---

[14] In the absence of any discussions with the underwriter, the accountants should outline in the draft letter those procedures specified in the underwriting agreement that they are willing to perform. In that event, the sentence to which this footnote refers should be revised as follows: "In the absence of any discussions with [*name of underwriter*], we have set out in this draft letter those procedures referred to in the draft underwriting agreement (of which we have been furnished a copy) that we are willing to follow." [Footnote renumbered by the issuance of Statement on Auditing Standards No. 76, September 1995.]

offerings during an extended period by filing one "shelf" registration statement. At the effective date of a shelf registration statement, the registrant may not have selected an underwriter (see footnote 12). A client or the legal counsel designated to represent the underwriting group might, however, ask the accountants to issue a comfort letter at the effective date of a shelf registration statement to expedite the due diligence activities of the underwriter when he or she is subsequently designated and to avoid later corrections of financial information included in an effective prospectus. However, as stated in paragraph .12, only the underwriter can determine the procedures that will be sufficient for his or her purposes. Under these circumstances, therefore, the accountants should not agree to furnish a comfort letter addressed to the client, legal counsel or a nonspecific addressee such as "any or all underwriters to be selected." The accountants may agree to furnish the client or legal counsel for the underwriting group with a draft comfort letter describing the procedures that the accountants have performed and the comments the accountants are willing to express as a result of those procedures. The draft comfort letter should include a legend, such as the following, describing the letter's purpose and limitations:

> This draft describes the procedures that we have performed and represents a letter we would be prepared to sign as of the effective date of the registration statement if the managing underwriter had been chosen at that date and requested such a letter. Based on our discussions with [*name of client or legal counsel*], the procedures set forth are similar to those that experience indicates underwriters often request in such circumstances. The text of the final letter will depend, of course, on whether the managing underwriter who is selected requests that other procedures be performed to meet his or her needs and whether the managing underwriter requests that any of the procedures be updated to the date of issuance of the signed letter.

A signed comfort letter may be issued to the underwriter selected for the portion of the issue then being offered when the underwriting agreement for an offering is signed and on each closing date. [Paragraph renumbered by the issuance of Statement on Auditing Standards No. 76, September 1995.]

.20 Accountants, when issuing a letter under the guidance provided in this section, may not issue any additional letters or reports, under any other section, to the underwriter or the other requesting parties identified in paragraphs .03, .04, and .05 (hereinafter referred to as the underwriter) in connection with the offering or placement of securities, in which the accountants comment on items for which commenting is otherwise precluded by this section, such as square footage of facilities. [Paragraph renumbered by the issuance of Statement on Auditing Standards No. 76, September 1995.]

.21 While the guidance in this section generally addresses comfort letters issued in connection with securities offerings registered pursuant to the Act, it also provides guidance on comfort letters issued in other securities transactions. However, the guidance that specifically refers to compliance of the information commented on with SEC rules and regulations, such as compliance with Regulation S-X[15] or S-K,[16] generally applies only to comfort letters

---

[15] Regulation S-X, "Form and Content of and Requirements for Financial Statements, Securities Act of 1933, Securities Exchange Act of 1934, Public Utility Holding Company Act of 1935, Investment Company Act of 1940, and Energy Policy and Conservation Act of 1975." [Footnote renumbered by the issuance of Statement on Auditing Standards No. 76, September 1995.]

[16] Regulation S-K, "Standard Instructions for Filing Forms Under Securities Act of 1933, Securities Exchange Act of 1934 and Energy Policy and Conservation Act of 1975." [Footnote renumbered by the issuance of Statement on Auditing Standards No. 76, September 1995.]

issued in connection with securities offerings registered pursuant to the Act. [Paragraph renumbered by the issuance of Statement on Auditing Standards No. 76, September 1995.]

Guidance on the Format and Contents of Comfort Letters

.22 This section (paragraphs .22 through .62) provides guidance on the format and possible contents of a typical comfort letter. It addresses how the comfort letter should be dated, to whom it may be addressed, and the contents of the introductory paragraph of the comfort letter. Further, it addresses the subjects that may be covered in a comfort letter:

a. The independence of the accountants (paragraphs .31 and .32)

b. Whether the audited financial statements and financial statement schedules included (incorporated by reference) in the registration statement comply as to form in all material respects with the applicable accounting requirements of the Act and the related published rules and regulations (paragraphs .33 and .34)

c. Unaudited financial statements, condensed interim financial information, capsule financial information, pro forma financial information, financial forecasts, and changes in selected financial statement items during a period subsequent to the date and period of the latest financial statements included (incorporated by reference) in the registration statement (paragraphs .35 through .53)

d. Tables, statistics, and other financial information included (incorporated by reference) in the registration statement (paragraphs .54 through .62)

e. Negative assurance as to whether certain non-financial statement information, included (incorporated by reference) in the registration statement complies as to form in all material respects with Regulation S-K (paragraph .57)

[Paragraph renumbered by the issuance of Statement on Auditing Standards No. 76, September 1995.]

Dating

.23 The letter ordinarily is dated on or shortly before the effective date (that is, the date on which the registration statement becomes effective). On rare occasions, letters have been requested to be dated at or shortly before the filing date (that is, the date on which the registration statement is first filed with the SEC). The underwriting agreement ordinarily specifies the date, often referred to as the "cutoff date," to which certain procedures described in the letter are to relate (for example, a date five days before the date of the letter). The letter should state that the inquiries and other procedures described in the letter did not cover the period from the cutoff date to the date of the letter. [Paragraph renumbered by the issuance of Statement on Auditing Standards No. 76, September 1995.]

.24 An additional letter may also be dated at or shortly before the closing date (that is, the date on which the issuer or selling security holder delivers the securities to the underwriter in exchange for the proceeds of the offering). If more than one letter is requested, it will be necessary to carry out the specified procedures and inquiries as of the cutoff date for each letter. Although comments contained in an earlier letter may, on occasion, be incorporated by reference in a subsequent letter (see example C [paragraph .64]), any subsequent letter should relate only to information in the registration statement as most recently amended. [Paragraph renumbered by the issuance of Statement on Auditing Standards No. 76, September 1995.]

Addressee

.25 The letter should not be addressed or given to any parties other than the client and the named underwriters,[17] broker-dealer, financial intermediary or buyer or seller. The appropriate addressee is the intermediary who has negotiated the agreement with the client, and with whom the accountants will deal in discussions regarding the scope and sufficiency of the letter. When a comfort letter is furnished to other accountants, it should be addressed in accordance with the guidance in this paragraph and copies should be furnished to the principal accountants and their client. [Paragraph renumbered by the issuance of Statement on Auditing Standards No. 76, September 1995.]

Introductory Paragraph

.26 It is desirable to include an introductory paragraph similar to the following:

> We have audited the [*identify the financial statements and financial statement schedules*] included (incorporated by reference) in the registration statement (no. 33-00000) on Form ________ filed by the company under the Securities Act of 1933 (the Act); our reports with respect thereto are also included (incorporated by reference) in that registration statement. The registration statement, as amended as of ____________, is herein referred to as the registration statement.

[Paragraph renumbered by the issuance of Statement on Auditing Standards No. 76, September 1995.]

.27 When the report on the audited financial statements and financial statement schedules included (incorporated by reference) in the registration statement departs from the standard report, for instance, where one or more explanatory paragraphs or a paragraph to emphasize a matter regarding the financial statements have been added to the report, the accountants should refer[18] to that fact in the comfort letter and discuss the subject matter of the paragraph.[19] In those rare instances in which the SEC accepts a qualified opinion on historical financial statements, the accountants should refer to the qualification in the opening paragraph of the comfort letter and discuss the subject matter of the qualification. (See also paragraph .35*f*.) [Paragraph renumbered by the issuance of Statement on Auditing Standards No. 76, September 1995.]

---

[17] An example of an appropriate form of address for this purpose is "The Blank Company and XYZ & Company, as Representative of the Several Underwriters." [Footnote renumbered by the issuance of Statement on Auditing Standards No. 76, September 1995.]

[18] The accountants may also refer in the opening paragraph to expansions of their report that do not affect their opinion on the basic financial statements, for example, expansions of their report regarding (*a*) interim financial information accompanying or included in the notes to audited financial statements (see section 722.41 and .42) or (*b*) required supplementary information described in section 558, *Required Supplementary Information*, paragraphs .08 through .10. See paragraph .30 of this section. [Footnote renumbered by the issuance of Statement on Auditing Standards No. 76, September 1995.]

[19] The accountants need not refer to or discuss explanatory paragraphs covering consistency of application of accounting principles. [Footnote renumbered by the issuance of Statement on Auditing Standards No. 76, September 1995.]

.28 The underwriter occasionally requests the accountants to repeat in the comfort letter their report on the audited financial statements included (incorporated by reference) in the registration statement. Because of the special significance of the date of the accountants' report, the accountants should not repeat their opinion.[20] The underwriter sometimes requests negative assurance regarding the accountants' report. Because accountants have a statutory responsibility with respect to their opinion as of the effective date of a registration statement, and because the additional significance, if any, of negative assurance is unclear and such assurance may therefore give rise to misunderstanding, accountants should not give such negative assurance. Furthermore, the accountants should not give negative assurance with respect to financial statements and financial statement schedules that have been audited and are reported on in the registration statement by other accountants. [Paragraph renumbered by the issuance of Statement on Auditing Standards No. 76, September 1995.]

.29 The accountants may refer in the introductory paragraphs of the comfort letter to the fact that they have issued reports on—[21]

a. Condensed financial statements that are derived from audited financial statements (see section 552, *Reporting on Condensed Financial Statements and Selected Financial Data*).

b. Selected financial data (see section 552).

c. Interim financial information (see section 722).

d. Pro forma financial information (see AT section 300, *Reporting on Pro Forma Financial Information*).

e. A financial forecast (see AT section 200, *Financial Forecasts and Projections*).

Such a reference should be to the accountants' reports that were previously issued, and if the reports are not included (incorporated by reference) in the registration statement, they may be attached to the comfort letter. In referring to previously issued reports, the accountants should not repeat their reports in the comfort letter or otherwise imply that they are reporting as of the date of the comfort letter or that they assume responsibility for the sufficiency of the procedures for the underwriter's purposes. However, for certain information on which they have reported, the accountants may agree to comment regarding compliance with published SEC requirements (see paragraphs .33 and .34). Accountants should not mention in a comfort letter reports issued in accordance with section 325, *Communication of Internal Control Related Matters Noted in an Audit*, or any restricted distribution reports issued to a client in connection with procedures performed on the client's internal control structure in accordance with AT section 400, *Reporting on an Entity's Internal Control Over Financial Reporting*. [Paragraph renumbered by the issuance of Statement on Auditing Standards No. 76, September 1995.]

.30 An underwriter may also request that the accountants comment in their comfort letter on (*a*) unaudited interim financial information required by item 302(a) of Regulation S-K, to which section 722 pertains or (*b*) required

---

[20] See section 530, *Dating of the Independent Auditor's Report*, paragraphs .03 through .08. [Footnote renumbered by the issuance of Statement on Auditing Standards No. 76, September 1995.]

[21] The accountants should not refer to or attach to the comfort letter any restricted distribution report, such as a report on agreed-upon procedures. [Footnote renumbered by the issuance of Statement on Auditing Standards No. 76, September 1995.]

supplementary information, to which section 558, *Required Supplementary Information*, pertains. Section 722 and section 558 provide that the accountants should expand the standard report on the audited financial statements to refer to such information when the scope of their procedures with regard to the information was restricted or when the information appears not to be presented in conformity with generally accepted accounting principles or, for required supplementary information, applicable guidelines. Such expansions of the accountants' standard report in the registration statement would ordinarily be referred to in the opening paragraph of the comfort letter (see also paragraph .35*f*). Additional comments on such unaudited information are therefore unnecessary. However, if the underwriter requests that the accountants perform procedures with regard to such information in addition to those performed in connection with their review or audit as prescribed by sections 722 and 558, the accountants may do so and report their findings. [Paragraph renumbered by the issuance of Statement on Auditing Standards No. 76, September 1995.]

Independence

.31 It is customary in conjunction with SEC filings for the underwriting agreement to provide for the accountants to make a statement in the letter concerning their independence. This may be done substantially as follows:

> We are independent certified public accountants with respect to The Blank Company, Inc., within the meaning of the Act and the applicable published rules and regulations thereunder.

Regulation S-K requires disclosure in the prospectus and registration statement of interests of named experts (including independent accountants) in the registrant. Regulation S-X precludes accountants who report on financial statements included (incorporated by reference) in a registration statement from having interests of the type requiring disclosure in the prospectus or registration statement. Therefore, if the accountants make a statement in a comfort letter that they are independent within the meaning of the Act and the applicable published rules and regulations thereunder, any additional comments on independence would be unnecessary. In a non-SEC filing, the accountants may refer to the AICPA's *Code of Professional Conduct* [ET section 101]. This may be done substantially as follows:

> We are independent certified public accountants with respect to The Blank Company, Inc., under rule 101 of the AICPA's *Code of Professional Conduct* and its interpretations and rulings.

[Paragraph renumbered by the issuance of Statement on Auditing Standards No. 76, September 1995.]

.32 When comfort letters are requested from more than one accountant (see paragraphs .17 and .18), each accountant must, of course, be sure he or she is independent within the meaning of the Act and the applicable published rules and regulations thereunder. The accountants for previously nonaffiliated companies recently acquired by the registrant would not be required to have been independent with respect to the company whose shares are being registered. In such a case, the accountants should modify the wording suggested in paragraph .31 and make a statement regarding their independence along the following lines.

> As of [*insert date of the accountants' most recent report on the financial statements of their client*] and during the period covered by the financial statements on which we reported, we were independent certified public account-

ants with respect to [*insert the name of their client*] within the meaning of the Act and the applicable published rules and regulations thereunder.

[Paragraph renumbered by the issuance of Statement on Auditing Standards No. 76, September 1995.]

Compliance With SEC Requirements

.33 The accountants may be requested to express an opinion on whether the financial statements covered by their report comply as to form with the pertinent published accounting requirements of the SEC.[22] This may be done substantially as follows:

> In our opinion [*include phrase "except as disclosed in the registration statement," if applicable*], the [*identify the financial statements and financial statement schedules*] audited by us and included (incorporated by reference) in the registration statement comply as to form in all material respects with the applicable accounting requirements of the Act and the related published rules and regulations.[23]

If there is a material departure from the pertinent published requirements, the departure should be disclosed in the letter.[24] An appropriate manner of doing this is shown in example K [paragraph .64]. [Paragraph renumbered by the issuance of Statement on Auditing Standards No. 76, September 1995.]

.34 Accountants may provide positive assurance on compliance as to form with requirements under published SEC rules and regulations only with respect to those rules and regulations applicable to the form and content of financial statements and financial statement schedules that they have audited. Accountants are limited to providing negative assurance on compliance as to form when the financial statements or financial statement schedules have not been audited. (For guidance in commenting on compliance as to form, see paragraph .37 regarding unaudited condensed interim financial information, paragraph .42 regarding pro forma financial information, paragraph .44 regarding a forecast, and paragraph .57 regarding Regulation S-K items.) [Paragraph renumbered by the issuance of Statement on Auditing Standards No. 76, September 1995.]

---

[22] The term *published* is used because accountants should not be expected to be familiar with, or express assurances on compliance with, informal positions of the SEC staff. [Footnote renumbered by the issuance of Statement on Auditing Standards No. 76, September 1995.]

[23] Certain financial statements may be incorporated in a registration statement under the Act by reference to filings under the Securities Exchange Act of 1934 (the 1934 Act). In those circumstances, the accountants may refer to whether the audited financial statements and financial statement schedules included (incorporated by reference) in the registration statement comply as to form in all material respects with the applicable accounting requirements of the 1934 Act and the related published rules and regulations (see example B [paragraph .64]). However, the accountants should not refer to compliance with the provisions of the 1934 Act regarding internal accounting control. See AT section 400, *Reporting on an Entity's Internal Control Over Financial Reporting*, paragraph .83. [Footnote renumbered by the issuance of Statement on Auditing Standards No. 76, September 1995.]

[24] Departures from published SEC requirements that require mention in a comfort letter ordinarily do not affect fair presentation in conformity with generally accepted accounting principles; however, if they do, the accountants will, of course, mention these departures in expressing their opinion and in consenting to the use of their report in the registration statement. If departures from published SEC requirements that require mention in a comfort letter either are not disclosed in the registration statement or have not been agreed to by representatives of the SEC, the accountants should carefully consider whether a consent to the use of their report in the registration statement should be issued. [Footnote renumbered by the issuance of Statement on Auditing Standards No. 76, September 1995.]

Commenting in a Comfort Letter on Information Other Than Audited Financial Statements

General

.35 Comments included in the letter will often concern (*a*) unaudited condensed interim financial information (see paragraphs .36 through .38),[25] (*b*) capsule financial information (see paragraphs .36 and .39 through .41), (*c*) pro forma financial information (see paragraphs .42 and .43), (*d*) financial forecasts (see paragraphs .36 and .44), and (*e*) changes in capital stock, increases in long-term debt, and decreases in other specified financial statement items (see paragraphs .36 and .45 through .53). For commenting on these matters, the following guidance is important:

a. As explained in paragraph .16, the agreed-upon procedures performed by the accountants should be set forth in the letter, except that when the accountants have been requested to provide negative assurance on interim financial information or capsule financial information, the procedures involved in an SAS No. 71 [section 722] review need not be specified (see paragraphs .37 through .41 of this section and paragraph 4 of example A [paragraph .64]).

b. To avoid any misunderstanding about the responsibility for the sufficiency of the agreed-upon procedures for the underwriter's purposes, the accountants should not make any statements, or imply that they have applied procedures that they have determined to be necessary or sufficient for the underwriter's purposes. If the accountants state that they have performed an SAS No. 71 [section 722] review, this does not imply that those procedures are sufficient for the underwriter's purposes. The underwriter may ask the accountants to perform additional procedures. For example, if the underwriter requests the accountants to apply additional procedures and specifies items of financial information to be reviewed and the materiality level for changes in those items that would necessitate further inquiry by the accountants, the accountants may perform those procedures and should describe them in their letter. Descriptions of procedures in the comfort letter should include descriptions of the criteria specified by the underwriter.

c. Terms of uncertain meaning (such as *general review*, *limited review*, *reconcile*, *check*, or *test*) should not be used in describing the work, unless the procedures comprehended by these terms are described in the comfort letter.

d. The procedures performed with respect to interim periods may not disclose changes in capital stock, increases in long-term debt or decreases in the specified financial statement items, inconsistencies in the application of generally accepted accounting principles, instances of noncompliance as to form with accounting requirements of the SEC, or other matters about which negative assurance is requested. An appropriate manner of making this clear is shown in the last three sentences in paragraph 4 of example A [paragraph .64].

---

[25] The SEC requirements specify condensed financial statements. However, the guidance in paragraphs .37 and .38 also applies to complete financial statements. For purposes of this section, interim financial statements may be for a twelve-month period ending on a date other than the entity's normal year end. [Footnote renumbered by the issuance of Statement on Auditing Standards No. 76, September 1995.]

e. Matters to be covered by the letter should be made clear in the meetings with the underwriter and should be identified in the underwriting agreement and in the draft comfort letter. Since there is no way of anticipating other matters that would be of interest to an underwriter, accountants should not make a general statement in a comfort letter that, as a result of carrying out the specified procedures, nothing else has come to their attention that would be of interest to the underwriter.

f. When the report on the audited financial statements and financial statement schedules in the registration statement departs from the auditor's standard report, and the comfort letter includes negative assurance with respect to subsequent unaudited condensed interim financial information included (incorporated by reference) in the registration statement or with respect to an absence of specified subsequent changes, increases, or decreases, the accountant should consider the effect thereon of the subject matter of the qualification, explanatory paragraph(s), or paragraph(s) emphasizing a matter regarding the financial statements. The accountant should also follow the guidance in paragraph .27. An illustration of how this type of situation may be dealt with is shown in example I [paragraph .64].

[Paragraph renumbered by the issuance of Statement on Auditing Standards No. 76, September 1995.]

Knowledge of Internal Control

.36 The accountants should not comment in a comfort letter on (*a*) unaudited condensed interim financial information, (*b*) capsule financial information, (*c*) a financial forecast when historical financial statements provide a basis for one or more significant assumptions for the forecast, or (*d*) changes in capital stock, increases in long-term debt and decreases in selected financial statement items, unless they have obtained knowledge of a client's internal control as it relates to the preparation of both annual and interim financial information. Knowledge of the client's internal control over financial reporting includes knowledge of the control environment, risk assessment, control activities, information and communication, and monitoring. Sufficient knowledge of a client's internal control as it relates to the preparation of annual financial information ordinarily would have been acquired, and may have been acquired with respect to interim financial information, by the accountants who have audited a client's financial statements for one or more periods. When the accountants have not audited the most recent annual financial statements, and thus have not acquired sufficient knowledge of the entity's internal control, the accountants should perform procedures to obtain that knowledge. [Paragraph renumbered by the issuance of Statement on Auditing Standards No. 76, September 1995; Revised, February 1997, to reflect conforming changes necessary due to the issuance of Statement on Auditing Standards No. 78.]

Unaudited Condensed Interim Financial Information

.37 Comments concerning the unaudited condensed interim financial information[26] included (incorporated by reference) in the registration statement provide negative assurance as to whether (*a*) any material modifications

---

[26] When accountants are engaged to perform procedures on interim financial information, they may have additional responsibilities under certain circumstances. The accountants should refer to section 722 for guidance. [Footnote renumbered by the issuance of Statement on Auditing Standards No. 76, September 1995.]

should be made to the unaudited condensed interim financial information for it to be in conformity with generally accepted accounting principles and (*b*) the unaudited condensed interim financial information complies as to form in all material respects with the applicable accounting requirements of the Act and the related published rules and regulations. Accountants may comment in the form of negative assurance only when they have conducted a review of the interim financial information in accordance with section 722. The accountants may (*a*) state in the comfort letter that they have performed the procedures identified in section 722 for a review of interim financial information (see paragraphs 4*a* and 5*a* of example A [paragraph .64] or (*b*) if the accountants have issued a report on the review, they may mention that fact in the comfort letter. If it is mentioned in the comfort letter, the accountants should attach the review report to the letter unless the review report is already included (incorporated by reference) in the registration statement. When the accountants have not conducted a review in accordance with section 722, the accountants may not comment in the form of negative assurance and are, therefore, limited to reporting procedures performed and findings obtained (see example O [paragraph .64]). [Paragraph renumbered by the issuance of Statement on Auditing Standards No. 76, September 1995.]

.38 The letter should specifically identify any unaudited condensed interim financial information and should state that the accountants have not audited the condensed interim financial information in accordance with generally accepted auditing standards and do not express an opinion concerning such information. An appropriate manner of making this clear is shown in paragraph 3 of example A [paragraph .64]. [Paragraph renumbered by the issuance of Statement on Auditing Standards No. 76, September 1995.]

Capsule Financial Information

.39 In some registration statements, the information shown in the audited financial statements or unaudited condensed interim financial information is supplemented by unaudited summarized interim information for subsequent periods (commonly called "capsule financial information"). This capsule financial information (either in narrative or tabular form) often is provided for the most recent interim period and for the corresponding period of the prior year. With regard to selected capsule financial information, the accountants—

a. May give negative assurance with regard to conformity with generally accepted accounting principles and may refer to whether the dollar amounts were determined on a basis substantially consistent with that of the corresponding amounts in the audited financial statements if (1) the selected capsule financial information is presented in accordance with the minimum disclosure requirements of Accounting Principles Board (APB) Opinion No. 28, paragraph 30 [AC section I73.146], and (2) the accountants have performed an SAS No. 71 [section 722] review of the financial statements underlying the capsule financial information. If those conditions have not been met, the accountants are limited to reporting procedures performed and findings obtained.

b. May give negative assurance as to whether the dollar amounts were determined on a basis substantially consistent with that of the corresponding amounts in the audited financial statements if the selected capsule financial information is more limited than the minimum disclosures described in APB Opinion 28, paragraph 30 (see example L [paragraph .64]), as long as the accountants have performed an SAS No. 71 [section 722] review of the financial statements underlying the capsule financial information. If an SAS No. 71 [section 722] review has not been performed, the accountants are limited to reporting procedures performed and findings obtained.

[Paragraph renumbered by the issuance of Statement on Auditing Standards No. 76, September 1995.]

.40 The underwriter occasionally asks the accountants to give negative assurance with respect to the unaudited interim financial statements or unaudited condensed interim financial information (see paragraph .37 and the interim financial information requirements of Regulation S-X) that underlie the capsule financial information and asks the accountants to state that the capsule financial information agrees with amounts set forth in such statements. Paragraphs 4*b* and 5*b* in example L [paragraph .64] provide an example of the accountants' comments in these circumstances. [Paragraph renumbered by the issuance of Statement on Auditing Standards No. 76, September 1995.]

.41 The underwriter might ask the accountants to give negative assurance on the unaudited condensed interim financial information, or information extracted therefrom, for a monthly period ending after the latest financial statements included (incorporated by reference) in the registration statement. In those cases, the guidance in paragraph .37 is applicable. The unaudited condensed interim financial information should be attached to the comfort letter so that it is clear what financial information is being referred to; if the client requests, the unaudited condensed interim financial information may be attached only to the copy of the letter intended for the managing underwriter. [Paragraph renumbered by the issuance of Statement on Auditing Standards No. 76, September 1995.]

Pro Forma Financial Information

.42 Accountants should not comment in a comfort letter on pro forma financial information unless they have an appropriate level of knowledge of the accounting and financial reporting practices of the entity (or, in the case of a business combination, of a significant constituent part of the combined entity). This would ordinarily have been obtained by the accountants auditing or reviewing historical financial statements of the entity for the most recent annual or interim period for which the pro forma financial information is presented. Accountants should not give negative assurance in a comfort letter on the application of pro forma adjustments to historical amounts, the compilation of pro forma financial information, whether the pro forma financial information complies as to form in all material respects with the applicable accounting requirements of rule 11-02 of Regulation S-X or otherwise provide negative assurance with respect to pro forma financial information unless they have obtained the required knowledge described above and they have performed an audit of the annual financial statements, or an SAS No. 71 [section 722] review of the interim financial statements, of the entity (or, in the case of a business combination, of a significant constituent part of the combined entity) to which the pro forma adjustments were applied. In the case of a business combination, the historical financial statements of each constituent part of the combined entity on which the pro forma financial information is based should be audited or reviewed. [Paragraph renumbered by the issuance of Statement on Auditing Standards No. 76, September 1995.]

.43 If the accountants have obtained the required knowledge as described in paragraph .36, but have not met the requirements for giving negative assurance, the accountants are limited to reporting procedures performed and findings obtained. (See example O [paragraph .64].) The accountants should comply with the relevant guidance on reporting the results of agreed-upon procedures in AT section 600. [Paragraph renumbered by the issuance of Statement on Auditing Standards No. 76, September 1995.]

Financial Forecasts

.44 For accountants to perform agreed-upon procedures on a financial forecast and comment thereon in a comfort letter, they should obtain the knowledge described in paragraph .36 and then perform procedures prescribed in AT section 200.68, for reporting on compilation of a forecast. Having performed these procedures, they should follow the guidance in AT section 200.16 and .17 regarding reports on compilations of prospective financial information and should attach their report[27] thereon to the comfort letter.[28] Then they can perform additional procedures and report their findings in the comfort letter (see examples E and O [paragraph .64]). Accountants may not provide negative assurance on the results of procedures performed. Further, accountants may not provide negative assurance with respect to compliance of the forecast with rule 11-03 of Regulation S-X unless they have performed an examination of the forecast in accordance with AT section 200. [Paragraph renumbered by the issuance of Statement on Auditing Standards No. 76, September 1995.]

Subsequent Changes

.45 Comments regarding subsequent changes typically relate to whether there has been any change in capital stock, increase in long-term debt or decreases in other specified financial statement items during a period, known as the "change period," subsequent to the date and period of the latest financial statements included (incorporated by reference) in the registration statement (see paragraph .50). These comments would also address such matters as subsequent changes in the amounts of (*a*) net current assets or stockholders' equity and (*b*) net sales and the total and per-share amounts of income before extraordinary items and of net income. The accountants ordinarily will be requested to read minutes and make inquiries of company officials relating to the whole of the change period.[29] For the period between the date of the latest financial statements made available and the cutoff date, the accountants must base their comments solely on the limited procedures actually performed with respect to that period (which, in most cases, will be limited to the reading of minutes and the inquiries of company officials referred to in the preceding sen-

---

[27] For purposes of issuing a comfort letter, if the forecast is included in the registration statement, the forecast must be accompanied by an indication that the accountants have not examined the forecast and therefore do not express an opinion on it. If a compilation report on the forecast has been issued in connection with the comfort letter, the report need not be included in the registration statement. [Footnote renumbered by the issuance of Statement on Auditing Standards No. 76, September 1995.]

[28] When a client's securities are subject to regulation by the SEC, the accountants should be aware of the SEC's views regarding independence when agreeing to perform a compilation of a forecast. Independence may be deemed to be impaired when services include preparation or assembly of financial forecasts. The SEC generally will not question the accountants' independence, however when services are limited to issuing a report on a forecast as a result of performing the procedures stated in paragraph 5 of AT section 200.68. [Footnote renumbered by the issuance of Statement on Auditing Standards No. 76, September 1995.]

[29] The answers to these inquiries generally should be supported by appropriate written representations of the company officials. [Footnote renumbered by the issuance of Statement on Auditing Standards No. 76, September 1995.]

tence), and their comfort letter should make this clear (see paragraph 6 of example A [paragraph .64]). [Paragraph renumbered by the issuance of Statement on Auditing Standards No. 76, September 1995.]

.46 If the underwriter requests negative assurance as to subsequent changes in specified financial statement items as of a date less than 135 days from the end of the most recent period for which the accountants have performed an audit or a review, the accountants may provide such negative assurance in the comfort letter. For instance—

- When the accountants have audited the December 31, 19X6, financial statements, the accountants may provide negative assurance on increases and decreases of specified financial statement items as of any date up to May 14 (135 days subsequent to December 31).
- When the accountants have audited the December 31, 19X6, financial statements and have also conducted an SAS No. 71 [section 722] review of the interim financial information as of and for the quarter ended March 31, 19X7, the accountants may provide negative assurance as to increases and decreases of specified financial statement items as of any date up to August 14, 19X7 (135 days subsequent to March 31).

An appropriate manner of expressing negative assurance regarding subsequent changes is shown in paragraphs 5*b* and 6 of example A [paragraph .64], if there has been no decrease and in example M [paragraph .64], if there has been a decrease. [Paragraph renumbered by the issuance of Statement on Auditing Standards No. 76, September 1995.]

.47 However, if the underwriter requests negative assurance as to subsequent changes in specified financial statement items as of a date 135 days or more subsequent to the end of the most recent period for which the accountants have performed an audit or a review, the accountants may not provide negative assurance but are limited to reporting procedures performed and findings obtained (see example O [paragraph .64]). [Paragraph renumbered by the issuance of Statement on Auditing Standards No. 76, September 1995.]

.48 In order that comments on subsequent changes be unambiguous and their determination be within accountants' professional expertise, the comments should not relate to "adverse changes," since that term has not acquired any clearly understood meaning. If there has been a change in an accounting principle during the change period, the accountants should note that fact in the letter. [Paragraph renumbered by the issuance of Statement on Auditing Standards No. 76, September 1995.]

.49 Comments on the occurrence of changes in capital stock, increases in long-term debt, and decreases in other specified financial statement items are limited to changes, increases, or decreases not disclosed in the registration statement. Accordingly, the phrase "except for changes, increases, or decreases that the registration statement discloses have occurred or may occur" should be included in the letter when it has come to the accountants' attention that a change, increase, or decrease has occurred during the change period, and the amount of such change, increase, or decrease is disclosed in the registration statement. This phrase need not be included in the letter when no changes, increases, or decreases in the specified financial statement items are disclosed in the registration statement. [Paragraph renumbered by the issuance of Statement on Auditing Standards No. 76, September 1995.]

.50 ***Change period.*** In the context of a comfort letter, a decrease occurs when the amount of a financial statement item at the cutoff date or for the change period (as if financial statements had been prepared at that date and for that period) is less than the amount of the same item at a specified earlier date or for a specified earlier period. With respect to the items mentioned in paragraph .45, the term *decrease* means (*a*) any combination of changes in amounts of current assets and current liabilities that results in decreased net current assets, (*b*) any combination of changes in amounts of assets and liabilities that results in decreased stockholders' equity, (*c*) decreased net sales, and (*d*) any combination of changes in amounts of sales, expenses and outstanding shares that results in decreased total and per-share amounts of income before extraordinary items and of net income (including, in each instance, a greater loss or other negative amount). The change period for which the accountants give negative assurance in the comfort letter ends on the cutoff date (see paragraph .23) and ordinarily begins, for balance sheet items, immediately after the date of the latest balance sheet in the registration statement and, for income statement items, immediately after the latest period for which such items are presented in the registration statement. The comparison relates to the entire period and not to portions of that period. A decrease during one part of the period may be offset by an equal or larger increase in another part of the period; however, because there was no decrease for the period as a whole, the comfort letter would not report the decrease occurring during one part of the period (see, however, paragraph .62). [Paragraph renumbered by the issuance of Statement on Auditing Standards No. 76, September 1995.]

.51 The underwriting agreement usually specifies the dates as of which, and periods for which, data at the cutoff date and data for the change period are to be compared. For balance sheet items, the comparison date is normally that of the latest balance sheet included (incorporated by reference) in the registration statement (that is, immediately prior to the beginning of the change period). For income statement items, the comparison period or periods might be one or more of the following: (*a*) the corresponding period of the preceding year, (*b*) a period of corresponding length immediately preceding the change period, (*c*) a proportionate part of the preceding fiscal year, or (*d*) any other period of corresponding length chosen by the underwriter. Whether or not specified in the underwriting agreement, the date and period used in comparison should be identified in the comfort letter in both draft and final form so that there is no misunderstanding about the matters being compared and so that the underwriter can determine whether the comparison period is suitable for his or her purposes. [Paragraph renumbered by the issuance of Statement on Auditing Standards No. 76, September 1995.]

.52 The underwriter occasionally requests that the change period begin immediately after the date of the latest audited balance sheet (which is, ordinarily, also the closing date of the latest audited statement of income) in the registration statement, even though the registration statement includes a more recent unaudited condensed balance sheet and condensed statement of income. The use of the earlier date may defeat the underwriter's purpose, since it is possible that an increase in one of the items referred to in paragraph .45 occurring between the dates of the latest audited and unaudited balance sheets included (incorporated by reference) in the registration statement might more than offset a decrease occurring after the latter date. A similar situation might arise in the comparison of income statement items. In these circumstances, the decrease occurring after the date of the latest unaudited condensed interim financial statements included (incorporated by reference) in the registration statement would not be reported in the comfort letter. It is desirable for the accountants to explain the foregoing considerations to the underwriter; however, if the underwriter nonetheless requests the use of a change period or periods other than those described in paragraph .50, the accountants may use the period or periods requested. [Paragraph renumbered by the issuance of Statement on Auditing Standards No. 76, September 1995.]

.53 When other accountants are involved and their letters do not disclose matters that affect the negative assurance given, an appropriate manner of expressing these comments is shown in example J [paragraph .64]. When appropriate, the principal accountants may comment that there were no decreases in the consolidated financial statement items despite the possibility that decreases have been mentioned by the other accountants. In such a case, the principal accountants could make a statement that "nothing came to our attention regarding the consolidated financial statements as a result of the specified procedures (which, so far as the related company was concerned, consisted solely of reading the other accountants' letter) that caused us to believe that...." [Paragraph renumbered by the issuance of Statement on Auditing Standards No. 76, September 1995.]

Tables, Statistics, and Other Financial Information

.54 The underwriting agreement sometimes calls for a comfort letter that includes comments on tables, statistics, and other financial information appearing in the registration statement. [Paragraph renumbered by the issuance of Statement on Auditing Standards No. 76, September 1995.]

.55 The accountants should refrain from commenting on matters to which their competence as independent accountants has little relevance. Accordingly, except as indicated in the next sentence, they should comment only with respect to information (*a*) that is expressed in dollars (or percentages derived from such dollar amounts) and that has been obtained from accounting records that are subject to the entity's controls over financial reporting or (*b*) that has been derived directly from such accounting records by analysis or computation. The accountants may also comment on quantitative information that has been obtained from an accounting record if the information is of a type that is subject to the same controls over financial reporting as the dollar amounts. Accountants should not comment on matters primarily involving the exercise of management's business judgment. For example, changes between periods in gross profit ratios or net income may be caused by factors that are not necessarily within the expertise of accountants. The accountants should not comment on matters merely because they happen to be present and are capable of reading, counting, measuring, or performing other functions that might be applicable. Examples of matters that, unless subjected to the entity's controls over financial reporting (which is not ordinarily the case), should not be commented on by the accountants include the square footage of facilities, number of employees (except as related to a given payroll period), and backlog information. The accountants should not comment on tables, statistics, and other financial information relating to an unaudited period unless (*a*) they have performed an audit of the client's financial statements for a period including or immediately prior to the unaudited period or have completed an audit for a later period or (*b*) they have otherwise obtained knowledge of the client's internal control as provided for in paragraph .36 herein. In addition, the accountants should not comment on information subject to legal interpretation, such as beneficial share ownership. [Paragraph renumbered by the issuance of Statement on Auditing Standards No. 76, September 1995.]

.56 As with comments relating to financial statement information, it is important that the procedures followed by the accountants with respect to other information be clearly set out in the comfort letter, in both draft and final form, so that there will be no misunderstanding about the basis of the comments on the information. Further, so that there will be no implication that the accountants are furnishing any assurance with respect to the sufficiency of the procedures for the underwriter's intended purpose, the comfort letter should contain a statement to this effect. An appropriate way of expressing this is shown in paragraph 10 of example F [paragraph .64] (see also paragraph .16 of this section). [Paragraph renumbered by the issuance of Statement on Auditing Standards No. 76, September 1995.]

.57 Certain financial information in registration statements is included because of specific requirements of Regulation S-K. Accountants may comment as to whether this information is in conformity with the disclosure requirements of Regulation S-K if the following conditions are met:

a. The information is derived from the accounting records subject to the entity's controls over financial reporting, or has been derived directly from such accounting records by analysis or computation.

b. This information is capable of evaluation against reasonable criteria that have been established by the SEC.

The following are the disclosure requirements of Regulation S-K that generally meet these conditions:

- Item 301, "Selected Financial Data"
- Item 302, "Supplementary Financial Information"
- Item 402, "Executive Compensation"
- Item 503(d), "Ratio of Earnings to Fixed Charges"

Accountants may not give positive assurance on conformity with the disclosure requirements of Regulation S-K; they are limited to giving negative assurance, since this information is not given in the form of financial statements and generally has not been audited by the accountants. Even with respect to the above-mentioned items, there may be situations in which it would be inappropriate to provide negative assurance with respect to conformity of this information with Regulation S-K because conditions (*a*) and (*b*) above have not been met. Since information relevant to Regulation S-K disclosure requirements other than those noted previously is generally not derived from the accounting records subject to the entity's controls over financial reporting, it is not appropriate for the accountants to comment on conformity of this information with Regulation S-K. The accountants' inability to comment on conformity with Regulation S-K does not preclude accountants from performing procedures and reporting findings with respect to this information. [Paragraph renumbered by the issuance of Statement on Auditing Standards No. 76, September 1995.]

.58 To avoid ambiguity, the specific information commented on in the letter should be identified by reference to specific captions, tables, page numbers, paragraphs, or sentences. Descriptions of the procedures followed and the findings obtained may be stated individually for each item of specific information commented on. Alternatively, if the procedures and findings are adequately described, some or all of the descriptions may be grouped or summarized, as long as the applicability of the descriptions to items in the registration statement is clear and the descriptions do not imply that the accountants assume responsibility for the adequacy of the procedures. It would also be appropriate to present a matrix listing the financial information and common procedures employed and indicating the procedures applied to the specific items. Another presentation that could be used identifies procedures performed with specified symbols and identifies items to which those procedures have been applied directly on a copy of the prospectus which is attached to the comfort letter. (See examples F, G, and H [paragraph .64]). [Paragraph renumbered by the issuance of Statement on Auditing Standards No. 76, September 1995.]

.59 Comments in the comfort letter concerning tables, statistics, and other financial information included (incorporated by reference) in the registration statement should be made in the form of a description of the procedures followed; the findings (ordinarily expressed in terms of agreement between items compared); and in some cases, as described below, statements with respect to the acceptability of methods of allocation used in deriving the figures commented on. Whether comments on the allocation of income or expense items between categories of sales (such as military and commercial sales) may appropriately be made will depend on the extent to which such allocation is made in, or can be derived directly by analysis or computation from, the client's accounting records. In any event, such comments, if made, should make clear that such allocations are to a substantial extent arbitrary, that the method of allocation used is not the only acceptable one, and that other acceptable methods of allocation might produce significantly different results. Furthermore, no comments should be made regarding segment information (or the appropriateness of allocations made to derive segment information) included in financial statements, since the accountants' report encompasses that information (see section 435, *Segment Information*).[30] Appropriate ways of expressing comments on tables, statistics, and other financial information are shown in examples F, G, and H [paragraph .64]. [Paragraph renumbered by the issuance of Statement on Auditing Standards No. 76, September 1995.]

.60 In comments concerning tables, statistics, and other financial information, the expression "presents fairly" (or a variation of it) should not be used. That expression, when used by independent accountants, ordinarily relates to presentations of financial statements and should not be used in commenting on other types of information. Except with respect to requirements for financial statements and certain Regulation S-K items discussed in paragraph .57, the question of what constitutes appropriate information for compliance with the requirements of a particular item of the registration statement form is a matter of legal interpretation outside the competence of accountants. Consequently, the letter should state that the accountants make no representations regarding any matter of legal interpretation. Since the accountants will not be in a position to make any representations about the completeness or adequacy of disclosure or about the adequacy of the procedures followed, the letter should so state. It should point out, as well, that such procedures would not necessarily disclose material misstatements or omissions in the information to which the comments relate. An appropriate manner of expressing the comments is shown in examples F, G, and H [paragraph .64]. [Paragraph renumbered by the issuance of Statement on Auditing Standards No. 76, September 1995.]

---

[30] See paragraph .30 regarding requests by an underwriter for comments on interim financial information required by item 302(*a*) of Regulation S-K and required supplementary information described in section 558. [Footnote renumbered by the issuance of Statement on Auditing Standards No. 76, September 1995.]

Concluding Paragraph

.61 In order to avoid misunderstanding of the purpose and intended use of the comfort letter, it is desirable that the letter conclude with a paragraph along the following lines:

> This letter is solely for the information of the addressees and to assist the underwriters[31] in conducting and documenting their investigation of the affairs of the company in connection with the offering of the securities covered by the registration statement, audit is not to be used, circulated, quoted, or otherwise referred to within or without the underwriting group for any other purpose, including, but not limited to, the registration, purchase, or sale of securities, nor is it to be filed with or referred to in whole or in part in the registration statement or any other document, except that reference may be made to it in the underwriting agreement or in any list of closing documents pertaining to the offering of the securities covered by the registration statement.

[Paragraph renumbered by the issuance of Statement on Auditing Standards No. 76, September 1995.]

Disclosure of Subsequently Discovered Matters

.62 Accountants who discover matters that may require mention in the final comfort letter but that are not mentioned in the draft letter that has been furnished to the underwriter, such as changes, increases, or decreases in specified items not disclosed in the registration statement (see paragraphs .45 and .49), will naturally want to discuss them with their client so that consideration can be given to whether disclosure should be made in the registration statement. If disclosure is not to be made, the accountants should inform the client that the matters will be mentioned in the comfort letter and should suggest that the underwriter be informed promptly. It is recommended that the accountants be present when the client and the underwriter discuss such matters. [Paragraph renumbered by the issuance of Statement on Auditing Standards No. 76, September 1995.]

Effective Date

.63 This section is effective for comfort letters issued on or after June 30, 1993. Early application of this section is encouraged. [Paragraph renumbered by the issuance of Statement on Auditing Standards No. 76, September 1995.]

---

[31] When the letter is furnished by the accountants for a subsidiary and they are not also accountants for the parent company, the letter should include the following phrase at this point: "and for the use of the accountants for [*name of issuer*] in furnishing their letter to the underwriters." [Footnote renumbered by the issuance of Statement on Auditing Standards No. 76, September 1995.]

.64

Appendix

Examples

1. The contents of comfort letters vary, depending on the extent of the information in the registration statement and the wishes of the underwriter or other requesting party. Shelf registration statements may have several closing dates and different underwriters. Descriptions of procedures and findings regarding interim financial statements, tables, statistics, or other financial information that is incorporated by reference from previous 1934 Act filings may have to be repeated in several comfort letters. To avoid restating these descriptions in each comfort letter, accountants may initially issue the comments in a format (such as an appendix) that can be referred to in, and attached to, subsequently issued comfort letters.

Example A: Typical Comfort Letter

2. A typical comfort letter includes—

a. A statement regarding the independence of the accountants (paragraphs .31 and .32).

b. An opinion regarding whether the audited financial statements and financial statement schedules included (incorporated by reference) in the registration statement comply as to form in all material respects with the applicable accounting requirements of the Act and related published rules and regulations (paragraphs .33 and .34).

c. Negative assurance on whether—

1. The unaudited condensed interim financial information included (incorporated by reference) in the registration statement (paragraph .37) complies as to form in all material respects with the applicable accounting requirements of the Act and the related published rules and regulations.
2. Any material modifications should be made to the unaudited condensed consolidated financial statements included (incorporated by reference) in the registration statement for them to be in conformity with generally accepted accounting principles.

d. Negative assurance on whether, during a specified period following the date of the latest financial statements in the registration statement and prospectus, there has been any change in capital stock, increase in long-term debt or any decrease in other specified financial statement items (paragraphs .45 through .53).

Example A is a letter covering all these items. Letters that cover some of the items may be developed by omitting inapplicable portions of example A.

Example A assumes the following circumstances.[1] The prospectus (part I of the registration statement) includes audited consolidated balance sheets as of December 31, 19X5 and 19X4, and audited consolidated statements of income, retained earnings (stockholders' equity), and cash flows for each of the three

[1] The example includes financial statements required by SEC regulations to be included in the filing. If additional financial information is covered by the comfort letter, appropriate modifications should be made.

years in the period ended December 31, 19X5. Part I also includes an unaudited condensed consolidated balance sheet as of March 31, 19X6, and unaudited condensed consolidated statements of income, retained earnings (stockholders' equity), and cash flows for the three-month periods ended March 31, 19X6 and 19X5, reviewed in accordance with section 722 but not previously reported on by the accountants. Part II of the registration statement includes audited consolidated financial statement schedules for the three years ended December 31, 19X5. The cutoff date is June 23, 19X6, and the letter is dated June 28, 19X6. The effective date is June 28, 19X6.

Each of the comments in the letter is in response to a requirement of the underwriting agreement. For purposes of example A, the income statement items of the current interim period are to be compared with those of the corresponding period of the preceding year.

June 28, 19X6

[*Addressee*]

Dear Sirs:

We have audited the consolidated balance sheets of The Blank Company, Inc. (the company) and subsidiaries as of December 31, 19X5 and 19X4, and the consolidated statements of income, retained earnings (stockholders' equity), and cash flows for each of the three years in the period ended December 31, 19X5, and the related financial statement schedules all included in the registration statement (no. 33-00000) on Form S-1 filed by the company under the Securities Act of 1933 (the Act); our reports with respect thereto are also included in that registration statement. The registration statement, as amended on June 28, 19X6, is herein referred to as the registration statement.[2]

In connection with the registration statement—

1. We are independent certified public accountants with respect to the company within the meaning of the Act and the applicable published rules and regulations thereunder.

2. In our opinion [*include the phrase "except as disclosed in the registration statement," if applicable*], the consolidated financial statements and financial statement schedules audited by us and included in the registration statement comply as to form in all material respects with the applicable accounting requirements of the Act and the related published rules and regulations.

3. We have not audited any financial statements of the company as of any date or for any period subsequent to December 31, 19X5; although we have conducted an audit for the year ended December 31, 19X5, the purpose (and therefore the scope) of the audit was to enable us to express our opinion on the consolidated financial statements as of December 31, 19X5, and for the year then ended, but not on the financial statements for any interim period within that year. Therefore, we are unable to and do not express any opinion on the unaudited condensed consolidated balance sheet as of March 31, 19X6, and the unaudited condensed consolidated statements of income, retained earnings

---

[2] The example assumes that the accountants have not previously reported on the interim financial information. If the accountants have previously reported on the interim financial information, they many refer to that fact in the introductory paragraph of the comfort letter as follows:

> Also, we have reviewed the unaudited condensed consolidated financial statements as of March 31, 19X6 and 19X5, and for the three-month periods then ended, as indicated in our report dated May 15, 19X6, which is included (incorporated by reference) in the registration statement.

The report may be attached to the comfort letter (see paragraph .29). The accountants may agree to comment in the comment letter on whether the interim financial information complies as to form in all material respects with the applicable accounting requirements of the published rules and regulations of the SEC.

(stockholders' equity), and cash flows for the three-month periods ended March 31, 19X6 and 19X5, included in the registration statement, or on the financial position, results of operations, or cash flows as of any date or for any period subsequent to December 31, 19X5.

4. For purposes of this letter we have read the 19X6 minutes of meetings of the stockholders, the board of directors, and [*include other appropriate committees, if any*] of the company and its subsidiaries as set forth in the minute books at June 23, 19X6, officials of the company having advised us that the minutes of all such meetings[3] through that date were set forth therein; we have carried out other procedures to June 23, 19X6, as follows (our work did not extend to the period from June 24, 19X6, to June 28, 19X6, inclusive):

a. With respect to the three-month periods ended March 31, 19X6 and 19X5, we have—

(i) Performed the procedures specified by the American Institute of Certified Public Accountants for a review of interim financial information as described in SAS No. 71, *Interim Financial Information*, on the unaudited condensed consolidated balance sheet as of March 31, 19X6, and unaudited condensed consolidated statements of income, retained earnings (stockholders' equity), and cash flows for the three-month periods ended March 31, 19X6 and 19X5, included in the registration statement.

(ii) Inquired of certain officials of the company who have responsibility for financial and accounting matters whether the unaudited condensed consolidated financial statements referred to in *a*(i) comply as to form in all material respects with the applicable accounting requirements of the Act and the related published rules and regulations.

b. With respect to the period from April 1, 19X6, to May 31, 19X6, we have—

(i) Read the unaudited consolidated financial statements[4] of the company and subsidiaries for April and May of both 19X5 and 19X6 furnished us by the company, officials of the company having advised us that no such financial statements as of any date or for any period subsequent to May 31, 19X6, were available.

(ii) Inquired of certain officials of the company who have responsibility for financial and accounting matters whether the unaudited consolidated financial statements referred to in *b*(i) are stated on a basis substantially consistent with that of the audited consolidated financial statements included in the registration statement.

The foregoing procedures do not constitute an audit conducted in accordance with generally accepted auditing standards. Also, they would not necessarily reveal matters of significance with respect to the comments in the following paragraph. Accordingly, we make no representations regarding the sufficiency of the foregoing procedures for your purposes.

---

[3] The accountants should discuss with the secretary those meetings for which minutes have not been approved. The letter should be modified to identify specifically the unapproved minutes of meetings that the accountants have discussed with the secretary.

[4] If the interim financial information is incomplete, a sentence similar to the following should be added: "The financial information for April and May is incomplete in that it omits the statements of cash flows and other disclosures."

5. Nothing came to our attention as a result of the foregoing procedures, however, that caused us[5] to believe that—

a. (i) Any material modifications should be made to the unaudited condensed consolidated financial statements described in 4*a*(i), included in the registration statement, for them to be in conformity with generally accepted accounting principles.[6]

(ii) The unaudited condensed consolidated financial statements described in 4*a*(i) do not comply as to form in all material respects with the applicable accounting requirements of the Act and the related published rules and regulations.

b. (i) At May 31, 19X6, there was any change in the capital stock, increase in long-term debt, or decrease in consolidated net current assets or stockholders' equity of the consolidated companies as compared with amounts shown in the March 31, 19X6, unaudited condensed consolidated balance sheet included in the registration statement, or (ii) for the period from April 1, 19X6, to May 31, 19X6, there were any decreases, as compared to the corresponding period in the preceding year, in consolidated net sales or in the total or per-share amounts of income before extraordinary items or of net income, except in all instances for changes, increases, or decreases that the registration statement discloses have occurred or may occur.

6. As mentioned in 4*b*, company officials have advised us that no consolidated financial statements as of any date or for any period subsequent to May 31, 19X6, are available; accordingly, the procedures carried out by us with respect to changes in financial statement items after May 31, 19X6, have, of necessity, been even more limited than those with respect to the periods referred to in 4. We have inquired of certain officials of the company who have responsibility for financial and accounting matters whether (*a*) at June 23, 19X6, there was any change in the capital stock, increase in long-term debt or any decreases in consolidated net current assets or stockholders' equity of the consolidated companies as compared with amounts shown on the March 31, 19X6, unaudited condensed consolidated balance sheet included in the registration statement or (*b*) for the period from April 1, 19X6, to June 23, 19X6, there were any decreases, as compared with the corresponding period in the preceding year, in consolidated net sales or in the total or per-share amounts of income before extraordinary items or of net income. On the basis of these inquiries and our reading of the minutes as described in 4, nothing came to our attention that caused us to believe that there was any such change, increase, or decrease, except in all instances for changes, increases, or decreases that the registration statement discloses have occurred or may occur.

7. This letter is solely for the information of the addressees and to assist the underwriters in conducting and documenting their investigation of the affairs of the company in connection with the offering of the securities covered by the registration statement, and it is not to be used, circulated, quoted, or otherwise referred to within or without the underwriting group for any purpose, including but not limited to the registration, purchase, or sale of securities, nor is it to be filed with or referred to in whole or in part in the registration statement or any other document, except that reference may be made to it in

---

[5] If there has been a change in accounting principle during the interim period, a reference to that change should be included herein.

[6] Section 722 does not require the accountants to modify the report on a review of interim financial information for a lack of consistency in the application of accounting principles provided that the interim financial information appropriately discloses such matters.

the underwriting agreement or in any list of closing documents pertaining to the offering of the securities covered by the registration statement.

Example B: Letter When a Short-Form Registration Statement Is Filed Incorporating Previously Filed Forms 10-K and 10-Q by Reference

3. Example B is applicable when a registrant uses a short-form registration statement (Form S-2 or S-3) which, by reference, incorporates previously filed Forms 10-K and 10-Q. It assumes that the short-form registration statement and prospectus include the Form 10-K for the year ended December 31, 19X5, and Form 10-Q for the quarter ended March 31, 19X6, which have been incorporated by reference. In addition to the information presented below, the letter would also contain paragraphs 6 and 7 of the typical letter in example A. A Form S-2 registration statement will often both incorporate and include the registrant's financial statements. In such situations, the language in the following example should be appropriately modified to refer to such information as being both incorporated and included.

June 28, 19X6

[*Addressee*]

Dear Sirs:

We have audited the consolidated balance sheets of The Blank Company, Inc. (the company) and subsidiaries as of December 31, 19X5 and 19X4, and the consolidated statements of income, retained earnings (stockholders' equity), and cash flows for each of the three years in the period ended December 31, 19X5, and the related financial statement schedules, all included (incorporated by reference) in the company's annual report on Form 10-K for the year ended December 31, 19X5, and incorporated by reference in the registration statement (no. 33-00000) on Form S-3 filed by the company under the Securities Act of 1933 (the Act); our report with respect thereto is also incorporated by reference in that registration statement. The registration statement, as amended on June 28, 19X6, is herein referred to as the registration statement.

In connection with the registration statement—

1. We are independent certified public accountants with respect to the company within the meaning of the Act and the applicable published rules and regulations thereunder.

2. In our opinion, the consolidated financial statements and financial statement schedules audited by us and incorporated by reference in the registration statement comply as to form in all material respects with the applicable accounting requirements of the Act and the Securities Exchange Act of 1934 and the related published rules and regulations.

3. We have not audited any financial statements of the company as of any date or for any period subsequent to December 31, 19X5; although we have conducted an audit for the year ended December 31, 19X5, the purpose (and therefore the scope) of the audit was to enable us to express our opinion on the consolidated financial statements as of December 31, 19X5, and for the year then ended, but not on the consolidated financial statements for any interim period within that year. Therefore, we are unable to and do not express any opinion on the unaudited condensed consolidated balance sheet as of March 31, 19X6, and the unaudited condensed consolidated statements of income, retained earnings (stockholders' equity), and cash flows for the three-month periods ended March 31, 19X6 and 19X5, included in the company's quarterly report on Form 10-Q for the quarter ended March 31, 19X6, incorporated by

reference in the registration statement, or on the financial position, results of operations, or cash flows as of any date or for any period subsequent to December 31, 19X5.

4. For purposes of this letter, we have read the 19X6 minutes of the meetings of the stockholders, the board of directors, and [*include other appropriate committees, if any*] of the company and its subsidiaries as set forth in the minute books at June 23, 19X6, officials of the company having advised us that the minutes of all such meetings[7] through that date were set forth therein; we have carried out other procedures to June 23, 19X6, as follows (our work did not extend to the period from June 24, 19X6, to June 28, 19X6, inclusive):

a. With respect to the three-month periods ended March 31, 19X6 and 19X5, we have—

(i) Performed the procedures specified by the American Institute of Certified Public Accountants for a review of interim financial information as described in SAS No. 71, *Interim Financial Information*, on the unaudited condensed consolidated financial statements for these periods, described in 3, included in the company's quarterly report on Form 10-Q for the quarter ended March 31, 19X6, incorporated by reference in the registration statement.

(ii) Inquired of certain officials of the company who have responsibility for financial and accounting matters whether the unaudited condensed consolidated financial statements referred to in *a*(i) comply as to form in all material respects with the applicable accounting requirements of the Securities Exchange Act of 1934 as it applies to Form 10-Q and the related published rules and regulations.

b. With respect to the period from April 1, 19X6, to May 31, 19X6, we have—

(i) Read the unaudited consolidated financial statements[8] of the company and subsidiaries for April and May of both 19X5 and 19X6 furnished us by the company, officials of the company having advised us that no such financial statements as of any date or for any period subsequent to May 31, 19X6, were available.

(ii) Inquired of certain officials of the company who have responsibility for financial and accounting matters whether the unaudited consolidated financial statements referred to in *b*(i) are stated on a basis substantially consistent with that of the audited consolidated financial statements incorporated by reference in the registration statement.

The foregoing procedures do not constitute an audit conducted in accordance with generally accepted auditing standards. Also, they would not necessarily reveal matters of significance with respect to the comments in the following paragraph. Accordingly, we make no representations about the sufficiency of the foregoing procedures for your purposes.

5. Nothing came to our attention as a result of the foregoing procedures, however, that caused us to believe that—

a. (i) Any material modifications should be made to the unaudited condensed consolidated financial statements described in 3, incorporated by reference in the registration statement, for them to be in conformity with generally accepted accounting principles.

---

[7] See footnote 3 of the Appendix.

[8] See footnote 4 of the Appendix.

(ii) The unaudited condensed consolidated financial statements described in 3 do not comply as to form in all material respects with the applicable accounting requirements of the Securities Exchange Act of 1934 as it applies to Form 10-Q and the related published rules and regulations.

b. (i) At May 31, 19X6, there was any change in the capital stock, increase in long-term debt, or any decreases in consolidated net current assets or stockholders' equity of the consolidated companies as compared with amounts shown in the March 31, 19X6 unaudited condensed consolidated balance sheet incorporated by reference in the registration statement or (ii) for the period from April 1, 19X6, to May 31, 19X6, there were any decreases, as compared with the corresponding period in the preceding year, in consolidated net sales or in the total or per-share amounts of income before extraordinary items or of net income, except in all instances for changes, increases, or decreases that the registration statement discloses have occurred or may occur.

Example C: Letter Reaffirming Comments in Example A as of a Later Date

4. If more than one comfort letter is requested, the later letter may, in appropriate situations, refer to information appearing in the earlier letter without repeating such information (see paragraph .24 and paragraph 1 of the Appendix). Example C reaffirms and updates the information in example A.

July 25, 19X6

[*Addressee*]

Dear Sirs:

We refer to our letter of June 28, 19X6, relating to the registration statement (no. 33-00000) of The Blank Company, Inc. (the company). We reaffirm as of the date hereof (and as though made on the date hereof) all statements made in that letter except that, for the purposes of this letter—

a. The registration statement to which this letter relates is as amended on July 13, 19X6 [*effective date*].

b. The reading of minutes described in paragraph 4 of that letter has been carried out through July 20, 19X6 [*the new cutoff date*].

c. The procedures and inquiries covered in paragraph 4 of that letter were carried out to July 20, 19X6 [*the new cutoff date*] (our work did not extend to the period from July 21, 19X6, to July 25, 19X6 [*date of letter*], inclusive).

d. The period covered in paragraph 4*b* of that letter is changed to the period from April 1, 19X6, to June 30, 19X6, officials of the company having advised us that no such financial statements as of any date or for any period subsequent to June 30, 19X6, were available.

e. The references to May 31, 19X6, in paragraph 5*b* of that letter are changed to June 30, 19X6.

f. The references to May 31, 19X6, and June 23, 19X6, in paragraph 6 of that letter are changed to June 30, 19X6, and July 20, 19X6, respectively.

This letter is solely for the information of the addressees and to assist the underwriters in conducting and documenting their investigation of the affairs of the company in connection with the offering of the securities covered by the registration statement, and it is not to be used, circulated, quoted, or otherwise referred to within the underwriting group for any other purpose, including but not limited to the registration, purchase, or sale of securities, nor is it to be filed with or referred to in whole or in part in the registration statement or any other document, except that reference may be made to it in the underwriting agreement or any list of closing documents pertaining to the offering of the securities covered by the registration statement.

Example D: Comments on Pro Forma Financial Information

5. Example D is applicable when the accountants are asked to comment on (*a*) whether the pro forma financial information included in a registration statement complies as to form in all material respects with the applicable accounting requirements of rule 11-02 of Regulation S-X, and (*b*) the application of pro forma adjustments to historical amounts in the compilation of the pro forma financial information (see paragraphs .42 and .43). The material in this example is intended to be inserted between paragraphs 6 and 7 in example A. The accountants have audited the December 31, 19X5, financial statements and have conducted an SAS No. 71 [section 722] review of the March 31, 19X6, interim financial information of the acquiring company. Other accountants conducted a review of the March 31, 19X6, interim financial information of XYZ Company, the company being acquired. The example assumes that the accountants have not previously reported on the pro forma financial information. If the accountants did previously report on the pro forma financial information, they may refer in the introductory paragraph of the comfort letter to the fact that they have issued a report, and the report may be attached to the comfort letter (see paragraph .29). In that circumstance, therefore, the procedures in 7*b*(i) and 7c ordinarily would not be performed, and the accountants should not separately comment on the application of pro forma adjustments to historical financial information, since that assurance is encompassed in the accountants' report on pro forma financial information. The accountants may, however, agree to comment on compliance as to form with the applicable accounting requirements of rule 11-02 of Regulation S-X.

7. At your request, we have—

a. Read the unaudited pro forma condensed consolidated balance sheet as of March 31, 19X6, and the unaudited pro forma condensed consolidated statements of income for the year ended December 31, 19X5, and the three-month period ended March 31, 19X6, included in the registration statement.

b. Inquired of certain officials of the company and of XYZ Company (the company being acquired) who have responsibility for financial and accounting matters about—

(i) The basis for their determination of the pro forma adjustments, and

(ii) Whether the unaudited pro forma condensed consolidated financial statements referred to in 7*a* comply as to form in all material respects with the applicable accounting requirements of rule 11-02 of Regulation S-X.

c. Proved the arithmetic accuracy of the application of the pro forma adjustments to the historical amounts in the unaudited pro forma condensed consolidated financial statements.

The foregoing procedures are substantially less in scope than an examination, the objective of which is the expression of an opinion on management's assumptions, the pro forma adjustments, and the application of those adjustments to historical financial information. Accordingly, we do not express such an opinion. The foregoing procedures would not necessarily reveal matters of significance with respect to the comments in the following paragraph. Accordingly, we make no representation about the sufficiency of such procedures for your purposes.

8. Nothing came to our attention as a result of the procedures specified in paragraph 7, however, that caused us to believe that the unaudited pro forma condensed consolidated financial statements referred to in 7*a* included in the registration statement do not comply as to form in all material respects with the applicable accounting requirements of rule 11-02 of Regulation S-X and that the pro forma adjustments have not been properly applied to the historical amounts in the compilation of those statements. Had we performed additional procedures or had we made an examination of the pro forma condensed consolidated financial statements, other matters might have come to our attention that would have been reported to you.

Example E: Comments on a Financial Forecast

6. Example E is applicable when accountants are asked to comment on a financial forecast (see paragraph .44). The material in this example is intended to be inserted between paragraphs 6 and 7 in example A. The example assumes that the accountants have previously reported on the compilation of the financial forecast and that the report is attached to the letter (see paragraph .29 and example O).

7. At your request, we performed the following procedure with respect to the forecasted consolidated balance sheet and consolidated statements of income and cash flows as of December 31, 19X6, and for the year then ending. With respect to forecasted rental income, we compared the occupancy statistics about expected demand for rental of the housing units to statistics for existing comparable properties and found them to be the same.

8. Because the procedure described above does not constitute an examination of prospective financial statements in accordance with standards established by the American Institute of Certified Public Accountants, we do not express an opinion on whether the prospective financial statements are presented in conformity with AICPA presentation guidelines or on whether the underlying assumptions provide a reasonable basis for the presentation.

Had we performed additional procedures or had we made an examination of the forecast in accordance with standards established by the American Institute of Certified Public Accountants, matters might have come to our attention that would have been reported to you. Furthermore, there will usually be differences between the forecasted and actual results, because events and circumstances frequently do not occur as expected, and those differences may be material.

Example F: Comments on Tables, Statistics, and Other Financial Information—Complete Description of Procedures and Findings

7. Example F is applicable when the accountants are asked to comment on tables, statistics, or other compilations of information appearing in a registration statement (paragraphs .54 through .60). Each of the comments is in response to a specific request. The paragraphs in example F are intended to follow paragraph 6 in example A.

7. For purposes of this letter, we have also read the following, set forth in the registration statement on the indicated pages.[9]

Item	Page	Description
a	4	"Capitalization." The amounts under the captions "Amount Outstanding as of June 15, 19X6" and "As Adjusted." The related notes, except the following in Note 2: "See 'Transactions With Interested Persons.' From the proceeds of this offering the company intends to prepay $900,000 on these notes, pro rata. See 'Use of Proceeds.'"
b	13	"History and Business—Sales and Marketing." The table following the first paragraph.
c	22	"Executive Compensation—19X5 Compensation."
d	33	"Selected Financial Data."[10]

8. Our audit of the consolidated financial statements for the periods referred to in the introductory paragraph of this letter comprised audit tests and procedures deemed necessary for the purpose of expressing an opinion on such financial statements taken as a whole. For none of the periods referred to therein, or any other period, did we perform audit tests for the purpose of expressing an opinion on individual balances of accounts or summaries of selected transactions such as those enumerated above, and, accordingly, we express no opinion thereon.

9. However, for purposes of this letter we have performed the following additional procedures, which were applied as indicated with respect to the items enumerated above.

Item in 7	Procedures and Findings
a	We compared the amounts and numbers of shares listed under the caption "Amount Outstanding as of June 15, 19X6" with the balances in the appropriate accounts in the company's general ledger at May 31, 19X6 (the latest date for which posting had been made), and found them to be in agreement. We were informed by company officials who have responsibility for financial and accounting matters that there have been no changes in such amounts and numbers of shares between May 31, 19X6, and June 15, 19X6. We compared the amounts and numbers of shares listed under the caption "Amount Outstanding as of June 15, 19X6," adjusted for the issuance of the debentures to be offered by means of the registration statement and for the proposed use of a portion of the proceeds thereof to prepay portions of certain notes, as described under "Use of Proceeds," with the amounts and numbers of shares shown under the caption "As Adjusted" and found such amounts and numbers of shares to be in agreement. (However, we make no comments regarding the reasonableness of the "Use of Proceeds" or whether such use will actually take place.) We compared the description of the securities and the information (except certain information in Note 2, referred to in 7) included in the notes to the table with the corresponding descriptions and information in the company's consolidated financial statements,

---

[9] In some cases it may be considered desirable to combine in one paragraph the substance of paragraphs 7 and 9. This may be done by expanding the identification of items in paragraph 9 to provide the identification information contained in paragraph 7. In such cases, the introductory sentences in paragraphs 7 and 9 and the text of paragraph 8 might be combined as follows: "For purposes of this letter, we have also read the following information and have performed the additional procedures stated below with respect to such information. Our audit of the consolidated financial statements. . ."

[10] In some cases the company or the underwriter may request that the independent accountants report on "selected financial data" as described in section 552, *Reporting on Condensed Financial Statements and Selected Financial Data*. When the accountants report on this data and the report is included in the registration statement, separate comments should not be included in the comfort letter (see paragraph .30).

Item in 7	Procedures and Findings
	including the notes thereto included in the registration statement, and found such description and information to be in agreement.
b	We compared the amounts of military sales, commercial sales, and total sales shown in the registration statement with the balances in the appropriate accounts in the company's accounting records for the respective fiscal years and for the unaudited interim periods and found them to be in agreement. We proved the arithmetic accuracy of the percentages of such amounts of military sales and commercial sales to total sales for the respective fiscal years and for the unaudited interim periods. We compared such computed percentages with the corresponding percentages appearing in the registration statement and found them to be in agreement.
c	We compared the dollar amounts of compensation (salary, bonus, and other compensation) for each individual listed in the table "Annual Compensation" with the corresponding amounts shown by the individual employee earnings records for the year 19X5 and found them to be in agreement. We compared the dollar amount of aggregate executive officers' cash compensation on page 22 with the corresponding amount shown in an analysis prepared by the company and found the amounts to be in agreement. We traced every item over $10,000 on the analysis to the individual employee records for 19X5. We compared the dollar amounts shown under the heading of "Long-Term Compensation" on page 24 for each listed individual and the aggregate amounts for executive officers with corresponding amounts shown in an analysis prepared by the company and found such amounts to be in agreement. We compared the executive compensation information with the requirements of item 402 of Regulation S-K. We also inquired of certain officials of the company who have responsibility for financial and accounting matters whether the executive compensation information conforms in all material respects with the disclosure requirements of item 402 of Regulation S-K. Nothing came to our attention as a result of the foregoing procedures that caused us to believe that this information does not conform in all material respects with the disclosure requirements of item 402 of Regulation S-K.
d	We compared the amounts of net sales, income from continuing operations, income from continuing operations per common share, and cash dividends declared per common share for the years ended December 31, 19X5, 19X4, and 19X3, with the respective amounts in the consolidated financial statements on pages 27 and 28 and the amounts for the years ended December 31, 19X2, and 19X1, with the respective amounts in the consolidated financial statements included in the company's annual reports to stockholders for 19X2 and 19X1 and found them to be in agreement. We compared the amounts of total assets, long-term obligations, and redeemable preferred stock at December 31, 19X5 and 19X4, with the respective amounts in the consolidated financial statements on pages 27 and 28 and the amounts at December 31, 19X3, and 19X2, and 19X1 with the corresponding amounts in the consolidated financial statements included in the company's annual reports to stockholders for 19X3, 19X2, and 19X1 and found them to be in agreement. We compared the information included under the heading "Selected Financial Data" with the requirements of item 301 of Regulation S-K. We also inquired of certain officials of the company who have responsibility for financial and accounting matters whether this information conforms in all material respects with the disclosure requirements of item 301 of Regulation S-K. Nothing came to our attention as a result of the foregoing procedures that caused us to believe that this information does not conform in all material respects with the disclosure requirements of item 301 of Regulation S-K.

10. It should be understood that we make no representations regarding questions of legal interpretation or regarding the sufficiency for your purposes of the procedures enumerated in the preceding paragraph; also, such procedures would not necessarily reveal any material misstatement of the amounts or percentages listed above. Further, we have addressed ourselves solely to the foregoing data as set forth in the registration statement and make no representations regarding the adequacy of disclosure or regarding whether any material facts have been omitted.

11. This letter is solely for the information of the addressees and to assist the underwriters in conducting and documenting their investigation of the affairs of the company in connection with the offering of the securities covered by the registration statement, and it is not be used, circulated, quoted, or otherwise referred to within or without the underwriting group for any other purpose, including but not limited to the registration, purchase, or sale of securities, nor is it to be filed with or referred to in whole or in part in the registration statement or any other document, except that reference may be made to it in the underwriting agreement or in any list of closing documents pertaining to the offering of the securities covered by the registration statement.

Example G: Comments on Tables, Statistics, and Other Financial Information—Summarized Description of Procedures and Findings Regarding Tables, Statistics, and Other Financial Information

8. Example G illustrates, in paragraph 9*a*, a method of summarizing the descriptions of procedures and findings regarding tables, statistics, and other financial information in order to avoid repetition in the comfort letter. The summarization of the descriptions is permitted by paragraph .58. Each of the comments is in response to a specific request. The paragraphs in example G are intended to follow paragraph 6 in example A.[11]

7. For purposes of this letter, we have also read the following, set forth in the registration statement on the indicated pages.

Item	Page	Description
a	4	"Capitalization." The amounts under the captions "Amount Outstanding as of June 15, 19X6" and "As Adjusted." The related notes, except the following in Note 2: "See 'Transactions With Interested Persons.' From the proceeds of this offering the company intends to prepay $900,000 on these notes, pro rata. See 'Use of Proceeds.'"
b	13	"History and Business—Sales and Marketing." The table following the first paragraph.
c	22	"Executive Compensation—19X5 Compensation."
d	33	"Selected Financial Data."[12]

8. Our audit of the consolidated financial statements for the periods referred to in the introductory paragraph of this letter comprised audit tests and procedures deemed necessary for the purpose of expressing an opinion on such financial statements taken as a whole. For none of the periods referred to there-

[11] Other methods of summarizing the descriptions may also be appropriately used. For example, the letter may present a matrix listing the financial information and common procedures employed and indicating the procedures applied to specific items.

[12] See footnote 10 of the Appendix.

in, or any other period, did we perform audit tests for the purpose of expressing an opinion on individual balances of accounts or summaries of selected transactions such as those enumerated above, and, accordingly, we express no opinion thereon.

9. However, for purposes of this letter and with respect to the items enumerated in 7 above—

a. Except for item 7*a*, we have (i) compared the dollar amounts either with the amounts in the audited consolidated financial statements described in the introductory paragraph of this letter or, for prior years, included in the company's annual report to stockholders for the years 19X1, 19X2, and 19X3, or with amounts in the unaudited consolidated financial statements described in paragraph 3 to the extent such amounts are included in or can be derived from such statements and found them to be in agreement; (ii) compared the amounts of military sales, commercial sales, and total sales and the dollar amounts of compensation for each listed individual with amounts in the company's accounting records and found them to be in agreement; (iii) compared other dollar amounts with amounts shown in analyses prepared by the company and found them to be in agreement; and (iv) proved the arithmetic accuracy of the percentages based on the data in the above-mentioned financial statements, accounting records, and analyses.

We compared the information in items 7*c* and 7*d* with the disclosure requirements of Regulation S-K. We also inquired of certain officials of the company who have responsibility for financial and accounting matters whether this information conforms in all material respects with the disclosure requirements of Regulation S-K. Nothing came to our attention as a result of the foregoing procedures that caused us to believe that this information does not conform in all material respects with the disclosure requirements of items 402 and 301, respectively, of Regulation S-K.

b. With respect to item 7*a*, we compared the amounts and numbers of shares listed under the caption "Amount Outstanding as of June 15, 19X6" with the balances in the appropriate accounts in the company's general ledger at May 31, 19X6 (the latest date for which postings had been made), and found them to be in agreement. We were informed by officials of the company who have responsibility for financial and accounting matters that there had been no changes in such amounts and numbers of shares between May 31, 19X6, and June 15, 19X6. We compared the amounts and numbers of shares listed under the caption "Amount Outstanding as of June 15, 19X6" adjusted for the issuance of the debentures to be offered by means of the registration statement and for the proposed use of a portion of the proceeds thereof to prepay portions of certain notes, as described under "Use of Proceeds," with the amounts and numbers of shares shown under the caption "As Adjusted" and found such amounts and numbers of shares to be in agreement. (However, we make no comments regarding the reasonableness of "Use of Proceeds" or whether such use will actually take place.) We compared the description of the securities and the information (except certain information in Note 2, referred to in 7) included in the notes to the table with the corresponding descriptions and information in the company's consolidated financial statements, including the notes thereto, included in the registration statement and found such descriptions and information to be in agreement.

10. It should be understood that we make no representations regarding questions of legal interpretation or regarding the sufficiency for your purposes of the procedures enumerated in the preceding paragraph; also, such procedures would not necessarily reveal any material misstatement of the amounts

or percentages listed above. Further, we have addressed ourselves solely to the foregoing data as set forth in the registration statement and make no representations regarding the adequacy of disclosure or regarding whether any material facts have been omitted.

11. This letter is solely for the information of the addressees and to assist the underwriters in conducting and documenting their investigation of the affairs of the company in connection with the offering of the securities covered by the registration statement, and it is not to be used, circulated, quoted, or otherwise referred to within or without the underwriting group for any other purpose, including but not limited to the registration, purchase, or sale of securities, nor is it to be filed with or referred to in whole or in part in the registration statement or any other document, except that reference may be made to it in the underwriting agreement or in any list of closing documents pertaining to the offering of the securities covered by the registration statement.

Example H: Comments on Tables, Statistics, and Other Financial Information: Descriptions of Procedures and Findings Regarding Tables, Statistics, and Other Financial Information—Attached Registration Statement (or Selected Pages) Identifies With Designated Symbols Items to Which Procedures Were Applied

9. This example illustrates an alternate format which could facilitate reporting when the accountant is requested to perform procedures on numerous statistics included in a registration statement. This format is permitted by paragraph .58. Each of the comments is in response to a specific request. The paragraph in example H is intended to follow paragraph 6 in example A.

7. For purposes of this letter, we have also read the items identified by you on the attached copy of the registration statement (prospectus), and have performed the following procedures, which were applied as indicated with respect to the symbols explained below:

[symbol] Compared the amount with the XYZ (Predecessor Company) financial statements for the period indicated and found them to be in agreement.

[symbol] Compared the amount with the XYZ (Predecessor Company) financial statements for the period indicated contained in the registration statement and found them to be in agreement.

✓ Compared the amount with ABC Company's financial statements for the period indicated contained in the registration statement and found them to be in agreement.

[symbol] Compared with a schedule or report prepared by the Company and found them to be in agreement.

The letter would also contain paragraphs 8, 10, and 11 of the letter in example F.

[*The following is an extract from a registration statement that illustrates how an accountant can document procedures performed on numerous statistics included in the registration statement.*]

The following summary is qualified in its entirety by the financial statements and detailed information appearing elsewhere in this Prospectus.

The Company

ABC Company (the "Company") designs, constructs, sells, and finances single-family homes for the entry-level and move-up homebuyer. The Company and its predecessor have built and delivered more single-family homes in the metropolitan area than any other homebuilder for each of the last five years. The Company delivered 1,000 Ⓓ homes in the year ending December 31, 19X5, and at December 31, 19X5, had 500 homes[13] under contract with an aggregate sales price of approximately $45,000,000. The Company's wholly owned mortgage banking subsidiary, which commenced operations in March 19X5, currently originates a substantial portion of the mortgages for homes sold by the Company.

The Company typically does not engage in land development without related home-building operations and limits speculative building. The Company purchases only that land which it is prepared to begin developing immediately for home production. A substantial portion of the Company's homes are under contract for sale before construction commences.

The DEF area has been among the top five markets in the country in housing starts for each of the last five years, with more than 90,000 single-family starts during that period. During the same period, the DEF metropolitan area has experienced increases in population, personal income, and employment at rates above the national average. The Company is a major competitive factor in three of the seven market areas, and is expanding significantly in a fourth area.

The Offering

Common Stock Offered by the Company	750,000 Ⓓ shares of Common Stock—$.01 par value (the "Common Stock")*
Common Stock to Be Outstanding	3,250,000 Ⓓ shares*
Use of Proceeds	To repay indebtedness incurred for the acquisition of the Company.
Proposed NASDAQ Symbol	ABC

* Assumes no exercise of the Underwriters' overallotment option. See "Underwriting."

Summary Financial Information
(In thousands, except per-share data)

	XYZ (Predecessor Company) Year Ended December 31,				ABC Company Year Ended December 31
Income Statement Data	*19X1*	*19X2*	*19X3*	*19X4*	*19X5*
Revenue from home sales	$106,603✓	$88,977✓	$104,110✓	$115,837✓	$131,032✓
Gross profit from sales	15,980✓	21,138✓	23,774✓	17,099✓	22,407✓
Income from home building net of tax	490✓	3,473✓	7,029✓	1,000✓	3,425✓
Earnings per share	—	—	—	—	$ 1.37✓

[13] See paragraph .55.

Example I: Alternate Wording When Accountants' Report on Audited Financial Statements Contains an Explanatory Paragraph

10. Example I is applicable when the accountants' report on the audited financial statements included in the registration statement contains an explanatory paragraph regarding a matter that would also affect the unaudited condensed consolidated interim financial statements included in the registration statement. The introductory paragraph of example A would be revised as follows:

> Our reports with respect thereto (which contain an explanatory paragraph that describes a lawsuit to which the Company is a defendant, discussed in note 8 to the consolidated financial statements) are also included in the registration statement.

The matter described in the explanatory paragraph should also be evaluated to determine whether it also requires mention in the comments on the unaudited condensed consolidated interim financial information (paragraph 5*b* of example A). If it is concluded that mention of such a matter in the comments on unaudited condensed consolidated financial statements is appropriate, a sentence should be added at the end of paragraph 5*b* in example A:

> Reference should be made to the introductory paragraph of this letter which states that our audit report covering the consolidated financial statements as of and for the year ended December 31, 19X5, includes an explanatory paragraph that describes a lawsuit to which the company is a defendant, discussed in note 8 to the consolidated financial statements.

Example J: Alternate Wording When More Than One Accountant Is Involved

11. Example J applies when more than one accountant is involved in the audit of the financial statements of a business and the principal accountants have obtained a copy of the comfort letter of the other accountants (see paragraph .18). Example J consists of an addition to paragraph 4*c*, a substitution for the applicable part of paragraph 5, and an addition to paragraph 6 of example A.

> [*4*]c. We have read the letter dated ________ of [*the other accountants*] with regard to [*the related company*].
>
> 5. Nothing came to our attention as a result of the foregoing procedures (which, so far as [*the related company*] is concerned, consisted solely of reading the letter referred to in 4*c*), however, that caused us to believe that....
>
> 6. . . .On the basis of these inquiries and our reading of the minutes and the letter dated ________ of [*the other accountants*] with regard to [*the related company*], as described in 4, nothing came to our attention that caused us to believe that there was any such change, increase, or decrease, except in all instances for changes, increases, or decreases that the registration statement discloses have occurred or may occur.

Example K: Alternate Wording When the SEC Has Agreed to a Departure From Its Published Accounting Requirements

12. Example K is applicable when (*a*) there is a departure from the applicable accounting requirements of the Act and the related published rules and regulations and (*b*) representatives of the SEC have agreed to the departure. Paragraph 2 of example A would be revised to read as follows:

2. In our opinion [*include the phrase "except as disclosed in the registration statement," if applicable*], the consolidated financial statements and financial statement schedules audited by us and included (incorporated by reference) in the registration statement comply as to form in all material respects with the applicable accounting requirements of the Act and the related published rules and regulations; however, as agreed to by representatives of the SEC, separate financial statements and financial statement schedules of ABC Company (an equity investee) as required by rule 3-09 of Regulation S-X have been omitted.

Example L: Alternate Wording When Recent Earnings Data Are Presented in Capsule Form

13. Example L is applicable when (*a*) the statement of income in the registration statement is supplemented by later information regarding sales and earnings (capsule financial information), (*b*) the accountants are asked to comment on that information (paragraphs .39 through .41), and (*c*) the accountants have conducted a review in accordance with section 722 of the financial statements from which the capsule financial information is derived. The same facts exist as in example A, except for the following:

a. Sales, net income (no extraordinary items), and earnings per share for the six-month periods ended June 30, 19X6 and 19X5 (both unaudited), are included in capsule form more limited than that specified by APB Opinion 28 [AC section I73.146].

b. No financial statements later than those for June 19X6 are available.

c. The letter is dated July 25, 19X6, and the cutoff date is July 20, 19X6.

Paragraphs 4, 5, and 6 of example A should be revised to read as follows:

4. For purposes of this letter we have read the 19X6 minutes of the meetings of the stockholders, the board of directors, and [*include other appropriate committees, if any*] of the company and its subsidiaries as set forth in the minute books at July 20, 19X6, officials of the company having advised us that the minutes of all such meetings[14] through that date were set forth therein; we have carried out other procedures to July 20, 19X6, as follows (our work did not extend to the period from July 21, 19X6, to July 25, 19X6, inclusive):

a. With respect to the three-month periods ended March 31, 19X6 and 19X5, we have—

(i) Performed the procedures specified by the American Institute of Certified Public Accountants for a review of interim financial information as described in SAS No. 71, *Interim Financial Information*, on the unaudited condensed consolidated balance sheet as of March 31, 19X6, and the unaudited condensed consolidated statements of income, retained earnings (stockholders' equity), and cash flows for the three-month periods ended March 31, 19X6 and 19X5, included in the registration statement.

(ii) Inquired of certain officials of the company who have responsibility for financial and accounting matters whether the unaudited condensed consolidated financial statements referred to in (i) comply as to form in all material respects with the applicable accounting requirements of the Act and the related published rules and regulations.

b. With respect to the six-month periods ended June 30, 19X6 and 19X5, we have—

(i) Read the unaudited amounts for sales, net income, and earnings per share for the six-month periods ended June 30, 19X6 and 19X5, as set forth in paragraph [*identify location*].

---

14 See footnote 3 of the Appendix.

(ii) Performed the procedures specified by the American Institute of Certified Public Accountants for a review of financial information as described in SAS No. 71, *Interim Financial Information*, on the unaudited condensed consolidated balance sheet as of June 30, 19X6 and the unaudited condensed consolidated statements of income, retained earnings (stockholders' equity), and cash flows for the six-month periods ended June 30, 19X6 and 19X5 from which the unaudited amounts referred to in *b*(i) are derived.

(iii) Inquired of certain officials of the company who have responsibility for financial and accounting matters whether the unaudited amounts referred to in (i) are stated on a basis substantially consistent with that of the corresponding amounts in the audited consolidated statements of income.

The foregoing procedures do not constitute an audit conducted in accordance with generally accepted auditing standards. Also, they would not necessarily reveal matters of significance with respect to the comments in the following paragraph. Accordingly, we make no representations regarding the sufficiency of the foregoing procedures for your purposes.

5. Nothing came to our attention as a result of the foregoing procedures, however, that caused us to believe that—

a. (i) Any material modifications should be made to the unaudited condensed consolidated financial statements described in 4*a*(i), included in the registration statement, for them to be in conformity with generally accepted accounting principles.

(ii) The unaudited condensed consolidated financial statements described in 4*a*(i) do not comply as to form in all material respects with the applicable accounting requirements of the Act and the related published rules and regulations.

b. (i) The unaudited amounts for sales, net income and earnings per share for the six-month periods ended June 30, 19X6 and 19X5, referred to in 4*b*(i) do not agree with the amounts set forth in the unaudited consolidated financial statements for those same periods.

(ii) The unaudited amounts referred to in *b*(i) were not determined on a basis substantially consistent with that of the corresponding amounts in the audited consolidated statements of income.

c. At June 30, 19X6, there was any change in the capital stock, increase in long-term debt or any decreases in consolidated net current assets or stockholders' equity of the consolidated companies as compared with amounts shown in the March 31, 19X6, unaudited condensed consolidated balance sheet included in the registration statement, except in all instances for changes, increases, or decreases that the registration statement discloses have occurred or may occur.

6. Company officials have advised us that no consolidated financial statements as of any date or for any period subsequent to June 30, 19X6, are available; accordingly, the procedures carried out by us with respect to changes in financial statement items after June 30, 19X6, have been, of necessity, even more limited than those with respect to the periods referred to in 4. We have inquired of certain officials of the company who have responsibility for financial and accounting matters regarding whether (*a*) at July 20, 19X6, there was any change in the capital stock, increase in long-term debt or any decreases in consolidated net current assets or stockholders' equity of the consolidated companies as compared with amounts shown on the March 31, 19X6 unaudited condensed consolidated balance sheet included in the registration statement; or (*b*) for the period from July 1, 19X6, to July 20, 19X6, there were any decreases, as compared with the corresponding period in the preceding year, in

consolidated net sales or in the total or per-share amounts of income before extraordinary items or of net income. On the basis of these inquiries and our reading of the minutes as described in 4, nothing came to our attention that caused us to believe that there was any such change, increase, or decrease, except in all instances for changes, increases, or decreases that the registration statement discloses have occurred or may occur.

Example M: Alternate Wording When Accountants Are Aware of a Decrease in a Specified Financial Statement Item

14. Example M covers a situation in which accountants are aware of a decrease in a financial statement item on which they are requested to comment (see paragraphs .45 through .53). The same facts exist as in example A, except for the decrease covered in the following change in paragraph 5*b*.

b. (i) At May 31, 19X6, there was any change in the capital stock, increase in long-term debt or any decrease in consolidated stockholders' equity of the consolidated companies as compared with amounts shown in the March 31, 19X6, unaudited condensed consolidated balance sheet included in the registration statement, or (ii) for the period from April 1, 19X6, to May 31, 19X6, there were any decreases, as compared with the corresponding period in the preceding year, in consolidated net sales or the total or per-share amounts of income before extraordinary items or of net income, except in all instances for changes, increases, or decreases that the registration statement discloses have occurred or may occur and except that the unaudited consolidated balance sheet as of May 31, 19X6, which we were furnished by the company, showed a decrease from March 31, 19X6, in consolidated net current assets as follows (in thousands of dollars):

	Current Assets	*Current Liabilities*	*Net Current Assets*
March 31, 19X6	$4,251	$1,356	$2,895
May 31, 19X6	3,986	1,732	2,254

6. As mentioned in 4*b*, company officials have advised us that no consolidated financial statements as of any date or for any period subsequent to May 31, 19X6, are available; accordingly, the procedures carried out by us with respect to changes in financial statement items after May 31, 19X6, have been, of necessity, even more limited than those with respect to the periods referred to in 4. We have inquired of certain officials of the company who have responsibility for financial and accounting matters regarding whether (*a*) there was any change at June 23, 19X6, in the capital stock, increase in long-term debt or any decreases in consolidated net current assets or stockholders' equity of the consolidated companies as compared with amounts shown on the March 31, 19X6, unaudited condensed consolidated balance sheet included in the registration statement; or (*b*) for the period from April 1, 19X6, to June 23, 19X6, there were any decreases, as compared with the corresponding period in the preceding year, in consolidated net sales or in the total or per-share amounts of income before extraordinary items or of net income. On the basis of these inquiries and our reading of the minutes as described in 4, nothing came to our attention that caused us to believe that there was any such change, increase, or decrease, except in all instances for changes, increases, or decreases that the registration statement discloses have occurred or may occur and except as described in the following sentence. We have been informed by officials of the company that there continues to be a decrease in net current assets that is estimated to be approximately the same amount as set forth in 5*b* [*or whatever other disclosure fits the circumstances*].

Example N: Alternate Wording of the Letter for Companies That Are Permitted to Present Interim Earnings Data for a Twelve-Month Period

15. Certain types of companies are permitted to include earnings data for a twelve-month period to the date of the latest balance sheet furnished in lieu of earnings data for both the interim period between the end of the latest fiscal year and the date of the latest balance sheet and the corresponding period of the preceding fiscal year. The following would be substituted for the applicable part of paragraph 3 of example A.

> 3. . . .was to enable us to express our opinion on the financial statements as of December 31, 19X5, and for the year then ended, but not on the financial statements for any period included in part within that year. Therefore, we are unable to and do not express any opinion on the unaudited condensed consolidated balance sheet as of March 31, 19X6, and the related unaudited condensed consolidated statements of income, retained earnings (stockholders' equity), and cash flows for the twelve months then ended included in the registration statement. . . .

Example O: Alternate Wording When the Procedures That the Underwriter Has Requested the Accountant to Perform on Interim Financial Information Are Less Than an SAS No. 71 Review

16. The example assumes that the underwriter has asked the accountants to perform specified procedures on the interim financial information and report thereon in the comfort letter. The letter is dated June 28, 19X6; procedures were performed through June 23, 19X6, the cutoff date. Since an SAS No. 71 [section 722] review was not performed on the interim financial information as of March 31, 19X6 and for the quarter then ended, the accountants are limited to reporting procedures performed and findings obtained on the interim financial information. In addition to the information presented below, the letter would also contain paragraph 7 of the typical comfort letter in example A.

June 28, 19X6

[*Addressee*]

Dear Sirs:

We have audited the consolidated balance sheets of The Blank Company, Inc. (the company) and the subsidiaries as of December 31, 19X5 and 19X4, and the consolidated statements of income, retained earnings (stockholders' equity), and cash flows for each of the three years in the period ended December 31, 19X5 and the related financial statement schedules all included in the registration statement (no. 33-00000) on Form S-1 filed by the company under the Securities Act of 1933 (the Act); our reports with respect thereto are included in that registration statement. The registration statement, as amended on June 28, 19X6, is herein referred to as the registration statement.

Also, we have compiled the forecasted balance sheet and consolidated statements of income, retained earnings (stockholders' equity), and cash flows as of December 31, 19X6 and for the year then ending, attached to the registration statement, as indicated in our report dated May 15, 19X6, which is attached.

In connection with the registration statement—

1. We are independent certified public accountants with respect to the company within the meaning of the Act and the applicable published rules and regulations thereunder.

2. In our opinion [*include the phrase "except as disclosed in the registration statement," if applicable*], the consolidated financial statements and financial statement schedules audited by us and included in the registration statement comply as to form in all material respects with the applicable accounting requirements of the Act and the related published rules and regulations.

3. We have not audited any financial statements of the company as of any date or for any period subsequent to December 31, 19X5; although we have conducted an audit for the year ended December 31, 19X5, the purpose (and therefore the scope) of the audit was to enable us to express our opinion on the consolidated financial statements as of December 31, 19X5, and for the year then ended, but not on the financial statements for any interim period within that year. Therefore, we are unable to and do not express any opinion on the unaudited condensed consolidated balance sheet as of March 31, 19X6, and the unaudited condensed consolidated statements of income, retained earnings (stockholders' equity), and cash flows for the three-month periods ended March 31, 19X6 and 19X5, included in the registration statement, or on the financial position, results of operations, or cash flows as of any date or for any period subsequent to December 31, 19X5.

4. For purposes of this letter, we have read the 19X6 minutes of meetings of the stockholders, the board of directors, and [*include other appropriate committees, if any*] of the company as set forth in the minute books at June 23, 19X6, officials of the company having advised us that the minutes of all such meetings[15] through that date were set forth therein; we have carried out other procedures to June 23, 19X6, as follows (our work did not extend to the period from June 24, 19X6, to June 28, 19X6, inclusive):

a. With respect to the three-month periods ended March 31, 19X6 and 19X5, we have—

(i) Read the unaudited condensed consolidated balance sheet as of March 31, 19X6, and unaudited condensed consolidated statements of income, retained earnings (stockholders' equity), and cash flows for the three-month periods ended March 31, 19X6 and 19X5, included in the registration statement, and agreed the amounts contained therein with the company's accounting records as of March 31, 19X6 and 19X5, and for the three-month periods then ended.

(ii) Inquired of certain officials of the company who have responsibility for financial and accounting matters whether the unaudited condensed consolidated financial statements referred to in *a*(i): (1) are in conformity with generally accepted accounting principles[16] applied on a basis substantially consistent with that of the audited consolidated financial statements included in the registration statement, and (2) comply as to form in all material respects with the applicable accounting requirements of the Act and the related published rules and regulations. Those officials stated that the unaudited condensed consolidated financial statements (1) are in conformity with generally accepted accounting principles applied on a basis substantially consistent with that of the audited financial statements, and (2) comply as to form in all material respects with the applicable accounting requirements of the Act and the related published rules and regulations.

b. With respect to the period from April 1, 19X6, to May 31, 19X6, we have—

[15] See footnote 3 of the Appendix.

[16] See footnote 5 of the Appendix.

(i) Read the unaudited condensed consolidated financial statements of the company[17] for April and May of both 19X5 and 19X6 furnished us by the company, and agreed the amounts contained therein to the company's accounting records. Officials of the company have advised us that no such financial statements as of any date or for any period subsequent to May 31, 19X6, were available.

(ii) Inquired of certain officials of the company who have responsibility for financial and accounting matters whether (1) the unaudited financial statements referred to in *b*(i) are stated on a basis substantially consistent with that of the audited consolidated financial statements included in the registration statement, (2) at May 31, 19X6, there was any change in the capital stock, increase in long-term debt or any decrease in consolidated net current assets or stockholders' equity of the consolidated companies as compared with amounts shown in the March 31, 19X6 unaudited condensed consolidated balance sheet included in the registration statement, and (3) for the period from April 1, 19X6, to May 31, 19X6, there were any decreases, as compared with the corresponding period in the preceding year, in consolidated net sales or in the total or per-share amounts of income before extraordinary items or of net income.

Those officials stated that (1) the unaudited consolidated financial statements referred to in 4*b*(i) are stated on a basis substantially consistent with that of the audited consolidated financial statements included in the registration statement, (2) at May 31, 19X6, there was no change in the capital stock, no increase in long-term debt, and no decrease in net current assets or stockholders' equity of the consolidated companies as compared with amounts shown in the March 31, 19X6, unaudited condensed consolidated balance sheet included in the registration statement, and (3) there were no decreases for the period from April 1, 19X6, to May 31, 19X6, as compared with the corresponding period in the preceding year, in consolidated net sales or in the total or per-share amounts of income before extraordinary items or of net income.

c. As mentioned in 4*b*(i), company officials have advised us that no financial statements as of any date or for any period subsequent to May 31, 19X6, are available; accordingly, the procedures carried out by us with respect to changes in financial statement items after May 31, 19X6, have, of necessity, been even more limited than those with respect to the periods referred to in 4*a* and 4*b*. We have inquired of certain officials of the company who have responsibility for financial and accounting matters whether (*a*) at June 23, 19X6, there was any change in the capital stock, increase in long-term debt or any decreases in consolidated net current assets or stockholders' equity of the consolidated companies as compared with amounts shown on the March 31, 19X6, unaudited condensed consolidated balance sheet included in the registration statement, or (*b*) for the period from April 1, 19X6, to June 23, 19X6, there were any decreases, as compared with the corresponding period in the preceding year, in consolidated net sales or in the total or per-share amounts of income before extraordinary items or of net income. Those officials stated that (1) at June 23, 19X6, there was no change in the capital stock, no increase in long-term debt and no decreases in consolidated net current assets or stockholders' equity of the consolidated companies as compared with amounts shown on the March 31, 19X6, unaudited condensed consolidated balance sheet,

[17] See footnote 4 of the Appendix.

and (2) for the period from April 1, 19X6, to June 23, 19X6, there were no decreases, as compared with the corresponding period in the preceding year, in consolidated net sales or in the total or per-share amounts of income before extraordinary items or of net income.

The foregoing procedures do not constitute an audit conducted in accordance with generally accepted auditing standards. We make no representations regarding the sufficiency of the foregoing procedures for your purposes. Had we performed additional procedures or had we conducted an audit or a review, other matters might have come to our attention that would have been reported to you.

5. At your request, we also performed the following procedures:

a. Read the unaudited pro forma condensed consolidated balance sheet as of March 31, 19X6, and the unaudited pro forma condensed consolidated statements of income for the year ended December 31, 19X5, and the three-month period ended March 31, 19X6, included in the registration statement.

b. Inquired of certain officials of the company and of XYZ Company (the company being acquired) who have responsibility for financial and accounting matters as to whether all significant assumptions regarding the business combination had been reflected in the pro forma adjustments and whether the unaudited pro forma condensed consolidated financial statements referred to in (*a*) comply as to form in all material respects with the applicable accounting requirements of rule 11-02 of Regulation S-X.

Those officials referred to above stated, in response to our inquiries, that all significant assumptions regarding the business combination had been reflected in the pro forma adjustments and that the unaudited pro forma condensed consolidated financial statements referred to in (*a*) comply as to form in all material respects with the applicable accounting requirements of rule 11-02 of Regulation S-X.

c. Compared the historical financial information for the company included on page 20 in the registration statement with historical financial information for the company on page 12 and found them to be in agreement.

We also compared the financial information included on page 20 of the registration statement with the historical information for XYZ Company on page 13 and found them to be in agreement.

d. Proved the arithmetic accuracy of the application of the pro forma adjustments to the historical amounts in the unaudited pro forma condensed consolidated financial statements.

The foregoing procedures are less in scope than an examination, the objective of which is the expression of an opinion on management's assumptions, the pro forma adjustments, and the application of those adjustments to historical financial information. Accordingly, we do not express such an opinion. We make no representation about the sufficiency of the foregoing procedures for your purposes. Had we performed additional procedures or had we made an examination of the pro forma financial information, other matters might have come to our attention that would have been reported to you.

6. At your request, we performed the following procedures with respect to the forecasted consolidated balance sheet and consolidated statements of income and cash flows as of December 31, 19X6, and for the year then ending. With respect to forecasted rental income, we compared the occupancy statistics about expected demand for rental of the housing units to statistics for existing comparable properties and found them to be the same.

Because the procedures described above do not constitute an examination of prospective financial statements in accordance with standards established by the American Institute of Certified Public Accountants, we do not express an opinion on whether the prospective financial statements are presented in conformity with AICPA presentation guidelines or on whether the underlying assumptions provide a reasonable basis for the presentation. Furthermore, there will usually be differences between the forecasted and actual results, because events and circumstances frequently do not occur as expected, and those differences may be material. We make no representations about the sufficiency of such procedures for your purposes. Had we performed additional procedures or had we made an examination of the forecast in accordance with standards established by the AICPA, matters might have come to our attention that would have been reported to you.

Example P: A Typical Comfort Letter in a Non-1933 Act Offering, Including the Required Underwriter Representations

17. Example P is applicable when a comfort letter is issued in a non-1933 Act offering. The underwriter has given the accountants a letter including the representations regarding their due diligence review process, as described in paragraphs .06 and .07, and the comfort letter refers to those representations. In addition, the example assumes that the accountants were unable, or were not requested, to perform an SAS No. 71 [section 722] review of a subsequent interim period and therefore no negative assurance has been given. See paragraph .47.

November 30, 19X5

[Addressee]

Dear Sirs:

We have audited the balance sheets of Example City, Any State Utility System as of June 30, 19X5 and 19X4, and the statements of revenues, expenses, and changes in retained earnings and cash flows for the years then ended, included in the Official Statement for $30,000,000 of Example City, Any State Utility System Revenue Bonds due November 30, 19Z5. Our report with respect thereto is included in the Official Statement. This Official Statement, dated November 30, 19X5, is herein referred to as the Official Statement.

This letter is being furnished in reliance upon your representation to us that—

a. You are knowledgeable with respect to the due diligence review process that would be performed if this placement of securities were being registered pursuant to the Securities Act of 1933 (the Act).

b. In connection with the offering of revenue bonds, the review process you have performed is substantially consistent with the due diligence review process that you would have performed if this placement of securities were being registered pursuant to the Act.

In connection with the Official Statement—

1. We are independent certified public accountants with respect to Example City, Any State and its Utility System under rule 101 of the AICPA's *Code of Professional Conduct*, and its interpretations and rulings.

2. We have not audited any financial statements of Example City, Any State Utility System as of any date or for any period subsequent to June 30, 19X5; although we have conducted an audit for the year ended June 30, 19X5, the purpose (and therefore the scope) of the audit was to enable us to express our opinion on the financial statements as of June 30, 19X5, and for the year then ended, but not on the financial statements for any interim period within that year. Therefore, we are unable to and do not express any opinion on the financial position, results of operations, or cash flows as of any date or for any period subsequent to June 30, 19X5, for the Example City, Any State Utility System.

3. For purposes of this letter we have read the 19X5 minutes of the meetings of the City Council of Example City, Any State as set forth in the minutes books as of November 25, 19X5, the City Clerk of Example City having advised us that the minutes of all such meetings[18] through that date were set forth therein.

4. With respect to the period subsequent to June 30, 19X5, we have carried out other procedures to November 25, 19X5, as follows (our work did not extend to the period from November 26, 19X5, to November 30, 19X5, inclusive):

- We have inquired of, and received assurance from, city officials who have responsibility for financial and accounting matters, that no financial statements as of any date or for any period subsequent to June 30, 19X5, are available.
- We have inquired of those officials regarding whether (*a*) at November 25, 19X5, there was any increase in long-term debt or any decrease in net current assets of Example City, Any State Utility System as compared with amounts shown on the June 30, 19X5, balance sheet, included in the Official Statement, or (*b*) for the period from July 1, 19X5, to November 25, 19X5, there were any decreases, as compared with the corresponding period in the preceding year, in total operating revenues, income from operations or net income. Those officials stated that (1) at November 25, 19X5, there was no increase in long-term debt and no decrease in net current assets of the Example City, Any State Utility System as compared with amounts shown in the June 30, 19X5, balance sheet; and (2) there were no decreases for the period from July 1, 19X5, to November 25, 19X5, as compared with the corresponding period in the preceding year, in total operating revenues, income from operations, or net income, except in all instances for changes, increases, or decreases that the Official Statement discloses have occurred or may occur.

5. For accounting data pertaining to the years 19X3 through 19X5, inclusive, shown on page 11 of the Official Statement, we have (i) for data shown in the audited financial statements, compared such data with the audited financial statements of the Example City, Any State Utility System for 19X3 through 19X5 and found them to be in agreement; and (ii) for data not directly shown in the audited financial statements, compared such data with the general ledger and accounting records of the Utility System from which such information was derived, and found them to be in agreement.

6. The procedures enumerated in the preceding paragraphs do not constitute an audit conducted in accordance with generally accepted auditing standards. Accordingly, we make no representations regarding the sufficiency of the foregoing procedures for your purposes.

7. This letter is solely for the information of the addressees and to assist the underwriters in conducting and documenting their investigation of the affairs of the Example City, Any State Utility System in connection with the offering of securities covered by the Official Statement, and it is not to be used, circulated, quoted, or otherwise referred to for any other purpose, including but not limited to the purchase or sale of securities, nor is it to be filed with or referred to in whole or in part in the Official Statement or any other document, except that reference may be made to it in the Purchase Contract or in any list of closing documents pertaining to the offering of securities covered by the Official Statement.

---

[18] See footnote 3 of paragraph .03.

Example Q: Letter to a Requesting Party That Has Not Provided the Representation Letter Described in Paragraphs .06 and .07

18. This example assumes that these procedures are being performed at the request of the placement agent on information included in an offering circular in connection with a private placement of unsecured notes with two insurance companies.[19] The letter is dated June 30, 19X6; procedures were performed through June 25, 19X6, the cutoff date. The statements in paragraphs 5 through 9 of the example should be included in any letter issued pursuant to paragraph .09.[20]

June 30, 19X6

[Addressee]

Dear Sirs:

We have audited the consolidated balance sheets of The Blank Company, Inc. (the company) and subsidiaries as of December 31, 19X5 and 19X4, and the consolidated statements of income, retained earnings (stockholders' equity), and cash flows for each of the three years in the period ended December 31, 19X5, included in the offering circular for $30,000,000 of notes due June 30, 20X6. Our report with respect thereto is included in the offering circular. The offering circular dated June 30, 19X6, is herein referred to as the offering circular.

We are independent certified public accountants with respect to the company under rule 101 of the AICPA's Code of Professional Conduct, and its interpretations and rulings.[21]

We have not audited any financial statements of the company as of any date or for any period subsequent to December 31, 19X5; although we have conducted an audit for the year ended December 31, 19X5, the purpose (and, therefore, the scope) of the audit was to enable us to express our opinion on the consolidated financial statements as of December 31, 19X5, and for the year then ended, but not on the financial statements for any interim period within that year. Therefore, we are unable to and do not express any opinion on the unaudited condensed consolidated balance sheet as of March 31, 19X6, and the unaudited condensed consolidated statements of income, retained earnings (stockholders' equity), and cash flows for the three-month periods ended March 31, 19X6 and 19X5, included in the offering circular, or on the financial position, results of operations, or cash flows as of any date or for any period subsequent to December 31, 19X5.

---

[19] This same example could be used in conjunction with a municipal bond offering in which the accountant has not received the representation letter described in paragraphs .06 and .07. [Footnote added, effective for letters issued pursuant to paragraph .09 of this section after April 30, 1996, by Statement on Auditing Standards No. 76.]

[20] This example may also be used in connection with a filing under the Securities Act of 1933 (the Act) when a party other than a named underwriter (for example, a selling shareholder) has not provided the accountant with the representation letter described in paragraphs .06 and .07. In such a situation, this example may be modified to include the accountant's comments on independence and compliance as to form of the audited financial statements and financial statement schedules with the applicable accounting requirements of the Act and the related published rules and regulations. Example paragraph 1*a*(ii) may include an inquiry, and the response of company officials, on compliance as to form of the unaudited condensed interim financial statements. [Footnote added, effective for letters issued pursuant to paragraph .09 of this section after April 30, 1996, by Statement on Auditing Standards No. 76.]

[21] See paragraphs .31 and .32 for guidance in commenting on independence. [Footnote added, effective for letters issued pursuant to paragraph .09 of this section after April 30, 1996, by Statement on Auditing Standards No. 76.]

1. At your request, we have read the 19X6 minutes of meetings of the stockholders, the board of directors, and [*include other appropriate committees, if any*] of the company as set forth in the minute books at June 25, 19X6, officials of the company having advised us that the minutes of all such meetings[22] through that date were set forth therein; we have carried out other procedures to June 25, 19X6 (our work did not extend to the period from June 26, 19X6, to June 30, 19X6, inclusive), as follows:

a. With respect to the three-month periods ended March 31, 19X6 and 19X5, we have—

(i) Read the unaudited condensed consolidated balance sheet as of March 31, 19X6, and the unaudited condensed consolidated statements of income, retained earnings (stockholders' equity), and cash flows,[23, 24] of the company for the three-month periods ended March 31, 19X6 and 19X5, included in the offering circular, and agreed the amounts contained therein with the company's accounting records as of March 31, 19X6 and 19X5, and for the three-month periods then ended.

(ii) Inquired of certain officials of the company who have responsibility for financial and accounting matters whether the unaudited condensed consolidated financial statements referred to in *a*(i) are in conformity with generally accepted accounting principles applied on a basis substantially consistent with that of the audited consolidated financial statements included in the offering circular. Those officials stated that the unaudited condensed consolidated financial statements are in conformity with generally accepted accounting principles applied on a basis substantially consistent with that of the audited consolidated financial statements.

b. With respect to the period from April 1, 19X6, to May 31, 19X6, we have—

(i) Read the unaudited condensed consolidated financial statements of the company for April and May of both 19X5 and 19X6, furnished us by the company, and agreed the amounts contained therein with the company's accounting records. Officials of the company have advised us that no financial statements as of any date or for any period subsequent to May 31, 19X6, were available.

(ii) Inquired of certain officials of the company who have responsibility for financial and accounting matters whether (1) the unaudited condensed consolidated financial statements referred to in *b*(i) are stated on a basis substantially consistent with that of the audited consolidated financial statements included in the offering circular, (2) at May 31, 19X6, there was any change in the capital stock, increase in long-term debt or any decrease in consolidated net current assets or stockholders' equity of the consolidated companies as compared with amounts shown in the March 31, 19X6, unaudited condensed consolidated balance sheet in-

[22] See footnote 3 of the Appendix. [Footnote added, effective for letters issued pursuant to paragraph .09 of this section after April 30, 1996, by Statement on Auditing Standards No. 76.]

[23] See footnotes 4 and 5 of the Appendix. [Footnote added, effective for letters issued pursuant to paragraph .09 of this section after April 30, 1996, by Statement on Auditing Standards No. 76.]

[24] Generally, accountants should recognize that the criteria for summarized financial information have not been established for entities other than SEC registrants. [Footnote added, effective for letters issued pursuant to paragraph .09 of this section after April 30, 1996, by Statement on Auditing Standards No. 76.]

cluded in the offering circular, and (3) for the period from April 1, 19X6, to May 31, 19X6, there were any decreases, as compared with the corresponding period in the preceding year, in consolidated net sales or in the total or per-share amounts of income before extraordinary items or of net income.

Those officials stated that (1) the unaudited condensed consolidated financial statements referred to in *b*(ii) are stated on a basis substantially consistent with that of the audited consolidated financial statements included in the offering circular, (2) at May 31, 19X6, there was no change in the capital stock, no increase in long-term debt, and no decrease in consolidated net current assets or stockholders' equity of the consolidated companies as compared with amounts shown in the March 31, 19X6, unaudited condensed consolidated balance sheet included in the offering circular, and (3) there were no decreases for the period from April 1, 19X6, to May 31, 19X6, as compared with the corresponding period in the preceding year, in consolidated net sales or in the total or per-share amounts of income before extraordinary items or of net income.

c. As mentioned in 1*b*, company officials have advised us that no financial statements as of any date or for any period subsequent to May 31, 19X6, are available; accordingly, the procedures carried out by us with respect to changes in financial statement items after May 31, 19X6, have, of necessity, been even more limited than those with respect to the periods referred to in 1*a* and 1*b*. We have inquired of certain officials of the company who have responsibility for financial and accounting matters whether (i) at June 25, 19X6, there was any change in the capital stock, increase in long-term debt, or any decreases in consolidated net current assets or stockholders' equity of the consolidated companies as compared with amounts shown on the March 31, 19X6, unaudited condensed consolidated balance sheet included in the offering circular or (ii) for the period from April 1, 19X6, to June 25, 19X6, there were any decreases, as compared with the corresponding period in the preceding year, in consolidated net sales or in the total or per-share amounts of income before extraordinary items or of net income.

Those officials referred to above stated that (i) at June 25, 19X6, there was no change in the capital stock, no increase in long-term debt, and no decreases in consolidated net current assets or stockholders' equity of the consolidated companies as compared with amounts shown on the March 31, 19X6, unaudited condensed consolidated balance sheet, and (ii) there were no decreases for the period from April 1, 19X6, to June 25, 19X6, as compared with the corresponding period in the preceding year, in consolidated net sales or in the total or per-share amounts of income before extraordinary items or of net income.

2. At your request, we have read the following items in the offering circular on the indicated pages.[25]

---

[25] In some cases it may be considered desirable to combine in one paragraph the substance of paragraphs 2 and 4. This may be done by expanding the identification of terms in paragraph 4 to provide the identification information contained in paragraph 2. In such cases the introductory sentences in paragraphs 2 and 4 and the text of paragraph 3 might be combined as follows: "At your request, we have also read the following information and have performed the additional procedures stated below with respect to such information. Our audit of the consolidated financial statements...." [Footnote added, effective for letters issued pursuant to paragraph .09 of this section after April 30, 1996, by Statement on Auditing Standards No. 76.]

Item	*Page*	*Description*
a	13	"History and Business—Sales and Marketing." The table following the first paragraph.
b	22	"Executive Compensation—19X5 Compensation."
c	33	"Selected Financial Data."[26]

3. Our audits of the consolidated financial statements for the periods referred to in the introductory paragraph of this letter comprised audit tests and procedures deemed necessary for the purpose of expressing an opinion on such financial statements taken as a whole. For none of the periods referred to therein, nor for any other period, did we perform audit tests for the purpose of expressing an opinion on individual balances of accounts or summaries of selected transactions such as those enumerated above, and, accordingly, we express no opinion thereon.

4. However, at your request, we have performed the following additional procedures, which were applied as indicated with respect to the items enumerated above.

Item in 2	*Procedures and Findings*
a	We compare the amounts of military sales, commercial sales, and total sales shown in the registration statement with the balances in the appropriate accounts in the company's accounting records for the respective fiscal years and for the unaudited interim periods and found them to be in agreement. We proved the arithmetic accuracy of the percentages of such amounts of military sales and commercial sales to total sales for the respective fiscal years and for the unaudited interim periods. We compared such computed percentages with the corresponding percentages appearing in the registration statement and found them to be in agreement.
b	We compared the dollar amounts of compensation (salary, bonus, and other compensation) for each individual listed in the table "Annual Compensation" with the corresponding amounts shown by the individual employee earnings records for the year 19X5 and found them to be in agreement. We compared the dollar amounts shown under the heading of "Long-Term Compensation" on page 24 for each listed individual and the aggregate amounts for executive officers with corresponding amounts shown in an analysis prepared by the company and found such amounts to be in agreement.
c	We compared the amounts of net sales, income from continuing operations, income from continuing operations per common share, and cash dividends declared per common share for the years ended December 31, 19X5, 19X4, and 19X3, with the respective amounts in the consolidated financial statements on pages 27 and 28 and the amounts for the years ended December 31, 19X2, and 19X1, with the respective amounts in the consolidated financial statements included in the company's annual reports to stockholders for 19X2 and 19X1 and found them to be in agreement.
	We compared the amounts of total assets, long-term obligations, and redeemable preferred stock at December 31, 19X5 and 19X4, with the respective amounts in the consolidated financial statements on pages 27 and 28 and the amounts at December 31, 19X3, and 19X2, and 19X1 with the corresponding amounts in the consolidated financial statements included in the company's annual reports to stockholders for 19X3, 19X2, and 19X1 and found them to be in agreement.

[26] See footnote 10 of the Appendix. [Footnote added, effective for letters issued pursuant to paragraph .09 of this section after April 30, 1996, by Statement on Auditing Standards No. 76.]

5. It should be understood that we have no responsibility for establishing (and did not establish) the scope and nature of the procedures enumerated in paragraphs 1 through 4 above; rather, the procedures enumerated therein are those the requesting party asked us to perform. Accordingly, we make no representations regarding questions of legal interpretation[27] or regarding the sufficiency for your purposes of the procedures enumerated in the preceding paragraphs; also, such procedures would not necessarily reveal any material misstatement of the amounts or percentages listed above as set forth in the offering circular. Further, we have addressed ourselves solely to the foregoing data and make no representations regarding the adequacy of disclosures or whether any material facts have been omitted. This letter relates only to the financial statement items specified above and does not extend to any financial statement of the company taken as a whole.

6. The foregoing procedures do not constitute an audit conducted in accordance with generally accepted auditing standards. Had we performed additional procedures or had we conducted an audit or a review of the company's March 31, April 30, or May 31, 19X6 and 19X5, condensed consolidated financial statements in accordance with standards established by the American Institute of Certified Public Accountants, other matters might have come to our attention that would have been reported to you.

7. These procedures should not be taken to supplant any additional inquiries or procedures that you would undertake in your consideration of the proposed offering.

8. This letter is solely for your information and to assist you in your inquiries in connection with the offering of the securities covered by the offering circular, and it is not to be used, circulated, quoted, or otherwise referred to for any other purpose, including but not limited to the registration, purchase, or sale of securities, nor is it to be filed with or referred to in whole or in part in the offering document or any other document, except that reference may be made to it in any list of closing documents pertaining to the offering of the securities covered by the offering document.

9. We have no responsibility to update this letter for events and circumstances occurring after June 25, 19X6.

[Paragraph renumbered and amended, effective for letters issued pursuant to paragraph .09 of this section after April 30, 1996, by the issuance of Statement on Auditing Standards No. 76.]

---

[27] See footnote 7 to paragraph .09. [Footnote added, effective for letters issued pursuant to paragraph .09 of this section after April 30, 1996, by Statement on Auditing Standards No. 76.]

AU Section 9634

Letters for Underwriters and Certain Other Requesting Parties: Auditing Interpretations of Section 634

1. Letters to Directors Relating to Annual Reports on Form 10-K[*]

.01 *Question*—Annual reports to the Securities and Exchange Commission (SEC) on Form 10-K must be signed by at least a majority of the registrant's board of directors. In reviewing the Form 10-K, directors may seek the involvement of the registrant's independent auditors and other professionals.

.02 What types of services could the auditor perform at the request of the board of directors in connection with the Form 10-K? For example, is it permissible for the auditor to comment on compliance of the registrant's Form 10-K with the requirements of the various SEC rules and regulations?[1]

.03 *Interpretation*—The auditor can express an opinion to the board of directors on whether the financial statements and financial statement schedules audited comply as to form with the applicable accounting requirements of the Securities Exchange Act of 1934 and the published rules and regulations thereunder (see section 634.33).[2]

.04 The auditor may affirm to the board of directors that under generally accepted auditing standards the auditor is required to read the information in addition to audited financial statements contained in the Form 10-K, for the purpose of considering whether such information may be materially inconsistent with information appearing in the financial statements (see section 550). However, the report to the board of directors should state that the auditor has no obligation to perform any procedures to corroborate such information.

.05 In addition, the auditor could perform, at the request of the board of directors, specified procedures and report the results of those procedures concerning various information contained in the Form 10-K such as tables, statistics and other financial information. There should be a clear understanding with the board as to the nature, extent and limitations of the procedures to be performed and as to the kind of report to be issued. Although the guidance provided in section 634 is intended primarily for auditors issuing a letter to underwriters and certain other requesting parties in connection with an offering of securities, the guidance in section 634.54–.60 would also be applicable when the auditor is asked to furnish a letter to the board of directors in connection with the filing of Form 10-K under the Securities Exchange Act of 1934.[3] The types of information on which auditors may comment are described in section 634.55. The auditor should comment only on that informa-

---

[*] Footnote deleted June 1993, by the issuance of Statement on Auditing Standards No. 72.

[1] Footnote deleted June 1993, by the issuance of Statement on Auditing Standards No. 72.

[2] The auditor should not provide any assurance on compliance with the provisions of the Securities Exchange Act of 1934 regarding controls. See the guidance provided in AT section 400, *Reporting on an Entity's Internal Control Over Financial Reporting*, paragraph .83.

[3] Section 634.12 states in part: "Accountants will normally be willing to assist the underwriter but the assistance accountants can provide by way of comfort letters is subject to limitations. One limitation is that independent accountants can properly comment in their professional capacity only on matters to which his professional expertise is substantially relevant."

tion if the criteria in section 634.55 and .57 have been met. The comments should be made in the form of description of procedures performed and findings obtained, ordinarily expressed in terms of agreement between items compared.

.06 Certain financial information in Form 10-K is included because of specific requirements of Regulation S-K. The auditor may comment as to whether this information is in conformity with the disclosure requirements of Regulation S-K if the conditions in section 634.57 are met. Section 634.57 identifies the disclosure requirements of Regulation S-K that generally meet those conditions. The auditor is limited to giving negative assurance, since this information is not given in the form of financial statements and generally has not been audited by the accountants. (See section 634.57.)

.07 The auditor should not comment on matters that are primarily subjective or judgmental in nature such as those included in Item 7 of Form 10-K, "Management's Discussion and Analysis of Financial Condition and Results of Operations." For example, changes between periods in gross profit ratios may be caused by factors that are not necessarily within the expertise of auditors. However, the auditor can comment on specific changes in comparative amounts that are included in management's discussion if the amounts used to compute such changes are obtained from the financial statements or accounting records as discussed in section 634.55, but cannot comment with respect to the appropriateness of the explanations.

.08 There are no criteria by which to measure the sufficiency of the procedures performed by the accountants for the directors' purposes. Ordinarily the auditor should discuss with the directors or the audit committee the procedures to be performed and may suggest procedures that might be meaningful in the circumstances. However, the auditor should clearly indicate to the board of directors that the auditor cannot make any representations as to whether the agreed-upon procedures are sufficient for the directors' purposes.

.09 It should not ordinarily be necessary for the auditor to reaffirm the auditor's independence to the board of directors. If such a representation is requested, however, the auditor may include in the letter a statement similar to that described in section 634.31.

[Issue Date: April 1981; Modified: May 1981; Revised: June 1993.]

[2.] Negative Assurance on Unaudited Condensed Interim Financial Statements Attached to Comfort Letters

[.10–.12] [Deleted April 1993 by Statement on Auditing Standards No. 72.]

AU Section 9642

Reporting on Internal Accounting Control: Auditing Interpretations of SAS No. 30

Many of the interpretations in this section were based on the concepts in Statement on Auditing Standards (SAS) No. 30, *Reporting on Internal Accounting Control*. SAS No. 30 was superseded in May 1993 by the issuance of Statement on Standards for Attestation Engagements (SSAE) No. 2, *Reporting on an Entity's Internal Control Over Financial Reporting*, effective for an examination of management's assertion on the effectiveness of an entity's internal control structure over financial reporting when the assertion is as of December 15, 1993 or thereafter. The AICPA's Auditing Standards Board decided at its October 1993 meeting to delete these interpretations. Notes have been included below to indicate where current guidance may be found in AICPA literature.

[1.] Pre-Award Surveys[*]

[.01–.03] [Deleted October 1993.] (See the guidance provided in SSAE No. 2, paragraphs 26 through 30 (AT section 400.22–.25).)

[2.] Award Survey Made in Conjunction With an Audit

[.04–.05] [Deleted October 1993.] (See the guidance provided in SSAE No. 2, paragraphs 26 through 30 (AT section 400.22–.25).)

[3.] Reporting on Matters Not Covered by Government-Established Criteria

[.06–.07] [Deleted October 1993.] (See the guidance provided in SSAE No. 2, paragraph 5 (AT section 400.05).)

[4.] Limited Scope

[.08–.09] [Deleted October 1993.] (See the guidance provided in SSAE No. 2, paragraph 72 (AT section 400.67).)

[5.] Compliance With the Foreign Corrupt Practices Act of 1977

[.10–.13] [Deleted October 1993.] (See the guidance provided in SSAE No. 2, paragraph 88 (AT section 400.83).)

[6.] Reports on Internal Accounting Control of Trust Departments of Banks

[.14–.17] [Deleted October 1993.] (See the guidance provided in SSAE No. 2, paragraph 72 (AT section 400.67).)

---

[*] [Footnote deleted, October 1993.]

[7.] Report Required by U.S. General Accounting Office[1-7]

[.18–.25] [Superseded by Statement on Auditing Standards No. 60, effective for audits of financial statements for periods beginning on or after January 1, 1989.] (See section 325.)

[8.] Form of Report on Internal Accounting Control Based Solely on a Study and Evaluation Made as Part of an Audit[8-10]

[.26–.32] [Superseded by Statement on Auditing Standards No. 60, effective for audits of financial statements for periods beginning on or after January 1, 1989.] (See section 325.)

[9.] Reporting on Internal Accounting Control Based Solely on an Audit When a Minimum Study and Evaluation Is Made

[.33–.34] [Superseded by Statement on Auditing Standards No. 60, effective for audits of financial statements for periods beginning on or after January 1, 1989.] (See section 325.)

[10.] Report Required by U.S. General Accounting Office Based on a Financial and Compliance Audit When a Study and Evaluation Does Not Extend Beyond the Preliminary Review Phase[11-15]

[.35–.36] [Superseded by Statement on Auditing Standards No. 60, effective for audits of financial statements for periods beginning on or after January 1, 1989.] (See section 325.)

[11.] Restricted Purpose Report Required by Law to Be Made Available to the Public[16]

[.37–.38] [Superseded by Statement on Auditing Standards No. 60, effective for audits of financial statements for periods beginning on or after January 1, 1989.] (See section 325.)

[12.] Reporting on Internal Accounting Control "Compliance With the Currency and Foreign Transactions Reporting Act"[*]

[.39–.41] [Deleted October 1993.]

[1-7] [Superseded by Statement on Auditing Standards No. 60, effective for audits of financial statements for periods beginning on or after January 1, 1989.] (See section 325.)

[8-10] [Superseded by Statement on Auditing Standards No. 60, effective for audits of financial statements for periods beginning on or after January 1, 1989.] (See section 325.)

[11-15] [Superseded by Statement on Auditing Standards No. 60, effective for audits of financial statements for periods beginning on or after January 1, 1989.] (See section 325.)

[16] [Superseded by Statement on Auditing Standards No. 60, effective for audits of financial statements for periods beginning on or after January 1, 1989.] (See section 325.)

[*] [Footnote deleted, October 1993.]

AU Section 700
SPECIAL TOPICS

. . . filings under federal securities statutes . . . interim financial information . . .

TABLE OF CONTENTS

Section		Paragraph
711	Filings Under Federal Securities Statutes	.01-.13
	Subsequent Events Procedures in 1933 Act Filings	.10-.11
	Response to Subsequent Events and Subsequently Discovered Facts	.12-.13
9711	Filings Under Federal Securities Statutes: Auditing Interpretations of Section 711	
	1. Subsequent Events Procedures for Shelf Registration Statements Updated After the Original Effective Date (5/83)	.01-.11
	2. Consenting to Be Named as an Expert in an Offering Document in Connection With Securities Offerings Other Than Those Registered Under the Securities Act of 1933 (issued 6/92; amended 3/95)	.12-.15
	3. Consenting to the Use of an Audit Report in an Offering Document in Securities Offerings Other Than One Registered Under the Securities Act of 1933 (6/92)	.16-.17
722	Interim Financial Information	.01-.44
	Introduction	.01-.02
	Applicability	.03-.06
	Understanding With the Client	.07
	Characteristics of Interim Financial Information	.08
	Objective of a Review of Interim Financial Information	.09
	The Accountant's Knowledge of Internal Control	.10-.11
	Procedures for a Review of Interim Financial Information	.12-.19
	Nature of Procedures	.13
	Timing of Procedures	.14
	Extent of Procedures	.15-.19
	Communication With Audit Committees	.20-.25
	The Accountant's Report on a Review of Interim Financial Information	.26-.34
	Form of Accountant's Review Report	.27-.29
	Modification of the Accountant's Review Report	.30-.32
	Other Information in Documents Containing Interim Financial Information	.33

Section | Paragraph

722 Interim Financial Information—continued

Subsequent Discovery of Facts Existing at the Date of the Accountant's Report .... .34

Client's Representation Concerning a Review of Interim Financial Information .... .35

Interim Financial Information Accompanying Audited Financial Statements .... .36-.43

Presentation of the Information and Application of Review Procedures .... .36-.39

Circumstances Requiring Modification of the Auditor's Report .... .40-.42

Other Matters .... .43

Effective Date .... .44

AU Section 711*

Filings Under Federal Securities Statutes

Source: SAS No. 37.

See section 9711 for interpretations of this section.

Issue date, unless otherwise indicated: April, 1981.

.01 As in the case of financial statements used for other purposes, management has the responsibility for the financial representations contained in documents filed under the federal securities statutes. In this connection the Securities and Exchange Commission has said:

> The fundamental and primary responsibility for the accuracy of information filed with the Commission and disseminated among the investors rests upon management. Management does not discharge its obligations in this respect by the employment of independent public accountants, however reputable. Accountants' certificates are required not as a substitute for management's accounting of its stewardship, but as a check upon the accounting.[1]

.02 When an independent accountant's report is included in registration statements, proxy statements, or periodic reports filed under the federal securities statutes, the accountant's responsibility, generally, is in substance no different from that involved in other types of reporting. However, the nature and extent of this responsibility are specified in some detail in these statutes and in the related rules and regulations. For example, section 11(*a*) of the Securities Act of 1933, as amended, imposes responsibility for false or misleading statements in an effective registration statement, or for omissions that render statements made in such a document misleading, on

> every accountant, engineer, or appraiser, or any person whose profession gives authority to a statement made by him, who has with his consent been named as having prepared or certified any part of the registration statement, or as having prepared or certified any report or valuation which is used in connection with the registration statement, report, or valuation, which purports to have been prepared or certified by him.

.03 Section 11 also makes specific mention of the independent accountant's responsibility as an expert when his report is included in a registration statement filed under that act.[2] Section 11(*b*) states, in part, that no person shall be liable as provided therein if that person sustains the burden of proof that

> as regards any part of the registration statement purporting to be made upon his authority as an expert or purporting to be a copy of or extract from a report or valuation of himself as an expert, (i) he had, after reasonable investigation,

---

* *Note:* This section supersedes Statement on Auditing Standards No. 1, section 710, *Filings Under Federal Securities Statutes*. The changes provide guidance for the accountant whose report based on a review of interim financial information is presented, or incorporated by reference, in a filing under the Securities Act of 1933.

[1] 4 S. E. C. 721 (1939).

[2] Under rules of the Securities and Exchange Commission, a report based on a review of interim financial information is not a report by the accountant under section 11 (see paragraph .06).

> reasonable ground to believe and did believe, at the time such part of the registration statement became effective, that the statements therein were true and that there was no omission to state a material fact required to be stated therein or necessary to make the statements therein not misleading, or (ii) such part of the registration statement did not fairly represent his statement as an expert or was not a fair copy of or extract from his report or valuation as an expert....

Section 11 further provides that, in determining what constitutes reasonable investigation and reasonable ground to believe, "the standard of reasonableness shall be that required of a prudent man in the management of his own property."

.04 This discussion of the independent accountant's responsibilities in connection with filings under the federal securities statutes is not intended to offer legal interpretations and is based on an understanding of the meaning of the statutes as they relate to accounting principles and auditing standards and procedures. The discussion is subject to any judicial interpretations that may be issued.

.05 Because a registration statement under the Securities Act of 1933 speaks as of its effective date, the independent accountant whose report is included in such a registration statement has a statutory responsibility that is determined in the light of the circumstances on that date. This aspect of responsibility is peculiar to reports used for this purpose (see paragraphs .10 through .12).

.06 Under rules of the Securities and Exchange Commission, an independent accountant's report based on a review of interim financial information is not a report by the accountant within the meaning of section 11. Thus, the accountant does not have a similar statutory responsibility for such reports as of the effective date of the registration statement (see paragraph .13).

.07 The other federal securities statutes, while not containing so detailed an exposition, do impose responsibility, under certain conditions, on persons making false or misleading statements with respect to any material fact in applications, reports, or other documents filed under the statute.

.08 In filings under the Securities Act of 1933, a statement frequently is made in the prospectus (sometimes included in a section of the prospectus called the *experts section*) that certain information is included in the registration statement in reliance upon the report of certain named experts. The independent accountant should read the relevant section of the prospectus to make sure that his name is not being used in a way that indicates that his responsibility is greater than he intends. The experts section should be so worded that there is no implication that the financial statements have been prepared by the independent accountant or that they are not the direct representations of management.

.09 The Securities and Exchange Commission requires that, when an independent accountant's report based on a review of interim financial information is presented or incorporated by reference in a registration statement, a prospectus that includes a statement about the independent accountant's involvement should clarify that his review report is not a "report" or "part" of the registration statement within the meaning of sections 7 and 11 of the Securities Act of 1933. In this respect, wording such as the following in a prospectus would ordinarily be considered a satisfactory description for the accountant's purposes of the status of his review report that was included in a Form 10-Q filing that was later incorporated by reference in a registration statement.[3]

---

[3] A similar description of the status of the accountant's report would also ordinarily be satisfactory for the accountant's purposes when the accountant's review report is presented in the registration statement rather than incorporated by reference. In that case, the description in the prospectus would specifically refer to that report in the registration statement.

Independent Public Accountants

The consolidated balance sheets as of December 31, 19X2 and 19X1, and the consolidated statements of income, retained earnings, and cash flows for each of the three years in the period ended December 31, 19X2, incorporated by reference in this prospectus, have been included herein in reliance on the report of _________ independent public accountants, given on the authority of that firm as experts in auditing and accounting.

With respect to the unaudited interim financial information for the periods ended March 31, 19X3 and 19X2, incorporated by reference in this prospectus, the independent public accountants have reported that they have applied limited procedures in accordance with professional standards for a review of such information. However, their separate report included in the company's quarterly report on Form 10-Q for the quarter ended March 31, 19X3, and incorporated by reference herein, states that they did not audit and they do not express an opinion on that interim financial information. Accordingly, the degree of reliance on their report on such information should be restricted in light of the limited nature of the review procedures applied. The accountants are not subject to the liability provisions of section 11 of the Securities Act of 1933 for their report on the unaudited interim financial information because that report is not a "report" or a "part" of the registration statement prepared or certified by the accountants within the meaning of sections 7 and 11 of the act.

The independent accountant should also read other sections of the prospectus to make sure that his name is not being used in a way that indicates that his responsibility is greater than he intends.

Subsequent Events Procedures in 1933 Act Filings

.10 To sustain the burden of proof that he has made a "reasonable investigation" (see paragraph .03), as required under the Securities Act of 1933, an auditor should extend his procedures with respect to subsequent events from the date of his audit report up to the effective date or as close thereto as is reasonable and practicable in the circumstances. In this connection, he should arrange with his client to be kept advised of the progress of the registration proceedings so that his review of subsequent events can be completed by the effective date. The likelihood that the auditor will discover subsequent events necessarily decreases following the completion of field work, and, as a practical matter, after that time the independent auditor may rely, for the most part, on inquiries of responsible officials and employees. In addition to performing the procedures outlined in section 560.12, at or near the effective date, the auditor generally should

a. Read the entire prospectus and other pertinent portions of the registration statement.

b. Inquire of and obtain written representations from officers and other executives responsible for financial and accounting matters (limited where appropriate to major locations) about whether any events have occurred, other than those reflected or disclosed in the registration statement, that, in the officers' or other executives' opinion, have a material effect on the audited financial statements included therein or that should be disclosed in order to keep those statements from being misleading.

.11 A registration statement filed with the Securities and Exchange Commission may contain the reports of two or more independent auditors on their audits of the financial statements for different periods. An auditor who has audited the financial statements for prior periods but has not audited the financial statements for the most recent audited period included in the registration statement has a responsibility relating to events subsequent to the date of the prior-period financial statements, and extending to the effective date, that bear materially on the prior-period financial statements on which he reported. Generally, he should

a. Read pertinent portions of the prospectus and of the registration statement.

b. Obtain a letter of representation from the successor independent auditor regarding whether his audit (including his procedures with respect to subsequent events) revealed any matters that, in his opinion, might have a material effect on the financial statements reported on by the predecessor auditor or would require disclosure in the notes thereto.

The auditor should make inquiries and perform other procedures that he considers necessary to satisfy himself regarding the appropriateness of any adjustment or disclosure affecting the prior-period financial statements covered by his report (see section 508).

Response to Subsequent Events and Subsequently Discovered Facts

.12 If, subsequent to the date of his report on audited financial statements, the auditor (including a predecessor auditor) (*a*) discovers, in performing the procedures described in paragraphs .10 and .11 above, subsequent events that require adjustment or disclosure in the financial statements or (*b*) becomes aware that facts may have existed at the date of his report that might have affected his report had he then been aware of those facts, he should follow the guidance in sections 560 and 561. If the financial statements are appropriately adjusted or the required additional disclosure is made, the auditor should follow the guidance in sections 530.05 and 530.07–.08, with respect to dating his report. If the client refuses to make appropriate adjustment or disclosure in the financial statements for a subsequent event or subsequently discovered facts, the auditor should follow the procedures in section 561.08–.09. In such circumstances, the auditor should also consider, probably with the advice of his legal counsel, withholding his consent to the use of his report on the audited financial statements in the registration statement.

.13 If an accountant concludes on the basis of facts known to him that unaudited financial statements or unaudited interim financial information presented or incorporated by reference in a registration statement are not in conformity with generally accepted accounting principles, he should insist on appropriate revision. Failing that,

a. If the accountant has reported on a review of such interim financial information and the subsequently discovered facts are such that they would have affected his report had they been known to him at the date of his report, he should refer to section 561, because certain provisions of that section may be relevant to his consideration of those matters (see section 722.34). [Reference changed by the issuance of Statement on Auditing Standards No. 71.]

b. If the accountant has not reported on a review of the unaudited financial statements or interim financial information, he should modify his report on the audited financial statements to describe the departure from generally accepted accounting principles contained in the unaudited financial statements or interim financial information.

In either case, the accountant should also consider, probably with the advice of his legal counsel, withholding his consent to the use of his report on the audited financial statements in the registration statement.

AU Section 9711

Filings Under Federal Securities Statutes: Auditing Interpretations of Section 711

1. Subsequent Events Procedures for Shelf Registration Statements Updated after the Original Effective Date

.01 *Question*—Rule 415 of Regulation C under the Securities Act of 1933 (1933 Act) permits companies to register a designated amount of securities for continuous or delayed offerings by filing one "shelf" registration statement with the SEC. Under this rule, a registrant can register an amount of securities it reasonably expects to offer and sell within the next two years, generally without the later need to prepare and file a new prospectus and registration statement for each sale.

.02 A Rule 415 shelf registration statement can be updated after its original effective date by—

a. The filing of a post-effective amendment,

b. The incorporation by reference of subsequently filed material, or

c. The addition of a supplemental prospectus (sometimes referred to as a "sticker").

.03 Section 711, *Filings Under Federal Securities Statutes*, paragraph .05, states, "Because a registration statement under the Securities Act of 1933 speaks as of its effective date, the independent accountant whose report is included in such a registration statement has a statutory responsibility that is determined in the light of the circumstances on that date." The independent accountant's statutory responsibility regarding information covered by his report and included in a registration statement is specified in Section 11 of the 1933 Act. Section 11(b)(3)(B) states that the accountant will not be held liable if he can sustain a burden of proof that "he had, after reasonable investigation, reasonable ground to believe and did believe, at the time such part of the registration statement became effective, that the statements therein were true and that there was no omission to state a material fact required to be stated therein or necessary to make the statements therein not misleading." To sustain the burden of proof that he has made a "reasonable investigation" as of the effective date, the accountant performs subsequent events procedures (as described in section 711.10 and .11) to a date as close to the effective date of the registration statement as is reasonable and practicable in the circumstances.

.04 In connection with Rule 415 shelf registrations, under what circumstances does the independent accountant have a responsibility to perform subsequent events procedures after the original effective date of the registration statement?

.05 *Interpretation*—As discussed in more detail below, in general, the accountant should perform the subsequent events procedures described in section 711.10 and .11, when either:

a. A post-effective amendment to the shelf registration statement, as defined by SEC rules, is filed pursuant to Item 512(a) of Regulation S-K,[1] or

b. A 1934 Act filing that includes or amends audited financial statements is incorporated by reference into the shelf registration statement.

.06 When a post-effective amendment is filed pursuant to the registrant's undertaking required by Item 512 of Regulation S-K, a shelf registration statement is considered to have a new effective date because Item 512(a)(2) of Regulation S-K states, ". . . for the purpose of determining any liability under the Securities Act of 1933, each such post-effective amendment shall be deemed to be a new registration statement. . . ." Accordingly, in such cases, the accountant should perform subsequent events procedures to a date as close to the new effective date of the registration statement as is reasonable and practicable in the circumstances.

.07 Item 512(b) of Regulation S-K states that for purposes of determining any liability under the Securities Act of 1933 each filing of a registrant's annual report (Form 10-K) and each filing of an employee benefit plan annual report (Form 11-K) that is incorporated by reference into a shelf registration statement is deemed to be a new registration statement relating to the securities offering. Accordingly, when a Form 10-K or Form 11-K is incorporated by reference into a shelf registration statement, the accountant should perform subsequent events procedures to a date as close to the date of the filing of the Form 10-K or Form 11-K as is reasonable and practicable in the circumstances and date his consent as of that date.

.08 In many circumstances, a Form 10-Q, Form 8-K, or other 1934 Act filing can be incorporated by reference into a shelf registration statement (sometimes this occurs automatically—for example, in a Form S-3 or Form S-8) without the need for a post-effective amendment. In those circumstances, the accountant has no responsibility to perform subsequent events procedures unless the filing includes or amends audited financial statements—for example, a Form 8-K that includes audited financial statements of an acquired company. In these latter circumstances, when the filing is incorporated into a registration statement, SEC rules require a currently dated consent of the accountant who audited those statements, and that accountant should perform subsequent events procedures to a date as close to the date of the incorporation by reference of the related material as is reasonable and practicable in the circumstances.[2]

.09 In addition, an accountant's report on a review of interim financial information contained in a Form 10-Q may also include his report on the information presented in the condensed year-end balance sheet that has also been included in the form and has been derived from the latest audited annual balance sheet. (See section 552, *Reporting on Condensed Financial Statements and Selected Financial Data*, paragraph .08.) When the Form 10-Q is incorpor-

---

[1] Item 512(a) of Regulation S-K provides that the registrant is required to undertake to file a post-effective amendment to a shelf registration statement to (*a*) file updated financial statements pursuant to section 10(*a*)(3) of the Securities Act of 1933, (*b*) reflect a "fundamental change" in the information in the registration statement arising from facts or events occurring after the effective date of the registration statement or previous post-effective amendments, or (*c*) include new material information regarding the plan of distribution.

[2] Typically in such cases, the affected audited financial statements are not those of the registrant, and accordingly, there would be no requirement for the registrant's auditor to update his subsequent events procedures with respect to the registrant's financial statements.

ated by reference into the shelf registration (which may occur automatically), the report on the year-end condensed balance sheet may be considered a report of an "expert." Because it is not clear what the accountant's responsibility is in those circumstances, the accountant should perform subsequent events procedures (as described in section 711.10 and .11) to a date as close to the date of the incorporation by reference of the Form 10-Q as is reasonable and practicable in the circumstances.

.10 One of the subsequent events procedures described in section 711 is to "read the entire prospectus and other pertinent portions of the registration statement." The reading of the entire prospectus (including any supplemental prospectuses and documents incorporated by reference—such as Form 10-Ks, 10-Qs, and 8-Ks) and the other procedures described in section 711.10 and .11, help assure that the accountant has fulfilled his statutory responsibilities under the 1933 Act to perform a "reasonable investigation."

.11 When a shelf registration statement is updated by a supplemental prospectus (or "sticker"), the effective date of the registration statement is considered to be unchanged since the supplemental prospectus does not constitute an amendment to the registration statement, and, consequently, no posteffective amendment has been filed. Accordingly, an accountant has no responsibility to update his performance of subsequent events procedures through the date of the supplemental prospectus or sticker. The accountant, however, may nevertheless become aware that facts may have existed at the date of his report that might have affected his report had he then been aware of those facts. Section 711.12 and .13, provide guidance on the accountant's response to subsequent events and subsequently discovered facts.

[Issue Date: May, 1983.]

2. Consenting to be Named as an Expert in an Offering Document in Connection With Securities Offerings Other Than Those Registered Under the Securities Act of 1933

.12 *Question*—Should the auditor consent to be named, or referred to, as an expert in an offering document in connection with securities offerings other than those registered under the Securities Act of 1933 (the Act)?

.13 *Interpretation*—No. The term "expert" has a specific statutory meaning under the Act.[3] The act states that anyone who purchases a security registered under the Act may sue specified persons if the registration statement contains an untrue statement or omits to state a material fact. Those persons who may be sued include "every accountant, engineer, or appraiser, or any person whose profession gives authority to a statement made by him, who has with his consent been named as having prepared or certified any part of the registration statement." These persons are typically referred to as "experts." Auditors sign a statement, known as a consent, in which they agree to be identified as experts in a section of the registration statement.

.14 Outside the 1933 Act arena, however, the term "expert" is typically undefined and the auditor's responsibility, as a result of the use of that term, is also undefined.

---

[3] If the term "expert" is defined under applicable state law, for instance, the accountant may agree to be named as an expert in an offering document in an intra-state securities offering. The accountant may also agree to be named as an expert, as that term is used by the Office of Thrift Supervision (OTS), in securities offering documents which are subject to the jurisdiction of the OTS.

.15 When a client wishes to make reference to the auditor's role in an offering document in connection with a securities offering that is not registered under the Act, the caption "Independent Auditors" should be used to title that section of the document; the caption "Experts" should not be used, nor should the auditors be referred to as experts anywhere in the document. The following paragraph should be used to describe the auditors role.

> Independent Auditors
>
> The financial statements as of December 31, 19XX and for the year then ended, included in this offering circular, have been audited by ABC, independent auditors, as stated in their report(s) appearing herein.

If the client refuses to delete from the offering document the reference to the auditors as experts, the auditor should not permit inclusion of the auditor's report in the offering document.

[Issue Date: June, 1992; Amended: March, 1995.]

3. Consenting to the Use of an Audit Report in an Offering Document in Securities Offerings Other Than One Registered Under the Securities Act of 1933

.16 *Question*—May the auditor consent to the use of his or her audit report in an offering document other than one registered under the Securities Act of 1933?

.17 *Interpretation*—When an auditor's report is included in an offering document other than one registered under the Securities Act of 1933, it is not usually necessary for the accountant to provide a consent. If the accountant is requested to provide a consent, he or she may do so. The following is example language the accountant might use:

> We agree to the inclusion in this offering circular of our report, dated February 5, 19XX, on our audit of the financial statements of [name of entity].

[Issue Date: June, 1992.]

AU Section 722

Interim Financial Information

(Supersedes SAS Nos. 36 and 66)

Source: SAS No. 71

Effective for interim periods within fiscal years beginning after September 15, 1992.

Introduction

.01 This section provides guidance on the nature, timing, and extent of procedures to be applied by the independent accountant in conducting a review of interim financial information, as defined in paragraph .02, and on the reporting applicable to such engagements. It also establishes certain communication requirements for an accountant who has been engaged to perform certain services related to interim financial information, as described in paragraph .05.

.02 For purposes of this section, the term *interim financial information* or *statements* means financial information or statements for less than a full year or for a twelve-month period ending on a date other than the entity's fiscal year end.

Applicability

.03 The guidance in this section applies only to—

a. Engagements to review interim financial information or statements of a public entity[1] that are presented alone either in the form of financial statements or in a summarized form that purports to conform with the provisions of Accounting Principles Board (APB) Opinion No. 28 [AC section I73].[2]

b. Interim financial information that accompanies, or is included in a note to, audited financial statements of a public entity.

c. Interim financial information that is included in a note to the audited financial statements of a nonpublic entity.[3]

---

[1] For purposes of this section, a public entity is any entity (*a*) whose securities trade in a public market either on a stock exchange (domestic or foreign) or in the over-the-counter market, including securities quoted only locally or regionally, (*b*) that makes a filing with a regulatory agency in preparation for the sale of any class of its securities in a public market, or (*c*) that is a subsidiary, corporate joint venture, or other entity controlled by an entity covered by (*a*) or (*b*) (see section 504, *Association With Financial Statements*). When a public entity does not have its annual financial statements audited, an accountant may be requested to review its annual or interim financial statements. In those circumstances, an accountant may make a review and, if so, should refer to the guidance in Statements on Standards for Accounting and Review Services (SSARSs) for the standards, procedures, and form of report applicable to such an engagement.

[2] SSARSs provide guidance in connection with the unaudited financial statements of a nonpublic entity.

[3] Nonpublic entities frequently include interim financial information as supplementary information.

If that information is included in an auditor-submitted document that contains basic financial statements, the accountant should refer to section 551, *Reporting on Information Accompanying the Basic Financial Statements in Auditor-Submitted Documents*, for guidance.

If the information is included in a client-prepared document that contains audited financial state-

(footnote continued)

.04 This section also provides guidance on reporting by the independent auditor when certain selected quarterly financial data required to be presented with audited annual financial statements by item 302(a) of Regulation S-K of the Securities and Exchange Commission (SEC) are not presented or are presented but have not been reviewed (see paragraph .41 for guidance).[4]

.05 The guidance requiring certain communications as described in paragraphs .20 through .22 applies only when (*a*) the accountant's report accompanied the entity's most recent audited annual financial statements filed with a specified regulatory agency,[5] or the accountant has been engaged to audit the entity's annual financial statements for the current period, as stated in a document filed by the entity with a specified regulatory agency, and (*b*) the accountant is engaged—

a. To assist the entity in preparing its interim financial information, or

b. To perform any of the procedures described in paragraph .13 on the interim financial information. However, mere reading of the interim financial information does not constitute a procedure sufficient to require consideration of the communication requirements described in paragraphs .20 through .22.

.06 This section does not apply to comparative presentations of audited and unaudited financial data as discussed in section 504.14 through .17.

Understanding With the Client

.07 A clear understanding should be established with the client regarding the nature of the procedures to be performed on the interim financial information. Accordingly, the accountant may wish to confirm the nature and scope of his or her engagement in a letter to the client. The letter usually would include (*a*) a general description of the procedures, (*b*) an explanation that such procedures are substantially less in scope than an audit performed in accordance with generally accepted auditing standards, (*c*) an explanation that the financial information is the responsibility of the company's management, and (*d*) a description of the form of the report, if any.

Characteristics of Interim Financial Information

.08 The characteristics of interim financial information necessarily affect the nature, timing, and extent of procedures that the accountant applies in conducting a review of that information. Timeliness is an important element of interim financial reporting. Interim financial information customarily is made available to investors and others more promptly than is annual financial information. Timely reporting of interim financial information ordinarily precludes the development by management of information and documentation un-

---

ments, the auditor should refer to the guidance in section 550, *Other Information in Documents Containing Audited Financial Statements*; if the information included in the client-prepared document is a complete set of financial statements, the accountant may perform a review in accordance with SSARSs and report thereon.

[4] Additional considerations of the accountant when unaudited interim financial information is presented or incorporated by reference in a filing under the Securities Act of 1933 are described in section 711, *Filings Under Federal Securities Statutes*. The accountants' involvement with such information in a comfort letter is described in section 634, *Letters for Underwriters and Certain Other Requesting Parties*. [Title of section 634 changed, February 1993, to reflect the issuance of Statement on Auditing Standards No. 72.]

[5] For purposes of this section, specified regulatory agencies are the SEC and the following agencies with which an entity files periodic reports pursuant to the Securities Exchange Act of 1934: Office of the Comptroller of the Currency, Federal Deposit Insurance Corporation, Federal Reserve System, and Office of Thrift Supervision.

derlying interim financial information to the same extent as that underlying annual financial information. Therefore, a characteristic of interim financial information is that many revenues, costs, and expenses are estimated to a greater extent than for annual reporting purposes. Another characteristic of interim financial information is its relationship to annual financial information. Deferrals, accruals, and estimates at the end of each interim period are frequently affected by judgments made at interim dates concerning anticipated results of operations for the remainder of the annual period.

Objective of a Review of Interim Financial Information

.09 The objective of a review of interim financial information is to provide the accountant, based on applying his or her knowledge of financial reporting practices to significant accounting matters of which he or she becomes aware through inquiries and analytical procedures, with a basis for reporting whether material modifications should be made for such information to conform with generally accepted accounting principles. The objective of a review of interim financial information differs significantly from the objective of an audit of financial statements in accordance with generally accepted auditing standards. The objective of an audit is to provide a reasonable basis for expressing an opinion regarding the financial statements taken as a whole. A review of interim financial information does not provide a basis for the expression of such an opinion, because the review does not contemplate (*a*) tests of accounting records through inspection, observation, or confirmation, (*b*) obtaining corroborating evidential matter in response to inquiries, or (*c*) the application of certain other procedures ordinarily performed during an audit. A review may bring to the accountant's attention significant matters affecting the interim financial information, but it does not provide assurance that the accountant will become aware of all significant matters that would be disclosed in an audit.

The Accountant's Knowledge of Internal Control

.10 To perform a review of interim financial information, the accountant needs to have sufficient knowledge of a client's internal control as it relates to the preparation of both annual and interim financial information to—

- Identify types of potential material misstatements in the interim financial information and consider the likelihood of their occurrence.
- Select the inquiries and analytical procedures that will provide the accountant with a basis for reporting whether material modifications should be made for such information to conform with generally accepted accounting principles.

Knowledge of the client's internal control includes knowledge of the control environment, risk assessment, control activities, information and communication, and monitoring. Sufficient knowledge of a client's internal control as it relates to the preparation of annual financial information would ordinarily have been acquired, and may have been acquired with respect to interim financial information, by the accountant who has audited a client's financial statements for one or more annual periods. When the accountant has not audited the most recent annual financial statements, and thus has not acquired sufficient knowledge of the entity's internal control, the accountant should perform procedures to obtain that knowledge. [Revised, February 1997, to reflect conforming changes necessary due to the issuance of Statement on Auditing Standards No. 78.]

.11 If internal control appears to contain deficiencies so significant that it is impracticable for the accountant to effectively apply his or her knowledge of accounting and financial reporting practices to the interim financial information, the accountant should consider whether this precludes completion of such a review (see paragraph .26).

Procedures for a Review of Interim Financial Information

.12 The procedures for a review of interim financial information are described in the following paragraphs concerning (*a*) the nature of procedures (paragraph .13), (*b*) the timing of procedures (paragraph .14), and (*c*) the extent of procedures (paragraphs .15 through .19).

Nature of Procedures

.13 Procedures for conducting a review of interim financial information generally are limited to inquiries and analytical procedures, rather than search and verification procedures, concerning significant accounting matters relating to the financial information to be reported. The procedures that the accountant ordinarily should apply are—

a. Inquiry concerning (1) internal control, including the control environment, risk assessment, control activities, information and communication, and monitoring, for both annual and interim financial information, and (2) any significant changes in internal control since the most recent financial statement audit or review of interim financial information to ascertain the potential effect of (1) and (2) on the preparation of interim financial information.

b. Application of analytical procedures to interim financial information to identify and provide a basis for inquiry about relationships and individual items that appear to be unusual. Analytical procedures, for purposes of this section, consist of (1) comparison of the interim financial information with comparable information for the immediately preceding interim period and for corresponding previous period(s), (2) evaluations of the interim financial information made by consideration of plausible relationships among both financial and, where relevant, nonfinancial data, and (3) comparisons of recorded amounts, or ratios developed from recorded amounts, to expectations developed by the accountant. The accountant develops such expectations by identifying and using plausible relationships that are reasonably expected to exist based on the accountant's understanding of the client and of the industry in which the client operates. Following are examples of sources of information for developing expectations:

- Financial information for comparable prior period(s) giving consideration to known changes
- Anticipated results—for example, budgets or forecasts including extrapolations from interim or annual data

- Relationships among elements of financial information within the period
- Information regarding the industry in which the client operates—for example, gross margin information
- Relationships of financial information with relevant nonfinancial information

In applying these procedures, the accountant should consider the types of matters that, in the preceding year or quarters, have required accounting adjustments. The accountant may find the guidance in section 329, *Analytical Procedures*, useful in performing a review of interim financial information. Section 329 provides guidance on the use of analytical procedures in a financial statement audit and requires the auditor to obtain corroborating evidential matter when analytical procedures are used as a substantive test. The accountant ordinarily would not obtain corroborating evidential matter of management's responses to the accountant's inquiries in performing a review of interim financial information. The accountant should, however, consider the consistency of management's responses in light of the results of other inquiries and the application of analytical procedures. Since many revenues, costs, and expenses are estimated to a greater extent in interim financial information than for annual financial reporting purposes, the accountant may wish to refer to the guidance in section 342, *Auditing Accounting Estimates*, paragraphs .05 and .06.

c. Reading the minutes of meetings of stockholders, the board of directors, and committees of the board of directors to identify actions that may affect the interim financial information.

d. Reading the interim financial information to consider whether, on the basis of information coming to the accountant's attention, the information to be reported conforms with generally accepted accounting principles.

e. Obtaining reports from other accountants, if any, who have been engaged to make a review of the interim financial information of significant components of the reporting entity, its subsidiaries, or its other investees.[6]

f. Inquiry of officers and other executives having responsibility for financial and accounting matters concerning (1) whether the interim financial information has been prepared in conformity with generally accepted accounting principles consistently applied, (2) changes in the entity's accounting practices, (3) changes in the entity's business activities, (4) matters about which questions have arisen in the course of applying the foregoing procedures, and (5) events subsequent to the date of the interim financial information that would have a material effect on the presentation of such information.

---

[6] When an accountant acts as principal auditor (see section 543, *Part of Audit Performed by Other Independent Auditors*) and makes use of the work or reports of other auditors in the course of the annual audit of the client's financial statements, the accountant ordinarily will be in a similar position in connection with a review of interim financial information. Thus, the accountant should take into account the same considerations in deciding whether to refer in his or her review report to the review performed by the other accountants.

g. Obtaining written representations from management concerning its responsibility for the financial information, completeness of minutes, subsequent events, and other matters about which the accountant believes written representations are appropriate in the circumstances. See section 333A, *Client Representations*, for guidance concerning client representations.

[Revised, February 1997, to reflect conforming changes necessary due to the issuance of Statement on Auditing Standards No. 78.]

Timing of Procedures

.14 Adequate planning by the accountant is essential to the timely completion of a review of interim financial information. Performance of some of the work before the end of the interim period may permit the work to be carried out in a more efficient manner and to be completed at an earlier date. Performing some of the work earlier in the interim period also permits early consideration of significant accounting matters affecting the interim financial information.

Extent of Procedures

.15 The extent to which the procedures referred to in paragraph .13 are applied depends on the considerations described in paragraphs .16 through .19.

.16 *The Accountant's Knowledge of Changes in Accounting Practices or in the Nature or Volume of Business Activity.* A review of interim financial information may bring to the accountant's attention significant changes in accounting practices or in the nature or volume of the client's business activities. Examples of changes that could affect the interim financial information to be reported include business combinations; disposal of a segment of the business; extraordinary, unusual, or infrequently occurring transactions; significant changes in related parties or related-party transactions; initiation of litigation or the development of other contingencies; trends in sales or costs that could affect accounting estimates relating to the valuations of receivables and inventories, realization of deferred charges, provisions for warranties and employee benefits, and unearned income; and changes in accounting principles or in the methods of applying them. If any such changes come to the accountant's attention, he or she should inquire about the manner in which the changes and their effects are to be reported in the interim financial information.

.17 *Inquiry Concerning Litigation, Claims, and Assessments.* A review of interim financial information does not involve obtaining corroborating evidential matter for responses to inquiries as a basis for issuing an unmodified accountant's report (see paragraph .09). Consequently, it ordinarily is not necessary to send an audit inquiry letter to a client's lawyer concerning litigation, claims, and assessments. However, if information comes to the accountant's attention that leads him or her to question whether the unaudited interim financial information departs from generally accepted accounting principles insofar as litigations, claims, or assessments may be concerned, and the accountant believes the client's lawyer may have information concerning that question, an inquiry of the lawyer concerning the specific question is appropriate.

.18 *Questions Raised in Performing Other Procedures.* If, in performing a review of interim financial information, the accountant becomes aware of information that leads him or her to question whether the interim financial information to be reported conforms with generally accepted accounting principles, the accountant should make additional inquiries or employ other procedures he or she considers appropriate to provide the limited assurance for a review engagement.

.19 *Modification of Review Procedures.* The procedures for a review of interim financial information may be modified, as appropriate, to take into consideration the results of auditing procedures applied in performing an audit conducted in accordance with generally accepted auditing standards.

Communication With Audit Committees

.20 As a result of performing the services described in paragraph .05, the accountant may become aware of matters that cause him or her to believe that interim financial information, filed or to be filed with a specified regulatory agency, is probably materially misstated as a result of a departure from generally accepted accounting principles. In such circumstances, the accountant should discuss the matters with the appropriate level of management as soon as practicable.

.21 If, in the accountant's judgment, management does not respond appropriately to the accountant's communication within a reasonable period of time, the accountant should inform the audit committee, or others with equivalent authority and responsibility (hereafter referred to as the audit committee), of the matters as soon as practicable. This communication may be oral or written. If information is communicated orally, the accountant should document the communication in appropriate memoranda or notations in the working papers.

.22 If, in the accountant's judgment, the audit committee does not respond appropriately to the accountant's communication within a reasonable period of time, the accountant should evaluate (*a*) whether to resign from the engagement related to interim financial information, and (*b*) whether to remain as the entity's auditor or stand for reelection to audit the entity's financial statements. The accountant may wish to consult with his or her attorney when making these evaluations.

.23 In performing the procedures in paragraphs .13 through .19, the accountant may become aware of fraud or illegal acts by clients. The accountant should assure himself or herself that the audit committee is adequately informed about—

a. Any fraud of which the accountant becomes aware during the review, unless it is clearly inconsequential. (See section 316, *Consideration of Fraud in a Financial Statement Audit*, paragraphs .38 through .40.)

b. Any illegal acts of which the accountant becomes aware during the review, unless those illegal acts are clearly inconsequential. (See section 317, *Illegal Acts by Clients*, paragraph .17.)

.24 In performing the procedures in paragraphs .13 through .19, the accountant may become aware of matters relating to internal control that may be of interest to the audit committee. The matters required for reporting to the audit committee are referred to as reportable conditions. Specifically, these are matters coming to the accountant's attention that, in his or her judgment, should be communicated to the audit committee because they represent significant deficiencies in the design or operation of internal control, which could adversely affect the organization's ability to record, process, summarize, and report financial data consistent with the assertions of management in the interim financial information. The accountant may also wish to submit recommendations for other matters of significance that come to the accountant's attention.[7]

.25 In performing the procedures in paragraphs .13 through .19, the accountant also should consider whether any of the matters described in section 380, *Communication With Audit Committees*, as they relate to the interim financial information, should be communicated to the audit committee. For instance, the accountant should determine that the audit committee is informed about the process used by management in formulating particularly sensitive accounting estimates or about a change in a significant accounting policy affecting the interim financial information.

The Accountant's Report on a Review of Interim Financial Information

.26 An accountant may permit the use of his or her name and inclusion of his or her report in a written communication setting forth interim financial information if he or she has made a review of such information as specified in the preceding paragraphs. If restrictions on the scope of a review of interim financial information preclude completion of such a review, the accountant should not permit the use of his or her name.[8] Restrictions on the scope of the review may be imposed by a client or may be caused by such circumstances as the timing of the accountant's work or an inadequacy in the accounting records.

Form of Accountant's Review Report

.27 The accountant's report accompanying interim financial information that he or she has reviewed should consist of—

a. A title that includes the word *independent*.

b. Identification of the interim financial information reviewed.

c. A statement that the financial information is the responsibility of the company's management.

d. A statement that the review of interim financial information was conducted in accordance with standards established by the AICPA.

e. A description of the procedures for a review of interim financial information.

f. A statement that a review of interim financial information is substantially less in scope than an audit conducted in accordance with generally accepted auditing standards, the objective of which is an expression of opinion regarding the financial statements taken as a whole, and accordingly, no such opinion is expressed.

g. A statement about whether the accountant is aware of any material modifications that should be made to the accompanying financial information so that it conforms with generally accepted accounting principles.

---

[7] Section 325, *Communication of Internal Control Related Matters Noted in an Audit*, provides guidance with respect to communicating reportable conditions in internal control.

[8] See paragraph .35 concerning a client's representation when the scope of a review of interim financial information has been restricted. Also, when the accountant is unable to complete such a review because of a scope limitation, he or she should consider the implications of that limitation with respect to the interim financial information issued by the client. In those circumstances, the accountant should also refer to paragraph .24 for guidance.

h. The manual or printed signature of the accountant's firm.

i. The date of the review report. The report may be addressed to the company whose financial information is being reviewed, its board of directors, or its stockholders. Generally, the report should be dated as of the date of completion of the review.[9] In addition, each page of the interim financial information should be clearly marked as unaudited.

.28 An example of such a report follows:[10]

Independent Accountant's Report

We have reviewed the accompanying [*describe the statements or information reviewed*] of ABC Company and consolidated subsidiaries as of September 30, 19X1, and for the three-month and nine-month periods then ended. These financial statements (information) are (is) the responsibility of the company's management.

We conducted our review in accordance with standards established by the American Institute of Certified Public Accountants. A review of interim financial information consists principally of applying analytical procedures to financial data and making inquiries of persons responsible for financial and accounting matters. It is substantially less in scope than an audit conducted in accordance with generally accepted auditing standards, the objective of which is the expression of an opinion regarding the financial statements taken as a whole. Accordingly, we do not express such an opinion.

Based on our review, we are not aware of any material modifications that should be made to the accompanying financial statements (information) for them (it) to be in conformity with generally accepted accounting principles.

[*Signature*]

[*Date*]

.29 The accountant may use and make reference to the report of another accountant on a review of interim financial information of a significant component of the reporting entity. This reference indicates a division of responsibility for performance of the review.[11] An example of a report including such a reference follows:

Independent Accountant's Report

We have reviewed the accompanying [*describe the statements or information reviewed*] of ABC Company and consolidated subsidiaries as of September 30, 19X1, and for the three-month and nine-month periods then ended. These financial statements (information) are (is) the responsibility of the company's management.

We were furnished with the report of other accountants on their review of the interim financial information of ADE subsidiary, whose total assets as of September 30, 19X1, and whose revenues for the three-month and nine-month periods then ended, constituted 15 percent, 20 percent, and 22 percent, respectively, of the related consolidated totals.

---

[9] Other reporting issues involved in the dating of reports or concerning subsequent events are similar to those encountered in an audit of financial statements (see section 530, *Dating of the Independent Auditor's Report*).

[10] If interim financial information of a prior period is presented with that of the current period and the accountant has conducted a review of that information, the accountant should report on his or her review of the prior period. An example of the first sentence of such a report follows: "We have reviewed ... of ABC Company and consolidated subsidiaries as of September 30, 19X1 and 19X2, and for the three-month and nine-month periods then ended...."

[11] See section 543.

We conducted our review in accordance with standards established by the American Institute of Certified Public Accountants. A review of interim financial information consists principally of applying analytical procedures to financial data and making inquiries of persons responsible for financial and accounting matters. It is substantially less in scope than an audit conducted in accordance with generally accepted auditing standards, the objective of which is the expression of an opinion regarding the financial statements taken as a whole. Accordingly, we do not express such an opinion.

Based on our review and the report of other accountants, we are not aware of any material modifications that should be made to the accompanying financial statements (information) for them (it) to be in conformity with generally accepted accounting principles.

[*Signature*]

[*Date*]

Modification of the Accountant's Review Report

.30 The accountant's report on a review of interim financial information should be modified for departures from generally accepted accounting principles,[12] which include inadequate disclosure and any changes in accounting principle that are not in conformity with generally accepted accounting principles. The existence of an uncertainty, substantial doubt about the entity's ability to continue as a going concern, or a lack of consistency in the application of accounting principles affecting interim financial information would not require the accountant to include an additional paragraph in the report, provided that the interim financial information appropriately discloses such matters. Although not required, the accountant may wish to emphasize such matters in a separate paragraph of the report.

.31 *Departure From Generally Accepted Accounting Principles.* If the accountant becomes aware that the interim financial information is materially affected by a departure from generally accepted accounting principles, he or she should modify the report. The modification should describe the nature of the departure and, if practicable, should state the effects on the interim financial information. An example of such a modification of the accountant's report follows:

[*Explanatory third paragraph*]

Based on information furnished us by management, we believe that the company has excluded from property and debt in the accompanying balance sheet certain lease obligations that should be capitalized to conform with generally accepted accounting principles. This information indicates that if these lease obligations were capitalized at September 30, 19X1, property would be increased by $_____, long-term debt by $_____, and net income and earnings per share would be increased (decreased) by $_______, $_______, $_______, and $_______, respectively, for the _______ and _______ periods then ended.

[*Concluding paragraph*]

Based on our review, with the exception of the matter(s) described in the preceding paragraph(s), we are not aware of any material modifications that should be made to the accompanying financial statements (information) for them (it) to be in conformity with generally accepted accounting principles.

---

[12] When the circumstances contemplated by Rule 203 [ET section 203.01] are present, the accountant should refer to the guidance in section 508, *Reports on Audited Financial Statements*, paragraph .15.

.32 *Inadequate Disclosure.* The information the accountant will conclude is necessary for adequate disclosure will be influenced by the form and context in which the interim financial information is presented. For example, the disclosures considered necessary for interim financial information presented in accordance with the minimum disclosure requirements of APB Opinion No. 28, paragraph 30 [AC section I73.146], are considerably less extensive than those necessary for annual financial statements that present financial position, results of operations, and cash flows in conformity with generally accepted accounting principles.[13] If information that the accountant believes is necessary for adequate disclosure in conformity with generally accepted accounting principles is not included in the interim financial information, the accountant should modify the report and, if practicable, include the necessary information. An example of such a modification of the accountant's report follows:

> [*Explanatory third paragraph*]
>
> Management has informed us that the company is presently contesting deficiencies in federal income taxes proposed by the Internal Revenue Service for the years 19XX through 19XY in the aggregate amount of approximately $_____, and that the extent of the company's liability, if any, and the effect on the accompanying statements (information) are (is) not determinable at this time. The statements (information) fail(s) to disclose these matters, which we believe are required to be disclosed in conformity with generally accepted accounting principles.
>
> [*Concluding paragraph*]
>
> Based on our review, with the exception of the matter(s) described in the preceding paragraph(s), we are not aware of any material modifications that should be made to the accompanying financial statements (information) for them (it) to be in conformity with generally accepted accounting principles.

Other Information in Documents Containing Interim Financial Information

.33 An entity may publish various documents that contain information in addition to interim financial information and the independent accountant's review report on that interim financial information. Under those circumstances, the accountant[14] may wish to refer to the guidance in section 550.

Subsequent Discovery of Facts Existing at the Date of the Accountant's Report

.34 Subsequent to the date of the accountant's review report, the accountant may become aware that facts existed at the date of the review report that might have affected the report had the accountant then been aware of those facts. Because of the variety of conditions that might be encountered, the specific actions to be taken by the accountant in a particular case may vary

---

[13] APB Opinion No. 28, paragraph 32 [AC section I73.148], states that "there is a presumption that users of summarized interim financial data will have read the latest published annual report, including the financial disclosures required by generally accepted accounting principles and management's commentary concerning the annual financial results, and that the summarized interim data will be viewed in that context."

[14] The principal accountant may also request the other accountant or accountants involved in the engagement to read the other information.

with the circumstances. In any event, the accountant should consider the guidance in section 561, *Subsequent Discovery of Facts Existing at the Date of the Auditor's Report*.

Client's Representation Concerning a Review of Interim Financial Information

.35 The accountant may be requested to conduct a review of interim financial information to permit the client to include a representation to that effect in documents issued to stockholders or third parties or in Form 10-Q, a quarterly report required to be submitted to the SEC pursuant to section 13 or 15(d) of the Securities Exchange Act of 1934. If the client represents in such a document setting forth interim financial information that the accountant has made a review of that information, the accountant should request that his or her report be included.[15] If the client will not agree to include the accountant's report or if the accountant has been unable to complete the review (see paragraph .26), the accountant should request that neither his or her name be associated with the interim financial information nor reference to him or her be made in the document. If the client does not comply, the accountant should advise the client that the accountant does not consent, either to the use of his or her name or to reference to him or her, and should consider what other actions might be appropriate.[16]

Interim Financial Information Accompanying Audited Financial Statements

Presentation of the Information and Application of Review Procedures

.36 Certain entities are required by item 302(a) of SEC Regulation S-K to include selected quarterly financial data in their annual reports or other documents filed with the SEC that contain audited financial statements.[17] If the independent accountant has audited the financial statements of annual periods for which selected quarterly financial data specified by Regulation S-K are required to be presented, he or she should apply the review procedures specified in paragraphs .13 through .19 to the selected quarterly financial data. The reporting guidance in paragraph .41 is appropriate if the independent accountant has not performed such a review.

.37 Other entities may voluntarily include in documents containing audited financial statements the selected quarterly financial data specified in item 302(a) of SEC Regulation S-K. When a public entity voluntarily includes such information, the procedures specified in paragraphs .13 through .19 are applicable, unless either the entity indicates that the quarterly data have not been reviewed or the auditor expands his or her report on the audited financial

---

[15] SEC regulations require that if the client includes a representation that the independent accountant has conducted a review, the accountant's report on the review must accompany the interim financial information.

[16] In considering what actions, if any, may be appropriate in these circumstances, the accountant may wish to consult his or her legal counsel.

[17] Item 302(a), "Supplementary Financial Information—Selected Quarterly Financial Data," states, in part, "Disclosure shall be made of net sales, gross profit ..., income (loss) before extraordinary items and cumulative effect of a change in accounting, per share data based upon such income (loss), and net income (loss) for each full quarter within the two most recent fiscal years and any subsequent interim period for which financial statements are included or are required to be included...."

statements to state that the data have not been reviewed (see paragraph .42).[18]

.38 The interim financial information ordinarily would be presented as supplementary information outside the audited financial statements. Each page of the interim financial information should be clearly marked as unaudited. If management chooses to present the interim financial information in a note to the audited financial statements, the information should also be clearly marked as unaudited.

.39 The accountant may perform the review procedures either at the time of an audit of the annual financial statements or quarterly before the issuance of the data. Performance of the procedures before issuance permits early consideration of significant accounting matters affecting the interim financial information and early modification of accounting procedures that the accountant believes might be improved. If review procedures are performed before the issuance of the quarterly data, they need not be repeated at the time an audit is performed.

Circumstances Requiring Modification of the Auditor's Report

.40 The auditor ordinarily need not modify the report on the audited financial statements to refer to his or her review or to refer to the interim financial information. The interim financial information has not been audited and is not required for presentation of financial position, results of operations, and cash flows in conformity with generally accepted accounting principles. Accordingly, the auditor need not report on the review of the interim financial information accompanying the audited financial statements.

.41 *Quarterly Data Required by SEC Regulation S-K.* The auditor's report on the audited financial statements should be expanded, however, if the selected quarterly financial data required by item 302(a) of Regulation S-K (*a*) are omitted or (*b*) have not been reviewed. For example, if the selected quarterly financial data required by item 302(a) are omitted, the auditor's report should include an additional paragraph, which might be worded as follows:

> The company has not presented the selected quarterly financial data, specified by item 302(a) of Regulation S-K, that the Securities and Exchange Commission requires as supplementary information to the basic financial statements.

If the selected quarterly financial data required by item 302(a) have not been reviewed, the auditor's report should include an additional paragraph, which might be worded as follows:

> The selected quarterly financial data on page xx contain information that we did not audit, and, accordingly, we do not express an opinion on that data. We attempted but were unable to review the quarterly data in accordance with standards established by the American Institute of Certified Public Accountants because we believe that the company's internal control for the preparation of interim financial information do not provide an adequate basis to enable us to complete such a review.

.42 *Voluntary or Required Presentations of Interim Financial Information.* The auditor's report on the audited financial statements should also be expanded in any of the following circumstances:

---

[18] If the interim financial information is included in an auditor-submitted document, the auditor should refer to section 551, for guidance.

a. Interim financial information included in a note to the financial statements of a public or nonpublic entity, including information that has been reviewed in accordance with the procedures specified in paragraphs .13 through .19, is not appropriately marked as unaudited.

b. Item 302(a) information that has not been reviewed is voluntarily presented by a public entity in a client-prepared document containing audited financial statements, and the information is not appropriately marked as not reviewed.

c. The interim financial information in *a* or *b* does not appear to be presented in conformity with generally accepted accounting principles (see paragraphs .30 through .32).

d. The interim financial information includes an indication that a review was made but fails to state that the review is substantially less in scope than an audit conducted in accordance with generally accepted auditing standards, the objective of which is an expression of opinion regarding the financial statements taken as a whole, and accordingly, no such opinion is expressed.

The auditor need not expand his or her report on the audited financial statements in the circumstances described in *c* and *d* if his or her separate review report, which refers to those circumstances, is presented with the information.

Other Matters

.43 It is not possible to specify the form or the content of the working papers the accountant should prepare in connection with a review of interim financial information because of the different circumstances of individual engagements. Ordinarily, the working papers should document the performance and results of the procedures set forth in paragraphs .13 through .19. See section 339, *Working Papers*, for further guidance concerning working papers.

Effective Date

.44 This section is effective for interim periods within fiscal years beginning after September 15, 1992. Reports issued or reissued after September 15, 1992 (including engagements based on procedures under SAS No. 36), should conform with the reporting guidance in this section. Earlier application is encouraged.

AU Section 800

COMPLIANCE AUDITING

. . . governmental entities and recipients of governmental financial assistance . . .

TABLE OF CONTENTS

Section		Paragraph
801	Compliance Auditing Considerations in Audits of Governmental Entities and Recipients of Governmental Financial Assistance	.01-.24
	Introduction and Applicability	.01-.02
	Effects of Laws on Financial Statements	.03-.07
	Government Auditing Standards	.08-.09
	Federal Audit Requirements	.10-.20
	Compliance Requirements Applicable to Federal Financial Assistance Programs	.12-.16
	Evaluating Results of Compliance Audit Procedures on Major Federal Financial Assistance Programs	.17-.20
	Communications Regarding Applicable Audit Requirements	.21-.23
	Effective Date	.24

AU Section 801

Compliance Auditing Considerations in Audits of Governmental Entities and Recipients of Governmental Financial Assistance

(Supersedes SAS No. 68)

Source: SAS No. 74; SAS No. 75.

Effective for audits of financial statements and of compliance with laws and regulations for fiscal periods ending after December 31, 1994, unless otherwise indicated.

Introduction and Applicability

.01 This section[1] is applicable when the auditor is engaged to audit a governmental entity under generally accepted auditing standards (GAAS), and engaged to test and report on compliance with laws and regulations under *Government Auditing Standards* (the Yellow Book) or in certain other circumstances involving governmental financial assistance,[2, 3] such as single or organization-wide audits or program-specific audits under certain federal or state audit regulations.[4]

---

[1] This section amends AT section 500, *Compliance Attestation*, to delete paragraph .02*d* and revise paragraph .02*c* as follows:

.02 This section does not—

c. Apply to engagements for which the objective is to report in accordance with AU section 801, *Compliance Auditing Considerations in Audits of Governmental Entities and Recipients of Governmental Financial Assistance*, unless the terms of the engagement specify an attestation report under this section.

Paragraphs .02*a* and.02*b* remain unchanged and paragraphs .02*e* and .02*f* are renumbered.

[2] Guidance for engagements related to management's written assertion about either (*a*) an entity's compliance with the requirements of specified laws, regulations, rules, or contracts not involving governmental financial assistance, or (*b*) the effectiveness of an entity's internal control structure over compliance with specified requirements is provided in AT section 500, *Compliance Attestation*.

[3] When engaged to perform an agreed-upon procedures engagement for which the objective is to report in accordance with this section, the auditor may consider the guidance in section 622, *Engagements to Apply Agreed-Upon Procedures to Specified Elements, Accounts, or Items of a Financial Statement*, or AT section 600, *Agreed-Upon Procedures Engagements*. [Footnote added, effective for reports on agreed-upon procedures engagements dated after April 30, 1996, by Statement on Auditing Standards No. 75.] (See section 622.)

[4] A single or organization-wide audit is an audit of an entity's financial statements and of compliance with regulations relating to governmental financial assistance. Examples are audits required by the Single Audit Act of 1984 and Office of Management and Budget (OMB) Circular A-128, *Audits of State and Local Governments*, OMB Circular A-133, *Audits of Institutions of Higher Education and Other Nonprofit Institutions*, or *the Connecticut Single Audit Act*. A program-specific audit is an audit of one governmental financial assistance program in accordance with federal or state laws, regulations or audit guides, such as the U.S. Department of Education's *Student Financial Assistance Audit Guide*, or the U.S. Department of Housing and Urban Development's (HUD's) *Consolidated Audit Guide for Audits of HUD Programs*, relative to that program. An auditor may also be engaged to test and report on compliance with other federal, state, and local laws and regulations that are beyond the scope of this section. (For additional guidance, see footnote 2.) [Footnote renumbered by the issuance of Statement on Auditing Standards No. 75, September 1995.]

.02 Specifically, this section provides general[5] guidance to the auditor to—

a. Apply the provisions of section 317, *Illegal Acts by Clients*, relative to detecting misstatements resulting from illegal acts related to laws and regulations that have a direct and material effect on the determination of financial statement amounts in audits of the financial statements of governmental entities and other recipients of governmental financial assistance (paragraphs .03 through .07).

b. Perform a financial audit in accordance with *Government Auditing Standards*, issued by the Comptroller General of the United States (paragraphs .08 and .09).[6]

c. Perform a single or organization-wide audit or a program-specific audit in accordance with federal audit requirements (paragraphs .10 through .20).

d. Communicate with management if the auditor becomes aware that the entity is subject to an audit requirement that may not be encompassed in the terms of his or her engagement (paragraphs .21 through .23).

Effects of Laws on Financial Statements

.03 The Governmental Accounting Standards Board's (GASB's) *Codification of Governmental Accounting and Financial Reporting Standards*, section 1200.103, recognizes that governmental entities generally are subject to a variety of laws and regulations that affect their financial statements.

> An important aspect of GAAP [generally accepted accounting principles] as applied to governments is the recognition of the variety of legal and contractual considerations typical of the government environment. These considerations underlie and are reflected in the fund structure, bases of accounting, and other principles and methods set forth here, and are a major factor distinguishing governmental accounting from commercial accounting.

For example, such laws and regulations may address the fund structure required by law, regulation, or bond covenant; procurement; debt limitations; and legal authority for transactions.

.04 Federal, state, and local governmental entities provide financial assistance to other entities, including not-for-profit organizations and business enterprises that are either primary recipients, subrecipients,[7] or beneficiaries.

---

[5] Specific guidance is provided in the AICPA Audit and Accounting Guide *Audits of State and Local Governmental Units*, and in Statement of Position (SOP) 92-9, *Audits of Not-for-Profit Organizations Receiving Federal Awards*. [Footnote renumbered by the issuance of Statement on Auditing Standards No. 75, September 1995.]

[6] In practice, *Government Auditing Standards*, or the Yellow Book, is sometimes referred to as *generally accepted government auditing standards* (GAGAS). *Government Auditing Standards* includes standards for financial and performance audits. The references to *Government Auditing Standards* in this section encompass only the standards that apply to financial audits, not the performance audit standards. The auditor should be aware that *Government Auditing Standards* is revised periodically and should ensure that the currently effective version is being followed. [Footnote renumbered by the issuance of Statement on Auditing Standards No. 75, September 1995.]

[7] A subrecipient is an entity that receives governmental financial assistance when the assistance is initially received by another entity (the primary recipient) that distributes the assistance for the government program that created and provided the assistance. As used in this section, *recipient* means either a primary recipient or a subrecipient. [Footnote renumbered by the issuance of Statement on Auditing Standards No. 75, September 1995.]

Among the forms of governmental financial assistance are grants of cash and other assets, loans, loan guarantees, and interest-rate subsidies.[8] By accepting such assistance, both governmental and nongovernmental entities may be subject to laws and regulations that may have a direct and material effect on the determination of amounts in their financial statements.

.05 Management is responsible for ensuring that the entity complies with the laws and regulations applicable to its activities. That responsibility encompasses the identification of applicable laws and regulations and the establishment of controls designed to provide reasonable assurance that the entity complies with those laws and regulations. The auditor's responsibility for testing and reporting on compliance with laws and regulations varies according to the terms of the engagement.

.06 Section 317 describes the auditor's responsibility, in an audit performed in accordance with GAAS, for considering laws and regulations and how they affect the audit. Thus, the auditor should design the audit to provide reasonable assurance that the financial statements are free of material misstatements resulting from violations of laws and regulations that have a direct and material effect on the determination of financial statement amounts.

.07 The auditor should obtain an understanding of the possible effects on financial statements of laws and regulations that are generally recognized by auditors to have a direct and material effect on the determination of amounts in an entity's financial statements. The auditor should also assess whether management has identified laws and regulations that have a direct and material effect on the determination of amounts in the entity's financial statements and obtain an understanding of the possible effects on the financial statements of such laws and regulations. The auditor may consider performing the following procedures in assessing such laws and regulations and in obtaining an understanding of their possible effects on the financial statements.

a. Consider knowledge about such laws and regulations obtained from prior years' audits.

b. Discuss such laws and regulations with the entity's chief financial officer, legal counsel, or grant administrators.

c. Obtain written representation from management regarding the completeness of management's identification.

d. Review the relevant portions of any directly related agreements, such as those related to grants and loans.

e. Review the minutes of meetings of the legislative body and governing board of the governmental entity being audited for the enactment of

---

[8] For purposes of this section, financial assistance, as defined by the Single Audit Act of 1984 and OMB Circular A-128, does not include contracts to provide goods or services to a governmental entity or arrangements in which a nongovernmental entity purchases insurance from the government. Federal awards, as defined by OMB Circular A-133, means financial assistance and federal cost-type contracts used to buy services or goods for the use of the federal government. Federal awards do not include procurement contracts to vendors under grants or contracts used to buy goods or services. For example, financial assistance does not include a contract to design and manufacture aircraft for the U.S. Air Force or the purchase of deposit insurance by a financial institution. In addition, although Medicaid funds paid by the federal government to states constitute financial assistance, most Medicaid arrangements between the states and health-care providers are contracts for services that are not considered to be financial assistance. [Footnote renumbered by the issuance of Statement on Auditing Standards No. 75, September 1995.]

laws and regulations that have a direct and material effect on the determination of amounts in the governmental entity's financial statements.

f. Inquire of the office of the federal, state, or local auditor, or other appropriate audit oversight organization about the laws and regulations applicable to entities within their jurisdiction, including statutes and uniform reporting requirements.

g. Review information about compliance requirements, such as the information included in the Compliance Supplements issued by OMB: *Compliance Supplement for Single Audits of State and Local Governments* and *Compliance Supplement for Audits of Institutions of Higher Learning and Other Non-Profit Institutions, Catalog of Federal Domestic Assistance*, issued by the Government Printing Office, and state and local policies and procedures.

Government Auditing Standards

.08 *Government Auditing Standards* contains standards for audits of government organizations, programs, activities, and functions and of government assistance received by contractors, not-for-profit organizations, and other nongovernment organizations. These standards, which include designing the audit to provide reasonable assurance of detecting material misstatements resulting from noncompliance with provisions of contracts or grant agreements that have a direct and material effect on the determination of financial statement amounts, are to be followed when required by law, regulation, agreement, contract, or policy.[9]

.09 For financial audits, *Government Auditing Standards* prescribes fieldwork and reporting standards beyond those required by GAAS. The general standards of *Government Auditing Standards* relate to qualifications of the staff, independence, due professional care, and quality control.

Federal Audit Requirements

.10 Although the scope and reporting requirements of an audit of a recipient of federal financial assistance in accordance with federal audit regulations vary, the audits generally have the following elements in common.

a. The audit is to be conducted in accordance with GAAS and *Government Auditing Standards.*

b. The auditor's consideration of internal control is to include obtaining and documenting an understanding of internal control established to ensure compliance with the laws and regulations applicable to the federal financial assistance. In some instances, federal audit regulations mandate a "test of controls" to evaluate the effectiveness of the design and operation of the policies and procedures in preventing or detecting material noncompliance.

---

[9] Some states have adopted regulations that require local governments within the states to have their audits conducted in accordance with *Government Auditing Standards*. In addition, some states require that recipients of state financial assistance be audited in accordance with *Government Auditing Standards*. [Footnote renumbered by the issuance of Statement on Auditing Standards No. 75, September 1995.]

c. The auditor is to issue a report on the consideration of internal control described above.

d. The auditor is to determine and report on whether the federal financial assistance has been administered in accordance with applicable laws and regulations (that is, compliance requirements).[10]

.11 A recipient of federal financial assistance may be subject to a single or organization-wide audit or to a program-specific audit. A number of federal audit regulations permit the recipient to "elect" to have a program-specific audit, whereas other federal audit regulations require a program-specific audit in certain circumstances. In planning the audit, the auditor should determine and consider the specific federal audit requirements[11] applicable to the engagement, including the issuance of additional reports. As noted in paragraph .10 of this section, federal audit regulations for both single or organization-wide audits and program-specific audits generally require consideration of internal control beyond what is normally required by GAAS and *Government Auditing Standards* and a determination of whether applicable compliance requirements have been met.

Compliance Requirements Applicable to Federal Financial Assistance Programs

.12 Compliance requirements applicable to federal financial assistance programs are usually one of two types: general and specific. General requirements involve national policy and apply to all or most federal financial assistance programs.[12]

.13 Specific requirements apply to a particular federal program and generally arise from statutory requirements and regulations. The OMB's Compliance Supplements set forth general and specific requirements for many of the federal programs awarded to state and local governments and to not-for-profit organizations, as well as suggested audit procedures to test for compliance with the requirements.

.14 For program-specific audits, the auditor should consult federal grantor agency audit guides to identify general requirements that are statutory and regulatory requirements pertaining to certain federal programs, specific requirements for a particular program, and suggested audit procedures to test for compliance with the requirements.

.15 In addition to those identified in the OMB's Compliance Supplements or federal grantor agency audit guides, specific requirements may also be enumerated in grant agreements or contracts.

.16 Generally, the auditor is required to determine whether the recipient has complied with the general and specific requirements. The form of the re-

---

[10] In accordance with section 333A, *Client Representations*, the auditor should obtain written representations from management about matters related to federal financial assistance as part of the compliance audit. [Footnote renumbered by the issuance of Statement on Auditing Standards No. 75, September 1995.]

[11] Such requirements may be set out in an engagement letter or audit contract. In some instances, a written engagement letter is required by the federal grantor agency. [Footnote renumbered by the issuance of Statement on Auditing Standards No. 75, September 1995.]

[12] General requirements also may be referred to as *common* requirements. Detailed guidance on evaluating the results of testing general requirements can be found in the AICPA Audit and Accounting Guide *Audits of State and Local Governmental Units*, and in SOP 92-9, [Footnote renumbered by the issuance of Statement on Auditing Standards No. 75, September 1995.]

port and the required level of assurance to be provided in the report may vary, depending on the requirements of a particular agency or program. For example, if reporting on compliance requirements, the auditor may be required to report findings relating to compliance with those requirements or the auditor may be required to express an opinion on whether the recipient has complied with the requirements applicable to its major[13] federal financial assistance programs.[14]

Evaluating Results of Compliance Audit Procedures on Major Federal Financial Assistance Programs

.17 In evaluating whether an entity has complied with laws and regulations that, if not complied with, could have a material effect on each major federal financial assistance program, the auditor should consider the effect of identified instances of noncompliance on each such program. In doing so, the auditor should consider—

a. The frequency of noncompliance identified in the audit.

b. The adequacy of a primary recipient's system for monitoring subrecipients and the possible effect on the program of any noncompliance identified by the primary recipient or the auditors of the subrecipients.

c. Whether any instances of noncompliance identified in the audit resulted in questioned costs, as discussed below, and, if they did, whether questioned costs are material to the program.[15]

.18 The criteria for classifying a cost as a questioned cost vary from one federal agency to another. In evaluating the effect of questioned costs on the opinion on compliance, the auditor considers the best estimate of total costs questioned for each major federal financial assistance program (hereafter referred to as *likely questioned costs*), not just the questioned costs specifically identified (hereafter referred to as *known questioned costs*). When using audit sampling, as defined in section 350, *Audit Sampling*, in testing compliance, the auditor should project the amount of known questioned costs identified in the sample to the items in the major federal financial assistance program from which the sample was selected.

.19 Regardless of the auditor's opinion on compliance, federal audit regulations may require him or her to report any instances of noncompliance found and any resulting questioned costs. In reporting instances of noncompliance, the auditor should follow the provisions of *Government Auditing Standards*. For purposes of reporting questioned costs, the auditor is not required to report likely questioned costs; rather, the auditor should report only known questioned costs.

---

[13] A major federal financial assistance program is defined by a federal regulation or law or by the federal grantor agency's audit guide. [Footnote renumbered by the issuance of Statement on Auditing Standards No. 75, September 1995.]

[14] Detailed testing and reporting guidance on single or organization-wide audits and program-specific audits is provided in the AICPA Audit and Accounting Guide *Audits of State and Local Governmental Units* and in SOP 92-9. [Footnote renumbered by the issuance of Statement on Auditing Standards No. 75, September 1995.]

[15] In auditing compliance with requirements governing major federal financial assistance programs, the auditor's consideration of materiality differs from that in an audit of the financial statements in accordance with GAAS. [Footnote renumbered by the issuance of Statement on Auditing Standards No. 75, September 1995.]

.20 When evaluating the results of compliance audit procedures on federal financial assistance programs, the auditor also should consider whether identified instances of noncompliance affect his or her opinion on the entity's financial statements (see paragraph .06).

Communications Regarding Applicable Audit Requirements

.21 Management is responsible for obtaining audits that satisfy relevant legal, regulatory, or contractual requirements. Auditors should exercise due professional care in ensuring that they and management understand the type of engagement to be performed. If a proposal, contract, or engagement letter is used, an auditor should consider including in it a statement about the type of engagement and whether the engagement is intended to meet specific audit requirements.

.22 GAAS do not require the auditor to perform procedures beyond those he or she considers necessary to obtain sufficient competent evidential matter to form a basis for the opinion on the financial statements. However, if during a GAAS audit of the financial statements the auditor becomes aware that the entity is subject to an audit requirement that may not be encompassed in the terms of the engagement, the auditor should communicate to management and the audit committee, or to others with equivalent authority and responsibility, that an audit in accordance with GAAS may not satisfy the relevant legal, regulatory, or contractual requirements.[16] For example, the auditor will be required to make this communication if an entity engages an auditor to perform an audit of its financial statements in accordance with GAAS and the auditor becomes aware that by law, regulation, or contractual agreement the entity also is required to have an audit performed in accordance with one or more of the following:

a. *Government Auditing Standards*

b. The Single Audit Act of 1984 and OMB Circular A-128, *Audits of State and Local Governments*

c. OMB Circular A-133, *Audits of Institutions of Higher Education and Other Nonprofit Institutions*

d. Other compliance audit requirements, such as state or local laws or program-specific audits under federal audit guides

.23 The communication required by paragraph .22 of this section may be oral or written. If the communication is oral, the auditor should document the communication in the working papers. The auditor should consider how the client's actions in response to such communication relate to other aspects of the audit, including the potential effect on the financial statements and on the auditor's report on those financial statements. Specifically, the auditor should consider management's actions (such as not arranging for an audit that meets the applicable requirements) in relation to the guidance in section 317.

---

[16] For entities that do not have an audit committee, "others with equivalent authority or responsibility" may include the board of directors, the board of trustees, the owner in owner-managed entities, the city council, or the legislative standing committee. [Footnote renumbered by the issuance of Statement on Auditing Standards No. 75, September 1995.]

Effective Date

.24 The provisions of this section are effective for audits of financial statements and of compliance with laws and regulations for fiscal periods ending after December 31, 1994. Early application of this section is encouraged.

AU Section 900

SPECIAL REPORTS OF THE COMMITTEE ON AUDITING PROCEDURE

. . . public warehouses—controls and auditing procedures for goods held . . .

TABLE OF CONTENTS

AU Section 901

Public Warehouses—Controls and Auditing Procedures for Goods Held*

Sources: SAS No. 1, section 901; SAS No. 43.

Issue date, unless otherwise indicated: November, 1972.

Introduction

.01 This section discusses controls of a public warehouse, the procedures of its independent auditor with respect to goods in the warehouse's custody, and auditing procedures performed by the independent auditor of the owner of goods in the warehouse.[1] [As amended, (by replacing paragraphs .01 through .05 with a new paragraph .01), effective after August 31, 1982, by Statement on Auditing Standards No. 43.]

General Considerations

.02 The management of a business has the responsibility for the proper recording of transactions in its books of account, for the safeguarding of its assets, and for the substantial accuracy and adequacy of its financial statements. The independent auditor is not an insurer or guarantor; his responsibility is to express a professional opinion on the financial statements he has audited.[2] [Formerly paragraph .06, number changed by issuance of Statement on Auditing Standards No. 43, effective after August 31, 1982.]

Summary of Recommendations

.03 The Committee recommends that the independent auditor of the warehouseman:

a. Obtain an understanding of controls, relating to the accountability for and the custody of all goods placed in the warehouse and perform tests of controls to evaluate their effectiveness.

b. Test the warehouseman's records relating to accountability for all goods placed in his custody.

c. Test the warehouseman's accountability under recorded outstanding warehouse receipts.

d. Observe physical counts of the goods in custody, wherever practicable and reasonable, and reconcile his tests of such counts with records of goods stored.

---

* Title revised, February 1997, to reflect conforming changes necessary due to the issuance of Statement on Auditing Standards No. 78.

[1] This section reports the conclusions of a 1966 study of the AICPA Committee on Auditing Procedure on the accountability of warehousemen for goods stored in public warehouses. [Footnote changed by issuance of Statement on Auditing Standards No. 43.]

[2] See section 110.

e. Confirm accountability (to the extent considered necessary) by direct communication with the holders of warehouse receipts.

The independent auditor should apply such other procedures as he considers necessary in the circumstances. [Formerly paragraph .07, number changed by issuance of Statement on Auditing Standards No. 43, effective after August 31, 1982. Subsequently, reference changed by the issuance of Statement on Auditing Standards No. 48.]

.04 Warehousing activities are diverse because the warehoused goods are diverse, the purposes of placing goods in custody are varied, and the scope of operations of warehouses is not uniform. The independent auditor has the responsibility to exercise his judgment in determining what procedures, including those recommended in this report, are necessary in the circumstances to afford a reasonable basis for his opinion on the financial statements.[3] [Formerly paragraph .08, number changed by issuance of Statement on Auditing Standards No. 43, effective after August 31, 1982.]

.05 The following sections of this report describe those aspects of warehousing operations of primary concern to independent auditors, suggest elements of internal control for warehousemen, and offer the Committee's recommendations as to procedures of the independent auditor. [Formerly paragraph .09, number changed by issuance of Statement on Auditing Standards No. 43, effective after August 31, 1982.]

Public Warehouse Operations

Types of Warehouses

.06 A warehouse may be described as a facility operated by a warehouseman whose business is the maintaining of effective custody of goods for others. [Formerly paragraph .10, number changed by issuance of Statement on Auditing Standards No. 43, effective after August 31, 1982.]

.07 Warehouses may be classified functionally as terminal warehouses or field warehouses:

Terminal Warehouse. The principal economic function of a terminal warehouse is to furnish storage. It may, however, perform other functions, including packaging and billing. It may be used to store a wide variety of goods or only a particular type of commodity.

Field Warehouse. A field warehouse is established in space leased by the warehouseman on the premises of the owner of the goods or the premises of a customer of the owner. In most circumstances all or most of the personnel at the warehouse location are employed by the warehouseman from among the employees of the owner (or customer), usually from among those who previously have been responsible for custody and handling of the goods. Field warehousing is essentially a financing arrangement, rather than a storage operation. The warehouse is established to permit the warehouseman to take and maintain custody of goods and issue warehouse receipts to be used as collateral for a loan or other form of credit.

Warehouses may be classified also by types of goods stored. Foods and other perishable products may be stored in refrigerated warehouses, constructed and equipped to meet controlled temperature and special handling requirements. Certain bulk commodities, such as various agricultural products and chemicals,

---

[3] See section 326. (Reference changed by issuance of Statement on Auditing Standards No. 31.)

are stored in commodity warehouses; these warehouses often are designed and equipped to store only one commodity, and fungible goods frequently are commingled without regard to ownership. A wide variety of goods, usually not requiring special storage facilities, is stored in general merchandise warehouses. Some warehouses confine their activities to storing furniture, other household goods, and personal effects. [Formerly paragraph .11, number changed by issuance of Statement on Auditing Standards No. 43, effective after August 31, 1982.]

Warehouse Receipts

.08 A basic document in warehousing is the warehouse receipt. Article 7 of the Uniform Commercial Code regulates the issuance of warehouse receipts, prescribes certain terms that must be contained in such receipts, provides for their negotiation and transfer, and establishes the rights of receipt holders. [Formerly paragraph .12, number changed by issuance of Statement on Auditing Standards No. 43, effective after August 31, 1982.]

.09 Warehouse receipts may be in negotiable form or non-negotiable form and may be used as evidence of collateral for loans or other forms of credit. Goods represented by a negotiable warehouse receipt may be released only upon surrender of the receipt to the warehouseman for cancellation or endorsement, whereas goods represented by a non-negotiable receipt may be released upon valid instructions without the need for surrender of the receipt. Other important ways in which the two kinds of receipts differ concern the manner in which the right of possession to the goods they represent may be transferred from one party to another and the rights acquired by bona fide purchasers of the receipts. [Formerly paragraph .13, number changed by issuance of Statement on Auditing Standards No. 43, effective after August 31, 1982.]

.10 Since goods covered by non-negotiable receipts may be released without surrender of the receipts, such outstanding receipts are not necessarily an indication of accountability on the part of the warehouseman or of evidence of ownership by the depositor. Since goods are frequently withdrawn piecemeal, the warehouseman's accountability at any given time is for the quantity of goods for which receipts have been issued minus the quantities released against properly authorized withdrawals. [Formerly paragraph .14, number changed by issuance of Statement on Auditing Standards No. 43, effective after August 31, 1982.]

.11 Article 7 of the Uniform Commercial Code, in addition to provisions with respect to the issuance and contents of warehouse receipts, contains provisions with respect to, among other things, the storage and release of warehoused goods, the standard of care to be exercised by the warehouseman, warehouseman's liability, and liens for the warehouseman's charges and expenses and the manner in which they may be enforced. [Formerly paragraph .15, number changed by issuance of Statement on Auditing Standards No. 43, effective after August 31, 1982.]

Government Regulation

.12 There are various other statutes and regulations, applicable in special situations, relating to the rights and duties of warehousemen and the operation of warehouses. Among the more important are (*a*) the United States Warehouse Act and the regulations adopted thereunder by the Department of Agriculture, providing for licensing and regulation of warehouses storing certain agricultural commodities, (*b*) the regulations adopted by commodity exchanges licensed under the United States Commodity Exchange Act, providing for issuance and registration of receipts and licensing and regulation of warehouses, and (*c*) the Internal Revenue Code and the Tariff Act of 1930, and regulations adopted thereunder, relating respectively to United States Revenue Bonded Warehouses and United States Customs Bonded Warehouses, providing for licensing, bonding, and regulation of such warehouses. In addition, there are statutes and regulations in various states relating to licensing, bonding, insurance, and other matters. [Formerly paragraph .16, number changed by issuance of Statement on Auditing Standards No. 43, effective after August 31, 1982.]

The Warehouseman

Controls

.13 Goods held in custody for others are not owned by the warehouseman and, therefore, do not appear as assets in his financial statements. Similarly, the related custodial responsibility does not appear as a liability. However, as in other businesses, the warehouseman is exposed to the risk of loss or claims for damage stemming from faulty performance of his operating functions. Faulty performance may take the form of loss or improper release of goods, improper issuance of warehouse receipts, failure to maintain effective custody of goods so that lenders' preferential liens are lost, and other forms. [Formerly paragraph .17, number changed by issuance of Statement on Auditing Standards No. 43, effective after August 31, 1982.]

.14 The recommendation herein that the independent auditor of the warehouseman obtain an understanding of relevant controls and perform tests of controls to evaluate their effectiveness is based upon the important relationship of such controls to the custodial responsibilities of the warehouseman, which are not reflected in his financial statements. Significant unrecorded liabilities may arise if these custodial responsibilities are not discharged properly. [Formerly paragraph .18, number changed by issuance of Statement on Auditing Standards No. 43, effective after August 31, 1982. Paragraph amended to reflect the conforming changes necessary due to the issuance of Statement on Auditing Standards Nos. 53 through 62.]

.15 Whether and to what extent the suggested controls that follow may be applicable to a particular warehouse operation will depend on the nature of the operation, of the goods stored, and of the warehouseman's organization. Appropriate segregation of duties in the performance of the respective operating functions should be emphasized.

Receiving, Storing, and Delivering Goods

Receipts should be issued for all goods admitted into storage.

Receiving clerks should prepare reports as to all goods received. The receiving report should be compared with quantities shown on bills of lading or other documents received from the owner or other outside sources by an employee independent of receiving, storing, and shipping.

Goods received should be inspected, counted, weighed, measured, or graded in accordance with applicable requirements. There should be a periodic check of the accuracy of any mechanical facilities used for these purposes.

Unless commingling is unavoidable, such as with fungible goods, goods should be stored so that each lot is segregated and identified with the pertinent warehouse receipt. The warehouse office records should show the location of the goods represented by each outstanding receipt.

Instructions should be issued that goods may be released only on proper authorization which, in the case of negotiable receipts, includes surrender of the receipt.

Access to the storage area should be limited to those employees whose duties require it, and the custody of keys should be controlled.

Periodic statements to customers should identify the goods held and request that discrepancies be reported to a specified employee who is not connected with receiving, storing, and delivery of goods.

The stored goods should be physically counted or tested periodically, and quantities agreed to the records by an employee independent of the storage function; the extent to which this is done may depend on the nature of the goods, the rate of turnover, and the effectiveness of other internal control structure policies and procedures.

Where the goods held are perishable, a regular schedule for inspection of condition should be established.

Protective devices such as burglar alarms, fire alarms, sprinkler systems, and temperature and humidity controls should be inspected regularly.

Goods should be released from the warehouse only on the basis of written instructions received from an authorized employee who does not have access to the goods.

Counts of goods released as made by stock clerks should be independently checked by shipping clerks or others and the two counts should be compared before the goods are released.

Warehouse Receipts

Prenumbered receipt forms should be used, and procedures established for accounting for all forms used and for cancellation of negotiable receipts when goods have been delivered.

Unused forms should be safeguarded against theft or misuse and their custody assigned to a responsible employee who is not authorized to prepare or sign receipts.

Receipt forms should be furnished only to authorized persons, and in a quantity limited to the number required for current use.

The signer of receipts should ascertain that the receipts are supported by receiving records or other underlying documents.

Receipts should be prepared and completed in a manner designed to prevent alteration.

Authorized signers should be a limited number of responsible employees.

Insurance

The adequacy, as to both type and amount, of insurance coverage carried by the warehouseman should be reviewed at appropriate intervals.

[Formerly paragraph .19, number changed by issuance of Statement on Auditing Standards No. 43, effective after August 31, 1982.]

Additional Controls for Field Warehouses

.16 As indicated earlier, the purpose of field warehousing differs from terminal warehousing. Operating requirements also may differ because a field warehouseman may operate at a large number of locations. [Formerly paragraph .20, number changed by issuance of Statement on Auditing Standards No. 43, effective after August 31, 1982.]

.17 In field warehousing, controls are applied at two points: the field location and the warehouseman's central office. At the field location, the controls as to receipt, storage, and delivery of goods and issuance of warehouse receipts generally will comprise the controls suggested above, with such variations as may be appropriate in light of the requirements, and available personnel, at the respective locations. Only non-negotiable warehouse receipts should be issued from field locations, and the receipt forms should be furnished to the field locations by the central office in quantities limited to current requirements. [Formerly paragraph .21, number changed by issuance of Statement on Auditing Standards No. 43, effective after August 31, 1982.]

.18 The central office should investigate and approve the field warehousing arrangements, and exercise control as to custody and release of goods and issuance of receipts at the field locations. Controls suggested for the central office are the following:

Consideration of the business reputation and financial standing of the depositor.

Preparation of a field warehouse contract in accordance with the particular requirements of the depositor and the lender.

Determination that the leased warehouse premises meet the physical requirements for segregation and effective custody of goods.

Satisfaction as to legal matters relative to the lease of the warehouse premises.

Investigation and bonding of the employees at the field locations.

Providing employees at field locations with written instructions covering their duties and responsibilities.

Maintenance of inventory records at the central office showing the quantity (and stated value, where applicable) of goods represented by each outstanding warehouse receipt.

Examination of the field warehouse by representatives of the central office. These examinations would include inspection of the facilities, observation as to adherence to prescribed procedures, physical counts or tests of goods in custody and reconcilement of quantities to records at the central office and at field locations, accounting for all receipt forms furnished to the field locations, and confirmation (on a test basis, where appropriate) of outstanding warehouse receipts with the registered holders.

[Formerly paragraph .22, number changed by issuance of Statement on Auditing Standards No. 43, effective after August 31, 1982.]

Procedures of the Independent Auditor

.19 The Committee recommends that the independent auditor of the warehouseman:

a. Obtain an understanding of controls, relating to the accountability for and the custody of all goods placed in the warehouse and perform tests of controls to evaluate their effectiveness.

b. Test the warehouseman's records relating to accountability for all goods placed in his custody.

c. Test the warehouseman's accountability under recorded outstanding warehouse receipts.

d. Observe physical counts of the goods in custody, wherever practicable and reasonable, and reconcile his tests of such counts with records of goods stored.

e. Confirm accountability (to the extent considered necessary) by direct communication with the holders of warehouse receipts.

The independent auditor should apply such other procedures as he considers necessary in the circumstances. [Formerly paragraph .23, number changed by issuance of Statement on Auditing Standards No. 43, effective after August 31, 1982. Subsequently, reference changed by the issuance of Statement on Auditing Standards No. 48.]

.20 The auditor's procedures relating to accountability might include, on a test basis, comparison of documentary evidence of goods received and delivered with warehouse receipts records, accounting for issued and unissued warehouse receipts by number, and comparison of the records of goods stored with billings for storage. In some circumstances, the auditor may consider it necessary to obtain confirmation from the printer as to the serial numbers of receipt forms supplied. [Formerly paragraph .24, number changed by issuance of Statement on Auditing Standards No. 43, effective after August 31, 1982. Subsequently, reference changed by the issuance of Statement on Auditing Standards No. 48.]

.21 In the case of a field warehouseman where goods are stored at many scattered locations, the independent auditor may satisfy himself that the warehouseman's physical count procedures are adequate by observing the procedures at certain selected locations. The amount of testing required will be dependent upon the effectiveness of both design and operation of controls. [Formerly paragraph .25, number changed by issuance of Statement on Auditing Standards No. 43, effective after August 31, 1982.]

.22 The confirmation of negotiable receipts with holders may be impracticable, since the identity of the holders usually is not known to the warehouseman. Confirmation with the depositor to whom the outstanding receipt was originally issued, however, would be evidential matter of the accountability for certain designated goods. It should be recognized, too, that as to both negotiable and non-negotiable receipts, confirmation may not be conclusive in the light of the possibility of issued but unrecorded receipts. In some circumstances, it may be desirable to request confirmations from former depositors who are not currently holders of record. [Formerly paragraph .26, number changed by issuance of Statement on Auditing Standards No. 43, effective after August 31, 1982.]

.23 The independent auditor should review the nature and extent of the warehouseman's insurance coverage and the adequacy of any reserves for losses under damage claims. [Formerly paragraph .27, number changed by issuance of Statement on Auditing Standards No. 43, effective after August 31, 1982.]

Controls and Auditing Procedures for Owner's Goods Stored in Public Warehouses

.24 The following paragraphs provide guidance on the controls for the owner of the goods and on the auditing procedures to be employed by his independent auditor. [As amended, (formerly paragraph .28) effective after August 31, 1982, by Statement on Auditing Standards No. 43.]

Controls

.25 The controls of the owner should be designed to provide reasonable safeguards over his goods in a warehouseman's custody. Ordinarily, the controls should include an investigation of the warehouseman before the goods are placed in custody, and a continuing evaluation of the warehouseman's performance in maintaining custody of the goods. [Formerly paragraph .29, number changed by issuance of Statement on Auditing Standards No. 43, effective after August 31, 1982.]

.26 Among the suggested controls that may be comprehended in an investigation of the warehouseman before the goods are placed in his custody are the following:

Consideration of the business reputation and financial standing of the warehouseman.

Inspection of the physical facilities.

Inquiries as to the warehouseman's controls and whether the warehouseman holds goods for his own account.

Inquiries as to type and adequacy of the warehouseman's insurance.

Inquiries as to government or other licensing and bonding requirements and the nature, extent, and results of any inspection by government or other agencies.

Review of the warehouseman's financial statements and related reports of independent auditors. [Formerly paragraph .30, number changed by issuance of Statement on Auditing Standards No. 43, effective after August 31, 1982.]

.27 After the goods are placed in the warehouse, suggested controls that may be applied periodically by the owner in evaluating the warehouseman's performance in maintaining custody of goods include the following:

Review and update the information developed from the investigation described above.

Physical counts (or test counts) of the goods, wherever practicable and reasonable (may not be practicable in the case of fungible goods).

Reconcilement of quantities shown on statements received from the warehouseman with the owner's records.

In addition, he should review his own insurance, if any, on goods in the custody of the warehouseman. [Formerly paragraph .31, number changed by issuance of Statement on Auditing Standards No. 43, effective after August 31, 1982.]

Procedures of the Independent Auditor

.28 Section 331.14, describes the procedures that the auditor should apply if inventories are held in public warehouses. [As amended, (formerly paragraph .32) by Statement on Auditing Standards No. 43, effective after August 31, 1982.]

AU
APPENDIXES

. . . historical background . . . analysis of international standards on auditing . . . cross-references for auditing interpretations . . . audit and accounting guides, and statements of position . . . changes in statements on auditing standards . . .

TABLE OF CONTENTS

AU Appendix A

Historical Background

The "Bulletins" of 1917, 1918, 1929, and 1936

In 1917, the American Institute of Certified Public Accountants, then known as the American Institute of Accountants, at the request of the Federal Trade Commission, prepared "a memorandum on balance-sheet audits," which the Commission approved and transmitted to the Federal Reserve Board.

The Federal Reserve Board, after giving the memorandum its provisional endorsement, published it in the *Federal Reserve Bulletin* of April 1917; reprints were widely disseminated for the consideration of "banks, bankers, banking associations; merchants, manufacturers, and associations of manufacturers; auditors, accountants, and associations of accountants" in pamphlet form with the title of "Uniform Accounting: a Tentative Proposal Submitted by the Federal Reserve Board."

In 1918, it was reissued under the same sponsorship, with a new title—"Approved Methods for the Preparation of Balance-Sheet Statements." There was practically no change from 1917 except that, as indicated by the respective titles and corresponding change in the preface, instead of the objective of "a uniform system of accounting to be adopted by manufacturing and merchandising concerns," the new objective was "the preparation of balance-sheet statements" for the same businesses.

In 1929, a special committee of the American Institute undertook revision of the earlier pamphlet in the light of the experience of the past decade; again under the auspices of the Federal Reserve Board, the revised pamphlet was issued in 1929 as "Verification of Financial Statements."

The preface of the 1929 pamphlet spoke of its predecessors as having been criticized, on the one hand, by some accountants for being "more comprehensive than their conception of the so-called balance-sheet audit," and, on the other hand, by other accountants because "the procedure would not bring out all the desired information." This recognition of opposing views evidenced the growing realization of the impracticability of uniform procedures to fit the variety of situations encountered in practice. Of significance is the appearance in the opening paragraph of "General Instructions" in the 1929 publication of the statement:

> The extent of the verification will be determined by the conditions in each concern. In some cases, the auditor may find it necessary to verify a substantial portion or all of the transactions recorded upon the books. In others, where the system of internal check is good, tests only may suffice. The responsibility for the extent of the work required must be assumed by the auditor.

Between 1932 and 1934, there was correspondence, dealing with both accounting and auditing matters, between the Institute's special committee on cooperation with stock exchanges and the committee on stock list of the New York Stock Exchange. The views expressed were an important development in the recognition of the position of accountancy in finance and business. The series of letters was published in 1934 under the title *Audits of Corporate Accounts*.

In 1936, a committee of the Institute prepared and published a further revision of the earlier pamphlets under the title of "Examination of Financial Statements by Independent Public Accountants." The Institute availed itself of the views of persons outside the ranks of the profession whose opinions would be helpful, but the authority behind and responsibility for the publication of the pamphlet rested wholly with the Institute as the authoritative representative of a profession that had by that time become well established in the business community.

In the 1936 revision, aside from the very briefly noted "Modifications of Program for Larger or Smaller Companies," the detailed procedures were restrictively stated to be an "outline of examination of financial statements of a small or moderate size company." Moreover, the nature and extent of such examinations were based on the purpose of the examination, the required detail to be reported on, the type of business, and, most important of all, the system of internal control; variations in the extent of the examination were specifically related to "the size of the organization and the personnel employed" and were said to be "essentially a matter of judgment which must be exercised by the accountant."

It is possible from the foregoing narrative to trace the development of the profession's view of an audit based on the experience of three decades. The succession of titles is illustrative. The earliest ambition for "uniform accounting" was quickly realized to be unattainable, and the same listed procedures were related instead to "balance-sheet statements." Then, with the gradually greater emphasis on periodic earnings, the earlier restrictive consideration of the balance sheet was superseded in the 1929 title, "Verification of Financial Statements," by according the income statement at least equal status. When in turn the 1936 revision was undertaken, there was a growing realization that, with the complexity of modern business and the need of the independent auditor to rely on testing, such a word as "verification" was not an accurate portrayal of the independent auditor's function. Accordingly, the bulletin of that year was stated to cover an "examination" of financial statements.

Statements on Auditing Procedure

The Committee on Auditing Procedure had its beginning on January 30, 1939, when the executive committee of the Institute authorized the appointment of a small committee "to examine into auditing procedure and other related questions in the light of recent public discussion."

On May 9 of that year, the report "Extensions of Auditing Procedure" of this special committee was adopted by the Council of the Institute and authority given for its publication and distribution, and in the same year the bylaws were amended to create a standing Committee on Auditing Procedure.

In 1941, the executive committee authorized the issuance to Institute members, in pamphlet form, of the "Statements on Auditing Procedure," prepared by the Committee on Auditing Procedure, previously published only in *The Journal of Accountancy*.

The "Statements on Auditing Procedure" were designed to guide the independent auditor in the exercise of his judgment in the application of auditing procedures. In no sense were they intended to take the place of auditing textbooks; by their very nature textbooks must deal in a general way with the description of procedures and refinement of detail rather than the variety of circumstances encountered in practice that require the independent auditor to exercise his judgment.

Largely to meet this need, the Institute began the series of Statements on Auditing Procedure. The first of these presented the report of the original special committee, as modified and approved, at the Institute's annual meeting on September 19, 1939, and issued under the title of "Extensions of Auditing Procedure."

Statement No. 1 presented conclusions drawn from the experience and tradition of the profession which largely furnished the foundation for the Committee's present structural outline of auditing standards; the other Statements on Auditing Procedure appropriately fit into that structural outline.

The "Codification of Statements on Auditing Procedure" was issued by the Committee on Auditing Procedure in 1951 to consolidate the features of the first 24 pronouncements which were of continuing usefulness.

When the Securities and Exchange Commission adopted the requirement that a representation on compliance with generally accepted auditing standards be included in the independent auditor's report on financial statements filed with the Commission, it became apparent that a pronouncement was needed to define these standards. Accordingly, the Committee undertook a special study of auditing standards (as distinguished from auditing procedures) and submitted a report that was published in October 1947 under the title "Tentative Statement of Auditing Standards—Their Generally Accepted Significance and Scope." The recommendations of this brochure ceased to be tentative when, at the September 1948 meeting, the membership of the Institute approved the summarized statement of auditing standards.

In 1954 the "tentative" brochure was replaced by the booklet *Generally Accepted Auditing Standards—Their Significance and Scope*, which was issued as a special report of the Committee on Auditing Procedure. This pronouncement also gave recognition to the approval of Statement on Auditing Procedure No. 23 (Revised), "Clarification of Accountant's Report When Opinion Is Omitted" (1949) and the issuance of the "Codification" (1951).

Statement on Auditing Procedure No. 33 was issued in 1963 as a consolidation of, and a replacement for, the following pronouncements of the Committee on Auditing Procedure: Internal Control (1949), Generally Accepted Auditing Standards (1954), Codification of Statements on Auditing Procedure (1951), and Statements on Auditing Procedure Nos. 25–32, which were issued between 1951 and 1963. Statement No. 33 was a codification of earlier Committee pronouncements which the Committee believed to be of continuing interest to the independent auditor.

Statements on Auditing Standards

After issuance of Statement on Auditing Procedure No. 33, 21 additional Statements on Auditing Procedure, Nos. 34 to 54, were issued by the Committee on Auditing Procedure. In November 1972, these pronouncements were codified in Statement on Auditing Standards No. 1, Codification of Auditing Standards and Procedures. Also, in 1972, the name of the Committee was changed to the Auditing Standards Executive Committee to recognize its role as the AICPA's senior technical committee charged with interpreting generally accepted auditing standards.

The Auditing Standards Executive Committee issued 22 additional statements through No. 23. These statements were incorporated in the AICPA's looseleaf service, *Professional Standards*, as issued. The looseleaf service began in 1974 and is administered by the AICPA staff. It provides a continuous codification of Statements on Auditing Standards.

The Auditing Standards Board

As a result of the recommendations of the Commission on Auditors' Responsibilities, an independent study group appointed by the AICPA, a special committee was formed to study the structure of the AICPA's auditing standard-setting activity. In May 1978, the AICPA Council adopted the recommendations of that committee to restructure the Committee. Accordingly, in October 1978 the Auditing Standards Board was formed as the successor to prior senior technical committees on auditing matters. The Board was given the following charge:

> The AICPA Auditing Standards Board shall be responsible for the promulgation of auditing standards and procedures to be observed by members of the AICPA in accordance with the Institute's rules of conduct.
>
> The board shall be alert to new opportunities for auditors to serve the public, both by the assumption of new responsibilities and by improved ways of meeting old ones, and shall as expeditiously as possible develop standards and procedures that will enable the auditor to assume those responsibilities.
>
> Auditing standards and procedures promulgated by the board shall—
>
> *a.* Define the nature and extent of the auditor's responsibilities.
>
> *b.* Provide guidance to the auditor in carrying out his duties, enabling him to express an opinion on the reliability of the representations on which he is reporting.
>
> *c.* Make special provision, where appropriate, to meet the needs of small enterprises.
>
> *d.* Have regard to the costs which they impose on society in relation to the benefits reasonably expected to be derived from the audit function.
>
> The auditing standards board shall provide auditors with all possible guidance in the implementation of its pronouncements, by means of interpretations of its statements, by the issuance of guidelines, and by any other means available to it.

AU Appendix B

Analysis of International Standards on Auditing

This analysis was prepared by Dr. Kay Tatum, University of Miami, and the Auditing Standards Division staff. This analysis is not authoritative; but is prepared for informational purposes only. It has not been acted on or reviewed by the Auditing Standards Board.

An independent auditor practicing in the United States may be engaged to audit financial statements in accordance with the International Standards on Auditing (ISAs) issued by the International Auditing Practice Committee of the International Federation of Accountants (IFAC). In those circumstances, the U.S. auditor should comply with both the ISAs and the Statements on Auditing Standards (SASs). An engagement of this nature is normally conducted by performing an audit in accordance with the U.S. SASs plus performing the additional procedures required by the ISAs. Because a U.S. auditor should plan and perform audit engagements in accordance with the SASs at a minimum, an analysis of where the SASs go beyond the ISAs has not been prepared.

The purpose of this Appendix is to assist the U.S. auditor in planning and performing an engagement in accordance with the ISAs. This document identifies the sections and paragraphs, if applicable, within the ISAs that may require additional procedures and documentation or that may be in conflict with the SASs. A brief description of how the international standard differs from the U.S. standard is provided. However, to fully understand how the ISA might affect the nature, timing, and extent of the procedures performed in an engagement in accordance with the SASs, *the auditor should read the international standard in its entirety*.

This analysis compares the ISAs included in the July 1995 *IFAC Handbook* (including ISAs 1-31) to the AICPA's *Codification of Statements on Auditing Standards*. This analysis segregates the guidance into general, fieldwork, and reporting sections. This guidance is summarized as follows.

General

ISA 2, *Terms of Audit Engagements* [ISA 210 (section 8210)]

ISA 210.02 [section 8210.02] states that the auditor and the client should agree on the terms of the engagement. The agreed terms would need to be recorded in an audit engagement letter or other suitable form of contract. In addition, ISA 210.17 [section 8210.17] states that where the terms of the engagement are changed the auditor and the client should agree on the new terms. U.S. SASs do not contain this guidance.

ISA 210.19 [section 8210.19] states that if the auditor is unable to agree to a change of the engagement [from an audit to a lower level of service] and is not permitted to continue the original engagement, the auditor should withdraw and consider whether there is any obligation, either contractual or otherwise, to report to other parties, such as the Board of Directors or shareholders, the circumstances necessitating the withdrawal. U.S. SASs do not include this guidance.

Field Work

ISA 31, *Consideration of Laws and Regulations in an Audit of Financial Statements* [ISA 250 (section 8250)], Compared to SAS No. 54, *Illegal Acts by Clients* [section 317]

ISA 250.02 [section 8250.02] states that when planning and performing audit procedures and in evaluating and reporting the results thereof, the auditor should recognize that noncompliance by the entity with laws and regulations may materially affect the financial statements. ISA 250.05 [section 8250.05] explains that laws and regulations vary considerably in their relation to the financial statements. Generally, the further removed noncompliance is from the events and transactions ordinarily reflected in financial statements, the less likely the auditor is to become aware of it or to recognize its possible noncompliance. However, ISA 250 [section 8250] does not distinguish between laws and regulations that have a direct versus an indirect effect on the financial statements. This approach to the auditor's responsibilities regarding noncompliance with laws and regulations is different from the approach set forth in SAS No. 54 [section 317].

ISA 4, *Planning* [ISA 300 (section 8300)], Compared to SAS No. 22, *Planning and Supervision* [section 311]

ISA 300.08 [section 8300.08] states that the auditor should develop and document an overall audit plan describing the expected scope and conduct of the audit. Similarly, the first standard of field work found in SAS No. 1, section 150, *Generally Accepted Auditing Standards*, paragraph .02 [section 150.02], requires the work to be adequately planned. According to SAS No. 22, paragraph 3 [section 311.03], audit planning involves developing an overall strategy for the expected conduct and scope of the audit. SAS No. 22, paragraph 4 [section 311.04] states that the auditor may wish to prepare a memorandum setting forth the preliminary audit plan, particularly for large and complex entities; however, the auditor is not required to do so.

Addenda to ISA 8: Part B, *Confirmation of Accounts Receivable* [ISA 501: Part B (section 8501.19–.30)], Compared to SAS No. 67, *The Confirmation Process* [section 330]

ISA 501.19 [section 8501.19] states that when the accounts receivable are material to the financial statements and when it is reasonable to expect debtors will respond, the auditor should ordinarily plan to obtain direct confirmation of accounts receivable or individual entries in an account balance. SAS No. 67, paragraph 34 [section 330.34] states that there is a presumption that the auditor will request the confirmation of accounts receivable during an audit unless one of the following is true:

- Accounts receivable are immaterial to the financial statements.
- The use of confirmations would be ineffective.
- The auditor's combined assessed level of inherent and control risk is low, and the assessed level, in conjunction with evidence expected to

be provided by analytical procedures or other substantive tests of details, is sufficient to reduce audit risk to an acceptably low level.

Thus, the two standards are similar, except that the international standard does not recognize the third exception found in the U.S. literature.

ISA 28, *Initial Engagements—Opening Balances* [ISA 510 (section 8510)], Compared to SAS No. 7, *Communications Between Predecessor and Successor Auditors* [section 315A]

When the successor is reviewing the working papers of the predecessor regarding opening balances, ISA 510.06 [section 8510.06] states that the successor would consider the professional competence and independence of the predecessor. The U.S. SASs do not contain comparable guidance.

ISA 12, *Analytical Procedures* [ISA 520 (section 8520)], Compared to SAS No. 56, *Analytical Procedures* [section 329]

ISA 520.15 [section 8520.15] states that the extent of reliance that the auditor places on the results of analytical procedures depends on the . . . materiality of the items involved. For example, when inventory balances are material, the auditor does not rely only on analytical procedures as substantive tests. However, the auditor may rely solely on analytical procedures for certain income and expense items when they are not individually material. In contrast, SAS No. 56, paragraph 9 [section 329.09] states that the auditor's reliance on substantive tests to achieve an audit objective related to a particular assertion may be derived from tests of details, from analytical procedures, or from a combination of both. The decision about which procedure or procedures to use to achieve a particular audit objective is based on the auditor's judgment on the expected effectiveness and efficiency of the available procedures. According to SAS No. 56, paragraph 15 [section 329.15], the expected effectiveness and efficiency of an analytical procedure in identifying potential misstatements depend on, among other things, . . . the precision of the expectation. The importance of the precision of the expectation is discussed in SAS No. 56, paragraph 17 [section 329.17].

ISA 23, *Going Concern* [ISA 570 (section 8570)], Compared to SAS No. 59, *The Auditor's Consideration of an Entity's Ability to Continue as a Going Concern* [section 341]

ISA 570.02 [section 8570.02] states that when planning and performing audit procedures and in evaluating the results thereof, the auditor should consider the appropriateness of the going concern assumption underlying the preparation of the financial statements. SAS No. 59, paragraph 3 [section 341.03] states that the auditor should evaluate whether there is substantial doubt about the entity's ability to continue as a going concern for a reasonable period of time. Thus, ISA 570 [section 8570] requires consideration of the going concern assumption throughout the engagement whereas SAS No. 59 [section 341] requires the auditor to consider information obtained during the course of the engagement that significantly contradicts the going concern assumption.

ISA 570 [section 8570] contains a Public Sector Perspective note stating that even where the going concern of a public sector entity is not in question, auditors are generally expected to provide an assessment of the general financial standing of the entity under audit in terms of its ability to meet its commitments and likely future demands. There is no counterpart in the U.S. SASs.

ISA 5, *Using the Work of Another Auditor* [ISA 600 (section 8600)], Compared to SAS No. 1, section 543, *Part of Audit Performed by Other Independent Auditors* [section 543]

ISA 600.09 [section 8600.09] states that the principal auditor would obtain written representations regarding the other auditor's compliance with the independence requirements and the accounting, auditing, and reporting requirements. SAS No. 1, section 543, paragraph .10 [section 543.10] states that the principal auditor should obtain a representation from the other auditor that he or she is independent. In addition, the principal auditor should ascertain through communication with the other auditor that he or she is familiar with accounting principles generally accepted in the United States and with the generally accepted auditing standards promulgated by the American Institute of Certified Public Accountants, and will conduct his or her audit and will report in accordance therewith. However, SAS No. 1, section 543 [section 543] does not require written representations regarding these matters.

ISA 600.14 [section 8600.14] states that the principal auditor would document in the audit working papers the components whose financial information was audited by other auditors, their significance to the financial statements of the entity as a whole, the names of the other auditors, and any conclusion reached that individual components are immaterial. The principal auditor would also document the procedures performed and the conclusions reached. SAS No. 1, section 543 [section 543] does not set forth specific documentation requirements regarding using the work of another auditor.

ISA 10, *Considering the Work of Internal Auditing* [ISA 610 (section 8610)], Compared to SAS No. 65, *The Auditor's Consideration of the Internal Audit Function in an Audit of Financial Statements* [section 322]

ISA 610.16 [section 8610.16] states that when the external auditor intends to use specific work of internal auditing, the external auditor should evaluate and test that work. In contrast, SAS No. 65, paragraph 26 [section 322.26] states that the auditor should test some of the internal auditors' work related to the significant financial statement assertions. These tests may be accomplished by either (*a*) examining some of the controls, transactions, or balances that the internal auditors examined or (*b*) examining similar controls, transactions, or balances not actually examined by the internal auditors.

ISA 18, *Using the Work of an Expert* [ISA 620 (section 8620)], Compared to SAS No. 73, *Using the Work of a Specialist* [section 336]

ISA 620.05 [section 8620.05] states that when the auditor uses the work of an expert employed by the auditor, that work is used in the employee's capacity as an expert rather than as an assistant on the audit as contemplated in ISA 7, *Quality Control for Audit Work* [section 8220]. Accordingly, in such circumstances the auditor will need to apply relevant procedures (as discussed in ISA 620, paragraphs 11 through 15 [section 8620.11–.15]) to the employee's work and findings but will not ordinarily need to assess the employee's skills and competence for each engagement. In contrast, SAS No. 73 [section 336] does not apply to situations in which a specialist employed by the auditor's firm participates in the audit. In that situation, SAS No. 22 [section 311] applies.

ISA 24, *The Auditor's Report on Special Purpose Audit Engagements* [ISA 800.18–.20 (section 8800.18–.20)], Compared to SAS No. 62, *Special Reports* [section 623.19–.21]

ISA 800.18–.20 [section 8800.18–.20] discusses a special-report engagement in which the auditor expresses an opinion on an entity's compliance with certain aspects of contractual agreements, such as bond indentures or local agreements. SAS No. 62, paragraphs 19 through 21 [section 623.19–.21], discusses a derivative report that an auditor may issue as part of performing an audit of financial statements. The SAS No. 62 [section 623] derivative report is in the form of negative assurance that is not enabled under the ISAs. Instead, Statement on Standards for Attestation Engagements No. 3, *Compliance Attestation* [AT section 500], provides guidance for such an engagement.

Reporting

ISA 21, *Subsequent Events* [ISA 560.08–.12 (section 8560.08–.12)], Compared to SAS No. 1, section 530, *Dating of the Independent Auditor's Report* [section 530.01–.05]

ISA 560.10 [section 8560.10] states that when management amends the financial statements for facts discovered after the date of the auditor's report but before the financial statements are issued, the auditor would provide management with a new report. The new auditor's report would be dated not earlier than the date the amended financial statements are signed or approved and, accordingly, the procedures referred to in ISA 560.04 [section 8560.04] and 560.05 [section 8560.05] would be extended to the date of the new auditor's report. In contrast, SAS No. 1, section 530, paragraph .03 [section 530.03] states that the date of the report ordinarily is not changed when the subsequent event requiring an adjustment to the financial statements is made without disclosure. In situations when the subsequent event requires disclosure, SAS No. 1, section 530, paragraph .05 [section 530.05] permits the auditor to dual-date the report or date the report as of the later date. In the former instance, the auditor's responsibility for events occurring subsequent to the completion of field work is limited to the specific event referred to in the note. In the latter instance, the independent auditor's responsibility for subsequent events extends to the date of the report and, accordingly, the procedures outlined in SAS No. 1, section 560, *Subsequent Events*, paragraph .12 [section 560.12], should be extended to that date.

ISA 23, *Going Concern* [ISA 570 (section 8570)], Compared to SAS No. 59, *The Auditor's Consideration of an Entity's Ability to Continue as a Going Concern* [section 341]

ISA 570.15 [section 8570.15] states that if, in the auditor's judgment, the going concern question is not satisfactorily resolved, the auditor would consider whether the financial statements—

a. Adequately describe the principal conditions that raise substantial doubt about the entity's ability to continue in operation for the foreseeable future

b. State that there is significant uncertainty that the entity will be able to continue as a going concern and, therefore, as appropriate, may be unable to realize its assets and discharge its liabilities in the normal course of business

c. State that the financial statements do not include any adjustments relating to the recoverability and classification of recorded asset amounts or to amounts and classification of liabilities that may be necessary if the entity is unable to continue as a going concern.

SAS No. 59, paragraph 10 [section 341.10] states that when, after considering management's plans, the auditor concludes there is substantial doubt about the entity's ability to continue as a going concern for a reasonable period of time, the auditor should consider the possible effects on the financial statements and the adequacy of the related disclosure. Examples of information that might be disclosed in the financial statements are provided; however, SAS No. 59, paragraph 10 [section 341.10] does not suggest the specific statements found in ISA 570.15*b* and *c* [section 8570.15*b* and *c*].

ISA 18, *Using the Work of an Expert* [ISA 620 (section 8620)], Compared to SAS No. 73, *Using the Work of a Specialist* [section 336]

ISA 620.17 [section 8620.17] states that if, as a result of the work of an expert, the auditor decides to issue a modified auditor's report, in some circumstances it may be appropriate, in explaining the nature of the modification, to refer to or describe the work of the expert. In these circumstances, the auditor would obtain the permission of the expert before making such a reference. SAS No. 73, paragraph 12 [section 336.12] discusses situations in which it is appropriate for the auditor to reference the specialist in the auditor's report; however, the auditor is not required to obtain the specialist's permission.

ISA 13, *The Auditor's Report on Financial Statements* [ISA 700 (section 8700)], Compared to SAS No. 58, *Reports on Audited Financial Statements* [section 508]

ISA 700.25 [section 8700.25] states that the report should name a specific location, which is ordinarily the city where the auditor maintains the office that has responsibility for the audit. SAS No. 58 [section 508] does not contain this guidance.

When the auditor's report contains an emphasis of matter paragraph, ISA 700.30 [section 8700.30] states that the paragraph would preferably be included after the opinion paragraph and would ordinarily refer to the fact that the auditor's opinion is not qualified in this respect. SAS No. 58 [section 508] does not contain comparable guidance on either of these matters regarding the emphasis paragraph.

ISA 700.41 [section 8700.41] states that when a limitation on the scope of the auditor's work is such that the auditor believes the need to express a disclaimer of opinion exists, the auditor would ordinarily not accept such a limited engagement, unless required by statute. SAS No. 58 [section 508] does not include this guidance.

ISA 24, *The Auditor's Report on Special Purpose Audit Engagement* [ISA 800.01–.11 (section 8800.01–.11)], Compared to SAS No. 62, *Special Reports* [section 623]

ISA 800.05(g) [section 8800.05(*g*)] states that the auditor's report on a special-purpose audit engagement should include the auditor's address. SAS No. 62 [section 623] does not contain this guidance.

ISA 24, *The Auditor's Report on Special Purpose Audit Engagement* [ISA 800.12–.17 (section 8800.12–.17)], Compared to SAS No. 62, *Special Reports* [section 623.11–.18]

ISA 800.15 [section 8800.15] states that the auditor would advise the client that the auditor's report on a component of financial statements is not to accompany the financial statements of the entity. SAS No. 62 [section 623] does not contain guidance regarding this matter.

ISA 24, *The Auditor's Report on Special Purpose Audit Engagements* [ISA 800.21–.25 (section 8800.21–.25)], Compared to SAS No. 42, *Reporting on Condensed Financial Statements and Selected Financial Data* [section 552.01–.08]

ISA 800.22 [section 8800.22] and .23 [section 8800.23] state that: (1) summarized financial statements need to clearly indicate the summarized nature of the information, and (2) summarized financial statements need to be appropriately titled to identify the audited financial statements from which they have been derived. SAS No. 42 [section 552] does not contain this guidance.

ISA 800.25 [section 8800.25] states that the auditor's report on summarized financial statements should include the following basic elements that are not included in SAS No. 42 [section 552]:

a. Addressee

b. A statement, or reference to the note within the summarized financial statements, which indicates that for a better understanding of an entity's financial performance and position and of the scope of the audit performed, the summarized financial statements should be read in conjunction with the unabridged financial statements and the audit report thereon

c. Auditor's address

AU Appendix C

Cross-Reference Table for Auditing Interpretations

(Sections of the text are cross-referenced to Auditing Interpretations)

Section	*Interpretation Subject (Interpretation No.)*	*Interpretation Section*
150.02	Auditor's Identification With Condensed Financial Data (No. 4)	9504.15-.18
220.04	Applicability of Guidance on Reporting When Not Independent (No. 5)	9504.19-.22
230	Responsibility of Assistants for the Resolution of Accounting and Auditing Issues (No. 3)	9311.35-.37
311.04	Communications Between the Auditor and Firm Personnel Responsible for Non-Audit Services (No. 1)	9311.01-.03
311.09	Audit Considerations for the Year 2000 Issue (No. 4)	9311.38-.47
311.14	Responsibility of Assistants for the Resolution of Accounting and Auditing Issues (No. 3)	9311.35-.37
312	The Nature and Extent of Auditing Procedures for Examining Related Party Transactions (No. 6)	9334.16-.21
313	Evidential Matter for an Audit of Interim Financial Statements (No. 1)	9326.01-.05
313.02	Evidential Matter for an Audit of Interim Financial Statements (No. 1)	9326.01-.05
315A	Determining the Predecessor Auditor (No. 1)	9315A.01-.05
315A	Restating Financial Statements Reported on by a Predecessor Auditor (No. 2)	9315A.06-.07
315A.04	Audits of Financial Statements That Had Been Previously Audited by a Predecessor Auditor (No. 3)	9315A.08-.18
315A.05	Audits of Financial Statements That Had Been Previously Audited by a Predecessor Auditor (No. 3)	9315A.08-.18
315A.06	Audits of Financial Statements That Had Been Previously Audited by a Predecessor Auditor (No. 3)	9315A.08-.18
315A.07	Audits of Financial Statements That Had Been Previously Audited by a Predecessor Auditor (No. 3)	9315A.08-.18
315A.08	Audits of Financial Statements That Had Been Previously Audited by a Predecessor Auditor (No. 3)	9315A.08-.18

Section	Interpretation Subject (Interpretation No.)	Interpretation Section
315A.09	Audits of Financial Statements That Had Been Previously Audited by a Predecessor Auditor (No. 3)	9315A.08-.18
317	Management Representations on Violations and Possible Violations of Laws and Regulations (No. 1)	9333.01-.04
317	Management Representations on Violations and Possible Violations of Laws and Regulations (No. 1)	9333A.01-.04
317	Material Weaknesses in Internal Control and the Foreign Corrupt Practices Act (No. 2)	9317.03-.06
317.22	Material Weaknesses in Internal Control Structure and the Foreign Corrupt Practices Act (No. 2)	9317.03-.06
319.19	Audit Considerations for the Year 2000 Issue (No. 4)	9311.38-.47
322	Audits of Financial Statements That Had Been Previously Audited by a Predecessor Auditor (No. 3)	9315A.08-.18
324.06	Service Organizations That Use the Services of Other Service Organizations (Subservice Organizations) (No. 2)	9324.04-.18
324.07	Service Organizations That Use the Services of Other Service Organizations (Subservice Organizations) (No. 2)	9324.04-.18
324.08	Service Organizations That Use the Services of Other Service Organizations (Subservice Organizations) (No. 2)	9324.04-.18
324.09	Service Organizations That Use the Services of Other Service Organizations (Subservice Organizations) (No. 2)	9324.04-.18
324.10	Service Organizations That Use the Services of Other Service Organizations (Subservice Organizations) (No. 2)	9324.04-.18
324.11	Service Organizations That Use the Services of Other Service Organizations (Subservice Organizations) (No. 2)	9324.04-.18
324.12	Service Organizations That Use the Services of Other Service Organizations (Subservice Organizations) (No. 2)	9324.04-.18
324.13	Service Organizations That Use the Services of Other Service Organizations (Subservice Organizations) (No. 2)	9324.04-.18
324.14	Service Organizations That Use the Services of Other Service Organizations (Subservice Organizations) (No. 2)	9324.04-.18
324.15	Service Organizations That Use the Services of Other Service Organizations (Subservice Organizations) (No. 2)	9324.04-.18

Section	Interpretation Subject (Interpretation No.)	Interpretation Section
324.16	Service Organizations That Use the Services of Other Service Organizations (Subservice Organizations) (No. 2)	9324.04-.18
324.44	Describing Tests of Operating Effectiveness and the Results of Such Tests (No. 1)	9324.01-.03
324.48	Service Organizations That Use the Services of Other Service Organizations (Subservice Organizations) (No. 2)	9324.04-.18
324.54	Service Organizations That Use the Services of Other Service Organizations (Subservice Organizations) (No. 2)	9324.04-.18
325	Reporting on the Existence of Material Weaknesses (No. 1)	9325.01-.07
325.02	Audit Considerations for the Year 2000 Issue (No. 4)	9311.38-.47
325.03	Audit Considerations for the Year 2000 Issue (No. 4)	9311.38-.47
325.17	Other References by Management to Internal Control Over Financial Reporting Including References to the Independent Auditor (No. 3)	9550.12-.15
326.03	Auditor's Consideration of the Completeness Assertion (No. 3)	9326.18-.21
326.11	Evidential Matter for an Audit of Interim Financial Statements (No. 1)	9326.01-.05
326.17	The Effect of an Inability to Obtain Evidential Matter Relating to Income Tax Accruals (No. 2)	9326.06-.17
326.21	The Use of Legal Interpretations As Evidential Matter to Support Management's Assertion That a Transfer of Financial Assets Has Met the Isolation Criterion in Paragraph 9(a) of Financial Accounting Standards Board Statement No. 125 (No. 1)	9336.01-.18
326.25	The Effect of an Inability to Obtain Evidential Matter Relating to Income Tax Accruals (No. 2)	9326.06-.17
331.09	Audits of Financial Statements That Had Been Previously Audited by a Predecessor Auditor (No. 3)	9315A.08-.18
331.09	Report of an Outside Inventory-Taking Firm as an Alternative Procedure for Observing Inventories (No. 1)	9508.01-.06
331.10	Audits of Financial Statements That Had Been Previously Audited by a Predecessor Auditor (No. 3)	9315A.08-.18
331.10	Report of an Outside Inventory-Taking Firm as an Alternative Procedure for Observing Inventories (No. 1)	9508.01-.06

Section	*Interpretation Subject (Interpretation No.)*	*Interpretation Section*
334.07	Exchange of Information Between Principal and Other Auditor on Related Parties (No. 4)	9334.12-.13
334.07	The Nature and Extent of Auditing Procedures for Examining Related Party Transactions (No. 6)	9334.16-.21
334.09	Examination of Identified Related Party Transactions With a Component (No. 5)	9334.14-.15
336	Audits of Financial Statements That Had Been Previously Audited by a Predecessor Auditor (No. 3)	9315A.08-.18
336.01	The Effect of an Inability to Obtain Evidential Matter Relating to Income Tax Accruals (No. 2)	9326.06-.17
336.06	The Use of Legal Interpretations As Evidential Matter to Support Management's Assertion That a Transfer of Financial Assets Has Met the Isolation Criterion in Paragraph 9(a) of Financial Accounting Standards Board Statement No. 125 (No. 1)	9336.01-.18
336.09	The Use of Legal Interpretations As Evidential Matter to Support Management's Assertion That a Transfer of Financial Assets Has Met the Isolation Criterion in Paragraph 9(a) of Financial Accounting Standards Board Statement No. 125 (No. 1)	9336.01-.18
336.13	The Use of Legal Interpretations As Evidential Matter to Support Management's Assertion That a Transfer of Financial Assets Has Met the Isolation Criterion in Paragraph 9(a) of Financial Accounting Standards Board Statement No. 125 (No. 1)	9336.01-.18
337	Specifying Relevant Date in an Audit Inquiry Letter (No. 1)	9337.01-.03
337	Alternative Wording of the Illustrative Audit Inquiry Letter to a Client's Lawyer (No. 5)	9337.10-.14
337	Client Has Not Consulted a Lawyer (No. 6)	9337.15-.17
337.05	Documents Subject to Lawyer-Client Privilege (No. 4)	9337.08-.09
337.05	Client Has Not Consulted a Lawyer (No. 6)	9337.15-.17
337.06	Client Has Not Consulted a Lawyer (No. 6)	9337.15-.17
337.06	Use of the Client's Inside Counsel in the Evaluation of Litigation, Claims, and Assessments (No. 8)	9337.24-.27
337.07	Client Has Not Consulted a Lawyer (No. 6)	9337.15-.17
337.08	Use of the Client's Inside Counsel in the Evaluation of Litigations, Claims, and Assessments (No. 8)	9337.24-.27

Section	Interpretation Subject (Interpretation No.)	Interpretation Section
337.09	Alternative Wording of the Illustrative Audit Inquiry Letter to a Client's Lawyer (No. 5)	9337.10-.14
337.09	Assessment of a Lawyer's Evaluation of the Outcome of Litigation (No. 7)	9337.18-.23
337.13	Documents Subject to Lawyer-Client Privilege (No. 4)	9337.08-.09
337.14	Assessment of a Lawyer's Evaluation of the Outcome of Litigation (No. 7)	9337.18-.23
337A	Relationship Between Date of Lawyer's Response and Auditor's Report (No. 2)	9337.04-.05
337A	Form of Audit Inquiry Letter When Client Represents That No Unasserted Claims and Assessments Exist (No. 3)	9337.06-.07
337A	Alternative Wording of the Illustrative Audit Inquiry Letter to a Client's Lawyer (No. 5)	9337.10-.14
337C	Alternative Wording of the Illustrative Audit Inquiry Letter to a Client's Lawyer (No. 5)	9337.10-.14
337C	Assessment of a Lawyer's Evaluation of the Outcome of Litigation (No. 7)	9337.18-.23
337C	Use of Explanatory Language Concerning Unasserted Possible Claims or Assessments in Lawyers' Responses to Audit Inquiry Letters (No. 10)	9337.31-.32
339.06	Providing Access to or Photocopies of Working Papers to a Regulator (No. 1)	9339.01-.15
339.08	Providing Access to or Photocopies of Working Papers to a Regulator (No. 1)	9339.01-.15
341.06	Eliminating a Going-Concern Explanatory Paragraph From a Reissued Report (No. 1)	9341.01-.02
341.07	Eliminating a Going-Concern Explanatory Paragraph From a Reissued Report (No. 1)	9341.01-.02
341.08	Eliminating a Going-Concern Explanatory Paragraph From a Reissued Report (No. 1)	9341.01-.02
341.09	Eliminating a Going-Concern Explanatory Paragraph From a Reissued Report (No. 1)	9341.01-.02
341.10	Eliminating a Going-Concern Explanatory Paragraph From a Reissued Report (No. 1)	9341.01-.02
341.11	Eliminating a Going-Concern Explanatory Paragraph From a Reissued Report (No. 1)	9341.01-.02
350.01	Applicability (No. 1)	9350.01-.02

Section	Interpretation Subject (Interpretation No.)	Interpretation Section
380	Applicability of Section 380 (No. 1).	9380.01-.03
380	The Auditor's Consideration of Management's Adoption of Accounting Principles for New Transactions or Events (No. 3).	9411.11-.15
380.01	Applicability of Section 380 (No. 1).	9380.01-.03
411	The Auditor's Consideration of Management's Adoption of Accounting Principles for New Transactions or Events (No. 3).	9411.11-.15
411.04	The Auditor's Consideration of Management's Adoption of Accounting Principles for New Transactions or Events (No. 3).	9411.11-.15
411.04	Evaluation of the Appropriateness of Informative Disclosures in Insurance Enterprises' Financial Statements Prepared on a Statutory Basis (No. 12).	9623.60-.79
411.09	The Auditor's Consideration of Management's Adoption of Accounting Principles for New Transactions or Events (No. 3).	9411.11-.15
411.11	The Auditor's Consideration of Management's Adoption of Accounting Principles for New Transactions or Events (No. 3).	9411.11-.15
411.13	The Auditor's Consideration of Management's Adoption of Accounting Principles for New Transactions or Events (No. 3).	9411.11-.15
420.02	The Effect of APB Opinion No. 28 on Consistency (No. 2).	9420.11-.15
420.02	The Effect of Accounting Changes by an Investee on Consistency (No. 8)	9420.52-.57
420.06	Auditors' Special Reports on Property and Liability Insurance Companies' Loss Reserves (No. 9).	9623.40-.46
420.14	Auditors' Special Reports on Property and Liability Insurance Companies' Loss Reserves (No. 9).	9623.40-.46
420.16	Change in Presentation of Accumulated Benefit Information in the Financial Statements of a Defined Benefit Pension Plan (No. 10)	9420.64-.65
420.21	Impact on the Auditor's Report of FIFO to LIFO Change in Comparative Financial Statements (No. 3).	9420.16-.23
504.03	Auditor's Identification With Condensed Financial Data (No. 4).	9504.15-.18
504.10	Applicability of Guidance on Reporting When Not Independent (No. 5)	9504.19-.22
508	Reports on Audited Financial Statements (No. 12).	9508.51-.52
508.16	Assessment of a Lawyer's Evaluation of the Outcome of Litigation (No. 7)	9337.18-.23

Section	Interpretation Subject (Interpretation No.)	Interpretation Section
508.16	Reporting on Financial Statements Prepared on a Liquidation Basis of Accounting (No. 8)	9508.33-.38
508.17	Assessment of a Lawyer's Evaluation of the Outcome of Litigation (No. 7)	9337.18-.23
508.17	Reporting on Financial Statements Prepared on a Liquidation Basis of Accounting (No. 8)	9508.33-.38
508.18	Assessment of a Lawyer's Evaluation of the Outcome of Litigation (No. 7)	9337.18-.23
508.18	Reporting on Financial Statements Prepared on a Liquidation Basis of Accounting (No. 8)	9508.33-.38
508.19	Assessment of a Lawyer's Evaluation of the Outcome of Litigation (No. 7)	9337.18-.23
508.19	The Impact on an Auditor's Report of an FASB Statement Prior to the Statement's Effective Date (No. 3)	9410.13-.18
508.19	Reporting on Financial Statements Prepared on a Liquidation Basis of Accounting (No. 8)	9508.33-.38
508.20	Assessment of a Lawyer's Evaluation of the Outcome of Litigation (No. 7)	9337.18-.23
508.20	Reporting on Financial Statements Prepared on a Liquidation Basis of Accounting (No. 8)	9508.33-.38
508.21	Assessment of a Lawyer's Evaluation of the Outcome of Litigation (No. 7)	9337.18-.23
508.21	Reporting on Financial Statements Prepared on a Liquidation Basis of Accounting (No. 8)	9508.33-.38
508.22	The Use of Legal Interpretations As Evidential Matter to Support Management's Assertion That a Transfer of Financial Assets Has Met the Isolation Criterion in Paragraph 9(a) of Financial Accounting Standards Board Statement No. 125 (No. 1)	9336.01-.18
508.22	Assessment of a Lawyer's Evaluation of the Outcome of Litigation (No. 7)	9337.18-.23
508.22	Reporting on Financial Statements Prepared on a Liquidation Basis of Accounting (No. 8)	9508.33-.38
508.23	The Use of Legal Interpretations As Evidential Matter to Support Management's Assertion That a Transfer of Financial Assets Has Met the Isolation Criterion in Paragraph 9(a) of Financial Accounting Standards Board Statement No. 125 (No. 1)	9336.01-.18

Section	Interpretation Subject (Interpretation No.)	Interpretation Section
508.23	Assessment of a Lawyer's Evaluation of the Outcome of Litigation (No. 7)	9337.18-.23
508.23	Reporting on Financial Statements Prepared on a Liquidation Basis of Accounting (No. 8)	9508.33-.38
508.24	The Effect of an Inability to Obtain Evidential Matter Relating to Income Tax Accruals (No. 2)	9326.06-.17
508.24	The Use of Legal Interpretations As Evidential Matter to Support Management's Assertion That a Transfer of Financial Assets Has Met the Isolation Criterion in Paragraph 9(a) of Financial Accounting Standards Board Statement No. 125 (No. 1)	9336.01-.18
508.24	Assessment of a Lawyer's Evaluation of the Outcome of Litigation (No. 7)	9337.18-.23
508.24	Report on an Outside Inventory-Taking Firm as an Alternative Procedure For Observing Inventories (No. 1)	9508.01-.06
508.24	Reporting on Financial Statements Prepared on a Liquidation Basis of Accounting (No. 8)	9508.33-.38
508.25	The Use of Legal Interpretations As Evidential Matter to Support Management's Assertion That a Transfer of Financial Assets Has Met the Isolation Criterion in Paragraph 9(a) of Financial Accounting Standards Board Statement No. 125 (No. 1)	9336.01-.18
508.25	Assessment of a Lawyer's Evaluation of the Outcome of Litigation (No. 7)	9337.18-.23
508.25	Reporting on Financial Statements Prepared on a Liquidation Basis of Accounting (No. 8)	9508.33-.38
508.26	The Use of Legal Interpretations As Evidential Matter to Support Management's Assertion That a Transfer of Financial Assets Has Met the Isolation Criterion in Paragraph 9(a) of Financial Accounting Standards Board Statement No. 125 (No. 1)	9336.01-.18
508.26	Assessment of a Lawyer's Evaluation of the Outcome of Litigation (No. 7)	9337.18-.23
508.26	Reporting on Financial Statements Prepared on a Liquidation Basis of Accounting (No. 8)	9508.33-.38
508.27	Assessment of a Lawyer's Evaluation of the Outcome of Litigation (No. 7)	9337.18-.23
508.27	The Impact on an Auditor's Report of an FASB Statement Prior to the Statement's Effective Date (No. 3)	9410.13-.18

Section	Interpretation Subject (Interpretation No.)	Interpretation Section
508.27	Reporting on Financial Statements Prepared on a Liquidation Basis of Accounting (No. 8)	9508.33-.38
508.28	Assessment of a Lawyer's Evaluation of the Outcome of Litigation (No. 7)	9337.18-.23
508.28	The Impact on an Auditor's Report of an FASB Statement Prior to the Statement's Effective Date (No. 3)	9410.13-.18
508.28	Reporting on Financial Statements Prepared on a Liquidation Basis of Accounting (No. 8)	9508.33-.38
508.29	Assessment of a Lawyer's Evaluation of the Outcome of Litigation (No. 7)	9337.18-.23
508.29	The Impact on an Auditor's Report of an FASB Statement Prior to the Statement's Effective Date (No. 3)	9410.13-.18
508.29	Reporting on Financial Statements Prepared on a Liquidation Basis of Accounting (No. 8)	9508.33-.38
508.30	Assessment of a Lawyer's Evaluation of the Outcome of Litigation (No. 7)	9337.18-.23
508.30	The Impact on an Auditor's Report of an FASB Statement Prior to the Statement's Effective Date (No. 3)	9410.13-.18
508.30	Reporting on Financial Statements Prepared on a Liquidation Basis of Accounting (No. 8)	9508.33-.38
508.31	Assessment of a Lawyer's Evaluation of the Outcome of Litigation (No. 7)	9337.18-.23
508.31	The Impact on an Auditor's Report of an FASB Statement Prior to the Statement's Effective Date (No. 3)	9410.13-.18
508.31	Reporting on Financial Statements Prepared on a Liquidation Basis of Accounting (No. 8)	9508.33-.38
508.32	Assessment of a Lawyer's Evaluation of the Outcome of Litigation (No. 7)	9337.18-.23
508.32	The Impact on an Auditor's Report of an FASB Statement Prior to the Statement's Effective Date (No. 3)	9410.13-.18
508.32	Reporting on Financial Statements Prepared on a Liquidation Basis of Accounting (No. 8)	9508.33-.38
508.33	Assessment of a Lawyer's Evaluation of the Outcome of Litigation (No. 7)	9337.18-.23
508.33	The Impact on an Auditor's Report of an FASB Statement Prior to the Statement's Effective Date (No. 3)	9410.13-.18

Section	Interpretation Subject (Interpretation No.)	Interpretation Section
508.33	Reporting on Financial Statements Prepared on a Liquidation Basis of Accounting (No. 8)	9508.33-.38
508.35	The Use of Legal Interpretations As Evidential Matter to Support Management's Assertion That a Transfer of Financial Assets Has Met the Isolation Criterion in Paragraph 9(a) of Financial Accounting Standards Board Statement No. 125 (No. 1)	9336.01-.18
508.35	Reporting on a Special-Purpose Financial Statement That Results in an Incomplete Presentation But is Otherwise in Conformity With Generally Accepted Accounting Principles (No. 13)	9623.80-.87
508.36	The Use of Legal Interpretations As Evidential Matter to Support Management's Assertion That a Transfer of Financial Assets Has Met the Isolation Criterion in Paragraph 9(a) of Financial Accounting Standards Board Statement No. 125 (No. 1)	9336.01-.18
508.36	Reporting on a Special-Purpose Financial Statement That Results in an Incomplete Presentation But is Otherwise in Conformity With Generally Accepted Accounting Principles (No. 13)	9623.80-.87
508.37	The Use of Legal Interpretations As Evidential Matter to Support Management's Assertion That a Transfer of Financial Assets Has Met the Isolation Criterion in Paragraph 9(a) of Financial Accounting Standards Board Statement No. 125 (No. 1)	9336.01-.18
508.37	Reporting on a Special-Purpose Financial Statement That Results in an Incomplete Presentation But is Otherwise in Conformity With Generally Accepted Accounting Principles (No. 13)	9623.80-.87
508.38	The Use of Legal Interpretations As Evidential Matter to Support Management's Assertion That a Transfer of Financial Assets Has Met the Isolation Criterion in Paragraph 9(a) of Financial Accounting Standards Board Statement No. 125 (No. 1)	9336.01-.18
508.38	Reporting on a Special-Purpose Financial Statement That Results in an Incomplete Presentation But is Otherwise in Conformity With Generally Accepted Accounting Principles (No. 13)	9623.80-.87

Section	Interpretation Subject (Interpretation No.)	Interpretation Section
508.39	The Use of Legal Interpretations As Evidential Matter to Support Management's Assertion That a Transfer of Financial Assets Has Met the Isolation Criterion in Paragraph 9(a) of Financial Accounting Standards Board Statement No. 125 (No. 1)	9336.01-.18
508.39	Reporting on a Special-Purpose Financial Statement That Results in an Incomplete Presentation But is Otherwise in Conformity With Generally Accepted Accounting Principles (No. 13)	9623.80-.87
508.40	The Use of Legal Interpretations As Evidential Matter to Support Management's Assertion That a Transfer of Financial Assets Has Met the Isolation Criterion in Paragraph 9(a) of Financial Accounting Standards Board Statement No. 125 (No. 1)	9336.01-.18
508.40	Reporting on a Special-Purpose Financial Statement That Results in an Incomplete Presentation But is Otherwise in Conformity With Generally Accepted Accounting Principles (No. 13)	9623.80-.87
508.41	The Use of Legal Interpretations As Evidential Matter to Support Management's Assertion That a Transfer of Financial Assets Has Met the Isolation Criterion in Paragraph 9(a) of Financial Accounting Standards Board Statement No. 125 (No. 1)	9336.01-.18
508.41	The Impact on an Auditor's Report of an FASB Statement Prior to the Statement's Effective Date (No. 3)	9410.13-.18
508.41	Reporting on a Special-Purpose Financial Statement That Results in an Incomplete Presentation But is Otherwise in Conformity With Generally Accepted Accounting Principles (No. 13)	9623.80-.87
508.42	The Use of Legal Interpretations As Evidential Matter to Support Management's Assertion That a Transfer of Financial Assets Has Met the Isolation Criterion in Paragraph 9(a) of Financial Accounting Standards Board Statement No. 125 (No. 1)	9336.01-.18
508.42	Reporting on a Special-Purpose Financial Statement That Results in an Incomplete Presentation But is Otherwise in Conformity With Generally Accepted Accounting Principles (No. 13)	9623.80-.87

Section	Interpretation Subject (Interpretation No.)	Interpretation Section
508.43	The Use of Legal Interpretations As Evidential Matter to Support Management's Assertion That a Transfer of Financial Assets Has Met the Isolation Criterion in Paragraph 9(a) of Financial Accounting Standards Board Statement No. 125 (No. 1)	9336.01-.18
508.43	Reporting on a Special-Purpose Financial Statement That Results in an Incomplete Presentation But is Otherwise in Conformity With Generally Accepted Accounting Principles (No. 13).....................	9623.80-.87
508.44	The Use of Legal Interpretations As Evidential Matter to Support Management's Assertion That a Transfer of Financial Assets Has Met the Isolation Criterion in Paragraph 9(a) of Financial Accounting Standards Board Statement No. 125 (No. 1)	9336.01-.18
508.44	Reporting on a Special-Purpose Financial Statement That Results in an Incomplete Presentation But is Otherwise in Conformity With Generally Accepted Accounting Principles (No. 13).....................	9623.80-.87
508.45	The Use of Legal Interpretations As Evidential Matter to Support Management's Assertion That a Transfer of Financial Assets Has Met the Isolation Criterion in Paragraph 9(a) of Financial Accounting Standards Board Statement No. 125 (No. 1)	9336.01-.18
508.46	The Use of Legal Interpretations As Evidential Matter to Support Management's Assertion That a Transfer of Financial Assets Has Met the Isolation Criterion in Paragraph 9(a) of Financial Accounting Standards Board Statement No. 125 (No. 1)	9336.01-.18
508.47	The Use of Legal Interpretations As Evidential Matter to Support Management's Assertion That a Transfer of Financial Assets Has Met the Isolation Criterion in Paragraph 9(a) of Financial Accounting Standards Board Statement No. 125 (No. 1)	9336.01-.18
508.48	The Use of Legal Interpretations As Evidential Matter to Support Management's Assertion That a Transfer of Financial Assets Has Met the Isolation Criterion in Paragraph 9(a) of Financial Accounting Standards Board Statement No. 125 (No. 1)	9336.01-.18
508.49	The Use of Legal Interpretations As Evidential Matter to Support Management's Assertion That a Transfer of Financial Assets Has Met the Isolation Criterion in Paragraph 9(a) of Financial Accounting Standards Board Statement No. 125 (No. 1)	9336.01-.18

Section	Interpretation Subject (Interpretation No.)	Interpretation Section
508.50	The Use of Legal Interpretations As Evidential Matter to Support Management's Assertion That a Transfer of Financial Assets Has Met the Isolation Criterion in Paragraph 9(a) of Financial Accounting Standards Board Statement No. 125 (No. 1)	9336.01-.18
508.51	The Use of Legal Interpretations As Evidential Matter to Support Management's Assertion That a Transfer of Financial Assets Has Met the Isolation Criterion in Paragraph 9(a) of Financial Accounting Standards Board Statement No. 125 (No. 1)	9336.01-.18
508.52	The Use of Legal Interpretations As Evidential Matter to Support Management's Assertion That a Transfer of Financial Assets Has Met the Isolation Criterion in Paragraph 9(a) of Financial Accounting Standards Board Statement No. 125 (No. 1)	9336.01-.18
508.53	The Use of Legal Interpretations As Evidential Matter to Support Management's Assertion That a Transfer of Financial Assets Has Met the Isolation Criterion in Paragraph 9(a) of Financial Accounting Standards Board Statement No. 125 (No. 1)	9336.01-.18
508.54	The Use of Legal Interpretations As Evidential Matter to Support Management's Assertion That a Transfer of Financial Assets Has Met the Isolation Criterion in Paragraph 9(a) of Financial Accounting Standards Board Statement No. 125 (No. 1)	9336.01-.18
508.55	The Use of Legal Interpretations As Evidential Matter to Support Management's Assertion That a Transfer of Financial Assets Has Met the Isolation Criterion in Paragraph 9(a) of Financial Accounting Standards Board Statement No. 125 (No. 1)	9336.01-.18
508.56	The Use of Legal Interpretations As Evidential Matter to Support Management's Assertion That a Transfer of Financial Assets Has Met the Isolation Criterion in Paragraph 9(a) of Financial Accounting Standards Board Statement No. 125 (No. 1)	9336.01-.18
508.57	The Use of Legal Interpretations As Evidential Matter to Support Management's Assertion That a Transfer of Financial Assets Has Met the Isolation Criterion in Paragraph 9(a) of Financial Accounting Standards Board Statement No. 125 (No. 1)	9336.01-.18

Section	Interpretation Subject (Interpretation No.)	Interpretation Section
508.58	The Use of Legal Interpretations As Evidential Matter to Support Management's Assertion That a Transfer of Financial Assets Has Met the Isolation Criterion in Paragraph 9(a) of Financial Accounting Standards Board Statement No. 125 (No. 1)	9336.01-.18
508.58	Reporting on a Special-Purpose Financial Statement That Results in an Incomplete Presentation But is Otherwise in Conformity With Generally Accepted Accounting Principles (No. 13)	9623.80-.87
508.59	The Use of Legal Interpretations As Evidential Matter to Support Management's Assertion That a Transfer of Financial Assets Has Met the Isolation Criterion in Paragraph 9(a) of Financial Accounting Standards Board Statement No. 125 (No. 1)	9336.01-.18
508.59	Reporting on a Special-Purpose Financial Statement That Results in an Incomplete Presentation But is Otherwise in Conformity With Generally Accepted Accounting Principles (No. 13)	9623.80-.87
508.60	The Use of Legal Interpretations As Evidential Matter to Support Management's Assertion That a Transfer of Financial Assets Has Met the Isolation Criterion in Paragraph 9(a) of Financial Accounting Standards Board Statement No. 125 (No. 1)	9336.01-.18
508.60	Reporting on a Special-Purpose Financial Statement That Results in an Incomplete Presentation But is Otherwise in Conformity With Generally Accepted Accounting Principles (No. 13)	9623.80-.87
508.61	The Use of Legal Interpretations As Evidential Matter to Support Management's Assertion That a Transfer of Financial Assets Has Met the Isolation Criterion in Paragraph 9(a) of Financial Accounting Standards Board Statement No. 125 (No. 1)	9336.01-.18
508.62	The Use of Legal Interpretations As Evidential Matter to Support Management's Assertion That a Transfer of Financial Assets Has Met the Isolation Criterion in Paragraph 9(a) of Financial Accounting Standards Board Statement No. 125 (No. 1)	9336.01-.18
508.63	The Use of Legal Interpretations As Evidential Matter to Support Management's Assertion That a Transfer of Financial Assets Has Met the Isolation Criterion in Paragraph 9(a) of Financial Accounting Standards Board Statement No. 125 (No. 1)	9336.01-.18

Section	Interpretation Subject (Interpretation No.)	Interpretation Section
530.05	Eliminating a Going-Concern Explanatory Paragraph From a Reissued Report (No. 1)	9341.01-.02
534	Financial Statements for General Use Only Outside of the United States in Accordance With International Accounting Standards and International Standards on Auditing (No. 1)	9534.01-.04
534.09	Financial Statements for General Use Only Outside of the United States in Accordance With International Accounting Standards and International Standards on Auditing (No. 1)	9534.01-.04
543	Audits of Financial Statements That Had Been Previously Audited by a Predecessor Auditor (No. 3)	9315A.08-.18
543.03	Inquiries of the Principal Auditor by the Other Auditor (No. 2)	9543.04-.07
543.10	Specific Procedures Performed by the Other Auditor at the Principal Auditor's Request (No. 1)	9543.01-.03
543.12	Examination of Identified Related Party Transactions With a Component (No. 5)	9334.14-.15
543.12	Application of Additional Procedures Concerning the Audit Performed by the Other Auditor (No. 6)	9543.18-.20
550	Performance and Reporting Guidance Related to Fair Value Disclosures (No. 1)	9342.01-.10
550	Letters to Directors Relating to Annual Reports on Form 10-K (No. 1)	9634.01-.09
550	Reports by Management on Internal Control Over Financial Reporting (No. 2)	9550.07-.11
550	Other References by Management to Internal Control Over Financial Reporting, Including References to the Independent Auditor (No. 3)	9550.12-.15
550	Other Information in Electronic Sites Containing Audited Financial Statements (No. 4)	9550.16-.18
550.02	Reports by Management on Internal Control Over Financial Reporting (No. 2)	9550.07-.11
550.02	Other References by Management to Internal Control Over Financial Reporting, Including References to the Independent Auditor (No. 3)	9550.12-.15
550.06	Reports by Management on Internal Control Over Financial Reporting (No. 2)	9550.07-.11
550.06	Other References by Management to Internal Control Over Financial Reporting, Including References to the Independent Auditor (No. 3)	9550.12-.15

Section	Interpretation Subject (Interpretation No.)	Interpretation Section
551.12	Performance and Reporting Guidance Related to Fair Value Disclosures (No. 1) . . .	9342.01-.10
551.13	Performance and Reporting Guidance Related to Fair Value Disclosures (No. 1) . . .	9342.01-.10
552.08	Subsequent Events Procedures for Shelf Registration Statements Updated After the Original Effective Date (No. 1).	9711.01-.11
558	Supplementary Oil and Gas Reserve Information (No. 1)	9558.01-.06
560.05	The Impact on an Auditor's Report of an FASB Statement Prior to the Statement's Effective Date (No. 3)	9410.13-.18
560.10	Relationship Between Date of Lawyer's Response and Auditor's Report (No. 2)	9337.04-.05
560.11	Relationship Between Date of Lawyer's Response and Auditor's Report (No. 2)	9337.04-.05
560.12	Relationship Between Date of Lawyer's Response and Auditor's Report (No. 2)	9337.04-.05
560.12	Eliminating a Going-Concern Explanatory Paragraph From a Reissued Report (No. 1) . . .	9341.01-.02
561	Restating Financial Statements Reported on by a Predecessor Auditor (No. 2).	9315A.06-.07
561	Auditor Association With Subsequently Discovered Information When the Auditor Has Resigned or Been Discharged (No. 1).	9561.01-.02
622	Other Information in Electronic Sites Containing Audited Financial Statements (No. 4).	9550.16-.18
622	Applying Agreed-Upon Procedures to All, or Substantially All, of the Elements, Accounts, or Items of a Financial Statement (No. 1)	9622.01-.02
622.06	Applying Agreed-Upon Procedures to All, or Substantially All, of the Elements, Accounts, or Items of a Financial Statement (No. 1)	9622.01-.02
622.16	Applying Agreed-Upon Procedures to All, or Substantially All, of the Elements, Accounts, or Items of a Financial Statement (No. 1)	9622.01-.02
622.26	Applying Agreed-Upon Procedures to All, or Substantially All, of the Elements, Accounts, or Items of a Financial Statement (No. 1)	9622.01-.02
623	Reports on the Financial Statements Included in Internal Revenue Form 990, "Return of Organizations Exempt From Income Tax" (No. 10).	9623.47-.54

Section	Interpretation Subject (Interpretation No.)	Interpretation Section
623.02	Evaluation of the Appropriateness of Informative Disclosures in Insurance Enterprises' Financial Statements Prepared on a Statutory Basis (No. 12)	9623.60-.79
623.04	Evaluation of the Appropriateness of Informative Disclosures in Insurance Enterprises' Financial Statements Prepared on a Statutory Basis (No. 12)	9623.60-.79
623.08	Reports on the Financial Statements Included in Internal Revenue Form 990, "Return of Organizations Exempt From Income Tax" (No. 10)	9623.47-.54
623.09	Evaluation of the Appropriateness of Informative Disclosures in Insurance Enterprises' Financial Statements Prepared on a Statutory Basis (No. 12)	9623.60-.79
623.10	Evaluation of the Appropriateness of Informative Disclosures in Insurance Enterprises' Financial Statements Prepared on a Statutory Basis (No. 12)	9623.60-.79
623.10	Evaluating the Adequacy of Disclosure in Financial Statements Prepared on the Cash, Modified Cash, or Income Tax Basis of Accounting (No. 14)	9623.88-.93
623.11	Auditors' Special Reports on Property and Liability Insurance Companies' Loss Reserves (No. 9)	9623.40-.46
623.12	Auditors' Special Reports on Property and Liability Insurance Companies' Loss Reserves (No. 9)	9623.40-.46
623.13	Auditors' Special Reports on Property and Liability Insurance Companies' Loss Reserves (No. 9)	9623.40-.46
623.14	Auditors' Special Reports on Property and Liability Insurance Companies' Loss Reserves (No. 9)	9623.40-.46
623.15	Auditors' Special Reports on Property and Liability Insurance Companies' Loss Reserves (No. 9)	9623.40-.46
623.16	Auditors' Special Reports on Property and Liability Insurance Companies' Loss Reserves (No. 9)	9623.40-.46
623.17	Auditors' Special Reports on Property and Liability Insurance Companies' Loss Reserves (No. 9)	9623.40-.46
623.18	Auditors' Special Reports on Property and Liability Insurance Companies' Loss Reserves (No. 9)	9623.40-.46

Section	Interpretation Subject (Interpretation No.)	Interpretation Section
623.22	Reporting on a Special-Purpose Financial Statement That Results in an Incomplete Presentation But is Otherwise in Conformity With Generally Accepted Accounting Principles (No. 13)	9623.80-.87
623.23	Reporting on a Special-Purpose Financial Statement That Results in an Incomplete Presentation But is Otherwise in Conformity With Generally Accepted Accounting Principles (No. 13)	9623.80-.87
623.24	Reporting on a Special-Purpose Financial Statement That Results in an Incomplete Presentation But is Otherwise in Conformity With Generally Accepted Accounting Principles (No. 13)	9623.80-.87
623.25	Reporting on a Special-Purpose Financial Statement That Results in an Incomplete Presentation But is Otherwise in Conformity With Generally Accepted Accounting Principles (No. 13)	9623.80-.87
623.26	Reporting on a Special-Purpose Financial Statement That Results in an Incomplete Presentation But is Otherwise in Conformity With Generally Accepted Accounting Principles (No. 13)	9623.80-.87
634	Letters to Directors Relating to Annual Reports on Form 10-K (No. 1)	9634.01-.09
634.12	Letters to Directors Relating to Annual Reports on Form 10-K (No. 1)	9634.01-.09
634.31	Letters to Directors Relating to Annual Reports on Form 10-K (No. 1)	9634.01-.09
634.33	Letters to Directors Relating to Annual Reports on Form 10-K (No. 1)	9634.01-.09
634.55	Letters to Directors Relating to Annual Reports on Form 10-K (No. 1)	9634.01-.09
634.56	Letters to Directors Relating to Annual Reports on Form 10-K (No. 1)	9634.01-.09
634.57	Letters to Directors Relating to Annual Reports on Form 10-K (No. 1)	9634.01-.09
634.58	Letters to Directors Relating to Annual Reports on Form 10-K (No. 1)	9634.01-.09
634.59	Letters to Directors Relating to Annual Reports on Form 10-K (No. 1)	9634.01-.09
634.60	Letters to Directors Relating to Annual Reports on Form 10-K (No. 1)	9634.01-.09

Section	Interpretation Subject (Interpretation No.)	Interpretation Section
711.05	Subsequent Events Procedures for Shelf Registration Statements Updated After the Original Effective Date (No. 1)	9711.01-.11
711.10	Subsequent Events Procedures for Shelf Registration Statements Updated After the Original Effective Date (No. 1)	9711.01-.11
711.11	Subsequent Events Procedures for Shelf Registration Statements Updated After the Original Effective Date (No. 1)	9711.01-.11
711.12	Subsequent Events Procedures for Shelf Registration Statements Updated After the Original Effective Date (No. 1)	9711.01-.11
711.13	Subsequent Events Procedures for Shelf Registration Statements Updated After the Original Effective Date (No. 1)	9711.01-.11

AU Appendix D

AICPA Audit and Accounting Guides and Statements of Position

Audit and Accounting Guides

Audit Sampling, Statistical Sampling Subcommittee.

Audits of Agricultural Producers and Agricultural Cooperatives, Agribusiness Special Committee; *Statement of Position*, Accounting by Agricultural Producers and Agricultural Cooperatives, Accounting Standards Division, April 1985.

Audits of Airlines, Civil Aeronautics Subcommittee; *Statement of Position*, Accounting for Developmental and Preoperating Costs, Purchases and Exchange of Take-off and Landing Slots, and Airframe Modifications, Accounting Standards Division, September 1988.

Audits of Casinos, Gaming Industry Special Committee.

Audits of Certain Nonprofit Organizations, Subcommittee on Nonprofit Organizations; *Statement of Position*, Accounting Principles and Reporting Practices for Certain Nonprofit Organizations, Accounting Standards Division, December 1978; *Statement of Position*, Accounting for Joint Costs of Informational Materials and Activities of Not-for-Profit Organizations That Include a Fund-Raising Appeal, Accounting Standards Division, August 1987; *Statement of Position*, Audits of Not-for-Profit Organizations Receiving Federal Awards, Not-for-Profit Organizations Committee, December 1992, as revised December 1995; *Statement of Position*, The Application of the Requirements of Accounting Research Bulletins, Opinions of the Accounting Principles Board, and Statements and Interpretations of the Financial Accounting Standards Board to Not-for-Profit Organizations, Not-for-Profit Organizations Committee, September 1994; *Statement of Position*, Reporting of Related Entities by Not-for-Profit Organizations, Not-for-Profit Organizations Committee, September 1994.

Audits of Colleges and Universities, Committee on College and University Accounting and Auditing; *Statement of Position*, Financial Accounting and Reporting by Colleges and Universities, Accounting Standards Division, August 1974; *Statement of Position*, Audits of Not-for-Profit Organizations Receiving Federal Awards, Not-for-Profit Organizations Committee, December 1992, as revised December 1995; *Statement of Position*, The Application of the Requirements of Accounting Research Bulletins, Opinions of the Accounting Principles Board, and Statements and Interpretations of the Financial Accounting Standards Board to Not-for-Profit Organizations, Not-for-Profit Organizations Committee, September 1994; *Statement of Position*, Reporting of Related Entities by Not-for-Profit Organizations, Not-for-Profit Organizations Committee, September 1994.

Audits of Credit Unions, Credit Unions Committee.

Audits of Employee Benefit Plans, Employee Benefit Plans Committee; *Statement of Position*, Accounting and Reporting by Health and Welfare Benefit Plans, Employee Benefit Plans Committee, August 1992; *Statement of Position*, Reporting of Investment Contracts Held by Health and Welfare

Audit and Accounting Guides—Continued

Benefit Plans and Defined-Contribution Pension Plans, Employee Benefit Plans Committee, September, 1994; *Practice Bulletin*, Reporting Separate Investment Fund Option Information of Defined-Contribution Pension Plans, Employee Benefit Plans Committee, September, 1994.

Audits of Entities With Oil and Gas Producing Activities, Oil and Gas Committee.

Audits of Federal Government Contractors, Government Contractors Guide Special Committee; *Statement of Position*, Accounting for Performance of Construction-Type and Certain Production-Type Contracts, Accounting Standards Division, July 1981.

Audits of Finance Companies (Including Independent and Captive Financing Activities of Other Companies), Finance Companies Guide Special Committee; *Statement of Position*, Disclosure of Certain Information by Financial Institutions About Debt Securities Held as Assets, Accounting Standards Executive Committee, November 1990; *Statement of Position*, Accounting for Foreclosed Assets, Accounting Standards Division, April 1992.

Audits of Investment Companies, Investment Companies Special Committee; *Statement of Position*, Reports on Audited Financial Statements of Investment Companies, Investment Companies Committee, January 1989; *Statement of Position*, Report on the Internal Control Structure in Audits of Investment Companies, Investment Companies Committee, December 1989; *Statement of Position*, Financial Accounting and Reporting for High-Yield Debt Securities by Investment Companies, Investment Companies Committee, January 1993; *Statement of Position*, Determination, Disclosure, and Financial Statement Presentation of Income, Capital Gain, and Return of Capital Distributions by Investment Companies, Investment Companies Committee, February 1993; *Statement of Position*, Foreign Currency Accounting and Financial Statement Presentation for Investment Companies, Investment Companies Committee, April 1993; *Statement of Position*, Financial Reporting by Nonpublic Investment Partnerships, Investment Companies Committee, May 1995; *Statement of Position*, Accounting for Certain Distribution Costs of Investment Companies, Investment Companies Committee, July 1995.

Audits of Property and Liability Insurance Companies, Insurance Companies Committee; *Statement of Position*, Auditing Property and Liability Reinsurance, Insurance Companies Committee, October 1982; *Statement of Position*, Accounting for Foreclosed Assets, Accounting Standards Division, April 1992; *Statement of Position*, Auditing Insurance Entities' Loss Reserves, Auditing Insurance Entities' Loss Reserves Task Force of the Insurance Companies Committee, May 1992; *Statement of Position*, Accounting for Foreign Property and Liability Reinsurance, Reinsurance Auditing and Accounting Task Force of the Insurance Companies Committee, June 1992; *Statement of Position*, Auditing Property/Casualty Insurance Entities' Statutory Financial Statements—Applying Certain Requirements of the NAIC Annual Statement Instructions, Insurance Companies Committee, October 1992; *Statement of Position*, Inquiries of State Insurance Regulators, Insurance Companies Committee, April 1994; *Statement of Position*, Disclosures of Certain Matters in the Finan-

Audit and Accounting Guides—Continued

cial Statements of Insurance Enterprises, Task Force on Insurance Companies' Disclosures of the Insurance Companies Committee, December 1994; *Statement of Position*, Letters for State Insurance Regulators to Comply With the NAIC Model Audit Rule, Insurance Companies Committee, November 1995; *Statement of Position*, Auditor's Reporting on Statutory Financial Statements of Insurance Enterprises, Insurance Companies Committee, December 1995; *Practice Bulletin*, Accounting by the Issuer of Surplus Notes, Insurance Companies Committee, January 1997; *Statement of Position*, Accounting by Insurance and Other Enterprises for Insurance-Related Assessments, Insurance Companies Committee, December 1997.

Audits of State and Local Governmental Units, Government Accounting and Auditing Committee.

Audits of Stock Life Insurance Companies,* Committee on Insurance Accounting and Auditing; *Statement of Position*, Confirmation of Insurance Policies in Force, Auditing Standards Division, August 1978; *Statement of Position*, Auditing Life Reinsurance, Auditing Standards Division, November 1984; *Statement of Position*, Accounting for Foreclosed Assets, Accounting Standards Division, April 1992; *Statement of Position*, The Auditor's Consideration of Regulatory Risk-Based Capital for Life Insurance Enterprises, Insurance Companies Committee, December 1993; *Statement of Position*, Inquiries of State Insurance Regulators, Insurance Companies Committee, April 1994; *Statement of Position*, Disclosures of Certain Matters in the Financial Statements of Insurance Enterprises, Task Force on Insurance Companies' Disclosures of the Insurance Companies Committee, December 1994; *Statement of Position*, Letters for State Insurance Regulators to Comply With the NAIC Model Audit Rule, Insurance Companies Committee, November 1995; *Statement of Position*, Auditor's Reporting on Statutory Financial Statements of Insurance Enterprises, Insurance Companies Committee, December 1995; *Statement of Position*, Accounting by Insurance and Other Enterprises for Insurance-Related Assessments, Insurance Companies Committee, December 1997.

Audits of Voluntary Health and Welfare Organizations, Committee on Voluntary Health and Welfare Organizations; *Statement of Position*, Accounting for Joint Costs of Informational Materials and Activities of Not-for-Profit Organizations That Include a Fund-Raising Appeal, Accounting Standards Division, August 1987; *Statement of Position*, Audits of Not-for-Profit Organizations Receiving Federal Awards, Not-for-Profit Organizations Committee, December 1992, as revised December 1995; *Statement of Position*, The Application of the Requirements of Accounting Research Bulletins, Opinions of the Accounting Principles Board, and Statements and Interpretations of the Financial Accounting Standards Board to Not-for-Profit Organizations, Not-for-Profit Organizations Committee, September 1994; *Statement of Position*, Reporting of Related Entities by Not-for-Profit Organizations, Not-for-Profit Organizations Committee, September 1994.

---

* Financial accounting and reporting principles and practices described in the indicated Audit and Accounting Guides and Statements of Position have been extracted by the FASB and issued as Statements of Financial Accounting Standards, which are enforceable under Rule 203 of the AICPA Rules of Conduct.

Audit and Accounting Guides—Continued

Banks and Savings Institutions, Banking and Savings Institutions Committee.

Brokers and Dealers in Securities, Stockbrokerage and Investment Banking Committee.

Common Interest Realty Associations, Common Interest Realty Associations Task Force; *Statement of Position*, Reporting on Required Supplementary Information Accompanying Compiled or Reviewed Financial Statements of Common Interest Realty Associations, Accounting and Review Services Committee, April 1993.

Consideration of Internal Control in a Financial Statement Audit, Control Risk Audit Guide Revision Task Force.

Construction Contractors, Construction Contractor Guide Committee; *Statement of Position*, Accounting for Performance of Construction-Type and Certain Production-Type Contracts, Accounting Standards Division, July 1981.

Guide for Prospective Financial Information, Financial Forecasts and Projections Task Force.

Guide for the Use of Real Estate Appraisal Information, Real Estate Committee.

Health Care Organizations, Health Care Committee and the Health Care Audit Guide Task Force.

Not-for-Profit Organizations, Not-for-Profit Organizations Committee.

Personal Financial Statements Guide, Personal Financial Statements Task Force; *Statement of Position*, Accounting and Financial Reporting for Personal Financial Statements, Accounting Standards Division, October 1982.

Statements of Position of the Auditing Standards Division

Confirmation of Insurance Policies in Force, Audits of Stock Life Insurance Companies 8/78

Auditing Property and Liability Reinsurance.................. 10/82

Auditing Life Reinsurance 11/84

Reports on Audited Financial Statements of Investment Companies.. 1/89

Questions Concerning Accountants' Services on Prospective Financial Statements.. 4/89

Report on the Internal Control Structure in Audits of Investment Companies.. 12/89

Accountants' Services on Prospective Financial Statements for Internal Use Only and Partial Presentations 1/90

Report on the Internal Control Structure in Audits of Futures Commission Merchants 2/90

Questions and Answers on the Term Reasonably Objective Basis *and Other Issues Affecting Prospective Financial Statements* 2/92

Auditing Insurance Entities' Loss Reserves................... 5/92

Statements of Position of the Auditing Standards Division—Continued

Auditing Property / Casualty Insurance Entities' Statutory Financial Statements—Applying Certain Requirements of the NAIC Annual Statement Instructions 10/92

Audits of Not-for-Profit Organizations Receiving Federal Awards (as revised) 12/95

Reporting on Required Supplementary Information Accompanying Compiled or Reviewed Financial Statements of Common Interest Realty Associations 4/93

The Auditor's Consideration of Regulatory Risk-Based Capital for Life Insurance Enterprises 12/93

Inquiries of State Insurance Regulators 4/94

Letters for State Insurance Regulators to Comply With the NAIC Model Audit Rule 11/95

Auditor's Reporting on Statutory Financial Statements of Insurance Enterprises 12/95

Statements of Position of the Accounting Standards Division

Accounting Practices of Real Estate Investment Trusts 6/75

Accounting Practices for Certain Employee Stock Ownership Plans 12/76

Accounting for Investments in Real Estate Ventures 12/78

Accounting for Performance of Construction-Type and Certain Production-Type Contracts 7/81

Accounting and Financial Reporting for Personal Financial Statements 10/82

Accounting by Agricultural Producers and Agricultural Cooperatives 4/85

Accounting for Developmental and Preoperating Costs, Purchases and Exchanges of Take-off and Landing Slots, and Airframe Modifications 9/88

Definition of the Term "Substantially the Same" for Holders of Debt Instruments as Used in Certain Audit Guides and a Statement of Position 2/90

Financial Reporting by Entities in Reorganization Under the Bankruptcy Code 11/90

Accounting for Real Estate Syndication Income 2/92

Accounting for Foreclosed Assets 4/92

Statements of Position of the Accounting Standards Division—Continued

Accounting for Foreign Property and Liability Reinsurance 6/92

Accounting and Reporting by Health and Welfare Benefit Plans ... 8/92

Financial Accounting and Reporting for High-Yield Debt Securities by Investment Companies 1/93

Determination, Disclosure, and Financial Statement Presentation of Income, Capital Gain, and Return of Capital Distributions by Investment Companies 2/93

Rescission of Accounting Principles Board Statements 3/93

Foreign Currency Accounting and Financial Statement Presentation for Investment Companies 4/93

Employers' Accounting for Employee Stock Ownership Plans 11/93

Reporting on Advertising Costs 12/93

Reporting of Related Entities by Not-for-Profit Organizations 9/94

Reporting of Investment Contracts Held by Health and Welfare Benefit Plans and Defined-Contribution Pension Plans 9/94

Disclosures of Certain Matters in the Financial Statements of Insurance Enterprises 12/94

Disclosure of Certain Significant Risks and Uncertainties 12/94

Accounting for Certain Insurance Activities of Mutual Life Insurance Enterprises 1/95

Financial Reporting by Nonpublic Investment Partnerships 5/95

Accounting for Certain Distribution Costs of Investment Companies 7/95

Environmental Remediation Liabilities 10/96

Accounting by Participating Mortgage Loan Borrowers 5/97

Software Revenue Recognition 10/97

Accounting by Insurance and Other Enterprises for Insurance-Related Assessments 12/97

AU Appendix E

Schedule of Changes in Statements on Auditing Standards

Section	*Par.*	*Changes*	*Date of Change*
110[1]	.02	New paragraph added by issuance of SAS 82	January, 1998
110[1]	.03	Amended[2]	April, 1989
110[1]	.03	Amended by SAS 78	February, 1997
110[1]	.06–.09	Superseded by SAS 16	January, 1977
150	.06	Amended by SAS 43	August, 1982
160	.25	Superseded by SAS 25	November, 1979
210	.05	Amended by SAS 5	July, 1975
230	.01–.03	Amended by SAS 82	January, 1998
230	.04	Amended by SAS 41	April, 1982
230	.04	Amended by SAS 82	January, 1998
230	.05–.13	New paragraphs added by issuance of SAS 82	January, 1998
310	.02	Amended by SAS 45	August, 1983
310	.03	Amended by SAS 45	August, 1983
310	.05–.09	Superseded by SAS 45	August, 1983
310[3]	.05–.07	New paragraphs added by issuance of SAS 83	October, 1997
311	.03	Amended by SAS 47	December, 1983
311	.03	Amended by SAS 48	July, 1984
311	.05	Amended by SAS 77	November, 1995
311[4]	.09	New paragraph added by issuance of SAS 48	July, 1984
311	.10	New paragraph added by issuance of SAS 48	July, 1984
312		Amended[2]	April, 1989
312	.02–.04	Amended by SAS 82	January, 1998
312[5]	.05–.08	New paragraphs added by issuance of SAS 82	January, 1998
312[5]	.11	Amended by SAS 82	January, 1998
312[5]	.13	Amended by SAS 82	January, 1998
312[5]	.16–.18	New paragraphs added by issuance of SAS 82	January, 1998
312[5]	.24	Amended by SAS 82	January, 1998
312[5]	.27	Amended by SAS 82	January, 1998
312[5]	.33	Amended by SAS 82	January, 1998
312[5]	.35	Amended by SAS 82	January, 1998

Section	Par.	Changes	Date of Change
312[5]	.40	New paragraph added by issuance of SAS 82	January, 1998
315[6]		Superseded by SAS 84	October, 1997
315A	.11	Superseded by SAS 15	December, 1976
316		Superseded by SAS 82	February, 1997
318	.07	Amended by SAS 48	July, 1984
318		Superseded by SAS 56	April, 1988
319		Amended by SAS 78	December, 1995
320[7]	.03	Superseded by SAS 48	July, 1984
320	.32	Amended by SAS 3	December,1974
320	.33	New paragraph added by issuance of SAS 48	July, 1984
320	.34	New paragraph added by issuance of SAS 48	July, 1984
320	.37	Amended by SAS 48	July, 1984
320	.50	Amended by SAS 43	August, 1982
320	.51	Amended by SAS 43	August, 1982
320	.52	Amended by SAS 43	August, 1982
320	.53	Amended by SAS 43	August, 1982
320	.54	Amended by SAS 43	August, 1982
320	.55	Amended by SAS 43	August, 1982
320	.56	Amended by SAS 43	August, 1982
320	.57	New paragraph added by issuance of SAS 48	July, 1984
320	.58	New paragraph added by issuance of SAS 48	July, 1984
320	.59	New paragraph added by issuance of SAS 43	August, 1982
320	.60	New paragraph added by issuance of SAS 43	August, 1982
320	.61	New paragraph added by issuance of SAS 43	August, 1982
320	.62	New paragraph added by issuance of SAS 43	August, 1982
320	.65	Amended by SAS 48	July, 1984
320	.66	New paragraph added by issuance of SAS 48	July, 1984
320	.67	Amended by SAS 48	July, 1984
320	.68	New paragraph added by issuance of SAS 48	July, 1984
320	.73	Amended by SAS 20	August, 1977
320	.73	Amended by SAS 30	July, 1980
320	.75	Amended by SAS 23	October, 1978
320	.77	Amended by SAS 39	June, 1981

Section	*Par.*	*Changes*	*Date of Change*
320	.79	Superseded by SAS 9	December, 1975
320		Superseded by SAS 55	April, 1988
320		Superseded by SAS 55	April, 1988
320A		Superseded by SAS 39	June, 1981
320B		Superseded by SAS 39	June, 1981
321		Superseded by SAS 48	July, 1984
322	.05	Superseded by SAS 55	April, 1989
322		Superseded by SAS 65	April, 1991
323	.01	Amended by SAS 24	March, 1979
323	.01	Amended by SAS 30	July, 1980
323	.08	Amended by SAS 30	July, 1980
323	.09	Amended by SAS 30	July, 1980
323		Superseded by SAS 60	April, 1988
324		Superseded by SAS 70	May, 1992
324	.07	Amended by SAS 78	February, 1997
324	.26	Amended by SAS 78	February, 1997
324	.42	Amended by SAS 78	February, 1997
325	.02	Amended by SAS 78	February, 1997
325	.04	Amended by SAS 78	February, 1997
326	.07	Amended by SAS 80	December, 1996
326[8]	.12	New paragraph added by issuance of SAS 48	August, 1984
326[8]	12–.13	Amended by SAS 80	December, 1996
326[9]	.14	New paragraph added by issuance of SAS 80	December, 1996
326[9]	.16–.17	Amended by SAS 80	December, 1996
326[9]	.18	New paragraph added by issuance of SAS 80	December, 1996
326[9]	.19–.22	Amended by SAS 80	December, 1996
326[9]	.25	Amended by SAS 80	December, 1996
327	.08	Amended by SAS 30	July, 1980
327		Superseded by SAS 53	April, 1988
328		Superseded by SAS 54	April, 1988
330		Superseded by SAS 31	August, 1980
330		SAS 67 added	November, 1991
331	.01	Amended by SAS 67	November, 1991
331	.03	Superseded by SAS 67	November, 1991
331	.04	Superseded by SAS 67	November, 1991
331	.05	Superseded by SAS 67	November, 1991
331	.06	Superseded by SAS 67	November, 1991
331	.07	Superseded by SAS 67	November, 1991
331	.08	Superseded by SAS 67	November, 1991

Section	Par.	Changes	Date of Change
331	.14	Amended by SAS 43	August, 1982
331[10]	.15	Deleted by SAS 43	August, 1982
331[10]	.15	Amended by SAS 2	December, 1974
332	.16	Amended by SAS 2	December, 1974
332		Superseded by SAS 81	December, 1996
333[11]		Superseded by SAS 85	November, 1997
334	.02	Revised by SOP 93-3	June, 1993
335	.01–.19	Superseded by SAS 45	August, 1983
336		Superseded by SAS 73	July, 1994
337	.14	Revised by SAS 79	February, 1997
338		Superseded by SAS 41	April, 1982
340		Superseded by SAS 59	April, 1988
341	.12	Amended by SAS 64	February, 1991
341	.13	Amended by SAS 77	November, 1995
350		Amended[2]	April, 1989
350	.08–.09	Amended by SAS 45	August, 1983
350	.11	Amended by SAS 45	August, 1983
350[12]	.46	Amended by SAS 43	June, 1982
350[12]	.47	Amended by SAS 45	August, 1983
410	.02	Amended by SAS 14	December, 1976
410	.03–.04	Superseded by SAS 5	July, 1975
411	.02	Revised by SOP 93-3	June, 1993
411	.05–.06	Amended by SAS 43	August, 1982
411	.05–.08	Amended by SAS 52	April, 1988
411[13]	.07–.08	New paragraphs added by issuance of SAS 43	August, 1982
411		Revised by SOP 93-3	June, 1993
411		Revised by SOP 93-3	June, 1993
411	.16	Revised by SOP 93-3	June, 1993
411		Superseded by SAS 69	January, 1992
420	.03	Revised by SOP 93-3	June, 1993
420	.08	Amended[2]	April, 1989
420[14]	.09	Added[2]	April, 1989
420[14]	.13	Added[2]	April, 1989
420[14]	.15	Amended by SAS 43	August, 1982
420[14]	.15	Deleted[2]	April, 1989
420	.16	Deleted by SAS 43	August, 1982
420[14]	.20	Deleted[2]	April, 1989
420	.23–.24	Added[2]	April, 1989
430	.04	Amended by SAS 21	December, 1977
430		Superseded by SAS 32	October, 1980

Section	*Par.*	*Changes*	*Date of Change*
504	.20	Amended by SAS 35	April, 1981
504	.20	Superseded by SAS 72	March, 1993
505	.05	Amended by SAS 43	August, 1982
505	.06	Amended by SAS 34	March, 1981
505	.13–.15	Superseded by SAS 26	November, 1979
505		Superseded by SAS 58	April, 1988
508	.11	Amended by SAS 79	December, 1995
508[15]	.16–.33	Deleted by SAS 79	December, 1995
508[15]	.37	Amended by SAS 79	December, 1995
508[15]	.29–.32	New paragraphs added by issuance of SAS 79	December, 1995
508[15]	.45–.49	New paragraphs added by issuance of SAS 79	December, 1995
508[15]	.70–.71	Amended by SAS 79	December, 1995
508[15]	.83	Amended by SAS 64	February, 1991
508[15]	.83–.85	Amended by SAS 79	December, 1995
509	.17	Amended by SAS 21	December, 1977
509	.18	Amended by SAS 5	July, 1975
509	.39	Amended by SAS 43	August, 1982
509	.45	Amended by SAS 26	November, 1979
509	.49	Superseded by SAS 15	December, 1976
509		Superseded by SAS 58	April, 1988
510		Superseded by SAS 2	December, 1974
511		Superseded by SAS 2	December, 1974
512		Superseded by SAS 2	December, 1974
513		Superseded by SAS 2	December, 1974
514		Superseded by SAS 2	December, 1974
515		Superseded by SAS 2	December, 1974
516	.02	Amended by SAS 2	December, 1974
516	.09	Amended by SAS 13	May, 1976
516	.09	Amended by SAS 24	March, 1979
516	.11	Amended by SAS 2	December, 1974
516	.11–.12	Superseded by SAS 15	December, 1976
516	.14	Amended by SAS 21	December, 1977
516		Superseded by SAS 26	November, 1979
517		Superseded by SAS 26	November, 1979
518	.03	Amended by SAS 14	December, 1976
518		Superseded by SAS 26	November, 1979
519		Superseded by SAS 24	March, 1979
534	.09–.10	Amended[2]	April, 1989
535		Superseded by SAS 2	December, 1974
540		Superseded by SAS 2	December, 1974

Section	*Par.*	*Changes*	*Date of Change*
541		Superseded by SAS 2	December, 1974
542	.01–.04	Superseded by SAS 2	December, 1974
542		Superseded by SAS 58	April, 1988
543	.16	Amended by SAS 64	February, 1991
543	.18	Superseded by SAS 7	November, 1975
544	.01	Superseded by SAS 2	December, 1974
544	.02	Amended by SAS 2	December, 1974
544	.02	Amended by SAS 14	December, 1976
544	.02	Amended by SAS 77	November, 1995
544	.04	Amended by SAS 14	December, 1976
544	.04	Amended by SAS 77	November, 1995
545	.01	Amended by SAS 21	December, 1977
545	.05	Amended by SAS 21	December, 1977
545		Superseded by SAS 58	April, 1988
546	.17	Amended by SAS 2	December, 1974
546		Superseded by SAS 58	April, 1988
547		Superseded by SAS 2	December, 1974
551	.15	Amended by SAS 52	April, 1988
552		Amended[2]	April, 1989
553	.02	Amended by SAS 33	October, 1980
553	.08	Amended by SAS 29	December, 1980
553	.11	Amended by SAS 29	December, 1980
553		Superseded by SAS 52	April, 1988
554		Superseded by SAS 52	April, 1988
555	.01–.06	Superseded by SAS 45	August, 1983
556		Superseded by SAS 52	April, 1988
557		Superseded by SAS 52	April, 1988
560	.12d	Amended by SAS 12	January, 1976
610		Superseded by SAS 29	December, 1980
620		Superseded by SAS 14	December, 1976
621		Superseded by SAS 63	April, 1989
621	.05	Amended by SAS 35	April, 1981
621	.15–.17	Superseded by SAS 35	April, 1981
622	.01	Amended by SAS 72	March, 1993
622		Superseded by SAS 75	September, 1995
623	.05	Amended by SAS 77	November, 1995
623	.08	Amended by SAS 77	November, 1995
623	.31	Revised by SAS 79	February, 1997
630		Superseded by SAS 38	April, 1981
631	.47	Amended by SAS 43	August, 1982
631	.51	Amended by SAS 43	August, 1982

Section	*Par.*	*Changes*	*Date of Change*
631	.56	Amended by SAS 43	August, 1982
631		Superseded by SAS 49	September, 1984
634	.33	Deleted[2]	April, 1989
634	.55	Deleted[2]	April, 1989
634		Superseded by SAS 72	March, 1993
634	.01	Amended by SAS 76	September, 1995
634	.09	Amended by SAS 76	September, 1995
634[16]	.10	New paragraph added by issuance of SAS 76	September, 1995
634[16]	.64	Amended by SAS 76	September, 1995
640	.01	Amended by SAS 20	August, 1977
640	.12–.13	Amended by SAS 20	August, 1977
640		Superseded by SAS 30	July, 1980
641		Superseded by SAS 30	July, 1980
642	.02	Amended by SAS 44	December, 1982
642	.47–.53	Superseded by SAS 60	April, 1988
642	.60	Amended by SAS 44	December, 1982
642		Superseded by SSAE 2	June, 1993
710	.11	Amended by SAS 15	December, 1976
710		Superseded by SAS 37	April, 1981
720	.22	Amended by SAS 13	May, 1976
720		Superseded by SAS 24	March, 1979
721	.02	Amended by SAS 26	November, 1979
721		Superseded by SAS 36	April, 1981
722	.01–.02	Amended by SAS 66	June, 1991
722[17]	.03–.04	New paragraphs added by issuance of SAS 66	June, 1991
722[17]	.31	Amended by SAS 66	June, 1991
722[17]	.32	Deleted by SAS 66	June, 1991
722[17]	.33–.35	New paragraphs added by issuance of SAS 66	June, 1991
722		Superseded by SAS 71	May, 1992
730		Withdrawn by Auditing Standards Board	April, 1981
801		Superseded by SAS 74	February, 1995
801	.01	Amended by SAS 75	September, 1995
901	.01	Amended by SAS 43	August, 1982
901[18]	.02	Deleted by SAS 43	August, 1982
901	.03	Deleted by SAS 43	August, 1982
901	.04	Deleted by SAS 43	August, 1982
901	.05	Deleted by SAS 43	August, 1982
901	.14	Amended[2]	April, 1989

Section	*Par.*	*Changes*	*Date of Change*
901	.24	Amended by SAS 43	August, 1982
901	.28	Amended by SAS 43	August, 1982

[1] Section 110 paragraphs .02 through .09 renumbered .03 through .10 by issuance of Statement on Auditing Standards No. 82.

[2] Paragraphs reflect the conforming changes necessary due to the issuance of Statement on Auditing Standards Nos. 53 through 62.

[3] Statement on Auditing Standards No. 1, section 310, as amended by Statement on Auditing Standards No. 45, *Omnibus Statement on Auditing Standards—1983*, "Substantive Tests Prior to the Balance-Sheet Date," has been moved to section 310A until the effective date of Statement on Auditing Standards No. 83.

[4] Section 311 paragraphs .09 through .13 renumbered .11 through .15 by issuance of Statement on Auditing Standards No. 48.

[5] Section 312 paragraphs .05 through .11 renumbered .09 through .15, .12 through .32 renumbered .19 through .39, and .33 renumbered .41 by issuance of Statement on Auditing Standards No. 82.

[6] Statement on Auditing Standards No. 7, as amended, has been moved to section 315A until the effective date of Statement on Auditing Standards No. 84.

[7] Section 320 paragraphs .56 through .75 renumbered .60 through .79 by issuance of Statement on Auditing Standards No. 43. Section 320 paragraphs .04 through .79 renumbered .03 through .84 by issuance of Statement on Auditing Standards No. 48.

[8] Section 326 paragraphs .12 through .23 renumbered .13 through .24 by issuance of Statement on Auditing Standards No. 48.

[9] Section 326 paragraphs .14 through .16 renumbered .15 through .17, and .17 through .24 renumbered .19 through .26 by issuance of Statement on Auditing Standards No. 80.

[10] Section 331 paragraph .16 (as amended by Statement on Auditing Standards No. 2) renumbered .15 by issuance of Statement on Auditing Standards No. 43.

[11] Statement on Auditing Standards No. 19, as originally issued in June 1977, has been moved to section 333A until the effective date of Statement on Auditing Standards No. 85. The former section 333A containing the appendix to Statement on Auditing Standards No. 19 has been incorporated into the new section 333A.14.

[12] Section 350 paragraph .32 added to reflect conforming changes necessary due to the issuance of Statement on Auditing Standards No. 53. Former paragraphs .32 through .47 renumbered .33 through .48.

[13] Section 411 paragraphs .07 through .09 renumbered .09 through .11 by issuance of Statement on Auditing Standards No. 43.

[14] Section 420 paragraphs .17 through .21 renumbered .16 through .20 by issuance of Statement on Auditing Standards No. 43. Paragraphs .09 through .11 renumbered .10 through .12, and paragraphs .12 through .20 renumbered .14 through .22 to reflect the conforming changes necessary due to the issuance of Statement on Auditing Standards Nos. 53 through 62.

[15] Section 508 paragraphs .34 through .46 renumbered .16 through .28, .47 through .58 renumbered .33 through .44, and .59 through .85 renumbered .50 through .76 by issuance of Statement on Auditing Standards No. 79.

[16] Section 634 paragraphs .10 through .63 renumbered .11 through .64 by issuance of Statement on Auditing Standards No. 76.

[17] Section 722 paragraphs .03 through .31 and .33 renumbered .05 through .32 and .36 through .37, respectively, by issuance of Statement on Auditing Standards No. 66.

[18] Section 901 paragraphs .06 through .32 renumbered .02 through .28 by issuance of Statement on Auditing Standards No. 43.

AU TOPICAL INDEX

References are to AU section and paragraph numbers.
Section numbers in the 9000 series refer to Auditing Interpretations.

A

References are to AU section and paragraph numbers.

References are to AU section and paragraph numbers.

References are to AU section and paragraph numbers.

References are to AU section and paragraph numbers.

AUDIT SAMPLING—continued

- Questioned Costs 801.18
- Risk—See Risk
- Sample Evaluation . . . . . 350.25–.30; 350.40–.43; 9350.02
- Sample Selection 350.24; 350.39
- Size of Sample . . . . . 350.19–.23; 350.38; 350.44
- Standards of Field Work 350.04; 350.19
- Statistical—See Statistical Sampling
- Substantive Tests . . . . . 350.12–.30; 350.43; 350.48; 9350.02
- Tests of Controls . . . . . 350.08–.10; 350.12–.14; 350.31–.43; 9350.02
- Tolerable Misstatement . . . . . 350.18; 350.21–.23; 350.26
- Tolerable Rate . . . . . 350.34–.35; 350.38; 350.41; 350.44
- Uncertainties 350.07–.11

AUDIT TESTS

- Compliance—See Compliance Tests
- Evaluation of Results 316.33–.36
- Evidential Matter 326.01–.26
- Examination at Interim Dates . . . 313.01–.10; 9326.03
- Fraud 311.03; 316.28–.36
- Illegal Act Detection 9317.01–.02; 9333.01–.04
- Information Provided to Specialist 9336.09–.16
- Material Misstatements 312.35
- Planning of Audit Work 311.03
- Prior to Balance Sheet Date 313.01–.10
- Related Party Transactions . . . . . 311.03; 334.01–.12; 9334.16–.21
- Relation to Internal Control 9317.01–.02
- Representation Letters 333.01–.18; 333A.01–.13
- Sampling—See Audit Sampling
- Segment Information 435.06
- Service Organizations—See Service Organizations
- Substantive—See Substantive Tests
- Use of Findings of Specialists 336.12; 9336.11–.12
- Work of Other Auditors 543.13
- Working Papers 339.03; 339.05

AUDITING INTERPRETATIONS

- Distribution of Reports 544.02–.04; 9623.51

AUDITING PROCEDURES

- Federal Financial Assistance Programs 801.13–.14; 801.17–.20
- Financial Statement Effects of Laws on Governmental Entities 801.07
- Representations From Management . . 333.03

AUDITING STANDARDS—See Generally Accepted Auditing Standards

AUDITOR, INDEPENDENT

- Accounting Estimates 342.01–.16
- Adequate and Appropriate Disclosure . . . . . 431.02; 9623.60–.77; 9623.88–.93
- Agreed-Upon Procedures Engagements . . 622.01–.49; 9622.01–.02
- Analytical Procedures 329.01–.23
- Appointment at Year-End . . 310.04; 310A.04
- Association With Financial Statements 504.01–.20
- Audit Risk and Materiality 312.01–.41
- Audit Sampling . . . 350.01–.48; 9350.01–.02
- Basis of Accounting Other Than GAAP . . . . . 534.01–.16; . . . . . 623.02–.10; 9534.01–.04; 9623.47–.54; 9623.88–.93
- Change of Auditors . . . . . 315.01–.25; 315A.01–.12; 9315A.01–.18
- Client Representations—See Representation Letters
- Comments on Audit 551.20
- Communication Regarding Applicable Audit Requirements 801.21–.23
- Communication When No Audit Committee Exists 9380.02–.03
- Communication With Audit Committees . . . 380.01–.15; 722.20–.25; 801.22; 9411.15
- Comparative Financial Statements 504.14–.17
- Completeness Assertion 9326.18–.21
- Compliance Auditing 801.01–.24
- Compliance Reports . . . . . 623.19–.21; 9634.01–.09
- Condensed Financial Information 9504.15–.18
- Condensed Financial Statements 552.01–.08
- Confirmation Process 330.01–.36
- Consideration of Management's Adoption of Accounting Principles for New Transactions or Events 9411.11–.15
- Consideration of Risk Factors in Assessing Risk of Material Misstatement Due to Fraud 316.12; 316.21–.25
- Continuing Auditor 508.65
- Current-Value Financial Statements 9623.55–.59
- Date of Engagement Acceptance 310.04; 310A.04
- Definition 311.02
- Design of Audit 801.06; 801.08
- Design of Substantive Tests 313.08
- Determination of Intent 316.03
- Direct v. Indirect Knowledge 326.21
- Due Professional Care 230.01–.13

References are to AU section and paragraph numbers.

AUDITOR, INDEPENDENT—continued
- · Estimation of Future Events 312.36
- · Evaluating Audit Test Results . . . 316.33–.36
- · Evaluating Results of Compliance Audit Procedures on Major Federal Financial Assistance Programs 801.17–.20
- · Evidential Matter . . . . . 312.12; 312.19–.20; . . . . 312.36–.38; 322.02; 326.01–.26; 9326.01–.21
- · Expertise in EDP 311.10
- · Firm—See Firm
- · First Year Audits 420.23–.24
- · Fraud 316.01–.41
- · Functions 110.01–.05; 110.10
- · GAAP—Sources 411.05–.13
- · Going Concern Assumption . . . . . 341.01–.17; 9341.01–.02
- · Illegal Acts by Client . . . . 312.05; 316.01; 317.01–.25
- · Incomplete Special-Purpose Financial Presentation 9623.80–.87
- · Independence . . . . 220.01–.07; 504.08–.10; 622.09; 634.31–.32; 9504.19–.22
- · Internal Audit Function Considerations 322.01–.29
- · Internal Auditor Competence and Objectivity Assessment 322.09–.11
- · Internal Auditor, Relationship 311.04
- · Internal Control Considerations . . . . 319.01–.84; 801.10; 9311.44–.47
- · Internal Control Reports—See Reports on Internal Control
- · Judgment—See Judgment
- · Knowledge of GAAP 722.09
- · Knowledge of Matters Outside Agreed-Upon Procedures 622.41
- · Legal Advice Regarding Access of Working Papers by Regulator 9339.12
- · Legal Liability 230.03
- · Letters for Underwriters 634.01–.64
- · Litigation, Claims, and Assessments . . . 337.01–.14; 9337.01–.32
- · Loss Reserves (Insurance) 9623.40–.46
- · Merger of Accounting Firms 508.65
- · Objective of Audit . . . . . 110.01; 326.09–.14; 326.22; 326.25
- · Observation of Inventories . . . . 310.04; . . . . 310A.04; 331.01–.02; 331.09–.12; 331.14; 9508.01–.06
- · Oil and Gas Reserve Information 9558.01–.05
- · Omitted Auditing Procedures . . . 390.01–.08
- · Opinions—See Opinions, Auditors'
- · Other Information in Electronic Sites Containing Audited Financial Statements 9550.16–.18
- · Planning of Audit Work . . . . 311.01; 312.01; 312.12–.33; 801.11; 9311.01–.34
- · Predecessor—See Predecessor Auditor
- · Preparation of Statements . . 110.03; 431.03
- · Principal Auditor . . 543.01–.17; 9543.18–.24

AUDITOR, INDEPENDENT—continued
- · Professional Skepticism . . . . 342.04; 342.07–.14
- · Proficiency—See Proficiency of Auditor
- · Public Warehouses, Procedures . . . . 901.01; 901.04; 901.24; 901.28
- · Publicly-Traded Companies 9504.01–.07
- · Qualifications 110.04–.05; 337.06
- · Quality Control Standards 161.01–.03
- · Reasonable Investigation . . . . 634.02; 634.12; 711.03
- · Registration Statements . . . . . . 711.01–.13; 9711.01–.11
- · Related Parties . . . . 334.01; 334.04; 334.09–.10; 9334.16–.21
- · Relation to Nonaudit Services 9311.01–.03
- · Relationship Between Appointment and Planning 310.01–.04; 310A.01–.04
- · Relationship of Confirmation Procedures to Risk Assessment . . . . 330.05; 330.07–.10; 330.20–.22
- · Reliance on Other Auditors—See Reports, Other Auditors'
- · Reliance on Representations . . . . 319.22; . . . . . . 326.03–.08; 326.22; 333.02–.04; 333A.02–.03; 350.25; 9326.18–.20
- · Report—See Auditors' Reports
- · Reporting on Internal Control 325.01–.21; 9325.01–.06
- · Resignation & Subsequent Discovery of Facts 9561.01–.02
- · Responses to Assessment of the Risk of Material Misstatement Arising From Fraudulent Financial Reporting 316.30
- · Responses to Assessment of the Risk of Material Misstatement Arising From Misappropriation of Assets 316.31
- · Responses to Assessment of the Risk of Material Misstatement Due to Fraud 316.29; 9550.16–.18
- · Responsibilities and Functions . . . . 110.01–.05; . . . . 110.10; 230.01–.13; 310.06; 311.02; . . . . 311.10; 312.05; 312.08; 316.01–.41; . . . . 317.05; 322.02; 322.19–.22; . . . . 324.22–.58; 336.03; 336.06–.17; . . . . 341.02–.04; 342.04; 380.06; . . . . 551.04–.11; 558.04–.05; 622.13–.15; . . . . . . 622.41; 801.01–.24; 9311.39–.41; . . . . 9333A.05–.06; 9336.01–.18; . . . . 9339.01–.15; 9341.01–.02; . . . . 9380.01–.03; 9550.07–.18; 9622.01–.02; 9623.86–.87
- · Responsibilities of Assistant for Audit Disagreements 9311.35–.37
- · Responsibility to Profession 110.10
- · Review of Form 10-K 9634.01–.09
- · Review of Interim Information . . . 722.01–.44
- · Risk 342.14
- · Risk Assessment—Internal Audit Function 322.14–.16

References are to AU section and paragraph numbers.

AUDITOR, INDEPENDENT—continued
- Risk Assessment—Response to Results of Assessment of Material Misstatement Due to Fraud 316.26–.32
- Role of Auditor 110.04; 322.02
- SEC Filings 711.01–.13; 9711.01–.17
- Segment Information 435.03
- Selected Financial Data 552.01–.02; 552.05; 552.09–.12
- Service Organization 324.01–.59; 9324.01–.18
- Special Reports—See Special Reports
- Special-Purpose Financial Presentations . . 623.22–.30; 9623.80–.87
- Successor—See Successor Auditor
- Supervision of Audit Work 311.01
- Supplementary Information 551.01–.22; 558.01–.10; 9558.01–.05
- Third-Party Additions 9623.85–.87
- Training—See Training and Education
- Understanding Financial Statement Effects of Laws on Governmental Entities 801.07
- Understanding Internal Audit Function 322.04–.08
- Understanding Internal Control . . 319.19–.44; 322.13
- Understanding Transactions 311.06; 334.09–.10
- Understanding With Client 310.05–.07; 622.03; 622.10–.11; 9339.04; 9339.12–.13
- Use of Illegal Interpretations to Support That Transfer of Assets Has Met Isolation Criteria in FASB Statement No. 125 . . . . . 9336.01–.18
- Use of Work of Specialists 311.10; 336.01–.17; 9326.13–.17; 9336.01–.18
- Weaknesses in Internal Control 9325.01–.06
- Withdrawal From Audit Engagement 316.26; 316.36; 504.13
- Work of Internal Auditors 322.12–.27
- Working Papers—See Working Papers
- Year 2000 Issue 9311.38–.47

AUDITOR, INTERNAL
- Auditor's Understanding of Function 322.04–.08
- Competence 322.09; 322.11
- Directly Assisting Auditor 322.27
- Effect on the Audit 322.12–.27
- Functions 322.03; 622.24–.25
- Internal Control 322.13
- Objectivity 322.03; 322.10–.11
- Planning of Audit Work 311.04
- Relation to Independent Auditors 311.04; 322.01–.29
- Relevance of Function to Audit of Entity's Financial Statements 322.06–.08
- Risk Assessment 322.14–.17
- Substantive Procedures 322.17

AUDITORS' OPINIONS—See Opinions, Auditors'

AUDITORS' REPORTS
- Accounting Changes 9410.13–.18; 9420.52–.54
- Addressee of Report 508.09
- Adverse Opinion 508.10; 508.58–.60
- Applicability of Guidance 508.01–.03
- Audit Risk and Materiality 312.01–.02
- Audited Financial Statements . . . 508.01–.76
- Auditor-Submitted Documents . . 551.01–.22
- Availability to Public 9623.47–.54
- Basis of Accounting Other Than GAAP 410.02; 623.02–.10; 9508.33–.37; 9623.47–.54; 9623.88–.93
- Change in Pension Plan Presentation 9420.64–.65
- Classification and Reclassification . . . 420.14
- Communication With Audit Committee 380.03–.04
- Comparability of Financial Statements 420.02; 420.05
- Comparative Financial Statements 504.14–.17; 508.08; 508.65–.74; 711.11–.12
- Compilation—See Compilation of Financial Statements
- Compliance Reports 9623.40–.46; 9634.03–.09
- Condensed Financial Statements 552.01–.08
- Consistency . . . . . 420.01–.24; 435.14; . . . 508.03; 508.16–.18; 623.31; 9420.20
- Consolidating Information 551.16–.19
- Current-Value Financial Statements Supplementing Historical-Cost Financial Statements 9623.55–.59
- Date of Report . . . 530.01–.08; 711.05–.06; 711.12; 9508.21–.24
- Departure—See Departure From Standard Report
- Departure From GAAP . 431.03; 508.14–.15; 508.35–.60; 711.13; 722.30–.32
- Differing Opinions 508.67–.69
- Disclaimer of Opinion 508.10
- Effect of Internal Audit Function 322.19–.22
- Effect of Specialists' Work 336.13–.14
- Emphasis of a Matter 508.19
- Explanatory Language Added 332.20; 508.10–.19; 623.31; 9550.10
- Explanatory Paragraph 341.12–.13; 9341.01–.02
- Expression of Opinion 110.01; 504.01
- Fair Presentation 110.01; 411.01–.16
- FIFO to LIFO Change 9420.16–.20
- Financial Statements for Use Outside U.S. 534.01–.16; 9534.01–.04
- Form for Qualified Opinion 508.21

References are to AU section and paragraph numbers.

AUDITORS' REPORTS—continued
- Form of Standard Report 508.07
- Going Concern Assumption..... 341.03–.04; 341.12–.16; 9341.01–.02
- Illustrations—See Illustrations
- Incomplete Special-Purpose Financial Presentation 9623.80–.87
- Interim Financial Information....... 711.01; .... 711.03; 711.06; 711.09; 711.13; 722.26–.34; 722.40–.42
- Internal Control—See Reports on Internal Control
- Introductory Paragraph..... 508.06; 508.12
- Lack of Independence .... 504.08–.10; 9504.19–.22
- Letters for Underwriters....... 634.27–.30; 634.59
- Litigation, Claims, and Assessments .... 337.01–.14; 9337.01–.32
- Management Responsibility for Financial Statements.............. 9508.51–.52
- Negative Assurance 504.18–.19
- Omitted Auditing Procedures 390.01–.08
- One Financial Statement Only ... 508.33–.34
- Opinion Paragraph 508.12
- Other Auditors'—See Reports, Other Auditors'
- Other Information in Documents... 550.01–.06; 551.04; 722.33
- Other Information in Electronic Sites Containing Audited Financial Statements.............. 9550.16–.18
- Planning of Audit Work............. 311.03–.04; 311.13
- Prescribed Forms............ 623.32–.33
- Prior Year's Statements..... 504.15–.17; 711.11–.13
- Qualified Opinion 508.10; 508.20–.57
- Reference to Specialists....... 336.15–.16
- Regulated Companies......... 544.02–.04
- Reissued—See Reissued Reports
- Report Form of a Foreign Country....... 534.07–.08; 534.11–.12; 534.15
- Reputation and Standing............ 543.01
- Restricted Distribution .... 9623.83; 9623.85–.87
- Review of Form 10-K 9634.01–.09
- Review Reports—See Review Reports
- Revision for Subsequent Discovery 561.06–.09
- Scope Limitation .... 333.13–.14; .... 333A.11–.12; 435.15–.16; .... 508.22–.34; 9326.06–.10; 9337.17; 9508.01
- SEC Filings....... 311.03; 504.14; 530.02; ...... 530.06; 711.01–.13; 722.35–.37; .... 722.41; 9711.03; 9711.09; 9711.12–.17
- Segment Information .... 435.08–.10; 435.13–.16; 435.18
- Selected Financial Data .... 552.01–.02; 552.05; 552.09–.12

AUDITORS' REPORTS—continued
- Service Organizations—See Service Organizations
- Special Reports—See Special Reports
- Special-Purpose Financial Presentations. . 623.22–.30; 9623.80–.87
- Standards of Reporting........... 150.02; 431.01–.04; 508.03–.05
- Statutory Reporting—See Statutory Reporting Requirements
- Subsequent Discovery of Facts............. 561.01–.10; 722.34; 9561.01–.02
- Summarized Comparative Information .. 508.65
- Supplementary Information .... 551.01–.22; 552.05; 558.01–.10; 9558.01–.05
- Third-Party Additions......... 9623.85–.87
- Time Lag in Reporting............ 332.20
- U.S. Report Form on Foreign Country's Accounting Principles........ 534.07–.10
- U.S. Report Form on Foreign Country's Financial Statements 534.14–.15
- Unaudited Financial Statements 504.05–.19; 508.02
- Uncertainties......... 337.14; 341.12–.13; 508.29–.32; 508.67; 9337.17
- Unqualified Opinion 508.10
- Updated Reports... 508.65–.66; 508.68–.69
- Working Papers 339.02; 339.04

AUTHORITIES, REGULATORY—See Regulatory Agencies

AUTHORIZATION
- Client's Permission to Predecessor Auditor..... 315.08; 315.11; 315.24–.25; 315A.05; 315A.09

B

BALANCE SHEETS—See Statements of Financial Position

BANKERS
- Inquiries Concerning Other Auditors..................... 543.10

BASIS OF ACCOUNTING
- Accrual—See Accrual Basis of Accounting
- Agreed-Upon Procedures .. 622.06; 622.09; 622.11; 622.14; 622.33
- Audit Risk and Materiality 312.03
- Cash Basis 623.08; 9623.88–.93
- Change in Bases............. 435.11–.14
- Description of Other Comprehensive Basis of Accounting.................. 623.04
- Income Tax Basis .... 623.08; 9623.47–.54; 9623.88–.93
- Liquidation Basis............ 9508.33–.37
- Management's Adoption of Accounting Principles for New Transactions or Events.................... 9411.12
- Modified Cash Basis 9623.88–.93

BASIS OF ACCOUNTING—continued

· Other Than GAAP......... 312.03; 410.02; .... 504.07; 623.02–.10; .... 9508.33–.37; 9623.47–.54; 9623.60–.77; 9623.88–.93

· Prescribed by Regulatory Agency... 623.08; 9623.47–.54; 9623.60–.77

· Representation Letters .... 333.05–.06; 333.10; 333.16; 333A.04–.05

· Sales or Transfers Between Segments.................... 435.07

BOARD OF DIRECTORS

· Control Environment ...... 319.18; 319.23; 319.25–.26

· Interim Financial Information............ 722.13; 722.27

· Internal Control 319.84

· Minutes of Meetings....... 333.06; 333.11; .... 333.16; 333A.04–.05; 333A.10; 334.08; 337.07; 722.13

· Planning of Audit Work........... 311.04

· Review of Form 10-K 9634.01–.09

BOOK VALUE—See Carrying Amount

BOOKS—See Records

BORROWING CONTRACT

· Compliance Reports........... 623.19–.21

· Going Concern Assumption 341.07

· Illustrative Special Report 623.30

· Litigation, Claims, and Assessments . 337.07

· Management Representations ..... 333.07; 333A.04; 333A.06

· Related Party Transactions.... 334.03; 334.08; 334.10

· Violation of Debt Covenant........ 9410.17

BUSINESS COMBINATIONS

· Auditing Firms 508.65; 508.74

· Letters for Underwriters........... 634.42

· Unaudited Information 508.28

BUSINESS ENTERPRISE

· Assertions by Management... 326.03–.08; 9326.06–.10

· Change in Reporting Entity..... 420.07–.10

· Closely Held Companies 334.07

· Components—See Components of a Business

· Going Concern—See Going Concern

· Nonbusiness—See Nonbusiness Organizations

· Nonpublic—See Nonpublic Enterprises

· Planning of Audit Work 311.01; 311.03–.10

· Publicly Traded—See Publicly Traded Companies

· Regulated—See Regulated Industries

· Segment Information 435.01–.18

· Types of Financial Statements 623.02

C

CAPITAL STRUCTURE

· Letters for Underwriters 634.35; 634.45; 634.49

CAPITAL, WORKING—See Working Capital

CAPITALIZATION

· Leases........................ 326.06

CAPSULE INFORMATION

· Letters for Underwriters....... 634.35; 634.39–.41

CARRYING AMOUNT

· Investments 332.23–.30

· Management Representations...... 333.06; 333.16–.17; 333A.04;

CASH

· Compensating Balances ... 333.17; 333A.04

CASH BASIS STATEMENTS—See Special Reports

CASH FLOWS

· Change in Presentation............ 420.13

· Management Representations...... 333.06; 333.16; 333.18

CHANGE OF AUDITORS

· Communication Between Auditors 315.01–.25; 315A.01–.12

CHANGES, ACCOUNTING

· Adverse Opinion .... 508.51; 508.53 .... 508.55–.56; 9410.15

· Alternatives 9410.13–.18

· Auditor's Evaluation 508.50–.51

· Change in Estimate 420.12; 420.14; 9623.46

· Change to GAAP From Other Basis 420.11; 508.50–.51

· Comparability............... 508.54–.55

· Comparability Between Years...... 420.02; 420.04; 9420.53

· Comparative Financial Statements .. 9420.16

· Concurrence by Auditor .... 508.16; 508.50–.52

· Consistency Affected .... 420.06–.11; 508.16–.18; 623.31; 9420.52–.54

· Consistency Not Affected .... 420.19; 552.05; 9420.20

· Correction of Error............... 420.11

· Cumulative Effect Adjustment....... 508.56

· Definition 420.04

· Departure From GAAP 508.55

· Disclosure 9420.19–.20

· Effects on Subsequent Years 508.18

· Elements of Financial Statements.............. 9623.45–.46

· Estimates...................... 420.14

· Future Change in Principle 9410.15–.18

· Illustrations of Reporting 508.17; 508.52; 9420.19

CHANGES, ACCOUNTING—continued
· Interim Financial Information 722.13; 722.16; 722.30
· Inventory Pricing Methods 9420.16–.20
· Investees 9420.52–.54
· Lacking Conformity With GAAP 508.50–.51; 722.30
· Management Justification...... 508.50–.52; 508.57
· Materiality 420.05; 420.19
· Pension Plans.............. 9420.64–.65
· Presentation of Cash Flows 420.13
· Qualified Opinion ..... 508.50; 508.52–.57; 9410.16–.17
· Reporting Entity 420.07–.10
· Reporting in Subsequent Years...... 508.18
· Restatement..................... 508.56
· Segment Information .. 435.08; 435.11–.14; 435.18
· Subsequent Years Reporting ... 508.53–.57

CHANGES, PRICE LEVEL—See Price Level Changes

CLAIMS
· Audit Procedures .... 333.06; 333A.04; .... 337.05–.07; 9337.15–.17; 9337.24–.27
· Client Has Not Consulted a Lawyer 9337.15–.17
· Inquiries of Client's Lawyers .... 337.08–.11; 722.17; 9337.01–.32
· Internal v. Outside Lawyers.... 9337.24–.27
· Limitations on Lawyer's Responses 337.12–.14
· Management Representations...... 333.06; 333.16–.17; 333A.04

CLASSIFICATION
· Adequate Disclosure.............. 431.02
· Auditor's Knowledge of Practices 722.13
· Comparability and Consistency...... 420.16
· Interim Financial Information........ 722.13
· Investments 332.07–.09; 332.11
· Management Representations... 326.03–.08; .... 333.06; 333.16–.17; 333A.04; 333A.06
· Pension Plans.............. 9420.64–.65
· Segment Information 435.06

CLIENTS
· Auditor-Submitted Documents 551.04; 552.01
· Auditor's Knowledge of Practices 722.13
· Authorization to Predecessor Auditor .... 315.08; 315.11; 315.24–.25; 315A.05; 315A.09
· Authorization to Provide Working Papers to Regulator 9339.04–.06; 9339.12–.13
· Change in Lawyers.............. 337.11
· Client-Prepared Documents .... 551.04; 552.01–.12

CLIENTS—continued
· Condensed Financial Information 9504.15–.18
· Confidential Information—See Confidential Client Information
· Disagreement With Auditor .... 315.07; .... 315.09; 315A.04–.07; 504.06; 504.13; 551.09; 722.35
· Disclosure of Discovery of Facts.......... 561.06–.09; 711.12–.13
· Failure to Disclose .... 504.11–.13; 508.41–.44; 561.08; 711.12
· Foreign Corrupt Practices Act 9317.01–.06
· Illegal Acts—See Illegal Acts
· Income Tax Accruals......... 9326.06–.17
· Integrity of Management 333A.02–.03
· Interim Financial Information .... 722.13; 722.35
· Investigation Requested by Auditor .. 561.04
· Lawyer-Client Communications ..... 337.13; 9337.10–.27
· Letters for Underwriters—See Letters for Underwriters
· Litigation, Claims, and Assessments............. 337.01–.14; 9337.01–.32
· Omitted Auditing Procedures....... 390.07
· Other Information in Documents .... 550.01–.06; 551.04; 558.04–.05; 9550.07–.15
· Other Information in Electronic Sites Containing Audited Financial Statements 9550.16–.18
· Personnel—See Employees
· Records—See Records
· Refusal to Accept Auditor's Report .. 504.13
· Registration Statements 711.10–.11
· Reissuance of Predecessor Auditor's Report.................. 508.70–.73
· Relationship With Predecessor Auditor...................... 508.73
· Relationship With Specialists 336.10–.11
· Relationships—See Relationship With Clients
· Representations—See Representation Letters
· Review Working Papers Prior to Access by Regulator................... 9339.14
· Scope Limitations .... 333.13–.14; .... 333A.11–.12; 508.22; .... 508.29–.32; 642.44; 722.26; 9326.06–.10; 9508.01–.06
· Segment Information... 435.10; 435.15–.16
· Special Reports—See Special Reports
· Supplementary Information—See Supplementary Financial Information
· Understanding With Accountant .... 310.05–.07; 622.03; 622.11; 9339.04; 9339.12–.13
· Use of Accountant's Name .... 504.06; 9504.15–.18; 9550.14–.15
· Use of Explanatory Language About Attorney-Client Privilege 9337.28–.30
· Working Papers .... 310.07; 339.06–.07; 622.30–.31

References are to AU section and paragraph numbers.

CLOSELY HELD COMPANIES
· Related Parties 334.07

CODE OF CONDUCT—See Conduct, Code of Professional

COLLATERAL
· Investments 332.30
· Management Representations ..... 333.06; 333.09; 333.17; 333A.04

COLLUSION—See Fraud

COMBINED FINANCIAL STATEMENTS
· Supplementary Information 551.16–.19

COMFORT LETTERS—See Letters for Underwriters

COMMITTEE
· Audit—See Audit Committee
· Directors—See Board of Directors
· Quality Control Standards 161.01

COMMON CARRIERS—See Regulated Industries

COMMUNICATION
· Access to Working Papers by Regulator 9339.04–.06; 9339.12–.13
· Accounting Policies to Audit Committee 380.07
· Agreed-Upon Procedures 622.10
· Applicable Audit Requirements ... 801.21–.23
· Audit Adjustments 380.09
· Audit Plan 311.04
· Auditor and Audit Committees .. 380.01–.15; 801.22; 9411.15
· Auditor—When No Audit Committee Exists 9380.02–.03
· Auditor's Responsibility Under GAAS ... 380.06
· Change of Auditors .... 315.01–.25; 315A.01–.12; 9315A.01–.18
· Continuing Accountant and Reporting Accountant 625.07
· Deficiencies in Internal Control 722.24
· Difficulties in Performing Audit 380.14
· Disagreements With Management ... 380.11
· Discussions With Management Prior to Retention 380.13
· Engagement Letters—See Engagement Letters
· Fraud 316.36; 316.38–.40; 722.33
· GAAS Audit Insufficient 801.22
· Illegal Acts 317.17; 722.23
· Interim Financial Information 722.05; 722.20–.26
· Lawyer-Client 337.13; 9337.10–.27
· Management Consultation With Other Accountants 380.12
· Management Judgments Regarding Accounting Estimates 380.08
· Material Weaknesses in Internal Control 325.15; 9325.01–.06
· Nonaudit Personnel 9311.01–.03

COMMUNICATION—continued
· Objectives to EDP Specialists 311.10
· Other Information in Documents 380.10
· Position Papers 625.04
· Principal and Other Auditor . 543.10; 543.17; 9334.12–.15; 9543.01–.17
· Principal and Reporting Accountant .. 625.07
· Privileged—See Confidential Client Information
· Reportable Conditions .... 316.39; 325.02–.03; 325.06; 325.09–.12
· Reporting on Internal Control 325.01–.21; 9325.01–.06
· Reports on Internal Control Over Financial Reporting 9550.07–.15
· Representations—See Representation Letters
· Responsibilities of Assistant for Audit Disagreements 9311.35–.37
· Service Organizations 324.23
· Timing Considerations 315.04; 315A.03
· Use of Accountant's Name .... 504.03; 504.06; 9504.15–.18
· Weakness in Internal Control Over Financial Reporting 9550.11; 9550.15
· Year 2000 Issue 9311.45–.47

COMPARABILITY
· Analytical Procedures 722.13
· Changes, Accounting ..... 420.02; 420.04; .... 508.16–.18; 508.54–.55; 9420.16; 9420.52–.54
· Classification and Reclassifications 420.04; 420.16
· Condensed Financial Statements 552.05; 552.08
· Emphasis in Auditor's Report 508.19
· Explanatory Language Added to Auditor's Standard Report 508.16–.18
· Factors Affecting 420.04–.05
· Interim v. Annual Data 313.08; 9420.14
· Lease Accounting 9420.24–.27
· Pooling of Interests 420.08
· Reissuance of Financial Statements .. 560.08
· Relation to Consistency .... 420.03; 552.05; 9420.20; 9420.52–.54

COMPARATIVE FINANCIAL STATEMENTS
· Auditors' Reports 508.65–.74
· Changes, Accounting .... 508.54; 508.57; 9420.16
· Condensed Financial Statements 552.08
· Consistency 420.08; 9420.20
· Going Concern Assumption 341.15–.16
· Illustration of Auditor's Report 508.08
· Interim Financial Information 722.13
· Liquidation Basis of Accounting 9508.35
· Predecessor Auditor's Report 508.70–.74; 711.11–.12
· Report Requirements 9420.20
· Reports With Differing Opinions . 504.16–.17; 508.67–.69; 623.31
· SEC Filings 504.14; 711.11–.12
· Segment Information 435.08
· Unaudited Financial Statements ... 504.14–.17

References are to AU section and paragraph numbers.

COMPENSATING BALANCES
- Management Representations...... 333.17; 333A.04
- Related Party Transactions......... 334.08

COMPETENCE
- Assistants to Auditor 311.10–.11
- Auditor, Independent 110.04–.05; 150.02; 210.01–.05; 634.55; 634.60; 9623.40
- Evidential Matter 312.12; 326.01–.02; 326.12; 326.21; 330.11; 350.06; 9326.03
- Internal Auditors.......... 322.09; 322.11
- Legal Matters................... 337.06
- Other Auditors 543.05; 543.10–.11
- Specialists......... 336.08; 9326.13–.17

COMPILATION OF FINANCIAL STATEMENTS
- Change From Audit Engagement..... 508.61
- Departures From Established Principles 552.02
- Omission of Disclosures........... 552.02
- Subsequent Period Audited......... 504.17

COMPLETENESS
- Assertions by Management........ 319.45; 326.03–.05; 326.09–.11; 9326.18–.19
- Consideration by Auditor 330.13–.14; 332.04; 9326.18–.21
- Evidential Matter 330.13–.14; 332.04; 9326.18–.21
- Reliance on Substantive Tests 9326.21
- Substantive Tests.... 313.05; 9326.20–.21

COMPLIANCE AUDITING
- Agreed-Upon Procedures Engagement.................. 801.01
- Applicability 801.01–.02
- Auditor's Responsibilities 801.01–.24
- Common Elements in Audit of Recipient of Federal Financial Assistance 801.10
- Communications Regarding Applicable Audit Requirements 801.21–.23
- Compliance Requirements Applicable to Federal Financial Assistance Programs 801.12–.16
- Compliance Supplements Requirements 801.13
- Design 801.06; 801.08
- Effects of Laws on Financial Statements of Governmental Entities 801.03–.07
- Evaluating Results of Compliance Audit Procedures on Major Federal Financial Assistance Programs 801.17–.20
- Federal Audit Requirements 801.10–.20
- Forms of Federal Financial Assistance 801.04
- Government Auditing Standards Requirements 801.08–.09
- Internal Control Considerations 801.10–.11

COMPLIANCE AUDITING—continued
- Management Representations 801.07; 801.10
- Management Responsibilities 801.05; 801.21
- Noncompliance....... 801.17; 801.19–.20
- Office of Management and Budget Standards and Requirements ... 801.07; 801.13–.15; 801.22
- Organization-Wide v. Program-Specific............... 801.11; 801.14
- Planning 801.11
- Procedures for Assessing Management Identification of Laws........... 801.07
- Questioned Costs 801.17–.19
- Terminology 801.01; 801.04; 801.08–.09; 801.12–.13
- Tests of Compliance ... 801.13–.14; 801.18
- Types of Compliance Requirements............. 801.12–.15
- Use of Audit Sampling............ 801.18
- Workpaper Documentation 801.23

COMPLIANCE REPORTS—See Special Reports

COMPLIANCE TESTS
- Compliance Auditing Applicable to Governmental Entities—See Compliance Auditing
- Reports—See Reports on Internal Control

COMPONENTS OF A BUSINESS
- Communication Between Auditors.......... 543.10; 9543.01–.17
- Consolidating Information 551.16–.19
- Emphasis in Auditor's Report....... 508.19
- Interim Financial Information 722.13
- Management....................... 543.13
- Related Party Transactions .. 334.07–.08; 9334.14–.15
- Uniformity...................... 543.10
- Work of Other Auditors.... 543.01–.02; 543.06; 543.10

COMPREHENSIVE BASIS OF ACCOUNTING
- Adequacy and Appropriateness of Disclosure 623.09–.10; 9623.60–.77; 9623.88–.93
- Audit Risk and Materiality 312.03
- Basic Financial Statements 551.02
- Definition 623.04
- Financial Statements Not Meeting Criteria 623.06
- Form of Auditor's Report.......... 623.05
- Illustrative Reports 623.08
- Limited Distribution Reports 623.05
- Omitted Auditing Procedures....... 390.01
- Regulatory Agencies............. 411.08
- Relation to Evidential Matter 326.25
- Reports on Application of Principles 625.01–.09
- Special Reports 410.02; 623.02–.10; 9623.60–.77; 9623.88–.93

References are to AU section and paragraph numbers.

CONDENSED FINANCIAL INFORMATION
· Identification of Auditor 9504.15–.18
· Letters for Underwriters—See Letters for Underwriters
· Parent Company 552.05

CONDENSED FINANCIAL STATEMENTS
· Adverse Opinion................ 552.07
· Auditor's Report............. 552.01–.08
· Comparability—See Comparability
· Comparative—See Comparative Financial Statements
· Consolidated—See Consolidated Financial Statements
· Date of Auditor's Report........... 552.05
· Disclosure................. 552.03–.04
· Filing With a Regulatory Agency........... 552.07–.08; 9711.07
· Financial Position............ 552.03–.04
· Generally Accepted Accounting Principles 552.03–.04
· Illustrations 552.06–.08
· Interim Periods 552.01; 552.08
· Letters for Underwriters—See Letters for Underwriters
· Qualified Opinion 552.05
· Reference to Another Auditor....... 552.05
· Results of Operations 552.03–.04
· Review Report 552.08; 9711.09
· SEC—See Securities and Exchange Commission
· Shelf Registration Statements 9711.09
· Unqualified Opinion 552.06
· Use of Auditor's Name........... 552.07

CONDUCT, CODE OF PROFESSIONAL
· Departures From GAAP 508.14–.15
· Disclosure of Confidential Information................... 315A.05
· Independence 220.04; 9504.19–.22
· Rules of Conduct—See Rules of Conduct

CONFIDENTIAL CLIENT INFORMATION
· Disclosure of Information... 315.06; 315.08; 315.25; 315A.05; 431.04
· Explanatory Language in Audit Inquiry Letter.................. 9337.28–.30
· Fraud........................... 316.40
· Illegal Acts by Client 317.23
· Information From Other Auditors ... 315A.02
· Lawyer-Client Communications.... 337.13; 9337.08–.09
· Subsequent Discovery of Facts 561.02
· Working Papers......... 339.06; 9339.03; 9339.05–.06; 9339.10; 9339.13

CONFIRMATIONS
· Alternative Procedures........ 330.31–.32
· Assertions................. 330.11–.14
· Compensating Balance Arrangements.................. 334.08

CONFIRMATIONS—continued
· Completeness 330.13–.14
· Definition 330.04
· Design 330.16–.27
· Evaluation of Results 330.33
· Evidential Matter .... 150.02; 326.17; .... 330.06–.14; 330.29; 330.33; 332.04; 350.04
· Guarantees Shown on Bank Confirmations................. 337.07
· Inventories.................. 331.09–.13
· Investments............. 332.04; 332.11
· Maintaining Control Requests and Responses 330.28–.30
· Nature of Information 330.24–.25
· Negative 330.20–.21
· Positive 330.17–.19
· Prior Experience................ 330.23
· Procedures 330.04
· Process 330.01–.36
· Professional Skepticism.... 330.15; 330.27
· Public Warehouses....... 331.14; 901.03; 901.19–.20; 901.22
· Receivables 330.34–.35; 9508.01
· Related Party Transactions..... 334.08–.10
· Relation to Risk Assessment....... 330.05; 330.07–.10; 330.20–.22
· Reliability 330.16–.27
· Respondent 330.26–.27
· Review of Interim Information 722.09
· Scope Limitation 508.24

CONFLICT OF INTERESTS
· Management Statements 334.08

CONSISTENCY
· Accounting Changes—See Changes, Accounting
· Accounting Records.............. 326.19
· Application of GAAP 508.67; 508.69
· Auditor's Report With Differing Opinion 508.67; 508.69
· Change of Auditors... 315.12–.13; 315A.08
· Condensed Financial Statements 552.05
· Departure From Standard Report ... 9623.52
· Disclosure 420.14–.19; 508.17–.18
· Elements of Financial Statements.............. 9623.45–.46
· Error Corrections................ 420.15
· Explanatory Paragraph............ 508.52
· FIFO to LIFO Change............. 9420.20
· First Year Audits............. 420.23–.24
· Form 990 (Internal Revenue)....... 9623.52
· Illustrative Auditor's Report......... 508.17
· Inconsistency............... 508.16–.48
· Interim Financial Information 722.13; 722.30
· Interim v. Annual Data 9420.11–.15
· Lease Accounting........... 9420.24–.27
· Objective 420.02; 9420.53
· Other Information in Documents 550.04–.06

References are to AU section and paragraph numbers.

CONSISTENCY—continued
· Other Information in Electronic Sites Containing Audited Financial Statements 9550.16–.18
· Periods to Which Standard Relates 420.21; 9420.20
· Pooling of Interests 420.08–.09
· Qualified Opinion 508.52
· Relation to Comparability . . . 420.03; 552.05
· Responsibilities of Auditor 110.01
· Review of Form 10-K 9634.04
· Segment Information . . 435.07; 435.11–.14
· Standard of Reporting .... 150.02; 420.01–.24; 508.03
· Supplementary Information......... 558.07

CONSOLIDATED FINANCIAL STATEMENTS
· Auditor's Opinion 551.19
· Basis of Accounting 534.02
· Communication Between Auditors 9543.01–.17
· Consolidating Information...... 551.16–.19
· Financial Statements Prepared for Use Outside U.S. 534.02
· Illustrations 552.07; 552.10
· Interim Financial Information........ 722.13
· Letters for Underwriters.... 634.18; 634.53
· Management Representations...... 333.16; 333.18; 333A.08
· Planning of Audit Work 311.03
· Relation to Condensed Financial Statements 552.05–.07
· Selected Financial Data 552.10
· Supplementary Schedules 552.05

CONSOLIDATING FINANCIAL STATEMENTS
· Auditor's Opinion 551.19

CONSOLIDATING INFORMATION
· Auditor's Opinion 551.16–.19

CONSULTATION
· Change of Auditors.............. 315A.09
· Planning of Audit Work 311.04

CONTINGENCIES
· Definition 337B
· Fines for Illegal Acts............. 9317.06
· Gain—See Gain Contingencies
· Income Taxes............. 9326.06–.17
· Litigation, Claims, and Assessments ... 337.03; 337B; 9337.07; 9337.11; 9337.19
· Loss—See Loss Contingencies
· Management Representations. . . 333.06–.08; .... 333.16–.17; 333A.04; 9333.01–.04; 9337.16
· Review by Successor Auditor 315.11
· Standards of Financial Accounting 337.03; 337B; 9337.07

CONTINGENT LIABILITIES
· Disclosure 317.06–.07; 317.14–.15
· Lawyers' Letters...... 337.08–.11; 560.12; 9337.01–.09
· Review by Successor Auditor 315A.09
· Subsequent Events.............. 561.03

CONTINUING AUDITOR
· Application of Accounting Principles . 625.03
· Definitions..................... 508.65

CONTINUING PROFESSIONAL EDUCATION—See Training and Education

CONTRACTS
· Compliance Reports 623.19–.21
· Estimates 311.06
· Evidential Matter................ 326.17
· Illustrative Auditor's Report 623.26
· Litigation, Claims, and Assessments .. 337.07
· Matters Requiring Specialists ...... 336.02; 336.07
· Representation Letters .... 333.06–.07; 333.10; 333A.04
· Special-Purpose Financial Presentations .. 623.22–.30; 9623.80–.87
· Underwriting Agreement ...... 634.14–.17; 634.19; 634.23; 634.35; 634.51

CONTROL
· Audit Risk 312.27–.33; 313.03–.07
· Internal—See Internal Control
· Management................... 110.03
· Quality—See Quality Control
· Related Parties 334.01; 334.04; 334.11

CONTROL RISK
· Assessed Level............. 312.27–.33; .... 319.47–.48; 319.54–.57; 319.59; 319.64–.78
· Assessment by Auditor .... 312.30–.31; ...... 319.03–.05; 319.47–.63; 319.78; ...... 322.14–.16; 324.11–.16; 326.14; 350.12–.14; 350.33; 350.43
· Completeness Assertion 9326.18–.21
· Considerations in Assessing 319.45–.57; 9311.42–.44
· Correlation With Detection Risk.............. 319.79–.82; 326.14
· Definition 319.46
· Documentation of Assessed Level. . . 319.57
· Dual-Purpose Samples 350.44
· Evidential Matter......... 312.30; 319.54; 319.60–.78; 324.12; 326.11–.14
· Factor in Planning Audit........... 311.03
· Financial Statement Assertions...... 319.47; 319.55; 319.57
· Internal Audit Considerations.... 322.14–.16
· Maximum Level....... 319.47–.48; 319.57; 319.60
· Reducing Control Risk...... 319.51; 319.61

CONTROL RISK—continued
- Reduction in Assessed Level 319.04; 319.61–.63
- Relationship of Understanding Internal Control to Assessing Control Risk 319.58–.63
- Service Organizations 324.11–.16
- Tests of Controls 319.47–.48; 326.14; 350.33
- Year 2000 Issue 9311.42–.44

CORRECTION OF ERROR
- Application of Principle 420.11
- Change to GAAP From Other Basis . . . 420.11
- Management Responsibilities 324.45
- Mathematical Mistakes 420.15

COST
- Allocation—See Allocation of Cost
- Audit Sampling 350.07; 350.46
- Carrying Value of Investments 332.23
- Historical—See Historical Cost
- Interim Financial Information 722.08
- Research and Development—See Research and Development Costs

COST METHOD
- Reports, Other Auditors 543.14

COST-BENEFIT RELATIONSHIPS
- Audit Sampling 350.07; 350.46
- Evidential Matter 326.23–.24
- Internal Control 319.17
- Quality Control Policies and Procedures 161.02
- Substantive Tests at Interim Dates . . . 313.04
- Weaknesses in Accounting Control 9317.03–.06
- Weaknesses in Internal Control 9317.03–.06

CREDITORS
- Inquiries Concerning Other Auditors 543.10

CURRENT LIABILITIES
- Refinancing Short-Term Obligations 333.17; 333A.06

CURRENT-VALUE FINANCIAL STATEMENTS
- Disclosure 9623.59
- Supplement to Historical-Cost Financial Statements 9623.55–.59

CUSTOMERS
- Segment Information 435.01; 435.04; 435.07; 435.15–.16

CUTOFF DATES
- Audit Sampling 9350.02
- Examination of Data 313.07; 560.11
- Letters for Underwriters 634.23–.24
- Substantive Tests at Interim Dates 313.07; 313.09–.10

D

DATA
- Audit Risk and Materiality 312.36
- Audit Sampling 350.07
- Auditor's Opinion on Supplementary Data 544.02; 551.10
- Availability 311.09
- Cutoffs 313.07; 560.11
- Interim Financial Information 313.01–.10; 722.36–.41
- Letters for Underwriters 504.18
- Pro Forma Financial Data 560.05
- Relation to Basic Financial Statements 551.03
- Reliability of Financial Records 326.16
- Selected Financial Data—See Selected Financial Data
- Subsequent Events 560.05; 560.11–.12
- Unaudited Financial Information 508.27–.28
- Working Papers 339.03

DATA PROCESSING
- Effects of Information Technology on Evidential Matter 326.12
- Effects of EDP on Internal Control 311.09
- Internal Control 311.09
- Method of Controlling 319.23
- Planning of Audit Work 311.09
- Review by Auditor 311.06
- Year 2000 Issue 9311.42–.44

DATE OF AUDITOR'S REPORT
- Coincident With Representation Letters 333A.09
- Comparative Financial Statements . . . 508.65
- Condensed Financial Statements 552.05
- Dual Dating 508.73; 530.05
- Establishment of Date 530.01
- Existence of Facts 561.04–.05; 9543.15–.17
- Letters for Underwriters 634.28
- Omitted Auditing Procedures 390.01
- Registration Statements 711.05–.06
- Reissuance of Auditor's Report 508.65; 508.73; 530.06–.08
- Relation to Date of Lawyer's Response 9337.04–.05; 9337.10–.14
- Review of Interim Information 722.27
- Subsequent Discovery of Facts 561.01–.10; 711.12; 722.34; 9561.01–.02
- Subsequent Events 530.03–.05; 552.05
- Versus Date of Representation Letter 333.09

DEBT
- Letters for Underwriters 634.35; 634.45; 634.49
- Securities—See Investments

References are to AU section and paragraph numbers.

DEFALCATIONS—See Fraud

DEFINED BENEFIT PENSION PLANS
- · Change in Presentation. 9420.64–.65

DEFINITIONS—See Terminology

DEPARTURE FROM STANDARD REPORT
- · Adverse Opinion 508.58–.60
- · Departure From GAAP . . . . 504.11–.13; 508.35–.60; 9420.17–.25
- · Emphasis of a Matter 9410.18
- · Letters for Underwriters 634.27; 634.35
- · Qualified Opinion 508.20–.57
- · Reports, Other Auditors' 543.15
- · Segment Information 435.09–.16
- · Special Reports—See Special Reports
- · Supplementary Information 558.08

DEPARTURES FROM ESTABLISHED PRINCIPLES
- · Accounting Changes. . . 420.08; 508.50–.51; 508.55
- · Accounting Estimates Unreasonable 508.48
- · Accounting Principles Inappropriate. 508.48
- · Compilation of Financial Statements 552.02
- · Effect of Specialist's Work 336.13–.14; 9336.18
- · Effect on Auditor's Opinion 341.14; 508.35–.60; 9336.18
- · Fair Value Disclosures 9342.03
- · Form 990 (Internal Revenue). . . 9623.47–.54
- · Illustrative Auditor's Report. 508.39–.40
- · Inadequate Disclosure 508.46
- · Interim Financial Information . . . . 711.13; 722.30–.32; 722.42
- · Justification for Departure 411.07
- · Letters for Underwriters 634.33
- · Nonprofit Organizations 9623.47–.54
- · Prior Year's Statements 508.55
- · Regulated Industries 544.02–.04
- · Related Parties 334.12
- · Special Reports 9623.47–.54
- · Unaudited Financial Statements 504.11–.13; 711.13

DEPRECIATION
- · Evaluation of Estimates 311.06
- · Segment Information 435.01

DESIGN
- · Audit in Compliance With Laws & Regulations 801.06; 801.08
- · Audit Sample . . 350.05–.06; 350.44; 350.46
- · Effects of EDP on System 311.09

DIRECTORS—See Board of Directors

DISAGGREGATION
- · Disclosure of Segment Information 435.01; 435.07

DISCIPLINARY SANCTIONS
- · Inquiries Concerning Firms 543.10

DISCLAIMER OF OPINION
- · Basis of Accounting Other Than GAAP . . 410.02
- · Departure From GAAP . . 504.11–.13; 508.61
- · Derecognition of Transferred Assets 9336.18
- · Elements of Financial Statements 622.33; 623.14
- · Evidential Matter . . . . 326.25; 508.63; 9315A.14; 9326.06–.10
- · Examples
- · · Insufficient Evidential Matter 508.63
- · · Lack of Independence 504.10
- · · Lack of Inventory Observation 508.67
- · · Scope Limitation 508.63
- · · Unaudited Financial Statements. . 504.05–.17
- · Expression of Opinion 110.01
- · Fraud 316.25
- · Illegal Acts by Client 317.19
- · Individual Financial Statement 508.05
- · Lack of Independence 504.08–.10
- · Negative Assurance 504.18
- · Permission to Use Legal Opinion Not Granted 9336.18
- · Piecemeal Opinion. 508.64
- · Principal Auditor's Report 543.11
- · Reasons for Opinion 508.62
- · Reports With Differing Opinions 508.67
- · Scope Limitations . . . . . 316.25; 333.13–.14; . . . . 333A.11–.12; 336.13; . . . . . . 508.22; 508.24; 508.27; 508.31; 508.61–.63; 9326.06–.10; 9336.18
- · Selected Financial Data 552.11
- · Service Organizations 324.10
- · Subsequent Events 530.03–.04
- · Supplementary Information . . . . 551.06; . . . . 551.10–.11; 551.13; 551.15; 558.03; 558.09
- · Unaudited Fair Value Disclosures. . . 9342.08
- · Unaudited Financial Statements . . 504.05–.07
- · Uncertainties. 341.12

DISCLOSURE
- · Accounting Changes . . . . 420.19–.20; 9410.15–.18; 9420.19–.20
- · Accounting Estimates 342.07
- · Adequacy and Appropriateness of Informative Disclosure . . . . 311.06; 431.01–.04; . . . . 504.11–.12; 623.09–.10; 9623.60–.77; 9623.88–.93
- · Adverse Opinions 508.59; 552.07
- · Agreements to Repurchase Assets Previously Sold 333.17
- · Assertions by Management 326.03–.08
- · Basis of Accounting Other Than GAAP . . . . . . 410.02; 623.05; 623.09–.10; . . . . 9508.33–.37; 9623.53; 9623.60–.77; 9623.88–.93
- · Capital Stock Repurchase Options, Agreements, Reservations 333.17

DISCLOSURE—continued
· Change in Auditor 317.23
· Change in Estimates 420.14
· Classification and Reclassifications . . 420.16
· Client Representations—See Representation Letters
· Comparability 420.05
· Compensating Balances. . . 333.17; 333A.04
· Compliance Reports. 623.20
· Condensed Financial Statements. 552.03–.04
· Consolidating Financial Statements . . 551.19
· Contingencies, Gain or Loss. 333.06; 333.16–.17
· Current-Value Financial Statements. 9623.59
· Elements of Financial Statements. . . . 623.15
· Environmental Remediation Liabilities 333.17
· Essential Information . . . . 508.41–.44; 9410.15–.18
· Fair Value—Performance and Reporting Guidance 9342.01–.10
· Financial Instruments With Off-Balance-Sheet Risk, Concentrations of Credit Risk 333.17
· Fourth Quarter Interim Data . . . 9504.01–.07
· Fraud. 316.38–.40
· Going Concern Assumption 341.10–.11; 341.14
· Illegal Acts by Clients. . 317.14–.15; 317.18; 317.23; 333A.04; 9333.01–.04
· Interim Financial Information . . . 722.30–.32
· Inventory Pricing Method Changed. 9420.19–.20
· Investments Accounted for Using the Equity Method. 332.15
· Investments, Application of Contrary Method of Accounting 332.15
· Investments, Fair-Value Estimates . . . 332.28
· Letters for Underwriters. . . . 634.33; 634.49; 634.54–.62
· Liabilities, Other. 333.06; 333.16
· Liquidation Basis of Accounting . . . 9337.31–.32; 9508.33–.37
· Litigation, Claims, and Assessments. . . . 333.06; 333.16; 333A.04; . . . . 337.05; 337.09; 337.13; . . . . 9337.04–.07; 9337.10–.18; 9337.24–.27; 9337.31–.32
· Loss Contingencies . . 333A.04; 9333.01–.04
· Loss Reserves (Insurance) 9623.40–.46
· Material Concentrations 333.06
· Notes to Financial Statements . . . . . 508.21; . . . . 508.27–.28; 9623.61; 9623.65–.66; 9623.88–.93
· Oil and Gas Reserves. 9558.01–.05
· Omission of Statements. 508.43–.44
· Omitted Auditing Procedures 390.02
· Other Auditors—See Reports, Other Auditors'
· Other Information in Documents. 550.01–.06

DISCLOSURE—continued
· Other Information in Electronic Sites Containing Audited Financial Statements 9550.16–.18
· Pension Plans. 9420.64–.65
· Pooling of Interests 420.09
· Privileged Communication . . . . 315.06; 315.08; 315.25; 315A.05; 431.04
· Pro Forma Financial Data 560.05
· Qualified Opinion Illustration 508.39–.40; 508.42
· Qualified Opinions. 552.05
· Reasonableness of Amounts. 334.09
· Reissuance of Auditors' Reports. 530.06–.08
· Related Parties. . . . . 333.03; 333.16; . . . . 333A.03–.04; 334.01; 334.04; 334.11–.12; 9334.17
· Revision of Auditors' Reports . . . 561.06–.09
· Segment Information . . . . 435.01–.02; 435.13; 435.18
· Service Organizations That Use the Services of Subservice Organizations . . . 9324.10–.13
· Significant Estimates 333.06
· Standard of Reporting 150.02; 431.01
· Statutory Basis—Insurance Enterprises 9623.60–.77
· Subsequent Discovery of Facts 561.06–.09; 711.12–.13
· Subsequent Events—See Subsequent Events
· Supplementary Information. . . . . 551.21; 9558.01–.05
· Titles of Financial Statements. 623.07
· Uncertainties 341.12; 508.45–.46
· Updated Auditor's Report 508.69
· Use of Findings of Specialists. . . 336.15–.16
· Violations of Laws and Regulations. 333.06; 333.16

DISCOVERY
· Communication Between Auditors 9315A.06–.07; 9543.15–.17
· Comparison With Subsequent Events. . . 561.03
· Date of Existence of Facts 561.04–.05
· Disclosure of Subsequent Discovery 561.06–.09; 711.12–.13
· Financial Statements of Predecessor . . . . 315.21; 315A.10; 9315A.06–.07
· Fraud 316.36
· Illegal Acts—See Illegal Acts
· Lawyer's Advice . . . . 315.22; 315A.10; 561.02; 561.08; 711.12–.13
· Reliability of Information 561.04–.05
· Review of Interim Information 711.13
· Subsequent Discovery of Facts . . . . 530.02; . . . . 561.01–.10; 634.62; 722.34; 9561.01–.02

DIVISION FOR CPA FIRMS (AICPA)
· Inquiries Concerning Firms 543.10
· Peer Review Reports 543.10

References are to AU section and paragraph numbers.

DUE PROFESSIONAL CARE
- Definition 230.05
- Fraud 230.10; 230.12–.13; 316.27
- General Standard 150.02; 230.01–.13
- Judgment 230.11
- Knowledge 230.06–.07
- Professional Skepticism 230.07–.09
- Reasonable Assurance 230.10–.13
- Responsibilities of Assistant for Audit Disagreements 9311.35–.37
- Subsequent Discovery of Facts 230.13

E

EARNED SURPLUS—See Retained Earnings

EARNINGS
- Forecast 334.06

ECONOMIC ACTIVITY
- Relation to Audit Objectives 326.09

ECONOMIC CONDITIONS
- Inventory Valuation Methods 9420.16
- Planning of Audit Work 311.07
- Timing of Substantive Tests 313.06

EDP—See Data Processing

EDP SERVICE CENTER—See Service Organizations

EDUCATION AND TRAINING—See Training and Education

EFFECTIVENESS
- Audit Sampling 350.46
- Auditing Procedures 350.13–.14
- Control Environment 319.49
- Internal Control.... 312.27; 312.30; 319.18; 319.47; 319.51–.53; 350.37
- Internal Control Over Financial Reporting 9550.07–.15
- Inventory Counting Procedures 9508.05–.06
- Substantive Tests..... 313.05–.06; 326.11; 350.13; 9326.03

EFFICIENCY
- Audit Sample 350.05; 350.13; 350.46
- EDP Applications 311.09
- Review of Interim Information 722.14
- Substantive Tests........ 326.11; 9326.03

ELECTRONIC SITE—See Information Technology

ELEMENTS OF FINANCIAL STATEMENTS
- Adequacy of Disclosure in Statements Prepared on Cash, Modified Cash, or Income Tax Basis of Accounting 9623.88–.93
- Applicability of Auditing Standards ... 552.09
- Based Upon Net Income or Stockholders' Equity 623.16
- Departure From Standard Report 623.17
- Engagements to Apply Agreed-Upon Procedures—See Agreed-Upon Procedures

ELEMENTS OF FINANCIAL STATEMENTS—continued
- Examples 623.11
- Form of Auditor's Report 623.15
- Illustrations 623.18
- Limited Distribution Reports 623.15
- Loss Reserves (Insurance) 9623.40–.46
- Materiality 623.13
- Piecemeal Opinions 623.14
- Special Reports 623.11–.18

EMPHASIS OF A MATTER
- Accounting Change 9410.18
- Explanatory Language...... 508.19; 623.31
- Financial Statements 508.19
- Unqualified Opinion 508.19; 9342.03

EMPLOYEES
- Communication of Audit Disagreements 9311.35–.37
- Definition 311.02
- Errors or Irregularities.......... 333A.04–.05
- Fraud .... 316.20; 316.25; 333.06; 333.08; 333.16
- Illegal Acts 317.02
- Internal Auditors 322.01–.29
- Legal Counsel 337.08
- Nonaudit Services 9311.01–.03
- Pensions—See Pension Plans
- Planning of Audit Work 311.04; 9311.01–.03
- Source of Audit Information 311.04; 311.08; 324.36
- Supervision of Audit Information.. 311.01–.02; 311.11–.14; 9311.35–.37
- Supplementary Information 551.11

ENGAGEMENT
- Attestation—See Attest Engagement
- Audit—See Audit Engagement
- Reports on Application of Accounting Principles 625.01–.09
- Reports on Condensed Financial Statements 552.04
- Reports on Selected Financial Data 552.09–.10
- Service Organizations—See Service Organizations
- Working Papers 339.01; 339.04

ENGAGEMENT LETTERS
- Elements of Financial Statements 310.05; 622.11
- Matters Communicated in 310.05–.07
- Recipients of Governmental Financial Assistance 310.05
- Review of Interim Information 310.05; 722.07

ENGINEERS
- SEC Filings 711.02
- Use of Work by Auditors 336.02; 336.07

References are to AU section and paragraph numbers.

ENVIRONMENTAL CONSULTANTS
· Use of Work by Auditors 336.02; 336.07

EQUITY METHOD
· Investments, Auditing.......... 332.13–.22
· Related Parties 334.01
· Reports, Other Auditors........... 543.14
· Unaudited Information 508.27

ERROR CORRECTION—See Correction of Error

ERRORS—See Fraud

ESTIMATION
· Analytical Procedures 342.08–.14
· Audit Risk 312.27
· Auditor's Professional Skepticism ... 342.04
· Changes 420.14
· Communication to Audit Committee .. 380.08
· Developments of Estimates 342.05–.06
· Disclosure.......... 342.07; 9342.01–.10
· Evaluation by Auditor...... 311.06; 312.36; 342.01–.16
· Evidential Matter 312.36; 342.07–.14
· Examples............... 342.02; 342.16
· Fair Value Disclosures 9342.01–.10
· Historical Financial Statements............... 342.01–.02
· Income Tax Accruals 9326.06–.17
· Interim Information......... 313.09; 722.08; 9326.01–.05
· Interim v. Annual Data 722.08; 9326.01
· Internal Controls 342.06
· Knowledge................. 342.08–.10
· Loss Reserve (Insurance)......... 9623.46
· Management Judgments 380.08
· Materiality 342.14
· Misstatements........ 312.25; 312.35–.36
· Oil and Gas Reserves......... 9558.02–.04
· Potential Losses 337.04; 337.09; 337.14; 9337.12
· Prepared in Accordance With GAAP 342.07
· Professional Skepticism....... 342.07–.14
· Reasonableness................ 312.36
· Representation Letter 342.09
· Risk........................ 342.14
· Sampling—See Audit Sampling
· Specialists..................... 342.11
· Subsequent Events 342.13
· Uncertainties 312.36; 337.14; 508.48–.49; 9508.13–.14; 9508.25–.28

ETHICS DIVISION—See Professional Ethics Division

EVENTS
· Auditor's Consideration of Management's Adoption of Accounting Principles for New Types................. 9411.11–.15
· Illegal Acts by Clients 9317.01–.06; 9333.01–.04
· Subsequent—See Subsequent Events

EVIDENTIAL MATTER
· Accounting Estimates......... 342.07–.14
· Analytical Procedures......... 326.19–.20; 329.02–.22
· Assertions 319.03–.04; 319.45–.57; 330.11–.14
· Audit Objectives 326.09–.14; 326.22; 326.25–.26; 9326.03
· Audit Sampling 350.03–.06; 350.16; 350.19; 350.45–.46; 9350.02
· Basis for Auditor's Opinion 319.22; 322.02; 322.18; 326.01–.26; 9326.01–.02; 9326.06–.17
· Change of Auditors.... 315.12; 315.17–.18; 315A.08–.09
· Competence......... 312.12; 326.01–.02; 326.11–.12; 326.21; 350.06; 9326.03
· Completeness 319.45; 326.03–.05; 326.09–.11; 330.13–.14; 9326.18–.21
· Confirmations........... 150.02; 326.17; 330.06–.14; 330.29; 330.33; 350.04
· Control Risk 312.30; 319.54; 319.64–.78
· Cost-Benefit Relationships 326.23–.24
· Definition 326.15
· Disclaimer of Opinion 326.25; 508.63; 9315A.14; 9326.06–.10
· Effects of Information Technology ... 326.12
· Electronic Form 326.18
· Estimation 312.36
· Evaluation 312.19; 326.25
· Events Affecting Prior Periods 508.72
· First Year Audits............. 420.23–.24
· Going Concern Assumption 341.02–.03; 341.08
· Illegal Acts by Clients .. 317.08–.11; 317.19
· Income Tax Accruals 9326.06–.17
· Inquiries............ 150.02; 326.17–.20; 350.04; 9315A.10–.11; 9326.06–.17
· Inside Counsel of Client 9337.24–.27
· Insufficient 508.24; 9336.14–.18
· Interim Financial Information........ 313.07
· Interim Financial Statements... 9326.01–.05
· Internal Audit Function 322.07; 322.17
· Internal Control 326.11–.14
· Interrelationship 319.74–.78
· Inventories...... 310.04; 310A.04; 326.04; 326.09; 326.26; 331.01–.02; 331.09–.14; 901.03; 9508.02
· Investment Transactions........... 332.04
· Investments Accounted for Using the Equity Method 332.14–.18; 332.22
· Judgment...................... 350.06
· Legal v. Audit Evidence 326.02

References are to AU section and paragraph numbers.

EVIDENTIAL MATTER—continued

- Litigation, Claims, and Assessments . . 337.04; . . . . 337.08; 337.13; 9337.08–.09; 9337.11–.27
- Material Misstatements . . . . 312.19–.20; 312.33; 312.36–.38; 326.11
- Materiality . . . . 312.12; 312.19–.20; 326.11; 9326.03; 9326.06–.10
- Nature 326.15–.20
- Omitted Auditing Procedures . . . 390.03–.07
- Planning 312.12–.20; 312.33
- Professional Skepticism 230.07–.09
- Qualified Opinion . . . . 326.25; 508.20; 9315A.14; 9326.06–.10
- Reasonable Assurance 230.10–.13
- Receivables 331.01–.08
- Records 326.16–.20
- Related Party Transactions 334.09–.11
- Relation to Comprehensive Basis of Accounting Other Than GAAP 326.25
- Relation to GAAP 326.25
- Relation to Risk . . . 312.12; 312.19; 312.30; 312.33; 313.07
- Relevance 326.11; 326.21
- Reliability 326.15–.22
- Reports, Other Auditors . . . . 543.14; 9315A.10–.11; 9543.18–.20
- Representations From Management . . . . . . 326.03–.08; 326.17; . . . . 326.22; 332.11; 333.02–.04; . . . . 333A.02–.03; 9326.06–.10; 9326.18–.19
- Restricted Use 9336.15–.18
- Review of Interim Information 722.09
- Scope Limitation . . . . 333A.11–.12; . . . . 508.22–.25; 508.29–.32; 9326.06–.10
- Service Organizations . . . . . 324.10; 332.04; 342.12; 324.16–.17; 324.27
- Source 319.68–.69
- Standards of Field Work . . . 150.02; 326.01; 9326.01–.02; 9326.06–.10
- Substantive Tests . . . . . 313.07; 326.09–.13; 326.26; 332.04–.33; 350.16–.30
- Sufficiency . . . . 312.19; 319.22; . . . . 326.13–.14; 326.22–.24; . . . . 350.46; 9315A.10–.11; 9315A.13–.14; 9336.09–.16
- Support of Assessed Level of Control Risk 319.64–.78
- Tests of Controls 319.03–.04
- Timeliness 319.70–.73; 326.02; 326.23
- Transfer of Financial Assets . . . 9336.01–.18
- Type 319.66–.67
- Uncertainties 337.14
- Use of Legal Interpretations to Support That Transfer of Assets Has Met Isolation Criteria in FASB Statement No. 125 . . . . 9336.01–.18

EVIDENTIAL MATTER—continued

- Use of Work of Specialists . . . . 336.03; . . . . 336.06; 336.12–.13; 9326.13–.17; 9336.01–.18
- Work of Internal Auditors 322.12–.22
- Working Papers . . 326.16–.20; 339.03–.05; 9315A.10–.11; 9326.06–.17

EXAMPLES—See Illustrations

EXCEPT FOR OPINION—See Qualified Opinion

EXPENSES

- Assertions by Management 326.07
- Going Concern Assumption 341.07
- Interim Financial Information 722.08

EXPERTS—See Specialists

EXPLANATORY LANGUAGE

- Attorney-Client Privilege 9337.28–.32
- Auditor's Reports 341.13; 508.11–.19
- Basis of Accounting Other Than GAAP 9508.35–.37
- Change in Accounting Principle . . . 420.05–.06; 420.08; 9420.52–.54
- Change in Financial Statement Classification 420.28–.31
- Change in Presentation of Cash Flows 420.13
- Change in Principle Inseparable From Change in Estimate 420.12
- Conditional Language 341.13
- Consistency . . . . 420.08–.09; 435.14; 508.16–.18; 623.31; 9623.45–.46
- Consistency of Interim & Annual Data 9420.11–.15
- Departures From GAAP 508.14–.15
- Emphasis of a Matter 508.19
- Fair Value Disclosures 9342.07
- Going Concern Assumption 341.13
- Illustrations . . 508.13; 508.17; 9508.36–.37
- Reports, Other Auditors . . 508.12–.13; 623.31
- Service Organizations . . . . 342.39–.40; 324.55–.56
- Special Reports 623.31
- Time Lag in Reporting 331.12; 332.20
- Uncertainties 341.13

EXPORT SALES

- Segment Information—See Segment Information

EXTERNAL AUDITOR—See Auditor, Independent

EXTRAORDINARY ITEMS

- Assertions by Management 326.08
- Interim Financial Information 722.16

F

FAIR PRESENTATION

- Adverse Opinion 508.58–.59
- Departure From GAAP 508.20–.21
- Essential Information . . . . 508.41–.42; 9410.15–.18

FAIR PRESENTATION—continued
· Financial Statements—See Financial Statements
· Fourth Quarter Interim Data . . . 9504.01–.07
· GAAP—See Generally Accepted Accounting Principles
· Inadequate Disclosure 508.41–.42
· Letters for Underwriters 634.60
· Management Responsibility . . . . 333.06; 333.16; 333A.04–.05; 504.03
· Material Misstatements 312.03–.04
· Materiality—See Materiality
· Meaning in Auditor's Report 411.01–.16
· Objective of Audit 110.01
· Qualified Opinion 508.21
· Regulated Companies 544.04
· Relation to Supplementary Information . . . . 551.03; 551.06; 551.12–.14; 558.06–.07
· Reservations 508.59
· Segment Information 435.18
· Summarization 508.65

FAIR VALUE—See Valuation

FAMILY RELATIONSHIPS
· Related Parties 334.01

FEDERAL FINANCIAL ASSISTANCE—See Compliance Auditing

FEDERAL INCOME TAXES—See Income Taxes

FIELD WORK—See Standards of Field Work—Audit

FINANCIAL ACCOUNTING STANDARDS BOARD
· Accounting for Contingencies . . . . 337.03; . . . . 337.05; 337.09; 337B; . . . . 9317.06; 9333.01–.04; . . . . 9337.07; 9337.11; 9337.13; 9337.16–.17; 9337.19; 9337.32
· Accounting for Nonprofit Organizations 9623.54
· Effective Date of Statements . . 9410.13–.18
· Management Representations . . . . . 333.06; 333.16–.17; 333A.04
· Related Party Disclosure 334.01–.12
· Relation to the Governmental Accounting Standards Board 9411.07–.09
· Research and Development Costs 9410.14; 9410.16
· Segments of a Business 435.01–.18
· Supplementary Information . . . . 551.04; 551.12; 551.15; 558.01–.10

FINANCIAL INFORMATION—See Financial Statements

FINANCIAL POSITION
· Condensed Financial Statements 552.03–.04

FINANCIAL STATEMENTS
· Accounting Estimates 342.01–.16
· Adequate Disclosure . . . . 431.01–.04; 623.09–.10; 9623.88–.93
· Audit Risk and Materiality 312.01–.41
· Audited . . . . 504.04; 504.14–.17; 508.01–.76; 9550.16–.18
· Auditor's Consideration of Internal Audit Function 322.01–.29
· Auditor's Responsibilities . . . . . . 110.02–.03; . . . . 504.01–.04; 508.04–.05; 550.04; . . . . 551.04–.11; 558.04–.05; 9311.39–.41; 9550.16–.18
· Audits at Interim Dates 313.01–.02
· Balance Sheets—See Statements of Financial Position
· Basic 508.06; 551.02
· Basis of Accounting Other Than GAAP . . . . 623.02–.10; 9623.47–.54; 9623.88–.93
· Cash Basis Statements—See Special Reports
· Change of Auditors . . . . 315.01–.25; 315A.01; 315A.08–.10
· Changes, Accounting—See Changes, Accounting
· Co-existing Statements 551.21
· Combined—See Combined Financial Statements
· Comparability—See Comparability
· Comparative—See Comparative Financial Statements
· Compliance Reports 623.19–.21
· Components . . . . . 543.01–.02; 551.16–.19; 9543.04–.07
· Condensed—See Condensed Financial Statements
· Conformity With GAAP . . . . 326.25; 411.01–.16; 9623.49
· Conformity With SEC Requirements . . 9634.03
· Consistency—See Consistency
· Consolidated—See Consolidated Financial Statements
· Consolidating—See Consolidating Financial Statements
· Current Value—See Current-Value Financial Statements
· Date of Auditor's Report 530.01–.08
· Definition 623.02
· Departure From GAAP . . . . 508.14–.15; . . . . 508.20; 508.68–.69; 544.02–.04; 9623.47–.54
· Disclosures—See Disclosure
· Effect of Laws on Governmental Entity 801.03–.07
· Effect of Misstatements 312.04

References are to AU section and paragraph numbers.

FINANCIAL STATEMENTS—continued
- Effects of EDP on Audit .... 311.09; 9311.38–.47
- Effects of Substantial Doubt in Going Concern Assumption 341.10–.11
- Elements—See Elements of Financial Statements
- Fair Presentation ..... 110.01; 312.03–.04; .... 312.12; 312.34; 326.19; 411.01–.16; 504.03; 634.60
- FIFO to LIFO Change............. 9420.19
- Going Concern Assumption.... 341.01–.17; 9341.01–.02
- Illegal Acts by Clients......... 317.01–.25; 9317.03–.06; 9333.01–.04
- Inadequate Disclosure 508.41–.42
- Income Statements—See Statements of Income
- Income Taxes.............. 9326.06–.10
- Incomplete Presentation...... 9623.80–.87
- Interim—See Interim Financial Statements
- Internal Audit Function, Relevance 322.06–.08
- Internal Control—See Internal Control
- Investors 9420.52–.54
- Items Requiring Adjustments 311.03
- Lack of Independence 9504.19–.22
- Letters for Underwriters....... 634.01–.64
- Liquidation Basis of Accounting 9508.33–.37
- Litigation, Claims, and Assessments .. 337.01–.14; 9337.01–.32
- Management's Responsibilities..... 110.03; 504.03; 9311.41; 9508.51–.52
- Material Misstatements .... 312.02–.11; .... 312.19; 312.24–.25; .... 312.27; 312.34; 319.55; .... 350.18; 350.30; 350.48; 551.09; 9550.09; 9550.13–.15
- Misleading—See Misleading Financial Statements
- Nonprofit Organizations ... 508.65; 550.02; 9623.47–.54
- Notes—See Notes to Financial Statements
- Objective of Audit..... 110.01; 558.04–.05; 722.09; 722.27–.29; 722.42
- Omitted Auditing Procedures ... 390.01–.08
- Opinions—See Opinions, Auditors'
- Other Information in Documents .... 380.10; 550.01–.06; 551.04; 9550.13–.15
- Other Information in Electronic Sites Containing Audited Financial Statements.............. 9550.16–.18
- Pension Plans.............. 6420.64–.65
- Preparation 110.03
- Prepared for Use in Another Country....... 534.01–.16; 9534.01–.04
- Prescribed Forms............ 623.32–.33
- Prior Period Compiled 504.17
- Prior Period Reviewed 504.17

FINANCIAL STATEMENTS—continued
- Prior Year's
  - Departure From GAAP 508.68–.69
  - Planning of Audit Work 312.23
  - Predecessor Auditor .... 508.70–.74; 9315A.06–.07
  - Responsibility Assumed 504.16
- Pro Forma—See Pro Forma Financial Statements
- Prospective—See Prospective Financial Statements
- Publicly-Traded Companies 9504.01–.07
- Reclassifications................ 420.16
- Reissuance of Report ..... 504.15; 508.65; .... 508.70–.74; 530.06–.08; 560.08; 561.06
- Related Party Transactions ... 334.01; 334.04; 334.09–.12; 9334.16–.21
- Reliance on Statements 312.10; 561.05–.09
- Representations of Management .... 326.03–.08; 326.20; ...... 333.02; 333.04–.06; 333.08–.12; ..... 333.14; 333.16–.18; 333A.02–.06; 9326.03; 9508.51–.52
- Restatement—See Restatements
- Revisions Required 561.06–.09
- SEC Filings ... 311.03; 504.14; 550.02–.03; ..... 561.03; 711.01–.13; 9634.01–.09; 9711.01–.11
- Segments of a Business—See Segment Information
- Special Reports—See Special Reports
- Special-Purpose .... 623.22–.30; 9623.80–.87
- Statements of Retained Earnings—See Statements of Retained Earnings
- Stockholders' Equity Changes...... 508.06
- Subsequent Discovery of Facts 561.01–.10; 9561.01–.02
- Subsequent Events—See Subsequent Events
- Subsequent Period Unaudited 504.16
- Subsidiaries 333.11; 333A.10
- Supplementary Information—See Supplementary Financial Information
- Titles of Statements 623.07; 623.24
- Types........................ 623.02
- Unaudited—See Unaudited Financial Statements
- Unaudited Information—See Unaudited Information
- Uncertainty—See Uncertainties
- Updating Reports .... 508.65–.66; 508.68–.69
- Use of Accountant's Name 504.03–.04
- Use of Findings of Specialists................ 336.12–.16
- Weaknesses in Internal Control 9317.03–.06
- Working Papers 339.04–.05
- Year 2000 Issue............ 9311.38–.47

FINES—See Penalties

FIRM
· Income Tax Accruals........ 9326.06–.17
· Inquiries Concerning Firms......... 543.10
· Merger With Another Firm................. 508.65; 508.74
· Personnel—See Employees
· Quality Control.............. 161.01–.03
· Work of Other Auditors........... 543.05

FIRST-IN, FIRST-OUT
· Effect of Change in Method... 9420.16–.20

FISCAL PERIOD
· Interim—See Interim Financial Statements

FIXED ASSETS—See Property

FOOTNOTES—See Notes to Financial Statements

FOREIGN CORRUPT PRACTICES ACT OF 1977
· Compliance Reports............. 9634.03
· Scope of Audit............. 9317.01–.02
· Weaknesses in Internal Control................. 9317.03–.06

FOREIGN COUNTRY
· Accounting Principles......... 534.01–.16; 9534.01–.04
· Auditing Standards.......... 534.01–.16; 9534.01–.04
· Reporting on Financial Statements.... 534.01–.16; 9534.01–.04
· Use of Specialist...... 534.05–.06; 534.12

FORGERY—See Fraud

FORM 10-K (SEC)
· Auditor's Report............ 9634.01–.09
· Negative Assurance............. 9634.06
· Regulation S-K................. 9634.06
· Shelf Registration Statements.... 9711.07; 9711.10

FORM 10-Q (SEC)
· Condensed Financial Statements.... 552.08
· Review of Interim Information..... 552.08; 711.09; 722.35
· Shelf Registration Statements... 9711.08–.11

FORM 990 (INTERNAL REVENUE)
· Nonprofit Organizations...... 9623.47–.54

FORM V. SUBSTANCE—See Substance v. Form

FRAUD
· Assessment of the Risk of Material Misstatement....... 312.16; 316.11–.25
· Assets, Susceptibility to Misappropriation........... 316.18–.20
· Audit Planning........... 316.03; 316.37
· Audit Procedures Modification...... 316.28
· Audit Tests................ 316.28–.36
· Auditor's Interest......... 312.07; 316.03

FRAUD—continued
· Auditor's Opinion................ 316.25
· Auditor's Responsibilities...... 316.01–.41
· Changes in Assessment, Conditions Resulting in.......................... 316.25
· Collusion...................... 316.08
· Communication to Management....... 316.36; 316.38–.40
· Communication With Audit Committees....... 316.36; 316.38–.40
· Concealment............... 316.07–.10
· Confidential Client Information...... 316.40
· Consideration in Financial Statement Audit........... 316.01–.41
· Considerations at the Account Balance, Class of Transactions, and Assertion Level......................... 316.29
· Definitions................. 316.04–.05
· Description and Characteristics..... 312.07; 316.03–.10
· Disclosure to Audit Committee... 316.38–.40
· Disclosure to Government Agency... 316.40
· Disclosure to Management..... 316.38–.40
· Disclosure to SEC............... 316.40
· Disclosure to Successor Auditor..... 316.40
· Distinguishing Factor...... 312.07; 316.03
· Due Professional Care............ 316.27
· Employees............. 316.20; 316.25
· Evaluation................. 316.33–.36
· Forgery........................ 316.07
· Improper Revenue Recognition...... 316.30
· Industry Conditions........... 316.16–.17
· Intent......................... 316.03
· Internal Control...... 316.16–.19; 316.23
· Inventory Quantities.............. 316.30
· Judgment.............. 316.10; 316.14; 316.21; 316.25–.27; 316.33
· Lawyer's Advice.......... 316.36; 316.40
· Management—See Management
· Management Representations....... 316.25
· Material Misstatements....... 312.01–.41 .... 316.01–.41
· Materiality—See Materiality
· Misstatements Arising From Fraudulent Financial Reporting............ 316.04; 316.16–.17; 316.30
· Misstatements Arising From Misappropriation of Assets... 316.05; 316.18–.20; 316.31
· Operating Characteristics and Financial Stability................. 316.16–.17
· Ownership Characteristics......... 316.22
· Perceived Opportunity to Commit.... 316.06
· Planning of Audit Work............ 311.03
· Pressure, Incentive to Commit...... 316.06
· Prevention and Detection... 316.02; 316.24
· Professional Skepticism........... 316.27
· Reportable Conditions............ 316.39
· Responses to Assessment Results.................. 316.26–.32

References are to AU section and paragraph numbers.

FRAUD—continued
- Responses to Detected Misstatements 312.08
- Risk—See Risk
- Scope of Audit 316.11; 316.25; 316.32
- Service Organizations 324.23; 324.57
- Subsequent Discovery 316.36
- Unauthorized Transactions 316.03
- Versus Error 312.06–.07; 316.03
- Withdrawal by Auditor 316.26; 316.36

G

GAIN CONTINGENCIES
- Definition 337B
- Management Representations 333.06; 333.08; 333A.04
- Standards of Financial Accounting 333.06; 333.08; 333A.04; 337.03; 337B

GENERAL STANDARDS, AUDIT
- Agreed-Upon Procedures Applied to Elements of Financial Statements 622.05
- Applicability 150.06
- Application of Accounting Principles .. 625.05
- Audit of Financial Statements for Use Outside U.S. 534.03–.06
- Due Professional Care 230.01–.13
- Independence 220.01–.07
- List of Standards 150.02
- Nature of Standards 201.01
- Training and Proficiency 210.01–.05

GENERALLY ACCEPTED ACCOUNTING PRINCIPLES
- Accounting Estimates 342.07
- Adherence 410.01–.02
- Alternative Principles 9410.14–.15
- Basis of Accounting Other Than GAAP 110.03; 504.07; 534.01–.16; 551.02; 623.02–.10; 9508.33–.37; 9623.47–54; 9623.60–.77; 9623.88–.93
- Change in Principle—See Changes, Accounting
- Co-Existing Financial Statements 551.21
- Condensed Financial Statements 552.03–.04
- Consistency 110.01; 315A.08
- Consolidating Financial Statements ... 551.19
- Definition 411.02
- Departures—See Departures From Established Principles
- Disagreement With Management 315A.06
- Fair Presentation 110.01; 312.03–.04; 312.12; 312.34; 411.01–.16; 504.03
- Foreign Country's Accounting Principles 543.03–.15
- Hierarchy 411.05–.13; 411.16

GENERALLY ACCEPTED ACCOUNTING PRINCIPLES—continued
- Inadequate Disclosure ... 431.03; 508.41–.44
- Interim Financial Information 711.13; 722.09; 722.13; 722.42
- Liquidation Basis of Accounting 9508.34–.37
- Litigation, Claims, and Assessments 337.02
- Management's Adoption for New Transactions or Events 9411.11–.15
- Material Misstatements 312.03–.04
- Nonprofit Organizations 508.65; 9623.47–.54
- Omitted Auditing Procedures 390.01–.02
- Other Information in Documents 550.03
- Performance Standards for Application of Accounting Principles 625.06
- Regulated Companies 544.02–.03
- Relation to Evidential Matter 326.25
- Relation to Supplementary Information 544.02; 551.03; 551.10; 551.19; 558.08
- Reports on Application 625.01–.09
- Reports, Other Auditors 543.10; 543.17
- Representation Letters 333.06; 333.16–.18; 333A.04–.05
- SEC Filings 711.04
- Segment Information 435.01–.02; 435.08; 435.10; 435.13; 435.18
- Sources of Established Principles 411.05–.13
- Standards of Reporting 150.02; 410.01–.02; 431.02–.04
- Substance of Transactions 411.06–.07; 411.09
- Summarized Prior Period Information 508.65
- Uncertainties 508.48
- Use of Work of Specialists 336.01–.17; 9336.01–.18

GENERALLY ACCEPTED AUDITING STANDARDS
- Analytical Procedures 329.04
- Applicability 150.06
- Applicability to Agreed-Upon Procedures Engagement 622.05
- Audit of Financial Statements for Use Outside U.S. 534.03–.13
- Audit Risk and Materiality 312.01–.02
- Auditor's Report 508.22; 508.35
- Basis for Opinion 110.05
- Change of Auditors 315A.01
- Communication of Auditor's Responsibility 380.06
- Consistency 315.12–.13
- Degree of Risk 150.05
- Disagreement With Management 315.07; 315.09
- Elements of Financial Statements .. 9623.41

References are to AU section and paragraph numbers.

GENERALLY ACCEPTED AUDITING STANDARDS—continued
· General Standards . . . 150.02
· Governmental Auditing Standards—See Governmental Auditing Standards
· Intercompany Transactions . . . 9543.01–.03
· Internal Control . . . 9317.01–.02
· Inventories . . . 150.04
· Lack of Independence . . . 504.09
· Litigation, Claims, and Assessments . . 337.01
· Loss Reserves (Insurance) . . . 9623.41
· Materiality . . . 150.03–.04
· Planning of Audit Work . . . 311.01; 311.06
· Receivables . . . 150.04
· Related Parties . . . 334.01; 334.04; 334.10
· Relation to Quality Control Standards . . . 161.01–.03
· Reports, Other Auditors . . . 543.10; 801.06–.08; 9543.18–.20; 110.10
· Responsibilities of Auditor . . . 110.01–.05; 110.10
· Review of Form 10-K . . . 9634.04
· Review of Interim Information . . 722.09; 722.42
· SEC Filings . . . 711.04
· Segment Information . . . 435.03; 435.18
· Special Reports . . . 623.05
· Standards of Field Work . . . 150.02; 9317.01–.02
· Standards of Reporting . . . 150.02; 431.01; 504.01–.02; 508.03–.05
· Standards v. Procedures . . . 150.01
· Supervision of Audit Work . . . 311.01
· Supplementary Information . . . 551.07; 558.01–.10
· Use of Accountant's Name . . . 504.01–.02
· Use of Work of Specialists . . . 336.01
· Weaknesses in Internal Control . . . 9317.03–.06
· Working Papers . . . 339.02

GENERALLY ACCEPTED FINANCIAL STATEMENTS
· Elements of Financial Statements . . . 623.12

GENERALLY ACCEPTED GOVERNMENTAL AUDITING STANDARDS—See Governmental Auditing Standards

GEOGRAPHIC AREAS
· Segment Information—See Segment Information

GEOLOGISTS
· Use of Work by Auditors . . . 336.02; 336.07

GOING CONCERN
· Audit Procedures . . . 341.05; 9341.01–.02
· Auditors' Report Explanatory Language . . 341.13; 623.31; 9341.01–.02
· Auditors' Reports . . . 341.03; 9341.01–.02
· Auditors' Responsibility . . . 341.02–.04; 9341.01–.02
· Comparative Financial Statements . . . 341.15–.16
· Conditions and Events . . . 341.06

GOING CONCERN—continued
· Contrary Information . . . 341.01
· Disclaimer of Opinion . . . 341.12
· Disclosure . . . 341.10–.11; 341.14
· Effect on Auditors' Reports . . . 341.12–.16
· Financial Statement Effects . . . 341.10–.11
· Indications of Financial Difficulties . . . 341.06
· Management Plans . . . 341.03; 341.07–.09
· Negative Trends . . . 341.06
· Prospective Financial Information . . . 341.09–.10
· Uncertainties . . . 623.31

GOVERNMENTAL ACCOUNTING STANDARDS BOARD
· Supplementary Information . . . 551.15; 558.01–.10

GOVERNMENTAL AGENCIES
· Disclosure of Illegal Acts . . . 317.23
· Litigation, Claims, and Assessments . . . 337.07
· SEC—See Securities and Exchange Commission
· Summarized Prior Period Information . . . 508.65

GOVERNMENTAL AUDITING STANDARDS
· Definition . . . 801.08–.09
· Description . . . 801.02

GOVERNMENTAL ENTITIES
· Compliance Auditing Considerations—See Compliance Auditing
· Sources of Established Principles . . . 411.12–.13; 411.16

GRANTS
· Compliance Auditing Applicable to Federal Financial Assistance . . . 801.04; 801.07–.08; 801.15

GUARANTEES AND WARRANTIES
· Future Events . . . 312.36
· Litigation, Claims, and Assessments . . . 337.07
· Related Party Transactions . . 334.08; 334.10

GUIDELINES
· Supplementary Information . . . 551.06; 551.15; 558.06
· Working Papers . . . 339.05; 9326.11–.12

H

HIERARCHY OF GAAP
· Sources of Established Accounting Principles . . . 411.05–.13
· Sources of Established Principles . . . 411.16

HISTORICAL COST
· Basis for Property . . . 326.07
· Supplemental Current Cost Financial Statements . . . 9623.55–.59

References are to AU section and paragraph numbers.

HISTORICAL SUMMARIES

· Relation to Basic Financial Statements 551.03

I

ILLEGAL ACTS

· Analytical Procedures .... 317.07–.11; 317.24
· Attest Engagement 317.24
· Audit Opinion 317.18–.21
· Audit Procedures 317.09–.11
· Auditor's Responsibilities .... 316.01; 317.01–.25
· Communication With Audit Committee 317.17; 722.23
· Confidentiality 317.23
· Definition 317.02
· Direct Effect on Financial Statements 317.05; 317.07
· Disclosure to Government Agency ... 317.23
· Disclosure to SEC 317.23
· Disclosures ... 317.14–.15; 317.18; 317.23
· Effects on Auditor's Report 317.18–.21
· Evaluation of Materiality 9333.01–.04
· Evidential Matter 317.08–.11; 317.19
· Examples 317.09
· Foreign Corrupt Practices Act .. 9317.01–.06
· Generally Accepted Audited Standards 317.07–.08
· Implications for Audit 317.16
· Indirect Effect on Financial Statements 317.06–.07
· Inquiries 317.08; 317.10
· Knowledge 317.03
· Laws and Regulations 317.05–.06
· Lawyers 317.03
· Management Representations ...... 333.06; 333A.04; 9333.01–.04
· Materiality .... 317.04–.06; 317.13–.15; 317.18
· Other Responsibilities 317.24
· Service Organizations 324.23
· Specialists .... 317.03; 317.10–.12; 317.22–.23
· Successor Auditor 317.23

ILLUSTRATIONS

· Accounting Estimates 342.16
· Accounts Receivable Report 623.18
· Adverse Opinions 508.60; 552.07
· Analytical Procedures .... 329.04–.05; 329.07; 329.12; 329.14–.15
· Audit Sampling .... 350.17; 350.26; 350.41; 350.48
· Balance-Sheet-Only Auditor's Report 508.34
· Cash Basis Statements 504.07; 623.08

ILLUSTRATIONS—continued

· Change in Accounting Principle 508.17; 9420.19
· Change in Inventory Pricing Method 9420.19
· Compliance Reports 623.21; 9623.42
· Condensed Financial Statements 552.06–.08
· Consolidated Financial Statements .. 552.07; 552.10
· Consolidating Information 551.18
· Date of Auditor's Report 530.05; 530.08
· Disclaimer of Opinion
· · Evidential Matter 508.63
· · Lack of Independence 504.10
· · Opening Inventory Not Observed .. 508.67
· · Scope Limitations 508.63
· · Supplementary Information .... 558.03; 558.09
· · Unaudited Financial Statements ... 504.05
· Evidential Matter for Inventories 326.26
· Explanatory Language Added to Auditor's Standard Report .... 508.13; 508.17; 9550.10
· Explanatory Paragraph for Uncertainty 341.13
· Explanatory Paragraphs 558.08
· FIFO to LIFO Change 9420.19
· Going Concern Explanatory Paragraph 341.13
· Illegal Acts by Clients 317.09; 317.14
· Income Tax Basis Statements 623.08
· Inquiry Letter to Legal Counsel ..... 337.05; 337A.01; 9337.04–.07; 9337.10–.16
· Inquiry Letter to Other Auditor 9543.08–.10
· Lawyer's Evaluation of Pending Litigation 9337.20–.23
· Letter to Regulator 9339.06
· Letters for Underwriters ... 634.16; 634.19; ... 634.26; 634.31–.33; 634.61; 634.64
· Liquidation Basis Reports 9508.36–.37
· Loss Reserves (Insurance) 9623.42
· Management Plans Relating to Going Concern Assumption 341.07
· Oil and Gas Reserve Information ... 9558.05
· Predecessor's Report Not Presented 508.74
· Principal Auditor 543.09; 543.16
· Profit Participation Report 623.18
· Qualified Opinions
· · Accounting Change 508.52
· · Departure From GAAP 508.39–.40
· · Inadequate Disclosure 508.42
· · Omission of Statement of Cash Flows 508.44
· · Scope Limitation 508.26
· Regulatory Agency Report .... 623.08; 623.26; 642.59; 9623.42

ILLUSTRATIONS—continued
· Related Parties 334.01; 334.03
· Rental Computation Report 623.18
· Report Based on Compliance With Contractual Agreement 623.26
· Report in Connection With a Proposed Acquisition 622.49
· Report in Connection With Claims of Creditors 622.49
· Reporting on Internal Control....... 325.12; 325.16; 9325.04
· Reporting on Supplementary Information......... 551.12–.15; 558.08
· Reports Following Pooling of Interests.................. 543.16
· Reports on Application of Accounting Principles 625.09
· Reports on Applying Agreed-Upon Procedures............ 622.34; 622.49
· Reports on Comparative Financial Statements.................. 508.08
· Reports on Current-Value Financial Statements Supplementing Historical-Cost Financial Statements.................. 9623.58
· Reports on Financial Statements for Use Outside United States........... 534.10
· Reports Prepared Pursuant to Loan Agreements 623.30
· Reports With Differing Opinions.............. 508.67; 508.69
· Representation Letters .... 333.16–.18; 333A.14
· Response to Inquiry by Principal Auditor 9543.11–.14
· Review of Interim Information...... 552.08; .... 711.09; 722.28–.29; 722.31–.32; 722.41
· Royalties Report 623.18
· Segment Information .... 435.09–.10; 435.13; 435.15–.16
· Selected Financial Data 552.10
· Service Organization Reports... 324.38–.40; 324.54–.56; 9324.16; 9324.18
· Special Purpose Financial Statements........... 623.26; 9623.52
· Special Reports .... 623.08; 623.18; 623.21; 623.26; 623.30
· Standard Report 508.08
· Substance v. Form............... 334.02
· Unqualified Opinion .... 508.08; 508.34; 508.69; 552.06

IMPAIRMENT
· Investments............... 332.31–.33
· Objectivity of Specialist 336.10–.11
· Substantive Tests 313.05

INCOME STATEMENTS—See Statements of Income

INCOME TAX RETURNS—See Tax Returns

INCOME TAXES
· Basis of Accounting 9623.47–.54
· Evidential Matter 9326.06–.17
· Form 990—See Form 990 (Internal Revenue)
· Interim Financial Information....... 9326.05
· Rates—See Rates (Income Taxes)
· Special Reports 9623.47–.54
· Technical Training 9326.13–.17
· Uncertainties 9326.06–.17

INDEPENDENCE
· Client's Legal Counsel 337.08
· General Standard .... 150.02; 220.01–.07; 504.08
· Lack of Independence 504.08–.10
· Other Auditors 543.04; 543.10
· Qualifications of Auditor 622.09; 634.18; 634.31–.32
· Reporting Requirements...... 9504.19–.22
· SEC Requirements 220.05; 9634.09
· Specialist Employed by Auditor's Firm 336.03

INDEPENDENT AUDITOR—See Auditor, Independent

INDUSTRY ACCOUNTING GUIDES—See Accounting Guides, Industry

INDUSTRY AUDIT GUIDES—See Audit Guides, Industry

INDUSTRY PRACTICES
· Relation to Evidential Matter........ 326.09

INFORMATION
· Availability 326.12
· Communication Between Auditors ...... 315A.02; 543.10; 550.04; .... 9315A.06–.07; 9315A.09; 9315A.11; ... 9315A.18; 9334.12–.15; 9543.01–.17
· Communication When No Audit Committee Exists 9380.02–.03
· Communication With Audit Committee 380.01–.15
· Confidential—See Confidential Client Information
· Consistency of Other Information .. 550.04–.06; 9550.13; 9634.04
· Consolidating—See Consolidating Information
· Description of Tests of Operating Effectiveness and the Results of Such Tests 9324.01–.03
· Discontinued Operations.......... 333A.03
· Discovery.................. 561.04–.05
· Discovery by Successor Auditor.... 315.21; 315A.10; 9315A.06–.07
· Electronic Form 326.14
· Essential for Fair Presentation .. 508.41–.42; 9410.15–.16
· Evidential Matter 326.15–.22
· Illegal Acts by Clients 9333.01–.04
· Income Tax Accruals 9326.06–.17
· Interim—See Interim Financial Information

References are to AU section and paragraph numbers.

INFORMATION—continued
- Legal Advice . . . 550.05–.06
- Litigation, Claims, and Assessments . . . 337.05–.06; 337.08; . . . 9337.01–.32
- Material Misstatements—See Materiality
- Oil and Gas Reserves . . . 9558.01–.05
- Omission by Management . . . 431.03
- Other Information in Electronic Sites Containing Audited Financial Statements . . . 9550.16–.18
- Planning of Audit Work . . . 311.03–.10; . . . 312.33
- Prescribed Report Forms . . 623.05; 623.15; . . . 623.20; 623.25; . . . 623.29; 623.32–.33
- Related Parties . . . 334.11
- Relationship to Audited Financial Statements . . . 508.11; 550.01–.04
- Reliability . . . 550.04–.06; 561.04–.05; . . . 561.09
- Reports to Stockholders . . . 550.02
- Segment—See Segment Information
- Sources—See Sources of Information
- Subsequent Discovery of Facts . . 561.01–.10
- Subservice Organization . . . 9324.08–.13
- Supplementary—See Supplementary Financial Information
- Systems—See Data Processing
- Unaudited—See Unaudited Information
- Voluntary Disclosure . . . 558.02

INFORMATION TECHNOLOGY
- Auditor's Responsibilities . . . 9550.16–.18
- Other Information in Electronic Sites Containing Audited Financial Statements . . . 9550.16–.18

INQUIRIES
- Analytical Procedures . . . 329.21
- Audit Procedure . . . 333.02–.03; . . . 333.06; 333A.02–.03
- Change of Client's Lawyers . . . 337.11
- Competence of Other Auditors . . 543.10–.11
- Current Business Developments . . . 311.04; 311.08
- Evidential Matter . . . 150.02; 326.17–.20; . . . 350.04; 9315A.10–.11; . . . 9326.06–.17
- Illegal Act Detection . . . 9317.03–.06; . . . 9333.01–.04
- Illegal Acts by Clients . . . 317.08; 317.10
- Illustrative Inquiry Letter to Legal Counsel . . . 337A.01; 9337.04–.07
- Internal Audit Function . . . 322.05
- Letter to Other Auditor . . . 9543.08–.10
- Letters for Underwriters . . . 634.23–.24; 634.45
- Litigation, Claims, and Assessments . . . 337.01–.14; 722.17; . . . 9337.01–.32

INQUIRIES—continued
- Oil and Gas Reserve Information . . . 9558.03–.05
- Qualifications of Specialists . . . 336.05
- Related Party Transactions . . . 9334.12–.13
- Response by Predecessor Auditor . . . 9315A.09; 9315A.18
- Response by Principal Auditor . . . 9543.11–.17
- Review of Interim Information . . 722.09–.10; . . . 722.13; 722.17; 722.18
- Segment Information . . . 435.07
- Subsequent Events . . . 560.12; 711.10
- Supplementary Information . . . 551.15; 558.07; . . . 9558.03–.05
- Unasserted Claims . . . 337.05–.06; . . . 9337.06–.07

INSTITUTE—See American Institute of CPAs

INSURANCE
- Companies—See Insurance Companies

INSURANCE COMPANIES
- Appropriateness of Informative Disclosures . . . 9623.60–.77
- Filing with Regulatory Agencies . . . 544.02; 9623.40–.46
- Loss Reserves . . . 9623.40–.46

INTENTIONAL MISSTATEMENT—See Fraud

INTERCOMPANY TRANSACTIONS
- Audit of Intercompany Balances . . . 9334.14–.15; 9543.01–.03
- Bases of Accounting . . . 435.07; 435.11–.14
- Communication Between Auditors . . . 543.10; 543.17
- Related Parties . . . 334.09–.10
- Unrealized Profits and Losses . . . 332.22

INTERIM FINANCIAL INFORMATION
- Accompanying Audited Financial Statements . . . 722.36–.42
- Accounting Changes . . . 722.13; 722.16
- Audit Sampling . . . 350.39
- Audit Tests Prior to Balance Sheet Date . . . 313.01–.10
- Changes in Business Activities . . . 722.16
- Characteristics . . . 722.08
- Communication . . . 722.05; 722.20–.25
- Comparability With Year-End Information . . . 313.08
- Condensed Financial Statements . . . 552.08
- Consistency . . . 722.13; 722.30
- Cutoffs . . . 313.07; 313.09–.10
- Definition . . . 722.02
- Departure From GAAP . . . 711.13; 722.30–.32; 722.42
- Design of Substantive Tests . . . 313.08
- Estimation . . . 313.09; 722.08
- Evidential Matter . . . 313.07
- Financial Statements—See Interim Financial Statements

INTERIM FINANCIAL INFORMATION—continued
· Income Taxes 9326.05
· Inquiries of Client's Lawyers. 722.17
· Investees. 722.13
· Letters for Underwriters. 634.29–.30; 634.35; 634.37–.38; 634.40–.41; 634.46; 722.04
· Material Misstatements 313.03; 313.09; 722.10; 722.20–.25
· Other Information in Documents. 722.33
· Presentation 722.02
· Representation Letters 333.17
· Review—See Review of Interim Financial Information
· SEC Filings 552.08
· Subsequent Discovery of Facts 722.34
· Subsequent Events 722.13; 722.34
· Substantive Tests 313.01–.10
· Supplemental Information 722.36–.39
· Timing of Audit Work . . . 313.04–.07; 313.10
· Uncertainties 722.30
· Understanding With Client 722.07
· Unusual Items 313.07–.08; 722.13; 722.16; 9326.04
· Use of Accountant's Name. 504.04

INTERIM FINANCIAL STATEMENTS
· Audit Risk and Materiality. 312.21
· Condensed Financial Statements 552.01
· Consistency With Annual Information. 9420.11–.15
· Evidential Matter 9326.01–.05
· Fourth Quarter Interim Data . . . 9504.01–.07
· Planning of Audit Work. 311.04; 312.21
· Representation Letters 333A.06
· Review—See Review of Interim Financial Information
· Subsequent Events 560.12
· Unaudited 504.04; 9504.01–.07
· Use of Accountant's Name. 504.04

INTERNAL AUDIT—See Auditor, Internal

INTERNAL AUDITOR—See Auditor, Internal

INTERNAL CONTROL
· Accounting Control
· · Auditors' Opinions. 324.18
· · Division of Procedures 324.10
· Accounting Estimates 342.06; 342.11
· Accounting System 319.34
· Agreed-Upon Procedures. 622.20
· Application of Components to a Financial Statement Audit 319.14–.15
· Application to Small and Midsized Entities. 319.40; 319.84
· Assertions 319.45–.57
. Assessing Control Risk 312.30–.31
· Audit Objectives. 325.04
· Audit Planning 325.07; 9311.42–.44
· Audit Sampling. 350.31–.44

INTERNAL CONTROL—continued
· Auditor's Consideration 319.01–.84
· Authorization for Transactions 319.84
· Board of Directors 319.84
· Communicating Related Matters. 325.07; 325.19
· Compliance Auditing of Major Programs 801.10–.11
· Considerations During Audit 319.01–.84; 322.13–.16
· Considerations in Planning an Audit. 319.19–.44
· Control Activities 319.07; 319.32–.33; 319.50; 319.84
· Control Environment. 319.07; 319.23; 319.25–.27; 319.49; 319.84
· Control Risk—See Control Risk
· Correction of Error—See Correction of Error
· Cost-Benefit Relationship 313.04–.05; 319.17
· Data Processing—See Data Processing
· Deficiencies 722.11
· Definition 319.06
· Design of Sample for Tests of Controls 350.33
· Detection Risk 312.27–.28; 312.32; 319.46; 319.55–.56; 319.79–.82
· Deviations 350.31–.42
· Documentation of Understanding. 319.44
· Effectiveness 312.27; 312.30; 319.18; 326.21; 350.37
· Effectiveness of Design 319.52–.54; 319.57; 319.59–.60
· Effects of EDP 311.09; 9311.44–.47
· Errors or Irregularities—See Fraud
· Evidential Matter 319.03–.04; 319.22; 319.45–.57; 326.11–.14
· Extent of Tests. 350.19
· Financial Reporting Objective 319.10
· Foreign Corrupt Practices Act 9317.01–.06; 9634.03
· Fraud—See Fraud
· Identifying Reportable Conditions. . 325.04–.06
· Information and Communication 319.07; 319.34–.36; 319.84
· Inherent Risk 312.27–.33; 319.23; 319.43; 319.46; 319.55
· Interim Testing 313.02; 313.04–.05; 313.08; 313.10; 722.10–.11
· Internal Audit Function . . 322.07; 322.13–.16
· Interrelated Components . . . 319.07; 319.84
· Letters for Underwriters. 634.36; 634.55; 634.57
· Limitations 312.27; 319.16–.18
· Management Responsibility 110.03
· Material Weakness . . . 325.15; 9325.01–.06
· Materiality 312.27; 333.08; 333A.05
· Monitoring 319.07; 319.37–.39; 319.84

References are to AU section and paragraph numbers.

INTERNAL CONTROL—continued
- Obtaining an Understanding .... 319.02; 319.09; 319.13; 319.19; 319.23–.40
- Operating Effectiveness ... 319.16; 319.21; .... 319.52–.54; 319.57; 319.59–.60
- Operations and Compliance Objectives 319.11–.12
- Organizational Structure.... 319.23; 319.84
- Placed in Operation ...... 319.21; 319.26; 319.41
- Planning the Audit............. 319.19–.44; 324.07–.10; 9311.42–.44
- Policies and Procedures........... 319.07
- Procedures to Obtain Understanding............. 319.41–.43
- Public Warehouses........... 901.01–.28
- Related Parties.................. 334.05
- Relationship Between Objectives and Components.............. 319.08–.15
- Reportable Conditions......... 325.02–.03; 325.06; 9311.45–.47
- Reports—See Reports on Internal Control
- Review of Interim Information ... 722.10–.14
- Risk Assessment................ 319.07; 319.28–.31; 319.84
- Risk of Fraud 150.05
- Risk of Material Misstatement...... 312.27; ...... 312.30–.31; 350.08; 350.11–.14; 350.20; 350.35–.36; 9311.42–.44
- Safeguarding of Assets 319.13
- Segment Information 435.06
- Segregation of Duties............. 319.84
- Service Organizations—See Service Organizations
- Special Reports—See Reports on Internal Control
- Standards of Field Work.......... 150.02; 319.01; 319.79
- Substantive Tests—See Substantive Tests
- Tests of Controls—See Tests of Controls
- Tolerable Rate 350.34–.35; 350.38
- Understanding .... 316.23; 319.19–.44; 319.58–.63; 322.04; 322.13
- Work of Other Auditors............ 543.12
- Working Papers 339.04–.05
- Year 2000 Issue............ 9311.42–.47

INTERNAL REVENUE SERVICE
- Audit Manual.................. 9326.06
- Form 990 (Internal Revenue)... 9623.47–.54

INTERPRETATIONS, AUDITING—See Auditing Interpretations

INVENTORIES
- Alternative Procedures....... 9508.01–.06
- Change in Pricing Methods.... 9420.16–.20
- Comparison With Records 9508.03
- Completeness 326.09
- Counted By Outside Firm 9508.01; 9508.05–.06

INVENTORIES—continued
- Disclaimer of Opinion 508.67
- Evidential Matter............ 331.01–.02; 331.09–.14; 9508.02
- First-in, First-out 9420.16–.20
- Illustrative Audit Objectives 326.26
- Last-in, First-out 9420.16–.20
- Management Representation....... 326.04; 333.17; 333A.04; 333A.07
- Matters Requiring Specialists 336.07
- Observation by Auditor ... 310.04; 310A.04; 9315A.17–.18; 9350.02
- Public Warehouses 331.14; 901.01–.28
- Role of Auditor 110.04
- Scope Limitation .... 310.04; 310A.04; 508.24; 9508.01
- Segment Information............ 435.06
- Substantive Tests 326.26; 9315A.18
- Valuation................ 110.04; 311.06

INVESTEES
- Accounting Changes 9420.52–.54
- Equity Method........ 332.13–.22; 543.14
- Interim Financial Information 722.13
- Scope Limitation................ 508.24
- Subsequent Events 332.21
- Unaudited Information 508.27

INVESTMENTS
- Accounting Policy Appropriateness 332.05–.06
- Auditor's Report .... 508.24; 543.14; 9420.52–.54
- Bank Trust Departments 9642.14
- Carrying Amount.............. 332.23–.30
- Classification 332.07–.09; 332.11
- Collateral 332.30
- Confirmations 332.04; 332.11
- Cost 332.23
- Disclosure 332.15; 332.28
- Equity Method........ 332.13–.22; 543.14
- Existence, Ownership, and Completeness 332.04
- Evidential Matter............. 332.03–.33
- Fair Value 332.12; 332.24–.30
- Fair-Value Estimates 332.27–.29
- FASB Statement No. 115 Application............... 332.07–.11
- FASB Statement No. 124 Application.................. 332.12
- Impairment in Valuation........ 332.31–.33
- Management's Intent.......... 332.08–.09
- Other Auditor's Report 543.01; 543.14
- Qualified Opinion 508.26
- Quoted Market Value.......... 332.24–.26
- Related Parties 334.01; 334.07–.08
- Representations From Management 332.11
- Scope Limitation.......... 508.24; 508.26
- Significant Influence ... 332.13–.14; 332.16

INVESTMENTS—continued
- Subsequent Events 332.18; 332.21
- Substantive Procedures 332.04–.33
- Time Lag in Reporting 332.20
- Unaudited Financial Information 332.18; 332.21
- Unrealized Intercompany Profits and Losses 332.22
- Use of a Specialist 332.19; 332.27; 332.29
- Valuation and Presentation 332.19; 332.23–.33

INVESTORS
- Accounting Changes 9420.52–.54
- Equity Method 332.13–.22; 543.14
- Unaudited Information 508.27

IRREGULARITIES—See Fraud

J

JUDGMENT
- Accounting Estimates 380.08
- Adverse Opinions 508.58
- Analytical Procedures 329.03; 329.05; 329.07; 329.09
- Audit Adjustments 380.09
- Audit Risk 312.13; 312.19; 312.24; 312.27–.33; 350.08
- Auditing Procedures 110.05
- Basis for Opinion 312.13; 326.02; 326.13–.14; 326.22–.23
- Basis of Accounting 623.03
- Evidential Matter 350.06
- Fair Presentation 411.03–.04
- Fraud 316.10; 316.14; 316.21; 316.25–.27; 316.33
- Generally Accepted Accounting Principles 311.06; 411.03–.04; 9411.11–.15
- Income Tax Accruals 9326.06–.17
- Independence 504.08
- Interim Financial Information 722.08; 722.20–.25
- Internal Control 319.23; 319.43
- Legal Matters 110.04; 337.06; 337.14; 9333.01–.04
- Management 634.55
- Material Weaknesses in Internal Control 325.15
- Materiality 312.10–.25; 312.33; 319.23; 319.43; 435.05; 435.08; 435.17; 508.36; 508.47; 623.24
- Matters Requiring Specialists 336.06–.07; 9336.01; 9336.04; 9336.06
- Observation of Inventories 9508.06
- Other Information in Documents 550.05–.06
- Planning—See Planning
- Related Party Transactions 334.11

JUDGMENT—continued
- Reportable Conditions 325.02–.05; 325.07; 325.15
- Reports on Application of Accounting Principles 625.05–.07
- Review of Form 10-K 9634.07
- Sampling Risk 350.12; 350.21–.23; 350.26
- Use of Legal Interpretations to Support That Transfer of Assets Has Met Isolation Criteria in FASB Statement No. 125 .... 9336.01; 9336.04; 9336.06
- Work of Internal Auditors 322.20; 322.24
- Work of Other Auditors 543.01–.02; 543.06; 543.13; 9543.18–.20
- Working Papers 339.04
- Year 2000 Issue 9311.44–.47

K

KINSHIP—See Family Relationships

KNOWLEDGE
- Accounting Estimates 342.08–.10
- Analytical Procedures 329.02–.03; 329.05–.06
- Auditor, Independent 110.03–.05; 326.21; 622.14; 634.36; 634.42–.44; 634.55; 9550.11; 9550.13
- Business of Entity 311.01; 311.06–.10; 312.15; 316.11; 341.02; 341.09
- Competence of Other Auditors 543.05
- Control Environment 319.26; 319.84
- Due Professional Care 230.06–.07
- Evidential Matter 326.21
- Foreign Country's Accounting Principles 534.05
- Foreign Country's Auditing Standards 534.06
- Illegal Acts 9333.01–.04
- Illegal Acts by Clients 317.03; 317.05–.06
- Income Tax Accruals 9326.06–.17
- Internal Control 319.19–.44; 722.10–.11
- Legal Matters 337.06; 337.14; 9337.26
- Loss Reserve Matters 336.07
- Matters Outside Agreed-Upon Procedures 622.41
- Principal Auditor 543.02; 9543.18–.20
- Reliance on Financial Statements 561.08
- Reliance on Representations 333.03; 333.09; 333.16; 333.18; 333A.02–.03
- Review of Interim Information 722.09–.11; 722.13
- Segment Information 435.15
- Specialists 336.08; 9336.03–.04; 9336.10
- Understanding EDP 311.10

References are to AU section and paragraph numbers.

KNOWLEDGE—continued

- Understanding Transactions .... 110.03; 311.06; 334.09; 350.02; 9334.19
- Use of Work of Specialists .... 336.01; 336.06; 9336.03–.04; 9336.10
- Weaknesses in Internal Control 9317.03–.06
- Weaknesses in Internal Control Over Financial Reporting 9550.11; 9550.15

L

LAST-IN, FIRST-OUT

- Effect of Change in Method ... 9420.16–.20

LAWS

- Compliance Auditing.......... 801.01–.24
- Design of Audit........... 801.06; 801.08
- Effects on Financial Statements .. 317.05–.06; 317.10; 317.21
- Effects on Financial Statements of Governmental Entities 801.03–.07
- Foreign Corrupt Practices Act 9317.01–.06
- GAAS Audit Insufficient............ 801.22
- Governmental Financial Assistance ... 801.04
- Planning of Audit Work 311.07
- Privileged Communication .... 337.13; 561.02; 9337.08–.09
- SEC Filings................. 711.01–.13
- Violations .. 333.06; 333A.04; 9333.01–.04

LAWSUITS—See Litigation

LAWYERS

- Advice on Discovery of Facts ...... 315.22; ... 315A.10; 561.02; 561.08; 711.12–.13
- Advice on Omitted Auditing Procedures........... 390.03; 390.07
- Advice on Other Information 550.05–.06
- Auditors' Reliance on Advice........ 110.04
- Code of Professional Responsibility..... 337.10; 337C; 9337.25
- Confidentiality of Communications 337.13; 9337.08–.09
- Correspondence and Invoices....... 337.05
- Date of Response 9337.01–.05; 9337.10–.14
- Disclosure of Illegal Acts 317.22–.23
- Explanatory Language About Attorney-Client Privilege 9337.28–.30
- Explanatory Language Concerning Unasserted Possible Claims or Assessments in Responses to Audit Inquiry Letters 9337.31–.32
- Foreign Corrupt Practices Act 9317.03–.06
- Illegal Act Investigation....... 9333.01–.04
- Illegal Acts.......... 317.03; 317.10–.12
- Improper Use of Auditor's Name.... 504.06; 722.35; 9550.15

LAWYERS—continued

- Income Tax Information....... 9326.13–.17
- Internal v. Outside Lawyers 9337.24–.27
- Letters of Audit Inquiry .... 333A.04; 337.08–.11; 337A.01; 9337.01–.32
- Limited Scope of Response..... 337.12–.14
- Policy on Audit Inquiries ..... 337.12; 337C; 9337.19–.22; 9337.30–.32
- Refusal to Furnish Information...... 337.13
- Related Party Transactions 334.10
- Responsibilities to Clients .... 337.09; 337.13; 9337.08–.09; 9337.25
- Uncertainties—See Uncertainties
- Use of Legal Interpretations to Support That Transfer of Assets Has Met Isolation Criteria in FASB Statement No. 125 .... 9336.01–.18
- Use of Work by Auditors ... 336.02; 336.07; 9336.01–.18

LEASES

- Assertions by Management........ 326.06

LEGAL MATTERS

- Audit Procedures .... 333A.04; 337.05–.07; .... 9317.03–.06; 9333.01–.04; 9337.15–.17
- Condensed Financial Statements.... 552.07
- Foreign Corrupt Practices Act..... 9634.03
- Invoices From Law Firms.......... 337.05
- Knowledge of Auditor 110.04; 337.06
- Legal v. Audit Evidence........... 326.02
- Letters for Underwriters 634.60
- Letters of Audit Inquiry .... 333A.04; .... 337.08–.11; 337A.01; 722.17; 9337.01–.32
- Litigation—See Litigation
- Matters Requiring Specialists ...... 336.02; 336.07; 9326.13–.17; 9336.01–.18
- Omitted Auditing Procedures....... 390.01; 390.03; 390.07
- Related Parties 334.02; 334.06; 334.08
- Review of Form 10-K............ 9634.03
- Selected Financial Data........... 552.11
- Substance v. Form 334.02
- Uncertainties—See Uncertainties
- Violation of Debt Covenant 9410.17

LETTERS FOR UNDERWRITERS

- Accountants' Limitations ... 634.12; 634.37; .... 634.39; 634.43; 634.45; 634.47
- Accountants' Report .... 504.19; 634.27–.30; 634.59
- Accounting Principle Changes...... 634.48
- Accounting Records ...... 634.55; 634.57; 634.59
- Acquisition Transactions 634.05
- Additional Letters or Reports 634.10; 634.20; 634.24
- Addressee 634.03; 634.19; 634.25
- Agreed-Upon Procedures .... 634.10; 634.35; 634.44

LETTERS FOR UNDERWRITERS—continued
· Allocation Methods 634.59
· Background Information....... 634.01–.21
· Business Combinations 634.42
· Capsule Information............ 634.35; 634.39–.41; 634.64
· Change in Specified Financial Statement Item 634.35; 634.45–.47; 634.49; 634.64
· Change Period........ 634.45; 634.48–.52
· Changes in Capital Structure 634.35; 634.45; 634.49
· Commenting on Information Other Than Audited Financial Statements . 634.35–.53
· Comparison Period 634.51
· Compliance With SEC Requirements .. 634.29; 634.33–.34; 634.60
· Concluding Paragraph 634.61
· Condensed Financial Statements ... 634.12; 634.29; 634.35; 634.37–.38; 634.40–.41
· Consolidated Financial Statements............ 634.18; 634.53
· Content of Typical Letter 634.64
· Cutoff Dates 634.23–.24; 634.50–.51
· Dating of Letter....... 634.19; 634.23–.24
· Departure From SEC Requirements................. 634.64
· Departure From Standard Accountants' Report 634.27; 634.35
· Disclosure Requirements......... 634.33; 634.49; 634.54–.62
· Draft Letter 634.16–.17; 634.19; 634.35; 634.51; 634.56; 634.62
· Financial Forecasts 634.29; 634.35; 634.44; 634.64
· Illustrations 634.16; 634.19; 634.26; 634.31–.33; 634.61; 634.64
· Independence of Accountants 634.18; 634.31–.32
· Inquiries............. 634.23–.24; 634.45
· Interim Financial Information ... 634.29–.30; 634.35; 634.37–.38; 634.40–.41; 634.46; 634.64
· Internal Control 634.36; 634.55
· Introductory Paragraph 634.26–.30
· Material Misstatements 634.60
· Minutes of Meetings.............. 634.45
· More Than One Accountant......... 634.17–.18; 634.32
· Negative Assurance....... 634.09; 634.12; 634.28; 634.34–.35; 634.37; 634.39–.42; 634.44; 634.46—.47; 634.50; 634.53; 634.57
· Opinions, Accountants'........ 634.27–.28; 634.33
· Positive Assurance 634.34
· Pro Forma Financial Information.... 634.29; 634.35; 634.42–.43; 634.64
· Procedures 634.12; 634.15–.19; 634.35–.43; 634.54–.60

LETTERS FOR UNDERWRITERS—continued
· Qualified Opinion 634.27
· Reasonable Investigation 634.02
· Reports, Other Accountants 634.18; 634.28; 634.53; 634.64
· Representation Letters........ 634.03–.07
· Requesting Party Other Than Named Underwriter........ 634.03–.10; 634.64
· Scope of Audit 634.30
· Secured Debt Offering 634.09
· Securities Act of 1933....... 634.01–.03; 634.11–.12; 634.14; 634.19; 634.21; 634.33–.34; 634.37; 634.44
· Securities Exchange Act of 1934 .... 634.33–.34; 634.57
· Securities Offerings 634.04; 634.12
· Segment Information 634.59
· Shelf Registration Statement 634.19
· Short Form Registration Statement.................... 634.64
· Statistical Summaries......... 634.54–.60; 634.64
· Subsequent Changes 634.35; 634.45–.53
· Subsequent Discovery of Facts 634.62
· Supplemental Financial Information 634.54–.60; 634.64
· Supplementary Information......... 634.30
· Time Periods 634.45–.47
· Unaudited Information 504.19; 634.12; 634.30; 634.35; 634.37–.38; 634.40–.41; 634.55
· Underwriting Agreement....... 634.14–.17; 634.19; 634.23–.24; 634.35; 634.51

LETTERS OF REPRESENTATION—See Representation Letters

LIABILITIES
· Assertions by Management 326.04–.07
· Contingent—See Contingent Liabilities
· Estimation 342.02
· Examination at Interim Dates ... 313.03–.07
· Litigations, Claims, and Assessments .. 337.01–.14; 9337.01–.32
· Loss Reserves (Insurance) 9623.42–.46
· Management Plans....... 333.06; 333A.04

LICENSES
· Specialists 336.08

LIENS
· Management Representations...... 333A.04

LIMITED REVIEW—See Review of Interim Financial Information

LINE OF CREDIT
· Management Representations...... 333.17; 333A.04

LINES OF BUSINESS—See Segment Information

References are to AU section and paragraph numbers.

LIQUIDATION
· Basis of Accounting 9508.33–.37
· Financial Statements 9508.33–.37
· Generally Accepted Accounting Principles 9508.34–.37
· Uncertainties 9508.34

LITERATURE—See Publications

LITIGATION
· Audit Procedures . . . . 337.05–.07; 9337.15–.17; 9337.24–.27
· Client Has Not Consulted a Lawyer 9337.15–.17
· Disclosure of Illegal Acts 317.23
· Inquiries From Successor Auditor . . . 315.05; . . . . . . 315.07–.10; 315.12; 315.14–.15; 315.20; 315.24; 315A.07
· Inquiries of Client's Lawyers . . . . 337.08–.11; 722.17; 9337.01–.32
· Internal vs. Outside Lawyers . . . 9337.24–.27
· Limitations on Lawyer's Responses 337.12–.14
· Loss Contingencies . . . . 9333.01–.04; 9337.11; 9337.17
· Related Parties. 334.06
· Stockholders vs. Management 334.06
· Uncertainties—See Uncertainties

LOAN AGREEMENTS—See Borrowing Contract

LOSS CONTINGENCIES
· Definitions 337B
· Disclosure . . . . 9333.01–.04; 9337.11; 9337.17
· Estimation . . . . 337.09; 337.14; 337B; 508.48–.49; 9337.12; 9337.17
· Illegal Acts . . . . 333.06; 333A.04; 9317.06; 9333.01–.04
· Management Representations. . . . . . 333.06; 333.16–.17; 333A.04
· Materiality Considerations 508.47
· Standards of Financial Accounting 337.03; 337B

LOSS RESERVES (INSURANCE)
· Illustration of Auditor's Report. 9623.42
· Special Reports 9623.40–.46
· Specialists 9623.40
· Subsequent Events. 9623.42

LOSSES
· Commitments. 333.17; 333A.04
· Estimation of Potential Losses . . . . . 337.09; 337.14; 337B; 9337.12; 9337.17
· Insurance Companies 9623.40–.46

M

MANAGEMENT
· Accounting Changes . . . 508.50–.52; 508.57
· Adoption of Accounting Principles for New Transactions or Events 9411.11–.15
· Advisory Services 9311.01–.03
· Assertions . . . . 326.03–.08; 9326.03; 9326.18–.19; 9334.17–.18
· Auditor Difficulties in Performance of Audit 380.14
· Auditor's Comments 551.20
· Characteristics 316.16–.17
· Classification of Investments. 332.08
· Communication With Audit Committee. 380.05
· Communications Regarding Applicable Audit Requirements. 801.21
· Components of a Business 543.13
· Conflict-of-Interests Statements. 334.08
· Consultation With Other Accountants. 380.12
· Control Environment . . . 316.16–.19; 319.18; 319.23; 319.25–.27; 319.84
· Control Objectives. 324.53
· Disagreement With Auditor . . . . 315.07; 315.09; 315A.06; 380.11; 504.13
· Errors or Irregularities. 333A.04–.05
· Estimation of Future Events. 337.14; 380.08
· Foreign Corrupt Practices Act 9317.03–.06
· Form 10-K. 9634.07
· Fraud . . . . 316.02; 316.13; . . . 316.36; 316.38–.40; 333.06; 333.16
· Going Concern Assumption 341.03; 341.07–.09
· Identification of Laws Affecting Governmental Entity Financial Statements 801.07
· Illegal Acts . . . . . . 317.02; 317.10; 317.17; 317.22; 9317.03–.06; 9333.01–.04
· Income Tax Information. 9326.06–.17
· Inquiries of Lawyers 337.08–.11
· Inquiry 316.13
· Integrity 319.22; 333A.02–.03
· Interim Financial Information 722.08
· Internal Audit Function. 322.05
· Internal Control . . . . 319.15–.18; 319.25–.27; 319.84
· Inventory Pricing Method 333A.07; 9420.16–.20
· Investigation Request by Auditor 561.04
· Issues Discussed With Auditor Prior to Retention. 380.13
· Judgment 342.03–.04; 634.55
· Justification for Accounting Changes 508.50–.52; 508.57

References are to AU section and paragraph numbers.

MANAGEMENT—continued
- Knowledge of Transactions 110.03; 311.06; 342.03–.06
- Litigation With Stockholders........ 334.06
- Litigations, Claims, and Assessments 337.02; 337.05; 9337.10–.17; 9337.24–.27
- Misstatement of Financial Statements............ 312.38; 313.06
- Oil and Gas Reserve Information ... 9558.03
- Omission of Information........... 431.03
- Operating Style 319.84
- Philosophy.................... 319.84
- Planning of Audit Work............ 311.04
- Plans............. 333.06; 333A.03–.04; 341.03; 341.07–.09
- References to Internal Control Over Financial Reporting 9550.12–.15
- Related Parties 334.01; 334.04–.09; 334.12; 9334.12–.13; 9334.16–.21
- Reportable Conditions 316.39; 325.06; 325.10
- Reports on Internal Control Over Financial Reporting 9550.07–.11
- Representations—See Representation Letters
- Responsibilities ... 110.03; 310.06; 316.02; 333.06; 333A.04–.05; 334.05; 337.02; 504.03; 551.05; 711.01; 711.08; 801.05; 801.21; 9311.41; 9508.51–.52
- Responsibility for Estimation ... 342.03–.06
- SEC Filings 711.01; 711.08
- Segment Information 435.07
- Selected Financial Data 552.09
- Source of Information on Legal Matters..................... 337.05
- Subsequent Events 560.12; 711.10
- Supplementary Information 551.05; 551.15; 558.07; 9558.03
- Transfer of Assets.......... 9336.01–.18
- Uncertainties.................... 337.14
- Weaknesses in Internal Control........... 722.11; 9317.03–.06
- Work of Other Auditors 543.13

MANUALS—See Publications

MARKETABLE SECURITIES—See Investments

MATCHING PRINCIPLE
- Effects of LIFO Method 9420.19
- Regulated Companies 544.03

MATERIALITY
- Accounting Estimates 342.14
- Accounting Principles, Adoption or Modification 420.18
- Adequate Disclosure 431.02
- Agreed-Upon Procedures......... 622.09; 622.27; 622.33
- Change in Accounting Estimate 420.14
- Change in Accounting Principle............ 9410.16; 9410.18

MATERIALITY—continued
- Classification Changes............ 420.16
- Compliance Auditing of Major Federal Financial Assistance Programs 801.17
- Concept................ 150.04; 411.04
- Consistent Standard Not Involved.... 420.18
- Definition 312.10
- Departure From GAAP 508.35–.36; 722.31–.32
- Effect on Audit 312.01–.02
- Effect on Financial Statements.............. 312.01–.41
- Elements of Financial Statements.... 623.13
- Evaluation of Illegal Acts...... 9333.01–.04
- Evidential Matter 312.12; 312.19–.20; 326.11; 9326.03; 9326.06–.10
- Factor in Planning Audit ... 311.03; 312.01; 312.12–.25; 312.33
- Fair Presentation 312.03–.04
- Fraud 316.34–.35
- Generally Accepted Auditing Standards.................... 312.01
- Illegal Acts 317.13–.15; 317.18–.19
- Inquiries of Client's Lawyers 337.09; 337.12
- Internal Control—See Internal Control
- Judgment—See Judgment
- Limits.... 312.40; 333.08; 333.10; 333.16; 333A.05; 9326.06–.10
- Management Representations...... 333.08; 333.16; 333A.05; 333A.11–.12; 9326.06–.10; 9333A.05–.06
- Matters Requiring Specialists 336.06; 336.13
- Misstatements ... 312.02–.11; 312.19–.20; 312.24–.27; 312.32–.40; 326.11; 350.11–.14; 350.18; 350.25; 350.30; 350.48; 550.05–06; 551.09; 634.60; 9550.09; 9550.11; 9550.13
- Other Auditor's Work 534.02; 543.05–.06; 543.15; 9543.01–.03; 9543.18–.20
- Other Information in Documents............... 550.04–.06
- Qualified Opinion 508.20–.21
- Related Party Transactions........ 334.04; 334.07–.08; 334.11–.12; 9334.12–.13
- Relation to Risk 312.24
- Review of Form 10-K 9634.04
- Review of Interim Information 722.09; 722.13
- Segment Information 435.05; 435.08; 435.17
- Special-Purpose Financial Presentations 623.24
- Subsequent Events........ 508.71; 560.05; 560.09; 711.11
- Supplementary Information..... 551.06–.09; 551.15
- Tolerable Misstatement 350.18

References are to AU section and paragraph numbers.

MATERIALITY—continued
- · Weaknesses in Internal Control 9317.03–.06
- · Weaknesses in Internal Control Over Financial Reporting 9550.11; 9550.15

MATHEMATICAL RELATIONSHIPS
- · Correction of Error 420.15
- · Reports, Other Auditors 543.07; 543.17

MEASUREMENT
- · Standards for Fair Presentation 411.02–.04
- · Supplementary Information . . . . 551.08; 558.06–.07

MEMBERSHIP
- · American Institute of CPAs 543.10

MERGERS—See Business Combinations

MINUTES OF MEETINGS
- · Evidential Matter 326.17
- · Letters for Underwriters 634.45
- · Litigations, Claims, and Assessments 337.07
- · Related Party Transactions 334.08
- · Representations of Management . . . . 333.06; 333.11; 333.16; 333A.04–.05; 333A.10
- · Review of Interim Information 722.08
- · Subsequent Events 560.12

MISAPPROPRIATION—See Fraud

MISLEADING FINANCIAL STATEMENTS
- · Changing Business Conditions 313.06
- · Disagreement With Predecessor Auditor 315.21–.22; 315A.10
- · Federal Securities Statutes 711.02–.03; 711.07
- · Interim v. Year-End Testing 313.06
- · Misstatements by Management 313.06
- · Rule 203, Accounting Principles . . . 508.14–.15
- · Segment Information 435.08–.10
- · Subsequent Discovery of Facts 561.09
- · Subsequent Events 711.10
- · Substantive Tests of Interim Information 313.06

MISTAKES—See Fraud

N

NATIONAL REVIEW BOARD
- · Inquiries Concerning Members 543.10

NEGATIVE ASSURANCE
- · Agreed-Upon Procedures . . . . 622.03; . . . 622.20; 622.26; 622.33; 9662.01–.02
- · Compliance Reports 623.19–.21
- · Definition 634.12
- · Disclaimer of Opinion 504.18
- · Letters for Underwriters—See Letters for Underwriters

NEGLIGENCE
- · Legal Liability 230.03

NET INCOME
- · Effect of Change to LIFO 9420.18–.19

NET REALIZABLE VALUE
- · Accounts Receivable 326.07
- · Inventories 333A.04

NONAUDIT SERVICES
- · Relation to Audit Planning 9311.01–.03

NONBUSINESS ORGANIZATIONS
- · Departures From Established Principles 9623.47–.54
- · Financial Accounting Standards Board 9623.54
- · Form 990 (Internal Revenue) . . . 9623.47–.54
- · Other Information in Documents 550.02
- · Summarized Prior Period Information 508.65

NONCLIENTS
- · Addressee of Report 508.09

NONCURRENT LIABILITIES
- · Assertions By Management 326.08

NONMONETARY TRANSACTIONS
- · Related Parties 334.03

NONPROFIT ORGANIZATIONS—See Nonbusiness Organizations

NONPUBLIC ENTERPRISES
- · Accountant Not Indpendent 504.10
- · Independence of CPAs 9504.22
- · Interim Financial Information 722.02
- · Segment Information 9508.01–.05
- · Selected Financial Data 552.01–.02; 552.09–.12
- · Use of Accountant's Name . . 504.02; 552.11

NONSTATISTICAL SAMPLING
- · Approach to Audit Sampling 350.03; 350.45–.46
- · Evidential Matter . . . 350.03–.06; 350.45–.46

NOTES TO FINANCIAL STATEMENTS
- · Accounting Changes 420.17; 9410.17
- · Basis of Presentation 504.07
- · Consolidating Financial Statements 551.19
- · Disclosure . . . . 420.09; 431.02; . . . . 623.09–.10; 9623.59; 9623.61; 9623.65–.66; 9623.88–.93
- · Interim Financial Information 722.02; 722.38
- · Pension Plans 9420.64–.65
- · Qualified Opinion . . . . 508.21; 508.25; 508.38; 508.40
- · Relation to Basic Financial Statements 551.02
- · Subsequent Discovery of Facts 561.06

NOTES TO FINANCIAL STATEMENTS—continued
- Subsequent Events . . . 508.28; 530.04–.05; 530.08; 711.11
- Unaudited Information . . . 504.07; 508.27–.28

NOTIFICATION
- Illegal Acts by Clients . . . 317.17

O

OBJECTIVES OF AUDIT
- Audit Sampling . . . 350.02; 350.05; 350.16–.22; 350.25
- Auditor's Expression of Opinion . . . 110.01; 310.06; 558.04; 722.09; 722.27–.29; 722.42
- Effects of Information Technology . . . 326.12
- Evidential Matter . . . 326.09–.13; 326.22; 326.25–.26; 9326.03
- Inventories . . . 326.26
- Relation to Substantive Tests . . . 313.08; 326.10–.14; 326.26
- Supplementary Information . . . 551.05
- Understanding With Client . . . 310.05–.07

OBJECTIVITY
- Evidential Matter . . . 326.02
- Internal Auditors . . . 322.03; 322.10–.11
- Specialists . . . 336.10–.11

OBLIGATIONS
- Assertions by Management . . . 326.03–.06
- Evidential Matter . . . 326.08

OBSOLESCENCE
- Estimation . . . 312.36
- Inherent Risk . . . 312.27
- Management Representations . . . 333.17; 333A.04
- Related Party Transactions . . . 334.06

OFFICE OF MANAGEMENT AND BUDGET (OMB)
- Audit & Reporting Requirements . . . 801.07; 801.13–.15; 801.22

OIL AND GAS RESERVES
- Audit Procedures . . . 9558.03–.05
- Disclosure Requirements . . . 9558.01–.05
- Estimation of Quantities . . . 9558.02–.04
- Illustrative Report . . . 9558.05
- Inquiries to Management . . . 9558.03–.05
- Limitations to Auditor . . . 9558.05
- Specialists . . . 9558.02; 9558.04

OMB—See Office of Management and Budget (OMB)

OMITTED AUDITING PROCEDURES
- Assessing Importance of Omitted Procedures . . . 390.04–.05
- Background Information . . . 390.01
- Effect on Previous Report . . . 390.06
- Legal Matters . . . 390.01; 390.03; 390.07
- Responsibilities of Auditor . . 390.02; 390.07
- Retrospective Review of Audit Work . . . 390.02

OPINIONS, ACCOUNTING PRINCIPLES BOARD
- Number 20 . . . 420.04; 420.06; 435.11; 561.06; 9420.18
- Number 28 . . . 9326.01; 9326.05; 9420.11–.12; 9420.14–.15; 9504.01–.06
- Number 9 . . . 561.06

OPINIONS, AUDITORS'
- Accounting Changes—See Changes, Accounting
- Adverse—See Adverse Opinions
- Application of Accounting Principles . . . 625.02; 625.07
- Appointment of Auditor . . . 310.04; 310A.04
- Audit Risk and Materiality . . . 312.02; 312.26
- Auditor-Submitted Documents . . 551.01–.22
- Basis for Judgment . . . 110.05; 312.13; 326.02; 326.13–.14; 326.22–.23; 411.04; 9411.14
- Basis of Accounting Other than GAAP . . . 410.02; 623.02–.10
- Change of Auditors . . . 315.12–.13; 315.15; 315.18; 315.25; 315A.08–.10
- Change to GAAP From Other Basis . . . 420.11
- Comparative Financial Statements . . . 508.65–.74
- Compliance Reports . . . 623.19–.21; 9623.40–.46
- Condensed Financial Statements . . . 552.05–.07
- Confidential Client Information . . . 431.04
- Consistency—See Consistency
- Consolidating Information . . . 551.16–.19
- Departure From GAAP . . . 504.11–.13; 508.35–.60
- Disclaimer—See Disclaimer of Opinion
- Disclosure Inadequate . . . 508.41–.44
- Elements of Financial Statements . . . 622.03; 622.33; 623.11–.18; 9623.41–.46
- Emphasis of a Matter . . . 508.19; 9410.18
- Evidential Matter—See Evidential Matter
- Examples—See Illustrations
- Explanatory Language . . . 9550.10
- Explanatory Paragraph . . . 508.69
- Expression of Opinion . . . 150.02; 312.26; 326.01–.02; 326.13–.14; 326.22–.23; 504.01
- Fair Presentation . . . 411.01–.16
- Filing With Regulatory Agencies . . . 9623.40–.46
- First Year Audits . . . 420.24
- Fraud . . . 316.25
- Generally Accepted Auditing Standards . . . 110.05; 508.03–.05
- Illegal Acts by Clients . . . 317.18–.21; 317.23
- Income Taxes . . . 9326.06–.17

References are to AU section and paragraph numbers.

OPINIONS, AUDITORS'—continued
- Included in Electronic Sites.... 9550.16–.18
- Incomplete Special-Purpose Financial Presentation.............. 9623.80–.87
- Individual Financial Statement......... 508.05; 508.33–.34
- Internal Control—See Reports on Internal Control
- Introductory Paragraph............ 508.63
- Lack of Conformity With Comprehensive Basis of Accounting Other Than GAAP.... 326.25
- Lack of Conformity With GAAP..... 326.25; 504.11–.13; 544.02–.04
- Lack of Independence 504.09
- Letters for Underwriters—See Letters for Underwriters
- Litigation, Claims, and Assessments 337.13–.14
- Loss Reserves (Insurance).... 9623.40–.46
- Material Misstatements 312.38
- Matters Requiring Specialists 336.13–.16; 9336.18
- Negative Assurance—See Negative Assurance
- Nonprofit Organizations 9623.47–.54
- Objective of Audit........ 110.01; 551.05; .... 558.04; 722.09; 722.27–.29; 722.42
- Omitted Auditing Procedures 390.04
- Opinion Paragraph 508.60
- Other Accountants—See Reports, Other Auditors'
- Other Information in Documents............. 550.03; 551.04
- Other Information in Electronic Sites Containing Audited Financial Statements.............. 9550.16–.18
- Piecemeal—See Piecemeal Opinions
- Principal Auditor...... 543.03–.09; 543.11
- Prior Year's Statements 504.15–.17
- Pro Forma Information 508.27
- Qualified—See Qualified Opinion
- Regulated Companies.......... 544.02–.04
- Related Parties................... 334.12
- Reports With Differing Opinions 508.67–.69
- Representations From Management....... 333.02; 333.13–.14; .... 333.16; 333.18; 333A.02; 333A.11–.12; 9508.51–.52
- Reservations—See Reservations
- Responsibility, Degree Assumed.... 110.03; .... 150.02; 504.01; 504.15; ...... 508.04–.05; 508.12; 543.03–.04; ..... 543.07–.09; 551.05; 9504.15–.18; 9543.04–.07; 9550.16–.18
- Restatements.................. 508.18
- Restricted Distribution .... 9623.83; 9623.85–.87
- Review of Form 10-K 9634.01–.09

OPINIONS, AUDITORS'—continued
- Scope—See Scope of Audit
- Segment Information............. 435.03; 435.09–.10; 435.13
- Selected Financial Data........ 552.09–.11
- Service Organizations..... 324.10; 324.29; .... 324.34; 324.37; 324.36–.40; .... 324.44; 324.49; 324.52; 324.55–.56
- Special Reports—See Special Reports
- Special-Purpose Financial Presentations............. 623.22–.30; 9623.80–.87
- Standard of Reporting............ 150.02
- Standard Report 508.07–.10
- Subject to—See Qualified Opinion
- Supplementary Data 544.02
- Supplementary Information .... 551.04–.19; 558.08
- Third-Party Additions......... 9623.85–.87
- Unqualified—See Unqualified Opinion
- Updated Auditor's Report 508.68–.69
- Working Papers 339.05

ORGANIZATIONAL STRUCTURE
- Internal Control........... 319.23; 319.84

ORGANIZATIONS, PROFESSIONAL
- Sources of Information 543.10

OTHER AUDITORS' REPORTS—See Reports, Other Auditors'

OVER-THE-COUNTER STOCKS
- Publicly Traded Companies........ 504.02

OWNERS—See Stockholders/Owners

OWNERS' EQUITY—See Stockholders' Equity

P

PARENT COMPANY
- Condensed Financial Information.... 552.05
- Management Representations...... 333.11; 333A.08; 333A.10

PAYABLES
- Assertions by Management........ 326.05
- Related Parties.................. 333.06; 333.16; 333A.04

PENALTIES
- Foreign Corrupt Practices Act..... 9317.06

PENSION PLANS
- Defined Benefit Plans—See Defined Benefit Pension Plans
- Related Parties........... 334.01; 334.07

PERSONNEL—See Employees

PIECEMEAL OPINIONS
- Prohibited..................... 508.64
- Report on Elements of Financial Statements 551.08; 623.14
- Supplementary Information .... 551.06; 551.10; 551.13

References are to AU section and paragraph numbers.

PLANNING
- Analytical Procedures .... 319.45; 329.01–.23
- Appointment of Independent Auditor 310.03–.04; 310A.03–.04
- Assertions 319.45
- Audit Program 311.05
- Audit Risk and Materiality ... 311.03; 312.01; 312.12–.33; 312.39–.40
- Audit Sampling .... 350.02–.03; 350.15–.23; 350.28; 350.31–.37
- Communication Between Auditors ...... 315.01–.25; 315A.01–.12; .... 543.10; 9315A.11–.13; 9315A.15; 9334.12–.15
- Compliance Auditing 801.11
- Designing Substantive Tests 319.19
- Effects of EDP on Audit .... 311.03; 311.09–.10; 9311.42–.44
- Elements of Financial Statements 623.12
- Evidential Matter ..... 312.12; 312.19–.20; 312.33; 326.09–.14
- Extent of Planning .... 310.03; 310A.03; .... 311.03; 312.15; 312.25; 312.33; 312.39
- Fraud .... 311.03; 312.12–.13; 312.16–.18; 316.03; 316.37
- Going Concern Assumption 341.02–.03; 341.08
- Interim Financial Statements—See Interim Financial Statements
- Internal Control Considerations ... 319.01–.05; 319.19–.44; 325.07
- Judgment .... 311.03; 312.13–.15; 312.19; 350.02–.03
- Lawyers' Letters 9337.01–.05
- Material Misstatements .... 312.05; .... 312.16; 312.19–.20; 312.23–.25; 350.18
- Prior Period Statements, Use of 312.23
- Relation to Nonaudit Services ... 9311.01–.03
- Relationship to Appointment of Auditor 310.01–.04; 310A.01–.04
- Review of Interim Information 722.14
- Scope of Audit .... 310.04; 310A.04; 311.03–.10; 312.26
- Segment Information 435.06
- Service Organization Processed Transactions 324.07–.10
- Sources of Information 312.33
- Standard of Field Work 150.02; 311.01
- Tests of Controls 319.59
- Timing of Audit Work .. 311.03–.05; 311.12; .... 312.15; 312.21; 312.25; 312.33; 312.39; 313.02
- Tolerable Misstatement 350.18
- Uncertainties, Control of 312.27
- Understanding Internal Audit Function 322.04
- Use of Specialist 311.10
- Work of Internal Auditors 311.04
- Working Papers 339.05
- Year 2000 Issue 9311.42–.44

POLICIES, ACCOUNTING
- Appropriateness 332.05–.06
- Communication to Audit Committee 380.07
- Departures From GAAP—See Departures From Established Principles
- Factor in Planning Audit 311.03
- Interim Financial Statements 9326.01
- Management Responsibility 110.03
- Relation to Basic Financial Statements 551.02
- Segment Information 435.06

POOLING OF INTERESTS
- Consistency 420.08–.09
- Restated Financial Statements .. 543.16–.17

POSITIVE ASSURANCE
- Letters for Underwriters—See Letters for Underwriters

PREDECESSOR AUDITOR
- Applicability of Section .... 315.01 .... 315A.01; 543.01
- Availability of Working Papers ... 315.11–.13; .... 315.15; 315.19–.20; 315.24–.25; 315A.08–.09
- Consultation With Successor 315A.09; 9315A.01–.18
- Contingencies 315.11; 315A.09
- Dating of Report 508.73
- Definition 315.02; 315A.01; 9315A.02
- Disagreement With Client .... 315.07; 315.09; 315A.04–.07
- Other Information in Documents 550.04
- Reference to Successor 508.71
- Reissuance of Report ... 508.70–.73; 530.06
- Representation Letter From Successor 508.71
- Responses to Successor Auditor ... 315.05; .... 315.08; 315.10; 315.24; 315A.04–.08; 9315A.05
- SEC Filings 711.11–.12
- Subsequent Discovery of Facts 561.01–.10; 9315A.06–.07
- Subsequent Events 508.71–.73

PRESCRIBED REPORT FORMS—See Special Reports

PRICE LEVEL CHANGES
- Minimizing Impact by LIFO 9420.19

PRINCIPLES ACCOUNTING—See Generally Accepted Accounting Principles

PRIOR PERIOD ADJUSTMENTS
- Restatements .... 9315A.06–.07; 9410.13–.18
- Subsequent Events 560.08

PRIOR PERIOD ITEMS
- Likely Misstatements 312.37
- Segment Information 435.12
- Subsequent Discovery of Facts 561.06
- Uncertainties 508.69

References are to AU section and paragraph numbers.

PRIVILEGED COMMUNICATION—See Confidential Client Information

PRO FORMA FINANCIAL STATEMENTS
- Effects of Accounting Changes 9420.19
- Letters for Underwriters 634.35; 634.42–.43; 634.64
- Subsequent Events 560.05; 9410.16
- Unaudited Information 508.27–.28

PROBABILITY
- Contingencies 337B
- Litigation, Claims, and Assessments 337.04; 337.09; 337.14; 9337.06–.07

PROFESSIONAL DEVELOPMENT—See Training and Education

PROFESSIONAL ETHICS DIVISION
- Inquiries Concerning Members 543.10

PROFESSIONAL ORGANIZATIONS—See Organizations, Professional

PROFESSIONAL SKEPTICISM
- Accounting Estimates 342.04; 342.07–.14
- Confirmation Process 330.15; 330.27
- Definition 230.07; 316.27
- Due Professional Care 230.07–.09
- Fraud 316.27

PROFICIENCY OF AUDITOR
- First General Standard 210.01–.15
- Knowledge of Entity's Business 311.06
- Qualifications 110.04–.05; 336.01

PROFIT AND LOSS STATEMENTS—See Statements of Income

PROGRAM, AUDIT
- Planning of Audit Work 311.01; 311.05
- Work of Other Auditors 543.12

PROPERTY
- Assertions by Management 326.07

PROSPECTIVE FINANCIAL STATEMENTS
- Going Concern Assumption 341.09–.10

PROSPECTUSES
- Consenting to Use of Audit Report 9711.12–.17
- Experts Section 711.08; 9711.12–.15
- Responsibility of Accountant 711.08–.09; 9711.12–.15
- Shelf Registration Statements ... 9711.01–.02; 9711.10–.11
- Subsequent Events 711.10–.11; 9711.01–.02; 9711.10–.11

PROVISIONS FOR CONTINGENCIES—See Contingencies

PROXY STATEMENTS
- Responsibilities of Accountant .. 711.02–.13

PUBLIC UTILITIES—See Utilities, Public

PUBLIC WAREHOUSES
- Accountability, Warehouseman's 901.03; 901.10; 901.19–.20
- Audit Procedures 901.01; 901.19–.23; 901.28
- Confirmations 901.03; 901.19–.20; 901.22
- Controls 901.01–.28
- Field Warehouses 901.07; 901.16–.18; 901.21
- General Considerations 901.02
- Government Regulation 901.08; 901.11–.12
- Insurance 901.15; 901.23; 901.27
- Inventories 331.14; 901.01–.28
- Observation of Inventories 901.03; 901.19; 901.21
- Operating Procedures 901.06–.12
- Recommendations 901.03–.05
- Reserve for Losses, Damage Claims ... 901.23
- Responsibility of Auditor 901.04
- Types
  - Commodity 901.07
  - Field 901.07
  - Terminal 901.07
- Warehouse Receipts
  - Accountability of Warehouseman 901.10; 901.19–.20
  - Confirmation 901.22
  - Description 901.08–.11
  - Field Warehousing 901.17
  - Internal Control 901.15
  - Negotiability 901.08
  - Pledged as Collateral 901.09
  - Release of Goods 901.09–.11
- Warehouseman 901.13–.23

PUBLICATIONS
- Auditor's Consideration of Management's Adoption of Accounting Principles for New Transactions or Events 9411.13
- IRS Audit Manual 9326.06

PUBLICLY TRADED COMPANIES
- Condensed Financial Statements 552.01–.12
- Definition 504.02; 722.02
- Disclosure of Fourth Quarter Data 9504.01–.17
- Interim Financial Information 722.02
- Oil and Gas Producing Companies 9558.01–.05
- Use of Accountant's Name 504.01–.19; 552.07–.08; 552.11

PURCHASES
- Assertions by Management 326.05

References are to AU section and paragraph numbers.

Q

QUALIFIED OPINION
· Accounting Estimates Unreasonable . . . 508.48–.49
· Accounting Principles Inappropriate . . . 508.48
· Changes, Accounting . . . 508.50; 508.52–.57; 9410.15
· Condensed Financial Statements . . . 552.05
· Consistency . . . 508.52
· Departure From GAAP . . . 334.12; 336.14; 508.35–.57; 508.68–.69; 9336.18; 9623.53
· Derecognition of Transferred Assets . . . 9336.18
· Disclosure . . . 552.05; 552.09
· Evidential Matter . . . 326.25; 9315A.14; 9326.06–.10
· Except for Opinions . . . 508.21
· Explanatory Paragraph . . . 508.21; 508.25; 508.37–.38; 508.40; 508.52
· Fraud . . . 316.25
· Illegal Acts by Clients . . . 317.18
· Illustrations
· · Accounting Charge . . . 508.52
· · Departure From GAAP . . . 508.39–.40
· · Inadequate Disclosure . . . 508.42
· · Management Unable to Justify Accounting Change . . . 508.52
· · Omission of Statement of Cash Flows . . . 508.44
· · Scope Limitation . . . 508.26
· · Uncertainties . . . 508.67
· Inadequate Disclosure . . . 431.03; 508.41–.44; 508.46; 9410.15
· Individual Financial Statement . . . 508.05
· Lack of Disclosure . . . 420.09
· Letters for Underwriters . . . 634.27
· Material Misstatements . . . 312.38
· Materiality . . . 508.20–.21
· Matters Requiring Specialists . . . 336.13–.14; 9336.18
· Nonprofit Organizations . . . 9623.53
· Notes to Financial Statements . . . 508.38; 508.40
· Omission of Statement of Cash Flows . . . 508.44
· Opinion Paragraph . . . 508.21; 508.25–.26; 508.37
· Regulated Companies . . . 544.02
· Related Parties . . . 334.12
· Report Form . . . 508.21
· Reports With Differing Opinions . . . 508.67–.69
· Reports, Other Auditors' . . . 543.08; 543.11
· Scope Limitations . . . 316.25; 313.13–.14; 333A.11–.12; 336.13; 308.20–.34; 9336.18; 9543.08–.10
· Scope Paragraph . . . 508.25
· Segment Information . . . 435.09–.10; 435.13; 435.15–.16

QUALIFIED OPINION—continued
· Service Organizations . . . 324.10; 9324.13
· Subject to Opinions . . . 508.21
· Subsequent Events . . . 530.03–.14
· Supplementary Information . . . 551.10; 551.14
· Titles of Financial Statements . . . 623.07
· Unaudited Information . . . 508.27–.28
· Uncertainties . . . 508.38

QUALITY CONTROL
· Audit Engagement . . . 161.01–.03
· Omitted Auditing Procedures . . . 390.02
· Relation to GAAS . . . 161.01–.03
· Uncertainties . . . 312.27
· Work of Other Auditors . . . 9543.18–.20

R

RATES (INCOME TAXES)
· Interim Financial Information . . . 9326.05

REAL ESTATE
· Current-Value Financial Statements . . . 9623.55–.59
· Related Party Transactions . . . 334.03

REALIZABLE VALUE, NET—See Net Realizable Value

RECEIVABLES
· Collectibility . . . 311.06; 312.36
· Confirmations . . . 330.34–.35; 9508.01
· Net Realizable Value . . . 326.07
· Related Parties . . . 333.06; 333.16; 333A.04
· Scope Limitation . . . 508.24; 9508.01

RECORDS
· Evidential Matter . . . 326.16–.20; 9326.06–.12
· Income Tax Accruals . . . 9326.06–.12
· Information for Auditor's Report . . . 431.03
· Interim Financial Information . . . 722.13
· Letters for Underwriters . . . 634.55; 634.57; 634.59
· Nonsampling Risk . . . 350.09–.11
· Reliability—See Reliability
· Sampling Risk . . . 350.12
· Working Papers . . . 339.01; 339.03–.08; 622.31–.32

REFUNDS—See Claims

REGISTRATION STATEMENTS
· Condensed Financial Information . . . 552.05
· Date of Reports . . . 711.05–.06; 9711.01–.11
· Discovery of Facts . . . 711.12–.13
· Letters for Underwriters—See Letters for Underwriters
· Negative Assurance . . . 504.19
· Responsibilities of Accountant . . . 552.05; 711.02–.13; 9711.01–.11
· Shelf Registration Statements . . . 9711.01–.11
· Subsequent Events . . . 711.10–.13; 9711.01–.11

References are to AU section and paragraph numbers.

REGULATED INDUSTRIES
- Basis of Accounting 544.02–.04
- Departure From GAAP 544.02–.04
- Disclosure of Illegal Actions 317.23
- Insurance Companies 544.02
- Public Utilities—See Utilities, Public
- Standards of Reporting 544.02
- Supplementary Data 544.02; 551.10

REGULATIONS
- Form 10-K (SEC) 9634.01–.09
- Form 10-Q (SEC) 711.09; 722.35
- Regulation S-K (SEC) ..... 552.09; 722.04; .... 722.36–.37; 722.41; 9634.06; 9711.05–.07
- Regulation S-X (SEC)........ 543.07; 552.08
- Rule 2-05 .... 543.07
- Working Papers 339.06

REGULATORY AGENCIES
- Basis of Accounting 9623.47–.54
- Compliance Reports .... 623.19–.21; 9623.40–.46
- Condensed Financial Statements 552.05; 552.07–.08
- Disclosure of Subsequent Discovery 561.06–.08
- Illustration of Auditor's Report...... 623.08; 623.26; 642.59; 9623.42
- Insurance Companies 9623.40–.46
- Interim Financial Information 722.04–.05
- Internal Revenue Service—See Internal Revenue Service
- Litigation, Claims, and Assessments. . 337.07
- Nonprofit Organizations 9623.47–.54
- Omitted Auditing Procedures 390.01; 390.07
- Other Information In Documents 550.03–.04
- Related Parties............... 334.07–.10
- Reports, Other Auditors 543.10
- Representation Letters........... 333.06; 333.16; 333A.04
- Requesting Access to or Photocopies of Working Papers........... 9339.01–.15
- SEC—See Securities and Exchange Commission
- Selected Financial Data 552.09
- Source of Established Principles..... 411.08
- Special-Purpose Financial Presentations 623.22–.30
- Supplementary Information........ 551.06; 551.10

REISSUED REPORTS
- Auditors' Reports ..... 504.15; 530.06–.08; 622.38; 9341.01–.02
- Dating of Reports.... 530.08; 9341.01–.02
- Distinguished From Updated........ 508.65
- Eliminating Going-Concern Explanatory Paragraph 9341.01–.02
- Predecessor Auditor........... 508.70–.73

RELATED PARTIES
- Accounting Considerations 334.02–.03
- Audit Procedures .... 150.05; 311.03; .... 333A.03; 334.04–.10; 9334.16–.21
- Audit Risk 9334.17–.19
- Communication Between Auditors................. 9334.12–.13
- Conditions Underlying Transactions.... 334.06
- Confirmations 334.08–.10
- Control 334.01; 334.04; 334.11
- Definition 334.01
- Departures From Established Principles.................... 334.12
- Determining Existence .... 334.07–.18; 9334.20–.21
- Disclosure Requirements.......... 334.01; 334.04; 334.11–.12
- Emphasis in Auditor's Report....... 508.19
- Evidential Matter 334.09–.11
- Examples 334.01; 334.03
- Guarantees.............. 334.08; 334.10
- Identification of Transactions ...... 334.08; 9334.14–.15
- Intercompany Balances....... 334.09–.10; 9334.14–.15
- Internal Control Structure 334.05
- Legal Matters..... 334.02; 334.06; 334.08
- Opinions, Auditors' 334.12
- Planning of Audit Work 311.03; 311.07
- Reliance on Representations...... 333A.03
- Representation Letters .... 333.03; 333.06; .... 333.11; 333.16; 333A.03–.04; 333A.10; 334.12
- Scope of Audit 334.05
- Sources of Information..... 334.07–.10; 9334.20–.21
- Substance v. Form 334.02
- Substantive Tests 9334.17
- Unrecorded Transactions 334.08
- Unusual Items....... 334.08; 9543.04–.07

RELATIONSHIP WITH CLIENTS
- Auditor-Submitted Documents...... 551.04
- Client-Prepared Documents........ 551.04; 552.01–.12
- Disagreement With Auditor .... 315.07; .... 315.09; 315A.04–.07; 504.13; 551.09; 722.35
- Engagement Letters—See Engagement Letters
- Evidential Matter 9326.06–.17
- Other Information in Documents 551.04
- Predecessor Auditor 508.73
- Representation Letters .... 333.01–.18; .... 333A.01–.14; 9333.01–.04; 9333A.05–.06
- Review of Interim Information 722.35
- Scope of Audit 9317.01–.02
- Segment Information 435.10; 435.15–.16

References are to AU section and paragraph numbers.

RELATIONSHIP WITH CLIENTS—continued
- Specialists . . . 336.10–.11
- Subsequent Discovery of Facts . . . 561.02
- Supplementary Information . . . 551.04; . . . 551.09–.11
- Weaknesses in Internal Control . . . 9317.03–.06
- Weaknesses in Internal Control Over Financial Reporting . . . 9550.11
- Withdrawal From Engagement . . . 504.13; 711.12–.13
- Working Papers . . . 339.06–.07

RELATIVES—See Family Relationships

RELEVANCE
- Evidential Matter . . . 326.11; 326.21; . . . 330.11
- Generally Accepted Auditing Standards . . . 150.06
- Internal Audit Function . . . 322.06–.08

RELIABILITY
- Confirmations . . . 330.16–.27
- Evidential Matter . . . 326.15–.22
- Financial Statements . . . 312.10
- Information . . . 550.04–.06; . . . 561.04–.05; 561.09
- Management of Client . . . 333.02–.04; . . . 333A.02–.03
- Relation to Risk . . . 350.45

RELIANCE ON WORK OF OTHERS
- Income Tax Matters . . . 9326.13–.17
- Other Auditors—See Reports, Other Auditors'
- Service Organizations—See Service Organizations
- Specialists—See Specialists

REPORTABLE CONDITIONS
- Agreed-Upon Criteria . . . 325.07–.08
- Agreement Between Auditor and Client . . . 325.08
- Audit Committee . . . 325.02–.03; . . . 325.06; 325.10
- Communication . . . 325.02–.03; 325.06; . . . 325.09–.12
- Communication When No Audit Committee Exists . . . 9380.02–.03
- Content of Report . . . 325.11
- Definition . . . 325.02
- Descriptions . . . 325.21
- Examples . . . 325.21
- Form of Reporting . . . 325.09
- Interim Communication . . . 325.18
- Internal Control . . . 325.02–.03
- Judgment . . . 325.02–.05; 325.07; 325.15
- Limited Distribution of Report . . . 325.10
- Management . . . 325.06; 325.10
- Material Weakness . . . 325.15; 9325.01–.06
- Reports on Internal Control . . . 325.09–.16
- Service Organizations . . . 324.20
- Year 2000 Issue . . . 9311.45–.47

REPORTS
- Auditors—See Auditors' Reports
- Internal Control—See Reports on Internal Control
- Other Auditors'—See Reports, Other Auditors'
- Review Reports—See Review Reports
- Special—See Special Reports
- Standard—See Auditors' Reports
- Stockholders—See Reports to Stockholders

REPORTS ON INTERNAL CONTROL
- Agreed-Upon Criteria . . . 325.07–.08
- Auditor's Responsibility . . . 9550.07–.15
- Communication . . . 325.01–.21; . . . 9325.01–.06
- Examples . . . 325.12; 325.16; 9325.04
- Form of and Level of Assurance in . . . 801.16
- Illustrations—See Illustrations
- Service Organizations . . . 324.02; 324.12; . . . 324.16; 324.18–.21; . . . 324.24–.56
- Users . . . 9550.14–.15
- Weaknesses in Internal Control Over Financial Reporting . . . 9550.11; 9550.15

REPORTS TO STOCKHOLDERS
- Interim Financial Information . . . 722.27; 722.35
- Other Information in Documents . . . 550.01–.06

REPORTS, OTHER AUDITORS'
- Affiliated Companies . . . 543.01–.02; . . . 543.06; 543.10
- Audit Program . . . 543.12
- Basis for Opinion . . . 508.12
- Condensed Financial Statements . . . 552.05
- Cost Method . . . 543.14
- Decision Not to Make Reference . . . 508.71; . . . 508.74; 543.04–.05; . . . 543.12–.13; 9334.14–.15; . . . 9543.18–.20
- Decision to Make Reference . . . 543.02–.03; 543.06–.09
- Departure From Standard Report . . . 543.15
- Disclaimer of Opinion . . . 543.11
- Disclosure of Reference . . . 508.12–.13; 543.07–.09
- Equity Method . . . 543.14
- Evidential Matter . . . 543.14; 9315A.10–.11; . . . 9543.18–.20
- Independence Requirements . . . 543.04; . . . 543.10
- Intercompany Account Balances . . . 543.10; 543.17; 9334.14–.15
- Internal Control . . . 543.12
- Letters for Underwriters . . . 634.18; 634.28
- Long-Term Investments . . . 543.14
- Materiality . . . 543.05–.06; 543.15; . . . 9543.01–.03; 9543.18–.20

References are to AU section and paragraph numbers.

REPORTS, OTHER AUDITORS'—continued
- Other Information in Documents 550.04
- Pooling of Interests 543.16–.17
- Predecessor—See Predecessor Auditor
- Procedures Applicable . . . . 543.10–.11; 9543.01–.03; 9543.18–.20
- Qualified Opinion . . . . 543.08; 543.11; 9543.08–.10
- Quality Control Policies. 9543.18–.20
- Related Party Transactions. . . . 9334.14–.15
- Representation Letters. 543.10
- Reputation and Standing. . . . . 543.01; 543.04–.05; 543.10–.11
- Responsibility of Auditor. 543.03
- Review of Interim Information 722.13; 722.29
- Scope of Audit 543.12; 9543.18–.20
- SEC Filings. 543.07; 711.11
- Selected Financial Data 552.09
- Successor—See Successor Auditor
- Working Papers 543.12

REPRESENTATION LETTERS
- Accounting Estimates. 342.09
- Agreed-Upon Procedures 622.39–.40
- Assertions by Management. 326.03–.08; 326.22
- Audit Requirement . . . . 333.01–.18; 333A.01–.14
- Change of Auditors. 508.71
- Compensating Balances . . . 333.17; 333A.04
- Completeness of Information 333.06
- Compliance Auditing of Federal Financial Assistance Programs 801.10
- Compliance With Laws 9333.01–.04
- Consolidated Financial Statements 333.16; 333.18; 333A.08
- Current Management Was Not Present During Period Under Audit 9333A.05–.06
- Dating of Letters 333.09; 333A.09
- Effective Date of Responses. . . 9337.01–.05
- Evaluation by Auditor 311.06
- Evidential Matter 326.17; 9326.06–.10
- Examples of Information Included . . . 333.06; 333.16–.18; 333A.04
- Illegal Acts by Clients 317.08
- Illustration . . . . 333.16–.18; 333A.14; 9337.16
- Independence of Other Auditors 543.10
- Interim Financial Information . . . . 722.13; 722.35
- Letters for Underwriters 634.03–.07
- Litigation, Claims, and Assessments 9337.16
- Related Party Transactions 334.12
- Reliance on Representations. . . . . . . 317.16; 333.02–.04; 333A.02–.03; 350.25
- Scope Limitations. . . . . 333.13–.14; 333A.11–.12; 9326.06–.10
- Service Organizations. 324.57

REPRESENTATION LETTERS—continued
- Signing of Letters 333.09; 333A.09
- Subsequent Events . . . . 333.06; 333.09; . . . . 333.12; 333.16–.18; 333A.04; 560.12; 711.10–.11
- Supplementary Information 558.07
- Unasserted Claims . . . . 337.05; 9337.06–.07; 9337.16
- Updating 333.12 333.18
- Violations of Laws. 9333.01–.04

REPRESENTATIONAL FAITHFULNESS
- Assertions by Management. . . . . 326.02; 326.13; 326.20–.21

RESEARCH AND DEVELOPMENT COSTS
- Accounting Changes 9410.14; 9410.16

RESERVATIONS
- Disclaimer of Opinion 508.62
- Fair Presentation. 508.59
- Titles of Financial Statements 623.07

RESERVES
- Income Tax Accruals. 9326.06–.17
- Loss Reserves (Insurance) 9623.40–.46

RESTATEMENTS
- Change in Accounting Principle . . . . . 420.13; 9410.13–.18; 9420.32–.43
- Correction of Error 420.11
- Financial Statements Reported on by Predecessor Auditor 9315A.06–.07
- Prior Period Financial Statements . . . . 508.68–.69; 508.74; 9315A.06–.07
- Reports Following Pooling of Interests 543.16–.17
- Segment Information. . . . . 435.07; 435.11–.14
- Subsequent Years' Reports 508.19

RESTRICTIONS
- Scope of Audit—See Scope of Audit

RESTRUCTURING OF DEBT
- Management Plans Relating to Going Concern Assumption 341.07

RESULTS OF OPERATIONS
- Condensed Financial Statements 552.03–.04
- Interim v. Annual 722.07; 9326.01

RETAINED EARNINGS
- Change in Accounting Principle 9420.18

RETROACTIVITY
- Change in Accounting Principle 9410.13–.18
- Segment Information. . . . . 435.07; 435.11–.14

References are to AU section and paragraph numbers.

REVENUE
- Assertions by Management 326.07

REVIEW OF FINANCIAL STATEMENTS
- Change From Audit Engagement 508.61
- Subsequent Period Audited 504.17

REVIEW OF INTERIM FINANCIAL INFORMATION
- Accompanying Audited Financial Statements. 722.36–.42
- Client Representations. 722.35
- Condensed Financial Statements. 552.08; 9711.09
- Date of Report. 722.27
- Deficiencies in Internal Control. 722.11
- Departure From GAAP 711.13; 722.30–.32; 722.42
- Disclosure Requirements 722.30–.32
- Discovery of Facts. 711.13
- Evidential Matter 722.09
- Examples of Reports . . . . . 552.08; 711.09; . . . . 722.28–.29; 722.31–.32; 722.41
- Extent of Procedures 722.10–.17
- Form 10-Q. 711.09; 722.35
- Fourth Quarter Interim Data . . . 9504.01–.07
- Inquiries—See Inquiries
- Internal Control 722.10–.11
- Letters for Underwriters—See Letters for Underwriters
- Limited Assurance. 722.18
- Litigation, Claims, and Assessments 722.17
- Modification of Procedures 722.19
- Objective of Review 722.09
- Other Information in Documents. 722.33
- Planning 722.14
- Procedures for Review. 722.12–.19
- Reports, Accountant's . . . . 722.26–.34; 722.40–.42
- Reports, Other Auditors' . . . 722.13; 722.29
- Scope of Audit. 722.26–.34
- Scope Restrictions 722.11; 722.26
- SEC Filings . . . . . . 552.08; 711.01; 711.03; . . . . 711.06; 711.09; 711.13; 722.04; 722.35–.37; 9711.09
- Shelf Registration Statements 9711.90
- Subsequent Discovery of Facts 722.34
- Subsequent Events 722.13
- Timing Considerations . . . . 722.08; 722.14; 722.26
- Use of Accountant's Name. 504.04
- Working Papers 722.43

REVIEW REPORTS
- Condensed Financial Statements 552.08

RIGHTS
- Assertions by Management 326.03–.06

RISK
- Accounting Estimates. 342.05; 342.14
- Analytical Procedures . . . 329.06; 329.09–.21
- Assessment for Internal Control 319.07; 319.28–.31; 319.84
- Assessment of Material Misstatement Due to Fraud 316.11–.25
- Audit . . . . 312.01–.41; 350.08–.11; 350.48; 9334.17–.19
- Changes in Assessment, Conditions Resulting in 316.25
- Consideration of Factors in Assessing Risk of Material Misstatement Due to Fraud 316.12; 316.21–.25
- Control—See Control Risk
- Control of Risk 313.03–.07
- Definition 312.02; 312.27–.28
- Detection Risk . . . . 312.27–.28; 312.32; . . . . 312.39–.40; 319.46; 319.55–.56; 319.79–.82; 326.13–.14
- Effect on Audit . . . . 150.05; 312.01–.02; 312.26; 9334.17–.19
- Effect on Financial Statements 312.01–.41
- Estimation 312.27
- Factor in Planning Audit . . . . 312.01; 312.12–.19; 312.26–.33; 312.39–.40
- Factors Relating to Misstatements Arising From Fraudulent Financial Reporting 316.16–.17
- Factors Relating to Misstatements Arising From Misappropriation of Assets 316.18–.20
- Generally Accepted Auditing Standards 150.03; 312.01–.02
- Illegal Acts by Clients 317.13–.15
- Inherent Risk . . . . 312.27–.33; 319.23; . . . . 319.43; 319.46; 319.55; 9326.20–.21
- Internal Audit Considerations . . . 322.14–.17
- Investments, Auditing 332.02
- Judgment—See Judgment
- Letters for Underwriters 634.12–.13
- Litigation, Claims, and Assessments 337.14
- Material Misstatements . . . . 312.02; . . . . 312.16–.17; 312.19; . . . . 312.24; 312.27–.33; 312.36–.40; . . . . 313.03; 326.11; 350.08–.14; . . . . 350.16–.23; 350.26; 350.35–.36; 350.48; 9326.03
- Nonsampling 350.09–.11
- Relation to Confirmation Procedures . . . 330.05; 330.07–.10; 330.20–.22
- Relation to Evidential Matter . . . . 312.12; . . . 312.19; 312.33; 313.07; 9326.20–.21
- Relation to Internal Control 312.27
- Relation to Materiality. 312.24
- Relation to Reliability 350.45
- Sampling . . . . 350.09–.14; 350.19–.23; . . . . 350.26; 350.33–.35; 350.41; 350.44
- Substantive Tests at Interim Dates 313.03–.07
- Uncertainties, as a Result of. 312.27

References are to AU section and paragraph numbers.

ROYALTIES
· Auditor's Report 551.11

RULES OF CONDUCT
· Rule 202 .... 161.01
· Rule 203 .... 411.05; 411.07
· Rule 301 .... 431.04
· Rules Supporting Standards 110.10

S

SALES
· Export Sales .... 435.01; 435.04; 435.07; 435.15–.16
· Intercompany 435.07; 435.11
· Transfer of Assets 9336.01–.18

SCOPE OF AUDIT
· Balance-Sheet-Only Audit 508.34
· Communication to Audit Commerce ... 380.02
· Degree of Risk .... 150.05; 312.01–.02; 312.26; 350.13
· Effect of Attorney-Client Privilege 9337.28–.30
· First Audits 315A.08–.09
· Foreign Corrupt Practices Act 9317.01–.02
· Fraud 316.11; 316.25; 316.32
· Generally Accepted Auditing Standards 150.06
· Lawyer's Responses to Inquiries .. 337.12–.13; 9337.28–.32
· Limitations
· · Disclaimer of Opinion .... 310.04; .... 310A.04; 316.25; 324.10; 508.27; 508.61–.63
· · Elements of Financial Statements .. 622.40
· · First Audits 315A.08–.09
· · Illustrative Auditor's Report 508.26
· · Income Taxes 9326.01–.10
· · Inventories 9508.01–.06
· · Investments 508.24; 508.26
· · Lawyer's Responses to Inquiries .... 337.12–.13; 9337.08–.09; 9337.28–.32
· · Letters for Underwriters 634.30
· · Matters Requiring Specialists 336.13; 9336.18
· · Permission to Use Legal Opinion Not Granted 9336.18
· · Piecemeal Opinions 508.64
· · Qualified Opinions ..... 310.04; 310A.04; 316.25; 324.10; 508.20–.34
· · Remedied 310.04; 310A.04
· · Representation Letters ...... 333.13–.14; 333A.11–.12
· · Review of Interim Information 722.11; 722.26
· · Segment Information 435.15–.16
· · Special Reports .... 623.05; 623.15; 623.25; 623.29
· · Uncertainties 9337.17

SCOPE OF AUDIT—continued
· Materiality, Effect 150.04; 312.01–.02
· Omitted Auditing Procedures 390.04
· Other Information in Documents 550.04
· Piecemeal Opinions—See Piecemeal Opinions
· Planning of Audit Work 311.03–.10
· Related Parties 334.05; 9543.04–.17
· Reports, Other Auditors' 9543.04–.17
· Review of Interim Information ...... 722.11; 722.26–.29; 722.42
· Segment Information 435.15–.16
· Supplementary Information .... 551.04–.11; 551.20
· Understanding With Client 310.05–.07
· Work of Other Auditor ... 543.12; 9543.18–.20

SECURITIES—See Investments

SECURITIES ACT OF 1933
· Filings Under Federal Securities Statutes .... 530.02; 711.01–.13; 9711.01–.17
· Interim Financial Information 722.04
· Letters for Underwriters—See Letters for Underwriters
· Other Information in Documents 550.03
· Shelf Registration Statements 9711.01–.11
· Subsequent Discovery of Facts 561.03

SECURITIES AND EXCHANGE COMMISSION
· Condensed Financial Information 552.05
· Condensed Financial Statements 552.07–.08
· Consenting to Use of Audit Report in Offering Document 9711.12–.17
· Disclosure of Illegal Acts 317.23
· Filings Under Securities Statutes .... 311.03; ...... 530.02; 530.06; 543.07; 552.05; ...... 552.07–.09; 561.03; 711.01–.13; 9634.01–.09; 9711.01–.17
· Form 10-K—See Form 10-K (SEC)
· Form 10-Q—See Form 10-Q (SEC)
· Independence Requirements... 220.05; 543.10; 9634.09
· Interim Financial Information .... 508.11; 552.08; 722.04; 722.35
· Letters for Underwriters—See Letters for Underwriters
· Negative Assurance 504.19
· Oil and Gas Reserves 9558.01–.05
· Prospectus—See Prospectuses
· Reissuance of Auditor's Report 530.06
· Reissuance of Financial Statements .. 560.08
· Related Parties 334.07–.08
· Responsibilities of Accountant.... 711.02–.13; 9711.01–.17
· Responsibilities of Management 711.01; 711.08
· SEC Engagement 380.01
· Selected Financial Data 552.09
· Shelf Registration Statements ... 9711.01–.11
· Subsequent Discovery of Facts 561.06–.08
· Unaudited Financial Statements 504.14

SECURITIES EXCHANGE ACT OF 1934

- Foreign Corrupt Practices Act . . . 9317.01–.02
- Letters for Underwriters—See Letters for Underwriters
- Other Information in Documents 550.02
- Review of Interim Information 722.35; 722.41
- Shelf Registration Statements 9711.05

SEGMENT INFORMATION

- Accounting Changes . . . 435.11–.14; 435.18
- Allocation of Costs 435.07; 435.09; 435.11
- Auditing Procedures 435.04–.07
- Auditor's Objective 435.03
- Consistency 435.07; 435.11–.14
- Definition 435.01
- Determination of Segments 435.07
- Disclosure 431.01; 435.01–.02; 435.13; 435.18
- Export Sales 435.01; 435.04; 435.07; 435.15–.16
- Foreign Operations 435.01; 435.04; 435.15–.16
- Geographic Areas 435.06–.07; 435.11–.12
- Illustration 435.09–.10; 435.13; 435.15–.16
- Industry Segments 435.01; 435.04–.07; 435.11–.12; 435.15–.16
- Letters for Underwriters 634.59
- Materialitiy 435.05; 435.08; 435.17
- Misstatement or Omission 435.09–.10
- Planning of Field Work 435.06
- Prior Periods 435.12
- Scope Limitation 435.15–.16
- Special Report 435.17–.18
- Unaudited Information 435.08; 435.10

SELECTED FINANCIAL DATA

- Auditor's Report 552.01–.02; 552.05; 552.09–.12
- Consolidated Financial Statements . . . 552.10
- Disclaimer of Opinion 552.11
- Filing With a Regulatory Agency 552.09
- Illustrations 552.10
- Letters for Underwriters 634.64
- Other Auditor's Report 552.05; 552.09

SERVICE ORGANIZATIONS

- Adverse Opinion 9324.13
- Agreed-Upon Procedures 324.19
- Alternative Methods of Presenting Controls and Subservice Organization Functions 9324.12–.18
- Carve-Out Method . . . 9324.12; 9324.15–.16
- Change in Controls Prior to Beginning of Fieldwork 324.28; 324.43
- Control Objectives 324.35–.36; 324.50–.51; 324.53

SERVICE ORGANIZATIONS—continued

- Control Risk Assessment 324.11–.16; 9324.05
- Deficiencies in Design or Operation of Controls 324.32; 324.40; 324.47
- Definition 324.02
- Description of Relevant Controls 324.26; 324.30; 324.33; 324.42; 324.45; 9324.08–.13
- Description of Tests of Operating Effectiveness and the Results of Such Tests 9324.01–.03
- Documentation 324.35; 324.41
- Effect of Subservice Organization Use on Auditor's Procedures 9324.04–.07
- Effect of Subservice Organization Use on User Organization's Financial Statement Assertions 9324.05
- Effect on User Organization's Controls 324.06–.10; 9324.05; 9324.07
- Elements Included in Description of Tests of Operating Effectiveness 9324.01
- Evidential Matter 324.10; 324.12; 324.16–.17; 324.27
- Examples 324.03
- Explanatory Paragraph 324.39–.40
- Fraud 324.23; 324.57
- Illustrative Reports 324.38–.40; 324.54–.56; 9324.16; 9324.18
- Inclusive Method . . . 9324.12; 9324.17–.18
- Internal Control Reports 324.02; 324.12; 324.16; 324.18–.21; 324.24
- Management Representations 324.57
- Modification of Service Auditor's Report 324.29; 324.31; 324.46
- Notation of Exceptions in Reports on Controls Placed in Operation and Tests of Operating Effectiveness 9324.03
- Opinions, Auditors' 324.10; 324.34; 324.37; 324.39–.40; 324.44; 324.49; 324.52; 324.55–.56; 324.79; 9324.13–.18
- Planning 324.07–.10; 9324.05
- Population Testing in Reports on Controls Placed in Operation and Tests of Operating Effectiveness 9324.03
- Qualified Opinion 9324.13
- Reportable Conditions 324.20
- Reports on Controls Placed in Operation 324.02; 324.12; 324.25–.40
- Reports on Controls Placed in Operation and Tests of Operating Effectiveness 324.02; 324.16; 324.41–.56; 9324.01–.03

References are to AU section and paragraph numbers.

SERVICE ORGANIZATIONS—continued
- Responsibilities of Service Auditor 324.22–.58
- Responsibility for Description of Controls 324.33; 324.48
- Scope Limitations................ 324.10
- Scope Paragraph 9324.16; 9324.18
- Service Auditor's Reports Affected by Method of Presentation 9324.14–.18
- Service Auditors............. 324.17–.58; .... 9324.01–.04; 9324.06; 9324.09; 9324.12–.18
- Sources of Information........ 324.25–.26; 324.41–.42
- Substantive Tests........ 324.15; 324.17; 324.58
- Tests of Controls 324.41
- Types of Reports 324.24
- Use of Service Auditor's Report.................. 324.18–.21
- Use of Subservice Organizations 9324.04–.18
- User Auditors .... 324.02; 324.05–.21; .... 9324.02–.05; 9324.07–.09; 9324.11–.12

SERVICES
- Nonaudit—See Nonaudit Services
- Service Organizations—See Service Organizations
- Subservice Organizations—See Service Organizations

SHAREHOLDERS—See Stockholders/Owners

SINGLE AUDIT ACT OF 1984
- Auditor's Responsibilities 317.24
- Illegal Acts by Clients 317.24

SOURCES OF INFORMATION
- Analytical Procedures....... 329.05; 329.16
- Business and Industry 311.08
- Competence of Other Auditors 543.10
- Established Accounting Principles 411.05–.13
- Governmental Entities.......... 411.12–.13; 411.16
- Income Tax Accruals 9326.06–.17
- Litigation, Claims, and Assessments 337.05; 337.08
- Nongovernmental Entities....... 411.10–.11; 411.16
- Planning...................... 312.33
- Professional Organizations 543.10
- Related Parties.............. 334.07–.10; 9334.20–.21
- Reliability 326.21
- Representation Letters......... 333.01–.18; 333A.01–.14
- Service Organizations.......... 324.25–.26; 324.41–.42
- Subsequent Discovery of Facts 561.04–.05
- Supplementary Financial Information 551.03

SPECIAL REPORTS
- Adequacy and Appropriateness of Disclosure ... 623.09–.10; 9623.60–.77; 9623.88–.93
- Agreed-Upon Procedures ..... 622.01–.49; 9622.01–.02
- Applicability 623.01
- Application of Accounting Principles.................. 625.01–.09
- Availability to Public 622.09; 622.33
- Basis of Accounting Other Than GAAP........................ 504.07; .... 623.02–.10; 9623.47–.54; 9623.60–.77; 9623.88–.93
- Combined or Included 622.47
- Compliance Reports ... 311.03; 623.19–.21; 9623.40–.46
- Current-Value Financial Statements Supplementing Historical-Cost Financial Statements 9623.55–.59
- Dating......................... 622.36
- Departure From Standard Report........... 623.17; 9623.45–.46
- Elements of Financial Statements ... 551.08; 622.01–.49; 9622.01–.02
- Explanatory Language..... 622.35; 623.31; 9623.45–.46
- Financial Statements Not Meeting Criteria for Basis of Accounting Other Than GAAP.......................... 623.06
- Form 990—See Form 990 (Internal Revenue)
- Form of Report for Application of Accounting Principles.................... 625.08
- Illustrations...... 622.34; 622.49; 623.08; .... 623.18; 623.21; 623.26; .... 623.30; 625.09; 9623.52; 9623.58
- Incomplete Financial Presentation 9623.80–.87
- Limited Distribution....... 623.05; 623.15; 623.20; 623.25; 623.29
- Loss Reserves (Insurance) 9623.40–.46
- Nonparticipant Parties as Specified Users......................... 622.38
- Nonprofit Organizations 9623.47–.54
- Other Auditor's Reports....... 9543.01–.03
- Other Information in Documents 550.03
- Prescribed Forms .... 623.05; 623.15; .... 623.20; 623.25; 623.29; 623.32–.33
- Qualified Opinions 623.07
- Restricted Distribution..... 622.04; 622.09; .... 622.33; 622.47; 9623.83; 9623.85–.87
- Restrictions on Performance of Procedures 622.37
- Scope Limitations......... 623.05; 623.15; 623.25; 623.29

SPECIAL REPORTS—continued
- Segment Information 435.17–.18
- Special-Purpose Financial Statement That Results in Incomplete Presentation But is Otherwise in Conformity With GAAP 9623.80–.87
- Special-Purpose Presentations to Comply With Contractual Agreements or Regulatory Provisions................. 623.22–.30
- Specialist Assistance.............. 622.22
- Third-Party Additions 9623.85–.87
- Titles of Financial Statements............ 623.07; 623.24
- Types of Financial Statements...... 623.02
- Use of Work of Specialists..... 336.01–.17

SPECIALISTS
- Accounting Estimates 342.11
- Actuaries—See Actuaries
- Agreed-Upon Procedures...... 622.21–.23
- Decision to Use Work .... 336.06–.07; 9336.03–.08
- Definition.............. 336.01; 9326.16
- EDP Applications 311.10
- Effects of Work on Auditors' Reports 336.13–.14; 9336.18
- Engineers—See Engineers
- Evidential Matter Relating to Tax Contingency Accruals................. 9326.13–.14
- Examples of Specialists........... 336.02
- Foreign Country's Accounting Principles 534.05; 534.12
- Foreign Country's Auditing Standards............. 534.06; 534.12
- Illegal Acts by Clients............ 317.03; 317.10–.12; 317.22–.23
- Inventories............. 110.04; 9508.01; 9508.05–.06
- Investments...... 332.19; 332.27; 332.29
- Lawyers—See Lawyers
- Legal........................ 9336.03
- Loss Reserves (Insurance)........... 336.07; 9623.40
- Matters Requiring Specialists... 336.06–.07; 622.21–.23; 622.33; 9336.01–.18
- Objectivity 336.10–.11
- Oil and Gas Reserves.... 9558.02; 9558.04
- Planning of Audit Work........... 311.04
- Qualifications........ 336.08–.09; 9558.04
- Reference in Auditors' Reports 336.15–.16
- Relationship With Clients 336.10–.11
- Responsibilities 336.12
- SEC Filings .... 711.02–.03; 711.08; 9711.12–.15
- Significant Influence.............. 336.10
- Transfers of Assets 9336.01–.18
- Use of Legal Interpretations to Support That Transfer of Assets Has Met Isolation Criteria in FASB Statement No. 125........ 9336.01–.18
- Use of Work by Auditors 336.01–.17; 9336.01–.18
- Work Experience 336.08–.09
- Work To Be Performed 336.09

STANDARD REPORTS—See Auditors' Reports

STANDARDS OF FIELD WORK—AUDIT
- Agreed-Upon Procedures Applied to Elements of Financial Statements........... 622.05
- Application of Accounting Principles 625.05
- Appointment of Independent Auditor 310.03–.04; 310A.03–.04
- Audit of Financial Statements for Use Outside U.S. 534.03–.06
- Audit Risk and Materiality 312.01
- Audit Sampling........... 350.04; 350.19
- Date of Auditor's Report....... 530.01–.08
- Evidential Matter .... 326.01; 9326.01–.02; 9326.06–.10
- Internal Control 9317.01–.02
- List of Standards 150.02
- Planning—See Planning
- Relationship Between Appointment and Planning 310.01–.04; 310A.01–.04
- Supervision—See Supervision
- Timing—See Timeliness
- Working Papers 339.02; 339.05

STANDARDS OF REPORTING—AUDIT
- Audit of Financial Statements for Use Outside U.S. 534.03–.06
- Audit Risk and Materiality 312.01
- Basis of Accounting Other Than GAAP 410.02; 504.07
- Consistency .... 420.01–.24; 508.03; 9420.20
- Disclosure 431.01
- Elements of Financial Statements............ 622.05; 623.12
- Expression of Opinion 508.04–.05; 508.65
- Generally Accepted Accounting Principles 410.01–.02; 411.02
- List of Standards 150.02
- Opinions, Auditors' 508.03–.05
- Regulated Companies............. 544.02
- Segment Information 435.18
- Supplementary Information..... 558.01–.10
- Unaudited Financial Statements 504.05
- Use of Accountant's Name 504.01–.02

STANDARDS, FINANCIAL ACCOUNTING
- Contingencies .... 337.03; 337.05; 337B; 9337.07
- Knowledge of Pronouncements 311.04
- SEC Filings..................... 711.04

STANDARDS, GENERAL—See General Standards—Audit

STATE AND LOCAL GOVERNMENTAL UNITS
- Regulatory Agencies—See Regulatory Agencies
- Sources of Established Principles 411.12–.13; 411.16
- Special Reports—See Special Reports

References are to AU section and paragraph numbers.

STATE BOARDS OF ACCOUNTANCY
- Independence of CPAs 9504.19–.22

STATE SOCIETIES, CPA
- Competence of Other Auditors 543.10
- Independence of CPAs 9504.19–.22

STATEMENTS OF CASH FLOWS
- Basic Financial Statements 508.06; 551.02
- Omission 508.43–.44
- Representations of Management .... 333.06; 333.16; 333.18; 333A.04–.05

STATEMENTS OF FINANCIAL POSITION
- Auditor's Report 508.34
- Basic Financial Statements......... 508.06
- Condensed Financial Statements ... 9711.09
- Disclosure of Legal Matters .... 337.05; .... 337.09; 337.13; 9337.04–.05
- Fair Value Disclosures 9342.05–.07
- Representations of Management .... 326.03–.08; 333.06; 333.16–.18; 333A.04–.05
- Review by Successor Auditor 315A.09
- SEC Filings.................... 9711.09
- Shelf Registration Statements 9711.09

STATEMENTS OF INCOME
- Basic Financial Statements 508.06; 551.02
- Representations of Management .... 326.03–.08; 333.16–.17; 333A.04–.05

STATEMENTS OF POSITION (AICPA)
- Nonprofit Organizations 9623.47
- Source of Established Principles.... 9623.47

STATEMENTS OF RETAINED EARNINGS
- Basic Financial Statements......... 508.06; 551.02

STATEMENTS OF STOCKHOLDERS' EQUITY
- Basic Financial Statement.......... 551.02

STATISTICAL SAMPLING
- Approach to Audit Sampling.......... 350.03; 350.45–.46
- Costs........................ 350.45
- Evidential Matter ..... 331.11; 350.03–.06; 350.45–.46; 9508.03
- Training and Education............ 350.46
- Use in Inventory Determination 331.11; 9508.03

STATISTICAL SUMMARIES
- Letters for Underwriters....... 634.54–.60
- Relation to Basic Financial Statements.................... 551.03

STATUTORY REPORTING REQUIREMENTS
- Compliance Reports .... 623.19–.21; 9623.40–.46
- Form 990 (Internal Revenue) 9623.47–.54
- Insurance Companies .... 9623.40–.46; 9623.60–.77
- Nonprofit Organizations 9623.47–.54
- Other Information 550.02–.03
- Public Distribution ... 544.02–.04; 9623.48; 9623.51–.53
- Public Record 9623.48; 9623.51
- SEC—See Securities and Exchange Commission
- Subsequent Events 9711.10

STEWARDSHIP—See Accountability

STOCK—See Inventories

STOCK EXCHANGES
- Publicly Traded Companies 504.02; 722.02
- Revision of Financial Statements 561.06–.08

STOCKHOLDERS' EQUITY
- Going Concern Assumption 341.07
- Separate Statement of Changes 508.06
- Violation of Debt Covenant 9410.17

STOCKHOLDERS/OWNERS
- Control Environment ...... 319.18; 319.23; 319.27
- Closely Held Companies 334.07
- Litigation With Management 334.06
- Minutes of Meetings ...... 333.06; 333.11; ....333.16; 333A.04–.05; 333A.10; 337.07; 722.13
- Related Parties .... 334.01; 334.04; 334.06–.07
- Reports—See Reports to Stockholders

SUBJECT TO OPINION—See Qualified Opinion

SUBSEQUENT DISCOVERY OF FACTS—See Discovery

SUBSEQUENT EVENTS
- Accounting Estimates 342.13
- Additional Evidence.............. 560.03
- Auditing Procedures in Subsequent Period 560.10–.12
- Changes in Estimates 560.03
- Comparison With Subsequent Discovery 561.03
- Cutoffs 560.11
- Date of Auditor's Report 530.01–.08
- Definition 560.01
- Disclosure ...... 530.01; 530.05; 530.08; 560.05–.06; 560.09; 711.10–.13
- Emphasis in Auditor's Report....... 508.19

SUBSEQUENT EVENTS—continued
· Events Not Requiring Adjustment 560.05–.06; 560.08
· Events Requiring Adjustment 530.03; 560.04; 560.07
· Examples, Type Two 560.06
· Inquiries 560.12; 711.10
· Interim Financial Information 560.12; 722.13
· Investment Transactions . . . 332.18; 332.21
· Lawyers' Letters . . . . 337.05; 560.12; 9337.04–.05
· Letters for Underwriters 634.45–.53
· Loss Reserves (Insurance) 9623.42
· Materiality 560.05; 560.09
· Minutes of Meetings 560.12
· Notes to Financial Statements . . 530.04–.05
· Omitted Auditing Procedures . . . 309.04–.06
· Predecessor Auditor's Report . . 508.71–.73
· Prior Period Adjustment 560.08
· Pro Forma Financial Data 560.05
· Realization of Assets 560.07
· Reissuance of Auditor's Report 530.06–.08
· Representation Letters . . . . 333.06; 333.09; . . . . 333.12; 333.16–.18; 333A.04; 560.12; 711.10–.11
· SEC Filings . . . . 530.02; 711.10–.13; 9711.01–.11
· Settlement of Liabilities 560.07
· Shelf Registration Statements 9711.01–.11
· Subsequent Period 560.10
· Type One Event 560.03–.04
· Type Two Event 560.05–.06
· Unaudited Information 508.28

SUBSTANCE V. FORM
· Examples 334.02
· Generally Accepted Accounting Principles 411.06–.07; 411.09
· Generally Accepted Accounting Principles Applied to New Transactions or Events 9411.12
· Related Parties 334.02

SUBSTANTIVE TESTS
· Analytical Procedures . . . . . 313.02; 313.08; . . . . 329.04; 329.09–.11; 329.20; 9326.20
· Audit Assurance 313.04; 313.08
· Audit at Interim Dates 313.01–.10
· Audit Sampling . . . . 350.12–.30; 350.43; 350.48; 9350.02
· Comparison of Information 313.08
· Completeness Assertion . . . . 313.05; 9326.20–.21
· Considerations Before Applying Tests 313.04–.07
· Cost-Effective 313.04
· Designing of 319.21; 319.23

SUBSTANTIVE TESTS—continued
· Documenting Assertions 313.05; 313.08
· Dual-Purpose Samples 350.44
· Effectiveness . . . . 313.05–.06; 326.11; 350.13; 9326.03
· Efficiency 326.11; 9326.03
· Evidential Matter . . . . . 313.07; 326.09–.14; 326.26; 350.16–.30; 9326.03
· Impairment 313.05
· Interim Financial Information 313.01–.10
· Interim v. Annual Data 313.03–.09
· Internal Auditor 322.17
· Inventories 326.26; 9315A.28
· Investments Assertions 332.04–.33
· Material Misstatements . . . 312.32; 312.35; 313.03; 313.09
· Planning 319.05
· Planning Samples 350.15–.23
· Prior to Balance Sheet Date 313.01–.10
· Related Populations 9326.21
· Relation to Audit Objectives . . . . . . 313.08; 326.10–.14; 326.26
· Relation to Detection Risk 319.56
· Relation to Economic Conditions 313.06
· Reliance on Substantive Tests 9326.21
· Risk of Misstatement 312.17; 312.32; 312.35; 313.03–.07; 350.08–.10; 350.20
· Sampling Risk 350.12–.13
· Service Organizations . . . . 324.15; 324.17; 324.58
· Tests of Details . . . 313.01–.10; 350.12–.30
· Timing and Extent . . . . 313.01–.10; 316.28; 319.05; 319.20
· Timing of Audit Work 313.10
· Use of Work of Specialists 336.03
· Year 2000 Issue 9311.42–.44

SUCCESSOR AUDITOR
· Acceptance of Engagement . . . 9315A.03; 9315A.08–.09
· Consultation With Predecessor 315A.09; 9315A.01–.18
· Contingencies 315.11; 315A.09
· Definition 315.02; 315A.01
· Evidential Matter From Predecessor . . . . 315.12; 315.17–.18; 315A.08–.09; 9315A.10–.11
· Existence of Inventories 9315A.17–.18
· Fraud 316.40
· Illegal Acts by Client 317.23
· Inquiries of Predecessor Auditor . . . . . 315.05; . . . . 315.07–.10; 315.12; 315.14–.15; . . . . 315.20; 315.24; 315A.04–.08; 9315A.03; 9315A.09–.11; 9315A.18

References are to AU section and paragraph numbers.

SUCCESSOR AUDITOR—continued
- Planning of Audit Work......... 9315A.11–.13; 9315A.15
- Predecessor's Report Not Presented.................... 508.74
- Reaudit.................... 315.14–.21
- Representation Letter for Predecessor.............. 508.71–.72
- Responsibilities 9315A.11–.12
- SEC Filings............ 711.11; 9315A.04
- Subsequent Discovery of Facts 9315A.06–.07
- Working Papers of Predecessor.. 315.11–.13; .... 315.15; 315.19–.20; 315.24–.25; .... 315A.08–.09; 9315A.10–.11; 9315A.15–.16; 9315A.18

SUMMARIZATION
- Interim Financial Information............ 722.02; 722.13
- Prior Period Financial Statements.... 508.65

SUPERVISION
- Due Professional Care 230.06
- Standard of Field Work........... 150.02; ... 210.03–.04; 310.01; 310A.01; 311.01
- Uncertainties, Control of........... 312.27
- Work of Assistants .... 311.11–.13; 9311.35–.37
- Work Performed by Others......... 543.05
- Working Papers 339.02; 339.04–.05

SUPPLEMENTARY FINANCIAL INFORMATION
- Adverse Opinion.......... 544.02; 551.10
- Auditor's Report...... 508.11; 551.12–.15; 552.05; 558.01–.10; 9558.01–.05
- Auditor's Responsibility........ 551.04–.11; 558.04–.05
- Combined Financial Statements . 551.16–.19
- Condensed Financial Information 552.05
- Consolidated Financial Statements ... 552.05
- Consolidating Information...... 551.16–.19
- Disclaimer .... 551.06; 551.10–.11; 551.13; 551.15; 558.03; 558.09
- Disclosure 551.21; 9558.01–.05
- Fair Value Disclosures 9342.07
- FASB Requirements 558.01–.10
- Future Accounting Changes 9410.16
- GASB Requirements.......... 558.01–.10
- Illustrations ... 551.12–.15; 551.18; 558.08
- Inquiries—See Inquiries
- Interim Financial Information.... 722.36–.39
- Letters for Underwriters....... 634.30; 634.54–.60
- Limited Procedures ... 551.06–.11; 558.08
- Material Misstatements 551.09
- Materiality—See Materiality
- Oil and Gas Reserve Information 9558.01–.05

SUPPLEMENTARY FINANCIAL INFORMATION—continued
- Omission of Information 551.15; 558.08
- Piecemeal Opinion........ 551.06; 551.10; 551.13
- Qualified Opinion.......... 551.10; 551.14
- Regulated Industries ...... 544.02; 551.06; 551.10
- Relation to GAAP......... 544.02; 551.03; 551.07; 551.10; 551.19
- Required by FASB.......... 551.04; 551.12; 551.15

SYSTEMATIC AND RATIONAL ALLOCATION
- Cost of Property................ 326.07

T

TAX RATES—See Rates (Income Taxes)

TAX RETURNS
- Accountant's Responsibility........ 504.03

TAXES
- Income—See Income Taxes
- Uncertainties................... 337.07

TAXPAYERS
- Income Tax Accruals......... 9326.06–.17

TERMINOLOGY
- Accountant.................... 622.01
- Accounting Estimates 342.01
- Agreed-Upon Procedures Engagement 622.03
- Analytical Procedures 329.02
- Assessed Level of Control Risk..... 319.54
- Assessing Control Risk 319.47
- Assistants.................... 311.02
- Audit Adjustments.............. 380.09
- Audit Committee............... 380.01
- Audit Risk .... 312.02; 312.27–.28; 350.08–.09; 350.48
- Audit Sampling 350.01; 9350.02
- Auditor 311.02; 622.01
- Available-for-Sale Securities........ 332.07
- Capsule Information 634.39
- Common Requirements........... 801.12
- Components of a Business 9334.14–.15
- Comprehensive Basis of Accounting................... 623.04
- Confirmations.................. 330.04
- Conflict-of-Interests Statements..... 334.08
- Contingencies.................... 337B
- Continuing Auditor.............. 508.65
- Contractual Agreement 623.22; 9623.82
- Control Activities.......... 319.07; 319.32
- Control Environment 319.07; 319.25
- Control Risk 319.46
- Detection Risk.................. 319.46
- Disclosure 431.02
- Due Professional Care............ 230.05
- Electronic Site 9550.16

TERMINOLOGY—continued
· Errors 312.06
· Evidential Matter 326.15
· Federal Awards 801.04
· Financial Assistance 801.04
· Financial Statements 622.07; 623.02
· Fraud 316.04–.05
· Gain Contingencies 337B
· General Requirements 801.12
· Generally Accepted Accounting Principles 411.02
· Government Auditing Standards 801.08–.09
· Held-to-Maturity Securities 332.07
· Illegal Acts 317.02
· Information and Communication 319.07; 319.34–.35
· Inherent Risk 319.46
· Interim Information 722.02
· Intermediaries 625.01
· Internal Control 319.06
· Known Questioned Costs 801.18
· Legal Specialist 9336.03
· Letters for Underwriters 634.12
· Likely Questioned Costs 801.18
· Loss Contingencies 337B
· Management 380.11
· Material Misstatement 319.46
· Material Weakness 325.15
· Materiality 312.10
· Maximum Level 319.47
· Misstatement in a Financial Statement Assertion 319.46
· Misstatements Arising From Fraudulent Financial Reporting 316.04
· Misstatements Arising From Misappropriation of Assets 316.05
· Monitoring 319.07; 319.38
· Offering Document 9623.81
· Operating Effectiveness 319.21
· Organization-Wide Audit 801.01
· Personnel 311.02
· Placed in Operation 319.21
· Predecessor Auditor 315.02; 315A.01
· Professional Skepticism 230.07; 316.27
· Program-Specific Audit 801.01
· Public Distribution 9623.51
· Public Entity 504.02; 722.02
· Public Record 623.05; 9623.51
· Reaudit 315.14; 9315A.08
· Recipient 801.04
· Regulator 9339.01
· Related Parties 334.01
· Report on Controls Placed in Operation 324.02
· Reportable Conditions 325.02
· Risk Assessment 319.07; 319.28
· Sampling Risk 350.12
· SEC Engagement 380.01

TERMINOLOGY—continued
· Segment Information 435.01
· Service Auditor 324.02
· Service Organizations 324.02
· Single Audit 801.01
· Specialists 336.01; 622.21; 9326.16
· Specific Requirements 801.13
· Specific Subject Matter 622.06
· Specified Elements, Accounts, or Items of a Financial Statement 622.06; 9622.01–.02
· Specified Users 622.04
· Subrecipient 801.04
· Subsequent Events 560.01
· Successor Auditor 315.02; 315A.01
· Test of Controls 319.52
· Tolerable Misstatement 350.18
· Tolerable Rate 350.34
· Trading Securities 332.07
· U.S. Entity 534.01
· Uncertainties 508.29
· Underwriters 634.14
· User Auditor 324.01
· User Organizations 324.02

TESTS OF CONTROLS
· Audit Sampling . . . 350.08–.10; 350.12–.14; 350.31–.43; 9350.02
· Design of Sample 350.33
· Documentation 319.57
· Dual-Purpose Samples 350.44
· Effectiveness of Design 319.52–.54; 319.57
· Evidential Matter 319.03–.04; 319.52; 319.58–.63; 326.14
· Financial Statement Assertions 319.52
· Operating Effectiveness 319.52–.54; 319.57
· Planning 319.59
· Risk Assessment 312.31; 326.14; 350.08–.14
· Service Organizations 324.41
· Year 2000 Issue 9311.42–.44

TIME PERIODS
· Letters for Underwriters 634.45

TIMELINESS
· Audit Procedures 311.03–.05; 313.04–.07; 313.10
· Cause for Legal Action 337.04
· Communication Between Auditors . . 315A:03; 9334.12–.13; 9543.08–.17
· Communication With Audit Committee 380.04–.05
· Evidential Matter 319.70–.73; 326.02; 326.23
· Interim Dates 9326.04
· Interim Financial Reporting 722.08

References are to AU section and paragraph numbers.

TIMELINESS—continued
- · Lawyers' Responses to Inquiries 9337.01–.05
- · Review of Interim Information ...... 722.14; 722.26
- · Scheduling Audit Work .... 310.03–.04; 310A.03–.04; 311.12; 9508.01–.04
- · Standard of Field Work .... 310.03; 310A.03; 311.03–.05
- · Substantive Tests............ 313.01–.10

TRAINING AND EDUCATION
- · General Standard 150.02; 210.01–.05
- · Income Taxes............. 9326.13–.17
- · Loss Reserve Matters............ 336.07
- · Qualifications 110.04–.05; 336.01
- · Statistical Sampling 350.46

TRANSACTIONS
- · Analytical Procedures........... 312.35; 313.02; 313.08
- · Assertions by Management..... 326.03–.08
- · Audit Risk and Materiality...... 312.24–.33; 312.39–.40
- · Auditor's Consideration of Management's Adoption of Accounting Principles for New Types 9411.11–.15
- · Estimation 312.36
- · Intercompany—See Intercompany Transactions
- · Interim Testing....... 313.02; 313.07–.08
- · Knowledge of Transactions........ 110.03; 311.06–.10
- · Lack of Control 315A.05
- · Material Misstatements .... 312.17–.20; 312.35
- · Nonmonetary—See Nonmonetary Transactions
- · Prior Periods 315.12; 315.20; 315A.08
- · Recording 722.13
- · Related Parties—See Related Parties
- · Sampling—See Audit Sampling
- · Substance v. Form.............. 334.02; 411.06–.07; 411.09
- · Substantive Tests........ 312.32; 313.02; 313.07–.08
- · Tests of Details 313.02; 313.08
- · Understanding Business Purpose 334.09–.10
- · Unrecorded 313.09; 333.06; 333A.04
- · Unusual Items—See Unusual Items

TRIAL BOARD
- · Inquiries Concerning Members 543.10

TRUSTS
- · Related Parties.................. 334.01

U

UNASSERTED CLAIMS—See Claims

UNAUDITED INFORMATION
- · Subsequent Events........ 332.18; 332.21

UNAUDITED FINANCIAL STATEMENTS
- · Accounting and Review Services 504.02
- · Departure From GAAP............. 504.11–.13; 711.13
- · Disclaimer of Opinion 504.05–.18
- · Fourth Quarter Interim Data.... 9504.01–.07
- · Investments 332.18
- · Lack of Independence........ 9504.19–.22
- · Letters for Underwriters—See Letters for Underwriters
- · Long-Term Investments........... 508.24; 508.26; 542.06
- · Negative Assurance 504.19
- · Presented With Audited Statements 504.14–.17
- · SEC Filings 504.14
- · Use of Accountant's Name............ 504.04; 9504.15–.18

UNAUDITED INFORMATION
- · Accounting and Review Services 504.02
- · Business Combinations........... 508.28
- · Condensed Financial Information 9504.15–.18
- · Departure From GAAP........... 711.13
- · Fair Value Disclosures........ 9342.08–.09
- · Interim Financial Information .... 504.04; ... 722.02; 722.17; 722.27; 722.36–.42
- · Letters for Underwriters—See Letters for Underwriters
- · Segment Information............ 435.08
- · Subsequent Events....... 332.18; 332.21; 508.28
- · Supplementary Information .... 551.04; 551.13; 558.01–.10

UNCERTAINTIES
- · Accounting Changes 9410.17
- · Accounting Estimates 508.48–.49
- · Accounting Principles 508.48
- · Audit Risk 312.27
- · Audit Sampling 350.07–.11
- · Auditor's Report 508.29–.32
- · Compliance Reports 623.21
- · Definition 508.29
- · Estimation—See Estimation
- · Explanatory Language in Auditor's Report..................... 341.13
- · Financial Statements............ 337.14
- · Going Concern Assumption..... 341.12–.13
- · Illustrations
  - · · Auditors' Reports 341.13
  - · · Lawyers' Response to Audit Inquiry................. 9337.20–.23
  - · · Letter to Client's Lawyer..... 9337.10–.16

UNCERTAINTIES—continued
· Income Taxes 9326.06–.17
· Interim Financial Information 722.30
· Liquidation Basis of Accounting 9508.34
· Litigation, Claims, and Assessments . . . . 337.04; 337.14; 9337.06–.07; 9337.17–.23
· Loss Contingencies 9333.01–.04
· Materiality Considerations 508.47
· Opinion on Illegal Acts 317.21
· Reporting 508.69
· Resolution 508.69
· Violation of Debt Covenant 9410.17

UNDERWRITERS
· Definition 634.14
· Letters—See Letters for Underwriters

UNIFORMITY
· Components of a Business 543.10

UNITED STATES
· Reports, Other Auditors 543.10

UNQUALIFIED OPINION
· Balance-Sheet-Only Audit 508.34
· Condensed Financial Statements 552.06
· Departure From GAAP 508.14–.15; 508.68–.69
· Emphasis of a Matter 508.19; 9342.03; 9410.18
· Explanatory Language Added 508.11–.19; 9342.07
· Fair Presentation 411.01–.16
· Fair Value Disclosures 9342.03; 9342.03–.07
· Illustrations 324.46; 508.69; 552.06
· Individual Financial Statement 508.05
· Nonprofit Organizations 9623.49
· Precluded by Lawyer's Refusal 337.13
· Reference to Specialists 336.16
· Reports With Differing Opinions 508.67–.69
· Reports, Other Auditors 508.12–.13
· Scope Limitation . . . . 333.13–.14; . . . . 333A.11–.12; 508.22; 508.30; 642.44; 9326.06–.10
· Uncertainties 508.30
· Updated Reports 508.68–.69

UNUSUAL ITEMS
· Analytical Procedures . . . . . 329.02; 329.06; 329.22
· Illegal Acts by Clients . . . . 317.01–.25; 9333.01–.04
· Interim Financial Information . . . 313.07–.08; 722.13; 722.16; 9326.04
· Related Party Transactions . . . . 334.08; 9334.14–.15; 9543.04–.07

USEFULNESS
· Evidential Matter . . . . 326.21; 326.24; 9326.04

USERS
· Identification 622.11; 622.33; 622.38
· Reports on Internal Control Over Financial Reporting 9550.14–.15
· Responsibilities in Agreed-Upon Procedures Engagement . . . . 622.03; 622.09–.12; . . . . 622.16; 622.22; 622.33; 622.38; 622.44
· Service Organizations . . . . 324.02; 324.05–.21

UTILITIES, PUBLIC
· Departures From GAAP 544.02–.04

V

VALIDITY—See Representational Faithfulness

VALUATION
· Assertions by Management 326.03–.07
· Estimates 332.27–.29
· Fair Value Disclosures 9342.01–.10
· Impairment 332.31–.33
· Investments 332.19; 332.23–.33
· Matters Requiring Specialists 336.07

VIOLATIONS OF LAW—See Illegal Acts

W

WAREHOUSES—See Public Warehouses

WARRANTIES—See Guarantees and Warranties

WITHDRAWAL FROM AUDIT ENGAGEMENT—See Audit Engagement

WORKING CAPITAL
· Lack of Sufficient Capital 334.06

WORKING PAPERS
· Access to Other Auditor's . . . . 9315A.15–.16; 9334.14–.15
· Assessed Level of Control Risk 319.57
· Assessed Risk of Material Misstatement Due to Fraud, and Response 316.37
· Confidential Client Information . . . . . 339.06; . . . . 9339.03; 9339.05–.06; 9339.10; 9339.13
· Custody . . . . 339.06–.08; 622.32; 9339.01; 9339.03
· Documentation of Oral Communication 380.03; 801.23
· Effective Date 339.09
· Evidential Matter . . . . 326.16–.20; . . . . 339.03–.05; 9315A.10–.11; 9326.06–.17
· Examples 339.03
· Financial Statements 339.04–.05

References are to AU section and paragraph numbers.

WORKING PAPERS—continued
- Form and Content..... 339.01; 339.03–.05; 622.29
- Functions.................. 339.02–.04
- Generally Accepted Auditing Standards.................. 339.02
- Guidelines......... 339.05; 9326.11–.12
- Income Tax Accruals........ 9326.06–.12
- Incomplete................ 9339.07–.08
- Internal Control....... 319.44; 339.04–.05
- Letter to Regulator.......... 9339.05–.06; 9339.08
- Letters for Underwriters........... 634.20
- Litigation, Claims, and Assessments................ 337.10
- Nature.................... 339.02–.04
- Nonaudit Services.......... 9311.01–.03
- Omitted Auditing Procedures............ 390.02; 390.04
- Ownership.......... 339.06–.08; 622.30; 9339.01; 9339.04
- Planning of Audit Work.... 311.04; 311.08; 339.05; 9311.01–.03
- Providing to Independent Party Access to or Photocopies of........... 9339.09–.10
- Providing to Regulator Access to or Photocopies of........... 9339.01–.15
- Records...... 339.01; 339.03–.08; 622.31
- Related Parties.................. 334.07

WORKING PAPERS—continued
- Retention....... 339.08; 622.32; 9339.01
- Review.......... 311.04; 311.08; 339.04
- Review by Client Prior to Access by Regulator.................. 9339.14
- Review by Predecessor Auditor..... 508.72
- Review by Principal Auditor........ 543.12
- Review by Successor Auditor.. 315.11–.13; .... 315.15; 315.19–.20; .... 315.24–.25; 315A.08–.09; 9315A.11; 9315A.16; 9315A.18
- Review of Interim Information...... 722.37
- Standards of Fieldwork..... 339.02; 339.05
- Supervision.......... 339.02; 339.04–.05; 9339.03; 9339.14
- Type and Content............ 339.03–.15
- Understanding With Client......... 310.05

YEAR 2000 ISSUE
- Audit Considerations......... 9311.38–.47
- Auditor Responsibilities....... 9311.39–.41
- Description.................... 9311.38
- Future Audit Periods............ 9311.41; 9311.43; 9311.45–.47
- Internal Control Deficiencies Related to.............. 9311.45–.47
- Management's Responsibilities.... 9311.41
- Manifestation and Effects........ 9311.38
- Planning Considerations...... 9311.42–.44
- Reportable Conditions........ 9311.45–.47

AT Section

STATEMENTS ON STANDARDS FOR ATTESTATION ENGAGEMENTS

CONTENTS

ATTESTATION STANDARDS

Introduction

The accompanying "attestation standards" provide guidance and establish a broad framework for a variety of attest services increasingly demanded of the accounting profession. The standards and related interpretive commentary are designed to provide professional guidelines that will enhance both consistency and quality in the performance of such services.

For years, attest services generally were limited to expressing a positive opinion on historical financial statements on the basis of an audit in accordance with generally accepted auditing standards (GAAS). However, certified public accountants increasingly have been requested to provide, and have been providing, assurance on representations other than historical financial statements and in forms other than the positive opinion. In responding to these needs, certified public accountants have been able to generally apply the basic concepts underlying GAAS to these attest services. As the range of attest services has grown, however, it has become increasingly difficult to do so.

Consequently, the main objective of adopting these attestation standards and the related interpretive commentary is to provide a general framework for and set reasonable boundaries around the attest function. As such, the standards and commentary (*a*) provide useful and necessary guidance to certified public accountants engaged to perform new and evolving attest services and (*b*) guide AICPA standard-setting bodies in establishing, if deemed necessary, interpretive standards for such services.

The attestation standards are a natural extension of the ten generally accepted auditing standards. Like the auditing standards, the attestation standards deal with the need for technical competence, independence in mental attitude, due professional care, adequate planning and supervision, sufficient evidence, and appropriate reporting; however, they are much broader in scope. (The eleven attestation standards are listed below.) Such standards apply to a growing array of attest services. These services include, for example, reports on descriptions of systems of internal control; on descriptions of computer software; on compliance with statutory, regulatory, and contractual requirements; on investment performance statistics; and on information supplementary to financial statements. Thus, the standards have been developed to be responsive to a changing environment and the demands of society.

These attestation standards apply only to attest services rendered by a certified public accountant in the practice of public accounting—that is, a practitioner as defined in footnote 1 of paragraph .01.

The attestation standards do not supersede any of the existing standards in Statements on Auditing Standards (SASs), Statements on Standards for Accounting and Review Services (SSARSs), and Statement on Standards for Accountants' Services on Prospective Financial Information. Therefore, the practitioner who is engaged to perform an engagement subject to these existing standards should follow such standards.

Attestation Standards

General Standards

1. The engagement shall be performed by a practitioner or practitioners having adequate technical training and proficiency in the attest function.
2. The engagement shall be performed by a practitioner or practitioners having adequate knowledge in the subject matter of the assertion.
3. The practitioner shall perform an engagement only if he or she has reason to believe that the following two conditions exist:
   - The assertion is capable of evaluation against reasonable criteria that either have been established by a recognized body or are stated in the presentation of the assertion in a sufficiently clear and comprehensive manner for a knowledgeable reader to be able to understand them.
   - The assertion is capable of reasonably consistent estimation or measurement using such criteria.
4. In all matters relating to the engagement, an independence in mental attitude shall be maintained by the practitioner or practitioners.
5. Due professional care shall be exercised in the performance of the engagement.

Standards of Fieldwork

1. The work shall be adequately planned and assistants, if any, shall be properly supervised.
2. Sufficient evidence shall be obtained to provide a reasonable basis for the conclusion that is expressed in the report.

Standards of Reporting

1. The report shall identify the assertion being reported on and state the character of the engagement.
2. The report shall state the practitioner's conclusion about whether the assertion is presented in conformity with the established or stated criteria against which it was measured.
3. The report shall state all of the practitioner's significant reservations about the engagement and the presentation of the assertion.
4. The report on an engagement to evaluate an assertion that has been prepared in conformity with agreed-upon criteria or on an engagement to apply agreed-upon procedures should contain a statement limiting its use to the parties who have agreed upon such criteria or procedures.

Introduction

AT

STATEMENTS ON STANDARDS FOR ATTESTATION ENGAGEMENTS

These Statements are issued by the Auditing Standards Board, the Accounting and Review Services Committee, and the Management Consulting Services Executive Committee under the authority granted them by the Council of the Institute to interpret Rule 201, General Standards, and Rule 202, Compliance With Standards, of the Institute's Code of Professional Conduct. Members should be prepared to justify departures from this Statement.

Interpretations are issued by the Audit Issues Task Force of the Auditing Standards Board to provide timely guidance on the application of pronouncements of that Board. Interpretations are reviewed by the Auditing Standards Board. An interpretation is not as authoritative as a pronouncement of that Board, but members should be aware that they may have to justify a departure from an interpretation if the quality of their work is questioned.

TABLE OF CONTENTS

Section		Paragraph
100	Attestation Standards	.01-.84
	Attest Engagement	.01-.05
	General Standards	.06-.27
	Standards of Fieldwork	.28-.43
	Standards of Reporting	.46-.71
	Examination	.54-.56
	Review	.57-.59
	Agreed-Upon Procedures	.64-.71
	Working Papers	.72-.76
	Attest Services Related to MAS Engagements	.77-.81
	Attest Services as Part of an MAS Engagement	.77-.79
	Assertions, Criteria, and Evidence	.80
	Nonattest Evaluations of Written Assertions	.81
	Effective Date	.82
	Appendix A: Comparison of the Attestation Standards With Generally Accepted Auditing Standards	.83

Section		Paragraph
100	Attestation Standards—continued	
	Appendix B: Analysis of Apparent or Possible Inconsistencies Between the Attestation Standards and Existing SASs and SSARSs	.84
9100	Attestation Standards: Attestation Engagements Interpretations of Section 100	
	1. Defense Industry Questionnaire on Business Ethics and Conduct (8/87)	.01-.32
	2. Responding to Requests for Reports on Matters Relating to Solvency (issued 5/88; amended 2/92)	.33-.44
	3. Applicability of Attestation Standards to Litigation Services (7/90)	.47-.55
	4. Providing Access to or Photocopies of Working Papers to a Regulator (5/96)	.56-.59
200	Financial Forecasts and Projections	.01-.69
	Definitions	.06
	Uses of Prospective Financial Statements	.07-.09
	Compilation of Prospective Financial Statements	.10-.26
	Working Papers	.15
	Reports on Compiled Prospective Financial Statements	.16-.23
	Modifications of the Standard Compilation Report	.24-.26
	Examination of Prospective Financial Statements	.27-.48
	Working Papers	.30
	Reports on Examined Prospective Financial Statements	.31-.35
	Modifications to the Accountant's Opinion	.36-.42
	Other Modifications to the Standard Examination Report	.43-.48
	Applying Agreed-Upon Procedures to Prospective Financial Statements	.49-.57
	Reports on the Results of Applying Agreed-Upon Procedures	.54-.57
	Other Information	.58-.65
	Effective Date	.66
	Appendix A: Minimum Presentation Guidelines	.67
	Appendix B: Training and Proficiency, Planning and Procedures Applicable to Compilations	.68
	Appendix C: Training and Proficiency, Planning and Procedures Applicable to Examinations	.69
300	Reporting on Pro Forma Financial Information	.01-.20
	Presentation of Pro Forma Financial Information	.04-.06
	Conditions for Reporting	.07
	Accountant's Objective	.08-.09
	Procedures	.10
	Reporting on Pro Forma Financial Information	.11-.14
	Effective Date	.15

Section		Paragraph
300	Reporting on Pro Forma Financial Information—continued	
	Examples of Reports on Pro Forma Financial Information	.16-.20
	Appendix A: Report on Examination of Pro Forma Financial Information	.16
	Appendix B: Report on Review of Pro Forma Financial Information	.17
	Appendix C: Report on Examination of Pro Forma Financial Information at Year End With a Review of Pro Forma Financial Information for a Subsequent Interim Date	.18
	Appendix D: Report on Examination of Pro Forma Financial Information Giving Effect to a Business Combination to be Accounted for as a Pooling of Interests	.19
	Appendix E: Other Example Reports	.20
400	Reporting on an Entity's Internal Control Over Financial Reporting	.01-.85
	Applicability	.01-.04
	Other Attest Services	.05-.07
	Nonattest Services	.08
	Conditions for Engagement Performance	.10-.11
	Components of an Entity's Internal Control	.12
	Limitations of an Entity's Internal Control	.13-.14
	Examination Engagement	.15-.33
	Planning the Engagement	.17-.20
	General Considerations	.17
	Multiple Locations	.18
	Internal Audit Function	.19
	Documentation	.20
	Obtaining an Understanding of the Internal Control	.21
	Evaluating the Design Effectiveness of Controls	.22-.25
	Testing and Evaluating the Operating Effectiveness of Controls	.26-.32
	Forming an Opinion on Management's Assertion	.33
	Deficiencies in an Entity's Internal Control	.34-.41
	Reportable Conditions	.35
	Material Weaknesses	.36-.39
	Communicating Reportable Conditions and Material Weaknesses	.40-.41
	Management's Representations	.42-.43
	Reporting Standards	.44-.49
	Management's Assertion Presented in a Separate Report	.45-.46
	Management's Assertion Presented Only in a Letter of Representation to the Practitioner	.47-.49
	Report Modifications	.50-.74

Section | Paragraph

400 Reporting on an Entity's Internal Control Over Financial Reporting—continued
Material Weaknesses 51-.57
Management Includes the Material Weakness in Its Assertion. 52-.53
Disagreements With Management 54-.56
Management's Assertion Includes the Material Weakness and Is Presented in a Document Containing the Audit Report 57
Scope Limitations 58-.61
Opinion Based in Part on the Report of Another Practitioner 62-.63
Subsequent Events 64-.66
Management's Assertion About the Effectiveness of a Segment of the Entity's Internal Control 67
Management's Assertion About the Suitability of Design of the Entity's Internal Control 68-.69
Management's Assertion Based on Criteria Specified by a Regulatory Agency. 70-.74
Other Information in a Client-Prepared Document Containing Management's Assertion About the Effectiveness of the Entity's Internal Control 75-.78
Relationship of the Practitioner's Examination of an Entity's Internal Control to the Opinion Obtained in an Audit 79-.82
Relationship to the Foreign Corrupt Practices Act. 83
Effective Date 84
Appendix 85

9400 Reporting on an Entity's Internal Control Over Financial Reporting: Attestation Engagements Interpretations of Section 400
1. Pre-Award Surveys (2/97) 01-.08

500 Compliance Attestation 01-.75
Introduction and Applicability 01-.03
Scope of Services 04-.08
Conditions for Engagement Performance. 09-.13
Responsibilities of Management 14
Agreed-Upon Procedures Engagement 15-.28
Examination Engagement 29-.69
Attestation Risk. 30-.34
Inherent Risk 32
Control Risk 33
Detection Risk. 34

Section — Paragraph

500 Compliance Attestation—continued
- Materiality .35-.36
- Performing an Examination Engagement .37-.38
- Obtaining an Understanding of the Specified Compliance Requirements .39
- Planning the Engagement .40-.43
- General Considerations .40
- Multiple Components .41
- Using the Work of a Specialist .42
- Internal Audit Function .43
- Consideration of Internal Control Over Compliance .44-.46
- Obtaining Sufficient Evidence .47-.48
- Consideration of Subsequent Events .49-.51
- Forming an Opinion on Management's Assertion .52
- Reporting .53-.60
- Report Modifications .61-.69
- Material Noncompliance .62-.68
- Material Uncertainty .69
- Management's Representations .70-.71
- Other Information in a Client-Prepared Document Containing Management's Assertion About the Entity's Compliance With Specified Requirements or the Effectiveness of Internal Control Over Compliance .72-.73
- Effective Date .74-.75

600 Agreed-Upon Procedures Engagements .01-.49
- Introduction and Applicability .01-.02
- Agreed-Upon Procedures Engagements .03-.04
- Standards .05
- Assertions and Related Subject Matter .06-.09
- Conditions for Engagement Performance .10-.12
- Agreement on and Sufficiency of Procedures .11
- Establishing an Understanding With the Client .12
- Nature, Timing, and Extent of Procedures .13-.25
- Users' Responsibility .13
- Practitioner's Responsibility .14-.16
- Procedures to Be Performed .17-.20
- Involvement of a Specialist .21-.23

AT Section 100

Attestation Standards

Sources: SSAE No. 1; SSAE No. 4; SSAE No. 5; SSAE No. 7.

See section 9100 for interpretations of this section.

Effective for attest reports issued on or after September 30, 1986, unless otherwise indicated.

Attest Engagement

.01 When a certified public accountant in the practice of public accounting[1] (herein referred to as "a practitioner") performs an attest engagement, as defined below, the engagement is subject to the attestation standards and related interpretive commentary in this pronouncement and to any other authoritative interpretive standards that apply to the particular engagement.[2]

> An attest engagement is one in which a practioner is engaged to issue or does issue a written communication that expresses a conclusion about the reliability of a written assertion[3] that is the responsibility of another party.[4]

.02 Examples of professional services typically provided by practitioners that would not be considered attest engagements include—

a. Management consulting engagements in which the practitioner is engaged to provide advice or recommendations to a client.

---

[1] A "certified public accountant in the practice of public accounting" includes any of the following who perform or assist in the attest engagement: (1) an individual public accountant; (2) a proprietor, partner, or shareholder in a public accounting firm; (3) a full- or part-time employee of a public accounting firm; and (4) an entity (for example, partnership, corporation, trust, joint venture, or pool) whose operating, financial, or accounting policies can be significantly influenced by one of the persons described in (1) through (3) or by two or more of such persons if they choose to act together.

[2] Existing authoritative standards that might apply to a particular attest engagement include SASs, SSARSs, and Statement on Standards for Accountants' Services on Prospective Financial Information. In addition, authoritative interpretive standards for specific types of attest engagements, including standards concerning the subject matter of the assertions presented, may be issued in the future by authorized AICPA senior technical committees. Furthermore, when a practitioner undertakes an attest engagement for the benefit of a government body or agency and agrees to follow specified government standards, guides, procedures, statutes, rules, and regulations, the practitioner is obliged to follow this section and the applicable authoritative interpretive standards as well as those governmental requirements.

[3] An *assertion* is any declaration, or set of related declarations taken as a whole, by a party responsible for it.

[4] The term *attest* and its variants, such as *attesting* and *attestation*, are used in a number of state accountancy laws, and in regulations issued by State Boards of Accountancy under such laws, for different purposes and with different meanings from those intended by this section. Consequently, the definition of *attest engagement* set out in this paragraph, and the attendant meaning of *attest* and *attestation* as used throughout the section should not be understood as defining these terms, and similar terms, as they are used in any law or regulation, nor as embodying a common understanding of the terms which may also be reflected in such laws or regulations.

b. Engagements in which the practitioner is engaged to advocate a client's position—for example, tax matters being reviewed by the Internal Revenue Service.

c. Tax engagements in which a practitioner is engaged to prepare tax returns or provide tax advice.

d. Engagements in which the practitioner compiles financial statements, because he is not required to examine or review any evidence supporting the information furnished by the client and does not express any conclusion on its reliability.

e. Engagements in which the practitioner's role is solely to assist the client—for example, acting as the company accountant in preparing information other than financial statements.

f. Engagements in which a practitioner is engaged to testify as an expert witness in accounting, auditing, taxation, or other matters, given certain stipulated facts.

g. Engagements in which a practitioner is engaged to provide an expert opinion on certain points of principle, such as the application of tax laws or accounting standards, given specific facts provided by another party so long as the expert opinion does not express a conclusion about the reliability of the facts provided by the other party.

.03 The practitioner who does not explicitly express a conclusion about the reliability of an assertion that is the responsibility of another party should be aware that there may be circumstances in which such a conclusion could be reasonably inferred. For example, if the practitioner issues a report that includes an enumeration of procedures that could reasonably be expected to provide assurance about an assertion, the practitioner may not be able to avoid the inference that the report is an attest report merely by omitting an explicit conclusion on the reliability of the assertion.

.04 The practitioner who has assembled or assisted in assembling an assertion should not claim to be the asserter if the assertion is materially dependent on the actions, plans, or assumptions of some other individual or group. In such a situation, that individual or group is the "asserter," and the practitioner will be viewed as an attester if a conclusion about the reliability of the assertion is expressed.

.05 An attest engagement may be part of a larger engagement—for example, a feasibility study or business acquisition study that includes an examination of prospective financial information. In such circumstances, these standards apply only to the attest portion of the engagement.

General Standards

.06 The first general standard is—*The engagement shall be performed by a practitioner or practitioners having adequate technical training and proficiency in the attest function.*

.07 Performing attest services is different from preparing and presenting an assertion. The latter involves collecting, classifying, summarizing, and communicating information; this usually entails reducing a mass of detailed data to a manageable and understandable form. On the other hand, performing attest services involves gathering evidence to support the assertion and objectively assessing the measurements and communications of the asserter. Thus, attest services are analytical, critical, investigative, and concerned with the basis and support for the assertions.

.08 The attainment of proficiency as an attester begins with formal education and extends into subsequent experience. To meet the requirements of a professional, the attester's training should be adequate in technical scope and should include a commensurate measure of general education.

.09 The second general standard is—*The engagement shall be performed by a practitioner or practitioners having adequate knowledge in the subject matter of the assertion.*

.10 A practitioner may obtain adequate knowledge of the subject matter to be reported on through formal or continuing education, including self-study, or through practical experience. However, this standard does not necessarily require a practitioner to personally acquire all of the necessary knowledge in the subject matter to be qualified to judge an assertion's reliability. This knowledge requirement may be met, in part, through the use of one or more specialists on a particular attest engagement if the practitioner has sufficient knowledge of the subject matter (*a*) to communicate to the specialist the objectives of the work and (*b*) to evaluate the specialist's work to determine if the objectives were achieved.

.11 The third general standard is—*The practitioner shall perform an engagement only if he or she has reason to believe that the following two conditions exist:*

a. The assertion is capable of evaluation against reasonable criteria that either have been established by a recognized body or are stated in the presentation of the assertion in a sufficiently clear and comprehensive manner for a knowledgeable reader to be able to understand them.

b. The assertion is capable of reasonably consistent estimation or measurement using such criteria.

.12 The attest function should be performed only when it can be effective and useful. Practitioners should have a reasonable basis for believing that a meaningful conclusion can be provided on an assertion.

.13 The first condition requires an assertion to have reasonable criteria against which it can be evaluated. Criteria promulgated by a body designated by Council under the AICPA Code of Professional Conduct are, by definition, considered to be reasonable criteria for this purpose. Criteria issued by regulatory agencies and other bodies composed of experts that follow due-process procedures, including procedures for broad distribution of proposed criteria for public comment, normally should also be considered reasonable criteria for this purpose.

.14 However, criteria established by industry associations or similar groups that do not follow due process or do not as clearly represent the public interest should be viewed more critically. Although established and recognized in some respects, such criteria should be considered similar to measurement and disclosure criteria that lack authoritative support, and the practitioner should evaluate whether they are reasonable. Such criteria should be stated in the presentation of the assertion in a sufficiently clear and comprehensive manner for knowledgeable readers to be able to understand them.

.15 Reasonable criteria are those that yield useful information. The usefulness of information depends on an appropriate balance between relevance and reliability. Consequently, in assessing the reasonableness of measurement and disclosure criteria, the practitioner should consider whether the assertions generated by such criteria have an appropriate balance of the following characteristics.

a. Relevance

- *Capacity to make a difference in a decision*—The assertions are useful in forming predictions about the outcomes of past, present, and future events or in confirming or correcting prior expectations.
- *Ability to bear upon uncertainty*—The assertions are useful in confirming or altering the degree of uncertainty about the result of a decision.
- *Timeliness*—The assertions are available to decision makers before they lose their capability to influence decisions.
- *Completeness*—The assertions do not omit information that could alter or confirm a decision.
- *Consistency*—The assertions are measured and presented in materially the same manner in succeeding time periods or (if material inconsistencies exist) changes are disclosed, justified, and, where practical, reconciled to permit proper interpretations of sequential measurements.

b. Reliability

- *Representational faithfulness*—The assertions correspond or agree with the phenomena they purport to represent.
- *Absence of unwarranted inference of certainty or precision*—The assertions may sometimes be presented more appropriately through the use of ranges or indications of the probabilities attaching to different values rather than as single point estimates.
- *Neutrality*—The primary concern is the relevance and reliability of the assertions rather than their potential effect on a particular interest.
- *Freedom from bias*—The measurements involved in the assertions are equally likely to fall on either side of what they represent rather than more often on one side than the other.

.16 Some criteria are reasonable in evaluating a presentation of assertions for only a limited number of specified users who participated in their establishment. For instance, criteria set forth in a purchase agreement for the preparation and presentation of financial statements of a company to be acquired, when materially different from generally accepted accounting principles (GAAP), are reasonable only when reporting to the parties to the agreement.

.17 Even when reasonable criteria exist, the practitioner should consider whether the assertion is also capable of reasonably consistent estimation or measurement using those criteria.[5] Competent persons using the same or sim-

---

[5] Criteria may yield quantitative or qualitative estimates or measurement.

ilar measurement and disclosure criteria ordinarily should be able to obtain materially similar estimates or measurements. However, competent persons will not always reach the same conclusion because (*a*) such estimates and measurements often require the exercise of considerable professional judgment and (*b*) a slightly different evaluation of the facts could yield a significant difference in the presentation of a particular assertion. An assertion estimated or measured using criteria promulgated by a body designated by Council under the AICPA Code of Professional Conduct is considered, by definition, to be capable of reasonably consistent estimation or measurement.

.18 A practitioner should not provide assurance on an assertion that is so subjective (for example, the "best" software product from among a large number of similar products) that people having competence in and using the same or similar measurement and disclosure criteria would not ordinarily be able to obtain materially similar estimates or measurements. A practitioner's assurance on such an assertion would add no real credibility to the assertion; consequently, it would be meaningless at best and could be misleading.

.19 The second condition does not presume that all competent persons would be expected to select the same measurement and disclosure criteria in developing a particular estimate or measurement (for example, the provision for depreciation on plant and equipment). However, assuming the same measurement and disclosure criteria were used (for example, the straight-line method of depreciation), materially similar estimates or measurements would be expected to be obtained.

.20 Furthermore, for the purpose of assessing whether particular measurement and disclosure criteria can be expected to yield reasonably consistent estimates or measurements, materiality must be judged in light of the expected range of reasonableness for a particular assertion. For instance, "soft" information, such as forecasts or projections, would be expected to have a wider range of reasonable estimates than "hard" data, such as the quantity of a particular item of inventory existing at a specific location.

.21 The second condition applies equally whether the practitioner has been engaged to perform an "examination" or a "review" of a presentation of assertions (see the second reporting standard). Consequently, it is inappropriate to perform a review engagement where the practitioner concludes that an examination cannot be performed because competent persons using the same or similar measurement and disclosure criteria would not ordinarily be able to obtain materially similar estimates or measurements. For example, practitioners should not provide negative assurance on the assertion that a particular software product is the "best" among a large number of similar products because they could not provide the highest level of assurance (a positive opinion) on such an assertion (were they engaged to do so) because of its inherent subjectivity.

.22 The fourth general standard is—*In all matters relating to the engagement, an independence in mental attitude shall be maintained by the practitioner or practitioners.*

.23 The practitioner should maintain the intellectual honesty and impartiality necessary to reach an unbiased conclusion about the reliability of an assertion. This is a cornerstone of the attest function. Consequently, practitioners performing an attest service should not only be independent in fact, but also should avoid situations that may impair the appearance of independence.

.24 In the final analysis, independence means objective consideration of facts, unbiased judgments, and honest neutrality on the part of the practitioner in forming and expressing conclusions. It implies not the attitude of a prosecutor but a judicial impartiality that recognizes an obligation for fairness. Independence presumes an undeviating concern for an unbiased conclusion about the reliability of an assertion no matter what the assertion may be.

.25 The fifth general standard is—*Due professional care shall be exercised in the performance of the engagement.*

.26 Due care imposes a responsibility on each practitioner involved with the engagement to observe each of the attestation standards. Exercise of due care requires critical review at every level of supervision of the work done and the judgment exercised by those assisting in the engagement, including the preparation of the report.

.27 *Cooley on Torts*, a treatise that has stood the test of time, describes a professional's obligation for due care as follows:

> Every man who offers his services to another and is employed, assumes the duty to exercise in the employment such skill as he possesses with reasonable care and diligence. In all those employments where peculiar skill is requisite, if one offers his services, he is understood as holding himself out to public as possessing the degree of skill commonly possessed by others in the same employment, and if his pretentions are unfounded, he commits a species of fraud upon every man who employs him in reliance on his public profession. But no man, whether skilled or unskilled, undertakes that the task he assumes shall be performed successfully, and without fault or error; he undertakes for good faith and integrity, but not for infallibility, and he is liable to his employer for negligence, bad faith, or dishonesty, but not for losses consequent upon mere errors of judgment.[6]

Standards of Fieldwork

.28 The first standard of fieldwork is—*The work shall be adequately planned and assistants, if any, shall be properly supervised.*

.29 Proper planning and supervision contribute to the effectiveness of attest procedures. Proper planning directly influences the selection of appropriate procedures and the timeliness of their application, and proper supervision helps ensure that planned procedures are appropriately applied.

.30 Planning an attest engagement involves developing an overall strategy for the expected conduct and scope of the engagement. To develop such a strategy, practitioners need to have sufficient knowledge to enable them to understand adequately the events, transactions, and practices that, in their judgment, have a significant effect on the presentation of the assertions.

.31 Factors to be considered by the practitioner in planning an attest engagement include (*a*) the presentation criteria to be used, (*b*) the anticipated level of attestation risk[7] related to the assertions on which he or she will re-

---

[6] D. Haggard, *Cooley on Torts*, 472 (4th ed., 1932).

[7] *Attestation risk* is the risk that the practitioner may unknowingly fail to appropriately modify his or her attest report on an assertion that is materially misstated. It consists of (*a*) the risk (consisting of inherent risk and control risk) that the assertion contains errors that could be material and (*b*) the risk that the practitioner will not detect such errors (detection risk).

port, (*c*) preliminary judgments about materiality levels for attest purposes, (*d*) the items within a presentation of assertions that are likely to require revision or adjustment, (*e*) conditions that may require extension or modification of attest procedures, and (*f*) the nature of the report expected to be issued.

.32 The practitioner should establish an understanding with the client regarding the services to be performed for each engagement.[8] Such an understanding reduces the risk that either the practitioner or the client may misinterpret the needs or expectations of the other party. For example, it reduces the risk that the client may inappropriately rely on the practitioner to protect the entity against certain risks or to perform certain functions that are the client's responsibility. The understanding should include the objectives of the engagement, management's responsibilities, the practitioner's responsibilities, and limitations of the engagement. The practitioner should document the understanding in the working papers, preferably through a written communication with the client. If the practitioner believes an understanding with the client has not been established, he or she should decline to accept or perform the engagement. [Paragraph added, effective for engagements for periods ending on or after June 15, 1998, by Statement on Standards for Attestation Engagements No. 7.]

.33 The nature, extent, and timing of planning will vary with the nature and complexity of the assertions and the practitioner's prior experience with the asserter. As part of the planning process, the practitioner should consider the nature, extent, and timing of the work to be performed to accomplish the objectives of the attest engagement. Nevertheless, as the attest engagement progresses, changed conditions may make it necessary to modify planned procedures. [Paragraph renumbered by the issuance of Statement on Standards for Attestation Engagements No. 7, October 1997.]

.34 Supervision involves directing the efforts of assistants who participate in accomplishing the objectives of the attest engagement and determining whether those objectives were accomplished. Elements of supervision include instructing assistants, staying informed of significant problems encountered, reviewing the work performed, and dealing with differences of opinion among personnel. The extent of supervision appropriate in a given instance depends on many factors, including the nature and complexity of the subject matter and the qualifications of the persons performing the work. [Paragraph renumbered by the issuance of Statement on Standards for Attestation Engagements No. 7, October 1997.]

.35 Assistants should be informed of their responsibilities, including the objectives of the procedures that they are to perform and matters that may affect the nature, extent, and timing of such procedures. The practitioner with final responsibility for the engagement should direct assistants to bring to his or her attention significant questions raised during the attest engagement so that their significance may be assessed. [Paragraph renumbered by the issuance of Statement on Standards for Attestation Engagements No. 7, October 1997.]

.36 The work performed by each assistant should be reviewed to determine if it was adequately performed and to evaluate whether the results are consistent with the conclusions to be presented in the practitioner's report.

---

[8] See Statement on Quality Control Standards No. 2, *System of Quality Control for a CPA Firm's Accounting and Auditing Practice*, paragraph 16 [QC section 20.16]. [Footnote added, effective for engagements for periods ending on or after June 15, 1998, by Statement on Standards for Attestation Engagements No. 7.]

[Paragraph renumbered by the issuance of Statement on Standards for Attestation Engagements No. 7, October 1997.]

.37 The second standard of fieldwork is—*Sufficient evidence shall be obtained to provide a reasonable basis for the conclusion that is expressed in the report.* [Paragraph renumbered by the issuance of Statement on Standards for Attestation Engagements No. 7, October 1997.]

.38 Selecting and applying procedures that will accumulate evidence that is sufficient in the circumstances to provide a reasonable basis for the level of assurance to be expressed in the attest report requires the careful exercise of professional judgment. A broad array of available procedures may be applied in an attest engagement. In establishing a proper combination of procedures to appropriately restrict attestation risk, the practitioner should consider the following presumptions, bearing in mind that they are not mutually exclusive and may be subject to important exceptions.

a. Evidence obtained from independent sources outside an entity provides greater assurance of an assertion's reliability than evidence secured solely from within the entity.

b. Information obtained from the independent attester's direct personal knowledge (such as through physical examination, observation, computation, operating tests, or inspection) is more persuasive than information obtained indirectly.

c. The more effective the internal control the more assurance it provides about the reliability of the assertions.

[Paragraph renumbered by the issuance of Statement on Standards for Attestation Engagements No. 7, October 1997.]

.39 Thus, in the hierarchy of available attest procedures, those that involve search and verification (for example, inspection, confirmation, or observation), particularly when using independent sources outside the entity, are generally more effective in reducing attestation risk than those involving internal inquiries and comparisons of internal information (for example, analytical procedures and discussions with individuals responsible for the assertion). On the other hand, the latter are generally less costly to apply. [Paragraph renumbered by the issuance of Statement on Standards for Attestation Engagements No. 7, October 1997.]

.40 In an attest engagement designed to provide the highest level of assurance on an assertion (an "examination"), the practitioner's objective is to accumulate sufficient evidence to limit attestation risk to a level that is, in the practitioner's professional judgment, appropriately low for the high level of assurance that may be imparted by his or her report. In such an engagement, a practitioner should select from all available procedures—that is, procedures that assess inherent and control risk and restrict detection risk—any combination that can limit attestation risk to such an appropriately low level. [Paragraph renumbered by the issuance of Statement on Standards for Attestation Engagements No. 7, October 1997.]

.41 In a limited assurance engagement (a "review"), the objective is to accumulate sufficient evidence to limit attestation risk to a moderate level. To accomplish this, the types of procedures performed generally are limited to inquiries and analytical procedures (rather than also including search and verification procedures). [Paragraph renumbered by the issuance of Statement on Standards for Attestation Engagements No. 7, October 1997.]

.42 Nevertheless, there will be circumstances when inquiry and analytical procedures (*a*) cannot be performed, (*b*) are deemed less efficient than other procedures, or (*c*) yield evidence indicating that the assertion may be incomplete or inaccurate. In the first circumstance, the practitioner should perform other procedures that he or she believes can provide him or her with a level of assurance equivalent to that which inquiries and analytical procedures would have provided. In the second circumstance, the practitioner may perform other procedures that he or she believes would be more efficient to provide him or her with a level of assurance equivalent to that which inquiries and analytical procedures would provide. In the third circumstance, the practitioner should perform additional procedures. [Paragraph renumbered by the issuance of Statement on Standards for Attestation Engagements No. 7, October 1997.]

.43 The extent to which attestation procedures will be performed should be based on the level of assurance to be provided and the practitioner's consideration of (*a*) the nature and materiality of the information to the presentation of assertions taken as a whole, (*b*) the likelihood of misstatements, (*c*) knowledge obtained during current and previous engagements, (*d*) the asserter's competence in the subject matter of the assertion, (*e*) the extent to which the information is affected by the asserter's judgment, and (*f*) inadequacies in the asserter's underlying data. [Paragraph renumbered by the issuance of Statement on Standards for Attestation Engagements No. 7, October 1997.]

[.44–.45] [Superseded by Statement on Standards for Attestation Engagements No. 4, effective for reports on agreed-upon procedures engagements dated after April 30, 1996 (see section 600). Paragraphs renumbered by the issuance of Statement on Standards for Attestation Engagements No. 7, October 1997.]

Standards of Reporting

.46 The first standard of reporting is—*The report shall identify the assertion being reported on and state the character of the engagement.* [Paragraph renumbered by the issuance of Statement on Standards for Attestation Engagements No. 7, October 1997.]

.47 The practitioner who accepts an attest engagement should issue a report on the assertions or withdraw from the attest engagement. When a report is issued, the assertions should be identified by referring to a separate presentation of assertions that is the responsibility of the asserter. The presentation of assertions should generally be bound with or accompany the practitioner's report. Because the asserter's responsibility for the assertions should be clear, it is ordinarily not sufficient merely to include the assertions in the practitioner's report. [Paragraph renumbered by the issuance of Statement on Standards for Attestation Engagements No. 7, October 1997.]

.48 The statement of the character of an attest engagement that is designed to result in a general-distribution report includes two elements: (*a*) a description of the nature and scope of the work performed and (*b*) a reference to the professional standards governing the engagement. When the form of the statement is prescribed in authoritative interpretive standards (for example, an examination in accordance with GAAS), that form should be used in the practitioner's report. However, when no such interpretive standards exist, (1) the terms *examination* and *review* should be used to describe engagements to provide, respectively, the highest level and a moderate level of assurance, and (2) the reference to professional standards should be accomplished by referring to "standards established by the American Institute of Certified Public Accountants." [Paragraph renumbered by the issuance of Statement on Standards for Attestation Engagements No. 7, October 1997.]

.49 The statement of the character of an attest engagement in which the practitioner applies agreed-upon procedures should refer to conformity with the arrangements made with the specified user(s). Such engagements are designed to accommodate the specific needs of the parties in interest and should be described by identifying the procedures agreed upon by such parties. [Paragraph renumbered by the issuance of Statement on Standards for Attestation Engagements No. 7, October 1997.]

.50 The second standard of reporting is—*The report shall state the practitioner's conclusion about whether the assertion is presented in conformity with the established or stated criteria against which it was measured.* [Paragraph renumbered by the issuance of Statement on Standards for Attestation Engagements No. 7, October 1997.]

.51 The practitioner should consider the concept of materiality in applying this standard. In expressing a conclusion on the conformity of a presentation of assertions with established or stated criteria, the practitioner should consider the omission or misstatement of an individual assertion to be material if the magnitude of the omission or misstatement—individually or when aggregated with other omissions or misstatements—is such that a reasonable person relying on the presentation of assertions would be influenced by the inclusion or correction of the individual assertion. The relative, rather than absolute, size of an omission or misstatement determines whether it is material in a given situation. [Paragraph renumbered by the issuance of Statement on Standards for Attestation Engagements No. 7, October 1997.]

.52 General-distribution attest reports should be limited to two levels of assurance: one based on a reduction of attestation risk to an appropriately low level (an "examination") and the other based on a reduction of attestation risk to a moderate level (a "review"). [Paragraph renumbered by the issuance of Statement on Standards for Attestation Engagements No. 7, October 1997.]

.53 In an engagement to achieve the highest level of assurance (an "examination"), the practitioner's conclusion should be expressed in the form of a positive opinion. When attestation risk has been reduced only to a moderate level (a "review"), the conclusion should be expressed in the form of negative assurance. [Paragraph renumbered by the issuance of Statement on Standards for Attestation Engagements No. 7, October 1997.]

Examination

.54 When expressing a positive opinion, the practitioner should clearly state whether, in his or her opinion, the presentation of assertions is presented in conformity with established or stated criteria. Reports expressing a positive opinion on a presentation of assertions taken as a whole, however, may be qualified or modified for some aspect of the presentation or the engagement (see the third reporting standard). In addition, such reports may emphasize certain matters relating to the attest engagement or the presentation of assertions. [Paragraph renumbered by the issuance of Statement on Standards for Attestation Engagements No. 7, October 1997.]

.55 The following is an illustration of an examination report that expresses an unqualified opinion on a presentation of assertions, assuming that no specific report form has been prescribed in authoritative interpretive standards.

> We have examined the accompanying [*identify the presentation of assertions—for example, Statement of Investment Performance Statistics of XYZ Fund for the year ended December 31, 19X1*]. Our examination was made in accordance with standards established by the American Institute of Certified Public Accountants and, accordingly, included such procedures as we considered necessary in the circumstances.
>
> [*Additional paragraph(s) may be added to emphasize certain matters relating to the attest engagement or the presentation of assertions.*]
>
> In our opinion, the [*identify the presentation of assertions—for example, Statement of Investment Performance Statistics*] referred to above presents [*identify the assertion—for example, the investment performance of XYZ Fund for the year ended December 31, 19X1*] in conformity with [*identify established or stated criteria—for example, the measurement and disclosure criteria set forth in Note1*].

[Paragraph renumbered by the issuance of Statement on Standards for Attestation Engagements No. 7, October 1997.]

.56 When the presentation of assertions has been prepared in conformity with specified criteria that have been agreed upon by the asserter and the user, the practitioner's report should also contain—

a. A statement of limitations on the use of the report because it is intended solely for specified parties (see the fourth reporting standard).

b. An indication, when applicable, that the presentation of assertions differs materially from that which would have been presented if criteria for the presentation of such assertions for general distribution had been followed in its preparation (for example, financial statements prepared in accordance with criteria specified in a contractual arrangement may differ materially from statements prepared in conformity with GAAP).

[Paragraph renumbered by the issuance of Statement on Standards for Attestation Engagements No. 7, October 1997.]

Review

.57 In providing negative assurance, the practitioner's conclusion should state whether any information came to the practitioner's attention on the basis of the work performed that indicates that the assertions are not presented in all material respects in conformity with established or stated criteria. (As discussed more fully in the commentary to the third reporting standard, if the assertions are not modified to correct for any such information that comes to the practitioner's attention, such information should be described in the practitioner's report.) [Paragraph renumbered by the issuance of Statement on Standards for Attestation Engagements No. 7, October 1997.]

.58 A practitioner's negative assurance report may also comment on or emphasize certain matters relating to the attest engagement or the presentation of assertions. Furthermore, the practitioner's report should—

a. Indicate that the work performed was less in scope than an examination.

b. Disclaim a positive opinion on the assertions.

c. Contain the additional statements noted in paragraph .56 when the presentation of assertions has been prepared in conformity with specified criteria that have been agreed upon by the asserter and user(s).

[Paragraph renumbered by the issuance of Statement on Standards for Attestation Engagements No. 7, October 1997.]

.59 The following is an illustration of a review report that expresses negative assurance where no exceptions have been found, assuming that no specific report form has been prescribed in authoritative interpretive standards:

> We have reviewed the accompanying [*identify the presentation of assertions—for example, Statement of Investment Performance Statistics of XYZ Fund for the year ended December 31, 19X1*]. Our review was conducted in accordance with standards established by the American Institute of Certified Public Accountants.
>
> A review is substantially less in scope than an examination, the objective of which is the expression of an opinion on the [*identify the presentation of assertions—for example, Statement of Investment Performance Statistics*]. Accordingly, we do not express such an opinion.
>
> [*Additional paragraph(s) may be added to emphasize certain matters relating to the attest engagement or the presentation of assertions.*]
>
> Based on our review, nothing came to our attention that caused us to believe that the accompanying [*identify the presentation of assertions—for example, Statement of Investment Performance Statistics*] is not presented in conformity with [*identify the established or stated criteria—for example, the measurement and disclosure criteria set forth in Note 1*].

[Paragraph renumbered by the issuance of Statement on Standards for Attestation Engagements No. 7, October 1997.]

Agreed-Upon Procedures

[.60–.63] [Superseded by Statement on Standards for Attestation Engagements No. 4, effective for reports on agreed-upon procedures engagements dated after April 30, 1996 (see section 600). Paragraphs renumbered by the issuance of Statement on Standards for Attestation Engagements No. 7, October 1997.][9]

[9] [Superseded by Statement on Standards for Attestation Engagements No. 4, effective for reports on agreed-upon procedures engagements dated after April 30, 1996 (see section 600). Footnote renumbered by the issuance of Statement on Standards for Attestation Engagements No. 7, October 1997.]

.64 The third standard of reporting is—*The report shall state all of the practitioner's significant reservations about the engagement and the presentation of the assertion.* [Paragraph renumbered by the issuance of Statement on Standards for Attestation Engagements No. 7, October 1997.]

.65 "Reservations about the engagement" refers to any unresolved problem that the practitioner had in complying with these attestation standards, interpretive standards, or the specific procedures agreed to by the specific user(s). The practitioner should not express an unqualified conclusion unless the engagement has been conducted in accordance with the attestation standards. Such standards will not have been complied with if the practitioner has been unable to apply all the procedures that he or she considers necessary in the circumstances or, when applicable, that have been agreed upon with the user(s). [Paragraph renumbered by the issuance of Statement on Standards for Attestation Engagements No. 7, October 1997.]

.66 Restrictions on the scope of an engagement, whether imposed by the client or by such other circumstances as the timing of the work or the inability to obtain sufficient evidence, may require the practitioner to qualify the assurance provided, to disclaim any assurance, or to withdraw from the engagement. The reasons for a qualification or disclaimer should be described in the practitioner's report. [Paragraph renumbered by the issuance of Statement on Standards for Attestation Engagements No. 7, October 1997.]

.67 The practitioner's decision to provide qualified assurance, to disclaim any assurance, or to withdraw because of a scope limitation depends on an assessment of the effect of the omitted procedure(s) on his or her ability to express assurance on the presentation of assertions. This assessment will be affected by the nature and magnitude of the potential effects of the matters in question, by their significance to the presentation of assertions, and by whether the engagement is an examination or a review. If the potential effects relate to many assertions within a presentation of assertions or if the practitioner is performing a review, a disclaimer of assurance or withdrawal is more likely to be appropriate. When restrictions that significantly limit the scope of the engagement are imposed by the client, the practitioner generally should disclaim any assurance on the presentation of assertions or withdraw from the engagement. [Paragraph renumbered by the issuance of Statement on Standards for Attestation Engagements No. 7, October 1997.]

.68 "Reservations about the presentation of assertions" refers to any unresolved reservation about the conformity of the presentation with established or stated criteria, including the adequacy of the disclosure of material matters. They can result in either a qualified or an adverse report depending on the materiality of the departure from the criteria against which the assertions were evaluated. [Paragraph renumbered by the issuance of Statement on Standards for Attestation Engagements No. 7, October 1997.]

.69 Reservations about the presentation of assertions may relate to the measurement, form, arrangement, content, or underlying judgments and assumptions applicable to the presentation of assertions and its appended notes, including, for example, the terminology used, the amount of detail given, the classification of items, and the bases of amounts set forth. The practitioner considers whether a particular reservation should be the subject of a qualified report or adverse report given the circumstances and facts of which he or she is aware at the time. [Paragraph renumbered by the issuance of Statement on Standards for Attestation Engagements No. 7, October 1997.]

.70 The fourth standard of reporting is—*The report on an engagement to evaluate an assertion that has been prepared in conformity with agreed-upon criteria or on an engagement to apply agreed-upon procedures should contain a statement limiting its use to the parties who have agreed upon such criteria or procedures.* [Paragraph renumbered by the issuance of Statement on Standards for Attestation Engagements No. 7, October 1997.]

.71 Certain reports should be restricted to specified users who have participated in establishing either the criteria against which the assertions were evaluated (which are not deemed to be "reasonable" for general distribution—see the third general standard) or the nature and scope of the attest engagement. Such procedures or criteria can be agreed upon directly by the user or through a designated representative. Reports on such engagements should clearly indicate that they are intended solely for the use of the specified parties and may not be useful to others. [Paragraph renumbered by the issuance of Statement on Standards for Attestation Engagements No. 7, October 1997.]

Working Papers

.72 The practitioner should prepare and maintain working papers in connection with an engagement under the attestation standards; such working papers should be appropriate to the circumstances and the practitioner's needs on the engagement to which they apply.[10] Although the quantity, type, and content of working papers will vary with the circumstances, they ordinarily should indicate that—

a. The work was adequately planned and supervised, indicating observance of the first standard of fieldwork.

b. Evidential matter was obtained to provide a reasonable basis for the conclusion or conclusions expressed in the practitioner's report.

[Paragraph added, effective for engagements beginning after December 15, 1995, by Statement on Standards for Attestation Engagements No. 5. Paragraph renumbered by the issuance of Statement on Standards for Attestation Engagements No. 7, October 1997.]

.73 Working papers are records kept by the practitioner of the work performed, the information obtained, and the pertinent conclusions reached in the engagement. Examples of working papers are work programs, analyses, memoranda, letters of confirmation and representation, abstracts of the entity's documents, and schedules or commentaries prepared or obtained by the practitioner. Working papers also may be in the form of data stored on tapes, films, or other media. [Paragraph added, effective for engagements beginning after December 15, 1995, by Statement on Standards for Attestation Engagements No. 5. Paragraph renumbered by the issuance of Statement on Standards for Attestation Engagements No. 7, October 1997.]

.74 Working papers are the property of the practitioner, and some states have statutes or regulations that designate the practitioner as the owner of the

---

[10] There is no intention to imply that the practitioner would be precluded from supporting his or her report by other means in addition to working papers. [Footnote added, effective for engagements beginning after December 15, 1995, by Statement on Standards for Attestation Engagements No. 5. Footnote renumbered by the issuance of Statement on Standards for Attestation Engagements No. 7, October 1997.]

working papers. The practitioner's rights of ownership, however, are subject to ethical limitations relating to the confidential relationship with the clients. [Paragraph added, effective for engagements beginning after December 15, 1995, by Statement on Standards for Attestation Engagements No. 5. Paragraph renumbered by the issuance of Statement on Standards for Attestation Engagements No. 7, October 1997.]

.75 Certain of the practitioner's working papers may sometimes serve as a useful reference source for his or her client, but the working papers should not be regarded as a part of or a substitute for the client's records. [Paragraph added, effective for engagements beginning after December 15, 1995, by Statement on Standards for Attestation Engagements No. 5. Paragraph renumbered by the issuance of Statement on Standards for Attestation Engagements No. 7, October 1997.]

.76 The practitioner should adopt reasonable procedures for safe custody of his or her working papers and should retain them for a period of time sufficient to meet the needs of his or her practice and to satisfy any pertinent legal requirements of records retention. [Paragraph added, effective for engagements beginning after December 15, 1995, by Statement on Standards for Attestation Engagements No. 5. Paragraph renumbered by the issuance of Statement on Standards for Attestation Engagements No. 7, October 1997.]

Attest Services Related to MAS Engagements[*]

Attest Services as Part of an MAS Engagement

.77 When a practitioner[11] provides an attest service (as defined in this section) as part of an MAS engagement, the Statements on Standards for Attestation Engagements[12] apply only to the attest service. Statements on Standards for Management Advisory Services (SSMASs) apply to the balance of the MAS engagement.[13] [Paragraph added, effective for attest reports issued on or after May 1, 1988, by Statement on Standards for Attestation Engagements, *Attest Services Related to MAS Engagements*. Paragraph renum-

[*] The terminology in this section is based on Statements on Standards for Management Advisory Services. The SSMASs were superseded by Statement on Standards for Consulting Services No. 1, *Consulting Services: Definitions and Standards* (SSCS), effective for engagements accepted on or after January 1, 1992. This section has not been revised to reflect the conforming changes necessary due to the issuance of SSCS.

[11] *Practitioner* is defined in this section to include a proprietor, partner, or shareholder in a public accounting firm and any full- or part-time employee of a public accounting firm, whether certified or not. [Footnote renumbered by the issuance of Statement on Auditing Standards No. 72, February 1993. Footnote subsequently renumbered by the issuance of Statement on Standards for Attestation Engagements No. 5, November 1995. Footnote subsequently renumbered by the issuance of Statement on Standards for Attestation Engagements No. 7, October 1997.]

[12] This refers to the SSAE *Attestation Standards* and subsequent statements in that series, as issued by the AICPA. [Footnote renumbered by the issuance of Statement on Auditing Standards No. 72, February 1993. Footnote subsequently renumbered by the issuance of Statement on Standards for Attestation Engagements No. 5, November 1995. Footnote subsequently renumbered by the issuance of Statement on Standards for Attestation Engagements No. 7, October 1997.]

[13] This refers to SSMAS No. 1, *Definitions and Standards for MAS Practice*, and subsequent statements in that series, as issued by the AICPA. [Footnote renumbered by the issuance of Statement on Auditing Standards No. 72, February 1993. Footnote subsequently renumbered by the issuance of Statement on Standards for Attestation Engagements No. 5, November 1995. Footnote subsequently renumbered by the issuance of Statement on Standards for Attestation Engagements No. 7, October 1997.]

bered by the issuance of Statement on Standards for Attestation Engagements No. 5, November 1995. Paragraph subsequently renumbered by the issuance of Statement on Standards for Attestation Engagements No. 7, October 1997.]

.78 When the practitioner determines that an attest service is to be provided as part of an MAS engagement, the practitioner should inform the client of the relevant differences between the two types of services and obtain concurrence that the attest service is to be performed in accordance with the appropriate professional requirements. The MAS engagement letter or an amendment should document the requirement to perform an attest service. The practitioner should take such actions because the professional requirements for an attest service differ from those for a management advisory service. [Paragraph added, effective for attest reports issued on or after May 1, 1988, by Statement on Standards for Attestation Engagements, *Attest Services Related to MAS Engagements*. Paragraph renumbered by the issuance of Statement on Standards for Attestation Engagements No. 5, November 1995. Paragraph subsequently renumbered by the issuance of Statement on Standards for Attestation Engagements No. 7, October 1997.]

.79 The practitioner should issue separate reports on the attest engagement and the MAS engagement and, if presented in a common binder, the report on the attest engagement or service should be clearly identified and segregated from the report on the MAS engagement. [Paragraph added, effective for attest reports issued on or after May 1, 1988, by Statement on Standards for Attestation Engagements, *Attest Services Related to MAS Engagements*. Paragraph renumbered by the issuance of Statement on Standards for Attestation Engagements No. 5, November 1995. Paragraph subsequently renumbered by the issuance of Statement on Standards for Attestation Engagements No. 7, October 1997.]

Assertions, Criteria, and Evidence

.80 An attest service may involve written assertions, evaluation criteria, or evidential matter developed during a concurrent or prior MAS engagement. A written assertion of another party developed with the practitioner's advice and assistance as the result of such an MAS engagement may be the subject of an attestation engagement, provided the assertion is dependent upon the actions, plans, or assumptions of that other party who is in a position to have an informed judgment about its accuracy. Criteria developed with the practitioner's assistance may be used to evaluate an assertion in an attest engagement, provided such criteria meet the requirements in this section. Relevant information obtained in the course of a concurrent or prior MAS engagement may be used as evidential matter in an attest engagement, provided the information satisfies the requirements of this section. [Paragraph added, effective for attest reports issued on or after May 1, 1988, by Statement on Standards for Attestation Engagements, *Attest Services Related to MAS Engagements*. Paragraph renumbered by the issuance of Statement on Standards for Attestation Engagements No. 5, November 1995. Paragraph subsequently renumbered by the issuance of Statement on Standards for Attestation Engagements No. 7, October 1997.]

Nonattest Evaluations of Written Assertions

.81 The evaluation of statements contained in a written assertion of another party when performing a management advisory service does not in and of itself constitute the performance of an attest service. For example, in the course of an engagement to help a client select a computer that meets the client's needs, the practitioner may evaluate written assertions from one or more vendors, performing some of the same procedures as required for an attest service. However, the MAS report will focus on whether the computer meets the client's needs, not on the reliability of the vendor's assertions. Also, the practitioner's study of the computer's suitability will not be limited to what is in the written assertions of the vendors. Some or all of the information provided in the vendors' written proposals, as well as other information, will be evaluated to recommend a system suitable to the client's needs. Such evaluations are necessary to enable the practitioner to achieve the purpose of the MAS engagement. [Paragraph added, effective for attest reports issued on or after May 1, 1988, by Statement on Standards for Attestation Engagements, *Attest Services Related to MAS Engagements*. Paragraph renumbered by the issuance of Statement on Standards for Attestation Engagements No. 5, November 1995. Paragraph subsequently renumbered by the issuance of Statement on Standards for Attestation Engagements No. 7, October 1997.]

Effective Date

.82 Paragraphs .01 through .31 and .33 through .71 are effective for attest reports issued on or after September 30, 1986. Earlier application is encouraged. Paragraph .32 is effective for engagements for periods ending on or after June 15, 1998. Earlier application is permitted. Paragraphs .72 through .76 are effective for engagements beginning after December 15, 1995. Paragraphs .77 through .81 are effective for attest reports issued on or after May 1, 1988. [Paragraph renumbered and amended, effective for attest reports issued on or after May 1, 1988, by the issuance of Statement on Standards for Attestation Engagements, *Attest Services Related to MAS Engagements*. Paragraph subsequently renumbered and amended, effective for engagements beginning after December 15, 1995, by the issuance of Statement on Standards for Attestation Engagements No. 5. Paragraph subsequently renumbered and amended, effective for engagements for periods ending on or after June 15, 1998, by the issuance of Statement on Standards for Attestation Engagements No. 7.]

This Appendix provides a historical analysis made as of March 1986. This Appendix has not been revised to reflect the new terminology from the issuance of Statement on Auditing Standards Nos. 53 through 72.

.83

Appendix A

Comparison of the Attestation Standards With Generally Accepted Auditing Standards

1. Two principal conceptual differences exist between the attestation standards and the ten existing GAAS. First, the attestation standards provide a framework for the attest function beyond historical financial statements. Accordingly, references to "financial statements" and "generally accepted accounting principles," which exist in GAAS, are omitted from the attestation standards. Second, as is apparent in the standards of fieldwork and reporting, the attestation standards accommodate the growing number of attest services in which the practitioner expresses assurances below the level that is expressed for the traditional audit ("positive opinion").

2. In addition to these two major differences, another conceptual difference exists. The attestation standards formally provide for attest services that are tailored to the needs of users who have participated in establishing either the nature and scope of the attest engagement or the specialized criteria against which the assertions are to be measured, and who will thus receive a limited-use report. Although these differences are substantive, they merely recognize changes that have already occurred in the marketplace and in the practice of public accounting.

3. As a consequence of these three conceptual differences, the composition of the attestation standards differs from that of GAAS. The compositional differences, as indicated in the table at the end of this Appendix, fall into two major categories: (*a*) two general standards not contained in GAAS are included in the attestation standards and (*b*) one of the fieldwork standards and two of the reporting standards in GAAS are not explicitly included in the attestation standards. Each of these differences is described in the remainder of this Appendix.

4. Two new general standards are included because, together with the definition of an attest engagement, they establish appropriate boundaries around the attest function. Once the subject matter of attestation extends beyond historical financial statements, there is a need to determine just how far this extension of attest services can and should go. The boundaries set by the attestation standards require (*a*) that the practitioner have adequate knowledge in the subject matter of the assertion (the second general standard) and (*b*) that the assertion be capable of reasonably consistent estimation or measurement using established or stated criteria (the third general standard).

5. The second standard of fieldwork in GAAS is not included in the attestation standards for a number of reasons. That standard calls for "a proper study and evaluation of the existing internal control as a basis for reliance thereon

and for the determination of the resultant extent of the tests to which auditing procedures are to be restricted." The most important reason for not including this standard is that the second standard of fieldwork of the attestation standards encompasses the study and evaluation of controls because, when performed, it is an element of accumulating sufficient evidence. A second reason is that the concept of internal control may not be relevant for certain assertions (for example, aspects of information about computer software) on which a practitioner may be engaged to report.

6. The attestation standards of reporting are organized differently from the GAAS reporting standards to accommodate matters of emphasis that naturally evolve from an expansion of the attest function to cover more than one level and form of assurance on a variety of presentations of assertions. There is also a new reporting theme in the attestation standards. This is the limitation of the use of certain reports to specified users and is a natural extension of the acknowledgement that the attest function should accommodate engagements tailored to the needs of specified parties who have participated in establishing either the nature and scope of the engagement or the specified criteria against which the assertions were measured.

7. In addition, two reporting standards in GAAS have been omitted from the attestation standards. The first is the standard that requires the auditor's report to state "whether such [accounting] principles have been consistently observed in the current period in relation to the preceding period." The second states that "informative disclosures in the financial statements are to be regarded as reasonably adequate unless otherwise stated in the report." Those two standards are not included in the attestation standards because the second attestation standard of reporting, which requires a conclusion about whether the assertions are presented in conformity with established or stated criteria, encompasses both of these omitted standards.

Attestation Standards Compared With Generally Accepted Auditing Standards

Attestation Standards	*Generally Accepted Auditing Standards*
General Standards	
1. The engagement shall be performed by a practitioner or practitioners having adequate technical training and proficiency in the attest function.	1. The examination is to be performed by a person or persons having adequate training and proficiency as an auditor.
2. The engagement shall be performed by a practitioner or practitioners having adequate knowledge in the subject matter of the assertion.	
3. The practitioner shall perform an engagement only if he or she has reason to believe that the following two conditions exist: • The assertion is capable of evaluation against reasonable criteria that either have been established by a recognized body or are stated in the presentation of the assertion in a sufficiently clear and comprehensive manner for a knowledgeable reader to be able to understand them. • The assertion is capable of reasonably consistent estimation or measurement using such criteria.	
4. In all matters relating to the engagement, an independence in mental attitude shall be maintained by the practitioner or practitioners.	2. In all matters relating to the assignment, an independence in mental attitude is to be maintained by the auditor or auditors.
5. Due professional care shall be exercised in the performance of the engagement.	3. Due professional care is to be exercised in the performance of the examination and the preparation of the report.
Standards of Fieldwork	
1. The work shall be adequately planned and assistants, if any, shall be properly supervised.	1. The work shall be adequately planned and assistants, if any, are to be properly supervised.
	2. There is to be a proper study and evaluation of the existing internal control as a basis for reliance thereon and for the determination of the resultant extent of the tests to which auditing procedures are to be restricted.

2. Sufficient evidence shall be obtained to provide a reasonable basis for the conclusion that is expressed in the report.	3. Sufficient competent evidential matter is to be obtained through inspection, observation, inquiries, and confirmations to afford a reasonable basis for an opinion regarding the financial statements under examination.

Standards of Reporting

1. The report shall identify the assertion being reported on and state the character of the engagement.	
2. The report shall state the practitioner's conclusion about whether the assertion is presented in conformity with the established or stated criteria against which it was measured.	1. The report shall state whether the financial statements are presented in accordance with generally accepted accounting principles.
	2. The report shall state whether such principles have been consistently observed in the current period in relation to the preceding period.
	3. Informative disclosures in the financial statements are to be regarded as reasonably adequate unless otherwise stated in the report.
3. The report shall state all of the practitioner's significant reservations about the engagement and the presentation of the assertion. 4. The report on an engagement to evaluate an assertion that has been prepared in conformity with agreed-upon criteria or on an engagement to apply agreed-upon procedures should contain a statement limiting its use to the parties who have agreed upon such criteria or procedures.	4. The report shall either contain an expression of opinion regarding the financial statements, taken as a whole, or an assertion to the effect that an opinion cannot be expressed. When an overall opinion cannot be expressed, the reasons therefore should be stated. In all cases where an auditor's name is associated with financial statements, the report should contain a clear-cut indication of the character of the auditor's examination, if any, and the degree of responsibility he is taking.

[Paragraph renumbered by the issuance of Statement on Standards for Attestation Engagements, *Attest Services Related to MAS Engagements*, December 1987. Paragraph subsequently renumbered by the issuance of Statement on Standards for Attestation Engagements No. 5, November 1995. Paragraph subsequently renumbered by the issuance of Statement on Standards for Attestation Engagements No. 7, October 1997.]

This Appendix provides a historical analysis made as of March 1986. This Appendix has not been revised to reflect the new terminology from the issuance of Statement on Auditing Standards Nos. 53 through 72 or SSAE No. 2.

.84

Appendix B

Analysis of Apparent or Possible Inconsistencies Between the Attestation Standards and Existing SASs and SSARSs

1. There are no identified inconsistencies between the attestation standards and the ten generally accepted auditing standards or those SASs that deal with audits of historical financial statements. However, certain existing interpretive standards (SASs and SSARSs) and audit and accounting guides that pertain to other attest services are modestly inconsistent with these attestation standards. The purpose of this Appendix is to identify apparent or possible inconsistencies between the attestation standards and existing SASs and SSARSs. It provides appropriate standard-setting bodies with a list of matters that may require their attention. The Auditing Standards Board and the Accounting and Review Services Committee will evaluate apparent or possible inconsistencies and consider whether any changes are necessary. The decision to propose changes, if any, to existing pronouncements will be the subject of the regular due-process procedures of AICPA standard-setting bodies.

2. The specific SASs, SSARSs, and other pronouncements in which apparent or possible inconsistencies exist (in whole or in part) have been classified into the following broad categories to assist readers in understanding and evaluating their potential significance:

a. Exception reporting

b. Failure to report on conformity with established or stated criteria

c. Failure to refer to a separate presentation of assertions that is the responsibility of the asserter

d. Lack of appropriate scope of work for providing a moderate level of assurance

e. Report wording inconsistencies

All existing authoritative pronouncements will remain in force while the Auditing Standards Board and the Accounting and Review Services Committee evaluate these apparent or possible inconsistencies.

Exception Reporting

3. Certain SASs (Nos. 27, 28, 36, 40, and 45) require the auditor to apply certain limited procedures to supplementary information required by the Financial Accounting Standards Board (FASB) but to separately report on such information only if exceptions arise. The purpose of these limited procedures

is to permit the auditor to reach a conclusion on the reliability of required supplementary information; consequently, this seems to amount to an attest service in the broadest sense of that term. However, because the auditor has not been engaged to express and normally does not express a conclusion in this particular circumstance, the limited procedures do not fully meet the definition of an attest engagement.

Failure to Report on Conformity With Established or Stated Criteria

4. SAS Nos. 29 and 42 provide guidance for auditors when they report on two specific types of assertions: information accompanying financial statements in an auditor-submitted document and condensed financial information, respectively. The apparent criterion against which the auditor is directed to report is whether the assertion is "fairly stated in all material respects in relation to the basic financial statements taken as a whole."

5. To some, such a form of reporting seems to be inconsistent with the second reporting standard, which requires the practitioner's report to state "whether the assertions are presented in conformity with the established or stated criteria against which they were measured." Although it seems reasonably clear that GAAP are the established criteria against which the information accompanying financial statements in an auditor-submitted document is evaluated, the report form required by SAS No. 29 does not specifically refer to GAAP. Such reference, if it were required, would effectively reduce the stated level of materiality from the "financial statements as a whole" to the specific assertions on which the practitioner is reporting, and a practitioner may not have obtained sufficient evidence to provide a positive opinion on the assertions in such a fashion.

6. The situation with respect to SAS No. 42 is somewhat different. Although some would argue that there are established criteria (for example, GAAP or Securities and Exchange Commission [SEC] regulations) for condensed financial statements and selected financial information, others do not agree with such a conclusion. The Auditing Standards Board took the latter position when this SAS was adopted because it did not provide for a reference to GAAP or SEC regulations in the standard auditor's report.

Failure to Refer to a Separate Presentation of Assertions That Is the Responsibility of the Asserter

7. SAS Nos. 14 and 30 provide for attest reports in which there is no reference to a separate presentation of assertions by the responsible party. In both cases, management's assertions—compliance with regulatory or contractual requirements and the adequacy of the entity's system of internal accounting control—are, at best, implied or contained in a management representation letter.

8. For instance, SAS No. 30 refers to an engagement to express an opinion on an entity's system of internal accounting control rather than on management's description of such a system (including its evaluation of the system's adequacy). Furthermore, the standard report gives the practitioner's opinion directly on the system. In an effort to better place the responsibility for the system where it really lies, the report does include some additional explanatory paragraphs that contain statements about management's responsibility and the inherent limitations of internal controls.

Lack of Appropriate Scope of Work for Providing a Moderate Level of Assurance

9. Portions of three SASs (SAS No. 14, on compliance with regulatory or contractual requirements; SAS No. 29, on information accompanying financial statements in an auditor-submitted document; and SAS No. 30, on a system of internal accounting control based on a financial statement audit) permit the expression of limited assurance on specific assertions based solely or substantially on those auditing procedures that happen to have been applied in forming an opinion on a separate assertion—the financial statements taken as a whole.

10. Such a basis for limited assurance seems inconsistent with the second fieldwork standard, which requires that limited assurance on a specific assertion must be based either on obtaining sufficient evidence to reduce attestation risk to a moderate level as described in the attestation standards or applying specific procedures that have been agreed upon by specified users for their benefit. The scope of work performed on the specific assertions covered in the three SASs identified above depends entirely, or to a large extent, on what happens to be done in the audit of another assertion and would not seem to satisfy the requirements of either of the bases for limited assurance provided in the second standard of fieldwork.

11. Four other SASs (Nos. 27, 28, 40, and 45) may be inconsistent with the requirements of the second fieldwork standard in that they prescribe procedures as a basis for obtaining limited assurance on a specific assertion that seem to constitute a smaller scope than those necessary to reduce attestation risk to a moderate level. These SASs either limit the prescribed procedures to specific inquiries or the reading of an assertion, or they acknowledge that an auditor may not be able to perform inquiries to resolve doubts about certain assertions.

Report Wording Inconsistencies

12. The four reporting standards require that an attest report contain specific elements, such as an identification of the assertions, a statement of the character of the engagement, a disclaimer of positive opinion in limited assurance engagements, and the use of negative assurance wording in such engagements. A number of existing SASs and SSARSs prescribe reports that do not contain some of these elements.

13. Because a compilation of financial statements as described in the SSARSs and a compilation of prospective financial statements as described in the Statement on Standards for Accountants' Services on Prospective Financial Information [section 200] do not result in the expression of a conclusion on the reliability of the assertions contained in those financial statements, they are not attest engagements. Therefore, such engagements do not have to comply with the attestation standards and there can be no inconsistencies. Although it does not involve the attest function, a compilation is nevertheless a valuable professional service involving a practitioner's expertise in putting an entity's financial information into the form of financial statements—an accounting (subject matter) expertise rather than attestation expertise.

14. Certain existing reporting and other requirements of SASs and SSARSs go beyond (but are not contrary to) the standards. Examples include the requirements to perform a study and evaluation of internal control, to re-

port on consistency in connection with an examination of financial statements, and to withdraw in a review of financial statements when there is a scope limitation. These requirements remain in force.

[Paragraph renumbered by the issuance of Statement on Standards for Attestation Engagements, *Attest Services Related to MAS Engagements*, December 1987. Paragraph subsequently renumbered by the issuance of Statement on Standards for Attestation Engagements No. 5, November 1995. Paragraph subsequently renumbered by the issuance of Statement on Standards for Attestation Engagements No. 7, October 1997.]

AT Section 9100

Attestation Standards: Attestation Engagements Interpretations of Section 100

1. Defense Industry Questionnaire on Business Ethics and Conduct

.01 *Question*—Certain defense contractors have made a commitment to adopt and implement six principles of business ethics and conduct contained in the *Defense Industry Initiatives on Business Ethics and Conduct (Initiatives)*. One of those principles concerns defense contractors' public accountability for their commitment to the Initiatives. That principle requires completion of a *Questionnaire on Business Ethics and Conduct (Questionnaire)*, which is appended to the six principles.

.02 The public accountability principle also requires the defense contractor's independent public accountant or similar independent organization to express a conclusion about the responses to the *Questionnaire* and issue a report thereon for submission to the External Independent Organization of the Defense Industry (EIODI). (Appendixes C and D to this Interpretation [paragraphs .29 and .30] provide background information about the *Initiatives*, the six principles, and the required *Questionnaire*.)

.03 A defense contractor may request its independent public accountant (practitioner) to examine or review its responses to the *Questionnaire* for the purpose of expressing a conclusion about the appropriateness of those responses in a report prepared for general distribution. Would such an engagement be an attest engagement as defined in section 100, *Attestation Standards*?

.04 *Interpretation*—Section 100 defines an attest engagement as one in which a practitioner is engaged to issue or does issue a written communication that expresses a conclusion about the reliability of a written assertion that is the responsibility of another party. The questions in the *Questionnaire* and the accompanying responses are written assertions of the defense contractor. When a practitioner is engaged by a defense contractor to express a written conclusion about the appropriateness of those responses, such an engagement involves a written conclusion about the reliability of an assertion that is the responsibility of the defense contractor. Consequently, section 100 applies to such engagements.

.05 *Question*—Section 100.11 specifies that a practitioner shall perform an attest engagement only if there are reasons to believe that "the assertion is capable of evaluation against reasonable criteria that either have been established by a recognized body or are stated in the presentation of the assertion in a sufficiently clear and comprehensive manner for a knowledgeable reader to be able to understand them." What are the criteria against which such assertions are to be evaluated and do such criteria provide a reasonable basis for the general distribution of the presentation of the assertions and a practitioner's report thereon?

.06 *Interpretation*—The criteria for evaluating the defense contractor's assertions are set forth in the *Initiatives* and *Questionnaire*. The reasonableness of those criteria must be evaluated by assessing whether the assertions they generate (the questions and responses in the *Questionnaire*) have an appropriate balance of the relevance and reliability characteristics discussed in section 100.15.

.07 The criteria set forth in the *Initiatives* and *Questionnaire* will, when properly applied, generate assertions that have an appropriate balance of relevance and reliability. Consequently, such criteria provide a reasonable basis for the general distribution of the *Questionnaire* and responses and the practitioner's report thereon. Although the criteria provide a reasonable basis for general distribution of the practitioner's report, they have not been established by the type of recognized body contemplated in section 100.13. Consequently, as required by section 100.14, the criteria must be stated in the presentation of assertions in a sufficiently clear and comprehensive manner for a knowledgeable reader to understand them. This requirement will be satisfied if the defense contractor attaches the *Initiatives* and *Questionnaire* to the presentation of the assertions.

.08 *Question*—What is the nature of the procedures that should be applied to the *Questionnaire* responses?

.09 *Interpretation*—The objective of the procedures performed in either an examination or review engagement is to obtain evidential matter that the defense contractor has designed and placed in operation policies and programs that conform with the criteria in the *Initiatives* and *Questionnaire* in a manner that supports the responses to the questions in the *Questionnaire* and that the policies and programs operated during the period covered by the defense contractor's assertion. The objective does not include providing assurance about whether the defense contractor's policies and programs operated effectively to ensure compliance with the defense contractor's code of business ethics and conduct on the part of individual employees or about whether the defense contractor and its employees have complied with federal procurement laws. In an examination, the evidential matter should be sufficient to limit the attestation risk for the assertions to a level that is appropriately low for the high degree of assurance imparted by an examination report. In a review, this evidential matter should be sufficient to limit the attestation risk to a moderate level.

.10 Examination procedures include obtaining evidential matter by reading relevant policies and programs, making inquiries of appropriate defense contractor personnel, inspecting documents and records, confirming defense contractor assertions with its employees or others, and observing activities. Illustrative examination procedures are presented in appendix A [paragraph .27]. Review procedures are generally limited to reading relevant policies and procedures and making inquiries of appropriate defense contractor personnel. Illustrative review procedures are presented in appendix E [paragraph .31]. When applying examination or review procedures, the practitioner should assess the appropriateness (including the comprehensiveness) of the policies and programs in meeting the criteria in the *Initiatives* and *Questionnaire*.

.11 A particular defense contractor's policies and programs may vary from those of other defense contractors. As a result, evidential matter obtained from the procedures performed cannot be evaluated solely on a quantitative basis. Consequently, it is not practicable to establish only quantitative guidelines for determining the nature or extent of the evidential matter that is necessary to provide the assurance required in either an examination or review. The qualitative aspects should also be considered.

.12 In an examination it will be necessary for a practitioner's procedures to go beyond reading relevant policies and programs and making inquiries of appropriate defense contractor personnel to determine whether the policies and programs that support a defense contractor's answers to specific questions in the *Questionnaire* operated during the period.

.13 In determining the nature, timing, and extent of examination or review procedures, the practitioner should consider information obtained in the performance of other services for the defense contractor, for example, the audit of the defense contractor's financial statements. For multi-location defense contractors, whether policies and programs operated during the period should be evaluated for both the defense contractor's headquarters and for selected defense contracting locations. The practitioner may consider using the work of the defense contractor's internal auditors. The guidance in AU section 322, *The Auditor's Consideration of the Internal Audit Function in an Audit of Financial Statements*, may be useful in that consideration.

.14 Examination procedures, and in some instances review procedures, may require access to information involving specific instances of actual or alleged noncompliance with laws. An inability to obtain access to such information because of restrictions imposed by a defense contractor (for example, to protect attorney-client privilege) may constitute a scope limitation. Section 100.64 through .67 provides guidance in such situations. The practitioner should assess the effect of the inability to obtain access to such information on his or her ability to form a conclusion about whether the related policy or program operated during the period. If the defense contractor's reasons for not permitting access to the information are reasonable (for example, the information is the subject of litigation or a governmental investigation) and have been approved by an executive officer of the defense contractor, the occurrences of restricted access to information are few in number, and the practitioner has access to other information about that specific instance or about other instances that is sufficient to permit a conclusion to be formed about whether the related policy or program operated during the period, the practitioner ordinarily would conclude that it is not necessary to disclaim assurance.

.15 If the practitioner's scope of work has been restricted with respect to one or more questions, the practitioner should consider the implications of that restriction on the practitioner's ability to form a conclusion about other questions. In addition, as the nature or number of questions on which the defense contractor has imposed scope limitations increases in significance, the practitioner should consider whether to withdraw from the engagement.

.16 *Question*—What is the form of report that should be issued to meet the requirements of section 100?

.17 *Interpretation*—The standards of reporting in section 100.46 through .71 provide guidance about report content and wording and the circumstances that may require report modification. Appendix B and appendix F [paragraphs .28 and .32] provide illustrative reports appropriate for various circumstances. Section 100.47 states that the practitioner's report should refer to a separate presentation of assertions that is the responsibility of the asserter. The completed *Questionnaire* constitutes the presentation of assertions that should be referred to in the practitioner's report. The defense contractor should prepare a statement to accompany the presentation of the completed *Questionnaire* that asserts that the responses to the *Questionnaire* are appropriately presented in conformity with the criteria. An illustrative defense contractor statement is also presented in appendix B and appendix F [paragraphs .28 and .32].

.18 The engagements addressed in this Interpretation do not include providing assurance about whether the defense contractor's policies and programs operated effectively to ensure compliance with the defense contractor's code of business ethics and conduct on the part of individual employees or about whether the defense contractor and its employees have complied with federal procurement laws. The practitioner's report should explicitly disclaim an opinion on the extent of such compliance.

.19 Because variations in individual performance and interpretation will affect the operation of the defense contractor's policies and programs during the period, adherence to all such policies and programs in every case may not be possible. In determining whether a reservation about a response in the *Questionnaire* is sufficiently significant to result in an opinion modified for an exception to that response, the practitioner should consider the nature, causes, patterns, and pervasiveness of the instances in which the policies and programs did not operate as designed and their implications for that response in the *Questionnaire*.

.20 When scope limitations have precluded the practitioner from forming an opinion on the responses to one or more questions, the practitioner's report should describe all such scope restrictions. If such a scope limitation was imposed by the defense contractor after the practitioner had begun performing procedures, that fact should be stated in the report.

.21 A defense contractor may request the practitioner to communicate to management, the board of directors, or one of its committees, either orally or in writing, conditions noted that do not constitute significant reservations about the answers to the *Questionnaire* but that might nevertheless be of value to management. Agreed-upon arrangements between the practitioner and the defense contractor to communicate conditions noted may include, for example, the reporting of matters of less significance than those contemplated by the criteria stated in the *Initiatives* and *Questionnaire*, the existence of conditions specified by the defense contractor, the results of further investigation of matters noted to identify underlying causes, or suggestions for improvements in various policies or programs. Under these arrangements, the practitioner may be requested to visit specific locations, assess the effectiveness of specific policies or programs, or undertake specific attestation procedures not otherwise planned. In addition, the practitioner is not precluded from communicating matters believed to be of value, even if no specific request has been made.

.22 *Question*—Will the defense contractor's responses to questions 19 and 20 meet the relevance and reliability criteria for reporting under the attestation standards?

.23 *Interpretation*—For the reasons described in paragraphs .06 and .07 the criteria set forth in the amendment to Principle 1 of the *Initiatives* described above and questions 19 and 20 will, when properly applied, generate assertions that have an appropriate balance of relevance and reliability for purposes of providing a reasonable basis for the practitioner's report thereon. Further, the requirement that the presentation of assertions be stated in a sufficiently clear and comprehensive manner for a knowledgeable reader to understand them will be satisfied if the defense contractor attaches the *Initiatives*, as amended, and the *Questionnaire*, including questions 19 and 20, to the presentation of assertions.

.24 *Question*—What is the nature of the examination or review procedures that should be applied to the responses to questions 19 and 20 of the *Questionnaire*?

.25 *Interpretation*—Appendix A [paragraph .27] includes illustrative procedures for an engagement to examine the responses to questions 1 through 18 of the *Questionnaire*. In an examination engagement, the practitioner should consider applying the following procedures to the responses to questions 19 and 20:

19. Does the Company have a code of conduct provision or associated policy addressing marketing activities?

    Read the Code or associated policy to determine whether it addresses the following marketing activities.

    a. The gathering of competitive information and the engagement and use of consultants (whether engaged in bid and proposal activity, marketing, research and development, engineering, or other tasks).

    b. A description of limitations on information which employees or consultants seek or receive.

20. Does the Company have a code of conduct provision or associated policy requiring that consultants are governed by, and oriented regarding, the Company's code of conduct and relevant associated policies?

    a. Read the Code or associated policy to determine whether consultants engaged in marketing activities are governed by it.

    b. Determine by inquiry of Company officials and/or by reading relevant documentation how the Company orients consultants engaged in marketing activities to the Code and relevant associated policies.

    c. Obtain additional evidential matter, by positive confirmation of a selected number of consultants engaged in marketing activities or by other means, that the Company oriented such consultants to the Code and relevant associated policies.

.26 Appendix E [paragraph .31] includes illustrative procedures for an engagement to review the responses to questions 1 through 18 of the *Questionnaire*. In a review engagement, the practitioner should consider applying the following procedures to the responses to questions 19 and 20:

19. Does the Company have a code of conduct provision or associated policy addressing marketing activities?

    Read the Code or associated policy to determine whether it addresses the following marketing activities:

    a. The gathering of competitive information and the engagement and use of consultants (whether engaged in bid and proposal activity, marketing, research and development, engineering, or other tasks).

    b. A description of limitations on information which employees or consultants seek or receive.

20. Does the Company have a code of conduct provision or associated policy requiring that consultants are governed by, and oriented regarding, the Company's code of conduct and relevant associated policies?

    a. Read the Code or associated policy to determine whether consultants engaged in marketing activities are governed by it.

b. Determine by inquiry of Company officials and/or by reading relevant documentation how the Company orients consultants engaged in marketing activities to the Code and relevant associated policies.

.27

Appendix A

Illustrative Procedures for Examination of Answers to Questionnaire

Defense Industry Questionnaire on Business Ethics and Conduct

Before performing procedures, the practitioner should read the *Defense Industry Initiatives on Business Ethics and Conduct*.

1. Does the Company have a written Code of Business Ethics and Conduct?

   Determine whether the Company has a written Code of Business Ethics and Conduct.

2. Is the Code distributed to all employees principally involved in defense work?

   a. Determine by inquiry of Company officials and/or by reading relevant documentation how the Company distributes the Code to all employees principally involved in defense work.

   b. Obtain additional evidential matter, by positive confirmation of a selected number of employees or by other means, that the Code was distributed to employees principally involved in defense work.

3. Are new employees provided any orientation to the Code?

   a. Determine by inquiry of Company officials and/or by reading relevant documentation how the Company provides an orientation to the Code to new employees.

   b. Obtain additional evidential matter, by positive confirmation of a selected number of employees hired during the reporting period or by other means, that an orientation to the Code was provided at time of employment.

4. Does the Code assign responsibility to operating management and others for compliance with the Code?

   Read the Code to determine whether it includes (*a*) the assignment of responsibility for compliance with the Code to operating management and others, and (*b*) a statement of the standards that govern the conduct of all employees in their relationships to the Company.

5. Does the Company conduct employee training programs regarding the Code?

   a. Determine by inquiry of Company officials and/or by reading relevant documentation how the Company conducts training programs regarding the Code.

   b. Obtain additional evidential matter, by positive confirmation of a selected number of employees or by other means, that the Company conducted employee training programs regarding the Code for employees principally involved in defense work.

6. Does the Code address standards that govern the conduct of employees in their dealings with suppliers, consultants and customers?

Read the Code to determine whether it addresses standards that govern the conduct of employees in their dealings with suppliers, consultants, and customers.

7. Is there a corporate review board, ombudsman, corporate compliance or ethics office or similar mechanism for employees to report suspected violations to someone other than their direct supervisor, if necessary?

   Determine by inquiry of Company officials, observation, and/or by reading relevant documentation whether a corporate review board, ombudsman, corporate compliance or ethics office, or similar mechanism exists for employees to report suspected violations.

8. Does the mechanism employed protect the confidentiality of employee reports?

   a. Determine by inquiry of members of the corporate review board, ombudsman, corporate compliance or ethics office, or similar mechanism established by the Company whether they understand the need to protect the confidentiality of employee reports.

   b. Determine by inquiry of Company officials and/or by reading relevant documentation how the procedures employed protect this confidentiality.

9. Is there an appropriate mechanism to follow-up on reports of suspected violations to determine what occurred, who was responsible, and recommended corrective and other actions?

   a. Determine by inquiry of Company officials and/or by reading relevant documentation how the follow-up procedures established by the Company operate and whether an appropriate mechanism exists to follow-up on reports of suspected violations reported to a corporate review board, ombudsman, corporate compliance or ethics office, or similar mechanism to determine what occurred, who was responsible, and recommended corrective and other action.

   b. Determine by inquiry of those responsible for performing such follow-up procedures how they document that the procedures were carried out.

   c. Obtain additional evidential matter that the follow-up mechanism was employed by examining a selected number of reports of suspected violations from the log or other record of reports used by the corporate review board, ombudsman, corporate compliance or ethics office, or similar mechanism.

10. Is there an appropriate mechanism for letting employees know the result of any follow-up into their reported charges?

   a. Determine by inquiry of Company officials and/or by reading relevant documentation whether an appropriate mechanism exists for letting employees know the result of any follow-up into their reported charges.

   b. For those items selected at Question 9 above, determine by inquiry of members of the corporate review board, ombudsman, corporate compliance or ethics office, or similar mechanism and by examining other evidential matter whether the results of the Company's follow-up of reported charges have been communicated to employees.

11. Is there an ongoing program of communication to employees, spelling out and re-emphasizing their obligations under the Code of conduct?

and

12. What are the specifics of such a program?
    - A. Written communication?
    - B. One-on-one communication?
    - C. Group meetings?
    - D. Visual aids?
    - E. Others?
        - *a.* Determine by inquiry of Company officials and/or by reading relevant documentation the extent of the Company's ongoing program of communication to employees, spelling out and re-emphasizing their obligations under the Code. Note the specific means of communication and compare to the Company's response to Question 12 of the *Questionnaire*.
        - *b.* Read announcements and other evidential matter in support of the actual program of re-emphasis.

13. Does the Company have a procedure for voluntarily reporting violations of federal procurement laws to appropriate governmental agencies?

    Determine by inquiry of Company officials and/or by reading relevant documentation how the Company's procedures operate for determining whether violations of federal procurement laws are to be reported to appropriate governmental agencies and examine evidential matter to determine whether such procedures are being implemented.

14. Is implementation of the Code's provisions one of the standards by which all levels of supervision are expected to be measured in their performance?
    - *a.* Determine by inquiry of Company officials and/or by reading relevant documentation, such as position descriptions and personnel policies, whether performance evaluations are to consider supervisors' efforts in the implementation of the Code's provisions as a standard of measurement of their performance.
    - *b.* Obtain additional evidential matter to determine that supervisors are responsible for implementation of the Code's provisions.

15. Is there a program to monitor on a continuing basis adherence to the Code of conduct and compliance with federal procurement laws?
    - *a.* Determine by inquiry of Company officials and/or by reading relevant documentation how the Company monitors, on a continuing basis, adherence to the Code and compliance with federal procurement laws.
    - *b.* Obtain additional evidential matter, for example by reading internal audit reports, of the Company's monitoring of compliance with the Code and federal procurement laws.

16. Does the Company participate in the industry's "Best Practices Forum"?

Examine evidence of the Company's participation in the "Best Practices Forum."

17. Are periodic reports on adherence to the principles made to the Company's board of directors or to its audit or other appropriate committee?

    Determine by inquiry of Company officials and/or by reading minutes of the board of directors or audit or other appropriate committee meetings or other relevant documentation whether Company officials have reported on adherence to the principles of business ethics and conduct.

18. Are the Company's independent public accountants or a similar independent organization required to comment to the board of directors or a committee thereof on the efficacy of the Company's internal procedures for implementing the Company's Code of conduct?

    Determine by inquiry of Company officials and/or by reading relevant documentation whether the Company's independent accountants or a similar independent organization are required to comment to the board of directors or a committee thereof on the efficacy of the Company's internal procedures for implementing the Company's Code.

19. Does the Company have a code of conduct provision or associated policy addressing marketing activities?

    Read the Code or associated policy to determine whether it addresses the following marketing activities.

    a. The gathering of competitive information and the engagement and use of consultants (whether engaged in bid and proposal activity, marketing, research and development, engineering, or other tasks).

    b. A description of limitations on information which employees or consultants seek or receive.

20. Does the Company have a code of conduct provision or associated policy requiring that consultants are governed by, and oriented regarding, the Company's code of conduct and relevant associated policies?

    a. Read the Code or associated policy to determine whether consultants engaged in marketing activities are governed by it.

    b. Determine by inquiry of Company officials and/or by reading relevant documentation how the Company orients consultants engaged in marketing activities to the Code and relevant associated policies.

    c. Obtain additional evidential matter, by positive confirmation of a selected number of consultants engaged in marketing activities or by other means, that the Company oriented such consultants to the Code and relevant associated policies.

.28

Appendix B

Illustrative Defense Contractor Assertions and Examination Reports

Defense Industry Questionnaire on Business Ethics and Conduct

Illustration 1: Unqualified Opinion

Defense Contractor Assertion

Statement of Responses to the Defense Industry Questionnaire on *Business Ethics and Conduct for the period from* __________ *to* __________.

The affirmative responses in the accompanying *Questionnaire on Business Ethics and Conduct with Responses by the XYZ Company for the period from* __________ *to* __________ are based on policies and programs in operation for that period and are appropriately presented in conformity with the criteria set forth in the *Defense Industry Initiatives on Business Ethics and Conduct*, including the Questionnaire.

Attachments:

Defense Industry Initiatives on Business Ethics and Conduct

Questionnaire on Business Ethics and Conduct with Responses by the XYZ Company for the period from __________ to __________.

Examination Report

To the Board of Directors of the XYZ Company

We have examined the XYZ Company's *Statement of Responses to the Defense Industry Questionnaire on Business Ethics and Conduct for the period from* __________ *to* __________, and the Questionnaire and responses attached thereto. Our examination was made in accordance with standards established by the American Institute of Certified Public Accountants and, accordingly, included such procedures as we considered necessary in the circumstances. Those procedures were designed to evaluate whether the XYZ Company had policies and programs in operation during that period that support the affirmative responses to the *Questionnaire*. The procedures were not designed, however, to evaluate whether the aforementioned policies and programs operated effectively to ensure compliance with the Company's *Code of Business Ethics and Conduct* on the part of individual employees or to evaluate the extent to which the Company or its employees have complied with federal procurement laws, and we do not express an opinion or any other form of assurance thereon.

In our opinion, the affirmative responses in the Questionnaire accompanying the *Statement of Responses to the Defense Industry Questionnaire on Business Ethics and Conduct for the period from* __________ *to* __________ referred to above are appropriately presented in conformity with the criteria set forth in the *Defense Industry Initiatives on Business Ethics and Conduct*, including the Questionnaire.

Illustration 2: Unqualified Opinion; Report Modified for Negative Responses

Defense Contractor Assertion

Statement of Responses to the Defense Industry Questionnaire on *Business Ethics and Conduct for the period from __________ to __________.*

The affirmative responses in the accompanying *Questionnaire on Business Ethics and Conduct with Responses by the XYZ Company for the period from __________ to __________* are based on policies and programs in operation for that period and are appropriately presented in conformity with the criteria set forth in the *Defense Industry Initiatives on Business Ethics and Conduct,* including the Questionnaire.

Attachments:

Defense Industry Initiatives on Business Ethics and Conduct

Questionnaire on Business Ethics and Conduct with Responses by the XYZ Company for the period from __________ to __________.

(The responses could include an explanation of negative responses if the defense contractor so desired.)

Examination Report

To the Board of Directors of the XYZ Company

We have examined the XYZ Company's *Statement of Responses to the Defense Industry Questionnaire on Business Ethics and Conduct for the period from __________ to __________*, and the Questionnaire and responses attached thereto. Our examination was made in accordance with standards established by the American Institute of Certified Public Accountants and, accordingly, included such procedures as we considered necessary in the circumstances. Those procedures were designed to evaluate whether the XYZ Company had policies and programs in operation during that period that support the affirmative responses to the *Questionnaire*. The procedures were not designed, however, to evaluate whether the aforementioned policies and programs operated effectively to ensure compliance with the Company's *Code of Business Ethics and Conduct* on the part of individual employees or to evaluate the extent to which the Company or its employees have complied with federal procurement laws, and we do not express an opinion or any other form of assurance thereon.

In our opinion, the affirmative responses in the Questionnaire accompanying the *Statement of Responses to the Defense Industry Questionnaire on Business Ethics and Conduct for the period from __________ to __________* referred to above are appropriately presented in conformity with the criteria set forth in the *Defense Industry Initiatives on Business Ethics and Conduct,* including the Questionnaire. The negative responses to Questions __________ and __________ in the Questionnaire indicate that the Company did not have policies and programs in operation during the period with respect to those areas.

Illustration 3: Opinion Modified for Exception on Certain Response

Defense Contractor Assertion

Statement of Responses to the Defense Industry Questionnaire on *Business Ethics and Conduct for the period from __________ to __________.*

The affirmative responses in the accompanying Questionnaire on Business Ethics and Conduct with Responses by the XYZ Company for the period from __________ to __________, are based on policies and programs in operation for that period and are appropriately presented in conformity with the criteria set forth in the *Defense Industry Initiatives on Business Ethics and Conduct*, including the Questionnaire.

Attachments:

Defense Industry Initiatives on Business Ethics and Conduct

Questionnaire on Business Ethics and Conduct with Responses by the XYZ Company for the period from __________ to __________.

Examination Report

To the Board of Directors of the XYZ Company

We have examined the XYZ Company's *Statement of Responses to the Defense Industry Questionnaire on Business Ethics and Conduct for the period from __________ to __________*, and the Questionnaire and responses attached thereto. Our examination was made in accordance with standards established by the American Institute of Certified Public Accountants and, accordingly, included such procedures as we considered necessary in the circumstances. Those procedures were designed to evaluate whether the XYZ Company had policies and programs in operation during that period that support the affirmative responses to the Questionnaire. The procedures were not designed, however, to evaluate whether the aforementioned policies and programs operated effectively to ensure compliance with the Company's Code of Business Ethics and Conduct on the part of individual employees or to evaluate the extent to which the Company or its employees have complied with federal procurement laws, and we do not express an opinion or any other form of assurance thereon.

In our opinion, except for the response to Question 10 as discussed in the following paragraph, the affirmative responses in the Questionnaire accompanying the *Statement of Responses to the Defense Industry Questionnaire on Business Ethics and Conduct for the period from __________ to __________* referred to above are appropriately presented in conformity with the criteria set forth in the Defense Industry Initiatives on Business Ethics and Conduct, including the Questionnaire.

Management believes that an appropriate mechanism exists for informing employees of the results of the Company's follow-up into charges of violations of the Company's Code of Business Ethics and Conduct, and has accordingly answered Question 10 in the affirmative. That mechanism consists principally of distributing newspaper articles and press releases of violations of federal procurement laws that have been voluntarily reported to the appropriate governmental agencies. We do not believe that such a mechanism is sufficient, in as much as it does not provide follow-up information on violations reported by employees that are not deemed reportable to a governmental agency. Consequently, in our opinion, the affirmative response to Question 10 in the Questionnaire is not appropriately presented in conformity with the criteria set forth in the *Defense Industry Initiatives on Business Ethics and Conduct*, including the Questionnaire.

Illustration 4: Opinion Modified for Exception on Certain Response; Report also Modified for Negative Responses

Defense Contractor Assertion

Statement of Responses to the *Defense Industry Questionnaire on Business Ethics and Conduct for the period from __________ to __________*.

The affirmative responses in the accompanying *Questionnaire on Business Ethics and Conduct with Responses by the XYZ Company for the period from* __________ *to* __________ are based on policies and programs in operation for that period and are appropriately presented in conformity with the criteria set forth in the *Defense Industry Initiatives on Business Ethics and Conduct*, including the Questionnaire.

Attachments:

Defense Industry Initiatives on Business Ethics and Conduct

Questionnaire on Business Ethics and Conduct with Responses by the XYZ Company for the period from __________ to __________.

(The responses could include an explanation of negative responses if the defense contractor so desired.)

Examination Report

To the Board of Directors of the XYZ Company

We have examined the XYZ Company's *Statement of Responses to the Defense Industry Questionnaire on Business Ethics and Conduct for the period from* __________ *to* __________, and the Questionnaire and responses attached thereto. Our examination was made in accordance with standards established by the American Institute of Certified Public Accountants and, accordingly, included such procedures as we considered necessary in the circumstances. Those procedures were designed to evaluate whether the XYZ Company had policies and programs in operation during that period that support the affirmative responses to the *Questionnaire*. The procedures were not designed, however, to evaluate whether the aforementioned policies and programs operated effectively to ensure compliance with the Company's *Code of Business Ethics and Conduct* on the part of individual employees or to evaluate the extent to which the Company or its employees have complied with federal procurement laws, and we do not express an opinion or any other form of assurance thereon.

In our opinion, except for the response to Question 10 as discussed in the following paragraph, the affirmative responses in the Questionnaire accompanying the *Statement of Responses to the Defense Industry Questionnaire on Business Ethics and Conduct for the period from* __________ *to* __________ referred to above are appropriately presented in conformity with the criteria set forth in the *Defense Industry Initiatives on Business Ethics and Conduct*, including the Questionnaire. The negative responses to Questions __________ and __________ in the Questionnaire indicate that the Company did not have policies and programs in operation during the period with respect to those areas.

Management believes that an appropriate mechanism exists for informing employees of the results of the Company's follow-up into charges of violations of the Company's Code of Business Ethics and Conduct, and has accordingly answered Question 10 in the affirmative. That mechanism consists principally of distributing newspaper articles and press releases of violations of federal procurement laws that have been voluntarily reported to the appropriate governmental agencies. We do not believe that such a mechanism is sufficient, in as much as it does not provide follow-up information on violations reported by employees that are not deemed reportable to a governmental agency. Consequently, in our opinion, the affirmative response to Question 10 in the Questionnaire is not appropriately presented in conformity with the criteria set forth in the Defense Industry Initiatives on Business Ethics and Conduct, including the Questionnaire.

Illustration 5: Opinion Disclaimed on Certain Responses Because of Scope Restrictions Imposed by Client

Defense Contractor Assertion

Statement of Responses to the Defense Industry Questionnaire on *Business Ethics and Conduct for the period from __________ to __________.*

The affirmative responses in the accompanying *Questionnaire on Business Ethics and Conduct with Responses by the XYZ Company for the period from __________ to __________* are based on policies and programs in operation for that period and are appropriately presented in conformity with the criteria set forth in the *Defense Industry Initiatives on Business Ethics and Conduct,* including the Questionnaire.

Attachments:

Defense Industry Initiatives on Business Ethics and Conduct

Questionnaire on Business Ethics and Conduct with Responses by the XYZ Company for the period from __________ to __________.

Examination Report

To the Board of Directors of the XYZ Company

We have examined the XYZ Company's *Statement of Responses to the Defense Industry Questionnaire on Business Ethics and Conduct for the period from __________ to __________,* and the Questionnaire and responses attached thereto. Except as explained in the following paragraph, our examination was made in accordance with standards established by the American Institute of Certified Public Accountants and, accordingly, included such procedures as we considered necessary in the circumstances. Those procedures were designed to evaluate whether the XYZ Company had policies and programs in operation during that period that support the affirmative responses to the *Questionnaire.* The procedures were not designed, however, to evaluate whether the aforementioned policies and programs operated effectively to ensure compliance with the Company's *Code of Business Ethics and Conduct* on the part of individual employees or to evaluate the extent to which the Company or its employees have complied with federal procurement laws, and we do not express an opinion or any other form of assurance thereon.

We were not permitted to read relevant documents and files or interview appropriate employees to determine that the affirmative answers to Questions 8, 9, and 10 are appropriate. The nature of those questions precluded us from satisfying ourselves as to the appropriateness of those answers by means of other examination procedures.

In our opinion, the affirmative responses to Questions 1 through 7 and 11 through 18 in the Questionnaire accompanying the *Statement of Responses to the Defense Industry Questionnaire on Business Ethics and Conduct for the period from __________ to __________* referred to above are appropriately presented in conformity with the criteria set forth in the *Defense Industry Initiatives on Business Ethics and Conduct,* including the Questionnaire. Because of the matters discussed in the preceding paragraph, the scope of our work was not sufficient to express, and we do not express, an opinion on the appropriateness of the affirmative responses to Questions 8, 9, and 10 in the Questionnaire.

.29

Appendix C

Background

Defense Industry Questionnaire on Business Ethics and Conduct

The June 1986 final report to the President of the United States, *A Quest for Excellence*, by the President's Blue Ribbon Commission on Defense Management (the "Packard Commission") included as an appendix the *Defense Industry Initiatives on Business Ethics and Conduct (Initiatives)* written by leaders in the defense industry and signed by many of the country's major defense contractors. The *Initiatives*, which were endorsed by the Packard Commission, set forth six principles of business ethics and conduct, which signatories to the *Initiatives* are committed to adopt and implement.

The sixth principle of business ethics and conduct specifies that "Each company must have public accountability for its commitment to these principles." The section of the *Initiatives* on implementation contains the following discussion of the sixth principle:

> The mechanism for public accountability will require each company to have its independent public accountants or similar independent organization complete and submit annually the attached questionnaire to an external independent body which will report the results for the industry as a whole and release the data simultaneously to the companies and the general public.
>
> This annual review, which will be conducted for the next three years, is a critical element giving force to these principles and adding integrity to this defense industry initiative as a whole. Ethical accountability, as a good-faith process, should not be affirmed behind closed doors. The defense industry is confronted with a problem of public perception—a loss of confidence in its integrity—that must be addressed publicly if the results are to be both real and credible, to the government and public alike. It is in this spirit of public accountability that this initiative has been adopted and these principles have been established.

Appendix D to this Interpretation [paragraph .30] reproduces in full the *Initiatives*, including the *Questionnaire on Business Ethics and Conduct (Questionnaire)*.

Representatives of the signatories to the *Initiatives* have agreed that the defense contractor assertion illustrated in Appendix B and Appendix F [paragraphs .28 and .32], with the attachments thereto, is the appropriate vehicle for meeting the sixth principle referred to above. They also have agreed that each signatory should adopt and implement a code of business ethics and conduct that, in a self-contained document, addresses all of the required provisions of the six principles. In 1987, representatives of the signatories to the Initiatives created the External Independent Organization of the Defense Industry (EIODI) as the body to receive responses to the Questionnaire, report the results for the defense industry as a whole, and release the data to the companies and the public. The Auditing Standards Division of the American Institute of Certified Public Accountants, the EIODI, and representatives of the signatories to the *Initiatives* have agreed to a framework, which is embodied in this Interpretation, in which practitioners can accept engagements to attest to the answers to the *Questionnaire* and issue reports on the results of those engagements.

.30

Appendix D

Defense Industry Initiatives on Business Ethics and Conduct and Questionnaire on Business Ethics and Conduct*

Business Ethics and Conduct

The defense industry companies who sign this document already have, or commit to adopt and implement, a set of principles of business ethics and conduct that acknowledge and address their corporate responsibilities under federal procurement laws and to the public. Further, they accept the responsibility to create an environment in which compliance with federal procurement laws and free, open, and timely reporting of violations become the felt responsibility of every employee in the defense industry.

In addition to adopting and adhering to this set of six principles of business ethics and conduct, we will take the leadership in making the principles a standard for the entire defense industry.

I. Principles

1. Each company will have and adhere to a written code of business ethics and conduct.
2. The company's code establishes the high values expected of its employees and the standard by which they must judge their own conduct and that of their organization; each company will train its employees concerning their personal responsibilities under the code.
3. Each company will create a free and open atmosphere that allows and encourages employees to report violations of its code to the company without fear of retribution for such reporting.
4. Each company has the obligation to self-govern by monitoring compliance with federal procurement laws and adopting procedures for voluntary disclosure of violations of federal procurement laws and corrective actions taken.
5. Each company has a responsibility to each of the other companies in the industry to live by standards of conduct that preserve the integrity of the defense industry.
6. Each company must have public accountability for its commitment to these principles.

II. Implementation: Supporting Programs

While all companies pledge to abide by the six principles, each company agrees that it has implemented or will implement policies and programs to meet its management needs.

Principle 1: Written Code of Business Ethics and Conduct

A company's code of business ethics and conduct should embody the values that it and its employees hold most important; it is the highest expression of a corporation's culture. For a defense contractor, the code represents the commitment of the company and its employees to work for its customers, shareholders, *and* the nation.

---

* From *A Quest for Excellence*, appendix, final report by the President's Blue Ribbon Commission on Defense Management, June 1986.

It is important, therefore, that a defense contractor's written code explicitly address that higher commitment. It must also include a statement of the standards that govern the conduct of all employees in their relationships to the company, as well as in their dealings with customers, suppliers, and consultants. The statement also must include an explanation of the consequences of violating those standards, and a clear assignment of responsibility to operating management and others for monitoring and enforcing the standards throughout the company.

Defense industry marketing practices, including the gathering of competitive information and the engagement and use of consultants (whether engaged in bid and proposal activity, marketing, research and development, engineering, or other tasks), should be explicitly addressed. There should be a description of limitations on information which employees or consultants seek or receive. Where consultants are engaged, the company's code of conduct or policies should require that the consultants are governed by, and oriented regarding, the company's code of conduct and relevant associated policies.

Principle 2: Employees' Ethical Responsibilities

A company's code of business ethics and conduct should embody the basic values and culture of a company and should become a way of life, a form of honor system, for every employee. Only if the code is embodied in some form of honor system does it become more than mere words or abstract ideals. Adherence to the code becomes a responsibility of each employee both to the company and to fellow employees. Failure to live by the code, or to report infractions, erodes the trust essential to personal accountability and an effective corporate business ethics system.

Codes of business ethics and conduct are effective only if they are fully understood by every employee. Communications and training are critical to preparing employees to meet their ethical responsibilities. Companies can use a wide variety of methods to communicate their codes and policies and to educate their employees as to how to fulfill their obligations. Whatever methods are used—broad distribution of written codes, personnel orientation programs, group meetings, videotapes, and articles—it is critical that they ensure total coverage.

Principle 3: Corporate Responsibility to Employees

Every company must ensure that employees have the opportunity to fulfill their responsibility to preserve the integrity of the code and their honor system. Employees should be free to report suspected violations of the code to the company without fear of retribution for such reporting.

To encourage the surfacing of problems, normal management channels should be supplemented by a confidential reporting mechanism.

It is critical that companies create and maintain an environment of openness where disclosures are accepted and expected. Employees must believe that to raise a concern or report misconduct is expected, accepted, and protected behavior, not the exception. This removes any legitimate rationale for employees to delay reporting alleged violations or for former employees to allege past offenses by former employers or associates.

To receive and investigate employee allegations of violations of the corporate code of business ethics and conduct, defense contractors can use a contract review board, an ombudsman, a corporate ethics or compliance office or other similar mechanism.

In general, the companies accept the broadest responsibility to create an environment in which free, open and timely reporting of any suspected violations becomes the felt responsibility of every employee.

Principle 4: Corporate Responsibility to the Government

It is the responsibility of each company to aggressively self-govern and monitor adherence to its code and to federal procurement laws. Procedures will be established by each company for voluntarily reporting to appropriate government authorities violations of federal procurement laws and corrective actions.

In the past, major importance has been placed on whether internal company monitoring has uncovered deficiencies before discovery by governmental audit. The process will be more effective if all monitoring efforts are viewed as mutually reinforcing and the measure of performance is a timely and constructive surfacing of issues.

Corporate and government audit and control mechanisms should be used to identify and correct problems. Government and industry share this responsibility and must work together cooperatively and constructively to ensure compliance with federal procurement laws and to clarify any ambiguities that exist.

Principle 5: Corporate Responsibility to the Defense Industry

Each company must understand that rigorous self-governance is the foundation of these principles of business ethics and conduct and of the public's perception of the integrity of the defense industry.

Since methods of accountability can be improved through shared experience and adaptation, companies will participate in an annual intercompany "Best Practices Forum" that will bring together operating and staff managers from across the industry to discuss ways to implement the industry's principles of accountability.

Each company's compliance with the principles will be reviewed by a Board of Directors committee comprised of outside directors.

Principle 6: Public Accountability

The mechanism for public accountability will require each company to have its independent public accountants or similar independent organization complete and submit annually the attached questionnaire to an external independent body which will report the results for the industry as a whole and release the data simultaneously to the companies and the general public.

This annual review, which will be conducted for the next three years, is a critical element giving force to these principles and adding integrity to this defense industry initiative as a whole. Ethical accountability, as a good-faith process, should not be affirmed behind closed doors. The defense industry is confronted with a problem of public perception—a loss of confidence in its integrity—that must be addressed publicly if the results are to be both real and credible, to the government and public alike. It is in this spirit of public accountability that this initiative has been adopted and these principles have been established.

Questionnaire

1. Does the company have a written code of business ethics and conduct?
2. Is the code distributed to all employees principally involved in defense work?

3. Are new employees provided any orientation to the code?
4. Does the code assign responsibility to operating management and others for compliance with the code?
5. Does the company conduct employee training programs regarding the code?
6. Does the code address standards that govern the conduct of employees in their dealings with suppliers, consultants and customers?
7. Is there a corporate review board, ombudsman, corporate compliance or ethics office or similar mechanism for employees to report suspected violations to someone other than their direct supervisor, if necessary?
8. Does the mechanism employed protect the confidentiality of employee reports?
9. Is there an appropriate mechanism to follow-up on reports of suspected violations to determine what occurred, who was responsible, and recommended corrective and other actions?
10. Is there an appropriate mechanism for letting employees know the result of any follow-up into their reported charges?
11. Is there an ongoing program of communication to employees, spelling out and re-emphasizing their obligations under the code of conduct?
12. What are the specifics of such a program?
    a. Written communication?
    b. One-on-one communication?
    c. Group meetings?
    d. Visual aids?
    e. Others?
13. Does the company have a procedure for voluntarily reporting violations of federal procurement laws to appropriate governmental agencies?
14. Is implementation of the code's provisions one of the standards by which all levels of supervision are expected to be measured in their performance?
15. Is there a program to monitor on a continuing basis adherence to the code of conduct and compliance with federal procurement laws?
16. Does the company participate in the industry's "Best Practices Forum"?
17. Are periodic reports on adherence to the principles made to the company's Board of Directors or to its audit or other appropriate committee?
18. Are the company's independent public accountants or a similar independent organization required to comment to the Board of Directors or a committee thereof on the efficacy of the company's internal procedures for implementing the company's code of conduct?
19. Does the Company have a code of conduct provision or associated policy addressing marketing activities?
20. Does the Company have a code of conduct provision or associated policy requiring that consultants are governed by, and oriented re-

garding, the Company's code of conduct and relevant associated policies?

Signatories to the *Initiatives* are required to initially respond to questions 19 and 20 in the *Questionnaire* for the reporting year ending September 30, 1989. The responses to questions 19 and 20 should cover at least the period from July 1, 1989 through September 30, 1989.

.31

Appendix E

Illustrative Procedures for Review of Answers to Questionnaire

Defense Industry Questionnaire on Business Ethics and Conduct

Before performing procedures, the practitioner should read the *Defense Industry Initiatives on Business Ethics and Conduct.*

1. Does the Company have a written Code of Business Ethics and Conduct?

   Determine whether the Company has a written Code of Business Ethics and Conduct.

2. Is the Code distributed to all employees principally involved in defense work?

   Determine by inquiry of Company officials and/or by reading relevant documentation how the Company distributes the Code to all employees principally involved in defense work.

3. Are new employees provided any orientation to the Code?

   Determine by inquiry of Company officials and/or by reading relevant documentation how the Company provides an orientation to the Code to new employees.

4. Does the Code assign responsibility to operating management and others for compliance with the Code?

   Read the Code to determine whether it includes (a) the assignment of responsibility for compliance with the Code to operating management and others, and (b) a statement of the standards that govern the conduct of all employees in their relationships to the Company.

5. Does the Company conduct employee training programs regarding the Code?

   Determine by inquiry of Company officials and/or by reading relevant documentation how the Company conducts training programs regarding the Code.

6. Does the Code address standards that govern the conduct of employees in their dealings with suppliers, consultants and customers?

   Read the Code to determine whether it addresses standards that govern the conduct of employees in their dealings with suppliers, consultants, and customers.

7. Is there a corporate review board, ombudsman, corporate compliance or ethics office or similar mechanism for employees to report suspected violations to someone other than their direct supervisor, if necessary?

   Determine by inquiry of Company officials and/or by reading relevant documentation whether a corporate review board, ombudsman, corporate compliance or ethics office, or similar mechanism exists for employees to report suspected violations.

8. Does the mechanism employed protect the confidentiality of employee reports?

a. Determine by inquiry of members of the corporate review board, ombudsman, corporate compliance or ethics office, or similar mechanism established by the Company whether they understand the need to protect the confidentiality of employee reports.

b. Determine by inquiry of Company officials and/or by reading relevant documentation how the procedures employed protect this confidentiality.

9. Is there an appropriate mechanism to follow-up on reports of suspected violations to determine what occurred, who was responsible, and recommended corrective and other actions?

   Determine by inquiry of Company officials and/or by reading relevant documentation how the follow-up procedures established by the Company operate and whether an appropriate mechanism exists to follow-up on reports of suspected violations reported to a corporate review board, ombudsman, corporate compliance or ethics office, or similar mechanism to determine what occurred, who was responsible, and recommended corrective and other action.

10. Is there an appropriate mechanism for letting employees know the result of any follow-up into their reported charges?

    a. Determine by inquiry of Company officials and/or by reading relevant documentation whether an appropriate mechanism exists for letting employees know the result of any follow-up into their reported charges.

    b. Determine by inquiry of members of the corporate review board, ombudsman, corporate compliance of ethics office, or similar mechanism whether the results of the Company's follow-up of reported charges have been communicated to employees.

11. Is there an ongoing program of communication to employees, spelling out and re-emphasizing their obligations under the Code of conduct?

and

12. What are the specifics of such a program?

    A. Written communication?

    B. One-on-one communication?

    C. Group meetings?

    D. Visual aids?

    E. Others?

    Determine by inquiry of Company officials and/or by reading relevant documentation the extent of the Company's ongoing program of communication to employees, spelling out and re-emphasizing their obligations under the Code. Note the specific means of communication and compare to the Company's response to Question 12 of the Questionnaire.

13. Does the Company have a procedure for voluntarily reporting violations of federal procurement laws to appropriate governmental agencies?

    Determine by inquiry of Company officials and/or by reading relevant documentation how the Company's procedures operate for determining whether violations of federal procurement laws are to be reported to appropriate governmental agencies.

14. Is implementation of the Code's provisions one of the standards by which all levels of supervision are expected to be measured in their performance?

    Determine by inquiry of Company officials and/or by reading relevant documentation, such as position descriptions and personnel policies, whether performance evaluations are to consider supervisors' efforts in the implementation of the Code's provisions as a standard of measurement of their performance.

15. Is there a program to monitor on a continuing basis adherence to the Code of Conduct and compliance with federal procurement laws?

    Determine by inquiry of Company officials and/or by reading relevant documentation how the Company monitors, on a continuing basis, adherence to the Code and compliance with federal procurement laws.

16. Does the Company participate in the industry's "Best Practices Forum"?

    Determine by inquiry of Company officials and/or by reading relevant documentation whether the Company participated in the "Best Practices Forum."

17. Are periodic reports on adherence to the principles made to the Company's Board of Directors or to its audit or other appropriate committee?

    Determine by inquiry of Company officials and/or by reading minutes of the Board of Directors or audit or other appropriate committee meetings or other relevant documentation whether Company officials have reported on adherence to the principles of business ethics and conduct.

18. Are the Company's independent public accountants or a similar independent organization required to comment to the Board of Directors or a committee thereof on the efficacy of the Company's internal procedures for implementing the Company's Code of Conduct?

    Determine by inquiry of Company officials and/or by reading relevant documentation whether the Company's independent accountants or a similar independent organization are required to comment to the Board of Directors or a committee thereof on the efficacy of the Company's internal procedures for implementing the Company's Code.

19. Does the Company have a code of conduct provision or associated policy addressing marketing activities?

    Read the Code or associated policy to determine whether it addresses the following marketing activities:

    a. The gathering of competitive information and the engagement and use of consultants (whether engaged in bid and proposal activity, marketing, research and development, engineering, or other tasks).

    b. A description of limitations on information which employees or consultants seek or receive.

20. Does the Company have a code of conduct provision or associated policy requiring that consultants are governed by, and oriented regarding, the Company's code of conduct and relevant associated policies?

a. Read the Code or associated policy to determine whether consultants engaged in marketing activities are governed by it.

b. Determine by inquiry of Company officials and/or by reading relevant documentation how the Company orients consultants engaged in marketing activities to the Code and relevant associated policies.

.32

Appendix F

Illustrative Defense Contractor Assertion and Review Report

Defense Industry Questionnaire on Business Ethics and Conduct

Defense Contractor Assertion

Statement of Responses to the Defense Industry Questionnaire on *Business Ethics and Conduct for the period from* __________ *to* __________ .

The affirmative responses in the accompanying *Questionnaire on Business Ethics and Conduct with Responses by the XYZ Company for the period from* __________ *to* __________ are based on policies and programs in operation during that period and are appropriately presented in conformity with the criteria set forth in the *Defense Industry Initiatives on Business Ethics and Conduct*, including the Questionnaire.

Attachments:

Defense Industry Initiatives on Business Ethics and Conduct

Questionnaire on Business Ethics and Conduct with Responses by the XYZ Company for the period from __________ to __________ .

Review Report

To the Board of Directors of the XYZ Company

We have reviewed the XYZ Company's *Statement of Responses to the Defense Industry Questionnaire on Business Ethics and Conduct for the period from* __________ *to* __________ , and the Questionnaire and responses attached thereto. Our review was made in accordance with standards established by the American Institute of Certified Public Accountants. Our review was designed to evaluate whether the XYZ Company had policies and programs in operation during that period that support the affirmative responses to the *Questionnaire*. Our review was not designed, however, to evaluate whether the aforementioned policies and programs operated effectively to ensure compliance with the Company's *Code of Business Ethics and Conduct* on the part of individual employees or to evaluate the extent to which the Company or its employees have complied with federal procurement laws, and we do not express an opinion or any other form of assurance thereon.

A review is substantially less in scope than an examination, the objective of which is the expression of an opinion on the affirmative responses in the Questionnaire accompanying the *Statement of Responses to the Defense Industry Questionnaire on Business Ethics and Conduct for the period from* __________ *to* __________ . Accordingly, we do not express such an opinion.

Based on our review, nothing came to our attention that caused us to believe that the affirmative responses in the Questionnaire accompanying the *Statement of Responses to the Defense Industry Questionnaire on Business Ethics and Conduct for the period from* __________ *to* __________ referred to above are not appropriately presented in conformity with the criteria set forth in the *Defense Industry Initiatives on Business Ethics and Conduct*, including the Questionnaire.

[Issue Date: August, 1987; amended: February, 1989; modified: May, 1989.]

2. Responding to Requests for Reports on Matters Relating to Solvency

.33 *Question*—Lenders, as a requisite to the closing of certain secured financings in connection with leveraged buyouts (LBOs), recapitalizations and certain other financial transactions, have sometimes requested written assurance from an accountant regarding the prospective borrower's solvency and related matters.[1] The lender is concerned that such financings not be considered to include a fraudulent conveyance or transfer under the Federal Bankruptcy Code[2] or the relevant state fraudulent conveyance or transfer statute.[3] If the financing is subsequently determined to have included a fraudulent conveyance or transfer, repayment obligations and security interests may be set aside or subordinated to the claims of other creditors.

.34 May an accountant provide assurance concerning "matters relating to solvency" as hereinafter defined?

.35 *Interpretation*—No. For reasons set forth below, an accountant should not provide any form of assurance, through examination, review or agreed-upon procedures engagements, that an entity

- Is not insolvent at the time the debt is incurred or would not be rendered insolvent thereby.
- Does not have unreasonably small capital.
- Has the ability to pay its debts as they mature.

In the context of particular transactions other terms are sometimes used or defined by the parties as equivalents of or substitutes for the terms listed above (e.g., fair salable value of assets exceeds liabilities). These terms, and those matters listed above, are hereinafter referred to as "matters relating to solvency." The prohibition extends to providing assurance concerning all such terms.

.36 The assertions on which an accountant can provide assurance are limited by the attestation standards included in section 100, *Attestation Stan-*

---

[1] While this interpretation describes requests from secured lenders and summarizes the potential effects of fraudulent conveyance or transfer laws upon such lenders, the interpretation is not limited to requests from lenders. All requests for assurance on matters relating to solvency are governed by this interpretation.

[2] Section 548 of the Federal Bankruptcy Code defines fraudulent transfers and obligations as follows:

"The trustee may avoid any transfer of an interest of the debtor in property or any obligation incurred by the debtor, that was made or incurred on or within one year before the date of the filing of the petition, if the debtor voluntarily or involuntarily—

"(1) made such transfer or incurred such obligation with actual intent to hinder, delay, or defraud any entity to which the debtor was or became, on or after the date that such transfer occurred or such obligation was incurred, indebted; or

"(2)(A) received less than a reasonably equivalent value in exchange for such transfer or obligation; and

"(2)(B)(i) was insolvent on the date that such transfer was made or such obligation was incurred, or became insolvent as a result of such transfer or obligation;

"(2)(B)(ii) was engaged in business or a transaction, or was about to engage in business or a transaction, for which any property remaining with the debtor was an unreasonably small capital; or

"(2)(B)(iii) intended to incur, or believed that the debtor would incur, debts that would be beyond the debtor's ability to pay as such debts matured." (Bankruptcy Law Reporter, 3 vols. [Chicago: Commerce Clearing House, 1986], vol. 1, 1339).

[3] State fraudulent conveyance or transfer statutes such as the Uniform Fraudulent Conveyance Act and the Uniform Fraudulent Transfer Act reflect substantially similar provisions. These state laws may be employed absent a declaration of bankruptcy or by a bankruptcy trustee under section 544(1) of the Federal Bankruptcy Code. While the statute of limitations varies from state to state, in some states financing transactions may be vulnerable to challenge for up to six years from closing.

dards. The third general attestation standard states that the practitioner shall perform the engagement only if he or she has reason to believe that the following conditions exist:

- The assertion is capable of evaluation against reasonable criteria that either have been established by a recognized body or are stated in the presentation of the assertion in a sufficiently clear and comprehensive manner for a knowledgeable reader to be able to understand them.
- The assertion is capable of reasonably consistent estimation or measurement using such criteria.

In addition, the second general attestation standard states that the engagement shall be performed by a practitioner or practitioners having adequate knowledge in the subject matter of the assertion.

.37 The matters relating to solvency mentioned in paragraph .36 above are subject to legal interpretation under, and varying legal definition in, the Federal Bankruptcy Code and various state fraudulent conveyance and transfer statutes. Because these matters are not clearly defined in an accounting sense, and are therefore subject to varying interpretations, they do not provide the accountant with the reasonable criteria required to evaluate the assertion under the third general attestation standard. In addition, lenders are concerned with legal issues on matters relating to solvency and the accountant is generally unable to evaluate or provide assurance on these matters of legal interpretation. Therefore, accountants are precluded from giving any form of assurance on matters relating to solvency or any financial presentation of matters relating to solvency.

.38 The rescinded auditing interpretation titled "Reporting on Solvency," issued in December 1984 (before section 100, which was effective in September 1986), indicated that accountants' solvency letters should contain definitions for the accountant to use in providing negative assurance. While lenders have defined matters relating to solvency in the context of a particular engagement, experience has shown that use of the lender's definitions by the accountant in a solvency letter could be misunderstood as an assurance by the accountant that a particular financing does not include a fraudulent conveyance or transfer under either federal or state law. Further, those who are not aware that the matters relating to solvency have been specifically defined for the engagement may, as a result of being informed that an accountant has issued a report on matters relating to solvency, infer unwarranted assurance therefrom.

.39 Under existing AICPA standards, the accountant may provide a client with various professional services that may be useful to the client in connection with a financing. These services include

- Audit of historical financial statements.
- Review of historical financial information (a review in accordance with AU section 722, *Interim Financial Information*, of interim financial information or in accordance with AR section 100, *Compilation and Review of Financial Statements*).
- Examination or review of pro forma financial information.
- Examination or compilation of prospective financial information (section 200, *Financial Forecasts and Projections*).

.40 In addition, under existing AICPA standards (AU section 622, *Engagements to Apply Agreed-Upon Procedures to Specified Elements, Accounts, or Items of a Financial Statement*, section 100, and section 200), the accountant can provide the client and lender with an agreed-upon procedures report. In such an engagement, a client and lender may request that specified procedures be applied to various financial presentations, such as historical financial information, pro forma financial information and prospective financial information, which can be useful to a client or lender in connection with a financing.

.41 The accountant should be aware that certain of the services described in paragraph .39 require that the accountant have an appropriate level of knowledge of the entity's accounting and financial reporting practices and its internal control structure. This has ordinarily been obtained by the accountant auditing historical financial statements of the entity for the most recent annual period or by otherwise obtaining an equivalent knowledge base. When considering acceptance of an engagement relating to a financing, the accountant should consider whether he or she can perform these services without an equivalent knowledge base.

.42 A report on agreed-upon procedures should not provide any assurances on matters relating to solvency or any financial presentation of matters relating to solvency (e.g., fair salable value of assets less liabilities or fair salable value of assets less liabilities, contingent liabilities and other commitments). An accountant's report on the results of applying agreed-upon procedures should

- State that the service has been requested in connection with a financing (no reference should be made to any solvency provisions in the financing agreement).
- State that the sufficiency of the procedures is the sole responsibility of the client and lender and disclaim responsibility for the sufficiency of those procedures.
- State that no representations are provided regarding questions of legal interpretation.
- State that no assurance is provided concerning the borrower's (1) solvency, (2) adequacy of capital or (3) ability to pay its debts.
- State that the procedures should not be taken to supplant any additional inquiries and procedures that the lender should undertake in its consideration of the proposed financing.
- Where applicable, state that an audit of recent historical financial statements has previously been performed and that no audit of any historical financial statements for a subsequent period has been performed. In addition, if other services have been performed pursuant to paragraph .39, they may be referred to.
- Describe the procedures applied (as applicable) to the historical financial information, prospective financial information or pro forma financial information and the accountant's findings.
- Where applicable, state that the procedures were less in scope than (1) an audit in accordance with generally accepted auditing standards; (2) an examination of pro forma financial information, the objective of which is the expression of an opinion on that information; (3) an examination of prospective financial statements in accordance with standards established by the AICPA, and include an appropriate disclaimer of opinion.

- If procedures have been applied to prospective financial information, state that there will usually be differences between the prospective financial information and actual results, because events and circumstances frequently do not occur as expected, and those differences may be material.
- State that had the accountant performed additional procedures or performed an audit or examination, additional matters might have come to his or her attention that would have been reported.
- State the limitations on the use of the report because it is intended solely for the use of specified parties.
- State that the accountant has no responsibility to update the report.

.43 The report ordinarily is dated at or shortly before the closing date. The financing agreement ordinarily specifies the date, often referred to as the cutoff date, to which the report is to relate (for example, a date three business days before the date of the report). The report should state that the inquiries and other procedures carried out in connection with the report did not cover the period from the cutoff date to the date of the report.

.44 The accountant might consider furnishing the client with a draft of the agreed-upon procedures report. The draft report should deal with all matters expected to be covered in the terms expected to be used in the final report. The draft report should be identified as a draft in order to avoid giving the impression that the procedures described therein have been performed. This practice of furnishing a draft report at an early point permits the accountant to make clear to the client and lender what they may expect the accountant to furnish and gives them an opportunity to change the financing agreement or the agreed-upon procedures if they so desire.

[.45–.46][Superseded, February 1993, by Statement on Auditing Standards No. 72.] (See AU section 634.)[4]

[Issue Date: May, 1988; Amended: February, 1993.]

3. Applicability of Attestation Standards to Litigation Services

.47 *Question*—Section 100, *Attestation Standards*, paragraph .02, provides examples of litigation services provided by practitioners that would not be considered attest engagements as defined by section 100. When does section 100 not apply to litigation service engagements?

.48 *Interpretation*—Section 100 does not apply to litigation services that involve pending or potential formal legal or regulatory proceedings before a "trier of fact"[5] in connection with the resolution of a dispute between two or more parties in any of the following circumstances when the:

a. Practitioner does not issue a written communication that expresses a conclusion about the reliability of a written assertion that is the responsibility of another party.

b. Service comprises being an expert witness.

c. Service comprises being a trier of fact or acting on behalf of one.

---

[4] [Footnote deleted.]

[5] A "trier of fact" in this section means a court, regulatory body, or government authority; their agents; a grand jury; or an arbitrator or mediator of the dispute.

d. Practitioner's work under the rules of the proceedings is subject to detailed analysis and challenge by each party to the dispute.

e. Practitioner is engaged by an attorney to do work that will be protected by the attorney's work product privilege and such work is not intended to be used for other purposes.

When performing such litigation services, the practitioner should comply with Rule 201, *General Standards*, of the AICPA *Code of Professional Conduct* [ET section 201.01].

.49 *Question*—When does section 100 apply to litigation service engagements?

.50 *Interpretation*—Section 100 applies to litigation service engagements when the practitioner:

a. Expresses a written conclusion about the reliability of a written assertion that is the responsibility of another party and that conclusion and assertion are for the use of others who, under the rules of the proceedings, do not have the opportunity to analyze and challenge such work, or

b. In connection with litigation services, is specifically engaged to perform a service in accordance with section 100.

.51 *Question*—Section 100.02*f* provides the following examples of litigation service engagements that are not considered attest engagements:

> Engagements in which a practitioner is engaged to testify as an expert witness in accounting, auditing, taxation, or other matters, given certain stipulated facts.

What does the term "stipulated facts" as used in section 100.02*f* mean?

.52 *Interpretation*—The term "stipulated facts" as used in section 100.02*f* means facts or assumptions that are specified by one or more parties to a dispute to serve as the basis for the development of an expert opinion. It is not used in its typical legal sense of facts agreed to by all parties involved in a dispute.

.53 *Question*—Does Interpretation of Attestation Standards No. 2, *Responding to Requests for Reports on Matters Relating to Solvency* (paragraphs .33 through .46), prohibit a practitioner from providing expert testimony, as described in section 100.02*f* and .02*g*, before a "trier of fact" on matters relating to solvency?

.54 *Interpretation*—No. Matters relating to solvency mentioned in paragraph .35 are subject to legal interpretation under, and varying legal definition in, the Federal Bankruptcy Code and various state fraudulent conveyance and transfer statutes. Because these matters are not clearly defined in an accounting sense, and therefore subject to varying interpretations, they do not provide the practitioner with the reasonable criteria required to evaluate the assertion. Thus, Interpretation of Attestation Standards No. 2, *Responding to Requests for Reports on Matters Relating to Solvency* (paragraphs .33 through .46), prohibits a practitioner from providing any form of assurance in reporting upon examination, review or agreed-upon procedures engagements about matters relating to solvency (as defined in paragraph .35).

.55 However, a practitioner who is involved with pending or potential formal legal or regulatory proceedings before a "trier of fact" in connection with the resolution of a dispute between two or more parties may provide an expert opinion or consulting advice about matters relating to solvency. The prohibition in paragraphs .33 through .46 does not apply in such engagements because as part of the legal or regulatory proceedings, each party to the dispute has the opportunity to analyze and challenge the legal definition and interpretation of the matters relating to solvency and the criteria the practitioner uses to evaluate matters related to solvency. Such services are not intended to be used by others who do not have the opportunity to analyze and challenge such definitions and interpretations.

[Issue Date: July, 1990.]

4. Providing Access to or Photocopies of Working Papers to a Regulator

.56 *Question*—Interpretation No. 1 to AU section 339, *Working Papers*, entitled "Providing Access to or Photocopies of Working Papers to a Regulator" [AU section 9339.01–.15], contains guidance relating to providing access to or photocopies of working papers to a regulator. Is this guidance applicable to an attestation engagement when a regulator requests access to or photocopies of the working papers?

.57 *Interpretation*—Yes. The guidance in Interpretation No. 1 to AU section 339 [AU section 9339.01–.15] is applicable in these circumstances; however, the letter to a regulator should be tailored to meet the individual engagement characteristics or the purpose of the regulatory request, for example, a quality control review. Illustrative letters for an examination engagement performed in accordance with section 500, *Compliance Attestation*, and an agreed-upon procedures engagement performed in accordance with section 600, *Agreed-Upon Procedures Engagements*, follow.

.58 Illustrative letter for examination engagement:

Illustrative Letter to Regulator[6]

(*Date*)

(*Name and Address of Regulatory Agency*)

Your representatives have requested access to our working papers in connection with our engagement to examine management's assertion that (*management's assertion*). It is our understanding that the purpose of your request is (*state purpose:* for example, "to facilitate your regulatory examination").[7]

Our examination was performed in accordance with standards[8] established by the American Institute of Certified Public Accountants, the objective of which is to form an opinion as to whether management's assertion is fairly stated, in all material respects, based on (*identify established or stated criteria*). Under these standards, we have the responsibility to plan and perform our examination to provide a reasonable basis for our opinion and to exercise due professional care in the performance of our examination. Our examination is subject to the inherent risk that material noncompliance, if it exists, would not be detected. In addition, our examination does not address the possibility that

---

[6] The practitioner should appropriately modify this letter when the engagement has been performed in accordance with the Statements on Standards for Attestation Engagements and also in accordance with additional attest requirements specified by a regulatory agency (for example, the requirements specified in *Government Auditing Standards* issued by the Comptroller General of the United States).

[7] If the practitioner is not required by law, regulation, or engagement contract to provide a regulator access to the working papers but otherwise intends to provide such access (see AU section 9339.11–.15), the letter should include a statement that: "Management of (*name of entity*) has authorized us to provide you access to our working papers for (*state purpose*)."

[8] Refer to footnote 6.

material noncompliance may occur in the future. Also, our use of professional judgment and the assessments of attestation risk and materiality for the purpose of our examination means that matters may have existed that would have been assessed differently by you. Our examination does not provide a legal determination on (*name of entity*)'s compliance with specified requirements.

The working papers were prepared for the purpose of providing the principal support for our opinion on management's assertion and to aid in the performance and supervision of our examination. The working papers document the procedures performed, the information obtained, and the pertinent conclusions reached in the examination. The procedures that we performed were limited to those we considered necessary under standards[9] established by the American Institute of Certified Public Accountants to provide us with reasonable basis for our opinion. Accordingly, we make no representation as to the sufficiency or appropriateness, for your purposes, of either the procedures or information documented in our working papers. In addition, any notations, comments, and individual conclusions appearing on any of the working papers do not stand alone and should not be read as an opinion on any part of management's assertion or the related subject matter.

Our examination was performed for the purpose stated above and was not planned or performed in contemplation of your (*state purpose*: for example, "regulatory examination"). Therefore, items of possible interest to you may not have been specifically addressed. Accordingly, our examination, and the working papers prepared in connection therewith, should not supplant other inquiries and procedures that should be undertaken by the (*name of regulatory agency*) for the purpose of monitoring and regulating (*name of entity*). In addition, we have not performed any procedures since the date of our report with respect to management's assertion, and significant events or circumstances may have occurred since that date.

The working papers constitute and reflect work performed or information obtained by us in the course of our examination. The documents contain trade secrets and confidential commercial and financial information of our firm and (*name of entity*) that is privileged and confidential, and we expressly reserve all rights with respect to disclosures to third parties. Accordingly, we request confidential treatment under the Freedom of Information Act or similar laws and regulations when requests are made for the working papers or information contained therein or any documents created by the (*name of regulatory agency*) containing information derived therefrom. We further request that written notice be given to our firm before distribution of the information in the working papers (or photocopies thereof) to others, including other governmental agencies, except when such distribution is required by law or regulation.[10]

[*If it is expected that photocopies will be requested, add:*

Any photocopies of our working papers we agree to provide you will contain a legend "Confidential Treatment Requested by (*name of practitioner, address, telephone number*)."]

Firm signature

---

[9] Refer to footnote 6.

[10] This illustrative paragraph may not in and of itself be sufficient to gain confidential treatment under the rules and regulations of certain regulatory agencies. The practitioner should consider tailoring this paragraph to the circumstances after consulting the regulations of each applicable regulatory agency and, if necessary, consult with legal counsel regarding the specific procedures and requirements necessary to gain confidential treatment.

.59 Example letter for agreed-upon procedures engagements:

Illustrative Letter to Regulator[11]

(*Date*)

(*Name and Address of Regulatory Agency*)

Your representatives have requested access to our working papers in connection with our engagement to perform agreed-upon procedures on management's assertion that (*management's assertion*). It is our understanding that the purpose of your request is (*state purpose*: for example, "to facilitate your regulatory examinations").[12]

Our agreed-upon procedures engagement was performed in accordance with standards[13] established by the American Institute of Certified Public Accountants. Under these standards, we have the responsibility to perform the agreed-upon procedures to provide a reasonable basis for the findings expressed in our report. We were not engaged to, and did not, perform an examination, the objective of which would be to form an opinion on management's assertion. Our engagement is subject to the inherent risk that material misstatement of management's assertion, if it exists, would not be detected. (*The practitioner may add the following*: "In addition, our engagement does not address the possibility that material misstatement of management's assertion may occur in the future.") The procedures that we performed were limited to those agreed to by the specified users, and the sufficiency of these procedures is solely the responsibility of the specified users of the report. Further, our engagement does not provide a legal determination on (*name of entity*)'s compliance with specified requirements.

The working papers were prepared to document the agreed-upon procedures performed, the information obtained, and the pertinent findings reached in the engagement. Accordingly, we make no representation, for your purposes, as to the sufficiency or appropriateness of the information documented in our working papers. In addition, any notations, comments, and individual findings appearing on any of the working papers should not be read as an opinion on management's assertion or the related subject matter, or any part thereof.

Our engagement was performed for the purpose stated above and was not performed in contemplation of your (*state purpose*: for example, "regulatory examination"). Therefore, items of possible interest to you may not have been specifically addressed. Accordingly, our engagement, and the working papers prepared in connection therewith, should not supplant other inquiries and procedures that should be undertaken by the (*name of regulatory agency*) for the purpose of monitoring and regulating (*name of client*). In addition, we have not performed any procedures since the date of our report with respect to management's assertion, and significant events or circumstances may have occurred since that date.

The working papers constitute and reflect work performed or information obtained by us in the course of our engagement. The documents contain trade secrets and confidential commercial and financial information of our firm and (*name of client*) that is privileged and confidential, and we expressly reserve

---

[11] The practitioner should appropriately modify this letter when the engagement has been performed in accordance with the Statements on Standards for Attestation Engagements and also in accordance with additional attest requirements specified by a regulatory agency (for example, the requirements specified in *Government Auditing Standards* issued by the Comptroller General of the United States).

[12] If the practitioner is not required by law, regulation or engagement contract to provide a regulator access to the working papers but otherwise intends to provide such access (see AU section 9339.11–.15) the letter should include a statement that: "Management of (*name of entity*) has authorized us to provide you access to our working papers for (*state purpose*)."

[13] Refer to footnote 6.

all rights with respect to disclosures to third parties. Accordingly, we request confidential treatment under the Freedom of Information Act or similar laws and regulations when requests are made for the working papers or information contained therein or any documents created by the (*name of regulatory agency*) containing information derived therefrom. We further request that written notice be given to our firm before distribution of the information in the working papers (or photocopies thereof) to others, including other governmental agencies, except when such distribution is required by law or regulation.[14]

[*If it is expected that photocopies will be requested, add:*

Any photocopies of our working papers we agree to provide you will contain a legend "Confidential Treatment Requested by (*name of practitioner, address, telephone number*)."]

Firm signature

[Issue Date: May, 1996.]

---

[14] This illustrative paragraph may not in and of itself be sufficient to gain confidential treatment under the rules and regulations of certain regulatory agencies. The practitioner should consider tailoring this paragraph to the circumstances after consulting the regulations of each applicable regulatory agency and, if necessary, consult with legal counsel regarding the specific procedures and requirements necessary to gain confidential treatment.

AT Section 200

Financial Forecasts and Projections

Source: SSAE No. 1; SSAE No. 4.

Effective for engagements in which the date of completion of the accountant's services on prospective financial statements is September 30, 1986, or later, unless otherwise indicated.

.01 This section sets forth standards and provides guidance to accountants concerning performance and reporting for engagements to examine (paragraphs .27 through .48), compile (paragraphs .10 through .26), or apply agreed-upon procedures to (paragraphs .49 through .57) prospective financial statements.[1] This section is not applicable to presentations that do not meet the minimum presentation guidelines in Appendix A [paragraph .67] of this section. Such partial presentations are not deemed to be "prospective financial statements."

.02 Whenever an accountant (*a*) submits, to his client or others, prospective financial statements that he has assembled, or assisted in assembling, that are, or reasonably might be, expected to be used by another (third) party[2] or (*b*) reports on prospective financial statements that are, or reasonably might be, expected to be used by another (third) party, he should perform one of the engagements described in the preceding paragraph. In deciding whether the prospective financial statements are, or reasonably might be, expected to be used by a third party, the accountant may rely on either the written or oral representation of the responsible party, unless information comes to his attention that contradicts the responsible party's representation. If such third party use of the prospective financial statements is not reasonably expected, the provisions of this section are not applicable unless the accountant has been engaged to examine, compile, or apply agreed-upon procedures to the prospective financial statements.

.03 This section does not provide standards or procedures for engagements involving prospective financial statements used solely in connection with litigation support services, although it provides helpful guidance for many aspects of such engagements and may be referred to as useful guidance in such engagements. *Litigation support services* are engagements involving pending or potential formal legal proceedings before a "trier of fact" in connection with the resolution of a dispute between two or more parties, for example, in circumstances where an accountant acts as an expert witness. This exception is provided because, among other things, the accountant's work in such proceedings is ordinarily subject to detailed analysis and challenge by each party to the dispute. This exception does not apply, however, if the prospective financial statements are for use by third parties who, under the rules of the proceedings, do not have the opportunity for such analysis and challenge. For example, creditors may not have such opportunities when prospective financial statements are submitted to them to secure their agreement to a plan of reorganization.

---

[1] Footnote deleted.

[2] However, paragraph .58 permits an exception to this for certain types of budgets.

.04 In reporting on prospective financial statements the accountant may be called on to assist the responsible party in identifying assumptions, gathering information, or assembling the statements.[3] The responsible party is nonetheless responsible for the preparation and presentation of the prospective financial statements because the prospective financial statements are dependent on the actions, plans, and assumptions of the responsible party, and only it can take responsibility for the assumptions. Accordingly, the accountant's engagement should not be characterized in his report or in the document containing his report as including "preparation" of the prospective financial statements. An accountant may be engaged to prepare a financial analysis of a potential project where the engagement includes obtaining the information, making appropriate assumptions, and assembling the presentation. Such an analysis is not, and should not be characterized as, a forecast or projection and would not be appropriate for general use. However, if the responsible party reviewed and adopted the assumptions and presentation, or based its assumptions and presentation on the analysis, the accountant could perform one of the engagements described in this section and issue a report appropriate for general use.

.05 The concept of materiality affects the application of this section to prospective financial statements as materiality affects the application of generally accepted auditing standards to historical financial statements. Materiality is a concept that is judged in light of the expected range of reasonableness of the information; therefore, users should not expect prospective information (information about events that have not yet occurred) to be as precise as historical information.

Definitions

.06 For the purposes of this section the following definitions apply.

Prospective financial statements. Either financial forecasts or financial projections including the summaries of significant assumptions and accounting policies. Although prospective financial statements may cover a period that has partially expired, statements for periods that have completely expired are not considered to be prospective financial statements. Pro forma financial statements[4] and partial presentations[5] are not considered to be prospective financial statements.

Financial forecast. Prospective financial statements that present, to the best of the responsible party's knowledge and belief, an entity's expected financial position, results of operations, and cash flows. A financial forecast is based on the responsible party's assumptions reflecting conditions it expects to exist and the course of action it expects to take. A financial forecast may be expressed in

---

[3] Some of these services may not be appropriate if the accountant is to be named as the person reporting on an examination in a filing with the Securities and Exchange Commission (SEC). SEC Release Nos. 33-5992 and 34-15305, "Disclosure of Projections of Future Economic Performance," state that for prospective financial statements filed with the commission, "a person should not be named as an outside reviewer if he actively assisted in the preparation of the projection."

[4] The objective of pro forma financial information is to show what the significant effects on the historical financial information might have been had a consummated or proposed transaction (or event) occurred at an earlier date. Although the transaction in question may be prospective, this section does not apply to such presentations because they are essentially historical financial statements and do not purport to be prospective financial statements. See section 300, *Reporting on Pro Forma Financial Information*. [Footnote revised, October 1991, to reflect the issuance of Statement on Standards for Attestation Engagements No. 1, *Attestation Standards*, "Reporting on Pro Forma Financial Information."]

[5] Partial presentations are presentations that do not meet the minimum presentation guidelines in paragraph .67 of this section.

specific monetary amounts as a single point estimate of forecasted results or as a range, where the responsible party selects key assumptions to form a range within which it reasonably expects, to the best of its knowledge and belief, the item or items subject to the assumptions to actually fall. When a forecast contains a range, the range is not selected in a biased or misleading manner, for example, a range in which one end is significantly less expected than the other. Minimum presentation guidelines for prospective financial statements are set forth in Appendix A [paragraph .67] of this section.

Financial projection. Prospective financial statements that present, to the best of the responsible party's knowledge and belief, given one or more hypothetical assumptions, an entity's expected financial position, results of operations, and cash flows. A financial projection is sometimes prepared to present one or more hypothetical courses of action for evaluation, as in response to a question such as "What would happen if . . . ?" A financial projection is based on the responsible party's assumptions reflecting conditions it expects would exist and the course of action it expects would be taken, given one or more hypothetical assumptions. A projection, like a forecast, may contain a range. Minimum presentation guidelines for prospective financial statements are set forth in Appendix A [paragraph .67] of this section.

Entity. Any unit, existing or to be formed, for which financial statements could be prepared in accordance with generally accepted accounting principles or another comprehensive basis of accounting.[6] For example, an entity can be an individual, partnership, corporation, trust, estate, association, or governmental unit.

Hypothetical assumption. An assumption used in a financial projection to present a condition or course of action that is not necessarily expected to occur, but is consistent with the purpose of the projection.

Responsible party. The person or persons who are responsible for the assumptions underlying the prospective financial statements. The responsible party usually is management, but it can be persons outside of the entity who do not currently have the authority to direct operations (for example, a party considering acquiring the entity).

Assembly. The manual or computer processing of mathematical or other clerical functions related to the presentation of the prospective financial statements. Assembly does not refer to the mere reproduction and collation of such statements or to the responsible party's use of the accountant's computer processing hardware or software.

Key factors. The significant matters on which an entity's future results are expected to depend. Such factors are basic to the entity's operations and thus encompass matters that affect, among other things, the entity's sales, production, service, and financing activities. Key factors serve as a foundation for prospective financial statements and are the bases for the assumptions.

Uses of Prospective Financial Statements

.07 Prospective financial statements are for either "general use" or "limited use." "General use" of prospective financial statements refers to use of the statements by persons with whom the responsible party is not negotiating directly, for example, in an offering statement of an entity's debt or equity in-

[6] AU section 623, *Special Reports*, discusses comprehensive bases of accounting other than generally accepted accounting principles.

terests. Because recipients of prospective financial statements distributed for general use are unable to ask the responsible party directly about the presentation, the presentation most useful to them is one that portrays, to the best of the responsible party's knowledge and belief, the expected results. Thus, only a financial forecast is appropriate for general use.

.08 "Limited use" of prospective financial statements refers to use of prospective financial statements by the responsible party alone or by the responsible party and third parties with whom the responsible party is negotiating directly. Examples include use in negotiations for a bank loan, submission to a regulatory agency, and use solely within the entity. Third-party recipients of prospective financial statements intended for limited use can ask questions of the responsible party and negotiate terms directly with it. Any type of prospective financial statements that would be useful in the circumstances would normally be appropriate for limited use. Thus, the presentation may be a financial forecast or a financial projection.

.09 Because a financial projection is not appropriate for general use, an accountant should not consent to the use of his name in conjunction with a financial projection that he believes will be distributed to those who will not be negotiating directly with the responsible party, for example, in an offering statement of an entity's debt or equity interests, unless the projection is used to supplement a financial forecast.

Compilation of Prospective Financial Statements

.10 A compilation of prospective financial statements is a professional service that involves—

a. Assembling, to the extent necessary, the prospective financial statements based on the responsible party's assumptions.

b. Performing the required compilation procedures,[7] including reading the prospective financial statements with their summaries of significant assumptions and accounting policies, and considering whether they appear to be (i) presented in conformity with AICPA presentation guidelines[8] and (ii) not obviously inappropriate.

c. Issuing a compilation report.

.11 A compilation is not intended to provide assurance on the prospective financial statements or the assumptions underlying such statements. Because of the limited nature of the accountant's procedures, a compilation does not provide assurance that the accountant will become aware of significant matters that might be disclosed by more extensive procedures, for example, those performed in an examination of prospective financial statements.

.12 The summary of significant assumptions is essential to the reader's understanding of prospective financial statements. Accordingly, the accountant should not compile prospective financial statements that exclude disclosure of the summary of significant assumptions. Also, the accountant should not compile a financial projection that excludes (*a*) an identification of the hypothetical assumptions or (*b*) a description of the limitations on the usefulness of the presentation.

---

[7] See paragraph .68, paragraph 5, for the required procedures.

[8] AICPA presentation guidelines are detailed in the AICPA *Guide for Prospective Financial Information*.

.13 The following standards apply to a compilation of prospective financial statements and to the resulting report:

a. The compilation should be performed by a person or persons having adequate technical training and proficiency to compile prospective financial statements.

b. Due professional care should be exercised in the performance of the compilation and the preparation of the report.

c. The work should be adequately planned, and assistants, if any, should be properly supervised.

d. Applicable compilation procedures should be performed as a basis for reporting on the compiled prospective financial statements. (See paragraph .68 for the procedures to be performed.)

e. The report based on the accountant's compilation of prospective financial statements should conform to the applicable guidance in paragraphs .16 through .26 of this section.

.14 The accountant should consider, after applying the procedures specified in paragraph .68, whether representations or other information he has received appear to be obviously inappropriate, incomplete, or otherwise misleading, and if so, the accountant should attempt to obtain additional or revised information. If he does not receive such information, the accountant should ordinarily withdraw from the compilation engagement.[9] (Note that the omission of disclosures, other than those relating to significant assumptions, would not require the accountant to withdraw, see paragraph .24.)

Working Papers

.15 Although it is not possible to specify the form or content of the working papers that an accountant should prepare in connection with a compilation of prospective financial statements because of the different circumstances of individual engagements, the accountant's working papers ordinarily should indicate that—

a. The work was adequately planned and supervised.

b. The required compilation procedures were performed as a basis for the compilation report.

Reports on Compiled Prospective Financial Statements

.16 The accountant's standard report on a compilation of prospective financial statements should include—

a. An identification of the prospective financial statements presented by the responsible party.

b. A statement that the accountant has compiled the prospective financial statements in accordance with standards established by the American Institute of Certified Public Accountants.

c. A statement that a compilation is limited in scope and does not enable the accountant to express an opinion or any other form of assurance on the prospective financial statements or the assumptions.

d. A caveat that the prospective results may not be achieved.

e. A statement that the accountant assumes no responsibility to update the report for events and circumstances occurring after the date of the report.

---

[9] The accountant need not withdraw from the engagement if the effect of such information on the prospective financial statement does not appear to be material.

.17 The following is the form of the accountant's standard report on the compilation of a forecast that does not contain a range.[10]

> We have compiled the accompanying forecasted balance sheet, statements of income, retained earnings, and cash flows of XYZ Company as of December 31, 19XX, and for the year then ending, in accordance with standards established by the American Institute of Certified Public Accountants.[11]
>
> A compilation is limited to presenting in the form of a forecast information that is the representation of management[12] and does not include evaluation of the support for the assumptions underlying the forecast. We have not examined the forecast and, accordingly, do not express an opinion or any other form of assurance on the accompanying statements or assumptions. Furthermore, there will usually be differences between the forecasted and actual results, because events and circumstances frequently do not occur as expected, and those differences may be material. We have no responsibility to update this report for events and circumstances occurring after the date of this report.

.18 When the presentation is a projection, the accountant's report should include a separate paragraph that describes the limitations on the usefulness of the presentation. The following is the form of the accountant's standard report on a compilation of a projection that does not contain a range.

> We have compiled the accompanying projected balance sheet, statements of income, retained earnings, and cash flows of XYZ Company as of December 31, 19XX, and for the year then ending, in accordance with standards established by the American Institute of Certified Public Accountants.[13]
>
> The accompanying projection and this report were prepared for [*state special purpose, for example, "the DEF National Bank for the purpose of negotiating a loan to expand XYZ Company's plant,"*] and should not be used for any other purpose.
>
> A compilation is limited to presenting in the form of a projection information that is the representation of management and does not include evaluation of the support for the assumptions underlying the projection. We have not examined the projection and, accordingly, do not express an opinion or any other form of assurance on the accompanying statements or assumptions. Furthermore, even if [*describe hypothetical assumption, for example, "the loan is granted and the plant is expanded,"*] there will usually be differences between the projected and actual results, because events and circumstances frequently do not occur as expected, and those differences may be material. We have no responsibility to update this report for events and circumstances occurring after the date of this report.

---

[10] The forms of reports provided in this section are appropriate whether the presentation is based on generally accepted accounting principles or on another comprehensive basis of accounting.

[11] When the presentation is summarized as discussed in paragraph .67 of this section, this sentence might read "We have compiled the accompanying summarized forecast of XYZ Company as of December 31, 19XX, and for the year then ending, in accordance with standards established by the American Institute of Certified Public Accountants."

[12] When the responsible party is other than management, the references to management in the standard reports provided in this section should be changed to refer to the party who assumes responsibility for the assumptions.

[13] When the presentation is summarized as discussed in paragraph .67 of this section, this sentence might read "We have compiled the accompanying summarized projection of XYZ Company as of December 31, 19XX, and for the year then ending, in accordance with standards established by the American Institute of Certified Public Accountants."

.19 When the prospective financial statements contain a range, the accountant's standard report should also include a separate paragraph that states that the responsible party has elected to portray the expected results of one or more assumptions as a range. The following is an example of the separate paragraph to be added to the accountant's report when he compiles prospective financial statements, in this case a forecast, that contain a range.

> As described in the summary of significant assumptions, management of XYZ Company has elected to portray forecasted [*describe financial statement element or elements for which the expected results of one or more assumptions fall within a range, and identify the assumptions expected to fall within a range, for example, "revenue at the amounts of $X,XXX and $Y,YYY, which is predicated upon occupancy rates of XX percent and YY percent of available apartments,"*] rather than as a single point estimate. Accordingly, the accompanying forecast presents forecasted financial position, results of operations, and changes in financial position [*describe one or more assumptions expected to fall within a range, for example, "at such occupancy rates."*] However, there is no assurance that the actual results will fall within the range of [*describe one or more assumptions expected to fall within a range, for example, "occupancy rates"*] presented.

.20 The date of completion of the accountant's compilation procedures should be used as the date of the report.

.21 An accountant may compile prospective financial statements for an entity with respect to which he is not independent.[14] In such circumstances, the accountant should specifically disclose his lack of independence; however, the reason for the lack of independence should not be described. When the accountant is not independent, he may give the standard compilation report but should include the following sentence after the last paragraph.

> We are not independent with respect to XYZ Company.

.22 Prospective financial statements may be included in a document that also contains historical financial statements and the accountant's report thereon.[15] In addition, the historical financial statements that appear in the document may be summarized and presented with the prospective financial statements for comparative purposes.[16] An example of the reference to the accountant's report on the historical financial statements when he audited, reviewed, or compiled those statements is presented below.

(concluding sentence of last paragraph)

> The historical financial statements for the year ended December 31, 19XX, (from which the historical data are derived) and our report thereon are set forth on pages xx-xx of this document.

.23 In some circumstances, an accountant may wish to expand his report to emphasize a matter regarding the prospective financial statements. Such information may be presented in a separate paragraph of the accountant's re-

---

[14] In making a judgment about whether he is independent, the accountant should be guided by the AICPA Code of Professional Conduct. Also, see the auditing interpretation "Applicability of Guidance on Reporting When Not Independent" (AU section 9504.19–.22).

[15] The accountant's responsibility with respect to those historical financial statements upon which he is not engaged to perform a professional service is described in AU section 504, *Association With Financial Statements*, in the case of public entities, and Statement on Standards for Accounting and Review Services (SSARS) No. 1, *Compilation and Review of Financial Statements*, paragraphs 5 through 7 [AR section 100.05–.07], in the case of nonpublic entities.

[16] AU section 552, *Reporting on Condensed Financial Statements and Selected Financial Data*, discusses the accountant's report where summarized financial statements are derived from audited statements that are not included in the same document.

port. However, the accountant should exercise care that emphasizing such a matter does not give the impression that he is expressing assurance or expanding the degree of responsibility he is taking with respect to such information.[17] For example, the accountant should not include statements in his compilation report about the mathematical accuracy of the statements or their conformity with presentation guidelines.

Modifications of the Standard Compilation Report

.24 An entity may request an accountant to compile prospective financial statements that contain presentation deficiencies or omit disclosures other than those relating to significant assumptions. The accountant may compile such prospective financial statements provided the deficiency or omission is clearly indicated in his report and is not, to his knowledge, undertaken with the intention of misleading those who might reasonably be expected to use such statements.

.25 Notwithstanding the above, if the compiled prospective financial statements are presented on a comprehensive basis of accounting other than generally accepted accounting principles and do not include disclosure of the basis of accounting used, the basis should be disclosed in the accountant's report.

.26 The following is an example of a paragraph that should be added to a report on compiled prospective financial statements, in this case a financial forecast, in which the summary of significant accounting policies has been omitted.

> Management has elected to omit the summary of significant accounting policies required by the guidelines for presentation of a forecast established by the American Institute of Certified Public Accountants. If the omitted disclosures were included in the forecast, they might influence the user's conclusions about the Company's financial position, results of operations, and changes in financial position for the forecast period. Accordingly, this forecast is not designed for those who are not informed about such matters.

Examination of Prospective Financial Statements

.27 An examination of prospective financial statements is a professional service that involves—

a. Evaluating the preparation of the prospective financial statements.

b. Evaluating the support underlying the assumptions.

c. Evaluating the presentation of the prospective financial statements for conformity with AICPA presentation guidelines.[18]

d. Issuing an examination report.

.28 As a result of his examination, the accountant has a basis for reporting on whether, in his opinion—

a. The prospective financial statements are presented in conformity with AICPA guidelines.

b. The assumptions provide a reasonable basis for the responsible party's forecast, or whether the assumptions provide a reasonable

---

[17] However, the accountant may provide assurance on tax matters in order to comply with the requirements of regulations governing practice before the Internal Revenue Service contained in 31 C.F.R. pt. 10 (Treasury Department Circular No. 230.)

[18] AICPA presentation guidelines are detailed in the AICPA *Guide for Prospective Financial Information.*

basis for the responsible party's projection given the hypothetical assumptions.

.29 The accountant should be independent; have adequate technical training and proficiency to examine prospective financial statements; adequately plan the engagement and supervise the work of assistants, if any; and obtain sufficient evidence to provide a reasonable basis for his examination report. (See paragraph .69 of this section for standards concerning such technical training and proficiency, planning the examination engagement, and the types of procedures an accountant should perform to obtain sufficient evidence for his examination report.)

Working Papers

.30 The accountant's working papers in connection with his examination of prospective financial statements should be appropriate to the circumstances and the accountant's needs on the engagement to which they apply. Although the quantity, type, and content of working papers vary with the circumstances, they ordinarily should indicate that—

a. The work was adequately planned and supervised.

b. The process by which the entity develops its prospective financial statements was considered in determining the scope of the examination.

c. Sufficient evidence was obtained to provide a reasonable basis for the accountant's report.

Reports on Examined Prospective Financial Statements

.31 The accountant's standard report on an examination of prospective financial statements should include—

a. An identification of the prospective financial statements presented.

b. A statement that the examination of the prospective financial statements was made in accordance with AICPA standards and a brief description of the nature of such an examination.

c. The accountant's opinion that the prospective financial statements are presented in conformity with AICPA presentation guidelines[19] and that the underlying assumptions provide a reasonable basis for the forecast or a reasonable basis for the projection given the hypothetical assumptions.

d. A caveat that the prospective results may not be achieved.

e. A statement that the accountant assumes no responsibility to update the report for events and circumstances occurring after the date of the report.

.32 The following is the form of the accountant's standard report on an examination of a forecast that does not contain a range.

> We have examined the accompanying forecasted balance sheet, statements of income, retained earnings, and cash flows of XYZ Company as of December 31, 19XX, and for the year then ending.[20] Our examination was made in accordance with standards for an examination of a forecast established by the Amer-

---

[19] The accountant's report need not comment on the consistency of the application of accounting principles as long as the presentation of any change in accounting principles is in conformity with AICPA presentation guidelines as detailed in the AICPA *Guide for Prospective Financial Information*.

[20] When the presentation is summarized as discussed in Appendix A [paragraph .67] of this section, this sentence might read "We have examined the accompanying summarized forecast of XYZ Company as of December 31, 19XX, and for the year then ending."

ican Institute of Certified Public Accountants and, accordingly, included such procedures as we considered necessary to evaluate both the assumptions used by management and the preparation and presentation of the forecast.

In our opinion, the accompanying forecast is presented in conformity with guidelines for presentation of a forecast established by the American Institute of Certified Public Accountants, and the underlying assumptions provide a reasonable basis for management's forecast. However, there will usually be differences between the forecasted and actual results, because events and circumstances frequently do not occur as expected, and those differences may be material. We have no responsibility to update this report for events and circumstances occurring after the date of this report.

.33 When an accountant examines a projection, his opinion regarding the assumptions should be conditioned on the hypothetical assumptions; that is, he should express an opinion on whether the assumptions provide a reasonable basis for the projection given the hypothetical assumptions. Also, his report should include a separate paragraph that describes the limitations on the usefulness of the presentation. The following is the form of the accountant's standard report on an examination of a projection that does not contain a range.

We have examined the accompanying projected balance sheet, statements of income, retained earnings, and cash flows of XYZ Company as of December 31, 19XX, and for the year then ending.[21] Our examination was made in accordance with standards for an examination of a projection established by the American Institute of Certified Public Accountants and, accordingly, included such procedures as we considered necessary to evaluate both the assumptions used by management and the preparation and presentation of the projection.

The accompanying projection and this report were prepared for [*state special purpose, for example, "the DEF National Bank for the purpose of negotiating a loan to expand XYZ Company's plant,"*] and should not be used for any other purpose.

In our opinion, the accompanying projection is presented in conformity with guidelines for presentation of a projection established by the American Institute of Certified Public Accountants, and the underlying assumptions provide a reasonable basis for management's projection [*describe the hypothetical assumption, for example, "assuming the granting of the requested loan for the purpose of expanding XYZ Company's plant as described in the summary of significant assumptions."*] However, even if [*describe hypothetical assumption, for example, "the loan is granted and the plant is expanded,"*] there will usually be differences between the projected and actual results, because events and circumstances frequently do not occur as expected, and those differences may be material. We have no responsibility to update this report for events and circumstances occurring after the date of this report.

.34 When the prospective financial statements contain a range, the accountant's standard report should also include a separate paragraph that states that the responsible party has elected to portray the expected results of one or more assumptions as a range. The following is an example of the separate paragraph to be added to the accountant's report when he examines prospective financial statements, in this case a forecast, that contain a range.

---

[21] When the presentation is summarized as discussed in paragraph .67 of this section, this sentence might read "We have examined the accompanying summarized projection of XYZ Company as of December 31, 19XX, and for the year then ending."

> As described in the summary of significant assumptions, management of XYZ Company has elected to portray forecasted [*describe financial statement element or elements for which the expected results of one or more assumptions fall within a range, and identify assumptions expected to fall within a range, for example, "revenue at the amounts of $X,XXX and $Y,YYY, which is predicated upon occupancy rates of XX percent and YY percent of available apartments,"*] rather than as a single point estimate. Accordingly, the accompanying forecast presents forecasted financial position, results of operations and changes in financial position [*describe one or more assumptions expected to fall within a range, for example, "at such occupancy rates."*] However, there is no assurance that the actual results will fall within the range of [*describe one or more assumptions expected to fall within a range, for example, "occupancy rates"*] presented.

.35 The date of completion of the accountant's examination procedures should be used as the date of the report.

Modifications to the Accountant's Opinion

.36 The following circumstances result in the following types of modified accountant's report involving the accountant's opinion:

a. If, in the accountant's opinion, the prospective financial statements depart from AICPA presentation guidelines, he should issue a qualified opinion (see paragraph .37) or an adverse opinion (see paragraph .39).[22] However, if the presentation departs from the presentation guidelines because it fails to disclose assumptions that appear to be significant the accountant should issue an adverse opinion (see paragraphs .39 and .40).

b. If the accountant believes that one or more significant assumptions do not provide a reasonable basis for the forecast, or a reasonable basis for the projection given the hypothetical assumptions, he should issue an adverse opinion (see paragraph .39).

c. If the accountant's examination is affected by conditions that preclude application of one or more procedures he considers necessary in the circumstances, he should disclaim an opinion and describe the scope limitation in his report (see paragraph .41).

.37 *Qualified Opinion.* In a qualified opinion, the accountant should state, in a separate paragraph, all of his substantive reasons for modifying his opinion and describe the departure from AICPA presentation guidelines. His opinion should include the words "except" or "exception" as the qualifying language and should refer to the separate explanatory paragraph. The following is an example of an examination report on a forecast that is at variance with AICPA guidelines for presentation of a financial forecast.

> We have examined the accompanying forecasted balance sheet, statements of income, retained earnings, and cash flows of XYZ Company as of December 31, 19XX, and for the year then ending. Our examination was made in accordance with standards for an examination of a forecast established by the American Institute of Certified Public Accountants and, accordingly, included such procedures as we considered necessary to evaluate both the assumptions used by management and the preparation and presentation of the forecast.
>
> The forecast does not disclose reasons for the significant variation in the relationship between income tax expense and pretax accounting income as required by generally accepted accounting principles.

---

[22] However, the accountant may issue the standard examination report on a financial forecast filed with the SEC that meets the presentation requirements of article XI of Regulation S-X.

> In our opinion, except for the omission of the disclosure of the reasons for the significant variation in the relationship between income tax expense and pretax accounting income as discussed in the preceding paragraph, the accompanying forecast is presented in conformity with guidelines for a presentation of a forecast established by the American Institute of Certified Public Accountants and the underlying assumptions provide a reasonable basis for management's forecast. However, there will usually be differences between the forecasted and actual results, because events and circumstances frequently do not occur as expected, and those differences may be material. We have no responsibility to update this report for events and circumstances occurring after the date of this report.

.38 Because of the nature, sensitivity, and interrelationship of prospective information, a reader would find an accountant's report qualified for a measurement departure,[23] the reasonableness of the underlying assumptions, or a scope limitation difficult to interpret. Accordingly, the accountant should not express his opinion about these items with language such as "except for . . ." or "subject to the effects of . . . ." Rather, when a measurement departure, an unreasonable assumption, or a limitation on the scope of the accountant's examination has led him to conclude that he cannot issue an unqualified opinion, he should issue the appropriate type of modified opinion described in paragraphs .39 through .42.

.39 *Adverse Opinion.* In an adverse opinion the accountant should state, in a separate paragraph, all of his substantive reasons for his adverse opinion. His opinion should state that the presentation is not in conformity with presentation guidelines and should refer to the explanatory paragraph. When applicable, his opinion paragraph should also state that, in the accountant's opinion, the assumptions do not provide a reasonable basis for the prospective financial statements. An example of an adverse opinion on an examination of prospective financial statements is set forth below. In this case, a financial forecast was examined and the accountant's opinion was that a significant assumption was unreasonable. The example should be revised as appropriate for a different type of presentation or if the adverse opinion is issued because the statements do not conform to the presentation guidelines.

> We have examined the accompanying forecasted balance sheet, statements of income, retained earnings, and cash flows of XYZ Company as of December 31, 19XX, and for the year then ending. Our examination was made in accordance with standards for an examination of a financial forecast established by the American Institute of Certified Public Accountants and, accordingly, included such procedures as we considered necessary to evaluate both the assumptions used by management and the preparation and presentation of the forecast.
>
> As discussed under the caption "Sales" in the summary of significant forecast assumptions, the forecasted sales include, among other things, revenue from the Company's federal defense contracts continuing at the current level. The Company's present federal defense contracts will expire in March 19XX. No new contracts have been signed and no negotiations are under way for new federal defense contracts. Furthermore, the federal government has entered into contracts with another company to supply the items being manufactured under the Company's present contracts.

---

[23] An example of a measurement departure is the failure to capitalize a capital lease in a forecast where the historical financial statements for the prospective period are expected to be presented in conformity with generally accepted accounting principles.

> In our opinion, the accompanying forecast is not presented in conformity with guidelines for presentation of a financial forecast established by the American Institute of Certified Public Accountants because management's assumptions, as discussed in the preceding paragraph, do not provide a reasonable basis for management's forecast. We have no responsibility to update this report for events or circumstances occurring after the date of this report.

.40 If the presentation, including the summary of significant assumptions, fails to disclose assumptions that, at the time, appear to be significant, the accountant should describe the assumptions in his report and issue an adverse opinion. The accountant should not examine a presentation that omits all disclosures of assumptions. Also, the accountant should not examine a financial projection that omits (*a*) an identification of the hypothetical assumptions or (*b*) a description of the limitations on the usefulness of the presentation.

.41 *Disclaimer of Opinion.* In a disclaimer of opinion the accountant's report should indicate, in a separate paragraph, the respects in which the examination did not comply with standards for an examination. The accountant should state that the scope of the examination was not sufficient to enable him to express an opinion with respect to the presentation or the underlying assumptions, and his disclaimer of opinion should include a direct reference to the explanatory paragraph. The following is an example of a report on an examination of prospective financial statements, in this case a financial forecast, for which a significant assumption could not be evaluated.

> We have examined the accompanying forecasted balance sheet, statements of income, retained earnings, and cash flows of XYZ Company as of December 31, 19XX, and for the year then ending. Except as explained in the following paragraph, our examination was made in accordance with standards for an examination of a financial forecast established by the American Institute of Certified Public Accountants and, accordingly, included such procedures as we considered necessary to evaluate both the assumptions used by management and the preparation and presentation of the forecast.
>
> As discussed under the caption "Income From Investee" in the summary of significant forecast assumptions, the forecast includes income from an equity investee constituting 23 percent of forecasted net income, which is management's estimate of the Company's share of the investee's income to be accrued for 19XX. The investee has not prepared a forecast for the year ending December 31, 19XX, and we were therefore unable to obtain suitable support for this assumption.
>
> Because, as described in the preceding paragraph, we are unable to evaluate management's assumption regarding income from an equity investee and other assumptions that depend thereon, we express no opinion with respect to the presentation of or the assumptions underlying the accompanying forecast. We have no responsibility to update this report for events and circumstances occurring after the date of this report.

.42 When there is a scope limitation and the accountant also believes there are material departures from the presentation guidelines, those departures should be described in the accountant's report.

Other Modifications to the Standard Examination Report

.43 The circumstances described below, although not necessarily resulting in modifications to the accountant's opinion, would result in the following types of modifications to the standard examination report.

.44 *Emphasis of a Matter.* In some circumstances, the accountant may wish to emphasize a matter regarding the prospective financial statements but nevertheless intends to issue an unqualified opinion. The accountant may present other information and comments he wishes to include, such as explanatory comments or other informative material, in a separate paragraph of his report.

.45 *Evaluation Based in Part on a Report of Another Accountant.* When more than one accountant is involved in the examination, the guidance provided for that situation in connection with examinations of historical financial statements is generally applicable. When the principal accountant decides to refer to the report of another accountant as a basis, in part, for his own opinion, he should disclose that fact in stating the scope of the examination and should refer to the report of the other accountant in expressing his opinion. Such a reference indicates the division of responsibility for the performance of the examination.

.46 *Comparative Historical Financial Information.* Prospective financial statements may be included in a document that also contains historical financial statements and an accountant's report thereon.[24] In addition, the historical financial statements that appear in the document may be summarized and presented with the prospective financial statements for comparative purposes.[25] An example of the reference to the accountant's report on the historical financial statements when he examined, reviewed, or compiled those statements is presented in paragraph .22.

.47 *Reporting When the Examination Is Part of a Larger Engagement.* When the accountant's examination of prospective financial statements is part of a larger engagement, for example, a financial feasibility study or business acquisition study, it is appropriate to expand the report on the examination of the prospective financial statements to describe the entire engagement.

.48 The following is a report that might be issued when an accountant chooses to expand his report on a financial feasibility study.[26]

a. The Board of Directors
Example Hospital
Example, Texas

b. We have prepared a financial feasibility study of Example Hospital's plans to expand and renovate its facilities. The study was undertaken to evaluate the ability of Example Hospital (the Hospital) to meet the Hospital's operating expenses, working capital needs, and other fi-

---

[24] The accountant's responsibility with respect to those historical financial statements upon which he is not engaged to perform a professional service is described in AU section 504, *Association With Financial Statements*, in the case of public entities, and SSARS No. 1, *Compilation and Review of Financial Statements*, paragraphs 5 through 7 [AR section 100.05–.07], in the case of nonpublic entities.

[25] AU section 552, *Reporting on Condensed Financial Statements and Selected Financial Data*, discusses the accountant's report for summarized financial statements derived from audited financial statements that are not included in the same document.

[26] Although the entity referred to in the report is a hospital, the form of report is also applicable to other entities such as hotels or stadiums. Also, although the illustrated report format and language should not be departed from in any significant way, the language used should be tailored to fit the circumstances that are unique to a particular engagement (for example, the description of the proposed capital improvement program, paragraph *c*; the proposed financing of the program, paragraphs *b* and *d*; the specific procedures applied by the accountant, paragraph *e*; and any explanatory comments included in emphasis-of-a-matter paragraphs, paragraph *i*, which deals with general matter; and paragraph *j*, which deals with specific matters).

nancial requirements, including the debt service requirements associated with the proposed $25,000,000 [*legal title of bonds*] issue, at an assumed average annual interest rate of 10.0 percent during the five years ending December 31, 19X6.

c. The proposed capital improvements program (the Program) consists of a new two-level addition, which is to provide fifty additional medical-surgical beds, increasing the complement to 275 beds. In addition, various administrative and support service areas in the present facilities are to be remodeled. The Hospital administration anticipates that construction is to begin June 30, 19X2, and to be completed by December 31, 19X3.

d. The estimated total cost of the Program is approximately $30,000,000. It is assumed that the $25,000,000 of revenue bonds that the Example Hospital Finance Authority proposes to issue would be the primary source of funds for the Program. The responsibility for payment of debt service on the bonds is solely that of the Hospital. Other necessary funds to finance the Program are assumed to be provided from the Hospital's funds, from a local fund drive, and from interest earned on funds held by the bond trustee during the construction period.

e. Our procedures included analysis of—

- Program history, objectives, timing and financing.
- The future demand for the Hospital's services, including consideration of—

  Economic and demographic characteristics of the Hospital's defined service area.

  Locations, capacities, and competitive information pertaining to other existing and planned area hospitals.

  Physician support for the Hospital and its programs.

  Historical utilization levels.
- Planning agency applications and approvals.
- Construction and equipment costs, debt service requirements, and estimated financing costs.
- Staffing patterns and other operating considerations.
- Third-party reimbursement policy and history.
- Revenue/expense/volume relationships.

f. We also participated in gathering other information, assisted management in identifying and formulating its assumptions, and assembled the accompanying financial forecast based on those assumptions.

g. The accompanying financial forecast for the annual periods ending December 31, 19X2, through 19X6, is based on assumptions that were provided by or reviewed with and approved by management. The financial forecast includes—

- Balance sheets.
- Statements of revenues and expenses.

- Statements of cash flows.
- Statements of changes in fund balance.

h. We have examined the financial forecast. Our examination was made in accordance with standards for an examination of a financial forecast established by the American Institute of Certified Public Accountants and, accordingly, included such procedures as we considered necessary to evaluate both the assumptions used by management and the preparation and presentation of the forecast.

i. Legislation and regulations at all levels of government have affected and may continue to affect revenues and expenses of hospitals. The financial forecast is based on legislation and regulations currently in effect. If future legislation or regulations related to hospital operations are enacted, such legislation or regulations could have a material effect on future operations.

j. The interest rate, principal payments, Program costs, and other financing assumptions are described in the section entitled "Summary of Significant Forecast Assumptions and Rationale." If actual interest rates, principal payments, and funding requirements are different from those assumed, the amount of the bond issue and debt service requirements would need to be adjusted accordingly from those indicated in the forecast. If such interest rates, principal payments, and funding requirements are lower than those assumed, such adjustments would not adversely affect the forecast.

k. Our conclusions are presented below.

- In our opinion, the accompanying financial forecast is presented in conformity with guidelines for presentation of a financial forecast established by the American Institute of Certified Public Accountants.
- In our opinion, the underlying assumptions provide a reasonable basis for management's forecast. However, there will usually be differences between the forecasted and actual results, because events and circumstances frequently do not occur as expected, and those differences may be material.
- The accompanying financial forecast indicates that sufficient funds could be generated to meet the Hospital's operating expenses, working capital needs, and other financial requirements, including the debt service requirements associated with the proposed $25,000,000 bond issue, during the forecast periods. However, the achievement of any financial forecast is dependent on future events, the occurrence of which cannot be assured.

l. We have no responsibility to update this report for events and circumstances occurring after the date of this report.

Applying Agreed-Upon Procedures to Prospective Financial Statements

.49 An accountant engaged to perform agreed-upon procedures on prospective financial statements should follow the guidance set forth herein and in section 600, *Agreed-Upon Procedures Engagements*. [As amended, effective for reports on agreed-upon procedures engagements dated after April 30, 1996, by Statement on Standards for Attestation Engagements No. 4.] (See section 600.)

.50 An accountant may perform an agreed-upon procedures attestation engagement to prospective financial statements[27] provided that—

a. The accountant is independent.

b. The accountant and the specified users agree upon the procedures performed or to be performed by the accountant.

c. The specified users take responsibility for the sufficiency of the agreed-upon procedures for their purposes.

d. The prospective financial statements include a summary of significant assumptions.

e. The prospective financial statements to which the procedures are to be applied are subject to reasonably consistent estimation or measurement.

f. Criteria[28] to be used in the determination of findings are agreed upon between the accountant and the specified users.

g. The procedures to be applied to the prospective financial statements are expected to result in reasonably consistent findings using the criteria.

h. Evidential matter related to the prospective financial statements to which the procedures are applied is expected to exist to provide a reasonable basis for expressing the findings in the accountant's report.

i. Where applicable, a description of any agreed-upon materiality limits for reporting purposes (see section 600.27).

j. Use of the report is to be restricted to the specified users.[29]

[As amended, effective for reports on agreed-upon procedures engagements dated after April 30, 1996, by Statement on Standards for Attestation Engagements No. 4.] (See section 600.)

.51 The accountant who accepts an engagement to apply agreed-upon procedures to prospective financial statements should (*a*) have adequate technical training and proficiency to apply agreed-upon procedures to prospective financial statements; (*b*) adequately plan the engagement and supervise the work of assistants, if any; and (*c*) obtain sufficient evidence to provide a reasonable basis for his report on the results of applying agreed-upon procedures. [As amended, effective for reports on agreed-upon procedures engagements dated after April 30, 1996, by Statement on Standards for Attestation Engagements No. 4.] (See section 600.)

---

[27] Accountants should follow the guidance in AU section 634, *Letters for Underwriters and Certain Other Requesting Parties*, when requested to perform agreed-upon procedures on a forecast and report thereon in a letter for an underwriter. (AU section 634.44). [Footnote added, effective for comfort letters issued on or after June 30, 1993, by the issuance of Statement on Auditing Standards No. 72.] (See AU section 634.)

[28] For example, accounting principles and other presentation criteria as discussed in chapter 8, "Presentation Guidelines," of the AICPA Audit and Accounting Guide *Guide for Prospective Financial Information*. [Footnote added, effective for reports on agreed-upon procedures engagements dated after April 30, 1996, by Statement on Standards for Attestation Engagements No. 4.] (See section 600.)

[29] An accountant may perform an engagement pursuant to which his report will be a matter of public record (see section 600.33). [Footnote added, effective for reports on agreed-upon procedures engagements dated after April 30, 1996, by Statement on Standards for Attestation Engagements No. 4.] (See section 600.)

.52 Generally, the accountant's procedures may be as limited or as extensive as the specified users desire, as long as the specified users take responsibility for their sufficiency. However, mere reading of prospective financial statements does not constitute a procedure sufficient to permit an accountant to report on the results of applying agreed-upon procedures to such statements. [As amended, effective for reports on agreed-upon procedures engagements dated after April 30, 1996, by Statement on Standards for Attestation Engagements No. 4.] (See section 600.)

.53 To satisfy the requirements that the accountant and the specified users agree upon the procedures performed or to be performed and that the specified users take responsibility for the sufficiency of the agreed-upon procedures for their purposes, ordinarily the accountant should communicate directly with and obtain affirmative acknowledgment from each of the specified users. For example, this may be accomplished by meeting with the specified users or by distributing a draft of the anticipated report or a copy of an engagement letter to the specified users and obtaining their agreement. If the accountant is not able to communicate directly with all of the specified users, the accountant may satisfy these requirements by applying any one or more of the following or similar procedures:

- Compare the procedures to be applied to written requirements of the specified users.
- Discuss the procedures to be applied with appropriate representatives of the specified users involved.
- Review relevant contracts with or correspondence from the specified users.

The accountant should not report on an engagement when specified users do not agree upon the procedures performed or to be performed and do not take responsibility for the sufficiency of the procedures for their purposes. (See section 600.38 for guidance on satisfying these requirements when the accountant is requested to add parties as specified users after the date of completion of the agreed-upon procedures.) [As amended, effective for reports on agreed-upon procedures engagements dated after April 30, 1996, by Statement on Standards for Attestation Engagements No. 4.] (See section 600.)

Reports on the Results of Applying Agreed-Upon Procedures

.54 The accountant's report on the results of applying agreed-upon procedures should be in the form of procedures and findings. The accountant's report should contain the following elements:

a. A title that includes the word *independent*

b. Identification of the specified users

c. Reference to the prospective financial statements covered by the accountant's report and the character of the engagement

d. A statement that the procedures performed were those agreed to by the specified users identified in the report

e. Reference to standards established by the American Institute of Certified Public Accountants

f. A statement that the sufficiency of the procedures is solely the responsibility of the specified users and a disclaimer of responsibility for the sufficiency of those procedures

g. A list of the procedures performed (or reference thereto) and related findings (The accountant should not provide negative assurance—see section 600.26.)

h. Where applicable, a description of any agreed-upon materiality limits (see section 600.27)

i. A statement that the accountant was not engaged to, and did not, perform an examination of prospective financial statements; a disclaimer of opinion on whether the presentation of the prospective financial statements is in conformity with AICPA presentation guidelines and on whether the underlying assumptions provide a reasonable basis for the forecast, or a reasonable basis for the projection given the hypothetical assumptions; and a statement that if the practitioner had performed additional procedures, other matters might have come to his or her attention that would have been reported

j. A statement of restrictions on the use of the report because it is intended to be used solely by the specified users (However, if the report is a matter of public record, the accountant should include the following sentence: "However, this report is a matter of public record and its distribution is not limited.")

k. Where applicable, reservations or restrictions concerning procedures or findings as discussed in section 600.35, .37, .41, and .42

l. A caveat that the prospective results may not be achieved

m. A statement that the accountant assumes no responsibility to update the report for events and circumstances occurring after the date of the report

n. Where applicable, a description of the nature of the assistance provided by a specialist as discussed in section 600.21 through .23

[As amended, effective for reports on agreed-upon procedures engagements dated after April 30, 1996, by Statement on Standards for Attestation Engagements No. 4.] (See section 600.)

[.55–.56] [Superseded by Statement on Standards for Attestation Engagements No. 4, effective for reports on agreed-upon procedures engagements dated after April 30, 1996.] (See section 600.)

.57 The following illustrates a report on applying agreed-upon procedures to the prospective financial statements.

Independent Accountant's Report
on Applying Agreed-Upon Procedures

Board of Directors—XYZ Corporation

Board of Directors—ABC Company

At your request, we have performed certain agreed-upon procedures, as enumerated below, with respect to the forecasted balance sheet and the related forecasted statements of income, retained earnings, and cash flows of DEF Company, a subsidiary of ABC Company, as of December 31, 19XX, and for the year then ending. These procedures, which were agreed to by the Boards of Directors of XYZ Corporation and ABC Company, were performed solely to assist you in evaluating the forecast in connection with the proposed sale of DEF Company to XYZ Corporation. This agreed-upon procedures engagement was performed in accordance with standards established by the American Institute of Certified Public Accountants. The sufficiency of these procedures is solely the responsibility of the specified users of the report. Consequently, we make no representation regarding the sufficiency of the procedures described below either for the purpose for which this report has been requested or for any other purpose.

> [*Include paragraphs to enumerate procedures and findings.*]
>
> We were not engaged to, and did not, perform an examination, the objective of which would be the expression of an opinion on the accompanying prospective financial statements. Accordingly, we do not express an opinion on whether the prospective financial statements are presented in conformity with AICPA presentation guidelines or on whether the underlying assumptions provide a reasonable basis for the presentation. Had we performed additional procedures, other matters might have come to our attention that would have been reported to you. Furthermore, there will usually be differences between the forecasted and actual results, because events and circumstances frequently do not occur as expected, and those differences may be material. We have no responsibility to update this report for events and circumstances occurring after the date of this report.
>
> This report is intended solely for the use of the Boards of Directors of ABC Company and XYZ Corporation and should not be used by those who have not agreed to the procedures and taken responsibility for the sufficiency of the procedures for their purposes.

[As amended, effective for reports on agreed-upon procedures engagements dated after April 30, 1996, by Statement on Standards for Attestation Engagements No. 4.] (See section 600.)

Other Information

.58 When an accountant's compilation, review, or examination report on historical financial statements is included in an accountant-submitted document containing prospective financial statements, the accountant should either examine, compile, or apply agreed-upon procedures to the prospective financial statements and report accordingly, unless (*a*) the prospective financial statements are labeled as a "budget," (*b*) the budget does not extend beyond the end of the current fiscal year, and (*c*) the budget is presented with interim historical financial statements for the current year. In such circumstances, the accountant need not examine, compile, or apply agreed-upon procedures to the budget; however, he should report on it and (*a*) indicate that he did not examine or compile the budget and (*b*) disclaim an opinion or any other form of assurance on the budget. In addition, the budgeted information may omit the summaries of significant assumptions and accounting policies required by the guidelines for presentation of prospective financial statements established by the American Institute of Certified Public Accountants, provided such omission is not, to the accountant's knowledge, undertaken with the intention of misleading those who might reasonably be expected to use such budgeted information, and is disclosed in the accountant's report. The following is the form of the standard paragraphs to be added to the accountant's report in this circumstance when the summaries of significant assumptions and accounting policies have been omitted.

> The accompanying budgeted balance sheet, statements of income, retained earnings, and cash flows of XYZ Company as of December 31, 19XX, and for the six months then ending, have not been compiled or examined by us, and, accordingly, we do not express an opinion or any other form of assurance on them.
>
> Management has elected to omit the summaries of significant assumptions and accounting policies required under established guidelines for presentation of prospective financial statements. If the omitted summaries were included in the budgeted information, they might influence the user's conclusions about the company's budgeted information. Accordingly, this budgeted information is not designed for those who are not informed about such matters.

.59 When the accountant's compilation, review, or examination report on historical financial statements is included in a client-prepared document containing prospective financial statements, the accountant should not consent to the use of his name in the document unless (*a*) he has examined, compiled, or applied agreed-upon procedures to the prospective financial statements and his report accompanies them, (*b*) the prospective financial statements are accompanied by an indication by the responsible party or the accountant that the accountant has not performed such a service on the prospective financial statements and that the accountant assumes no responsibility for them, or (*c*) another accountant has examined, compiled, or applied agreed-upon procedures to the prospective financial statements and his report is included in the document. In addition, if the accountant has examined the historical financial statements and they accompany prospective financial statements that he did not examine, compile, or apply agreed-upon procedures to in certain[30] client-prepared documents, he should refer to AU section 550, *Other Information in Documents Containing Audited Financial Statements*.

.60 The accountant whose report on prospective financial statements is included in a client-prepared document containing historical financial statements should not consent to the use of his name in the document unless (*a*) he has compiled, reviewed, or examined the historical financial statements and his report accompanies them, (*b*) the historical financial statements are accompanied by an indication by the responsible party or the accountant that the accountant has not performed such a service on the historical financial statements and that the accountant assumes no responsibility for them, or (*c*) another accountant has compiled, reviewed, or examined the historical financial statements and his report is included in the document.

.61 An entity may publish various documents that contain information other than historical financial statements in addition to the compiled or examined prospective financial statements and the accountant's report thereon. The accountant's responsibility with respect to information in such a document does not extend beyond the financial information identified in the report, and he has no obligation to perform any procedures to corroborate other information contained in the document. However, the accountant should read the other information and consider whether such information, or the manner of its presentation, is materially inconsistent with the information, or manner of its presentation, appearing in the prospective financial statements.

.62 If the accountant examines prospective financial statements included in a document containing inconsistent information, he might not be able to conclude that there is adequate support for each significant assumption. The accountant should consider whether the prospective financial statements, his report, or both require revision. Depending on the conclusion he reaches, the accountant should consider other actions that may be appropriate, such as issuing an adverse opinion, disclaiming an opinion because of a scope limitation, withholding the use of his report in the document, or withdrawing from the engagement.

---

[30] AU section 550 applies only to such prospective financial statements contained in (*a*) annual reports to holders of securities or beneficial interests, annual reports of organizations for charitable or philanthropic purposes distributed to the public, and annual reports filed with regulatory authorities under the Securities Exchange Act of 1934 or (*b*) other documents to which the auditor, at the client's request, devotes attention. AU section 550 does not apply when the historical financial statements and report appear in a registration statement filed under the Securities Act of 1933 (in which case, see AU section 711, *Filings Under Federal Securities Statutes*). [Footnote renumbered by the issuance of Statement on Auditing Standards No. 72, February 1993. Footnote subsequently renumbered by the issuance of Statement on Standards for Attestation Engagements No. 4, September 1995.]

.63 If the accountant compiles the prospective financial statements included in the document containing inconsistent information, he should attempt to obtain additional or revised information. If he does not receive such information, the accountant should withhold the use of his report or withdraw from the compilation engagement.

.64 If, while reading the other information appearing in the document containing the examined or compiled prospective financial statements, as described in the preceding paragraphs, the accountant becomes aware of information that he believes is a material misstatement of fact that is not an inconsistent statement, he should discuss the matter with the responsible party. In connection with this discussion, the accountant should consider that he may not have the expertise to assess the validity of the statement made, that there may be no standards by which to assess its presentation, and that there may be valid differences of judgment or opinion. If the accountant concludes that he has a valid basis for concern, he should propose that the responsible party consult with some other party whose advice might be useful, such as the entity's legal counsel.

.65 If, after discussing the matter as described in paragraph .64, the accountant concludes that a material misstatement of fact remains, the action he takes will depend on his judgment in the particular circumstances. He should consider steps such as notifying the responsible party in writing of his views concerning the information and consulting his legal counsel about further appropriate action in the circumstances.

Effective Date

.66 This section is effective for engagements in which the date of completion of the accountant's services on prospective financial statements is September 30, 1986, or later. Earlier application is encouraged.

.67

Appendix A*

Minimum Presentation Guidelines

1. Prospective information presented in the format of historical financial statements facilitates comparisons with financial position, results of operations, and cash flows of prior periods, as well as those actually achieved for the prospective period. Accordingly, prospective financial statements preferably should be in the format of the historical financial statements that would be issued for the period(s) covered unless there is an agreement between the responsible party and potential users specifying another format. Prospective financial statements may take the form of complete basic financial statements[1] or may be limited to the following minimum items (where such items would be presented for historical financial statements for the period).[2]

a. Sales or gross revenues

b. Gross profit or cost of sales

c. Unusual or infrequently occurring items

d. Provision for income taxes

e. Discontinued operations or extraordinary items

f. Income from continuing operations

g. Net income

h. Primary and fully diluted earnings per share

i. Significant changes in financial position[3]

j. A description of what management intends the prospective financial statements to present, a statement that the assumptions are based on information about circumstances and conditions existing at the time the prospective information was prepared, and a caveat that the prospective results may not be achieved

k. Summary of significant assumptions

l. Summary of significant accounting policies

2. A presentation that omits one or more of the applicable minimum items *a* through *i* above is a partial presentation, which would not ordinarily be appropriate for general use. If an omitted applicable minimum item is derivable from the information presented, the presentation would not be deemed to be a partial presentation.[4] A presentation that contains the applicable minimum items *a* through *i* above, but omits minimum items *j* through *l* above is not a partial presentation, and an engagement involving such a presentation is subject to the provisions of this section.

---

* ***Note:*** This appendix describes the minimum items that constitute a presentation of a financial forecast or a financial projection, as specified in the AICPA *Guide for Prospective Financial Information*. Complete presentation guidelines for entities that choose to issue prospective financial statements, together with illustrative presentations, are included in the guide.

[1] The details of each statement may be summarized or condensed so that only the major items in each are presented. The usual footnotes associated with historical financial statements need not be included as such. However, significant assumptions and accounting policies should be disclosed.

[2] Similar types of financial information should be presented for entities for which these terms do not describe operations. Further, similar items should be presented if a comprehensive basis of accounting other than generally accepted accounting principles is used to present the prospective financial statements. For example, if the cash basis were used, item *a* would be cash receipts.

[3] This item does not require a balance sheet or a statement of changes in financial position. Examples are included in the AICPA *Guide for Prospective Financial Information*.

[4] Footnote deleted.

.68

Appendix B

Training and Proficiency, Planning and Procedures Applicable to Compilations

Training and Proficiency

1. The accountant should be familiar with the guidelines for the preparation and presentation of prospective financial statements. The guidelines are contained in the AICPA *Guide for Prospective Financial Information*.

2. The accountant should possess or obtain a level of knowledge of the industry and the accounting principles and practices of the industry in which the entity operates, or will operate, that will enable him to compile prospective financial statements that are in appropriate form for an entity operating in that industry.

Planning the Compilation Engagement

3. To compile the prospective financial statements of an existing entity, the accountant should obtain a general knowledge of the nature of the entity's business transactions and the key factors upon which its future financial results appear to depend. He should also obtain an understanding of the accounting principles and practices of the entity to determine if they are comparable to those used within the industry in which the entity operates.

4. To compile the prospective financial statements of a proposed entity, the accountant should obtain knowledge of the proposed operations and the key factors upon which its future results appear to depend and that have affected the performance of entities in the same industry.

Compilation Procedures

5. In performing a compilation of prospective financial statements the accountant should, where applicable—

a. Establish an understanding with the client regarding the services to be performed. The understanding should include the objectives of the engagement, the client's responsibilities, the accountant's responsibilities, and limitations of the engagement. The accountant should document the understanding in the working papers, preferably through a written communication with the client. If the accountant believes an understanding with the client has not been established, he or she should decline to accept or perform the engagement.

b. Inquire about the accounting principles used in the preparation of the prospective financial statements.

- For existing entities, compare the accounting principles used to those used in the preparation of previous historical financial statements and inquire whether such principles are the same as those expected to be used in the historical financial statements covering the prospective period.
- For entities to be formed or entities formed that have not commenced operations, compare specialized industry accounting principles used, if any, to those typically used in the industry. Inquire about whether the accounting principles used for the prospective financial statements are those that are expected to be used when, or if, the entity commences operations.

c. Ask how the responsible party identifies the key factors and develops its assumptions.

d. List, or obtain a list of, the responsible party's significant assumptions providing the basis for the prospective financial statements and consider whether there are any obvious omissions in light of the key factors upon which the prospective results of the entity appear to depend.

e. Consider whether there appear to be any obvious internal inconsistencies in the assumptions.

f. Perform, or test the mathematical accuracy of, the computations that translate the assumptions into prospective financial statements.

g. Read the prospective financial statements, including the summary of significant assumptions, and consider whether—

- The statements, including the disclosures of assumptions and accounting policies, appear to be not presented in conformity with the AICPA presentation guidelines for prospective financial statements.[1]

- The statements, including the summary of significant assumptions, appear to be not obviously inappropriate in relation to the accountant's knowledge of the entity and its industry and, for a—

Financial forecast, the expected conditions and course of action in the prospective period.

Financial projection, the purpose of the presentation.

h. If a significant part of the prospective period has expired, inquire about the results of operations or significant portions of the operations (such as sales volume), and significant changes in financial position, and consider their effect in relation to the prospective financial statements. If historical financial statements have been prepared for the expired portion of the period, the accountant should read such statements and consider those results in relation to the prospective financial statements.

i. Confirm his understanding of the statements (including assumptions) by obtaining written representations from the responsible party. Because the amounts reflected in the statements are not supported by historical books and records but rather by assumptions, the accountant should obtain representations in which the responsible party indicates its responsibility for the assumptions. The representations should be signed by the responsible party at the highest level of authority who the accountant believes is responsible for and knowledgeable, directly or through others, about matters covered by the representations.

- *For a financial forecast*, the representations should include a statement that the financial forecast presents, to the best of the responsible party's knowledge and belief, the expected financial position, results of operations, and cash flows for the forecast period and that

---

[1] Presentation guidelines for entities that issue prospective financial statements are set forth and illustrated in the AICPA *Guide for Prospective Financial Information*.

the forecast reflects the responsible party's judgment, based on present circumstances, of the expected conditions and its expected course of action. If the forecast contains a range, the representation should also include a statement that, to the best of the responsible party's knowledge and belief, the item or items subject to the assumption are expected to actually fall within the range and that the range was not selected in a biased or misleading manner.

- *For a financial projection*, the representations should include a statement that the financial projection presents, to the best of the responsible party's knowledge and belief, the expected financial position, results of operations, and cash flows for the projection period given the hypothetical assumptions, and that the projection reflects its judgment, based on present circumstances, of expected conditions and its expected course of action given the occurrence of the hypothetical events. The representations should also (i) identify the hypothetical assumptions and describe the limitations on the usefulness of the presentation, (ii) state that the assumptions are appropriate, (iii) indicate if the hypothetical assumptions are improbable, and (iv) if the projection contains a range, include a statement that, to the best of the responsible party's knowledge and belief, given the hypothetical assumptions, the item or items subject to the assumption are expected to actually fall within the range and that the range was not selected in a biased or misleading manner.

j. Consider, after applying the above procedures, whether he has received representations or other information that appears to be obviously inappropriate, incomplete, or otherwise misleading and, if so, attempt to obtain additional or revised information. If he does not receive such information, the accountant should ordinarily withdraw from the compilation engagement.[2] (Note that the omission of disclosures, other than those relating to significant assumptions, would not require the accountant to withdraw; see paragraph .24 of this section.)

[2] The accountant need not withdraw from the engagement if the effect of such information on the prospective financial statements does not appear to be material.

.69

Appendix C

Training and Proficiency, Planning and Procedures Applicable to Examinations

Training and Proficiency

1. The accountant should be familiar with the guidelines for the preparation and presentation of prospective financial statements. The guidelines are contained in the AICPA *Guide for Prospective Financial Information*.

2. The accountant should possess or obtain a level of knowledge of the industry and the accounting principles and practices of the industry in which the entity operates, or will operate, that will enable him to examine prospective financial statements that are in appropriate form for an entity operating in that industry.

Planning an Examination Engagement

3. Planning the examination engagement involves developing an overall strategy for the expected scope and conduct of the engagement. To develop such a strategy, the accountant needs to have sufficient knowledge to enable him to adequately understand the events, transactions, and practices that, in his judgment, may have a significant effect on the prospective financial statements.

4. Factors to be considered by the accountant in planning the examination include (*a*) the accounting principles to be used and the type of presentation, (*b*) the anticipated level of attestation risk[1] related to the prospective financial statements, (*c*) preliminary judgments about materiality levels, (*d*) items within the prospective financial statements that are likely to require revision or adjustment, (*e*) conditions that may require extension or modification of the accountant's examination procedures, (*f*) knowledge of the entity's business and its industry, (*g*) the responsible party's experience in preparing prospective financial statements, (*h*) the length of the period covered by the prospective financial statements, and (*i*) the process by which the responsible party develops its prospective financial statements.

5. The accountant should obtain knowledge of the entity's business, accounting principles, and the key factors upon which its future financial results appear to depend. The accountant should focus on such areas as—

a. The availability and cost of resources needed to operate. Principal items usually include raw materials, labor, short-term and long-term financing, and plant and equipment.

b. The nature and condition of markets in which the entity sells its goods or services, including final consumer markets if the entity sells to intermediate markets.

---

[1] *Attestation risk* is the risk that the accountant may unknowingly fail to appropriately modify his examination report on prospective financial statements that are materially misstated, that is, that are not presented in conformity with AICPA presentation guidelines or have assumptions that do not provide a reasonable basis for management's forecast, or management's projection given the hypothetical assumptions. It consists of (*a*) the risk (consisting of inherent risk and control risk) that the prospective financial statements contain errors that could be material and (*b*) the risk (detection risk) that the accountant will not detect such errors.

c. Factors specific to the industry, including competitive conditions, sensitivity to economic conditions, accounting policies, specific regulatory requirements, and technology.

d. Patterns of past performance for the entity or comparable entities, including trends in revenue and costs, turnover of assets, uses and capacities of physical facilities, and management policies.

Examination Procedures

6. The accountant should establish an understanding with the responsible party regarding the services to be performed. The understanding should include the objectives of the engagement, the responsible party's responsibilities, the accountant's responsibilities, and limitations of the engagement. The accountant should document the understanding in the working papers, preferably through a written communication with the responsible party. If the accountant believes an understanding with the responsible party has not been established, he or she should decline to accept or perform the engagement. If the responsible party is different than the client, the accountant should establish the understanding with both the client and the responsible party, and the understanding also should include the client's responsibilities.

7. The accountant's objective in an examination of prospective financial statements is to accumulate sufficient evidence to limit attestation risk to a level that is, in his professional judgment, appropriate for the level of assurance that may be imparted by his examination report. In a report on an examination of prospective financial statements, he provides assurance only about whether the prospective financial statements are presented in conformity with AICPA presentation guidelines and whether the assumptions provide a reasonable basis for management's forecast, or a reasonable basis for management's projection given the hypothetical assumptions. He does not provide assurance about the achievability of the prospective results because events and circumstances frequently do not occur as expected and achievement of the prospective results is dependent on the actions, plans, and assumptions of the responsible party.

8. In his examination of prospective financial statements, the accountant should select from all available procedures—that is, procedures that assess inherent and control risk and restrict detection risk—any combination that can limit attestation risk to such an appropriate level. The extent to which examination procedures will be performed should be based on the accountant's consideration of (*a*) the nature and materiality of the information to the prospective financial statements taken as a whole; (*b*) the likelihood of misstatements; (*c*) knowledge obtained during current and previous engagements; (*d*) the responsible party's competence with respect to prospective financial statements; (*e*) the extent to which the prospective financial statements are affected by the responsible party's judgment, for example, its judgment in selecting the assumptions used to prepare the prospective financial statements; and (*f*) the adequacy of the responsible party's underlying data.

9. The accountant should perform those procedures he considers necessary in the circumstances to report on whether the assumptions provide a reasonable basis for the—

a. *Financial forecast.* The accountant can form an opinion that the assumptions provide a reasonable basis for the forecast if the responsible party represents that the presentation reflects, to the best of its knowledge and belief, its estimate of expected financial position, results of operations, and cash flows for the prospective period[2] and the accountant concludes, based on his examination, (i) that the responsible party has explicitly identified all factors expected to materially affect the operations of the entity during the prospective period and has developed appropriate assumptions with respect to such factors[3] and (ii) that the assumptions are suitably supported.

b. *Financial projection* given the hypothetical assumptions. The accountant can form an opinion that the assumptions provide a reasonable basis for the financial projection given the hypothetical assumptions if the responsible party represents that the presentation reflects, to the best of its knowledge and belief, expected financial position, results of operations, and cash flows for the prospective period given the hypothetical assumptions[4] and the accountant concludes, based on his examination, (i) that the responsible party has explicitly identified all factors that would materially affect the operations of the entity during the prospective period if the hypothetical assumptions were to materialize and has developed appropriate assumptions with respect to such factors and (ii) that the other assumptions are suitably supported given the hypothetical assumptions. However, as the number and significance of the hypothetical assumptions increase, the accountant may not be able to satisfy himself about the presentation as a whole by obtaining support for the remaining assumptions.

10. The accountant should evaluate the support for the assumptions.

a. *Financial forecast*—The accountant can conclude that assumptions are suitably supported if the preponderance of information supports each significant assumption.

b. *Financial projection*—In evaluating support for assumptions other than hypothetical assumptions, the accountant can conclude that they are suitably supported if the preponderance of information supports each significant assumption given the hypothetical assumptions. The accountant need not obtain support for the hypothetical assumptions, although he should consider whether they are consistent with the purpose of the presentation.

11. In evaluating the support for assumptions, the accountant should consider—

a. Whether sufficient pertinent sources of information about the assumptions have been considered. Examples of external sources the accountant might consider are government publications, industry publications, economic forecasts, existing or proposed legislation, and reports of changing technology. Examples of internal sources are budgets, labor agreements, patents, royalty agreements and records, sales backlog records, debt agreements, and actions of the board of directors involving entity plans.

---

[2] If the forecast contains a range, the representation should also include a statement that, to the best of the responsible party's knowledge and belief, the item or items subject to the assumption are expected to actually fall within the range and that the range was not selected in a biased or misleading manner.

[3] An attempt to list all assumptions is inherently not feasible. Frequently, basic assumptions that have enormous potential impact are considered to be implicit, such as conditions of peace and absence of natural disasters.

[4] If the projection contains a range, the representation should also include a statement that, to the best of the responsible party's knowledge and belief, given the hypothetical assumptions, the item or items subject to the assumption are expected to actually fall within the range and that the range was not selected in a biased or misleading manner.

b. Whether the assumptions are consistent with the sources from which they are derived.

c. Whether the assumptions are consistent with each other.

d. Whether the historical financial information and other data used in developing the assumptions are sufficiently reliable for that purpose. Reliability can be assessed by inquiry and analytical or other procedures, some of which may have been completed in past examinations or reviews of the historical financial statements. If historical financial statements have been prepared for an expired part of the prospective period, the accountant should consider the historical data in relation to the prospective results for the same period, where applicable. If the prospective financial statements incorporate such historical financial results and that period is significant to the presentation, the accountant should make a review of the historical information in conformity with the applicable standards for a review.[5]

e. Whether the historical financial information and other data used in developing the assumptions are comparable over the periods specified or whether the effects of any lack of comparability were considered in developing the assumptions.

f. Whether the logical arguments or theory, considered with the data supporting the assumptions, are reasonable.

12. In evaluating the preparation and presentation of the prospective financial statements, the accountant should perform procedures that will provide reasonable assurance that the—

a. Presentation reflects the identified assumptions.

b. Computations made to translate the assumptions into prospective amounts are mathematically accurate.

c. Assumptions are internally consistent.

d. Accounting principles used in the—

- *Financial forecast* are consistent with the accounting principles expected to be used in the historical financial statements covering the prospective period and those used in the most recent historical financial statements, if any.

- *Financial projection* are consistent with the accounting principles expected to be used in the prospective period and those used in the most recent historical financial statements, if any, or that they are consistent with the purpose of the presentation.[6]

e. Presentation of the prospective financial statements follows the AICPA guidelines applicable for such statements.[7]

f. Assumptions have been adequately disclosed based on AICPA presentation guidelines for prospective financial statements.

---

[5] If the entity is a public company, the accountant should perform the procedures in AU section 722, *Interim Financial Information*, paragraphs .13 through .19. If the entity is nonpublic, the accountant should perform the procedures in SSARS No. 1, *Compilation and Review of Financial Statements*, paragraphs 24 through 31 [AR section 100.24–.31]. [Reference changed by the issuance of Statement on Auditing Standards No. 71.]

[6] The accounting principles used in a financial projection need not be those expected to be used in the historical financial statements for the prospective period if use of different principles is consistent with the purpose of the presentation.

[7] Presentation guidelines for entities that issue prospective financial statements are set forth and illustrated in the AICPA *Guide for Prospective Financial Information*.

13. The accountant should consider whether the prospective financial statements, including related disclosures, should be revised because of (*a*) mathematical errors, (*b*) unreasonable or internally inconsistent assumptions, (*c*) inappropriate or incomplete presentation, or (*d*) inadequate disclosure.

14. The accountant should obtain written representations from the responsible party acknowledging its responsibility for both the presentation and the underlying assumptions. The representations should be signed by the responsible party at the highest level of authority who the accountant believes is responsible for and knowledgeable, directly or through others in the organization, about the matters covered by the representations. Paragraph .68, subparagraph 5*i* describes the specific representations to be obtained for a financial forecast and a financial projection.

AT Section 300

Reporting on Pro Forma Financial Information

Source: SSAE No. 1; SAS No. 76.

Effective for reports on an examination or a review of pro forma financial information issued on or after November 1, 1988, unless otherwise indicated.

.01 This section provides guidance to an accountant who is engaged to examine or review and report on pro forma financial information. Such an engagement should comply with the general and fieldwork standards set forth in section 100, *Attestation Standards*, and the specific performance and reporting standards set forth in this statement.[1]

.02 When pro forma financial information is presented outside the basic financial statements but within the same document, and the accountant is not engaged to report on the pro forma financial information, the accountant's responsibilities are described in AU section 550, *Other Information in Documents Containing Audited Financial Statements*, and AU section 711, *Filings Under Federal Securities Statutes*.

.03 This section does not apply in those circumstances when, for purposes of a more meaningful presentation, a transaction consummated after the balance sheet date is reflected in the historical financial statements (such as a revision of debt maturities or a revision of earnings per share calculations for a stock split).[2]

Presentation of Pro Forma Financial Information

.04 The objective of pro forma financial information is to show what the significant effects on historical financial information might have been had a consummated or proposed transaction (or event) occurred at an earlier date. Pro forma financial information is commonly used to show the effects of transactions such as a—

- Business combination.
- Change in capitalization.

---

[1] AU section 634, *Letters for Underwriters and Certain Other Requesting Parties*, identifies, in paragraphs .03 through .05, certain parties who may request a letter. When one of those parties requests a letter or asks the accountant to perform agreed-upon procedures on pro forma financial information in connection with an offering, the accountant should follow the guidance in AU section 634 (see paragraphs .03 through .10, .36, .42, and .43). [As amended, effective for letters issued pursuant to AU section 634.09 after April 30, 1996, by Statement on Auditing Standards No. 76.] (See AU section 634.)

[2] In certain circumstances, generally accepted accounting principles may require the presentation of pro forma financial information in the financial statements or accompanying notes. That information includes, for example, pro forma financial information required by APB Opinion 16, *Business Combinations* (paragraphs 61, 65, and 96 [AC B50.120, .124, and .165]); APB Opinion 20, *Accounting Changes* (paragraph 21 [AC A06.117]); or, in some cases, pro forma financial information relating to subsequent events (see AU section 560.05). For guidance in reporting on audited financial statements that include pro forma financial information for a business combination or subsequent event, see AU section 508, *Reports on Audited Financial Statements*, paragraph .28.

- Disposition of a significant portion of business.
- Change in the form of business organization or status as an autonomous entity.
- Proposed sale of securities and the application of proceeds.

.05 This objective is achieved primarily by applying pro forma adjustments to historical financial information. Pro forma adjustments should be based on management's assumptions and give effect to all significant effects directly attributable to the transaction (or event).

.06 Pro forma financial information should be labeled as such to distinguish it from historical financial information. This presentation should describe the transaction (or event) that is reflected in the pro forma financial information, the source of the historical financial information on which it is based, the significant assumptions used in developing the pro forma adjustments, and any significant uncertainties about those assumptions. The presentation also should indicate that the pro forma financial information should be read in conjunction with related historical financial information and that the pro forma financial information is not necessarily indicative of the results (such as financial position and results of operations, as applicable) that would have been attained had the transaction (or event) actually taken place earlier.[3]

Conditions for Reporting

.07 The accountant may agree to report on an examination or a review of pro forma financial information if the following conditions are met:

a. The document that contains the pro forma financial information includes (or incorporates by reference) complete historical financial statements of the entity for the most recent year (or for the preceding year if financial statements for the most recent year are not yet available) and, if pro forma financial information is presented for an interim period, the document also includes (or incorporates by reference) historical interim financial information for that period (which may be presented in condensed form).[4] In the case of a business combination, the document should include (or incorporate by reference) the appropriate historical financial information for the significant constituent parts of the combined entity.

b. The historical financial statements of the entity (or, in the case of a business combination, of each significant constituent part of the combined entity) on which the pro forma financial information is based have been audited or reviewed.[5] The accountant's attestation risk relating to the pro forma financial information is affected by the scope of the engagement providing the accountant with assurance about the underlying historical financial information to which the

[3] For further guidance on the presentation of pro forma financial information included in filings with the Securities and Exchange Commission (SEC), see Article 11 of Regulation S-X.

[4] For pro forma financial information included in an SEC Form 8-K, historical financial information previously included in an SEC filing would meet this requirement. Interim historical financial information may be presented as a column in the pro forma financial information.

[5] The accountant's audit or review report should be included (or incorporated by reference) in the document containing the pro forma financial information. The review may be that as defined in AU section 722, *Interim Financial Information*, for public companies, or as defined in Statement on Standards for Accounting and Review Services 1, *Compilation and Review of Financial Statements* [AR section 100], for nonpublic companies.

pro forma adjustments are applied. Therefore, the level of assurance given by the accountant on the pro forma financial information, as of a particular date or for a particular period, should be limited to the level of assurance provided on the historical financial statements (or, in the case of a business combination, the lowest level of assurance provided on the underlying historical financial statements of any significant constituent part of the combined entity). For example, if the underlying historical financial statements of each significant constituent part of the combined entity have been audited at year end and reviewed at an interim date, the accountant may perform an examination or a review of the pro forma financial information at year end but is limited to performing a review of the pro forma financial information at the interim date.

c. The accountant who is reporting on the pro forma financial information should have an appropriate level of knowledge of the accounting and financial reporting practices of each significant constituent part of the combined entity. This would ordinarily have been obtained by the accountant auditing or reviewing historical financial statements of each entity for the most recent annual or interim period for which the pro forma financial information is presented. If another accountant has performed such an audit or a review, the need, by the accountant reporting on the pro forma financial information, for an understanding of the entity's accounting and financial reporting practices is not diminished, and that accountant should consider whether, under the particular circumstances, he or she can acquire sufficient knowledge of these matters to perform the procedures necessary to report on the pro forma financial information.

Accountant's Objective

.08 The objective of the accountant's examination procedures applied to pro forma financial information is to provide reasonable assurance as to whether—

- Management's assumptions provide a reasonable basis for presenting the significant effects directly attributable to the underlying transaction (or event).
- The related pro forma adjustments give appropriate effect to those assumptions.
- The pro forma column reflects the proper application of those adjustments to the historical financial statements.

.09 The objective of the accountant's review procedures applied to pro forma financial information is to provide negative assurance as to whether any information came to the accountant's attention to cause him or her to believe that—

- Management's assumptions do not provide a reasonable basis for presenting the significant effects directly attributable to the transaction (or event).
- The related pro forma adjustments do not give appropriate effect to those assumptions.
- The pro forma column does not reflect the proper application of those adjustments to the historical financial statements.

Procedures

.10 Other than the procedures applied to the historical financial statements,[6] the procedures the accountant should apply to the assumptions and pro forma adjustments for either an examination or a review engagement are as follows:

a. Obtain an understanding of the underlying transaction (or event), for example, by reading relevant contracts and minutes of meetings of the board of directors and by making inquiries of appropriate officials of the entity, and, in some cases, of the entity acquired or to be acquired.

b. Obtain a level of knowledge of each significant constituent part of the combined entity in a business combination that will enable the accountant to perform the required procedures. Procedures to obtain this knowledge may include communicating with other accountants who have audited or reviewed the historical financial information on which the pro forma financial information is based. Matters that may be considered include accounting principles and financial reporting practices followed, transactions between the entities, and material contingencies.

c. Discuss with management their assumptions regarding the effects of the transaction (or event).

d. Evaluate whether pro forma adjustments are included for all significant effects directly attributable to the transaction (or event).

e. Obtain sufficient evidence in support of such adjustments. The evidence required to support the level of assurance given is a matter of professional judgment. The accountant typically would obtain more evidence in an examination engagement than in a review engagement. Examples of evidence that the accountant might consider obtaining are purchase, merger or exchange agreements, appraisal reports, debt agreements, employment agreements, actions of the board of directors, and existing or proposed legislation or regulatory actions.

f. Evaluate whether management's assumptions that underlie the pro forma adjustments are presented in a sufficiently clear and comprehensive manner. Also, evaluate whether the pro forma adjustments are consistent with each other and with the data used to develop them.

g. Determine that computations of pro forma adjustments are mathematically correct and that the pro forma column reflects the proper application of those adjustments to the historical financial statements.

h. Obtain written representations from management concerning their—

- Responsibility for the assumptions used in determining the pro forma adjustments.
- Belief that the assumptions provide a reasonable basis for presenting all of the significant effects directly attributable to the transaction (or event), that the related pro forma adjustments

[6] See paragraph .07(*b*).

give appropriate effect to those assumptions, and that the pro forma column reflects the proper application of those adjustments to the historical financial statements.

- Belief that the significant effects directly attributable to the transaction (or event) are appropriately disclosed in the pro forma financial information.

i. Read the pro forma financial information and evaluate whether—

- The underlying transaction (or event), the pro forma adjustments, the significant assumptions and the significant uncertainties, if any, about those assumptions have been appropriately described.

- The source of the historical financial information on which the pro forma financial information is based has been appropriately identified.

Reporting on Pro Forma Financial Information

.11 The accountant's report on pro forma financial information should be dated as of the completion of the appropriate procedures. The accountant's report on pro forma financial information may be added to the accountant's report on historical financial information, or it may appear separately. If the reports are combined and the date of completion of the procedures for the examination or review of the pro forma financial information is after the date of completion of the fieldwork for the audit or review of the historical financial information, the combined report should be dual-dated. (For example, "February 15, 19X2, except for the paragraphs regarding pro forma financial information as to which the date is March 20, 19X2.")

.12 An accountant's report on pro forma financial information should include—

a. An identification of the pro forma financial information.

b. A reference to the financial statements from which the historical financial information is derived and a statement as to whether such financial statements were audited or reviewed. The report on pro forma financial information should refer to any modification in the accountant's report on the historical financial statements.

c. A statement that the examination or review of the pro forma financial information was made in accordance with standards established by the American Institute of Certified Public Accountants. If a review is performed, the report should include the following statement:

A review is substantially less in scope than an examination, the objective of which is the expression of an opinion on the pro forma financial information. Accordingly, we do not express such an opinion.

d. A separate paragraph explaining the objective of pro forma financial information and its limitations.

e. (1) If an examination of pro forma financial information has been performed, the accountant's opinion as to whether management's assumptions provide a reasonable basis for presenting the significant effects directly attributable to the transaction (or event), whether the related pro forma adjustments give appropriate effect to those assumptions, and whether the pro forma column reflects the proper application of those adjustments to the historical financial statements (see paragraphs .16 and .18).

(2) If a review of pro forma financial information has been performed, the accountant's conclusion as to whether any information came to the accountant's attention to cause him or her to believe that management's assumptions do not provide a reasonable basis for presenting the significant effects directly attributable to the transaction (or event), or that the related pro forma adjustments do not give appropriate effect to those assumptions, or that the pro forma column does not reflect the proper application of those adjustments to the historical financial statements (see paragraphs .17 and .18).

.13 Because a pooling-of-interests business combination is accounted for by combining historical amounts retroactively, pro forma adjustments for a proposed transaction generally affect only the equity section of the pro forma condensed balance sheet. Further, because of the requirements of the Accounting Principles Board Opinion No. 16, *Business Combinations* [AC B50], a business combination effected as a pooling of interests would not ordinarily involve a choice of assumptions by management. Accordingly, a report on a proposed pooling transaction need not address management's assumptions unless the pro forma financial information includes adjustments to conform the accounting principles of the combining entities (see paragraph .19).

.14 Restrictions on the scope of the engagement, significant uncertainties about the assumptions that could materially affect the transaction (or event), reservations about the propriety of the assumptions and the conformity of the presentation with those assumptions (including inadequate disclosure of significant matters), or other reservations may require the accountant to qualify the opinion, render an adverse opinion, disclaim an opinion or withdraw from the engagement.[7] The accountant should disclose all substantive reasons for any report modifications. Uncertainty as to whether the transaction (or event) will be consummated would not ordinarily require a report modification (see paragraph .20).

Effective Date

.15 This section is effective for reports on an examination or a review of pro forma financial information issued on or after November 1, 1988. Earlier application of the provisions of this section is permissible.

---

[7] See paragraph 66 of the SSAE, *Attestation Standards* [section 100.67].

Examples of Reports on Pro Forma Financial Information

.16

Appendix A

Report on Examination of Pro Forma Financial Information

We have examined the pro forma adjustments reflecting the transaction [*or event*] described in Note 1 and the application of those adjustments to the historical amounts in [*the assembly of*][8] the accompanying pro forma condensed balance sheet of X Company as of December 31, 19X1, and the pro forma condensed statement of income for the year then ended. The historical condensed financial statements are derived from the historical financial statements of X Company, which were audited by us, and of Y Company, which were audited by other accountants,[9] appearing elsewhere herein [*or incorporated by reference*].[10] Such pro forma adjustments are based upon management's assumptions described in Note 2. Our examination was made in accordance with standards established by the American Institute of Certified Public Accountants and, accordingly, included such procedures as we considered necessary in the circumstances.

The objective of this pro forma financial information is to show what the significant effects on the historical financial information might have been had the transaction [*or event*] occurred at an earlier date. However, the pro forma condensed financial statements are not necessarily indicative of the results of operations or related effects on financial position that would have been attained had the above-mentioned transaction [*or event*] actually occurred earlier.

[*Additional paragraph(s) may be added to emphasize certain matters relating to the attest engagement.*]

In our opinion, management's assumptions provide a reasonable basis for presenting the significant effects directly attributable to the above-mentioned transaction [*or event*] described in Note 1, the related pro forma adjustments give appropriate effect to those assumptions, and the pro forma column reflects the proper application of those adjustments to the historical financial statement amounts in the pro forma condensed balance sheet as of December 31, 19X1, and the pro forma condensed statement of income for the year then ended.

---

[8] This wording is appropriate when one column of pro forma financial information is presented without separate columns of historical financial information and pro forma adjustments.

[9] If either accountant's report includes an explanatory paragraph or is other than unqualified, that fact should be referred to within this report.

[10] If the option in footnote 4 to paragraph .07*a* is followed, the report should be appropriately modified.

.17

Appendix B

Report on Review of Pro Forma Financial Information

We have reviewed the pro forma adjustments reflecting the transaction [*or event*] described in Note 1 and the application of those adjustments to the historical amounts in [*the assembly of*][11] the accompanying pro forma condensed balance sheet of X Company as of March 31, 19X2, and the pro forma condensed statement of income for the three months then ended. These historical condensed financial statements are derived from the historical unaudited financial statements of X Company, which were reviewed by us, and of Y Company, which were reviewed by other accountants,[12, 13] appearing elsewhere herein [*or incorporated by reference*].[14] Such pro forma adjustments are based on management's assumptions as described in Note 2. Our review was conducted in accordance with standards established by the American Institute of Certified Public Accountants.

A review is substantially less in scope than an examination, the objective of which is the expression of an opinion on management's assumptions, the pro forma adjustments and the application of those adjustments to historical financial information. Accordingly, we do not express such an opinion.

The objective of this pro forma financial information is to show what the significant effects on the historical information might have been had the transaction [*or event*] occurred at an earlier date. However, the pro forma condensed financial statements are not necessarily indicative of the results of operations or related effects on financial position that would have been attained had the above-mentioned transaction [*or event*] actually occurred earlier.

[*Additional paragraph(s) may be added to emphasize certain matters relating to the attest engagement.*]

Based on our review, nothing came to our attention that caused us to believe that management's assumptions do not provide a reasonable basis for presenting the significant effects directly attributable to the above-mentioned transaction [*or event*] described in Note 1, that the related pro forma adjustments do not give appropriate effect to those assumptions, or that the pro forma column does not reflect the proper application of those adjustments to the historical financial statement amounts in the pro forma condensed balance sheet as of March 31, 19X2, and the pro forma condensed statement of income for the three months then ended.

---

[11] This wording is appropriate when one column of pro forma financial information is presented without separate columns of historical financial information and pro forma adjustments.

[12] If either accountant's report includes an explanatory paragraph or is modified, that fact should be referred to within this report.

[13] Where one set of historical financial statements is audited and the other set is reviewed, wording similar to the following would be appropriate:

The historical condensed financial statements are derived from the historical financial statements of X Company, which were audited by us, and of Y Company, which were reviewed by other accountants, appearing elsewhere herein [*or incorporated by reference*].

[14] If the option in footnote 4 to paragraph .07*a* is followed, the report should be appropriately modified.

.18

Appendix C

Report on Examination of Pro Forma Financial Information at Year End With a Review of Pro Forma Financial Information for a Subsequent Interim Date

We have examined the pro forma adjustments reflecting the transaction [*or event*] described in Note 1 and the application of those adjustments to the historical amounts in [*the assembly of*][15] the accompanying pro forma condensed balance sheet of X Company as of December 31, 19X1, and the pro forma condensed statement of income for the year then ended. The historical condensed financial statements are derived from the historical financial statements of X Company, which were audited by us, and of Y Company, which were audited by other accountants,[16] appearing elsewhere herein [*or incorporated by reference*].[17] Such pro forma adjustments are based upon management's assumptions described in Note 2. Our examination was made in accordance with standards established by the American Institute of Certified Public Accountants and, accordingly, included such procedures as we considered necessary in the circumstances.

In addition, we have reviewed the related pro forma adjustments and the application of those adjustments to the historical amounts in [*the assembly of*][15] the accompanying pro forma condensed balance sheet of X Company as of March 31, 19X2, and the pro forma condensed statement of income for the three months then ended. The historical condensed financial statements are derived from the historical financial statements of X Company, which were reviewed by us, and Y Company, which were reviewed by other accountants,[18] appearing elsewhere herein [*or incorporated by reference*].[17] Such pro forma adjustments are based upon management's assumptions described in Note 2. Our review was made in accordance with standards established by the American Institute of Certified Public Accountants.

The objective of this pro forma financial information is to show what the significant effects on the historical information might have been had the transaction [*or event*] occurred at an earlier date. However, the pro forma condensed financial statements are not necessarily indicative of the results of operations or related effects on financial position that would have been attained had the above-mentioned transaction [*or event*] actually occurred earlier.

[*Additional paragraph(s) may be added to emphasize certain matters relating to the attest engagements.*]

In our opinion, management's assumptions provide a reasonable basis for presenting the significant effects directly attributable to the above-mentioned

---

[15] This wording is appropriate when one column of pro forma financial information is presented without separate columns of historical financial information and pro forma adjustments.

[16] If either accountant's report includes an explanatory paragraph or is other than unqualified, that fact should be referred to within this report.

[17] If the option in footnote 4 to paragraph .07*a* is followed, the report should be appropriately modified.

[18] Where one set of historical financial statements is audited and the other set is reviewed, wording similar to the following would be appropriate:

> The historical condensed financial statements are derived from the historical financial statements of X Company, which were audited by us, and of Y Company, which were reviewed by other accountants, appearing elsewhere herein [*or incorporated by reference*].

transaction [*or event*] described in Note 1, the related pro forma adjustments give appropriate effect to those assumptions, and the pro forma column reflects the proper application of those adjustments to the historical financial statement amounts in the pro forma condensed balance sheet as of December 31, 19X1, and the pro forma condensed statement of income for the year then ended.

A review is substantially less in scope than an examination, the objective of which is the expression of an opinion on management's assumptions, the pro forma adjustments and the application of those adjustments to historical financial information. Accordingly, we do not express such an opinion on the pro forma adjustments or the application of such adjustments to the pro forma condensed balance sheet as of March 31, 19X2, and the pro forma condensed statement of income for the three months then ended. Based on our review, however, nothing came to our attention that caused us to believe that management's assumptions do not provide a reasonable basis for presenting the significant effects directly attributable to the above-mentioned transaction [*or event*] described in Note 1, that the related pro forma adjustments do not give appropriate effect to those assumptions, or that the pro forma column does not reflect the proper application of those adjustments to the historical financial statement amounts in the pro forma condensed balance sheet as of March 31, 19X2, and the pro forma condensed statement of income for the three months then ended.

.19

Appendix D

Report on Examination of Pro Forma Financial Information Giving Effect to a Business Combination to be Accounted for as a Pooling of Interests

We have examined the pro forma adjustments reflecting the proposed business combination to be accounted for as a pooling of interests described in Note 1 and the application of those adjustments to the historical amounts in the accompanying pro forma condensed balance sheet of X Company as of December 31, 19X1, and the pro forma condensed statements of income for each of the three years in the period then ended. These historical condensed financial statements are derived from the historical financial statements of X Company, which were audited by us,[19] and of Y Company, which were audited by other accountants, appearing elsewhere herein [*or incorporated by reference*].[20] Our examination was made in accordance with standards established by the American Institute of Certified Public Accountants and, accordingly, included such procedures as we considered necessary in the circumstances.

The objective of this pro forma financial information is to show what the significant effects on the historical information might have been had the proposed transaction occurred at an earlier date.

[*Additional paragraph(s) may be added to emphasize certain matters relating to the attest engagement.*]

In our opinion, the accompanying condensed pro forma financial statements of X Company as of December 31, 19X1, and for each of the three years in the period then ended give appropriate effect to the pro forma adjustments necessary to reflect the proposed business combination on a pooling of interests basis as described in Note 1 and the pro forma column reflects the proper application of those adjustments to the historical financial statements.

---

[19] If either accountant's report includes an explanatory paragraph or is other than unqualified, that fact should be referred to within this report.

[20] If the option in footnote 4 to paragraph .07*a* is followed, the report should be appropriately modified.

.20

Appendix E

Other Example Reports

An example of a report qualified because of a scope limitation follows:

We have examined the pro forma adjustments reflecting the transaction [*or event*] described in Note 1 and the application of those adjustments to the historical amounts in [*the assembly of*][21] the accompanying pro forma condensed balance sheet of X Company as of December 31, 19X1, and the pro forma condensed statement of income for the year then ended. The historical condensed financial statements are derived from the historical financial statements of X Company, which were audited by us, and of Y Company, which were audited by other accountants,[22] appearing elsewhere herein [*or incorporated by reference*].[23] Such pro forma adjustments are based upon management's assumptions described in Note 2. Our examination was made in accordance with standards established by the American Institute of Certified Public Accountants and, accordingly, included such procedures as we considered necessary in the circumstances, except as explained in the following paragraphs.

We are unable to perform the examination procedures we considered necessary with respect to assumptions relating to the proposed loan described as Adjustment E in Note 2.

[*Same paragraph as second paragraph in examination report in paragraph .16*]

In our opinion, except for the effects of such changes, if any, as might have been determined to be necessary had we been able to satisfy ourselves as to the assumptions relating to the proposed loan, management's assumptions provide a reasonable basis for presenting the significant effects directly attributable to the above-mentioned transaction [*or event*] described in Note 1, the related pro forma adjustments give appropriate effect to those assumptions, and the pro forma column reflects the proper application of those adjustments to the historical financial statement amounts in the pro forma condensed balance sheet as of December 31, 19X1, and the pro forma condensed statement of income for the year then ended.

An example of a report modified because of an uncertainty follows:

[*Same first and second paragraphs as examination report in paragraph .16*]

In our opinion, management's assumptions provide a reasonable basis for presenting the significant effects directly attributable to the above-mentioned transaction described in Note 1, the related pro forma adjustments give appropriate effect to those assumptions, and the pro forma column reflects the proper application of those adjustments to the historical financial statement amounts in the pro forma condensed balance sheet as of December 31, 19X1, and the pro forma condensed statement of income for the year then ended.

It has been assumed that the transaction described in Note 1 is nontaxable. Such determination is dependent on an Internal Revenue Service (IRS) ruling

---

[21] This wording is appropriate when one column of pro forma financial information is presented without separate columns of historical financial information and pro forma adjustments.

[22] If either accountant's report includes an explanatory paragraph or is other than unqualified, that fact should be referred to within this report.

[23] If the option in footnote 4 to paragraph .07*a* is followed, the report should be appropriately modified.

that has been requested but not yet received by management. The ultimate decision by the IRS cannot be determined at this time.

An example of a report qualified for reservations about the propriety of assumptions on an acquisition transaction follows:

[*Same first and second paragraphs as examination report in paragraph .16*]

As discussed in Note 2 to the pro forma financial statements, the pro forma adjustments reflect management's assumption that X Division of the acquired company will be sold. The net assets of this division are reflected at their historical carrying amount; generally accepted accounting principles require these net assets to be recorded at estimated net realizable value.

In our opinion, except for inappropriate valuation of the net assets of X Division, management's assumptions described in Note 2 provide a reasonable basis for presenting the significant effects directly attributable to the above-mentioned transaction [or event] described in Note 1, the related pro forma adjustments give appropriate effect to those assumptions, and the pro forma column reflects the proper application of those adjustments to the historical financial statement amounts in the pro forma condensed balance sheet as of December 31, 19X1, and the pro forma condensed statement of income for the year then ended.

An example of a disclaimer of opinion because of a scope limitation follows:

We were engaged to examine the pro forma adjustments reflecting the transaction [*or event*] described in Note 1 and the application of those adjustments to the historical amounts in [*the assembly of*][24] the accompanying pro forma condensed balance sheet of X Company as of December 31, 19X1, and the pro forma condensed statement of income for the year then ended. The historical condensed financial statements are derived from the historical financial statements of X Company, which were audited by us,[25] and of Y Company which were audited by other accountants, appearing elsewhere herein [*or incorporated by reference*].[26] Such pro forma adjustments are based upon management's assumptions described in Note 2.

As discussed in Note 2 to the pro forma financial statements, the pro forma adjustments reflect the management's assumptions that the elimination of duplicate facilities would have resulted in a 30 percent reduction in operating costs. Management could not supply us with sufficient evidence to support this assertion.

[*Same paragraph as second paragraph in examination report in paragraph .16*]

Since we were unable to evaluate management's assumptions regarding the reduction in operating costs and other assumptions related thereto, the scope of our work was not sufficient to express and, therefore, we do not express an opinion on the pro forma adjustments, management's underlying assumptions regarding those adjustments and the application of those adjustments to the historical financial statement amounts in pro forma condensed financial statement amounts in the pro forma condensed balance sheet as of December 31, 19X1, and the pro forma condensed statement of income for the year then ended.

---

[24] See footnote 21.

[25] See footnote 22.

[26] See footnote 23.

[illegible]

[illegible]

[illegible]

[illegible]

[illegible]

[illegible]

[illegible]

[illegible]

[illegible]

AT Section 400

Reporting on an Entity's Internal Control Over Financial Reporting

(Supersedes AU section 642)

Source: SSAE No. 2; SSAE No. 4; SSAE No. 6.

See section 9400 for interpretations of this section.

Effective for an examination of management's assertion on the effectiveness of an entity's internal control over financial reporting when the assertion is as of December 15, 1993 or thereafter, unless otherwise indicated.

> *In January 1989, the Statements on Standards for Attestation Engagements (SSAE)* Attestation Standards *(AT section 100)*, Financial Forecasts and Projections *(AT section 200), and* Reporting on Pro Forma Financial Information *(AT section 300), were codified in* Codification of Statements on Standards for Attestation Engagements. *In April 1993, the codified sections became SSAE No. 1*, Attestation Standards. *This section, therefore, becomes SSAE No. 2*, Reporting on an Entity's Internal Control Over Financial Reporting.

Applicability

.01 This section provides guidance to the practitioner who is engaged to examine and report on management's written assertion about the effectiveness of an entity's internal control over financial reporting[1] as of a point in time.[2] Specifically, guidance is provided regarding the following:

a. Conditions that must be met for a practitioner to examine and report on management's assertion about the effectiveness of an entity's internal control (paragraph .10); the prohibition of acceptance of an engagement to review and report on such a management assertion (paragraph .06)

b. Engagements to examine and report on management's assertion about the design and operating effectiveness of an entity's internal control (paragraphs .15 through .66)

c. Engagements to examine and report on management's assertion about the design and operating effectiveness of a segment of an entity's internal control (paragraph .67)

---

[1] This section does not change the auditor's responsibility for considering the entity's internal control in an audit of the financial statements. See paragraphs .79 through .82 of this section.

[2] Ordinarily, management will present its assertion about the effectiveness of the entity's internal control over financial reporting as of the end of the entity's fiscal year; however, management may select a different date for its assertion. A practitioner may also be engaged to examine and report on management's assertion about the effectiveness of an entity's internal control during a period of time. In that case, the guidance in this section should be modified accordingly.

d. Engagements to examine and report on management's assertion about only the suitability of design of an entity's internal control (no assertion is made about the operating effectiveness of the internal control) (paragraphs .68 and .69)

e. Engagements to examine and report on management's assertion about the design and operating effectiveness of an entity's internal control based on criteria established by a regulatory agency (paragraphs .70 through .74)

This section does *not* provide guidance for the following:

a. Engagements to examine and report on management's assertion about controls over operations or compliance with laws and regulations[3]

b. Agreed-upon procedures engagements (except as noted in paragraph .05)

c. Certain other services in connection with an entity's internal control covered by other authoritative guidance (paragraph .07 and the appendix [paragraph .85])

d. Consulting engagements (paragraph .08)

e. Engagements to gather data for management (paragraphs .11 and .20)

.02 An entity's internal control over financial reporting[4] includes those policies and procedures that pertain to an entity's ability to record, process, summarize, and report financial data consistent with the assertions embodied in either annual financial statements or interim financial statements, or both. A practitioner engaged to examine and report on management's assertion about the effectiveness of an entity's internal control should comply with the general, fieldwork, and reporting standards in section 100, and the specific performance and reporting standards set forth in this section.[5]

.03 Management may present its written assertion about the effectiveness of the entity's internal control in either of two forms:

a. A separate report that will accompany the practitioner's report

b. A representation letter to the practitioner (in this case, however, the practitioner should restrict the use of his or her report to management and others within the entity and, if applicable, to specified regulatory agencies)

---

[3] A practitioner engaged to examine management's assertion about the effectiveness of an entity's internal control over operations or compliance with laws and regulations should refer to the guidance in section 100, *Attestation Standards*. A practitioner engaged to perform agreed-upon procedures on management's assertion relating to an entity's internal control over operations or compliance with laws and regulations should refer to the guidance in section 600, *Agreed-Upon Procedures Engagements*. In addition, the guidance in section 500, *Compliance Attestation*, may be helpful when performing an engagement relating to internal control over compliance with laws and regulations. Further, the guidance in this section may be helpful in attestation engagements to report on management's assertion about internal control over operations or compliance with laws and regulations. [As amended, effective for an examination of management's assertion when the assertion is as of or for the period ending on December 15, 1996, or thereafter, by Statement on Standards for Attestation Engagements No. 6.]

[4] Throughout this section, an entity's internal control over financial reporting is referred to as its "internal control."

[5] Practitioners engaged to examine and report on the design and/or operating effectiveness of the internal control of a service organization should refer to AU section 324, *Reports on the Processing of Transactions by Service Organizations*.

A practitioner should not consent to the use of his or her examination report on management's assertion about the effectiveness of an entity's internal control in a general-use document unless management presents its written assertion in a separate report that will accompany the practitioner's report.

.04 Management's written assertion about the effectiveness of an entity's internal control structure may take various forms. Throughout this section, for example, the phrase, "management's assertion that W Company maintained effective internal control over financial reporting as of [*date*]," illustrates such an assertion. Other phrases, such as "management's assertion that W Company's internal control over financial reporting is sufficient to meet the stated objectives" may also be used. However, a practitioner should not provide assurance on an assertion that is so subjective (for example, "very effective" internal control) that people having competence in and using the same or similar measurement and disclosure criteria would not ordinarily be able to arrive at similar conclusions.

Other Attest Services

.05 A practitioner may also be engaged to provide other types of services in connection with an entity's internal control. For example, he or she may be engaged to *perform agreed-upon procedures* relating to management's assertion about the effectiveness of the entity's internal control. For such engagements, the practitioner should refer to the guidance in *Attestation Standards*. However, notwithstanding the guidance set forth in *Attestation Standards*, a practitioner's report on agreed-upon procedures related to management's assertion about the effectiveness of the entity's internal control should be in the form of procedures and findings. The practitioner should not provide negative assurance about whether management's assertion is fairly stated.

.06 Although a practitioner may *examine* or *perform agreed-upon procedures* relating to management's assertion about the effectiveness of the entity's internal control, he or she should not accept an engagement to *review* and report on such a management assertion.

.07 The appendix [paragraph .85] presents a listing of authoritative guidance for a practitioner engaged to provide other services in connection with an entity's internal control. Under the Securities Exchange Act of 1934, certain reports on the entity's internal control are required. Rule 17a-5 requires such a report for a broker or dealer in securities. The American Institute of Certified Public Accountants (AICPA) Statement of Position (SOP) 89-4, *Reports on the Internal Control Structure of Brokers and Dealers in Securities*, contains a sample report that a practitioner might use in such circumstances. In addition, Form N-SAR requires a report on the internal control of an investment company. A sample report that a practitioner might use in such situations is included in the Audit and Accounting Guide *Audits of Investment Companies*, published by the AICPA. Such information, included in the appendix [paragraph .85] to this section, in Rule 17a-5, and in Form N-SAR, is not covered by this section.

Nonattest Services

.08 The guidance in this section does not apply if management does not present a written assertion. In this situation, there is no assertion by management on which the practitioner can provide assurance. However, management may engage the practitioner to provide certain nonattest services in connection with the entity's internal control. For example, management may engage the practitioner to provide recommendations on improvements to the entity's internal control. A practitioner engaged to provide such nonattest services should refer to the guidance in the Statement on Standards for Consulting Services [CS section 100].

[.09] [Superseded by Statement on Standards for Attestation Engagements No. 4, effective for reports on agreed-upon procedures engagements dated after April 30, 1996.] (See section 600.)

Conditions for Engagement Performance

.10 A practitioner may *examine* and report on management's assertion about the effectiveness of an entity's internal control if the following conditions are met:

a. Management accepts responsibility for the effectiveness of the entity's internal control.

b. Management evaluates the effectiveness of the entity's internal control using reasonable criteria for effective internal control established by a recognized body. Such criteria are referred to as "control criteria" throughout this section.[6]

c. Sufficient evidential matter exists or could be developed to support management's evaluation.

d. Management presents its written assertion, as discussed in paragraph .03, about the effectiveness of the entity's internal control based upon the control criteria referred to in its report.

.11 Management is responsible for establishing and maintaining effective internal control. In some cases, management may evaluate and report on the effectiveness of internal control without the practitioner's assistance. However, management may engage the practitioner to gather information to enable management to evaluate the effectiveness of the entity's internal control.

Components of an Entity's Internal Control

.12 The components that constitute an entity's internal control are a function of the definition and description of internal control selected by management for the purpose of assessing its effectiveness. For example, management may select the definition and description of internal control based on the internal control framework set forth in *Internal Control—Integrated Framework*,[7] published by the

[6] Criteria issued by the AICPA, regulatory agencies, and other bodies composed of experts that follow due process procedures, including procedures for broad distribution of proposed criteria for public comment, usually should be considered reasonable criteria for this purpose. For example, the Committee of Sponsoring Organizations (COSO) of the Treadway Commission's report, *Internal Control—Integrated Framework*, provides reasonable criteria against which management may evaluate and report on the effectiveness of the entity's internal control.

Criteria established by groups that do not follow due process or groups that do not as clearly represent the public interest should be viewed more critically. The practitioner should judge whether such criteria are reasonable for general distribution reporting by evaluating them against the elements in section 100.15. If the practitioner determines that such criteria are reasonable for general distribution reporting, such criteria should be stated in the presentation of the assertion in a sufficiently clear and comprehensive manner for a reader to be able to understand them.

Some criteria are reasonable for only the parties who have participated in establishing them; for example, criteria established by a regulatory agency for its specific use. When such criteria are used, they are not suitable for general distribution reporting and the practitioner should modify his or her report by adding a paragraph that limits the report distribution to the specific parties who have participated in establishing the criteria.

[7] As noted in footnote 6, this report also contains control criteria. [Footnote added, effective for an examination of management's assertion when the assertion is as of or for the period ending on December 15, 1996, or thereafter, by Statement on Standards for Attestation Engagements No. 6.]

Committee of Sponsoring Organizations of the Treadway Commission.[8] *Internal Control—Integrated Framework* describes an entity's internal control as consisting of five components: control environment, risk assessment, control activities, information and communication, and monitoring. If management selects another definition and description of internal control, these components may not be relevant. [As amended, effective for an examination of management's assertion when the assertion is as of or for the period ending on December 15, 1996, or thereafter, by Statement on Standards for Attestation Engagements No. 6.]

Former paragraphs .13 through .16 have been deleted and all subsequent paragraphs renumbered by the issuance of Statement on Standards for Attestation Engagements No. 6, effective for an examination of management's assertion when the assertion is as of or for the period ending on December 15, 1996, or thereafter.

Limitations of an Entity's Internal Control

.13 Internal control, no matter how well designed and operated, can provide only reasonable assurance to management and the board of directors regarding achievement of an entity's control objectives. The likelihood of achievement is affected by limitations inherent to internal control. These include the realities that human judgment in decision-making can be faulty, and that breakdowns in internal control can occur because of such human failures as simple error or mistake. Additionally, controls can be circumvented by the collusion of two or more people or management override of internal control. [Paragraph renumbered and amended, effective for an examination of management's assertion when the assertion is as of or for the period ending on December 15, 1996, or thereafter, by the issuance of Statement on Standards for Attestation Engagements No. 6.]

.14 Custom, culture, and the corporate governance system may inhibit irregularities by management, but they are not absolute deterrents. An effective control environment, too, may help mitigate the probability of such irregularities. For example, an effective board of directors, audit committee, and an internal audit function may constrain improper conduct by management. Alternatively, an ineffective control environment may negate the effectiveness of the other components. For example, when the presence of management incentives creates an environment that could result in material misstatement of financial statements, the effectiveness of control activities may be reduced. The effectiveness of an entity's internal control might also be adversely affected by such factors as a change in ownership or control, changes in management or other personnel, or developments in the entity's market or industry. [Paragraph renumbered and amended, effective for an examination of management's assertion when the assertion is as of or for the period ending on December 15, 1996, or thereafter, by the issuance of Statement on Standards for Attestation Engagements No. 6.]

---

[8] This definition and description is consistent with the definition contained in AU section 319, *Consideration of Internal Control in a Financial Statement Audit*. However, AU section 319 is not intended to provide criteria for evaluating internal control effectiveness. [Footnote added, effective for an examination of management's assertion when the assertion is as of or for the period ending on December 15, 1996, or thereafter, by Statement on Standards for Attestation Engagements No. 6.]

Examination Engagement

.15 The practitioner's objective in an engagement to examine and report on management's assertion about the effectiveness of the entity's internal control is to express an opinion about whether management's assertion regarding the effectiveness of the entity's internal control is fairly stated, in all material respects, based upon the control criteria. The practitioner's opinion relates to the fair presentation of management's assertion about the effectiveness of the entity's internal control taken as a whole, and not to the effectiveness of each individual component (control environment, risk assessment, control activities, information and communication, and monitoring) of the entity's internal control.[9] Therefore, the practitioner considers the interrelationship of the components of an entity's internal control in achieving the objectives of the control criteria. To express an opinion on management's assertion, the practitioner accumulates sufficient evidence about the design effectiveness and operating effectiveness of the entity's internal control to attest to management's assertion, thereby limiting attestation risk to an appropriately low level. When evaluating the design effectiveness of specific controls, the practitioner considers whether the control is suitably designed to prevent or detect material misstatements on a timely basis. When evaluating operating effectiveness, the practitioner considers how the control was applied, the consistency with which it was applied, and by whom it was applied. [Paragraph renumbered by the issuance of Statement on Standards for Attestation Engagements No. 6, December 1995.]

.16 Performing an examination of management's assertion about the effectiveness of an entity's internal control involves (*a*) planning the engagement, (*b*) obtaining an understanding of internal control, (*c*) evaluating the design effectiveness of the controls, (*d*) testing and evaluating the operating effectiveness of the controls and (*e*) forming an opinion about whether management's assertion regarding the effectiveness of the entity's internal control is fairly stated, in all material respects, based on the control criteria. [Paragraph renumbered and amended, effective for an examination of management's assertion when the assertion is as of or for the period ending on December 15, 1996, or thereafter, by the issuance of Statement on Standards for Attestation Engagements No. 6.]

Planning the Engagement

General Considerations

.17 Planning an engagement to examine and report on management's assertion about the effectiveness of the entity's internal control involves developing an overall strategy for the scope and performance of the engagement. When developing an overall strategy for the engagement, the practitioner should consider factors such as the following:

- Matters affecting the industry in which the entity operates, such as financial reporting practices, economic conditions, laws and regulations, and technological changes.
- Knowledge of the entity's internal control obtained during other professional engagements

[9] However, as discussed in paragraph .67, management's assertion may relate to a segment of its internal control. [Footnote renumbered by the issuance of Statement on Standards for Attestation Engagements No. 6, December 1995.]

- Matters relating to the entity's business, including its organization, operating characteristics, capital structure, and distribution methods
- The extent of recent changes, if any, in the entity, its operations, or its internal control
- Management's method of evaluating the effectiveness of the entity's internal control based upon control criteria
- Preliminary judgments about materiality levels, inherent risk, and other factors relating to the determination of material weaknesses
- The type and extent of evidential matter supporting management's assertion about the effectiveness of the entity's internal control
- The nature of specific controls designed to achieve the objectives of the control criteria, and their significance to internal control taken as a whole
- Preliminary judgments about the effectiveness of internal control

[Paragraph renumbered by the issuance of Statement on Standards for Attestation Engagements No. 6, December 1995.]

Multiple Locations

.18 A practitioner planning an engagement to examine management's assertion about the effectiveness of the internal control of an entity with operations in several locations should consider factors similar to those he or she would consider in performing an audit of the financial statements of an entity with multiple locations. It may not be necessary to understand and test controls at each location. In addition to the factors listed in paragraph .17, the selection of locations should be based on factors such as (*a*) the similarity of business operations and internal control at the various locations, (*b*) the degree of centralization of records, (*c*) the effectiveness of control environment policies and procedures, particularly those that affect management's direct control over the exercise of authority delegated to others and its ability to effectively supervise activities at the various locations, and (*d*) the nature and amount of transactions executed and related assets at the various locations. [Paragraph renumbered by the issuance of Statement on Standards for Attestation Engagements No. 6, December 1995.]

Internal Audit Function

.19 Another factor the practitioner should consider when planning the engagement is whether the entity has an internal audit function. An important responsibility of the internal audit function is to monitor the performance of an entity's controls. One way internal auditors monitor such performance is by performing tests that provide evidence about the effectiveness of the design and operation of specific controls. The results of these tests are often an important basis for management's assertions about the effectiveness of the entity's internal control. A practitioner should consider the guidance in AU section 322, *The Auditor's Consideration of the Internal Audit Function in an Audit of Financial Statements*, when assessing the competence and objectivity of internal auditors, the extent of work to be performed, and other matters. [Paragraph renumbered by the issuance of Statement on Standards for Attestation Engagements No. 6, December 1995.]

Documentation

.20 Controls and the control objectives that they were designed to achieve should be appropriately documented to serve as a basis for management's and the practitioner's reports. Such documentation is generally prepared by management. However, at management's request, the practitioner may assist in preparing or gathering such documentation. This documentation may take various forms: entity policy manuals, accounting manuals, narrative memoranda, flowcharts, decision tables, procedural write-ups, or completed questionnaires. No one particular form of documentation is necessary, and the extent of documentation may vary depending upon the size and complexity of the entity. [Paragraph renumbered by the issuance of Statement on Standards for Attestation Engagements No. 6, December 1995.]

Obtaining an Understanding of the Internal Control

.21 A practitioner generally obtains an understanding of the design of specific controls by making inquiries of appropriate management, supervisory, and staff personnel; by inspecting entity documents; and by observing entity activities and operations. The nature and extent of the procedures a practitioner performs vary from entity to entity and are influenced by factors such as those discussed in paragraph .12. [Paragraph renumbered by the issuance of Statement on Standards for Attestation Engagements No. 6, December 1995.]

Evaluating the Design Effectiveness of Controls

.22 To evaluate the design effectiveness of an entity's internal control, the practitioner should obtain an understanding of the controls within each component of internal control.[10] [Paragraph renumbered and amended, effective for an examination of management's assertion when the assertion is as of or for the period ending on December 15, 1996, or thereafter, by the issuance of Statement on Standards for Attestation Engagements No. 6.]

> Former paragraph .27 has been deleted and all subsequent paragraphs renumbered by the issuance of Statement on Standards for Attestation Engagements No. 6, effective for an examination of management's assertion when the assertion is as of or for the period ending on December 15, 1996, or thereafter.

.23 Any of the elements of internal control may include controls designed to achieve the objectives of the control criteria. Some controls may have a pervasive effect on achieving many overall objectives of these criteria. For example, computer general controls over program development, program changes, computer operations, and access to programs and data help assure that specific controls over the processing of transactions are operating effectively. In contrast, other controls are designed to achieve specific objectives of the control criteria. For example, management generally establishes specific

[10] As discussed in paragraph .12, the components that constitute an entity's internal control are a function of the definition and description of internal control selected by management. Paragraph .12 lists the components the practitioner should understand if management decides to evaluate and report on the entity's internal control based on the definition of internal control in *Internal Control—Integrated Framework*, published by the Committee of Sponsoring Organizations of the Treadway Commission. If management selects another definition, these components may not be relevant. [Footnote added, effective for an examination of management's assertion when the assertion is as of or for the period ending on December 15, 1996, or thereafter, by Statement on Standards for Attestation Engagements No. 6.]

controls, such as accounting for all shipping documents, to ensure that all valid sales are recorded. [Paragraph renumbered by the issuance of Statement on Standards for Attestation Engagements No. 6, December 1995.]

.24 The practitioner should focus on the significance of controls in achieving the objectives of the control criteria rather than on specific controls in isolation. The absence or inadequacy of a specific control designed to achieve the objectives of a specific criterion may not be a deficiency if other controls specifically address the same criterion. Further, when one or more control achieves the objectives of a specific criterion, the practitioner may not need to consider other controls designed to achieve those same objectives. [Paragraph renumbered by the issuance of Statement on Standards for Attestation Engagements No. 6, December 1995.]

.25 Procedures to evaluate the effectiveness of the design of a specific control are concerned with whether that control is suitably designed to prevent or detect material misstatements in specific financial statement assertions. Such procedures will vary depending upon the nature of the specific control, the nature of the entity's documentation of the specific control, and the complexity and sophistication of the entity's operations and systems. [Paragraph renumbered by the issuance of Statement on Standards for Attestation Engagements No. 6, December 1995.]

Testing and Evaluating the Operating Effectiveness of Controls

.26 To evaluate the operating effectiveness of an entity's internal control, the practitioner performs tests of relevant controls to obtain sufficient evidence to support the opinion in the report. Tests of the operating effectiveness of a control are concerned with how the control was applied, the consistency with which it was applied, and by whom it was applied. The tests ordinarily include procedures such as inquiries of appropriate personnel, inspection of relevant documentation, observation of the entity's operations, and reapplication or reperformance of the control. [Paragraph renumbered by the issuance of Statement on Standards for Attestation Engagements No. 6, December 1995.]

.27 The evidential matter that is sufficient to support a practitioner's opinion on management's assertion is a matter of professional judgment. However, the practitioner should consider matters such as the following:

- The nature of the control
- The significance of the control in achieving the objectives of the control criteria
- The nature and extent of tests of the operating effectiveness of the controls performed by the entity, if any
- The risk of noncompliance with the control, which might be assessed by considering the following:
  - — Whether there have been changes in the volume or nature of transactions that might adversely affect control design or operating effectiveness
  - — Whether there have been changes in controls
  - — The degree to which the control relies on the effectiveness of other controls (for example, control environment policies and procedures or computer general controls)
  - — Whether there have been changes in key personnel who perform the control or monitor its performance

— Whether the control relies on performance by an individual or by electronic equipment
— The complexity of the control
— Whether more than one control achieves a specific objective

[Paragraph renumbered by the issuance of Statement on Standards for Attestation Engagements No. 6, December 1995.]

.28 Management or other entity personnel may provide the practitioner with the results of their tests of the operating effectiveness of certain controls. Although the practitioner should consider the results of such tests when evaluating the operating effectiveness of controls, it is the practitioner's responsibility to obtain sufficient evidence to support his or her opinion and, if applicable, corroborate the results of such tests. When evaluating whether sufficient evidence has been obtained, the practitioner should consider that evidence obtained through his or her direct personal knowledge, observation, reperformance, and inspection is more persuasive than information obtained indirectly, such as from management or other entity personnel. Further, judgments about the sufficiency of evidence obtained and other factors affecting the practitioner's opinion, such as the materiality of identified control deficiencies, should be those of the practitioner. [Paragraph renumbered by the issuance of Statement on Standards for Attestation Engagements No. 6, December 1995.]

.29 The nature of the controls influences the nature of the tests of controls the practitioner can perform. For example, the practitioner may examine documents regarding controls for which documentary evidence exists. However, documentary evidence regarding some control environment policies and procedures (such as management's philosophy and operating style) often does not exist. In these circumstances, the practitioner's tests of controls would consist of inquiries of appropriate personnel and observation of entity activities. The practitioner's preliminary judgments about the effectiveness of control environment policies and procedures often influence the nature, timing, and extent of the tests of controls to be performed to obtain evidence about the operating effectiveness of controls in the accounting system and other controls. [Paragraph renumbered by the issuance of Statement on Standards for Attestation Engagements No. 6, December 1995.]

.30 The period of time over which the practitioner should perform tests of controls is a matter of judgment; however, it varies with the nature of the controls being tested and with the frequency with which specific controls operate and specific policies are applied. Some controls operate continuously (for example, controls over sales) while others operate only at certain times (for example, controls over the preparation of interim financial statements and controls over physical inventory counts). The practitioner should perform tests of controls over a period of time that is adequate to determine whether, as of the date selected by management for its assertion, the controls necessary for achieving the objectives of the control criteria are operating effectively. [Paragraph renumbered by the issuance of Statement on Standards for Attestation Engagements No. 6, December 1995.]

.31 Management may present a written assertion about the effectiveness of controls related to the preparation of interim financial information. Depending on management's assertion, the practitioner should perform tests of controls in effect during one or more interim periods to form an opinion about the effectiveness of such controls in achieving the related interim reporting objectives. [Paragraph renumbered by the issuance of Statement on Standards for Attestation Engagements No. 6, December 1995.]

.32 Prior to the date as of which it presents its assertion, management may change the entity's controls to make them more effective or efficient, or to address control deficiencies. In these circumstances, the practitioner may not need to consider controls that have been superseded. For example, if the practitioner determines that the new controls achieve the related objectives of the control criteria and have been in effect for a sufficient period to permit the practitioner to assess their design and operating effectiveness by performing tests of controls, the practitioner will not need to consider the design and operating effectiveness of the superseded controls. [Paragraph renumbered by the issuance of Statement on Standards for Attestation Engagements No. 6, December 1995.]

Forming an Opinion on Management's Assertion

.33 When forming an opinion on management's assertion about the effectiveness of an entity's internal control, the practitioner should consider all evidence obtained, including the results of the tests of controls and any identified control deficiencies, to evaluate the design and operating effectiveness of the controls based on the control criteria. [Paragraph renumbered by the issuance of Statement on Standards for Attestation Engagements No. 6, December 1995.]

Deficiencies in an Entity's Internal Control

.34 During the course of the engagement, the practitioner may become aware of significant deficiencies in the entity's internal control. The practitioner's responsibility to communicate such deficiencies is described in paragraphs .40 and .41. [Paragraph renumbered by the issuance of Statement on Standards for Attestation Engagements No. 6, December 1995.]

Reportable Conditions

.35 AU section 325, *Communication of Internal Control Related Matters Noted in an Audit*, defines reportable conditions as matters coming to an auditor's attention that represent significant deficiencies in the design or operation of internal control that could adversely affect the entity's ability to record, process, summarize, and report financial data consistent with the assertions of management in the financial statements. [Paragraph renumbered by the issuance of Statement on Standards for Attestation Engagements No. 6, December 1995.]

Material Weaknesses

.36 A reportable condition may be of such magnitude as to be considered a material weakness. AU section 325 defines a material weakness as a condition in which the design or operation of one or more of the internal control [components] does not reduce to a relatively low level the risk that misstatements caused by error or fraud in amounts that would be material in relation to the financial statements may occur and not be detected within a timely period by employees in the normal course of performing their assigned functions. Therefore, the presence of a material weakness will preclude management from asserting that the entity has effective internal control. However, depending on the significance of the material weakness and its effect on the achievement of the objectives of the control criteria, management may qualify its assertion (that is, assert that internal control is effective "except for" the material weakness noted).[11] [Paragraph renumbered by the issuance of Statement on Standards for Attestation Engagements No. 6, December 1995.]

.37 When evaluating whether a reportable condition is also a material weakness, the practitioner should recognize that—

a. The amounts of misstatements caused by error or fraud that might occur and remain undetected range from zero to more than the gross financial statement amounts or transactions that are exposed to the reportable condition.

b. The risk of misstatement due to error or fraud is likely to be different for the different possible amounts within that range. For example, the risk of misstatement due to error or fraud in amounts equal to the gross exposure might be very low, but the risk of smaller amounts might be progressively greater.

[Paragraph renumbered by the issuance of Statement on Standards for Attestation Engagements No. 6, December 1995.]

.38 In evaluating whether the combined effect of individual reportable conditions results in a material weakness, the practitioner should consider—

a. The range or distribution of the amounts of misstatement caused by error or fraud that may result during the same accounting period from two or more individual reportable conditions.

b. The joint risk or probability that such a combination of misstatements would be material.

[Paragraph renumbered by the issuance of Statement on Standards for Attestation Engagements No. 6, December 1995.]

.39 Evaluating whether a reportable condition is also a material weakness is a subjective process that depends on such factors as the nature of the accounting system and of any financial statement amounts or transactions exposed to the reportable condition, the overall control environment, other controls, and the judgment of those making the evaluation. [Paragraph renumbered by the issuance of Statement on Standards for Attestation Engagements No. 6, December 1995.]

Communicating Reportable Conditions and Material Weaknesses

.40 A practitioner engaged to examine and report on management's assertion about the effectiveness of the entity's internal control should communicate reportable conditions to the audit committee[12] and identify the reportable conditions that are also considered to be material weaknesses. Such a communication should preferably be made in writing. Because of the potential for misinterpretation of the limited degree of assurance associated with the auditor issuing a written report representing that no reportable conditions were

---

[11] Paragraphs .51 through .57 contain guidance the practitioner should consider when reporting on a management assertion that contains, or should contain, a description of a material weakness. [Footnote renumbered by the issuance of Statement on Standards for Attestation Engagements No. 6, December 1995.]

[12] If the entity does not have an audit committee, the practitioner should communicate with individuals whose authority and responsibility are equivalent to those of an audit committee, such as the board of directors, the board of trustees, an owner in an owner-managed entity, or those who engaged the practitioner. [Footnote renumbered by the issuance of Statement on Standards for Attestation Engagements No. 6, December 1995.]

noted during the examination, the auditor should not issue such representations. [Paragraph renumbered by the issuance of Statement on Standards for Attestation Engagements No. 6, December 1995.]

.41 Because timely communication may be important, the practitioner may choose to communicate significant matters during the course of the examination rather than after the examination is concluded. The decision about whether an interim communication should be issued would be influenced by the relative significance of the matters noted and the urgency of corrective follow-up action. [Paragraph renumbered by the issuance of Statement on Standards for Attestation Engagements No. 6, December 1995.]

Management's Representations

.42 The practitioner should obtain written representations from management—[13]

a. Acknowledging management's responsibility for establishing and maintaining internal control.

b. Stating that management has performed an evaluation of the effectiveness of the entity's internal control and specifying the control criteria used.

c. Stating management's assertion about the effectiveness of the entity's internal control based upon the control criteria.

d. Stating that management has disclosed to the practitioner all significant deficiencies in the design or operation of internal control which could adversely affect the entity's ability to record, process, summarize, and report financial data consistent with the assertions of management in the financial statements and has identified those that it believes to be material weaknesses in internal control.

e. Describing any material fraud and any other fraud that, although not material, involve management or other employees who have a significant role in the entity's internal control.

f. Stating whether there were, subsequent to the date of management's report, any changes in internal control or other factors that might significantly affect internal control, including any corrective actions taken by management with regard to significant deficiencies and material weaknesses.

[Paragraph renumbered by the issuance of Statement on Standards for Attestation Engagements No. 6, December 1995.]

.43 Management's refusal to furnish all appropriate written representations constitutes a limitation on the scope of the examination sufficient to require a qualified opinion or disclaimer of opinion on management's assertion about the effectiveness of the entity's internal control. Further, the practitioner should consider the effects of management's refusal on his or her ability

---

[13] AU section 333A, *Client Representations*, paragraph .09, provides guidance on the date as of which management should sign such a representation letter and which member(s) of management should sign it. [Footnote renumbered by the issuance of Statement on Standards for Attestation Engagements No. 6, December 1995.]

to rely on other management representations. [Paragraph renumbered by the issuance of Statement on Standards for Attestation Engagements No. 6, December 1995.]

Reporting Standards

.44 The form of the practitioner's report depends on the manner in which management presents its written assertion.

a. If management's assertion is presented in a separate report that accompanies the practitioner's report, the practitioner's report is considered appropriate for general distribution and the practitioner should use the form of report discussed in paragraphs .45 and .46.

b. If management presents its assertion only in a representation letter to the practitioner, the practitioner should restrict the distribution of his or her report to management, to others within the entity, and, if applicable, to specified regulatory agencies, and the practitioner should use the form of report discussed in paragraphs .47 through .49.

[Paragraph renumbered by the issuance of Statement on Standards for Attestation Engagements No. 6, December 1995.]

Management's Assertion Presented in a Separate Report

.45 When management presents its assertion in a separate report that will accompany the practitioner's report, the practitioner's report should include—

a. A title that includes the word *independent.*

b. An identification of management's assertion about the effectiveness of the entity's internal control over financial reporting.

c. A statement that the examination was made in accordance with standards established by the AICPA and, accordingly, that it included obtaining an understanding of internal control over financial reporting, testing and evaluating the design and operating effectiveness of internal control, and performing other such procedures as the practitioner considered necessary in the circumstances. In addition, the report should include a statement that the practitioner believes the examination provides a reasonable basis for his or her opinion.

d. A paragraph stating that, because of inherent limitations of any internal control, error or fraud may occur and not be detected. In addition, the paragraph should state that projections of any evaluation of internal control over financial reporting to future periods are subject to the risk that internal control may become inadequate because of changes in conditions, or that the degree of compliance with the policies or procedures may deteriorate.

e. The practitioner's opinion on whether management's assertion about the effectiveness of the entity's internal control over financial reporting as of the specified date is fairly stated, in all material respects, based on the control criteria.

[Paragraph renumbered by the issuance of Statement on Standards for Attestation Engagements No. 6, December 1995.]

.46 The following is the form of report a practitioner should use when he or she has examined management's assertion about the effectiveness of an entity's internal control as of a specified date.

Independent Accountant's Report

[*Introductory paragraph*]

We have examined management's assertion [*identify management's assertion, for example, that W Company maintained effective internal control over financial reporting as of December 31, 19XX*] included in the accompanying [*title of management report*].[14]

[*Scope paragraph*]

Our examination was made in accordance with standards established by the American Institute of Certified Public Accountants and, accordingly, included obtaining an understanding of the internal control over financial reporting, testing and evaluating the design and operating effectiveness of the internal control, and such other procedures as we considered necessary in the circumstances. We believe that our examination provides a reasonable basis for our opinion.

[*Inherent limitations paragraph*]

Because of inherent limitations in any internal control, errors or irregularities may occur and not be detected. Also, projections of any evaluation of the internal control over financial reporting to future periods are subject to the risk that the internal control may become inadequate because of changes in conditions, or that the degree of compliance with the policies or procedures may deteriorate.

[*Opinion paragraph*]

In our opinion, management's assertion [*identify management's assertion, for example, that W Company maintained effective internal control over financial reporting as of December 31, 19XX*] is fairly stated, in all material respects, based upon [*identify stated or established criteria*].[15]

[Paragraph renumbered by the issuance of Statement on Standards for Attestation Engagements No. 6, December 1995.]

Management's Assertion Presented Only in a Letter of Representation to the Practitioner

.47 Sometimes, management may present its written assertion about the effectiveness of the entity's internal control in a representation letter to the practitioner but not in a separate report that accompanies the practitioner's report. For example, an entity's board of directors may request the practitioner to report on management's assertion without requiring management to present a separate written assertion. [Paragraph renumbered by the issuance of Statement on Standards for Attestation Engagements No. 6, December 1995.]

---

[14] The practitioner should identify the management report examined by referring to the title used by management in its report. Further, he or she should use the same description of the entity's internal control as management uses in its report, including the types of controls (that is, controls over the preparation of annual financial statements, interim financial statements, or both) on which management is reporting. [Footnote renumbered by the issuance of Statement on Standards for Attestation Engagements No. 6, December 1995.]

[15] For example, "criteria established in *Internal Control—Integrated Framework* issued by the Committee of Sponsoring Organizations of the Treadway Commission (COSO)." [Footnote renumbered by the issuance of Statement on Standards for Attestation Engagements No. 6, December 1995.]

.48 When management does not present a written assertion that accompanies the practitioner's report, the practitioner should modify the report to include management's assertion about the effectiveness of the entity's internal control and add a paragraph that limits the distribution of the report to management, to others within the entity, and, if applicable, to a specified regulatory agency. [Paragraph renumbered by the issuance of Statement on Standards for Attestation Engagements No. 6, December 1995.]

.49 A sample report that a practitioner might use in such circumstances follows.

Independent Accountant's Report

[Introductory paragraph]

We have examined management's assertion, included in its representation letter dated February 15, 19XY, that [*identify management's assertion, for example, W Company maintained effective internal control over financial reporting as of December 31, 19XX*].

[Standard scope, inherent limitations, and opinion paragraphs]

[Limitation on distribution paragraph]

This report is intended solely for the information and use of the board of directors and management of W Company [*and, if applicable, a specified regulatory agency*] and should not be used for any other purpose.[16]

[Paragraph renumbered by the issuance of Statement on Standards for Attestation Engagements No. 6, December 1995.]

Report Modifications

.50 The practitioner should modify the standard reports in paragraphs .46 and .49 if any of the following conditions exist:

a. There is a material weakness in the entity's internal control (paragraphs .51 through .57).

b. There is a restriction on the scope of the engagement (paragraphs .58 through .61).

c. The practitioner decides to refer to the report of another practitioner as the basis, in part, for the practitioner's own report (paragraphs .62 and .63).

d. A significant subsequent event has occurred since the date of management's assertion (paragraphs .64 through .66).

e. Management presents an assertion about the effectiveness of only a segment of the entity's internal control (paragraph .67).

f. Management presents an assertion only about the suitability of design of the entity's internal control (paragraphs .68 and .69).

g. Management's assertion is based upon criteria established by a regulatory agency without following due process (paragraphs .70 through .74).

---

[16] If the report is a matter of public record, the following sentence should be added: "However, this report is a matter of public record and its distribution is not limited." [Footnote renumbered by the issuance of Statement on Standards for Attestation Engagements No. 6, December 1995.]

[Paragraph renumbered by the issuance of Statement on Standards for Attestation Engagements No. 6, December 1995.]

Material Weaknesses

.51 If the examination discloses conditions that, individually or in combination, result in one or more material weaknesses (paragraphs .36 through .39), the practitioner should modify the report. The nature of the modification depends on whether management includes, in its assertion, a description of the weakness and its effect on the achievement of the objectives of the control criteria. [Paragraph renumbered by the issuance of Statement on Standards for Attestation Engagements No. 6, December 1995.]

Management Includes the Material Weakness in its Assertion

.52 If management includes in its assertion a description of the weakness and its effect on the achievement of the objectives of the control criteria, and if it appropriately modifies its assertion about the effectiveness of the entity's internal control in light of that weakness,[17] the practitioner should both modify the opinion paragraph by including a reference to the material weakness and add an explanatory paragraph (following the opinion paragraph) that describes the weakness. [Paragraph renumbered by the issuance of Statement on Standards for Attestation Engagements No. 6, December 1995.]

.53 The following is the form of the report, modified with explanatory language, that a practitioner should use when management includes in its assertion a description of the weakness and its effect on the achievement of the objectives of the control criteria, and when it appropriately modifies its assertion about the effectiveness of the entity's internal control in light of that weakness.

Independent Accountant's Report

[*Standard introductory, scope, and inherent limitations paragraphs*]

[*Opinion paragraph*]

In our opinion, management's assertion that, except for the effect of the material weakness described in its report, [*identify management's assertion, for example, W Company maintained effective internal control over financial reporting as of December 31, 19XX*] is fairly stated, in all material respects, based upon [*identify established or stated criteria*].

[*Explanatory paragraph*]

As discussed in management's assertion, the following material weakness exists in the design or operation of the internal control of W Company in effect at [*date*]. [*Describe the material weakness and its effect on the achievement of the objectives of the control criteria.*][18] A material weakness is a condition that

[17] As stated in paragraph .36, the existence of a material weakness precludes management from asserting that an entity's internal control is effective. [Footnote renumbered by the issuance of Statement on Standards for Attestation Engagements No. 6, December 1995.]

[18] The language used by the practitioner ordinarily should conform with management's description of the effect of the material weakness on the effectiveness of the entity's internal control. [Footnote renumbered by the issuance of Statement on Standards for Attestation Engagements No. 6, December 1995.]

precludes the entity's internal control from providing reasonable assurance that material misstatements in the financial statements will be prevented or detected on a timely basis.[19]

[Paragraph renumbered by the issuance of Statement on Standards for Attestation Engagements No. 6, December 1995.]

Disagreements With Management

.54 In some circumstances, management may disagree with the practitioner over the existence of a material weakness and, therefore, not include in its assertion a description of such a weakness and its effect on the achievement of the objectives of the control criteria. In other circumstances, management may describe a material weakness but not modify its assertion that the entity's internal control is effective.[20] In such cases, the practitioner should express an adverse opinion on management's assertion. [Paragraph renumbered by the issuance of Statement on Standards for Attestation Engagements No. 6, December 1995.]

.55 The following is the form of the report a practitioner should use when he or she concludes that an adverse opinion is appropriate in the circumstances.

Independent Accountant's Report

[*Standard introductory, scope and inherent limitations paragraphs*]

[*Explanatory paragraph*]

Our examination disclosed the following condition, which we believe is a material weakness in the design or operation of the internal control of W Company in effect at [*date*]. [*Describe the material weakness and its effect on achievement of the objectives of the control criteria.*] A material weakness is a condition that precludes the entity's internal control from providing reasonable assurance that material misstatements in the financial statements will be prevented or detected on a timely basis.

[*Opinion paragraph*]

In our opinion, because of the effect of the material weakness described above on the achievement of the objectives of the control criteria, management's assertion [*identify management's assertion, for example, that W Company maintained effective internal control over financial reporting as of December 31, 19XX*] is not fairly stated based upon [*identify established or stated criteria*].

[Paragraph renumbered by the issuance of Statement on Standards for Attestation Engagements No. 6, December 1995.]

.56 If management's assertion contains a statement that management believes the cost of correcting the weakness would exceed the benefits to be derived from implementing new controls, the practitioner should disclaim an opinion on management's cost-benefit statement. The practitioner may use the

---

[19] This description of a material weakness differs from the definition of material weakness discussed in paragraph .36. Although a practitioner should consider the definition contained in paragraph .36 when determining whether a material weakness exists, the description above should be used to describe a material weakness in the practitioner's report. [Footnote renumbered by the issuance of Statement on Standards for Attestation Engagements No. 6, December 1995.]

[20] See footnote 18. [Footnote renumbered by the issuance of Statement on Standards for Attestation Engagements No. 6, December 1995.]

following sample language as the last paragraph of the report to disclaim an opinion on management's cost-benefit statement:

> We do not express an opinion or any other form of assurance on management's cost-benefit statement.

However, if the practitioner believes that management's cost-benefit statement is a material misstatement of fact, he or she should consider the guidance in paragraphs .77 and .78 and take appropriate action. [Paragraph renumbered by the issuance of Statement on Standards for Attestation Engagements No. 6, December 1995.]

Management's Assertion Includes the Material Weakness and Is Presented in a Document Containing the Audit Report

.57 If the practitioner issues an examination report on management's assertion about the effectiveness of the entity's internal control within the same document that includes his or her audit report on the entity's financial statements, the following sentence should be included in the paragraph of the examination report that describes the material weakness:

> These conditions were considered in determining the nature, timing, and extent of audit tests applied in our audit of the 19XX financial statements, and this report does not affect our report dated [*date of report*] on these financial statements.

The practitioner may also include the preceding sentence in situations where the two reports are not included within the same document. [Paragraph renumbered by the issuance of Statement on Standards for Attestation Engagements No. 6, December 1995.]

Scope Limitations

.58 An unqualified opinion on management's assertion about the effectiveness of the entity's internal control can be expressed only if the practitioner has been able to apply all the procedures he or she considers necessary in the circumstances. Restrictions on the scope of the engagement, whether imposed by the client or by the circumstances, may require the practitioner to qualify or disclaim an opinion. The practitioner's decision to qualify or disclaim an opinion because of a scope limitation depends on his or her assessment of the importance of the omitted procedure(s) to his or her ability to form an opinion on management's assertion about the effectiveness of the entity's internal control. [Paragraph renumbered by the issuance of Statement on Standards for Attestation Engagements No. 6, December 1995.]

.59 For example, management may have implemented controls to correct a material weakness identified prior to the date of its assertion. However, unless the practitioner has been able to obtain evidence that the new controls were appropriately designed and have been operating effectively for a sufficient period of time,[21] he or she should refer to the material weakness described in the report and qualify his or her opinion on the basis of a scope limitation. The following is the form of the report a practitioner should use when restrictions on the scope of the examination cause the practitioner to issue a qualified opinion.

---

[21] See guidance in paragraph .30. [Footnote renumbered by the issuance of Statement on Standards for Attestation Engagements No. 6, December 1995.]

Independent Accountant's Report

[*Standard introductory paragraph*]

[*Scope paragraph*]

Except as described below, our examination was made in accordance with standards established by the American Institute of Certified Public Accountants and, accordingly, included obtaining an understanding of the internal control over financial reporting, testing, and evaluating the design and operating effectiveness of the internal control, and such other procedures as we considered necessary in the circumstances. We believe that our examination provides a reasonable basis for our opinion.

[*Standard inherent limitations paragraph*]

[*Explanatory paragraph*]

Our examination disclosed the following material weaknesses in the design or operation of the internal control of W Company in effect at [*date*]. A material weakness is a condition that precludes the entity's internal control from providing reasonable assurance that material misstatements in the financial statements will be prevented or detected on a timely basis. Prior to December 20, 19XX, W Company had an inadequate system for recording cash receipts, which could have prevented the Company from recording cash receipts on accounts receivable completely and properly. Therefore, cash received could have been diverted for unauthorized use, lost, or otherwise not properly recorded to accounts receivable. Although the Company implemented a new cash receipts system on December 20, 19XX, the system has not been in operation for a sufficient period of time to enable us to obtain sufficient evidence about its operating effectiveness.

[*Opinion paragraph*]

In our opinion, except for the effect of matters we may have discovered had we been able to examine evidence about the effectiveness of the new cash receipts system, management's assertion [*identify management's assertion, for example, that W Company maintained effective internal control over financial reporting as of December 31, 19XX*] is fairly stated, in all material respects, based upon [*identify established or stated criteria*].

[Paragraph renumbered by the issuance of Statement on Standards for Attestation Engagements No. 6, December 1995.]

.60 When restrictions that significantly limit the scope of the examination are imposed by the client, the practitioner generally should disclaim an opinion on management's assertion about the effectiveness of the entity's internal control. [Paragraph renumbered by the issuance of Statement on Standards for Attestation Engagements No. 6, December 1995.]

.61 The following is the form of report that a practitioner should use when restrictions that significantly limit the scope of the examination are imposed by the client and cause the practitioner to issue a disclaimer of opinion.

Independent Accountant's Report

[*Introductory paragraph*]

We were engaged to examine management's assertion [*identify management's assertion, for example, that W Company maintained effective internal control over financial reporting as of December 31, 19XX*] included in the accompanying [*title of management's report*].

[*Scope paragraph should be omitted*]

[Explanatory paragraph]

[Include paragraph to describe scope restrictions]

[Opinion paragraph]

Since management [*describe scope restrictions*] and we were unable to apply other procedures to satisfy ourselves as to management's assertion about the entity's internal control over financial reporting, the scope of our work was not sufficient to enable us to express, and we do not express, an opinion on management's assertion.

[Paragraph renumbered by the issuance of Statement on Standards for Attestation Engagements No. 6, December 1995.]

Opinion Based in Part on the Report of Another Practitioner

.62 When another practitioner has examined management's assertion about the effectiveness of the internal control of one or more subsidiaries, divisions, branches, or components of the entity, the practitioner should consider whether he or she may serve as the principal practitioner and use the work and reports of the other practitioner as a basis, in part, for his or her opinion on management's assertion. If the practitioner decides it is appropriate for him or her to serve as the principal practitioner, he or she should then decide whether to make reference in the report to the examination performed by the other practitioner. In these circumstances, the practitioner's considerations are similar to those of the independent auditor who uses the work and reports of other independent auditors when reporting on an entity's financial statements. AU section 543, *Part of Audit Performed by Other Independent Auditors*, provides guidance on the auditor's considerations when deciding whether he or she may serve as the principal auditor and, if so, whether to make reference to the examination performed by the other practitioner. [Paragraph renumbered by the issuance of Statement on Standards for Attestation Engagements No. 6, December 1995.]

.63 When the practitioner decides to make reference to the report of the other practitioner as a basis, in part, for the practitioner's opinion on management's assertion, the practitioner should disclose this fact when describing the scope of the examination and should refer to the report of the other practitioner when expressing the opinion. The following form of the report is appropriate in these circumstances.

Independent Accountant's Report

[Introductory paragraph]

We have examined management's assertion [*identify management's assertion, for example, that W Company maintained effective internal control over financial reporting as of December 31, 19XX*] included in the accompanying [*title of management report*]. We did not examine management's assertion about the effectiveness of the internal control over financial reporting of B Company, a wholly owned subsidiary, whose financial statements reflect total assets and revenues constituting 20 and 30 percent, respectively, of the related consolidated financial statement amounts as of and for the year ended December 31, 19XX. Management's assertion about the effectiveness of B Company's internal control over financial reporting was examined by other accountants whose report has been furnished to us, and our opinion, insofar as it relates to management's assertion about the effectiveness of B Company's internal control over financial reporting, is based solely on the report of the other accountants.

[Scope paragraph]

Our examination was made in accordance with standards established by the American Institute of Certified Public Accountants and, accordingly, included obtaining an understanding of the internal control over financial reporting, testing, and evaluating the design and operating effectiveness of the internal control, and such other procedures as we considered necessary in the circumstances. We believe that our examination and the report of the other accountants provide a reasonable basis for our opinion.

[Standard inherent limitations paragraph]

[Opinion paragraph]

In our opinion, based on our examination and the report of the other accountants, management's assertion [*identify management's assertion, for example, that W Company maintained effective internal control over financial reporting as of December 31, 19XX*] is fairly stated, in all material respects, based upon [*identify established or stated criteria*].

[Paragraph renumbered by the issuance of Statement on Standards for Attestation Engagements No. 6, December 1995.]

Subsequent Events

.64 Changes in internal control or other factors that might significantly affect internal control may occur subsequent to the date of management's assertion but before the date of the practitioner's report. As described in paragraph .42, the practitioner should obtain management's representations relating to such matters. Additionally, to obtain information about whether changes have occurred that might affect management's assertion about the effectiveness of the entity's internal control and, therefore, the practitioner's report, he or she should inquire about and examine, for this subsequent period, the following:

a. Relevant internal auditor reports issued during the subsequent period

b. Independent auditor reports (if other than the practitioner's) of reportable conditions or material weaknesses

c. Regulatory agency reports on the entity's internal control

d. Information about the effectiveness of the entity's internal control obtained through other professional engagements

[Paragraph renumbered by the issuance of Statement on Standards for Attestation Engagements No. 6, December 1995.]

.65 If the practitioner obtains knowledge about subsequent events that he or she believes significantly affect management's assertion about the effectiveness of the entity's internal control as of the date of management's assertion, the practitioner should ascertain that management has adequately described in its assertion these events and their effect on internal control. If management has not included such a description and appropriately modified its assertion, the practitioner should add to his or her report an explanatory paragraph that includes such a description. [Paragraph renumbered by the issuance of Statement on Standards for Attestation Engagements No. 6, December 1995.]

.66 The practitioner has no responsibility to keep informed of events subsequent to the date of his or her report; however, the practitioner may later become aware of conditions that existed at that date that might have affected the practitioner's opinion had he or she been aware of them. The practitioner's consideration of such subsequent information is similar to an auditor's consideration of information discovered subsequent to the date of the report on an audit of financial statements described in AU section 561, *Subsequent Discovery of Facts Existing at the Date of the Auditor's Report*. The guidance in that section requires the auditor to determine whether the information is reliable and whether the facts existed at the date of his or her report. If so, the auditor considers (*a*) whether the facts would have changed the report if he or she had been aware of them and (*b*) whether there are persons currently relying on or likely to rely on management's assertion about the effectiveness of the entity's internal control. Based on these considerations, detailed guidance is provided for the auditor in AU section 561.06. [Paragraph renumbered by the issuance of Statement on Standards for Attestation Engagements No. 6, December 1995.]

Management's Assertion About the Effectiveness of a Segment of the Entity's Internal Control

.67 When engaged to report on management's assertion about the effectiveness of only a segment of an entity's internal control (for example, internal control over financial reporting of an entity's operating division or its accounts receivable), a practitioner should follow the guidance in this section and issue a report using the guidance in paragraphs .45 through .61, modified to refer to the segment of the entity's internal control examined. In this situation, the practitioner may use a report such as the following.

Independent Accountant's Report

[*Introductory paragraph*]

We have examined management's assertion [*identify management's assertion, for example, that W Company's retail division maintained effective internal control over financial reporting as of December 31, 19XX*], included in the accompanying [*title of management report*].

[*Standard scope and inherent limitations paragraphs*]

[*Opinion paragraph*]

In our opinion, management's assertion [*identify management's assertion, for example, that W Company's retail division maintained effective internal control over financial reporting as of December 31, 19XX*] is fairly stated, in all material respects, based upon [*identify established or stated criteria*].

[Paragraph renumbered by the issuance of Statement on Standards for Attestation Engagements No. 6, December 1995.]

Management's Assertion About the Suitability of Design of the Entity's Internal Control

.68 Management may present an assertion about the suitability of the design of the entity's internal control for preventing or detecting material misstatements on a timely basis and request the practitioner to examine and report on the assertion. For example, prior to granting a new casino a license to operate, a regulatory agency may request a report on whether the internal control that management plans to implement will provide reasonable assurance that the control objectives specified in the regulatory agency's regulations will be achieved. When evaluating the suitability of design of the entity's internal control for the regulatory agency's purpose, the practitioner should obtain an understanding of the components of internal control[22] that management should implement to meet the control objectives of the regulatory agency and identify the controls that are relevant to those control objectives. [Paragraph renumbered by the issuance of Statement on Standards for Attestation Engagements No. 6, December 1995.]

.69 The following is a suggested form of report a practitioner may issue. The actual form of the report should be modified, as appropriate, to fit the particular circumstances.[23]

<u>Independent Accountant's Report</u>

[*Introductory paragraph*]

We have examined management's assertion [*identify management's assertion, for example, that W Company's internal control over financial reporting is suitably designed to prevent or detect material misstatements in the financial statements on a timely basis as of December 31, 19XX*] included in the accompanying [*title of management report*].

[*Scope paragraph*]

Our examination was made in accordance with standards established by the American Institute of Certified Public Accountants and, accordingly, included obtaining an understanding of the internal control over financial reporting, evaluating the design of the internal control, and such other procedures as we considered necessary in the circumstances. We believe that our examination provides a reasonable basis for our opinion.

[*Standard inherent limitations paragraph*]

[*Opinion paragraph*]

In our opinion, management's assertion [*identify management's assertion, for example, that W Company's internal control over financial reporting is suitably designed to prevent or detect material misstatements in the financial statements on a timely basis as of December 31, 19XX*] is fairly stated, in all material respects, based upon [*identify established or stated criteria*].

When management presents such an assertion about an entity's internal control that has already been placed in operation, the practitioner should modify his or her report by adding the following to the scope paragraph of the report:

> We were not engaged to examine and report on the operating effectiveness of W Company's internal control over financial reporting as of December 31, 19XX, and, accordingly, we express no opinion on operating effectiveness.

---

[22] See paragraph .22. [Footnote renumbered by the issuance of Statement on Standards for Attestation Engagements No. 6, December 1995.]

[23] This report assumes that the control criteria of the regulatory agency have been subjected to due process and, therefore, are considered reasonable criteria for reporting purposes. Therefore, there is no limitation on the distribution of this report. [Footnote renumbered by the issuance of Statement on Standards for Attestation Engagements No. 6, December 1995.]

[Paragraph renumbered by the issuance of Statement on Standards for Attestation Engagements No. 6, December 1995.]

Management's Assertion Based on Criteria Specified by a Regulatory Agency

.70 A governmental or other agency that exercises regulatory, supervisory, or other public administrative functions may establish its own criteria and require reports on the internal control of entities subject to its jurisdiction. Criteria established by a regulatory agency may be set forth in audit guides, questionnaires, or other publications. The criteria may encompass specified aspects of an entity's internal control and specified aspects of administrative control or compliance with grants, regulations, or statutes. If such criteria have been subjected to due process procedures, including the broad distribution of proposed criteria for public comment, a practitioner should use the form of report illustrated in paragraph .46 or .49, depending on the manner in which management presents its assertion. If, however, such criteria have not been subjected to due process procedures, the practitioner should modify the report by adding a separate paragraph that limits the distribution of the report to the regulatory agency and to those within the entity. [Paragraph renumbered by the issuance of Statement on Standards for Attestation Engagements No. 6, December 1995.]

.71 For purposes of these reports, a material weakness is—

a. A condition in which the design or operation of one or more of the specific internal control components does not reduce to a relatively low level the risk that errors or irregularities in amounts that would be material in relation to the applicable grant or program might occur and not be detected on a timely basis by employees in the normal course of performing their assigned functions.

b. A condition in which the lack of conformity with the regulatory agency's criteria is material in accordance with any guidelines for determining materiality that are included in such criteria.

[Paragraph renumbered by the issuance of Statement on Standards for Attestation Engagements No. 6, December 1995.]

.72 The following report illustrates one that a practitioner might use when he or she has examined management's assertion about the effectiveness of the entity's internal control based upon criteria established by a regulatory agency that did not follow due process.

Independent Accountant's Report

[*Introductory paragraph*]

We have examined management's assertion included in its representation letter dated February 15, 19XY, [*identify management's assertion, for example, that W Company's internal control over financial reporting as of December 31, 19XX is adequate to meet the criteria established by _______ agency, as set forth in its audit guide dated _______*].

[*Standard scope and inherent limitations paragraphs*]

[*Opinion paragraph*]

We understand that the agency considers the controls over financial reporting that meet the criteria referred to in the first paragraph of this report adequate for its purpose. In our opinion, based on this understanding and on our examination, management's assertion [*identify management's assertion, for example, that W Company's internal control over financial reporting is adequate to meet the criteria established by agency* __________] is fairly stated, in all material respects, based upon such criteria.

[*Limitation on distribution paragraph*]

This report is intended for the information and use of the board of directors and management of W Company and [*agency*] and should not be used for any other purpose.[24]

[Paragraph renumbered by the issuance of Statement on Standards for Attestation Engagements No. 6, December 1995.]

.73 When the practitioner issues this form of report, he or she does not assume any responsibility for the comprehensiveness of the criteria established by the regulatory agency. However, the practitioner should report any condition that comes to his or her attention during the course of the examination that he or she believes is a material weakness, even though it may not be covered by the criteria. [Paragraph renumbered by the issuance of Statement on Standards for Attestation Engagements No. 6, December 1995.]

.74 If a regulatory agency requires management to report all conditions (whether material or not) that are not in conformity with the agency's criteria, the practitioner should determine whether all conditions of which he or she is aware have been reported by management. If the practitioner concludes that management has not reported all such conditions, he or she should describe them in the report. [Paragraph renumbered by the issuance of Statement on Standards for Attestation Engagements No. 6, December 1995.]

Other Information in a Client-Prepared Document Containing Management's Assertion About the Effectiveness of the Entity's Internal Control

.75 An entity may publish various documents that contain other information in addition to management's assertion on the effectiveness of the entity's internal control and the practitioner's report thereon. The practitioner may have performed procedures and issued a report covering some or all of this other information (for example, an audit report on the entity's financial statements), or another practitioner may have done so. Otherwise, the practitioner's responsibility with respect to other information in such a document does not extend beyond the management report identified in his or her report, and the practitioner has no obligation to perform any procedures to corroborate any other information contained in the document. However, the practitioner should read the other information not covered by the practitioner's report or by the report of the other practitioner and consider whether it, or the manner of its

---

[24] If the report is a matter of public record, the following sentence should be added: "However, this report is a matter of public record and its distribution is not limited." [Footnote renumbered by the issuance of Statement on Standards for Attestation Engagements No. 6, December 1995.]

presentation, is materially inconsistent with the information appearing in management's report, or whether such information contains a material misstatement of fact. [Paragraph renumbered by the issuance of Statement on Standards for Attestation Engagements No. 6, December 1995.]

.76 If the practitioner believes that the other information is inconsistent with the information appearing in management's report, he or she should consider whether management's report, the practitioner's report, or both require revision. If the practitioner concludes that these do not require revision, he or she should request management to revise the other information. If the other information is not revised to eliminate the material inconsistency, the practitioner should consider other actions, such as revising his or her report to include an explanatory paragraph describing the material inconsistency, withholding the use of his or her report in the document, or withdrawing from the engagement. [Paragraph renumbered by the issuance of Statement on Standards for Attestation Engagements No. 6, December 1995.]

.77 If the practitioner discovers in the other information a statement that he or she believes is a material misstatement of fact, he or she should discuss the matter with management. In connection with this discussion, the practitioner should consider whether he or she possesses the expertise to assess the validity of the statement, whether standards exist by which to assess the manner of presentation of the information, and whether there may not be valid differences of judgment or opinion. If the practitioner concludes that a material misstatement exists, the practitioner should propose that management consult with some other party whose advice might be useful, such as the entity's legal counsel. [Paragraph renumbered by the issuance of Statement on Standards for Attestation Engagements No. 6, December 1995.]

.78 If, after discussing the matter, the practitioner concludes that a material misstatement of fact remains, the action taken will depend on his or her judgment in the circumstances. The practitioner should consider steps such as notifying the entity's management and audit committee in writing of his or her views concerning the information and consulting his or her legal counsel about further action appropriate in the circumstances. [Paragraph renumbered by the issuance of Statement on Standards for Attestation Engagements No. 6, December 1995.]

Relationship of the Practitioner's Examination of an Entity's Internal Control to the Opinion Obtained in an Audit

.79 The purpose of a practitioner's examination of management's assertion about the effectiveness of an entity's internal control is to express an opinion about whether management's assertion that the entity maintained effective internal control as of a point in time is fairly stated in all material respects, based on the control criteria. In contrast, the purpose of an auditor's consideration of internal control in an audit of financial statements conducted in accordance with generally accepted auditing standards is to enable the auditor to plan the audit and determine the nature, timing, and extent of tests to be performed. Ultimately, the results of the auditor's tests will form the basis for the auditor's opinion on the fairness of the entity's financial statements in conformity with generally accepted accounting principles. The auditor's responsibility in considering the entity's internal control is discussed in AU section 319. [Paragraph renumbered by the issuance of Statement on Standards for Attestation Engagements No. 6, December 1995.]

.80 In a financial statement audit, the auditor obtains an understanding of internal control by performing procedures such as inquiries, observations, and inspection of documents. After he or she has obtained this understanding, the auditor assesses the control risk for assertions related to significant account balances and transaction classes. The auditor assesses control risk for an assertion at maximum if he or she believes that controls are unlikely to pertain to the assertion, that controls are unlikely to be effective, or that an evaluation of their effectiveness would be inefficient. When the auditor assesses control risk for an assertion at below maximum, he or she identifies the controls that are likely to prevent or detect material misstatements in that assertion and performs tests of controls to evaluate the effectiveness of such controls. [Paragraph renumbered by the issuance of Statement on Standards for Attestation Engagements No. 6, December 1995.]

.81 An auditor's consideration of internal control in a financial statement audit is more limited than that of a practitioner engaged to examine management's assertion about the effectiveness of the entity's internal control. However, knowledge the practitioner obtains about the entity's internal control as part of the examination of management's assertion may serve as the basis for his or her understanding of internal control in an audit of the entity's financial statements. Similarly, the practitioner may consider the results of tests of controls performed in connection with an examination of management's assertion, as well as any material weaknesses identified, when assessing control risk in the audit of the entity's financial statements. [Paragraph renumbered by the issuance of Statement on Standards for Attestation Engagements No. 6, December 1995.]

.82 While an examination of management's assertions about the effectiveness of the entity's internal control and an audit of the entity's financial statements may be performed by the same practitioner, each can be performed by a different practitioner. If the audit of the entity's financial statements is performed by another practitioner, the practitioner may wish to consider any material weaknesses and reportable conditions identified by the auditor and any disagreements between management and the auditor concerning such matters. [Paragraph renumbered by the issuance of Statement on Standards for Attestation Engagements No. 6, December 1995.]

Relationship to the Foreign Corrupt Practices Act

.83 The Foreign Corrupt Practices Act of 1977 (FCPA) includes provisions regarding internal accounting control for entities subject to the Securities Exchange Act of 1934. Whether an entity is in compliance with those provisions of the FCPA is a legal determination. A practitioner's examination report issued under this section does not indicate whether an entity is in compliance with those provisions. [Paragraph renumbered by the issuance of Statement on Standards for Attestation Engagements No. 6, December 1995.]

Effective Date

.84 This section is effective for an examination of management's assertion on the effectiveness of an entity's internal control over financial reporting when the assertion is as of December 15, 1993 or thereafter. Earlier application of this section is encouraged. [Paragraph renumbered by the issuance of Statement on Standards for Attestation Engagements No. 6, December 1995.]

.85

Appendix

The following documents contain guidance for practitioners engaged to provide other services in connection with an entity's internal control.

- AU section 325, *Communication of Internal Control Related Matters Noted in an Audit*, provides guidance on identifying and communicating reportable conditions that come to the auditor's attention during an audit of financial statements.
- AU section 324, *Reports on the Processing of Transactions by Service Organizations*, provides guidance to auditors of a service organization on issuing a report on certain aspects of the service organization's internal control that can be used by other auditors, as well as guidance on how other auditors should use such reports.
- Audit and Accounting Guide *Audits of State and Local Governmental Units* provides auditors of state and local governmental entities with a basic understanding of the work they should do and the reports they should issue for audits under *Government Auditing Standards* (1994 Revision), issued by the Comptroller General of the United States, the Single Audit Act of 1984, and Office of Management and Budget (OMB) Circular A-128, "Audits of State and Local Governments."
- SOP 92-9, *Audits of Not-for-Profit Organizations Receiving Federal Awards*, provides auditors with a basic understanding of the work they should do and the reports they should issue for audits under *Government Auditing Standards* (1994 Revision), issued by the Comptroller General of the United States and OMB Circular A-133, *Audits of Institutions of Higher Education and Other Nonprofit Organizations.*

[Revised March, 1995 by the Auditing Standards Division due to the issuance of Statement on Auditing Standards No. 74. Paragraph renumbered by the issuance of Statement on Standards for Attestation Engagements No. 6, December 1995.]

AT Section 9400

Reporting on an Entity's Internal Control Over Financial Reporting: Attestation Engagements Interpretations of Section 400

1. Pre-Award Surveys

.01 *Question*—As part of the process of applying for a government grant or contract, an entity may be required to submit a written pre-award assertion (survey) by management about the effectiveness (suitability) of the design of an entity's internal control or a portion thereof for the government's purposes, together with a practitioner's report thereon. May a practitioner issue such a report based on the consideration of internal control in an audit of the entity's financial statements?

.02 *Interpretation*—No. The purpose of the consideration of an entity's internal control in a financial statement audit is to obtain an understanding sufficient to plan the audit and to determine the nature, timing and extent of audit tests to be performed and not to provide assurance on internal control. The consideration made in a financial statement audit does not provide the practitioner with a sufficient basis to issue a report expressing any assurance about the effectiveness of the design of internal control or any portion thereof.

.03 *Question*—How may a practitioner report on the design effectiveness of an entity's internal control or a portion thereof?

.04 *Interpretation*—In order to issue such a report, the practitioner should perform an examination of or apply agreed-upon procedures to management's written assertion about the effectiveness (suitability) of the design of an entity's internal control as described in section 400, *Reporting on an Entity's Internal Control Over Financial Reporting*, paragraphs .22 through .25 and .68 through .74. When the engagement involves the application of agreed-upon procedures to a written assertion about the design effectiveness of the entity's internal control over compliance with specified requirements, the practitioner should also follow the provisions of section 500, *Compliance Attestation*, paragraphs .09 and .14 through .28, and section 600, *Agreed-Upon Procedures Engagements*.

.05 *Question*—What are a practitioner's responsibilities when requested to sign a form prescribed by a government agency in connection with a pre-award survey?

.06 *Interpretation*—The practitioner should refuse to sign such a prescribed form unless he or she has performed an attestation engagement, as discussed in paragraph .04. If the practitioner has performed such an attestation engagement, he or she should consider whether the wording of the prescribed form conforms to the requirements of professional standards. For example, the prescribed form may contain a description of the practitioner's responsibilities or the practitioner's conclusions that is not in conformity with those standards. Some prescribed forms can be made acceptable by inserting additional or deleting existing wording; others can be made acceptable only by complete revision. When a prescribed form contains a statement or wording not in conformity with professional standards, the practitioner should either reword the form to conform to those standards or attach a separate report conforming with such standards in place of the prescribed form.

.07 *Question*—An entity may also be required to submit a written pre-award assertion (survey) about its *ability* to establish suitably designed internal control with an accompanying practitioner's report. May a practitioner issue such a report based on the consideration of existing internal control in an audit of an entity's financial statements or the performance of an attestation engagement?

.08 *Interpretation*—No. Neither the consideration of internal control in an audit of an entity's financial statements nor the performance of an attestation engagement provides the practitioner with a basis for issuing a report on the ability of an entity to establish suitably designed internal control. The assertion about *ability* is not capable of reasonably consistent estimation or measurement. The requesting agency may be willing to accept a report of the practitioner on a nonattest service as described in section 100, *Attestation Standards*, paragraphs .02 and .81. The practitioner should consider including in the nonattest service report—

a. A statement that the practitioner is unable to perform an attest engagement on the entity's ability to establish suitably designed internal control because there are no criteria that are capable of reasonably consistent estimation or measurement for assessing such an assertion;

b. A description of the nature and scope of the practitioner's services; and

c. The practitioner's findings.

The practitioner may refer to the guidance in CS section 100, *Consulting Services: Definitions and Standards.*

[Issue Date: February, 1997.]

AT Section 500

Compliance Attestation

Source: SSAE No. 3; SAS No. 74; SSAE No. 4.

Effective for engagements in which management's assertion is as of, or for a period ending, June 15, 1994, or thereafter, unless otherwise indicated.

> *In January 1989, the Statements on Standards for Attestation Engagements (SSAE)* Attestation Standards *(AT section 100),* Financial Forecasts and Projections *(AT section 200), and* Reporting on Pro Forma Financial Information *(AT section 300), were codified in* Codification of Statements on Standards for Attestation Engagements. *In April 1993, the codified sections became SSAE No. 1,* Attestation Standards. *In May 1993, SSAE No. 2,* Reporting on an Entity's Internal Control Over Financial Reporting, *was issued.*

Introduction and Applicability

.01 This section provides guidance for engagements related to management's written assertion about either (*a*) an entity's compliance with requirements of specified laws, regulations, rules, contracts, or grants or (*b*) the effectiveness of an entity's internal control structure over compliance with specified requirements.[1] Management's assertions may relate to compliance requirements that are either financial or nonfinancial in nature. An attestation engagement conducted in accordance with this section should comply with the general, fieldwork, and reporting standards in section 100, *Attestation Standards*, and the specific standards set forth in this section.

.02 This section does not—

a. Affect the auditor's responsibility in an audit of financial statements performed in accordance with generally accepted auditing standards (GAAS).

b. Apply to situations in which an auditor reports on specified compliance requirements based solely on an audit of financial statements, as addressed in AU section 623, *Special Reports*, paragraphs .19 through .21.

---

[1] Throughout this section—

a. An entity's compliance with requirements of specified laws, regulations, rules, contracts, or grants is referred to as compliance with specified requirements.

b. An entity's internal control over compliance with specified requirements is referred to as its internal control over compliance. The internal control addressed in this section may include parts of, but is not the same as, internal control over financial reporting.

c. Apply to engagements for which the objective is to report in accordance with AU section 801, *Compliance Auditing Considerations in Audits of Governmental Entities and Recipients of Governmental Financial Assistance*, unless the terms of the engagement specify an attestation report under this section.

d. Apply to engagements covered by AU section 634, *Letters for Underwriters and Certain Other Requesting Parties*.

e. Apply to the report that encompasses the internal control over compliance for a broker or dealer in securities as required by rule 17a-5 of the Securities Exchange Act of 1934.[2]

[As amended, effective for audits of financial statements and of compliance with laws and regulations for fiscal periods ending after December 31, 1994, by Statement on Auditing Standards No. 74.] (See AU section 801.)

.03 A report issued in accordance with the provisions of this section does not provide a legal determination on an entity's compliance with specified requirements. However, such a report may be useful to legal counsel or others in making such determinations.

Scope of Services

.04 The practitioner may be engaged to perform agreed-upon procedures to assist users in evaluating management's written assertion about (*a*) the entity's compliance with specified requirements, (*b*) the effectiveness of the entity's internal control over compliance,[3] or (*c*) both. The practitioner also may be engaged to examine management's written assertion about the entity's compliance with specified requirements.

.05 An important consideration in determining the type of engagement to be performed is expectations by users of the practitioner's report. Since the users decide the procedures to be performed in an agreed-upon procedures engagement, it often will be in the best interests of the practitioner and users (including the client) to have an agreed-upon procedures engagement rather than an examination engagement. When deciding whether to accept an examination engagement, the practitioner should consider the risks discussed in paragraphs .30 through .34.

.06 A practitioner may be engaged to examine management's assertion about the effectiveness of the entity's internal control over compliance. However, in accordance with section 100, the practitioner cannot accept an engagement unless management uses reasonable criteria that have been established by a recognized body or are stated in the presentation of management's as-

---

[2] An example of this report is contained in AICPA Statement of Position 89-4, *Reports on the Internal Control Structure in Audits of Brokers and Dealers in Securities*.

[3] An entity's internal control over compliance is the process by which management obtains reasonable assurance of compliance with specified requirements. Although the comprehensive internal control may include a wide variety of objectives and related policies and procedures, only some of these may be relevant to an entity's compliance with specified requirements (see footnote 1*b*). The components of internal control over compliance vary based on the nature of the compliance requirements. For example, internal control over compliance with a capital requirement would generally include accounting procedures, whereas internal control over compliance with a requirement to practice nondiscriminatory hiring may not include accounting procedures.

sertion.[4] If a practitioner determines that such criteria do exist for internal control over compliance, he or she should perform the engagement in accordance with section 100. Additionally, section 400, *Reporting on an Entity's Internal Control Over Financial Reporting*, may be helpful to a practitioner in such an engagement.

.07 A practitioner should not accept an engagement to perform a review, as defined in section 100.41, of management's assertion about an entity's compliance with specified requirements or about the effectiveness of an entity's internal control over compliance.

.08 The guidance in this section does not apply unless management presents a written assertion. In the absence of a written assertion, management may engage the practitioner to provide certain nonattest services in connection with the entity's compliance with specified requirements or the entity's internal control over compliance. For example, management may engage the practitioner to provide recommendations on how to improve the entity's compliance or the related internal control. A practitioner engaged to provide such nonattest services should refer to the guidance in the Statement on Standards for Consulting Services, *Consulting Services: Definitions and Standards* [CS section 100].

Conditions for Engagement Performance

.09 A practitioner may perform an engagement related to management's written assertion about an entity's compliance with specified requirements or about the effectiveness of internal control over compliance if both of the following conditions, along with the applicable conditions in paragraph .11, are met:

a. Management accepts responsibility for the entity's compliance with specified requirements and the effectiveness of the entity's internal control over compliance.

b. Management evaluates the entity's compliance with specified requirements or the effectiveness of the entity's internal control over compliance.

See also section 600, *Agreed-Upon Procedures Engagements*.

[.10] [Superseded by Statement on Standards for Attestation Engagements No. 4, effective for reports on agreed-upon procedures engagements dated after April 30, 1996.] (See section 600.)

.11 A practitioner may perform an examination if, in addition to the conditions listed in paragraph .09, the following conditions are met:

a. Management makes an assertion about the entity's compliance with specified requirements. If the practitioner's report is intended for

---

[4] Criteria issued by regulatory agencies and other bodies composed of experts that follow due-process procedures, including procedures for broad distribution of proposed criteria for public comment, normally should be considered reasonable criteria for this purpose. For example, the Committee of Sponsoring Organizations (COSO) of the Treadway Commission's report, *Internal Control—Integrated Framework*, provides a general framework for effective internal control. However, more detailed criteria relative to specific compliance requirements may have to be developed and an appropriate threshold for measuring the severity of control deficiencies needs to be developed in order to apply the concepts of the COSO report to internal control over compliance.

Criteria established by a regulatory agency that does not follow such due-process procedures also may be considered reasonable criteria for use by the regulatory agency. However, the practitioner's report generally would have to include a limitation of its use to those within the entity and the regulatory agency. (See section 100.14 through .16, .71, and .77.)

general use, the assertion should be in a representation letter to the practitioner and in a separate report that will accompany the practitioner's report.[5] If use of the practitioner's report will be restricted to those within the entity and a specified regulatory agency, the assertion might be only in a representation letter.

b. Management's assertion is capable of evaluation against reasonable criteria that either have been established by a recognized body or are stated in the assertion in a sufficiently clear and comprehensive manner for a knowledgeable reader to understand them, and the assertion is capable of reasonably consistent estimation or measurement using such criteria.[6]

c. Sufficient evidential matter exists or could be developed to support management's evaluation.

[.12] [Superseded by Statement on Standards for Attestation Engagements No. 4, effective for reports on agreed-upon procedures engagements dated after April 30, 1996.] (See section 600.)

.13 In an examination engagement, management's written assertion may take various forms but should be specific enough that users having competence in and using the same or similar measurement and disclosure criteria ordinarily would be able to arrive at materially similar conclusions. For example, an acceptable assertion about compliance with specified requirements might state, "Z Company complied with restrictive covenants contained in paragraphs 13, 14, 15, and 16*a-d*, of its Loan Agreement with Y Bank, dated January 1, 19X1, as of and for the three months ended June 30, 19X2." However, the practitioner should not examine an assertion that is too broad or subjective (for example, "X Company complied with laws and regulations applicable to its activities" or "X Company sufficiently complied") to be capable of reasonably consistent estimation or measurement.

Responsibilities of Management

.14 Management is responsible for ensuring that the entity complies with the requirements applicable to its activities. That responsibility encompasses (*a*) identifying applicable compliance requirements, (*b*) establishing and maintaining internal control structure policies and procedures to provide reasonable assurance that the entity complies with those requirements, (*c*) evaluating and monitoring the entity's compliance, and (*d*) specifying reports that satisfy legal, regulatory, or contractual requirements. Management's evaluation may include documentation such as accounting or statistical data, entity policy manuals, accounting manuals, narrative memoranda, procedural write-ups, flowcharts, completed questionnaires, or internal auditors' reports. The form and extent of documentation will vary depending on the nature of the compliance requirements and the size and complexity of the entity. Management may engage the practitioner to gather information to assist it in evaluating the entity's compliance. Regardless of the procedures performed by the practitioner, management must accept responsibility for its assertion and must not base such assertion solely on the practitioner's procedures.

---

[5] Management's report may be in the form of an assertion addressed to a third party or in the form of a prescribed schedule or declaration submitted to a third party.

[6] See footnote 4.

Agreed-Upon Procedures Engagement

.15 The objective of the practitioner's agreed-upon procedures is to present specific findings to assist users in evaluating management's assertion about an entity's compliance with specified requirements or about the effectiveness of an entity's internal control over compliance based on procedures agreed upon by the users of the report. A practitioner engaged to perform agreed-upon procedures on management's assertion about an entity's compliance with specified requirements or about the effectiveness of an entity's internal control over compliance should follow the guidance set forth herein and in section 600. [As amended, effective for reports on agreed-upon procedures engagements dated after April 30, 1996, by Statement on Standards for Attestation Engagements No. 4.] (See section 600.)

.16 The practitioner's procedures generally may be as limited or as extensive as the specified users desire, as long as the specified users (*a*) agree upon the procedures performed or to be performed and (*b*) take responsibility for the sufficiency of the agreed-upon procedures for their purposes.[7] [As amended, effective for reports on agreed-upon procedures engagements dated after April 30, 1996, by Statement on Standards for Attestation Engagements No. 4.] (See section 600.)

.17 To satisfy the requirements that the practitioner and the specified users agree upon the procedures performed or to be performed and that the specified users take responsibility for the sufficiency of the agreed-upon procedures for their purposes, ordinarily the practitioner should communicate directly with and obtain affirmative acknowledgment from each of the specified users. For example, this may be accomplished by meeting with the specified users or by distributing a draft of the anticipated report or a copy of an engagement letter to the specified users and obtaining their agreement. If the practitioner is not able to communicate directly with all of the specified users, the practitioner may satisfy these requirements by applying any one or more of the following or similar procedures:

- Compare the procedures to be applied to written requirements of the specified users.
- Discuss the procedures to be applied with appropriate representatives of the specified users involved.
- Review relevant contracts with or correspondence from the specified users.

The practitioner should not report on an engagement when specified users do not agree upon the procedures performed or to be performed and do not take responsibility for the sufficiency of the procedures for their purposes. (See section 600.38 for guidance on satisfying these requirements when the practitioner is requested to add parties as specified users after the date of completion of the agreed-upon procedures.) [As amended, effective for reports on agreed-upon procedures engagements dated after April 30, 1996, by Statement on Standards for Attestation Engagements No. 4.] (See section 600.)

.18 In an engagement to apply agreed-upon procedures to management's assertion about an entity's compliance with specified requirements or about the effectiveness of an entity's internal control over compliance, the practitioner is required to perform only the procedures that have been agreed to by

[7] [Footnote deleted by the issuance of Statement on Standards for Attestation Engagements No. 4, September 1995.]

users.[8] However, prior to performing such procedures, the practitioner should obtain an understanding of the specified compliance requirements, as discussed in paragraph .19. [As amended, effective for reports on agreed-upon procedures engagements dated after April 30, 1996, by Statement on Standards for Attestation Engagements No. 4.] (See section 600.)

.19 To obtain an understanding of the requirements specified in management's assertion about compliance, a practitioner should consider the following:

a. Laws, regulations, rules, contracts, and grants that pertain to the specified compliance requirements, including published requirements

b. Knowledge about the specified compliance requirements obtained through prior engagements and regulatory reports

c. Knowledge about the specified compliance requirements obtained through discussions with appropriate individuals within the entity (for example, the chief financial officer, internal auditors, legal counsel, compliance officer, or grant or contract administrators)

d. Knowledge about the specified compliance requirements obtained through discussions with appropriate individuals outside the entity (for example, a regulator or a third-party specialist)

.20 When circumstances impose restrictions on the scope of an agreed-upon procedures engagement, the practitioner should attempt to obtain agreement from the users for modification of the agreed-upon procedures. When such agreement cannot be obtained (for example, when the agreed-upon procedures are published by a regulatory agency that will not modify the procedures), the practitioner should describe such restrictions in his or her report or withdraw from the engagement.

.21 The practitioner has no obligation to perform procedures beyond the agreed-upon procedures. However, if noncompliance related to management's assertion comes to the practitioner's attention by other means, such information ordinarily should be included in his or her report.

.22 The practitioner may become aware of noncompliance related to management's assertion that occurs subsequent to the period addressed by management's assertion but before the date of the practitioner's report. The practitioner should consider including information regarding such noncompliance in his or her report. However, the practitioner has no responsibility to perform procedures to detect such noncompliance other than obtaining management's representation about noncompliance in the subsequent period, as described in paragraph .70.

.23 The practitioner's report on agreed-upon procedures related to management's assertion about an entity's compliance with specified requirements or about the effectiveness of an entity's internal control over compliance should be in the form of procedures and findings. The practitioner should not provide

---

[8] AU section 322, *The Auditor's Consideration of the Internal Audit Function in an Audit of Financial Statements*, does not apply to agreed-upon procedures engagements. [As amended, effective for reports on agreed-upon procedures engagements dated after April 30, 1996, by Statement on Standards for Attestation Engagements No. 4.] (See section 600.)

negative assurance about whether management's assertion is fairly stated. The practitioner's report should contain the following elements:

a. A title that includes the word *independent*

b. Identification of the specified users

c. A reference to management's assertion about the entity's compliance with specified requirements, or about the effectiveness of an entity's internal control over compliance, including the period or point in time addressed in management's assertion,[9] and the character of the engagement

d. A statement that the procedures, which were agreed to by the specified users identified in the report, were performed to assist the users in evaluating management's assertion about the entity's compliance with specified requirements or about the effectiveness of its internal control over compliance

e. Reference to standards established by the American Institute of Certified Public Accountants

f. A statement that the sufficiency of the procedures is solely the responsibility of the specified users and a disclaimer of responsibility for the sufficiency of those procedures

g. A list of the procedures performed (or reference thereto) and related findings[10] (The practitioner should not provide negative assurance—see section 600.26.)

h. Where applicable, a description of any agreed-upon materiality limits (see section 600.27)

i. A statement that the practitioner was not engaged to, and did not, perform an examination of management's assertion about compliance with specified requirements or about the effectiveness of an entity's internal control over compliance, a disclaimer of opinion on the assertion, and a statement that if the practitioner had performed additional procedures, other matters might have come to his or her attention that would have been reported

j. A statement of restrictions on the use of the report because it is intended to be used solely by the specified users (However, if the report is a matter of public record, the practitioner should include the following sentence: "However, this report is a matter of public record and its distribution is not limited.")

k. Where applicable, reservations or restrictions concerning procedures or findings as discussed in section 600.35, .37, .41, and .42

l. Where applicable, a description of the nature of the assistance provided by the specialist as discussed in section 600.21 through .23

---

[9] Generally, management's assertion about compliance with specified requirements will address a *period* of time, whereas an assertion about internal control over compliance will address a *point* in time. [As amended, effective for reports on agreed-upon procedures engagements dated after April 30, 1996, by Statement on Standards for Attestation Engagements No. 4.] (See section 600.)

[10] [Footnote deleted by the issuance of Statement on Standards for Attestation Engagements No. 4, September 1995.]

[As amended, effective for reports on agreed-upon procedures engagements dated after April 30, 1996, by Statement on Standards for Attestation Engagements No. 4.] (See section 600.)

.24 The following is an illustration of an agreed-upon procedures report on management's assertion about an entity's compliance with specified requirements in which the procedures and findings are enumerated rather than referenced.

Independent Accountant's Report
on Applying Agreed-Upon Procedures

We have performed the procedures enumerated below, which were agreed to by [*list specified users of report*], solely to assist the users in evaluating management's assertion about [*name of entity*]'s compliance with [*list specified requirements*] during the [*period*] ended [*date*], included in the accompanying [*title of management report*].[11, 12] This agreed-upon procedures engagement was performed in accordance with standards established by the American Institute of Certified Public Accountants. The sufficiency of these procedures is solely the responsibility of the specified users of the report. Consequently, we make no representation regarding the sufficiency of the procedures described below either for the purpose for which this report has been requested or for any other purpose.

[*Include paragraphs to enumerate procedures and findings.*]

We were not engaged to, and did not, perform an examination, the objective of which would be the expression of an opinion on management's assertion. Accordingly, we do not express such an opinion. Had we performed additional procedures, other matters might have come to our attention that would have been reported to you.

This report is intended solely for the use of [*list or refer to specified users*] and should not be used by those who have not agreed to the procedures and taken responsibility for the sufficiency of the procedures for their purposes.

[As amended, effective for reports on agreed-upon procedures engagements dated after April 30, 1996, by Statement on Standards for Attestation Engagements No. 4.] (See section 600.)

.25 Evaluating compliance with certain requirements may require interpretation of the laws, regulations, rules, contracts, or grants that establish those requirements. In such situations, the practitioner should consider whether he or she is provided with the reasonable criteria required to evaluate an assertion under the third general attestation standard. If these interpretations are significant, the practitioner may include a paragraph stating the de-

[11] If management's assertion is in a representation letter rather than a separate, attached report, the first sentence of this paragraph would state: "We have performed the procedures enumerated below, . . . , included in its representation letter dated [*date*]." [As amended, effective for reports on agreed-upon procedures engagements dated after April 30, 1996, by Statement on Standards for Attestation Engagements No. 4.] (See section 600.)

[12] If the agreed-upon procedures have been published by a third-party user (for example, a regulator in regulatory policies or a lender in a debt agreement), this sentence might begin: "We have performed the procedures included in [*title of publication or other document*] and enumerated below, which were agreed to by [*list users of report*], solely to assist the users in evaluating management's assertion about . . . . " [As amended, effective for reports on agreed-upon procedures engagements dated after April 30, 1996, by Statement on Standards for Attestation Engagements No. 4.] (See section 600.)

scription and the source of interpretations made by the entity's management. An example of such a paragraph, which should precede the procedures and findings paragraph(s), follows:

> We have been informed that, under [*name of entity*]'s interpretation of [*identify the compliance requirement*], [*explain the nature and source of the relevant interpretation*].

.26 The following is an illustration of an agreed-upon procedures report on management's assertion about the effectiveness of an entity's internal control over compliance in which the procedures and findings are enumerated rather than referenced.

Independent Accountant's Report
on Applying Agreed-Upon Procedures

> We have performed the procedures enumerated below, which were agreed to by [*list specified users*], solely to assist the users in evaluating management's assertion about the effectiveness of [*name of entity*]'s internal control over compliance with [*list specified requirements*] as of [*date*], included in the accompanying [*title of management report*].[13] This agreed-upon procedures engagement was performed in accordance with standards established by the American Institute of Certified Public Accountants. The sufficiency of these procedures is solely the responsibility of the specified users of the report. Consequently, we make no representation regarding the sufficiency of the procedures described below either for the purpose for which this report has been requested or for any other purpose.
>
> [*Include paragraphs to enumerate procedures and findings.*]
>
> We were not engaged to, and did not, perform an examination, the objective of which would be the expression of an opinion on management's assertion. Accordingly, we do not express such an opinion. Had we performed additional procedures, other matters might have come to our attention that would have been reported to you.
>
> This report is intended solely for the use of [*list or refer to specified users*] and should not be used by those who have not agreed to the procedures and taken responsibility for the sufficiency of the procedures for their purposes.[14], [15]

[As amended, effective for reports on agreed-upon procedures engagements dated after April 30, 1996, by Statement on Standards for Attestation Engagements No. 4.] (See section 600.)

.27 In some agreed-upon procedures engagements, management's assertion may address both compliance with specified requirements and the effectiveness of internal control over compliance. In these engagements, the practitioner may issue one report that addresses both assertions. For example, the first sentence of the introductory paragraph would state—

> We have performed the procedures enumerated below, which were agreed to by [*list users of report*], solely to assist the users in evaluating management's

---

[13] See footnotes 11 and 12. [As amended, effective for reports on agreed-upon procedures engagements dated after April 30, 1996, by Statement on Standards for Attestation Engagements No. 4.] (See section 600.)

[14] [Footnote deleted by the issuance of Statement on Standards for Attestation Engagements No. 4, September 1995.]

[15] [Footnote deleted by the issuance of Statement on Standards for Attestation Engagements No. 4, September 1995.]

assertions about [*name of entity*]'s compliance with [*list specified requirements*] during the [*period*] ended [*date*] and about the effectiveness of [*name of entity*]'s internal control over compliance with the aforementioned compliance requirements as of [*date*], included in the accompanying [*title of management report*].

.28 The date of completion of the agreed-upon procedures should be used as the date of the practitioner's report.

Examination Engagement

.29 The objective of the practitioner's examination procedures applied to management's assertion about an entity's compliance with specified requirements is to express an opinion about whether management's assertion is fairly stated in all material respects based on established or agreed-upon criteria. To express such an opinion, the practitioner accumulates sufficient evidence in support of management's assertion about the entity's compliance with specified requirements, thereby limiting attestation risk to an appropriately low level.

Attestation Risk

.30 In an engagement to examine management's assertion about compliance with specified requirements, the practitioner seeks to obtain reasonable assurance that management's assertion is fairly stated in all material respects based on established or agreed-upon criteria. This includes designing the examination to detect both intentional and unintentional noncompliance that is material to management's assertion. Absolute assurance is not attainable because of factors such as the need for judgment, the use of sampling, and the inherent limitations of internal control over compliance and because much of the evidence available to the practitioner is persuasive rather than conclusive in nature. Also, procedures that are effective for detecting noncompliance that is unintentional may be ineffective for detecting noncompliance that is intentional and is concealed through collusion between client personnel and third parties or among management or employees of the client. Therefore, the subsequent discovery that material noncompliance exists does not, in and of itself, evidence inadequate planning, performance, or judgment on the part of the practitioner.

.31 Attestation risk is the risk that the practitioner may unknowingly fail to modify appropriately his or her opinion on management's assertion. It is composed of inherent risk, control risk, and detection risk. For purposes of a compliance examination, these components are defined as follows:

a. Inherent risk—The risk that material noncompliance with specified requirements could occur, assuming there are no related internal control structure policies or procedures.

b. Control risk—The risk that material noncompliance that could occur will not be prevented or detected on a timely basis by the entity's internal control structure policies and procedures.

c. Detection risk—The risk that the practitioner's procedures will lead him or her to conclude that material noncompliance does not exist when, in fact, such noncompliance does exist.

Inherent Risk

.32 In assessing inherent risk, the practitioner should consider factors affecting risk similar to those an auditor would consider when planning an audit of financial statements. Such factors are discussed in AU section 316, *Consideration of Fraud in a Financial Statement Audit*, paragraphs .16 through .19. In addition, the practitioner should consider factors relevant to compliance engagements, such as the following:

- The complexity of the specified compliance requirements
- The length of time the entity has been subject to the specified compliance requirements
- Prior experience with the entity's compliance
- The potential impact of noncompliance

Control Risk

.33 The practitioner should assess control risk as discussed in paragraphs .44 and .45. Assessing control risk contributes to the practitioner's evaluation of the risk that material noncompliance exists. The process of assessing control risk (together with assessing inherent risk) provides evidential matter about the risk that such noncompliance may exist. The practitioner uses this evidential matter as part of the reasonable basis for his or her opinion on management's assertion.

Detection Risk

.34 In determining an acceptable level of detection risk, the practitioner assesses inherent risk and control risk and considers the extent to which he or she seeks to restrict attestation risk. As assessed inherent risk or control risk decreases, the acceptable level of detection risk increases. Accordingly, the practitioner may alter the nature, timing, and extent of compliance tests performed based on the assessments of inherent risk and control risk.

Materiality

.35 In an examination of management's assertion about an entity's compliance with specified requirements, the practitioner's consideration of materiality differs from that in an audit of financial statements in accordance with GAAS. In an examination of management's assertion about an entity's compliance with specified requirements, the practitioner's consideration of materiality is affected by (*a*) the nature of management's assertion and the compliance requirements, which may or may not be quantifiable in monetary terms, (*b*) the nature and frequency of noncompliance identified with appropriate consideration of sampling risk, and (*c*) qualitative considerations, including the needs and expectations of the report's users.

.36 In some situations, the terms of the engagement may provide for a supplemental report of all or certain noncompliance discovered. Such terms should not change the practitioner's judgments about materiality in planning and performing the engagement or in forming an opinion on management's assertion about an entity's compliance with specified requirements.

Performing an Examination Engagement

.37 The practitioner should exercise (*a*) due care in planning, performing, and evaluating the results of his or her examination procedures and (*b*) the proper degree of professional skepticism to achieve reasonable assurance that material noncompliance will be detected.

.38 In an examination of management's assertion about the entity's compliance with specified requirements, the practitioner should—

a. Obtain an understanding of the specified compliance requirements (paragraph .39).

b. Plan the engagement (paragraphs .40 through .43).

c. Consider relevant portions of the entity's internal control structure over compliance (paragraphs .44 through .46).

d. Obtain sufficient evidence including testing compliance with specified requirements (paragraphs .47 through .48).

e. Consider subsequent events (paragraphs .49 through .51).

f. Form an opinion about whether management's assertion about the entity's compliance with specified requirements is fairly stated in all material respects based on the established or agreed-upon criteria (paragraph .52).

Obtaining an Understanding of the Specified Compliance Requirements

.39 A practitioner should obtain an understanding of the requirements specified in management's assertion about compliance. To obtain such an understanding, a practitioner should consider the following:

a. Laws, regulations, rules, contracts, and grants that pertain to the specified compliance requirements, including published requirements

b. Knowledge about the specified compliance requirements obtained through prior engagements and regulatory reports

c. Knowledge about the specified compliance requirements obtained through discussions with appropriate individuals within the entity (for example, the chief financial officer, internal auditors, legal counsel, compliance officer, or grant or contract administrators)

d. Knowledge about the specified compliance requirements obtained through discussions with appropriate individuals outside the entity (for example, a regulator or a third-party specialist)

Planning the Engagement

General Considerations

.40 Planning an engagement to examine management's assertion about the entity's compliance with specified requirements involves developing an overall strategy for the expected conduct and scope of the engagement. The practitioner should consider the planning matters discussed in section 100.28 through .33.

Multiple Components

.41 In an engagement to examine management's assertion about an entity's compliance with specified requirements when the entity has operations in several components (for example, locations, branches, subsidiaries, or programs), the practitioner may determine that it is not necessary to test compliance with requirements at every component. In making such a determination and in selecting the components to be tested, the practitioner should consider factors such as the following: (*a*) the degree to which the specified compliance requirements apply at the component level, (*b*) judgments about materiality, (*c*) the degree of centralization of records, (*d*) the effectiveness of control environment policies and procedures, particularly those that affect management's direct control over the exercise of authority delegated to others and its ability to supervise activities at various locations effectively, (*e*) the nature and extent of operations conducted at the various components, and (*f*) the similarity of operations and controls over compliance for different components.

Using the Work of a Specialist

.42 In some compliance engagements, the nature of the specified compliance requirements may require specialized skill or knowledge in a particular field other than accounting or auditing. In such cases, the practitioner may use the work of a specialist and should follow the relevant performance and reporting guidance in AU section 336, *Using the Work of a Specialist*.

Internal Audit Function

.43 Another factor the practitioner should consider when planning the engagement is whether the entity has an internal audit function and the extent to which internal auditors are involved in monitoring compliance with the specified requirements. A practitioner should consider the guidance in AU section 322, *The Auditor's Consideration of the Internal Audit Function in an Audit of Financial Statements*, when addressing the competence and objectivity of internal auditors, the nature, timing, and extent of work to be performed, and other related matters.

Consideration of Internal Control Over Compliance

.44 The practitioner should obtain an understanding of relevant portions of internal control over compliance sufficient to plan the engagement and to assess control risk for compliance with specified requirements. In planning the examination, such knowledge should be used to identify types of potential noncompliance, to consider factors that affect the risk of material noncompliance, and to design appropriate tests of compliance.

.45 A practitioner generally obtains an understanding of the design of specific controls by performing: inquiries of appropriate management, supervisory, and staff personnel; inspection of the entity's documents; and observation of the entity's activities and operations. The nature and extent of procedures a practitioner performs vary from entity to entity and are influenced by factors such as the newness and complexity of the specified requirements, the practitioner's knowledge of internal control over compliance obtained in previous professional engagements, the nature of the specified compliance requirements, an understanding of the industry in which the entity operates, and judgments about materiality. When seeking to assess control risk below the maximum, the practitioner should perform tests of controls to obtain evidence to support the assessed level of control risk.

.46 During the course of an engagement to examine management's assertion, the practitioner may become aware of significant deficiencies in the design or operation of internal control over compliance that could affect adversely the entity's ability to comply with specified requirements. A practitioner's responsibility to communicate these deficiencies in an examination of management's assertion about an entity's compliance with specified requirements is similar to the auditor's responsibility described in AU section 325, *Communication of Internal Control Related Matters Noted in an Audit*.

Obtaining Sufficient Evidence

.47 The practitioner should apply procedures to provide reasonable assurance of detecting material noncompliance. Determining these procedures and evaluating the sufficiency of the evidence obtained are matters of professional judgment. When exercising such judgment, practitioners should consider the guidance contained in section 100.37 through .40, and AU section 350, *Audit Sampling*.

.48 For engagements involving compliance with regulatory requirements, the practitioner's procedures should include reviewing reports of significant examinations and related communications between regulatory agencies and the entity and, when appropriate, making inquiries of the regulatory agencies, including inquiries about examinations in progress.

Consideration of Subsequent Events

.49 The practitioner's consideration of subsequent events in an examination of management's assertion about the entity's compliance with specified requirements is similar to the auditor's consideration of subsequent events in a financial statement audit, as outlined in AU section 560, *Subsequent Events*. The practitioner should consider information about such events that comes to his or her attention after the end of the period addressed by management's assertion and prior to the issuance of his or her report.

.50 Two types of subsequent events require consideration by management and evaluation by the practitioner. The first consists of events that provide additional information about the entity's compliance during the period addressed by management's assertion and may affect management's assertion and, therefore, the practitioner's report. For the period from the end of the reporting period (or point in time) to the date of the practitioner's report, the practitioner should perform procedures to identify such events that provide additional information about compliance during the reporting period. Such procedures should include, but may not be limited to, inquiring about and considering the following information:

- Relevant internal auditors' reports issued during the subsequent period
- Other practitioners' reports identifying noncompliance, issued during the subsequent period
- Regulatory agencies' reports on the entity's noncompliance, issued during the subsequent period
- Information about the entity's noncompliance, obtained through other professional engagements for that entity

.51 The second type consists of noncompliance that occurs subsequent to the period addressed by management's assertion but before the date of the practitioner's report. The practitioner has no responsibility to detect such noncompliance. However, should the practitioner become aware of such noncompliance, it may be of such a nature and significance that disclosure of it is required to keep management's assertion from being misleading. In such cases, the practitioner should include, in his or her report, an explanatory paragraph describing the nature of the noncompliance if it was not disclosed in management's assertion accompanying the practitioner's report.

Forming an Opinion on Management's Assertion

.52 In evaluating whether management's assertion is stated fairly in all material respects, the practitioner should consider (*a*) the nature and frequency of the noncompliance identified and (*b*) whether such noncompliance is material relative to the nature of the compliance requirements, as discussed in paragraph .35.

Reporting

.53 The form of the practitioner's report depends on, among other things, the method in which management presents its written assertion:

- If management's assertion is presented in a separate report that will accompany the practitioner's report, the practitioner should use the form of report discussed in paragraphs .54 and .55.
- If management presents its assertion only in a representation letter to the practitioner, the practitioner should use the form of report discussed in paragraphs .56 and .57.

.54 When management presents its assertion in a separate report that will accompany the practitioner's report, the practitioner's report, which is ordinarily addressed to the entity, should include—

a. A title that includes the word *independent.*

b. A reference to management's assertion about the entity's compliance with specified requirements, including the period covered by management's assertion.[16]

c. A statement that compliance with the requirements addressed in management's assertion is the responsibility of the entity's management and that the practitioner's responsibility is to express an opinion on management's assertion about compliance with those requirements based on the examination.

d. A statement that the examination was made in accordance with standards established by the American Institute of Certified Public Accountants and, accordingly, included examining, on a test basis, evidence about the entity's compliance with those requirements and performing such other procedures as the practitioner considered necessary in the circumstances. In addition, the report should include a statement that the practitioner believes the examination provides a reasonable basis for his or her opinion and a statement that the examination does not provide a legal determination on the entity's compliance.

---

[16] A practitioner also may be engaged to report on management's assertion about an entity's compliance with specified requirements as of a point in time. In this case, the illustrative reports in this section should be adapted as appropriate.

e. The practitioner's opinion on whether management's assertion is fairly stated, in all material respects, based on established or agreed-upon criteria.[17, 18]

.55 The following is the form of report a practitioner should use when he or she has examined management's assertion about an entity's compliance with specified requirements during a period of time.

Independent Accountant's Report

[*Introductory paragraph*]

We have examined management's assertion about [*name of entity*]'s compliance with [*list specified compliance requirements*] during the [*period*] ended [*date*] included in the accompanying [*title of management report*].[19] Management is responsible for [*name of entity*]'s compliance with those requirements. Our responsibility is to express an opinion on management's assertion about the Company's compliance based on our examination.

[*Scope paragraph*]

Our examination was made in accordance with standards established by the American Institute of Certified Public Accountants and, accordingly, included examining, on a test basis, evidence about [*name of entity*]'s compliance with those requirements and performing such other procedures as we considered necessary in the circumstances. We believe that our examination provides a reasonable basis for our opinion. Our examination does not provide a legal determination on [*name of entity*]'s compliance with specified requirements.

[*Opinion paragraph*]

In our opinion, management's assertion [*identify management's assertion—for example, that Z Company complied with the aforementioned requirements for the year ended December 31, 19X1*] is fairly stated, in all material respects.[20]

.56 When management presents its written assertion about an entity's compliance in a representation letter to the practitioner and not in a separate report to accompany the practitioner's report, the practitioner should modify his or her report to include management's assertion about the entity's compliance and add a paragraph that limits the use of the report to specified parties. For example, a regulatory agency may request a report from the practitioner on management's assertion about the entity's compliance with specified requirements but not request a separate written assertion from management.

---

[17] Frequently, criteria will be contained in the compliance requirements, in which case it is not necessary to repeat the criteria in the practitioner's report; however, if the criteria are not included in the compliance requirement, the practitioner's report should identify the criteria. For example, if a compliance requirement is to "maintain $25,000 in capital," it would not be necessary to identify the $25,000 in the report; however, if the requirement is to "maintain adequate capital," the practitioner should identify the criteria used to define "adequate."

[18] Although the practitioner's report generally will be for general use when management presents its assertion in an accompanying report, the practitioner is not precluded from restricting the use of the report.

[19] The practitioner should identify the management report examined by reference to the report title used by management in its report. Further, he or she should use the same description of the compliance requirements as management uses in its report.

[20] If it is necessary to identify criteria (see footnote 17), the criteria should be identified in the opinion paragraph (for example, ". . . in all material respects, based on the criteria set forth in Attachment 1").

.57 The following is the form of report that a practitioner should use in such circumstances.

Independent Accountant's Report

[*Introductory paragraph*]

We have examined management's assertion, included in its representation letter dated [*date*], that [*name of entity*] complied with [*list specified compliance requirements*] during the [*period*] ended [*date*]. As discussed in that representation letter, management is responsible for [*name of entity*]'s compliance with those requirements. Our responsibility is to express an opinion on management's assertion about the Company's compliance based on our examination.

[*Standard scope and opinion paragraphs*]

[*Limitation on use paragraph*]

This report is intended solely for the information of the audit committee, management, and [*specify legislative or regulatory body*].[21]

.58 When the presentation of assertions has been prepared in conformity with specified criteria that have been agreed upon by management and the users, the practitioner's report also should contain a statement of limitations on the use of the report because it is intended solely for specified parties.[22]

.59 Evaluating compliance with certain requirements may require interpretation of the laws, regulations, rules, contracts, or grants that establish those requirements. In such situations, the practitioner should consider whether he or she is provided with the reasonable criteria required to evaluate an assertion under the third general attestation standard. If these interpretations are significant, the practitioner may include a paragraph stating the description and the source of interpretations made by the entity's management. The following is an example of such a paragraph, which should directly follow the scope paragraph:

We have been informed that, under [*name of entity*]'s interpretation of [*identify the compliance requirement*], [*explain the source and nature of the relevant interpretation*].

.60 The date of completion of the examination procedures should be used as the date of the practitioner's report.

Report Modifications

.61 The practitioner should modify the standard reports in paragraphs .55 and .57, if any of the following conditions exist:

- There is material noncompliance with specified requirements (paragraphs .62 through .68).

---

[21] If the report is part of the public record, the following sentence should be included in the report: "However, this report is a matter of public record and its distribution is not limited."

[22] In certain situations, however, criteria that have been specified by management and other report users may be "reasonable" for general distribution. See section 100.71.

- There is a matter involving a material uncertainty (paragraph .69).
- There is a restriction on the scope of the engagement.[23]
- The practitioner decides to refer to the report of another practitioner as the basis, in part, for the practitioner's report.[24]

Material Noncompliance

.62 When an examination of management's assertion about an entity's compliance with specified requirements discloses noncompliance with the applicable requirements that the practitioner believes have a material effect on the entity's compliance, the practitioner should modify the report. The nature of the report modification depends on whether management discloses, in its assertion, a description of the noncompliance with requirements.

.63 If management discloses the noncompliance and appropriately modifies its assertion about the entity's compliance with specified requirements, the practitioner should modify the opinion paragraph by including a reference to the noncompliance and add an explanatory paragraph (after the opinion paragraph) that emphasizes the noncompliance.

.64 The following is the form of report, modified with explanatory language, that a practitioner should use when he or she has identified noncompliance and management has appropriately modified its assertion for the noncompliance.

Independent Accountant's Report

[*Standard introductory and scope paragraphs*]

[*Opinion paragraph*]

In our opinion, management's assertion [*identify management's assertion, for example, that except for noncompliance with (list requirements) Z Company complied with the aforementioned requirements for the year ended December 31, 19X1*], described in management's report, is fairly stated, in all material respects.

[*Explanatory paragraph*]

As discussed in management's assertion, the following material noncompliance occurred at [*name of entity*] during the [*period*] ended [*date*]. [*Describe noncompliance.*]

.65 In some circumstances, management may disagree with the practitioner over the existence of material noncompliance and, therefore, not include in its assertion a description of such noncompliance. Alternatively, management may describe noncompliance but not modify its assertion that the entity complied with specified requirements. In such cases, the practitioner should express either a qualified or adverse opinion on management's assertion, depending on the materiality of the noncompliance. In deciding whether to modify the opinion, and whether a modification should be a qualified or ad-

[23] The practitioner should refer to section 400.58 through .61 for guidance on a report modified for a scope restriction and adapt such guidance to the standard reports in this section.

[24] The practitioner should refer to section 400.62 through .63 for guidance on an opinion based in part on the report of another practitioner and adapt such guidance to the standard reports in this section.

verse opinion, the practitioner should consider such factors as the significance of the noncompliance to the entity and the pervasiveness of the noncompliance.

.66 The following is the form of report a practitioner should use when he or she concludes that a qualified opinion is appropriate in the circumstances.

> Independent Accountant's Report
>
> [*Standard introductory and scope paragraphs*]
>
> [*Explanatory paragraph*]
>
> Our examination disclosed the following material noncompliance with [*type of compliance requirement*] applicable to [*name of entity*] during the [*period*] ended [*date*]. [*Describe noncompliance.*]
>
> [*Opinion paragraph*]
>
> In our opinion, except for the material noncompliance described in the third paragraph, management's assertion [*identify management's assertion, for example, that Z Company complied with the aforementioned requirements for the year ended December 31, 19X1*] is fairly stated, in all material respects.

.67 The following is the form of report a practitioner should use when he or she concludes that an adverse opinion is appropriate in the circumstances.

> Independent Accountant's Report
>
> [*Standard introductory and scope paragraphs*]
>
> [*Explanatory paragraph*]
>
> Our examination disclosed the following material noncompliance with [*type of compliance requirement*] applicable to [*name of entity*] during the [*period*] ended [*date*]. [*Describe noncompliance.*]
>
> [*Opinion paragraph*]
>
> In our opinion, because of the material noncompliance described in the third paragraph, management's assertion [*identify management's assertion, for example, that Z Company complied with the aforementioned requirements for the year ended December 31, 19X1*] is not fairly stated.

.68 If the practitioner issues an examination report on management's assertion about the entity's compliance with specified requirements in the same document that includes his or her audit report on the entity's financial statements, the following sentence should be included in the paragraph of an examination report that describes material noncompliance:

> These conditions were considered in determining the nature, timing, and extent of audit tests applied in our audit of the 19XX financial statements, and this report does not affect our report dated [*date of report*] on those financial statements.

The practitioner also may include the preceding sentence when the two reports are not included within the same document.

Material Uncertainty

.69 In certain instances, the outcome of future events that may affect the determination of compliance with specified requirements during a previous period is not susceptible to reasonable estimation by management. When such uncertainties exist, it cannot be determined whether an entity complied with specified requirements and, therefore, whether management's assertion is fairly stated. For example, an entity may be involved in litigation or a regulatory investigation that may, at the time of the engagement, cause the determination of compliance to be uncertain. When such a matter exists and is included in management's assertion, the practitioner should add an explanatory paragraph in his or her report describing the uncertainty. When such a matter exists but is not included in management's assertion, the practitioner should add an explanatory paragraph in his or her report and consider the need for a qualified or adverse opinion.

Management's Representations

.70 In an agreed-upon procedures engagement or an examination engagement, the practitioner should obtain management's written representations[25]—

a. Acknowledging management's responsibility for complying with the specified requirements.

b. Acknowledging management's responsibility for establishing and maintaining effective internal control over compliance.

c. Stating that management has performed an evaluation of (1) the entity's compliance with specified requirements or (2) the entity's controls for ensuring compliance and detecting noncompliance with requirements, as applicable.

d. Stating management's assertion about the entity's compliance with the specified requirements or about the effectiveness of internal control over compliance, as applicable, based on the stated or established criteria.

e. Stating that management has disclosed to the practitioner all known noncompliance.

f. Stating that management has made available all documentation related to compliance with the specified requirements.

g. Stating management's interpretation of any compliance requirements that have varying interpretations.

h. Stating that management has disclosed any communications from regulatory agencies, internal auditors, and other practitioners concerning possible noncompliance with the specified requirements, including communications received between the end of the period addressed in management's assertion and the date of the practitioner's report.

i. Stating that management has disclosed any known noncompliance occurring subsequent to the period for which, or date as of which, management selects to make its assertion.

.71 Management's refusal to furnish all appropriate written representations also constitutes a limitation on the scope of the engagement that requires the practitioner to withdraw from an agreed-upon procedures engagement and issue a qualified opinion or disclaimer of opinion in an examination

---

[25] AU section 333A, *Client Representations*, paragraph .09 provides guidance on the date as of which management should sign such a representation letter and on which member(s) of management should sign it.

engagement. Further, the practitioner should consider the effects of management's refusal on his or her ability to rely on other management representations. [As amended, effective for reports on agreed-upon procedures engagements dated after April 30, 1996, by Statement on Standards for Attestation Engagements No. 4.] (See section 600.)

Other Information in a Client-Prepared Document Containing Management's Assertion About the Entity's Compliance With Specified Requirements or the Effectiveness of Internal Control Over Compliance

.72 An entity may publish various documents that contain information ("other information") in addition to management's assertion (report) on either (*a*) the entity's compliance with specified requirements or (*b*) the effectiveness of the entity's internal control over compliance and the practitioner's report thereon. The practitioner may have performed procedures and issued a report covering the other information. Otherwise, the practitioner's responsibility with respect to other information in such a document does not extend beyond the management report identified in his or her report, and the practitioner has no obligation to perform any procedures to corroborate other information contained in the document. However, the practitioner should read the other information and consider whether such information, or the manner of its presentation, is materially inconsistent with the information appearing in management's report or whether such information contains a material misstatement of fact.

.73 The practitioner should follow the guidance in section 400.76 through .78 if he or she believes the other information is inconsistent with the information appearing in management's report or if he or she becomes aware of information that he or she believes is a material misstatement of fact.

Effective Date

.74 This section is effective for engagements in which management's assertion is as of, or for a period ending, June 15, 1994, or thereafter, except as noted in paragraph .75. Earlier application of this section is encouraged.

.75 For engagements to perform agreed-upon procedures to test a financial institution's compliance with specified safety and soundness laws in accordance with the Federal Deposit Insurance Corporation Improvement Act of 1991, this section should be implemented when management's assertion is as of, or for a period ending, December 31, 1993 or thereafter.

Other Information in a Client-Prepared Document Containing Management's Assertion About the Entity's Compliance With Specified Requirements or the Effectiveness of Internal Control Over Compliance

AT Section 600

Agreed-Upon Procedures Engagements[1]

Source: SSAE No. 4.

Effective for reports on agreed-upon procedures engagements dated after April 30, 1996.

Introduction and Applicability

.01 This section sets forth attestation standards and provides guidance to a practitioner concerning performance and reporting in all agreed-upon procedures engagements, except as noted in paragraph .02.[1] A practitioner also should refer to the following Statements on Standards for Attestation Engagements (SSAEs), which provide additional guidance for certain types of agreed-upon procedures engagements:

a. Section 200, *Financial Forecasts and Projections*

b. Section 500, *Compliance Attestation*

.02 This section does not apply to[2] —

a. Situations in which an auditor reports on the application of agreed-upon procedures to one or more specified elements, accounts, or items of a financial statement,[3] pursuant to AU section 622, *Engagements to Apply Agreed-Upon Procedures to Specified Elements, Accounts, or Items of a Financial Statement.*[4]

b. Situations in which an auditor reports on specified compliance requirements based solely on an audit of financial statements, as addressed in AU section 623, *Special Reports*, paragraphs .19 through .21.

c. Engagements for which the objective is to report in accordance with AU section 801, *Compliance Auditing Considerations in Audits of Governmental Entities and Recipients of Governmental Financial Assistance*, unless the terms of the engagement specify that the engagement be performed pursuant to SSAEs.

---

[1] This section *supersedes* section 100, *Attestation Standards*, paragraphs .43, .44, and .59 through .62, and section 200, *Financial Forecasts and Projections*, paragraphs .53, .55, and .56. This section also supersedes section 400, *Reporting on an Entity's Internal Control Over Financial Reporting*, paragraph .09, and section 500, *Compliance Attestation*, paragraphs .10 and .12.

It also *amends* section 200.49 through .52, .54, and .57 and section 500, paragraphs .15 through .18, .23, .26, .71, and footnote 8 to paragraph .18.

Furthermore, as a consequence of the foregoing changes to existing standards, this section requires conforming changes to certain Statements on Auditing Standards (SASs) and related interpretations and to certain SSAEs and the interpretation "Responding to Requests for Reports on Matters Relating to Solvency" (section 9100.33–.44). In addition, the guidance in certain Audit and Accounting Guides and in Statement of Position (SOP) 90-1, *Accountants' Services on Prospective Financial Statements for Internal Use Only and Partial Presentations*, will be updated.

[2] The attest interpretation "Responding to Requests for Reports on Matters Relating to Solvency" (section 9100.33–.44) prohibits the performance of any attest engagements concerning assertions on matters of solvency or insolvency.

[3] When engaged to perform agreed-upon procedures on prospective financial information, the practitioner should follow the guidance in this section and in section 200.

[4] The practitioner may issue combined reports on engagements to apply agreed-upon procedures pursuant to paragraph .48 of this section and AU section 622.47.

d. Circumstances covered by AU section 324, *Reports on the Processing of Transactions by Service Organizations*, paragraph .58, when the service auditor is requested to apply substantive procedures to user transactions or assets at the service organization and he or she makes specific reference in his or her service auditor's report to having carried out designated procedures. (However, this section applies when the service auditor provides a separate report on the performance of agreed-upon procedures in an attestation engagement.)

e. Engagements covered by AU section 634, *Letters for Underwriters and Certain Other Requesting Parties*.

f. An engagement for which there is no written assertion, as defined in paragraph .06. In such a situation, a practitioner may provide certain nonattest services involving advice or recommendations to a client. A practitioner engaged to provide such nonattest services should refer to the guidance in the Statement on Standards for Consulting Services, *Consulting Services: Definitions and Standards* [CS section 100], or other applicable professional standards.

g. Certain professional services that would not be considered as falling under this section as described in section 100, *Attestation Standards*, paragraph .02.

Agreed-Upon Procedures Engagements

.03 An agreed-upon procedures engagement is one in which a practitioner is engaged by a client to issue a report of findings based on specific procedures performed on the subject matter of an assertion, as defined in paragraph .06. The client engages the practitioner to assist users in evaluating an assertion as a result of a need or needs of users of the report. Because users require that findings be independently derived, the services of a practitioner are obtained to perform procedures and report his or her findings. The users and the practitioner agree upon the procedures to be performed by the practitioner that the users believe are appropriate. Because users' needs may vary widely, the nature, timing, and extent of the agreed-upon procedures may vary as well; consequently, the users assume responsibility for the sufficiency of the procedures since they best understand their own needs. In an engagement performed under this section, the practitioner does not perform an examination or review (see section 100) and does not provide an opinion or negative assurance (see paragraph .26 of this section) about the assertion. Instead, the practitioner's report on agreed-upon procedures should be in the form of procedures and findings. (See paragraph .33 of this section.)

.04 As a consequence of the users' role in agreeing upon the procedures performed or to be performed, a practitioner's report on such engagements should clearly indicate that its use is restricted to those users. Those users, including the client, are hereinafter referred to as *specified users*.

Standards

.05 The general, fieldwork, and reporting standards for attestation engagements as set forth in section 100, together with interpretive guidance regarding their application as addressed throughout this section, should be followed by the practitioner in performing and reporting on agreed-upon procedures engagements.

General Standards

a. The first general standard is—*The engagement shall be performed by a practitioner or practitioners having adequate technical training and proficiency in the attest function.* (section 100.06)

b. The second general standard is—*The engagement shall be performed by a practitioner or practitioners having adequate knowledge in the subject matter of the assertion.* (section 100.09)

c. The third general standard is—*The practitioner shall perform an engagement only if he or she has reason to believe that the following two conditions exist:*

1. *The assertion is capable of evaluation against reasonable criteria that either have been established by a recognized body or are stated in the presentation of the assertion in a sufficiently clear and comprehensive manner for a knowledgeable reader to be able to understand them.*
2. *The assertion is capable of reasonably consistent estimation or measurement using such criteria.* (section 100.11)

(Refer to paragraph .06 of this section.)

d. The fourth general standard is—*In all matters relating to the engagement, an independence in mental attitude shall be maintained by the practitioner.* (section 100.22)[5]

e. The fifth general standard is—*Due professional care shall be exercised in the performance of the engagement.* (section 100.25)

Standards of Fieldwork

a. The first standard of fieldwork is—*The work shall be adequately planned and assistants, if any, shall be properly supervised.* (section 100.28)

b. The second standard of fieldwork is—*Sufficient evidence shall be obtained to provide a reasonable basis for the conclusion that is expressed in the report.* (section 100.37)

(Refer to paragraph .18 of this section.)

Standards of Reporting

a. The first standard of reporting is—*The report shall identify the assertion being reported on and state the character of the engagement.* (section 100.46)

(Refer to paragraph .33 of this section.)

b. The second standard of reporting is—*The report shall state the practitioner's conclusion about whether the assertion is presented in conformity with the established or stated criteria against which it was measured.* (section 100.50)

(Refer to paragraphs .06, .26 through .28, and .33 of this section.)

c. The third standard of reporting is—*The report shall state all of the practitioner's significant reservations about the engagement and the presentation of the assertion.* (section 100.64)

(Refer to paragraphs .35, .37, .41, and .42 of this section.)

---

[5] Practitioners performing attest engagements must be *independent* pursuant to rule 101 of the *Code of Professional Conduct* [ET section 101.01]. Interpretation 11 to rule 101 [ET section 101.13] provides guidance about its application in certain attest engagements (see ET section 101.13).

d. The fourth standard of reporting is—*The report on an engagement to evaluate an assertion that has been prepared in conformity with agreed-upon criteria or on an engagement to apply agreed-upon procedures should contain a statement limiting its use to the parties who have agreed upon such criteria or procedures.* (section 100.70)

(Refer to paragraphs .04 and .38 of this section.)

Assertions and Related Subject Matter

.06 An *assertion* is any declaration, or set of related declarations taken as a whole, by a party responsible for it. The *subject matter of an assertion* is any attribute, or subset of attributes, referred to or contained in an assertion and may in and of itself constitute an assertion. An assertion may be capable of reasonably consistent estimation or measurement using reasonable criteria as discussed in the third general standard; or an assertion may be one that is not measurable against reasonable criteria, possibly because the assertion is too broad or because such criteria do not exist. In an agreed-upon procedures engagement, it is the *specific subject matter of the assertion to which the agreed-upon procedures are to be applied* (referred to in this section as *specific subject matter*) that must satisfy the conditions set forth in the third general standard. Since the procedures are agreed upon between the practitioner and the specified users, the criteria against which the specific subject matter needs to be measurable may be recited within the procedures enumerated or referred to in the practitioner's report.

.07 The assertion should be presented in writing in a representation letter or another written communication from the responsible party (see paragraph .39). A written assertion may be presented to a practitioner in a number of ways, such as in a statement, narrative description, or schedule appropriately identifying what is being presented and the point in time or the period of time covered.

.08 Examples of written assertions include—

- A statement that an entity maintained effective internal controls over financial reporting based upon established criteria as of a certain date.
- A narrative description about an entity's compliance with requirements of specified laws, regulations, rules, contracts, or grants during a specified period (see section 500 for additional guidance).
- A representation by management that all investment securities owned by an entity during a specified period were traded on one or more of the markets specified in the entity's investment policy.
- A statement that the documentation of employee evaluations included in personnel files as of a certain date is dated within the time frame set forth in the entity's personnel policy.
- A schedule of statistical production data prepared in accordance with the policies of an identified entity for a specified period.

.09 In certain circumstances, the assertion may not have been finalized before determination that an attestation engagement will be undertaken by the practitioner and before all procedures have been agreed upon. This is a consequence of the evolving nature of these engagements, often to the point that the assertion is not finalized until shortly before the practitioner prepares his or her report. Typically, however, there is information identified to the practitioner from which an assertion will be formulated. In any event, the responsible party should furnish the written assertion to the practitioner prior to issuance of his or her report on an agreed-upon procedures engagement.

Conditions for Engagement Performance

.10 The practitioner may perform an agreed-upon procedures attestation engagement provided that—

a. The practitioner is *independent.*

b. The responsible party will provide the assertion in writing to the practitioner prior to the issuance of his or her report.

c. The practitioner and the specified users agree upon the procedures performed or to be performed by the practitioner.

d. The specified users take responsibility for the sufficiency of the agreed-upon procedures for their purposes.

e. The specific subject matter to which the procedures are to be applied is subject to reasonably consistent estimation or measurement.

f. Criteria to be used in the determination of findings are agreed upon between the practitioner and the specified users.

g. The procedures to be applied to the specific subject matter are expected to result in reasonably consistent findings using the criteria.

h. Evidential matter related to the specific subject matter to which the procedures are applied is expected to exist to provide a reasonable basis for expressing the findings in the practitioner's report.

i. Where applicable, the practitioner and the specified users agree on any materiality limits for reporting purposes. (See paragraph .27.)

j. Use of the report is restricted to the specified users.[6]

k. For agreed-upon procedures engagements on prospective financial information, the prospective financial statements include a summary of significant assumptions (see section 200.50).

l. For agreed-upon procedures engagements performed pursuant to section 500, management evaluates the entity's compliance with specified requirements or the effectiveness of the entity's internal control structure over compliance (see section 500.09).

Agreement on and Sufficiency of Procedures

.11 To satisfy the requirements that the practitioner and the specified users agree upon the procedures performed or to be performed and that the specified users take responsibility for the sufficiency of the agreed-upon procedures for their purposes, ordinarily the practitioner should communicate directly with and obtain affirmative acknowledgment from each of the specified users. For example, this may be accomplished by meeting with the specified users or by distributing a draft of the anticipated report or a copy of an engagement letter to the specified users and obtaining their agreement. If the practitioner is not able to communicate directly with all of the specified users, the practitioner may satisfy these requirements by applying any one or more of the following or similar procedures:

---

[6] A practitioner may perform an engagement pursuant to which his or her report will be a matter of public record. (See paragraph .33.)

- Compare the procedures to be applied to written requirements of the specified users.
- Discuss the procedures to be applied with appropriate representatives of the specified users involved.
- Review relevant contracts with or correspondence from the specified users.

The practitioner should not report on an engagement when specified users do not agree upon the procedures performed or to be performed and do not take responsibility for the sufficiency of the procedures for their purposes. (See paragraph .38 for guidance on satisfying these requirements when the practitioner is requested to add parties as specified users after the date of completion of the agreed-upon procedures.)

Establishing an Understanding With the Client

.12 The practitioner should establish an understanding with the client regarding the services to be performed.* When the practitioner documents the understanding through a written communication with the client (an "engagement letter"), such communication should be addressed to the client, and in some circumstances also to all specified users. Matters that might be included in such an understanding include the following:

- Nature of the engagement
- Identification of or reference to the assertion to be received and the party responsible for the assertion
- Identification of specified users (see paragraph .38)
- Specified users' acknowledgment of their responsibility for the sufficiency of the procedures
- Responsibilities of the practitioner (see paragraphs .14 through .16 and .42)
- Reference to applicable AICPA standards
- Agreement on procedures by enumerating (or referring to) the procedures (see paragraphs .17 through .20)
- Disclaimers expected to be included in the practitioner's report
- Use restrictions
- Assistance to be provided to the practitioner (see paragraphs .24 and .25)
- Involvement of a specialist (see paragraphs .21 through .23)
- Agreed-upon materiality limits (see paragraph .27)

Nature, Timing, and Extent of Procedures

Users' Responsibility

.13 Specified users are responsible for the sufficiency (nature, timing, and extent) of the agreed-upon procedures, because they best understand their own needs. The specified users assume the risk that such procedures might be insufficient for their purposes. In addition, the specified users assume the risk that they might misunderstand or otherwise inappropriately use findings properly reported by the practitioner.

---

* Section 100.32, which provides guidance on establishing an understanding with the client regarding the services to be performed, applies to agreed-upon procedures engagements. [Footnote added, January 1998, to reflect conforming changes necessary due to the issuance of Statement on Standards for Attestation Engagements No. 7.]

Practitioner's Responsibility

.14 The responsibility of the practitioner is to carry out the procedures and report the findings in accordance with the general, fieldwork, and reporting standards as discussed and interpreted in this section. The practitioner assumes the risk that misapplication of the procedures may result in inappropriate findings being reported. Furthermore, the practitioner assumes the risk that appropriate findings may not be reported or may be reported inaccurately. The practitioner's risks can be reduced through adequate planning and supervision and due professional care in performing the procedures, determining the findings, and preparing the report.

.15 The practitioner should have adequate knowledge in the specific subject matter to which the agreed-upon procedures are to be applied. He or she may obtain such knowledge through formal or continuing education, practical experience, or consultation with others.[7]

.16 The practitioner has no responsibility to determine the differences between the agreed-upon procedures to be performed and the procedures that the practitioner would have determined to be necessary had he or she been engaged to perform another form of attest engagement. The procedures that the practitioner agrees to perform pursuant to an agreed-upon procedures engagement may be more or less extensive than the procedures that the practitioner would determine to be necessary had he or she been engaged to perform another form of engagement.

Procedures to Be Performed

.17 The procedures that the practitioner and specified users agree upon may be as limited or as extensive as the specified users desire. However, mere reading of an assertion or specified information does not constitute a procedure sufficient to permit a practitioner to report on the results of applying agreed-upon procedures. In some circumstances, the procedures agreed upon evolve or are modified over the course of the engagement. In general, there is flexibility in determining the procedures as long as the specified users acknowledge responsibility for the sufficiency of such procedures for their purposes. Matters that should be agreed upon include the nature, timing, and extent of the procedures.

.18 The practitioner should not agree to perform procedures that are overly subjective and thus possibly open to varying interpretations. Terms of uncertain meaning (such as *general review, limited review, reconcile, check,* or *test*) should not be used in describing the procedures unless such terms are defined within the agreed-upon procedures. The practitioner should obtain evidential matter from applying the agreed-upon procedures to provide a reasonable basis for the finding or findings expressed in his or her report, but need not perform additional procedures outside the scope of the engagement to gather additional evidential matter.

.19 Examples of appropriate procedures include—

- Execution of a sampling application after agreeing on relevant parameters.
- Inspection of specified documents evidencing certain types of transactions or detailed attributes thereof.

---

[7] Section 500.18 and .19 provide guidance about obtaining an understanding of certain requirements in an agreed-upon procedures engagement involving management's assertion on compliance.

- Confirmation of specific information with third parties.
- Comparison of documents, schedules, or analyses with certain specified attributes.
- Performance of specific procedures on work performed by others (including the work of internal auditors—see paragraphs .24 and .25).
- Performance of mathematical computations.

.20 Examples of inappropriate procedures include—

- Mere reading of the work performed by others solely to describe their findings.
- Evaluating the competency or objectivity of another party.
- Obtaining an understanding about a particular subject.
- Interpreting documents outside the scope of the practitioner's professional expertise.

Involvement of a Specialist[8]

.21 The practitioner's education and experience enable him or her to be knowledgeable about business matters in general, but he or she is not expected to have the expertise of a person trained for or qualified to engage in the practice of another profession or occupation. In certain circumstances, it may be appropriate to involve a specialist to assist the practitioner in the performance of one or more procedures. For example—

- An attorney might provide assistance concerning the interpretation of legal terminology involving laws, regulations, rules, contracts, or grants.
- A medical specialist might provide assistance in understanding the characteristics of diagnosis codes documented in patient medical records.

.22 The practitioner and the specified users should explicitly agree to the involvement of the specialist in assisting a practitioner in the performance of an agreed-upon procedures engagement. This agreement may be reached when obtaining agreement on the procedures performed or to be performed and acknowledgment of responsibility for the sufficiency of the procedures, as discussed in paragraph .11. The practitioner's report should describe the nature of the assistance provided by the specialist.

.23 A practitioner may agree to apply procedures to the report or work product of a specialist that does not constitute assistance by the specialist to the practitioner in an agreed-upon procedures engagement. For example, the practitioner may make reference to information contained in a report of a specialist in describing an agreed-upon procedure. However, it is inappropriate for the practitioner to agree to merely read the specialist's report solely to describe or repeat the findings, or to take responsibility for all or a portion of any procedures performed by a specialist or the specialist's work product.

---

[8] A *specialist* is a person (or firm) possessing special skill or knowledge in a particular field other than the attest function. As used herein, a specialist does not include a person employed by the practitioner's firm who participates in the attestation engagement.

Internal Auditors and Other Personnel[9]

.24 The agreed-upon procedures to be enumerated or referred to in the practitioner's report are to be performed entirely by the practitioner except as discussed in paragraphs .21 through .23. However, internal auditors or other personnel may prepare schedules and accumulate data or provide other information for the practitioner's use in performing the agreed-upon procedures. Also, internal auditors may perform and report separately on procedures that they have carried out. Such procedures may be similar to those that a practitioner may perform under this section.

.25 A practitioner may agree to perform procedures on information documented in the working papers of internal auditors. For example, the practitioner may agree to—

- Repeat all or some of the procedures.
- Determine whether the internal auditors' working papers contain documentation of procedures performed and whether the findings documented in the working papers are presented in a report by the internal auditors.

However, it is inappropriate for the practitioner to—

- Agree to merely read the internal auditors' report solely to describe or repeat their findings.
- Take responsibility for all or a portion of any procedures performed by internal auditors by reporting those findings as the practitioner's own.
- Report in any manner that implies shared responsibility for the procedures with the internal auditors.

Findings

.26 A practitioner should present the results of applying agreed-upon procedures to specific subject matter in the form of findings. The practitioner should not provide negative assurance about whether the assertion is fairly stated in accordance with established or stated criteria. For example, the practitioner should not include a statement in his or her report that "nothing came to my attention that caused me to believe that the assertion is not fairly stated in accordance with (established or stated) criteria."

.27 The practitioner should report all findings from application of the agreed-upon procedures. The concept of materiality does not apply to findings to be reported in an agreed-upon procedures engagement unless the definition of materiality is agreed to by the specified users. Any agreed-upon materiality limits should be described in the practitioner's report.

.28 The practitioner should avoid vague or ambiguous language in reporting findings. Examples of appropriate and inappropriate descriptions of findings resulting from the application of certain agreed-upon procedures follow:

[9] AU section 322, *The Auditor's Consideration of the Internal Audit Function in an Audit of Financial Statements*, does not apply to agreed-upon procedures engagements.

Procedures Agreed Upon	*Appropriate Description of Findings*	*Inappropriate Description of Findings*
Inspect the shipment dates for a sample (agreed-upon) of specified shipping documents and determine whether any such dates were subsequent to December 31, 19XX.	No shipment dates shown on the sample of shipping documents inspected were subsequent to December 31, 19XX.	Nothing came to my attention as a result of applying the procedure.
Calculate the number of blocks of streets paved during the year ended September 30, 19XX, shown on contractors' certificates of project completion; compare the resultant number to the number in an identified chart of performance statistics.	The number of blocks of street paved in the chart of performance statistics was Y blocks more than the number calculated from the contractors' certificates of project completion.	The number of blocks of streets paved approximated the number of blocks included in the chart of performance statistics.
Calculate the rate of return on a specified investment (according to an agreed-upon formula) and verify that the resultant percentage agrees to the percentage in an identified schedule.	No exceptions were found as a result of applying the procedure.	The resultant percentage approximated the predetermined percentage in the identified schedule.
Inspect the quality standards classification codes in identified performance test documents for products produced during a specified period; compare such codes to those shown in an identified computer printout.	All classification codes inspected in the identified documents were the same as those shown in the computer printout except for the following: [*List all exceptions*.]	All classification codes appeared to comply with such performance test documents.

Working Papers

.29 The practitioner should prepare and maintain working papers in connection with an agreed-upon procedures engagement under the attestation standards; such working papers should be appropriate to the circumstances and the practitioner's needs on the engagement to which they apply.[10] Al-

[10] There is no intention to imply that the practitioner would be precluded from supporting his or her report by other means in addition to working papers.

though the quantity, type, and content of working papers vary with the circumstances, ordinarily they should indicate that—

a. The work was adequately planned and supervised.

b. Evidential matter was obtained to provide a reasonable basis for the finding or findings expressed in the practitioner's report.

.30 Working papers are the property of the practitioner, and some states have statutes or regulations that designate the practitioner as the owner of the working papers. The practitioner's rights of ownership, however, are subject to ethical limitations relating to confidentiality.[11]

.31 Certain of the practitioner's working papers may sometimes serve as a useful reference source for his or her client, but the working papers should not be regarded as a part of, or a substitute for, the client's records.

.32 The practitioner should adopt reasonable procedures for safe custody of his or her working papers and should retain them for a period of time sufficient to meet the needs of his or her practice and satisfy any pertinent legal requirements of records retention.

Reporting

Required Elements

.33 The practitioner's report on agreed-upon procedures should be in the form of procedures and findings. The practitioner's report should contain the following elements:

a. A title that includes the word *independent*

b. Identification of the specified users (see paragraph .38)

c. Reference to the assertion[12] and the character of the engagement

d. A statement that the procedures performed were those agreed to by the specified users identified in the report

e. Reference to standards established by the American Institute of Certified Public Accountants

f. A statement that the sufficiency of the procedures is solely the responsibility of the specified users and a disclaimer of responsibility for the sufficiency of those procedures

g. A list of the procedures performed (or reference thereto) and related findings (The practitioner should not provide negative assurance—see paragraph .26.)

h. Where applicable, a description of any agreed-upon materiality limits (see paragraph .27)

i. A statement that the practitioner was not engaged to, and did not, perform an examination of the assertion, a disclaimer of opinion on the assertion, and a statement that if the practitioner had performed additional procedures, other matters might have come to his or her attention that would have been reported[13]

---

[11] For guidance on requests from regulators for access to working papers, see the interpretation "Providing Access to or Photocopies of Working Papers to a Regulator" (AU section 9339.01–.15).

[12] In some agreed-upon procedures engagements, management may present more than one assertion. In these engagements, the practitioner may issue one report that refers to all assertions presented. (See section 500.27.)

[13] When the practitioner consents to the inclusion of his or her report on an agreed-upon procedures engagement in a document or written communication containing the entity's financial statements, he or she should refer to AU section 504, *Association With Financial Statements*, or to

(footnote continued)

j. A statement of restrictions on the use of the report because it is intended to be used solely by the specified users[14] (However, if the report is a matter of public record, the practitioner should include the following sentence: "However, this report is a matter of public record and its distribution is not limited.")

k. Where applicable, reservations or restrictions concerning procedures or findings as discussed in paragraphs .35, .37, .41, and .42

l. For an agreed-upon procedures engagement on prospective financial information, all items included in section 200.54

m. Where applicable, a description of the nature of the assistance provided by a specialist as discussed in paragraphs .21 through .23

Illustrative Report

.34 The following is an illustration of an agreed-upon procedures report.

Independent Accountant's Report
on Applying Agreed-Upon Procedures

To the Audit Committees and Managements of ABC Inc. and XYZ Fund:

We have performed the procedures enumerated below, which were agreed to by the audit committees and managements of ABC Inc. and XYZ Fund, solely to assist you in evaluating the accompanying Statement of Investment Performance Statistics of XYZ Fund (prepared in accordance with the criteria specified therein) for the year ended December 31, 19X1. This agreed-upon procedures engagement was performed in accordance with standards established by the American Institute of Certified Public Accountants. The sufficiency of these procedures is solely the responsibility of the specified users of the report.

Consequently, we make no representation regarding the sufficiency of the procedures described below either for the purpose for which this report has been requested or for any other purpose.

[*Include paragraphs to enumerate procedures and findings.*]

We were not engaged to, and did not, perform an examination, the objective of which would be the expression of an opinion on the accompanying Statement of Investment Performance Statistics of XYZ Fund. Accordingly, we do not express such an opinion. Had we performed additional procedures, other matters might have come to our attention that would have been reported to you.

Statement on Standards for Accounting and Review Services (SSARS) 1, *Compilation and Review of Financial Statements* [AR section 100], as appropriate, for guidance on his or her responsibility pertaining to the financial statements.

The practitioner should follow (*a*) AU section 504.04 when the financial statements of a public or nonpublic entity are audited (or reviewed in accordance with AU section 722, *Interim Financial Information*), or (*b*) AU section 504.05 when the financial statements of a public entity are unaudited. The practitioner should follow SSARS 1, paragraph 6 [AR section 100.06] when (*a*) the financial statements of a nonpublic entity are reviewed or compiled or (*b*) the financial statements of a nonpublic entity are *not* reviewed or compiled and are not submitted by the accountant (as defined in SSARS 1, paragraph 7 [AR section 100.07]).

In addition, including or combining a report that is restricted to specified users with a report for general distribution results in restriction of all included reports to the specified users (see section 100.71).

[14] The purpose of the restriction on use of a practitioner's report on applying agreed-upon procedures is to limit its use to only those parties that have agreed upon the procedures performed and taken responsibility for the sufficiency of the procedures. Paragraph .38 describes the process for adding parties who were not originally contemplated in the agreed-upon procedures engagement.

This report is intended solely for the use of the audit committees and managements of ABC Inc. and XYZ Fund, and should not be used by those who have not agreed to the procedures and taken responsibility for the sufficiency of the procedures for their purposes.

Explanatory Language

.35 The practitioner also may include explanatory language about matters such as the following:

- Disclosure of stipulated facts, assumptions, or interpretations (including the source thereof) used in the application of agreed-upon procedures (for example, see section 500.25)
- Description of the condition of records, controls, or data to which the procedures were applied
- Explanation that the practitioner has no responsibility to update his or her report
- Explanation of sampling risk

Dating of Report

.36 The date of completion of the agreed-upon procedures should be used as the date of the practitioner's report.

Restrictions on the Performance of Procedures

.37 When circumstances impose restrictions on the performance of the agreed-upon procedures, the practitioner should attempt to obtain agreement from the specified users for modification of the agreed-upon procedures. When such agreement cannot be obtained (for example, when the agreed-upon procedures are published by a regulatory agency that will not modify the procedures), the practitioner should describe any restrictions on the performance of procedures in his or her report or withdraw from the engagement.

Adding Parties as Specified Users (Nonparticipant Parties)

.38 Subsequent to the completion of the agreed-upon procedures engagement, a practitioner may be requested to consider the addition of another party as a specified user (a nonparticipant party). The practitioner may agree to add a nonparticipant party as a specified user, based on consideration of such factors as the identity of the nonparticipant party and the intended use of the report.[15] If the practitioner does agree to add the nonparticipant party, he or she should obtain affirmative acknowledgment, normally in writing, from the nonparticipant party agreeing to the procedures performed and of its taking responsibility for the sufficiency of the procedures. If the nonparticipant party is added after the practitioner has issued his or her report, the report may be reissued or the practitioner may provide other written acknowledgment that the nonparticipant party has been added as a specified user. If the report is reissued, the report date should not be changed. If the practitioner provides written acknowledgment that the nonparticipant party has been added as a specified user, such written acknowledgment ordinarily should state that no procedures have been performed subsequent to the date of the report.

Representations by Asserters

.39 As discussed in paragraph .07, the written assertion should be presented in a representation letter or another written communication from the

[15] When considering whether to add a nonparticipant party, the guidance in AU section 530, *Dating of the Independent Auditor's Report*, paragraphs .06 and .07, may be helpful.

responsible party. The responsible party's refusal to furnish a written assertion constitutes a limitation on the performance of the engagement that requires the practitioner to withdraw from the engagement.

.40 A practitioner also may find a representation letter to be a useful and practical means of obtaining other representations from the responsible party. The need for such a letter may depend on the nature of the engagement and the specified users. For example, section 500.70 requires a practitioner to obtain a representation letter in an agreed-upon procedures engagement related to compliance with specified requirements. Examples of matters that might appear in a representation letter include a statement that the responsible party has disclosed to the practitioner—

- All known matters contradicting the assertion.
- Any communication from regulatory agencies affecting the assertion.

.41 The responsible party's refusal to furnish written representations determined by the practitioner to be appropriate for the engagement constitutes a limitation on the performance of the engagement. In such circumstances, the practitioner should do one of the following:

a. Disclose in his or her report the inability to obtain representations from the responsible party.

b. Withdraw from the engagement.[16]

c. Change the engagement to another form of engagement.

Knowledge of Matters Outside Agreed-Upon Procedures

.42 The practitioner need not perform procedures beyond the agreed-upon procedures. However, in connection with the application of agreed-upon procedures, if matters come to the practitioner's attention by other means that significantly contradict the assertion referred to in the practitioner's report, the practitioner should include this matter in his or her report. For example, if, during the course of applying agreed-upon procedures regarding management's assertion relating to the entity's internal control, the practitioner becomes aware of a material weakness by means other than performance of the agreed-upon procedure, the practitioner should include this matter in his or her report.

Change to an Agreed-Upon Procedures Engagement From Another Form of Engagement

.43 A practitioner who has been engaged to perform another form of attest engagement or a nonattest service engagement may, before the engagement's completion, be requested to change the engagement to an agreed-upon procedures engagement under this section. A request to change the engagement may result from a change in circumstances affecting the client's requirements, a misunderstanding about the nature of the original services or the alternative services originally available, or a restriction on the performance of the original engagement, whether imposed by the client or caused by circumstances.

---

[16] For an agreed-upon procedures engagement performed pursuant to section 500, management's refusal to furnish all required written representations also constitutes a limitation on the scope of the engagement that requires the practitioner to withdraw from the engagement. (See section 500.71.)

.44 Before a practitioner who was engaged to perform another form of engagement agrees to change the engagement to an agreed-upon procedures engagement, he or she should consider the following:

a. The possibility that certain procedures performed as part of another type of engagement are not appropriate for inclusion in an agreed-upon procedures engagement

b. The reason given for the request, particularly the implications of a restriction on the scope of the original engagement or the matters to be reported

c. The additional effort required to complete the original engagement

d. If applicable, the reasons for changing from a general-distribution report to a restricted-use report

.45 If the specified users acknowledge agreement to the procedures performed or to be performed and assume responsibility for the sufficiency of the procedures to be included in the agreed-upon procedures engagement, either of the following would be considered a reasonable basis for requesting a change in the engagement—

a. A change in circumstances that requires another form of engagement

b. A misunderstanding concerning the nature of the original engagement or the available alternatives

.46 In all circumstances, if the original engagement procedures are substantially complete or the effort to complete such procedures is relatively insignificant, the practitioner should consider the propriety of accepting a change in the engagement.

.47 If the practitioner concludes, based on his or her professional judgment, that there is reasonable justification to change the engagement, and provided he or she complies with the standards applicable to agreed-upon procedures engagements, the practitioner should issue an appropriate agreed-upon procedures report. The report should not include reference to either the original engagement or performance limitations that resulted in the changed engagement. (See paragraph .42.)

Combined or Included Reports

.48 When a practitioner performs services pursuant to an engagement to apply agreed-upon procedures to specific subject matter as part of or in addition to another form of service, this section applies only to those services described herein; other Standards would apply to the other services. Other services may include an audit, review, or compilation of a financial statement, another attest service performed pursuant to the SSAEs, or a nonattest service.[17] Reports on applying agreed-upon procedures to specific subject matter may be included or combined with reports on such other services, provided the types of services can be clearly distinguished and the applicable Standards for each service are followed. However, since a practitioner's report on applying agreed-upon procedures to specific subject matter is restricted to the specified users, including or combining such a report with reports on other services results in restriction of all the included reports to the specified users.

---

[17] See section 100.77 through .79 for requirements relating to attest services provided as part of an MAS engagement.

Effective Date

.49 The effective date for this section is for reports on agreed-upon procedures engagements dated after April 30, 1996. Earlier application is encouraged.

AT TOPICAL INDEX

References are to AT section and paragraph numbers.

A

ACCOUNTABILITY
· Defense Industry Questionnaire on Business Ethics and Conduct........ 9100.01–.02

ADVERSE OPINIONS
· Compliance Attestation..... 500.65; 500.67; 500.69
· Disagreement With Management.............. 400.54–.56
· Prospective Financial Statements............... 200.39–.40

AGREED-UPON PROCEDURES
· Additional Procedures..... 200.54; 500.23; 600.18; 600.33
· Agreement on and Sufficiency of Procedures........ 200.50; 200.53–.54; 500.23; 600.03; 600.10–.12; 600.17; 600.22; 600.27; 600.33; 600.45
· Assertions and Related Subject Matter.................. 600.06–.09
· Change From Another Form of Engagement............. 600.43–.47
· Character of the Engagement...... 100.49
· Combined or Included Reports.............. 600.33; 600.48
· Compliance Attestation....... 500.04–.05; .... 500.15–.28; 500.70–.71; 9400.03–.04
· Conditions for Engagement Performance.......... 200.50; 200.53; 600.10–.12
· Conformity With Assertions........ 100.56
· Dating of Report................ 600.36
· Definition....................... 600.03
· Disclaimer of Opinion........ 200.54; 600.12; 600.33
· Elements of Report....... 600.03; 600.33
· Engagement............... 600.01–.49
· Engagement Letters.............. 600.12
· Evidential Matter........ 200.50; 600.10; 600.18
· Explanatory Language in Report..... 600.35
· Findings.................. 600.26–.28
· Illustrative Report................ 600.34
· Internal Auditors and Other Personnel................ 600.24–.25
· Internal Control Effectiveness....... 400.05; 9400.03–.04
· Involvement of a Specialist......... 200.54; 600.12; 600.21–.23; 600.33
· Letter to Regulator............ 9100.56–.59
· Limited Distribution of Reports..... 100.56; .... 100.70–.71; 200.50; 200.54; .... 500.23; 600.04; 600.10; 600.12; 600.33; 600.48

AGREED-UPON PROCEDURES—continued
· Management's Representations... 500.70–.71
· Materiality....... 200.50; 500.23; 600.10; 600.12; 600.27; 600.33
· Matters Outside................. 600.42
· Matters Relating to Solvency...... 9100.35
· Nature, Timing, and Extent............ 600.03; 600.13–.25
· Negative Assurance...... 600.03; 600.26; 600.33
· Nonparticipant Parties as Specified Users...................... 600.38
· Objective......................... 500.15
· Performing a Review.............. 600.03
· Performing an Examination......... 600.03
· Practitioner Responsibilities....... 200.54; 600.14–.16; 600.42
· Practitioner's Reservations About Assertions.................. 100.64
· Practitioner's Reservations About Engagement............. 100.64–.67
· Pro Forma Financial Information..... 300.01
· Procedures Performed. 200.52; 600.17–.20
· Prospective Financial Statements.... 600.10
· Reporting.................. 600.33–.38
· Reports on Attest Engagements—See Reports on Attest Engagements
· Reports on Compliance Attestation............... 500.23–.27
· Reports on Prospective Financial Statements—See Reports on Prospective Financial Statements
· Representations by Asserters......... 600.07; 600.39–.41
· Restrictions on Performance of Procedures.................. 600.37
· Scope Limitation......... 600.39; 600.41
· Scope of Engagement........ 100.66–.67; 500.16; 500.20
· Scope Restrictions—Compliance Attestation..... 500.20; 500.71; 600.41
· Services Provided in Connection With a Financing.................. 9100.40
· Standards and Procedures........ 200.49–.53; 600.05
· Summary of Significant Assumptions................. 200.50
· Understanding With Client...... 200.50–.53; 500.16–.18; 600.12
· User Responsibilities.. 200.50; 200.52–.54; .... 600.03; 600.10–.13; 600.17; 600.22; 600.33; 600.38; 600.45
· Working Papers... 600.29–.32; 9100.56–.59

References are to AT section and paragraph numbers

ANALYTICAL PROCEDURES
- Attest Engagement.......... 100.41–.43

ATTEST ENGAGEMENTS
- Agreed-Upon Procedures......... 100.56; .... 100.70–.71; 400.05; ... 500.04–.05; 500.15–.28; 500.70–.71; 600.01–.49; 9100.35; 9100.37–.41
- Assert v. Attest 100.07
- Assertion Measurement .... 100.11–.21; 9100.36
- Assertions From Concurrent or Prior MAS Engagements 100.80
- Attestation Risk ...... 100.31; 100.38–.43; 100.52–.53; 500.30–.34
- Competence of Evidential Matter................... 100.38–.39
- Compliance Attestation........ 500.01–.75
- Conduct, Code of Professional 100.13; 100.17
- Control Risk 500.33; 500.44–.45
- Criteria for Performance....... 100.11–.21; 100.31; 100.80; 9100.36
- Defense Industry Questionnaire on Business Ethics and Conduct—See Defense Industry Questionnaire on Business Ethics and Conduct
- Definition 100.01
- Detection Risk 500.34
- Disclosure 100.68–.69
- Evidential Matter ..... 100.37–.43; 100.80; 400.15; 400.27–.29
- Examination .... 100.40; 100.52–.56; .... 400.10; 400.15–.33; .... 500.04–.06; 500.11; 500.13; 500.29–.71; 9100.35
- Expert Testimony on Matters Related to Solvency................ 9100.53–.55
- Inherent Risk 500.32
- Legal Interpretation on Matters Relating to Solvency.................... 9100.37
- Levels of Assurance... 100.43; 100.52–.53; 300.07
- Limitation of an Entity's Internal Control 400.13–.14
- Limitations 100.32
- Litigation Services 9100.47–.53
- Management Advisory Service Engagements 100.77–.82
- MAS v. Attest Services........... 100.78
- Materiality 100.31; 500.35–.36
- Matters Relating to Solvency 9100.35
- Nonattest Evaluations of Written Assertions...................... 100.81
- Other Information in Client-Prepared Document...... 400.75–.78; 500.72–.73
- Part of Larger Engagement .... 100.05; 100.77–.79; 600.48
- Planning......... 100.28–.33; 500.40–.51
- Practitioner 100.01–.84
- Practitioner's Reservations About Assertions......... 100.64; 100.68–.69
- Practitioner's Reservations About Engagement 100.64–.67

ATTEST ENGAGEMENTS—continued
- Pro Forma Financial Information 300.01–.20
- Relevance of Assertions 100.15–.21
- Reliability of Assertions........ 100.15–.21
- Report on Solvency.......... 9100.33–.44
- Reporting on an Entity's Internal Control Over Financial Reporting......... 400.01–.85; 9400.01–.08
- Reports—See Reports on Attest Engagements
- Review .... 100.21; 100.41–.43; .... 100.52–.53; 100.57–.59; 400.06; 500.17; 9100.36
- Scope of Engagement............ 100.46
- Sources of Authoritative Guidance for Internal Control Engagements 400.07; 400.85
- Standards—See Attestation Standards
- Subsequent Events 400.64–.66
- Supervision....... 100.28–.29; 100.34–.36
- Timeliness 100.29
- Use of Specialists............... 100.09
- Usefulness of Assertions....... 100.15–.21
- Versus Audit Engagement—Internal Control 400.79–.82
- Withdrawal by Practitioner...... 100.66–.67
- Work of Assistants 100.34–.36
- Work of Other Practitioners..... 100.63–.64
- Working Papers ...... 100.32; 100.72–.76; 9100.56–.59

ATTESTATION STANDARDS
- Apparent Inconsistencies With GAAS & SSARS 100.84
- Comparison With GAAS........... 100.83
- General Standards 100.06–.27; 600.05
- Interpretations
  - Applicability to Litigation Services 9100.47–.55
  - Defense Industry Questionnaire 9100.01–.32
  - Matters Relating to Solvency . 9100.33–.44
- Practitioner................. 100.01–.84
- Standards of Fieldwork.......... 100.28–.43; 600.05
- Standards of Reporting....... 100.46–.59; 100.64–.71; 600.05

AUDIT ENGAGEMENT
- Services Provided in Connection With a Financing.................. 9100.39

AUDITOR, INDEPENDENT
- Attest Engagements—See Practitioner
- Compilation of Prospective Financial Statements 200.21
- Prospective Financial Statements 200.01–.69
- Understanding With Client 200.50–.53

AUDITOR, INTERNAL
- Agreed-Upon Procedures 600.24–.25
- Compliance Attestation........... 500.43

References are to AT section and paragraph numbers

B

BANKRUPTCY
· Fraudulent Transfers and Obligations 9100.33

BORROWING CONTRACT
· Report on Solvency 9100.33–.44

BUDGETS
· Prospective Financial Statements.... 200.58

C

CASH
· Solvency—See Solvency

CLIENTS
· Draft of Agreed-Upon Procedures Report 9100.44
· Professional Services in Connection With a Financing 9100.39–.40
· Understanding With Accountant........ 100.32; 200.50–.53; 600.03; 600.12
· Working Papers ... 100.74–.75; 600.30–.31

COMMUNICATION
· Agreed-Upon Procedures......... 200.53; 600.11–.12
· Reportable Conditions and Material Weaknesses.............. 400.40–.41

COMPETENCE
· Attest Engagement .... 100.06–.08; 100.38–.39
· Evidential Matter 100.38–.39
· Practitioners 100.06–.08

COMPILATION OF PROSPECTIVE FINANCIAL STATEMENTS
· Basis of Accounting Other Than GAAP 200.25
· Content of Report 200.16
· Date of Accountant's Report 200.20
· Inconsistent Information........... 200.63
· Lack of Independence 200.21
· Misleading Information or Representations 200.14
· Planning the Engagement.......... 200.68
· Reports—See Reports on Prospective Financial Statements
· Responsibility of Auditor 200.23
· Services Provided in Connection With a Financing 9100.39
· Standards and Procedures......... 200.10–.14; 200.68
· Summary of Significant Assumptions........ 200.12; 200.24–.26
· Withdrawal From Engagement........... 200.14; 200.63
· Working Papers 200.15

COMPLIANCE ATTESTATION
· Adverse Opinion... 500.65; 500.67; 500.69
· Agreed-Upon Procedures...... 500.04–.05; .... 500.15–.28; 500.70–.71; 600.10; 9400.03–.04
· Agreed-Upon Procedures Report 500.23–.27

COMPLIANCE ATTESTATION—continued
· Attestation Risk 500.30–.34
· Authority of Reports Issued 500.03
· Conditions for Engagement 500.09; 500.11; 500.13
· Considerations for Understanding Compliance Requirements 500.19; 500.39
· Control Risk 500.33; 500.44–.45
· Deficiencies in Internal Control 500.46
· Detection Risk 500.34
· Disclaimer of Opinion 500.71
· Documentation.................. 500.14
· Evidential Matter 500.11; 500.47–.48
· Examination Engagement .. 500.04; 500.06; 500.11; 500.13; 500.29–.71
· Examination Engagement—Practitioner's Report.................... 500.53–.71
· Illustrative Reports .... 500.24–.27 .... 500.55; 500.57; 500.59; 500.64; 500.66–.68
· Inherent Risk 500.32
· Internal Audit Function 500.43
· Internal Control ...... 500.04; 500.06–.07; 500.09; 500.44–.46
· Interpretations of Laws & Regulations............ 500.25; 500.59
· Limited Distribution Reports........... 500.23; 500.56–.58
· Management Representations... 500.70–.71
· Management Responsibilities 500.14
· Materiality 500.23; 500.35–.36
· Nonattest Engagement.............. 500.08
· Noncompliance .... 500.21–.22; 500.51–.52; 500.62–.68
· Other Information in Client-Prepared Document 500.72–.73
· Planning.................... 500.40–.51
· Practitioner's Responsibilities in Performing Examination 500.37–.38
· Pre-Award Surveys 9400.03–.04
· Qualified Opinions 500.65–.66; 500.69; 500.71
· Report Included With Audit Report.... 500.68
· Report Modification Conditions......... 500.61–.62; 500.65
· Reports on Assertions 500.11
· Representation Letters..... 500.11; 500.56
· Review Engagement.............. 500.07
· Scope of Services 500.04–.08; 500.16
· Scope Restrictions 500.20; 500.71
· Specialists 500.42
· Subsequent Events.... 500.22; 500.49–.51
· Uncertainties 500.69

CONDUCT, CODE OF PROFESSIONAL
· Attest Engagement........ 100.13; 100.17

CONSISTENCY
· Attestation Standards & GAAS and SSARS 100.84
· General Standards ... 100.11–.21; 9100.36

CONTROL RISK
· Compliance Attestation............ 500.33; 500.44–.45

CUTOFF DATES
· Agreed-Upon Procedures Report.... 9100.43
· Solvency Report................ 9100.43

D

DATE OF REPORT
· Agreed-Upon Procedures .... 500.28; 600.36; 9100.43
· Compilation of Prospective Financial Statements.................. 200.20
· Compliance Attestation..... 500.28; 500.60
· Dual-Dating..................... 300.11
· Examination..................... 500.60
· Examination of Prospective Financial Statements.................. 200.35
· Pro Forma Financial Statements..... 300.11

DEFENSE INDUSTRY QUESTIONNAIRE ON BUSINESS ETHICS AND CONDUCT
· Accountability Principle....... 9100.01–.02
· Application of Attestation Standards to Engagement................ 9100.04
· Attest Engagements......... 9100.01–.32
· Attestation Risk 9100.09
· Background 9100.29
· Contractor Assertions and Examination Reports
· · Disclaimer of Opinion........... 9100.28
· · Opinion Modified for Exception and Negative Response.................. 9100.28
· · Opinion Modified for Exception on Certain Response.......... 9100.19; 9100.28
· · Unqualified Opinion 9100.28
· · Unqualified Opinions Modified for Negative Responses................ 9100.28
· Criteria for Evaluating Contractor's Assertions.... 9100.05–.07; 9100.22–.23
· Defense Contractor Assertion and Review Report.................... 9100.32
· Disclaimer of Opinion on Extent of Compliance................... 9100.18
· Evidential Matter 9100.09–.15
· Examination 9100.08–.15; 9100.24–.25
· Form of Practitioner's Report .. 9100.06–.21
· General Distribution Reports... 9100.03–.07
· Illustrative Procedures for Examination of Questionnaire Answers 9100.27
· Initiatives and Questionnaire....... 9100.30
· Practitioner 9100.01–.32
· Procedures Applied to Questionnaire Responses .... 9100.08–.15; 9100.24–.25; 9100.31
· Relevance 9100.04–.07; 9100.22–.23
· Reliability 9100.04–.07; 9100.22–.23
· Review ... 9100.08–.15; 9100.24; 9100.26
· Scope Limitation 9100.14–.15
· Withdrawal by Practitioner 9100.13

DEFINITIONS—See Terminology

DISCLAIMER OF OPINION
· Agreed-Upon Procedures ... 600.12; 600.33
· Compliance Attestation............ 500.71
· Cost-Benefit Statement............. 400.56
· Extent of Compliance With Defense Contractor's Code of Ethics...... 9100.18

DISCLAIMER OF OPINION—continued
· Prospective Financial Statements 200.41; 200.58
· Scope Limitations..... 200.41–.42; 400.43; 400.58; 400.60–.61

DISCLOSURE
· Attest Engagement........... 100.68–.69
· Basis of Accounting Other Than GAAP......................... 200.25
· Summary of Significant Assumptions .... 200.12; 200.24–.26; 200.38–.41

DOCUMENTATION
· Compliance Attestation............ 500.14

DUE PROFESSIONAL CARE
· General Standards 100.25–.27

E

EMPHASIS OF A MATTER
· Prospective Financial Statements Compilation.................. 200.23
· Prospective Financial Statements Examination.................. 200.44

ENGAGEMENT
· Agreed-Upon Procedures—See Agreed-Upon Procedures
· Attestation—See Attest Engagement
· Pro Forma Financial Statements—See Pro Forma Financial Statements
· Prospective Financial Statements— See Prospective Financial Statements

ENTITY, ACCOUNTING
· Definition 200.06
· Reporting on an Entity's Internal Control Over Financial Reporting—See Internal Control

ERRORS—See Fraud

EVIDENTIAL MATTER
· Competence................. 100.38–.39
· Compliance Attestation—Examination........ 500.11; 500.47–.48
· Defense Industry Questionnaire on Business Ethics and Conduct 9100.09–.15
· Fieldwork Standards 100.37–.43
· Internal Control....... 400.15; 400.27–.29
· Pro Forma Financial Statements 300.10
· Relation to Attestation Risk 100.38–.43

EXAMPLES—See Illustrations

F

FIELDWORK—See Standards of Fieldwork, Attest

FINANCIAL FORECASTS—See Forecasts

References are to AT section and paragraph numbers

FINANCIAL PROJECTIONS
· Compilation 200.12; 200.18
· Definition 200.06
· Examination Report Example 200.33
· Hypothetical Assumptions .. 200.06; 200.12; 200.33; 200.40
· Limited Use 200.08; 200.18; 200.33; 200.40
· Range 200.06
· Use of Accountant's Name 200.09

FINANCIAL STATEMENTS
· Historical Associated With Prospective Financial Statements..... 200.22; 200.46; 200.58–.60
· Pro Forma—See Pro Forma Financial Statements
· Prospective Financial Statements—See Prospective Financial Statements
· Services Provided in Connection With a Financing 9100.39–.40

FORECASTS
· Adverse Opinion 200.39
· Agreed-Upon Procedures 200.57
· Compilation Report 200.17; 200.19
· Definition 200.06
· Disclaimer of Opinion 200.41
· Examination Report 200.32; 200.34
· General Use 200.07–.08
· Limited Use 200.07–.08
· Qualified Opinion 200.37
· Range 200.06

FOREIGN CORRUPT PRACTICES ACT OF 1977
· Compliance Reports 400.83

FRAUD
· Internal Control Considerations and Representations .... 400.36–.38; 400.42; 400.45

G

GENERAL STANDARDS, ATTEST
· Agreed-Upon Procedures Engagement 600.05
· Attestation Standards v. GAAS...... 100.83
· Criteria for Performance........ 100.11–.21; 100.31
· Due Professional Care 100.25–.27
· Independence 100.22–.24
· Knowledge.......... 100.09–.10; 9100.36
· Training and Proficiency....... 100.06–.08

GENERALLY ACCEPTED AUDITING STANDARDS
· Apparent Inconsistencies With Attestation Standards 100.84
· Comparison With Attestation Standards 100.83

H

HISTORICAL FINANCIAL STATEMENTS
· Condition for Reporting on Pro Forma Financial Statements 300.07
· Pro Forma Adjustments 300.05; 300.10

I

ILLUSTRATIONS
· Adverse Opinion 200.39; 500.67
· Adverse Opinions Due to Disagreement With Management 400.55
· Association With Historical Financial Statements 200.22
· Compliance Attestation—Agreed-Upon Procedures Reports 500.24–.27
· Compliance Attestation—Examination Reports........ 500.55; 500.57; 500.59; 500.64; 500.66–.69
· Defense Contractor Assertion and Review Report 9100.32
· Defense Contractor Assertions and Examination Reports 9100.28
· Defense Industry Initiatives and Questionnaire on Business Ethics and Conduct .. 9100.30
· Disclaimer of Opinion 200.41
· Disclaimer of Opinion Due to Scope Limitation 400.61
· Disclaimer of Opinion on Management's Cost Benefit Statement 400.56
· Disclaimer of Opinion on Pro Forma Financial Statements With Scope Limitation .. 300.20
· Examination Report on Management's Assertion Including Material Weakness Presented With Audit Report 400.57
· Financial Feasibility Study 200.48
· Financial Projections—Compilation Report 200.18
· Financial Projections—Examination Report 200.33
· Forecasts—Agreed-Upon Procedures 200.57
· Forecasts—Compilation Report 200.17; 200.19
· Forecasts—Examination Report 200.32; 200.34
· Lack of Independence 100.21
· Letters to Regulators 9100.58–.59
· Limited Distribution 500.57
· Management's Assertion Based on Criteria Specified by Regulatory Agency ... 400.72
· Modifications to Standard Practitioner's Report on Internal Control 400.53
· Modified Report on Pro Forma Financial Statements With Uncertainty 300.20
· Omission of Significant Accounting Policies 200.26
· Opinion Based in Part on the Report of Another Practitioner 400.63
· Practitioner's Report on Management's Assertion About the Suitability of Design of Entity's Internal Control 400.69
· Practitioner's Report Presented Separately From Management's Assertions on Internal Control 400.46
· Practitioner's Report When Management's Assertions on Internal Control are Presented in Representation Letter 400.49

References are to AT section and paragraph numbers

ILLUSTRATIONS—continued
· Procedures Applied to Defense Industry Questionnaire Responses 9100.31
· Procedures for Examination of Answers to Defense Industry Questionnaire . . . 9100.27
· Qualified Opinion 200.37; 500.66
· Qualified Opinions Resulting From Scope Limitations 400.59
· Qualified Report on Pro Forma Financial Statements With Scope Limitation . . 300.20
· Report on Examination at Year End & Review at Interim Date of Pro Forma Financial Statements 300.18
· Report on Examination of Pro Forma Financial Information 300.16
· Report on Pro Forma Financial Statements Accounted for as Pooling of Interests 300.19
· Report on Pro Forma Financial Statements Qualified for Reservations About Propriety of Assumptions 300.20
· Report on Review of Pro Forma Financial Information 300.17
· Reports on Applying Agreed-Upon Procedures 200.57–.58; 600.34
· Review Report 100.59
· Segment Reporting on Management's Assertion on Internal Control 400.67
· Statement Added to Report for Review of Pro Forma Financial Statements....... 300.12
· Unqualified Opinion................ 100.55

INDEPENDENCE
· General Standards 100.22–.24

INDUSTRY PRACTICES
· Criteria for Performance of Attest Engagement 100.14

INQUIRIES
· Attest Engagement........... 100.41–.43
· Compilation Procedures 200.14

INTERIM FINANCIAL INFORMATION
· Effectiveness of Controls 400.31

INTERIM FINANCIAL STATEMENTS
· Pro Forma Financial Statements..... 300.07

INTERNAL CONTROL
· Agreed-Upon Procedures .... 400.05; 9400.03–.04
· Compliance Attestation—See Compliance Attestation
· Components........... 400.02; 400.12; 400.22–.25
· Deficiencies 400.34–.41
· Design Effectiveness Evaluation . . . 400.22–.25; 9400.01–.06
· Entity's Ability to Establish Suitable Design........... 9400.07–.08
· Evidential Matter 400.15; 400.27–.29
· Examination .... 400.10; 400.15–.33; 9400.03–.04
· Foreign Corrupt Practices Act....... 400.83
· Form of Management's Written Assertion 400.03–.04; 400.44
· Forming an Opinion on Management's Assertion 400.33

INTERNAL CONTROL—continued
· Fraud 400.36–.38; 400.42; 400.45
· Interim Financial Information 400.31
· Limitations 400.13–.14
· Management Representations . . . 400.42–.43
· Management Responsibilities ...... 400.11; 500.14
· Nonattest Services .... 400.08; 500.08; 9400.07–.08
· Obtaining an Understanding 400.21
· Other Information in Client-Prepared Document 400.75–.78; 500.72–.73
· Planning 400.17–.20
· Practitioner's Report 400.44–.74
· · Adverse Opinion Due to Disagreement With Management............. 400.54–.56
· · Disclaimer of Opinion Due to Scope Limitation . . . 400.58; 400.60–.61
· · Disclaimer of Opinion on Cost-Benefit Statement.................. 400.56
· · Illustrations .... 400.46; 400.49; 400.53; .... 400.55–.57; 400.59; 400.61; 400.63; 400.67; 400.69; 400.72
· · Included With Audit Report 400.57
· · Limited Distribution Reports 400.70
· · Management's Assertion About Suitability of Design 400.68–.69
· · Management's Assertion Based on Criteria Specified by Regulatory Agency 400.70–.74
· · Management's Assertions in Separate Report 400.45–.46
· · Modifications to Standard Report 400.50–.74
· · Modified Report Resulting From Management's Inclusion of Material Weaknesses in Assertion.... 400.52–.53
· · Opinion Based in Part on the Report of Another Practitioner 400.62–.63
· · Pre-Award Surveys......... 9400.01–.08
· · Qualified Opinions 400.58–.59
· · Representation Letter........ 400.47–.49
· · Segment Reporting 400.67
· · Subsequent Events.......... 400.64–.66
· Pre-Award Surveys 9400.01–.08
· Prescribed Forms 9400.05–.06
· Purpose of Consideration in a Financial Statement Audit.............. 9400.02
· Reportable Conditions and Material Weaknesses ... 400.35–.41; 400.51–.57; 400.71; 400.73–.74; 400.81–.82
· Reporting on an Entity's Internal Control Over Financial Reporting.......... 400.01–.85
· Scope Limitations 400.43; 400.58–.61
· Sources of Authoritative Guidance.............. 400.07; 400.58
· Superseded Controls 400.32
· Testing and Evaluating Operating Effectiveness............... 400.26–.32
· Tests of Controls 400.29–.30
· Versus Audit Engagement—Internal Control 400.79–.82

IRREGULARITIES—See Fraud

K

KNOWLEDGE
· Business of Entity 300.07; 300.10; 9100.41
· Compliance Attestation .... 500.19; 500.39; 500.44; 600.15
· General Standards 100.09–.10; 9100.36
· Matters Outside Agreed-Upon Procedures 600.42
· Subject Matter to Apply Agreed-Upon Procedures 600.15
· Use of Work of Specialists 100.09

L

LAWS—See Compliance Attestation
LEGAL MATTERS
· Applicability of Attestation Standards to Litigation Service 9100.47–.55
· Compliance Attestation—See Compliance Attestation
· Foreign Corrupt Practices Act 400.83
· Relating to Solvency 9100.37
LEVERAGED BUYOUT
· Attest Engagement 9100.33–.44
LOAN AGREEMENTS—See Borrowing Contract

M

MANAGEMENT
· Advisory Services 100.77–.82
· Disagreements With Practitioner..... 400.54–.56; 500.65–.67
· Reporting on an Entity's Internal Control Over Financial Reporting—See Internal Control
· Representations in Compliance Attestation 500.70–.71
· Representations on Pro Forma Financial Statements.................... 300.10
· Representations Relating to Internal Control........ 400.42–.43; 400.47–.49
· Responsibilities 500.14
MAS ENGAGEMENTS
· Assertions Involved in Attest Services...................... 100.80
· Attest Services 100.77–.82
· Attest V. MAS Services 100.78
· Criteria Involved in Attest Services... 100.80
· Evidential Matter 100.80
· Nonattest Evaluations of Written Assertions 100.81; 400.08
· Reports on Attest Services 100.79
MATERIALITY
· Agreed-Upon Procedures Engagement.... 200.50; 500.23; 600.10; 600.12; 600.27; 600.33
· Attest Engagement 100.51
· Compliance Attestation 500.35–.36
· Effect on Prospective Financial Statements.................. 200.05
MEASUREMENT
· Reasonableness Criteria for Assertions......... 100.11–.21; 9100.36

N

NEGATIVE ASSURANCE
· Agreed-Upon Procedures..... 600.03; 600.26; 600.33
· Pro Forma Financial Statements..... 300.09
· Reports on Attest Engagements—See Reports on Attest Engagements
NONATTEST SERVICES
· Compliance Attestation............ 500.08
· Internal Control 400.08; 9400.07–.08
· MAS Engagements............... 100.81

O

OPINIONS, AUDITORS'
· Adverse—See Adverse Opinions
· Agreed-Upon Procedures ... 600.03; 600.33
· Examples—See Illustrations
· Prospective Financial Statements... 200.28; 200.36–.42; 200.54; 200.57
· Qualified—See Qualified Opinion
· Unqualified—See Unqualified Opinion

P

PLANNING
· Compliance Attestation........ 500.40–.49
· · Evidential Matter 500.47–.48
· · Internal Audit Function 500.43
· · Internal Control Considerations 500.44–.46
· · Multiple Components............ 500.41
· · Subsequent Events 500.49–.51
· · Use of Specialists 500.42
· Engagement to Examine and Report on Management's Assertions of Effectiveness of Internal Control.......... 400.17–.20
· · Documentation 400.20
· · Entity's Operations in Multiple Locations.................. 400.18
· · Internal Audit Function 400.19
· Fieldwork Standards.......... 100.28–.33
PRACTITIONER
· Agreed-Upon Procedures Engagements 600.01–.49
· Agreed-Upon Procedures Report Included With Financial Statements............ 600.33
· Attest Engagements .. 100.01–.84; 9100.01–.55
· Attest Services Related to MAS Engagements 100.77–.82
· Compliance Attestation........ 500.01–.75
· Conclusion About Reliability of Assertion 100.03–.04
· Defense Industry Questionnaire on Business Ethics and Conduct........ 9100.01–.32
· Definition 100.01
· Evidential Matter 100.37–.43; 200.51
· Examples of Services Not Considered Attest Engagements 100.02

PRACTITIONER—continued
- Expert Testimony on Matters Relating to Solvency 9100.53–.55
- Illustrative Reports—See Illustrations
- Independence. . 100.22–.24; 200.50; 600.10
- Knowledge 100.09–.10; 600.15; 600.42
- Litigation Services 9100.47–.55
- Planning and Supervision 100.28–.36; 200.51
- Pre-Award Surveys 9400.01–.08
- Pro Forma Financial Statements 300.01–.20
- Reasonableness Criteria for Assertions................ 100.11–.21
- Relevance of Assertions 100.15–.21
- Reliability of Assertions 100.15–.21
- Reporting on an Entity's Internal Control Over Financial Reporting—See Internal Control
- Reporting on Attest Engagements 100.46–.59; 100.64–.71
- Requests for Assurance on Solvency 9100.33–.44
- Responsibilities and Functions .... 600.14–.16; 600.42; 9400.01–.08
- Services in Connection With a Financing 9100.39–.40
- Training and Proficiency 100.06–.08; 200.51
- Understanding With Client......... 100.32; 200.49–.53; 600.03; 600.11–.12

PRE-AWARD SURVEYS
- Ability of Entity to Establish Suitably Designed Internal Control 9400.07–.08
- Agreed-Upon Procedures 9400.03–.04
- Compliance Attestation....... 9400.03–.04
- Design Effectiveness of Entity's Internal Control 9400.01–.04
- Examination 9400.03–.04
- Internal Control............ 9400.07–.08
- Practitioner's Responsibility ... 9400.01–.08
- Prescribed Forms........... 9400.05–.06

PRESCRIBED REPORT FORMS—See Special Reports

PRO FORMA FINANCIAL STATEMENTS
- Adjustments............. 300.05; 300.10
- After Balance Sheet Date 300.03
- Agreed-Upon Procedures . . 300.01; 9100.41
- Attestation Risk 300.07
- Conditions for Reporting........... 300.07
- Definition 200.06
- Evidential Matter 300.10
- Examination Procedures........... 300.08
- Knowledge Requirement........... 300.07
- Letter for Underwriters and Certain Other Requesting Parties 300.01
- Management Representations....... 300.10
- Objective 300.04; 300.08–.09
- Outside Basic Financial Statements .. 300.02
- Presentation................ 300.04–.06
- Procedures to Apply to Assumptions or Adjustments 300.10
- Reports—See Reports on Pro Forma Financial Statements

PRO FORMA FINANCIAL STATEMENTS—continued
- Review Procedures 300.09
- Services Provided in Connection With a Financing 9100.39–.40
- Types of Transactions Included..... 300.04

PROSPECTIVE FINANCIAL STATEMENTS
- Agreed-Upon Procedures ..... 200.49–.54; 200.57; 600.10
- Assembly 200.06
- Association With Historical Financial Statements . 200.22; 200.46; 200.58–.60
- Attestation Risk................. 200.69
- Budgets 200.58
- Compilation—See Compilation of Prospective Financial Statements
- Definition 200.06
- Examination Procedures 200.27–.48; 200.69
- Financial Feasibility Study 200.47–.48
- Financial Projections—See Financial Projections
- Forecasts—See Forecasts
- Format 200.67
- General Use 200.07
- Inconsistent Information 200.62
- Key Factors 200.06
- Limited Use 200.08
- Litigation Support Services 200.03
- Material Misstatements 200.64–.65
- Materiality, Effect . . 200.05; 200.50; 200.54
- Misleading Information or Representations.............. 200.14
- Presentation Guidelines.... 200.37; 200.39; 200.41–.42; 200.67
- Pro Forma Financial Statements 200.06
- Range....................... 200.06
- Reports on the Results of Applying Agreed-Upon Procedures . . 200.54; 200.57
- Reports, Other Auditors 200.45
- Responsible Party..... 200.06–.09; 200.17; 200.50; 200.52–.54
- Services Provided in Connection With a Financing............... 9100.39–.40
- Standards and Procedures for Agreed-Upon Procedures 200.49–.54
- Standards and Procedures for Examination............... 200.27–.29
- Summary of Significant Assumptions ...... 200.12; 200.24–.26; 200.38–.41; 200.50; 200.58
- Training and Education 200.68–.69
- Use by Third Party 200.02–.03
- Use of Accountant's Name 200.59–.60
- Working Papers 200.15; 200.30

Q

QUALIFIED OPINION
- Compliance Attestation. . 500.65–.66; 500.69; 500.71
- Prospective Financial Statements 200.37–.38
- Scope Limitations........ 200.38; 400.43; 400.58–.59

R

REGULATIONS—See Compliance Attestation

REGULATORY AGENCIES

- Compliance Attestation—See Compliance Attestation
- Internal Control Assertions 400.70–.74
- Requesting Access to or Photocopies of Working Papers 9100.56–.59

RELEVANCE

- Usefulness of Assertions . . . . . . 100.15–.21; 9100.04–.07; 9100.22–.23

RELIABILITY

- Usefulness of Assertions . . . . . . 100.15–.21; 9100.04–.07; 9100.22–.23

REPORTABLE CONDITIONS & MATERIAL WEAKNESSES

- Internal Control . . . 400.35–.41; 400.51–.57; 400.71; 400.73–.74; 400.81–.82

REPORTS

- Attest Engagement—See Reports on Attest Engagements
- Internal Control—See Internal Control
- Pro Forma Financial Statements—See Reports on Pro Forma Financial Statements
- Prospective Financial Statements—See Reports on Prospective Financial Statements

REPORTS ON ATTEST ENGAGEMENTS

- Accountability Principle 9100.02
- Adverse Report . . . . . . 100.68–.69; 500.65; 500.67; 500.69
- Agreed-Upon Procedures . . . . . . 100.70–.71; . . . . 400.05; 500.23–.28; 600.33–.38; 9100.40; 9100.42–.44
- Assertions Conform to Agreed-Upon Criteria 100.56; 100.58
- Assertions Conform to Established Criteria 100.54–.55; 100.57–.59
- Attest Services as Part of MAS Engagement 100.79; 600.48
- Availability to Public 600.10; 600.33
- Combined or Included 600.48
- Compliance Attestation . . . . 500.03; 500.11; 500.23–.28; 500.53–.69; 500.71
- Content of Agreed-Upon Procedures Report 9100.42
- Content of Examination Report 100.56
- Content of Review Report 100.58
- Date of Report . . . . 500.25; 500.60; 600.36; 9100.43
- Defense Contractor Assertion and Review Report 9100.32
- Defense Contractor Assertions and Examination Reports 9100.28
- Departure From Established Criteria 100.68
- Disclaimer of Assurance 100.66–.67
- Disclaimer of Opinion on Defense Industry Questionnaire 9100.18; 9100.28
- Disclaimer of Opinion—Compliance Attestation 500.71
- Draft Report Furnished to Client 9100.44

REPORTS ON ATTEST ENGAGEMENTS—continued

- Emphasis of a Matter 100.54; 100.58
- Examination . . . . 100.52–.56; 400.10; 500.53–.69; 500.71
- Explanatory Language 600.35
- Form of Practitioner's Opinion on Defense Industry Questionnaire 9100.16–.17
- General Distribution . . . . . . 100.48; 100.52; 100.56; 9100.03–.07
- Illustrations—See Illustrations
- Included With Audit Report 500.68
- Internal Control—See Internal Control
- Limited Distribution . . . 100.56; 100.70–.71; . . . . 400.70; 500.56–.58; . . . . 600.04; 600.10; 600.12; 600.33; 600.48
- Negative Assurance . . . . 100.41–.43; 100.52–.53; 100.57–.59
- Nonattest Services Report 9400.08
- Nonparticipant Parties as Specified Users 600.38
- Omission of an Assertion 100.51
- Other Information in Client-Prepared Document . . . . 400.75–.78; 500.72–.73
- Positive Opinion 100.52–.56
- Practitioner's Reservations About Assertions 100.64; 100.68–.69
- Practitioner's Reservations About Engagement 100.64–.67
- Pre-Award Surveys 9400.01–.08
- Pro Forma Financial Information—See Reports on Pro Forma Financial Statements
- Qualified Assurance 100.66–.69
- Qualified Opinion 500.65–.66; 500.71
- Reporting on an Entity's Internal Control Over Financial Reporting—See Internal Control
- Reporting on Assertions . . . . 100.46–.59; 100.64–.71; 500.11
- Reporting on the Character of the Engagement 100.46–.49
- Responses to Defense Industry Questionnaire 9100.03–.15
- Restrictions on Performance of Procedures 600.37
- Review . . 100.52–.53; 100.57–.59; 9100.32
- Scope Limitation . . . . 100.66–.67; 9100.20; 9100.28
- Solvency Reports 9100.42
- Specialist Assistance 600.22
- Unqualified Opinion 100.55; 9100.28

REPORTS ON INTERNAL CONTROL—See Internal Control

REPORTS ON PRO FORMA FINANCIAL STATEMENTS

- Contents of Report 300.12
- Date of Report 300.11
- Examination 300.12; 300.16; 300.18
- Illustrations—See Illustrations
- Pooling-of-Interests Transaction 300.13; 300.19
- Presentation 300.11

References are to AT section and paragraph numbers

REPORTS ON PRO FORMA FINANCIAL STATEMENTS—continued
· Qualified for Reservations About Propriety of Assumptions 300.14; 300.20
· Review 300.12; 300.17–.18
· Scope Limitations......... 300.14; 300.20
· Uncertainties 300.14; 300.20

REPORTS ON PROSPECTIVE FINANCIAL STATEMENTS
· Adverse Opinion 200.39–.40
· Agreed-Upon Procedures..... 200.50; 200.57; 9100.40
· Availability to Public 200.50; 200.54
· Basis of Accounting Other Than GAAP 200.25
· Compilation Report........... 200.16–.23
· Contents of Agreed-Upon Procedures Report..................... 200.54
· Contents of Examination Report 200.31
· Date of Accountant's Report .. 200.20; 200.35
· Disclaimer of Opinion 200.41; 200.54; 200.58
· Examination as Part of Larger Engagement 200.47
· Examination Report 200.31–.35
· Financial Feasibility Study...... 200.47–.48
· Illustrations—See Illustrations
· Lack of Independence 200.21
· Modifications to Compilation Report.................. 200.24–.26
· Modifications to Examination Report................. 200.36–.48
· Preparation and Presentation of Financial Statements 200.04
· Qualified Opinion 200.37–.38
· Restricted Use 200.50; 200.54
· Tax Matters 200.23

REPORTS, OTHER AUDITORS'
· Examination of Prospective Financial Statements 200.45

REPRESENTATION LETTERS
· Agreed-Upon Procedures........ 600.07; 600.39–.41
· Compliance Attestation..... 500.11; 500.56
· Management's Written Assertion on Effectiveness of Internal Control .... 400.03–.04; 400.42–.43; 400.47–.49; 500.11; 500.56

REVIEW OF FINANCIAL STATEMENTS
· Services Provided in Connection With a Financing 9100.39

REVIEW REPORTS
· Defense Industry Questionnaire on Business Ethics and Conduct........ 9100.08–.15; 9100.24; 9100.26; 9100.32
· Evidential Matter 100.41–.43
· General Standard—Consistency..... 100.21
· Levels of Assurance.......... 100.52–.53
· Negative Assurance ... 100.57–.59; 300.09
· Pro Forma Financial Statements........ 300.12; 300.17–.18

RISK
· Attestation Risk........ 100.31; 100.38–.43; .... 100.52–.53; 200.69; 300.07; 400.15; 500.30–.34; 9100.09
· Control Risk 500.33; 500.44–.45
· Detection Risk................. 500.34
· Inherent Risk.................. 500.32

S

SCOPE OF EXAMINATION
· Limitations ... 100.32; 100.66–.67; 200.38; .... 200.41–.42; 300.14; 400.43; 400.48; 400.58–.61; 9100.14–.15
· Understanding With Client 100.32

SECURITIES EXCHANGE ACT OF 1934
· Foreign Corrupt Practices Act...... 400.83

SOLVENCY
· Agreed-Upon Procedures 9100.40; 9100.42–.44
· Attest Engagements .... 9100.33–.44; 9100.53–.55
· Auditor's Knowledge of Entity 9100.41
· Expert Testimony 9100.53–.55
· Fraudulent Transfers and Obligations 9100.01; 9100.05
· Legal Matters 9100.37; 9100.53–.55
· Requests for Assurance 9100.33–.44
· Services Provided in Connection With a Financing............... 9100.39–.40
· Use of Lender's Definitions 9100.38

SOURCES OF INFORMATION
· Attest Engagement........... 100.38–.39
· Reliability 100.38–.39

SPECIAL REPORTS
· Pre-Award Surveys 9400.05–.06
· Conformity With Professional Standards 9400.06

SPECIALISTS
· Agreed-Upon Procedures .. 200.54; 600.12; 600.21–.23; 600.33
· Compliance Attestation........... 500.42
· Matters Requiring Specialists ... 600.21–.23
· Use in Attest Engagements........ 100.10

STANDARDS OF FIELDWORK, ATTEST
· Agreed-Upon Procedures Engagement 600.05
· Attestation Standards v. GAAS 100.83
· Evidential Matter............. 100.37–.43
· Planning 100.28–.33
· Supervision....... 100.28–.29; 100.34–.36

STANDARDS OF REPORTING, ATTEST
· Agreed-Upon Procedures Engagement 600.05
· Attestation Standards v. GAAS 100.83
· Character of the Engagement ... 100.46–.49
· Expression of Assurance 100.50–.59; 100.64
· Identifying Assertions 100.46–.49
· Limited Distribution of Reports .. 100.70–.71
· MAS Engagement 100.79

STANDARDS OF REPORTING, ATTEST—continued
· Practitioner's Reservations About Assertions 100.64; 100.68–.69
· Practitioner's Reservations About Engagement 100.64–.67

STANDARDS, ATTESTATION—See Attestation Standards

STATEMENTS ON STANDARDS FOR ACCOUNTING AND REVIEW SERVICES
· Apparent Inconsistencies With Attestation Standards 100.84

SUBSEQUENT EVENTS
· Compliance Attestation . . . . 500.22; 500.49–.51
· Management's Assertion of Effectiveness of Internal Control 400.64–.66

SUPERVISION
· Due Professional Care 100.25–.27
· Fieldwork Standards 100.28–.29; 100.34–.36
· Work of Assistants 100.34–.36

T

TERMINOLOGY
· Agreed-Upon Procedures Engagement 600.03
· Assertions 100.01; 600.06
· Attest Engagement 100.01; 9100.04
· Attestation Risk 100.31; 200.69
· Entity 200.06
· Financial Forecast 200.06
· Financial Projection 200.06
· Fraudulent Transfers and Obligations 9100.33
· Hypothetical Assumption 200.06
· Litigation Support Services 200.03
· Practitioner 100.01
· Pro Forma Financial Statements 200.06
· Prospective Financial Statements 200.06
· Specialist 600.21
· Specified Users 600.04

TERMINOLOGY—continued
· Stipulated Facts 9100.51–.53
· Subject Matter of an Assertion 600.06
· Trier of Fact 9100.48
· Working Papers 100.73

TIMELINESS
· Attest Engagement 100.29

TRAINING AND EDUCATION
· General Standards 100.06–.08

U

UNCERTAINTIES
· Compliance Attestation 500.69

UNQUALIFIED OPINION
· Defense Industry Questionnaire on Business Ethics and Conduct 9100.28
· Presentation of Assertions 100.55–.56

USEFULNESS
· Relevance of Assertions 100.15–.21
· Reliability of Assertions 100.15–.21

USERS
· Identification . . . . 200.54; 500.23; 600.12; 600.33; 600.38
· Responsibilities in Agreed-Upon Procedures Engagement . . . . 200.50; 200.52–.54; . . . . 600.03; 600.10–.13; 600.17; 600.22; 600.33; 600.38; 600.45

W

WORKING PAPERS
· Agreed-Upon Procedures 600.29–.32
· Attestation Engagements . . . . 100.32; 100.72–.76; 9100.56–.59
· Custody 100.76; 600.32
· Definition 100.73
· Examples 100.73
· Form and Content 100.72–.73; 600.29
· Ownership 100.74; 600.30
· Prospective Financial Statements 200.15; 200.30
· Providing to Regulator Access to or Photocopies of 9100.56–.59
· Records 100.75; 600.31
· Regulator Access 600.30
· Retention 100.76; 600.32
· Understanding With Client 100.32